Florida

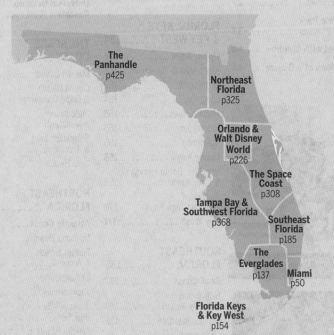

The Panhandle
p425

Northeast Florida
p325

Orlando & Walt Disney World
p226

The Space Coast
p308

Tampa Bay & Southwest Florida
p368

Southeast Florida
p185

The Everglades
p137

Miami
p50

Florida Keys & Key West
p154

THIS EDITION WRITTEN AND RESEARCHED BY

Adam Karlin, Jennifer Rasin Denniston,

Paula Hardy, Benedict Walker

Contents

SOUTH BEACH, MIAMI P51

ROSEATE SPOONBILL P499

Contents

Welcome to Florida

A hundred worlds – from magic kingdoms and Latin American and Caribbean capitals to mangrove islands, wild wetlands and artist colonies – are all contained within this flat peninsula.

Seaside Fantasy

Maybe there's no mystery to what makes the Florida peninsula so intoxicating. Beaches as fine and sweet as powdered sugar, warm waters, rustling mangroves: all conspire to melt our workaday selves. We come to Florida to let go – of worries and winter, of inhibitions and reality. Some desire a beachy getaway of swimming, seafood and sunsets. Others seek the hedonism of South Beach, spring break and Key West. Still more hope to lose themselves within the phantasmagorical realms of Walt Disney World and Orlando's theme parks.

Sexy Swamps

Within Florida's semitropical wilderness, alligators prowl beside waterways, herons strut through ponds, manatees winter in springs and sea turtles nest in summer. Osprey and eagles, dolphins and tarpon, coral-reef forests, oceans of sawgrass: despite the best efforts of 21st-century humans, overwhelming portions of Florida remain untamed, sometimes disconcertingly so. We come to Florida to experience this taste of wildness, to paddle so close to our toothsome Jurassic-era friends that our palms tingle. To meet loggerheads and manatees underwater, eye to eye.

Tropical Mosaic

While many know Florida for beaches and theme parks, few understand this is one of the most populous states in the country, a bellwether for the American experiment. And that experiment – and this state - is more diverse than ever. From rural hunters and trappers in her geographically northern, culturally Southern climes, to Jewish transplants sitting side by side with Latin arrivals from every Spanish-speaking nation in the world, it's hard to beat Florida when it comes to experiencing the human tapestry at its most colorful and vibrant.

Culture By the Coast

Tan, tropical Florida is smarter and more culturally savvy then her appearance suggests. This state, particularly South Florida, has a reputation for attracting eccentrics and idiosyncratic types from across the United States, Latin America and Europe. Many of these folks, and their descendants, have gone on to create or provide patronage for the arts, as evidenced by enormous concert spaces in Miami, a glut of museums on the Gulf Coast, and a long, literary tradition – Florida has produced more than her fair share of great American authors.

Why I Love Florida

By Adam Karlin, Author

I was raised on wetlands and I'm drawn to wetlands, and I can't think of a state that better combines that favored biome with some of my other great travel loves – namely, good food, ethnic entrepôts, warm weather and nice beaches. What can I say? Give me the ocean on one hand, swamps on the other and some fried conch and ice tea for lunch and I'm happy as a clam (which are great fried at a dockside restaurant, by the way...).

For more about our authors, see page 536

Above: The Everglades (p137)

Florida

Gulf Islands National Seashore
Stunning beaches (p433)

Apalachicola
Mecca for sweet Florida
oysters (p448)

Crystal River
Kayak & swim with wintering
manatees (p396)

St Petersburg
Artful encounters at the
Salvador Dalí Museum (p381)

Sanibel Island
Upscale beach getaway,
legendary shelling (p417)

Everglades National Park
Kayak in the swamp with
the gators (p140)

Key West
Everyone's welcome at this
party (p171)

ELEVATION

400ft

0

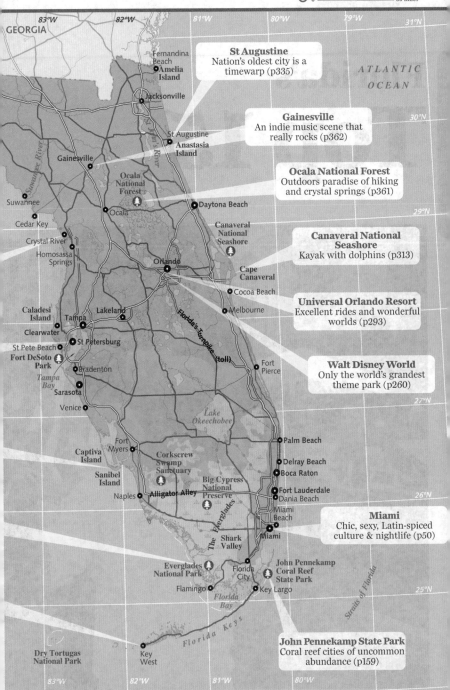

St Augustine
Nation's oldest city is a timewarp (p335)

Gainesville
An indie music scene that really rocks (p362)

Ocala National Forest
Outdoors paradise of hiking and crystal springs (p361)

Canaveral National Seashore
Kayak with dolphins (p313)

Universal Orlando Resort
Excellent rides and wonderful worlds (p293)

Walt Disney World
Only the world's grandest theme park (p260)

Miami
Chic, sexy, Latin-spiced culture & nightlife (p50)

John Pennekamp State Park
Coral reef cities of uncommon abundance (p159)

GEORGIA

ATLANTIC OCEAN

Fernandina Beach
Amelia Island
Jacksonville
St Augustine
Anastasia Island
Gainesville
Ocala National Forest
Suwannee
Cedar Key
Ocala
Daytona Beach
Crystal River
Homosassa Springs
Canaveral National Seashore
Orlando
Cape Canaveral
Cocoa Beach
Caladesi Island
Lakeland
Melbourne
Tampa
Clearwater
St Petersburg
St Pete Beach
Fort DeSoto Park
Fort Pierce
Tampa Bay
Bradenton
Sarasota
Venice
Lake Okeechobee
Fort Myers
Palm Beach
Captiva Island
Corkscrew Swamp Sanctuary
Delray Beach
Boca Raton
Sanibel Island
Big Cypress National Preserve
Fort Lauderdale
Dania Beach
Naples
Alligator Alley
Miami Beach
Miami
The Everglades
Shark Valley
Everglades National Park
Florida City
John Pennekamp Coral Reef State Park
Flamingo
Key Largo
Florida Bay
Straits of Florida
Dry Tortugas National Park
Key West
Florida Keys
Florida's Turnpike (toll)

0   100 km
0   60 miles

Florida's
Top 15

Capital of the Americas

1 Many Latin Americans resent when citizens of the United States call themselves, simply, 'Americans.' 'Are we not citizens of the *Americas* too?' they ask. Yes, and in this vein, Miami (p50) is the capital of America, North and South. No other city blends the Anglo attitude of North America with the Latin energy of South America and the Caribbean. Throw in an African American heritage, gastronomic edge, pounding nightlife, a skyline plucked from a patrician's dream and miles of gorgeous sand, and say hello to the Magic City. Bottom left: Carnaval Miami (p100) celebrations in Calle Ocho

The Magic of Disney

2 Want to set the bar of expectations high? Call yourself 'The Happiest Place on Earth.' Walt Disney World (p260) does, and then pulls out all the stops to deliver the exhilarating sensation that you are the most important character in the show. Despite all the frantic rides, entertainment and nostalgia, the magic is watching a child swell with belief after they have made Goofy laugh, been curtsied to by Cinderella, guarded the galaxy with Buzz Lightyear and battled Darth Maul like a Jedi knight. Bottom right: Cinderella's Castle (p263), Magic Kingdom, Walt Disney World

JEFF GREENBERG / GETTY IMAGES ©

PAUL THOMPSON / GETTY IMAGES ©

Coral Reef Symphony

3 Florida's most breathtaking scenery is underwater. The bowl of the peninsula's spoon is edged by more coral reefs than anywhere else in North America, and their quality and diversity rival Hawaii and the Caribbean. The prime protected areas are Biscayne National Park (p152), John Pennekamp Coral Reef State Park (p159) and Looe Key (p168). Not only can you see the reefs and their denizens by glass-bottom boat, snorkeling and diving, you can spend the night with the fishes (at John Pennekamp) if you just can't bear to surface. Below: *Christ of the Abyss* (p159) by Guido Galletti

St Augustine: Fun with History

4 According to legend, the USA's oldest city (p335) possesses Ponce de León's elusive fountain of youth. Though apocryphal, this anecdote indicates the breadth of the historic legacy so lovingly preserved along St Augustine's cobblestoned streets. Tour Spanish cathedrals, forts, and ludicrously ornate resorts. Watch costumed reenactors demonstrate cannon firing, and how to shackle and chain prisoners. Then sip a cup of eternal youth, 'cause you never know. Right: Cathedral Basilica of St Augustine (p339)

IMAGE SOURCE / GETTY IMAGES ©

Kayaking the Everglades

5 The Everglades (p137) are unnerving.
They don't reach majestically skyward
or fill your heart with the aching beauty of
a glacier-carved valley. They ooze, flat and
watery, a river of grass mottled by hammocks, cypress domes and mangroves.
You can't hike them, not really. To properly
explore the Everglades – and meet its prehistoric residents up close – you must leave
the safety of land. You must push a canoe
or kayak off a muddy bank, tamp down your
fear and explore the shallow waterways on
the Everglades' own, unforgettable terms.

The Conch Republic

6 Florida is not one place but many,
each nearly a self-contained world
unto itself. Or so wish the Conchs (p172)
of Key West, a separate island unteth-
ered from the nation, the state and even
the rest of the island chain, except by a
flimsy bridge one hurricane away from
being swallowed by the Gulf. A bring-on-
the-night crazy party animates Mallory
Square and Duval St nightly, part drunken
cabal and part authentic tolerance for the
self-expression of every impolite, noncon-
formist impulse known to humanity. Above:
Mallory Square (p171), Key West

Culture-Clash St Petersburg

7 It's all too easy to overuse the adjective 'surreal' when discussing Florida. In the case of the Salvador Dalí Museum, surreal is exactly right. Dalí has no connection to Florida whatsoever; this magnificent collection of 96 oil paintings and an overwhelming slew of ephemera landed in St Petersburg (p381) almost by chance. But then, all sorts of cultural offerings are flowering across 'St Pete,' from fine dining to live music to excellent art museums. Here is proof the Gulf Coast can be as cerebral as it is relaxing. Below: Salvador Dalí Museum (p384), designed by architect Yann Weymouth

Gulf Islands National Seashore

8 Near Pensacola, the Panhandle's barrier islands occupy about as much real estate as a string bikini, particularly the sensual stretches that form the Gulf Islands National Seashore (p433). While the region is well known for its activity-fueled beach towns, these are quickly left behind along the park's white quartz-sand beaches, gleaming like new snow. If you really need an activity, tour the crumbling wreckage of historic Fort Pickens or hike the woods, but really, isn't this why you came, to nap and tan in paradise?

ANNE RIPPY / GETTY IMAGES ©

VISIONSOFAMERICA/JOE SOHM / GETTY IMAGES ©

Swimming with Manatees

9 Is there any giant mammal as lovable, approachable and altogether nonthreatening as Florida's West Indian manatees? These lumbering, intelligent creatures seek Florida's warm-water springs and rivers each winter, and many places offer the chance to snorkel beside them. Top of the list, though, is Kings Bay, near Crystal River (p396) on the Gulf Coast, where upwards of 500 may gather on a cold January day. But while manatees sometimes approach swimmers with their own curious wonder, one thing to avoid is touching them.

Canaveral National Seashore

10 If you've been to Florida's Atlantic Coast before, you know it is one extremely built-up and crowded stretch of sand. This is partly why the 24 miles of Canaveral National Seashore's unspoiled barrier island (p313) are so special. Here, virtually in the shadow of Kennedy's shuttle launchpad, the dunes, lagoons and beaches look much as they did 500 years ago when the Spaniards landed. Kayak among the mangroves with bottlenose dolphins and manatees, observe nesting sea turtles, swim on pristine beaches and camp in solitude.

Sanibel Island: 'Stooping' to Shell

11 Gorgeous Sanibel Island (p417) is famous for the bounty of colorful and exotic shells that wash up along its beaches; the 'Sanibel stoop' is the name for the distinctive profile of avid shellers (who these days save their backs with long-handled scoops). But the dirty little secret is this: like fishing and golf, shelling is just an excuse to do nothing but let the mind wander the paths of its own reckoning. Yet delightfully, when you awake, you're rewarded with a handful of spiral calcium treasures. Above: Shells on Sanibel Island

MICHAEL SZÖNYI / GETTY IMAGES ©

YVETTE CARDOZO / GETTY IMAGES ©

Hiking the Ocala National Forest

12 We love the Everglades, but there are moments within the subtropical forests, cypress stands, sinkholes and crystal springs of the Ocala National Forest (p361) and its adjacent state parks that are just as otherworldly and strange. You can get happily lost along hundreds of miles of forested trails and among countless lakes, while hopping between campgrounds and soaking up oodles of Old Florida atmosphere. It's easy enough to dabble, but for dedicated outdoor enthusiasts, draw a big circle around Florida's heart and come here.

Apalachicola Oysters

13 Apalachicola (p448) is more than a pretty seaside town, although it is, indeed, a very pretty seaside – well, Gulfside – town. It's an experience and introduction to the laid-back folkways and crusty exterior of 'Cracker' Florida. The only thing that blazes across this town are rich orange sunsets and glistening plates of oysters. Oh, those plump, sweet, delicious oysters; Apalachicola supplies 90% of Florida's oysters, and is one of the last places in the US where 'tongers' still harvest them wild.

Universal Orlando Resort

14 We're not trying to overload you on theme parks, but this is Florida, after all. And Universal Orlando Resort (p293) is something else. The theming, the creativity of the rides, the ease of the Express Pass system, the adrenalin rushes, the silly fun – it's the smart class clown to Disney's teacher's pet. With some planning you can enjoy attractions such as the Wizarding World of Harry Potter (one of the greatest artificial worlds ever created) without waiting hours to get in or for the rides. Top far right: Wizarding World of Harry Potter (p296)

Gainesville Rocks

15 If local boy Tom Petty and transplant Bo Diddley are the patron saints of Gainesville's rock-music scene (p365), the University of Florida – the nation's second-largest university – is the engine that keeps it going strong. Bands span about every iteration of rock, from Florida's own gator-swamp rockabilly to post-punk industrial, but blues, bluegrass, reggae and hip-hop get their due on any given night. Lots of Florida cities get loud, but Gainesville has the state's hungriest, most vibrant music scene.
Right: Gainesville band Less Than Jake

Need to Know

For more information, see Survival Guide (p505)

Currency
US dollars ($)

Language
English, also Spanish in Tampa, Miami and South Florida and Haitian Creole in South Florida.

Visas
Nationals qualifying for Visa Waiver Program allowed a 90-day stay without a visa; all others need visa.

Money
ATMs widely available everywhere.

Cell Phones
Europe and Asia's GSM 900/1800 standard is incompatible with USA's cell-phone systems. Confirm phone can be used before arriving.

Time
East of the Apalachicola River, Florida is in the US Eastern Time Zone (GMT minus five hours). West of the Apalachicola is US Central Time (GMT minus six hours).

When to Go

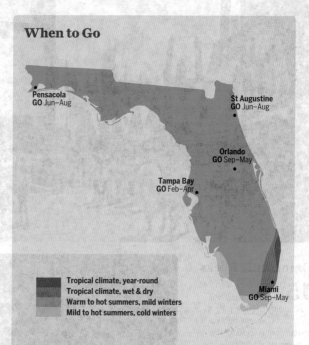

Pensacola
GO Jun–Aug

St Augustine
GO Jun–Aug

Orlando
GO Sep–May

Tampa Bay
GO Feb–Apr

Miami
GO Sep–May

Tropical climate, year-round
Tropical climate, wet & dry
Warm to hot summers, mild winters
Mild to hot summers, cold winters

High Season
(Mar–Aug)

➡ South Florida beaches peak with spring break.

➡ Panhandle and northern beaches peak in summer.

➡ Orlando theme parks peak in summer.

➡ Summer wet season hot and humid (May to September).

Shoulder
(Feb & Sep)

➡ In South Florida, February has ideal dry weather, but no spring-break craziness.

➡ With school in September, northern beaches/theme parks less crowded, still hot.

➡ Prices drop from peak by 20% to 30%.

Low Season
(Oct–Jan)

➡ Beach towns quiet until winter snowbirds arrive.

➡ Hotel prices can drop from peak by 50%.

➡ November-to-April dry season is best time to hike/camp.

➡ Holidays spike with peak rates.

17

PLAN YOUR TRIP NEED TO KNOW

Useful Websites

Visit Florida (www.visitflorida.com) Official state tourism website.

My Florida (www.myflorida.com) Portal to state government.

Florida Smart (www.floridasmart.com) Comprehensive Florida links.

Miami Herald (www.miamiherald.com) Main daily newspaper.

Florida State Parks (www.floridastateparks.org) Primary resource for state parks.

Lonely Planet (www.lonelyplanet.com/florida) Pretrip planning and fellow-traveler advice.

Important Numbers

Country code	☏1
International access code	☏011
Emergency	☏911
Directory assistance	☏411

Exchange Rates

Australia	A$1	$0.93
Canada	C$1	$0.92
Europe	€1	$1.35
Japan	Y100	$0.97
New Zealand	NZ$1	$0.85
UK	UK£1	$1.67

For current exchange rates see www.xe.com.

Daily Costs

Budget: Less than $120

➡ Dorm beds/camping: $30–50

➡ Supermarket self-catering and cheap eats

➡ Beaches are free

➡ Avoid a car; stick to one place and cycle

Midrange: $120–$250

➡ Hotels: $80–200

➡ Mix of in-room meals and seafood feasts

➡ Target theme park/beach shoulder seasons

➡ Rental car: $40–50

Top End: More than $250

➡ High-season beach hotel/resort: $250–400

➡ Miami gourmet dinners (for two): $150–300

➡ All-inclusive, four- to seven-day theme-park blowout: $1500–4000

Opening Hours

Standard business hours:

Banks 8:30am to 4:30pm Monday to Thursday, to 5:30pm Friday; some 9am to 12:30pm Saturday.

Bars Most bars 5pm to midnight; to 2am Friday and Saturday.

Businesses 9am to 5pm Monday to Friday.

Post Offices 9am to 5pm Monday to Friday; sometimes 9am to noon Saturday.

Restaurants Breakfast 7am to 10:30am and lunch 11:30am to 2:30pm Monday to Friday; dinner 5pm to 9:30pm, later Friday and Saturday.

Shops 10am to 6pm Monday to Saturday, noon to 5pm Sunday; malls keep extended hours.

Arriving in Florida

Miami International Airport (p516) Metrobus runs every 30 minutes 6am to 11pm; Miami Beach 35 minutes. Shuttle vans cost $15 to $24. A taxi to South Beach is $32.

Orlando International Airport (p516) Lynx buses ($2) run from 6am to 10pm. Public bus #11 services downtown Orlando (40 minutes); #42 services International Dr (one hour) and #111 services SeaWorld (45 minutes). Complimentary luggage handling and airport transport for guests staying at a Walt Disney World resort (Disney's Magical Express). Shuttle vans cost $20 to $30. Taxi costs: Disney area, $50 to $60; International Dr and Universal Orlando Resort, $35 to $40; downtown Orlando, $35; Winter Park, $45.

Getting Around

Transport in Florida revolves around the car.

Car The most common means of transport. Car-hire offices can be found in almost every town. Drive on the right.

Bus Greyhound and Megabus are cheap, if slow, and serve larger cities.

Train Amtrak's *Silver Service/Palmetto* runs between Miami and Tampa, and from there connects to a nationwide network. The *Auto Train* runs from Washington, DC to Sanford, near Orlando.

Cycling Flat Florida is good for cycling, although hot weather and a lack of highway bike lanes are hindrances.

For much more on **getting around**, see p518.

What's New

New Fantasyland

The Magic Kingdom is the oldest part of Walt Disney World, and Fantasyland has long been the most nostalgic corner of the Magic Kingdom. But by the time you read this, the New Fantasyland will be open and offering a Snow White–themed roller coaster and Be Our Guest – the only restaurant in the Magic Kingdom that serves booze (wine and beer only). Parents rejoice! (p263)

Pérez Art Museum Miami

After many years, Miami's homegrown art museum and its accompanying Museum Park is open to the public. The tropical-moderne facade is already an iconic part of Miami's waterfront. (p78)

DecoBike

Peddle around South Beach in style (and help combat the emissions belched out by all of those classic cars and Hummers) on your own lovely DecoBike. (p94)

Coliseum Ballroom

After an extensive renovation, St Petersburg's historic Coliseum Ballroom is reopening to the public. Don't miss the lavish interior of this events space, originally built in 1924. (p387)

Legacy Trail

See blue waterways and green subtropical woodland on two unhurried wheels on the Legacy Trail, a bike path that runs from Sarasota to Venice. (p407)

Great Calusa Blueway

Experience the serenity of Southwest Florida's gentle waters on the Buck Key Paddling Trail, a reopened ecological playground of mangroves, beaches and wetlands within the Great Calusa Blueway. (p411)

Gale South Beach Hotel

The Gale manages to blend the nostalgia of South Beach's swinging, deco-era youth with the ultra-modern facade of modern Miami's cosmopolitan cachet. (p106)

Springfield

If you've wanted to walk the streets of Springfield, drink a Duff, quaff a Flaming Moe and down a Krusty Burger, don't miss this *Simpsons*-themed addition to Universal Orlando Resort. (p298)

Wood Tavern

This welcome addition to the Miami nightlife scene manages to combine casual service, a huge outdoor area, artsy clientele and an enormous beer menu. (p126)

Wet Walks

Want to see the Everglades up close and personal? Embark on a wet walk into the heart of the wetlands. Nothing says adventure like an alligator-adjacent stroll. (p148)

For more recommendations and reviews, see lonelyplanet.com/usa/florida

If You Like...

Secluded Islands

The Florida peninsula is ringed with barrier islands and mangrove-fringed keys. Many are accessible by causeways and bridges, but to really leave the crowds behind, go by boat. That's the only way to get to these beauties.

Cayo Costa Island Undeveloped and majestic; for real solitude, book a cabin or campsite and spend the night. (p409)

Caladesi Island A 20-minute ferry ride to three miles of sugary, seashell-strewn goodness. (p394)

St Vincent Island Just off the Panhandle coastline, with great hikes, wildlife and beaches. (p451)

Cedar Keys National Wildlife Refuge Cedar Key is like a frontier town, with kayaking among dozens of tiny wildernesses. (p461)

Dry Tortugas Far off Key West in the middle of the sea: camp, stargaze, snorkel coral reefs, and barter beers with fishermen for lobster. (p179)

Roadside Attractions

Florida boasts mermaids, Hogwarts, Haitian *botanicas* (shops that deal in herbs and charms), and at least three alleged fountains of youth, making the state a roadside-attraction hall of fame. For these, you needn't travel north of I-75.

Coral Castle In Homestead, this monument to unrequited love defies explanation and belief. (p148)

Robert Is Here Also in Homestead, it's just a farm stand with a petting zoo, but feels like...an event. (p149)

Skunk Ape Research Headquarters Apparently, Bigfoot's relatives live in the swamp, and they don't smell too good. (p144)

Ochopee Post Office Not just the tiniest post office in the USA, the world's most patient postal worker. (p144)

Cycling

Flat, warm and did we mention flat? Florida can be a cyclist's dream, although she may be a bore to mountain bikers (which isn't quite fair, as there are some nice off-road paths out there!).

Florida Keys Overseas Heritage Trail Ride alongside the shoulder of the road above the teal horizons of the ocean and Florida Bay. (p160)

Paisley Woods Bicycle Trail Think Florida has nothing for mountain bikers? You'll think again after pounding the scrub on this 22-mile ride through Ocala National Forest. (p361)

West Orange Trail This 24-mile trail passes through about 10 miles of lovely horse-country just west of theme-park-studded Orlando. (p241)

Sanibel Island This calm little refuge, with its distinct lack of highway development, is laced with dozens of bicycle paths. (p417)

Nature Walks

Florida's backyard is an American original – slash pine, clear springs, snowy sands, and miles of reptile-rich wetlands bordered by a hairy fringe of spidery mangroves. The following spots get deep in the subtropical mix.

Historic Spanish Point This gorgeous 30-acre historic site is anchored by a 1-mile walking tour that runs between the historic attractions that pepper the unspoilt coastal habitat. (p406)

Egan's Creek Greenway Over 300 acres of grassy paths run by the forests, clear streams and diverse wildlife of Amelia Island. (p354)

Canaveral National Seashore
With 24 miles of wilderness beaches, this is the longest stretch of undeveloped coastline on the eastern Florida seaboard. (p313)

Wekiwa Springs State Park
Hop on the boardwalk and take in the National Wild and Scenic Rivers–designated Wekiva River. (p244)

Manatees

From November through March, Florida's West Indian manatees seek the warmth of the peninsula's freshwater rivers, its 72°F (22°C) crystal springs and the warm-water discharge canals of power plants. Yeah, it's bizarre, but these canals are now protected sanctuaries. That's our modern world.

Crystal River Kings Bay is perhaps the best place to swim with these magnificent mammals. (p396)

Homosassa Springs The state park's underwater observatory gets you nose-to-prehensile-nose with them. (p396)

Lee County Manatee Park Manatees can crowd this Fort Myers discharge canal; they're almost close enough to touch. (p413)

Space Coast Manatees like the intercoastal waters of Canaveral National Seashore, Mosquito Lagoon, Indian River Lagoon and others. (p309)

Blue Spring State Park This spring near Orlando can draw up to 200 manatees during cold spells. (p358)

Live Music

With loud, fist-pumping rock, gator-swamp rockabilly and sweaty blues, Florida's northern cities flex

Top: Manatee, off the Gulf Coast
Bottom: Fort Jefferson (p179), Dry Tortugas National Park

their Southern roots. The state has a rich, diverse musical heritage, with lots of great venues.

Jacksonville Freebird Live is a shrine to Lynyrd Skynyrd and one of the nation's best small music venues. (p352)

Gainesville Tom Petty's hometown has a first-rate and extensive college-music scene, including some fantastic punk clubs. (p365)

Tallahassee The city is known for blues; just head for the Bradfordville Blues Club, a local legend. (p457)

Naples The Naples Philharmonic is one of those unexpected gems of a regional orchestra. (p424)

West Palm Beach Perhaps surprisingly, West Palm Beach really rocks; its several venues include a BB King's blues outpost. (p219)

Miami Yes, Miami is mainly about its DJ-driven nightclubs, but rock and Latin bands still pump up the volume, especially out in Wynwood. (p122)

Locavore Gourmet

The explosion of Florida's gourmet food scene has led, naturally, to an increasing embrace of today's locavore ethics and the arrival of accomplished chefs passionate about using products grown no further away than the charge of an electric car.

Up the Creek Raw Bar If you're into oysters, get fresh ones from the source at this Apalachicola eatery. (p449)

Indigenous This Sarasota restaurant is a James Beard semi-finalist and excellent purveyor of Gulf Coast culinary goodness. (p401)

Dixie Crossroads One of the few spots on the Space Coast that sells locally sourced shrimp. (p313)

Orlando There's an entire foodie sub-scene here that is embracing the locavore thing with a passion. (p252)

Baseball

Major League Baseball's spring training – with almost daily exhibition games – is a long-standing Florida tradition drawing hordes of fans. The 'grapefruit league' (www.florida grapefruitleague.com) has 15 pro teams, and two stay when the season starts: the Tampa Bay Rays and Miami Marlins.

Tampa Bay area The Tampa Bay Rays play the regular season in St Petersburg at Tropicana Field (p388), and the New York Yankees have spring training in Tampa at Steinbrenner Field (p378).

Fort Myers Both the Boston Red Sox and Minnesota Twins hold spring training here. (p414)

Jupiter The St Louis Cardinals have spring training at Roger Dean Stadium, and then the Marlins' minor-league team plays. (p221)

Orlando area The Atlanta Braves play within Walt Disney World, and the Houston Astros hold court in nearby Kissimmee. (p244)

Miami Catch a Miami Marlins game amid the South Florida swelter. (p131)

The Circus

Sarasota is no longer the winter home of the Ringling Bros and Barnum &

Bailey Circus, but it once was, and this has left a circus legacy in Florida that is equal parts nostalgia, palm-tingling performance and DIY thrills.

Ringling's Circus Museum Truly, this shrine to Ringling's showmanship and the wonder of the circus is as entertaining and thrilling as the thing itself. (p398)

PAL Sailor Circus Performed entirely by kids, and focusing on acrobatics, this may be the country's most unique circus. It's certainly the most heartwarming. (p400)

South Florida Circus Arts School Weren't those kids amazing? Now *you* try the flying trapeze. Seriously. Climb the ladder. Stand on the platform. Graaaab the bar... (p98)

Cirque du Soleil La Nouba Walt Disney World designed the intimate theater to house this Cirque show, which, not surprisingly, is the best live entertainment Disney offers. (p258)

Gay Nightlife

As much as Manhattan, San Francisco and LA, Florida is a destination for gay travelers. It hosts some of the wildest parties and has some of the best-organized gay communities in the country.

Key West The Conch Republic is all about letting your freak flag fly. How established is gay life here? There's even a gay trolley tour. (p183)

Miami In South Beach especially, gay nightlife is almost synonymous with 'nightlife.' Be as out as you like among the fashionistas and celebrities. (p122)

Fort Lauderdale The Lauderdale scene is less snooty patootie than South Beach, and welcomes

Diver exploring the wreck of the USS *Oriskany* (p433)

hordes of sun-seeking gay travelers to its B&Bs and bars. (p196)

West Palm Beach Palm Beach's hipper sister has a notable and noticeable gay scene. (p212)

Orlando Orlando is gay-friendly year-round, but everyone comes out for Gay Days in early June. (p245)

Pensacola Surprise! Attend Pensacola's Memorial Day party, and you might not recognize the Panhandle. (p436)

Craft Drinks

Florida's drinking profile has increased a fair bit since the early-21st-century heyday of the mighty *mojito*. Be they muddled, shaken, stirred or strained, craft booze is appearing with delicious, inebriating frequency in bars across the state.

Broken Shaker Miami Beach throws its hat in the fancy cocktail ring with this excellent outdoor outpost. (p124)

Stache Craft drinks and beautiful Fort Lauderdale clientele. (p195)

Blackbird Ordinary This downtown Miami bar doesn't play when it comes to seriously powerful mixed drinks. (p125)

Point5 Lounge Get past the dross of meathead bars in Key West and enjoy a fine libation in this lounge. (p182)

Wreck Diving

Skrrrriiiitch! What was that sound? Just another oceangoing vessel striking reef and going down off Florida's coast. A few are even shallow enough for snorkelers to access.

Panama City Beach The 'Wreck Capital of the South' boasts more than a dozen boats, barges, tugs and a WWII Liberty ship, plus natural reefs. (p444)

Pensacola Dive a 900ft-long aircraft carrier, the *Oriskany*, deliberately sunk in 2006. (p433)

Fort Pierce Snorkel a Spanish galleon, the *Urca de Lima*, under only 10ft to 15ft of water. (p224)

Fort Lauderdale Freighters, steamers, tugs and barges litter the sea floor near Fort Lauderdale. (p191)

Biscayne National Park The Maritime Heritage Trail has six ships, and a two-masted schooner is shallow enough for snorkelers. (p153)

Troy Springs The Civil War–era steamboat *Madison* was scuttled out here, and makes for some nice scenery on your dip. (p367)

Month by Month

TOP EVENTS
Carnaval Miami,
March

Fantasy Fest, October

SunFest, May

Goombay Festival,
June

Gay Days, June

January

January is smack in the middle of Florida's 'dry' season, winter. In northern Florida, cool temps make this off-season. In southern Florida, after New Year's, January becomes beach resort shoulder season.

☆ College Football Bowl Games

On January 1, New Year's Day, Floridians go insane for college football. Major bowls are played in Orlando (Capital One Bowl), Tampa (Outback Bowl) and Jacksonville (Gator Bowl), while Miami's Orange Bowl (January 3) often crowns the collegiate champion.

February

Ideal month for less-crowded South Florida beaches; high season ramps up. Still too cool for tourists up north.

☆ Speed Weeks

During the first two weeks of February, up to 200,000 folks rev their engines for two major car races – the Rolex 24 Hour Race and Daytona 500 – and party full throttle.

🎆 Edison Festival of Light

(www.edisonfestival.org) For two weeks, Fort Myers celebrates the great inventor Thomas Edison with a block party, concerts and a huge science fair. February 11, Edison's birthday, culminates in an incredible Parade of Light. (p413)

☆ Florida State Fair

More than a century old, Tampa's Florida State Fair is classic Americana: two mid-February weeks of livestock shows, greasy food, loud music and old-fashioned carnival rides. (p373)

🎆 Street Painting Festival

You'll never see the streets of Lake Worth quite the same after this festival, which kicks off in late February. The art that is produced isn't just chalk on asphalt; veritable curbside Sistine Chapels blanket Lake Worth's urban landscape. (p204)

✕ South Beach Wine & Food Festival

(www.sobefest.com) No paper-plate grub-fest, this late-February event is a Food Network–sponsored culinary celebration of food, drink and celebrity chefs. (p100)

🎆 Mardi Gras

Whether it falls in late February or early March, Fat Tuesday inspires parties statewide, yet Pensacola Beach, closest to New Orleans, is Florida's best.

March

Beach resort high season over, due to spring break. Modest temps and dry weather make for an ideal time to hike and camp. Last hurrah for manatees.

🍷 Spring Break

Throughout March to mid-April, American colleges release students for one-week 'spring breaks.' Coeds pack Florida beaches for debaucherous drunken binges – but hey, it's all good fun. The biggies? Panama City Beach, Pensacola, Daytona and Fort Lauderdale.

⭐ Baseball Spring Training

Through March, Florida hosts Major League Baseball's spring training 'Grapefruit League' (www.floridagrapefruitleague.com): 15 pro teams train and play exhibition games in the Orlando area, the Tampa Bay area and the Southeast.

🎭 Carnaval Miami

(www.carnavalmiami.com) Miami's premier Latin festival takes over for nine days in early March: there's a Latin drag-queen show, in-line-skate competition, domino tournament, the immense Calle Ocho street festival, Miss Carnaval Miami and more.

🍷 Bike Week

Enjoy doing 12oz curls while admiring hogs and tatts? Join bikers for Daytona's Bike Week, a fortnight in early March. Everyone returns in mid-October for Biketoberfest.

🎭 Captain Robert Searle's Raid

St Augustine re-creates Robert Searle's infamous 1668 pillaging of the town in March. Local pirates dress up again in June for Sir Francis Drake's Raid. Volunteers are welcome! (p339)

🎭 St Patrick's Day

Ireland's patron saint gets his due across Florida on March 17 (any excuse to drink, right?). Miami turns the greenest.

⭐ Winter Music Conference

(www.wmcon.com) For five days in late March, DJs, musicians, promoters and music-industry execs converge on Miami to party, strike deals, listen to new dance music and coo over the latest technology.

April

As spring-break madness fades, prices drop. Last hurrah for the winter dry season.

⭐ Florida Film Festival

Held in Winter Park, near Orlando, this celebration of independent films is fast becoming one of the largest in the southeast. Sometimes held in late March. (p244)

🎭 Interstate Mullet Toss

In late April on Perdido Key, near Pensacola, locals are famous for their annual ritual of tossing dead fish over the Florida–Alabama state line. Distance trumps style, but some have lots of style. (p438)

May

Summer 'wet' season begins: rain, humidity, bugs all increase with temps. Northern beach season ramps up; southern beaches enter off-season.

🏃 Sea Turtle Nesting

Beginning in May and extending through October, sea turtles nest on Florida beaches; after two months (from midsummer through fall), hatchling runs see the kids totter back to sea.

🎭 Isle of Eight Flags Shrimp Festival

On May's first weekend, Amelia Island celebrates shrimp, art and pirates, with an invasion and lots of scurvy pirate talk – aaarrrrgh!

⭐ SunFest

(www.sunfest.com) Over five days in early May, West Palm Beach holds South Florida's largest waterfront music and arts festival.

⭐ Memorial Day Circuit Party

For late May's Memorial Day weekend, Pensacola becomes one massive three-day gay party, with lots of DJs, dancing and drinking.

🍴 Palatka Blue Crab Festival

For four late-May days, Palatka celebrates the blue crab and hosts the state championship for chowder and gumbo. That's some serious bragging rights.

June

Oh my it's getting hot. It's also the start of hurricane season, which peaks in September/October. School's out for summer, so theme parks become insanely crowded.

⭐ Gay Days

(www.gaydays.com) Starting on the first Saturday of June, and going for a week, upwards of 40,000 gays and lesbians descend on the Magic Kingdom and other Orlando theme parks, hotels and clubs. Wear red.

✨ Goombay Festival

In Miami's Coconut Grove, this massive four-day, early-June street party draws well over 300,000 to celebrate the city's Bahamian culture with music, dancing and parades; it's one of America's largest black-culture festivals.

July

Northern-beach and theme-park high season continues. Swamp trails are unbearably muggy and buggy; stick to crystal springs and coastlines.

✨ Fourth of July

America's Independence Day is cause for parades and fireworks, large and small, across the state. Miami draws the biggest crowd for the best fireworks and laser show.

✗ Steinhatchee Scallop Season

The opening day of scallop season in Steinhatchee can draw a thousand folks, who take to the waters to harvest this delectable bivalve by hand. Anyone can join the following two-month treasure hunt.

August

Floridians do nothing but crank the air-con inside while foolish tourists swelter and burn on the beaches – and run from afternoon thundershowers.

✗ Miami Spice

Miami's restaurants join together in August to offer prix-fixe lunches and

Top: Musician taking part in Key West's Goombay Festival (p178)
Bottom: Loggerhead turtle hatchling

dinners in an attempt to draw city residents from their apartments.

September

☆ Mickey's Not-So-Scary Halloween Party

At Disney World on select evenings over two months (starting in September), kids can trick or treat in the shadow of Cinderella's Castle, with costumed Disney favorites and a Halloween-themed parade. (p277)

October

Temperatures drop, rains abate, school returns, crowds leave. Prices dip all over. The last hurricanes strike.

✿✿ Universal's Halloween Horror Nights

Magnificently spooky haunted houses, gory thrills and over-the-top Halloween shows. Watch for goblins, monsters and mummies roaming the streets, creeping up behind you, and remember, this is Universal, not Disney: parents should think carefully before bringing children 13 and under. (p300)

✿✿ Fantasy Fest

Key West pulls out all the stops for this weeklong costumed extravaganza culminating in Halloween. Everyone's even crazier than usual, and Key West's own Goombay Festival competes for attention the same week. (p178)

☆ MoonFest

West Palm Beach throws a rockin', riotous block party for Halloween, October 31. Guests are encouraged to come in costume, and dozens of the best local bands play for free.

November

Florida's 'dry' winter season begins. Northern 'snowbirds' start flocking to their Florida condos. It's safe to hike again. Thanksgiving holidays spike tourism for a week.

✿✿ Tampa Cigar Heritage Festival

(www.cigarheritagefestival. com) Tampa's Ybor City has a long history as the cigar-making capital of the US. That heritage, and the cigars themselves, are celebrated in this one-day festival.

✿✿ St Arrrgustine Pirate Gathering

Put on an eye patch and dust off your pirate lingo for this hokey celebration of scurvy dogs and seafaring rascals in St Augustine for three days in November.

☆ White Party

(www.whiteparty.net) A raucous gay and lesbian celebration (and HIV/AIDS fundraiser), the White Party is actually a series of parties and nightclub events in Miami Beach and Fort Lauderdale over a week in late November. And yes, wear white.

December

High season begins for South Florida beaches. Manatees arrive in warm-water springs.

✿✿ Art Basel Miami Beach

(www.artbaselmiamibeach. com) Very simply, early December sees one of the biggest international art shows in the world, with more than 150 art galleries represented and four days of parties).

☆ Victorian Christmas Stroll

The landmark 1891 Tampa Bay Hotel (now a museum) celebrates Christmas, Victorian-style, for three weeks in December, with folks in period costume acting out fairy tales.

✿✿ King Mango Strut

(www.kingmangostrut. org) Miami's Coconut Grove rings in the New Year with this wacky, freak-alicious, after-Christmas parade, which spoofs current events and local politics.

Itineraries

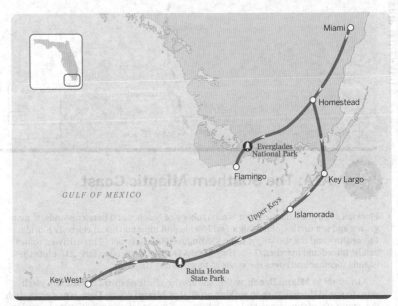

 Iconic Florida

For sheer iconic box-ticking, you can't do better than spending a week taking in Miami, the Everglades and the Florida Keys. First off, explore **Miami** for three solid days (more if you can). South Beach's pastel art-deco hotels and hedonistic beach culture? Check. Cuban sandwiches, Haitian *botanicas,* modern art? Check. Charming the velvet ropes, Latin hip-hop, *mojitos*? Hey, we're doing good.

Then take one day and visit the sunning alligators (check) of **Everglades National Park**. On the way, **Homestead** has prime Florida roadside attractions (Coral Castle, Robert Is Here – check and check!), and the **Flamingo** visitor center offers opportunities to kayak among the mangroves (check).

Now spend three days (or more) in the Florida Keys. Stop first in **Key Largo**, for Key lime pie, conch fritters and jaw-dropping coral reefs (check x 3). Enjoy tarpon fishing in **Islamorada** (check), beach napping at **Bahia Honda State Park** (check), and finally, hit **Key West** to ogle the Mallory Sq freak show (check) and raise a libation as the tangerine sun drops into an endless ocean – *salut!*

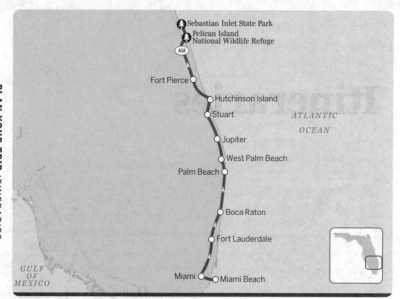

A1A: The Southern Atlantic Coast

Florida's southern Atlantic Coast is a symphony of beaches and barrier islands, of mangroves and sea turtles, of nostalgic Old Florida and nip-and-tucked celebrity Florida, of the wealthy and the you've-got-to-be-kidding-me obscenely rich. Three driving routes can be mixed and matched (I-95, Hwy 1 and A1A), but scenic, two-lane A1A knits the islands together and edges the sands as much as any road can.

A1A starts in **Miami Beach**, within the art-deco historic district. Naturally, you'll want to spend three days or so soaking up all that **Miami** offers. Then, rent a convertible, don your Oakley sunglasses, and nest a Dior scarf around your neck: it's time to road trip.

Whoops! There already? First stop is **Fort Lauderdale**. Preen along the promenade among the skating goddesses and be-thonged gay men, ride a romantic gondola in the canals, enjoy fine art and gourmet cuisine: it's a suite of pleasures the Gold Coast specializes in.

After two or three days, stagger on. Pause for a quiet interlude on the gorgeous beaches of **Boca Raton**, then repeat your Lauderdale experience in **Palm Beach**. Ogle the uberwealthy as they glide between mansion and Bentley and beach, stop by the Flagler Museum to understand how this all got started, and each day decamp to **West Palm Beach**, the hipper, more happening sister city.

After several days, it's time to detox. Heading north, the Treasure Coast is known for unspoiled nature, not condos and cosmopolitans. Stop first in **Jupiter**; among its pretty parks, don't miss the seaside geyser at Blowing Rocks Preserve.

Even better, spend several days in **Stuart**. From here, you can kayak the Loxahatchee River, book a fishing charter, snorkel the reefs at St Lucie Inlet, and escape the crowds on nearby **Hutchinson Island** beaches.

If you only have two weeks, then you may have to skip the next offerings. At **Fort Pierce**, admire manatees in winter and snorkel a Spanish galleon. Surfers should pause at **Sebastian Inlet State Park**, and birders detour to the nation's first national wildlife refuge, **Pelican Island**. We've come a long way from Miami, yes?

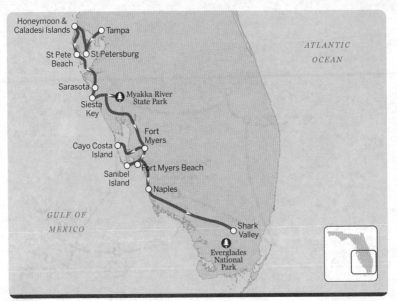

Gulf Coast Swing

Many prefer Florida's Gulf Coast: the beaches aren't as built up, soporifically warm waters lap blindingly white sand, and the sun sets (rather than rises) over the sea. Plus, it's easy to mix urban sophistication with seaside getaways and swampy adventures – just like around Miami, only even more family- (and budget-) friendly.

On this trip, spend your first three to four days in **Tampa** and **St Petersburg**. Stroll the museums and parks along Tampa's sparkling Riverwalk, and spend a day enjoying historic Ybor City's Spanish cuisine, cigars and nightclubs. St Pete offers similar city fun, but above all, don't miss its Salvador Dalí Museum.

Now head west for the barrier islands. Take their full measure by spending one day on unspoiled **Honeymoon and Caladesi Islands**, then enjoy the hyper, activity-fueled atmosphere of **St Pete Beach**.

Next, drive down to **Sarasota** for three days. You'll need that long to take in the magnificent Ringling Museum Complex, the orchid-rich Marie Selby Botanical Gardens, perhaps catch the opera and still allow plenty of time to build sandcastles on the amazing white-sand beaches of **Siesta Key**. If you have extra time, visit **Myakka River State Park** and kayak among the alligators.

Then skip down to **Fort Myers** for two days of regional exploring. Take the ferry to **Cayo Costa Island** for a beach of unforgettable solitude, or go the party route and hit the crowded strands of **Fort Myers Beach**.

You need to save at least two days for **Sanibel Island**. World famous for its shelling, it's also a bike-friendly island stocked with great eats and wildlife-filled bays ripe for kayaking.

Finally, end with two to three days in **Naples**, the quintessence of Gulf Coast beach towns: upscale, artistic, and welcoming of every age demographic, with perhaps all of Florida's most pristine city beach. You can eat and shop to your heart's content, and no question: fit in a day trip to the **Everglades**. It's easy – zip along the Tamiami Trail to **Shark Valley**, and take a tram tour or bike ride among the sawgrass plains and sometimes countless alligators.

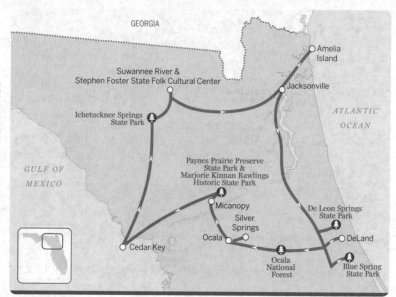

3 WEEKS North Florida Backroads

North Florida appeals to outdoor-lovers who prefer that days be filled with forests and springs and rivers and fishing, and that evenings be spent reliving these adventures around campfires.

Fly into **Jacksonville**, and spend the first day embracing the Atlantic Ocean on Jax beaches. For a full dose of Florida's Southern personality, have dinner at Clark's Fish Camp and see a show at Freebird Live.

Drive south to small-town-idyllic **DeLand**. Explore **Blue Spring State Park**, which attracts manatees in winter, or **De Leon Springs State Park** and its crystal-springs kayaking. The big daddy down here is the **Ocala National Forest**, with epic hiking and biking through Florida's fascinating limestone karst terrain.

Next, scoot over to **Ocala**. Here, the Old Florida glass-bottom boat tours of **Silver Springs** and high-revving dragster energy of the Don Garlits Museums beckon. Then go north to **Micanopy**, 'the town that time forgot,' for more eerie hikes at **Paynes Prairie Preserve State Park** and a taste of Cracker history at **Marjorie Kinnan Rawlings Historic State Park**.

For the next two to four days, string together these outdoor highlights: drive to **Cedar Key**, where you can kayak among seabirds and unspoiled mangrove-fringed islands; further north is **Ichetucknee Springs State Park**, which warrants a half-day of tubing.

Save at least a day for a river trip along the **Suwannee River**, a muddy-brown moss-draped meander that's North Florida all over. Reserve ahead for a multiday river-camping trip, and visit the **Stephen Foster State Folk Cultural Center**.

Nothing personal, but it's clean-up time. Drive back to Jacksonville, and spend a final day or three on **Amelia Island**. Spoil yourself with a Victorian B&B and some gourmet seafood.

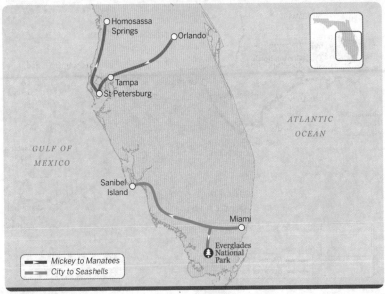

 *Mickey to Manatees*

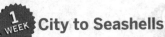 *City to Seashells*

Mickey to Manatees
1 WEEK

The kids want Disney, but Mom and Dad want beach time, a good meal and some culture. Oh, and you've only got a week.

Presto change-o – here you go! For the first three or four days, stay in **Orlando**. Rather than give in entirely to Walt Disney World, spend two days there and another day at Universal Orlando Resort, particularly if you've read any of those *Harry Potter* books.

For the next three or four days, hit Tampa Bay. On one day in **Tampa** choose between its tremendous zoo and aquarium and its fantastic museums, then end in historic Ybor City, for Spanish cuisine with a side of flamenco. In **St Petersburg**, even kids will find the Salvador Dalí Museum intriguing. Then squeeze in a day trip north for the mermaid shows at Weeki Wachee and the manatees of **Homosassa Springs**. Everybody's happy!

City to Seashells
1 WEEK

Geez, you really don't want to miss sexy, high-energy Miami, but if you don't get some sandy, leave-me-alone-with-my-novel downtime you'll never make it when you return to work in [insert name of major metropolis here]. Oh, and you've only got a week.

Presto change-o – here you go! Spend the first three days in **Miami** and have a party. Tour the art-deco-district hotels, enjoy the sophisticated art museums, shop for tailored shirts and racy designer dresses, and prance past the velvet ropes to celebrity-spot and dance all night to Latin hip-hop.

Next, spend one day peering at alligators through dark sunglasses in the **Everglades**, just so everyone back home won't be all 'What? You went to Florida and didn't even *go?*'

For the last three days, chill on **Sanibel Island**. Get a hotel on a private stretch of beach and do nothing but sun, sleep, read and collect handfuls of beautiful seashells as you kick along. Maybe take a bike ride and have a gourmet dinner. But each night, dig your toes in the sand and enjoy the setting sun in romantic solitude.

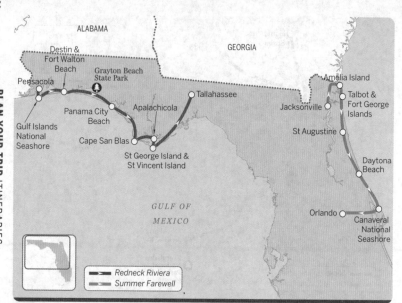

ALABAMA

GEORGIA

Destin &
Fort Walton
Beach
Grayton Beach
State Park
Pensacola
Amelia Island
Talbot &
Fort George
Islands
Tallahassee
Jacksonville
Panama City
Beach
Apalachicola
Gulf Islands
National
Seashore
St Augustine
Cape San Blas
St George Island &
St Vincent Island
Daytona
Beach

GULF OF
MEXICO

Orlando
Canaveral
National
Seashore

Redneck Riviera
Summer Farewell

10 DAYS Redneck Riviera

Sure, Florida's Panhandle gets rowdy, yet there's family-friendly warmth and unexpected sophistication along with its spectacular bone-white beaches.

Start your tour with a few days in **Pensacola**. Relax on the beaches of the **Gulf Islands National Seashore**, and enjoy Pensacola's historic village and its naval aviation history. The Blue Angels may even put on a show.

Spend another two days in the tourist towns of **Destin** and **Fort Walton Beach**, but don't miss the world-class sand of **Grayton Beach State Park**. If you have kids, a day among the hyperactive boardwalk amusements of **Panama City Beach** is virtually a must.

Afterward, shuffle along to the secluded wilderness of **Cape San Blas** and quaint **Apalachicola**, whose romantic historic village is perhaps not what you were expecting. The local specialty? Delectably fresh oysters.

St George and **St Vincent Islands** provide more secluded getaways, but if time is short, spend your last day around **Tallahassee**. Unwind and get a little rowdy in some local live-music joints.

10 DAYS Summer Farewell

Let's say you want the warmest weather but the fewest people. Hello, September! This trip is good anytime, but Florida's north is particularly sweet as school starts and summer fades.

Fly into **Jacksonville**, but don't hesitate: go straight to **Amelia Island** for several days of romantic B&Bs, luscious food and pretty sand. The good vibes continue as you kayak and explore the undeveloped beaches of **Talbot and Fort George Islands**, just south.

Then spend two to three days in **St Augustine**. America's oldest city preserves its heritage very well, with plenty of pirate tales enlivening the Spanish forts and basilicas.

When you've had enough of fine dining and costumed reenactors, spend a few days in **Daytona Beach**. High-octane thrills include the Speedway as well as the activity-filled beach scene. Perhaps you will even spy nesting sea turtles.

At this point, you've filled a week, but a few more days means more kayaking in **Canaveral National Seashore**, and perhaps a day or two in the theme parks of **Orlando**. Where are the kids when they're not in school? In line.

Plan Your Trip
Theme Park Trip Planner

Walt Disney World and Universal Orlando Resort draw millions of visitors to Orlando, the theme-park capital of the world, every year, and there are a handful of lesser-known parks beyond their gates. Here's the bottom line on what's what and how to tackle them.

Florida's Theme Parks
Walt Disney World

Walt Disney World (WDW) encompasses 40 sq miles and includes four completely separate and distinct theme parks, all with rides and shows: Magic Kingdom, Epcot, Hollywood Studios and Animal Kingdom. There are also two water parks (Typhoon Lagoon and Blizzard Beach), more than 20 hotels, almost 140 restaurants, and two shopping and nightlife districts (Downtown Disney and Disney's BoardWalk), as well as four golf courses, two miniature-golf courses, lagoons with water sports, and a spectator-sports complex, all connected by a system of free buses, boats and monorails.

For classic Disney at its best, head to the iconic Magic Kingdom, home to Cinderella's Castle, fairy-tale rides and quintessential Disney parades, shows and fireworks. Garden-filled Epcot is another favorite; one half is themed around technology and the future, and the other features recreated countries of the world spread along a small lake. Hollywood Studios offers some don't-miss highlights, but they're peppered among filler and muffled by *Hannah Montana* and *American Idol*–style energy. Africa-inspired Animal Kingdom fuses rides and shows with zoo encounters, animal conservation and, oddly, a dash of dinosaur. This is where you'll find *Finding Nemo: The Musical,* one of Disney's best live performances.

When to Go
Peak Periods

Crowds and prices soar during US school vacations, including summer (June through August), spring break (March through mid-April), Thanksgiving weekend (late November) and, especially, the week between Christmas and New Year's. If at all possible, do not visit during these high seasons.

Slow Times

The slowest times are mid-January through February, September through mid-October, the first half of May, and the few weeks in between Thanksgiving weekend and mid-December.

Special Events

Some events worth planning for are the Epcot International Food & Wine Festival (late September through early November), Mickey's Very Merry Christmas Party (November to mid-December), and Universal Orlando's Halloween Horror Nights (October).

Universal Orlando Resort

In contrast to WDW, Universal Orlando is a more intimate and walkable complex, with two excellent theme parks (Islands of Adventure and Universal Studios), four first-rate resorts, and a carnival-like restaurant and nightlife district (CityWalk), connected by gardened paths and a quiet wooden boat shuttle.

Universal's theme parks offer shamelessly silly, laugh-out-loud 'wow' for the whole family, with some of Orlando's best thrills, incredibly designed simulated experiences and water rides that leave you soaked.

At Islands of Adventure, each section has its own distinct tone and vibe. Seuss Landing surrounds visitors with the characters and landscapes of the celebrated children's books, and the Wizarding World of Harry Potter – Hogsmeade has proven a well-deserved runaway hit.

Universal Studios, just next door, has primarily movie- and TV-themed rides and scheduled shows, emphasizing comic-book superheroes and contemporary favorites like *Despicable Me* and *The Simpsons,* but it also has a sweet Barney Show, a mini-museum dedicated to Lucille Ball and an excellent kids' play area. In the summer of 2014, Universal Studios unveiled Diagon Alley, a much-anticipated expansion of Potter-themed attractions. Guests with tickets for both theme parks can ride the Hogwarts Express through the British countryside between Hogsmeade and Diagon Alley.

Other Orlando Parks

In Orlando, roughly equidistant from Disney and Universal are three major parks, clustered together, all owned by the same parent company:

ESSENTIAL THEME-PARK STRATEGIES

In Advance...

➡ **Purchase advance tickets** While ticket prices at Disney are always the same, prices for other parks cost $10 to $20 less if purchased in advance and certain tickets change day-by-day. Online calendars allow you to peruse prices over several months.

➡ **Purchase multiple day-admission tickets and be flexible** It's absolutely exhausting tackling the parks at 110% day after day. You'll better enjoy the fun if you allow room for down-time by the pool or beyond.

➡ **Reserve Disney's FastPass+ attractions up to 60 days in advance** This guarantees a short wait at three rides or character spots per day through the separate 'Fastpass+ line.' Note that you cannot reserve attractions until you have purchased theme-park tickets.

➡ **Reserve Disney dining up to 180 days in advance** Select a few don't-miss eating experiences as the backbone of your Disney plans, and be sure to take location into consideration.

➡ **Stay at an on-site resort if going to Universal Orlando's Wizarding World of Harry Potter** The quality of the accommodations, amenities and service, combined with the time- and stress-saving perks they offer plus easy access to the parks, make this a no-brainer if you can swing it. On-site guests can enter Harry Potter–themed attractions one hour earlier than the general public.

Once There...

➡ **Arrive early** Come before park gates open, march straight to popular rides before lines get long, and consider leaving by lunch, when crowds are worst. This probably won't work every day, but a few efficient mornings make a palpable difference.

➡ **Pack snacks** Something as simple as peanut-butter sandwiches and an apple stuffed in your bag will save time, money and stress.

➡ **Factor travel time** When planning each day, carefully consider travel to and within the parks. At Disney especially, transportation logistics can waste hours and leave you drained.

→ **SeaWorld** (p232) Fantastic marine animal shows, a handful of great rides including a charming tiny tot section, and animal-interaction programs.

→ **Aquatica** (p235) Water park with a marine animal twist.

→ **Discovery Cove** (p236) All-day package includes unlimited snorkeling, beachside lagoon swimming, lazy river floats through an aviary and optional swimming with dolphins.

Other Orlando parks include:

→ **Gatorland** (p237) Old Florida throwback favorite that's an extravaganza of alligators – feed them hot dogs, watch kitschy gator shows and zip-line over the park.

→ **Wet 'n Wild** (p237) Another extremely popular Orlando water park, owned by and just down the road from Universal Orlando Resort.

Around Orlando

→ **Legoland** (p240) In Winter Haven about 45 minutes south of Disney, Florida's newest theme park aims at the 12-and-under set.

→ **Kennedy Space Center** (p311) On the Atlantic Coast about an hour's drive from Orlando and next to the wild beaches of Canaveral National Seashore, it makes for a fascinating all-day immersion in the US space program, but there are no traditional rides.

Tampa Bay Area

→ **Busch Gardens** (p376) African-themed wildlife encounters, various shows and musical entertainment, and some of the state's wildest roller coasters.

→ **Adventure Island** (p377) Top-notch water park adjacent to and owned by Busch Gardens.

→ **Weeki Wachee Springs** (p395) One hour north of Tampa, this Old Florida original is world-famous for its spangly-tailed, long-haired mermaid shows. Plus, there's a small spring-fed water park, animal presentations and river canoeing.

Tickets

At Disney and Universal, per-day theme-park admission costs plummet the more days you buy; go to park websites for details on current specials, accommodation packages and dining plans that can save loads.

You do not need admission to enter the resort complexes themselves. Admission tickets are only required to get into the theme and water parks, and there are all kinds of entertainment and activities beyond theme-park gates (especially at WDW).

Prices are without tax, children aged three to nine cost about $10 less, and kids under three are free. Multiday tickets are good anytime within 14 days of the first visit, and expire 14 days after first use.

Walt Disney World

Base tickets, called Magic Your Way in Disney jargon, range from one to 10 days ($94 to $354) and allow unlimited entry to any one of Disney's four parks per day. To this, you can *add* one-time purchase options:

→ **Park Hopper** ($49-60) Allows you to 'hop' between all four WDW parks within one day and for the length of your base ticket.

→ **Water Park Fun & More** ($60) For each day of base ticket, this gives one pass to your choice of Disney's two water parks, two miniature-golf courses, the 9-hole walking golf course, DisneyQuest or ESPN Wide World of Sports, to be used any time and in any combination. For example, if you have a five-day ticket and have purchased this option, you can go to a water park and miniature golf one day and a water park the second day, and you will have used three of your five designated passes. Counterintuitively, the price is the same whether you add it to a two-day or a 10-day ticket.

→ **Park Hopper and Water Park Fun & More** ($86) Save money by combining the above two options.

Universal Orlando Resort

Universal Orlando tickets come in one- to four-day Single Park or Park-to-Park tickets; note that in order to ride the Hogwarts Express directly between the two sections of the Wizarding World of Harry Potter, you must purchase a *Park-to-Park* ticket.

The Express Pass, purchased separately from park admission, allows access to a separate Express Pass line that rarely has a wait longer than 15 minutes. Guests at any of Universal Orlando Resort's three recommended deluxe hotels automatically receive an Unlimited Express Pass, which means you can use the Express Pass line at the same ride again and again.

➤ **Single Park Ticket** ($96-160) Unlimited entrance to one theme park each day.

➤ **Park-to-Park Ticket** ($136-196) Unlimited entrance to both parks each day.

➤ **Park-to-Park Ticket plus Unlimited Express** ($190-420) Prices vary according to season; a one-day ticket ranges from $190 to $225, and a four-day ticket from $340 to $420. When you purchase this option online, a calender shows day-to-day prices as well as black-out dates, and you must *reserve a specific day as your first day.*

➤ **Park-to-Park Ticket plus Wet 'n Wild** ($212-232) Includes admission to Universal's water park, a 15-minute walk from the theme parks.

In addition, there are add-on options:

➤ **Express Pass** (single park $35-70/ park-to-park $40-90) Access to the Express Pass line *one time per ride.* Quantities are limited, price is based on demand, and you must purchase a separate Express Pass for each specific day of your visit. Between Christmas and New Year's, prices soar to about $120.

➤ **CityWalk Dining, Movies and Mini-Golf** Various packages for clubs and entertainment at CityWalk.

SeaWorld, Aquatica, Discovery Cove & Busch Gardens Tampa

➤ **SeaWorld** ($92) Seasonal midweek tickets can be significantly less.

➤ **Aquatica** ($56) The Splash & Save (from $28) requires the advance purchase of a specific date for your visit.

➤ **Discovery Cove** Rates vary by day, season and demand, like airline tickets. The only difference between the Resort Package ($129-169) and the Dolphin Swim Package ($169-319) is that the latter includes a 30-minute dolphin interaction. *Both tickets include unlimited 14-day admission to Aquatica and SeaWorld.*

➤ **Busch Gardens** ($92) See website for packages that include admission to Adventure Island water park.

The following combination tickets offer unlimited access over 14 consecutive days: SeaWorld & Aquatica ($119); SeaWorld & Busch Gardens ($130); SeaWorld, Aquatica & Busch Gardens ($150, including complimentary advanced-reservation bus between Busch Gardens and SeaWorld).

MYMAGIC+

MyMagic+ is Disney's three-fold system designed to help guests both plan and navigate their Disney vacation. It includes My Disney Experience, FastPass+ and MagicBands.

➤ **My Disney Experience** Accessible through the Walt Disney World website (www.disneyworld.disney.go.com) and the free app, My Disney Experience allows guests to create itineraries for visits to WDW. Once you create an account, you can link family and friends, view all your room and ticket reservations, make dining reservations, reserve FastPass+ selections, peruse current character spots and parade times, view wait times and more.

➤ **FastPass+** An electronic system that allows theme-park guests to reserve access to FastPass+ lines for rides, character spots, movies and other attractions either through My Disney Experience or at kiosks inside the theme parks. You reserve a one-hour window, arrive at the attraction within that window, scan your ticket at the FastPass+ line and va-voom, you zip right onto the ride with minimal wait. Though you can reserve only three attractions per day in advance, once you have used all three of your FastPass+ reservations for the day, you can reserve more same-day attractions if there are reservations available. Note that a FastPass+ for a show does not guarantee a specific seat.

➤ **MagicBand** This rubber-like wristband electronically stores all your dining, entertainment and FastPass+ reservations, functions as a theme-park ticket and, if you are staying at a Disney hotel, serves as a room key and a room charge at hotels, restaurants and stores throughout WDW. MagicBands will be sent to Disney hotel guests in advance of their visit, or will be waiting upon arrival. If you're staying at an off-site hotel, you can purchase a MagicBand for $13; if you don't have a MagicBand, your FastPass+ reservations will be stored in your paper ticket.

Top: Kumba roller coaster (p377), Busch Gardens Tampa

Bottom: Spaceship Earth, Epcot (p269), Walt Disney World

WENDELL METZEN / GETTY IMAGES ©

Purchase Quick Queue Unlimited at SeaWorld ($19 to $30) and Busch Gardens ($35 to $60) for front-of-the-line access.

Orlando FlexTicket

The Orlando FlexTicket (adult/child $324/304) gives 14-day unlimited entry to CityWalk clubs, Universal Studios, Islands of Adventure, Wet 'n Wild, SeaWorld and Aquatica. Add Tampa's Busch Gardens for about $40 more. Look online for discounts.

Staying in the Resorts

Disney and Universal provide great perks for their hotel guests and both offer budget accommodations, so if you'll be spending several days exploring their parks, there's no compelling reason not to stay on-site.

If, however, you choose to stay off-site, resorts and national chains surround the parks, and many offer theme-park packages. Convenient locations to Disney parks are Lake Buena Vista, Kissimmee and the town of Celebration. International Drive is more convenient for Universal Orlando Resort and SeaWorld. Most hotels offer shuttles to some or all of the theme parks, but be warned that they can be a pain. They leave at prearranged times, make lots of stops, often require advance booking, and, for Disney in particular, you may need to take additional Disney transportation once the hotel shuttle drops you off. Always ask for *precise details* about shuttle logistics.

Disney and Universal hotel rates vary wildly by season and demand, as do hotel rates in Orlando in general, and prices can change (as in hundreds of dollars) within 24 hours. Stay flexible, be persistent and always ask about packages and specials. Most hotels sleep at least four at no extra charge and several have bunk beds, suites and villas to accommodate larger parties.

Walt Disney World Resort Hotels

With two dozen resort hotels, Disney has lodging for every budget, from camping to villas, from motel-style complexes to full-service resorts. You're paying for convenience, location, recreational amenities and theming; quality-wise, except for the very best deluxe resorts, rooms are no better than good midrange chains elsewhere, and even the most expensive options pale in comparison to comparably priced luxury resorts elsewhere in Florida.

Guest Perks

➜ **Extra Magic Hours** Each day, one theme park opens early and closes late for guests at Disney hotels only.

➜ **FastPass+ Advanced Reservations** Reserve a one-hour window to FastPass+ lines at three attractions per person, per day up to 60 days in advance, thus slashing wait times. Guests staying off-site can reserve attractions up to 30 days in advance. This doesn't seem like much, but it makes a difference.

➜ **Disney transportation** Despite the frustration of tackling Disney buses, boats and monorails, they can be more convenient than off-site hotel shuttles.

➜ **Free parking** No fee at theme parks or hotels.

➜ **Disney's Magical Express** Complimentary baggage handling and deluxe bus transportation from Orlando International Airport.

➜ **Baggage transfer** If you change to a different Disney hotel during your stay, leave your bags in the morning and they'll be at your new hotel by evening.

➜ **Dining plans** Only resort guests have access to the meal plans.

Universal Orlando Resort Hotels

Universal has only four resort hotels, but they are top quality, extremely well situated within their more-intimate resort, and highly recommended.

Guest Perks

➜ **Early admission to Wizarding World of Harry Potter** Theme-park gates open one hour early for access to Harry Potter–themed attractions.

➜ **Unlimited Express Pass** Up to five guests per room at Universal's three deluxe resort hotels automatically receive unlimited access to Express Pass lines. This is a huge plus, worth hundreds of dollars, but note that the two major attractions at the Wizarding World of Harry Potter do not have Express Pass lines.

➜ **Universal transportation** Small boats run between the parks and deluxe resort hotels, and there's complimentary shuttle service to Cabana Bay (an on-site resort), Wet 'n Wild, Aquatica and SeaWorld.

➜ **Priority Seating** Deluxe-resort guests get first-available seating at select restaurants.

WEBSITES & APPS

Google 'WDW' and you'll find pages upon pages of websites with detailed menus, crowd calenders, touring plans, photographs, discounts and more, and there are dozens and dozens of apps to help you navigate the parks in real-time. While it's easy to get buried in and stressed by information overload, they can be helpful. Here are some of our favorites – all but two offer both apps and websites:

➡ **Walt Disney World** (www.disneyworld.disney.go.com) Official WDW website.

➡ **Universal Orlando Resort** (www.universalorlando.com) Official Universal website.

➡ **SeaWorld Parks** (www.seaworldparks.com) Official SeaWorld parks website.

➡ **My Disney Experience** (www.disneyworld.disney.go.com) Indispensible Disney app for creating WDW itineraries; reserve FastPass+ and meal reservations.

➡ **Orlando Informer** (www.orlandoinformer.com) Go-to for all things Universal Orlando, including crowd calender.

➡ **Theme Park Insider** (www.themeparkinsider.com) News from theme parks around the world, with painstaking details.

➡ **Undercover Tourist** (www.undercovertourist.com) Disney, Universal and Sea-World discounts, car rental, wait times etc.

➡ **All Ears** (www.allears.net) Menus and advice.

➡ **WDW Info** (www.wdwinfo.com) Go-to source.

➡ **MouseSavers** (www.mousesavers.com) Money-saving tips.

➡ **Our Laughing Place** (www.ourlaughingplace.com) WDW Transportation Wizard (TW) plots best routes. Several apps, including planning, TW and dining.

➡ **Mom's Panel** (https://disneyparksmomspanel.disney.go.com) Perky Disney-sponsored discussion boards run by moms. Website only.

➡ **Touring Plans** (https://touringplans.com) Tips on best use of FastPass+.

➡ **Disney Tourist Blog** (www.disneytouristblog.com) Ride guides and more. Website only.

Dining & Character Meals

Eating at the theme parks falls into two general categories: quick service (a euphemism for 'fast-food') and table service. Beyond this, your primary considerations are price, quality and theming fun. Sip on a Flaming Moe or Butterbeer at Universal Orlando Resort, eat under asteroid showers or in a mock drive-in theater at WDW, watch giraffes and ostriches over African fare at Disney's Animal Kingdom Lodge. At Disney's Epcot, it's particularly fun to sample food and drink from around the world.

Beyond Disney and Universal, the creative twists to dining fade. There's certainly a nod to healthy and interesting, but generally it's the usual over-priced burgers and pizza served cafeteria-style. With the exception of Magic Kingdom, which serves alcohol at only one restaurant (wine and beer only), you'll find plenty of tantalizing cocktails and cold beer throughout the parks.

Disney allows table-service restaurant reservations 180 days in advance, and for a Disney character meal, dinner show, or some of the more popular restaurants, you'll need to reserve the moment your 180-day window opens. Seriously. Some of the most coveted seats include Cinderella's Royal Table (p271) inside the Castle, the *Beauty and the Beast*–themed Be Our Guest (p283), dinner at California Grill (p287) with fireworks views, and the ultra-chic no-kids-allowed Victoria and Albert's (p287). Always ask about cancellation policies; generally, you can cancel with no penalty up to 24 hours in advance.

Snagging a table at Universal isn't nearly the trouble it is at Disney. Each park has two table-service restaurants that take advance reservations, and there are only three character dining options.

Note that restaurants inside theme parks require theme-park admission, but there are plenty of excellent ones, including several that offer character meals, at entertainment districts and resort hotels in both WDW and Universal Orlando Resort.

Plan Your Trip

Travel with Children

The Sunshine State makes it so easy for families to have a good time that many return year after sandy, sunburned year. But with so many beaches, theme parks and kid-perfect destinations and activities, the challenge is deciding exactly where to go and what to do.

Best Regions for Kids

Orlando
Spinning wheel of theme-park fun and oodles of family entertainment beyond their gates.

Tampa Bay & Gulf Coast
Great zoos, aquariums and museums, plus some of Florida's prettiest, most family-friendly beaches and alluring island getaways.

Florida Keys
Snorkeling, diving, fishing, boating and all-around no-worries vibe.

Space Coast (Hwy A1A)
World-class surfing, nature preserves and sleepy beach towns combine with vintage airplanes and all-things-space to make this 75-mile stretch of barrier islands a favorite.

Emerald Coast
Panhandle coastline with stunningly white sand beaches, crystal water and pockets of frenetic boardwalk amusements.

Miami
Kid-focused zoos and museums, but also Miami itself, one of the USA's great multicultural cities.

Florida for Kids

Kids love Florida. And what's not to like? Sandcastles and waves, dolphins and alligators, Cinderella and Harry Potter. There are the classics and the don't misses, the obvious and the cliché, but just as memorable, and often far less stressful and less expensive, are the distinctly Floridian under-the-radar discoveries. Roadside attractions, mom-and-pop animal rescues, intimate wildlife expeditions, street festivals and more...and when you've had enough, there's plenty of opportunities to do a whole lot of nothing in the sun.

Theme Parks

The self-contained resort complexes of Walt Disney World and Universal Orlando Resort offer multiple theme and water parks, on-site hotels and transportation systems, and just beyond their gates you'll find SeaWorld, Discovery Cove and Legoland; the only big-hitter theme park beyond Orlando is Busch Gardens.

To do theme parks justice, they have their own chapter (see p33). This chapter focuses on all the *other* things families can do in Florida.

Beaches

While the prototypical Florida family beach is fronted by crowded commercial centers, you'll find loads of beaches that echo that quintessential Old Florida feel. Many are protected in state parks, wildlife preserves and island sanctuaries, and there are pockets of road-trip-perfect coastline, with mile upon mile of beautiful emptiness dotted with flip-flop friendly low-rise towns. Remember that there's a distinct difference between Gulf and Atlantic beaches – many find the shallows and gentle surf of the Gulf perfect for little ones, but Atlantic ones often lie on barrier islands that are flanked by calm water rivers and inlets to the west. Currents can be dangerously strong along both coasts; always pay attention to rip-tide warnings.

Zoos & Museums

Up-close animal encounters have long been a Florida tourist staple, and the state has some of the best zoos and aquariums in the country as well as all kinds of small-scale jewels and Old Florida favorites that offer hands-on interactions and quirky shows. Florida's cities also have top-quality children's museums, and art museums and centers throughout the state almost always offer excellent kids' programs.

Getting into Nature

It's easy to get out into nature in Florida – there are wilderness preserves and state parks up and down the state, and you don't have to drive far, hike long or paddle hard to get away from it all. Best part is, once you get there, you're almost guaranteed to see some pretty cool critters.

Florida is exceedingly flat, so rivers and trails are frequently ideal for short legs and little arms. Placid rivers and intercoastal bays are custom-made for first-time paddlers, and often are so shallow and calm you can just peek over the boat and see all kinds of marine life. Never snorkeled or surfed? Florida has gentle places to learn. Book a sea-life cruise, a manatee swim or nesting-sea-turtle watch, or simply stroll along raised boardwalks through alligator-filled swamps, perfect for pint-size adventurers.

Children's Highlights

Believe it or not, these extensive highlights merely cherry-pick the best of the best.

Family Beach Towns

On the Atlantic...

➡ **St Augustine** (p335) Pirates, forts, jails and reenactors.

➡ **Daytona Beach** (p327) Tons of Southern-fried activities and amusements, ATVs on the beach, water park.

➡ **Cocoa Beach** (p315) Surfing rattle-and-hum energy along the Atlantic with lessons for kids and easy access to lovely Banana River kayaking.

➡ **Vero Beach** (p322) Carefully zoned with grassy parks, a pedestrian-friendly downtown and wide, life-guarded beaches.

➡ **Indialantic** (p320) Flip-flop Old Florida beach life with a BoHo vibe.

➡ **Lauderdale-by-the-Sea** (p197) Less snooty than towns just south; great butterfly park.

➡ **Stuart** (p222) For outdoors-eager families, plus getaway beaches and a Smithsonian Marine Station on Hutchinson Island.

➡ **Amelia Island** (p353) Easygoing and upscale.

On the Gulf...

➡ **Anna Maria Island** (p404) Old Florida, with low-rise beachfront, independent hotels and an historic fishing pier.

➡ **Florida Keys** (p154) The whole island chain brims with activities for all ages; check out the street performances at Key West's Mallory Sq.

➡ **Naples** (p420) Upscale downtown bustles each evening; easy access to miles of beautiful wide beaches.

➡ **Sanibel Island** (p417) Bike, kayak and shell the days away; undeveloped beaches but no pedestrian-friendly downtown.

➡ **Siesta Key** (p403) Crescent of soft white sand, plenty of activities and a lively village scene at night.

➡ **Fort Myers Beach** (p415) Party atmosphere, lots to do, yet quieter beaches just south (we like Lovers Key State Park).

➡ **Gasparilla Island** (p408) Intimate, easy, and blissfully free of high-rises and chain restaurants and hotels; ditch the car and toot around in a golf-cart.

➡ **St Pete Beach** (p389) Activity-filled social epicenter of Tampa Bay area.

➡ **Pensacola Beach** (p428) Mix of unspoiled strands and low-key tourist center.

➡ **Fort Walton Beach & Destin** (p438) Family-perfect Panhandle beauty.

➡ **Apalachicola** (p448) Tiny historic fishing town on Apalachicola Bay; close to excellent beachside state parks.

Zoos

➜ **Lowry Park Zoo** (p371, Tampa) Fantastic zoo with up-close encounters.

➜ **Homosassa Springs Wildlife State Park** (p396, Gulf Coast, 70 miles north of Tampa) Old Florida don't-miss staple emphasizing Florida wildlife; underwater manatee observatory.

➜ **Zoo Miami** (p92, Miami) Extensive, with all the big-ticket species.

➜ **Monkey Jungle** (p93, Miami) The tagline 'Where humans are caged and monkeys run wild' says it all. Unforgettable classic, opened in 1933; don't miss the wild monkey swimming pool.

➜ **Jungle Island** (p93, Miami) Tropical birds and exotic species such as the liger, a tiger-and-lion crossbreed.

➜ **Lion Country Safari** (p213, West Palm Beach) An enormous drive-through safari park and rehabilitation center.

➜ **Brevard Zoo** (p320, Melbourne) On the Space Coast; little old-school favorite; feed giraffes and lorikeets.

Aquariums

➜ **Florida Aquarium** (p371, Tampa) Another stellar aquarium, with an excellent recreated swamp, swim programs and sea-life tours.

➜ **Mote Marine Laboratory** (p399, Sarasota) Visit sharks, manatees, dolphins and sea turtles up close at this center for shark study.

➜ **Clearwater Marine Aquarium** (p393) Intimate rehabilitation center and home to Winter, of *Dolphin Tale* fame; sea-life safari boat trips, dolphin encounters and more.

➜ **Florida Oceanographic Coastal Science Center** (p223, Stuart) 30 miles south of Vero Beach; great tanks and a sea-turtle-spotting program.

Nature Centers, Wildlife Parks & Preserves

➜ **Everglades National Park** (p140) Don't miss the Anhinga Trail, an easy boardwalk past alligators and beautiful birds; for family-friendly kayaking, head to Everglades City and Flamingo centers.

➜ **Marjory Stoneman Douglas Biscayne Nature Center** (p83, Key Biscayne) Kid-friendly intro to subtropical South Florida.

➜ **Environmental Learning Center** (p323, Vero Beach) Florida ecosystems and touch-tanks.

➜ **Loggerhead Marinelife Center** (p221, Juno Beach) 18 miles north of West Palm Beach; excellent little turtle rescue and rehabilitation center with children's programs.

➜ **McCarthy's Wildlife Sanctuary** (p217, West Palm Beach) First-rate animal rescue featuring endangered animals and discarded exotic pets in botanical surrounds and up-close interactions.

➜ **Florida Keys Eco-Discovery Center** (p172, Key West) Entertaining displays pull together Florida Keys ecology.

➜ **JN 'Ding' Darling National Wildlife Refuge** (p417, Sanibel Island) Easy tram tours and the park's education center is tops.

➜ **Nancy Forrester's Secret Garden** (p173, Key West) Intimate labor-of-love parrot rescue and rehab sanctuary in a private garden, with education, bird interaction and storytelling.

➜ **Naples Botanical Garden** (p421) Designed especially with kids in mind.

Wildlife Encounters on Land

➜ **National Key Deer Refuge** (p169, Big Pine Key, Florida Keys) Kids love spotting these cute-as-Bambi mini deer.

➜ **Bill Baggs Cape Florida State Park** (p83, Key Biscayne) Accessible island-ecology walk.

➜ **John D Macarthur State Park** (p220, West Palm Beach) Ranger-led sea-turtle watches, beautiful beaches, calm-water kayaking.

➜ **Corkscrew Swamp Sanctuary** (p420) 30 miles northeast of Naples; maybe the most diverse and rewarding swampy boardwalk trail.

➜ **Myakka River State Park** (p406, Sarasota) Tram and air-boat tours, canoeing, short hikes and hundreds of alligators.

➜ **Lee County Manatee Park** (p413, Fort Myers) Easy way to see wintering manatees.

➜ **Six Mile Cypress Slough Preserve** (p412, Fort Myers) Another ideal, shady boardwalk trail often packed with wildlife.

➜ **Paynes Prairie Preserve State Park** (p365, Gainesville) Hiking trails through prairies, woods and wetlands, with alligators, armadillo and more.

➜ **Leon Sinks Geological Area** (p458, Tallahassee) Bizarre sinkhole terrain is bound to make an impression.

➜ **St George Island State Park** (p450, Apalachicola) Loggerhead nesting.

➜ **Merritt Island National Wildlife Refuge** (p312, Cocoa Beach) Black Point Wildlife Dr and excellent visitors center.

➡ **Butterfly World** (p198, Coconut Creek, outside Lauderdale-by-the-Sea) Sanctuary of butterflies and exotic birds.

Wildlife Encounters by Water

➡ **Biscayne National Park** (p152, Homestead) 30 miles south of Miami; glass-bottom boat tours, snorkeling over epic reef.

➡ **John Pennekamp Coral Reef State Park** (p159, Key Largo, Florida Keys) Great coral reefs, by snorkel or glass-bottom boat tour.

➡ **Loxahatchee River** (p222, Jupiter) 20 miles north of West Palm Beach; one of Florida's two National Wild and Scenic Rivers, this placid eight-mile river is great for kayaking and canoeing.

➡ **Canaveral National Seashore** (p313, Titusville) 35 miles south of Daytona; easy paddling on the Indian River and sea-turtle watches along 24 miles of undeveloped Atlantic Coast beaches.

➡ **Crystal River National Wildlife Refuge** (p396) Eighty miles north of Tampa; legendary manatee spot where you can boat and swim among them.

➡ **Ichetucknee Springs State Park** (p367, Fort White) 37 miles northwest of Gainesville; inner-tube along crystal-clear slow-moving water with manatees, otters and turtles.

➡ **Blue Spring State Park** (p358, Deland) 35 miles north of Orlando; canoe and cruise among manatees.

➡ **Suwannee River State Park** (p461) 75 miles east of Tallahassee; great muddy river dotted with crystal-clear springs for swimming.

➡ **Dolphin Study** (p422, Naples) Dolphin-spotting ecotours.

➡ **Fin Expeditions** (p317, Cocoa Beach) Kayak through the mangroves with small-group nature tours tailor-made for kids.

Children's Museums

➡ **Glazer Children's Museum** (p372, Tampa) Charming interactive extravaganza.

➡ **Museum of Science & Industry** (p372, Tampa) Huge hands-on science fun, with an IMAX and planetarium.

➡ **Miami Children's Museum** (p93) Extensive role-playing environments.

➡ **Golisano Children's Museum of Naples** (p421) Modern facility geared towards kids under eight.

Planning

If you're a parent, you already know that luck favors the prepared. But in Florida's crazy-crowded, overbooked high-season tourist spots, a little bit of planning can make all the difference. Sort out where to go, where to stay, and a few pillars of plans to hang the trip on in advance – book that manatee cruise, schedule a day at the Kennedy Space Center, reserve a character-meal at Disney, but always check about cancellation policies. Once there, it may turn out that all anyone wants to do is play in the sun and sand.

PLAN YOUR TRIP TRAVEL WITH CHILDREN

FOSSIL HUNTING

Not all of Florida's wildlife encounters are with animals of the here and now. Much of central and southern Florida was underwater as recently as 100,000 years ago, and as a result, the rocks and sands of the state are teeming with remnants of ancient marine life. Look carefully and it's not hard to find fossilized shells of clams, sand dollars and corals. More rare, but not uncommon if you know where to look, are shark teeth (including those of the Megalodon, a school-bus-sized relative of the Great White) as well as bones of extinct Ice Age mammals.

Mark Renz, an expert on Florida fossils, has been leading family-friendly fossil-hunting expeditions for more than 20 years. Small-group kayak and river-walking trips with his **Fossil Expeditions** (☑239-368-3252; www.fossilexpeditions.com) include screen-washing and snorkeling in knee-deep water, and Mark is great with kids – even little ones enjoy digging around in the mud and muck. Trips are usually in streams between Arcadia and Wauchula, and in the Peace River, 45 to 70 miles north of Fort Myers.

BABYSITTING & CHILDCARE CENTERS

Traveling with children doesn't necessarily mean doing *everything* as a family. Several childcare services, including **Sunshine Babysitting** (www.sunshinebabysitting.com) and the Disney- and Universal-recommended Kid's Nite Out (p290), offer in-hotel babysitting by certified sitters, and full-service resorts often have childcare centers, organized kids' camps and local sitter recommendations. At Walt Disney World, you don't need to be a resort guest to reserve a spot at a Disney's Children Activity Center (p290); five centers, located at resort hotels, welcome kids aged three to 12.

Accommodations

Resorts & Hotels

The vast majority of Florida hotels stand ready to aid families. They have cribs, rollaway beds and sleeper-sofas, suites and adjoining rooms, refrigerators and microwaves, and most do not charge extra for kids under 18. Most full-service resorts offer children's programs, including beach-walks, art activities and educational workshops exploring Florida sea life, and at theme-park hotels in Orlando you'll find poolside screenings of family-friendly movies.

Properties catering specifically to families are marked by a family-friendly icon (⚄).

Renting a House or Condo

Though staying in a hotel may feel like more of a vacation for harried parents, and it's awfully nice to have room service, on-site children's activities and daily housekeeping services, renting a private house or condo can save thousands of dollars. And it can, in fact, ultimately be much more relaxing than staying in a hotel. You have plenty of room to spread out, you don't have to worry about eating in restaurants for every meal, and many homes are right on the beach or boast private pools. On top of that, Florida is particularly overflowing with vacation-home rentals – you'll find options in every nook and cranny of the state, from riverside cabins to urban bungalows to Mickey-themed extravaganzas. Be sure to peruse the listing details carefully and always ask about cancellation policies before committing to a rental.

➡ **VRBO** (www.vrbo.com) Reputable and user-friendly vacation-home rental.

➡ **Airbnb** (www.airbnb.com) Quirky and eclectic selection and your best bet for rentals of less than a week.

➡ **Home Away** (www.homeaway.com) Easy-to-use with a dizzying number of choices.

What to Bring

Pack light rain gear, a snuggly fleece (for air-conditioning and cool nights), water sandals (for beaches, fountains and water parks), mosquito repellent and a simple first-aid kit with band-aids, antibiotic cream, tweezers (for splinters), anti-itch cream, children's Tylenol and Vaseline (perfect for little faces after too much sun and wind). If you have infants, a pack-and-play can be helpful, especially if you're road-tripping or sticking to amenity-poor, budget-range motels.

Most importantly, bring and use sunscreen. We've tried them all, from thick white goos that never seem to rub in to fancy stuff from the cosmetic aisle, and our hands-down favorite is the made-in-Florida Sun Bum and their naturally-sourced Baby Bum line.

Florida car-seat laws require that children must be in a rear-facing car-seat until they are 20lb and one year, a separate or integrated child-safety seat until five, and a booster until the seat-belts fit properly (over 4ft 9in and 80lb). Rental-car companies are legally required to provide child seats, but only if you reserve them in advance. Avoid surprises by bringing your own.

Don't sweat it if you forget something. Except for your child's can't-sleep-without stuffed blue elephant and favorite blanket, you'll be able to find anything you need in Florida.

Renting Baby Gear

If you prefer to travel light and save the hassle of lugging loads of essentials, several services offer baby-gear rental (cribs, strollers, car seats etc) and infant supplies (diapers, baby food etc), all delivered to your hotel; some deliver to the airport.

➡ **Babies Travel Lite** (www.babiestravellite.com)

➡ **Baby's Away** (www.babysawayrentals.com)

➡ **Jet Set Babies** (www.jetsetbabies.com)

➡ **Traveling Baby Company** (www.travelingbabyco.com)

Regions at a Glance

Miami

Museums
Nightlife
Food

Museums & the Arts

Miami is practically a real-time performance-art piece. There are the major cultural institutions – the Bass, the Adrienne Arsht Center, the Lowe – as well as vibrant gallery districts such as Wynwood and architectural masterpieces such as South Beach's deco district.

Miami's Vice

Mix indulgence, a love of beauty, youth and good times and you get the Miami nightlife cocktail. It's not all glam celebrity-spotting, drag shows and bottle service. Authentic Cuban dancehalls and grotty dive bars keep things refreshingly real, while artsy bars and bohemian lounges are peppered throughout.

Ethnic/Gourmet

Miami offers an ideal gastronomic mix of wealth, immigrants and agricultural abundance. Trendy, celebrity-chef-driven laboratories of gourmet perfection dot Miami Beach and Coral Gables, and they are balanced out by hole-in-the-wall ethnic eateries that will leave you gasping for more.

p50

The Everglades

Wildlife-Watching
Activities
Old Florida

Find-the-Fauna

There are 1.5 million alligators in Florida, and in the Everglades, sometimes nearly half of them seem to be within a 100 yards. More than that, the Everglades can turn anyone into an avid amateur birder: more than 350 species call the swamps home.

Outdoor Adventures

Even a ramble along raised wooden boardwalks can feel like an adventure. Jump into a kayak or canoe and let yourself be swallowed by the Everglades' watery wilderness for an unforgettable – yet surprisingly easy – experience of a lifetime.

Roadside Attractions

Bizarre food, strange legends of mythical beasts, offbeat roadside stands, monuments to scorned love? Yep, all these and then some pepper the land in this part of the world, which happily marches to its own quirky beat.

p137

Florida Keys & Key West

Activities
Beaches
Nightlife

Islands & Outdoors

Except for drinking and partying, people come to the Keys to do stuff: fish, snorkel, dive, kayak, hike, bike, fish some more, snorkel again, feed tarpon, spot Key deer, hell, let's fish again. North America's best coral reefs provide brag-worthy expeditions.

Mangroves & Sand

Except for Bahia Honda, which often makes Florida's 'best beach' lists, Keys beaches aren't as uniformly perfect as elsewhere, and yet they provide all one needs: a comfortable place to sleep off the night before.

Crazy Key West

No nightlife scene in Florida matches Key West's peculiar mix of off-beat craziness, self-conscious performance, gay humor and drunken loutishness. Hemingway found his perfect bar at the end of the world here; maybe you can too.

p154

Southeast Florida

Beaches
Activities
Entertainment

Buttery Beaches

With monikers such as the Gold Coast and the Treasure Coast, you know where the money's at. Some of these towns – Palm Beach, Boca Raton, Fort Lauderdale – are so wealthy it's practically obscene. But do they take care of their beaches? Very well, thank you very much.

Sightseeing

Canal and gondola tours around Fort Lauderdale, river trips on the Loxahatchee, epic wreck diving, snorkeling Spanish galleons, good surfing, sportfishing charters, turtle watches: your menu is full of stuff to do in Southeast Florida.

Waterfront Fun

Southeast beach towns are simply good fun, whether people-watching along the Hollywood Broadwalk, partying in Fort Lauderdale bars, chilling out in Jupiter or simply gaping at the mansions of Palm Beach.

p185

Orlando & Walt Disney World

Theme Parks
Entertainment
Activities

Magic Kingdoms

If theme parks are worlds, then Orlando contains a veritable galaxy. Walt Disney World is itself a solar system of amusements; Universal Orlando Resort may be smaller but is equally entertaining and has a bit more attitude.

Family Parties

Start with Disney, which packs evenings with a magical light parade and Cirque du Soleil. Or maybe head to Universal, which dishes up a luau and the Blue Man Group. Orlando itself is rife with bars, movies and live music.

Outdoor Exploring

In and around Orlando are plentiful opportunities to bike, golf, kayak, go river tubing and even 'skydive' indoors, not to mention the water play at park resorts.

p226

The Space Coast

Activities
Beaches
History

Surfing & Kayaking

Surfing and kayaking are the Space Coast's unbeatable one-two punch, and when it comes to the former, Cocoa Beach is the scene's epicenter. Meanwhile, the wildlife to be seen among the protected, unspoiled lagoons and intercoastal waterways includes manatees, dolphins and more.

Cosmic Coast

Space Coast beaches are truly swell, with a relaxed and low-key vibe that you'll rarely find to the north or south. Seek out cute Vero Beach and escape on beautiful Apollo Beach.

Kennedy Space Center

The shuttle launches may have ended, but the Space Center is still a top-notch, immersive experience that throws you into the US space program and the life of an astronaut.

p308

Northeast Florida

Activities
Old Florida
Beaches

Outdoor Adventures

Ocala National Forest beckons with a veritable wealth of forested hikes, crystal springs, rivers and tons of camping. But the region's interior state parks are all prime, and there's splendid kayaking among northeast waterways.

Old & Oldest Florida

Old Florida can be found in Micanopy and Cross Creek, where Cracker (backwoods Florida pioneer) life is lovingly preserved in Marjorie Kinnan Rawlings Historic State Park. 'Oldest' Florida means Spanish-founded St Augustine, a splendid time warp back to the days of Spanish explorers, missionaries and real pirates of the Caribbean.

Sun & Sand

For romantic getaways, choose Amelia Island; for high-octane, amusement-rich family fun, pick Daytona. These beach towns bookend a string of great beaches in-between.

p325

Tampa Bay & Southwest Florida

Beaches
Food
Museums

Gulf Breezes

The Gulf Coast from Tampa south enjoys some of Florida's best white-sand beaches. There's too much to choose from, but Siesta Key, Fort Myers Beach, Honeymoon Island, Naples, Fort DeSoto, St Pete Beach and Sanibel are all great.

Coastal Cuisine

Tampa has a big-city foodie scene, with several gourmet destinations, and St Petersburg is no slouch. The sophisticated towns of Sarasota, Naples and Sanibel also provide their fair share of excellent cuisine.

Arts & Culture

The region has two of Florida's best museums – the Salvador Dalí Museum and the Ringling Museum complex – and each are worth trekking from Miami and Orlando to see. Yet sophisticated art and cultural institutions are highlights in Tampa, St Petersburg, Sarasota, Fort Myers and Naples, too.

p368

The Panhandle

Beaches
Activities
Entertainment

Country Coast

The Panhandle, dubbed the 'Redneck Riviera,' could just as easily be called 'pristine snow-white sands lapped by gentle emerald waters.' The beaches are unbelievably beautiful, and the sometimes raucous beach towns can be sought out or avoided as you wish.

Springs & Sinkholes

Kayaking the waterways around Cedar Key is wonderful, and canoeing the Suwannee River is classic Florida. Meanwhile, there's swimming, snorkeling and diving in crystal springs, and great hiking and biking in the Apalachicola National Forest. Seek out the sinkholes of Leon Sinks Geological Area.

Beaches & Blues

Enjoy the blues clubs of Tallahassee, the frantic boardwalk amusements of Panama City Beach, the glass-bottom boat tours of nature-as-entertainment Wakulla Springs State Park, and Pensacola's Blue Angels and beach-bar nightlife.

p425

On the Road

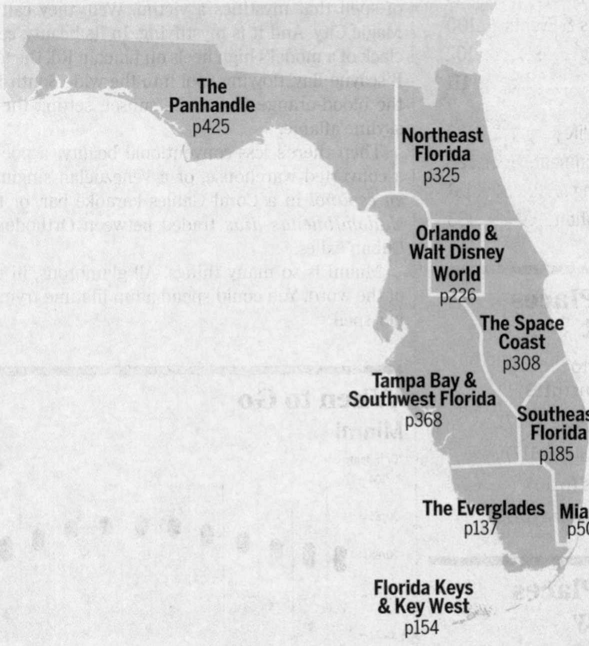

The Panhandle p425

Northeast Florida p325

Orlando & Walt Disney World p226

The Space Coast p308

Tampa Bay & Southwest Florida p368

Southeast Florida p185

The Everglades p137

Miami p50

Florida Keys & Key West p154

Miami

Best Places to Eat

➡ Exquisito Restaurant (p119)

➡ Chef Creole (p117)

➡ Blue Collar (p117)

➡ Choices (p116)

➡ Steve's Pizza (p115)

Best Places to Stay

➡ Shore Club (p106)

➡ Gale South Beach (p106)

➡ The Standard (p106)

➡ Raleigh Hotel (p106)

➡ Pelican Hotel (p104)

Why Go?

Miami is so many things, but to most visitors, it's mainly glamour, condensed into urban form.

They're right. The archaic definition of 'glamour' is a kind of spell that mystifies a victim. Well, they call Miami the Magic City. And it is mystifying. In its beauty, certainly: the clack of a model's high heels on Lincoln Rd, the teal sweep of Biscayne Bay, flowing cool into the wide South Florida sky; the blood-orange fire of the sunset, setting the downtown skyline aflame.

Then there's less-conventional beauty: a poetry slam in a converted warehouse, or a Venezuelan singing Metallica *en español* in a Coral Gables karaoke bar, or the passing *shalom/buenas días* traded between Orthodox Jews and Cuban exiles.

Miami is so many things. All glamorous, in every sense of the word. You could spend a fun lifetime trying to escape her spell.

When to Go
Miami

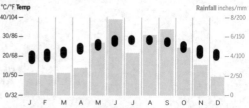

Jan–Mar Warm and dry, with lots of tourists: snowbirds from the northeast and Europeans.

Apr–Jun Not as muggy as deep summer, but lusher and greener than winter.

Jul–Oct Prices plummet. When it's not as hot as an oven, there are storms: it's hurricane season.

History

It's always been the weather that's attracted Miami's two most prominent species: developers and tourists. But it wasn't the sun per se that got people moving here – it was an ice storm. The great Florida freeze of 1895 wiped out the state's citrus industry; at the same time, widowed Julia Tuttle bought out parcels of land that would become modern Miami, and Henry Flagler was building his Florida East Coast Railroad. Tuttle offered to split her land with Flagler if he extended the railway to Miami, but the train man didn't pay her any heed until north Florida froze over and Tuttle sent him an 'I told you so' message: an orange blossom clipped from her Miami garden.

The rest is a history of boom, bust, dreamers and opportunists. Generally, Miami has grown in leaps and bounds following major world events and natural disasters. Hurricanes (particularly the deadly Great Miami Hurricane of 1926) have wiped away the town, but it just keeps bouncing and building back better than before. In the late 19th and early 20th centuries, Miami earned a reputation for attracting design and city-planning mavericks such as George Merrick, who fashioned the artful Mediterranean village of Coral Gables, and James Deering, designer of the fairy-tale Vizcaya mansion.

Miami Beach blossomed in the early 20th century when Jewish developers recognized the potential American Riviera in their midst. Those hoteliers started building resorts that were branded with a distinctive art-deco facade by daring architects willing to buck the more staid aesthetics of the northeast. The world wars brought soldiers who were stationed at nearby naval facilities, many of whom liked the sun and decided to stay. Latin American and Caribbean revolutions introduced immigrants from the other direction, most famously from Cuba. Cuban immigrants arrived in two waves: first, the anti-Castro types of the '60s, and those looking for a better life since the late 1970s, such as the arrivals on the 1980 Mariel Boatlift during a Cuban economic crisis. The glam and overconsumption of the 1980s, as shown in movies like *Scarface* and *Miami Beach,* attracted a certain breed of the rich and beautiful, and their associated models, designers, hoteliers and socialites, all of whom transformed South Beach into the beautiful beast it is today.

Political changes in Latin America continue to have repercussions in this most Latin of cities – as former mayor Manny Diaz once said, 'When Venezuela or Argentina sneezes, Miami catches a cold.' In the last half of the 'aughts,' Miami embarked on a Manhattanization of its skyline that – barring a brief pause from 2008 to 2010 due to the financial crisis – hasn't really let up. Miami has, as of this writing, the third-biggest skyline in the USA (after New York and Chicago), most clearly evident in the area around Brickell.

Maps

McNally, AAA and Dolph's all make great maps of the Miami area. The best free map is from the Greater Miami & the Beaches Convention & Visitors Bureau (p134).

◉ Sights

Miami's major sights aren't concentrated in one neighborhood. The most frequently visited area is South Beach, home to hot nightlife, beautiful beaches and art-deco hotels, but you'll find historic sites and museums downtown, art galleries in Wynwood and the Design District, old-fashioned hotels and eateries in Mid-Beach (in Miami Beach), more beaches on Key Biscayne, and peaceful neighborhood attractions in Coral Gables and Coconut Grove.

Water and income – canals, bays and bank accounts – are the geographic and social boundaries that divide Miami. Of course, the great water that divides here is Biscayne Bay, holding the city of Miami apart from its preening sibling Miami Beach (along with the fine feathers of South Beach). Don't forget, as many do, that Miami Beach is not Miami's beach, but its own distinct town.

◉ South Beach

The most iconic neighborhood in Greater Miami, South Beach encompasses the region south of 21st St in the city of Miami Beach, though hoteliers have been known to push that up as high as 40th St and on our maps it is below 23rd St. Collins Ave, the main artery, is famous for its long string of art-deco hotels. The chic outdoor cafes and restaurants of Ocean Dr overlook the wide Atlantic shorefront, while pedestrian-only Lincoln Rd Mall is a shopper's heaven. Anything south of 5th St is called 'SoFi.'

★**Art Deco Historic District** NEIGHBORHOOD
(Map p64) South Beach's heart is its Art Deco Historic District, from 18th St and south along Ocean Dr and Collins Ave. It's ironic that in a

Miami Highlights

① Mingling with the beautiful hipsters amid the jaw-dropping **Wynwood Walls** (p81) murals.

② Cigar smoke and dominoes; saying *bienvenido* a Little Havana in **Máximo Gómez Park** (p85).

③ Taking in a show at the gorgeous **Adrienne Arsht Center for the Performing Arts** (p76).

④ Splashing about the faux grottoes and coral cliffs in the magnificent **Venetian Pool** (p89).

⑤ Dancing to Caribbean beats and chowing down on curried conch and goat at the monthly **Big Night in Little Haiti** (p81).

ATLANTIC OCEAN

A1A

Golden Beach

Collins Ave

Aventura

Oleta River State Park

Collins Ave

Collins Ave

Indian Creek

Dade Blvd

Alton Rd

See Northern Miami Beach Map (p72)

JFK/79th St Causeway

Ives Dairy Rd

NORTH MIAMI BEACH

NE 163rd St

Southern Memorial Park

909

W Dixie Hwy

Biscayne Blvd

Morningside Park

NE 6th Ave

Griffing Blvd

NE 2nd Ave
N Miami Ave

DESIGN DISTRICT

See Wynwood, Design District & Little Haiti Map (p80)

441

NW 2nd Ave

NW 7th Ave

⑤

LITTLE HAITI

Big Night in Little Haiti

Julia Tuttle Cswy

9

OPA-LOCKA

NW 119th St

NW 79th St

LIBERTY CITY

NW 54th St

MIAMI

NW 27th Ave

Little River Canal

NW 36th St

821

NW 37th Ave

Palmetto Expwy

N Le Jeune Rd

E 4th Ave

112

924

CAROL CITY

Gratigny Pkwy

W 4th Ave

NW 57th Ave

HIALEAH

826

Palmetto Expwy

75

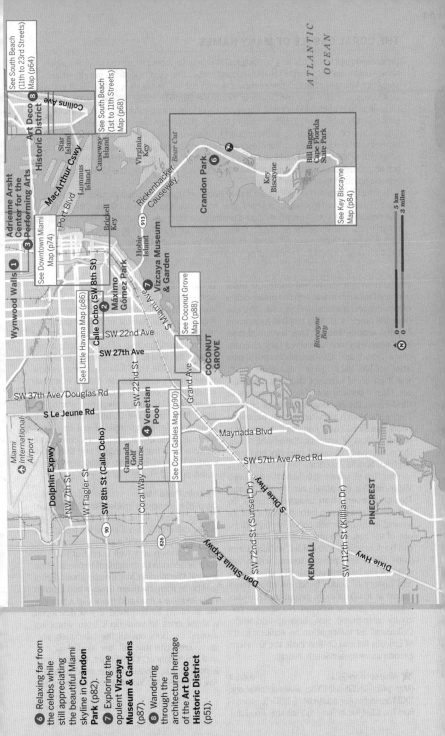

6 Relaxing far from the celebs while still appreciating the beautiful Miami skyline in **Crandon Park** (p82).

7 Exploring the opulent **Vizcaya Museum & Gardens** (p87).

8 Wandering through the architectural heritage of the **Art Deco Historic District** (p51).

See South Beach (11th to 23rd Streets) Map (p64)

8 Art Deco Historic District

See South Beach (1st to 11th Streets) Map (p68)

1 Wynwood Walls

3 Adrienne Arsht Center for the Performing Arts

MacArthur Cswy

Collins Ave

Star Island

Lummus Island

Port Blvd

Causeway Island

Virginia Key

See Downtown Miami Map (p74)

Brickell Key

Hobie Island

Rickenbacker Causeway

Bear Cut

Key Biscayne

Bill Baggs Cape Florida State Park

6 Crandon Park

See Key Biscayne Map (p84)

2 Máximo Gómez Park

Calle Ocho (SW 8th St)

913

7 Vizcaya Museum & Garden

See Little Havana Map (p86)

SW 22nd Ave

SW 27th Ave

S Miami Ave

See Coconut Grove Map (p88)

COCONUT GROVE

Grand Ave

Biscayne Bay

ATLANTIC OCEAN

Miami International Airport

Dolphin Expwy

NW 7th St

W Flagler St

SW 8th St (Calle Ocho)

Granada Golf Course

Coral Way

SW 37th Ave/Douglas Rd

S Le Jeune Rd

SW 22nd St

4 Venetian Pool

See Coral Gables Map (p90)

Maynada Blvd

SW 57th Ave/Red Rd

90

826

Don Shula Expwy

SW 72nd St (Sunset Dr)

S Dixie Hwy

KENDALL

PINECREST

SW 112th St (Killian Dr)

Dixie Hwy

N

0   5 km

0   3 miles

THE CORAL CASTLE OF MANY NAMES

On a street full of fairly opulent buildings, 1114 Ocean Dr, a cream-colored Mediterranean-revival castle built of hewn coral and exposed timber that could rightly be the center set piece of a *Pirates of the Caribbean* movie, stands out. The three-story palace, built in the 1930s, was modeled after the Governor's House in Santo Domingo, where Christopher Columbus' son once laid his head. For years it was known as the Amsterdam Palace – until one day, in the early 1980s, it caught the eye of a certain fashion designer named Gianni Versace. Versace bought the property, renamed it the Versace Mansion and promptly locked horns with local preservationists after announcing plans to tear down a neighboring hotel so he could build a pool. After a battle, the moneyed designer won – but also struck a deal that would allow for law changes, saving more than 200 other historic hotels in the process.

None of it mattered in 1997, when stalker Andrew Cunanan gunned Versace down in front of the beloved mansion. For years after, the house was known as Casa Casuarina and operated as a members-only club. Currently it is the site of The Villa by Barton G hotel (p105). Ironically, the death of a European fashion guru here has attracted lots of, well, European fashion gurus. Tourists still shuffle by, armed with morbid curiosity and a thirst for celebrity-related photos of any kind.

city built on speculative real estate, the main engine of urban renewal was the preservation of a unique architectural heritage. See, all those beautiful hotels, with their tropical-Americana facades, scream 'Miami.' They screamed it so loud when they were preserved they gave this city a brand, and this neighborhood a new lease on life. Back in the day, South Beach was a ghetto of vagrants, druggies and retirees. Then it became one of the largest areas in the USA on the National Register of Historic Places, and then it attracted models, photographers, hoteliers, chefs and...well, today it's a pastel medina of cruisers, Euro-fashionistas, the occasionally glimpsed celebrity and tourists from Middle America.

Your first stop here should be the Art Deco Welcome Center (p134), run by the Miami Design Preservation League (MDPL). To be honest, it's a bit of a tatty gift shop, but it's located in the old beach-patrol headquarters, one of the best deco buildings out there. You can book excellent $20 guided walking tours (plus audio and private tours), which are some of the best introductions to the layout and history of South Beach on offer. Tours depart at 10:30am daily, except on Thursday when they leave at 6:30pm. No advance reservations required; just show up and smile. Call ahead for information on walking tours of Lincoln Rd and Collins Park, the area that encompasses upper South Beach.

★ **Wolfsonian-FIU**　　　　MUSEUM
(Map p68; ☑ 305-531-1001; www.wolfsonian.org; 1001 Washington Ave; adult/child 6-12 $7/5; ☺ noon-6pm Thu & Sat-Tue, to 9pm Fri) Visit this excellent design museum early in your stay to put the aesthetics of Miami Beach into fascinating context. It's one thing to see how wealth, leisure and the pursuit of beauty manifests in Miami Beach, it's another to understand the roots and shadings of local artistic movements. By chronicling the interior evolution of everyday life, the Wolfsonian reveals how these trends were architecturally manifested in SoBe's exterior deco. Which reminds us of the Wolfsonian's own noteworthy facade. Remember the Gothic-futurist apartment-complex-cum-temple-of-evil in *Ghostbusters*? Well, this imposing structure, with its grandiose 'frozen fountain' and lion-head-studded grand elevator, could serve as a stand-in for that set.

Lincoln Road Mall　　　　ROAD
(Map p64; ☺ farmers market 9am-6:30pm Sun) Calling Lincoln Rd a mall, which many do, is like calling Big Ben a clock: it's technically accurate but misses the point. Yes, you can shop, and shop very well here. But this outdoor pedestrian thoroughfare between Alton Rd and Washington Ave is really about seeing and being seen; there are times when Lincoln feels less like a road and more like a runway. We wouldn't be surprised if you developed a slight crick in your neck from whipping around to check out all the fabulously gorgeous creatures that call 'the road' their natural environment. Carl Fisher, the father of Miami Beach, envisioned the road as a '5th Ave of the South.' Morris Lapidus, one of the

(continued on p63)

GLOWIMAGES / GETTY IMAGES ©

Art Deco Miami

South Beach may be known for celebrity spotting, but the area's original cachet owes less to paparazzi and more to preservation. The art-deco design movement, the architectural and aesthetic backbone of SoBe, is powerfully distinctive and finds expression in soft lines, bright pastels and the integration of neon into structural facades.

Contents

Above Detail of a carved art-deco wall, Miami.

MAISANT LUDOVIC / HEMIS.FR / GETTY IMAGES ©

Classical Deco

In the past, South Beach architects distinguished themselves through decorative finials, parapets and neon signage. Miami Beach deco relies on 'stepped-back' facades that disrupt the harsh, flat Florida light. Cantilevered 'eyebrows' jut out above windows to protect interiors from the sun.

Cardozo Hotel

This lovely building (p107), along with the neighboring Carlyle Hotel, was the first to be rescued by the original Miami Beach Preservation League when developers threatened to raze South Beach's deco buildings in the 1980s.

Carlyle Hotel

Located at 1250 Ocean Dr, the Carlyle comes with futuristic styling, triple parapets, a *Jetsons* vibe and some cinematic cachet: *The Birdcage* was filmed here.

Essex House Hotel

Porthole windows lend the feel of a grand cruise ship, while the hotel's spire looks like a rocket ship, recalling art deco's roots as an aesthetic complement to modernism and industrialism. Terrazzo floors cool the lobby (p105).

Lifeguard Stations on South Beach

Besides being cubist-inspired exemplars of the classical deco movement, with their sharp, pleasing geometric lines, these stations are painted in dazzling colors. They're along the beach from 1st St to 17th St.

Jerry's Famous Deli

Housed in the Hoffman Cafeteria Building, this spacious 1939 gem (p113) has a front that resembles the prow of a *Buck Rogers*–inspired ship. The carved owls on the roof scare off pigeons – and their poo.

1. Cardozo Hotel **2.** Lifeguard station on South Beach **3.** Essex House Hotel

Deco Elements

As individualized as South Beach's buildings are, they share quirks and construction strategies. Canopy porches provide cool places to sit. To reflect heat, buildings were originally painted white, and later, pastels, with accent colors highlighting smaller elements. Some hotels resemble Mesoamerican temples; others evoke cruise liners.

Crescent Hotel

Besides having one of Miami Beach's most recognizable neon facades, the Crescent (at 1420 Ocean Dr) has signage that draws the eye down into its lobby (the better to pack guests in), rather than up to its roof.

Waldorf Towers Hotel

Deco guru L Murray Dixon designed the tower of this hotel (at 860 Ocean Dr) to resemble a lighthouse, surely meant to illuminate the way home from drunken Ocean Dr revels.

Colony Hotel

The Colony, at 736 Ocean Dr, is the oldest deco hotel in Miami Beach, and has what may be the most iconic facade on Ocean Dr. It was the first hotel in Miami to incorporate its sign (a neon wonder) as part of its overall design. Inside the lobby, a space-age interior includes Saturn-shaped lamps and *Flash Gordon* elevators.

Cavalier South Beach

The step-pyramid sides and geometric carvings that grace the front of this classic (p105) are some of the best examples of the Mayan or Incan-inspired 'temple-as-hotel' school of design.

Wolfsonian-FIU

The lobby of this museum (p54) contains a phenomenally theatrical example of a 'frozen fountain.' The gold-leaf fountain, which formerly graced a movie-theater lobby, shoots up vertically and flows downward symmetrically.

1. Colony Hotel **2.** Waldorf Towers Hotel **3.** Cavalier South Beach

1. Hotel Victor **2.** James Royal Palm Hotel
3. Delano Hotel among the Collins Ave streetscape **4.** The Tides

DENNIS K. JOHNSON / GETTY IMAGES ©

'New' Deco Hotels

Hoteliers such as Ian Schrager combine faith in technology – flat-screen TVs, Lucite 'ghost chairs,' computer-controlled lobby displays – with an air of fantastical glamour. Newer hotels such as the W and Gansevoort South have deco roots, but have expanded the architectural sense of scale, integrating deco style into Miami Modern's (enormous) proportions.

Hotel Victor

Forward-thinking management (who give a nod to the past) have done an excellent job of turning this L Murray Dixon original (p104) into an undersea wonderland of jellyfish lamps and sea-green terrazzo floors.

Delano Hotel

The top tower evokes old-school deco rocket-ship fantasies, but the theater-set-on-acid interior is a flight of pure modern fancy. The enormous backyard pool mixes Jazz Age elegance with pure Miami muscular opulence. (p107)

Tides

The biggest deco structure of its day was a temple to the deco movement. Today, the lobby of the Tides (p107) feels like Poseidon's audience chamber, while rooms exemplify contemporary boutique aesthetics.

James Royal Palm Hotel

There's no better place to feel a sense of sea-borne movement than the *Titanic*-esque, ocean-liner themed back lobby of this massive and beautifully restored hotel (p108). The mezzanine has enormous modern dimensions but classic deco styling.

Surfcomber

One of the best deco renovations on the beach is offset by sleek, transit-lounge inspired lines in the lobby and a lovely series of rounded shades over room windows. (p108)

Vintage Ford Thunderbird outside the Avalon Hotel

Quirky Deco Delights

Tropical deco is mainly concerned with stimulating the imagination. Painted accents lifted from archaeology sites might make a passerby think of travel, maybe on a cruise ship. And hey, isn't it funny the windows resemble portholes? Almost all of the preserved buildings here still inspire this childlike sense of wonder.

Bas-Relief & Friezes

Although art deco was inspired by stripped-down modernist aesthetics, it also rebelled against utilitarianism. Its bas-relief and frieze work is noticeable on the exterior of many South Beach hotels.

Portholes

The deco movement came about in the early 20th century, when affordable travel became a reality for the developed world. Sea journeys were the height of luxury and many deco buildings are decorated with nautical porthole windows.

Berkeley Shore Hotel

One of the older hotels in South Beach, the Berkeley Shore, at 1610 Collins Ave, has a striking exterior set off by a cylindrical 'prow' rising out of shade-providing 'eyebrows,' plus elegant exterior friezes.

Avalon Hotel

The exterior of the Avalon, at 700 Ocean Dr, is a fantastic example of classical art-deco architecture – clean lines, old-school signage lit up in tropical green, with a 1950s Oldsmobile parked outside.

11th Street Diner

It doesn't get much more deco than dining in a classical Pullman train car. Many buildings on Miami Beach evoke planes, trains and automobiles – this diner (p111) is actually in one.

(continued from p54)

founders of the loopy, neo-baroque Miami Beach style, designed much of the mall, including several shady overhangs, waterfall structures and traffic barriers that look like the marbles a giant might play with. Other architectural icons of note include the Lincoln Theatre (Map p64; 541 Lincoln Rd), designed by renowned theater and cinema architect Thomas W Lamb (now an H&M), and the wonderfully deco Colony Theater (p128). There's also an excellent farmers market and the Antique & Collectible Market (www.antiquecollectiblemarket.com; ☺8am-6pm, every 2nd Sun Oct-May), both held along Lincoln.

1111 Lincoln Rd
BUILDING

(Map p64; www.1111lincolnroad.com; Ⓟ) The west side of Lincoln Rd is anchored by what may be the most impressive parking garage you'll ever lay eyes on, a geometric pastiche of sharp angles, winding corridors and incongruous corners that looks like a lucid fantasy dreamed up by Pythagoras after a long night out. In fact, the building was designed by Swiss architecture firm Herzog & de Meuron, who describe the structure as 'all muscle without cloth.' Besides parking, 1111 Lincoln is filled with retail shops and residential units.

ArtCenter/South Florida
GALLERY

(Map p64; ☑305-674-8278; www.artcentersf.org; 924 Lincoln Rd) Established in 1984 by a small but forward-thinking group of artists, this compound is the creative heart of South Beach. In addition to some 52 artists' studios (many of which are open to the public), ArtCenter offers an exciting lineup of classes and lectures. The residences are reserved for artists who do not have major exposure, so this is a good place to spot up-and-coming talent. Monthly rotating exhibitions keep the presentation fresh and pretty avant-garde.

Miami Beach Community Church
CHURCH

(Map p64; http://miamibeachcommunitychurch.com; 1620 Drexel Ave) In rather sharp and refreshing contrast to all the ubermodern structures muscling their way into the art-deco design of South Beach, this community church puts one in mind of an old Spanish mission – humble, modest and elegantly understated in an area where overstatement is the general philosophy. Fourteen stained-glass windows line the relatively simple interior, while the exterior is built to resemble coral stone in a Spanish Revival style. The congregation is LGBT friendly and welcomes outside visitors; sermons are at 10:30am on Sunday and 6pm nightly.

New World Center
BUILDING

(Map p64; ☑305-673-3331; www.newworldcenter.com; 500 17th St; tours $5; ☺tours 4pm Tue & Thu, noon Fri & Sat) Miami has a penchant for sumptuous performing-arts venues and the New World Center is certainly competing with the Arsht Center for most impressive concert hall in the city. Designed by Frank Gehry, the Center rises majestically out of a manicured lawn just above Lincoln Rd, looking somewhat like a tissue box from the year 3000 with a glass facade; note the 'fluttering' stone waves that pop out of the exterior. The grounds form a 2½-acre public park; performances inside the center are projected to those outside via a 7000-sq-ft projection wall (like you're in the classiest drive-in movie theater in the universe). Inside, the folded layers of white walls feel somewhere between organic and origami. Tours are led by docents; call ahead to book, as space is limited.

Ocean Drive
ROAD

(Map p68; from 1st to 11th St) This is the great cruising strip of Miami; an endless parade of classic cars, testosterone-sweating young men, peacocklike young women, street performers, vendors, those guys who yell unintelligible crap at everyone, celebrities pretending to be tourists, tourists who want to play celebrity, beautiful people, ugly people, people people and the best ribbon of art-deco preservation on the beach. Say 'Miami.' That image in your head? Probably Ocean Dr.

South Pointe Park
PARK

(Map p68; 1 Washington Ave; ☺sunrise-10pm) The very southern tip of Miami Beach has been converted into a lovely park, replete with manicured grass for lounging; views over a remarkably teal and fresh ocean; a restaurant; a refreshment stand; warm, scrubbed-stone walkways; and lots of folks who want to enjoy the great weather and views sans the South Beach strutting. That said, we saw two model photo shoots here in under an hour, so it's not all casual relaxation.

A1A
ROAD

'Beachfront Avenue!' The A1A causeway, coupled with the Rickenbacker Causeway in Key Biscayne, is one of the great bridges in America, linking Miami and Miami Beach via the glittering turquoise of Biscayne Bay. To drive this road in a convertible or with the windows down, with a setting sun behind you, enormous cruise ships to the side, the palms swaying in the ocean breeze, and

MIAMI

South Beach (11th to 23rd Streets)

200 m
0.1 miles

Collins Ave

37

31

35
67
32

66

4

Collins Park

23rd St

Park Ave

21st St

21st St

20th St

Liberty Ave

19th St

70

29
22

28

33
24
27
30

25
60

20

James Ave

18th St

42

12

Washington Ave

Miami Beach
High School

Miami Beach Convention Center

68
63

Prairie Ave

10

P

N Meridian Ave

8

Convention Center Dr

Sheridan Ave

Miami Beach
Botanical Garden

6

Meridian Ct

19th St

18th St

17th St

Miami
Beach
City Hall

Meridian Ave

P

Bayshore
Municipal
Golf Course

i

Jefferson Ave

Lincoln La N

18th St

P

N Bay Rd

Alton Rd

Michigan Ave

16

Collins Canal

19th St

Lenox Ave

P

Sunset Islands

W 24th St

Number 3

W 23rd St

Sunset Dr

W 22nd St

Number 4

W 21st St

Alton Rd

West Ave

20th St

18th St

Bay Rd

Sheridan Ave

75
15

51

41

Purdy Ave

Island
View
Park

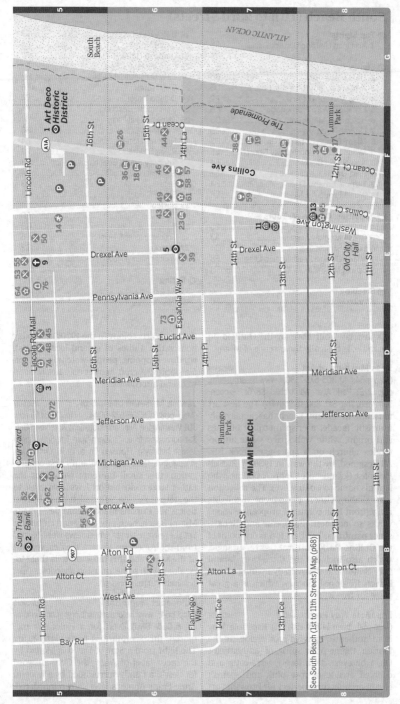

ATLANTIC OCEAN

South
Beach

**1 Art Deco
Historic
District**

The Promenade

Lummus
Park

Lincoln Rd

16th St

15th St

14th La

Collins Ave

Ocean Dr

Drexel Ave

14th St

Drexel Ave

Old City
Hall

Washington Ave

Ocean Ct

12th St

Collins Ct

13th St

12th St

11th St

Pennsylvania Ave

Española Way

Euclid Ave

14th Pl

Meridian Ave

Lincoln Rd Mall

16th St

15th St

Meridian Ave

Jefferson Ave

Flamingo
Park

MIAMI BEACH

Jefferson Ave

Courtyard

Michigan Ave

14th St

13th St

12th St

Lincoln La S

Lenox Ave

Sun Trust
2 Bank

Alton Rd

15th Tce

15th St

14th Ct

Alton La

14th St

Alton Ct

Alton Ct

West Ave

Flamingo
Way

14th Tce

13th Tce

Lincoln Rd

Bay Rd

See South Beach (1st to 11th Streets) Map (p68)

5   6   7   8

South Beach (11th to 23rd Streets)

let's just say 'Your Love' by the Outfield on the radio, is basically the essence of Miami.

Bass Museum of Art MUSEUM
(Map p64; ☑ 305-673-7530; www.bassmuseum.org; 2121 Park Ave; adult/child $8/6; ⊙noon-5pm Wed, Thu, Sat, Sun, to 9pm Fri) The best art museum in Miami Beach has a playfully futuristic facade, a crisp interplay of lines and bright, white wall space – like an Orthodox church on a space-age Greek isle. All designed, by the way, in 1930 by Russell Pancoast (grandson of John A Collins, who lent his name to Collins Ave). The collection isn't shabby either: permanent highlights range from 16th-century European religious works to northern European and Renaissance paintings. The Bass forms one point of the **Collins Park Cultural Center** triangle, which also includes the three-story **Miami City Ballet** and the lovingly inviting **Miami Beach Regional Library**, which is a great place for free wi-fi.

Española Way Promenade PROMENADE
(Map p64; btwn 14th & 15th Sts) Española Way is an 'authentic' Spanish promenade...in the Florida theme-park spirit of authenticity. Oh, whatever; it's a lovely, terra-cotta and cobbled arcade of rose pink and Spanish cream architecture, perfect for browsing art

(it was an arts colony in the 1920s and today houses the studios of several local artists), window-shopping, people-watching and coffee-sipping. A craft market operates here on weekend afternoons.

Jewish Museum of Florida MUSEUM
(Map p68; ☑ 305-672-5044; http://jmof.fiu.edu; 301 Washington Ave; adult/student & senior $6/5, Sat admission free; ⊙10am-5pm Tue-Sun, closed Jewish holidays) Housed in a 1936 Orthodox synagogue that served Miami's first congregation, this small museum chronicles the rather large contribution Jews have made to the state of Florida. After all, it could be said that while Cubans made Miami, Jews made Miami Beach, both physically and culturally. Yet there were times when Jews were barred from the American Riviera they carved out of the sand, and this museum tells that story, along with some amusing anecdotes (like seashell Purim dresses).

Holocaust Memorial MEMORIAL
(Map p64; www.holocaustmmb.org; cnr Meridian Ave & Dade Blvd) Even for a Holocaust memorial, this sculpture is particularly grim. The light from a Star of David is blotted by the racist label of *Jude* (the German word for 'Jew'); a family surrounded by a hopeful Anne Frank quote is later shown murdered,

MIAMI IN...

Two Days

There's more to Miami than South Beach, but we're assuming you're starting – and sleeping – here. Have breakfast at **Puerto Sagua** (p111) and, gorged, waddle to the **Wolfsonian-FIU** (p54) to get some background on the surrounding art-deco architecture. Now stroll around **Lincoln Road** (p54), hotel-spot on Collins Ave or check out South Beach's most flamboyant structures, like the **Delano Hotel** (p107), **Tides** (p107) and the **Shore Club** (p106).

Get in some beach time and as evening sets in consider an excellent deco district tour with the **Art Deco Welcome Center** (p134). For a nice Haitian dinner try **Tap Tap** (p111). Afterwards, grab a craft cocktail at **Broken Shaker** (p124).

The next day potter around either of the excellent ethnic enclaves of **Little Haiti** (p82) or **Little Havana** (p85) before dining in the trendy **Design District** (p117). End your trip rocking out in one of Midtown's excellent venues, like **Bardot** (p127) or **Wood Tavern** (p126).

Four Days

Follow the two-day itinerary and visit whichever one of the 'Littles' (Haiti or Havana) you missed the first time round. If you can, visit Coral Gables, making sure not to miss the **Biltmore Hotel** (p89), the **Venetian Pool** (p89) and a shopping stroll down Miracle Mile. If all that isn't opulent enough for you, see what happens when Mediterranean revival, baroque stylings and a lot of money gets mashed together at the **Vizcaya Museum & Gardens** (p87). Top off a visit to these elegant manses with dinner at one of the best restaurants in Miami in, no kidding, a gas station at **El Carajo** (p121).

On day four, head downtown and take a long ride on the free **Metromover** (p76), hopping on and off to see the gorgeous **Adrienne Arsht Center for the Performing Arts** (p76). Have your last meal at **Blue Collar** (p117) on emergent N Biscayne Blvd before having a farewell drink under the stars in the courtyard of the **Blackbird Ordinary** (p125).

South Beach (1st to 11th Streets)

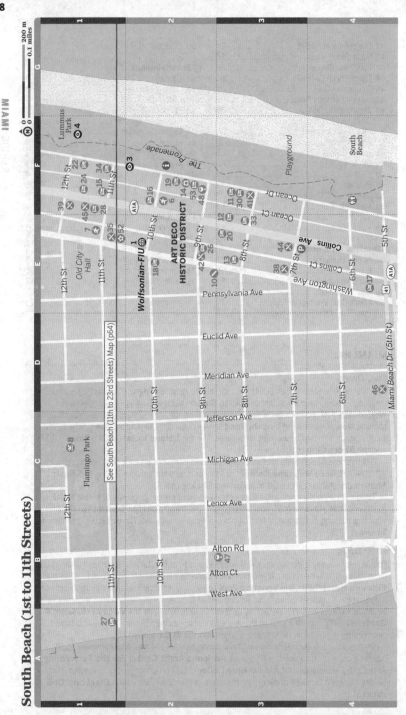

N
0 — 200 m
0 — 0.1 miles

Lummus Park
⊙ 4

Old City Hall
Flamingo Park

Wolfsonian-FIU

ART DECO HISTORIC DISTRICT

The Promenade

Playground

South Beach

See South Beach (11th to 23rd Streets) Map (p64)

12th St
11th St
10th St
9th St
8th St
7th St
6th St
5th St

Pennsylvania Ave
Euclid Ave
Meridian Ave
Jefferson Ave
Michigan Ave
Lenox Ave
Alton Rd
Alton Ct
West Ave

Washington Ave
Collins Ave
Collins Ct
Ocean Ct
Ocean Dr

Miami Beach Dr (5th St)

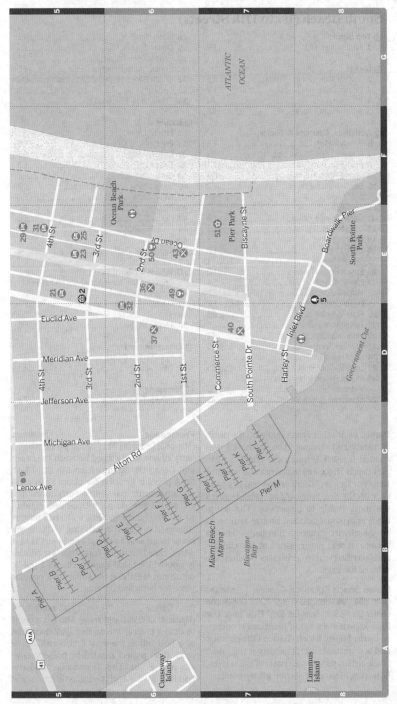

South Beach (1st to 11th Streets)

framed by another Frank quote on the death of ideals and dreams. The memorial was created in 1984 through the efforts of Miami Beach Holocaust survivors and sculptor Kenneth Treister. There are several key pieces, with the *Sculpture of Love and Anguish* the most visible to passers-by. The sculpture's enormous, oxidized bronze arm bears an Auschwitz tattooed number – chosen because it was never issued at the camp – and terrified camp prisoners scaling the sides of the arm.

Miami Beach Botanical Garden   GARDENS
(Map p64; www.mbgarden.org; 2000 Convention Center Dr; ⊙9am-5pm Tue-Sat) This lush but little-known 4½ acres of plantings is operated by the Miami Beach Garden Conservancy, and is a veritable secret garden in the midst of the urban jungle – an oasis of palm trees, flowering hibiscus trees and glassy ponds.

Promenade   PROMENADE
(Map p68; Ocean Dr) This beach promenade, a wavy ribbon sandwiched between the beach and Ocean Dr, extends from 5th St to 15th St. A popular location for photo shoots, especially during crowd-free early mornings, it's also a breezy, palm-tree-lined conduit for in-line skaters, cyclists, volleyball players (there's a net at 11th St), dog walkers, yahoos, locals and tourists. The beach that it edges, called Lummus Park, sports six floridly colored lifeguard stands. There's a public bathroom at 11th St; the sinks are a popular place for homeless bathing.

Post Office   HISTORIC BUILDING
(Map p64; 1300 Washington Ave) Make it a point to mail a postcard from this 1937 deco gem of a post office, the very first South Beach renovation project tackled by preservationists in the '70s. This Depression moderne building in the 'stripped classic' style was

constructed under President Roosevelt's reign and funded by the Works Progress Administration (WPA) initiative, which supported artists who were out of work during the Great Depression. On the exterior, note the bald eagle and the turret with iron railings, and inside, a large wall mural of Florida's Seminole Wars.

Temple Emanu-El   RELIGIOUS

(Map p64; www.tesobe.org; Washington Ave at 17th St) An art-deco temple? Not exactly, but the smooth, bubbly dome and sleek, almost aerodynamic profile of this Conservative synagogue, established in 1938, fits right in on SoBe's deco parade of moderne this and streamline that. Shabbat services are on Friday at 7pm and on Saturday at 10am.

World Erotic Art Museum   MUSEUM

(Map p64; www.weam.com; 1205 Washington Ave; over 18yr $15; ⊙ 11am-10pm Mon-Thu, to midnight Fri-Sun) In a neighborhood where no behavior is too shocking, the World Erotic Art Museum screams, 'Hey! We have a giant golden penis!' Back in 2005, then 70-year-old Naomi Wilzig turned her 5000-piece private erotica collection into a South Beach attraction. WEAM takes itself very seriously, which is part of the charm of this collection of fascinating erotica through the ages, from ancient sex manuals to Victorian peep-show photos to, yes, a big golden phallus by the exit.

⊙ Northern Miami Beach

Maps refer to the area above South Beach as Miami Beach, but locals use the jargon Mid-Beach (around the 40th streets) and North Beach (70th St and above). Communities like Surfside, Bal Harbour, Sunny Isles and Aventura are further north and can be included in spirit. Indian Creek waterway separates the luxury hotels and high-rise condos from the residential districts in the west. Keep in mind that the separate city of North Miami Beach (as opposed to the *region* of Northern Miami Beach) is not, technically, on the spit of land known as Miami Beach – it's on the mainland. Confused? So are most residents.

Boardwalk   BEACH

(Map p72; 21st St to 46th St) What's trendy in beachwear this season? Seventeenth-century Polish gabardine coats, apparently. There are plenty of skimpily dressed hotties on the Mid-Beach boardwalk, but there are also Orthodox Jews going about their business in the midst of joggers, strolling tourists and sunbathers. Nearby are numerous condo buildings occupied by middle-class Latinos and Jews, who walk their dogs and play with their kids here, giving the entire place a laid-back, real-world vibe that contrasts with the nonstop glamour of South Beach.

Little Buenos Aires   NEIGHBORHOOD

(Map p72; 71st St west of Collins Ave) The area stretching in a 10-block radius around 71st Ave and Collins Ave may be one of the best places outside Mendoza to people-watch with a *cortada* (Argentine espresso) before digging into traditional pasta and steak dishes. With that said, today the Argentines compete with their neighbors the Uruguayans, their rivals the Brazilians, and even a big crop of Colombians, for first place in the Normandy Isle ethnic-enclave stakes. Not that there's tension; this is as prosperous and pleasant as Miami gets. On Saturday mornings the small village green hosts a lovely farmers market.

Fontainebleau   HISTORIC BUILDING

(Map p72; www.fontainebleau.com; 4441 Collins Ave) As you proceed north on Collins, the condos and apartment buildings grow in grandeur and embellishment until you enter an area nicknamed Millionaire's Row. The most fantastic jewel in this glittering crown is the Fontainebleau hotel. The hotel – mainly the pool, which has since been renovated – features in Brian de Palma's classic *Scarface*. This iconic 1954 leviathan is a brainchild of the great Miami Beach architect Morris Lapidus and has undergone many renovations; in some ways, it is utterly different from its original form, but it retains that early glamour.

KEEPING IT KOSHER IN MIAMI BEACH

They're no shtetls, but Arthur Godfrey Rd (41st St) and Harding Ave between 91st and 96th Sts in Surfside are popular thoroughfares for the Jewish population of Miami Beach. Just as Jews have shaped Miami Beach, so has the beach shaped its Jews: you can eat lox *y arroz con moros* (salmon with rice and beans) and while the Orthodox men don *yarmulkes* and the women wear headscarves, many have nice tans and drive flashy SUVs.

Northern Miami Beach

N ⬆ 0 —————————— 1 km
0 —————————— 0.5 miles

A **B** **C** **D**

Normandy
Isle

N Shore Dr

77th St

Harding Ave

Collins Ave

21

Normandy
Shores
Golf Course

71st St
Bridge

71st St

⊗14

S Shore Dr

79th St

18

⊗15

Trouville Esplanade

◎4

16 ⊗

11

5

Normandy Dr

6

*Aquatic Rental
Center & Sailing
School (0.8 mi)*

20

JFK/79th St Causeway

22

**NORTH BAY
VILLAGE**

W 63rd St

La Gorce
Country
Club

A1A

7

*Biscayne
Bay*

La Gorce Dr
Pine Tree Dr

Indian Creek

Collins Ave

Alton Rd

Dade Blvd

907

2

3

A1A

41st St/Arthur Godfrey Rd

19

Julia Tuttle Cswy
195

Sheridan Ave

Pine Tree Dr

Indian Creek Dr

9

South
Beach

N Bay Rd
Alton Rd

N Chase Ave

13

12

*Sunset
Islands*

N Chase Ave

*Bayshore
Municipal
Golf Course*

W 28th St

Collins Ave

⊗1

10

17

Northern Miami Beach

**Eden Roc Renaissance
Miami Beach**   HISTORIC BUILDING
(Map p72; www.edenrocmiami.com; 4525 Collins Ave) The Eden Roc Resort was the second groundbreaking resort from Morris Lapidus, and it's a fine example of the architecture known as MiMo (Miami Modern). It was the hangout for the 1960s Rat Pack – Sammy Davis Jr, Dean Martin, Frank Sinatra and crew. Extensive renovation has eclipsed some of Lapidus' style, but with that said, the building is still an iconic piece of Miami Beach architecture, and an exemplar of the brash beauty of Millionaire's Row.

Haulover Beach Park   PARK
(www.miamidade.gov/parks/parks/haulover_park. asp; 10800 Collins Ave; per car $4; ☉ sunrise-sunset; ⓟ) Where are all those tanned men in gold chains and Speedos going? That would be the clothing-optional beach in this 40-acre park hidden from condos, highways and prying eyes by vegetation. There's more to do here than get in the buff, though; most of the beach is 'normal' (there's even a dog park) and is one of the nicer spots for sand in the area (also note the colorful deco-ish shower 'cones'). The park is located on Collins Ave about 4.5 miles north of 71st St.

Oleta River State Park   PARK
(www.floridastateparks.org/oletariver; 3400 NE 163rd St; per person/car $2/6; ☉ 8am-sunset; ⓟⓐ) Tequesta people were boating the Oleta River estuary as early as 500 BC, so you're just following in a long tradition if you canoe or kayak in this park. At almost 1000 acres, this is the largest urban park in the state and one of the best places in Miami to escape the maddening throng. Boat out to the local mangrove island, watch the eagles fly by, or just chill on the pretension-free beach. On-site Blue Moon Outdoor Center (p97) offers single kayaks ($18 per 1½ hours, $25 per three hours), tandem kayaks ($25.50 per 1½ hours, $40 per three hours) and bike rental ($18 per 1½ hours, $25 per three hours). The park is off 163rd St NE/FL-826 in Sunny Isles, about 8 miles north of North Miami Beach.

Arch Creek Park   PARK
(www.miamidade.gov/parks/parks/arch_creek. asp; 1855 NE 135 St; ☉ 9am-5pm Wed-Sun; ⓟⓐ) This compact-and-cute park, located near Oleta River, encompasses a cozy habitat of tropical hardwood species that surrounds a pretty, natural limestone bridge. Naturalists can lead you on kid-friendly ecotours of the area, which include a lovely butterfly garden, or visitors can peruse a small but well-stocked museum of Native American and pioneer artifacts. The excellent Miami-Dade Eco-Adventures (☏ 305-365-3018; www.miamidade.gov/ecoadventures) ⌖ is based here. The park is just off North Biscayne Blvd, 7 miles north of the Design District.

⊙ Downtown Miami

Downtown Miami, the city's international financial and banking center, is split between tatty indoor shopping arcades on the one hand, and new condos and high-rise luxury hotels in the area known as Brickell on the other. The lazy, gritty Miami River divides downtown into north and south. Miami is

Downtown Miami

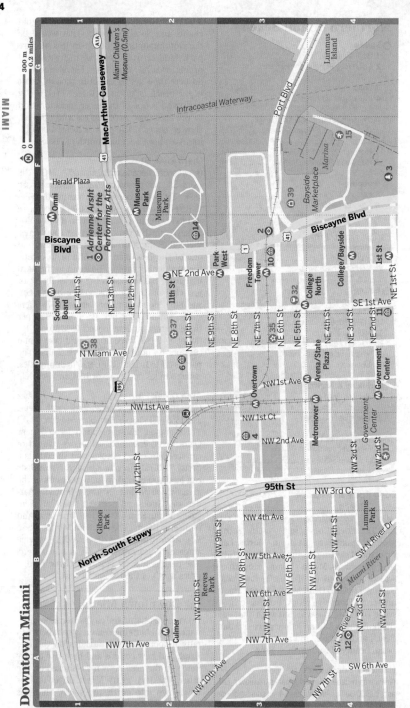

MIAMI

0 ___ 300 m
0 ___ 0.2 miles

MacArthur Causeway

A1A

Miami Children's Museum (0.5mi)

Lummus Island

Intracoastal Waterway

Port Blvd

Herald Plaza

Museum Park

Museum Park

Bayside Marketplace

15

3

39

14

Biscayne Blvd

Biscayne Blvd

Omni

1 Adrienne Arsht Center for the Performing Arts

Biscayne Blvd

Park West

Freedom Tower

2

41

College/Bayside

1st St

School Board

NE 14th St

NE 13th St

NE 12th St

11th St

NE 2nd Ave

10

College North

NE 1st St

SE 1st Ave

38

N Miami Ave

37

NE 10th St

NE 9th St

NE 8th St

NE 7th St

NE 6th St

NE 5th St

NE 4th St

NE 3rd St

NE 2nd St

32

35

6

Overtown

NW 1st Ave

NW 1st Ct

4

NW 2nd Ave

Arena/State Plaza

Metromover

Government Center

Government Center

11

17

NW 1st Ave

NW 3rd St

NW 2nd St

95th St

NW 3rd Ct

Gibson Park

NW 12th St

North-South Expwy

NW 4th Ave

Lummus Park

NW 9th St

NW 8th St

NW 5th Ave

NW 6th St

NW 5th St

NW 4th St

26

Miami River

SW N River Dr

Reeves Park

NW 10th St

NW 6th Ave

NW 7th St

SW S River Dr

NW 3rd St

NW 2nd St

Culmer

NW 7th Ave

NW 7th Ave

NW 10th Ave

12

SW 6th Ave

NW 7th St

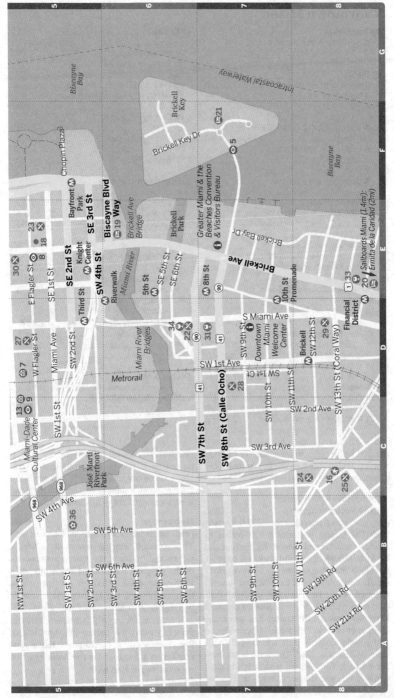

Downtown Miami

defined by an often frenetic pace of growth; when you visit, chances are the fruits of said growth will be visible in this area.

★ **Adrienne Arsht Center
for the Performing Arts** BUILDING
(Map p74; www.arshtcenter.com; 1300 N Biscayne Blvd) The largest performing-arts center in Florida (and second largest, by area, in the USA) is Miami's beautiful, beloved baby. It is also a major component of downtown's urban equivalent of a face-lift and several regimens of Botox. Designed by Cesar Pelli (the man who brought you Kuala Lumpur's Petronas Towers), the center has two main components: the Ziff Ballet Opera House and Knight Concert Hall, which span both sides of Biscayne Blvd. The venues are connected by a thin, elegant pedestrian bridge, while inside the theaters there's a sense of

ocean and land sculpted by wind; the rounded balconies rise up in spirals that resemble a sliced-open seashell. If you have the chance, catch a show here; the interior alone is easily a highlight of any Miami trip.

Metromover MONORAIL
(www.miamidade.gov/transit/metromover.asp) This elevated, electric monorail is hardly big enough to serve the mass-transit needs of the city, and has become something of a tourist attraction. Whatever its virtues as a commuting tool, the Metromover is a really great (and free!) way to see central Miami from a height (which helps, given the skyscraper-canyon nature of downtown). Because it's gratis, Metromover has a reputation as a hangout for the homeless, but commuters use it as well.

Bayfront Park
PARK

(Map p74; www.bayfrontparkmiami.com; 301 N Biscayne Blvd) Few American parks can claim to front such a lovely stretch of turquoise (Biscayne Bay), but Miamians are lucky like that. Lots of office workers catch quick naps under the palms at a little beach that does you the favor of setting out 'sit and chill' chairs. Notable park features are two performance venues: the Klipsch Amphitheater, which boasts excellent views over Biscayne Bay, is a good spot for live-music shows, while the smaller 200-seat (lawn seating can accommodate 800 more) Tina Hills Pavilion hosts free springtime performances. Look north for the JFK Torch of Friendship, and a fountain recognizing the accomplishments of longtime US congressman Claude Pepper. There's a huge variety of activities here, including yoga classes, trapeze classes and, we hear, flying-trapeze yoga classes (seriously).

Noted artist and landscape architect Isamu Noguchi redesigned much of Bayfront Park in the 1980s and dotted the grounds with three sculptures. In the southwest corner is the Challenger Memorial, a monument designed for the astronauts killed in the 1986 space-shuttle explosion, built to resemble both the twisting helix of a human DNA chain and the shuttle itself. The Light Tower is a 40ft, somewhat abstract allusion to Japanese lanterns and moonlight over Miami. Our favorite is the Mantra Slide, a twisting spiral of marble that doubles as a playground piece for the kids.

American Airlines Arena
BUILDING

(Map p74; www.aaarena.com; 601 N Biscayne Blvd) Just north of the park, and resembling a massive spaceship that perpetually hovers at the edge of Biscayne Bay, this arena has been the home of the Miami Heat basketball team since 2000. The Waterfront Theater, Florida's largest, is housed inside; throughout the year it hosts concerts, Broadway performances and the like. A giant airplane is painted on top of the arena; you may spot it (it looks like the shadow of a plane from afar) when you fly out of the city, or if you're Superman.

HistoryMiami
MUSEUM

(Map p74; www.historymiami.org; 101 W Flagler St; adult/child $8/5; ⊙10am-5pm Tue-Fri, from noon Sat & Sun) South Florida – a land of escaped slaves, guerilla Native Americans, gangsters, land grabbers, pirates, tourists, drug dealers and alligators – has a special history, and it takes a special kind of museum to capture that narrative. This place, located in the Miami-Dade Cultural Center, does just that, weaving together the stories of the region's successive waves of population, from Native Americans to Nicaraguans. Get off the Metromover at the Government Center stop.

Brickell Avenue Bridge & Brickell Key
ISLAND

(Map p74) Crossing the Miami River, the lovely Brickell Avenue Bridge between SE 4th St and SE 5th St was made wider and higher several years ago, which was convenient for the speedboat-driving drug runners being chased by Drug Enforcement Administration agents on the day of the bridge's grand reopening! Note the 17ft bronze statue by Cuban-born sculptor Manuel Carbonell of a Tequesta warrior and his family, which sits atop the towering Pillar of History column. Walking here is the best way to get a sense of the sculptures and will allow you to avoid one of the most confusing traffic patterns in Miami. Brickell Key looks more like a floating porcupine, with glass towers for quills, than an island. To live the life of Miami glitterati, come here, pretend you belong, and head into a patrician hangout like the Mandarin Oriental Miami

---

DOWNTOWN'S INTERNATIONAL BAZAARS

Downtown Miami has a reputation for being a bit rough around the edges. We think this is a bit undeserved; the area is dodgy at night but safe by day, if a little down-at-heel. Part of this ratty atmosphere is due to large amounts of cheap, knock-off electronics, fashion and jewelry shops that cluster in half-abandoned malls and shopping arcades. These stores are almost all run by immigrants, from West Africa, East Asia, South America and the Middle East (did we cover all the directions?). While we doubt you need cheap consumer goods of dubious origin, we do think it's fun to check out one of these markets, like the 777 International Mall (Map p74; 145 E Flagler St). This may be as close as you'll get to the messy, shouting, sweaty and exciting bazaars of the developing world, where folks yell at you to seal a deal and haggling is often an option. It's not as pretty as shopping in Miami Beach or the Design District, but it's a fascinating slice of this city's life.

hotel, where the lobby and intimate lounges afford sweeping views of Biscayne Bay.

Pérez Art Museum Miami
MUSEUM

(PAMM; Map p74; ☑ 305-375-3000; www.pamm. org; 1103 Biscayne Blvd; $12/8 adult/senior & student; ☺ 10am-6pm Tue, Wed & Fri-Sun, to 9pm Thu) The Pérez can claim fine rotating exhibits that concentrate on post-WWII international art, but just as impressive are its location and exterior. This art institution inaugurated Museum Park, a patch of land that overseas the broad blue swath of Biscayne Bay. Swiss architects Herzog & de Meuron designed the structure, which integrates tropical foliage, glass and metal – a melding of tropical vitality and fresh modernism that is a nice architectural analogy for Miami itself.

Gusman Center for the Performing Arts
BUILDING

(Map p74; ☑ 305-374-2444; www.gusmancenter. org; 174 E Flagler St) Miami loves modern, but the Olympia Theater at the Gusman Center for the Performing Arts is vintage-classic beautiful. The ceiling, which features 246 twinkling stars and clouds cast over an indigo-deep night, frosted with classical Greek sculpture and Vienna Opera House–style embellishment, will melt your heart. The theater opened in 1925; today the lobby serves as the Downtown Miami Welcome Center, doling out visitor information and organizing tours of the historic district; at night you can still catch theater and music performances.

MDC Museum of Art & Design
MUSEUM

(Freedom Tower; Map p74; ☑ 305-237-7700; www. mdcmoad.org; 600 Biscayne Blvd; free; ☺ noon-5pm Wed-Sun) Miami-Dade College operates a small but well-curated art museum downtown; the permanent collection includes works by Matisse, Picasso and Chagall and focuses on minimalism, pop art and contemporary Latin American art. The museum's home building is art itself: the Freedom Tower, an iconic slice of Miami's old skyline, is one of two surviving towers modeled after the Giralda bell tower in Spain's Cathedral of Seville. The 'Ellis Island of the South,' it served as an immigration processing center for almost half a million Cuban refugees in the 1960s. Placed on the National Register of Historic Places in 1979, it was also home to the *Miami Daily News* for 32 years.

Miami Center for Architecture & Design
MUSEUM

(Old US Post Office; Map p74; ☑ 305-448-7488; www.miamicad.org; 100 NE 1st Ave; ☺ 10am-5pm Mon-Fri) It makes sense that the Miami branch of the American Institute of Architects would pick the Old US Post Office as headquarters of its Center for Architecture & Design. Constructed in 1912, this was the first federal building in Miami. It features a low-pitched roof, elaborate doors and carved entryways, and was purchased in 1937 to serve as the country's first savings and loan. Today, it houses lectures and events related to architecture, design and urban planning, and hosts a small but vibrant exhibition on all of the above subjects.

Black Archives Historic Lyric Theater Welcome Center
HISTORIC BUILDING

(Lyric Theater; Map p74; ☑ 305-636-2390; www. theblackarchives.org; 819 NW 2nd Ave) Duke Ellington and Ella Fitzgerald once walked across the stage of the Lyric, a major stop on the 'Chitlin' Circuit' – the black live-entertainment trail of preintegration USA. As years passed both the theater and the neighborhood it served, Overtown, fell into disuse. Then the Black Archives History & Research Foundation of South Florida took over the building. Today the theater hosts occasional shows, while the Archives serves as an information center for those interested in Miami's African American heritage.

Cisneros Fontanal Arts Foundation
MUSEUM

(CIFO; Map p74; ☑ 305-455-3380; www.cifo.org; 1018 N Miami Ave; ☺ 10am-4pm Thu-Sun) This arts foundation displays the work of contemporary Latin American artists, and has an impressive showroom to boot. Even the exterior blends postindustrial rawness with a lurking, natural ambience, offset by the extensive use of Bisazza tiles to create an overarching tropical motif. The opening hours only apply during exhibition showings, although informal tours can be arranged if you call ahead.

Miami-Dade Public Library
LIBRARY

(Map p74; www.mdpls.org; 101 W Flagler St; ☺ 9am-6pm Mon-Wed & Fri, 9am-9pm Thu, 1-5pm Sun) To learn more about Florida (especially South Florida), take a browse through the extensive Florida Dept, or ask to see the Romer Collection, an archive of some 17,500 photos and prints that chronicles the history of the city from its early years to the 1950s.

Miami River
RIVER

(Map p74) For a taste of a seedy Old Florida, come to the lazy, sultry and still kinda spicy Miami River. Much of the shore is lined with makeshift warehouses, where you-can-only-imagine-what is loaded and unloaded onto small tugboats bound for you-can-only-imagine-where. Fisherfolk float in with their daily catch, fancy yachts 'slumming it' dock at restaurants and all in all, it just seems like a matter of time before the music from *Buena Vista Social Club* starts drifting over the scene.

Dade County Courthouse
HISTORIC BUILDING

(Map p74; 73 W Flagler St) If you end up on trial here, at least you'll get a free tour of one of the most imposing courthouses in the USA. Built between 1925 and 1929, this a very... appropriate building: if structures were people, the courthouse would definitely be a judge. Some trivia: back in the day, the top nine floors served as a 'secure' prison, from which more than 70 prisoners escaped.

◉ Wynwood, Design District & Little Haiti

Now rebranded as 'Midtown', Wynwood and the Design District are Miami's official arts neighborhoods, plus the focal points of much of the new art, food and nightlife in Greater Miami. This area still abuts some of the city's poorer 'hoods, and if you come here via city streets instead of the highway you'll see the rough edges that once characterized the vicinity. The Midtown mall is the area's natural center of gravity. Wynwood is the place for dedicated art galleries, while the small collection of posh retail outlets in the Design District are filled with things as beautiful as any canvas. Between the Italian-designed chairs, Russian Romanov-era cabinets and Dale Chihuly–esque chandeliers, the Design District tends to be expensive (we're talking thousands for a single item), although there are some relative bargains to be found if you look.

MIAMI SIGHTS

FINDING ART IN WYNWOOD

At the time of writing, there are over 60 art galleries in Wynwood, with new spaces opening on what sometimes feels like a weekly basis. The stomping grounds of 'Wypsters' (Wynwood hipsters, those who enjoy, staff and provide content for the neighborhood's galleries) shift month by month as 'guerilla' galleries, new murals, graffiti, cafes, restaurants and studio spaces spread across Midtown. In general, art galleries can be found in a square bound by NW 20th and NW 37th Sts to the south and north, and N Miami Ave and NW 3rd Ave to the east and west. It's difficult for us to recommend one specific set of galleries given the diversity of what's on offer, but the following are some of our favorites.

Artopia (Map p80; ☑305-374-8882; www.artopiamiami.com; 1753 NE 2nd Ave; ⊗call for hours) Proves the extents for Wynwood we mention above are flexible – Artopia is physically in Overtown, but culturally part of the gallery circuit. This was the old studio space of the late, renowned self-taught artist Purvis Young, who grew up near the studio. His folk-arty works and similar pieces are often displayed, as are pieces by up-and-coming artists, local or otherwise.

PanAmerican Art Projects (Map p80; ☑305-573-2400; www.panamericanart.com; 2450 NW 2nd Ave; ⊗9:30am-5:30pm Tue-Fri, noon-5:30pm Sat) Despite the name, PanAmerican also showcases work from European and Chinese artists. But much of what is on display comes from fine artists representing Latin America, the Caribbean and the USA.

Brisky Gallery (Map p80; ☑786-409-3585; www.briskygallery.com; 130 NW 24th St; ⊗call for hours) Coming to Miami by way of its original location in Germany, Brisky boasts an enormous 4500-sq-ft warehouse that houses a museum's worth of local and international art. Need more creativity? Head outside to a 5000-sq-ft back lot filled with murals, curated graffiti, art installations and sculpture.

There are literally dozens of other galleries to check out; a nice way of seeing them and getting in some free wine and cheese is attending the famous **Wynwood Art Walks**, or if you're around at the right time, the Art Wynwood (p100) festival. Check out websites such as www.beachedmiami.com, wynwoodartwalk.com and www.miamiartguide.com for more information.

Wynwood, Design District & Little Haiti

New Yorker (0.7 mi);
Michy's (0.8 mi); Jimmy's
East Side Diner (1 mi);
Motel Blu (1.1mi);
Magnum Lounge
(1.3 mi); Boteco (1.5mi)

Wynwood, Design District & Little Haiti

Unlike Wynwood, the Design District is pretty compact and walkable. Little Haiti is not to be missed and sits above the Design District. In between the two lies the leafy, lovely residential neighborhood of Buena Vista, where restaurants, bars, gay hot spots and gentrification are rapidly spreading.

★ **Wynwood Walls**   PUBLIC ART
(Map p80; www.thewynwoodwalls.com; NW 2nd Ave, btwn 25th & 26th Sts; ⊘noon-8pm Wed-Sat) In the midst of rusted warehouses and concrete blah, there's a pastel-and-graffiti explosion of urban art. Wynwood Walls is a collection of murals and paintings laid out over an open courtyard that invariably bowls people over with its sheer color profile and unexpected location. What's on offer tends to change with the coming and going of major arts events such as Art Basel, but it's always interesting stuff.

Little Haiti Cultural Center   GALLERY
(Map p80; ☑305-960-2969; www.miamigov.com/ LHCulturalcenter; 212 NE 59th Tce; ⊘9am-5pm) Miami has the largest community of Ayisyens (Haitians) in the world outside Haiti, and this is the place to learn about their story. The cultural center is a study in playful island designs and motifs that houses a small but vibrant art gallery, crafts center

and activities space – dance classes, drama productions and similar events are held here year-round. The best time to visit is for the **Big Night in Little Haiti** (www.rhythm-foundation.com/series/big-night-in-little-haiti), a street party held on the third Friday of every month from 6pm to 10pm. The celebration is rife with music, mouth-watering Caribbean food and beer, and is one of the safest, easiest ways of accessing the culture of Haiti outside of that island.

Rubell Family Art Collection   MUSEUM
(Map p80; ☑305-573-6090; www.rfc.museum; 95 NW 29th St; adult/student & under 18yr $10/5; ⊘10am-6pm Tue-Sat Dec-Aug) The Rubell family – specifically, the niece and nephew of the late Steve, better known as Ian Schrager's Studio 54 partner – operates some top-end hotels in Miami Beach, but they've also amassed an impressive contemporary-art collection that spans the last 30 years. The most admirable quality of this collection is its commitment to not just displaying one or two of its artists' pieces; the museum's aim is to showcase a contributor's entire career.

Miami City Cemetery   CEMETERY
(Map p80; 1800 NE 2nd Ave; ⊘7am-3:30pm Mon-Fri, 8am-4:30pm Sat & Sun) This quiet grave-yard, the final resting place of some of

DON'T MISS

LITTLE HAITI

If you haven't been to Port-au-Prince, then Little Haiti (La Petite Haïti), one of the most evocative neighborhoods in Miami, is the next best thing. Young men in tank tops listen to Francophone rap, while broad-necked women wearing bright wraps gossip in front of the *botanicas* – which, by the way, are not selling plants. A *botanica* here is a *vodou* shop. The neighborhood is one of Miami's poorest and it's not advisable to walk around here alone after dark, but by day or if visiting the Little Haiti Cultural Center you'll be fine.

Botanicas are perhaps the most 'foreign' sight in Little Haiti. Storefronts promise to help in matters of love, work and sometimes 'immigration services,' but trust us, there are no marriage counselors or Immigration & Naturalization agents in here. As you enter you'll probably get a funny look, but be courteous, curious and respectful and you should be welcomed. Before you browse, forget stereotypes about pins and dolls. Like many traditional religions, *vodou* recognizes supernatural forces in everyday objects, and powers that are both distinct from and part of one overarching deity. Ergo, you'll see shrines to Jesus next to altars to traditional *vodou* deities. Notice the large statues of what look like people; these actually represent *loa* (pronounced lwa), intermediary spirits that form a pantheon below God in the *vodou* religious hierarchy. Drop a coin into a *loa* offering bowl before you leave, especially to Papa Legba, spirit of crossroads and, by our reckoning, travelers.

For a more cerebral taste of Haitian culture, peruse the shelves at **Libreri Mapou** (Map p80; www.librerimapou.com; 5919 NE 2nd Ave), bursting with thousands of titles (including periodicals) in English, French and Creole, as well as crafts and recorded music.

Miami-Dade's most important citizens, is a sort of narrative of the history of the city cast in bone, dirt and stone. The dichotomy of the past and modernity gets a nice visual representation in the form of looming condos shadowing the last abode of the Magic City's late, great ones. More than 9000 graves are divided into separate white, black and Jewish sections. Buried here are mayors, veterans (including about 90 Confederate soldiers) and the godmother of South Florida, Julia Tuttle, who purchased the first orange groves that attracted settlers to the area.

Living Room PUBLIC ART
(Map p80; cnr NW 40th St & N Miami Ave) Just to remind you that you're entering the Design District is a big, honking public-art installation of, yep, a living room – just the sort of thing you're supposed to shop for while you're here. Actually this Living Room, by Argentine husband-and-wife team Roberto Behar and Rosario Marquardt, is an 'urban intervention' meant to be a criticism of the disappearance of public space, but we think it serves as a nice metaphor for the Design District as a whole: a contemporary interior plopped into the middle of urban decay.

Bacardi Building ARCHITECTURE
(Map p80; 2100 Biscayne Blvd; ⊘9am-3:30pm or 4pm Mon-Fri) FREE You don't need to down 151 to appreciate the former Miami head-quarters of the world's largest family-owned spirits company, Bacardi. The main event is a beautifully decorated tower that looks like the mosaic pattern of a tropical bathhouse multiplied by infinity.

◉ Key Biscayne

The scenic drive along the Rickenbacker Causeway leads first to small Virginia Key, then over to Key Biscayne, an island that's just 7 miles long with unrivaled views of the Miami skyline. As you drive over the causeway, note the small public beaches, picnic areas and fishing spots arranged on its margins. The road turns into Crandon Blvd, the key's only real main road, which runs to the Cape Florida Lighthouse at the island's southernmost tip.

Crandon Park PARK
(Map p84; ☑305-361-5421; www.miamidade.gov/parks/parks/crandon_beach.asp; 6747 Crandon Blvd; per car $5; ⊘sunrise-sunset; P⛱☺) ✦ This 1200-acre park boasts Crandon Park Beach, a glorious but crowded beach that stretches for 3 miles. Much of the park consists of a dense coastal hammock (hardwood forest) and mangrove swamps. Pretty cabanas at the south end of the park can be rented by the day ($37.45). The 2-mile-long beach here is clean, uncluttered with tourists, faces a lovely sweep of teal goodness and is regularly named one of the best beaches in the USA.

Miami Seaquarium AQUARIUM
(Map p84; ☑305-361-5705; www.miamiseaquar-ium.com; 4400 Rickenbacker Causeway; adult/child $40/30; ☺9:30am-6pm, last entry 4:30pm; ℗🚼) The Seaquarium was one of the country's first facilities dedicated to marine life, and its mission remains one of protecting aquatic creatures and educating the public about its charges. There are dozens of shows and exhibits, including a tropical reef; the Shark Channel, with feeding presentations; and Discovery Bay, a natural mangrove habitat that serves as a refuge for rehabilitating rescued sea turtles. Check out the Pacific white-sided dolphins or West Indian manatees being nursed back to health; some are released into the wild.

With that said, the big attraction at the Seaquarium is also its most controversial: dolphin and whale shows, including swim-with-the-dolphin programs. While the Seaquarium says it is are protecting cetaceans (sea mammals) and educating the public about them, animal-welfare organizations claim any form of captivity and human interaction is debilitating to dolphins and whales. If you decide you want to swim with dolphins, note that people under 5ft 2in cannot participate and children under three cannot enter the observation area. Last entry is at 4:30pm.

Marjory Stoneman Douglas Biscayne Nature Center MUSEUM
(Map p84; ☑305-261-6767; www.biscaynena-turecenter.org; Crandon Park, 6767 Crandon Blvd; ☺10am-4pm; ℗🚼) 🆓FREE Marjory Stoneman Douglas was a beloved environmental crusader and worthy namesake of this child-friendly nature center. The structure is a perfect introduction and exploration of the continental USA's own subtropical ecosystem: South Florida. There are weekend hikes and nature lessons that let kids wade into the water in search of marine wildlife; check the website for a full breakdown of the many activities on offer, most of which cost $12 per person.

Bill Baggs Cape Florida State Park PARK
(Map p84; ☑305-361-5811; www.floridastateparks.org/capeflorida; 1200 S Crandon Blvd; per car/person $8/2; ☺8am-sunset; ℗🚼🐾) 🖉 If you don't make it to the Florida Keys, come to this park for a taste of their unique island ecosystems. The 494-acre space is a tangled clot of tropical fauna and dark mangroves – look for the 'snorkel' roots that provide air for half-submerged mangrove trees – all interconnected by sandy trails and wooden boardwalks, and surrounded by miles of pale ocean. A concession shack rents kayaks, bikes, in-line skates, beach chairs and umbrellas.

At the state recreation area's southernmost tip, the 1845 brick **Cape Florida Lighthouse** is the oldest structure in Florida (it replaced another lighthouse that was severely damaged in 1836 during the Second Seminole War). Free tours run at 10am and 1pm Monday to Thursday.

Biscayne Community Center & Village Green Park PARK
(Map p84; ☑305-365-8900; www.keybiscayne.fl.gov/pr; Village Green Way, off Crandon Blvd; ☺community center 6am-10pm Mon-Fri, 8am-8pm Sat & Sun; 🚼🐾) 🆓FREE An unmissable park for

---

STILTSVILLE

Head to the southern shore of Bill Baggs Cape Florida State Park and you'll see, way out in the distance, a collection of seven houses that stands on pilings in Biscayne Bay. The buildings, known as Stiltsville, have been around since the early 1930s, ever since 'Crawfish Eddie Walker' built a shack on the waves. More buildings were added over the years, and the 'village' was, at times, a gambling den, smuggling haven and, during the 1960s, a bikini club where women drank for free if they wore a two piece, and anything could famously go.

At its peak in 1960, there were 27 'homes' in Stiltsville, but as one mght guess, hurricanes and erosions took their toll. No one lives in Stiltsville today, but it is possible to take a **boat tour** (☑305-379-5119; www.islandqueencruises.com/stiltsville.htm; tours $49) out here with the illustrious historian Dr Paul George.

In 2003 the nonprofit Stiltsville Trust was set up by the National Parks Service to rehabilitate the buildings into as-yet-unknown facilities; proposals include a National Parks Service visitor center, artist-in-residence colony or community center. Not much work seems to have progressed toward this idea, but if you'd like more information, check out www.stiltsvilletrust.org.

Key Biscayne

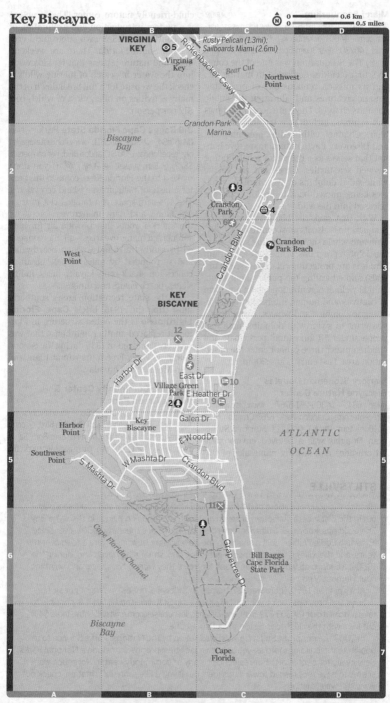

Key Biscayne

kids: there's a swimming pool, jungle gyms, an activity room with a play set out of a child's happiest fantasies and an African baobab tree that's over a century old and teeming with tropical birdlife. Did we mention it's free?

◉ Little Havana

Little Havana's main thoroughfare, Calle Ocho (SW 8th St), doesn't just cut through the heart of the neighborhood; it *is* the heart of the neighborhood. In a lot of ways, this is every immigrant enclave in the USA – full of restaurants, mom-and-pop convenience shops and phonecard kiosks. Admittedly, the Cubaness of Little Havana is slightly exaggerated for visitors, and many of the Latin immigrants here are actually from Central America. With that said, this is an atmospheric place with a soul that's rooted outside the USA. Be on the lookout for the **Cuban Walk of Fame**, a series of sidewalk-implanted stars emblazoned with the names of Cuban celebrities that runs up and down much of 8th St.

The biggest event in the neighborhood's yearly calendar is the Carnaval Miami (Calle Ocho Festival, p100), a street party that showcases Miami's Latin culture over 10 frenetic days.

★**Máximo Gómez Park**   PARK
(Map p86; SW 8th St at SW 15th Ave; ⊙9am-6pm) Little Havana's most evocative reminder of Old Cuba is Máximo Gómez Park, or 'Domino Park,' where the sound of elderly men trash-talking over games of chess is harmonized by the quick clack-clack of slapping dominoes. The jarring backtrack, plus the heavy smell of cigars and a sunrise-bright mural of the 1993 Summit of the Americas, combine to make Máximo Gómez one of the most sensory sites in Miami (although it is admittedly one of the most tourist-heavy ones as well).

Cuban Memorials   MONUMENT
(Map p86) The two blocks of SW 13th Ave south of Calle Ocho contain a series of monuments to Cuban and Cuban American heroes, including those that died in the Cuban War of Independence and anti-Castro conflicts. The memorials include the **Eternal Torch in Honor of the 2506th Brigade**, for the exiles who died during the Bay of Pigs Invasion; a huge **Cuba brass relief** depicting a map of Cuba, dedicated to the 'ideals of people who will never forget the pledge of making their Fatherland free'; a **José Martí memorial**; and a **Madonna statue**, which is supposedly illuminated by a shaft of holy light every afternoon. Bursting out of the island in the center of the boulevard is a massive ceiba tree, revered by followers of Santeria. The tree is an unofficial reminder of the poorer *Marielitos* (those who fled Cuba in the 1980 Mariel Boatlift) and successive waves of desperate-for-work Cubans, many of whom are *santeros* (Santeria practitioners) who have come to Miami since the 1980s.

Just away from the main drag are a fountain and monument, collectively entitled **La Plaza de la Cubanidad** (cnr W Flagler St & NW 17th Ave), which is a tribute both to the Cuban provinces and to migrants who drowned in 1994 while trying to leave Cuba on a ship, *13 de Marzo,* which was sunk by Castro's forces just off the coast.

Cuba Ocho   GALLERY
(Map p86; ☑305-285-5880; www.cubaocho.com; 1465 SW 8th St; ⊙11:30am-3am Tue-Sat) The jewel of the Little Havana Art District, Cuba Ocho functions as a community center, art gallery and research outpost for all things Cuban. The interior resembles a cool old Havana cigar bar, yet the walls are decked out in artwork that references both the classical past of Cuban art and its avant-garde future. Frequent live music, films, drama performances, readings and other events go off every week. The center opens during the evening for these events; check online for more information.

Little Havana

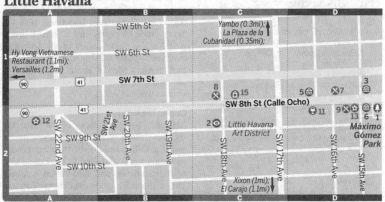

Little Havana Art District   GALLERY

(Map p86; Calle Ocho, btwn SW 15th & 17th Aves)
OK, it's not Wynwood. In fact, it's more 'Art
Block' than district. But this little strip of
galleries and studios does house one of the
best concentrations of Latin American art
(particularly from Cuba) in Miami. Any one
of the studios is worth a stop and a browse.
This particular stretch of Little Havana
is the epicenter of the Viernes Culturales
(p129) celebration.

Bay of Pigs Museum & Library   LIBRARY

(Map p86; www.bayofpigsmuseum.org; 1821 SW
9th St; ⊙9am-4pm Mon-Sat) This small museum is more of a memorial to the 2506th
Brigade, otherwise known as the crew of the
ill-fated Bay of Pigs invasion. Whatever your
thoughts on Fidel Castro and Cuban Americans, pay a visit here to flesh out one side
of this contentious story. You'll likely chat
with survivors of the Bay of Pigs, who like
to hang out here surrounded by pictures of
comrades who never made it back to the
USA.

Tower Theater   HISTORIC BUILDING

(Map p86; ☑305-643-8706; www.towertheater-
miami.com; 1508 SW 8th St) This renovated
1926 landmark theater has a proud deco
facade and a newly done interior, thanks to
support from the Miami-Dade Community
College. In its heyday it was the center of
Little Havana social life, and via the films
it showed served as a bridge between immigrant society and American pop culture.
Today the space frequently shows independent and Spanish-language films (sometimes both) and hosts varied art exhibitions
in the lobby.

◉ Coconut Grove

Coconut Grove was once a hippie colony, but
these days its demographic is middle-class,
mall-going Miami and college students. It's
a pleasant place, especially in the evenings,
bursting with shops and restaurants. 'The
Grove' unfolds along S Bayshore Dr as it
hugs the shoreline; US Hwy 1 (S Dixie Hwy)
acts as the northern boundary.

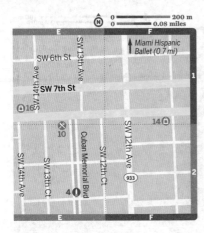

Hwy, on the other side of the road, there's a small Buddhist temple shaded by large groves of banyan trees.

Miami Museum of Science & Planetarium
MUSEUM

(☑305-646-4200; www.miamisci.org; 3280 S Miami Ave; adult/child, student & senior $15/11; ⊙10am-6pm; **P**🕭) The Miami Museum of Science is a dedicated if small institution with exhibits ranging from weather phenomena to creepy crawlies, coral reefs and vital-microbe displays. The planetarium hosts space lessons and telescope-viewing sessions, as well as old-school laser shows with trippy flashes set to the music of the Beatles and Pink Floyd. A new facility is being built next to the Pérez Art Museum Miami (p78) in downtown's Museum Park.

★Vizcaya Museum & Gardens
HISTORIC BUILDING

(☑305-250-9133; www.vizcayamuseum.org; 3251 S Miami Ave; adult/6-12yr/student & senior $18/6/10; ⊙9:30am-4:30pm Wed-Mon; **P**) They call Miami the Magic City, and if it is, this Italian villa, the housing equivalent of a Fabergé egg, is its most fairy-tale residence. In 1916 industrialist James Deering started a long and storied Miami tradition by making a ton of money and building ridiculously grandiose digs. He employed 1000 people (then 10% of the local population) for four years to fulfill his desire for a home that looked centuries old. He was so obsessed with creating an atmosphere of old money that he had the house stuffed with 15th- to 19th-century furniture, tapestries, paintings and decorative arts; had a monogram fashioned for himself; and even had paintings of fake ancestors commissioned. The 30-acre grounds are full of splendid gardens and Florentine gazebos, and both the house and gardens are used for the display of rotating contemporary-art exhibitions.

Barnacle Historic State Park
PARK

(Map p88; www.floridastateparks.org/thebarnacle; 3485 Main Hwy; admission $2, house tours $3; ⊙park 9am-4pm Fri-Mon, house tours 10am, 11:30am, 1pm, 2:30pm Fri-Mon; 🕭) In the center of the village is the 1891, 5-acre pioneer residence of Ralph Monroe, Miami's first honorable snowbird. The house is open for guided tours, and the park it's located on is a lovely, shady oasis for strolling. Barnacle hosts frequent (and lovely) moonlight concerts, from jazz to classical. A little way down Main

Kampong
HISTORIC SITE, GARDENS

(☑305-442-7169; www.ntbg.org/gardens/kampong.php; 4013 Douglas Rd; ⊙tours by appointment only 9am-4pm Mon-Fri) David Fairchild, Indiana Jones of the botanical world and founder of Fairchild Tropical Gardens, would rest at the Kampong (Malay/Indonesian for 'village') in between journeys in search of beautiful and economically viable plant life. Today this lush garden is listed on the National Register of Historic Places and the lovely grounds serve as a classroom for the National Tropical Botanical Garden. Free self-guided tours

---

RESURRECTING THE COCONUT GROVE PLAYHOUSE

Miami's oldest theater is the Coconut Grove Playhouse (Map p88), which sits at 3500 Main Hwy in the heart of the Grove. Back in the day this was a grand dame of a building, with a snazzy marquee and a celebrity vibe balanced by a good deal of artsy cred; Samuel Beckett's *Waiting for Godot* had its US premiere here in 1956 (the show was apparently a disaster). Sadly, the theater was shut down during its 50th-anniversary season due to major debt issues and still sits, today, like a sad shell over Main Hwy. At the time of writing, the theater had been acquired by Miami-Dade County; the building's future remains in question, but plans for turning it into a regional theater house have been discussed.

Coconut Grove

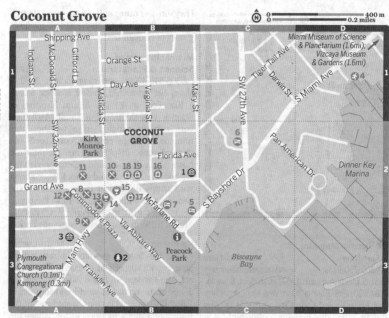

Coconut Grove

(allow at least an hour) are available by appointment, as are $20 two-hour guided tours.

Coconut Grove Arts Precinct GALLERY
Coconut Grove, like many of Miami's neighborhoods, has been making a big deal of promoting its homegrown art galleries. You can walk among them – they're concentrated near **CocoWalk** and **Streets of Mayfair** malls (with a few exceptions) – on the first Saturday night (from 7pm) of every month;

the Coconut Grove Art Walk is decidedly the most family friendly of Miami's many neighborhood art walks.

AC Fine Art GALLERY
(Map p88; ☎ 305-742-7071; www.acfineartsite.com; 2911 Grand Ave; ◎ 10am-6pm) One our favorite galleries, AC Fine Art specializes in limited editions and originals (!) of masters like Dalí, Picasso, Lautrec, Warhol, Basquiat and Lichtenstein.

EVA MUNROE'S GRAVE

Tucked into a small gated area near the Coconut Grove Library (2875 McFarlane Rd), you'll find the humble headstone of one Ms Eva Amelia Hewitt Munroe. Eva, who was born in New Jersey in 1856 and died in Miami in 1882, lies in the oldest American grave in Miami-Dade County (a sad addendum: local African American settlers died before Eva, but their deaths were never officially recorded). Eva's husband Ralph entered a deep depression, which he tried to alleviate by building the Barnacle (p87), now one of the oldest historic homes in the area.

Plymouth Congregational Church CHURCH
(www.plymouthmiami.com; 3400 Devon Rd; P) This 1917 coral church is striking, from its solid masonry to a hand-carved door from a Pyrenees monastery, which looks like it should be kicked in by Antonio Banderas carrying a guitar case full of explosives and Salma Hayek on his arm. Architecturally, this is one of the finest Spanish Mission–style churches in a city that does not lack for examples of the genre.

Ermita de la Caridad MONUMENT
(☑305-854-2404; www.ermitadelacaridad.org; 3609 S Miami Ave) The Catholic diocese purchased some of the bayfront land from Deering's Villa Vizcaya estate and built a shrine here for its displaced Cuban parishioners. Symbolizing a beacon, it faces the homeland, exactly 290 miles due south. There is also a mural that depicts Cuban history. After visiting Vizcaya or the science museum, consider picnicking at this quiet sanctuary on the water's edge.

⊙ Coral Gables

The lovely city of Coral Gables, filled with Mediterranean-style buildings, is bordered by Calle Ocho to the north, Sunset Dr to the south, Ponce de Leon Blvd to the east and Red Rd to the west. The main campus of the University of Miami is located just south of the enormous Biltmore Golf Course and the main pedestrian drag is Miracle Mile – heaven for the shopping obsessed.

Venetian Pool OUTDOORS
(Map p90; ☑305-460-5306; www.coralgablesvenetianpool.com; 2701 De Soto Blvd; adult/child $11.50/7.70; ⊙hours vary; ⊛) Just imagine: it's 1923, tons of rock have been quarried for one of the most beautiful neighborhoods in Miami, but now an ugly gash sits in the middle of the village. What to do? How about pump the irregular hole full of water, mosaic and tile up the whole affair, and make it look like a Roman emperor's aquatic playground? Result: one of the few pools listed on the National Register of Historic Places, a wonderland of coral rock caves, cascading waterfalls, a palm-fringed island and Venetian-style moorings. Take a swim and follow in the footsteps (fin-steps?) of stars like Esther Williams and Johnny 'Tarzan' Weissmuller. Opening hours vary depending on the season; call or check the website for details.

Biltmore Hotel HISTORIC BUILDING
(Map p90; ☑855-311-6903; www.biltmorehotel.com; 1200 Anastasia Ave; P) In the most opulent neighborhood of one of the showiest cities in the world, the Biltmore peers down her nose and says, 'hrmph.' It's one of the greatest of the grand hotels of the American Jazz Age, and if this joint were a fictional character from a novel, it'd be, without question, Jay Gatsby. Al Capone had a speakeasy on-site, and the Capone Suite is still haunted by the spirit of Fats Walsh, who was murdered here (for more ghost details, join in the weekly storytelling in the lobby, 7pm Thursday). Back in the day, imported gondolas transported celebrity guests like Judy Garland and the Vanderbilts around because, of course, there was a private canal system out the back. It's gone now, but the largest hotel pool in the continental USA, which resembles a sultan's water garden from *One Thousand and One Nights,* is still here.

Lowe Art Museum MUSEUM
(www.lowemuseum.org; 1301 Stanford Dr; adult/student $10/5; ⊙10am-4pm Tue-Sat, noon-4pm Sun) Your love of the Lowe, located on the campus of the University of Miami, depends on your taste in art. If you're into modern and contemporary works, it's good. If you're into the art and archaeology of cultures from Asia, Africa and the South Pacific, it's great. And if you're into pre-Columbian and Mesoamerican art, it's fantastic. That isn't to discount the lovely permanent collection of Renaissance and baroque art, Western sculpture from the 18th to 20th centuries, and paintings by Gauguin, Picasso and Monet.

Coral Gables

Merrick House   HISTORIC BUILDING
(Map p90; ☎ 305-460-5361; 907 Coral Way; adult/child/senior $5/1/3; ⊙ tours 1pm, 2pm & 3pm Sun & Wed) It's fun to imagine this simple homestead, with its little hints of Med style, as the core of what would eventually become the gaudy Gables. When George Merrick's father purchased this plot, site unseen, for $1100, it was all dirt, rock and guavas. The property is now used for meetings and receptions, and you can tour both the house and its pretty organic garden. The modest family residence looks as it did in 1925, outfitted with family photos, furniture and artwork.

Entrances & Watertower   LANDMARK
Coral Gables designer George Merrick planned a series of elaborate entry gates to the city, but the real-estate bust meant that projects went unfinished. Among the completed gates worth seeing, which resemble the entrance pavilions to grand Andalucian estates, are the **Country Club Prado**; the

Douglas Entrance; the **Granada Entrance** (Map p90; cnr Alhambra Circle & Granada Blvd); the **Alhambra Entrance** (Map p90; cnr Alhambra Circle & Douglas Rd) and the **Coral Way Entrance** (Map p90; cnr Red Rd & Coral Way). The **Alhambra Watertower** (Map p90; Alhambra Circle), where Greenway Ct and Ferdinand St meet Alhambra Circle, resembles a Moorish lighthouse.

Coral Gables City Hall   HISTORIC BUILDING
(Map p90; 405 Biltmore Way) This grand building has housed boring city-commission meetings since it opened in 1928. It's impressive from any angle, certainly befitting its importance as a central government building. Check out Denman Fink's *Four Seasons* ceiling painting in the tower, as well as his framed, untitled painting of the underwater world on the 2nd-floor landing. There's a small farmers market on-site from 8am to 1pm, January to March.

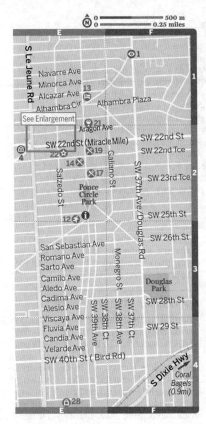

Coral Gables

Coral Gables
Congregational Church   CHURCH
(Map p90; www.coralgablescongregational.org;
3010 De Soto Blvd) George Merrick's father was
a New England Congregational minister, so
perhaps that accounts for him donating the
land for the city's first church. Built in 1924
as a replica of a church in Costa Rica, the
yellow-walled, red-roofed exterior is as far
removed from New England as...well, Miami. The interior is graced with a beautiful
sanctuary and the grounds are landscaped
with stately palms.

Coral Gables Museum   MUSEUM
(Map p90; ☏ 305-603-8067; www.coralgablesmu-
seum.org; 285 Aragon Ave; adult/student/child
$7/5/3; ⊙ noon-6pm Tue-Fri, 11am-5pm Sat, noon-
5pm Sun) This museum is a well-plotted introduction to the oddball narrative of the
founding and growth of the City Beautiful
(Coral Gables). The collection includes historical artifacts and mementos from suc-
ceeding generations in this tight-knit, eccentric little village. The main building is
the old Gables police and fire station, itself
a lovely architectural blend of Gables' Mediterranean revival and a more Miami Beach–
esque, muscular Depression-moderne style.

◎ Greater Miami – North

Museum of Contemporary Art
North Miami   MUSEUM
(MoCA; www.mocanomi.org; 770 NE 125th St; adult/
student & senior $5/3; ⊙ 11am-5pm Tue-Sun; 🅿)
The Museum of Contemporary Art has long

HIBISCUS, PALM & STAR ISLANDS

Floating off the edge of the A1A, in the heart of Biscayne Bay (and posh exclusivity), Hibiscus Island, Palm Island and Star Island are little floating Primrose Hills. There aren't many famous people living here – just wealthy ones – although Star Island is home to Gloria Estefan and for a short time Al Capone lived (and died) on Palm Island. In the 1970s and '80s a mansion on Star Island was the headquarters of the Ethiopian Zion Coptic Church, a Rastafari sect eventually convicted of smuggling large amounts of marijuana into the US. That incident prompted a media circus that focused on both the indictments and neighborly disputes between the long-haired, bearded white Rastas and their aristocratic Star Island neighbors, who complained about the fog of cannabis smoke constantly emanating from the EZCC's compound.

Today the drives for the islands are guarded by a security booth, but the roads are public, so if you ask politely and don't look sketchy, you can get in. Star Island is little more than one elliptical road lined with royal palms, sculpted ficus hedges and fancy gates guarding houses you can't see.

been a reason to hike up to the far reaches of North Miami. Its galleries feature excellent rotating exhibitions of contemporary art by local, national and international artists.

Ancient Spanish Monastery CHURCH
(☑ 305-945-1461; www.spanishmonastery.com; 16711 W Dixie Hwy; adult/child $8/4; ⊙ 10am-4:30pm Mon-Sat, from 11am Sun; ℗) The Episcopal Church of St Bernard de Clairvaux is a stunning early-Gothic and Romanesque building. Constructed in 1141 in Segovia, Spain, it was converted into a granary 700 years later, and eventually bought by newspaper tycoon William Randolph Hearst. He had it dismantled and shipped to the USA in more than 10,000 crates, intending to reconstruct it at his sprawling California estate. But construction was never approved by the government, and the stones sat in boxes until 1954, when a group of Miami developers purchased the dismantled monastery from Hearst and reassembled it. Now it's a lovely, popular oasis (busy for weddings especially, so call before going) and allegedly the oldest building in the western hemisphere. Church services are held at 8am, 10:30am and noon on Sunday, and a healing service is held at 10am on Wednesday.

Hialeah Park PARK
(www.hialeahparkracing.com; 2200 E 4th Ave; ⊙ 9am-5pm Mon-Fri; ℗) Hialeah is more Havanan than Little Havana (more than 90% of the population speak Spanish as a first language), and the symbol and center of this working-class Cuban community is this grand former racetrack. Today a walk through the grounds is recommended, if only to gaze at the grand staircases and pastel-painted concourse, and imagine the thunder of racing hooves. Look for the caps, boots and saddle carved into the window below the administration building, and the oft-photographed central fountain.

Greater Miami – South

Fairchild Tropical Garden GARDENS
(www.fairchildgarden.org; 10901 Old Cutler Rd; adult/child/senior $25/12/18; ⊙ 7:30am-4:30pm; ℗ ⓙ) If you need to escape Miami's madness, consider a green day in the country's largest tropical botanical garden. A butterfly grove, jungle biospheres, and gentle vistas of marsh and keys habitats, plus frequent art installations from folks like Roy Lichtenstein, are all stunning. In addition to easy-to-follow, self-guided walking tours, a free 40-minute tram tours the entire park on the hour from 10am to 3pm. Located 5 miles south of Coral Gables.

Deering Estate at Cutler LANDMARK
(☑ 305-235-1668; www.deeringestate.org; 16701 SW 72nd Ave; adult/child under 14yr $12/7; ⊙ 10am-5pm; ℗ ⓙ) The Deering estate is sort of 'Vizcaya lite,' which makes sense as it was built by Charles, brother of James Deering (of Vizcaya fame). The 150-acre grounds are awash with tropical growth, an animal-fossil pit of bones dating back 50,000 years and the remains of Native Americans who lived here 2000 years ago. There's a free tour of the grounds included in admission, and the estate often hosts jazz evenings under the stars. Last tickets sold at 4pm.

Zoo Miami ZOO
(Miami Metrozoo; ☑ 305-251-0400; www.miamimetrozoo.com; 12400 SW 152nd St; adult/child

$16/12; ☺9:30am-5:30pm, last entry 4pm; P ⓓ) Miami's tropical weather makes strolling around the Metrozoo almost feel like a day in the wild. Look for Asian and African elephants, rare and regal Bengal tigers prowling in an evocative Hindu temple and a pair of Komodo dragons from Indonesia. For a quick overview (and because the zoo is so big), hop on the Safari Monorail; it departs every 20 minutes. There's a glut of grounds tours, and kids will love feeding the Samburu giraffes ($2). Last admission at 4pm.

Jungle Island   ZOO

(✆305-400-7000; www.jungleisland.com; 1111 Parrot Jungle Trail, off MacArthur Causeway; adult/senior/child $35/33/27; ☺10am-5pm; P ⓓ) Jungle Island, packed with tropical birds, alligators, orangutans, chimps, lemurs, a (wait for it *Napoleon Dynamite* fans) liger (a cross between a lion and a tiger) and a Noah's Ark of other animals, is a ton of fun. It's one of those places kids (justifiably) beg to go, so just give up and prepare for some bright-feathered, bird-poopie-scented fun in this artificial, self-contained jungle.

Monkey Jungle   ZOO

(✆305-235-1611; www.monkeyjungle.com; 14805 SW 216th St; adult/child $30/24; ☺9:30am-5pm, last entry 4pm; P ⓓ) The Monkey Jungle tag line is: 'Where humans are caged and monkeys run free.' Indeed, you'll be walking through screened-in trails, with primates swinging, screeching and chattering all around you. It's incredibly fun, and just a bit odorous. The big show of the day takes place at feeding time, when crab-eating monkeys and Southeast Asian macaques dive into the pool for fruit and other treats. There's a lovely aviary for clouds of beautiful rescued parrots.

Pinecrest Gardens   PARK

(www.pinecrest-fl.gov/gardens; 11000 SW 57th Ave; adult/child $3/2; ☺9am-5pm fall & winter, to 6pm spring & summer; P ⓓ) When Parrot Jungle (now Jungle Island) flew the coop for the big city, the village of Pinecrest purchased the property in order to keep it as a municipal park. It's now a quiet oasis with some of the best tropical gardens this side of the Gulf of Mexico, topped off by a gorgeous centerpiece banyan tree. Outdoor movies and jazz concerts are held here, and in all this is a total gem that is utterly off the tourism trail.

Fruit & Spice Park   PARK

(✆305-247-5727; www.fruitandspicepark.org; 24801 SW 187th Ave; adult/child/under 6 $8/2/free;

☺9am-5pm; P) Set just on the edge of the Everglades, this 35-acre tropical public park grows all those great tropical fruits you usually have to contract dysentery to enjoy. The park is divided into 'continents' (Africa, Asia etc) and admission to the grounds includes a free tour; you can't pick the fruit, but you can eat anything that falls to the ground. If you're coming down this far, you may want to consider taking a day trip into Everglades National Park.

Gold Coast Railroad Museum   MUSEUM

(✆305-253-0063; www.gcrm.org; 12450 SW 152nd St; adult/child 3-11yr $8/6; ☺10am-4pm Mon-Fri, from 11am Sat & Sun; P) Primarily of interest to train buffs, this museum displays more than 30 antique railway cars, including the Ferdinand Magellan presidential car, where President Harry Truman famously brandished a newspaper with the erroneous headline 'Dewey Defeats Truman.' On weekends the museum offers 20-minute rides on old cabooses ($6), standard gauge cabs ($12) and, for kids, on a small 'link' train ($2.50). It's advised you call ahead to make an appointment to ride.

Miami Children's Museum   MUSEUM

(✆305-373-5437; www.miamichildrensmuseum. org; 980 MacArthur Causeway; admission $16; ☺10am-6pm; ⓓ) This museum, located between South Beach and downtown Miami, isn't exactly a museum. It feels more like an uberplayhouse, with areas for kids to practice all sorts of adult activities – banking and food shopping, caring for pets, reporting scoops as a TV news anchor in a studio, and acting as a local cop or firefighter.

Matheson Hammock Park   PARK

(www.miamidade.gov/parks/parks/matheson_ beach.asp; 9610 Old Cutler Rd; per car $5; ☺sunrise-sunset; P ⓓ) This 100-acre county park is the city's oldest and one of its most scenic. It offers good swimming for children in an enclosed tidal pool, lots of hungry raccoons, dense mangrove swamps and (pretty rare) alligator-spotting.

Wings Over Miami   MUSEUM

(✆305-233-5197; www.wingsovermiami.com; Kendall-Tamiami Executive Airport, 14710 SW 128th St; adult/child under 12yr/senior $10/6/7; ☺10am-5pm Wed-Sun) Plane-spotters will be delighted by this Kendall-Tamiami Executive Airport museum, which chronicles the history of aviation. Highlights include a propeller collection, J47 jet engine, a Soviet bomber from

Smolensk and the nose section of a B-29 called *Fertile Myrtle,* the same type of aircraft used to drop atomic bombs on Hiroshima and Nagasaki. An impressive exhibit on the Tuskegee Airmen features videos of the African American pilots telling their own stories.

Activities

Miami doesn't lack for ways to keep yourself busy. From sailing her teal waters to hiking through her tropical undergrowth, yoga in her parks and (why not?) trapeze artistry above her head, the Magic City rewards those who want an active holiday.

Biking

**Miami-Dade County Parks
& Recreation Dept** CYCLING
(Map p74; ☑ 305-755-7800; www.miamidade.gov/
parksmasterplan/bike_trails_map.asp) ✐ Leads
frequent ecobike tours through parklands
and along waterfront paths, and offers a list
of traffic-free cycling paths on its website.
For less strenuous rides, try the side roads
of South Beach or the shady streets of Coral
Gables and Coconut Grove. Some good trails
include:

Old Cutler Bike Path Starts at the end
of Sunset Dr in Coral Gables and leads
through Coconut Grove to Matheson Hammock Park and Fairchild Tropical Garden.

Rickenbacker Causeway This route
takes you up and over the bridge to Key
Biscayne for an excellent workout combined with gorgeous water views.

Oleta River State Park (3400 NE 163rd
St) Has a challenging dirt trail with hills
for off-road adventures.

Bowling

Strike Miami BOWLING
(☑ 305-594-0200; www.bowlmor.com/
strike-miami; 11401 NW 12th St; ☺ 4pm-midnight
Tue-Thu, noon-3am Fri, 11am-3am Sat, 11am-midnight Sun, 4pm-1am Mon) In the Dolphin Mall,
this is a good example of what happens
when Miami's talent for glitz and glamor
meets some humble 10-pins.

Lucky Strike BOWLING
(Map p64; ☑ 305-532-0307; www.bowlluckystrike.
com; 1691 Michigan Ave; ☺ 11:30am-1am Mon-Thu,
to 2am Fri, 11am-2am Sat, 11am-1am Sun) Just off
Lincoln Rd, this is Miami Beach's answer to
high-end bowling, full of house and hip-hop
music, electric-bright cocktails and beautiful
club kids.

Day Spas

As you may have guessed, Miami offers
plenty of places to get pampered. Some of
the most luxurious spas in town are found
at high-end hotels, where you can expect to
pay $300 to $400 for a massage and/or acupressure, and $200 for a body wrap. Notable
spas are listed here.

Spa at Mandarin Oriental Miami SPA
(Map p74; ☑ 305-913-8332; www.mandarinoriental.com; 500 Brickell Key Dr, Mandarin Oriental
Miami; manicures $75, spa treatments $150-400;
☺ 8:30am-9:30pm) Calling this spa over the
top is an understatement. Treatments utilize
materials like bamboo and rice paper, and
services include Ayurvedic herbal baths,
aromatherapy, oiled massages and plenty
more decadence.

DOING THE DECOBIKE

Miami Beach is flat, warm, and covered in concrete. In other words, it's about perfect
for cycling. Yet cycling infrastructure has been slow to develop on the beach, leading to
traffic snarls, gridlock and the inevitable slow roll of a Hummer blasting electronic dance
music at every stop light on Collins Ave.

Well no more (although the cars blasting dance music will probably be with us for a
long time). DecoBike saves the day, sort of. This bike-sharing program, modeled after
similar initiatives in New York, London and Paris, makes cycling from South Beach to
Surfside a relative breeze. Just rock up to a solar-powered DecoBike station (a handy
dandy map can be found at www.decobike.com/map-location), insert a credit card and
ride away. You can return your bike at any DecoBike location.

Pricing varies; you'll pay $4 for 30 minutes, $6 for an hour, $10 for two hours, or $24
for a whole day's riding. If you keep your bicycle past the allotted time, you're charged $4
per half-hour. So get out there! Bike away! Get in shape so you don't feel self-conscious
on South Beach while biking around South Beach. Winning all around.

City Walk
Art-Deco
Miami Beach

START ART DECO WELCOME CENTER
END OCEAN'S TEN
LENGTH 1.2 MILES; TWO TO THREE HOURS

Start at the **1 Art Deco Welcome Center** (p134), at the corner of Ocean Dr and 10th St (named Barbara Capitman Way here after the founder of the Miami Design Preservation League). Step in for an exhibit on art-deco style, then head out and go north along Ocean Dr; between 12th St and 14th St you'll see three examples of deco hotels: the **2 Leslie**, a boxy shape with cantilevered sun shades wrapped around the side of the building; the **3 Carlyle**, featured in the film *The Birdcage* and boasting modernistic styling; and the graceful **4 Cardozo Hotel** (p107), built by Henry Hohauser, owned by Gloria Estefan and featuring sleek, rounded edges. At 14th St, peek inside the sun-drenched **5 Winter Haven Hotel** (p108) to see its fabulous floors of terrazzo, made of stone chips set in mortar that is polished when dry. Turn left and head down 14th St to Washington Ave and the **6 US Post Office** (p70), at 13th St. It's a curvy block of white deco in the stripped classic style. Step inside to admire the wall mural, domed ceiling and marble stamp tables. Stop for lunch at the **7 11th St Diner** (p111), a gleaming aluminum Pullman car that was imported in 1992 from Wilkes-Barre, Pennsylvania. Get a window seat and gaze across the avenue to the corner of 10th St and the stunningly restored **8 Hotel Astor** (p103), designed in 1936 by T Hunter Henderson. After your meal, walk half a block east from there to the imposing **9 Wolfsonian-FIU** (p54), an excellent museum of design, formerly the Washington Storage Company. Wealthy snowbirds of the '30s stashed their pricey belongings here before heading back up north. Continue walking Washington Ave, turn left on 7th St and then continue north along Collins Ave to the **10 Hotel** (p104), featuring an interior and roof deck by Todd Oldham. L Murray Dixon designed the hotel as the Tiffany Hotel, with a deco spire, in 1939. Turn right on 9th St and go two blocks to Ocean Dr and nonstop deco beauties; at 960 Ocean Dr (the middling **11 Ocean's Ten restaurant**) you'll see an exterior designed in 1935 by deco legend Henry Hohauser.

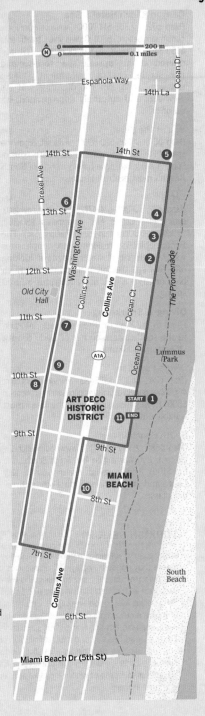

Canyon Ranch Hotel & Spa   SPA

(Map p72; ☑305-514-7000; www.canyonranch.com/miamibeach; 6801 Collins Ave; treatments $150-350; ☺8am-8pm) Check out the 'rituals' offered at this upscale spa: rose-scented rice scrubs, chakra realignment, shiatsu massage, reiki, chi coordinating – if it's New Age and culturally appropriated, it's on offer.

Spa at the Setai   SPA

(Map p64; ☑305-520-6900; www.setai.com/the spa; 101 20th St; treatments $150-380; ☺9am-9pm) A silky Balinese haven in one of South Beach's most beautiful hotels.

Lapis   SPA

(Map p72; ☑305-674-4772; www.fontainebleau.com; 4441 Collins Ave; treatments $80-350; ☺9:30am-6:30pm Sun-Fri, to 7:30pm Sat) The Fontainebleau's resident spa emphasizes water, with 'ritual water journeys' kicking off every spa treatment. Dip into a Turkish bath or enjoy a soak in a eucalyptus-infused spring.

Diving & Snorkeling

Head to the Keys or Biscayne National Park, in the southeastern corner of Dade county. Operators in Miami:

Divers Paradise   DIVING

(Map p84; ☑305-361-3483; www.kbdivers.com; 4000 Crandon Blvd; private open-water certification $500) In Key Biscayne, one of the area's most reliable outfits.

South Beach Divers   DIVING

(Map p68; ☑305-531-6110; www.southbeachdivers.com; 850 Washington Ave, South Beach; dive trip $100) Runs regular excursions to Key Largo and around Miami, plus offers three-day classes.

Fishing

Places to drop a line: South Pointe Park; Rickenbacker Causeway; Key Biscayne Beach. Fishing charters are commonplace but expensive; expect to pay at least $1000 for a day of sportfishing:

Ace Blue Waters Charters   FISHING

(Map p74; ☑305-373-5016; www.fishingmiami.net; Bayside Marketplace, 401 Biscayne Blvd) Fish around Miami and Key Biscayne with this Bayfront Marina–based operation.

Kelley Fleet   FISHING

(☑305-945-3801; www.miamibeachfishing.com; Haulover Beach Park, 10800 Collins Ave, Bal Harbour) Catch a group-fishing party boat with the Kelley Fleet.

Golf

At high-end resorts expect to pay between $150 and $350 to tee off, depending on the season and time of day (it's more expensive in winter and daylight hours).

Biltmore Golf Course   GOLF

(Map p90; ☑855-311-6903; www.biltmorehotel.com/golf; 1210 Anastasia Ave, Coral Gables) Designed by the golfer of that name and boasting the immaculate company of the Biltmore Hotel.

Doral Golf Course   GOLF

(☑800-713-6725; www.trumphotelcollection.com/miami; 4400 NW 87th Ave) Very highly rated, which may explain why it's difficult to get in and also why it once hosted the PGA Ford Championship.

Crandon Golf Course   GOLF

(Map p84; ☑305-361-9129; www.crandongolfclub.com; 6700 Crandon Blvd, Key Biscayne; daylight Dec-Apr $140, twilight May-Nov $30) Overlooks the bay from its perch on Key Biscayne.

TURKISH DELIGHT

Just because you enjoy a good back rub doesn't mean you need to go to some glitzy spa where they constantly play soft house music on a repetitive loop. Right? Why not head to a favorite 'hot' spot among folks who want a spa experience without the glamour, the Russian & Turkish Baths (Map p72; ☑305-867-8316; www.russianandturkishbaths.com; 5445 Collins Ave; ☺noon-midnight). Enter this little labyrinth of *banyas* (steam rooms) and there's a plethora of spa choices. You can be casually beaten with oak-leaf brooms called *venik* in a lava-hot spa (for $40; it's actually really relaxing...well, interesting anyway). There's Dead Sea salt and mud exfoliation ($50), plus, the on-site cafe serves delicious borscht, blintzes, dark bread with smoked fish and, of course, beer. The crowd is interesting too: hipsters, older Jews, model types, Europeans and folks from Russia and former Soviet states, some of whom look like, um, entirely legitimate businessmen and we're leaving it at that.

LOCAL KNOWLEDGE

MIAMI CRITICAL MASS

If you're in Miami at the beginning of the weekend late in any given month, you may spot hordes of cyclists and, less frequently, some skateboarders, roller skaters and other self-propelled individuals. To quote the great Marvin Gaye, 'what's going on?'

It's Miami Critical Mass. The event, put on by the Miami Bike Scene (www.themiamibikescene.com) is meant to raise awareness of cycling and indirectly advocate for increased bicycle infrastructure in the city. Anyone is welcome to join; the mass ride gathers at Government Center (by HistoryMiami, p77) at 6:30pm on the last Friday of each month.

The whole shebang departs on the 12-to-18-mile trek at 7:15pm. The average speed of the ride is a not-too-taxing 12mph, and you will be expected to keep up (at the same time, you're not to go faster than the pacesetters). All in all, a fun experience, and a good way to meet members of the local cycling community.

Haulover Golf Course GOLF
(☑ 305-947-3525; www.miamidade.gov/parks/ haulover; 10800 Collins Ave, Bal Harbour; $21-43) A nine-hole, par-three course that's great for beginners.

Kayaking, Paddleboarding & Windsurfing

Kayaking through mangroves, one of the coolest ecosystems on earth, is magical: all those slender roots kiss the water while the ocean breeze cools your flanks. Try these places: Haulover Beach Park (p98); Bill Baggs Cape Florida State Park (p83); Oleta River State Park (p73).

Blue Moon Outdoor Center WATER SPORTS
(☑ 305-957-3040; http://bluemoonoutdoor.com; 3400 NE 163rd St; ⊗9am-sunset Mon-Fri, from 8am Sat & Sun) Offers single kayaks ($23 per 1½ hours, $41 per three hours), tandem kayaks ($33 per 1½ hours, $51 per three hours) and bike rental ($18 per 1½ hours, $26 per three hours).

Sailboards Miami WATER SPORTS
(☑ 305-892-8992; www.sailboardsmiami.com; 1 Rickenbacker Causeway; ⊗10am-6pm Fri-Tue) Also rents kayaks. You can purchase 10 hours' worth of kayaking for $90. This is also a good spot to rent (and learn how to operate) windsurfing gear (lessons from $35, gear per hour $30).

Aquatic Rental Center & Sailing School WATER SPORTS
(☑ 305-751-7514, evening 305-279-7424; www. arcmiami.com; 1275 NE 79th St; sailboats per 2hr/3hr/4hr/day $85/125/150/225; ⊗9am-9pm) If you're a bona fide seaworthy sailor, this place will rent you a sailboat. If you're not, it can teach you how to operate one (sailing courses $400, $500 for two people).

Bayshore Landing Marina SAILING
(Map p88; ☑ 305-854-7997; 2550 S Bayshore Dr) Key Biscayne sailing is a pure joy, as is gliding along the waters just about anywhere else off Miami. A good starting point is Monty's Marina, which is perfect if you have your own boat.

Rodeo

Rodeo in South Florida? You just have to head a little way out of Miami. Check websites or call ahead for specific rodeo times. If the idea of performing animals and spurs in the same arena makes you ill at ease, you may want to avoid local rodeos.

Bergeron Rodeo Grounds RODEO
(☑ 954-680-3555; www.davie-fl.gov/gen/daviefl_ spclprjcts/bergeronrodeo; 4271 Davie Rd, Fort Lauderdale) In Davie, about 20 miles north of downtown Miami.

Homestead Rodeo RODEO
(☑ 305-247-3515; http://homesteadrodeo.com; 1034 NE 8th St, Homestead) In Homestead, about an hour south of downtown.

Running

Running is quite popular, and the beach is very good for jogging, as it's flat, wide and hard-packed (apparently with amazingly hot joggers). A great resource for races, special events and other locations is the Miami Runners Club (☑ 305-255-1500; www. miamirunnersclub.com).

Some good places for a run include the Flamingo Park track, located east of Alton Rd between 11th St and 12th St, for serious runners; Promenade in South Beach for its style; the boardwalk on Mid-Beach for great people-watching and scenery; and South Bayshore Dr in Coconut Grove for its shady banyan trees.

SOUTH FLORIDA CIRCUS ARTS SCHOOL

Admit it: you always wanted to fly on the trapeze, clamber out of the clown car, tame a lion. Well, we can't really help you with those last two activities, but if you want to learn some circus-worthy acrobatics, contortion and flexibility skills, come to the South Florida Circus Arts School (SFCAS; ☑ 954-540-1344; www.sfcas.com; 15161 NE 21st Ave) in North Miami, off North Biscayne Blvd, about 8 miles north of the Design District. SFCAS claims to be the only institution of its kind offering all-levels accessible education in the skills of the circus. It's a ton of fun and pretty unique; classes include aerial fitness, trapeze skills and the extremely popular flying yoga course (just try it), with fees ranging from $15 to $75 for an hour of instruction. See you in the center ring...

Skating

Serious crowds have turned promenades into obstacle courses for anyone crazy enough to strap on some blades or get on a board. Leave the crowded strips to experts and try the ocean side of Ocean Dr, or Lincoln Rd before the shoppers descend.

Fritz's Skate, Bike & Surf   SKATING
(Map p64; ☑ 305-532-1954; www.fritzsmiami beach.com; 1620 Washington Ave; bike & skate rentals per hour/day/week $10/24/69; ☉ 10am-9pm Mon-Sat, to 8pm Sun) Rent your wheels from Fritz's, which also offers free lessons on Sunday at 10:30am – just about the only time there's ever room on the mall anymore.

Surfing

Miami is not a good place for surfing. The Bahamas block swells, making the water very calm; many will tell you it's best to head about 100 miles north to Jupiter or Palm Beach to catch decent waves (not big waves, just surf consistent enough to hold a board upright). Plus, Miami surfers have worse reputations than Miami drivers when it comes to aggressive, territorial behavior. If you want to ride waves here, the best surfing is just north of South Pointe Park, where you can sometimes find 2ft to 5ft waves and a nice, sandy bottom. Unfortunately it's usually closer to 2ft than 5ft, it can get a little mushy (so longboards are the way to go), and it's swamped with weekend swimmers and surfers. Conditions are better further north, near Haulover Beach Park (10800 Collins Ave, Bal Harbour) or anywhere north of 70th St, like Sunny Isles Beach (Sunny Isles Causeway). Check in with Island Water Sports (☑ 305-944-0104; www. iwsmiami.com; 16231 Biscayne Blvd) for gear, SoBe Surf (☑ 786-216-7703; www.sobesurf.com) for lessons (private instructors will meet with you somewhere on the beach) and www.dadecosurf.com for general information.

Swimming

All of the following pools have lap lanes. Call the Venetian Pool (p89) beforehand, as its lap hours change often.

Flamingo Park Swimming Pool   SWIMMING
(Map p68; ☑ 305-673-7750; 999 11th St, South Beach; adult/child $10/6; ☉ laps 6:30-8:30am & 7-8:30pm) Has a swimming pool with lap lanes.

Normandy Isle Park & Pool   SWIMMING
(Map p72; ☑ 305-673-7750; 7030 Trouville Esplanade; adult/child $10/6; ☉ laps 6:30-8:30am & 7-8:30pm) Family-friendly pool; also offers lap swimming.

Yoga

The beach is definitely not the only place to salute the sun in Miami. There's a lovely 'yoga by the sea' course offered at the Barnacle Historic State Park (per class $13; ☉ classes 6-7:15pm Mon & Wed) in Coconut Grove. If you don't feel like breaking out your wallet, try the free yoga classes at Bayfront Park (☉ classes 6-7:15pm Mon & Wed, 9-10:15am Sat), held outdoors at Tina Hills Pavilion, at the south end of the park, three times a week.

All of the following studios offer a large range of classes; bring your own mat.

Green Monkey Yoga   YOGA
(Map p64; ☑ 305-397-8566; www.greenmonkey. net; 1827 Purdy Ave; classes from $20) Miami Beach; also has a branch in South Miami.

Brickell Hot Yoga   YOGA
(Map p74; ☑ 305-856-1387; www.brickellyoga. com; 301 SW 17th Rd, Brickell; 1-/5-/10-class pass $22/95/180) Downtown.

Prana Yoga Center   YOGA
(Map p90; ☑ 305-567-9812; www.pranayogamiami. com; 247 Malaga Ave, Coral Gables; 1-/5-/10-class pass $20/99/169) In Coral Gables.

Bikram Yoga Miami Beach YOGA
(Map p68; ☑ 305-534-2727; www.bikramyogami-ami.com; 235 11th St, Miami Beach; per day/week $25/50) South Beach.

☞ Tours

Miami Design Preservation League WALKING
(Map p64; ☑ 305-531-3484; http://www.mdpl.org; 1001 Ocean Dr, South Beach; guided tour per adult/senior & student $20/15; ⊙ tours 10:30am Fri-Wed, 6:30pm Thu) Tells the stories and history behind the art-deco buildings in South Beach, either with a lively guide from the Miami Design Preservation League, or a well-presented recording and map for self-guided walks (try the guides). Tours last 90 minutes. Also offers tours of Jewish Miami Beach, Gay & Lesbian Miami Beach and other themed walks; check website for details.

Dr Paul George WALKING
(☑ 305-375-1492; www.historymiami.org/tours/walking-tours; tours from $30) For great historical perspective, call the lively Dr George, a historian for HistoryMiami (p77). George leads several popular tours – including those that focus on Stiltsville, Miami crime, Little Havana and Coral Gables at twilight – between September and late June; hours vary. Dr George also offers private tours by appointment.

Miami Food Tours WALKING
(Map p68; ☑ 888-291-2970; www.miamifoodtours.com; 429 Lennox Ave; adult/student/child from $53/35/17.50; ⊙ tours 11am-2pm Mon-Sat) You'll be visiting five of South Beach's best restaurants, but hey, it's a walking tour – you're burning calories, right?

Urban Tour Host WALKING
(Map p74; ☑ 305-416-6868; www.miamiculturaltours.com; 25 SE 2nd Ave, Suite 1048; tours from $20) Has a rich program of custom tours that provides face-to-face interaction in all of Miami's neighborhoods. A deluxe city tour includes Coral Gables, South Beach, downtown Miami and Coconut Grove.

EcoAdventure Bike Tours CYCLING
(☑ 305-365-3018; www.miamidade.gov/ecoadventures; tours from $28) The Dade County parks system leads excellent bike tours through peaceful areas of Miami and Miami Beach, including along beaches, on Key Biscayne and into the Everglades.

Island Queen BOAT TOUR
(Map p74; ☑ 305-379-5119; www.islandqueencruises.com; 401 Biscayne Blvd; adult/child from $28/19) Boat tours of Millionaire's Row, the Miami River and Stiltsville, among other locations.

MIAMI FOR CHILDREN

Well really, it's Florida, folks; your kids will be catered to. Many of the attractions run toward animal experiences, starting with the Miami Seaquarium (p83), which boasts a large collection of crocodiles, dolphins and sea lions and a killer whale, most of which perform. Next comes the Metrozoo (p92), a 740-acre zoo with plenty of natural habitats (thank you, tropical weather). Should your little ones like colorful animal shows, the outdoors and the smell of animal poo in all its myriad varieties, Miami shall not disappoint. Monkey Jungle (p93) acts as a habitat for endangered species and is everything you'd expect: screeching primates, covered pathways and a grand finale show of crab-eating monkeys diving for fruit. Jungle Island (p93), on the other hand, tends to entertain with brilliant bird shows. Next door is the new Miami Children's Museum (p93), an indoor playland where youngsters can try out the roles of TV anchor, banker and supermarket customer, among others. Coral Gables draws the water-wise to its way-fun, lagoonlike Venetian Pool (p89). For a more educational experience, let your kids explore the Marjory Stoneman Douglas Biscayne Nature Center (p83) on Key Biscayne. Coconut Grove is probably the most child-friendly neighborhood in Miami, with its malls, easy-to-digest (on every level) mainstream dining, and events put on at places such as Barnacle Historic State Park (p87).

Childcare

When it's time to head out for some adult time, check with your hotel, as many offer childcare services – any larger resort worth its salt should be able to provide such services. Or call the local **Nanny Poppinz** (☑ 305-607-1170; www.nannypoppinz.com). For more information, advice and anecdotes, read Lonely Planet's *Travel with Children*.

Miami Nice Tours BUS TOUR
(☑ 305-949-9180; www.miami-nice.com; tours from $50) Has a wide range of guided bus excursions to the Everglades, the Keys and Fort Lauderdale, as well as trips around Miami.

🎉 Festivals & Events

There's something special happening year-round in Miami, with well-touted events bringing in niche groups from serious DJs (Winter Music Conference) to obsessed foodies (Miami Spice Restaurant Month). Addresses are given where there is a fixed festival location.

January

The beginning of the new year also happens to be the height of the tourist season in these parts. Expect fair weather, crowds of visitors, higher prices than usual and a slew of special events.

Orange Bowl FOOTBALL
(www.orangebowl.org; Sun Life Stadium, 2269 Dan Marino Blvd, Miami Gardens) Hordes of football fans descend on Miami for the Super Bowl of college football.

Art Deco Weekend CULTURE
(www.artdecoweekend.com; Ocean Dr, btwn 1st St & 23rd St) This weekend fair featuring guided tours, concerts, classic-auto shows, sidewalk cafes, arts and antiques is held in mid-January.

Miami Jewish Film Festival FILM
(www.miamijewishfilmfestival.com; 4200 Biscayne Blvd) A great chance to cinematically schmooze with one of the biggest Jewish communities in the USA.

February

The last hurrah for northerners needing to escape the harsh winter, February brings arts festivals and street parties, as well as warm days and cool nights.

Art Wynwood ART
(www.artwynwood.com) The dozens of galleries spread throughout Wynwood strut their artistic stuff during this festival, which showcases the best of the Midtown's burgeoning arts scene. There's a palpable commercial bent to this artistic event; big wallet buyers are wooed and marketed to. Expect murals and installations to appear throughout the area. Held on the second weekend in February.

Coconut Grove Arts Festival CULTURE
(www.coconutgroveartsfest.com; Biscayne Blvd, btwn NE 1st St & 5th St, Coconut Grove) One of the most prestigious arts festivals in the country, this late-February fair features more than 300 artists.

**Original Miami Beach
Antiques Show** ANTIQUES
(www.originalmiamibeachantiqueshow.com; Miami Beach Convention Center) One of the largest events of its kind in the USA, with over 800 dealers from more than 20 countries.

South Beach Wine & Food Festival FOOD
(www.sobefest.com) A festival of fine dining and sipping to promote South Florida's culinary image. Expect star-studded brunches, dinners and barbecues.

March

Spring arrives, bringing warmer weather, world-class golf and tennis, outdoor festivals and St Patrick's Day. Expect some Spring Breakers to behave badly on the beach.

Miami International Film Festival FILM
(www.miamifilmfestival.com) This event, sponsored by Miami-Dade College, is a two-week festival showcasing documentaries and features from all over the world.

Calle Ocho Festival CULTURE
(Carnaval Miami; www.carnavalmiami.com) This massive street party in March is the culmination of Carnaval Miami, a 10-day celebration of Latin culture.

South Beach Comedy Festival COMEDY
(www.southbeachcomedyfestival.com) Some of the best comedic talent in the world does stand-up in venues across the city.

Miami Fashion Week FASHION
(www.miamifashionweek.com; Miami Beach Convention Center) Models are as abundant as fish in the ocean as designers descend on the city and catwalks become ubiquitous.

Winter Music Conference MUSIC
(www.wmcon.com) Party promoters, DJs, producers and revelers come from around the globe to hear new artists, catch up on technology and party the nights away.

April

Welcome to the shoulder season, bringing quieter days, lower prices, balmier temperatures and a few choice events.

Billboard Latin Music Awards   MUSIC
(www.billboardevents.com) This prestigious awards show in late April draws top industry execs, star performers and a slew of Latin music fans.

Miami Gay & Lesbian Film Festival   FILM
(www.mglff.com) Held in late April to early May, this annual event features shorts, feature films and documentaries screened at various South Beach theaters.

May & June
May and June boast increased heat, fewer visitors and several cultural events.

Sweatstock   MUSIC
(www.sweatrecordsmiami.com) Sweat Records puts on an annual music festival aimed at locals, with headline acts performing indie rock, punk and electronica.

Goombay Festival   CULTURE
(www.goombayfestivalcoconutgrove.com) A massive festival, held in the first week of June, which celebrates Bahamian culture.

Miami Museum Month   CULTURE
(www.miamimuseummonth.com) An excellent chance to see and hang out in some of the best museums in the city in the midst of happy hours, special exhibitions and lectures.

July & August
The most beastly, humidity-drenched days are during these months, when locals either vacation elsewhere or spend their days melting on the beach.

Independence Day Celebration   HOLIDAY
(Bayfront Park) July 4 is marked with excellent fireworks, a laser show and live music that draw more than 100,000 people to breezy Bayfront Park.

Miami Spice Restaurant Month   FOOD
(www.llovemiamispice.com) Top restaurants around Miami offer prix-fixe lunches and dinners to try to lure folks out during the heat wave.

September & October
The days and nights are still steamy and the start of school brings back college students.

International Ballet Festival   DANCE
(www.internationalballetfestival.org) Some of the most important ballet talent in the world performs at venues across the city.

Great Grove Bed Race   RACE
(www.thegreatgrovebedrace.com) Between the pajama pub crawl and drag-racing beds through Coconut Grove, this is one of Miami's wackier celebrations.

November
Tourist season kicks off at the end of the month, bringing more crowds and slightly cooler days.

Miami Book Fair International   CULTURE
(www.miamibookfair.com; 401 NE 2nd Ave) Occurring in mid- to late November, this is among the most important and well-attended book fairs in the USA. Hundreds of nationally known writers join hundreds of publishers and hundreds of thousands of visitors.

White Party   MUSIC
(www.whiteparty.net) If you're gay and not here, there's a problem. This weeklong extravaganza draws more than 15,000 gay men and women for nonstop partying at clubs and venues all over town.

December
Tourist season is in full swing, with northerners booking rooms so they can bask in the sunshine and be here for holiday festivities. New Year's Eve brings fireworks and festivals to South Beach and downtown Miami's bayfront.

Art Basel Miami Beach   ART
(www.artbaselmiamibeach.com) One of the most important international art shows in the world, with works from more than 150 galleries and a slew of trendy parties.

Design Miami   ART
(www.designmiami.com/) Held in conjunction with Art Basel, usually in early December, Design Miami is a high-profile party hosting some of the world's top design professionals and assorted entourages. Design-inspired lectures and showcases center on the Miami Beach Convention Center.

King Mango Strut   PARADE
(www.kingmangostrut.org; Main Ave & Grand Ave, Coconut Grove) Held each year just after Christmas since 1982, this quirky Coconut Grove parade is a politically charged, fun freak that began as a spoof on current events and the now-defunct Orange Bowl Parade.

Art Miami   ART
(www.art-miami.com) Held in December or January, this massive fair displays modern

and contemporary works from more than 100 galleries and international artists.

🛏 Sleeping

It's in this category, more than any other, where all the hype surrounding Miami, and particularly South Beach, is justified. What sets South Beach apart – what defines it as a travel destination – is the deco district, and the deco district's backbone is hotels. This is one of the largest concentrations of boutique hotels in the country. And the Beach's glam only grows with every new accommodation lauded by the travel glossies, which brings the designers, which brings the fashionistas, which brings the models, which brings the tourists, which brings the chefs and...well, you get the idea.

South Beach hotels are some of the most expensive in Florida. Also, if you opt for hotel parking, expect to be charged $25 to $40 a day for the privilege. It may be easier to park in the large public garages scattered all around South Beach.

Note that the following rates can vary widely based on what events are occuring around town and how far you book in advance.

🛏 South Beach (1st to 11th Streets)

Miami Beach International Hostel HOSTEL **$**
(Map p68; ☎305-534-1740, 305-534-0268; www.hostelmiamibeach.com; 236 9th St; dm/r from $27/32; ✴@🛜) An extensive makeover has turned this reliable old hostel into something like a boutique club with dorm rooms. Bright plaster, marble accents, deco-and-neon decor and hip, clean rooms all make for a hostel to remember. There's a party-friendly social vibe throughout.

South Beach Hostel HOSTEL **$**
(Map p68; ☎305-534-6669; www.sobe-hostel.com; 235 Washington Ave; dm/r from $18/60;

NORTHERN CAPITAL OF THE LATIN WORLD

Miami may technically be part of the USA, but it's widely touted as the 'capital of the Americas' and the 'center of the New World.' That's a coup when it comes to marketing Miami to the rest of the world, and especially to the USA, where Latinos are now the largest minority. Miami's pan-Latin mixture makes it more ethnically diverse than any Latin American city. At the turn of the 21st century, the western suburbs of Hialeah Gardens and Hialeah were numbers one and two respectively on the list of US areas where Spanish is spoken as a first language (over 90% of the population).

How did this happen? Many of Miami's Latinos arrived in this geographically convenient city as political refugees – Cubans fleeing Castro from around the '60s, Venezuelans fleeing President Hugo Chávez (or his predecessors), Brazilians and Argentines running from economic woes, Mexicans and Guatemalans arriving to find work. And gringos, long fascinated with Latin American flavors, can now visit Miami to get a taste of the pan-Latin stew without having to leave the country.

This has all led to the growth of Latin American businesses in Miami, which has boosted the local economy. Miami is the US headquarters of many Latin companies, including Lan Chile, a Chilean airline; Televisa, a Mexican TV conglomerate; and Embraer, a Brazilian aircraft manufacturer. Miami is also home to Telemundo, one of the biggest Spanish-language broadcasters in the US, as well as MTV Networks Latin America and the Latin branch of the Universal Music Group. Miami is the host city of the annual Billboard Latin Music Conference & Awards.

Cubans have a strong influence on local and international politics in Miami. Conservative exile groups have often been characterized as extreme, many refusing to visit Cuba while the Castro family remains in power. A newer generation, however – often referred to as the 'YUCAs' (Young Urban Cuban Americans) – are more willing to see both sides of issues in Cuba.

While many of the subtleties may escape you as a visitor, one thing is obvious: the Latino influence, which you can experience by seeking it out or waiting for it to fall in your lap. Whether you're dining out, listening to live music, overhearing Spanish conversations, visiting Little Havana or Little Buenos Aires, or simply sipping a chilled *mojito* at the edge of your hotel pool, the Latin American energy is palpable, beautiful and everywhere you go.

✳@🛜) On a quiet end of SoFi (the area south of 5th St, South Beach), this hostel has a happening common area and spartan rooms. It may not be too flashy, but the staff are friendly and the on-site bar (open to 5am) seems to stay busy.

Deco Walk
HOSTEL $

(Map p68; 📞305-531-5511; http://decowalkhostel. com; 928 Ocean Dr; dm $35; P✳🛜) The Deco Walk is shooting hard for the title of hippest hostel on the beach, and it's making a good run of it. Pop-art-decorated dorms and a rooftop bar with requisite Jaccuzi and club-esque lounge area are well thought out, but as is often the case with hostels, this place is as good as the crowd staying there.

Jazz on South Beach
HOSTEL $

(Map p68; 📞305-672-2137; www.jazzhostels.com/ jazzlocations/jazz-on-south-beach; 321 Collins Ave; dm $13-24, d $65; ✳@🛜) A nice addition to the expanding SoBe backpacker scene. The hip vibe attracts lots of scenesters and club kids.

★Hotel St Augustine
BOUTIQUE HOTEL $$

(Map p68; 📞305-532-0570; www.hotelstaugustine. com; 347 Washington Ave; r $155-289; P✳🛜) Wood that's blonder than Barbie and a crisp-and-clean deco theme combine to create one of SoFi's most elegant yet stunningly modern sleeps. Color schemes blend beige, caramel, white and cream – the sense is the hues are flowing into one eye-smoothing palette. The familiar, warm service is the cherry on top for this hip-and-homey standout, although the soothing lighting and glass showers – that turn into personal steam rooms at the flick of a switch – are pretty appealing too.

Kent Hotel
BOUTIQUE HOTEL $$

(Map p68; 📞305-604-5068; www.thekentho-tel.com; 1131 Collins Ave; r from 140; P✳🛜) Young party types will probably get a kick out of this lobby, filled with fuchsia- and electric-colored geometric furniture plus Lucite toy blocks, which makes for an aggressively playful welcome. Interior rooms are well appointed with earthy hardwood floors, pretty beds and bright paint palettes.

Hotel Astor
BOUTIQUE HOTEL $$

(Map p68; 📞305-531-8081; www.hotelastor. com; 956 Washington Ave; r/ste from $210/350; P✳🛜≋) They lay the retro-punk on thick in the Astor lobby, glamorizing and exag-

gerating the Age of Transportation into a hip caricature of itself: a gigantic industrial fan blows over a ceiling studded with psychedelic 'lamp balls,' all suspended over a fanciful daydream of an old-school pilots' club. The earth-toned rooms are relaxing, and the small pool gets covered at night to make room for clubgoers who bop on the back-patio lounge.

Fashionhaus
BOUTIQUE HOTEL $$

(Map p68; 📞305-673-2550; www.fashionhaus hotel.com; 534 Washington Ave; r $130-250; P✳🛜≋) The Fashionhaus doesn't just sound like a Berlin avant-garde theater; it kinda feels like one, with its smooth geometric furnishings, 48 individualized rooms decked out in original artwork – from abstract expressionism to washed out photography – and its general blending of comfort, technology and design. Popular with Europeans, fashionistas, artists (and European fashionista artists) and those who just want to emulate that lifestyle.

Nash Hotel
BOUTIQUE HOTEL $$

(Map p68; 📞305-674-7800; www.nashsouth-beach.com; 1120 Collins Ave; r $164-204, ste from $360; P✳🛜≋) This used to be the Lords Hotel, an epicenter of South Beach's gay scene. Today the Nash is still a pretty cream puff of a hotel, with rooms decked out in lemony yellow and whites offset by graphic and pop art. At time of writing, it seemed less LGBT-focused than in the past, if still popular with the boys.

Clinton Hotel
BOUTIQUE HOTEL $$

(Map p68; 📞305-938-4040; www.clintonsouth-beach.com; 825 Washington Ave; r $150-180, ste from $205; P✳🛜) Washington Ave is the quietest of the three main drags in SoBe, but the Clinton doesn't mind. This joint knows it would be the hottest girl in the most crowded party, with her velveteen banquettes and Zen sun porches. Balcony rooms offer a nice view onto the hip courtyard.

Hotel Shelley
BOUTIQUE HOTEL $$

(Map p68; 📞305-531-3341; www.hotelshelley. com; 844 Collins Ave; r from $170; ✳🛜) Gossamer curtains, a lively lounge and a sublimely relaxing violet-and-blue color scheme combine with orblike lamps that look like bunched-up glass spiderwebs. The rooms are as affordably stylish as the rest of the offerings in the South Beach Group selection of hotels (see www.southbeachgroup.com).

Lord Balfour Hotel
BOUTIQUE HOTEL $$

(Map p68; ☑ 305-673-0401; www.lordbalfourmiami.com; 350 Ocean Dr; r $196-300; P❄🔊) Why not name a hotel for a minor, generally ill-regarded British prime minister? Name choice aside, the Lord Balfour features the usual minimalist-plus-pop-art rooms Miami beach is famous for, along with Corinelli bed linens and an overarching Cool Britannia theme. The lobby/bar area is a gem, mixing retro accoutrements with sweeping, modernist lines.

Hotel Breakwater
HOTEL $$

(Map p68; ☑ 305-532-2362; www.esplendorbreakwatersouthbeach.com; 940 Ocean Dr; r $190-250, ste from $360; ❄🔊🏊) A towering blue marquee offset by a stylistically geometric deco facade advertises the Breakwater to all of Ocean Dr. The breezy pool is a good spot to hang before retiring to rooms splashed with citrus-tropical colors and splashes of vintage art.

Ocean Five Hotel
BOUTIQUE HOTEL $$

(Map p68; ☑ 305-532-7093; www.oceanfive.com; 436 Ocean Dr; r/ste from $155/210; P❄🔊) This boutique hotel is all pumpkin-bright; deco dressed up on the outside, with cozy, quiet rooms that reveal a maritime-meets-vintage theme on the inside, with a dash of Old West ambience on top. Think mermaid murals on pale stucco walls. Good value for South Beach.

★ Pelican Hotel
BOUTIQUE HOTEL $$$

(Map p68; ☑ 305-673-3373; www.pelicanhotel.com; 826 Ocean Dr; r $165-425, ste $295-555; ❄🔊) When the owners of Diesel jeans purchased the Pelican in 1999, they started scouring garage sales for just the right ingredients to fuel a mad experiment: 30 themed rooms that come off like a fantasy-suite hotel dipped in hip. From the cowboy-hipster chic of 'High Corral, OK Chaparral' to the jungly electric tiger stripes of 'Me Tarzan, You Vain,' all the rooms are completely different (although all have beautiful recycled-oak floors), fun and even come with their own 'suggested soundtrack.'

★ Sense South Beach
BOUTIQUE HOTEL $$$

(Map p68; ☑ 305-538-5529; www.sensesobe.com; 400 Ocean Dr; r $300; P❄🔊🏊) The Sense is fantastically atmospheric – smooth white walls disappearing behind melting blue views of South Beach, wooden paneling arranged around lovely sharp angles that feel inviting, rather than imposing, and rooms that contrast whites and dark grays into straight duochromatic cool. Pop art hangings and slender furnishings round out the MacBook-esque air.

Mondrian South Beach
RESORT $$$

(Map p68; ☑ 305-514-1500; www.mondrian-miami.com; 1100 West Ave; r/ste from $329/430; P❄🔊🏊) Morgan Hotel Group hired Dutch design star Marcel Wanders to basically crank it up to 11 at the Mondrian. The theme is inspired by *Alice in Wonderland* (if it had been penned by Crockett from *Miami Vice*) – columns carved like giant table legs, chandelier showerheads, imported Delft tiles with beach scenes instead of windmills, and magic walls with morphing celebrity faces (perhaps because the morphing nature of celebrity is what fuels South Beach's glamour?). Oh, and there's a private island (naturally).

Hotel Victor
BOUTIQUE HOTEL $$$

(Map p68; ☑ 305-428-1234; www.hotelvictorsouthbeach.com; 1144 Ocean Dr; r/ste from $335/505; P❄🔊🏊) The Victor wins – the 'hot design' stakes, that is. And the 'fishtanks full of jellyfish' competition. And the 'damn that room is fly' pageant too. Designed by L Murray Dixon in 1938, the redone Victor was opened in 2005, marking a wave of remastered deco classics. Room interiors have a blocky, geometry-meets-minimalism sense of style.

The Hotel
BOUTIQUE HOTEL $$$

(Map p68; ☑ 305-531-2222; www.thehotelofsouthbeach.com; 801 Collins Ave; r $260-425; P❄🔊🏊) This place is stylin' – and why shouldn't it be, when Todd Oldham designed the boldly beautiful rooms? The themed palette of 'sand, sea and sky' adds a dash of eye candy to the furnishings, as do the mosaic doorknobs and brushed-steel sinks. The Hotel boasts a fine rooftop pool, overshadowed only by a lovely deco spire (which says 'Tiffany,' because that was the name of this place before the blue-box jewelry chain threatened a lawsuit).

Chesterfield Hotel
BOUTIQUE HOTEL $$$

(Map p68; ☑ 305-531-5831; www.thechesterfieldhotel.com; 855 Collins Ave; r $200-250, ste $300-600; P❄🔊) Hip-hop gets funky with zebra-stripe curtains and cushions in the small lobby, which hosts a chill happy hour when the sun goes down at the in-house Safari Bar. Rooms mix up dark wood furniture with bright-white beds and vaguely tropical colors swathed throughout. Make sure to enoy the view from the roof deck.

Dream South Beach
BOUTIQUE HOTEL $$$

(Map p68; ☑ 305-673-4747; www.dreamsouthbeach.com; 1111 Collins Ave; r/ste from $250/527;

P ✳ ⚘) How to explain the Dream? From the outside it looks like an ice-cube box of clean white lines, but come inside and it feels like a cross between the interior of an Indian palace, an electric blue tube of toothpaste and a set piece from *Tron*. The rooftop bar is a perfect place to kick back and pretend you're some kind of film-industry mogul, before returning to your room and pretending to be a futuristic mogul. Very popular with LGBT clientele.

Essex House Hotel
BOUTIQUE HOTEL **$$$**

(Map p68; ☑ 305-534-2700; www.essexhotel.com; 1001 Collins Ave; r/ste from $220/280; ✳ ⚘ ⚒) When you gaze at this lobby, one of the best-preserved interiors in the deco district, you're getting a glimpse of South Beach's gangster heyday. Beyond that the Essex has helpful staff, rooms furnished with soft, subdued colors and a side verandah filled with rattan furnishings that's a particularly pleasant people-watching perch.

The Villa by Barton G
RESORT **$$$**

(Map p68; ☑ 305-576-8003; www.thevillabybartong.com; 1116 Ocean Dr; r from $900; P ✳ ⚘ ⚒) Formerly the Versace Mansion (see p54), it has been turned into one of South Beach's most upscale resorts by Barton G, replete with a mosaic pool plucked from ancient Rome, marble bathrooms, linen spun from angel hair and rooms that resemble the guest wing of a minor South American oligarch's personal compound.

Casa Grande Hotel
BOUTIQUE HOTEL **$$$**

(Map p68; ☑ 305-672-7003; www.casagrandesuitehotel.com; 834 Ocean Dr; r $220-380; P ✳ ⚘ ⚘) Fall colors and a splash of bright citrus start the show in the lobby, but the main event is the snow white elegance of the so-chic rooms, each one an ultramodern designer's dream – although we've got to say the big, marble Virgin Mary in the room we visited was way out of place. Pets are welcome (and pampered!) for $50 per critter.

🛏 South Beach (11th to 23rd Streets)

Tropics Hotel & Hostel
HOTEL **$**

(Map p64; ☑ 305-531-0361; www.tropicshotel.com; 1550 Collins Ave; dm $27, r from $65; ✳ ⚒) The Tropics looks a little ratty on the outside, but the interior is nice enough. It sports a big swimming pool and a patio area that seems consistently packed with chatting travelers. The four-bed dorms have attached bathrooms; private rooms are basic and serviceable.

Townhouse Hotel
BOUTIQUE HOTEL **$$**

(Map p64; ☑ 305-534-3800; www.townhousehotel.com; 150 20th St at Collins Ave; r $145-195, ste from $350; ✳ ⚘ ⚒) You'd think the Townhouse was designed by the guy who styled the iPod but no, it was Jonathan Morr and India Mahdavi who fashioned a cool white lobby and igloolike rooms with random scarlet accents and a breezy, white rooftop lounge. Who needs mints on pillows when the Townhouse provides beach balls? One of the better-value hotels on South Beach.

Aqua Hotel
BOUTIQUE HOTEL **$$**

(Map p64; ☑ 305-538-4361; www.aquamiami.com; 1530 Collins Ave; r $150-180, ste from $200; P ✳ ⚘ ⚒) A front desk made of shiny surfboard sets the mellow tone at this former motel – the old, family kind where the rooms are set around a pool. That old-school vibe barely survives under the soft glare of aqua spotlights and an alfresco lounging area. The sleekness of the rooms is offset by quirky furniture and deep blue sea bathrooms.

Catalina Hotel
BOUTIQUE HOTEL **$$**

(Map p64; ☑ 877-762-3477, 305-674-1160; www.catalinahotel.com; 1732 Collins Ave; r from $200; P ✳ ⚘ ⚒) The Catalina is a lovely example of midrange deco style. Most appealing, besides the playfully minimalist rooms, is the vibe – the Catalina doesn't take itself too seriously, and staff and guests all seem to be having fun as a result. The back pool, concealed behind the main building's crisp white facade, is particularly attractive and shaded by a large grove of tropical trees.

Clay Hotel
HOTEL **$$**

(Map p64; ☑ 305-534-2988; www.clayhotel.com; 1438 Washington Ave; r $100-190; ✳ @ ⚘) Hotels are always nicer when they come packaged in a 100-year-old Spanish-style villa. The Clay has clean and comfortable rooms, not too flashy but hardly spartan, located in a medina-like maze of adjacent buildings. If you're on a budget but don't want dorm-y hostel atmosphere, head here. This is one Miami place where Al Capone got some shut-eye.

Cavalier South Beach
BOUTIQUE HOTEL **$$**

(Map p64; ☑ 305-531-3555; www.cavaliersouthbeach.com; 1320 Ocean Dr; r $129-155, ste $229;

P✳🛜) The exterior is a rare Ocean Dr example of the Mayan/Incan inspiration that graced some deco facades (look for Mesoamerican details like the step pattern on the sides of the building). Inside? The Cavalier sacrifices ultrahip for Old Florida casualness, which is refreshing.

★ **Shore Club**   BOUTIQUE HOTEL $$$
(Map p64; ☎305-695-3100; www.shoreclub.com; 1901 Collins Ave; r/ste from $348/455; P✳🖥🈂) Imagine a Zen ink-brush painting; what's beautiful isn't what's there, but what gets left out. If you could turn that sort of art into a hotel room, it might look like the stripped-down-yet-serene digs of the Shore Club. Yeah, yeah: it has the 400-thread-count Egyptian cotton sheets, Mexican sandstone floors etc, but what the Shore Club does like no other hotel is arrange these elements into a greater whole that's impressive in its understatement; the aesthetic is compelling because it comes across as an afterthought.

★ **Gale South Beach**   HOTEL $$$
(Map p64; ☎855-532-2212; galehotel.com; 1690 Collins Ave; r from $310; P✳🖥🛜🈂) The Gale's exterior is an admirable re-creation of classic boxy deco aesthetic expanded to the grand dimensions of a modern SoBe super resort. This blend of classic and haute South Beach carries on indoors, where you'll find bright rooms with clean colors and sharp lines and a retro-chic vibe inspired by the mid-Century Modern movement.

MIAMI'S BEST HOTEL POOLS

Miami has some of the most beautiful hotel pools in the world, and they're more about seeing and being seen than swimming. Most of these pools double as bars, lounges or even clubs. Some hotels have a guests-only policy when it comes to hanging out at the pool, but if you buy a drink at the poolside bar you should be fine.

➡ Delano Hotel (p107)

➡ Shore Club (p106)

➡ Epic Hotel (p109)

➡ Biltmore Hotel (p111)

➡ Raleigh Hotel (p106)

➡ Fontainebleau (p108)

★ **The Standard**   BOUTIQUE HOTEL $$$
(☎305-673-1717; www.standardhotels.com/miami; 40 Island Ave; r/ste from $240/480; P✳🖥🈂) Look for the upside-down 'Standard' sign on the old Lido building on Belle Island (between South Beach and downtown Miami) and you'll find the Standard – which is anything but. This excellent boutique blends a bevy of spa services, hipster funk and South Beach sex, and the result is a '50s motel gone glam. There are organic wooden floors, raised white beds, and gossamer curtains, which open onto a courtyard of earthly delights, including a heated hammam (Turkish bath).

★ **Raleigh Hotel**   BOUTIQUE HOTEL $$$
(Map p64; ☎305-534-6300; www.raleighhotel. com; 1775 Collins Ave; r/ste from $280/420; P✳🛜🈂) While everyone else was trying to get all modern, the Raleigh painstakingly tried to restore itself to prewar glory. It succeeded in a big way. Celebrity hotelier André Balazs has managed to capture a tobacco-and-dark-wood men's club ambience and old-school elegance while sneaking in modern design and amenities. Have a swim in the stunning pool; Hollywood actress Esther Williams used to.

National Hotel   HOTEL $$$
(Map p64; ☎888-897-5959, 305-532-2311; www. nationalhotel.com; 1677 Collins Ave; r $240-420, ste from $500; P✳🛜🈂) The National is an old-school deco icon, with its bell-tower-like cap and slim yet muscular facade. Inside the hotel itself you'll find off-white rooms fashioned to fit more traditional, as opposed to ubermodern, tastes. The lobby and halls are riots of geometric design, while outside a lovely infinity pool beckons guests and visitors. The decadent cabana suites are exercises in luxury, offering unfettered access to said pool, private terraces and on-site tropical gardens.

Sagamore   BOUTIQUE HOTEL $$$
(Map p64; ☎305-535-8088; www.sagamorehotel. com; 1671 Collins Ave; r $240-360, ste from $400; P✳@🈂) This hotel-cum-exhibition hall likes to blur the boundaries between interior decor, art and conventional hotel aesthetics. Almost every space within this hotel, from the lobbies to the rooms, doubles as an art gallery thanks to a talented curator and an impressive roster of contributing artists. Rooms? Stark whites, accented by artsy photography and sleek designer accents.

Setai
BOUTIQUE HOTEL $$$

(Map p64; ☑ 305-520-6000; www.setai.com; 101 20th St; ste $840-6000; P ❄ 🤖 ☀) There's a *linga* in the lobby – nothing says high-end luxury like a Hindu phallus. It's all part of the aesthetic at this exclusive sleep, where a well-realized theme mixes Southeast Asian temple architecture, Chinese furniture, contemporary luxury and an overarching Anywhere Asia concept. Each floor is staffed by teams of 24-hour butlers, while rooms were decked out in chocolate teak wood, clean lines, and Chinese and Khmer embellishments.

W Hotel
RESORT $$$

(Map p64; ☑ 305-938-3000; www.wsouthbeach. com; 2201 Collins Ave; r from $470, ste $700-5700; P ❄ 🤖 ☀) There's an astounding variety of rooms available at the South Beach outpost of the W chain, which brings the whole W-brand mix of luxury, hipness and overblown cool to Miami Beach in a big way. The 'spectacular studios' balance long panels of reflective glass with cool tablets of cipollino marble; the Oasis suite lets in so much light you'd think the sun had risen in your room; the Penthouse may as well be the setting of an MTV video (and given the sort of celebrities who stay here, that assessment might not be far off). The attendant bars, restaurants, clubs and pool built into this complex are some of the most well regarded on the beach.

Cadet Hotel
BOUTIQUE HOTEL $$$

(Map p64; ☑ 305-672-6688; www.cadethotel.com; 1701 James Ave; r from $209; ❄ 🤖 ☀) From paper lanterns hanging from ceilings to furry throw rugs; from clamshell designs encapsulating large mirrors to classical Asian furniture;; and, as always, a great art-deco facade, the Cadet has the aesthetics right. Check out the shaded verandah at the back, lifted from a fantasy idea of what a plantation should feel like.

Betsy Hotel
BOUTIQUE HOTEL $$$

(Map p64; ☑ 305-531-6100; www.thebetsyhotel. com; 1440 Ocean Dr; r from $330; P ❄ 🤖 ☀) The Betsy's rooms present a sort of blend of Caribbean plantation and modern IKEA store; pastel and tropical color schemes blot into the usual South Beach monochrome white, which makes for an elegant but friendly vibe. The exterior suggests much the same spirit, but given the elite set this hotel attracts, areas like the lobby and the pool feel more exclusive and self-assured. The shutter-style doors that frame the windows within the rooms are a nice touch, as are the walnut floors and bath mirrors with inbuilt LCD TVs.

Cardozo Hotel
BOUTIQUE HOTEL $$$

(Map p64; ☑ 305-535-6500; www.cardozohotel. com; 1300 Ocean Dr; r $230-290, ste $320-460; P ❄ 🤖) The Cardozo and its neighbor, the Carlyle, were the first deco hotels saved by the Miami Design Preservation League, and in the case of the Cardozo, we think they saved the best first. It's the combination of the usual contemporary sexiness (white walls, hardwood floors, high-thread-count sheets) and playful embellishments: leopard-print details, handmade furniture and a general sense that, yes, you are cool if you stay here, but you don't have to flaunt it. Oh – remember the 'hair gel' scene in *There's Something About Mary*? Filmed here.

Delano Hotel
BOUTIQUE HOTEL $$$

(Map p64; ☑ 305-672-2000; www.delano-hotel. com; 1685 Collins Ave; r $430-650, ste from $899; P ❄ 🤖 ☀) The Delano opened in the 1990s and immediately started ruling the South Beach roost. If there's a quintessential 'I'm too sexy for this song' South Beach moment, it's when you walk into the Delano's lobby, which has all the excess of an overbudgeted theater set. 'Magic mirrors' in the halls disclose weather info, tide charts and inspirational quotes. The pool area resembles the courtyard of a Disney princess's palace and includes a giant chess set; there are floor-to-ridiculously-high-ceiling curtains in the two-story waterfront rooms; and the bedouin tent cabanas are outfitted with flat-screen TVs. Rooms are almost painfully white and bright; all long, smooth lines, reflective surfaces and sexy, modern, luxurious amenities.

Tides
BOUTIQUE HOTEL $$$

(Map p64; ☑ 305-604-5070; www.tidessouth-beach.com; 1220 Ocean Dr; r $280-625, ste $1000-4000; P ❄ 🤖 ☀) The Tides' ocean-fronting rooms are icy cool, with their jumbled vintage, ocean organic and indie vibe. The pure-white bedding is overlaid by beige, tan and shell, and offset with cream accents. Rooms come with telescopes for planetary (or Hollywood) stargazing, and the lobby, bedecked with nautical embellishments, looks like a modern sea god's palace.

Redbury South Beach
BOUTIQUE HOTEL $$$

(Map p64; ☑ 855-220-1776; http://theredbury. com/southbeach; 1776 Collins Ave; r from $260; ❄ ☀) What sets the Redbury apart is its refusal to toe the line of identikit South Beach minimalist rooms. Rather, the interior here references art across the 20th century, 1960s psychedelia and sleek comfort. A rooftop pool makes for some chilled out lounging, while the lobby has an early-20th-century, Gatsby-era-glam vibe.

Winter Haven Hotel BOUTIQUE HOTEL $$$
(Map p64; ☑ 305-531-5571; www.winterhavenhotel-sobe.com; 1400 Ocean Dr; r $215-330; P ❄ 🎧 ☎) Al Capone used to stay here; maybe he liked the deco ceiling lamps in the lobby, with their sharp, retro sci-fi lines and grand-Gothic proportions, and the oddly placed oriental mirrors (which have nothing to do with art deco whatsoever). The rooms, with their dark-wood accents and ice-white bedspreads, are a bit warmer than your average South Beach digs.

Surfcomber HOTEL $$$
(Map p64; ☑ 305-532-7715; www.surfcomber.com; 1717 Collins Ave; r $190-350, ste from $430; P ❄ 🎧 ☎) Simply put, the Surfcomber is one of the best deco structures in Miami. Note the movement-suggestive lines on the exterior and semicircular, shade-providing 'eyebrows' that jut out of the windows. The rounded, aeronautical feel of the lobby suggests you're entering a 1930s airline lounge but no, you're just going to your room, which replicates the classic deco and modern design marriage of the front.

James Royal Palm Hotel HOTEL $$$
(Map p64; ☑ 305-604-5700; www.jameshotels.com/miami; 1545 Collins Ave; r/ste from $240/500; P ❄ 🎧 ☎) Even the trolleys here have a touch of curvy deco flair, to say nothing of the chunky staircase and mezzanine, which are the best South Beach examples of the building-as-cruise-liner deco theme. The shipboard theme carries into the rooms, which are also offset by bright whites and minty color accents.

Northern Miami Beach

Circa 39 BOUTIQUE HOTEL $$
(Map p72; ☑ 305-538-4900; www.circa39.com; 3900 Collins Ave; r $130-170; P ❄ @ ☎) If you love South Beach style but loathe South Beach attitude, Circa has got your back. The lobby, with its molded furniture and wacky embellishments, is one of the funkiest in Miami. Chic rooms, bursting with tropical lime green and subtle earth tones, are hip enough for the design-obsessed scenesters.

Freehand Miami BOUTIQUE HOTEL $$
(Map p72; ☑ 305-531-2727; http://thefreehand.com; 2727 Indian Creek Dr; dm/r from $50/220; ❄ 🎧 ☎) The Freehand is the brilliant re-imagining of the old Indian Creek Hotel, a classic of the Miami Beach scene. Rooms are comfortably minimalist, with just the right amount of local artwork and wooden tones to strike a nice balance between warm funky and cool hip. Dorms serve the hostel crowd, and the on-site Broken Shaker (p124) is one of the best bars in town.

Red South Beach BOUTIQUE HOTEL $$
(Map p72; ☑ 800-528-0823; www.redsouthbeach.com; 3010 Collins Ave; r $130-200; ❄ 🎧 ☎) Red is indeed the name of the game, from the cushions on the sleek chairs in the lobby to the flashes dancing around the marble pool to deep, blood crimson headboards and walls wrapping you in warm sexiness in the small but beautiful guest rooms. The Red is excellent value for money and come evening the pool-bar complex is a great place to unwind and meet fellow guests.

Daddy O Hotel BOUTIQUE HOTEL $$
(☑ 305-868-4141; www.daddyohotel.com; 9660 E Bay Harbor Dr; r $150-260; P ❄ 🎧 ☎) The Daddy O is a cheerful, hip option that looks, from the outside, like a large B&B that's been fashioned for MTV and Apple employees. This vibe continues in the lobby and the rooms: cool, clean lines offset by bright, bouncy colors, plus a nice list of amenities: flat-screen TVs, custom wardrobes, free wi-fi and the rest. It's located about 3 miles north of North Miami Beach.

Mimosa BOUTIQUE HOTEL $$
(Map p72; ☑ 305-868-4141; www.themimosa.com; 6525 Collins Ave; r $120-220; ❄ 🎧 ☎) The Mimosa is decked out in mid-20th-century modern furniture, offset by deco embellishment like portico-style mirrors, dark-and-light room color schemes and a tangerine-and-cream lobby with a citrus-bright vibe. The pool is smallish, but overlooks a lovely stretch of the Atlantic Ocean.

Fontainebleau RESORT $$$
(Map p72; ☑ 305-535-3283; www.fontainebleau.com; 4441 Collins Ave; r $344-461, ste from $550; P ❄ 🎧 ☎) The grand Fontainebleau opened in 1954, when it became a celeb-sunning spot. Numerous renovations have added beachside cabanas, seven tennis courts, a grand ballroom, a shopping mall and a fabulous swimming pool. The rooms are

surprisingly bright and cheerful – we expected more hard-edged attempts to be cool, but the sunny disposition of these chambers is a welcome surprise.

Eden Roc Renaissance
RESORT $$$

(Map p72; ☑ 305-531-0000, 855-433-3676; www.edenrocmiami.com; 4525 Collins Ave; r/ste from $305/440; [P][✳][⚲][≋]) The Roc's immense inner lobby draws inspiration from the Rat Pack glory days of Miami Beach cool, and rooms in the Ocean Tower boast lovely views over the Intracoastal Waterway. All the digs here have smooth, modern embellishments and amenities ranging from MP3 players to HDTV, ergonomic furniture and turndown service, among others.

Claridge Hotel
HOTEL $$$

(Map p72; ☑ 305-604-8485; www.claridgemiamibeach.com; 3500 Collins Ave; r from $220; [✳][@][≋]) This 1928 Mediterranean-style palace feels like an (Americanized) Tuscan villa, with a honey-stone courtyard enclosing a sparkling pool, framed by palms, frescoed walls and gleaming stone floors. The soothing, old-world rooms are set off by rich earth tones, and staff are eager to please.

Palms Hotel
HOTEL $$$

(Map p72; ☑ 305-534-0505; www.thepalmshotel.com; 3025 Collins Ave; r $200-380, ste from $440; [P][✳][@][≋]) The lobby of the Palms manages to be imposing and comfortable all at once; the soaring ceiling, cooled by slow-spinning giant rattan fans, makes for a colonial-villa-on-convention-center-steroids vibe. Upstairs the rooms are perfectly fine, a mix of pastel colors and comfortable, if slightly bland, furnishings.

🛏 Downtown Miami

Epic
HOTEL $$$

(Map p74; ☑ 866-760-3742, 305-424-5226; www.epichotel.com; 270 Biscayne Blvd; r $240-510, ste from $570; [P][✳][⚲][≋]) Epic indeed! This massive Kimpton hotel is one of the more attractive options downtown and it possesses a coolness cred that could match any spot on Miami Beach. Of particular note is the outdoor pool and sun deck, which overlooks a gorgeous sweep of Brickell and the surrounding condo canyons. The rooms are outfitted in designer-chic furnishings and some have similarly beautiful views of greater Miami-Dade. There's a youthful energy throughout that's lacking in other corporate-style downtown hotels.

MIMO ON BIBO

That cute little phrase means 'Miami Modern on Biscayne Boulevard,' and refers to the architectural style of buildings on North Biscayne Blvd past 55th Street. Specifically, there are some great roadside motels here with lovely, Rat Pack–era '50s neon beckoning visitors in. This area was neglected for a long time, and some of these spots are seedy (when we asked one owner why she advertised rooms for only $25, she smiled and said, 'Por hora' – by the hour). But north BiBo is also one of Miami's rapidly gentrifying areas, and savvy motel owners are cleaning up their act and looking to attract the hipsters, artists and gay population flocking to the area. There's already exciting food here. Now the lodgings are getting stimulating too. All these hotels provide South Beach comfort at half the price.

New Yorker (☑ 305-759-5823; www.hotelnewyorkermiami.com; 6500 Biscayne Blvd; r $75-130; [P][✳][⚲]) This hotel has been around since the 1950s and it shows – in a good way. If you could turn a classic Cadillac into a hotel with a modern interior and hipster cred, then bam, there's the New Yorker in a nutshell. Staff are friendly and the rooms – done up with pop art, geometric designs and solid colors – would make Andy Warhol proud.

Motel Blu (☑ 877-784-6835; www.motelblumiami.com; 7700 Biscayne Blvd; r $52-150; [P][✳][⚲][≋]) Situated above Miami's Little River, the Blu may not look like much from the outside, but inside you'll find freshly done-up rooms with a host of modern amenities. Rooms are comfortable and have a soothing lime-and-lemon interior.

Motel Bianco (Map p80; ☑ 305-751-8696; www.motelbianco.com; 5255 Biscayne Blvd; r $80-110; [P][✳][⚲]) The Bianco situates several orange-and-milky-white rooms around a glittery courtyard where coffee is served and guests can get to know each other. Contemporary art designs swirl through the larger rooms and wicker furniture abounds throughout.

Mandarin Oriental Miami HOTEL $$$

(Map p74; ☑ 866-888 6780, 305-913-8383; www.mandarinoriental.com/miami; 500 Brickell Key Dr; r $380-750, ste from $950; P❋☎✸) The Mandarin shimmers on Brickell Key, which is actually annoying – you're a little isolated from the city out here. Not that it matters; there's a luxurious world within a world inside this exclusive compound, from swank restaurants to a private beach and skyline views that look back at Miami from the far side of Biscayne Bay. Rooms are good in a luxury-chain kind of way, but nothing sets them apart from other sleeps in this price range.

Four Seasons Miami HOTEL $$$

(Map p74; ☑ 305-358-3535; www.fourseasons.com/miami; 1435 Brickell Ave; r/ste from $330/450; P❋☎✸) The marble common areas double as art galleries, a massive spa caters to corporate types and there are sweeping, could-have-been-a-panning-shot-from-*Miami-Vice* views over Biscayne Bay in some rooms. The 7th-floor terrace bar, Bahia, is pure *mojito*-laced, Latin-loved swankiness, especially on Thursdays and Fridays from 6pm to 8pm, when ladies drink free.

🛏 Key Biscayne

Silver Sands Beach Resort RESORT $$

(Map p84; ☑ 305-361-5441; www.silversandsbeachresort.com; 301 Ocean Dr; r $169-189, cottages $279-349; P❋✸) Silver Sands: aren't you cute, with your one-story, stucco tropical tweeness? How this little, Old Florida–style independent resort has survived amid the corporate competition is beyond us, but it's definitely a warm, homey spot for those seeking some intimate, individual attention – to say nothing of the sunny courtyard, garden area and outdoor pool.

Ritz-Carlton Key Biscayne RESORT $$$

(Map p84; ☑ 305-365-4500; www.ritzcarlton.com; 455 Grand Bay Dr; r/ste from $320/1200; P❋☎✸) Many Ritz-Carlton outposts feel a little cookie-cutter, but the Key Biscayne outpost of the empire is pretty unique. There's the magnificent lobby, vaulted by four giant columns lifted from a Cecil B DeMille set – hell, the whole hotel is lifted from a DeMille set. Tinkling fountains, the view of the bay and the marble grandeur speak less of a chain hotel and more of early-20th-century glamour. Rooms and amenities are predictably excellent.

🛏 Coconut Grove

Sonesta Hotel & Suites Coconut Grove HOTEL $$

(Map p88; ☑ 305-529-2828; www.sonesta.com/coconutgrove; 2889 McFarlane Rd; r $140-400, ste $210-660; P❋☎✸) The Coco Grove outpost of this luxury chain of hotels has decked out its rooms in almost all white with a splash of color (South Beach style). The amenities, from flat-screen TVs to minikitchenettes, add a layer of luxury to this surprisingly hip chain. Make your way to the top of the building to enjoy a wonderful outdoor deck pool.

Mutiny Hotel HOTEL $$$

(Map p88; ☑ 888-868-8469, 305-441-2100; mutinyhotel.com; 2951 S Bayshore Dr; ste $150-351; P❋☎✸) This small, luxury bayfront hotel, with one- and two-bedroom suites featuring balconies, boasts an indulgent staff, high-end bedding, gracious appointments, fine amenities and a small heated pool. Although it's on a busy street, you won't hear the traffic once inside. The property boasts fine views over the water.

Ritz-Carlton Coconut Grove RESORT $$$

(Map p88; ☑ 305-365-4500; www.ritzcarlton.com; 3300 SW 27th Ave; r & ste $270-399; P❋☎✸🐾) Another member of the Ritz-Carlton organization in Miami, this one overlooks the bay, has immaculate rooms and offers butlers for every need, from shopping and web-surfing to dog-walking and bathing. The massive spa is stupendous.

Grove Isle Club & Resort RESORT $$$

(☑ 305-858-8300; www.groveisle.com; 4 Grove Isle Dr; r $250-529, ste $389-879; P❋☎✸) One of those 'I've got my own little island' type places, Grove Island is off the coast of Coconut Grove. This stunning boutique hotel has colonial elegance, lush tropical gardens, its own jogging track, decadent pool, sunset views over Biscayne Bay, amenities galore and the cachet of staying in your own floating temple of exclusivity.

🛏 Coral Gables

Hotel St Michel HOTEL $$

(Map p90; ☑ 305-444-1666; www.hotelstmichel.com; 162 Alcazar Ave; r $120-225; P❋☎) The Michel is more Metropole than Miami, and we mean that as a compliment. The old-world wooden fixtures, refined sense of tweedy style and dinner-jacket ambience don't get in the way of friendly service. The lovely restaurant and cool bar-lounge are as elegant as the hotel they occupy.

★**Biltmore Hotel**   HISTORIC HOTEL **$$$**
(Map p90; ☎855-311-6903; www.biltmorehotel. com; 1200 Anastasia Ave; r from $209; P❄🐾🏊) Though the Biltmore's standard rooms can be small, a stay here is a chance to sleep in one of the great laps of US luxury. The grounds are so palatial it would take a solid week to explore everything the Biltmore has to offer – we highly recommend reading a book in the Romanesque/Arabian Nights opulent lobby, sunning underneath enormous columns and taking a dip in the largest hotel pool in the continental USA.

🛏 Greater Miami

Inn at the Fisher Island Club   RESORT **$$$**
(☎305-535-6000;   www.fisherislandclub.com; r $600-2250; ❄🐾🏊) If you're not Jeb Bush (who lives here), the only way to glimpse Fisher Island is to stay at this luxurious resort. Whether in 'simple' rooms or Vanderbilt-era cottages, your money will be well spent: one of the best-rated spas in the country is here, as well as eight restaurants (which seems like overkill given the size of the island) and enough royal perks to please a pharaoh.

🍴 Eating

Miami is a major immigrant entrepôt and a sucker for food trends. Thus you get a good mix of cheap ethnic eateries and high-quality top-end cuisine here. There's admittedly a lot of dross too, especially on Miami Beach, where people can overcharge tourists and get away with it. The best new spots for dining are in Wynwood and Design District (Midtown); Coral Gables is also an established foodie hot spot.

🍴 South Beach
(1st to 11th Streets)

Puerto Sagua   CUBAN **$**
(Map p68; ☎305-673-1115; 700 Collins Ave; mains $6-20; ⊙7:30am-2am) There's a secret colony of older working-class Cubans and construction workers hidden among South Beach's sex-and-flash, and evidently, they eat here (next to a Benetton). Puerto Sagua challenges the US diner with this reminder: Cubans can greasy-spoon with the best of them. Portions of favorites such as *picadillo* (spiced ground beef with rice, beans and plantains) are stupidly enormous. The Cuban coffee here is not for the faint of heart – strong stuff.

11th St Diner   DINER **$**
(Map p68; 1065 Washington Ave; mains $9-18; ⊙24hr except midnight-7am Wed) You've seen the art-deco landmarks. Now eat in one: a Pullman-car diner trucked down from Wilkes-Barre, Pennsylvania – as sure a slice of Americana as a *Leave It to Beaver* marathon. If you've been drinking all night, we'll split a three-egg omelet with you and the other drunkies at 6am – if there's a diner where you can replicate Edward Hopper's *Nighthawks,* it's here.

Pizza Rustica   PIZZERIA **$**
(Map p68; www.pizza-rustica.com; 863 Washington Ave; slices $5, mains $8-10; ⊙11am-6pm) South Beach's favorite pizza place has several locations to satisfy the demand for crusty Roman-style slices topped with an array of exotic offerings. A slice is a meal unto itself and goes down a treat when you need something to soak up the beer.

News Cafe   AMERICAN **$**
(Map p68; www.newscafe.com; 800 Ocean Dr; mains $7-17; ⊙24hr) News Cafe is an Ocean Dr landmark that attracts thousands of travelers. We find the food to be pretty uninspiring, but the people-watching is good, so take a perch, eat some over-the-average but not-too-special food and enjoy the anthropological study that is South Beach as she skates, salsas and otherwise shambles by.

★**Tap Tap**   HAITIAN **$$**
(Map p68; ☎305-672-2898; www.taptaprestaurant. com; 819 5th St; mains $9-20; ⊙noon-11:30pm) In Haiti, tap-taps are brightly colored pickup trucks turned public taxis, and their tropi-psychedelic paint schemes inspire the decor in this excellent Haitian eatery. This is no Manhattan-style South Beach lounge – here you dine under bright murals of Papa Legba, guardian of the dead, emerging from a Port-au-Prince cemetery. Meals are a happy marriage of West African, French and Caribbean: spicy pumpkin soup, snapper in a scotch-bonnet lime sauce, curried goat and charcoal-grilled Turks and Caicos conch. Make sure you try the *mayi moulen*, a signature side of cornmeal smothered in a rich bean sauce – bloody delicious! If you need some liquid courage, shoot some Barbancourt rum, available in several grades (all strong).

BUILDING A CUBAN SANDWICH

The traditional Cuban sandwich, also known as a *sandwich mixto*, is not some slapdash creation. It's a craft best left to the experts – but here's some insight into how they do it. Correct bread is crucial – it should be Cuban white bread: fresh, soft and easy to press. The insides (both sides) should be buttered and layered (in the following order) with sliced pickles, slices of roast Cuban pork, ham (preferably sweet-cured ham) and baby Swiss cheese. Then it all gets pressed in a hot *plancha* (sandwich press) until the cheese melts. Mmmm.

Cafe Mistral
FRENCH $$

(Map p68; ✆305-763-8184; 110 Washington Ave; mains $11-18; ✆9am-11pm Tue-Sat; ✐) Mistral's simple French fare makes this spot a favorite breakfast and lunch spot in SoFi. You're on Miami Beach but removed from its worst excesses, and treated instead to tasty croque monsieurs, garden salads, the 'Fruban' (which of course blends a Cuban sandwich and a baguette) and killer coffee.

Big Pink
DINER $$

(Map p68; ✆305-532-4700; 157 Collins Ave; mains $11-26; ✆8am-midnight Sun-Wed, to 2am Thu, to 5am Fri & Sat) Big Pink does American comfort food with joie de vivre and a dash of whimsy. The Americana menu is consistently good throughout the day; pulled Carolina pork holds the table next to a nicely done reuben. The interior is somewhere between a '50s sock hop and a South Beach club; expect to be seated at a long communal table.

Grazie
ITALIAN $$$

(Map p68; ✆305-673-1312; www.grazieitaliancuisine.com; 702 Washington Ave; mains $19-34; ✆noon-3pm Mon-Fri, 6pm-midnight daily) Thanks indeed; Grazie is top class and comfortably old-school northern Italian. There's a distinct lack of gorgeous, clueless waitstaff and unwise menu experimentation. Instead there's attentive service, solid and delicious mains, and extremely decent prices given the quality of the dining and high-end nature of the location. The porcini risotto is simple in construction yet deeply complex in execution – one of the best Italian dishes on the beach.

Prime 112
STEAKHOUSE $$$

(Map p68; ✆305-532-8112; www.prime112.com; 112 Ocean Dr; mains $29-75; ✆noon-3pm Mon-Fri, 5:30pm-midnight Sun-Thu, to 1am Sat & Sun) Sometimes, you need a steak: well aged, juicy, marbled with the right bit of fat, served in a spot where the walls sweat testosterone, the bar serves Manhattans and the hostesses are models. Chuck the above into Miami Beach's oldest inn – the beautiful 1915 Browns Hotel – and there's Prime 112. Dress up, because there's a good chance you'll be dining next to a celebrity.

Joe's Stone Crab Restaurant
AMERICAN $$$

(Map p68; ✆305-673-0365; www.joesstonecrab.com; 11 Washington Ave; mains $11-60; ✆11:30am-2pm Wed-Sun, except in summer, & 6-10pm Wed-Sun year-round) The wait is long, the prices high. But if those aren't deal-breakers, queue up to don a bib in Miami's most famous restaurant and enjoy deliciously fresh stone-crab claws.

South Beach (11th to 23rd Streets)

Burger & Beer Joint
BURGERS $

(Map p64; ✆305-672-3287; www.bnbjoint.com; 1766 Bay Rd; mains $5.50-9; ✆11:30am-midnight Sun-Thu, to 2am Fri & Sat; ✐) Gourmet burgers. Microbrew beer. Clearly, the folks at B&B did their marketing research. Because who doesn't love both? Oh yes, vegetarians, you're catered to as well: the 'Dear Prudence', a mix of portobello, red pepper, walnut pesto and zucchini fries will keep herbivores happy. Oh, there's a turkey and stuffing burger with gravy served *between turkey patties*, an ahi tuna burger, a patty of wagyu beef with foie gras...you get the idea. Did we mention the microbrew beer?

Flamingo Restaurant
NICARAGUAN $

(Map p64; ✆305-673-4302; 1454 Washington Ave; mains $2.50-7; ✆7am-9pm Mon-Sat) This tiny Nicaraguan storefront-cafe serves the behind-the-scenes laborers who make South Beach function. You will very likely be the only tourist eating here. Workers devour hen soup, pepper chicken and cheap breakfasts prepared by a meticulous husband-and-wife team.

Paul
BAKERY $

(Map p64; 450 Lincoln Rd; mains $5.50-11; ✆8:30am-8pm; ✐) Paul sells itself as a 'Maison de Qualite', which in other words means you can get some very fine bread here, the sort of crusty-outside and pillow-soft-inside bread you associate with a Parisian *boulangerie*. Gourmet sandwiches and light pastries make for a refreshing Lincoln Rd lunch stop.

Gelateria 4D
ICE CREAM $

(Map p64; ☑ 305-538-5755; 670 Lincoln Rd; ice creams $3.85-8; ⊙ 9am-midnight Sun-Thu, to 1:30am Fri & Sat) It's hot. You've been walking all day. You need ice cream, stat. Why hello, 4D! This is an excellent spot for creamy, pillowy waves of European-style frozen goodness, and based on the crowds it's the favorite ice cream on South Beach.

★ Pubbelly
FUSION $$

(Map p64; ☑ 305-532-7555; 1418 20th Street; mains $11-26; ⊙ 6pm-midnight Tue-Thu & Sun, to midnight Fri & Sat) Pubbelly's dining genre is hard to pinpoint, besides delicious. It skews between Asian, North American and Latin American, gleaning the best from all cuisines. Examples? Try duck and scallion dumplings, or the mouth-watering udon 'carbonara' with pork belly, poached eggs and parmesan. Hand-crafted cocktails wash down the dishes a treat.

Jerry's Famous Deli
DELI $$

(Map p64; ☑ 305-532-8030; www.jerrysfamous-deli.com; 1450 Collins Ave; mains $9-18; ⊙ 24hr) Important: Jerry's delivers. Why? Because when you've gorged on the pastrami on rye, turkey clubs and other mile-high sandwiches at this enormous Jewish deli (housed in what used to be the Warsaw nightclub), you'll be craving more of the above 24/7.

Spiga
ITALIAN $$

(Map p68; ☑ 305-534-0079; www.spigarestaurant.com; Impala Hotel, 1228 Collins Ave; mains $15-28; ⊙ 6pm-midnight) This romantic nook is a perfect place to bring your partner and gaze longingly at one another over candlelight, before you both snap out of it and start digging into excellent traditional Italian such as lamb in olive oil and rosemary, and baby clams over linguine.

Jimmy'z Kitchen
LATIN AMERICAN $$

(Map p64; ☑ 305-534-8216; 1542 Alton Rd; mains $8-18; ⊙ 11am-10pm Sat-Thu, to 11pm Fri; ☑) It's hard to find Nuevo Latino cuisine that comfortably fits a midrange budget and is still tasy, but in steps Jimmy'z. Make sure to try the *mofongo*, a ridculously filling fried plantain dish from Puerto Rico. Make sure to top the evening off with some decadent guava cheesecake.

Van Dyke Cafe
FUSION $$

(Map p64; ☑ 305-534-3600; 846 Lincoln Rd; mains $12-28; ⊙ 8am-1am) One of Lincoln Rd's most touristed spots, the Van Dyke is an institution akin to the News Cafe, serving adequate food in a primo spot for people-watching. It's usually packed and takes over half the sidewalk. Service is friendly and efficient, and you get free preening models with your burgers and eggplant parmigiana. There's excellent nightly jazz upstairs.

Guru
INDIAN $$

(Map p68; ☑ 305-534-3996; 232 12th St; mains $15-23; ⊙ noon-11:30pm; ☑) A sexy, soft-lit interior of blood reds and black wood sets the stage for this Indian eatery, where local ingredients like lobster swim into the korma. Goan fish curry goes down a treat but the service often seems rushed and the kitchen can be inconsistent. Try coming at lunchtime for the *thali* special, an assemble-your-own meal extravaganza.

Balans
FUSION $$

(Map p64; ☑ 305-534-9191; 1022 Lincoln Rd; mains $13-36; ⊙ 8am-midnight) Kensington, Chiswick...South Beach? Oi, give this Brit-owned fusion favorite a go. Where else do veal saltimbocca and lamb *jalfrezi* share a menu? After you down the signature lobster club, you'll agree tired stereotypes about English cooking need to be reconsidered.

Nexxt Cafe
FUSION $$

(Map p64; ☑ 305-532-6643; 700 Lincoln Rd; mains $7-23; ⊙ 11:30am-11pm Mon-Thu, to midnight Fri & Sat, 11am-11pm Sun) There's a lot of cafes arranged around Lincoln Rd that offer good people-watching along one of Miami Beach's most fashionable stretches. Many of these spots are of questionable quality. Nexxt is the best of the bunch, with a huge menu that jumps between turkey chili, gourmet burgers and low-cal salads the size of your face. Speaking of which, the menu is simply enormous, and though nothing is really excellent, everything is pretty good.

Front Porch Cafe
AMERICAN $$

(Map p64; ☑ 305-531-8300; 1418 Ocean Dr; mains $10-18; ⊙ 7am-11pm) A blue-and-white escape from the madness of the cruising scene, the Porch has been serving excellent salads, sandwiches and the like since 1990 (eons by South Beach standards). Weekend brunch is justifiably mobbed; the big omelets are delicious, as are the fat pancakes and strong coffees.

★ **Osteria del Teatro**   ITALIAN $$$
(Map p64; ☑ 305-538-7850; 1443 Washington Ave; mains $17-45; ⊘6-11pm Mon-Thu, to 1am Fri-Sun) There are few things to swear by but the specials board of Osteria, one of the oldest and best Italian restaurants in Greater Miami, ought to be one. When you get here, let the gracious Italian waiters seat you, coddle you and then basically order for you off the board. They never pick wrong.

Yardbird   SOUTHERN $$$
(Map p64; ☑ 305-538-5220; 1600 Lenox Ave; mains $26-42; ⊘11:30am-11pm Mon-Thu, to midnight Fri, 10am-midnight Sat, 10am-11pm Sun) Yardbird is one of the most popular practitioners of Miami's surprisingly deep wave of haute Southern comfort food. The restaurant dishes out some nice Salisbury steak, St Louis ribs, grits and kale, but it's most famous for a signature chicken and waffles dish that strikes a nice balance of salty, savory and sweet.

Casa Tua   ITALIAN $$$
(Map p64; ☑ 305-673-1010; www.casatualife-style.com/miami; 1700 James Ave; mains $23-58; ⊘11:30am-3pm Mon-Fri, 7:30-11pm daily) Casa Tua is way too cool to have a sign out front. You'll know it by the oh-so-fabulous crowd streaming in, the hovering limos and what you can see of the beautiful building itself (much of it hidden behind a high hedge). If you manage to get a table in the magnificent, 1925 Mediterranean-style villa, you can linger over delicious prosciutto, Dover sole, risotto with lobster and veal cheeks.

Juvia   FUSION $$$
(Map p64; ☑ 305-763-8272; 1111 Lincoln Rd; mains $23-55; ⊘noon-3pm & 6pm-midnight daily, to 1am Fri & Sat; ☑) Juvia blends the trendsetters that have staying power in Miami's culinary world: namely, France, Latin America and Japan. Chilean seabass comes cooked in soy butter, while sea scallops are dressed with shiitakes and garlic chips. The big, bold, beautiful dining room, which sits on the high floors of 1111 Lincoln Rd (p63), is quintessential South Beach glam.

Mr Chow Chinese   CHINESE, FUSION $$$
(Map p64; ☑ 305-695-1695; www.mrchow.com; 2201 Collins Ave; mains $30-45; ⊘6pm-midnight) Located in the W Hotel (p107), Mr Chow takes Chinese American comfort food to gourmet heights. The setting is almost intimidatingly cool, with dangling moderne-style chandeliers and an enormous bar plucked out of *Sex and the City*, yet service is friend-

ly and the food lovely: velvet chicken served with diced chilies; stinky, spicy tofu; squid sautéed with asparagus.

Yuca   LATIN AMERICAN $$$
(Map p64; ☑ 305-532-9822; 501 Lincoln Rd; mains $22-48; ⊘noon-11:30pm) This was one of the first Nuevo Latino hot spots in Miami and it's still going strong, even if locals say it has lost a little luster over the years. The Yuca *rellena* (a mild chili stuffed with truffle-laced mushroom *picadillo*) and the tender guava ribs still make our mouth water.

✗ **Northern Miami Beach**

Roasters' n Toasters   DELI $
(Map p72; ☑ 305-531-7691; 525 Arthur Godfrey Rd; mains $8-16; ⊘6:30am-3:30pm) Given the crowds and the satisfied smiles of customers, Roasters' n Toasters meets the demanding standards of Miami Beach's large Jewish demographic, thanks to juicy deli meat, fresh bread, crispy bagels and warm *latkes*. Sliders (mini-sandwiches) are served on challah bread, an innovation that's as charming as it is tasty.

Josh's Deli   DELI $
(☑ 305-397-8494; 9517 Harding Ave; mains $6-14; ⊘8:30am-3:30pm) Josh's is simplicity itself. Here in the heart of Jewish Miami, it serves Jewish deli meat, and that deli meat is delicious. Corned beef, pastrami, rye bread, mustard – truly, what more do we need from life?

Shuckers   AMERICAN $
(Map p72; ☑ 305-866-1570; 1819 79th St Causeway; mains $8-19; ⊘11am-late) With excellent views overlooking the waters from the 79th St Causeway, Shuckers has to be one of the best-positioned restaurants around. The food is pub grub: burgers, fried fish and the like. We come here for one reason: the chicken wings. They're basted in several mouthwatering sauces, deep-fried and grilled again. We could sit here and devour a flock of poultry if our willpower was low.

Chivitoteca   URUGUAYAN $
(Map p72; ☑ 305-864-5252; 6987 Collins Ave; mains $5.50-16; ⊘noon-11:30pm Mon-Thu, to 1am Fri & Sat, to midnight Sun) Heart, meet the *chivito*: a Uruguayan sandwich of steak, ham, cheese, fried eggs and mayonnaise (there may have been lettuce, peppers and tomatoes too, but the other ingredients just laughed at them). Now run, heart, run away! That's just the basics, by the way, and

it comes with fries. You can also get pizza served by the meter, because honestly, at this stage you should just let yourself go.

La Perrada de Edgar FAST FOOD $
(Map p72; ☑ 305-866-4543; 6976 Collins Ave; hot dogs $4-7; ☻noon-midnight) Back in the day, Colombia's most (in)famous export to Miami was cocaine. But seriously, what's powder got on La Perrada and its kookily delicious hot dogs that were devised by some Dr Evil of the frankfurter world? Don't believe us? Try an *especial*, topped with plums, pineapple and whipped cream. How about shrimp and potato sticks? Apparently these are normal hot-dog toppings in Colombia. The homemade lemonade also goes down a treat.

★ Steve's Pizza PIZZERIA $$
(☑ 305-891-0202; www.stevespizzas.net; 12101 Biscayne Blvd; slices $3, pizzas $10-16; ☻ 11am-3am Sun-Wed, to 4am Thu & Fri, to 2am Sat) So many pizza chains compete for the attention of tourists in South Beach, but ask a Miami Beach local where to get the best pizza and they'll tell you about Steve's. This is New York–style pizza, thin crust and handmade with care and good ingredients. New branches of Steve's are opening elsewhere in Miami, all in decidedly nontouristy areas, which preserves that feeling of authenticity. Steve's flagship is in South Miami; the closer North Miami outpost listed here caters to nighthawks, and is located about 6 miles (15 minutes' drive) north of the Design District.

Indomania INDONESIAN $$
(Map p72; ☑ 305-535-6332; 131 26th St; mains $17-28; ☻6-10:30pm Tue-Sun) There's a lot of watered-down Asian cuisine in Miami; Indomania bucks this trend with an authentic execution of dishes from Southeast Asia's largest nation. Dishes reflect Indonesia's diversity, ranging from chicken in coconut curry to snapper grilled in banana leaves to gut-busting *rijsttafel*, a sort of buffet of small, tapas-style dishes that reflects the culinary character of particular Indonesian regions.

Cafe Prima Pasta ARGENTINE $$
(Map p72; ☑ 305-867-0106; 414 71st St; mains $13-24; ☻5pm-midnight Mon-Sat, 4-11pm Sun) We're not sure what's better at this Argentine-Italian place: the much-touted pasta, which deserves every one of the accolades heaped on it (try the gnocchi), or the atmosphere, which captures the dignified sexiness of Buenos Aires. Actually, it's no contest: you're the winner, as long as you eat here.

Fifi's Place SEAFOOD $$
(Map p72; ☑ 305-865-5665; 6934 Collins Ave; mains $13-30; ☻noon-midnight) Latin seafood is the name of the game here – Fifi's does delicious seafood paella, a dish that mixes the supporting cast of *The Little Mermaid* with Spanish rice, and an equally good seafood *parrillada*, which draws on the same ingredients and grills them with garlic butter. Awesome.

🍴 Downtown Miami

La Moon COLOMBIAN $
(Map p74; ☑ 305-379-5617; www.lamoonrestaurantmiami.com; 144 SW 8th St; meals $6-15; ☻9am-midnight Mon-Wed, 9am-6am Thu-Sun) Nothing – and we're not necessarily saying this in a good way – soaks up the beer like a Colombian hot dog topped with eggs and potato sticks. Or fried pork belly and pudding. These delicacies are the preferred food and drink of Miami's party people, and the best place for this wicked fare is here, within stumbling distance of bars like Tobacco Road. To really fit in, order a *refajo:* Colombian beer (Aguila) with Colombian soda (preferably the red one).

Soya e Pomodoro ITALIAN $
(Map p74; ☑ 305-381-9511; 120 NE 1st St; lunch $9-16, dinner $13-22; ☻11:30am-4pm Mon-Fri, 7-11:30pm Thu-Sat) Soya e Pomodoro feels like a bohemian retreat for Italian artists and filmmakers, who can dine on bowls of fresh pasta under vintage posters, rainbow paintings and wall-hangings. Think what would happen if hippies were dropped into the set of *Casablanca*. As per this vibe, readings, jazz shows and other arts events take place here on select evenings.

Fresco California MEDITERRANEAN $
(Map p74; ☑ 305-858-0608; 1744 SW 3rd Ave; mains $9-16; ☻11:30am-3:30pm Mon-Fri, 5-10:30pm Mon-Thu, to 11pm Fri, 11am-11pm Sat) Fresco serves all kinds of West Coast takes on the Mediterranean palate. Relax in the candlelit backyard dining room, which feels like an Italian porch in summer when the weather is right (ie almost always). Pear and walnut salad and portobello sandwiches are lovely, while the pumpkin-stuffed ravioli is heaven on a platter.

Mini Healthy Deli DELI $
(Map p74; ☑ 305-523-2244; Station Mall, 48 E Flagler St; mains $6-10; ☻11am-3pm; ☑) This excellent cafe, tucked into a half-vacant

mini-mall, is where chef Carlos Bedoya works solo and churns out remarkably fresh and delicious specials such as grilled tilapia, fresh salad, and rice and beans. There are only two little tables, but it's worth waiting – or standing while you eat.

Granny Feelgoods
HEALTH FOOD $

(Map p74; ☑ 305-377-9600; 25 W Flagler St; mains $9-15; ☉ 7am-5pm Mon-Fri; ☑) If you need karmic balance (or just tasty vegetarian fare), try this neighborhood health-food staple. Located next to the courthouse, Granny's must have the highest lawyer-to-bean-sprouts ratio in the USA. Try simple, vegetarian dishes such as tofu sandwiches and spinach lasagna. Carnivores are catered for too – there's a turkey burger.

★Choices
VEGETARIAN $$

(Map p74; ☑ 305-400-8895; 379 SW 15th Rd; mains $10-16; ☉ 8am-9pm Mon-Fri, to 9pm Sat; ☑) ✐ The description everyone writes when vegan food tastes good is that you're not missing the meat. This trope actually holds true at Choices. With clever ingredient combinations like walnut 'meat' and daiya cheese, this restaurant lives up to its name, offering burgers, tacos and pizza – all 100% vegan, and all delicious.

Bonding
FUSION $$

(Map p74; ☑ 786-409-4796; 638 S Miami Ave; mains $12-28; ☉ noon-11pm Mon-Fri, to midnight Sat, 5pm-midnight Sun; ☑) Multiple Asian cuisines, including Thai, Japanese and Korean, come together into an excellent whole at Bonding. Chicken is expertly tossed with

chilis and basil, red curry is deliciously fiery and sushi rolls are given a South Florida splash with ingredients like mango salsa and spicy mayo. The bar here keeps some excellent sake under the counter.

OTC
AMERICAN $$

(Map p74; ☑ 305-374-4612; 1250 S Miami Ave; mains $10-22; ☉ 11:30am-11:30pm Mon-Wed, to midnight Thu, to 1am Fri, 10:30am-1am Sat, to 11pm Sun) Miami loves its food trends, and the movement of the moment is 'rustic' farm-to-table food served alongside craft beer. Brickell's OTC is an exemplar of these practices, serving up truffle steak frites and the like, although it's hard to feel connected to the land in Brickell's high-rise canyons. Whatever; the food is damn tasty.

Garcia's Seafood Grille & Fish Market
SEAFOOD $$

(Map p74; ☑ 305-375-0765; 398 NW River Dr; mains $9-22; ☉ 11am-9:30pm) Crowds of Cuban office workers lunch at Garcia's, which feels more like you're in a smugglers' seafood shack than the financial district. Expect occasionally spotty service (a bad thing), freshly caught-and-cooked fish (a good thing) and pleasantly seedy views of the Miami River.

Carol's Resaurant
ITALIAN $$

(Map p74; ☑ 305-373-7622; 245 SE 1st St; mains $10-22; ☉ 6-10pm Sun & Mon, to 11pm Tue-Thu, to midnight Fri & Sat, 11am-3pm Sat & Sun; ☑) Carol's is a rare bird in Miami's restaurant aviary: an affordable Italian place with quality food. Wild mushroom ravioli goes down a treat with some red wine, while the duck

---

KEEP ON TRUCKIN'

Food trucks are a huge deal in Miami. There's far too many to list here, but if you want a taste (pun intended) of what's good on four wheels, head to the Biscayne Triangle Truck Round-Up (BTTR). Like a herd of gastronomic wildebeests, the city's food trucks gather for the BTTR every Tuesday from 5:30pm to 10pm at the Johnson & Wales University campus in North Miami (127th St & Biscayne Blvd). Otherwise, here's some of our favorite purveyors of mobile cuisine; we've included Twitter handles so you can follow their locations online:

Purple People Eatery (www.purpleppleatery.com; @purpleppleatery; mains $4-8) Battered mahimahi, herb-crusted mac 'n' cheese and gourmet bison burgers.

gastroPod (www.gastropodmiami.com/food; @gastropodmiami; mains $5-11) Sliders, short ribs, corn cakes and more.

Jefe's Original Fish Tacos & Burgers (www.jefesoriginal.com; @jefesoriginal; mains $2.50-6.50) As you may guess, the fish taco is the way to go.

Slow Food Truck (www.slowfoodtruck.com; @SlowFoodTruck; mains $4-8) Seasonal, local food – a changing menu ensures variety and straight deliciousness.

confit risotto comes out practically perfect. The interior, done up in warm wooden tones offset by plenty of natural light, is as attractive as the food.

Azul
FUSION $$$

(Map p74; ☑ 305-913-8288; 500 Brickell Key Dr; mains $25-40; ⊙ 7-11pm Tue-Sat) Falling-water windows, clean metallic spaces and curving copper facades complement one of the nicest views of the city. The Scandi-tastic decor works in harmony with a menu that marries the Mediterranean to Asia; try the oysters wrapped in beef and *hamachi* carpaccio.

Wynwood, Design District & Little Haiti

★ Chef Creole
HAITIAN $

(Map p80; ☑ 305-754-2223; 200 NW 54th St; mains $7-20; ⊙ 11am-11pm Mon-Sat) When you need Caribbean food on the cheap, head to the edge of Little Haiti and this excellent takeout shack. Order up fried conch, oxtail or fish, ladle rice and beans on the side, and you'll be full for a week. Enjoy the food on nearby picnic benches while Haitian music blasts out of tinny speakers – as island an experience as they come.

Cheese Course
CHEESE $

(Map p80; ☑ 786-220-6681; www.thecheesecourse.com; 3451 NE 1st Ave; mains $5-15; ⊙ 10:30am-9pm Sun-Wed, to 10pm Thu, to 11pm Fri & Sat; ☑) We love the idea at this place – pick out a few cheeses with the help of the staff and have them assemble a platter for you with fresh bread, candied walnuts, cornichons or whatever other accoutrement you so desire. There are also nice sandwiches, spreads and preserves, but for our money you can't beat a perfect lunch here of fermented dairy goodness.

La Latina
LATIN AMERICAN $

(Map p80; ☑ 305-571-9655; 3509 NE 2nd Ave; mains $4-10; ⊙ 10am-10pm Tue-Thu, to 5am Fri & Sat, to 4pm Sun; ☑) One of the best budget meals in the immediate Design District vicinity can be found at La Latina, a Venezuelan diner that's popular with Midtown locals and artsy transplants to the area. Cheese and avocado arepas are a treat for vegetarians, but there's a lot of meat, rice, beans and sweet plantains filling out the menu.

Lemoni Café
CAFE $

(Map p80; ☑ 305-571-5080; www.mylemonicafe.com; 4600 NE 2nd Ave; mains $6-10; ⊙ 11am-10:30pm; ☑) Lemoni is as bright as its name suggests, a cute, cozy hole in the wall that serves up superlative sandwiches, wraps and salads. The salami sandwich with greens and olive oil is a simple revelation, and we'd probably rob a bank to get another slice of its key lime pie. Located in the pretty Buena Vista neighborhood, this is a perfect place to grab a sidewalk alfresco lunch or dinner.

Enriqueta's
LATIN AMERICAN $

(Map p80; ☑ 305-573-4681; 186 NE 29th St; mains $5-8; ⊙ 6:30am-3:45pm Mon-Fri, to 2pm Sat) Back in the day, Puerto Ricans, not installation artists, ruled Wynwood. Have a taste of those times in this perpetually packed roadhouse, where the Latin-diner ambience is as strong as the steaming shots of *cortadito* (Cuban-style coffee) served at the counter. Balance the local gallery fluff with a steak-and-potato-stick sandwich.

★ Blue Collar
AMERICAN $$

(☑ 305-756-0366; www.bluecollarmiami.com; 6730 Biscayne Blvd; mains $15-22; ⊙ 11:30am-3:30pm Mon-Fri, 11am-3:30pm Sat & Sun, 6-10pm Sun-Thu, 6-11pm Fri & Sat; ☑☑☑) It's not easy striking a balance between laid back and delicious in a city like Miami, where even 'casual' eateries can feel like nightclubs, but Blue Collar has the formula nailed. Friendly staff serve All-American fare sexied the hell up, from crispy snapper to smoky ribs to a superlatively good cheeseburger. A well-curated veg board keeps noncarnivores happy.

Oak Tavern
AMERICAN $$

(Map p80; ☑ 786-391-1818; 35 NE 40th St; mains $12-26; ⊙ noon-10:30pm Mon-Thu, to midnight Fri, 6pm-midnight Sat, 11am-9:30pm Sun; ☑☑) Oak is a fine addition to the burgeoning dining scene in leafy Buena Vista. Grilled grouper sandwiches, wood-fired pizzas, farm-fresh vegetables, mushroom-crusted strip steaks and some great burgers are ostensibly hearty, but presented with sleek Miami attitude in a dining room that successfully pulls off sexy and rustic simultaneously.

Gigi
ASIAN $$

(Map p80; ☑ 305-573-1520; 3470 North Miami Ave; mains $14-28; ⊙ noon-midnight Sun & Mon, to 3am Tue-Thu, to 5am Fri & Sat; ☑) Gigi does Asian cuisine, but it's the sort of Asian you'd expect to find on the border of the ultrahip Design District. Ribs come glazed in hoisin and South American aji, the sweet-and-savory cornbread is an excellent complement and the pad Thai is divine. Does sushi go with country chicken? Surprisingly well.

The Federal AMERICAN $$
(Map p80; ☎305-758-9559; 5132 Biscayne Blvd; mains $12-25; ☺5-10pm Tue-Thu & Sun, to 11pm Fri & Sat; ☒) Down-home rustic Americana dining on the upper edges of Buena Vista? Sign us up. Especially when the offerings include chili laced with slow-cooked venison, beer-braised Florida clams and a host of vegetarian options such as crispy brussels sprouts. A chilled-out bar space makes for an easy, social ambience – the buzz here is friendly and easy to fall in love with.

Egg & Dart GREEK $$
(Map p80; ☎786-431-1022; 4029 N Miami Ave; small plates $4-16, mains $15-36; ☺4-11:30pm Tue-Thu, to midnight Fri, 11am-11:30pm Sat & Sun; ☒☒) Miami has a habit of sexing up the presentation of most ethnic cuisines, but we have to admit, we hadn't seen Greek done with glam till Egg & Dart. The effort is marvelous. Crafted cocktails (try the orange *mojito*) loosen up the palate for small plates like grilled *halloumi* and zucchini croquettes, and big mains like lovingly grilled lamb and a delicious beet-and-cheese stack.

The Butcher Shop AMERICAN $$
(Map p80; ☎305-846-9120; 165 NW 23rd St; mains $11-32; ☺11am-11pm Sun-Thu, to 2am Fri & Sat)

We suppsoe there *is* a vegetarian option here – you could order a bread and cheese plate. But this Wynwood joint is called the Butcher Shop for a reason, and that's because it's unashamedly aimed at carnivores. From bone-in rib eyes to smoked sausages to full charcuterie, meat lovers have reason to rejoice. Beer lovers too; this butcher's doubles as a beer garden.

The Embassy SPANISH $$
(Map p80; ☎305-571-8446; 4600 NE 2nd Ave; mains $17-23; ☺6pm-midnight Tue-Thu, to 3am Fri & Sat, 10am-3pm Sun; ☒) Embassy is a gastropub with Miami attitude, a Midtown veneer and an emphasis on Spanish tapas. Seared chicken with olive mashed potatoes and roasted snapper with fennel make a strong showing, as do regular vegan platters. The Buena Vista setting projects understated hip, as does the clientele.

Fiorito ARGENTINE $$
(Map p80; ☎305-754-2899; 5555 NE 2nd Ave; mains $14-21; ☺noon-10pm) Sometimes you need simple Latin American fare that's a cut above the average fried-plantains diner. Enter Fiorito, an excellent Argentine steakhouse that will fill your stomach way before it empties your wallet. Pastas, steaks, braised pork and some gorgeous hand-cut fries had us rolling happily out the door. Grab some excellent empanadas on the way out.

NORTH BISCAYNE BOULEVARD

As North Biscayne Blvd continues to gentrify, better and better restaurants are opening up. Here are some winners from this foodie find:

Michy's (☎305-759-2001; http://michysmiami.com; 6927 Biscayne Blvd; meals $29-38; ☺6-10:30pm Tue-Thu, to 11pm Fri & Sat, to 10pm Sun; ☒) Blue-and-white pop decor. Organic, locally sourced ingredients. A stylish, fantastical bar where Alice could drink before painting Wonderland red. Welcome to Michelle 'Michy' Bernstein's culinary lovechild – one of the brightest stars in Miami's culinary constellation. The emphasis is on good food and fun. The 'half plates' concept lets you halve an order and mix up delicious gastronomic fare, such as foie gras on corn cakes, chicken pot pie with wild mushrooms, white almond gazpacho, and blue-cheese croquettes.

Honey Tree (Map p80; ☎305-756-1696; 5138 Biscayne Blvd; mains under $10; ☺8am-8pm Mon-Thu, to 7pm Fri, 9am-6pm Sat; ☒) The Honey Tree is a health-food store that happens to serve excellent juices, smoothies and what many consider to be Miami's best vegan lunch. What's on offer varies day by day, but rest assured it will be cheap (it's priced by weight) and delicious. Lunch is usually served from noon to 2pm, but keep in mind that food often runs out due to high demand.

Jimmy's East Side Diner (☎305-754-3692; 7201 Biscayne Blvd; mains $5-13; ☺6:30am-4pm) Come to Jimmy's, a classic greasy spoon (that happens to be very gay friendly; note the rainbow flag out front), for big cheap breakfasts of omelets, French toast or pancakes, and turkey clubs and burgers later in the day.

Mandolin GREEK $$
(Map p80; ☑ 305-576-6066; 4312 NE 2nd Ave;
mains $12-26; ⊘noon-11pm Mon-Sat, to 10pm
Sun; 🖉) Mandolin doesn't just provide good
Greek food – although that is present in the
form of fresh fish grilled in lemon and olive
oil, tomato and Turkish chorizo sandwiches
and light mezes such as smoked eggplant
and creamy yogurt. What Mandolin also pro-
vides is excellent Greek atmosphere. It's all
Aegean whites and blues, colors that come
to life under the strong, melting Miami sun,
especially if you sit in the back courtyard,
shaded by the same trees that stretch over
the surrounding Buena Vista neighborhood.

Harry's Pizzeria PIZZERIA $$
(Map p80; ☑ 786-275-4963; 3918 North Miami Ave;
pizzas $15; ⊘11:30am-11pm Mon-Thu, to midnight
Fri & Sat, to 10pm Sun; 🖉) A stripped-down yet
sumptuous dining experience awaits (pizza)
pie lovers in Midtown. Harry's tiny kitch-
en and dining room dishes out deceptively
simple wood-fired pizzas that are a perfect
date meal; we're big fans of the braised fen-
nel pie. Look out for nonpizza daily specials
such as Friday's oven-roasted local fish.

Lost & Found Saloon MEXICAN $$
(Map p80; ☑ 305-576-1008; www.thelostandfound-
saloon-miami.com; 185 NW 36th St; mains $10-17;
⊘11am-3am; 🖉) The service is as friendly
as the omelets and burritos are awesome
(which is to say, very), at this little Wynwood
spot, the sort of saloon where microbrews
are on tap and the wine list reads like a year
abroad. Come the evening, this turns into a
fun hipster kind of bar.

🗡 Key Biscayne

Oasis CUBAN $
(Map p84; ☑ 305-361-9009; 19 Harbor Dr; mains
$5-12; ⊘6am-9pm) This excellent Cuban cafe
has a customer base that ranges from the
working poor to city players, and the socio-
economic barriers come tumbling down fast
as folks sip high-octane Cuban coffee. Be-
tween the superstrong coffee and *masas de
puerco* – marinated pork chunks, which go
great with hot sauce – we're in hole-in-the-
wall heaven.

Boater's Grill SEAFOOD $$
(Map p84; ☑ 305-361-0080; 1200 S Crandon Blvd;
mains $12-29; ⊘9am-9pm) Located in Cran-
don Park, this waterfront restaurant (actually there's water below and all around) feels
like a Chesapeake Bay sea house from up

north, except the menu is packed with South
Florida maritime goodness: stone crabs, mahimahi and lobster paella.

Rusty Pelican SEAFOOD $$$
(☑305-361-3818; 3201 Rickenbacker Causeway;
mains $18-42; ⊘11am-11pm Sun-Thu, to midnight
Fri & Sat) More than the fare itself, it's the
panoramic skyline views – among the best in
Miami – that draw the faithful and roman-
tic to this restaurant. But if you come for a
sunset drink, the fresh air could certainly
seduce you into staying for some of the surf
'n' turf menu, which is packed with high-end
grilled steaks and seafood.

🗡 Little Havana

★**Exquisito Restaurant** CUBAN $
(Map p86; ☑ 305-643-0227; 1510 SW 8th St; mains
$7-13; ⊘7am-11pm) For great Cuban cuisine in
the heart of Little Havana, this place is exqui-
site (ha ha). The roast pork has a tangy cit-
rus kick and the *ropa vieja* (pulled braised
brisket) is wonderfully rich and filling. Even
standard sides like beans and rice and roast-
ed plantains are executed with a little more
care and tastiness. Prices are a steal too.

**Hy Vong Vietnamese
Restaurant** VIETNAMESE $
(☑305-446-3674; 3458 SW 8th; mains $7-22; ⊘6-
11pm Wed-Sun, closed mid-late Aug) In a neigh-
borhood full of exiles from a communist
regime, it makes sense to find a Vietnamese
restaurant. And it's telling that despite all
the great Latin food around, Little Havan-
ans wait hours for a seat here. Why? Because
this spot serves great Vietnamese food with
little touches of Florida, like Florida-style
mango marinade.

Islas Canarias CUBAN $
(☑305-559-6666; 285 NW 27th Ave; mains $8-19;
⊘7am-11pm) Islas may not look like much, sit-
ting in a strip mall, but it serves some of the
best Cuban in Miami. The *ropa vieja* is deli-
cious and there are nice Spanish touches on
the menu (the owner's father is from the Ca-
nary Islands, hence the restaurant's name).
Don't pass up the signature homemade
chips, especially the ones cut from plantains.

El Cristo CUBAN $
(Map p86; ☑ 305-643-9992; 1543 SW 8th St;
mains $6-18; ⊘7am-11pm; 🖬) A popular
hangout among locals, the down-to-earth
El Cristo has options from all over the
Spanish-speaking world. Lots of people say

it's as good as Calle Ocho gets. The menu has daily specials, but the standout is fish – try it fried for a local version of fish and chips, or take away some excellent fish empanadas and *croquetas* (deep-fried in breadcrumbs).

Yambo
LATIN AMERICAN $

(1643 SW 1st St; mains $4-11; ◎24hr) If you're a bit drunk in the middle of the night and can find a cab or a friend willing to drive all the way out to Little Havana, direct them to Yambo. We've never actually been here during the day, although the restaurant is surely a pretty place for lunch or breakfast. At night Yambo does a roaring stock in trade selling trays and take-away boxes about to burst with juicy slices of carne asada, piles of rice and beans and sweet fried plantains. If you're going to soak up beer, this is a great sponge.

Los Pinareños Frutería
FRUIT STAND $

(Map p86; 1334 SW 8th St; snacks & drinks $2-4; ◎7am-7pm Mon-Sat, to 2pm Sun) Nothing says refreshment on a sweat-stained Miami afternoon like a long, cool glass of fruit smoothie at this popular juice and veggie stand – try the sugarcane juice for something particularly sweet and bracing. The produce is pretty fresh and flavorful too.

El Rey de Las Fritas
BURGERS $

(Map p86; www.reydelasfritas.com; 1821 SW 8th St; snacks $2-3; ◎8am-10:30pm Mon-Sat) If you've never had a *frita* (Cuban-style burger) make your peace with McDonald's and come down to El Rey with the lawyers, developers, construction workers and every other slice of Miami's Latin life. These *fritas* are big, juicy and served under a mountain of shoestring fries. Plus, the *batidos* (Latin American milkshakes) definitely bring the boys to the yard.

Versailles
CUBAN $$

(◎305-444-0240; 3555 SW 8th St; mains $5-26; ◎8am-1am) Versailles (ver-*sigh*-yay) is an institution, one of the mainstays of Miami's Cuban gastronomic scene. Try the ground beef in a gratin sauce or chicken breast cooked in creamy garlic sauce. Older Cubans and Miami's Latin political elite still love coming here, so you've got a real chance to rub elbows with a who's who of Miami's most prominent Latin citizens.

🍴 Coconut Grove

Coral Bagels
DELI $

(◎305-854-0336; 2750 SW 26th Ave; mains $3.75-9; ◎6:30am-3pm Mon-Fri, 7am-4pm Sat & Sun;

P ◎) At the risk of engaging in hyperbole, we can't imagine a better way of starting the day than a garlic bagel at this little deli. Breakfast (bagels and more traditional eggs, meat and potatoes) is the way to go; you'll be hard pressed to spend double digits, and you'll leave satisfied.

Last Carrot
VEGETARIAN $

(Map p88; ◎305-445-0805; 3133 Grand Ave; mains $6; ◎10am-6pm Mon-Fri, to 4pm Sun; ◎) Folks of all walks, corporate suits included, come here for fresh juice, delicious wraps (veggie options are great but the tuna melt is divine) and old-Grove neighborliness. The Carrot's endurance next to massive CocoWalk is testament to the quality of its good-for-your-body food served in a good-for-your-soul setting.

LoKal
AMERICAN $

(Map p88; ◎305-442-3377; 3190 Commodore Plaza; burgers $11-14; ◎noon-10pm Sun-Thu, to 11pm Fri & Sat; ✳◎🖐) ◢ This little Coconut Grove joint does two things very well: burgers and smart ingredient sourcing. The former come in several variations, all utilizing excellent beef (bar the oat-bran-based veggie version); we love the frita, which adds in guava sauce. The latter comes in the form of genuine farm-to-table relationships; there's a reason the avocado slices are so beautiful.

Xixon
SPANISH $$

(◎305-854-9350; 2101 SW 22nd St; tapas $8-15; ◎11am-10pm Mon-Thu, to 11pm Fri & Sat; ◎) It takes a lot to stand out in Miami's crowded tapas-spot stakes. Bread that has a crackling crust and a soft center, delicate explosions of *bacalao* (cod) fritters and the best eels cooked in garlic we've ever eaten secure Xixon's status as a top tapas contender. The *bocadillo* (sandwiches), with their blood red Serrano ham and salty Manchego cheese, are great picnic fare.

Lulu
AMERICAN $$

(Map p88; ◎305-447-5858; 3105 Commodore Plaza; mains $9-25; ◎11:30am-10:45pm Sun-Thu, to 11:45pm Fri & Sat; ◎) Lulu is the Grove's exemplar of using local, organic ingredients to provide gourmet versions of comfort food in a nice outdoor setting. Well, there is an interior dining space, and it is lovely, but the outdoor seating, shaded by the spreading boughs of Coconut Grove's many trees, is where we prefer to be. The truffle mac 'n' cheese is rich and immensely satisfying, while the Lulu burger is to die for.

Green Street Cafe
AMERICAN $$

(Map p88; ☑305-567-0662; 3468 Main Hwy; mains $10-23; ☉7:30am-1am) Sidewalk spots don't get more popular (and many say more delicious) than Green Street, where the Grove's young and gorgeous congregate at sunset. There's an excellent mix of lamb burgers with goat's cheese, salmon salads, occasional art shows and general indie defiance of Grove gentrification, which makes for an idiosyncratic dining experience.

Jaguar
LATIN AMERICAN $$

(Map p88; ☑305-444-0216; www.jaguarspot.com; 3067 Grand Ave; mains $17-32; ☉11:30am-11pm Mon-Thu, to 11:30pm Fri & Sat, 11am-11pm Sun) The menu spans the Latin world, but really, everyone's here for the ceviche 'spoon bar.' The idea: pick from six styles of ceviche (raw, marinated seafood), ranging from swordfish with cilantro to corvina in lime juice, and pull a culinary version of DIY. It's novel and fun, and the $2 ceviche varieties are pretty damn delicious. Other mains include different kinds of grilled meats and fish – endearing in their simplicity, but lacking the tasty complexity of the ceviche.

George's in the Grove
FRENCH $$

(Map p88; ☑305-444-7878; 3145 Commodore Plaza; mains $13-29; ☉10am-11pm Mon-Fri, 8am-11pm Sat & Sun) George's has a manically over-the-top menu that throws in everything from French to Italian to Latin plus the kitchen sink. This all comes packaged with manic, over-the-top decor that looks like a cozy attic just exploded all over Coconut Grove. Mains are rich in the best rural French culinary tradition; standbys include steak *frites*, duck confit and grilled branzino.

✗ Coral Gables

Matsuri
JAPANESE $

(Map p90; ☑305-663-1615; 5759 Bird Rd; mains $7-23; ☉11:30am-2:30pm Tue-Fri, 5:30-10:30pm Tue-Sat) Note the customers here: Matsuri, tucked into a nondescript shopping center, is consistently packed with Japanese customers. They don't want scene; they want a taste of home, although many of the diners are actually South American Japanese who order *unagi* (eels) in Spanish. Spicy *toro* (fatty tuna) and scallions, grilled mackerel with natural salt, and an ocean of raw fish are all *oishii* (delicious).

★ El Carajo
SPANISH $$

(☑305-856-2424; www.elcarajointernationaltapasandwines.com; 2465 SW 17th Ave; tapas $4.50-17; ☉noon-10pm Mon-Wed, to 11pm Thu-Sat, 1-9pm Sun) Pass the Penzoil please. We know it is cool to tuck restaurants into unassuming spots, but the Citgo station on SW 17th Ave? Really? Really. Walk past the motor oil into a Granadan wine cellar and try not to act too fazed. And now the food, which is absolutely incredible: chorizo in cider blends burn, smoke and juice; frittatas are comfortably filling; and *sardinas* and *boquerones*...wow. These sardines and anchovies cooked with a bit of salt and olive oil are dizzyingly delicious.

Swine
SOUTHERN $$

(Map p90; ☑786-360-6433; 2415 Ponce De Leon Blvd; mains $16-40; ☉11:30am-11pm Tue-Thu, to midnight Fri, 10am-midnight Sat, 10am-10pm Sun, 11:30am-10pm Mon) Rustic smoked pork and whiskey comes to chic Coral Gables courtesy of Swine. Well, to be fair, there's more than pig on the menu; confit rabbit legs, Florida shrimp and grits, country-fried bacon and burgers all make an appearance, and by heavens they're some kind of delicious. Pair with a craft cocktail from the expertly run bar.

Bulla
SPANISH $$

(Map p90; ☑305-441-0107; 2500 Ponce de Leon Blvd; small plates $4-17; ☉noon-10pm Sun-Thu, to late Fri & Sat; ☑) Bulla serves up tapas, which is nothing new in Miami, let alone Coral Gables. But it does so in a gastropub atmosphere, which adds a touch of debauchery to an already hedonistic gastronomic experience, and the tapas themselves are a cut above the rest. Cheeses, grilled fish and Iberico ham croquettes will keep a smile on your face.

Seasons 52
FUSION $$

(Map p90; ☑305-442-8552; 321 Miracle Mile; mains $14-32; ☉11:30am-11pm Mon-Thu, to midnight Fri & Sat, to 10pm Sun) ✔ We love the concept and the execution at Seasons 52. The concept? A menu that partially rotates on a weekly basis depending on what is seasonally available (now the title makes sense). The execution? Warm flatbreads overlaid with sharp melted cheese and steak; tiger shrimp tossed in a light pasta and chili that manages elegance and heartiness all at once.

Caffe Abbracci
ITALIAN $$

(Map p90; ☑305-441-0700; www.caffeabbracci.com; 318 Aragon Ave; mains $17-37; ☉11:30am-3:30pm Mon-Fri, 6pm-midnight daily) Perfect moments in Coral Gables come easy. Here's a simple formula: you, a loved one, a muggy Miami evening, some delicious pasta and a glass of red at a sidewalk table at Abbracci – one of the finest Italian restaurants in the Gables.

La Palme d'Or   FRENCH $$$

(Map p90; ☑ 305-913-3200; Biltmore Hotel, 1200 Anastasia Ave; 5-/9-course tasting menu $105/175; ⏰ 6:30-10:30pm Tue-Sat) One of the most acclaimed French restaurants in the USA, the Palme is the culinary match for the Jazz Age opulence that ensconces it. With its white-gloved, old-world class and US attention to service, unmuddled by pretensions of hipness, this place captures, in one elegant stroke, all the exclusivity a dozen South Beach restaurants could never grasp.

Pascal's on Ponce   FRENCH $$$

(Map p90; ☑ 305-444-2024; www.pascalmiami. com; 2611 Ponce de Leon Blvd; mains $30-42; ⏰ 11:30am-2:30pm Mon-Fri, 6-10pm Mon-Thu, to 11pm Fri & Sat) They're fighting the good fight here: sea scallops with beef short rib, crème brûlée and other French fine-dining classics set the elegant stage at this neighborhood hangout, a favorite night out among Coral Gables foodies who appreciate time-tested standards. The menu and the atmosphere rarely changes, and frankly we think this a good thing: if it ain't broke...

Greater Miami

Lots of Lox   DELI $

(www.originallotsoflox.com; 14995 S Dixie Hwy; mains $4-13; ⏰ 8am-2:30pm) In a city with no shortage of delis, especially in mid–Miami Beach, who would have thought some of the best chopped liver on rye could be found in this unassuming place all the way down in Palmetto Bay? It is bustling, friendly and the excellent lunch meats sneer at their cousins over on Arthur Godfrey Rd, secure in their dominance of Greater Miami's deli ranks.

Fritanga Montelimar   NICARAGUAN $

(☑ 305-388-8841; 15722 SW 72nd St; buffet $9-13; ⏰ 9am-11pm) A *fritanga* is a Nicaraguan cafe, and if you've never eaten at one, here's a warning: Nicaraguans are not scared of big portions. This beloved spot, located deep in Kendall, serves up grilled pork, chicken stew, meltingly soft beef and other goodies on Styrofoam plates collapsing under the weight of beans and rice. Delicious and cheaper than chips.

Drinking & Nightlife

Too many people assume Miami's nightlife is all about being superattractive, super-rich and supersnooty. Disavow yourself of this notion, which only describes a small slice of the scene in South Beach. Miami has an intense variety of bars to pick from that range from grotty dives to beautiful – but still laid-back – lounges and nightclubs. Not to say you can't spot celebrities if you want to...

In South Beach and the big Miami superclubs, covers range from $20 to $30 (sometimes higher!), so get your wallet ready.

Gay and lesbian nightlife used to be the province of South Beach, but today the scene is pretty integrated into straight Miami. Some clubs are still found in South Beach, while more casual gay bars are in Midcity, North Biscayne Blvd and Northern Miami Beach.

South Beach

★ Room   BAR

(Map p68; www.theotheroom.com; 100 Collins Ave; ⏰ 7pm-5am) The Room's a gem: a crowded, dimly lit boutique beer bar where you can guzzle the best (brew) Miami has to offer and gawk at the best (hotties) South Beach has to show off. It's hip as hell, but the attitude is as low-key as the sexy mood lighting. Just beware, it gets crowded and it can be tough to find seats as the night goes on.

Kill Your Idol   BAR

(Map p64; ☑ 305-672-1852; 222 Española Way; ⏰ 8pm-5am) Kill Your Idol is a self-conscious dive that aims snooty condescension at South Beach's celebrity scene with one hand (see: the name of the place) while sipping a PBR with the other. Precocious? But it does have sweet postmodern art, graffiti and undeniably cute hipsters, and it's adjoined to that most unselfconscious of dives, Lost Weekend.

Abbey Brewery   BAR

(Map p64; www.abbeybrewinginc.com; 1115 16th St; ⏰ 1pm-5am) The only brewpub in South Beach is on the untouristed end of South Beach (near Alton Rd). It's friendly and packed with folks listening to the Grateful Dead and slinging back some excellent home brew: give Father Theo's stout or the Immaculate IPA a shot.

Ted's Hideaway   SPORTS BAR

(Map p68; 124 2nd St; ⏰ noon-5am) Somewhere in the Florida panhandle is a bumpin', fabulous gay club, which clearly switched places with Ted's, a no-nonsense, pool-table and sports-showin' 'lounge' smack in the middle of SoFi's elegance.

Rose Bar at the Delano
BAR
(Map p64; ☎305-672-2000; 1685 Collins Ave, Delano Hotel; ⊙noon-2am) The ultrachic Rose Bar at this elegant Ian Schrager original is a watering hole for beautiful creatures (or at least those with a healthy ego). Get ready to pay up for the privilege – but also prepare to enjoy it. The tiki bar in the back of the Delano is another winner; wait for staff to set out a wrought-iron table in the shallow end of the pool and you'll start rethinking your definition of opulence.

B Bar
BAR
(Map p64; Betsy Hotel, 1440 Ocean Dr; ⊙10pm-3am Wed-Sat) This smallish basement bar, tucked under the Betsy Hotel, has two salient features. One is a crowd of the beautiful, in-the-know SoBe-tastic types you expect at South Beach nightspots. The other is an odd, low-hanging reflective ceiling, built out of a sort of wobbly material that sinks in like soft Jell-O and ripples like a stone in a pond when you touch it. It's a pretty cool thing to witness, especially when all sorts of drunk, beautiful people try to (literally) raise the roof.

Lost Weekend
BAR
(Map p64; 218 Española Way; ⊙noon-5am) The Weekend is a grimy, sweaty, slovenly dive, filled with pool tables, cheap domestics and – hell yeah – Golden Tee arcade games and Big Buck Hunter. God bless it. Popular with local waiters, kitchen staff and bartenders.

Pool Bar at the Sagamore
BAR
(Map p64; 1671 Collins Ave) Head out to the back pool and sip a beer (or a nice cocktail) in the shadow of the artsy funk and hip geometric lines of the Sagamore hotel (p106).

Mac's Club Deuce Bar
BAR
(Map p64; 222 14th St; ⊙8am-5am) The oldest bar in Miami Beach (established in 1926), the Deuce is a real neighborhood bar and hype-free zone. It's just straight-up seediness, which, depending on your outlook, can be quite refreshing. Plan to see everyone from transgendered ladies to construction workers – some hooking up, some talking rough, all having a good time.

Chesterfield Hotel Bar
BAR
(Map p68; Chesterfield Hotel, 855 Collins Ave; ⊙usually noon-3am) Perch on some prime Collins people-watching real estate and get crunk on the hip-hop and zebra-stripe theme they've got going. You'd think this would be a start-the-night-out sort of place, but the setting's so fly, folks end up stationary, sipping on martinis until they stumble into their rooms.

Dewey's Tavern
BAR
(Map p68; 852 Alton Rd; ⊙11am-5am) Dewey's is an art-deco dive (really; the exterior is a little gem of the genre) and it's as unpretentious as the best sordid watering holes get. Come here to get wasted and menace the crowds seeking serenity on quiet Alton Rd (just kidding – behave yourself!).

Mango's Tropical Café
BAR
(Map p68; ☎305-673-4422; www.mangostropicalcafe.com; 900 Ocean Dr; cover $10-20; ⊙11:45am-5am Mon-Fri, 10am-5am Sat & Sun) Cuba meets

---

MIAMI DRINKING & NIGHTLIFE

SOUTH BEACH SIPPIN'

Starbucks has a pretty iron grip on the Miami coffee scene (we don't count stand-up Cuban coffee counters, as you can't sit there and read a book or work on your laptop, although if you speak Spanish, they're a good place for hearing local gossip). That said, there are some options besides Starbucks in Miami Beach.

A La Folie (Map p64; www.alafoliecafe.com; 516 Española Way; mains $5-15; ⊙11am-8pm; 🖉) A *tres* French cafe where the waiters have great accents. Why yes, we would like 'zee moka.'

Segafredo L'Originale (Map p64; 1040 Lincoln Rd; mains $5-15; ⊙10:30am-1am; 🖉) Immensely popular with Europeans and South Americans, this chic cafe always seems packed with gorgeous people. Credited with being the first Lincoln Rd business to open its trade to the outside street.

Nespresso (Map p64; 1111 Lincoln Rd; mains $5-15; ⊙10:30am-11pm; 🖉) This futuristic cafe, all done up in geometric swirls and shapes, has excellent (if overpriced) coffee.

Coyote Ugly Saloon in this tourist hot spot, where a staff of gorgeous and/or ripped bodies (take your pick) dances, gyrates and puts some serious booty on the floor. Of course, you're here for anthropological reasons: to study the nuances of Latin dance. Not to watch the bartender do that thing Shakira does with her butt.

Skybar
CLUB
(Map p64; ☑ 305-695-3100; Shore Club, 1901 Collins Ave; 4pm-2am Mon-Wed, to 3am Thu-Sat) Skybar is one of those SoBe spots that is so impossibly full of beautiful people you wonder if you've walked into a dream – and it's not just the clientele who are gorgeous. The setting: the Moroccan garden of delights that is the courtyard of the Shore Club hotel. Chill alfresco in a sultan's pleasure garden under enormous, wrought-iron lanterns, gaze at the patricians lounging around the pool, or try (and fail, if you're an unlisted travel writer) to get into the all-crimson, all-A-list Red Room.

Twist
CLUB
(Map p68; ☑ 305-538-9478; www.twistsobe.com; 1057 Washington Ave; 1pm-5am) Never a cover, always a groove, and right across from the police station, this two-story gay club has some serious staying power and a little bit of something for everyone: six different bars; go-go dancers; drag shows; lounging areas and a small dance floor.

Nikki Beach Club
CLUB
(Map p68; ☑ 305-538-1111; www.nikkibeach.com; 1 Ocean Dr; cover from $25; noon-6pm Mon-Thu, noon-11pm Fri & Sat, 11am-11pm Sun) Get your groove on outdoors, wandering from immaculate gossamer beach cabana to cabana at Nikki's, which feels like an incredibly upscale full-moon party. On Sunday (Sunday?!), starting around 4pm, it's the hottest party in town, as folks clamor to get in and relive whatever it was they did the night before.

FDR
CLUB
(Map p64; ☑ 305-924-4071; 1685 Collins Ave; 11pm-5am Fri-Mon) Indigo mood lighting, lots of models, scenester DJs and general sex in the air: this is as exclusive as clubs get in Miami Beach. Show up before 11pm, be a celebrity or be on the list to get in. Located below the Delano Hotel.

Cameo
CLUB
(Map p64; ☑ 305-532-2667; www.cameomiami.com; 1445 Washington Ave; 11pm-5am Tue, Fri & Sat) This enormous, touristy club, where Gwen

Stefani tracks get smooshed into Oakenfold, is where the sexy times are to be had – if by sexy times you're thinking thumping music, a packed crowd and sweat to slip on. Sunday's gay night (the specific party name frequently changes) is one of the best in town.

Mansion
CLUB
(Map p64; ☑ 305-532-1525; www.mansionmiami.com; 1235 Washington Ave; cover from $20; 11pm-5am Wed-Sat) Every night the lines stretch around the block as plebs beg, cajole and strut in a vain attempt to get past that damned red rope. Inside? Well, they don't call it 'Mansion' for nothing. Expect megaclub grandiosity, plenty of attitude, waiting in line for hours and the chance to see young celebs do something tabloid-worthy.

Mynt
CLUB
(Map p64; ☑ 305-695-1705; www.myntlounge.com; 1921 Collins Ave; noon-5am) Join the partying stars – Justin Timberlake, Vin Diesel, Britney Spears etc – by bottle servicing yourself into the VIP section. Otherwise, make friends with the red rope until you can order a drink and then try not to spill it, which is tough in the sweaty scrum of models, Moët and *mojitos*.

Score
GAY
(Map p64; ☑ 305-535-1111; www.scorebar.net; 727 Lincoln Rd; 9pm-5am Tue, Thu & Sun, 6pm-5am Fri & Sat) Muscle boys with mustaches, glistening six-packs gyrating on stage, and a crowd of men who've decided shirts really aren't their thing: do we need to spell out the orientation of Score's customer base? It's still the best dedicated – and decadent – gay bar on the beach.

Northern Miami Beach

★ Broken Shaker
BAR
(Map p72; ☑ 305-531-2727; 2727 Indian Creek Dr; 6pm-2am Sun-Thu, 2pm-2am Fri & Sat) Craft cocktails are having their moment in Miami, and if mixology is in the spotlight, you can bet Broken Shaker is sharing the glare. Expert bartenders run this spot, located in the back of the Freehand Miami hotel (p108), which takes up one closet-sized indoor niche and a sprawling outdoor courtyard of excellent drinks and beautiful people.

Circa 39 Bar
LOUNGE
(Map p72; 3900 Collins Ave; 4pm-midnight) Tucked off to the back of Circa 39's moody front lobby, the designer dream bar has a warm, welcoming feel to it. Definitely stop

GETTING PAST THE RED ROPE

If you're going out in Miami, ask yourself: what do I want? Do I want to dance? Hear good tunes? Score? See celebrities? If you answered 'yes' to the first two questions, the downtown Miami and Wynwood scene might be more to your liking. If you answered 'yes' to the last two questions, you may want to stay in South Beach.

Also, ask yourself another question: What do I bring? If it's good looks, money or promoter connections, the world is your oyster. If you have none of the above you can still party, but be prepared for some ego-crushing. Best overheard conversation in the course of this research:

Guy A: [Looking at model] 'How do you approach a girl like that?'

Guy B: 'In a Mercedes.'

Here's how it breaks down: the South Beach club scene plays on the appeal of celebrity. More famous customers equal more regular customers. Eventually, a strange equilibrium works out where enough regular customers make people assume famous people are there, even if they're not. But those regular customers can't appear too regular, so a little social engineering is committed by club owners and the titans of the cultural scene (bouncers) in the form of the red rope. How do you get by it?

→ **Be polite** Don't be skittish, but don't act like you're J Lo either. And whatever you do, don't yell at the doorman – or touch him or yank on his clothing – to try to get his attention.

→ **Get guest-listed** Ask the concierge at your hotel to help you out, or simply call the club and leave your name; it's often that simple.

→ **Remain confidently aloof** Don't stare at the doorman. Look elsewhere – but look hot doing it.

→ **Be aggressive. Failing that, be rich** If there's a clamoring crowd, standing at the back of it and hoping it'll part is about as effective as being meek when you need a seat on the New York subway. Push your way through to the front. Or order bottle service (an overpriced bottle of spirits), which usually guarantees you a pass to the front.

→ **Come correct** For women, showing a sophisticated amount of skin is effective, although 'sophisticated' depends on the wearer. We've seen chic women in barely-there tops look less trashy than folks sporting a standard miniskirt ensemble. Men, don't wear T-shirts and jeans, unless you're one of those guys who can and still look put together. Also, this is Miami – be a little more daring than a button-up shirt and slacks if you want to stand out.

→ **Get there early** Do you want to be cool or do you want to get in? From 10:30pm to 11pm is a golden time for bouncer leniency, but you can't club-hop with this strategy.

→ **If you're a man, bring a woman** A man alone is not worth much (unless you're at a gay club, natch); up your value by having a beautiful woman – or two or three – on your arm.

Though our listings represent the hottest parties as of press time, we urge you to do some follow-up research when you arrive: talk to friends and your concierge, and pick up a copy of the local arts weekly, *Miami New Times*.

---

in for a cosmopolitan if you're up this way, before sauntering across the street and checking out the nighttime ocean.

Lou's Beer Garden PUB
(Map p72; ☎ 305-704-7879; 7337 Harding Ave; ⊙5pm-2am Mon-Fri, noon-2am Sat & Sun) Miami is pretty much made for beer gardens. The weather is perfect, nothing cools you off like a breeze and a beer and, well, yeah... the weather is perfect. Gather around long tables under tropical trees, order a cheese plate or a Kobe beef burger and down pints of Belgian craft ales. What could be better?

 Downtown Miami

★**Blackbird Ordinary** BAR
(Map p74; ☎ 305-671-3307; 729 SW 1st Ave; ⊙3pm-5am Mon-Fri, 6pm-5am Sat & Sun) The Ordinary is almost that...well, no. It isn't ordinary at all – this is an excellent bar, with great cocktails (the London Sparrow, with

gin, cayenne, lemon juice and passion fruit, goes down well) and an enormous courtyard. But it is 'ordinary' in the sense that it's a come-as-you-are joint that eschews judgment for easy camaraderie.

Tobacco Road
BAR

(Map p74; ☑305-374-1198; 626 S Miami Ave; ☺11:30am-5am) Miami's oldest bar has been on the scene since the 1920s, and boasts the first liquor license issued in the city. These days it's a little touristy, but it has stayed in business for a reason: old wood, blue lights, cigarette smoke and sassy bartenders greet you like a buddy. Film buffs may recognize it as the place where Kurt Russell has a drink in *The Mean Season* (1985).

DRB
BAR

(Map p74; 501 NE 1st Ave; ☺ noon-2am Mon-Wed, to 5am Thu & Fri, 4pm-5am Sat, 4pm-2am Sun) The acronym stands for Democratic Republic of Beer, and that's what's on offer here: a good variety of microbrews and hard-to-score imports, served in a small, understated bar area or outside on comfy couches in the heart of downtown Miami.

Level 25
BAR

(Map p74; Conrad Miami, 1395 Brickell Ave; ☺11:30am-11pm Sun-Thu, to midnight Fri & Sat) When Neo buys Morpheus a drink, they probably meet at this Conrad Miami spot (guess which floor), where it's all long white lines, low black couches, pinstriped gorgeousity and God's-eye views over Biscayne Bay.

Grand Central
CLUB

(Map p74; ☑305-377-2277; 697 N Miami Ave; ☺10pm-5am Fri & Sat) As enormous clubs go, Grand Central is good. Yes, the bouncers have way more attitude here than other clubs, and yes, the cost of everything, from drinks to covers, borders on criminal. But the promoters consistently book big DJs and musical acts, and when things are hopping, the energy is undeniable.

Garret
CLUB

(Map p74; ☑305-377-2277; 697 N Miami Ave; ☺10pm-4am Tue, 8pm-1am Wed, 11pm-5am Thu-Sat) Upstairs from Grand Central, the Garret is the hipster half of the big club scene downstairs. Electro pop and synth-y sounds are pumped out on Friday nights, while Saturdays feature indie dance nights and third Thursdays are devoted to a riotous Latin funk mix.

Vagabond
CLUB

(Map p74; ☑305-379-0508; 30 NE 14th St; ☺10pm-3am Tue, 10pm-5am Thu-Sat) The folks at Vagabond are still attractive, but they're funkier, definitely more local and the music is more experimental than what you'll find on Miami Beach. The animal-print furniture and flying, loopy lines and curves are made to be gawked at, which is possible as no one keeps the Vagabond too dimly lit.

Space
CLUB

(Map p74; ☑305-375-0001; www.clubspace.com; 34 NE 11th St; ☺24hr) This multilevel warehouse is Miami's main megaclub. With 30,000 sq ft to fill, dancers have room to strut, and an around-the-clock liquor license redefines the concept of after-hours. DJs usually pump each floor with a different sound – hip-hop, Latin, heavy trance – while the infamous rooftop lounge is the place to be for sunrise.

Wynwood, Design District & Little Haiti

★ Wood Tavern
BAR

(Map p80; ☑305-748-2828; 2531 NW 2nd Ave; ☺5pm-2am Tue-Sun) So many new bars in Miami want to be casual but cool; Wood is one of the few locales achieving this Golden Mean of atmosphere and aesthetic. The crowd is local Miami kids who don't want a dive, but don't want the long lines and attitude of South Beach. Ergo: Anglo kids joking with Latinos in an outdoor space that includes picnic benches, a wooden stage complete with bleachers and giant Jenga game, and an attached art gallery with rotating exhibits. Food specials are cheap, the beer selection is excellent and the crowd is friendly – this Wood's got the right grain.

Panther Coffee
CAFE

(Map p80; ☑305-677-3952; 2390 NW 2nd Ave; ☺7am-9pm Mon-Sat, 8am-9pm Sun) The coffee is great at Panther, but what's better are frequent poetry readings, performance-art sessions and general artsy events that fill a packed schedule of events. If there's a non-alcoholic lynchpin to the Wynwood creative scene, it can be found here.

Gramps
BAR

(Map p80; ☑786-752-6693; 176 NW 24th St; ☺6pm-3am Sun-Thu, 5pm-3am Fri & Sat) Besides being a kick-butt bar that hosts great quiz nights, Gramps has an enormous outdoor backyard that's perfect for alfresco drinking and socializing. It helps that the cocktails are strong and the beer menu is as extensive as a complete encyclopedia set.

Churchill's
BAR

(Map p80; ☑ 305-757-1807; www.churchillspub.com; 5501 NE 2nd Ave; ☺ 10pm-3am) Churchill's is a Brit-owned pub in the midst of what could be Port-au-Prince. There's a lot of live music here, mainly punk, indie and more punk. Not insipid modern punk either: think the Ramones meets the Sex Pistols. While everyone's getting their ya-yas off, Haitians are waiting outside to park your car or sidle in and enjoy the gig and a beer with you.

Magnum Lounge
GAY & LESBIAN

(☑ 305-757-3368; 709 NE 79th St; ☺ 5pm-2am Tue-Thu, to 3am Fri & Sat) This gay piano lounge is all dark shadows and deep reds but not to the point you're blind, and the clientele is a nice mix: gays, lesbians, straights on dates or just looking for something different – and by the way, the drinks are stiff, the prices are reasonable and the piano music is quite good.

The Social Lubricant
LOUNGE

(Map p80; ☑ 786-409-2241; 167 NW 23rd St; ☺ 6pm-3am) Enter The Social Lubricant and you'll feel like you've entered the backstage of some surreal caberet that blends the Middle East, the Caribbean and (of course) a Miami nightclub. Sushi is served in the back, movies are shown on a big screen and DJs spin chill music to soothe the beautiful crowds.

Boteco
BAR

(www.botecomiami.com; 916 NE 79th St; ☺ 11am-midnight) If you're missing São Paolo, come to Boteco on Friday evening to see the biggest Brazilian expat reunion in Miami. *Cariocas* (Rio natives) and their countrymen flock here to listen to samba and bossa nova, and chat each other up over the best caipirinhas in town.

Bardot
CLUB

(Map p80; ☑ 305-576-5570; 3456 N Miami Ave; ☺ 8pm-3am Tue & Wed, to 5am Thu-Sat) You really should see the interior of Bardot before you leave the city. It's all sexy French vintage posters and furniture seemingly plucked from a private club that serves millionaires by day, and becomes a scene of decadent excess by night. The entrance looks to be on N Miami Ave, but it's actually in a parking lot behind the building.

Little Havana

Casa Panza Bar
TAVERNA

(Map p86; ☑ 305-644-3444; 1620 SW 8th St; ☺ 11am-11pm) It doesn't get cornier than this 'authentic' Spanish taverna where the live shows, flamenco dancers, Spanish guitarists and audience participation reach new heights of sangria-soaked fun. Drop your cynicism, enter and enjoy.

Coconut Grove

Everything here closes at 3am.

Taurus
BAR

(Map p88; ☑ 305-529-6523; 3540 Main Hwy; ☺ 4pm-3am) The oldest bar in Coconut Grove is a cool mix of wood paneling, smoky leather chairs, about 100 beers to choose from and a convivial vibe – as neighborhood bars go in Miami, this is one of the best.

Tavern in the Grove
BAR

(Map p88; ☑ 305-447-3884; 3416 Main Hwy; ☺ 3pm-3am) To say this sweatbox is popular with University of Miami students is like saying it rains sometimes in England. More of a neighborhood dive on weekdays.

ART WALKS: THE NEW CLUBBING?

It's hipsters gone wild! Or to put it another way: it's free wine! And artsy types, and galleries open till late, and the eye candy of a club, and the drunken momentum of a pub crawl and – best of all – no red ropes. The Wynwood & Design District Art Walks are one of the best nightlife experiences in Miami. The experience of strolling from gallery to gallery ('That piece is *gorgeous*. Pour me another'), perusing the paintings ('No, I don't think there's a bathroom behind the performance artist') and delving into the nuances of aesthetic styles ('The wine's run out? Let's bounce') is as genuinely innovative as...well, the best contemporary art. Just be careful, as a lot of galleries in Wynwood are separated by short drives (the Design District is more walkable). Art Walks take place on the second Saturday of each month, from 7pm to 10pm (some galleries stretch to 11pm); when it's all over, lots of folks repair to Wood Tavern or Bardot. Visit artofmiami.com/maps/art-walks for information on participating galleries.

Barracuda
BAR

(Map p88; ☎305-918-9013; 3035 Fuller St; ⏱noon-3am) The other place in the Grove to get overloaded on backwards baseball caps and coeds in miniskirts.

Coral Gables

Seven Seas
BAR

(Map p90; ☎305-266-6071; 2200 SW 57th Ave; ⏱noon-1am Sun-Thu, to late Fri & Sat) Seven Seas is a genuine Miami neighborhood dive, decorated on the inside like a nautical theme park and filled with University of Miami students, Cuban workers, gays, straights, lesbians and folks from around the way. Come for the best karaoke in Miami on Tuesday, Thursday and Saturday – there's plenty of Spanish-language music, which adds Latin spice.

The Bar
BAR

(Map p90; ☎305-442-2730; 172 Giralda Ave; ⏱11:30am-3am) All in a name, right? Probably the best watering hole in the Gables, The Bar is just what the title says (which is unusual in this neighborhood of extravagant embellishment). If you're in the 'hood on Friday, come here for happy hour (5pm to 8pm), when young Gables professionals take their ties off and let loose long into the night.

MIAMI'S SMALL CINEMAS

Miami has a glut of art-house cinemas showing first-run, independent and foreign films. Here are some of our favorites:

Cosford Cinema (☎305-284-4861; www.cosfordcinema.com; Memorial Classroom Bldg, 5030 Brunson Dr, University of Miami) On the University of Miami campus, this renovated art house was launched in memory of the *Miami Herald* film critic Bill Cosford.

Coral Gables Art Cinema (Map p90; ☎786-385-9689; www.gablescinema.com; 260 Aragon Ave) Indie and foreign films in a 144-seat cinema.

Tower Theater (Map p86; ☎305-643-8706; www.mdc.edu/culture/tower; 1508 SW 8th St) In a gem of a deco building, managed by Miami Dade College.

O Cinema (Map p80; ☎305-571-9970; www.o-cinema.org; 90 NW 29th St) Indie screenings in Wynwood.

Titanic
BAR

(☎305-668-1742; 5813 Ponce de Leon Blvd; ⏱11:30am-1am Sun-Thu, to 2am Fri & Sat) By day, it's an all-American-type bar and grill, but at night Titanic turns into a popular University of Miami watering hole. Thursday tends to be a big night. Located by the University entrance near Dixie Hwy and Red Rd (SW 57th Ave).

Greater Miami

La Covacha
CLUB

(☎305-594-3717; www.lacovacha.com; 10730 NW 25th St, Doral; ⏱9:30pm-4am Thu-Sun, from 5pm Fri) Drive out about halfway to the Everglades (just kidding, but only just) and you'll find Covacha, the most hidden, most hip Latin scene in Miami. Actually, it's not hidden; all the young Latinos know about Covacha and love it well, and we do too. It's an excellent spot to see new bands, upcoming DJs (almost all local), an enormous crowd and few tourists. Covacha is out in Doral, a good 14 miles west of downtown Miami.

☆ Entertainment

Miami's artistic merits are obvious, even from a distance. Could there be a better creative base? There's Southern homegrown talent, migratory snowbirds bringing the funding and attention of northeastern galleries, and immigrants from across the Americas. These disparate cultures communicate their values via the language of expression. Creole, Spanish and English, after all, are poor languages compared to dance, music and theater.

Performing Arts

Adrienne Arsht Center for the Performing Arts
PERFORMING ARTS

(Map p74; www.arshtcenter.org; 1300 Biscayne Blvd) This magnificent venue manages to both humble and enthrall visitors. Today the Arsht is where the biggest cultural acts in Miami come to perform; a show here is a must-see on any Miami trip. Get off the Metromover at the Omni stop.

Colony Theater
PERFORMING ARTS

(Map p64; ☎305-434-7091; www.colonytheatre miamibeach.com; 1040 Lincoln Rd) The Colony is an absolute art-deco gem, with a classic marquee and Inca-style crenellations, which looks like the sort of place gangsters would go to watch *Hamlet*. Built in 1935, this used to be the main cinema house in upper South

Beach before it fell into disrepair in the mid-20th century. It was renovated and revived in 1976 and now boasts 465 seats and great acoustics. This treasure serves as a major venue for performing arts – from comedy and occasional musicals to theatrical dramas, off-Broadway productions and ballet – as well as hosting movie screenings and small film festivals.

Gusman Center for the Performing Arts
PERFORMING ARTS

(Map p74; ✆ 305-374-2444; www.gusmancenter.org; 174 E Flagler St) This elegantly renovated 1920s movie palace services a huge variety of performing arts including film festivals, symphonies, ballets and touring shows. The acoustics are excellent.

Fillmore Miami Beach/ Jackie Gleason Theater
PERFORMING ARTS

(Map p64; ✆ 305-673-7300; www.fillmoremb.com/index; 1700 Washington Ave) Built in 1951, South Beach's premier showcase for touring Broadway shows, orchestras and other big musical productions has 2700 seats and excellent acoustics. Jackie Gleason chose to make the theater his home for the long-running 1960s TV show, but now you'll find an eclectic line-up of shows – Elvis Costello or Albita one night, the Dutch Philharmonic or an over-the-top musical the next.

Miami Light Project
PERFORMING ARTS

(Map p80; ✆ 305-576-4350; www.miamilightproject.com; 3000 Biscayne Blvd) The Miami Light Project is a nonprofit cultural foundation that represents innovative shows from theater troupes and performance artists from around the world. Shows are performed across the city, but the project is housed at Light Box Theatre.

Theater

See www.southfloridatheatre.com for a comprehensive directory of playhouses in greater South Florida.

Actors Playhouse
THEATER

(Map p90; ✆ 305-444-9293; www.actorsplayhouse.org; Miracle Theater, 280 Miracle Mile; tickets $20-50) Housed within the 1948 deco Miracle Theater in Coral Gables, this three-theater venue stages musicals and comedies, children's theater on its kids stage and more avant-garde productions in its small experimental black-box space.

Gablestage
THEATER

(Map p90; ✆ 305-445-1119; www.gablestage.org; 1200 Anastasia Ave; tickets $15-40) Founded as the Florida Shakespeare Theatre in 1979 and now housed on the property of the Biltmore Hotel in Coral Gables, this company still performs an occasional Shakespeare play, but mostly presents contemporary and classical pieces.

Jerry Herman Ring Theatre
THEATER

(✆ 305-284-3355; www.miami.edu/ring; University of Miami, 1321 Miller Dr; tickets $8-15) This University of Miami troupe stages musicals, dramas and comedies, with recent productions including Falsettos and Baby. Alumni actors include Sylvester Stallone, Steven Bauer, Saundra Santiago and Ray Liotta.

Dance

Miami City Ballet
DANCE

(Map p64; ✆ 305-929-7000; www.miamicityballet.org; 2200 Liberty Ave) Formed in 1985, this troupe is based out of a lovely three-story headquarters designed by famed local architectural firm Arquitectonica. The facade allows passers-by to watch the dancers rehearsing through big picture windows, which makes you feel like you're in a scene from Fame, except the weather is better and people don't spontaneously break into song.

MIAMI ENTERTAINMENT

THE FULL MOON DRUM CIRCLE

If there's a full moon, check out the beach between 79th and 85th Sts – a big, boisterous drum circle is held here that doubles as a full-moon party. The beat tends to start between 8:30pm and 9:30pm, and can run well into the wee hours. That said, drinking (and the consumption of other substances) is technically illegal on the beach, and police have broken up the event before. Still, it tends to be a pretty fun party that shouldn't be missed if you're in the area and want to see an incredible moonset. Check www.miamidrums.com for more information. The drum circle also goes off periodically in Coconut Grove, in the tropical overgrowth of the Barnacle (p87).

Ifé-Ilé Afro-Cuban Dance   DANCE

(☑ 305-476-0832; www.ife-ile.org) Ifé-Ilé is a nonprofit organization that promotes cultural understanding through dance and performs in a range of styles – traditional Afro-Cuban, mambo, rumba, conga, *chancleta*, *son* (a salsalike dance that originated in Oriente, Cuba), salsa and ritual pieces. Call for further information.

Miami Hispanic Ballet   DANCE

(Map p74; ☑ 305-549-7711; www.miamihispanicballet.org; 111 SW 5th Ave) Directed by Cuban-trained Pedro Pablo Peña, this troupe presents mainly classical ballets based out of the Miami Hispanic Cultural Arts Center, also known as 'The White House of Ballet.'

Classical

Miami Symphony Orchestra   CLASSICAL MUSIC

(☑ 305-284-6477, 305-275-5666; www.themiso.org; venues vary; tickets $15-30) Its yearly series features world-renowned soloists at shows held around the city, including the University of Miami and the Adrienne Arsht Center for the Performing Arts. Performances run from November to May.

New World Symphony   CLASSICAL MUSIC

(NWS; Map p64; ☑ 305-673-3330; www.nws.edu; 500 17th St) Housed in the New World Center (a funky explosion of cubist lines and geometric curves, fresh white against the blue Miami sky), the acclaimed New World Symphony holds performances from October to May. The deservedly heralded NWS serves as a three- to four-year preparatory program for talented musicians from prestigious music schools.

Chopin Foundation of the United States   CLASSICAL MUSIC

(Map p72; ☑ 305-868-0624; www.chopin.org; 1440 JFK/79th St Causeway) This national organization hosts a treasure trove of performances for Chopin fans – the Chopin Festival, a series of free monthly concerts and the less-frequent National Chopin Piano Competition, an international contest held in Miami every five years.

Florida Grand Opera   OPERA

(Map p74; ☑ 800-741-1010; www.fgo.org; 1300 Biscayne Blvd) Founded in the 1940s, this highly respected opera company, which stages many shows including *Madame Butterfly*, *La Boheme* and *Tosca*, performs throughout the year at the Adrienne Arsht Center for the Performing Arts and Fort Lauderdale.

Live Music

The Stage   LIVE MUSIC

(Map p80; ☑ 305-576-9577; www.thestagemiami.com; 170 NE 38th St; ⊙10pm-2am Tue, 9pm-2am Wed & Sun, 9pm-5am Fri & Sat) The Stage is many things: edgy art gallery, live-music venue, arts and crafts bazaar, occasional bar, and sometimes all of these things at once. Check the website to see what shows are playing and try to catch a party here – you may see a more bohemian, creative side of Miami than you initially expected.

Hoy Como Ayer   LIVE MUSIC

(Map p86; ☑ 305-541-2631; www.hoycomoayer.us; 2212 SW 8th St; ⊙8:30pm-4am Thu-Sat) This Cuban hot spot – with authentic music, unstylish wood paneling and a small dance floor – is enhanced by cigar smoke and Havana transplants. Stop in nightly for *son*, *boleros* (a Spanish dance in triple meter) and modern Cuban beats.

Sports

Miami Heat   BASKETBALL

(☑ 786-777-1000; www.nba.com/heat; American Airlines Arena, 601 Biscayne Blvd; tickets from $26) The city's NBA franchise plays at American Airlines Arena.

Miami Dolphins   FOOTBALL

(☑ 305-943-8000; www.miamidolphins.com; Sun Life Stadium, 2269 Dan Marino Blvd; tickets from $35) 'Dol-fans' are respectably crazy about their team, even if a Super Bowl showing has evaded them since 1985. Games are

---

wildly popular and the Dolphins are painfully successful, in that they always raise fans' hopes but never quite fulfill them. Sun Life Stadium is in Miami Gardens, 15 miles north of downtown.

University of Miami Hurricanes FOOTBALL
(☎800-462-2637; www.hurricanesports.com; tickets $22-60) The Hurricanes were once undisputed titans of university football, but had experienced a slow decline since 2004. They've recovered a bit as of the time of writing, and attending a game surrounded by UM's pack of fanatics is lots of fun. Their season is from August to December.

Miami Marlins BASEBALL
(http://miami.marlins.mlb.com; Marlins Park, 501 Marlins Way; tickets from $15) The MLB regular season runs from April to September.

University of Miami Hurricanes BASKETBALL
(☎800-462-2637; www.hurricanesports.com; tickets $20) From November to April you can catch the beloved college Hurricanes shooting hoops at the BankUnited Center at the University of Miami.

🔒 Shopping

There are two main shopping strips in South Beach – Lincoln Rd Mall, a pedestrian road lined with a great mix of indie shops and chain stores; and the southern end of Collins Ave, below 9th St. Here you'll find mostly high-end chains like A/X, Ralph Lauren and Barney's Co-op. Shooting way north of here, you'll find two extremely popular

CRICKET – IT'S A PITCH

Cricket in South Florida? Really? Oh yes. There's a huge West Indian and Jamaican community in South Florida, plus a very sizable British expat population. As such cricket is actually quite popular in these parts. The South Florida Cricket Alliance (☎954-805-2922; www.southfloridacricket.com) is one of the largest cricket clubs in the US, the Cricket Council of the USA (www.cricketcouncilusa.com) is based in Boca Raton, and the first dedicated cricket pitch in the country opened in Lauderhill (where the population is 25% West Indian), north of Fort Lauderdale, in 2008. Contact any of the above if you'd like to watch a match or join a team.

shopping malls: the Aventura Mall (www.shopaventuramall.com; 19501 Biscayne Blvd, Aventura), a mainstream collection including JC Penney and Bloomingdale's, and the chichi Bal Harbour Shops (www.balharbourshops.com; 9700 Collins Ave), a classy scene boasting Prada, Gucci, Chanel and Saks Fifth Avenue outposts. Bal Harbour is located about 3 miles north of North Miami Beach; Aventura is 9 miles north of North Miami Beach.

Move over to the mainland and there are a few options, the hippest being the Design District where you'll find a glut of art and homewares plus clothing and accessories hawkers. You'll have an easier time at the touristy, chain-store-drenched Bayside Marketplace (Map p74; www.baysidemarketplace.com; 401 Biscayne Blvd), on the shores of downtown Miami. Find more outdoor malls in Coconut Grove, at the ever-popular Coco-Walk (Map p88; 3015 Grand Ave) and Streets of Mayfair (Map p88; www.mayfairinthegrove.net; 2911 Grand Ave); Coral Gables meanwhile, has its Miracle Mile and the classy Village of Merrick Park (Map p90; www.villageofmerrickpark.com; 358 San Lorenzo Ave), located a mile south of the Miracle Mile, near the intersection of S Le Jeune Rd and Dixie Hwy.

Art

GO! Shop ART
(Map p80; ☎305-576-8205; 2516 NW 2nd Ave; ⊙noon-8pm Thu-Sat) If you fancy the art at the Wynwood Walls (p81), make sure to pop into the GO! shop, located within the street-art complex. Original artwork, prints and other arts accoutrements are presented on a rotating basis; the stuff for sale is either produced by or related to the works created by the current crop of Wynwood Walls artists.

Española Way Art Center ART
(Map p64; ☎305-673-0946; 405 Española Way) There are three levels of studios here, plus excellent original work and prints for sale, all by local artists. Hours vary by studio.

Clothing & Accessories

Consign of the Times VINTAGE
(Map p64; ☎305-535-0811; www.consignofthetimes.com; 1635 Jefferson Ave; ⊙11am-9pm) Cute vintage boutique that carries labels as lovely as Gucci (patent-leather shoes!), Von Furstenberg (leather slingbacks!) and Versace (silver bustier!).

C Madeleine's VINTAGE
(☎305-945-7770; 13702 Biscayne Blvd; ⊙11am-6pm Mon-Sat, noon-5pm Sun) The undisputed

queen of vintage Miami, C Madeleine's is more than your standard used-clothes write-off. This is a serious temple to classical style, selling Yves Saint Laurent couture and classic Chanel suits. Come here for the sort of timeless looks that are as beautiful now as when they first appeared on the rack.

Base
CLOTHING

(Map p64; ☑ 305-531-4982; www.baseworld.com; 939 Lincoln Rd; ⊙ 11am-10pm) This groovy hip-hop outlet has everything you need to be a good clubber – the latest Pumas, edgy streetwear, designer baseball caps, men's shaving and skincare products from gourmet labels, and a whole range of thumpa-thumpa and bom-chika-bom-chika CDs available for sampling at storefront listening stations.

Hip.e
CLOTHING

(Map p90; ☑ 305-445-3693; 359 Miracle Mile; ⊙ 11am-7pm Mon-Sat) A bit more hip than hippie, the clothes and jewelry here manage to mix up indie and hip-hop aesthetics in an admirably wearable way. Think Lucite bangles just slightly embellished by bling and you've got an idea of the vibe.

Alchemist
CLOTHING

(Map p64; ☑ 305-531-4653; 1111 Lincoln Rd; ⊙ 10am-10pm) This high-end boutique eschews bling and snootiness for friendly attitude, minimalism and simply beautiful clothes – standout labels include Zara and Proenza Schouler.

Pepe Y Berta
CLOTHING

(Map p86; ☑ 305-857-3771, 305-266-1007; 1421 SW 8th St; ⊙ 10am-6:30pm Mon-Fri, 9am-7pm Sat) The most gorgeous collection of *guayaberas* (Cuban dress shirts) in Miami can be found in this family-run shop, where the friendly owner will hand measure you and tailor a shirt to your tastes.

Boy Meets Girl
CHILDREN

(Map p90; ☑ 305-445-9668; 355 Miracle Mile; ⊙ 10am-7pm Mon-Fri, 11am-6pm Sat) Fantastically upscale and frankly expensive clothing for wee ones – if the kids are getting past puberty, look elsewhere, but otherwise they'll be fashionable far before they realize it.

Olin
MATERNITY

(Map p90; ☑ 305-446-2306; 356 Miracle Mile; ⊙ 9am-6pm Mon-Fri) Flagship of the Olin empire and Miami's premier maternity boutique, this is where expecting mommies can outfit themselves to look as glam as any South Beach model.

U Rock Couture
CLOTHING

(Map p68; ☑ 305-538-7625; 928 Ocean Dr; ⊙ 10am-1am Sun-Fri, to 2am Sat) U Rock is the quintessential Miami Beach clothing store. Loud, flashy and in your face, it resembles a mangled clash of rhinestones, tight clothes, revealing dresses, deep tans, euro accents and the cast of *Jersey Shore*. Somehow, this is all strangely appealing…rather like Lincoln Rd itself.

Gifts

Books and Books
BOOKS

(Map p90; ☑ 305-442-4408; 265 Aragon Ave; ⊙ 9am-11pm Sun-Thu, 9am-midnight Fri & Sat) The best indie bookstore in South Florida is a massive emporium of all things literary. Hosts frequent readings and is generally just a fantastic place to hang out. Has other outposts on Lincoln Road (☑ 305-532-3222; 927 Lincoln Rd) and at the Bal Harbour shops.

Metta Boutique
GIFTS

(Map p64; ☑ 305-763-8230; 1845 Purdy Ave; ⊙ 9am-8pm Mon-Thu, to 9pm Fri & Sat, 11am-6pm Sun) ✐ A cute store that brings some sustainability to South Beach. All of the goodies – clothes, journals, accessories, gifts and tchotchkes – are decidedly green/organic/sustainable/fair trade.

Celestial Treasures
GIFTS

(Map p88; ☑ 305-461-2341; 3444 Main Hwy; ⊙ noon-8pm Sun-Thu, to 10pm Fri & Sat) ✐ Your one-stop shop for spiritual and metaphysical needs, this shop has books, cards and components for those interested in Zen, Buddhism, Hinduism, Wicca, kabbalah and yoga. Also has staff psychics on hand.

Bookstore in the Grove
BOOKS

(Map p88; ☑ 305-483-2855; 3399 Virginia St; ⊙ 7am-10pm Mon-Fri, 8am-10pm Sat & Sun) Coconut Grove's independent bookstore is a good spot for all kinds of lit, and has a great cafe (try the empanadas) to boot.

Taschen
BOOKS

(Map p64; ☑ 305-538-6185; 1111 Lincoln Rd; ⊙ 11am-9pm Mon-Thu, to 10pm Fri & Sat, noon-9pm Sun) Ridiculously cool, well-stocked collection of art, photography, design and coffee-table books to make your hip home look that much smarter.

Ricky's NYC
GIFTS

(Map p64; ☑ 305-674-8511; 536 Lincoln Rd; ⊙ 10am-midnight Sun-Fri, to 1am Sat) This South Beach standby boasts hundreds of tacky gifts (boxing-nun puppets), pop-art paraphernalia and, well, 'adult' accoutrements such as sex toys, games, costumes and other unmentionables.

El Crédito Cigars
TOBACCONIST

(Map p86; ☑ 305-858-4162; 1106 SW 8th St; ☺ 8am-6pm Mon-Fri, to 4pm Sat) In one of the most popular cigar stores in Miami, and one of the oldest in Florida, you'll be treated as a venerated member of the stogie-chomping club.

M&N Variedades
BOTANICA

(Map p86; ☑ 305-649-3040; 1753 SW 8th St; ☺ 9am-8pm) This Santeria *botanica* (see p82) offers spell components, magic candles, *consultas espirituales* (spiritual consultation) and computer repair.

Eyes on Lincoln
EYEWEAR

(Map p64; ☑ 305-532-0070; 708 Lincoln Rd; ☺ 10am-11pm) The most sexy, impressive collection of glasses, sunglasses and optical accoutrements we've seen in South Florida.

Genius Jones
TOYS

(Map p80; ☑ 866-436-4875; 49 NE 39th St; ☺ 10am-7pm Mon-Sat, noon-6pm Sun) High-end toys, dolls and gear for babies and toddlers and their parents. Fatboy 'beanbag' chairs, Primo Viaggio car seats and Bugaboo strollers – geek out, parents.

Music

Sweat Records
MUSIC

(Map p80; ☑ 786-693-9309; 5505 NE 2nd Ave; ☺ noon-10pm Tue-Sat, to 5pm Sun) Sweat's almost a stereotypical indie record store – there's funky art and graffiti on the walls, it has big purple couches, it sells weird Japanese toys and there are skinny guys with thick glasses arguing over LPs and EPs you've never heard of, and, of course, there's coffee and vegan snacks.

ℹ Information

DANGERS & ANNOYANCES

There are a few areas considered by locals to be dangerous: Liberty City, in northwest Miami; Overtown, from 14th St to 20th St; Little Haiti and stretches of the Miami riverfront. In these and other reputedly 'bad' areas you should avoid walking around alone late at night – use common sense and travel in groups. In doubt, it's best to take a taxi and to know your address.

Deserted areas below 5th St in South Beach are more dangerous at night, but your main concerns are aggressive drunks or the occasional strung-out druggie, rather than muggers. In downtown Miami, use caution near the Greyhound station and around causeways, bridges

and overpasses where homeless people and some refugees have set up shanty towns.

Natural dangers include the strong sun (use a high-SPF sunscreen), mosquitoes (use a spray-on repellent) and hurricanes (between June and November). There's a **hurricane hotline** (☑ 305-468-5400), which will give you information about approaching storms, storm tracks, warnings and estimated time to touchdown – all the things you will need to know to make a decision about if and when to leave.

EMERGENCY

Ambulance (☑ 911)

Beach Patrol (☑ 305-673-7714)

Hurricane Hotline (☑ 305-468-5400)

Poison Information Center (☑ 305-585-5250)

Rape Hotline (☑ 305-585-7273)

Suicide Intervention (☑ 305-358-4357)

INTERNET ACCESS

Most hotels and hostels (and increasingly, even camping grounds) offer wi-fi access. Free wi-fi is also available in libraries, Starbucks and McDonald's.

MEDIA

Beach Channel (www.thebeachchannel.tv) Local 24-hour TV station on channel 19, like a quirky infomercial about goings-on in Miami Beach.

Diario Las Americas (www.diariolasamericas. com) Spanish-language daily.

El Nuevo Herald (www.elnuevoherald.com) Spanish-language daily of the *Herald*.

Miami Herald (www.miamiherald.com) Major daily covering local, national and international news.

Miami New Times (www.miaminewtimes.com) Free alternative weekly paper.

Miami Sun Post (www.miamisunpost.com) In-depth news and lifestyle coverage.

Sun-Sentinel (www.sun-sentinel.com) Daily covering South Florida.

WLRN (www.wlrn.org) Local National Public Radio affiliate, at 91.3FM on the dial.

MEDICAL SERVICES

Beach Dental Center (☑ 877-353-8845; 333 Arthur Godfrey Rd) For dental needs.

Coral Gables Hospital (☑ 305-445-8461; 3100 Douglas Rd, Coral Gables) A community-based facility with many bilingual doctors.

Eckerd Drugs (☑ 305-538-1571; 1421 Alton Rd, South Beach; ☺ 24hr) One of many 24-hour Eckerd pharmacies.

Miami Beach Community Health Center (Stanley C Meyers Center; ☑ 305-538-8835; 710 Alton Rd, South Beach) Walk-in clinic with long lines.

Mount Sinai Medical Center (☑305-674-2121; emergency room 305-674-2200; 4300 Alton Rd) The area's best emergency room. Beware that you must eventually pay, and fees are high.

Visitor's Medical Line (☑305-674-2222; ☺24hr) For physician referrals.

MONEY

Bank of America has branch offices all over Miami and Miami Beach. To get currency exchanged you can go to Amex.

POST

The following branches have hours extended until evening thanks to self-serve machines in the lobbies:

Post office Mid-Beach (Map p72; 445 W 40th St; ☺8am-5pm Mon-Fri, 8:30am-2pm Sat); South Beach (Map p64; 1300 Washington Ave; ☺8am-5pm Mon-Fri, 8:30am-2pm Sat)

TOURIST INFORMATION

Art Deco Welcome Center (Map p68; ☑305-672-2014; www.mdpl.org; 1001 Ocean Dr, South Beach; ☺9:30am-5pm Fri-Wed, to 7pm Thu) Run by the Miami Design Preservation League (MDPL); has tons of art-deco district information and organizes excellent walking tours.

Black Archives History & Research Center of South Florida (☑305-636-2390; www. theblackarchives.org; 5400 NW 22nd Ave, Suite 101, Liberty City; ☺9am-5pm Mon-Fri) Information about black culture.

Coconut Grove Chamber of Commerce (Map p88; ☑305-444-7270; www.coconutgrove-chamber.com; 2820 McFarlane Rd, Coconut Grove; ☺9am-5pm Mon-Fri)

Coral Gables Chamber of Commerce (Map p90; ☑305-446-1657; www.coralgables-chamber.org; 224 Catalonia Ave, Coral Gables; ☺9am-5pm Mon-Fri)

Downtown Miami Welcome Center (Map p74; ☑786-472-5930; www.downtownmiami.com; 900 S Miami Ave; ☺9am-5pm Mon-Fri) Provides maps, brochures and tour information for the downtown area.

Greater Miami & the Beaches Convention & Visitors Bureau (Map p74; ☑305-539-3000; www.miamiandbeaches.com; 701 Brickell Ave, 27th fl; ☺8:30am-5pm Mon-Fri) Located in an oddly intimidating high-rise building.

Miami Beach Chamber of Commerce (Map p64; ☑305-674-1300; www.miamibeach-chamber.com; 1920 Meridian Ave; ☺9am-5pm Mon-Fri) You can purchase a Meter Card here. Denominations come in $10, $20 and $25 (and meters cost $1 per hour).

USEFUL WEBSITES

Art Circuits (www.artcircuits.com) The best insider info on art events; includes excellent neighborhood-by-neighborhood gallery maps.

Beached Miami (www.beachedmiami.com) The best independent arts website in Miami.

Meatless Miami (www.meatlessmiami.com) Vegetarians in need of an eating guide, look no further.

Miami Beach 411 (www.miamibeach411.com) A great guide for Miami Beach visitors, covering just about all concerns.

Miami Nights (www.mianinights.com) Get a good, opinionated lowdown on Miami's ever-shifting after-dark scene.

Short Order (http://blogs.miaminewtimes.com/shortorder) The *New Times* food blog that always seems ahead of the curve on eating events in the Magic City.

That's So Miami (http://thatssomiami.tumblr.com/) Quirky, weird and fun Miami.

❶ Getting There & Away

AIR

Miami is served by all major carriers via two main airports: Miami International Airport (MIA) and the Fort Lauderdale-Hollywood International Airport (FLL), half an hour north of MIA. **MIA** (☑305-876-7000; www.miami-airport.com) is the third-busiest airport in the country. Just 6 miles west of downtown Miami, the airport is open 24 hours and is laid out in a horseshoe design. There are left-luggage facilities on two concourses at MIA, between B and C, and on G; prices vary according to bag size.

The Fort Lauderdale-Hollywood International Airport (p516), about 15 miles north of Miami just off I-95, often serves as a lower-cost alternative to MIA, especially because it's serviced by popular, cut-rate flyers including Southwest Airlines and JetBlue.

BOAT

Though it's doubtful you'll be catching a steamer to make a trans-Atlantic journey, it is quite possible that you'll arrive in Miami via a cruise ship, as the **Port of Miami** (☑305-347-4800; www.miamidade.gov/portofmiami), which received nearly four million passengers in 2013, is known as the 'cruise capital of the world.' Arriving in the port will put you on the edge of downtown Miami; taxis and public buses to other local points are available from nearby Biscayne Blvd. The Key West Express ferry plies to Key West from Miami.

BUS

Greyhound (Map p74; ☑800-231-2222; www.greyhound.com) is the major carrier in and out of town. There are four major terminals: **Airport terminal** (☑305-871-1810; 4111 NW 27th St); **Main Downtown terminal** (☑305-374-6160; 1012 NW 1st Ave); **North Miami terminal** (☑305-945-0801; 16560 NE 6th Ave); and the **Southern Miami terminal** (Cutler Bay, ☑305-296-9072; Cutler Ridge Mall, 20505 S Dixie Hwy), also known as the Cutler Bay terminal. There are several buses daily that head both up the East Coast and across the panhandle through the Gulf Coast.

TRAIN

The main Miami terminal of **Amtrak** (☑ 305-835-1222; www.amtrak.com; 8303 NW 37th Ave) connects the city with the rest of continental USA and Canada. Travel time between New York and Miami is a severe 27 to 30 hours. The Miami Amtrak station has a left-luggage facility, which costs $2 per bag.

🛈 Getting Around

TO/FROM THE AIRPORT
Miami International Airport

It's a cinch to get from the airport to just about anywhere in Miami, especially Mid-Beach. If you're driving, follow Rte 112 from the airport, then head east on the Julia Tuttle Causeway or the I-195 to get to South Beach. Other options include the free shuttles offered by most hotels, or a taxi ($32 flat rate from the airport to South Beach). Alternatively, catch the Airport Owl night-only public bus, or the **SuperShuttle** (☑ 305-871-8210; www.supershuttle.com) shared-van service, which will cost about $26 to South Beach. Be sure to reserve a seat the day before. Metro buses leave from across Concourse E and run throughout the city; fares are $1.50, plus 50 cents for transfers.

Fort Lauderdale-Hollywood International Airport

Put the money you save on flights toward getting to Miami once you land; either rent a car at one of the many Fort Lauderdale agencies, or take the free shuttle from terminals 1 and 3 to the **Tri-Rail station** (☑ 800-874-7245; www.tri-rail.com; 1-way $2-5.50); you can ride this commuter train into Miami. The schedule is infrequent, though, so you may want to opt for the **GOShuttle** (☑ 877-544-4646; https://goairportshuttle.com), which will cost about $30 to South Beach.

BICYCLE

A bike-share program on Miami Beach makes cycling around the beaches, at least, a cinch.

The Miami area may be as flat as a pancake, but it's also plagued by traffic backups and speedy thoroughfares, so judge the bikeability of your desired route carefully.

The city of Miami Beach offers the DecoBike (p94) bike-share program. Bike stations are located in dozens of spots around Miami Beach (there's a map on the website, plus a link to an iPhone app that tells you where the nearest station is).

Places that rent bicycles include the following:

BikeAndRoll (Map p68; ☑ 305-604-0001; www.bikeandroll.com; 210 10th St; per hour/day from $5/15; ⏱9am-7pm) Also does bike tours.

Mangrove Cycles (Map p84; ☑ 305-361-5555; 260 Crandon Blvd, Key Biscayne; per 2hr/day/week from $20/25/75; ⏱10am-6pm Tue-Sun) Rents bicycles.

BUS

The local bus system is called **Metrobus** (☑ 305-891-3131; www.miamidade.gov/transit/routes.asp; tickets $2). An easy-to-read route map is available online. You may spend more time waiting for a bus than you will riding on one.

In South Beach, an excellent option is the **South Beach Local Circulator** (☑ 305-891-3131; 25¢) – also called the South Beach Local – a looping shuttle bus with disabled-rider access that operates along Washington between S Pointe Dr and 17th St and loops back around on Alton Rd on the west side of the beach. Rides come along every 10 to 15 minutes.

CAR & MOTORCYCLE

If you drive around Miami there are a few things to keep in mind. Miami Beach is linked to the mainland by four causeways built over Biscayne Bay. They are, from south to north: the MacArthur (the extension of US Hwy 41 and Hwy A1A); Venetian ($1.50 toll); Julia Tuttle; and John F Kennedy. There's also a $1.75 toll over the Rickenbacker Causeway to Key Biscayne.

The most important north–south highway is I-95, which ends at US Hwy 1 south of downtown Miami. US Hwy 1, which runs from Key West all the way north to Maine, hugs the coastline. It's called Dixie Hwy south of downtown Miami and Biscayne Blvd north of downtown Miami. The Palmetto Expwy (Hwy 826) makes a rough loop around the city and spurs off below SW 40th St to the Don Shula Expwy (Hwy 874, a toll road). Florida's Turnpike Extension makes the most western outer loop around the city. Hwy A1A becomes Collins Ave in Miami Beach.

Miami has an annoying convention of giving major roads multiple names. So for example, Bird Rd is also SW 40th St and Hwy 976. Hwy 826 is the Palmetto Expwy. US 1 is the Dixie Hwy – except in downtown, when it becomes Biscayne Blvd. Hwy 836 is the Dolphin Expwy, while in Miami Beach 5th St becomes A1A. Calle Ocho is SW 8th St, as well as the Tamiami Trail, and US 41 (phew), and Hwy 959 is Red Rd, except when it's SW 57th St. Somehow, this isn't as confusing as it reads on paper – most signage indicates every name a route may have, but it can be frustrating to first-time Miami drivers.

Besides the causeways to Miami Beach, the major east–west roads are SW 8th St; Hwy 112 (also called Airport Expwy); and Hwy 836 (also called Dolphin Expwy), which slices through downtown Miami and connects with I-395 and the MacArthur Causeway, and which runs west to the Palmetto Expwy and Florida's Turnpike Extension.

Miami drivers are...how can we put this delicately?...aggressive, tailgating jerks who'd cut off their grandmother if they could figure out how to properly change lanes. We are, of course, kidding. Not all Miami drivers fit the above description, but there are enough of these maniacs about to make driving here an occasional (and sometimes not-so-occasional) nightmare.

Parking

Parking is pretty straightforward. Regulations are well signposted and meters are plentiful (except perhaps on holiday-weekend evenings in South Beach). Downtown, near the Bayside Marketplace, parking is cheap but a bit confusing: you must find a place in the head-on parking lots (backing into the parking space not allowed), buy a ticket from a central machine and display it in your windshield.

On South Beach there's metered street parking along most streets (except Lincoln Rd and residential areas). Meters are enforced from 9am to as late as 3am in some parts of South Beach. Most allow you to pay for up to three hours, although some have increased that range to 12 hours. Most Miami Beach meter machines include a credit-card option; parking rates vary, but it rarely costs more than $1.50 per hour.

There are many municipal parking garages, which are usually the easiest and cheapest option – look for giant blue 'P' signs. You'll find several located along Collins Ave and Washington Ave. If you park illegally or if the meter runs out, parking fines are about $30, but a tow could cost much more.

TAXI

Central Cabs (☑ 305-532-5555)
Flamingo Taxis (☑ 305-759-8100)
Metro (☑ 305-888-8888)
Miami Taxi Service (☑ 305-525-2455)
Sunshine (☑ 305-445-3333)
Yellow (☑ 305-400-0000)

TRAIN

The **Metromover** (www.miamidade.gov/transit/metromover.asp), which is equal parts bus, monorail and train, is helpful for getting around downtown Miami. It offers visitors a great perspective on the city and a free orientation tour of the area.

Metrorail (www.miamidade.gov/transit/metrorail.asp) is a 21-mile-long heavy-rail system that has one elevated line running from Hialeah through downtown Miami and south to Kendall/Dadeland. Trains run every five to 15 minutes from 6am to midnight. The fare is $2, or $1 with a Metromover transfer.

The regional **Tri-Rail** (☑ 800-874-7245; www.tri-rail.com) double-decker commuter trains run the 71 miles between Dade, Broward and Palm Beach counties. Fares are calculated on a zone basis; the shortest distance traveled costs $4.40 round-trip; the most you'll ever pay is for the ride between MIA and West Palm Beach ($11.55 round-trip). No tickets are sold on the train, so allow time to make your purchase before boarding. All trains and stations are accessible to riders with disabilities. For a list of stations, log on to the Tri-Rail website.

The Everglades

Best Places to Eat

➡ Robert is Here (p149)

➡ Joannie's Blue Crab Café (p145)

➡ JT's Island Grill & Gallery (p146)

➡ Rosita's (p149)

➡ Oyster House (p146)

Best Places to Stay

➡ Everglades International Hostel (p149)

➡ Everglades City Motel (p146)

➡ Ivey House Bed & Breakfast (p146)

➡ Wilderness Camping (p151)

➡ Swamp Cottage (p145)

Why Go?

There is no wilderness in America quite like the Everglades. Called the 'River of Grass' by its initial Native American inhabitants, this is not just a wetland, or a swamp, or a lake, or a river, or a prairie, or a grassland – it is all of the above, twisted together into a series of soft horizons, long vistas, sunsets that stretch across your entire field of vision and the creeping grin of a large population of dinosaur-era reptiles.

When you watch anhinga flexing their wings before breaking into a corkscrew dive, or the slow, Jurassic flap of a great blue heron gliding over its domain, or the sun kissing miles of unbroken saw grass as it sets behind humps of skeletal cypress domes, you'll have an idea of what we're speaking of. In a nation where natural beauty is measured by its capacity for drama, the Everglades subtly, contentedly flows on.

When to Go
Everglades City

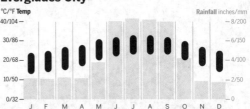

Dec–Mar Dry season: top wildlife viewing along watercourses, but some kayaking will be difficult.

Apr–Jun Although the weather gets pretty hot, there's a good mix of water and wildlife.

Jul–Nov Lots of heat, lots of bugs and (except in October and November) chances of hurricanes.

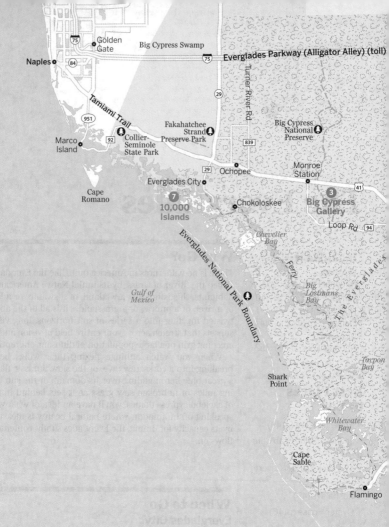

Everglades Highlights

1 Watching the sun set over the ingress road to **Pa-hay-okee Overlook** (p151) from the roof of your car.

2 Canoeing or kayaking into **Hell's Bay Paddling Trail** (p151), a tangled morass of red creeks, slow blackwater and the heavy vegetative curtain of a preserved marsh.

3 Checking out some of the best photography of the surrounding swamps, forests, beaches and sea at **Big Cypress Gallery** (p141).

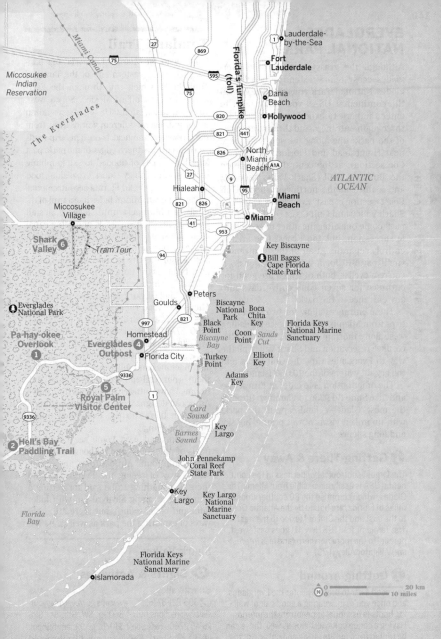

EVERGLADES NATIONAL PARK

Although the grassy waters – the Everglades ecosystem – extend outside Everglades National Park (the third-largest in the continental USA), you really need to enter the park to experience it. There are three main entrances and three main areas of the park: one along the southeast edge near Homestead and Florida City (Ernest Coe section); at the central-north side on the Tamiami Trail (Shark Valley section); and a third at the northwest shore (Gulf Coast section), past Everglades City. The Shark Valley and Gulf Coast sections of the park come one after the other in geographic succession, but the Ernest Coe area is entirely separate. At all of these entrances you'll pay $10 for a vehicle pass, or $5 if you're a cyclist, both of which are good for entrance for seven consecutive days into any entrance in the park.

These entrances allow for two good road trips from Miami. The first choice is heading west along the Tamiami Trail, past the Miccosukee reservation and Shark Valley, all the way to Everglades City, the Gulf Coast and the crystal waters of the 10,000 Islands.

The other option is to enter at Ernest Coe and take State Rd 9336 to Flamingo through the most 'Glades-y' landscape in the park, with unbroken vistas of wet prairie, big sky and long silences.

❶ Getting There & Away

The largest subtropical wilderness in the continental USA is easily accessible from Miami. The Glades, which comprise the 80 southernmost miles of Florida, are bound by the Atlantic Ocean to the east and the Gulf of Mexico to the west. The Tamiami Trail (US Hwy 41) goes east–west, parallel to the more northern (and less interesting) Alligator Alley (I-75).

❶ Getting Around

You need a car to properly enter the Everglades and once you're in, wearing a good pair of walking boots is essential to penetrate the interior. Having a canoe or kayak helps as well; these can be rented from outfits inside and outside of the park, or else you can seek out guided canoe and kayak tours. Bicycles are well suited to the flat roads of Everglades National Park, particularly in the area between Ernest Coe and Flamingo Point. Road shoulders in the park tend to be dangerously small.

Tamiami Trail

Calle Ocho, in Miami's Little Havana happens to be the eastern end of the Tamiami Trail/US 41, which cuts through the Everglades to the Gulf of Mexico. So go west, young traveler, along US 41, a few dozen miles and several different worlds away from the city where the heat is on. This trip leads you onto the northern edges of the park, past long landscapes of flooded forest, gambling halls, swamp-buggy tours, roadside food shacks and other Old Florida accoutrements.

Past Hialeah, Miami fades like a trail of diminishing Starbucks until...*whoosh*...it's all huddled forest, open fields and a big canal off to the side (evidence of US 41's diversion of the Glades' all-important sheet flow). The surest sign the city is gone and the Glades have begun is the Confederate flag decals on **Pit BBQ**, which serves decent if not memorable smoked pork and dishes of that ilk. The empty road runs past the **Miccosukee Resort & Convention Center** (☎305-222-4600, 877-242-6464; www.miccosukee.com; 500 SW 177th Ave; r Dec-Mar/Apr-Nov $150/120; ❇☎). It's essentially a casino-hotel complex full of slot machines and folks chunking coins into them – not really an ecological wonderland. Rooms have attractive geometric Native American designs worked into the furniture, but again, there's no need to stay here unless you're gambling.

As you head west you'll see fields and fields of pine forest and billboards advertising swamp tours. Airboat tours are an old-school way of seeing the Everglades (and there is something to be said for getting a tour from a raging Skynyrd fan with killer tatts and better camo), but there are other ways of exploring the park as well.

Shark Valley

◉ Sights & Activities

Shark Valley   PARK
(☎305-221-8776; www.nps.gov/ever/planyourvisit/svdirections.htm; 36000 SW 8th St, GPS 25°45'27.60; car/cyclist $10/5; ☉9:15am-5:15pm; Ⓟ⌖) ☙ Shark Valley sounds like it should be the headquarters for the villain in a James Bond movie, but it is in fact a slice of National Park Service grounds heavy with informative signs and knowledgeable rangers. Shark Valley is located in the cypress-and-hardwood-and-riverine section

of the Everglades, a more traditionally jungly section of the park than the grassy fields and forest domes surrounding the Ernest Coe visitor center. A 15-mile/24km paved trail takes you past small creeks, tropical forest and 'borrow pits' (manmade holes that are now basking spots for gators, turtles and birdlife). The pancake-flat trail is perfect for bicycles, which can be rented at the entrance for $7.50 per hour. Bring water with you.

If you don't feel like exerting yourself, the most popular and painless way to immerse yourself in the Everglades is via the two-hour **tram tour** (☑305-221-8455; www.sharkvalleytramtours.com; adult/child under 12yr/senior $22/19/12.75; ☺departures May-Dec 9:30am, 11am, 2pm, 4pm, Jan-Apr 9am-4pm every hr on the hr) that runs along Shark Valley's entire 15-mile trail. If you only have time for one Everglades activity, this should be it, as guides are informative and witty, and you'll likely see gators sunning themselves on the road. Halfway along the trail is the 50ft-high Shark Valley Observation Tower, an ugly concrete tower that offers dramatically beautiful views of the park.

At the park entrance, the easy **Bobcat Boardwalk Trail** (800m) makes a loop through a thick copse of tropical hardwoods before emptying you out right back into the Shark Valley parking lot. A little ways past is the **Otter Cave Trail** (400m) which heads over a limestone shelf that has been Swiss-cheesed into a porous sponge by rainwater. Animals now live in the eroded holes (although it's not likely you'll spot any) and Native Americans used to live on top of the shelf.

Miccosukee Village PARK
(☑305-222-4600, 877-242-6464; www.miccosukee.com; Mile 70, Hwy 41; adult/child/5yr & under $10/6/free; ☺9am-5pm; ⓟ▲) Just across the road from Shark Valley, this 'village' is an informative open-air museum that showcases the culture of the Miccosukee via guided tours of traditional homes, a crafts gift store, dance and music performances, an airboat ride into a hammock-cum-village of raised 'chickee' (wooden platforms built above the waterline) huts and (natch) gator wrestling. There's a somewhat desultory on-site restaurant if you get hungry. The art and handmade crafts from the on-site art gallery make good souvenirs.

Big Cypress & Ochopee

The better part of the Tamiami Trail is fronted on either side by long cypress trees overhung with moss and endless vistas of soft prairie, flooded in the wet season into a boggy River of Grass.

⊙ Sights & Activities

Big Cypress Gallery GALLERY
(☑941-695-2428; www.clydebutcher.com; Tamiami Trail; swamp walk 1.5hr adult/child $50/35, 45min adult/child $35/25; ☺10am-5pm; ⓟ) ✎
The highlight of many Everglades trips, this gallery showcases the work of Clyde Butcher, an American photographer who follows in the great tradition of Ansel Adams. His large-format black-and-white images elevate the swamps to a higher level. Butcher has found a quiet spirituality in the brackish waters and you might, too, with the help of his eyes. Every Labor Day (first weekend in

AIRBOATS & SWAMP BUGGIES

Airboats are flat-bottomed skiffs that use powerful fans to propel themselves through the water. Their environmental impact has not been determined, but one thing is clear: airboats can't be doing much good, which is why they're not allowed in the park. Swamp buggies are enormous balloon-tired vehicles that can go through wetlands, creating ruts and damaging wildlife.

Airboat and swamp-buggy rides are offered all along US Hwy 41 (Tamiami Trail). Think twice before going on a 'nature' tour. Loud whirring fanboats and marsh jeeps really don't do the quiet serenity of the Glades justice. That said, many tourists in the Everglades are there (obviously) because of their interest in the environment, and they demand environmentally knowledgeable tours. The airboat guys are pretty good at providing these – their livelihood is also caught up in the preservation of the Glades, and they know the back country well. We recommend going with the guys at **Cooperstown** (☑305-226-6048; http://coopertownairboats.com; 22700 SW 8th St; adult/child $23/11; ▲), one of the first airboat operators you encounter heading west on 41. Just expect a more touristy experience than the National Park grounds.

THE EVERGLADES: AN OVERVIEW

It's tempting to think of the Everglades as a swamp, but 'prairie' may be a more apt description. The Glades, at the end of the day, are grasslands that happen to be flooded for most of the year: visit during the dry season (winter) and you'd be forgiven for thinking the Everglades was the Everfields.

So where's the water coming from? Look north on a map of Florida, all the way to Lake Okeechobee and the small lakes and rivers that band together around Kissimmee. Florida dips into the Gulf of Mexico at its below-sea-level tip, which happens to be the lowest part of the state geographically and topographically. Run-off water from central Florida flows down the peninsula via streams and rivers, over and through the Glades, and into Florida Bay. The glacial pace of the flood means this seemingly stillest of landscapes is actually in constant motion. Small wonder the Calusa Indians called the area Pa-hay-okee (grassy water). Famous conservationist Marjory Stoneman Douglas (1890–1998) called it the River of Grass; in her famous book of the same title, she revealed that Gerard de Brahm, a colonial cartographer, named the region the River Glades, which became Ever Glades on later English maps.

So what happens when nutrient-rich water creeps over a limestone shelf? The ecological equivalent of a sweaty orgy. Beginning at the cellular level, organic material blooms in surprising ways, clumping and forming into algal beds, nutrient blooms and the ubiquitous periphyton, which are basically clusters of algae, bacteria and detritus (ie stuff). Periphyton ain't pretty: in the water they resemble puke streaks and the dried version looks like hippo turds. But you should kiss them when you see them (well, maybe not), because in the great chain of the Everglades, this slop forms the base of a very tall organic totem pole. The smallest tilt in elevation alters the flow of water and hence the content of this nutrient soup, and thus the landscape itself: all those patches of cypress and hardwood hammock (not a bed for backpackers; in this case, hammock is a fancy Floridian way of saying a forest of broadleaf trees, mainly tropical or subtropical) are areas where a few inches of altitude create a world of difference between biosystems.

Fight for the Green Grassy Waters

The Everglades were utter wilderness for thousands of years. Even Native Americans avoided the Glades; the 'native' Seminole and Miccosukee actually settled here as exiles escaping war and displacement from other parts of the country. But following European settlement of Florida, some pioneers saw the potential for economic development of the Grassy Waters.

Cattle ranchers and sugar growers, attracted by mucky waters and Florida's subtropical climate (paradise for sugarcane), successfully pressured the government to make land available to them. In 1905, Florida governor Napoleon Bonaparte Broward personally dug the first shovelful of a diversion that connected the Caloosahatchee River to Lake Okeechobee. Hundreds of canals were cut through the Everglades to the coastline to 'reclaim' the land, and the flow of lake water was restricted by a series of dikes. Farmland began to claim areas previously uninhabited by humans.

Unfortunately, the whole 'River of Grass' needs the river to survive. And besides being a pretty place to watch the birds, the Everglades acts as a hurricane barrier and kidney. Kidney? Yup: all those wetlands leeched out pollutants from the Florida Aquifer (the state's freshwater supply). But when farmland wasn't diverting the sheet flow, it was adding fertilizer-rich wastewater to it. Result? A very sweaty (and well-attended) biological orgy. Bacteria, and eventually plant life, bloomed at a ridiculous rate (they call it fertilizer for a reason), upsetting the fragile balance of resources vital to the Glades' survival.

Enter Marjory Stoneman Douglas, stage left. Ms Douglas gets the credit for almost single-handedly pushing the now age-old Florida issue of Everglades conservation.

Despite the tireless efforts of Douglas and other environmentalists, today the Florida Aquifer is in serious danger of being contaminated and drying up. In 2011, the water level in Okeechobee was almost 2.7 inches below normal level. The number of wading birds nesting has declined by 90% to 95% since the 1930s. Currently, there are 67 threatened and endangered plant and animal species in the park.

The diversion of water away from the Glades and run-off pollution are the main culprits behind the region's environmental degradation. This delicate ecosystem is the neighbor of one of the fastest-growing urban areas in the US. The current water-drainage system in South Florida was built to handle the needs of two million people; the local population topped six million in 2010. And while Miami can't grow north or south into Fort Lauderdale or Homestead, it can move west, directly into the Everglades. At this stage, scientists estimate the wetlands have been reduced by 50% to 75% of their original size.

Humans are not the only enemy of the Everglades. Nature has done its share of damage as well. During 2005's Hurricane Wilma, for example, six storm-water treatment areas (artificial wetlands that cleanse excess nutrients out of the water cycle) were lashed and heavily damaged by powerful winds. Without these natural filtration systems, the Glades are far more susceptible to nutrient blooms and external pollution. In 2011, wildfires caused by drought incinerated huge patches of land near the Tamiami Trail.

Restoration of the Everglades

Efforts to save the Everglades began in the late 1920s, but were sidelined by the Great Depression. In 1926 and 1928, two major hurricanes caused Lake Okeechobee to overflow; the resulting floods killed hundreds. The Army Corps of Engineers did a really good job of damming the lake. A bit too good: the Glades were essentially cut off from their source, the Kissimmee watershed.

In the meantime, conservationists began donating land for protection, starting with 1 sq mile of land donated by a garden club. The Everglades was declared a national park in 1947, the same year Marjory Stoneman Douglas' *The Everglades: River of Grass* was published.

By draining the wetlands through the damming of the lake, the Army Corps made huge swaths of inland Florida inhabitable. But the environmental problems created by shifting water's natural flow, plus the area's ever-increasing population, now threaten to make the whole region uninhabitable. The canal system sends, on average, over 1 billion gallons of water into the ocean every day. At the same time, untreated run-off flows unfiltered into natural water supplies. Clean water is disappearing from the water cycle while South Florida's population gets bigger by the day.

Enter the **Comprehensive Everglades Restoration Plan** (CERP; www.evergladesplan.org). CERP is designed to address the root of all Everglades issues: water – where to get it, how to divert it and ways to keep it clean. The plan is to unblock the Kissimmee, restoring remaining Everglades lands to predevelopment conditions, while maintaining flood protection, providing freshwater for South Florida's populace and protecting earmarked regions against urban sprawl. It sounds great, but political battles have significantly slowed the implementation of CERP. The cost of the project has increased over the years, and a mix of political red tape and maneuvering courtesy of federal and state government has delayed CERP's implementation.

Not to throw another acronym at you, but a major portion of the CERP is the **Central Everglades Planning Project** (CEPP), the rare public works project that is supported by environmentalists and industry alike. The CEPP's aim is to clean polluted water from Florida's agricultural central heartland and redirect it towards the 'Glades. The River of Grass would be re-watered, and toxic run-off would no longer flow to the sea. But as of the time of writing, the CEPP's implementation was being delayed by the Army Corps of Engineers. Governmental gridlock may damage the Glades in the 21st century as much as government policies did in the 20th.

Bringing back the Everglades is one of the biggest, most ambitious environmental restoration projects in US history, one that combines the needs of farmers, fishers, urban residents, local governments and conservationists. The success or failure of the program will be a bellwether for the future of the US environmental movement.

CANOE CAMPING ON 10,000 ISLANDS

One of the best ways to experience the serenity of the Everglades – somehow desolate yet lush, tropical and foreboding – is by paddling the network of waterways that skirt the northwest portion of the park. The 10,000 Islands consist of many (but not really 10,000) tiny islands and a mangrove swamp that hugs the southwestern-most border of Florida. The Wilderness Waterway, a 99-mile path between Everglades City and Flamingo, is the longest canoe trail in the area, but there are shorter trails near Flamingo.

Most islands are fringed by narrow beaches with sugar-white sand, but note that the water is brackish, and very shallow most of the time. It's not Tahiti, but it's fascinating. You can camp on your own island for up to a week.

Getting around the 10,000 Islands is pretty straightforward if you religiously adhere to National Oceanic & Atmospheric Administration (NOAA) tide and nautical charts. Going against the tides is the fastest way to have a miserable trip. The Gulf Coast Visitor Center (p145) sells nautical charts and gives out free tidal charts. You can also purchase charts prior to your visit – call ☎ 305-247-1216 and ask for charts 11430, 11432 and 11433.

September), the gallery holds a gala event, which includes a fun $20 swamp walk onto his 30-acre property; the party attracts swamp-stompers from across the state.

Take a walk on the wet and wild side with a swamp walk behind the gallery. If you don't mind getting soggy, this is one of our favorite ways of exploring the Everglades. You'll slog under a blooming, moss-draped canopy of wispy cypress leaves and blooming flowers, squishing your way near the spidery trunks of the trees that interlace the Western Everglades. Call ahead to reserve a tour.

Big Cypress National Preserve PARK
(☎239-695-4758; 33000 Tamiami Trail E; ⊙8:30am-4:30pm; P ♿) The 1139-sq-mile Big Cypress Preserve (named for the size of the park, not its trees) is the result of a compromise between environmentalists, cattle ranchers and oil-and-gas explorers. The area is integral to the Everglades' ecosystem: rains that flood the Preserve's prairies and wetlands slowly filter down through the Glades. About 45% of the cypress swamp (actually mangrove islands, hardwood hammocks, orchid flowers, slash pine, prairies and marshes) is protected. Great bald cypress trees are nearly gone, thanks to pre-Preserve lumbering, but dwarf pond cypress trees fill the area with their own understated beauty. The helpful Oasis Visitor Center (☎941-695-1201; ⊙8am-4:30pm Mon-Fri; ♿), about 20 miles west of Shark Valley, has great exhibits for the kids and a water-filled ditch that's popular with alligators.

Ochopee VILLAGE
(GPS 25.901529, -81.306023) Drive to the hamlet of Ochopee (population about four)... no...wait...turn around, you missed it! Then pull over and break out the cameras: Ochopee's claim to fame is the country's smallest post office. It's housed in a former toolshed and set against big park skies; a friendly postal worker patiently poses for snapshots.

Skunk Ape Research Headquarters PARK
(☎239-695-2275; www.skunkape.info; 40904 Tamiami Trail E; ⊙7am-7pm,'zoo' closes around 4pm; P) This only-in-Florida roadside attraction is dedicated to tracking down Southeastern USA's version of Bigfoot, the eponymous Skunk Ape (a large gorilla-man who supposedly stinks to high heaven). We never saw a Skunk Ape, but you can see a corny gift shop and, in the back, a reptile-and-bird zoo run by a true Florida eccentric, the sort of guy who wraps albino pythons around his neck for fun. Donate a few bucks at the entrance.

Florida National Scenic Trail HIKING
(www.fs.usda.gov/fnst) There are some 31 miles of the Florida National Scenic Trail within Big Cypress National Preserve. From the southern terminus, which can be accessed via Loop Rd, the trail runs 8.3 miles north to US 41. The way is flat, but it's hard going: you'll almost certainly be wading through water, and you'll have to pick through a series of solution holes (small sinkholes) and thick hardwood hammocks. There is often no shelter from the sun, and the bugs are... *plentiful*. There are three primitive campsites with water wells along the trail; pick up

a map at the visitor center. Most campsites are free, and you needn't register. **Monument Lake** (May-Dec 14 free, Dec 15-Apr $16) has water and toilets.

Tours

Everglades Adventure Tours   TOUR
(EAT; ☑ 800-504-6554; www.evergladesadventuretours.com; tours from $69) We already like the guys at EAT for being based out of the same headquarters as the Skunk Ape people; we like them even more for offering some of the best private tours of the Everglades we've found. Swamp hikes, 'safaris,' airboats and, best of all, being poled around in a canoe or skiff by some genuinely funny guys with genuine local knowledge of the Grassy Waters; it's an absolute treat. The EAT guys have set up a campsite at Skunk Ape HQ; it costs $30 to camp here, and there's wi-fi throughout the camp.

🛏 Sleeping & Eating

Swamp Cottage   COTTAGE **$$**
(☑ 239-695-2428; www.clydebutchersbigcypressgallery.com/swamp-cottage; cottage $275; P 🐾) 🐾 Want to get as close to the swamp as possible without giving up on the amenities? This two-bedroom cottage, which sits behind the Big Cypress Gallery (p141), may be the answer you're seeking. It's like a beach cottage, except the 'beach' is one of America's great wetlands. It's comfortably appointed, and if not luxurious, it's certainly cozy.

Joannie's Blue Crab Café   AMERICAN **$$**
(☑ 239-695-2682; Tamiami Trail; mains $9-17; ☺ 9am-5pm) This quintessential shack, east of Ochopee, with open rafters, shellacked picnic tables and alligator kitsch, serves delicious food of the 'fried everything' variety on paper plates. There's live music most days.

Everglades City

The end of the track is an old Florida fishing village of raised houses, turquoise water and scattershot emerald-green mangrove islands. Hwy 29 runs south through town into the peaceful residential island of Chokoloskee, past a great psychedelic mural of a gator on a shed. 'City' is an ambitious name for Everglades City, but this is a friendly fishing town where you can easily lose yourself for a day or three.

◉ Sights & Activities

Museum of the Everglades   MUSEUM
(☑ 239-695-0008;   www.evergladesmuseum.org; 105 W Broadway; ☺ 9am-5pm Tue-Fri, to 4pm Sat; P) This small museum, located in an old library, has some placards and information on the settlement of the Everglades – the focus is more concerned with the human history of the area than the natural environment. It's a decidedly community museum, with rotating local art and the feel of an attic full of everyone's interesting stuff and heirlooms, but charming for all that.

Gulf Coast Visitor Center   BOATING
(☑ 239-695-2591,   239-695-3311;   http://evergladesnationalparkboattoursgulfcoast.com; 815 Oyster Bar Lane, off Hwy 29; per day canoe/single kayak/tandem kayak $24/45/55; ☺ 9am-4:30pm mid-Apr–mid-Nov, 8am-4:30pm mid-Nov–mid-Apr; ♿) 🐾 This is the northwestern-most ranger station for Everglades National Park, and provides access to the 10,000 Islands area. Boat tours depart from the downstairs marina into the mangrove flats and green islands – if you're lucky you may see dolphins springing up beside your craft. This tangled off-shore archipelago was a major smuggling point for drugs into the mainland USA during the late 1970s and early '80s; bales of marijuana were nicknamed 'square grouper' by local fishermen.

It's great fun to go kayaking and canoeing around here; boats can be rented from the marina, but make sure to take a map with you (they're available for free in the visitor center). Boaters will want to reference NOAA Charts 11430 and 11432.

🖝 Tours

North American Canoe Tours   CANOEING
(NACT; ☑ 239-695-3299, 877-567-0679; www.evergladesadventures.com; Ivey House Bed & Breakfast, 107 Camellia St; tours $99, rentals from $35; ☺ Nov–mid-Apr) 🐾 If you're up for a tour, try Everglades Adventure Tours, or the guys at North American Canoe Tours rent out camping equipment and canoes ($35 per day) and touring kayaks ($45 to $65). You get 20% off most of these services and rentals if you're staying at the Ivey House Bed & Breakfast (p146), which runs the tours. Tours shuttle you to places like Chokoloskee Island, Collier-Seminole State Park, Rabbit Key or Tiger Key for afternoon or overnight excursions (from $99).

🛏 Sleeping

All lodging is family-friendly, and comes with air-conditioning and parking.

★ Everglades City Motel   MOTEL **$**
(☎ 239-695-4224, 800-695-8353; www.evergladescitymotel.com; 310 Collier Ave; r from $80; P ✳ 🛜) With large renovated rooms that have flat-screen TVs, arctic air-conditioning and a fantastically friendly staff that will hook you up with whatever tours your heart desires, this is an exceptionally good-value lodge for those looking to spend some time near the 10,000 Islands.

Parkway Motel & Marina   MOTEL **$**
(☎ 239-695-3261; www.parkwaymotelandmarina.com; 1180 Chokoloskee Dr; r $99-120; P ✳) An extremely friendly owner (and an even friendlier dog) runs this veritable testament to the old-school Floridian lodge: cute small rooms and one cozy apartment in a one-story motel building.

Ivey House Bed & Breakfast   B&B **$$**
(☎ 239-695-3299, 877-567-0679; www.iveyhouse.com; 107 Camellia St; lodge $89-120, inn $99-219; P ✳ 🛜) This family-run tropical inn serves good breakfasts in its small Ghost Orchid Grill. Plus it operates some of the best nature trips around (North American Canoe Tours (p145)). Ivey offers an entire range of package vacations (see the website), from day trips to six-day excursions including lodging, tours and some meals; trips run from $300 to $2290.

Rod & Gun Club Lodge   B&B **$$**
(☎ 239-695-2101; www.evergladesrodandgun.com; 200 Riverside Dr; r Jul–mid-Oct $95, mid-Oct–Jun $110-140; P ✳) Built in the 1920s as a hunting lodge by Barron Collier (who needed a

place to chill after watching workers dig his Tamiami Trail), this masculine place, fronted by a lovely porch, has a restaurant that serves anything that moves in them thar waters.

🍴 Eating

JT's Island Grill & Gallery   AMERICAN **$**
(238 Mamie St, Chokoloskee; mains $5-16; ⊙ 11am-3pm late Oct-May) Just a mile or so past the edge of town, this awesome cafe-cum-art-gallery sits in a restored 1890 general store. It's outfitted with bright retro furniture and piles of kitschy books, pottery, clothing and maps (all for sale). But the best part is the food (lunch only) – fresh crab cakes, salads, fish platters and veggie wraps, made with locally grown organic vegetables.

Triad Seafood Cafe   SEAFOOD **$**
(☎ 239-695-0722; 401 School Dr; mains $9-16; ⊙ 10:30am-6pm Sun-Thu, to 7pm Fri & Sat) Triad is famous for its all-you-can-eat stone crab legs, but they serve up all kinds of seafood gleaned from the swamp and the sea (well, the Gulf of Mexico). Should you impress the friendly owners with your ability to devour arthropod legs, you get the dubious honor of having your picture hung on the Glutton Board.

Oyster House   SEAFOOD **$**
(on Chokoloskee Causeway; mains $8-22; ⊙ 10am-11pm) Besides serving the Everglades staples of excellent fried seafood and burgers, Oyster House has a friendly bar with a screened-in porch where you can drink, slap mosquitoes and have a chat with friendly local boozehounds.

Seafood Depot   SEAFOOD **$**
(102 Collier Ave; mains $6-20; ⊙ 10:30am-9pm) Don't totally sublimate your desire for fried

---

DETOUR: LOOP ROAD

Loop Rd, off Tamiami Trail (Hwy 41), offers some unique sites. One: the homes of the Miccosukee, some of which have been considerably expanded by gambling revenue. You'll see some traditional chickee-style huts and some trailers with massive add-on wings that are bigger than the original trailer – all seem to have shiny new pickup trucks parked out front. Two: great pull-offs for viewing flooded forests, where egrets that look like pterodactyls perch in the trees. Three: houses with large Confederate flags and 'Stay off my property' signs; these homes are as much a part of the landscape as the swamp. And four: the short, pleasantly jungly Tree Snail Hammock Nature Trail. Be warned: the Loop is a rough, unpaved road; you'll need a 4WD vehicle (there has been talk of repaving the road, so it may have improved by the time you read this). True to its name, the road loops right back onto the Tamiami; expect a good long jaunt on the Loop to add two hours to your trip.

AH-TAH-THI-KI MUSEUM

If you want to learn about Florida's Native Americans, come to the **Ah-Tah-Thi-Ki Seminole Indian Museum** (📞877-902-1113; www.ahtahthiki.com; Big Cypress Seminole Indian Reservation, Clewiston; adult/child/senior $9/6/6; ⊙9am-5pm), 17 miles north of I-75. All of the excellent educational exhibits on Seminole life, history and the tribe today were founded on gaming proceeds, which provide most of the tribe's multimillion-dollar operating budget.

The museum is located within a cypress dome cut through with an interpretive boardwalk, so from the start it strikes a balance between environmentalism and education. The permanent exhibit has several dioramas with life-sized figures depicting various scenes out of traditional Seminole life, while temporary exhibits have a bit more academic polish (past ones have included lengthy forays into the economic structure of the Everglades). There's an old-school 'living village' and recreated ceremonial grounds as well. The Ah-Tah-Thi-Ki is making an effort to not be a cheesy Native American theme park, and the Seminole tribe is to be commended for its effort in this regard.

food, because the gator tail and frogs legs here offer an excellent way to honor the inhabitants of the Everglades: douse them in Tabasco and devour them.

Camellia Street Grill SEAFOOD $$
(📞239-695-2003; 202 Camellia St; mains $10-20; ⊙noon-9pm Sun-Thu, to 10pm Fri & Sat) Camellia is as fancy as Everglades City gets, although even then it's easily accessible and down to earth. The food is inspired by both the American South and the Mediterranean; grouper, for example, is seared with caramelized onions but also comes with a nice bouquet of herbs. Enjoy it while watching the sun melt like honey on the water.

ℹ️ Information

Everglades Area Chamber of Commerce
(📞239-695-3941; cnr US Hwy 41 & Hwy 29; ⊙9am-4pm) General information about the region is available here.

Everglades City to Naples

Fakahatchee Strand Preserve PARK
(www.floridastateparks.org/fakahatcheestrand; Coastline Dr, Copeland; ⊙8am-sunset; P🚻) 🆓FREE
The Fakahatchee Strand, besides having a fantastic name, also houses a 20-mile by 5-mile estuarine wetland that could have emerged directly out of the *Jurassic Park* franchise. A 2000ft boardwalk traverses this wet and wild wonderland, where panthers still stalk their prey amid the black waters. While it's unlikely you'll spot any, there's a great chance you will see a large variety blooming orchids, bird life and reptiles ranging in size from tiny skinks to grinning alligators.

Homestead to Flamingo Point

Head south of Miami to drive into the heart of the park and the best horizons of the Everglades. Plus, there are plenty of side paths and canoe creeks to detour onto. You'll see some of the most quietly exhilarating scenery the park has to offer on this route, and have better access to an interior network of trails for those wanting to push off the beaten track into the buggy, muggy solar plexus of the wetlands.

Homestead & Florida City

Homestead is not the prettiest town in the USA. After getting battered into rubble by Hurricane Andrew in 1992 and becoming part of the expanding subdivisions of South Miami, it's been poorly planned around fast-food stops, car dealerships and gas stations. A lot of Mexicans have moved here seeking farm work (or moved here providing services for farm laborers), and as a result, if you speak Spanish, it's impossible not to notice the shift in accent as Cuban Spanish gives way to Mexican. Radio stations also shift from Cuban reggaeton and hip-hop to brass-style mariachi music.

You could pass a mildly entertaining afternoon walking around Homestead's almost quaint Main Street (www.homestead-mainstreet.org) which essentially comprises a couple of blocks of Krome Ave extending north and south of Old Town Hall (41 N Krome Ave). It's a good effort at injecting some character into 'downtown' Homestead.

GLADES GUARDIAN

In a state known for iconoclasts, no one can hold a candle to Marjory Stoneman Douglas. Not just for her quirks, but for her drive. A persistent, unbreakable force, she fueled one of the longest conservation battles in US history.

Born in 1890, Douglas moved to Florida after her failed first marriage. She worked for the *Miami Herald* and eventually as a freelance writer, producing short stories that are notable for both the quality of the writing and their progressive themes: *Plumes* (1930) and *Wings* (1931), published in the *Saturday Evening Post,* addressed the issue of Glades bird-poaching when the business was still immensely popular (the feathers were used to decorate ladies' hats).

In the 1940s, Douglas was asked to write about the Miami River for the Rivers of America Series and promptly chucked the idea in favor of capturing the Everglades in her classic, *The Everglades: River of Grass.* Like all of Douglas' work the book is remarkable for both its exhaustive research and lyrical, rich language.

River of Grass immediately sold out of its first print-run, and public perception of the Everglades shifted from 'nasty swamp' to 'national treasure.' Douglas went on to be an advocate for environmental causes, women's rights and racial equality, fighting, for example, for basic infrastructure in Miami's Overtown.

Today she is remembered as Florida's favorite environmentalist. Always immaculately turned out in gloves, dress, pearls and floppy straw hat, she would bring down engineers, developers, politicians and her most hated opponents, sugar farmers by force of her oratory alone. She kept up the fight, speaking and lecturing without fail, until she died in 1998 at the age of 108.

Today it seems every environmental institution in Florida is named for Douglas, but were she around, we doubt she'd care for those honors. She'd be too busy planting herself in the CERP office, making sure everything was moving along on schedule.

With that said, let us give Homestead huge props: it houses two of the great attractions of the Florida roadside, one of its best hostels and an incredible farmers' market. Yup: four 'top picks' in one town.

⊙ Sights & Activities

★ Coral Castle
CASTLE
(☑305-248-6345; www.coralcastle.com; 28655 S Dixie Hwy; adult/senior/child $15/12/7; ⊙8am-6pm Sun-Thu, to 8pm Fri & Sat) 'You will be seeing unusual accomplishment,' reads the inscription on the rough-hewn quarried wall. That's an understatement. There is no greater temple to all that is weird and wacky about South Florida. The legend: a Latvian gets snubbed at the altar. Comes to the US. Moves to Florida. Hand carves, unseen, in the dead of night, a monument to unrequited love: a rock compound that includes a 'throne room,' a sun dial, a stone stockade (his intended's 'timeout area') and a revolving boulder gate that engineers around the world, to this day, cannot explain. Oh, and there are audio stations situated around the place that explain the site in a replicated Latvian accent, so it feels like you're getting a narrated tour by Borat.

Everglades Outpost
WILDLIFE RESERVE
(☑305-247-8000; www.evergladesoutpost.org; 35601 SW 192nd Ave; recommended donation $20; ⊙10am-5pm Mon, Tue & Fri-Sun, by appointment Wed & Thu) The Everglades Outpost houses, feeds and cares for wild animals that have been seized from illegal traders, abused, neglected or donated by people who could not care for them. Residents of the outpost include gibbons, a lemur, wolves, cobras, alligators and a pair of majestic tigers (one of whom was bought by an exotic dancer who thought she could incorporate it into her act). Your money goes into helping the outpost's mission.

★ Everglades Hostel Tours
TOUR
(☑305-248-1122, 800-372-3874; www.evergladeshostel.com; 20 SW 2nd Ave; half-day/full-day tours from $65/120) ◢ Everglades Hostel offers fantastic tours of the Eastern Everglades. You can either paddle into the bush, or if you don't mind getting a little damp, embark on a 'wet walk' into a flowered and fecund cypress dome, stepping through black water and around the edges of an alligator wallow.

🛏 Sleeping

There are plenty of chains such as Best Western, Days Inn and similar hotels and motels all along Rt 1 Krome Ave.

★ **Everglades**
International Hostel   HOSTEL $
(☎ 305-248-1122, 800-372-3874; www.ever-gladeshostel.com; 20 SW 2nd Ave, Florida City; camping $18, dm $28, d $61-75, ste $125-225; P ⊛ 🛜 ⛟) Located in a cluttered, comfy 1930s boarding house, this friendly hostel has good-value dorms, private rooms and 'semi-privates' (you have an enclosed room within the dorms and share a bathroom with dorm residents). But what they've done with their backyard – wow. It's a serious garden of earthly delights. There's a tree house; a natural rock-cut pool with a waterfall; a Bedouin pavilion that doubles as a dancehall; a gazebo; an open-air tented 'bed room'; an oven built to resemble a tail-molting tadpole. It all needs to be seen to be believed, and best of all you can sleep anywhere in the back for $18. Sleep in a treehouse! We think that's an amazing deal. We should add the crowd is made up of all those funky international traveler types that made you fall in love with backpacking in the first place, and the hostel conducts some of the best tours into the Everglades around.

🍴 Eating

★ **Robert is Here**   MARKET $
(www.robertishere.com; 19200 SW 344th St, Homestead; mains $3-8; ⊘ 8am-7pm Nov-Aug) More than a farmers' stand, Robert's is an institution. This is Old Florida at its kitschy best, in love with the Glades and the agriculture that surrounds it. There's a petting zoo for the kids, live music at night, plenty of homemade preserves and sauces, and while everyone goes crazy for the milkshakes – as they should – do not leave without having the fresh orange juice. It's the best in the world.

Rosita's   MEXICAN $
(☎ 305-246-3114; 199 W Palm Dr, Florida City; mains $6-10; ⊘ 8:30am-9pm) There's a working-class Mexican crowd here, testament to the sheer awesomeness of the tacos and burritos. Everyone is friendly, and best of all, they'll give you a takeaway plate if you're staying at the next-door Everglades International Hostel.

ℹ Information

Chamber of Commerce (☎ 305-247-2332; www.chamberinaction.com; 455 N Flagler Ave, Homestead; ⊘ 9am-noon & 1-5pm Mon-Fri)

Ernest Coe & Royal Palm to Flamingo

Drive past Florida City, through miles of paper-flat farmland and past an enormous, razor-wired jail (it seems like an escapee heads for the swamp at least once a year) and turn left when you see the signs for Robert Is Here – or stop in so the kids can pet a donkey at Robert's petting zoo.

👁 Sights & Activities

Ernest Coe Visitor Center   PARK
(☎ 305-242-7700; www.nps.gov/ever; State Rd 9336; ⊘ 9am-5pm) As you go past Homestead and Florida City, the farmland loses its uniformity and the flat land becomes more tangled, wild and studded with pine and cypress. After a few more miles you'll enter Everglades National Park at this friendly visitor center. Have a look at the excellent exhibits, including a diorama of 'typical' Floridians (the fisherman looks like he should join ZZ Top).

Royal Palm Visitor Center   PARK
(☎ 305-242-7700; State Rd 9336; ⊘ 8am-4:15pm) Four miles past Ernest Coe Visitor Center, Royal Palm offers the easiest access to the Glades in these parts. Two trails, the **Anhinga** and **Gumbo Limbo** (the latter named for the gumbo-limbo tree, also known as the 'tourist tree' because its bark peels like a sunburned Brit), take all of an hour to walk and put you face to face with a panoply of Everglades wildlife. Gators sun on the shoreline, anhinga spear their prey and wading birds stalk haughtily through the reeds. Come at night for a ranger walk on the boardwalk and shine a flashlight into the water to see one of the coolest sights of your life: the glittering eyes of dozens of alligators prowling the waterways.

Flamingo Visitor Center   PARK
(☎ 239-695-3101, 239-695-2945; ⊘ marina 7am-7pm, from 6am Sat & Sun) The most isolated portion of the park is a squat **marina** where you can go on a backcountry boat tour or rent boats. Due to its isolation, this area is subject to closure during bad weather. Boat tours to Florida Bay or into the swampy backcountry run for $32.25/16.13 per adult/

PYTHONS, GATORS & CROCS, OH MY!

Gators

Alligators are common in the park, although not so much in the 10,000 Islands, as they tend to avoid saltwater. If you do see an alligator, it probably won't bother you unless you do something overtly threatening or angle your boat between it and its young. If you hear an alligator making a loud hissing sound, get the hell out of Dodge. That's a call to other alligators when a young gator is in danger. Finally, never feed an alligator – it's stupid and illegal.

Crocs

Crocodiles are less common in the park, as they prefer coastal and saltwater habitats. They are more aggressive than alligators, however, so the same rules apply. With perhaps only a few hundred remaining in the USA, they are also an endangered species.

Panthers

The Florida panther is critically endangered, and although it is the state's official animal its survival in the wild is by no means assured. There are an estimated 100 panthers left in the wild, and although that number has increased from around 20 to 30 since the 1980s, it's not cause for big celebration either. As usual, humans have been the culprit behind this predator's demise. Widespread habitat reduction (ie the arrival of big subdivisions) is the major cause of concern. In the past, poor data on panther populations and the approval of developments that have been harmful to the species' survival have occurred; environmental groups contend the shoddy information was linked to financial conflicts of interest. Breeding units, which consist of one male and two to five females, require about 200 sq miles of ground to cover, and that often puts panthers in the way of one of Florida's most dangerous beasts: drivers. Fifteen panthers were killed by cars in 2013.

If you're lucky enough to see one (and you gotta be pretty damn lucky), Florida panthers are rather magnificent brown hunting cats (they are, in fact, cougars). They are extremely elusive and only inhabit 5% of their historic range. Many are relatively concentrated in Big Cypress National Preserve (p144).

Weather

Thunderstorms and lightning are more common in summer than in winter. But in summer the insects are so bad you won't want to be outside anyway. In emergency weather, rangers will search for registered campers, but under ordinary conditions they won't unless they receive information that someone's missing. If camping, have a friend or family member ready to contact rangers if you do not report back by a certain day.

Insects

You can't overestimate the problem of mosquito and no-see-ums (tiny biting flies) in the Everglades; they are, by far, the park's worst feature. While in most national parks there are warning signs showing the forest-fire risk, here the charts show the mosquito level (call ☎305-242-7700 for a report). In summer and fall, the sign almost always says 'extremely high.' You'll be set upon the second you open your car door. The only protections are 100% DEET or, even better, a pricey net suit.

Snakes in a Glade!

There are four types of poisonous snake in the Everglades: diamondback rattlesnake (*Crotalus adamanteus*); pigmy rattlesnake (*Sistrurus miliarius*); cottonmouth or water moccasin (*Agkistrodon piscivorus conanti*), which swims along the surface of water; and the coral snake (*Micrurus fulvius*). Wear long thick socks and lace-up boots – and keep the hell away from them. Oh, and now there are Burmese pythons prowling the water too. Pet owners who couldn't handle the pythons have dumped the animals into the swamp, where they've adapted like...well, a tropical snake to a subtropical forest. The python is an invasive species that is badly mucking up the natural order of things.

child, while canoes (two hours/four hours/ full day $16/22/40) and sea kayaks (half-/ full day $35/45) are available for rental; if you do rent, you're largely left to explore the channels and islands of Florida Bay on your own. During rough weather be cautious, even when on land, as storm surges can turn an attractive spread of beach into a watery stretch of danger fairly quickly.

Kayaking & Canoeing   BOATING
The real joy here in this part of the park is canoeing into the bracken heart of the swamp. There are plenty of push-off points, all with names that sound like they were read off Frodo's map to Mordor, including Hell's Bay, the Nightmare, Snake Bight and Graveyard Creek. Our favorite is Hell's Bay. 'Hell to get into and hell to get out of,' was how this sheltered launch was described by old Gladesmen, but damn if it isn't heaven inside: a capillary network of mangrove creeks, saw-grass islands and shifting mudflats, where the brambles form a green tunnel and all you can smell is sea salt and the dark organic breath of the swamp. Three chickee sites are spaced along the trail.

Hiking Trails   HIKING
State Rd 9336 cuts through the soft heart of the park, past long fields of marsh prairie, white, skeletal forests of bald cypress and dark clumps of mahogany hammock. There are plenty of trails to detour down; all of the following are half a mile (800m) long.

Mahogany Hammock leads into an 'island' of hardwood forest floating on the water-logged prairie, while the Pinelands takes you through a copse of rare spindly swamp pine and palmetto forest. Further on, Pahay-okee Overlook is a raised platform that peeks over one of the prettiest bends in the River of Grass. The West Lake Trail runs through the largest protected mangrove forest in the Northern Hemisphere. Further down you can take a good two-hour, 1.8-mile (2.9km) hike to Christian Point. This dramatic walk takes you through several Glades environments: under tropical forest, past columns of white cypress and over a series of mudflats (particularly attractive on grey, cloudy days), and ends with a dramatic view of the windswept shores of Florida Bay.

🛏 Sleeping

National Park
Service Campsites   CAMPGROUND $
(NPS; ☑ 800-365-2267; www.nps.gov/ever/plan-yourvisit/camping; sites May-Oct free, Nov-Apr $16) There are campgrounds run by the NPS located throughout the park. Sites are primitive and do not have hookups. Depending on the time of year, cold-water showers are either bracing or a welcome relief. The NPS information office at Royal Palm can provide a map of all campsites, as does the park website.

WILDERNESS CAMPING

Three types of backcountry campsites are available: beach sites, on coastal shell beaches and in the 10,000 Islands; ground sites, which are basically mounds of dirt built up above the mangroves; and 'chickees,' wooden platforms built above the waterline where you can pitch a free-standing (no spikes) tent. Chickees, which have toilets, are the most civilized – there's a serenity found in sleeping on what feels like a raft levitating above the water. Ground sites tend to be the most bug-infested.

Warning: if you're paddling around and see an island that looks pleasant for camping but isn't a designated campsite, beware – you may end up submerged when the tides change.

From November to April, backcountry camping permits cost $10, plus $2 per person per night; from May to October sites are free, but you must still self-register at Flamingo and Gulf Coast Visitor Centers or call ☑ 239-695-2945.

Some backcountry tips:

➡ Store food in a hand-sized, raccoon-proof container (available at gear stores).

➡ Bury your waste at least 10in below ground, but keep in mind some ground sites have hard turf.

➡ Use a backcountry stove to cook. Ground fires are only permitted at beach sites, and you can only burn dead or drowned wood.

Long Pine Key Campground CAMPGROUND $
(☑305-242-7873; camp/RV site $16/30) This is a good bet for car campers, just west of Royal Palm Visitor Center.

Flamingo Campground CAMPGROUND $
(☑877-444-6777; www.recreation.gov; camp/RV site $16/30) There are 41 car-camping sites at the Flamingo Visitor Center that have electrical hookups.

BISCAYNE NATIONAL PARK

Just to the east of the Everglades is Biscayne National Park, or the 5% of it that isn't underwater. Let us explain: a portion of the world's third-largest reef sits here off the coast of Florida, along with mangrove forests and the northernmost Florida Keys. Fortunately this unique 300-sq-mile park is easy to explore independently with a canoe, or via a glass-bottom boat tour.

A bit shadowed by the Everglades, Biscayne is unique as national parks go, requiring both a little extra planning and a lot more reward for your effort. The offshore keys, accessible only by boat, offer pristine opportunities for camping. Generally, summer and fall are the best times to visit the park; you'll want to snorkel when the water is calm. This is some of the best reef-viewing and snorkeling you'll find in the US, outside Hawaii and nearby Key Largo.

⊙ Sights

Biscayne National Park PARK
(☑786-335-3612, 305-230-7275; www.nps.gov/bisc; 9700 SW 328th St) The park itself offers canoe rentals, transportation to the offshore keys, snorkeling and scuba-diving trips, and glass-bottom boat viewing of the exceptional

---

MANATEES' BIGGEST THREAT

Manatees are shy, utterly peaceful mammals that are, for all intents, the poster children of Floridian environmentalism. They look like obese seals with vaguely elephantine noses. Back in the day, sailors apparently mistook them for mermaids and sirens, which suggests these guys had been at sea for entirely too long.

Jokes aside, the manatee is a major environmental concern for Florida. Pollution is a problem for these gentle giants, but their biggest killers are boaters, and of those, the worst offenders are pleasure boaters.

Manatees seek warm, shallow water and feed on vegetation. South Florida is surrounded by just such an environment, but it also has one of the highest concentrations of pleasure boats in the world. Despite pleas from environmental groups, wildlife advocates and the local, state and federal governments, which have declared many areas 'Manatee Zones,' some pleasure boaters routinely exceed speed limits and ignore simple practices that would help protect the species.

After grabbing a bite, manatees come up for air and often float just beneath the surface, chewing and hanging around. When speedboats zoom through the area, manatees are hit by the hulls and either knocked away or pushed under the boat, whose propeller then gashes the mammal as the boat passes overhead. Few manatees get through life without propeller scars, which leave slices in their bodies similar to the diagonal slices on a loaf of French bread.

There are several organizations throughout the state that rescue and rehabilitate injured manatees, but they're fighting what would appear to be a losing battle. Some of these organizations include Save the Manatee (www.savethemanatee.org) and the Miami Seaquarium. Divers, animal experts and veterinarians of Seaquarium's Marine Mammal Rescue Team patrol South Florida waters, responding to reports of stranded manatees, dolphins and whales. While the Seaquarium's program has been successful, pleasure boaters still threaten the manatees' survival. In 2010, the Florida Fish & Wildlife Commission reported that 83 manatees were killed by watercraft.

In February of 2011, a man was charged with killing a nursing manatee mother while speeding his boat through a slow-water area. He was put on probation for a year and had his boat seized by authorities. The ruling was welcomed by conservationists, but decisions like this are few and far between – the speeder was caught in the act of killing the manatee, but most such incidents are not reported.

reefs. All tours require a minimum of six people, so call to make reservations. Three-hour glass-bottom boat trips ($45) depart at 10am and are very popular; if you're lucky you may spot some dolphins or manatees. Canoe rentals cost $12 per hour and kayaks $16; they're rented from 9am to 3pm. Three-hour snorkeling trips ($45) depart at 1:15pm daily; you'll have about 1½ hours in the water. Scuba trips ($99) depart at 8:30am Friday to Sunday. You can also arrange a private charter boat tour around the park for $300.

Offshore Keys
ISLANDS

Long **Elliott Key** has picnicking, camping and hiking among mangrove forests; tiny **Adams Key** has only picnicking; and equally tiny **Boca Chita Key** has an ornamental lighthouse, picnicking and camping. These little islands were settled under the Homestead Act of 1862, which gave land freely to anyone willing to take five years at turning a scratch of the tropics into a working pineapple and Key-lime farm. No-see-ums (tiny flies) are invasive, and their bites are devastating. Make sure your tent is devoid of minuscule entry points.

Maritime Heritage Trail
DIVE SITE

The Maritime Heritage Trail takes 'hikers' through one of the only trails of its kind in the USA. If you've ever wanted to explore a sunken ship, this may well be the best opportunity in the country. Six are located within the park grounds; the trail experience involves taking visitors out, by boat, to the site of the wrecks where they can swim and explore among derelict vessels and clouds of fish – there are even waterproof information site cards placed among the ships. Five of the vessels are suited for scuba divers, but one, the *Mandalay,* a lovely two-masted schooner that sank in 1966, can be accessed by snorkelers.

🏃 Activities

Boating and **fishing** are naturally very popular and often go hand in hand, but to do either you'll need to get some paperwork in order. Boaters will want to get tide charts from the park (or from www.nps.gov/bisc/planyourvisit/tide-predictions.htm). And make sure you comply with local slow-speed zones, designed to protect the endangered manatee.

The slow zones currently extend 1000ft out from the mainland, from Black Point south to Turkey Point, and include the marinas at Black Point and Homestead Bayfront Parks. Another slow zone extends from Sands Cut to Coon Point; maps of all of the above can be obtained from rangers, and are needed for navigation purposes in any case.

Although Biscayne is a national park, it is governed by state law when it comes to fishing, so if you want to cast a line, you'll need a state license. These come in varieties many and sundry, all of which can be looked up at http://myfwc.com/fishing, which also provides a list of places where licenses can be obtained. At the time of writing, nonresident seven-day saltwater and freshwater fishing permits cost $50 each.

For information on boat tours and rental, contact **Biscayne Underwater** (www.biscayneunderwater.com), which can help arrange logistics.

The water around Convoy Point is regarded as prime **windsurfing** territory. Windsurfers may want to contact outfits in Miami

🛏 Sleeping

Primitive camping on Elliott and Boca Chita Keys costs $15 per tent, per night; you pay on a trust system with exact change on the harbor (rangers cruise the Keys to check your receipt). Bring all supplies, including water, and carry everything out. There's no water on Boca Chita, only saltwater toilets, and since it has a deeper port, it tends to attract bigger (and louder) boats (and boaters). Bring your own water to both islands; while there is potable water on Elliot Key, it's best to be prepared. It costs $20 to moor your boat overnight at Elliott or Boca Chita harbors, but that fee covers the use of one campsite for up to six people and two tents.

ℹ Information

Dante Fascell Visitor Center (☑ 305-230-7275; www.nps.gov/bisc; 9700 SW 328th St; ☺ 8:30am-5pm) Located at Convoy Point, this center shows a great introductory film for an overview of the park, and has maps, information and excellent ranger activities. The grounds around the center are a popular picnic spot on weekends and holidays, especially for families from Homestead. Also showcases local artwork.

ℹ Getting There & Away

To get here, you'll have to drive about 9 miles east of Homestead (the way is pretty well signposted) on SW 328th St (North Canal Dr) into a long series of green-and-gold flat fields and marsh.

Florida Keys & Key West

Best Places to Eat

➡ Café Solé (p182)

➡ Nine One Five (p182)

➡ Midway Cafe (p164)

➡ Key Largo Conch House (p161)

Best Places to Stay

➡ Deer Run Bed & Breakfast (p170)

➡ Lighthouse Court Inn (p180)

➡ Mermaid & the Alligator (p180)

➡ Tropical Inn (p180)

Why Go?

If Florida is a state apart from the USA, the Keys are islands apart from Florida – in other words, it's different down here. They march to the beat of their own drum, or Alabama country band, or Bahamanian steel calypso set... This is a place where those who reject everyday life on the mainland escape. What do they find? About 113 mangrove-and-sandbar islands where the white sun melts over tight fists of deep green mangroves; long, gloriously soft mudflats and tidal bars; water as teal as Arizona turquoise; and a bunch of people often like themselves: freaks, geeks and lovable weirdoes all.

Key West is still defined by its motto, which we love – One Human Family – an ideal that equals a tolerant, accepting ethos where anything goes and life is always a party (or at least a hungover day after). The color scheme: watercolor pastels cooled by breezes on a sunset-kissed Bahamian porch. Welcome to the End of the USA.

Have a drink.

When to Go
Key West

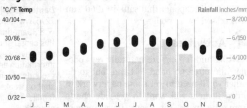

°C/°F **Temp** · **Rainfall** inches/mm

Dec–Mar It's dry, the sun is out, the weather is grand and the lodging is at its most expensive.

Apr–Jun Sea breezes help to keep the summer heat down, and hotel rates drop precipitously.

Jul–Nov There's some rain (and maybe even some hurricanes), but plenty of festivals too.

History

Calusa and Tequesta peoples plied these waters for thousands of years, but that era came to a depressingly predictable end with the arrival of the Spanish, the area's first European settlers. Upon finding Native American burial sites, Spanish explorers named Key West Cayo Hueso (pronounced kah-ya way-so, meaning Bone Island), a title since anglicized into its current incarnation. From 1760 to 1763, as the Spaniards transferred control of Florida to Great Britain, all of the islands' indigenous peoples were transferred to Cuba, where they either died in exile or integrated into the local ethnic mélange.

Key West itself was purchased by John Simonton in 1821, and developed as a naval base in 1822. For a long while, the area's cycle of boom and bust was tied to the military, salt manufacturing, lime production (from coral), shipwrecks, and sponges, which were harvested, dried and turned into their namesake bath product.

In the late 1800s the area became the focus of mass immigration as Cubans fled Spanish rule and looked to form a revolutionary army. Along with them came cigar manufacturers, who turned Key West into the USA's cigar-manufacturing center. That would end when workers' demands convinced several large manufacturers, notably Vicente Martínez Ybor and Ignacio Haya, to relocate to Tampa in southwest Florida. Immigrants from the Caribbean settled in the Keys in this period, and as a result, today's local African Americans tend to be descended from Bahamian immigrants rather than Southern slaves – something of a rarity in the US.

During the Spanish-American War (1898), Key West was an important staging point for US troops, and the military presence lasted through to WWI. In the late 1910s, with Prohibition on the horizon, Key West became a bootlegging center, as people stocked up on booze. The Keys began to boom around 1938 when Henry Flagler constructed his Overseas Hwy, replacing the by-then defunct Overseas Railroad.

Key West has always been a place where people buck trends. A large society of artists and craftspeople congregated here at the end of the Great Depression because of cheap real estate, and that community continues to grow (despite today's pricey real estate). While gay men have long been welcomed, the gay community really picked up in earnest in the 1970s; today it's one of the most renowned and best organized gay communities in the country.

Climate

Though it's warm and tropical in the Keys, it never gets higher than about 97°F. The peak in summer is usually about 89°F, with the temperature staying a few degrees cooler than Miami because the Keys are surrounded by ocean (and refreshing ocean breezes). The coldest it gets is usually in the 50s (when some people dress like a blizzard has descended), and water temperature stays in the 80s most of the time. The thunderstorm season begins by late May, and then everyone buckles down for the feared hurricanes – if they arrive, expect them in late summer and early fall.

ⓘ Information

The Monroe County Tourist Development Council's **Florida Keys & Key West Visitors Bureau** (☎800-352-5397; www.fla-keys.com) runs an excellent website, which is packed with information on everything the Keys has to offer.

Check www.keysnews.com for good daily online news and information about the islands.

ⓘ Getting There & Away

Getting here can be half the fun – or, if you're unlucky, a whopping dose of frustration. Imagine a tropical-island hop, from one bar-studded mangrove islet to the next, via one of the most unique roads in the world: the Overseas Hwy (US Hwy 1). On a good day, driving down the Overseas with the windows down, the wind in your face and the twin sisters of Florida Bay and the Atlantic stretching on either side, is the US road trip in tropical perfection. On a bad day, you end up sitting in gridlock behind some guy who is riding a midlife-crisis Harley.

Greyhound (☎800-229-9424; www.greyhound.com) buses serve all Keys destinations along US Hwy 1 and depart from downtown Miami and Key West; you can pick up a bus along the way by standing on the Overseas Hwy and flagging one down. If you fly into Fort Lauderdale or Miami, the **Keys Shuttle** (☎888-765-9997) provides door-to-door service to most of the Keys ($70/80/90 to the Upper and Middle Keys/Lower Keys/Key West). Reserve at least a day in advance.

UPPER KEYS

No, really, you're in the islands!

It is a bit hard to tell when you first arrive, though. The huge, rooty blanket of mangrove

0 — 20 km
0 — 12 miles

Gulf of Mexico

Everglades National Park Boundary

Shark Point

INSET

Hospital Key
Middle Key
East Key
Loggerhead Key
Bush Key
Garden Key
Long Key
8 Dry Tortugas National Park

Note: Same scale as main map

Florida Keys National Marine Sanctuary

Marquesas Keys

Key West National Wildlife Refuge

See Inset

Florida Keys National Marine Sanctuary

Marquesas Keys

Key West National Wildlife Refuge

Great White Heron National Wildlife Refuge

Snipe Keys

Boca Chica Key

Sugarloaf Key

Summerland Key

Cudjoe Key

Big Torch Key

Little Torch Key

Big Pine Key

Big Pine

Ramrod Key

Little Pine Key

No Name Key

Seven Mile Bridge

Bahia Honda Key

Pigeon Key

Boot Key

Bahia Honda State Park

Looe Key National Marine Sanctuary

Great White Heron National Wildlife Refuge

Key West
5 4 1
Key West
Key West International Airport

Lower Keys

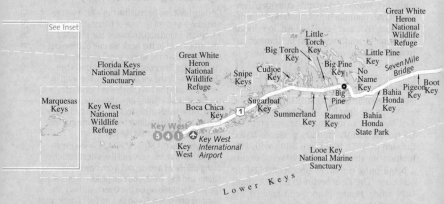

Florida Keys & Key West Highlights

1 Watching the sun set over the ocean as you sit and take in the raucous show at **Mallory Square** (p171).

2 Diving around the rainbow reefs of **John Pennekamp**

Coral Reef State Park (p159).

3 Paddling out to eerie, lonely, beautiful **Indian Key Historic State Park** (p162).

4 Donning a purple-and-green crocodile costume and partying in the streets at Key West's **Fantasy Fest** (p178).

5 Scratching Papa's six-toed cats behind their ears at the

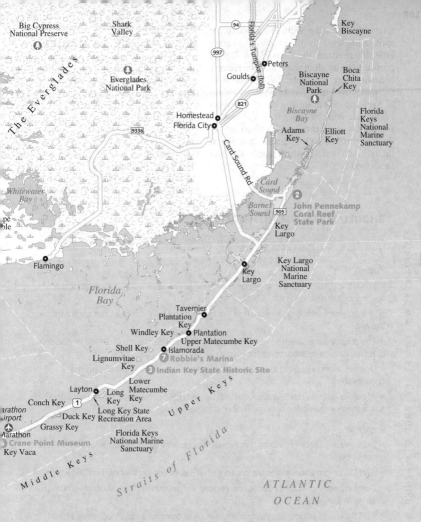

lovely **Hemingway House**
(p172).

⑥ Strolling through the
palm-hammock and pineland
scrub at eco-educational

Crane Point Museum
(p166).

⑦ Feeding the giant tarpon
swimming in circles at
Robbie's Marina (p163).

⑧ Making an island-hopping
day trip and detour to **Dry
Tortugas National Park**
(p179).

forest that forms the South Florida coastline spreads like a woody morass into Key Largo; little differentiates the island from Florida proper. Keep heading south and the scenery becomes more archipelagically pleasant as the mangroves give way to wider stretches of road and ocean, until – bam – you're in Islamorada and the water is everywhere. If you want to avoid traffic on US 1, you can try the less trafficked FL 997 and Card Sound Rd to FL 905 (toll $1), which passes Alabama Jack's (p162).

Key Largo & Tavernier

We ain't gonna lie: Key Largo (both the name of the town and the island it's on) is slightly underwhelming at a glance. 'Under' is the key word, as its main sights are under the water, rather than above. As you drive onto the islands, Key Largo resembles a long line of low-lying hammock (raised areas) and strip development. But that's just from the highway: head down a side road and duck into this warm little bar, or that converted Keys plantation house, and the island idiosyncrasies become more pronounced.

SHOULD YOU SWIM WITH DOLPHINS?

There are five swim-with-the-dolphin (SWTD) centers in the Keys, and many more arguments for and against the practice.

For

➡ While SWTD sites are commercial, they are also research entities devoted to learning more about their charges.

➡ The dolphins raised on-site are legally obtained and have not been not captured from the wild.

➡ The dolphins are safe from environmental hazards often found in the wild – accidental catches, run-ins with boats and pollution.

➡ Dolphin swim programs increase visitors' knowledge of dolphins and promote conservation.

➡ At places such as the Dolphin Research Center (p165), the dolphins can actually swim out of their pens into the open water, but choose not to.

Against

➡ Dolphins are social creatures that require interaction, which is impossible to provide in captivity.

➡ SWTD tourism encourages the capture of wild dolphins in other parts of the world.

➡ Dolphin behavior is never 100% predictable. Dolphins can seriously injure a human, even while playing.

➡ SWTD centers encourage customers to think of dolphins as anthropomorphized 'friends,' rather than wild animals.

➡ Dolphins never appreciate captivity. Those that voluntarily remain in SWTD sites do so to remain close to food.

SWTD Centers

If you decide to swim or see dolphins in the Keys, you can contact one of the following:

Theater of the Sea (✆305-664-2431; www.theaterofthesea.com; MM 84.7 bayside; adult/child 3-10 $30/21; ◷9:30am-5pm) has been here since 1946. Structured dolphin swims and sea-lion programs ($135) include 30 minutes of instruction and a 30-minute supervised swim. You can also swim with stingrays ($55).

Dolphins Plus (✆305-451-1993, 866-860-7946; www.dolphinsplus.com; off MM 99.5 bayside; swim programs $135-220), a Key Largo center, specializes in recreational and educational unstructured swims. They expect you know a good deal before embarking upon the swim, even though a classroom session is included.

There is also dolphin swimming at Grassy Key's Dolphin Research Center (p165) and Hawk's Cay Resort (p165).

The 33-mile-long Largo, which starts at MM 106, is the longest island in the Keys, and those 33 miles have attracted a lot of marine life, all accessible from the biggest concentration of dive sites in the islands. The town of Tavernier (MM 93) is just south of the town of Key Largo.

If you approach Key Largo from FL 905, you'll be driving through Crocodile Lake National Wildlife Refuge (www.fws.gov/nationalkeydeer/crocodilelake; FL 905), one of the last wild sanctuaries for the threatened American crocodile, indigo snake and Key Largo woodrat – the latter is an enterprising fellow who likes to build 4ft by 6ft homes out of forest debris. That said, the wildlife areas are closed to the public, and your chances of seeing the species we've mentioned from the road are negligible.

◎ Sights & Activities

Florida Keys Wild Bird Rehabilitation Center WILDLIFE RESERVE
(www.fkwbc.org; 93600 Overseas Hwy, MM 93.6; suggested donation $5; ⊙sunrise-sunset; P⁣⬛) ✈ This sanctuary is the first of many animal hospitals you'll come across built by critter-loving Samaritans throughout the Keys. You'll find an alfresco bird hospital that cares for birds that have swallowed fish hooks, had wings clipped in accidents, been shot by BB pellets etc. A pretty trail leads back to a nice vista of Florida Bay and a wading bird pond. Just be warned, it does smell like bird doo back here.

Harry Harris Park PARK
(MM 93.5; ⊙sunrise-sunset; ⬛) This small park is a good place to take the kids – there's a small playground, a picnic table and other such accoutrements. Rare for the Keys, there's also a good patch of white sand fronting a warm lagoon that's excellent for swimming.

Caribbean Club Bar FILM LOCATION
(⌨http://www.caribbeanclubkl.com; MM 104 bayside; ⊙7am-4am) Here's one for the movie fans, particularly Bogie buffs: the Caribbean Club Bar is, in fact, the only place in Key Largo where Key Largo, starring Humphrey Bogart and Lauren Bacall, was filmed (the rest of the island was a Hollywood soundstage). If that's not enough, the original African Queen, of the same-titled movie, is docked in a channel at the Holiday Inn at MM 100 – just walk around the back and there she is.

John Pennekamp Coral Reef State Park PARK
(☏305-451-6300; www.pennekamppark.com; MM 102.6 oceanside; car/motorcycle/cyclist or pedestrian $8/4/2; ⊙8am-sunset, aquarium to 5pm; ⬛) ✈ John Pennekamp has the singular distinction of being the first underwater park in the USA. There's 170 acres of dry parkland here and over 48,000 acres (ie 75 sq miles) of wet: the vast majority of the protected area is the ocean. Before you get out in that water, make sure to dig around some pleasant beaches and stroll over the nature trails.

The Mangrove Trail is a good boardwalk introduction to this oft-maligned, ecologically awesome arboreal species (the trees, often submerged in water, breathe via long roots that act as snorkels – neat). Stick around for nightly campfire programs and ranger discussions.

The visitor center is well run and informative and has a small, cute aquarium (8am to 5pm) that gives a glimpse of what's under them thar waters. To really get beneath the surface of this park (pun intended), you should take a 2½-hour glass-bottom boat tour (☏305-451-6300; adult/child $24/17; ⊙9:15am, 12:15pm & 3:15pm). You won't be ferried around in some rinky-dink fishing boat; you're brought out in a safe, modern 38ft catamaran from which you'll ooh and aah at filigreed flaps of soft coral, technicolor schools of fish, dangerous-looking barracuda and massive, yet ballerina-graceful, sea turtles. Besides the swirl of natural coral life, interested divers can catch a glimpse of the Christ of the Abyss, a submerged 8.5ft, 4000lb bronze sculpture of Jesus – a copy of a similar sculpture off the coast of Genoa, Italy, in the Mediterranean Sea.

If you want to go even deeper, try straight-up snorkeling trips (☏305-451-6300; adult/child $30/25) or diving excursions (☏305-451-6322; $55). DIYers may want to take out a canoe ($20 per hour) or kayak (single/double per hour $12/$17) to journey through a 3-mile network of trails. Call ☏305-451-6300 for boat-rental information.

To learn more about the reef in this area, go to www.southeastfloridareefs.net.

FLORIDA KEYS OVERSEAS HERITAGE TRAIL

One of the best ways to see the Keys is by bicycle. The flat elevation and ocean breezes are perfect for cycling, and the Florida Keys Overseas Heritage Trail (FKOHT; www.dep.state.fl.us/gwt/state/keystrail) will connect all the islands from Key Largo to Key West.

If you are keen to ride, it's currently possible to bike through the Keys by shoulder riding (it takes three days at a good clip). There are particularly pleasant rides around Islamorada, and if you're uncomfortable riding on the shoulder, you can contact the FKOHT through its website for recommended bike excursions.

Jacob's Aquatics Center   WATERPARK
(☎305-453-7946; http://jacobsaquaticcenter.org; 320 Laguna Ave, MM 99.6; adult/child/student/family $10/6/8/25; ⏱11am-6pm Mon-Fri, 10am-7pm Sat & Sun; 🖝) Jacob's is a complex of all kinds of aquatic fun. There's an eight-lane pool for lap and open swimming, a therapy pool with handicapped access, courses on water aerobics. For the kids there's a small waterpark with waterslides, a playground and, of course, kiddie-sized pools.

🛏 Sleeping

One of our favorite small hotels on the island, Largo Lodge (☎305-451-0424; www.largolodge.com; MM 102 bayside; cottages $150-265; P), was undergoing extensive renovations at the time of research, and was scheduled to re-open in early 2015.

Air-con is standard in virtually all Key accommodations. Lodgings have higher rates during the high season (mid-December to April). In addition, many properties add a 'shoulder' (midseason) that runs from May to June; rates may fall somewhere between low (July to November) and high during midseason. Many hotels (especially smaller properties) enforce two-night minimum stays. Expect rates to be extremely high during events such as New Year's and Fantasy Fest, when some places enforce up to seven-night minimum stays.

John Pennekamp Coral Reef State Park   CAMPGROUND $
(☎800-326-3521; www.pennekamppark.com; camp/RV site both $36; P) You don't even have to leave Pennekamp at closing time if you opt for tent or RV camping, but be sure to make a reservation, as the sites fill up fast.

Stone Ledge Paradise Inn   HOTEL $
(☎305-852-8114; www.stoneledgeparadiseinn.com; 95320 Overseas Hwy; r $78-118, villas $185-300; P) This is a pink palace (well, squat bunch of motel blocks) of old-school US seaside kitsch. The wooden fish hung on every door are only the tip of the nautical-kitsch iceberg, but the real joy is the sweeping view over Florida Bay at the back of the property. Rooms are pretty simple on the inside.

Hilton Key Largo Resort   HOTEL $$
(☎305-852-5553; www.keylargoresort.com; MM 102 bayside; r from $179, ste from $315; P🕸🏊) This Hilton has a ton of character. Folks just seem to get all laid-back when lounging in clean, designer rooms outfitted in blues, greens and (why not?) blue-green. Throw in some beiges and you've got a supremely soothing sleeping experience. The grounds are enormous and include an artificial waterfall-fed pool and frontage to a rather large stretch of private white-sand beach.

Dove Creek Lodge   HOTEL $$
(☎800-401-0057; www.dovecreeklodge.com; 147 Seaside Ave; r $169-269, ste from $350; P🕸🏊) This midsized hotel offers bright rooms decked out in citrus-shaded colors and a grounds that fronts the Atlantic Ocean. It's a family-friendly spot with an old-school resort feel. Can help with booking tours and excursions in the area.

Key Largo House Boatel   HOTEL $$
(☎305-766-0871; www.keylargohouseboat.com; Shoreland Dr, MM 103.5 oceanside; houseboat small/medium/large from $75/100/150; P) There are five well-decorated houseboats available, with the largest one spacious enough to sleep six people comfortably. The boats are right on the docks (and across from a bar), so there's no possibility of being isolated from land (or booze).

Kona Kai Resort & Gallery   HOTEL $$$
(☎305-852-7200; www.konakairesort.com; MM 97.8 bayside; r $220-439; P🕸🏊) This hideaway is one of the only botanical gardens we can think of that integrates a hotel onto their grounds – or is that the other way around? Either way, this spot is lush. The 13 airy rooms and suites (with full kitchens) are all bright and comfortable, with good natural light and linoleum floors. Kona Kai also houses a lovely art gallery.

Guided tours of the extensive gardens are offered for nonguests Tuesday through Saturday for $25 (if you're staying, the gardens are free, because they're your backyard).

Jules' Undersea Lodge
HOTEL $$$

(☎305-451-2353; www.jul.com; 51 Shoreland Dr, MM 103.2 oceanside; group of 3-4 per person $350, s $675) There's lots of talk about underwater hotels getting built in Dubai and Fiji, but as of this writing, Jules' Undersea Lodge is still the only place in the world outside of a submarine where you and your significant other can join the 'five-fathom club' (we're not elaborating). Once a research station, this module has been converted into a delightfully cheesy Keys motel, but wetter.

In addition to two private guest rooms, there are common rooms, a kitchen-dining room and a wet room with hot showers and gear storage. Telephones and an intercom connect guests with the surface. Guests must be at least 10 years old and you gotta dive to get here – plus, there's no smoking or alcohol. If you just want to visit, you can pop in for a three-hour visit (with pizza!) for $150.

Eating

Mrs Mac's Kitchen
AMERICAN $

(☎305-451-3722; www.mrsmacskitchen.com; MM 99.4 bayside; breakfast & lunch $8-12, dinner $9-22; ☺7am-9:30pm Mon-Sat; P ♠) When Applebee's stuffs its wall full of license plates, it's tacky. When Mrs Mac's does it, it's homey. Probably because the service is warm and personable, and the breakfasts are delicious. Plus, the food packs in the locals, tourists, their dogs and pretty much everyone else on the island (plus, admittedly, a fair few calories, but that's why it tastes good).

DJ's Diner
AMERICAN $

(☎305-451-2999; 99411 Overseas Hwy; mains $6-14; ☺7am-9pm to 3pm Sat & Sun; P ♠) You're greeted by a mural of Humphrey Bogart, James Dean *and* Marilyn Monroe – that's a lot of Americana. It's all served with a heapin' helpin' of diner faves, vinyl-boothed ambience and South Florida staples like *churrasco* (skirt steak) and conch.

Key Largo Conch House
FUSION $$

(☎305-453-4844; www.keylargoconchhouse.com; MM 100.2 oceanside; mains $8-26; ☺8am-10pm; P ♠ ♠) This wi-fi hotspot, coffeehouse and innovative kitchen likes to sex up local classics (conch in a lime and white-wine sauce, or in a vinegar sauce with capers). Set in a restored old-school Keys mansion wrapped in a *Gone With the* Wind veranda, it's hard not to love the way the period architecture blends in seamlessly with the local tropical fauna.

A justifiably popular spot with tourists and locals. The fish tacos are intensely good.

Fish House
SEAFOOD $$

(☎305-451-4665; www.fishhouse.com; MM 102.4 oceanside; mains $9-24; ☺11:30am-10pm; P ♠) The Fish House delivers on the promise of its title – very good fish, bought whole from local fishermen and prepared fried, broiled, jerked, blackened or char-grilled. Because the Fish House only uses fresh fish, the menu changes daily based on what is available. We prefer the original Fish House over the more sushi-centered Fish House Encore next door.

FLORIDA KEYS FOR CHILDREN

Check out some of the following options to entertain the kids:

Florida Keys Eco-Discovery Center (p172) Get an understanding of the region's environment.

Glass-bottom boat tours at John Pennekamp Coral Reef State Park (p159) Your own window to the underwater world.

Key West Butterfly & Nature Conservatory (p172) Pretty flying things.

Turtle Hospital (p166) Save (or watch) the turtles.

Conch Tour Train (p177) Kitschy, corny, enjoyable tour.

Ghost tours (p177) Only slightly spooky; younger kids may find this one a bit scary.

Key-deer spotting (p169) Kids go crazy for cute mini-deer.

Key West Cemetery (p172) Get Gothic with these often humorous tombs.

Robbie's Marina (p163) All sorts of activities, including the ever-popular tarpon (giant fish) feeding frenzy.

KEY LIME PIE

Many places claim to serve the original Key lime pie, but no one knows who discovered the tart treat. Types of crust vary, and whether or not the pie should be topped with meringue is debated. However, the color of Key lime pie is not open to question. Beware of places serving green Key lime pie: Key limes are yellow, not green. Restaurants that add green food coloring say that tourists expect it to be green. Steer clear.

Snook's Bayside
AMERICAN $$

(☑305-453-5004; 99470 Overseas Hwy; lunch mains $9-18, dinner mains $19-42; ☺11:30am-9:30pm; 🅿🐾) Floridians love their waterfront dining establishments crossed with a tiki bar, and Snook's is Key Largo's contribution to the genre. The surf-and-turf-style menu is good, but the view onto the water – and the accompanying artificial sandy beach – is better.

🍸 Drinking

Alabama Jack's
BAR

(58000 Card Sound Rd; ☺11am-7pm) Welcome to your first taste of the Keys: zonked-out fishermen, exiles from the mainland and Harley heads getting drunk on a mangrove bay. This is the line where Miami-esque South Florida gives way to the country-fried American South. Wildlife-lovers: you may spot the rare mulleted version of *Jacksonvillia Redneckus*!

But seriously, everyone raves about the conch fritters, and the fact they have to close because of nightly onslaughts of mosquitoes means this place is as authentically Florida as they come. Country bands take the stage on weekends from 2pm to 5pm.

ℹ️ Information

Chamber of Commerce (☑305-451-1414; www.keylargochamber.org; MM 106 bayside; ☺9am-6pm) Visit the chamber of commerce for maps and brochures.

Mariner Hospital (☑305-434-3000; www.baptisthealth.net; Tavernier, MM 91.5 bayside)

ℹ️ Getting There & Away

The Greyhound bus stops at MM 99.6 oceanside.

Islamorada

Islamorada (eye-luh-murr-*ah*-da) is also known as 'The Village of Islands.' Doesn't that sound pretty? Well, it really is. This little string of pearls (well, keys) – Plantation, Upper and Lower Matecumbe, Shell and Lignumvitae (lignum-*vite*-ee) – shimmers as one of the prettiest stretches of the islands. This is where the scrubby mangrove is replaced by unbroken horizons of ocean and sky, one perfect shade of blue mirroring the other. Islamorada stretches across some 20 miles, from MM 90 to MM 74.

⊙ Sights & Activities

★Anne's Beach
BEACH

(MM 73.5 oceanside) Anne's is one of the best beaches in these parts. The small ribbon of sand opens upon a sky-bright stretch of tidal flats and a green tunnel of hammock and wetland. Nearby mudflats are a joy to get stuck in, and will be much loved by the kids.

Indian Key Historic State Park
ISLAND

(☑305-664-2540; www.floridastateparks.org/indiankey; MM 78.5 oceanside; $2.50; ☺8am-sunset) This quiet island was once a thriving city, complete with a warehouse, docks, streets, a hotel and about 40 to 50 permanent residents. There's not much left at the historic site – just the foundation, some cisterns and jungly tangle. Robbie's Marina used to bring boats this way, and still does boat rentals (around $30 for a kayak or canoe). You can also see the island from the water on an ecotour with Robbie's ($37.50).

By 1836, Indian Key was the first seat of Dade County, but four years later the inhabitants of the island were killed or scattered by a Native American attack during the Second Seminole War. Trails follow the old layout of the city streets, or you can walk among ruins and paddle around spotting rays and dolphins in utter isolation in a canoe or kayak.

Lignumvitae Key Botanical State Park
ISLAND

(☑305-664-2540; www.floridastateparks.org/lignumvitaekey; admission/tour $2.50/2; ☺tours 10am & 2pm Fri-Sun) This key, only accessible by boat, encompasses a 280-acre island of virgin tropical forest and is home to roughly a zillion jillion mosquitoes. The official attraction is the 1919 Matheson House, with its windmill and cistern; the real draw is a nice sense of shipwrecked isolation. Guided walking tours (1¼ hours) are given at 10am and 2pm Friday to Sunday. You'll have to get here via Robbie's Marina; boats depart for tours to here and Indian Key.

Strangler figs, mastic, gumbo-limbo, poisonwood and lignum vitae trees form a dark canopy that feels more South Pacific than South Florida.

Florida Keys History of Diving Museum
MUSEUM

(☏305-664-9737; www.divingmuseum.org; MM 83; adult/child $12/6; ☉10am-5pm; P ♿) You can't miss the diving museum – it's the building with the enormous mural of swimming manatees on the side – and we mean that in every sense of the phrase. In other words, don't miss this museum, a collection of diving paraphernalia from around the world. This is the sort of charmingly eccentric museum that really reflects the quirks of the Keys. The hall of diving helmets from around the world, from Denmark to Japan, is particularly impressive.

We're also wowed by the exhibitions of diving 'suits' and technology from the 19th century. Folks in the museum can also provide information on diving in a vintage Mark V diving suit (the ones with the bulbous onion-heads connected to surface pumps). Hosts lectures on diving entitled (of course) 'Immerse Yourself' at 7pm on the third Wednesday of every month.

Windley Key Fossil Reef Geological State Site
PARK

(☏305-664-2540; www.floridastateparks.org/windleykey; MM 85.5 oceanside; admission/tour $2.50/2; ☉8am-5pm Thu-Mon) To get his railroad built across the islands, Henry Flagler had to quarry out some sizable chunks of the Keys. The best evidence of those efforts can be found at this former quarry-cum-state-park. Besides having a mouthful of a name, Windley has leftover quarry machinery scattered along an 8ft former quarry wall. The wall offers a cool (and rare) public peek into the stratum of coral that forms the substrate of the Keys.

Ranger tours are offered at 10am and 2pm Friday to Sunday for $3.

Rain Barrel
ARTS CENTER

(☏305-852-3084, 305-852-8935; 86700 Overseas Hwy; ☉9am-5pm) We want to tell you the Rain Barrel, Islamorada's local artists' village, strikes a balance between the beautiful and the tacky. But you're more likely to find souvenir-y tourist tat here than a truly striking work of art. That said, strolling around the seven studios and galleries that make up the Rain Barrel is nice, and who knows, you may find the piece of your dreams, or at least a hand-painted sign that says, 'It's always 5 o'clock somewhere.'

★ Robbie's Marina
MARINA

(☏305-664-8070; www.robbies.com; MM 77.5 bayside; kayak & SUP rentals $40-75; ☉9am-8pm; ♿) More than a boat launch, Robbie's is a local flea market, tacky tourist shop (all the shells you ever wanted), sea pen for tarpons (very big-ass fish) and jump-off for fishing expeditions, all wrapped into one driftwood-laced compound. Boat-rental and tour options are also available. The party boat (half-day/night trips $40/45) is just that: a chance to drink, fish and basically achieve Keys Zen.

For real Zen (ie the tranquil kind as opposed to drunken kind), take an ecotour ($35) on an electrically propelled silent boat deep into the mangroves, hammocks and lagoons. Snorkeling trips are a good deal; for $37.50 you get a few hours on a very smooth-riding Happy Cat vessel and a chance to bob amid some of the USA's only coral reefs. If you don't want to get on the water, at least feed the freakishly large tarpons from the dock ($2.79 per bucket, $1 to watch).

🛏 Sleeping

Conch On Inn
MOTEL $

(☏305-852-9309; conchoninn.com; MM 89.5, 103 Caloosa St; apt $59-129; P) A simple motel popular with yearly snowbirds, Conch On Inn has basic, clean and comfortable rooms.

Ragged Edge Resort
RESORT $$

(☏305-852-5389; www.ragged-edge.com; 243 Treasure Harbor Rd; apt $69-259; P ❄ 🛜) This popular low-key efficiency and apartment complex, far from the maddening traffic, has friendly hosts and 10 quiet units. The larger studios have screened-in porches. There's no beach, but you can swim off the dock and at the pool.

Casa Morada
HOTEL $$$

(☏305-664-0044, 888-881-3030; www.casamorada.com; 136 Madeira Rd, off MM 82.2; ste incl breakfast $279-659; P ❄ 🛜 ≋) Contemporary chic comes to Islamorada, but it's not gentrifying away the village vibe. Rather, the Casa adds a welcome dab of sophistication to Conch chill: a keystone standing circle, freshwater pool, artificial lagoon, plus a *Wallpaper*-magazine-worthy bar that overlooks Florida Bay – all make this boutique hotel worth a reservation. Go to the bar to catch a drink and a sunset.

La Siesta Resort & Marina
RESORT $$$

(☏305-664-2132; www.lasiestaresort.com; MM 80.5 oceanside; ste $190-340; P 🛜 ≋) This pretty option consists of renovated suites and apartments that let in generous amounts of light and are decorated to feel modern and classy, but still refreshingly un-hip and family friendly. Service is amiable, the pool is busy and the ocean views are lovely.

Chesapeake Resort
RESORT $$$

(☑ 305-664-4662; www.chesapeake-resort.com; 83409 Overseas Hwy; r $200-330, ste $350-550; P 🛜 ☲) This all-inclusive resort is packed with activities and rooms that have more tropical character than the average Keys accommodation. An on-site tennis court is good for exercise, while the charter boat dock and marina keeps you linked in to the local world of recreational fishing and sea exploring. You won't lack for amenities.

✖ Eating

★ Midway Cafe
CAFE $

(☑ 305-664-2622; 80499 Overseas Hwy; dishes $2-11; ⊙ 7am-3pm Thu-Tue, to 2pm Sun; P 🖶) The lovely folks who run this cafe – stuffed with every variety of heart-warming art the coffee-shop trope can muster – roast their own beans, make baked goods that we would swim across the Gulf for, and are friendly as hell. You're almost in the Middle Keys: celebrate making it this far with a cup of joe.

Bob's Bunz
CAFE $

(www.bobsbunz.com; MM 81.6 bayside; mains $6-12; ⊙ 6am-2pm; P 🖶) The service at this cute cafe is energetic and friendly in an only-in-America kinda way, and the food is fine, filling and cheap. Key lime pie is a classic Keys dish and Key-lime anything at this bakery is highly regarded, so buy that souvenir pie here.

Lorelei
AMERICAN $$

(☑ 305-664-2692; MM 82 bayside; mains $9-22; ⊙ 7am-midnight; P 🖶) Need a sunset and some excellent seafood? Maybe a touch of steak? Lorelei has got you covered. The sunsets really are magnificent, an experience compounded by yummy fish sandwiches, cracked conch and some frankly gorgeous ribs. Look for the big mermaid sign.

Pierre's
FRENCH $$$

(☑ 305-664-3225; www.pierres-restaurant.com; MM 81.6 bayside; mains $28-42; ⊙ 5-10pm Sun-Thu, to 11pm Fri & Sat; P) Why hello two-story waterfront plantation – what are you serving? A tempura-ed spiny lobster tail...good, decadent start. Hogfish meunière? Well, that's rich enough to knock out a rhino. A filet mignon with black truffle mash potatoes? Splurge, traveler, on possibly the best food between Miami and Key West.

Beach Cafe at Morada Bay
AMERICAN $$$

(☑ 305-664-0604; www.moradabay-restaurant. com; MM 81.6 bayside; mains $14-33; ⊙ 11:30am-10pm; P) If you can ignore the service from staff who can get overwhelmed by customers and the awful bands that occasionally 'headline' the lunch rush, this is a lovely, laid-back Caribbean experience, complete with an imported, powder-white sandy beach, nighttime torches, tapas and fresh seafood.

🍷 Drinking & Nightlife

Hog Heaven
BAR

(☑ 305-664-9669; MM 85 oceanside; ⊙ 11am-3:30am) We're tempted to place this joint in an eating section, as the seafood nachos are so good. But it deserves pride of place in any list of best places to drink in town, thanks to the huge crowds that trip all the way down from Fort Lauderdale for back-porch, alfresco imbibing.

Morada Bay
BAR

(☑ 305-664-0604; www.moradabay.com; MM 81.6 bayside; ⊙ 5pm-midnight) In addition to its excellent food, the Bay holds monthly full-moon parties that attract the entire party-people population of the Keys. The whole shebang typically starts around 9pm and goes until whenever the last person passes out; check website for dates.

ℹ Information

Chamber of Commerce (☑ 305-664-4503; www.islamoradachamber.com; MM 83.2 bayside; ⊙ 9am-5pm Mon-Fri, to 4pm Sat, to 3pm Sun) Located in an old caboose.

Post Office (☑ 305-664-4738; MM 82.9 oceanside)

ℹ Getting There & Away

The Greyhound bus stops at the Burger King at MM 82.5 oceanside.

Long Key

The 965-acre **Long Key State Recreation Area** (☑ 305-664-4815; www.floridastateparks.org/longkey; MM 67.5 oceanside; per car/motorcycle/cyclist $5/4/2; P) 🏊 takes up much of Long Key. It's about 30 minutes south of Islamorada, and comprises a tropical clump of gumbo-limbo, crabwood and poisonwood trees; a picnic area fronting a long, lovely sweep of teal water; and lots of wading birds in the mangroves. Two short nature trails head through distinct plant communities. The park also has a 1.5-mile canoe trail through a saltwater tidal lagoon and rents out ocean-going kayaks (two hours single/double $17.50/21.50).

If you want to stay here, make reservations this minute: it's tough to get one of the 60 sites at the campground (☎800-326-3521; www.reserveamerica.com; MM 67.5 oceanside; sites $36; P). They're all waterfront, making this the cheapest (and probably most unspoiled) ocean view – short of squatting on a resort – you're likely to find in Florida.

MIDDLE KEYS

As you truck down the Keys, the bodies of water get wider until you reach the big boy: Seven Mile Bridge, one of the world's longest causeways and a natural divider between the Middle and Lower Keys. In this stretch of islands you'll cross specks like Conch Key and Duck Key; green, quiet Grassy Key; and finally Key Vaca (MM 54 to MM 47), where Marathon, the second-largest town and most Key-sy community in the islands, is located.

Grassy Key

At first blush Grassy Key seems pretty sedate. Well spotted; Grassy is very much an island of few attractions and lots of RV lots and trailer parks. These little villages were once the heart of the Keys, where retirees, escapists, fishermen and the waitstaff who served them lived, drank and dreamed (of a drink). Some of these communities remain, but development is relentless, and so, it seems, is the migration of the old Conch trailer towns.

◉ Sights & Activities

Curry Hammock State Park   PARK
(☎305-289-2690; www.floridastateparks.org/curry-hammock; MM 56.2 bayside; car/motorcycle/cyclist $5/4/2; ☺8am-sunset; P) ❧ This park is small but sweet and the rangers are just lovely. Like most parks in the Keys, it's a good spot for preserved tropical hardwood and mangrove habitat – a 1.5-mile hike takes you through both environments. Rent a kayak (single/double for two hours $17.20/21.50) or, when the wind is up, join the windsurfers and kiteboarders. You can also camp at the park for $36 per night – sites have toilets and electric hookups.

Local waters are blissfully free of power boats, which is a blessing down here.

Dolphin Research Center   WILDLIFE RESERVE
(☎305-289-0002; www.dolphins.org; MM 59 bayside; adult/under 4yr/4-12yr/senior $20/free/15/17.50, swim program $120-675; ☺9am-4pm; ❧) By far the most popular activity on this island is swimming with the descendants of

Flipper. Dolphins are free to leave the grounds and a lot of marine-biology research goes on behind the (still pretty commercial) tourist activities, such as getting a dolphin to paint your T-shirt or playing 'trainer for a day' ($675). Still, swimming with dolphins is an activity that raises animal rights questions (see p158).

🛏 Sleeping & Eating

Grassy Key Outpost   AMERICAN $$
(☎305-743-7373; 58152 Overseas Hwy; mains $8-28; ☺7am-10pm; P❧) The Outpost is an interesting spot that skews between fine dining and Keys casualness, both in terms of atmosphere and cuisine. There's a Southern flair to the gastronomy; shrimp and grits comes rich and smoky, while the mac'n'cheese is laced with decadent slathers of rich lobster.

Wreck Galley & Grill   AMERICAN $$
(☎305-743-8282; MM 59 bayside; mains $10-25; ☺11am-10pm; P) The Wreck is a Keys classic, where fisherman types knock back brew and feast on wings. It's definitely a local haunt, where island politicos like to prattle about the issues (fishing). The food is excellent; it grills one of the best burgers in the Keys, and the aforementioned wings go down a treat with a tall beer.

Hawk's Cay Resort   RESORT $$$
(☎305-743-7000, 888-395-5539; www.hawkscay.com; 61 Hawk's Cay Blvd, Duck Key, off MM 61 oceanside; r & ste winter $350-1600, summer $150-500; P☎☀) The Cay is an enormous luxury compound that could well have its own zip code, and besides a series of silky-plush rooms and nicely appointed townhouses, it has a variety of island activities. The Cay has its own dolphin pool, sailing school, snorkeling tours, tennis courts and boat rentals.

Rainbow Bend   HOTEL $$$
(☎800-929-1505; www.rainbowbend.com; MM 58 oceanside; r $165-270; P☀) You'll be experiencing intensely charming Keys-kitsch in these big pink cabanas, where the apartments and suites are bright, the tiki huts are shady, the bedsheets are ghastly, the beach swing is...um, swing-y and the ocean is (splash)...right there. Half-day use of the Bend's Boston whalers (motorboats), kayaks and canoes is complimentary.

Marathon

Marathon sits right on the halfway point between Key Largo and Key West, and it's a good place to stop on a road trip across the islands. It's perhaps the most 'developed' key outside Key West (that's really pushing the definition of the word 'developed') in the sense that it has large shopping centers and a population of a few thousand. Then again it's still a place where exiles from the mainland fish, booze it up and have a good time, so while Marathon is more family-friendly than Key West, it's hardly G-rated.

Sights

Crane Point Museum   MUSEUM

(📞305-743-9100; www.cranepoint.net; MM 50.5 bayside; adult/child $12.50/8.50; ⊙9am-5pm Mon-Sat, from noon Sun; P 🕭) 🞉 This is one of the nicest spots on the island to stop and smell the roses. And the pinelands. And the palm hammock – a sort of palm jungle (imagine walking under giant, organic Japanese fans) that only grows between MM 47 and MM 60. There's also Adderly House, a preserved example of a Bahamian immigrant cabin (which must have *baked* in summer) and 63 acres of green goodness to stomp through.

This is a great spot for the kids, who'll love the pirate exhibits in an on-site museum and yet another bird hospital.

Sombrero Beach   BEACH

(Sombrero Beach Rd, off MM 50 oceanside; P) One of the few white-sand, mangrove-free beaches in the Keys. It's a good spot to lay out or swim, and it's free.

Turtle Hospital   WILDLIFE RESERVE

(📞305-743-2552; www.theturtlehospital.org; 2396 Overseas Hwy; adult/child $15/7.50; ⊙9am-6pm; P 🕭) 🞉 Be it a victim of disease, boat propeller strike, flipper entanglement with fishing lines or any other danger, an injured sea turtle in the Keys will hopefully end up in this motel-cum-sanctuary. We know we shouldn't anthropomorphize animals, but these turtles just seem so sweet. It's sad to see the injured and sick ones, but heartening to see them so well looked after. Tours are educational, fun and offered on the hour from 10am-4pm.

Pigeon Key National
Historic District   ISLAND

(📞305-743-5999; www.pigeonkey.net; MM 47 oceanside; adult/child/under 5yr $12/9/free; ⊙tours 10am, noon & 2pm) For years, tiny Pigeon Key, located 2 miles west of Marathon (basically below the Old Seven Mile Bridge) housed the rail workers and maintenance men who built the infrastructure that connected the Keys. Today you can tour the

structures of this National Historic District or relax on the beach and get in some snorkeling. Ferries leave Knight's Key (to the left of the Seven Mile Bridge if you're traveling south) to Pigeon; the last one returns at 4pm.

The Old Seven Mile Bridge, meanwhile, is closed to traffic and now serves as 'the World's Longest Fishing Bridge'; park at the northeastern foot of the bridge and have a wander.

Activities

Marathon Community
Park & Marina   MARINA

(12222 Overseas Hwy) Has athletic fields and a skate park for disaffected adolescents. The marina, better known as Boot Key Harbor (📞305-289-8877; www.bootkeyharbor.com; VHF 16), is one of the best maintained working waterfronts in the Keys, and an excellent spot to book charter-fishing and diving trips. Come during Christmas to see a 'boat parade' of boats decked out with Christmas lights.

Marathon Kayak   KAYAKING

(📞305-395-0355; www.marathonkayak.com; 3hr tours $60) Does guided mangrove ecotours, sunset tours and boat rentals. The three-hour paddle through a canopy of red mangroves is highly recommended.

Wheels-2-Go   RENTAL

(📞305-289-4279; http://wheels-2-go.com; 5994 Overseas Hwy; see-through kayaks/bicycles per day $40/10; ⊙9am-5pm) Friendly kayak and bicycle rental services.

Tilden's Scuba Center   DIVING

(📞305-743-7255; www.tildensscubacenter.com; 4650 Overseas Hwy) Offers snorkeling and diving expeditions through nearby sections of the coral reef.

Sombrero Reef Explorers   DIVING

(📞305-743-0536; www.marathoncharters.com; 19 Sombrero Rd, off MM 50 oceanside) Offers snorkeling and diving expeditions through nearby sections of the coral reef.

Sleeping

Siesta Motel   MOTEL $

(📞305-743-5671; www.siestamotel.net; MM 51 oceanside; r $85-115; P 🕭) Head here for one of the cheapest, cleanest spots in the Keys, located in a friendly cluster of cute Marathon homes – and it's got great service, to boot.

Seascape Motel & Marina   MOTEL $$

(📞305-743-6212; www.seascapemotelandmarina. com; 1275 76th St Ocean E, btwn MM 51 & 52; r $99-

250; P✻🛜⌘) The classy, understated luxury in this B&B manifests in its nine rooms, all of which have a different feel – from old-fashioned cottage to sleek boutique. Seascape also has a waterfront pool, kayaks for guests to use and a lovely lobby-lounge where you'll find breakfast and afternoon wine and snacks (all included).

Sea Dell Motel
MOTEL $$

(☎305-743-5161; 5000 Overseas Hwy; r $89-209; P@) The Sea Dell is a Keys classic: low-slung huts containing linoleum-floored rooms and tropical bedspreads. The rooms are more or less self-sufficient small apartments, and can comfortably accommodate small families.

Tranquility Bay
RESORT $$$

(☎888-755-7486; www.tranquilitybay.com; MM 48.5 bayside; r $280-650; P🛜⌘) If you're serious about going upscale, you should be going here. Tranquility Bay is a massive condo-hotel resort with plush townhouses, high-thread-count sheets and all-in-white chic. The grounds are enormous and activity-filled; the owners really don't want you to leave.

Tropical Cottages
COTTAGES $$

(☎305-743-6048; www.tropicalcottages.net; 243 61st St; cottages from $130; P🐾) These pretty pastel cottages are a good option, especially if you're traveling in a larger group. The individual cottages aren't particularly plush, but they're cozy, comfortable and offer a nice bit of privacy, along with some Old Florida atmosphere. There's a daily $10 fee per pet.

🍴 Eating

★Keys Fisheries
SEAFOOD $

(☎305-743-4353; www.keysfisheries.com; 3502 Louisa St; mains $7-16; ☺8am-9pm; P🐾) The lobster Reuben is the stuff of legend here. Sweet, chunky, creamy, so good it'll make you leave unsightly drool all over the place mat. But you can't go wrong with any of the excellent seafood here, all served with sass. Expect pleasant levels of seagull harassment as you dine on a working waterfront.

As an odd bonus, to order you have to identify your favorite car, color, etc; a question that depends on the mood of the guy behind the counter.

Wooden Spoon
AMERICAN $

(7007 Overseas Hwy; dishes $2-10; ☺5:30am-1:30pm; P) It's the best breakfast around, served by sweet Southern women who know their way around a diner. The biscuits are fluffy, and they drown so well in that thick, delicious sausage gravy, and the grits are the most buttery soft starch you'll ever have the pleasure of seeing beside your eggs.

Hurricane
AMERICAN $$

(☎305-743-2200; 4650 Overseas Hwy; mains $9-19; ☺11am-midnight; P🎵) Besides being our favorite bar in Marathon, the Hurricane also

---

GROOVY GROVES

It's easy to think of the Keys, environmentally speaking, as a little boring. The landscape isn't particularly dramatic (with the exception of those sweet sweeps of ocean visible from the Overseas Hwy); it tends toward low brush and...well, more low brush.

Hey, don't judge a book by its cover. The Keys have one of the most unique, sensitive environments in the US. The difference between ecosystems here is measured in inches, but once you learn to recognize the contrast between a hammock and a wetland, you'll see the islands in a whole new tropical light. Some of the best introductions to the natural Keys can be found at Crane Point Museum and the Florida Keys Eco-Discovery Center (p172).

But we want to focus on the mangroves – the coolest, if not most visually arresting, habitat in the islands. They rise from the shallow shelf that surrounds the Keys (which also provides that lovely shade of Florida teal), looking like masses of spidery fingers constantly stroking the waters. Each mangrove traps the sediment that has accrued into the land your tiki barstool is perched on. That's right, no mangroves = no Jimmy Buffett.

The three different types of mangrove trees are all little miracles of adaptation. Red mangroves, which reside on the water's edge, have aerial roots, called propagules, allowing them to 'breathe' even as they grow into the ocean. Black mangroves, which grow further inland, survive via 'snorkel' roots called pneumatophores. Resembling spongy sticks, these roots grow out from the muddy ground and consume fresh air. White mangroves grow furthest inland and actually sweat out the salt they absorb through air and water to keep healthy.

The other tree worth a mention here isn't a mangrove. The lignum vitae, which is limited to the Keys in the US, is just as cool. Its sap has long been used to treat syphilis, hence the tree's Latin name, which translates to 'tree of life.'

serves a menu of creative South Florida–inspired goodness. Snapper stuffed with crabmeat comes after an appetizer of conch sliders (miniburgers) jerked in Caribbean seasoning. Save room for the chicken wings, an amazing blend of hot, sweet and plain delicious. The $5 lunch specials are great deal.

 Drinking & Nightlife

★**Hurricane** BAR
(☑305-743-2200; MM 49.5 bayside; ☺11am-12am) The staff is sassy and warm. The drinks will kick your ass out the door and have you back begging for more. Locals, tourists, mad fishermen, rednecks and the odd journalist saddle up for endless Jägerbombs before dancing the night away to any number of consistently good live acts. It's the best bar before Key West, and it deserves a visit.

Island Fish Company BAR
(☑305-743-4191; MM 54 bayside; ☺11:30am-10pm) The Island has a friendly staff pouring strong cocktails on a sea-breeze-kissed tiki island overlooking Florida Bay. Chat with your friendly Czech or Georgian bartender – tip well, and they'll top up your drinks without you realizing it. The laidback, by-the-water atmosphere is quintessentially Keys.

Brass Monkey BAR
(☑305-743-4028; Marathon, MM 52; ☺10am-4am) When Colonel Kurtz whispered, 'The horror, the horror,' in *Apocalypse Now* he was probably thinking about the night he got trashed in this scuzziest of dives, frequented by off-the-clock bar- and waitstaff in Marathon.

Marathon Cinema & Community Theater CINEMA
(☑305-743-0288; www.marathontheater.org; 5101 Overseas Hwy) A good, old-school, single-stage theater that shows movies and plays in big reclining seats (with even bigger cup-holders).

ⓘ **Information**

Fisherman's Hospital (☑305-743-5533; www.fishermanshospital.com; 3301 Overseas Hwy) Has a major emergency room.
Marathon Visitors Center Chamber of Commerce (☑305-743-5417, 800-262-7284; www.floridakeysmarathon.com; MM 53.5 bayside; ☺9am-5pm) Sells Greyhound tickets.

ⓘ **Getting There & Away**

You can fly into the **Marathon Airport** (☑305-289-6060; MM 50.5 bayside) or go Greyhound, which stops at the airport.

LOWER KEYS

The people of the Lower Keys vary between winter escapees and native Conchs. Some local families have been Keys castaways for generations, and there are bits of Big Pine that feel more Florida Panhandle than Overseas Hwy. It's an odd contrast, the islands get at their most isolated, rural and quintessentially 'Keez-y' before opening onto (relatively) cosmopolitan, heterogeneous (yet strongly homosexual) Key West.

Big Pine, Bahia Honda & Looe Keys

Big Pine is home to endless stretches of quiet roads, Key West employees who found a way around astronomical real-estate rates, and packs of wandering Key deer. Bahia Honda has everyone's favorite sandy beach, while the coral-reef system of Looe offers amazing reef-diving opportunities.

⊙ **Sights & Activities**

Bahia Honda State Park PARK
(☑305-872-3210; www.bahiahondapark.com; MM 36.8; car/motorcycle/cyclist $5/4/2; ☺8am-sunset; ⊞) This park, with its long, white-sand (and seaweed-strewn) beach, named Sandspur Beach by locals, is the big attraction in these parts. As Keys beaches go, this one is probably the best natural stretch of sand in the island chain, but we wouldn't vote it best beach in the continental USA (although Condé Nast did...in 1992). As a tourist, the more novel experience is walking on the old Bahia Honda Rail Bridge, which offers nice views of the surrounding islands.

You can also check out the nature trails (ooh, butterflies!) and science center, where helpful park employees help you identify stone crabs, fireworms, horseshoe crabs and comb jellies. The park concession offers daily 1½-hour snorkeling trips at 9:30am and 1:30pm (adult/child $30/25). Reservations are a good idea in high season.

Looe Key National Marine Sanctuary MARINE PARK
(☑305-809-4700; floridakeys.noaa.gov) Looe (pronounced 'loo') Key, located five nautical miles off Big Pine, isn't a key at all but a reef, part of the Florida Keys National Marine Sanctuary. This is an area of some 2800 sq nautical miles of 'land' managed by the National Oceanic & Atmospheric Administration. The reef here can only be visited

KEY DEER

While we can't guarantee you'll see one, if you head down the side roads of Big Pine Key, there's a pretty good chance you'll spot the Key deer, a local species roughly the size of a large dog. Once mainland dwellers, the Key deer were stranded on the Keys during the formation of the islands. Successive generations grew smaller and had single births, as opposed to large litters, to deal with the reduced food resources in the archipelago. While you won't see thundering herds of dwarfish deer, the little cuteballs are pretty easy to spot if you're persistent and patient. In fact, they're so common you need to pay careful attention to the reduced speed limits. Note: speed limits drop further at night, because cars are still the biggest killer of Key deer.

To visit the official Key deer refuge (although the deer can be spotted almost anywhere on Big Pine) take Key Deer Blvd (it's a right at the lights off the Overseas Hwy at the southern end of Big Pine) north for 3.5 miles from MM 30.5.

through a specially arranged charter-boat trip, best arranged through any Keys diving outfit, the most natural one being **Looe Key Dive Center** (☑ 305-872-2215; www.diveflakeys.com; snorkel/dive $40/70).

The marine sanctuary is named for an English frigate that sank here in 1744, and the Looe Key reef contains the 210ft MV *Adolphus Busch*, used in the 1957 film *Fire Down Below* and then sunk (110ft deep) in these waters in 1998.

National Key Deer Refuge Headquarters   WILDLIFE RESERVE

(☑ 305-872-2239; www.fws.gov/nationalkeydeer; Big Pine Shopping Center, MM 30.5 bayside; ⊙ 8am-5pm Mon-Fri; 🖻) What would make Bambi cuter? Mini Bambi. Introducing: the Key deer, an endangered subspecies of white-tailed deer that prance about primarily on Big Pine and No Name Keys. The folks here are an incredibly helpful source of information on the deer and all things Keys. The refuge sprawls over several islands, but the sections open to the public are on Big Pine and No Name.

The headquarters also administers the **Great White Heron National Wildlife Refuge** – 200,000 acres of open water and mangrove islands north of the main Keys that is only accessible by boat. There's no tourism infrastructure in place to get out here, but you can inquire about nautical charts and the heron themselves at the office.

Blue Hole   POND

(off MM 30.5; ⊙ 24hr) This little pond (and former quarry) is now the largest freshwater body in the Keys. That's not saying much, but the hole is a pretty little dollop of blue (well, algal green) surrounded by a small path and information signs. The water is home to turtles, fish and wading birds. A

quarter mile further along the same road is **Watson's Nature Trail** (less than 1 mile long) and **Watson's Hammock**, a small Keys forest habitat.

Apparently people have taken to (illegally) feeding the wildlife here; please don't follow in their footsteps.

No Name Key   ISLAND

Perhaps the best-named island in the Keys, No Name gets few visitors, as it's basically a residential island. It's one of the most reliable spots for Key deer watching. From Overseas Hwy, go on to Watson Blvd, turn right, then left onto Wilder Blvd. Cross Bogie Bridge and you'll be on No Name.

Veterans Memorial Park & Beach   PARK

(MM 39 oceanside; ⊙ sunrise-sunset; 🖻) This small park has covered picnic tables and good access to the mudflat and mangrove habitat that makes up most of the Keys' coastline. The views onto the ocean are pristine.

Big Pine Flea Market   MARKET

(MM 30.5 oceanside; ⊙ 8am-sunset Sat & Sun) This market, which attracts folks from across the Keys, rivals local churches for weekly attendance. You know how we keep harping on about how weird Keys residents are? Well, imagine rummaging through their closets and seeing their deepest, darkest secrets – on sale for 50¢?!

Strike Zone Charters   SNORKELING, DIVING

(☑ 305-872-9863; www.strikezonecharter.com; MM 29.5 bayside) Runs snorkeling ($38) and diving trips ($48) aboard glass-bottom boats, in which you can explore the thousands of varieties of colorful tropical fish, coral and sea life in the Looe Key sanctuary. Get open water PADI certification for $395.

🛌 Sleeping

⭐ Bahia Honda
State Park Campground   CAMPGROUND $
(☎305-872-2353; www.reserveamerica.com; MM 37, Bahia Honda Key; sites/cabins $38.50/122.50; ℗) 🏊 Bahia Honda has the best camping in the Keys. There's nothing quite like waking up to the sky as your ceiling and the ocean as your shower (Ow! Damned sand flies. OK, it's not paradise…). The park has six cabins, each sleeping six people, and 200 sites a short distance from the beach. Reserve well in advance.

Barnacle Bed & Breakfast   B&B $$
(☎305-872-3298; www.thebarnacle.net; 1557 Long Beach Dr, Big Pine Key; r $165-235; ℗🏊) The Barnacle welcomes you into its atrium with the promise of fresh ocean breezes. Wander around the pool and Jacuzzi, past the swinging hammocks, and into highly individualized rooms that all share a lovingly mad design sense. Tropical knickknacks and big windows that let in lots of Keys sunlight are standard. Meals should be enjoyed on the deck, which overlooks the sea.

Parmer's Resort   HOTEL $$
(☎305-872-2157; www.parmersresort.com; 565 Barry Ave, Little Torch Key, off MM 28.5 bayside; r winter $159-304, summer $99-209; ℗🛜🏊) Appearing deceptively small from the outside, this 5-acre property takes up a nice chunk of Little Torch Key and fills it with inviting rooms that overlook local waterways and channels. The rooms are spacious, although you'd be mad not to step outside them and enjoy a view of the islands from your balcony.

⭐ Deer Run Bed & Breakfast   B&B $$$
(☎305-872-2015; www.deerrunfloridabb.com; 1997 Long Beach Dr, Big Pine Key, off MM 33 oceanside; r $255-375; ℗🛜🏊) 🏊 This state-certified green lodge and vegetarian B&B is isolated on a lovely stretch of Long Beach Dr. It's a garden of quirky delights, complemented by love-the-earth paraphernalia, street signs and four simple but cozy rooms. The helpful owners will get you out on a boat or into the heated pool for relaxation while they whip up delicious vegetarian meals.

Little Palm Island Resort & Spa   RESORT $$$
(☎305-515-3019, 800-343-8567; www.littlepalmisland.com; packages from $890; @🛜🏊) How do you get here? By boat or by plane, accompanied by a big wad of money. If you can afford to get here you can afford to spoil yourself, and this exclusive island, with its Zen gardens, blue lagoons and general Persian Empire air of decadent luxury, is very good at spoiling you.

🍴 Eating

No Name Pub   PIZZERIA $
(☎305-872-9115; N Watson Blvd, Big Pine Key, off MM 30.5 bayside; mains $7-18; ⏰11am-11pm; ℗) The No Name's one of those off-the-track places that everyone seems to know about. It feels isolated, it looks isolated, yet somehow, the tourists are all here – and this doesn't detract in the slightest from the kooky ambience, friendly service, excellent locally brewed beer and primo pizzas served up at this colorful semidive.

Note: the name of this place implies that it is located on No Name Key, but it is on Big Pine Key, just over the causeway.

Coco's Kitchen   DINER $
(Big Pine Key Shopping Center, MM 30.5 bayside; mains & sandwiches $10.50; ⏰7am-2pm & 4-7pm Tue-Sat; ℗♿) Enter through the oddly mirrored storefront into this tiny luncheonette, where local fishers join shoppers from the Winn Dixie next door for diner fare and local gossip. Serves a good mix of American standards and Cuban diner fare such as picadillo (ground beef cooked in Cuban spices).

Good Food Conspiracy   VEGETARIAN $
(☎305-872-3945; Big Pine Key, MM 30 oceanside; mains under $10; ⏰9:30am-7pm Mon-Sat, 11am-5pm Sun; ℗🖊) 🏊 Rejoice, health-food nuts: all the greens, sprouts, herbs and tofu you've been dreaming about during that long, fried-food-studded drive down the Overseas are for sale in this friendly little macrobiotic organic shop. There is a good smoothie and fresh-juice bar on site. Note the big pink shrimp out front – Keezy kitsch as its best.

ℹ️ Information

Lower Keys Chamber of Commerce (☎305-872-2411; www.lowerkeyschamber.com; MM 31 oceanside; ⏰9am-5pm Mon-Fri, to 3pm Sat) Stocked with brochures and tourist information.

Sugarloaf & Boca Chica Keys

This is the final stretch before the holy grail of Key West. There's not much going on – just bridges over lovely swathes of teal and turquoise, a few good eats and a thoroughly batty roadside attraction.

This lowest section of the Keys goes from about MM 20 to the start of Key West.

◎ Sights

Perky's Bat Tower TOWER
(Sugarloaf Key, MM17) It resembles an Aztec-inspired fire lookout, but this wooden tower is actually one real-estate developer's vision gone utterly awry. In the 1920s Richter C Perky had the bright idea to transform this area into a vacation resort. There was just one problem: mosquitoes. His solution? Build a 35ft tower and move in a colony of bats (he'd heard they eat mosquitoes). He imported the flying mammals, but they promptly took off, leaving the tower empty.

Sheriff's Animal Farm ZOO
(☑ 305-293-7300; 5501 College Rd, Stock Island; ⊙1-3pm second & fourth Sun of the month or by appt; P ♿) ✔ Just before you hit Key West, you may be tempted to stop at this farm, located near the Monroe County Sheriff's Office and Detention Center (no, really). This shelter for Monroe County animals that have been abandoned or given up is a lovely place to take the kids (call ahead to visit and farmer Jeanne Selander will be happy to show you around). There are tortoises, South American cavvies (a kind of rodent), birds, llamas and an albino python.

⌁ Sleeping

Sugarloaf Lodge HOTEL $$
(☑ 305-745-3211, 800-553-6097; www.sugarloaflodge.net; Sugarloaf Key, MM 17; r $120-170; P ✚) The 55 motel-like rooms are nothing special, though every single one has a killer bay view. There is also an on-site restaurant, a tiki bar, a marina and an airstrip, from which you can charter a seaplane tour or go skydiving.

✗ Eating

Baby's Coffee CAFE $
(☑ 305-744-9866; MM 15 oceanside; ⊙7am to 6pm Mon-Fri, 7am to 5pm Sat & Sun) This very cool coffeehouse has an on-site bean-roasting plant and sells bags of the aromatic stuff along with excellent hot and cold java brews – many locals consider this to be some of the best coffee in the islands. Other essentials are sold, from yummy baked goods to Dr Bronner's liquid soap.

Mangrove Mama's CARIBBEAN $$
(☑ 305-745-3030; MM 20 oceanside; lunch $10-15, dinner $15-29; ⊙11:30am-3:30pm & 5:30-10pm; P ♿) This groovy roadside eatery serves Caribbean-inspired seafood – coconut shrimp, spicy conch stew, lobster – best enjoyed on the backyard patio and accompanied by a little live reggae.

KEY WEST

The Keys, like any frontier, have always been defined by two 'E's': edge and eccentric. And when it came to the far frontier, the very edge, the last outpost of America – out here, only the most eccentric would dare venture. And thus, Key West: the most beautifully strange (or is it strangely beautiful?) island in the US. This place is seriously screwy, in a (mostly) good way. There's no middle separating the high and low brow, that's for sure. On one side of the road, literary festivals, Caribbean villas, tropical noir and expensive art galleries. On the other, an S&M fetishist parade, frat boys vomiting on their sorority girlfriends and 'I Love to Fart' T-shirts (seriously).

Where the other Keys are a bit more country-fried, Key West, a historical haven for homosexuals and artists, remains a little more left of center. The locals revel in their funky nonconformity here, probably because weirdness is still integral to the Key West brand. But past these idiosyncrasies is simply a beautiful tropical island, where the moonflowers bloom at night and the classical Caribbean homes are so sad and romantic it's hard not to sigh at them.

◎ Sights

★ Mallory Square SQUARE
(♿) Take all those energies, subcultures and oddities of Keys life and focus them into one torchlit, family-friendly (but playfully edgy), sunset-enriched street party. The child of all these raucous forces is Mallory Sq, one of the greatest shows on Earth. It all begins as the sun starts to set, a sign for the madness that it's OK to break out. Watch a dog walk a tightrope, a man swallow fire, British acrobats tumble and sass each other.

Have a beer. And a conch fritter. And wait for the sun to dip behind the ocean and for the carnival to really get going.

Duval Street STREET
Key West locals have a love-hate relationship with the most famous road in Key West (if not the Keys). Duval, Old Town Key West's main drag, is a miracle mile of booze, tacky everything and awful behavior. But it's fun. The 'Duval Crawl' is one of the wildest pub

crawls in the country. The mix of neon drink, drag shows, T-shirt kitsch, local theaters, art studios and boutiques is more charming than jarring.

Hemingway House
HOUSE

(☎ 305-294-1136; www.hemingwayhome.com; 907 Whitehead St; adult/child $13/6; ⊙ 9am-5pm) Key West's biggest darling, Ernest Hemingway, lived in this gorgeous Spanish colonial house from 1931 to 1940. Papa moved here in his early 30s with wife No 2, a Vogue fashion editor and (former) friend of wife No 1 (he left the house when he ran off with wife No 3). *The Short Happy Life of Francis Macomber* and *The Green Hills of Africa* were produced here, as well as many six-toed cats, whose descendants basically run the grounds.

Florida Keys Eco-Discovery Center
MUSEUM

(☎ 305-809-4750; http://eco-discovery.com/ecokw.html; 35 East Quay Rd; ⊙ 9am-4pm Tue-Sat; P ♿) FREE So, you've been making your way down the Keys, thinking, Gosh, could there be a place that ties all the knowledge of this unique ecological phenomenon into one fun, well-put-together educational exhibit? OK, maybe those weren't your exact thoughts, but this is exactly what you get at this excellent center. This place does a marvelous job of filling in all the wild details of the natural Keys. The kids love it.

Fort Zachary Taylor Historic State Park
PARK

(☎ 305-292-6713; www.floridastateparks.org/fort-taylor; Truman Annex; per car/motorcycle/pedestrian & cyclist $6/4/2; ⊙ 8am-sunset) 'America's Southernmost State Park,' this park is oft-neglected by authorities and visitors, which is a shame. The actual fort walls are still standing, and within the compound those most-blessed of nerds – historical re-enactors – sometimes act out scenes of pirate and Civil War battles. The beach here is the best one Key West has to offer – it's got white sand to lounge on, water deep enough to swim in and tropical fish under the waves.

Key West Cemetery
CEMETERY

(cnr Margaret & Angela Sts; ⊙ 7am - 6pm; ♿) A darkly alluring Gothic labyrinth beckons at the center of this pastel town. Built in 1847, the cemetery crowns Solares Hill, the highest point on the island (with an elevation of 16ft). Some of the oldest families in the Keys rest in peace – and close proximity – here. With body space at a premium, mausoleums stand practically shoulder to shoulder. Island quirkiness penetrates the gloom: seashells and macramé adorn headstones with inscriptions like, 'I told you I was sick.'

Get chaperoned by a guide from the Historic Florida Keys Foundation, with guided tours for $10 per person at 9:30am on Tuesday and Thursday; departs from the main gate at Margaret and Angela Sts.

Key West Butterfly & Nature Conservatory
ANIMAL SANCTUARY

(☎ 305-296-2988; www.keywestbutterfly.com; 1316 Duval St; adult/4-12yr $12/8.50; ⊙ 9am-5pm; ♿) This vast domed conservatory lets you stroll through a magic garden of flowering plants, colorful birds and up to 1800 fluttering butterflies, all live imports from around the globe.

THE CONCH REPUBLIC: ONE HUMAN FAMILY

Conchs (pronounced 'conk' as in 'bonk,' not 'contsh' as in 'bunch') are people who were born and raised in the Keys. It's a rare title to achieve. Even transplants can only rise to the rank of 'freshwater Conch.' You will hear reference to, and see the flag of, the Conch Republic everywhere in the islands, which brings us to an interesting tale.

In 1982 US border patrol and customs agents erected a roadblock at Key Largo to catch drug smugglers and illegal aliens. As traffic jams and anger mounted, many tourists disappeared. They decided they'd rather take the Shark Valley Tram in the Everglades, thank you very much. To voice their outrage, a bunch of fiery Conchs decided to secede from the USA. After forming the Conch Republic, they made three declarations (in this order): secede from the USA; declare war on the USA and surrender; and request $1 million in foreign aid. The roadblock was eventually lifted, and every February, Conchs celebrate the anniversary of those heady days with nonstop parties, and the slogan 'We Seceded Where Others Failed.'

Today the whole Conch Republic thing is largely a marketing gimmick, but that doesn't detract from its official motto: 'One Human Family.' This emphasis on tolerance and mutual respect has kept the Keys' head and heart in the right place, accepting gays, straights, and peoples of all colors and religions.

Nancy Forrester's Secret Garden GARDEN
(www.nfsgarden.com; 518 Elizabeth St; admission adult/child $10/5; ⊙10am-3pm; 🎨) Nancy, a local artist and fixture of the Keys community, invites you to bring lunch (but no cell phones!) into her oasis of lush palms, orchids and chatty rescued parrots and macaws. Although the place is called a secret garden, Nancy considers it to be a piece of art in and of itself – the last acre of undeveloped (although tended and cared for by human hands) natural space within the heart of Key West. Children are welcome and seem to love the local bird life.

**Museum of Art & History
at the Custom House** MUSEUM
(📞305-295-6616; www.kwahs.com/customhouse; 281 Front St; adult/child $9/5; ⊙9:30am-4:30pm) There is art at the end of the road, and you'll find the best at this museum, which is worth a look-see if only for its gorgeous home – the grand Customs House, long abandoned until its impressive renovation in the '90s. The permanent display includes massive portraits and some of the best showcases of international (particularly Caribbean) art in the region.

**Fort East Martello
Museum & Gardens** MUSEUM
(📞305-296-3913; www.kwahs.com/martello. htm; 3501 S Roosevelt Blvd; adult/child $9/5; ⊙9:30am-4:30pm) This old fortress was built to resemble an old Italian Martello-style coastal watchtower (hence the name), a design that quickly became obsolete with the advent of the explosive shell. Now the fort serves a new purpose: preserving the old. There's historical memorabilia, artifacts, the folk art of Mario Sanchez, and 'junk' sculptor Stanley Papio, who worked with scrap metal and a genuinely creepy haunted doll.

Perhaps the most haunted thing in Key West, 'Robert the doll' is a terrifying child's toy from the 19th century who reportedly causes much misfortune to those who question his powers. Honest, he looks like something out of a Stephen King novel; see www.robertthedoll.org for more information.

Studios of Key West GALLERY
(TSKW; 📞305-296-0458; www.tskw.org; 600 White St; ⊙10am-6pm) This nonprofit showcases about a dozen artists' studios in a gallery space located in the old Armory building, which includes a lovely sculpture garden. Besides its public visual-arts displays, TSKW hosts readings, literary and visual workshops, concerts, lectures and community discussion groups.

Essentially, it has become the accessible heart of this city's enormous arts movement, and offers a good point-of-entry for visitors who want to engage in Key West's creative scene but don't have a clue where to start.

Little White House HISTORIC BUILDING
(📞305-294-9911; www.trumanlittlewhitehouse. com; 111 Front St; adult/child 5-12yr/senior $16/5/14; ⊙9am-4:30pm, gardens 7am-6pm) While we were first tempted here by the prospect of a Lego-sized model of the presidential digs, this is in fact the spot where ex-president Harry S Truman used to vacation when he wasn't molding post-WWII geopolitics. It's lushly luxurious and open only for guided tours, although you are welcome to walk around the surrounding botanical gardens for free. Plenty of Truman's possessions are scattered about, but the real draw is the guides, who are intensely intelligent, quirky and helpful.

San Carlos Institute HISTORIC BUILDING
(📞305-294-3887; www.institutosancarlos.org; 516 Duval St) Founded in 1871 by Cuban exiles, the San Carlos is a gorgeous building constructed in classical Spanish mission style. The current structure dates from 1924. The interior is spackled with Cuban tile work, Italian marble and statues of Cuban luminaries, including Jose Marti, who spoke here and dubbed the building 'La Casa Cuba.' Today the building serves as library, art gallery, lecture hall and theater; it is only open during events, but these occur often.

Bahama Village NEIGHBORHOOD
Bahama Village was the old Bahamian district of the island, and in days past had a colorful Caribbean feel about it, which is resurrected a bit during the Goombay Festival (p178). But today the village is pretty gentrified; many areas have been swallowed into a sort of pseudo-Duval periphery zone, but some retain Caribbean charm. At the **Office of the Secretary General of the Conch Republic** (📞305-296-0213; www.conchrepublic.com; 613 Simonton St) you can see all manner of Conch Republic tat – flags, souvenirs and such.

Casa Antigua HISTORIC BUILDING
(314 Simonton St; ⊙10am-6pm) This was technically Hemingway's first house in Key West and where he wrote *A Farewell to Arms,* but it isn't all that notable, except for a lush garden in the back and a very kitschy 'guided tour'. For $2, they'll let you into a peaceful green area out the back, where a recorded

Key West

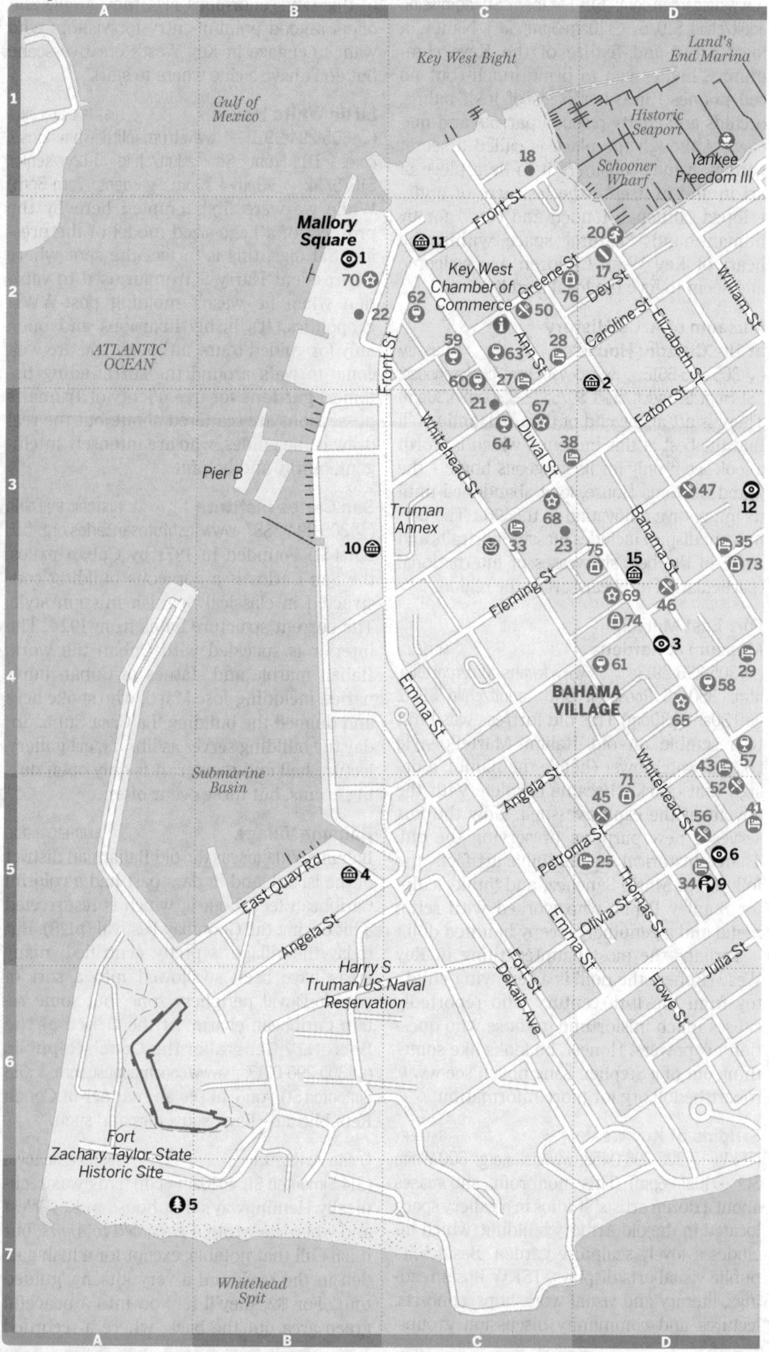

Key West Bight
Land's End Marina
Gulf of Mexico
Historic Seaport
Schooner Wharf
Yankee Freedom III
Front St
Mallory Square
Key West Chamber of Commerce
Greene St
Dey St
William St
Caroline St
Elizabeth St
ATLANTIC OCEAN
Ann St
Front St
Eaton St
Whitehead St
Duval St
Pier B
Truman Annex
Bahama St
Fleming St
BAHAMA VILLAGE
Emma St
Submarine Basin
Angela St
Whitehead St
Petronia St
East Quay Rd
Angela St
Olivia St
Thomas St
Emma St
Julia St
Harry S Truman US Naval Reservation
Fort St
Dekalb Ave
Howe St
Fort Zachary Taylor State Historic Site
Whitehead Spit
A
B
C
D
1
2
3
4
5
6
7
1
2
3
4
5
6
9
10
11
12
15
17
18
20
21
22
23
25
27
28
29
33
34
35
38
41
43
45
46
47
50
52
56
57
58
59
60
61
62
63
64
65
67
68
69
70
71
73
74
75
76

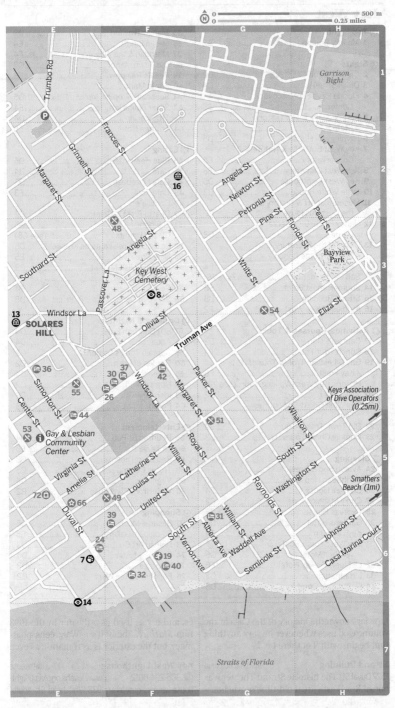

Key West

tape lays down the history of the Casa at the volume God uses whenever he says anything that begins with 'Let there be...'

Strand Building HISTORIC BUILDING
(527 Duval St) The historic Strand Theater was one of Key West's great old-time movie hous-

es, and it was used as a theater in the 1993 film *Matinee*. Today it's a Walgreens pharmacy, but the exterior is as romantic as ever.

Key West Lighthouse LIGHTHOUSE
(☏ 305-294-0012; www.kwahs.org/visit/lighthouse-keepers-quarters/; 938 Whitehead St; adult/

student over 7yr/senior $10/5/9; ⊘9:30am-4:30pm) You can climb up 88 steps to the top of this lighthouse, built in 1846, for a decent view. But honestly, it's just as enjoyable to gaze up at the tower from the leafy street below.

Southernmost Point LANDMARK
(cnr South & Whitehead Sts) The most photographed spot on the island, this red-and-black buoy isn't even the southernmost point in the USA (that's in the off-limits naval base around the corner). This is the most overrated attraction in Key West.

🏃 Activities

Beaches
Key West is *not* about beach going. In fact, for true sun 'n' surf, locals go to Bahia Honda whenever possible. Still, the three city beaches on the southern side of the island are lovely and narrow, with calm and clear water. **South Beach**, at the end of Simonton St. **Higgs Beach**, at the end of Reynolds St and Casa Marina Ct, has barbecue grills, picnic tables and a big crowd of gay sunbathers. **Smathers Beach**, further east off S Roosevelt Blvd, is more popular with jet-skiers, parasailers, teens and college students. The best local beach, though, is at Fort Zachary Taylor; it's worth the admission to enjoy the white sand and relative calm.

Boating
Check www.charterboatkeywest.com for a directory of the many fishing and cruising charters offered in Key West.

★ Jolly Rover CRUISE
(☑305-304-2235; www.schoonerjollyrover.com; cnr Greene & Elizabeth Sts, Schooner Wharf; cruise $45) This outfit has a gorgeous, tanbark (reddish-brown) 80ft schooner that embarks on daily sunset cruises under sail. It looks like a pirate ship and has the cannons to back the image up.

Reelax Charters KAYAKING
(☑305-304-1392; www.keyskayaking.com; MM 17 Sugarloaf Key Marina; all inclusive kayak trips $240) Get your paddle on and slip silently into the surrounding mangroves and mudflats of the Lower Keys with Andrea Paulson. Based on Sugarloaf Key.

Diving & Snorkeling
The diving is better in Key Largo and Biscayne National Park, but there is some decent wreck diving near Key West.

The website of the **Keys Association of Dive Operators** (www.divekeys.com; 3128 N Roosevelt Blvd) is a clearing house for information on diving opportunities in the islands; it also works on enhancing local sustainable underwater activities by creating artificial reefs and encouraging safe boating and diving practices.

Captain's Corner DIVING
(☑305-296-8865; 631 Greene St; snorkel/scuba from $40/75) This dive outfit leads snorkeling and scuba trips to local reefs and wrecks.

Dive Key West DIVING
(☑305-296-3823; www.divekeywest.com; 3128 N Roosevelt Blvd; snorkel/scuba from $60/75) Largest dive facility on the island. Wreck-diving trips cost $135 with all equipment and air provided.

👉 Tours
Worth noting is *Sharon Wells' Walking & Biking Guide to Historic Key West*, a booklet of self-guided walks available free at inns and businesses around town, written by a local. See www.walkbikeguide.com.

Old Town Trolley Tours TOUR
(☑888-910-8687; www.trolleytours.com/key-west; adult/child under 13yr/senior $30/free/27; ⊘tours 9am-4:30pm; ☑) These tours are a great introduction to the city. The 90-minute, hop-on, hop-off narrated tram tour starts at Mallory Sq and makes a loop around the whole city, with nine stops along the way. Trolleys depart every 15 to 30 minutes from 9am to 4:30pm daily. The narration is hokey, but you'll get a good overview of Key West history.

Conch Tour Train TOUR
(☑305-294-5161; www.conchtourtrain.com; adult/child under 13yr/senior $30/free/27; ⊘tours 9am-4:30pm; ☑) Run by the same company as Trolley Tours, this one seats you in breezy linked train cars with no on/off option. Offers discounted admission to sights such as the Hemingway House.

Historic Key West Walking Tour WALKING TOUR
(☑800-844-7601; www.trustedtours.com; 1 Whitehead St; adult/child $18/9) A walking tour that takes in some of the major architecture and historical sights of the island. Takes about two hours. You need to book in advance.

Key West Ghost & Mysteries Tour TOUR
(☑305-292-2040; www.keywestghostandmysteriestour.com; tours depart from Duval & Caroline; adult/child $18/10; ⊘tours 9pm) A playfully

creepy ghost tour that's as family friendly as this sort of thing gets – in other words, no big chills or pop-out screaming.

Original Ghost Tours TOUR
(☎ 305-294-9255; www.hauntedtours.com; adult/child $15/10; ⊙ 8pm & 9pm) Stories about souls who inhabit locations that include about half the bars and hotels on the island.

✪ Festivals & Events

Contact the **Key West Art & Historical Society** (☎ 305-295-6616; www.kwahs.com) to get the skinny on upcoming studio shows, literary readings, film festivals and the like.

Key West Literary Seminar LITERARY
(www.kwls.org) Now in its 23rd year, draws top writers from around the country each January (although it costs hundreds of dollars to attend).

Robert Frost Poetry Festival LITERARY
Held in April. Contact the Studios of Key West (p173) for details.

Hemingway Days Festival CULTURE
(www.fla-keys.com/hemingwaymedia/) Held in late July, brings parties, a 5km run and an Ernest look-alike contest.

WomenFest LESBIAN & TRANSEXUAL
(www.womenfest.com) Nothing says dignified sexiness like this festival, held in early September, which attracts thousands of lesbians who just want to party.

Fantasy Fest CULTURE
(www.fantasyfest.net) You gotta see this festival held throughout the week leading up to Halloween. It's when all the inns get competitive about decorating their properties, and everyone gets decked out in the most outrageous costumes they can cobble together (or decked down in daring body paint).

Goombay Festival CULTURE
(www.goombay-keywest.org) Held during the same out-of-control week as Fantasy Fest, this is a Bahamian celebration of food, crafts and culture.

Parrot Heads in Paradise Convention MUSIC
(www.phip.com/motm.asp) This festival in November is for, you guessed it, Jimmy Buffett fans (rabid ones only, naturally).

🛏 Sleeping

There's a glut of boutique hotels, cozy B&Bs and four-star resorts here at the end of the USA, so sleepers won't want for accommodations. Although some options are more central than others, the fact is that any hotel in Old Town will put you within walking distance of all the action. Most hotels in Key West are gay friendly.

Caribbean House GUESTHOUSE $
(☎ 305-296-0999; www.caribbeanhousekw.com; 226 Petronia St; summer $89, winter $119-139; P ❋ @) This is a cute, canary-yellow Caribbean cottage in the heart of Bahama Village. The 10 small, brightly colored guest rooms aren't too fancy, but it's a happy, cozy bargain.

Key West Youth Hostel & Seashell Motel HOSTEL $
(☎ 305-296-5719; www.keywesthostel.com; 718 South St; dm from $54, motel r from $95; P ❋) This isn't our favorite hostel, but it's about the only youth-oriented budget choice on the island. That said, both dorms and motel rooms are overpriced.

Mango Tree Inn B&B $$
(☎ 305-293-1177; www.mangotree-inn.com; 603 Southard St; $150-200; ❋ ☎ ⛵) This down-to-earth B&B offers a courtyard pool and elegant accommodation in a number of airy rooms, each decorated with swathes of tropical-chic accoutrement, from rattan furniture to flowering hibiscus. Rates are a deal for this kind of downtown proximity.

Seascape Tropical Inn B&B $$
(☎ 305-296-7776, 800-765-6438; www.seascape-tropicalinn.com; 420 Olivia St; r $184-250; ❋ ☎ ⛵) Had this B&B existed back in the day, Hemingway could have stumbled into it after one of his epic drinking binges – it's within spitting distance of his old house. Now you can crash in one of six rooms, appointed with cool, airy interiors and warm accents like floral comforters and high-thread-count sheets.

Old Town Manor BOUTIQUE HOTEL $$
(☎ 305-292-2170; www.oldtownmanor.com; 511 Eaton St; $185-275; ❋ ☎ ⛵) While it bills itself as a B&B (and breakfast is included), the Old Town feels more like a boutique operation that offers a wide variety of rooms – 14, to be exact, spread amid lush gardens. The digs come in the usual tropically inspired palette, but they're a little more subdued than the Keys norm. Service is friendly and on point.

L'Habitation GUESTHOUSE $$
(☎ 305-293-9203; www.lhabitation.com; 408 Eaton St; r $119-189; ❋ ☎) A beautiful, classical Keys cottage with cute rooms kitted

DRY TORTUGAS NATIONAL PARK

After all those keys, connected by all that convenient road, the nicest islands in the archipelago require a little extra effort. Ponce de León named them Las Tortugas (The Turtles) for the sea turtles that roamed here. A lack of freshwater led sailors to add a 'dry.' Today the **Dry Tortugas** (☎ 305-242-7700; www.nps.gov/drto; adult/15yr & under $5/free) are a national park under the control of the National Park Service and are accessible by boat or plane.

Originally the Tortugas were the US's naval perch into the Gulf of Mexico. But by the Civil War, **Fort Jefferson**, the main structure on the islands, had become a prison for Union deserters and at least four people, among them Dr Samuel Mudd, who had been arrested for complicity in the assassination of Abraham Lincoln. Hence, a new nickname: Devil's Island. The name was prophetic; in 1867 a yellow-fever outbreak killed 38 people, and after an 1873 hurricane the fort was abandoned. It reopened in 1886 as a quarantine station for smallpox and cholera victims, was declared a national monument in 1935 by President Franklin D Roosevelt, and was upped to national park status in 1992 by George Bush Sr.

The park is open for day trips and overnight camping, which provides a rare phenomenon: a quiet Florida beach. Garden Key has 13 campsites ($3 per person, per night), which are given out on a first-come, first-served basis. Reserve early by calling the National Park Service. There are toilets, but no freshwater showers or drinking water; bring everything you'll need. The sparkling waters offer excellent snorkeling and diving opportunities. A **visitor center** is located within fascinating Fort Jefferson.

If you're hungry, watch for Cuban American fishing boats trolling the waters. They'll happily trade for lobster, crab and shrimp; you'll have the most leverage trading beverages. Just paddle up and bargain for your supper. In March and April, there is stupendous bird-watching, including aerial fighting. Star-gazing is mind-blowing any time of the year.

Getting There

If you have your own boat, the Dry Tortugas are covered under National Ocean Survey chart No 11438. Otherwise, the **Yankee Freedom III** (☎ 800-634-0939; www.drytortugas.com/; Historic Seaport) operates a fast ferry between Garden Key and the Historic Seaport (at the northern end of Margaret St). Round-trip fares cost $165/120 per adult/child. Reservations are recommended. Continental breakfast, a picnic lunch, snorkeling gear and a 45-minute tour of the fort are all included.

Key West Seaplanes (☎ 305-294-0709; www.seaplanesofkeywest.com) can take up to 10 passengers (flight time 40 minutes each way). A four-hour trip costs $295/free/$236 per adult/child under two years/child over two; an eight-hour trip costs $515/free/$412. Again, reserve at least a week in advance.

The $5 park admission fees are included in the above prices.

out in light tropical shades, with lamps that look like contemporary art pieces and Skittles-bright quilts. The friendly bilingual owner welcomes guests in English or French. The front porch, shaded by palms, is a perfect place to stop and engage in Keys people-watching.

Avalon Bed & Breakfast
B&B **$$**

(☎ 305-294-8233, 800-848-1317; www.avalonbnb.com; 1317 Duval St; r low season $109-229, high season $189-289; ❀❈⊛) A restored Victorian house on the quiet end of Duval blends attentive service with stately old ceiling fans, tropical lounge-room rugs and black-and-white photos of old-timey Key West. Music the cat likes to greet guests at reception.

Pearl's Rainbow
B&B **$$**

(☎ 305-292-1450, 800-749-6696; www.pearlsrainbow.com; 525 United St; r incl breakfast $161-318; ❀❈⊛) Pearl's is one of the best low-key lesbian resorts in the country, an intimate garden of tropical relaxation and enticing rooms scattered across a few cottages. A clothing-optional backyard pool bar is the perfect spot for alfresco happy hour, or to enjoy your breakfast.

Chelsea House
HOTEL **$$**

(☎ 305-296-2211; www.historickeywestinns.com/the-inns/chelsea-house; 707 Truman Ave; r low season $150-210, high season from $250; ❒❀@❈⊛) This perfect pair of Victorian mansions beckons with large, vaulted rooms and big, comfy beds, with the whole shebang done out in floral (but not dated) chic. The old-school villa ambience clashes – in a nice way – with the happy vibe of the guests and the folks at reception.

★ Tropical Inn
BOUTIQUE HOTEL $$$

(☎ 888-651-6510; www.tropicalinn.com; 812 Duval St; r $175-360; ❄️🌐🏊) The Tropical Inn has excellent service and a host of individualized rooms spread out over a historic home property. Each room comes decked out in bright pastels and shades of mango, lime and seafoam. A delicious breakfast is included and can be enjoyed in the jungly courtyard next to a lovely sunken pool. Two attached cottages offer romance and privacy for couples.

Curry Mansion Inn
HOTEL $$$

(☎ 305-294-5349; www.currymansion.com; 511 Caroline St; r winter $240-365, summer $205-310; P❄️🌐🏊) In a city full of stately homes, the Curry Mansion is especially handsome. It has all the elements of an aristocratic American home, from plantation-era Southern colonnades to a New England–style widow's walk and, of course, bright Floridian rooms with canopied beds. Enjoy bougainvillea and breezes on the veranda.

Mermaid & the Alligator
GUESTHOUSE $$$

(☎ 305-294-1894; www.kwmermaid.com; 729 Truman Ave; r winter $278-348, summer $188-248; P❄️@🌐🏊) It takes a real gem to stand out amid the jewels of Keys hotels, but this place, located in a 1904 mansion, more than pulls off the job. Each of the nine rooms is individually designed with a mix of modern comfort, Keys Colonial ambience and playful laughs.

The treetop suite, with its exposed beams and alcoved bed and bathroom, is our pick of this idiosyncratic litter.

La Mer & Dewey Hotel
BOUTIQUE HOTEL $$$

(☎ 305-296-6577, 800-354-4455; www.southernmostresorts.com/lamer; 504 South St; r from $400; ❄️🌐) Nineteen rooms are spread across two historic homes, one Victorian, the other fashioned like an old-school Keys cottage. Inside, rooms come equipped with a mix of European twee antiques and sleek, modern amenities. Your porch looks out onto the Atlantic Ocean, whose breezes make for nice natural air-conditioning (not that you can't crank up the air-con in your room).

Santa Maria
BOUTIQUE HOTEL $$$

(☎ 305-600-5165; www.santamariasuites.com; 1401 Simonton St; r $300-450; P❄️🌐🏊) The Santa Maria looks like it took a wrong turn on South Beach, Miami, and ended up in Key West. It's an incredible deco edifice – the exterior should be studied by architecture students looking to identify the best of deco design, and the interior rooms call to mind a 1950s leisure lounge. The courtyard holds one of the finest hotel pools in Key West.

Gardens Hotel
HOTEL $$$

(☎ 305-294-2661, 800-526-2664; www.gardenshotel.com; 526 Angela St; r & ste low season $165-425, high season $325-665; P❄️@🏊) Would we be stating the obvious if we mentioned this place has really nice gardens? In fact, the 17 rooms are located in the Peggy Mills Botanical Gardens, which is a longish way of saying 'tropical paradise.' Inside, Caribbean accents mesh with the fine design to create a sense of green-and-white-and-wood space that never stops massaging your eyes.

Lighthouse Court Inn
BOUTIQUE HOTEL $$$

(☎ 305-294-5229, 800-549-4430; www.historickeywestinns.com/the-inns/lighthouse-court; 902 Whitehead St; r from $250; ❄️🌐🏊) The rooms at the Lighthouse Court, which sits near the Hemingway House, may be the most handsomely appointed in town. They're elegant in their simplicity, with the warm earth tones of hardwood floors set off by just the right amount of tropical breeziness and cool colors. Affiliated with Historic Key West Inns.

Silver Palms Inn
BOUTIQUE HOTEL $$$

(☎ 800-294-8783; www.silverpalmsinn.com; 830 Truman Ave; r from $319; P❄️🌐🏊) 🚲 Royal blues, sweet teals, bright limes and lemon-yellow color schemes douse the interior of this boutique property, which also boasts bicycle rentals, a saltwater swimming pool and a green certification from the Florida Department of Environmental Protection. Overall, the Silver Palms offers more of a modern, large-hotel vibe with a candy-colored dose of Keys tropics attitude.

Cypress House
HOTEL $$$

(☎ 305-294-5229, 800-549-4430; www.cypresshousekw.com; 601 Caroline St; r $219-329; P❄️🌐🏊) This plantation-like getaway has wraparound porches, leafy grounds, a secluded swimming pool and spacious, individually designed bedrooms with four-poster beds. It's lazy, lovely luxury in the heart of Old Town, and one of the most extensively renovated and converted mansions we've seen anywhere. We recommend rooms in the Main House and Simonton House over the blander guest studios.

Truman Hotel
HOTEL $$$
(☎ 866-487-8626; www.trumanhotel.com; 611 Truman Ave; r low season $195-285, high season $240-365; P✳︎❄︎❋︎⚓︎) Close to the main downtown drag, these playful rooms have huge flat-screen TVs, kitchenettes, zebra-print throw rugs and mid-century modern furniture. The bouncy, fluff-errific beds will serve you well after the inevitable Duval Crawl (which is only steps from your door). Make sure to grab a drink by the courtyard pool at the bar, which looks as if it's carved from a single stone.

Merlin Inn
GUESTHOUSE $$$
(☎ 800-549-4430; www.historickeywestinns.com/the-inns/merlin-guesthouse; 811 Simonton St; r from $240; P✳︎@⚓︎) Set in a secluded garden with a pool and elevated walkways, everything here is made from bamboo, rattan and wood. Throw in the rooms' high ceilings and exposed rafters, and this hotel oozes Colonial-tropical atmosphere.

Key Lime Inn
HOTEL $$$
(☎ 800-549-4430; www.historickeywestinns.com; 725 Truman Ave; r from $240; P❋︎⚓︎) These cozy cottages are all scattered around a tropical hardwood backdrop. Inside, the blissfully cool rooms are greener than a jade mine, with wicker furniture and tiny flat-screens on hand to keep you from ever leaving.

✕ Eating

For such a small island, Key West has a superlative range of places to eat, from delicious neighborhood holes in the wall to top-end purveyors of haute cuisine that could easily compete with the best restaurants in Miami.

For a night in, head to **Key West Food to Go** (www.keywestfoodtogo.com), which connects you to over two dozen restaurants that offer delivery service across the island.

Duetto Pizza & Gelato
ITALIAN $
(☎ 305-848-4981; 540 Greene St; mains under $10; ⏱︎8am-11pm; ✿🏠) This little pizza and gelato stand is a good-value stop for a quick slice or scoop, especially compared to the greasy cardboard pie served elsewhere in town.

Café
VEGETARIAN $
(509 Southard St; mains $7-17; ⏱︎11am-10pm Mon-Sat; ✿) The Café is the only place in Key West that exclusively caters to herbivores (OK, they have one fish dish). By day, it's a cute, sunny, earthy-crunchy luncheonette; by night, with flickering votive candles and a classy main dish (grilled, blackened tofu and polenta cakes), it's a sultry-but-healthy dining destination.

Six Toed Cat
AMERICAN $
(☎ 305-294-3318; 823 Whitehead St; mains $8-16; ⏱︎8:30am-5pm) Simple, fresh and filling breakfast and lunch fare is served here within spitting distance of the Hemingway House (p172) and the restaurant is indeed named for the author's six-toed felines. A lobster Benedict with avocado should satisfy the day's protein needs, but if you're here for lunch, don't miss the lovely fried shrimp sandwich.

Pierogi Polish Market
EASTERN EUROPEAN $
(☎ 305-292-0464; 1008 White St; mains $5-10; ⏱︎10am-8pm Mon-Sat, 11am-6pm Sun; P✿) The Keys have an enormous seasonal population of temporary workers largely drawn from Central and Eastern Europe. This is where those workers can revisit the motherland, via pierogis, dumplings, blinis (pancakes) and a great sandwich selection. Although it's called a Polish market, there's food here that caters to Hungarians, Czechs and Russians (among others).

Glazed Donuts
BAKERY $
(☎ 305-294-9142; 420 Eaton St; under $4; ⏱︎7am-3pm; ✿🏠) Doughnuts make the world go round, and you'll find some excellent examples of the genre at this cute bakery. The flavors are as eccentric as Key West itself, and reflect seasonal ingredients; past examples include blood orange marmalade, mango hibiscus and (of course) piña colada.

Seven Fish
SEAFOOD $$
(☎ 305-296-2777; www.7fish.com; 632 Olivia St; mains $17-20; ⏱︎6-10pm Wed-Mon) This simple yet elegant, tucked-away spot is the perfect place for a romantic feast of homemade gnocchi or sublime banana chicken. All that said, the way to go here is to order the fresh fish of the day. The dining room might be the Zen-est interior in the islands.

Camille's
FUSION $$
(☎ 305-296-4811; www.camilleskeywest.com; 1202 Simonton St; breakfast & lunch $4-13, dinner $15-25; ⏱︎8am-3pm & 6-10pm; ✿) This healthy and tasty neighborhood joint is a locals' place where players on the high school softball team are served by friends from science class. For 20 years the homey facade of Camille's has concealed a sharp kitchen that makes a mean chicken-salad sandwich,

stone crab claws with Dijon mayo and a macadamia-crusted yellowtail.

Point5 Lounge
FUSION $$

(☎305-296-0669; 915 Duval St; small plates $5-17; ☺5pm-midnight, to 2am Sat; ✈) Like stylish Nine One Five (p182) (which it sits above), Point5 is a good deal more sophisticated than the typical Duval St trough or frozen drink hall. It trades in fusion-style tapas with global influence, ranging from Asia (Vietnamese chicken rolls) to Europe (a cone of Belgian-style *frites*) to local (Key West shrimp). All, consequently, delicious.

Le Bistro/Croissants de France
FRENCH $$

(☎305-294-2624; 816 Duval St; mains $12-16; ☺7:30am-10pm; ✈) France comes to the Caribbean at this lovely bistro, with predictably tasty results. *Galettes* (buckwheat crepes) are filled with scallops, shrimp and crab or smoked salmon and sour cream; sweet crepes come with grilled bananas, rum and almonds, or you can just enjoy a hearty cheeseburger or some brie and baguette. The setting perfectly seizes Key West's cozy-Caribbean-chic aesthetic.

El Siboney
CUBAN $$

(900 Catherine St; mains $8-16; ☺11am-9:30pm) This is a rough-and-ready Cuban joint where the portions are big and there's no screwing around with high-end embellishment or bells and whistles. It's rice, it's beans, it's shredded beef and roasted pork, it's cooked with pride, and it's good.

Café Solé
FRENCH $$$

(☎305-294-0230; www.cafesole.com; 1029 Southard St; dinner $20-34; ☺5:30-10pm) Conch carpaccio with capers? Yellowtail fillet and foie gras? Oh yes. This locally and critically acclaimed venue is known for its cozy backporch ambience and innovative menus, cobbled together by a chef trained in southern French techniques who works with island ingredients. The memory of the anchovies on crostini makes us smile as we type.

Nine One Five
FUSION $$$

(☎305-296-0669; www.915duval.com; 915 Duval St; mains $18-34; ☺6pm-midnight; ✈) Classy Nine One Five certainly stands out from the nearby Duval detritus of alcoholic aggression and tribal band tattoos. Ignore all that and enter this immaculate, modern and elegant space, which serves a creative, New American-dips-into-Asia menu. It's all quite rich – imagine a butternut squash and almond risotto, or local lobster accompanied by duck confit potatoes.

Blue Heaven
AMERICAN $$$

(☎305-296-8666; http://blueheavenkw.homestead.com; 729 Thomas St; dinner $17-35; ☺8am-4pm, until 2pm Sun & 5-10:30pm daily; ✈) Proof that location is *nearly* everything, this is one of the quirkiest venues on an island of oddities. Customers (and a local chicken) flock to dine in the spacious courtyard where Hemingway once officiated boxing matches. This place gets packed with customers who wolf down Southern-fried takes on Keys cuisine. Restrooms are in the adjacent former brothel.

Cafe Marquesa
FUSION $$$

(☎305-292-1244; 600 Fleming St; mains $32-43; ☺6-10pm; ✈) The Marquesa is as elegant as it gets in Key West, all white tablecloths, candle light and good food to boot. The mains are French-inspired with little Floridan and Asian twists, like ginger-and-coconut-crusted mahi-mahi and a rack of Australian lamb served over a bed of couscous.

🍷 Drinking & Nightlife

Basically, Key West is a floating bar. 'No, no, it's a nuanced, multilayered island with a proud nautical and multicultural histo...' *bzzzt*! Floating bar. Bars close around 3am.

★ Green Parrot
BAR

(www.greenparrot.com; 601 Whitehead St; ☺10am-4am) The oldest bar on an island of bars, this rogues' cantina opened in the late 19th century and hasn't closed yet. The owner tells you the parachute on the ceiling is 'weighed down with termite turds,' while defunct business signs and local artwork litter the walls and the city attorney shows off her new tattoo at the pool table.

Men: check out the Hieronymus Bosch-like painting *Proverbidioms* in the restroom, surely the most entertaining urinal talk-piece on the island.

Porch
BAR

(www.theporchkw.com; 429 Caroline St; ☺10am-2am Mon-Sat, noon-2am Sun) If you're getting tired of the frat-boy bars on the Duval St strip, head to the Porch. It's a friendly little artisan beer bar that's more laid back (but hardly civilized) than your average Keys watering hole. The knowledgeable bartenders will trade jokes with you and point you in the right direction for some truly excellent brew.

Garden of Eden BAR
(224 Duval St; ⊘12pm-4am) Go to the top of this building and discover Key West's own clothing-optional drinking patio. Lest you get too excited, cameras aren't allowed, most people come clothed, and those who do elect to go *au naturel* are often...erm...older.

Captain Tony's Saloon BAR
(www.capttonyssaloon.com; 428 Greene St; ⊘10am-2am) Propagandists would have you believe the nearby megabar complex of Sloppy Joe's was Hemingway's original bar, but the physical place where the old man drank was right here, the original Sloppy Joe's location (before it was moved onto Duval St and into frat-boy hell). Hemingway's third wife (a journalist sent to profile Papa) seduced him in this very bar.

Irish Kevin's BAR
(211 Duval St; ⊘10am-2:30am) One of the most popular megabars on Duval, Kevin's has a pretty good entertainment formula pinned down: nightly live acts that are a cross between a folk singer, radio shock jock and pep-rally cheerleader. The crowd consistently goes ape-poo for acoustic covers of favorites from around 1980 onward mixed with boozy, Lee Greenwood-esque patriotic exhortations.

Basically, this is a good place to see people do tequila shots, scream 'Livin' on a Prayer'

at the top of their lungs and then inexplicably sob into their Michelobs. It's more fun than it sounds.

Hog's Breath BAR
(400 Front St; ⊘10am-2am) A good place to start the infamous Duval Pub Crawl, the Hog's Breath is a rockin' outdoor bar with good live bands and better cold Coronas.

★ Entertainment

La Te Da CABARET
(www.lateda.com; 1125 Duval St) While the outside bar is where locals gather for mellow chats over beer, you can catch high-quality drag acts – big names come here from around the country – upstairs at the fabulous Crystal Room on weekends. More low-key cabaret acts grace the downstairs lounge.

Virgilio's JAZZ
(www.virgilioskeywest.com; 524 Duval St) This bar-stage is as un-Keys as they come, and frankly, thank God for a little variety. This town needs a dark, candlelit martini lounge where you can chill to jazz and get down with some salsa, and Virgilio's handsomely provides. Enter on Applerouth Lane.

Red Barn Theatre THEATER
(☑305-296-9911; www.redbarntheatre.org; 319 Duval St) An occasionally edgy and always fun, cozy little local playhouse.

GAY & LESBIAN KEY WEST

Key West's position at the edge of the USA has always attracted artists and eccentrics, and with them a refreshing dose of tolerance. The island had one of the earliest 'out' communities in the USA, and though less true than in the past, visiting Key West is still a rite of passage for many LGBT Americans. In turn, this community has had a major impact on the local culture. Just as there is a straight trolley tour, you can hop aboard the **Gay & Lesbian Trolley Tour of Key West** (☑305-294-4603; tour $25), departing from the corner of South St and Simonton St at 11am on Saturday. The tour provides commentary on local gay lore and businesses (you'll also see the site of the infamous Monster club). It's organized by the Key West Business Guild, which represents many gay-owned businesses; the guild is housed at the **Gay & Lesbian Community Center** (☑305-292-3223; www.glcckeywest.org; 513 Truman Ave), where you can access free internet on one of the few computers, plus pick up loads of information about local gay life. For details on gay parties and events, log onto www.gaykeywestfl.com.

Gay nightlife, in many cases, blends into mainstream nightlife, with everybody kind of going everywhere these days. But the backbone of the gay bar scene can be found in a pair of cruisey watering holes that sit across the street from one another, **Bourbon St Pub** (724 Duval St) and **801 Bourbon Bar** (www.801bourbon.com; 801 Duval St), and can be summed up in five words: drag-queen-led karaoke night. For a peppier scene that includes dancing and occasional drag shows, men and women should head to **Aqua** (☑305-294-0555; www.aquakeywest.com; 711 Duval St) while women will enjoy the backyard pool bar at the women's inn Pearl's Rainbow (p179).

Tropic Cinema
CINEMA

(📞877-761-3456; www.tropiccinema.org; 416 Eaton St) Great art-house movie theater with deco frontage.

Waterfront Playhouse
THEATER

(📞305-294-5015; www.waterfrontplayhouse. com; Waterfront Playhouse, Mallory Sq) Catch high-quality musicals and dramas from the oldest-running theater troupe in Florida. The season runs November through April.

🛍 Shopping

Bright and breezy art galleries, excellent cigars, leather fetish gear and offensive T-shirts – Key West, what don't you sell?

Montage
SOUVENIRS

(512 Duval St; ⊘9am-10pm) Had a great meal or wild night at some bar or restaurant in the Keys? Well, this store probably sells the sign of the place (along with lots of Conch Republic tat), which makes for a nice souvenir.

Peppers of Key West
FOOD

(602 Greene St; ⊘10am-8pm Mon-Sat) For a downright shopping party, you should bring your favorite six-pack with you into this store and settle in at the tasting bar, where the entertaining owners use double entendres to hawk seriously mouth-burning hot sauces, like their own Right Wing Sauce (use liberally).

Bésame Mucho
GIFTS

(315 Petronia St; ⊘10am-6pm, to 4pm Sun) This place is well stocked with high-end beauty products, eclectic jewelry, clothing and housewares.

Leather Master
LEATHER

(415 Applerouth Lane; ⊘11am-10pm, to 11pm Fri & Sat, noon-5pm Sun) Besides the gladiator outfits, studded jockstraps and S&M masks, they do very nice bags and shoes here. Which is what you came for, right?

Frangipani Gallery
ARTS & CRAFTS

(1102 Duval St; ⊘10am-6pm) One of the best galleries of local artists' work.

Haitian Art Co
ARTS & CRAFTS

(📞305-296-8932; 605 Simonton St; ⊘10am-7pm) Haitian arts and crafts.

ℹ Information

Bank of America (📞305-296-1204; 510 Southard St)

Citizen (www.keysnews.com) A well-written, oft-amusing daily.

Key West Chamber of Commerce (📞305-294-2587; www.keywestchamber.org; 510 Greene St; ⊘8:30am-6:30pm Mon-Sat, to 6pm Sun) An excellent source of information.

Lower Keys Medical Center (📞305-294-5531, 800-233-3119; www.lkmc.com; 5900 College Rd, Stock Island, MM 5) Has a 24-hour emergency room.

Post Office (400 Whitehead St; ⊘8:30am-9pm Mon-Fri, 9:30am-noon Sat)

Solares Hill (www.solareshill.com) Weekly, slightly activist take on community interests.

South Med (📞305-295-3838; www.southmed. us; 3138 Northside Dr) Dr Scott Hall caters especially to the gay community, but serves all visitors.

ℹ Getting There & Around

Key West International Airport (EYW) is off S Roosevelt Blvd on the east side of the island. You can fly into Key West from some major US cities such as Miami and New York. Flights from Los Angeles and San Francisco usually have to stop in Tampa, Orlando or Miami first. **American Airlines** (📞800-433-7300) and **US Airways** (📞800-428-4322) have several flights a day. From the Key West airport, a quick and easy taxi ride into Old Town will cost about $20.

Greyhound (📞305-296-9072; www.greyhound.com; 3535 S Roosevelt Blvd) has two buses daily between Key West and downtown Miami. Buses leave Miami for the 4¼-hour journey at 12:35pm and 6:50pm and Key West at 8:55am and 5:45pm going the other way (from US$33 each way).

You can boat from Miami to the Keys on the **Key West Express** (📞888-539-2628; www. seakeywestexpress.com; adult/child round trip $147/85, one way $86/60), which departs from Fort Myers beach daily at 8:30am and does a 3½-hour cruise to Key West. Returning boats depart the seaport at 6pm. You'll want to show up 1½ hours before your boat departs. During winter and fall the Express also leaves from Marco Island (adult/child round-trip $147/85, one-way $86/60).

Once you're in Key West, the best way to get around is by bicycle (rentals from the Duval St area, hotels and hostels are about $12 a day). Other options include the **City Transit** (📞305-292-8160; tickets 75¢), with color-coded buses running about every 15 minutes; mopeds, which generally rent for $35 for four hours ($50 for a six-hour day); or the ridiculous electric tourist cars, or 'Conch cruisers,' which travel at 35mph and cost about $60/220 per hour/day.

Southeast Florida

Best Places to Eat

➜ Green Bar & Kitchen (p194)
➜ Sea (p199)
➜ Paradiso Ristorante (p205)
➜ Būccan (p210)
➜ Garage VV (p217)

Best Places to Stay

➜ Pillars (p192)
➜ Parliament Inn (p202)
➜ Brazilian Court (p209)
➜ Grandview Gardens (p216)
➜ Old Colorado Inn (p223)

Why Go?

Zooming north from Miami's tanned and diamond-draped clutches, you'll find an endearing collection of beach towns – some classy, others quirky, all unique. From activity-packed, gay- and family-friendly Fort Lauderdale to quiet, exclusive, semireclusive Palm Beach, laid-back Lauderdale-by-the-Sea and the rugged coast of Jupiter, you'll find more adventure and nightlife than you can handle. This chunk of coast also includes some of Florida's wealthiest enclaves – enjoy gawking at the castle-like beachfront mansions, but don't rear-end that $350,000 Bentley when parallel parking in front of the Gucci store in Palm Beach!

For those looking for a more down-to-earth setting, the region's numerous natural gems – secluded islands, moss-draped mangrove swamps, wild rivers, empty dunes – will surely satisfy your demands for nonmaterial pleasures.

So please, whatever you do, don't skip over this region on your journey from Miami to Disney World.

When to Go
Palm Beach

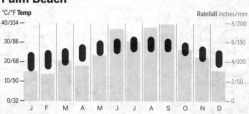

Mar & Apr Spring break hits, packing beaches with party-happy twenty-somethings.

Jun & Jul Low-season prices and turtle-nesting season.

Dec–Feb Perfect beach weather and Delray's tennis tournament.

Southeast Florida Highlights

1 Glide through mangroves past undisturbed beaches in the **John U Lloyd Beach State Park** (p187).

2 Catch some culture along **Riverwalk** (p189), Fort Lauderdale's most beautiful mile.

3 Sip *matcha* green tea at Delray Beach's serene **Morikami Museum and Japanese Gardens** (p201).

4 Dig Lake Worth's outsized nightlife scene with music at **Bamboo Room** (p205) and community theatre at the **Playhouse** (p205).

5 Enjoy the Palm Beach high-life for free: window-shop **Worth Avenue** (p207), stroll the **Lake Trail** (p207) and catch some rays at the **Municipal Beach** (p207).

6 Learn to fish, paint, sculpt and play croquet in fun-filled **West Palm Beach** (p212).

7 Get up close and personal with loggerheads and leatherback turtles as they recuperate at **Loggerhead Marinelife Center** (p221).

8 Kayak Jupiter's 'Wild and Scenic' **Loxahatchee River** (p222), for close-up views of cypress knees, mangrove forests and sunning alligators.

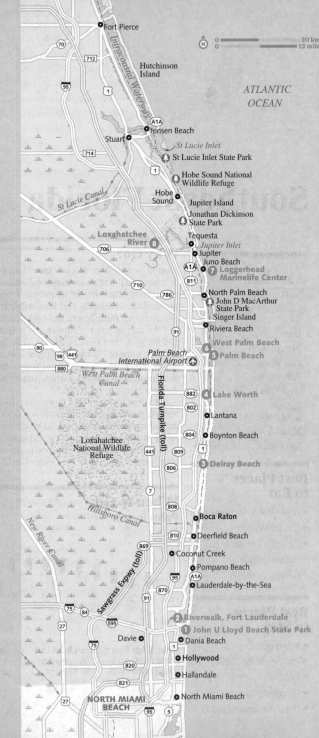

ATLANTIC OCEAN

Fort Pierce

Hutchinson Island

Jensen Beach

Stuart

St Lucie Inlet

St Lucie Inlet State Park

Hobe Sound National Wildlife Refuge

Hobe Sound

Jupiter Island

Jonathan Dickinson State Park

Tequesta

Jupiter Inlet

Jupiter

Juno Beach

Loggerhead Marinelife Center

North Palm Beach

John D MacArthur State Park

Singer Island

Riviera Beach

West Palm Beach

Palm Beach International Airport

West Palm Beach

Palm Beach

Florida Turnpike (toll)

Lake Worth

Lantana

Boynton Beach

Delray Beach

Loxahatchee National Wildlife Refuge

Boca Raton

Deerfield Beach

Coconut Creek

Pompano Beach

Lauderdale-by-the-Sea

Riverwalk, Fort Lauderdale

John U Lloyd Beach State Park

Davie

Dania Beach

Hollywood

Hallandale

North Miami Beach

NORTH MIAMI BEACH

St Lucie Canal

Loxahatchee River

West Palm Beach Canal

Hillsboro Canal

New River Canal

Sawgrass Expwy (toll)

0   20 km
0   12 miles

History

Two words: Henry Flagler. If it weren't for this deep-pocketed visionary, southeast Florida may still be overrun with cabbage palms, bloodthirsty mosquitoes and territorial gators snapping at trembling canoers. After transforming northeastern Florida into a winter wonderland in the 1870s, Flagler set his sights further south. By the mid-1890s had already completed two world-class hotels (including the 1100-room Royal Poinciana Hotel in Lake Worth, at the time the largest wooden structure in the world); established both Palm Beach and West Palm Beach; and began pushing on to Miami and the Keys.

GOLD COAST

Though the 70-or-so miles of sparkling Atlantic shoreline from Hollywood to Jupiter earned its nickname from the gold salvaged from area shipwrecks, it could easily have come from the mix of sapphire skies, cinnamony sands and bejeweled, wealthy residents.

Here, the coastline has a split personality. First, there's slow-going, ocean-fronting Rte 1, a pleasant drive revealing infinite vistas of unspoiled beaches...though occasionally it feels like driving through a condo canyon. Second, there's older Dixie Hwy, running parallel to Rte 1 but further inland, past dive bars and working-class communities. Drive both stretches; each is rich with divergent offerings.

Hollywood & Dania Beach

Two 'suburban Fort Lauderdale' communities have managed to make names for themselves. Hollywood, a bustling waterfront town that positions itself as a gateway to Fort Lauderdale, has earned a sizable wedge of the spring break market since Lauderdale gave revelers the boot. The resulting influx brings with it concerts in the sand, beach-volleyball tourneys and assorted debauchery each March. These days, the city's trying to glam up its image with several new South Beach–style developments.

In contrast, Dania (*dane*-ya) remains a mellow little town, with a fledgling antiques district and a breezy fishing pier.

⊙ Sights & Activities

Hollywood is divided into two distinct zones: the hotel-lined beach strip and a characterful downtown listed on the National Register of Historic Places.

Hollywood Beach & Broadwalk   BEACH
Reminiscent of California's famed Venice Beach, this beach and adjacent promenade teem with scantily clad Rollerbladers and fanny-pack-wearing tourists. The Broadwalk itself is a 2.2 mile, six-person-wide path, extending from pretty **North Beach Park** (3601 N Ocean Dr; ⊙11am-5pm) **FREE**, where the route is lined with seagrapes, all the way to **South Surf Road**. It's regularly clogged with skaters, strollers and entire families pedaling enormous group bikes. The latter like to stop at **Charnow Park** (300 Garfield St), where there's shaded seating and a popular interactive fountain.

If you feel like rolling along it, a dozen or so Broadwalk vendors rent bikes (per hour/day $10/30), Rollerblades and other beach gear.

John U Lloyd
Beach State Park   KAYAKING, DIVING
(www.floridastateparks.org/lloydbeach; 6503 North Ocean Dr, Dania Beach; per vehicle/cyclist $6/2; ⊙8am-sundown) Once an important stop for Prohibition-era bootleggers, lush Whiskey Creek (get it?) is now a kayaking hot spot. The dense mangrove-lined route meanders 1.5 miles through the park, and is shallow and calm. There's also 2.5 miles of undisturbed beach to enjoy. At the northern end is the Port Everglades inlet, where cruise ships and yachts sail past, while at the southern end you'll find the **Dania Beach fishing pier**. The park also offers some of the best offshore snorkeling and diving in the county and is an important turtle nesting area.

The **Loggerhead Cafe** at the north end of the park provides kayak and canoe rentals.

West Lake Park   KAYAKING, HIKING
(☏954-357-5161; www.broward.org/parks/west-lakepark; 1200 Sheridan St, Hollywood; per person/car $1.50/8; ⊙9am-5pm) This 1500 acre park is a rarity in Broward County. It's wild. Fortunately, environmentalists in the 1970s managed to save it from development, forever preserving its tangle of mangroves, wetlands and wildlife. These days it's one of the most accessible natural places for kayaking, biking and hiking within a largely built-up

SOUTHEAST FLORIDA HOLLYWOOD & DANIA BEACH

area. From Thursday to Friday, canoeists and kayakers can rent boats (1/2/4 hours $14/24/30) from the marina and paddle through the mangrove trails, maps of which are provided at the gatehouse.

On the north side of Sheridan Street the **Anne Kolb Nature Centre** (751 Sheridan St; admission $2; ⊙ 9am-5pm) encompasses a further 1501 acres of coastal mangroves crisscrossed with hiking trails and offering views over the lake. A variable schedule of environmental boat trails also departs from here (adult/under-18s $5/3).

🛏 Sleeping

Although both Hollywood and Dania abound with characterful period motels and guesthouses, in 2013 a large chunk of the Broadwalk was signed over in a public–private partnership to develop the new Jimmy Buffett Margaritaville Beach Resort. Scheduled for completion in 2015, the 6-acre, island-themed resort will feature a 350-room hotel, multiple restaurants, shopping outlets and and an extensive water recreation area.

★ Hollywood Beach
Hotel & Hostel   HOTEL, HOSTEL $
(🏠 954-391-9441; www.hollywoodbeachhostel. com; 334 Arizona St, Hollywood; dm/r from $22/88; ✳ @ 🛜) This slick complex combines dorms with a warren of whitewashed, vaguely Moroccan-looking motel units. Friendly staff, a clean and bright common kitchen, bike and surfboard rentals, and a deck with hammock chairs add sociability. This is generally a quiet place, however, which appeals to families as well as the traditional backpacker types.

Walkabout Beach Resort   BOUTIQUE HOTEL $$
(🏠 954-272-6000; www.walkaboutbeachresort. com; 2500 North Surf Rd; d $174-259; ✳🛜) If you blink you might just miss this classic, baby-pink art-deco hotel which sits curvaceously on the Broadwalk gazing out to sea. There are just eight rooms, all of which are equipped with kitchenette, dining table and foldout couch. Wooden and terrazzo floors, vintage black-and-white photographs and furnishings, and a miniature on-site tiki bar all combine to create a retro beachside getaway. Come the 4th July, you even have front-row seats for the fireworks.

Seminole Hard Rock
Hotel & Casino   HOTEL $$$
(🏠 866-502-7529; www.seminolehardrockholly-wood.com; 1 Seminole Way, Hollywood; r $169-519;

✳🛜📺) This Mediterranean-style monster provides everything you'd ever need under one massive roof. In this case, it's casinos, eateries, theaters, a day spa, 500 swank guestrooms and some of the most alluring concert bills in the state. It's all very Vegas. Except for the 4.5 acre lagoon-style pool surrounding a bar – *that's* out of this world.

🍴 Eating

Unless you find yourself starving in the middle of your inline-skating session, give most of the Broadwalk restaurants a miss – they're overpriced, overcrowded and mediocre. There are better eats to be found along Ocean Dr or in downtown Hollywood.

If you're in town on a Monday, head downtown to the **ArtsPark** (Young Circle, off US1), where you'll find a gathering of food trucks from 5.30pm to 10pm.

★ Tarks of Dania Beach   SEAFOOD $
(🏠 954-925-8275; www.tarks.com; 1317 S Federal Hwy, Dania Beach; mains $2-9) This jaunty clam stand has been going strong since 1966 and is now a local landmark. Most of the tiny interior is taken up with the cooking counter, where they broil, fry and steam daily specials. These usually include a combination of steamed, fried and raw clams alongside shrimp, oysters, snow crab and spicy chicken wings. It can get crazy busy, but food usually vanishes so fast you won't be waiting long.

Jaxson's Ice Cream Parlor   ICE CREAM $
(www.jaxsonsicecream.com; 128 S Federal Hwy, Dania; ice cream from $4; ⊙ 11:30am-11pm Sun-Thu, to midnight Fri & Sat; 🚸) Established in 1956, this place has 80-plus flavors of homemade ice cream.

Taco Beach Shack   MEXICAN $
(www.tacobeachshack.com; 334 Arizona St, Hollywood; tacos $4-10; ⊙ 11:30am-10pm Mon-Thu, to midnight Fri & Sat) Hipsters and hangers-on lounge around on wicker chaises at this open-air taqueria. The menu (written on a surfboard) has a very of-the-moment mix of ethnic flavors – try the Korean short rib and kimchi tacos. You'll feel cooler just by eating one.

Le Comptoir   FRENCH $$
(🏠 786-718-9441; www.lecomptoir.menubaron. com; 1902 Harrison St; mains $17.50-26; ⊙ 5-10pm) It's worth making the trip Downtown for this classic bistro. You'll dine on bowls heaped high with mussels stewed in white wine and Provençal sauces, and dusted

with vibrant green parsley. Other signature French dishes include duck with an orange glaze, escargot bathed in garlic and succulent peppered steak.

🔒 Shopping

Josh's Organic Garden   FOOD
(cnr Harrison & S Broadwalk, Hollywood; ⊙9am-5:30pm Sun) 🌿 Beneath tents overlooking the ocean, Josh sells 100% certified organic fruits, veggies, nuts and juices in PLA cups (made from corn, and so compostable, like the bags he provides). Buy lots, because it's good for you, but don't worry: whatever remains is donated to a homeless shelter. An adjacent juice stand whips up killer smoothies.

ℹ️ Information

Greater Dania Beach Chamber of Commerce (☑ 954-926-2323; www.daniabeachchamber. org; 102 W Dania Beach Blvd; ⊙9am-5pm)
Hollywood Office of Tourism (☑ 954-924-2980; www.visithollywoodfl.org; 330 N Federal Hwy; ⊙9am-5pm)

ℹ️ Getting There & Around

An old-fashioned trolley travels between downtown Hollywood and the beach from 10am to 10pm Wednesday through Sunday. Fares are $1; bright-colored signs mark the stops.

Broward County Transit (www.broward.org/bct) buses serve Hollywood and Dania, connecting them with Fort Lauderdale. Fares are $1.75.

To shoot north to West Palm Beach or south to Miami from either city, head to the Fort Lauderdale-Hollywood International Airport on BCT bus 1 and jump on **Tri-Rail** (www.tri-rail.com; 200 Terminal Dr).

Parking at the beach in Hollywood is hellacious – if you can't find on-street parking (per hour $2), try the parking deck on Johnson St.

Fort Lauderdale

After years of building a reputation as *the* destination for beer-swilling college students on raucous spring breaks, Fort Lauderdale now angles for a slightly more mature and sophisticated crowd. Think martinis rather than tequila shots, jazz concerts instead of wet T-shirt contests. But don't worry, there's still plenty of carrying-on within the confines of area bars and nightclubs.

Few visitors venture far inland – except maybe to dine and shop along Las Olas Blvd; most spend the bulk of their time on the coast. It's understandable. Truly, it's hard to compete with beautiful beaches, a system of Venice-like waterways, an international yachting scene, spiffy new hotels and top-notch restaurants.

The city's Port Everglades is one of the busiest cruise-ship ports in the world, with megaships departing daily for the Caribbean, Mexico and beyond.

⊙ Sights

⭐**Riverwalk**
& Las Olas Riverfront   WATERFRONT
Curving along the New River, the meandering **Riverwalk** (Map p194; www.goriverwalk.com) runs from Stranahan House to the Broward Center for the Performing Arts. Host to culinary tastings and other events, the walk connects a number of sights, restaurants and shops. **Las Olas Riverfront** (Map p194; cnr SW 1st Ave & Las Olas Blvd) is basically a giant alfresco shopping mall with stores, restaurants and live entertainment nightly; it's also the place to catch many river cruises.

Fort Lauderdale Beach
& Promenade   BEACH
Fort Lauderdale's promenade – a wide, brick, palm-tree-dotted pathway swooping along the beach and the A1A – is a magnet for runners, in-line skaters, walkers and cyclists. The white-sand beach, meanwhile, is one of the nation's cleanest and best. Stretching 7 miles to Lauderdale-by-the-Sea, it has dedicated family-, gay- and dog-friendly sections. Boating, diving, snorkeling and fishing are all extremely popular.

Bonnet House   HISTORIC BUILDING
(Map p190; ☑954-563-5393; www.bonnethouse. org; 900 N Birch Rd; adult/child $20/16, grounds only $10; ⊙10am-4pm Tue-Sat, from 11am Sun) This pretty plantation-style property was once the home of artists and collectors Frederic and Evelyn Bartlett. It is now open to guided tours that swing through its art-filled rooms and studios. Beyond the house, 35 acres of lush, subtropical gardens protect a pristine barrier-island ecosystem, including one of the finest orchid collections in the country.

Stranahan House   HISTORIC BUILDING
(Map p194; ☑954-524-4736; www.stranahanhouse. org; 335 SE 6th Ave; adult/student $12/7; ⊙tours 1pm, 2pm & 3pm) Constructed from Dade County pine, grand Stranahan House is a fine example of Florida vernacular design, and one

SOUTHEAST FLORIDA FORT LAUDERDALE

Fort Lauderdale Beach

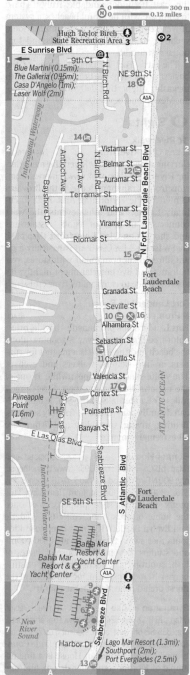

of the state's oldest homes. It served as both home and store for Ohio transplant Frank Stranahan, who built a small empire trading with the Seminoles before committing suicide by jumping into the New River after real-estate and stock-market losses in the late 1920s. The house, with many original furnishings, is open daily for three hour-long tours.

Docents from the house also guide a fun hour-long River Ghost Tour ($25 per person) in conjunction with the water taxi. Tours depart from the house (and include a tour inside) at 7:30pm every Sunday.

Museum of Art Fort Lauderdale MUSEUM
(Map p194; www.moafl.org; 1 E Las Olas Blvd; adult/student/child $10/5/free; ⊙11am-5pm Mon-Sat, noon-5pm Sun) A curvaceous Florida standout known for its William Glackens collection (among Glackens fans) and its exhibitions on wide-ranging themes from northern European art to contemporary Cuban art, American pop art and contemporary photography. On Thursday evenings, the museum stays open late and hosts lectures, films

and performances, as well as a happy hour in the museum cafe. Day courses and workshops are also available. Check the website for details.

Hugh Taylor Birch
State Recreation Area PARK
(Map p190; 3109 E Sunrise Blvd; per vehicle/bike $6/2; ⊙8am-sunset) This lusciously tropical park contains one of the last significant maritime hammocks in Broward County. There are mangroves and a freshwater lagoon system (great for birding) and several endangered plants and animals (including the golden leather fern and gopher tortoise). You can fish, picnic, stroll the short Coastal Hammock Trail or cycle the 1.9 mile park drive. Canoe rentals, to be used on the half-mile trail, cost about $6 per hour. Kayaks cost $10 per hour for use in the lagoon and $20 per hour in the ocean.

Museum of Discovery & Science MUSEUM
(Map p194; www.mods.org; 401 SW 2nd St; adult/child $14/12; ⊙10am-5pm Mon-Sat, noon-6pm Sun; 🐾) A 52ft kinetic-energy sculpture greets you here, and fun exhibits include Gizmo City and Runways to Rockets – where it actually *is* rocket science. Plus there's an Everglades exhibit and IMAX theater.

🏃 Activities

Fort Lauderdale lies on the same reef system as the Keys. Snorkeling is a popular pastime but the real action in the water lies within a 50-minute boat ride at the site of some two-dozen wrecks. Here divers can nose around the *Mercedes* freighter and the Tenneco Towers artificial reef made up from an old oil platform. Soft corals bloom prolifically and barracuda, jacks and parrotfish duck and dive between the wreckage.

Besides the underwater scenery, everything from Waverunners to parasailing to deep-sea fishing charters is available at the beach. If you want to tool around in your own boat, try **Best Boat Club** (Map p190; 954-779-3866; www.fortlauderdaleboatrentals.com; Bahia Mar Yachting Center, 801 Seabreeze Blvd; per day from $100), which rents everything from single-engine 21ft Bowriders to luxurious 27ft Crownlines.

⭐ Sea Experience BOATING, SNORKELING
(Map p190; 954-770-3483; www.seaxp.com; 801 Seabreeze Blvd; snorkeling adult/child $35/21; ⊙10:15am & 2:15pm daily; 🐾) Takes guests in a 40ft glass-bottom boat along the Intracoast-al and into the ocean to snorkel on a natural reef, thriving with marine life, in 10ft to 20ft of water. Also offers scuba trips to multiple wreck sites and the Tenneco Towers from $55.

Fish Lauderdale FISHING
(Map p190; 954-805-3474; www.fishlauderdale.com; 1005 Seabreeze Blvd; up to 6 people per hr $125; ⊙8am-sunset) The waters off Fort Lauderdale are rich with marlin, sailfish, snapper, tarpon, wahoo and more. Naturally, there are plenty of fishing charters available – this outfit has four boats to take you trolling for dinner.

Fort Lauderdale Parasail PARASAILING
(Map p190; 954-462-7266; www.ftlauderdaleparasail.com; 1005 Seabreeze Blvd; flights $70-95) If you're curious how the mansions along Millionaires' Row look from above, sign up for a parasailing trip. You'll soar between 600ft and 1000ft above the waves while strapped securely to an enormous smiley-face parachute.

🧭 Tours

Fort Lauderdale's miles of canals make it one of the top spots in Florida for boat tours.

⭐ Atlantic Coast
Kayak Company KAYAKING
(954-781-0073; www.atlanticcoastkayak.com; Richardson Historical Park Boat Dock, 1937 Wilton Dr; single/double per hr $16/24, single/double per half-day $40/60; ⊙9am-5pm) An excellent alternative to tour-boat cruises is to rent your own kayak in Richardson Park and paddle the 7.5 mile (roughly 2.5 to three hours) Middle River loop around the Island City yourself. Day, sunset and moonlight tours, including basic instruction and gourmet sandwiches and soft drinks, are also available on a scheduled calendar. All you need to do is turn up.

Paddleboard instruction and rental is also available.

Carrie B BOAT TOUR
(Map p194; 954-642-1601; www.carriebcruises.com; 440 N New River Dr E; tours adult/child $23/13; ⊙tours 11am, 1pm & 3pm) Hop aboard this replica 19th-century riverboat for a narrated 90-minute 'lifestyles of the rich and famous' tour of the ginormous mansions along the Intracoastal and New River. Tours leave from Las Olas at SE 5th Ave.

Jungle Queen Riverboat BOAT TOUR
(Map p190; 954-462-5596; www.junglequeen.com; 801 Seabreeze Blvd; adult/child $20/13;

SOUTHEAST FLORIDA FORT LAUDERDALE

⊙tours 9:30am & 1:30pm) Runs three-hour tours along the waterfront, Millionaires' Row and part of the Everglades on a Mississippi-style paddle-wheeler. In addition to taking daily sightseeing cruises, you can also hop aboard the four-hour evening barbecue cruise at 6pm. It has all-you-can-eat shrimp or ribs, and entertainment (adult/child $43/23).

Gondola Man
BOAT TOUR

(Map p194; ☑201-919-1999; www.gondolaman. com; SE 1st Ave; tour $150) Explore the 'Venice of America' with a romantic ride in an original Venetian gondola, accompanied by Italian music. The tour lasts roughly 75 minutes and takes you past the homes of the rich and famous.

🛌 Sleeping

The splashiest hotels are found along the beach. Of course, those places are also the priciest. Meander inland and you'll discover some wonderful inns with Old Florida charm, many of which exclusively welcome gay guests. For more budget-friendly accommodation, check out Lauderdale-by-the-Sea.

Sea Club Resort
MOTEL $

(Map p190; ☑954-564-3211; www.seaclubresort. com; 619 Fort Lauderdale Beach Blvd; r from $93; P❄🛎🖭) After extensive remodeling this funky beachfront motel, which looks to all intents and purposes as if a spaceship has landed beachside, now sports fashion-forward rooms with plum-colored accents, new carpets and even plump pillowtop mattresses. With ocean views, free beach towels and chairs, and a resident parrot named Touki, it's unique.

★ Island Sands Inn
B&B $$

(☑954-990-6499; www.islandsandsinn.com; 2409 NE 7th Ave, Wilton Manors; r $129-209; P❄🛎🖭) It's hard to say whether it's the ultrathick beach towels, the luxurious bed and bedding, the thoughtful attention to details (tissues, bath products, mini-bar, microwave – you name it, they've thought about it) or the utterly unpretentious *ease* of the place that makes Island Sands Inn so comfortable and accommodating. Certainly your charming hosts, Mike and Jim, unobtrusively ensure that you get the best from your stay, whether it's serving up that 'just-so' bloody Mary or supplying you with great recommendations for tried-and-tested Wilton Manors hot spots.

Riverside Hotel
HOTEL $$

(Map p194; ☑954-467-0671; www.riversidehotel. com; 620 E Las Olas Blvd; r $129-239; P❄🛎🖭🖭)

This Fort Lauderdale landmark (c 1936), fabulously located downtown on Las Olas, has three room types: larger, executive rooms in the newer 12-story tower, and 'traditional' and 'classic' rooms in the historic 1936 building. The classic rooms overlooking Las Olas are the pick of the bunch.

Alhambra Beach Resort
HOTEL $$

(Map p190; ☑954-525-7601; www.alhambra-beachresort.com; 3021 Alhambra St; r $119-199; P❄🛎🖭) Beloved for its reasonable prices and warm-hearted owners, this charming 1930s-era inn has modest-but-immaculate rooms and suites painted in cheerful buttercup yellow, and a pleasant pool deck amid a manicured garden of palms and hibiscus. A gate adds a private feel, though the beach is only half a block away. Lots of return-guests means the place books up quickly.

Tranquilo
MOTEL $$

(Map p190; ☑954-565-5790; www.tranquilofort-lauderdale.com; 2909 Vistamar St; d $119-189, ste $119-219; P❄🛎🖭) With a successful white-on-white decorative facelift, this retro 1950s motel offers fantastic value for families. Rooms range over three buildings, each with their own pool, and include newly refurbed kitchens along with access to outdoor grills and laundry services. Complimentary shuttle service to the beach, three blocks away.

Sheraton Fort Lauderdale Beach Hotel
HOTEL $$

(Map p190; ☑954-524-5551; www.sheratonft-lauderdalebeach.com; 1140 Seabreeze Blvd; r $169-500; P❄🛎🖭) Defining the southern end of Seabreeze Blvd, this Sheraton hotel straddles the uberpopular South Beach and offers breezy ocean views from the majority of its aqua-and-white styled rooms. Built by M Tony Sherman in 1956, it looks like a giant cruise ship tethered to the sidewalk. Its 'hull', the Wreck Bar (p196), offers porthole views on the underwater world of the swimming pool. Come at the weekend and you'll be able to catch the mermaid show.

★ Pillars
B&B $$$

(Map p190; ☑954-467-9639; www.pillarshotel. com; 111 N Birch Rd; r $199-569; P❄🛎🖭) From the harp in the sitting area to the private balconies and the intimate prearranged dinners for two, this tiny boutique B&B radiates hushed good taste and is often booked months in advance. A block from the beach, it faces one of the best sunsets in town.

Pineapple Point   GUESTHOUSE **$$$**
(☑888-844-7295; www.pineapplepoint.com; 315
NE 16th Tce; r $298, ste $429-449; P❊@🛜🏊)
Tucked away in a quiet residential neighbor-
hood, this guesthouse caters exclusively to
a loyal gay male clientele. Suites and apart-
ments are bright and beachy, all clustered
around a handful of pools, hot tubs and
tree-shaded sitting areas. Daily happy hours
ensure mingling, and the super-friendly
staff know all the best restaurants and gay
bars in town. Located six blocks north of E
Las Olas Blvd, east off SE 16th Ave.

W   HOTEL **$$$**
(Map p190; ☑954-414-8200; www.wfortlauderd-
alehotel.com; 401 N Fort Lauderdale Beach Blvd; r
$249-865; P❊@🛜🏊) With an exterior re-
sembling two giant sails and an interior that
looks like the backdrop for a J Lo video, this
is where the glitterati stay – bust out your
stiletto heels/skinny ties and join them. The
massive lobby is built for leisure, with a sil-
ver-and-aqua lounge area, a moodily lit bar,
and a deck lined with wicker chaises. Swank,
modern rooms are done up in a monochro-
matic palette of sand, silver and cream.

Lago Mar Resort   RESORT **$$$**
(☑800-524-6627, 954-523-6511; www.lagomar.
com; 1700 S Ocean Lane; r $205-560; P❊@🏊)
🏊 On the south end of South Beach, this
wonderfully noncorporate resort has it all:
a private beach, over-the-top grand lobby,
massive island-style rooms, a full-service
spa, on-site eateries, a lagoon-style pool set
amid tropical plantings and the personal
touch of family ownership.

✖ Eating

Fort Lauderdale's food scene is heavily influ-
enced by the area's large Italian American
population. Las Olas Blvd has the bulk of
the nicer eating places, especially the stretch
between 5th and 16th Aves.

★Gran Forno   ITALIAN **$**
(Map p194; http://gran-forno.com; 1235 E Las Olas
Blvd; mains $6-12; ⊙7am-6pm Tue-Sun) This de-
lightfully old-school Milanese-style bakery
and cafe is the best lunch spot in downtown
Fort Lauderdale: warm crusty pastries, bub-
bling pizzas, and fat golden loaves of ciabat-
ta, sliced and stuffed with ham, roast pep-
pers, pesto and other delicacies.

11th Street Annex   AMERICAN **$**
(☑954-767-8306; www.twouglysisters.com; 14 SW
11th St; lunch $9; ⊙11:30am-2pm Mon-Fri; 🍴) In
this off-the-beaten-path peach cottage, the
'two ugly sisters' serve whatever strikes their
fancy: perhaps brie mac 'n' cheese, chicken
confit and sour cream chocolate cake. Most
of the vegetables are grown from the cot-
tage's garden, and there's always a vegetarian
option on the menu. It's located a mile south
of E Las Olas Blvd, just off S Andrews Ave.

Lester's Diner   DINER **$**
(http://lestersdiner.com; 250 W State Rd 84; mains
$4-17; ⊙24hr; 🍴) Hailed endearingly as a
greasy spoon, campy Lester's Diner has been

SOUTHEAST FLORIDA FORT LAUDERDALE

BAHAMAS DAY TRIPS

Just 55 miles east of Florida, the Bahamian island of Grand Bahama is close enough for
a day trip or overnight cruises. A couple of operators ply the 'quickie cruise' territory,
although the reality is most overnight trips take the form of a booze cruise rather than
conjuring ocean-borne gentility. The best overnight provider, Bahamas Celebration
(☑800-314-7735; www.bahamascelebration.com; trips from $120) leaves Palm Beach in the
afternoon, spends the night at sea, then docks in Grand Bahama the following morning
for a day of island activities before returning that evening. It's furnished with several
bars, a casino, four restaurants, a spa and a kids club, and cabins range from bare-bones
to luxe. For a more relaxed and luxurious experience, consider at least a three- or four-
night excursion with either Princess Cruises (☑0843-374-4444; www.princess.com) or
Royal Caribbean (☑0844-493-4005; www.royalcaribbean.com). They start around $120
per night, depart Fort Lauderdale in the early evening and dock in Nassau the following
morning before returning to the US. This way you get at least a whole day in the Baha-
mas and do all your sailing overnight.

Peak season is between February and August, when many cruises sell out. For the best
deals search out fall cruises, particularly for weekday sailings. International travellers
should note the drinking age in US waters is 21 and in international waters 18. Yes, you
need a passport.

Fort Lauderdale

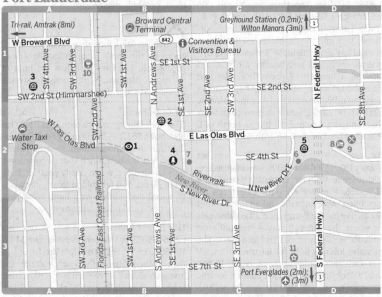

keeping folks happy since the late 1960s. Everyone makes their way here at some point, from business types on cell phones to clubbers and blue-haired ladies with third husbands. Lester's is between downtown Fort Lauderdale and the airport.

★ **Green Bar & Kitchen** VEGAN **$$**
(📞954-533-7507; www.greenbarkitchen.com; 1075 SE 17th St; mains $8-14; ⊗11am-9pm Mon-Sat, 9am-3pm Sun; 🍽) Discover bright flavors and innovative dishes at this cult vegan eatery. Instead of pasta-layered lasagna, slithers of zucchini are layered with macadamia ricotta and sundried tomatoes. Almond milk replaces dairy in cold-pressed fruit smoothies, and the delectable cashew cup gives Reese's a run for its money. To reach it from the beach continue south on A1A and cross the Intracoastal Waterway to Southport. After two miles turn right into the shopping mall.

Casablanca Cafe MEDITERRANEAN **$$**
(Map p190; 📞954-764-3500; www.casablanca-cafeonline.com; 3049 Alhambra St; mains $10-30; ⊗11:30am-2am) Try to score a seat on the upstairs balcony of this Moroccan-style home where Mediterranean-inspired food and Florida-style ocean views are served. Live music Wednesdays through Sundays.

Southport Raw Bar SEAFOOD **$$**
(📞954-525-2526; www.southportrawbar.com; 1536 Cordova Rd; mains $5.50-18; ⊗11-2am; 🅿) A local favorite serving spiced shrimp, cheese steaks, roast pork hoagies and pitchers of beer – all Southport staples. Clams and oysters are shucked to order, and there's a whole variety

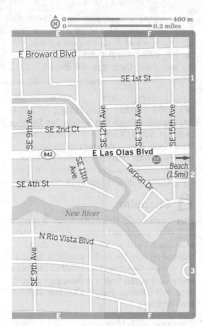

15th Street Fisheries
SEAFOOD $$$

(📞 954-763-2777; www.15streetfisheries.com; 1900 SE 15th St; bar mains $6-16, restaurant mains $26-38; P) Tucked away in Lauderdale Marina with a broad, open-fronted deck offering a front row view of yachts and motor boats, this place is hard to beat for waterfront dining. The warm wooden interior is kitted out like an Old Florida boathouse with a fine-dining restaurant upstairs and a more informal dockside bar serving shrimp, crab cakes and grilled mahi mahi beside the water. At the weekends there's live music from 6pm to 10pm.

You can also reach the Fisheries via the water taxi.

Eduardo de San Angel
MEXICAN $$$

(📞 954-772-4731; www.eduardodesanangel.com; 2822 E Commercial Blvd; mains $24-34; ⊘ 5:30am-10pm Mon-Sat) Dreamy upscale Mexican food full of romantic ingredients – squash blossoms! Chocolate-chili! Guava syrup! – served in a warmly elegant dining room full of Mexican folk art. The restaurant is north of downtown, nearly in Lauderdale-by-the-Sea.

🍷 Drinking & Entertainment

Fort Lauderdale bars can stay open until 4am on weekends and 2am during the week. A handful of bars and pubs are found in the Himmarshee Village area on SW 2nd St, while the beach offers plenty of open-air boozing.

⭐ Stache
COCKTAIL BAR

(Map p194; 📞 954-449-1044; http://stacheftl.com; 109 SW 2nd Ave; ⊘ 5pm-4am) Stache is a sexy 1920s drinking den serving crafted cocktails and rocking a crossover classic rock/funk/soul/R&B blend. At weekends there's live music, dancing and burlesque. Dress up; this is where the cool cats come to play.

Laser Wolf
BAR

(www.laserwolf.com; 901 Progresso Dr, Suite 101) We don't want to call Laser Wolf sophisticated, but its extensive booze menu and pop-art styling definitely attracts Fort Lauderdale's cerebral set. But they're a cerebral set that *loves* to party, so if this wolf is sophisticated, it knows how to let its hair down. To run with the pack, head 2 miles west along Sunrise Blvd before turning left onto NE 4th Ave, which merges with Progresso Dr.

Blue Martini
COCKTAIL BAR

(📞 954-653-2583; www.bluemartinilounge.com; 2432 E Sunrise Blvd, Ste 1008; cover $10; ⊘ 2pm-2am) Live music, hot staff and high-energy bands. The half-price happy hour is the best in town.

of fried baskets and seafood platters, including blackened mahi mahi. The cavernous interior is dark and usually crowded; wait for outdoor seating and marina views.

Rustic Inn
SEAFOOD $$

(📞 954-584-1637; www.rusticinn.com; 4331 Ravenswood Rd; mains $9.50-30; ⊘ 11:30am-10:30pm Mon-Sat, noon-9:30pm Sun) Hungry locals at this messy, noisy crab house use wooden mallets at long, newspaper-covered tables to get at the Dungeness, blue and golden crabs drenched in garlic. The Inn is located on the Dania Cut-Off Canal on the west side of the airport. To reach it take I-95 S and exit 23 onto Ravenswood Rd.

⭐ Casa D'Angelo
ITALIAN $$$

(📞 954-564-1234; http://casa-d-angelo.com; 1201 N Federal Hwy; mains $25-50; ⊘ 5:30-10:30pm) Chef Angelo Elia presides over an impressive kitchen specializing in Tuscan and southern Italian dishes, many handed down by his mother. Seasonality and quality translate into intense flavors and delightful textures: the sunburst taste of just-ripe tomatoes, peppery arugula, silken sea bass and surprisingly spicy cinnamon gelato. The restaurant stocks one of the finest wine lists in the state. The restaurant sits canal-side on North Federal Hwy, 1.4 miles north of East Sunrise Blvd.

Wreck Bar
BAR

(Map p190; Sheraton Fort Lauderdale; ☑954-524-5551; 1140 Seabreeze Blvd; ⊗5:30-11:30pm) After one too many cocktails you might wonder whether you're seeing things as you look through the Wreck Bar's 'portholes' to see MeduSirena, Fort Lauderdale's fire-eating mermaid, start her Friday and Saturday shows. Advice: keep drinking and enjoy this piece of priceless Florida kitsch. The show begins at 6:30pm, but you'll want to get there early for a seat.

Lulu's Bait Shack
BAR

(Map p190; www.lulusbaitshack.com; 17 S Atlantic Blvd; ⊗11am-1am) Lures 'em in with buckets of beer, bowls of mussels and fishbowl drinks at the ocean's edge.

★Cinema Paradiso
CINEMA

(Map p194; ☑954-525-3456; www.fliff.com/Cinema_Paradiso; 503 SE 6th St) This funky church-turned-cinema offers plush velvet seats, film festival entries, independent and European films, and plenty of kid-friendly programs. It's a great rainy-day standby. Events and films are posted on its Facebook page.

Blue Jean Blues
JAZZ

(☑954-306-6330; www.bluejeanblues.net; 3220 NE 33rd St; pizza $4-13; ⊗11-2am Sun-Thu, to 3am Fri & Sat) Get away from the beach for a low-key evening of jazz and blues at this cool little neighborhood bar. There's live music seven nights a week and four afternoons, featuring a who's who of the southern Florida music scene. It also serves a mean pizza. From East Sunrise Blvd head north for 2.3 miles and then turn left onto NE 33rd Street.

Tonic Lounge & Club
CLUB

(Map p190; www.tonicclubandlounge.com; 837 N Fort Lauderdale Beach Blvd; ⊗5pm-2am Sun-Thu, to 3am Fri & Sat) Ocean views and sky-slicing laser displays provide a perfect backdrop for your beachside party at this rooftop lounge. More-focused drinkers can retire for pub-style drinking downstairs in McSorley's.

🔒 Shopping

Fort Lauderdale Beach Blvd has a gaggle of T-shirt shops and sunglasses huts, while Las Olas is lined with swanky boutiques and antiques shops. For outlet shopping, head to the massive Sawgrass Mills Mall or the more centrally located Galleria (www.galleriamall-fl.com; 2414 E Sunrise Blvd; ⊗10am-9pm Mon-Sat, noon-6pm Sun).

Sawgrass Mills Mall
MALL

(www.simon.com/mall/sawgrass-mills; 12801 W Sunrise Blvd, Sunrise; ⊗10am-9:30pm Mon-Sat, 11am-8pm Sun) America's sixth-largest mall, Sawgrass features 350-plus name-brand stores and outlets, so budget a whole day. The mall is 13 miles northwest of downtown.

GAY & LESBIAN FORT LAUDERDALE

Sure, South Beach is a mecca for gay travelers, but lately Fort Lauderdale has been nipping at the high heels of its southern neighbor. Compared to South Beach, Lauderdale is a little more rainbow-flag oriented and a little less exclusive. And for the hordes of gay boys who flock here, either to party or to settle down, therein lies the charm.

Fort Lauderdale is home to several dozen gay bars and clubs, as many gay guesthouses, and a couple of way-gay residential areas. Victoria Park is the established gay hub just northeast of downtown Fort Lauderdale. A bit further north, Wilton Manors is a more recently gay-gentrified area boasting endless nightlife options. Look for Bill's (www.billsfillingstation.com; 2209 Wilton Dr; ⊗4pm-2am), a friendly 'bear' bar; Rosie's (☑954-563-0123; www.rosiesbarandgrill.com; 2449 Wilton Dr; ⊗11am-11pm), a low-key neighborhood watering hole; The Manor (www.themanorcomplex.com; 2345 Wilton Dr; ⊗8pm-4am), for nationally recognized performers and an epic dance floor; and Georgie's Alibi (www.georgiesalibi.com; 2266 Wilton Dr; ⊗11-2am), best for its Wednesday comedy night with Cashetta, a fabulous female impersonator. There's even a gay sports bar, Sidelines (☑954-563-8001; www.sidelinessports.com; 2031 Wilton Dr; ⊗4pm-2am), which has a super-fun Wednesday darts tournament, and a leather/bear/cowboy club, Ramrod (www.ramrodbar.com; 1508 Wilton Dr; ⊗3pm-2am).

Gay guesthouses are plentiful; visit www.gayftlauderdale.com. Consult the glossy weekly rag Hot Spots (www.hotspotsmagazine.com) to keep updated on gay nightlife. For the most insanely comprehensive list of everything gay, log on to www.jumponmarkslist.com.

Swap Shop
MARKET

(www.floridaswapshop.com; 3291 W Sunrise Blvd; ⊙9am-5pm) Perhaps the most fun shopping in town, the state's biggest flea market has acres of stalls selling everything from underwear to antique cookie jars to pink lawn flamingos, and a carnival atmosphere of mariachi music, hot-dog trucks and a 14-screen drive-in movie theater. The flea market is slightly northwest of downtown.

❶ Information

Convention & Visitors Bureau (☑954-765-4466; www.sunny.org; 100 E Broward Blvd, Suite 200; ⊙8:30-5pm Mon-Fri) Has an excellent array of visitor information about the greater Fort Lauderdale region.

Post Office (1404 E Las Olas Blvd, Suite B) Not the main branch, but well located.

❶ Getting There & Away

AIR

Fort Lauderdale-Hollywood International Airport (p516) is located off I-95 between Lauderdale and Hollywood. The airport is served by more than 35 airlines, including many low-cost carriers and nonstop flights from Europe. In progress is a $2.3 billion dollar renovation, which will see the existing three terminals upgraded, the construction of a new southern runway and the rebuilding of the fourth terminal, which should be completed by 2017.

From the airport, it's a short 20-minute drive to downtown, or a $20 cab ride.

BOAT

Port Everglades (www.porteverglades.net; 1850 Eller Drive) cruise port is the second busiest port in the country after Miami and is currently undergoing renovation and expansion, with added baggage and parking areas, and a newly extended slip to accommodate larger cruise ships. From the port, walk to SE 17th St and take bus 40 to the beach or to Broward Central Terminal.

If you're heading to Fort Lauderdale in your own boat (not that unlikely here), head for the **Bahia Mar Resort & Yacht Center** (☑954-627-6309; www.bahiamarhotel.com; 801 Seabreeze Blvd; ⊙7am-6pm).

BUS

The **Greyhound station** (☑954-764-6551; www.greyhound.com; 515 NE 3rd St) is about four blocks from Broward Central Terminal, the central transfer point for buses in the area.

TRAIN

Tri-Rail (☑954-783-6030; www.tri-rail.com; 6151 N Andrews Ave) runs between Miami and Fort Lauderdale (one-way $5, 45 minutes). A feeder system of buses has connections at no charge. Free parking is provided at most stations. Provide ample cushion for delays. **Amtrak** (☑800-872-7245; www.amtrak.com; 200 SW 21st Tce) also uses Tri-Rail tracks.

❶ Getting Around

If you're driving here, I-95 and Florida's Turnpike run north–south. I-595, the major east–west artery, intersects I-95, Florida's Turnpike and the Sawgrass Expressway. It also feeds into I-75, which runs to Florida's west coast.

Sun Trolley (www.suntrolley.com; single fare/day pass $1/3) runs between Las Olas and the beaches between 9:30am and 6:30pm Friday to Monday. **Broward County Transit** (BCT; www.broward.org/bct; single fare/day pass $1.75/4) operates between downtown, the beach and Port Everglades. From **Broward Central Terminal** (101 NW 1st Ave), take bus 11 to upper Fort Lauderdale Beach and Lauderdale-by-the-Sea; bus 4 to Port Everglades; and bus 40 to 17th St and the beaches.

The fun, yellow **water taxi** (☑954-467-6677; www.watertaxi.com; all-day pass adult/child $22/11) travels the canals and waterways between 17th St to the south, Atlantic Blvd/Pompano Beach to the north, the Riverfront to the west and the Atlantic Ocean to the east. There are also services to Hollywood ($11 per person).

Lauderdale-by-the-Sea & Deerfield Beach

In the late 1800s southern Florida was a wild frontier, home to a few dozen Seminole families and some hardy settlers. Remnants of this early history can be found in the flow of beachside communities north of Fort Lauderdale along the Intracoastal Waterway. The high-rises thin out, giving way to the sleepy, family-oriented communities of Lauderdale-by-the-Sea, Pompano and Deerfield Beach.

◉ Sights

Deerfield Beach Historical Society
MUSEUM

(☑954-429-0378; www.deerfieldhistory.org; 380 E Hillsboro Rd; ⊙10am-2pm) FREE This volunteer-run organization oversees several sites from Deerfield Beach's early days in the 1920s. Back then the community was 1300 people strong and the town consisted of four or five stores, a lodge, a post office and two hotels. The Old Deerfield School, Kester Cottage and the Butler House museum are all open for tours on the first and third Saturday of the month.

Butterfly World
NATURE RESERVE

(www.butterflyworld.com; 3600 W Sample Rd, Coconut Creek; adult/child $25/20; ⊙9am-5pm Mon-Sat, from 11am Sun; 🖪) The first indoor butterfly park in the US is also one of the largest butterfly exhibits anywhere. It features thousands of live, exotic species, such as the bright-blue morphos or camouflaged owl butterfly. Various exhibits highlight different creatures – from butterflies to hummingbirds. Butterfly World is an excellent place to spend the better part of a day, especially with wide-eyed children or trigger-happy shutterbugs.

🏃 Activities

Wherever you go along this coastline you'll be spoilt for choice for beaches. The best of the bunch is Deerfield Beach.

A popular fishing pier is **Anglin's Pier** in Lauderdale-by-the-Sea, where you'll find a 24-hour tackle shop, night fishing lights and rod rental for $15.

Deerfield Beach
BEACH

(www.deerfield-beach.com) Deerfield Beach is an award-wining 'Blue Wave' beach with pristine water, nine lifeguard towers and a designated surfing area north of the pier and south of Tower 7. The **pier** (200 NE 21st Ave) itself is well known for large catches such as king mackerel. Rods rent for $16.

Quiet Waters Park
WATER PARK

(www.broward.org/parks/quietwaterspark; 401 S Powerline Rd, Deerfield Beach; admission per person/car $1.50/8; 🖪) Hardly quiet, this 430 acre county park rings with the squeals of kids (and grown-ups) enjoying all kinds of wet 'n' wild fun. There's **Splash Adventure** (per person $5), a water playground with a shallow pool and fountains spraying every which way. Then there's the **Ski Rixen** (www.skirixenusa.com; cable pass per hr/half-day $25/40; ⊙noon-8pm Tue-Sun), a super-cool cable water-ski system. Using an innovative cabling system suspended from towers surrounding a half-mile course, water-skiers (and wake-boarders) are pulled over a wake-free watercourse. For lower-octane adventures, the park has fishing, kayak rental, hiking and a mountain-bike trails.

South Florida Diving Headquarters
DIVING

(☑954-783-2299; www.southfloridadiving.com; 101 N Riverside Dr, Pompano Beach; 2-tank dives $55, snorkeling $30) Dive natural and artificial reefs, or float along one of the area's famous drift dives with this PADI-certified company. Forty-five-minute snorkeling trips will keep nondivers happy.

🛏 Sleeping

Lauderdale-by-the-Sea and Deerfield Beach have no shortage of sweet, family-run motels and guesthouses. **Quiet Waters Park** (☑955-357-5100; tent sites $35) offers 'rent-a-tent' tepees for camping.

★ Blue Seas Courtyard
HOTEL $$

(☑954-772-3336; http://blueseascourtyard.com; 4525 El Mar Dr, Lauderdale-by-the-Sea; r $124-179; P❋🛜🏊) Standing out from the crowd with a hacienda-style roof of clay barrel tiles, a bright yellow exterior and hand-stenciled decoration, Blue Seas seems to embody the sunny, laid-back disposition of Lauderdale-by-the-Sea. Owners Marc and Cristie have been at the helm since the 1970s, and provide a truly attentive and personalized service that keeps rooms booked up weeks in advance.

Cottages by the Ocean
GUESTHOUSE $$

(☑954-283-1111; www.4rentbythebeach.com; 3309 SE Third St, Pompano Beach; studio $99-209, apt $125-240; P❋🛜🏊) These breezy, beachy 1940s cottages set in well-tended tropical gardens just minutes from Pompano Beach are perfect for longer getaways. Studios and one-bed apartments are decorated with a retro nautical theme (think quilts, ceiling fans and a blue-and-white color scheme) and come with a full-service kitchen, a patio or porch, a BBQ, beach chairs and access to a coin laundry. Three-night minimum stay.

High Noon Resort
MOTEL $$

(☑954-776-1121; www.highnoonresort.com; 4424 El Mar Dr, Lauderdale-by-the-Sea; r $140-190, cabana $350-390; ❋@🛜🏊) Spilling onto the beach, this ultraclean motel-resort includes two sister properties, the Sea Foam (apartment-style stays) and the Nautilus (for those seeking seclusion). Guests can enjoy the property's seven tiki huts, two pools and shuffleboard court, while just steps from bars and restaurants. Nothing says Florida like relaxing under numerous palm trees and listening to a sea breeze rustle the leaves.

Seacrest Hotel
HOTEL $$

(☑954-530-8854; www.hotelseacrest.com; 4562 Bougainvillea Dr, Lauderdale-by-the-Sea; r $109-149; P❋🛜🏊) One of the best-kept secrets in Lauderdale-by-the-Sea the Seacrest is set back from the beach and offers the polished standards of a hotel within the intimate confines of a converted home. Pad across cool travertine marble floors to enormous beds with plump pillowtops before flicking on your favorite HBO show. There's a generous private pool, and the beach is just five minutes' walk away.

✕ Eating & Drinking

★**Tucker Duke's Lunchbox**   BURGERS $
(☑954-708-2035; www.tuckerdukeslunchbox.com; 1101 S Powerline Rd, Deerfield Beach; mains $4-11; ⊙10:30am-10pm Sun-Wed, to 11pm Thu-Sat) Superior burgers and southern comfort food made from local, seasonal ingredients. The brain behind the brand is Florida native and 'Cutthroat Kitchen' winner chef Brian Cartenuto, who is passionate about getting back to basics in the kitchen. Check out the website for blogged recipes, including the invaluable 'Hangover Breakfast Tacos'.

You'll find it just south of Quiet Waters Park.

La Spada's Original Hoagies   SANDWICHES $
(www.laspadashoagies.com; 4346 Sea Grape Dr, Lauderdale-by-the-Sea; sandwiches $7-10; ⊙10am-8pm) This strip-mall spot is a hush-hush cult favorite for crazy-good Philly-style hoagies and a staff of fun-loving jokers who can toss a slice of turkey like a Frisbee and make it land on your bread. Pssst: try the Monster.

Aruba Beach Cafe   CARIBBEAN $$
(www.arubabeachcafe.com; 1 Commercial Blvd, Lauderdale-by-the-Sea; mains $10-22; ⊙11am-11pm Mon-Sat, 9am-11pm Sun; 🐾) The food isn't the only reason people flock here (though the conch fritters *are* divine). There's also live music nightly, daily drink specials served from three separate bars, and just a bank of sliding glass doors separating you and the beach.

★**Sea**   SEAFOOD $$$
(☑954-533-2580; www.seatherestaurant.com; 235 Commercial Blvd, Lauderdale-by-the-Sea; menu $25-45; ⊙noon-2:30pm & 5-10pm Tue-Fri) See if you can squeeze into Sea for a perfectly executed three-course fixed-price menu featuring succulent blackened grouper, tender conch, Florida snapper or hummus-encrusted sea bass. Chef Tony Sindaco has a Michelin-starred pedigree and presides over the kitchen with a fanatical attention to detail. If it's on the menu, don't miss his signature whiskey cake in a starburst of raspberry coulis.

Village Pump   BAR
(www.villagegrille.com; 4404 El Mar Dr, Lauderdale-by-the-Sea) Serving sturdy drinks in a nautical wood-paneled room since 1949.

❶ Information

Deerfield Beach Chamber of Commerce
(☑954-427-1050; www.deerfieldchamber.com; 1601 E Hillsboro Blvd; ⊙9am-3pm Mon-Fri Apr-Dec, to 3pm Mon-Sat & noon-4pm Sun Jan-Mar)

Lauderdale-by-the-Sea Chamber of Commerce (☑954-776-1000; www.lbts.com; 4201 N Ocean Dr; ⊙9am-5pm) Info on businesses throughout the area.

❶ Getting There & Around

Tri-Rail (www.tri-rail.com) heads north from Fort Lauderdale. If you're driving, try to take A1A (sometimes called Ocean Blvd): the drive's glorious.

Boca Raton

The name Boca Raton may mean 'mouth of the rat,' but there's nothing ratty about this proud-to-be-posh coastal town. What began as a sleepy residential community was transformed in the mid-1920s by architect Addison Mizner, who relied on his love of Spanish architecture to build the place into a fancy-pants town. His fingerprints remain on numerous structures throughout the area, though his name is most often invoked when talking about the popular anchor of town – the alfresco mall, Mizner Park. The rest of Boca is a mostly mainstream collection of chain stores and restaurants and, as you near the ocean, some peaceful beaches and parks. Most people don't come to Boca on vacation unless they have family here, as there are almost no beachfront hotels.

◉ Sights & Activities

Since Boca lacks a cohesive downtown, **Mizner Park** (www.miznerpark.com) generally serves as the city's center. At the north end, the Count de Hoernle Amphitheater accommodates more than 4000 people for symphonies, ballet, rock concerts and other cultural events.

★ **Gumbo Limbo Nature Center** PARK
(☎ 561-544-8605; www.gumbolimbo.org; 1801 N
Ocean Blvd; suggested $5 donation; ⊙ 9am-4pm
Mon-Sat, noon-4pm Sun; ⊕) Boca's best asset is
this stretch of waterfront parkland. It's a preserve of tropical hammock and dunes ecosystems, and a haven for all manner of sea
creatures and birds. Dedicated to educating
the public about sea turtles and other local
fauna, the natural-history displays include
saltwater tanks full of critters. The highlight
is the brand-new sea-turtle rehabilitation
center, which is open for 90-minute tours
(10am and 1pm from Monday to Saturday;
1pm Sundays).

The preserve also has a number of secluded
hikes. These take you along elevated boardwalks through tropical foliage and along an
artificial mangrove wetland, reclaimed using
filtered wastewater from the city.

Boca Raton Museum of Art MUSEUM
(☎ 561-392-2500; www.bocamuseum.org; 501 Plaza Real; adult/student $14/6; ⊙ 10am-5pm Tue-Fri,
noon-5pm Sat & Sun) In Mizner Park, this elegant museum showcases the minor works
of modern masters such as Picasso, Chagall
and Modigliani. It also has a genuinely
worthwhile collection of pieces by 20th- and
21st-century American and European painters, sculptors and photographers.

Red Reef Beach BEACH
(1 N Ocean Blvd; per vehicle Mon-Fri $16, Sat & Sun
$18; ⊙ 8am-sunset; ⊕) Sadly Hurricane Sandy
buried most of the artificial reef, but this
beach is still tops for water-lovers. There are
lifeguards and great shallow pools for begin-
ner snorkelers. Together with neighboring
South Beach Park, the beaches encompass
some 60 acres of wild shores.

🛏 Sleeping & Eating

Boca has a startling lack of hotels, the result
of zoning laws that have privileged condo development over tourism. There are a
handful of chains off I-95, but if you're looking for unique beachfront digs, you'll have
to lay your head just north in Delray Beach.

Boca Raton Resort & Club RESORT $$$
(☎ 888-498-2622; www.bocaresort.com; 501 E
Camino Real; r $249-709; ❉ 🛜 ☲) A collection
of palatial Mediterranean-style buildings,
this Addison Mizner–built resort is as old-
school glam as it gets. Well-heeled northern-
ers make the pilgrimage here each year to

winter in its spacious suites and cottages,
enjoying two 18-hole golf courses, a 32-slip
marina, a private beach and an otherworldly
spa. Add in the five pools, 10 restaurants and
priceless historic vibe and you'll find you
can stay a week and never leave the grounds.

Ben's Kosher Deli DELI $
(www.bensdeli.net; 9942 Clint Moore Rd; mains $5-
12; ⊙ 11am-9pm) The Florida outpost of a well-
loved New York–based deli, Ben's sprawling
menu covers all the Jewish classics – corned-
beef sandwiches, knishes (potato-stuffed
pastries), sweet-and-sour beef tongue and
eggs with smoked salmon. The deli is about
20 minutes' drive northwest of Mizner Park.

Six Tables MODERN AMERICAN $$$
(☎ 561-347-6260; www.sixtablesbocaraton.com;
Mizner Plaza, 112 NE 2nd St; menu $79; ⊙ 7-10pm
Wed-Sat) Chef Jonathan Fyhrie offers an elegant and romantic dining experience for
just six lucky tables. The evening starts with
the chef drawing the curtains and locking
the door, then a shared glass of bubbles,
some cheese puffs and a presentation. Settle in for a flavorful five-course fixed price
menu, which often includes a peerless lobster bisque and chateaubriand. It's necessary to book a few weeks in advance.

ⓘ Information

Chamber of Commerce (☎ 561-395-4433;
www.bocaratonchamber.com; 1800 N Dixie
Hwy; ⊙ 8:30am-5pm) Helpful, with racks of
pamphlets and a map.

ⓘ Getting There & Around

Boca Raton is more or less equidistant from Fort
Lauderdale-Hollywood International Airport
(FLL) and Palm Beach International Airport
(PBI), and sprawls several miles east and west
of I-95.

The **Tri-Rail Station** (www.tri-rail.com;
680 Yamato Rd) has shuttle services to both
airports. PalmTran bus 94 connects downtown
Boca with the Tri-Rail station.

PalmTran (www.palmtran.org) serves southeast Florida from North Palm Beach to Boca
Raton. It costs $2 to ride. From the Tri-Rail sta-
tion, bus 2 takes you to PBI and bus 94 to Florida
Atlantic University, where you can transfer to
bus 91 to Mizner Park. From Mizner Park, take
bus 92 to South Beach Park.

Boca Raton Taxi (☎ 561-392-2727; www.
bocaratontaxi.com) serves the area. Cabs to the
Fort Lauderdale or Palm Beach airports are $64.

EVERGLADES TOURS

The southeast coast isn't all glossy development and glitzy malls. Sandwiched between the Hillsboro Canal and I-98 the Loxahatchee National Wildlife Refuge encompasses the northern reaches of the Everglades. To explore this 221 square mile wilderness, filled with swamp ferns, cypress and nodding nixies, you need a guide. Stop at the visitors center for exhibits, a movie and maps of walking and cycling trails.

To really get a feel for this forgotten corner of the southeast, Wild Lyle's Loxahatchee Everglades Tours (☑561-482-6107; www.evergladesairboattours.com; 15490 Loxahatchee Rd; adult/child under 12yr $55/24.50; ◷9:30am-4pm) offers hourly ecoexplorations on one of eight custom airboats. Guests enjoy an adventure ride through swampy marsh, around papyrus and hurricane grass, past long-winged birds, turtles and gators sunning themselves. At the halfway point, Lyle stops the boat, discusses the importance of the Everglades and answers questions. You can't stump this guy. With nearly 40 years' experience, Lyle's explored the area thoroughly and even conducted rescue missions recovering downed planes. Kid-friendly but science-drenched, an airboat ride with Lyle is a great way to get to know a part of the world that most people don't understand.

Delray Beach

Founded by Seminoles, and later settled in the 18th and 19th centuries by African Americans and Japanese agriculturists, who farmed pineapples just east of I-95, this melting pot retooled itself for the tourist trade when the railroads chugged through Delray Beach in 1896. Local hotels and clubs turned a blind eye to prohibition laws and accommodated everyone. Perhaps this eclectic mix of early residents – from the industrious to the lawless – is the reason Delray so effortlessly juggles a casual seaside vibe and a suave urban sophistication.

◉ Sights & Activities

Atlantic Ave, the town's main drag, is lined with boutiques, bistros, hotels and more. A few blocks away, a stretch of NE 2nd Ave known as Pineapple Grove has a lower-key hipster vibe.

Among the best beaches are the Atlantic Dunes Beach (1600 Ocean Blvd), with 7 acres of shorefront sporting clean restroom facilities, volleyball courts and picnic areas, and the public beach (Ocean Blvd, at Atlantic), a hip gathering spot for young locals and visitors, with excellent surf for swimming. Coin-operated meters charge $1.25 per hour for parking.

Delray Beach is also home to the International Tennis Championships, a professional tournament held annually at the Delray Beach Tennis Club.

★Morikami Museum
& Japanese Gardens   MUSEUM, GARDENS
(☑561-495-0233; www.morikami.org; 4000 Morikami Park Rd; adult/child $14/9; ◷10am-5pm Tue-Sun) Japanese immigrant and pineapple farmer Sukjei 'George' Morikami, a member of the original Yamato settlement of Delray, donated his spectacularly landscaped 200 acre property for the establishment of a museum showcasing Japanese culture. Today you can wander more than a mile of pine-lined nature trails around koi-filled ponds, experiencing different Japanese gardens from bonsai to a 12th-century *shinden* (pleasure) garden modelled on a noble estate. To complement the gardens, the outstanding museum showcases more than 5000 Japanese antiques, objects and works of fine art.

On the third Saturday of the month you can take part in a tea ceremony in the Seishin-An Teahouse ($5 with admission to the museum). Classes, cultural and educational events are also offered. Check out the website for details.

The museum's Cornell Cafe (mains $7-10; ◷11am-3pm) serves neo-Japanese cuisine such as sweet-potato tempura, ginger-roasted duck and sushi rolls. It is considered one of the best museum restaurants in the country.

Delray Center for the Arts   ARTS CENTER
(Old School Square; ☑561-243-7922; http://delray-centerforthearts.org; 51 N Swinton Ave) Otherwise known as Old School Square, this highly successful preservation project encompasses Delray's 1913 elementary school, 1925 high school and 1926 gymnasium. Now these

buildings house the **Cornell Museum of Art & American Culture** (adult/child $10/3; ◷ 10am-4:30pm Tue-Sat, from 1pm Sun), showcasing rotating exhibitions of local, national and international arts and crafts; the **Crest Theatre**; and a vibrant **School of Creative Arts**, sponsoring a program of classes, events, theater and exhibitions.

Delray Beach Tennis Center TENNIS
(☑ 561-243-7360; www.delraytennis.com; 201 W Atlantic Ave; hard/clay courts $10/15) With capacity for more than 8000 spectators, Delray's tennis center hosts pro tennis tournaments with big-name stars such as Serena and Venus Williams. Both kids and adults can also play or take lessons on the 14 clay courts and 7 Har-Tru courts, and the club offers a wide variety of clinics and camps. Spotlights are available for night play ($7).

The club has a second location, the **Delray Swim & Tennis Club** (☑ 561-243-7079; 2350 Jaeger Dr; ◷ 11am-4pm). It has a further 24 courts and a pool (adult/child $3/2).

Delray Yacht Cruises BOAT TOUR
(☑ 561-243-0686; www.delraybeachcruises. com; launches from 777 Atlantic Plaza; adult/child $24/21) The Intracoastal from Delray Beach south to Boca Raton is pretty swanky. Get to know the area better with a narrated sightseeing cruise aboard the 105ft luxury *Lady Atlantic*. Departs from the canal side of Veterans Park.

🛏 Sleeping

Delray has tons of sleeping options, from family-run motels to swanky B&Bs.

★**Parliament Inn** GUESTHOUSE $$
(☑ 561-276-6245; www.florida-info.com; 1236 George Bush Blvd; 2-person ste $93-192, 4-person ste $100-199; 🅿 ❋ 🛜 🌊) This lushly planted hideaway is tucked away just off Delray's spectacular 2 mile beach. It's easy to miss given the eight lemon-yellow, single-story units are situated in a gorgeous tropical garden shaded by towering palms. The trees are strung with hammocks from where you can idly contemplate the turquoise pool. Each unit has a full kitchen, ample living space and a private porch, and there's an endless supply of books and beach chairs, which you can borrow for beachside outings.

Crane's Beach House GUESTHOUSE $$
(☑ 561-278-1700; www.cranesbeachhouse.com; 82 Gleason St; r & ste $150-350; 🅿 ❋ @ 🛜 🌊) Through a jasmine-entwined arch, this

hidden garden guesthouse has 27 spacious rooms and suites, brightly appointed in colorful Key West style with loads of funky local art. Palm-shaded grotto swimming pools and a weekend tiki bar add a fun, sociable spirit. The ultrafriendly staff love to chat and help out with tips and restaurant recommendations.

Wright by the Sea HOTEL $$
(☑ 561-278-3355; www.wbtsea.com; 1901 S Ocean Blvd; r winter $259-336, summer $129-169; 🅿 ❋ 🛜 🌊) With a spiffy green lawn and retro blue shutters, this shipshape little seaside hotel recalls the glory days of American family travel. Suites are spacious and clean, with pullout couches and private hallways leading from the living room to the bathroom, a boon for those traveling with children.

Colony Hotel & Cabana Club HOTEL $$
(☑ 561-276-4123; www.thecolonyhotel.com; 525 Atlantic Ave; r from $125-259; ❋ 🌊) If you dig historical detail, you'll love this 1926 Atlantic Ave classic, complete with an attendant-operated cage elevator. Rooms are more simple than grand, with hardwood floors and old-fashioned white-tiled bathrooms. Though it's in the center of downtown Delray, its private oceanfront Cabana Club is only 2 miles away by free shuttle.

Sundy House Inn B&B $$$
(☑ 561-272-5678; www.sundyhouse.com; 106 S Swinton Ave; r winter $299-349, summer $139-189; ❋ 🛜 🌊) Stepping through the front gate at this sumptuous B&B feels like being transported to Bali. Pathways twine through a dense 1-acre garden of trumpet flowers, hibiscus and coconut palms, the vegetation occasionally parting to reveal vintage bird cages or Chinese lion statues. Guestrooms are British-colonial chic, with heavy wood furniture and dark shutters. But the true highlight is the freshwater pool, designed to look like a jungle pond, complete with darting fish. Even if you sleep elsewhere, don't miss the on-site Sundy House Restaurant.

🍴 Eating

Delray's got one of the area's best eating scenes, with everything from Parisian-style cafes to funky lunch counters to swanky seafood bistros.

Doc's All-American BURGERS, AMERICAN $
(10 N Swinton Ave; mains $6-15; ◷ 11am-11pm Sun-Thu, to 1am Fri & Sat; ♿) Great, greasy burgers

and thick, frosty shakes are summertime classics at this beloved open-air '50s-style walk-up counter.

Bamboo Fire
CARIBBEAN **$$**

(www.bamboofirecafe.com; 149 NE 4th Ave; mains $9-15; ☺ 6:30-11pm Wed-Thu, to 11:30pm Fri, noon-11:30pm Sat) On a quiet shopping street a few blocks from the main Delray action, this arty little hole-in-the-wall is a cult favorite for authentic Caribbean fare such as conch fritters, jerk chicken and oxtail stew. Veggies and vegans will be in tofu heaven – try it curried, grilled or fried.

Tryst
PUB **$$**

(☏ 561-921-0201; www.trystdelray.com; 4 E Atlantic Ave; mains $12-26; ☺ 11:30am-10pm Mon-Fri, 5:30-11pm Fri & Sat, 4-10pm Sun) Cashing in on the local-seasonal-organic trend to great success, this upmarket gastropub is a hit for casual bistro food with modern twists: fish 'n' chips with smoked sea salt, *steak frites* with blue cheese. On Sunday evenings, it all comes accompanied by live jazz.

★ Joseph's Wine Bar
MEDITERRANEAN **$$$**

(☏ 561-272-6100; www.josephswinebar.com; 200 NE 2nd Ave #107; lunch mains $9-14, dinner mains $21-36; ☺ 11am-10pm) Hosted by the gregarious Joseph, lunch or dinner at this friendly eatery is an elegant and convivial affair. Everything is made fresh to order so relax, take a wine recommendation from Joseph and await a vibrant selection of dips (including a deliciously smokey baba ghanoush), salads and wraps at lunchtime, and a sophisticated selection of mains in the evening. The baked rack of lamb in an unctuous Chianti sauce is a particular highlight.

J&J Raw Bar
SEAFOOD **$$$**

(☏ 561-272-3390; www.jjseafooddelray.com; 634 E Atlantic Blvd; mains $21-34; ☺ 11:30am-10:30pm) Perennially popular raw bar serving up generous platters of little neck clams, Gulf Coast oysters and seasonal stone crab claws. The J&J Seafood Trio appetizer, with shrimps, scallops and crab cakes, is enough for a main. Otherwise opt for the nut-crusted snapper in a sweet lime and rum butter sauce.

Sundy House Restaurant
MODERN AMERICAN **$$$**

(☏ 561-272-5678; 106 S Swinton Ave; mains $25-41; ☺ 11:30am-2:30pm Tue-Sat, 6-10pm Tue-Sun, brunch 10:30am-2pm Sun) Nibble goat's cheese salads and fennel-pollen seared salmon at Delray's most romantic restaurant, over-looking the primeval Taru Gardens at the Sundy House Inn. Sunday brunch, complete with made-to-order crepes and a prime rib-carving station, is an extravaganza.

☤ Drinking & Entertainment

Most hipsters head to West Palm to party, but there are a few places worth haunting right here in town.

★ Dada
PUB, CAFE

(☏ 561-330-3232; http://sub-culture.org/dada; 52 N Swinton Ave; ☺ 5pm-2am) Join the cool cats lounging in this two-story bungalow to sip cocktails, hear poetry readings or live bands, and nibble on fare including ravioli, salads and hummus. The front porch, outdoor lanterns and boho vibe all add to the romantic charm.

Boston's on the Beach
BAR

(www.bostonsonthebeach.com; 40 S Ocean Blvd; ☺ 11-2am Mon, Fri & Sat, to 1am Tue, to midnight Wed-Thu & Sun) This perennial beachfront favorite has nightly live music, great sea views and a party-happy vibe.

★ Arts Garage
ARTS CENTER

(☏ 561-450-6357 ; www.artsgarage.org; 180 Northeast 1st St; ☺ box office 10am-6pm) Delray's new community arts center hosts anything from bands and musical performances to radio shows and theater. Patrons can bring their own wine and snacks and, given the intimate size, there isn't a bad seat in the house.

⌂ Shopping

Atlantic Ave is one of South Florida's best shopping districts. Look for everything from doggie gift shops to vintage thrift stores and jewelry shops selling necklaces made from shells and sea glass. For those looking for a good beach read, **Murder on the Beach** (☏ 561-279-7790; www.murderonthebeach.com; 273 NE 2nd Ave, Pineapple Grove) bookstore is a popular stop for Floridian mystery authors on book tours. You can also pick up other general interest books on Florida here.

❶ Information

Chamber of Commerce (☏ 561-279-1380; www.delraybeach.com; 140 NE 1st St; ☺ 9am-5pm) For maps, guides and local advice.

❶ Getting There & Around

Delray Beach is about 20 miles south of West Palm Beach and 45 miles north of Miami on I-95, US Hwy 1 or Hwy A1A.

The **Greyhound station** (561-272-6447; www.greyhound.com; 1587 SW 4th Ave) is served by PalmTran. Bus 2 takes you to Palm Beach International Airport or Boca Raton; bus 81 services the Tri-Rail station, Amtrak and downtown Delray. **Amtrak** (800-872-7245; www.amtrak.com; 345 S Congress Ave), half a mile south of Atlantic Ave, shares a station with **Tri-Rail** (800-874-7245; www.tri-rail.com).

Lake Worth

Billing itself as 'Where the tropics begin,' this bohemian community sits further east than any place in South Florida. Meanwhile, just offshore, the Gulf Stream flows further west than anywhere along the coast. This geographical good fortune means Lake Worth has warm weather year-round. Add to that a distinct artsy vibe, a cool collection of eateries, a robust local music scene and a spectacular sliver of public-access beachfront, and you have one of the great hidden treasures of the Southeast Coast.

If you're visiting in February don't miss the fantastic **Street Painting Festival** (www.streetpaintingfestivalinc.org; ⊙ Feb), when artists come from far and wide to cover Lake Worth's pedestrianized main streets with more than 200 surreal images of super heroes and Old Masters. Wander the open-air gallery while snacking on BBQ fare, tacos or cheese sandwiches, and then settle down for a program of live music in the park.

⊙ Sights & Activities

Lake Worth is light on sights; most people come here for the beach and the laid-back vibe, or use the town as a budget-priced jumping-off point to explore nearby Delray Beach or Palm Beach.

★ **Snook Islands Natural Area**   PARK
(www.lakeworth.org/visitors/parks; Lake Avenue Bridge) Twenty-mile long Lake Worth lagoon is the largest estuary in Palm Beach county and is an important warm-water refuge for manatees. Years of development have surrounded the lagoon with premium property, resulting in some lamentable environmental degradation. To reverse some of the damage the $18 million Snook Islands Natural Area was created in a biologically dead zone, stretching 1.2 miles north from Lake Avenue into the lagoon. Restoring miles of mangroves and laying down new oyster beds to encourage the growth of sea grasses,

a favorite manatee snack, has enabled the return of a startling number of birds and marine life.

A 545ft boardwalk traces the line of mangroves, while floating boat docks and a sloping grass bank for kayaks make the water easily accessible. There's even a new **fishing pier**, which is open from 6am until midnight.

Vehicles can access the area from the westbound lanes on the north side of Lake Avenue Bridge.

Lake Worth Beach   BEACH
This stretch of sand is universally agreed to be the finest between Fort Lauderdale and Daytona. Surfers come from miles to tame the waves; everyone else comes to enjoy the fine white sand.

Kayak Lake Worth   KAYAKING
(561-225-8250; http://kayaklakeworth.com; kayaks 2.5/4hr $35/40, tours per person $40-65) This mobile kayak and paddleboard operator can kit you up with all the necessary equipment for kayaking, paddleboarding and fishing, mainly in the areas of Snook Islands Natural Area and Bingham Islands. Two- to three-hour eco sunset and moonlight tours are also available with knowledgeable local guides Bryce and Emily.

Wet Pleasures   DIVING
(561-547-4343; www.wetpleasuresfla.com; 312 W Lantana Rd; ⊙ 9am-6:30pm Mon-Sat, to 4pm Sun) Lake Worth enjoys some excellent snorkeling and diving opportunities. Head to this (unfortunately named) dive shop for lessons, equipment and advice. They'll also hook you up with charters to take you diving as far south as the Keys.

Bar Jack Fishing   FISHING
(561-588-7612; http://barjackfishing.com; 314 E Ocean Ave; 4hr trips adult $37) Deep-sea-fishing day trips aboard the *Lady K,* with departures at 8am, 1:30pm and 6:30pm. All gear included.

🛌 Sleeping

Mango Inn   B&B $$
(561-533-6900; www.mangoinn.com; 128 N Lakeside Dr; r $130-190, ste $190-250; P ❄ 🤍 ☲) All three buildings composing the Mango Inn were built between 1915 and 1920 in a residential area. As a result, this lushly landscaped inn today boasts one of the most secluded settings around. Only three blocks from town and a 15-minute walk to the beach, accommodation ranges from single

rooms (many with private entrances) to an adorable cottage with French doors opening on to the heated pool.

Sabal Palm B&B
B&B $$

(📞 561-582-1090; www.sabalpalmhouse.com; 109 N Golfview Rd; r winter $159-239, summer $119-199; 🅿 ❄ 🛜) A classic knickknack-and-floral-print B&B, this 1936 house has rooms named after artists. To escape the frilliness, try the Dali Room, which has an art deco-y modern vibe.

🍴 Eating

Pelican
DINER, INDIAN $

(610 Lake Ave; mains $3-10; ⊙ 6:30am-2pm; 🍴) This early-risers' place offers hearty portions of perfectly prepared breakfast, plus a carnival of vegetarian-friendly specials, many with Mediterranean or Middle Eastern flavors (the owners are Pakistani). It also offers divine Indian dinners on Fridays from 6pm to 10pm, including a range of potent curries and masalas.

Mother Earth Sanctuary Café
AMERICAN, CAFE $

(📞 561-460-8647; www.motherearthsanctuarycafe. com; 410 2nd Ave N; mains $4.50-10; ⊙ 8:30am-4pm Tue-Sat, 10am-2pm Sun) Since when do you have option-paralysis over *which* veggie burger to eat? At the Sanctuary Café you can feed your body and soul on hearty yamburgers, black-bean burgers and sweet-potato chakra burgers. These are served alongside an array of organic salads topped with locally grown micro-greens, and chicken dishes. This cafe is also the only purveyor of fairtrade Larry's Beans, and the homemade Mighty Leaf Chai is heavenly.

To create your own sacred kitchen, join Patti for cookery classes on Thursday evenings ($50 per person).

Downtown Pizza
PIZZERIA $$

(📞 561-586-6448; 608 Lake Ave; pizza $11-20; ⊙ 11am-11pm) In business for more than 20 years, this slither of a restaurant serves up delicious 14-inch, 16-inch and 18-inch thin-crust pizza with generous toppings. Meat-lovers should try the Philly cheese steak pizza with shredded steak tips, peppers and onions.

★ Paradiso Ristorante
ITALIAN $$$

(📞 561-547-2500; www.paradisolakeworth.com; 625 Lucerne Ave; 3-course lunch menu $21, mains $32-56; ⊙ 11:30am-3pm & 5:30-10pm) From the elegant interiors to the exquisitely present-ed dishes of homemade pasta, sheep ricotta gnocchi and succulent veal fillet, this is a dining experience to savor. Seasonal delights such as truffles, chestnuts and huckleberries call for specialty menu. Scheduled wine dinners and theatre packages are arranged in conjunction with the Lake Worth Playhouse.

Reservations are recommended.

🍷 Drinking & Entertainment

Nightlife is where Lake Worth truly shines, with its outsized wealth of great bars and music venues.

Havana Hideout
BAR

(www.havanahideout.com; 509 Lake Ave; ⊙ 11-2am) The most happening place in town, open-air, palm-fringed Havana has live music most nights, a thoughtful draft-beer selection and an on-site taqueria. Countless stomachs get filled on Taco Tuesdays, when tacos are $1.50 apiece.

Igot's Martiki Bar
BAR

(📞 561-582-4468; 702 Lake Ave; ⊙ noon-2am) Get acquainted with Lake Worth's most eccentric locals at this surf-themed dive bar. It's open-sided so you can either sit at the high tops at the bar and watch the ball game or take a pew streetside and watch the sidewalk scene. Drinks are poured strong, and there's live acoustic guitar on Thursday.

★ Bamboo Room
LIVE MUSIC

(📞 561-585-2583; www.bamboorm.com; 25 S J St; ⊙ 7pm-3am Thu-Sat) This favorite spot has an intimate roadhouse feel and features regional and internationally known blues, rockabilly, alt-country and jam bands, drawing music-lovers from miles around.

★ Lake Worth Playhouse
THEATER

(📞 561-586-6410; www.lakeworthplayhouse.org; 713 Lake Ave; tickets $15-32) Housed in a restored 1924 vaudeville venue, this intimate spot stages classic community theater. The attached Stonzek Studio Theatre screens independent films (tickets cost from $6 to $8). The Dinner + Theater package with Paradiso Ristorante is an absolute bargain at $55.

Lake Worth Drive-In
CINEMA

(📞 561-965-4517; 3438 Lake Worth Rd) When was the last time you went to the drive-in? Screening first-run movies under the stars seven nights a week – drive in, tune in and sit back. Coolers are welcome; dogs are not.

ℹ Information

Chamber of Commerce (📞 561-790-6200; www.cpbchamber.com; 501 Lake Ave; ⏰ 9am-5pm)

City Hall (📞 561-586-1600; www.lakeworth. org/visitors; 7 North Dixie Hwy) Useful website with an up-to-date calendar of events.

ℹ Getting There & Around

The **Tri-Rail Station** (www.tri-rail.com; 1703 Lake Worth Rd) is at the intersection of A St. PalmTran bus 61 connects the station to downtown.

Palm Beach

The third-wealthiest city in America, Palm Beach is home to 24 billionaires and looks every inch the playground for the rich and famous that it is. Palatial Greco-Roman mansions line the shore; Bentleys and Porsches cruise the wide avenues of downtown; streets look clean enough to eat off. Life here revolves around charity balls, Beverly Hills–style shopping and wine-soaked three-hour lunches. Though all the bling may feel a bit intimidating, fear not – much of Palm Beach is within the reach of budget travelers. Stroll along the truly gold Gold Coast beach, ogle the massive gated compounds on A1A or window-shop in uber-ritzy Worth Ave – all for free.

History

The first tourists to visit Palm Beach in the late 19th century came for fishing and hunting, not fancy balls. The area was largely swampland made famous by a man named Alligator Joe, who wrestled alligators to entertain the visitors for the princely sum of 25¢.

Historic **Sea Gull Cottage** (60 Cocoanut Row), built in 1886 by RR McCormick, a Denver railroad and land developer, dates from the period and is the oldest house on the island. Built in the Florida vernacular style, the shingle cottage was famous as the 'show-place along the shores,' so pretty was its stained glass windows, its Georgian marble floors and commanding viewing turret. Oil magnate and railroad entrepreneur Henry Flagler was immediately taken with it and bought it from McCormick as his winter retreat, that is until he completed his adjacent Whitehall Mansion in 1902. In the interim, he extended his railroad to its service town West Palm Beach in 1894 and started attracting a more monied crowd to his two hotels, the 1100-room Royal Poinciana Hotel (opened 1894 and closed in 1934) and the Palm Beach Inn, now more famously known as the Breakers (p209).

◎ Sights

Along the eastern side of the island, the **Lake Trail** offers views over Lake Worth, while Atlantic-facing **Ocean Blvd** (Hwy A1A) is lined with millionaire mansions. Take a drive down here for an eye-popping lesson in exactly how much money can buy. The most famous mansion overlooking this stretch of surf and sand is Donald Trump's over-the-top **Mar-a-Lago** (1100 S Ocean Blvd), purchased in 1985 for $8 million and soon turned into a private club.

★ **Flagler Museum** MUSEUM
(📞 561-655-2833; www.flaglermuseum.us; 1 Whitehall Way; adult/child $18/10; ⏰ 10am-5pm Tue-Sat, noon-5pm Sun) This museum is housed in the spectacular 1902 mansion built by Henry Flagler as a gift for his bride, Mary Lily Keenan. The beaux-arts-styled Whitehall was one of the most modern houses of its era and quickly became the locus of the winter season in Palm Beach. Designed by John Carrere and Thomas Hastings, both students of the École des Beaux-Arts in Paris and collaborators on other Gilded Age landmarks such as the New York Public Library, the elaborate 75-room house was the first residential home to feature both a heating system and an air-con system. Its modish, pink aluminum-leaf wallpaper was more expensive, at the time, than gold.

Downstairs, public rooms such as the 4750-sq-ft Grand Hall, the Library with its painted cast plaster ceiling and the silk- and wood-lined Drawing Room wow visitors with their detailed craftsmanship and opulence. Upstairs, intimate bedrooms give an insight into family life. Of particular interest is the **Flagler/Kenan History Room**, which chronicles, through letters, newspaper clippings and photographs, Flagler's personal and professional life and Mary Lily's family history.

If you'd like more than to simply wander around the house, take a look at the website for a whole host of lectures, talks and exhibits, as well as the critically acclaimed **Music Series** that features intimate chamber concerts in the Music Room followed by a champagne reception ($60 per person).

Time your visit right and you can segue into a 'Gilded Age Style' lunch in the **Café des Beaux-Arts** ($40; ⊙ 11:30am-2:30pm Tue-Sat, noon-3pm Sun), which is housed in the **Pavilion**, a 19th-century, iron-and-glass railway palace, which also displays Flagler's private railroad car. Here you can dine on finger sandwiches, scones and custom-blended teas while looking out over Lake Worth.

Worth Avenue   STREET
(www.worth-avenue.com) This quarter-mile, palm-tree-lined strip of more than 200 high-end brand shops is like the Rodeo Dr of the east. You can trace its history back to the 1920s when the now-gone Everglades Club staged weekly fashion shows and launched the careers of designers from Bonwit Teller to Elizabeth Arden. Even if you don't have the slightest urge to sling a swag of glossy bags over your arm, the people-watching is priceless.

Bethesda-by-the-Sea   CHURCH
(☑ 561-655-4554; www.bbts.org; 141 S County Rd; ⊙ 9am-5pm Mon-Sat, 7am-4pm Sun) After visiting Tiffany's windows on Worth Ave, head to Bethesda-by-the-Sea to admire its glorious Tiffany window and grand Gothic architecture. Built in 1926 to replace the first Protestant church of Palm Beach, it has a long community history and has hosted many a celebrity wedding, including those of Donald Trump and Michael Jordan. To the side is a tranquil English-style cloister and the lovely **Cluett Memorial Garden**.

🏃 Activities

⭐ **Palm Beach Lake Trail**   WALKING, CYCLING
(Royal Palm Way, at the Intracoastal Waterway) The first 'road' in Palm Beach ran along the Intracoastal Waterway, and provided a five-mile paved path stretching from Worth Ave (in the south) to Indian Rd (in the north) for Flagler's hotel guests to stretch their legs and scope out the social scene. Nicknamed 'The Trail of Conspicuous Consumption,' it is sandwiched between two amazing views: Lake Worth lagoon to the west, and an unending series of mansions to the east.

To get here from Worth Ave, walk west to S Lake Dr and follow the path north to the Sailfish Club. For an abbreviated version, park in the metered lot off Royal Palm Way (or in the supermarket's lot on Sunset Ave) and head west to pick up the trail. Another nice stretch runs along N County Rd. Park on Sunset Ave and head north on the path

running to Palm Beach Country Club. At just under 2 miles, the route is lined with houses and magnificent trees and there are plenty of exotic side streets to explore.

If bike rentals are not available at your hotel, head to Palm Beach Bike Shop. There's a 10 mph speed limit on the trail.

Palm Beach Municipal Beach   BEACH
(Ocean Blvd, btwn Royal Palm Way & Hammon Ave; ⊙ sunrise-sunset) This is one of Palm Beach's two beautiful public beaches, both of which are kept pleasantly seaweed-free by the town. Metered beachfront parking costs an absurd $5 per hour – head inland to snag free streetfront parking downtown. This beach can get crowded.

For privacy, head north along S Ocean Blvd and turn left onto Barton Ave. There's free two-hour parking near the church before S County Rd and public access to the beach across from Clarke Ave.

Phipps Ocean Park   BEACH
South of Southern Blvd on Ocean Blvd, before the Lake Worth Bridge, this is another place to catch rays.

Palm Beach Bike Shop   BICYCLE RENTAL
(☑ 561-659-4583; www.palmbeachbicycle.com; 223 Sunrise Ave; ⊙ 9am-5:30pm Mon-Sat, 10am-5pm Sun) This shop rents all manner of wheeled transportation, including bikes ($39 per day), skates ($39 per day) and scooters ($100 per day).

Seaview Park Tennis Center   TENNIS
(☑ 561-838-5404; www.palmbeachtennis.us; 340 Seaview Ave; court fee adult/junior $16/8.50; ⊙ 8am-8pm) 🚶 Located in the heart of Palm Beach, this award-winning tennis center features seven hard courts, a full-service Pro Shop and a stadium court for events. The center offers coaching as well as daily drop-ins.

👣 Tours

Island Living Tours   CULTURAL TOUR
(☑ 561-868-7944; www.islandlivingpb.com; tours $35-150) Intriguing walking and cycling tours led by local resident Leslie Divers give a hint at some of the personal stories and history behind all the glitz.

🛏 Sleeping

If you're looking for a deal, head west. Palm Beach properties aren't cheap. Most pet-friendly hotels charge a nonrefundable pet fee of $75.

Palm Beach

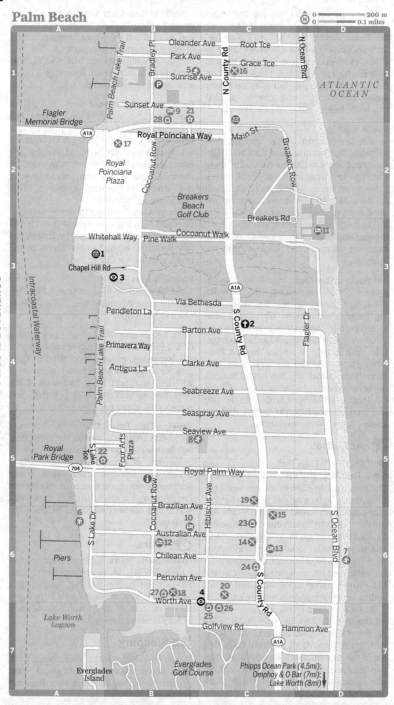

0 — 200 m
0 — 0.1 miles

Oleander Ave
Park Ave
Sunrise Ave
Root Tce
Grace Tce
16
5

Sunset Ave
9 **21**
28

Flagler
Memorial Bridge

Royal Poinciana Way
Main St

17

Royal
Poinciana
Plaza

Breakers
Beach
Golf Club

Breakers Rd
11

Whitehall Way
Cocoanut Walk
Pine Walk

1

Chapel Hill Rd
3

Via Bethesda

Pendleton La

Barton Ave
2

Primavera Way
Clarke Ave

Antigua La
Seabreeze Ave

Seaspray Ave

Seaview Ave
8

Royal
Park Bridge
22

Four Arts Plaza

Royal Palm Way

Brazilian Ave
19

10
23 **15**

Australian Ave
14 **13**

12

Chilean Ave

6
24

Peruvian Ave
20

27 **18**
4
Worth Ave
25 **26**

Golfview Rd
Hammon Ave

Lake Worth
Lagoon

Piers

Everglades
Island
Everglades
Golf Course

Phipps Ocean Park (4.5mi);
Omphoy & O Bar (7mi);
Lake Worth (8mi)

N County Rd
N Ocean Blvd
Bradley Pl
Cocoanut Row
Breakers Row
S County Rd
Flagler Dr
S Ocean Blvd
S Lake Dr
Cocoanut Row
Hibiscus Ave
S County Rd

ATLANTIC
OCEAN

Intracoastal Waterway
Palm Beach Lake Trail
Palm Beach Lake Trail

7

Palm Beach

★ **Palm Beach Historic Inn**   B&B **$$**
(☑ 561-832-4009; www.palmbeachhistoricinn.
com; 365 S County Rd; r $159-239, ste $189-329;
❄ 🐾 🐶) Housed on the 2nd floor of a land-
mark building brimming with character,
this intimate European-style hotel has airy,
light-filled rooms with hardwood floors
and period Palm Beach furnishings. Soak in
enamel tubs and sleep like a baby beneath
goose-down comforters. Stroll a block to the
beach or two to Worth Ave. It's excellent val-
ue and the location can't be beaten.

Bradley Park Hotel   HOTEL **$$**
(☑ 561-832-7050; www.bradleyparkhotel.com;
2080 Sunset Ave; r $99-229, ste $129-575;
🅿 ❄ 🐾) The midrange Bradley offers large,
gold-hued rooms, some with small kitchens
and characterful furniture that looks like it's
been bought at local estate sales. There's no
lobby to speak of, but rooms with kitchens
feel like mini-apartments, and it's located
just a short walk from the shops and restaurants of Royal Poinciana Way.

★ **Breakers**   RESORT **$$$**
(☑ 561-655-6611; www.thebreakers.com; 1 S Coun-
ty Rd; r $329-1330; 🅿 ❄ @ 🐾 🐾 🐶) Originally
built by Henry Flagler (in 1904 rooms cost
$4 per night, including meals), today this
550-room resort sprawls across 140 acres
and boasts a staff of 2300, fluent in 56
languages. Just feet from the county's best

snorkeling, this palace has two 18-hole golf
courses, a mile of semiprivate beach, four
pools, two croquet courts and the best
brunch around. For opulence, elegance and
old-world charm, there's no other choice.
Green Lodging certified.

★ **Brazilian Court**   HOTEL **$$$**
(☑ 561-655-7740; www.thebraziliancourt.com;
301 Australian Ave; r $199-422, ste $341-774;
🅿 ❄ 🐾 🐾 🐶) Built in 1926, this elegant resort is an excellent choice for those who
want pampering but not obsequiousness.
Trendy but timeless, it's got a lovely Mediterranean style, a romantic courtyard and
fashionable suites that effortlessly blend
sleek lines and soft comfort. The on-site
Frédéric Fekkai salon and renowned (and
ultraromantic) French Café Boulud (p210)
are major draws, too.

Heading to the beach? Hitch a ride in the
hotel's Jeep – your driver will supply you
with chairs, umbrellas, towels, bottled water
and magazines. Bliss.

Chesterfield   HOTEL **$$$**
(☑ 561-659-5800; www.chesterfieldpb.com;
363 Cocoanut Row; r $185-385, ste $410-735;
🅿 ❄ 🐾 🐾 🐶) From its old-fashioned room
keys to the cookie jar in the lobby, this ho-
tel aims for an old-world elegance that's
much appreciated by its loyal guests, many
of whom have been returning for decades.

SOUTHEAST FLORIDA PALM BEACH

Room decor is very 'Great White Hunter,' with English plaid wallpaper and murals of monkeys gamboling around the jungle. The hotel's Leopard Lounge, with its painted ceilings and tiger-print banquettes, is a perennial favorite for long lunches and evening piano music.

✗ Eating

Dining out in Palm Beach is a high-end affair, though there is a reasonable selection of budget bites. After all, just because you can afford to eat foie gras and Kobe beef every night doesn't mean you never crave a big, greasy burger with fries, right?

Green's Pharmacy   DINER $

(151 N County Rd; mains $4-11; ☉8am-6pm Mon-Fri, to 4pm Sat) Housed inside a working pharmacy, this place hasn't changed since John F Kennedy, looking to slip away from the Secret Service, would stroll across the mint-green linoleum to grab a bite. Choose between a table or a stool at the Formica counter and order from the paper menu just like everyone else, from trust-fund babies slumming it to college girls headed to the beach.

Surfside Diner   DINER, BREAKFAST $

(☑561-659-7495; 314 S County Rd; mains $4.50-14; ☉7:30am-3:30pm) This great remake of a classic diner serves one of the better brunch options in town. Pancakes, chicken breakfast burritos and French toast are all tasty. For lunch there's a healthy offering of grilled cheese and tomato soup, BLTs, PB&Js and sliders.

★ Būccan   MODERN AMERICAN $$

(☑561-833-3450; www.buccanpalmbeach.com; 350 S County Rd; small plates $4.50-36; ☉5pm-midnight Mon-Sat, to 11pm Sun) With its modern American menu and James Beard–nominated chef, Clay Conley, at the helm, Būccan is taking Palm Beach by storm. Flavor-hop with a selection of small plates, including exquisite short-rib empanadas, harissa and mint lamb sliders, and jumbo shrimp with housemade *tasso* (smoked, seasoned ham) and popcorn grits. Reservations recommended.

Palm Beach Grill   MODERN AMERICAN $$

(☑561-835-1077; www.hillstone.com; 340 Poinciana Way; mains $12-36; ☉5-10pm Sun-Thu, to 11pm Fri & Sat) This restaurant is a great compromise between Palm Beach chic and casual.

During the season it's perpetually packed thanks to good food and a buzzing bar. Securing one of the dining room's leather booths can be nearly impossible at the weekend, so book well ahead.

Pizza al Fresco   PIZZERIA $$

(☑561-832-0032; www.pizzaalfresco.com; 14 Via Mizner; pizzas $15-23, salads $6.50-12.50; ☉9am-10pm; ☛) If Worth Ave shopping is making you feel fatigued, duck into quaint Via Mizner and take the strain off your feet at this alfresco pizza place. Light-spangled palm trees provide evening romance, while efficient wait staff whisk out orders of whole wheat and traditional flat crusts lathered with generous and inventive toppings. It also serves a good selection of salads and sandwiches.

★ Café Boulud   FRENCH $$$

(☑561-655-6060; www.thebraziliancourt.com; 301 Australian Ave; mains $16-46, fixed-price menu lunch/dinner $25/45; ☉7am-2:30pm daily, 5:30-10pm Sun-Thu) Created by renowned New York chef Daniel Boulud, the restaurant at the Brazilian Court is one of the few places in Palm Beach that truly justifies the sky-high prices. The warm gold-and-coral dining room and 60-seat terrace complements a rich menu of classic French and fusion dishes, all displaying Boulud's signature sophistication and subtlety.

Kinder on the purse, the Boulud breakfast is a delicious feast of mini Belgian waffles with caramelized banana and walnut compote; wild mushroom omelets with *mâche* (corn salad) drizzled with truffle vinaigrette; or a classic all-American fry-up.

Happy hour is from 4pm to 7:30pm in the lounge and there's live music on Thursday and Friday nights.

Circle   AMERICAN, EUROPEAN $$$

(☑561-659-8440; www.thebreakers.com; 1 S County Rd; adult/child $95/45; ☉11am-2:30pm Sun) Sure, it's steep, but brunch at the Breakers' storied restaurant will certainly rank among the most amazing you'll ever enjoy. Beneath soaring 30ft frescoed ceilings, surrounded by ocean views and entertained by a roving harpsichordist, guests begin their feast at the breakfast bar, which features homemade doughnuts, tropical fruits and on-demand omelets.

In-season you'll need to reserve weeks in advance.

SOUTHEAST FLORIDA PALM BEACH

Cafe L'Europe
EUROPEAN $$$

(☎ 561-655-4020; www.cafeleeurope.com; 331 S County Rd; mains $30-46; ⊙ 11am-2:30pm Tue-Fri, 5-10pm Tue-Sun) Reservations are essential if you hope to sample the fab caviar, poached salmon, lamb chops or snapper here. The dining room is transcendent, and the owners friendly.

Ta-Boo
MODERN AMERICAN $$$

(☎ 561-835-3500; www.taboorestaurant.com; 221 Worth Ave; mains $16-45; ⊙ 11:30am-10pm) If you believe the legend, the Bloody Mary was invented here, mixed to soothe the hangover of Woolworth heiress Barbara Hutton. Today the restaurant boasts the most coveted window seats on Worth Ave and competition to get in is as stiff as the heiress' drinks. But get past the intricate woodwork and jungle murals, and you'll enjoy a well-executed American bistro meal.

🍷 Drinking & Entertainment

Palm Beach doesn't party much (must be tired from all that shopping and afternoon wine-sipping), but all the large hotels have swanky bars. If you want to get wild, head across the bridge to West Palm.

O Bar
BAR

(www.omphoy.com; 2842 S Ocean Blvd, Omphoy Hotel) Moneyed hipster types sip 'Aum-Foys' (Lillet Blanc, ruby grapefruit, sparkling white wine), guava margaritas and other chic cocktails at this sleek, moodily lit bar in the trendalicious Omphoy hotel.

Cucina Dell'arte
CLUB

(http://cucinadellarte.com; 257 Royal Poinciana Way; ⊙ 7am-3am) Reminiscent of a Florentine cafe, this high-end eatery overflows with warm colors, art and some of the finest glitterati in Palm Beach. Around 10pm they shove the tables out of the way and blast the music. Pretentious enough to be fun; if you arrive wearing a serious face, you'll be sorry.

Leopard Lounge
LOUNGE

(www.chesterfieldpb.com/dining/bar; 363 Cocoanut Row; ⊙ 6:30pm-1am) This swanky fresco-and-leopard-print place attracts a mature crowd and the occasional celeb (neither photos nor autograph hounds are allowed). Live music nightly.

Society of the Four Arts
PERFORMING ARTS

(☎ 561-655-7226; www.fourarts.org; 2 Four Arts Plaza) The concert series here includes cabaret, the Palm Beach Symphony, chamber orchestras, string quartets and piano performances.

🛍 Shopping

The quarter-mile palm-tree-lined Worth Ave is Florida's answer to Rodeo Dr. It's lined with global marques such as Cartier, Armani, Gucci, Chanel, Dior, Tiffany and Hermes, and the gilding drips down onto the sidewalk scene. Among these giants, tucked down side alleys, you'll find smaller independent purveyors and galleries. Half the shops close for summer, but it's fun to stroll and window-shop (and celeb-spot), whether you want to lay down your plastic or not. Royal Poinciana Way is another shopping hot spot, with a slightly more accessible price range.

C. Orrico
FASHION

(☎ 561-659-1284; www.corrico.com; 336 S County Rd; ⊙ 10am-6pm Mon-Sat, 11am-6pm Sun) Lilly Pulitzer, the Palm Beach princess of prints who created a fashion uniform for wealthy socialites, passed away in February 2013, aged 81. Pay homage to this enduring Palm Beach style icon by purchasing one of her lurid print dresses from C. Orrico, and pair it with similarly psychedelic sandals and jewelry.

Stubbs & Wootton
SHOES

(☎ 561-655-6857; www.stubbsandwootton.com; 1 Via Parigi; ⊙ 9:30am-5:30pm Mon-Sat, noon-4pm Sun) If you want to fit in with the no-socks Palm Beach set, head straight to this high-end slippers and sandals shop. Wedges made from woven raffia handcrafted in Spain, hand-embroidered velvet slippers with custom-designed monograms and cool chambray cotton espadrilles are all uniquely Palm Beach.

Daniela Ortiz
ACCESSORIES

(☎ 561-366-0008; www.daniellaortiz.com; 256 Worth Ave; ⊙ 10:30am-5:30pm Mon-Sat) Shoppers in Daniela Ortiz are like kids in a candy store – they're unable to decide between the rainbow-colored collection of totes, purses, shoulder bags and clutches. Detailed hand-stitching, contrast color linings and jeweled locks and buckles make for a beautiful finish. And the best bit? They retail for around a quarter of the price of the big brands on Worth Ave.

Il Sandalo
SHOES

(☎ 561-805-8674; www.ilsandalo.com; Via Gucci Courtyard, 240 Worth Ave; ⊙ 10am-6pm Mon-Sat) Handcrafted leather sandals from Neapolitan brothers Fabio and Pier Paolo Tesorone. Classic styles are embellished with glittering laminates, coral and, in some cases, semi-precious stones. If you can't find anything you like, have a pair made on-site to your exact specifications.

Church Mouse CONSIGNMENT
(☑561-659-2154; www.bbts.org/churchmouse; 374 S County Rd; ☺10am-5pm Mon-Sat) Sponsored by Bethesda-by-the-Sea, this little consignment shop has raised more than $4.5 million dollars for Palm Beach charities in the last 20 years. It stocks 'gently' used castaways, and if you browse carefully you can find Palm Beach classics from Lilly Pulitzer or Chanel.

Tropical Fruit Shop FOOD
(www.tropicalfruitshop.com; 261 Royal Poinciana Way; ☺8:30am-6pm) Since 1915 this dim little storefront has been shipping the finest Indian River oranges and grapefruits to friends and family of Palm Beach vacationers. Stop in to pick out a gift basket for a deserving loved one, or simply to buy some retro orange candies.

ℹ Information

Note that many shops and restaurants are only open from Thanksgiving to Easter. For 'everyday' needs, such as internet cafes and laundries, head to West Palm Beach.

Chamber of Commerce (☑561-655-3282; www.palmbeachchamber.com; 400 Royal Palm Way, Suite 106) Excellent maps, racks of pamphlets and a new android app of the *Palm Beach Guide*.

ℹ Getting There & Around

PalmTran (www.palmtran.org) bus 41 covers the bulk of the island, from Lantana Rd to Sunrise Ave; transfer to bus 1 at Publix to go north or south along US 1. A single fare costs adult/child $2/1. To get to Palm Beach International Airport (p219) in West Palm Beach, take bus 41 to the downtown transfer and hop on bus 44.

Though it's a fairly compact city, the two major downtown neighborhoods, centered on Royal Poinciana Way and Worth Ave, are a fair hike apart.

West Palm Beach

☑561 / POP 99,920

When Henry Flagler decided to develop what is now West Palm Beach, he knew precisely what it would become: a working-class community for the labor force that would support his glittering resort town across the causeway. And so the fraternal twins were born – Palm Beach, considered the fairer of the two, and West Palm Beach, a cooler work-hard-play-hard community. West Palm has a surprisingly diverse collection of restaurants, friendly inhabitants (including a strong gay community) and a gorgeous waterway that always seems to reflect the perfect amount of starlight.

◉ Sights

Long before the CityPlace (p219) complex came along, there was **Clematis St**, a hip, bohemian strip bustling with locals, diners and scads of bar-hoppers come nightfall. The most eclectic strip in town, much of it's also a **historic district** with a jumbled collection of architecture – Greek Revival, Venetian Revival, Mediterranean Revival and art deco. Every Thursday night, Clematis plays host to West Palm's signature event, Clematis by Night (p216).

Another area worth a wander or drive is the **El Cid District** south of Okeechobee Blvd. Facing Palm Beach across the water, this lovely neighborhood is packed with multimillion-dollar homes – ranging from Mediterranean Revival to classic Florida bungalows.

★**Norton Museum of Art** MUSEUM
(☑561-832-5196; www.norton.org; 1451 S Olive Ave; adult/child $12/5; ☺10am-5pm Tue-Sat, to 9pm Thu, 11am-5pm Sun) The largest art museum in Florida, the Norton opened in 1941 to display the enormous art collection of industrialist Ralph Hubbard Norton and his wife Elizabeth. The Nortons' permanent collection of more than 5000 pieces (including works by Matisse, Warhol and O'Keeffe) is displayed alongside important Chinese, pre-Columbian Mexican and US Southwestern artifacts, plus some wonderful contemporary photography and regular traveling exhibitions.

To enhance your visit you can join one of the free docent-led tours through the galleries. Alternatively, drop by on Thursday evenings for the fun 'Art After Dark' series, which includes anything from lectures and live music to conversations with curators and wine tastings.

★**Ann Norton Sculpture Garden** GARDEN
(www.ansg.org; 253 Barcelona Rd; adult/child $10/5; ☺10am-4pm Wed-Sun) This serene collection of sculptures is a real West Palm gem. The historic house, verdant grounds and enormous sculptures are all the work of Ralph Norton's second wife, Ann. After

establishing herself as an artist in New York in the mid-1930s, she became the first sculpture teacher at the Norton School of Art in West Palm, and created this luxurious garden as a place of repose.

After poking through Norton's antique-filled home, you can wander the grounds and uncover her soaring feats of granite, brick, marble and bronze. Perhaps most awe-inspiring is the 1965 *Cluster*, a collection of seven burka-clad women in pink granite. Before leaving, be sure to peek into Norton's light-filled studio, where dusty tools lie just as she left them.

Artists are free to bring their easels and indulge in a spot of plein air painting in the garden for $15.

International Polo Club   POLO
(☑ 561-204-5687; www.internationalpoloclub.com; 3667 120th Ave S, Wellington; general admission $11.50, lawn seating $22-32.50; ☺ Sun Jan-Apr) Between January and April the International Polo Club hosts 16 weeks of polo and glamour. As one of the finest polo facilities in the world, it not only attracts the most elite players but also the local and international glitterati who whoop it up in head-turning fashion over champagne brunches (tickets $120). Why not join the fun?

Lion Country Safari   WILDLIFE RESERVE
(☑ 561-793-1084; www.lioncountrysafari.com; 2003 Lion Country Safari Rd; adult/child $29.95/21.95; ☺ 9:30am-5:30pm; ⓓ) The first cageless drive-through safari in the country, this incredible animal park puts you in the cage (ie your car) as 900 creatures roam freely, staring at *you*. Equal parts conservation area and safari, the park's 500 acres are home to bison, zebra, white rhinos, chimpanzees and, of course, lions. You tour in your car (unless it's a convertible, in which case short-term rentals are available), driving slowly, hoping the animals approach the vehicle. The best time to go is when it rains, because the animals are more active when it's cool.

The park is about half an hour's drive west of downtown West Palm.

Palm Beach County Museum   MUSEUM
(☑ 561-832-4164; www.historicalsocietypbc.org; 300 N Dixie Hwy; ☺ 10am-5pm Tue-Sat) FREE For all the region's activities and museums, it can be hard for outsiders to get an insight into the history and people of the Sunshine State. This small museum housed in the restored 1916 courthouse and staffed by volunteers aims to change. Quirky exhibits –

featuring models, photographs and period artifacts – highlight individuals who have contributed to the growth and prosperity of Palm Beach County. Informative plaques on everyone from Flagler and Mizner to Alligator Joe and the first settlers make the tour a fascinating one.

Peanut Island   PARK
(www.pbcgov.com/parks/peanutisland) Plopped right off the northeastern corner of West Palm, Peanut Island was created in 1918 by dredging projects. Originally named Inlet Island, the spit was renamed for a peanut-oil-shipping operation that failed in 1946. It has long been a popular spot for boaters to moor and party by day, and in 2005 the county invested $13 million into island rehabilitation, resulting in Peanut Island Park, which includes a pier, an artificial reef and some pretty sweet campsites.

There are no roads to the island. Visitors must either have their own boats or take the water taxi.

Ragtops Motorcars Museum   MUSEUM
(www.ragtopsmotorcars.com; 2119 S Dixie Hwy; donations appreciated; ☺ 10am-5pm Tue-Sat) This spot was originally a classic-car dealership with three convertible Mercedes, but Ty Houck's incredible automobile collection quickly grew, compelling area automotive enthusiasts to stop by for a look-see. Today, you can test-drive many of the vehicles on display, though it helps to have serious intent to buy. Otherwise, you're free to browse the rarities displayed, including an amphibious 1967 Triumph, a regal 1935 Bentley and a 1959 Edsel station wagon.

🏃 Activities

You'll find several parks around town, many equipped with paved trails suitable for cycling, blading or running.

★ National Croquet Center   CROQUET
(☑ 561-478-2300; www.nationalcroquetclub.com; 700 Florida Mango Rd; ☺ 9am-5pm) FREE Get a real taste of the upper-crust Palm Beach lifestyle at the National Croquet Center, the largest croquet facility in the world. Here, genteel sportspeople dressed in crisp whites hit balls through wickets on 12 of the world's biggest, greenest, most manicured lawns. It's members-only, but the public is invited to free lessons on Saturday mornings at 10am. The pro shop, inside the plantation-style

West Palm Beach

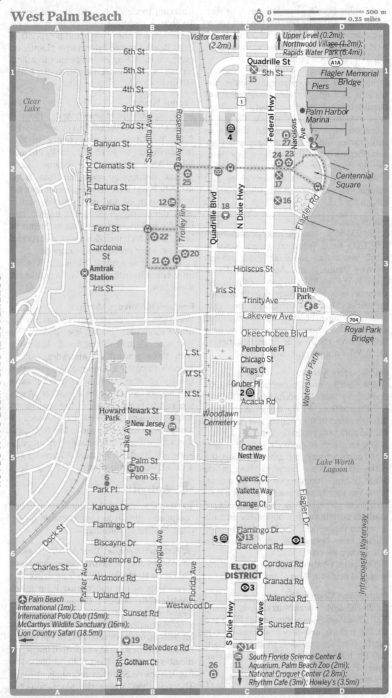

SOUTHEAST FLORIDA WEST PALM BEACH

0 ——————— 500 m
0 ——————— 0.25 miles

Visitor Center
(2.2mi)

Upper Level (0.2mi);
Northwood Village (1.2mi);
Rapids Water Park (6.4mi)

6th St
5th St
4th St
3rd St
2nd St

Quadrille St

Flagler Memorial
Bridge

Clear
Lake

Banyan St
Clematis St
Datura St
Evernia St

Fern St

Gardenia
St

Amtrak
Station

Iris St

S Tamarind Ave

Rosemary Ave

Sapodilla Ave

Quadrille Blvd

N Dixie Hwy

Federal Hwy

Narcissus Ave

Flagler Dr

Trolley line

5th St
15

Piers

Palm Harbor
Marina

27

7

24 23

17

16

25

12

18

22

21 20

Centennial
Square

Hibiscus St

Iris St

TrinityAve

Lakeview Ave

Okeechobee Blvd

L St

M St

N St

Pembrooke Pl
Chicago St
Kings Ct
Gruber Pl
2
Acacia Rd

Trinity
Park

8

704

Royal Park
Bridge

Waterside Path

Howard
Park

Newark St

New Jersey
St

Palm St

Penn St

6
Park Pl

9

10

Woodlawn
Cemetery

Cranes
Nest Way

Queens Ct
Vallette Way
Orange Ct

Lake Worth
Lagoon

Lake Ave

Dock St

Charles St

Kanuga Dr
Flamingo Dr
Biscayne Dr
Claremore Dr
Ardmore Rd
Upland Rd

Georgia Ave

Florida Ave

Flamingo Dr

Barcelona Rd

Cordova Rd

Granada Rd

5 13

1

EL CID
DISTRICT

3

Flagler Dr

Intracoastal Waterway

Parker Ave

Palm Beach
International (1mi);
International Polo Club (15mi);
McCarthys Wildlife Sanctuary (16mi);
Lion Country Safari (18.5mi)

Sunset Rd

Westwood Dr

19

Gotham Ct

Lake Blvd

S Dixie Hwy

Valencia Rd

Sunset Rd

Olive Ave

Belvedere Rd

26

11

South Florida Science Center &
Aquarium, Palm Beach Zoo (2mi);
National Croquet Center (2.8mi);
Rhythm Cafe (3mi); Howley's (3.5mi)

14

A1A

clubhouse, has all the latest in mallets and croquet wear.

The center is about a 10-minute drive southwest of downtown West Palm.

Armory Art Center COURSE
(☎561-832-1776; 1700 Parker Ave) **FREE** When the Norton Museum of Art closed down their educational programs, the not-for-profit Armory took over as the county's leading visual arts education and exhibition center. In the process they saved the wonderful 1939 art deco Armory building, which was built by architect William Manley King and occupied by the National Guard until 1989. With more than a dozen state-of-the-art studios, the center now hosts more than a hundred adult and youth courses in ceramics, jewelry, painting, drawing, printmaking, photography and sculpture.

Special events, lectures and rotating gallery exhibits also aim to educate and enrich. From June to early August, the Armory hosts a Summer Art Camp for kids between the ages of five and 17.

FishCastings FISHING
(☎561-352-8011; www.fishcastings.com; 900 E Blue Heron Blvd, Riviera Beach) Hard-to-beat fishing know-how dished up by long-time local Captain James who knows all the best places to hook monster barracuda, blue runners, king mackerel and even shark. Boats are limited to six fishers. Spearfishing trips are possible for certified free divers. Most

trips leave from Riviera Beach, 5.5 miles north of downtown on the Intracoastal Waterway to Singer Island.

Okeeheelee County Park CYCLING, WATER SPORTS
(☎561-233-1400; www.pbcgov.com/parks; 7715 Forest Hill Blvd; ⊗9am-4pm) Five miles south of town, this park has a 6-mile paved path, plus BMX track, golf course, water-ski park, nature center and equestrian trail. The most scenic walk – a smooth, waterside path – is the one that edges the Intracoastal Waterway along Flagler Dr.

⭐ Tours

Palm Beach Water Taxi BOAT TOUR
(☎561-683-8294; www.sailfishmarina.com; 98 Lake Dr, Singer Island) Water taxis run between downtown West Palm and Singer Island ($15), as well as to Peanut Island (round-trip $12), leaving from Singer Island. Additionally, the outfit offers guided tours along the Intracoastal, including 90-minute narrated tours of Palm Beach mansions (adult/child $30/15).

Diva Duck BOAT TOUR
(☎561-844-4418; www.divaduck.com; adult/child $25/15; ⊛) This hybrid bus-boat gives quacky 75-minute narrated tours of downtown's historic district, CityPlace, the surrounding waterways and the shores of Peanut Island. Yes, the bus really does float in the water. Tours start at CityPlace.

✹ Festivals & Events

SunFest
ARTS

(www.sunfest.com; ☺May) Florida's largest waterfront music and art festival, SunFest attracts more than 250,000 visitors for five days in early May, raising money for scholarships for art students.

Clematis by Night
MUSIC

(www.clematisbynight.net; ☺6-9:30pm Thu) Every Thursday night the city shuts down the eastern terminus of Clematis St, brings in food carts and crafts vendors, and stages a free outdoor music festival under the stars.

🛌 Sleeping

Skip the depressing chain hotels near the airport and try one of West Palm's cool spots.

Peanut Island
CAMPGROUND $

(☎561-845-4445; www.pbcgov.com/parks/peanutisland; tent sites $30) This tiny island has 20 developed campsites by reservation only and a host of primitive sites right on the sand on a first-come, first-served basis. There are some restrictions, so call or hit the website.

Hotel Biba
MOTEL $

(☎561-832-0094; www.hotelbiba.com; 320 Belvedere Rd; r $75-149; ❇🐾🛜🏊) 🏄 Funky, retro Hotel Biba has injected an ordinary motel with pop-art flair. This groovy spot has lots going for it – spare-chic decor in vibrantly colored rooms; a leafy little courtyard with a hidden-away pool; and a hip, sexy bar where you'll find a thriving lounge scene at night. A block from the Intracoastal, the Biba is perched on the edge of the El Cid district.

★ Grandview Gardens
B&B $$

(☎561-833-9023; www.grandview-gardens.com; 1608 Lake Ave; r $125-209; P❇🛜🏊) Book a room at this intimate resort and you'll feel like a local in no time. Hidden in a tropical garden on Howard Park, the enormous suites with their wrought-iron and four-poster beds access the pool patio through French doors. They're decorated to reflect the Spanish Mediterranean style that is so popular in these parts. The house is a period 1925 structure typical of the historic neighborhood and it sits opposite the Armory Art Center, so is perfect for longer stays for the arts-inclined.

Palm Beach Hibiscus
B&B $$

(☎561-833-8171; www.palmbeachhibiscus.com; 213 S Rosemary Ave; r $110-280; ❇🛜) Fabulously located just a block from CityPlace, this pair of 1917 homes has four-poster beds, floral prints, abundant light and a cool front porch with wicker chairs. Take a load off and watch the world – including the city trolley, which stops out front – roll by. Reserve ahead for lunch and dinner in the shady tiki bar lounge.

Upper Level
B&B $$

(☎561-429-8169; www.theupperlevel.me; 1011 N Dixie Hwy; r $150-200; P❇🛜) Great value for West Palm Beach, this 1920s art deco house is part way between an upmarket hostel and a stylish B&B. It has 10 bedrooms, five gleaming bathrooms and two showers. Although guests share washing facilities you barely notice it, and the rooms are styled with white-on-white decor and interesting contemporary artworks.

Casa Grandview
B&B, COTTAGE $$$

(☎561-313-9695; www.casagrandview.com; 1410 Georgia Ave; r $149-299; ❇🛜🏊) Hidden behind hedgerows in the historic Grandview Heights neighborhood, this intimate little compound has five B&B rooms, seven cottages and five suite apartments. B&B rooms are in the main house, which has a charming-if-odd medieval-Spanish feel, with a narrow stone staircase and elf-sized wooden doors in the walls. We love the cozy Library Suite – small but plush. Luxurious cottages have a stylized 1940s beach chic, with vintage signs and bright tiled kitchens – great for families.

🍴 Eating

The food scene here is an eclectic affair – ethnic eats mixed with quirky spaces and quaint tearooms – with many affordable options. Clematis St and CityPlace are both teaming with restaurants, and a drive north to the up-and-coming Northwood Village (http://wpb.org/northwood) will reward with some stellar dining and shopping. Every fourth Friday, the village hosts the popular 'Art and Wine Promenade,' where visitors stroll between studios and galleries discovering local artists.

★ Curbside Gourmet
FOOD TRUCK $

(☎561-371-6565; http://curbsidegourmet.com; 2000 S Dixie Hwy) This bright, peppermint truck is Palm Beach's first mobile food truck dedicated to bringing good, seasonal staples to resident gourmands. The short, sweet menu includes a breakfast burrito, BLTs, crabcake sliders, fresh fish and pork tacos, and a daily panini or frittata. Fries are hand cut; add-ons include heritage tomatoes and Applewood smoked bacon; and dessert is caramelized grapefruit. Yum.

On Mondays, Wednesdays and Fridays the truck parks at South Dixie; on Tuesdays and Thursdays at Trinity Park.

★ **Mediterranean**
Market & Deli   MIDDLE EASTERN $
(☎561-659-7322; www.mediterraneanmarketandbakery.com; 327 5th St; mains $2-11.50) Don't be put off by the nondescript warehouse exterior – this Middle Eastern deli serves up some of the most flavorful lunches in town. Fresh baked pita is stuffed with homemade hummus, feta and kefta accompanied by zingy lima bean salad and tabbouleh. You can then order honey-drenched baklava or lady fingers to go.

Paris Bakery & Cafe   FRENCH $
(www.parisbakerycafe.com; 212 S Olive Ave; mains $4-13; ☺8am-2:30pm Mon & Tue, to 2:30pm & 5-9pm Wed-Fri, 9am-2pm & 5-9pm Sat) French owned and operated, this cute patisserie serves Continental breakfasts of crepes any style, well-priced lunches of salmon soaked in white wine and beef tornadoes, and sandwiches stuffed with paysanne chicken. On Saturday, queues form down the block for 'Le Frunch'.

★ **Garage VV**   MODERN AMERICAN $$
(☎561-802-4441; www.garagevv.com; 409 Northwood Rd; mains $12-25.50; ☺11am-11pm Mon-Thu, to midnight Fri & Sat, to 4pm Sun) You can tell Northwood is on the up by this latest addition to its culinary landscape. The brainchild of Vivian Bordieri Moir, partner to Mike Moir of Jupiter's famous Little Moir's Food Shack (p222), and partners Nina Wasserman and Kimberly Levine, industrial-styled Garage focuses on inventive fish dishes crusted and marinated with an array of interesting spices, nuts and herbs. Fresh baked breads and pastas made on the premises are also available to buy from the small market inside the restaurant.

Rocco's Tacos & Tequila Bar   MEXICAN $$
(www.roccostacos.com; 224 Clematis St; mains $12-23; ☺11:30am-11pm Sun-Wed, to midnight Thu-Sat) This saucy Nuevo Mexican restaurant, in the heart of West Palm's Clematis St, is not your typical taqueria. Under the warm twinkle of funky chandeliers, you can enjoy guacamole prepared tableside, fresh-made ceviche, or a range of tacos from pork to mushroom to cactus paddle. And, oh yeah, there are 175 different kinds of tequila to choose from.

WEST PALM BEACH FOR CHILDREN

Besides the beach scene, there's a ton of activities laid on for kids in West Palm Beach, ranging from funparks and bike parks to wildlife reserves and a full scale safari experience (p213).

Palm Beach Zoo (☎561-533-0887; www.palmbeachzoo.com; 1301 Summit Blvd; adult/child $18.95/12.95; ☺9am-5pm; 🚸) The highlight of this compact zoo is the Tropics of the Americas exhibit, a 3-acre recreation of a rainforest, stocked with jaguars, monkeys, snakes, macaws and other tropical creatures. Gator feedings occur regularly and are advertised. The zoo is a brief drive south of downtown.

McCarthys Wildlife Sanctuary (☎561-790-2116.; www.mccarthyswildlifesanctuary.com; 12943 61st St N; adult/child $25/15; ☺tours 11am, noon, 1pm Tue-Sat) By reservation only, this wildlife sanctuary takes unwanted exotics and treats dozens of native animals, and then releases them back into the wild. On the two-hour guided tour you'll get to see white tigers, panthers and barred owls, all from 3ft away. Children under five are not permitted.

South Florida Science Center & Aquarium (☎561-832-1988; www.sfsm.org; 4801 Dreher Trail N; adult/child museum $9/6, planetarium plus $4/2; ☺10am-5pm Mon-Fri, to 6pm Sat, noon-6pm Sun) A hands-on science center, aquarium and planetarium with weekend programs, travelling exhibits, a science trail and mini galaxy golf. On the last Friday of the month the museum stays open until 9pm so you can view the night sky from the observatory. It's a short drive south of downtown.

Rapids Water Park (☎561-842-8756; www.rapidswaterpark.com; 6566 North Military Trail, Riviera Beach; weekday/weekend $39.99/43.99, after 4pm $22; ☺10am-5pm) This water park features 30 action-packed acres of wet and wild rides. Don't let the squeals of fear and delight from the Big Thunder funnel put you off. It's a short drive northwest of downtown.

SINGER ISLAND

To reach Singer from West Palm Beach, take Olive Ave north over the bridge (where it's called Broadway) until you hit Blue Heron Blvd; cross the causeway, turn right on Lake Dr and follow it to the **Sailfish Marina** (📞561-842-8449; www.sailfishmarina.com; 98 Lake Dr; mains $6-38; ⊙7am-10pm), which serves brunch on weekends between 8am and 1pm. Grab a seat close to the water, slowly chew your smoked salmon, tropical fruit or fresh Belgian waffles, and watch the resident pelicans paddle around the yachts, searching for their own breakfast.

Full? Good. Get in the car and head east to S Ocean Ave, then head north to Beach Rd and scoot into the parking lot. Park and head past the surf shop and gently rolling dunes. You're probably thinking, 'Where are all the people?' Yup, that's why we're here. Pick a spot, spread your towel, lie down and let breakfast digest. Read a magazine. Stroll the beach. Take a dip.

If you're thirsty, nearby **Tiki Waterfront Sea Grill** (📞561-845-5532; 200 E 13th St; mains $10-30; ⊙11am-10pm Mon-Fri, from 8am Sat & Sun), a dive teeming with sunburned boaters, has a loud, fun bar, great fish tacos and regular live music. To get there, head back along Blue Heron to Broadway, turn left (south) and then left onto E 13th St. The Tiki Grill is at the end of the street. Enjoy your tacos; dance awhile. You're in Florida.

Howley's
AMERICAN $$

(4700 S Dixie Hwy; mains $14-25; ⊙11am-2pm Mon-Thu, to 5am Fri & Sat) Open almost all night, this mint-green 1950s diner's tagline is 'cooked in sight, must be right.' The food (shake 'n' bake pork chops, crab hash, tiki-style tuna burgers and banana pancakes) might be described as 'upscale retro' and certainly tastes right – especially at 2am.

★ O-BŌ
MODERN AMERICAN $$$

(📞561-366-1185; 422 Northwood Rd; plates $8-32; ⊙5pm-12:30am Tue-Sat) At O-BŌ art gallerist Jeffery Thompson and chef Bob Reilly have come up with a perfect combination of retro-cool interior, delectable small plates, a carefully curated wine and beer list and soulful live music. House specials include black-and-white lobster ravioli, spicy short rib spring rolls and the unique Saketini – a white hot sake martini. Check out the Facebook page for live acts and events

★ Rhythm Cafe
FUSION $$$

(📞561-833-3406; www.rhythmcafe.cc; 3800 S Dixie Hwy; mains $17-30; ⊙5:30-10pm Tue-Sat, to 9pm Sun) There's no lack of flair at this colorful, upbeat bistro set in a converted drugstore in West Palm's antiques district. It's strung with Christmas lights and hung with bright, bobbing paper lanterns. The menu is equally vibrant, bopping from goat's cheese pie to 'the best tuna tartar ever' to the pomegranate-infused catch of the day. Dessert's a star – the chocolate butter-cream cake is advertized as 'so good you'll slap your momma!' We don't advise that, but do taste the cake.

Kitchen
MODERN AMERICAN $$$

(📞561-249-2281; http://kitchenpb.com; 319 Belvedere Road #2; mains $20-34; ⊙6-10pm Mon-Sat) Book well ahead if you want to snag a seat at one of the 10 tables in chef Matthew Byrne's contemporary American brasserie. The concept is simple: take the freshest ingredients, present them in the simplest, most flavorful manner possible, and *voilà*! You get highlights such as organic chicken schnitzel dressed in Panko breadcrumbs and topped with charred lemon and a sunny fried egg. Aliza, Bryne's wife, hosts and there's a chef's table that seats up to ten.

🍸 Drinking & Entertainment

Clematis and CityPlace have a revolving door of ultrachic bar-lounges and late-night dance clubs; they're also home to a couple of great, casual, stalwart hangouts.

On Fridays and Saturdays, CityPlace hosts **free outdoor concerts** (www.cityplace.com) from 6pm to 10pm. Bands stick to familiar rock, R&B and occasional country sounds.

Blind Monk
WINE BAR

(📞561-833-3605; http://theblindmonk.com; 410 Evernia St #107; ⊙4pm-late) With a team of knowledgeable sommeliers behind it, the Blind Monk is arguably the best wine bar in West Palm. It offers an extensive list of wines by the glass, including international labels and local craft beers. Small plates of cheese, salami, grapes, pickles and nuts soak up the vino, while silent old movies play on the wall.

HG Roosters
GAY

(http://roosterswpb.com; 823 Belvedere Rd; ⊙3pm-3am Mon-Sat, noon-3am Sun) A mainstay of West Palm's thriving gay community, this bar has been offering wings, bingo and hot young male dancers since 1984.

Pawnshop
CLUB

(http://pawnshopwpb.com; 219 Clematis St; cover $10; ☺5pm-3am Tue-Thu, to 4am Fri & Sat) This former Miami dance club and celebrity haunt opened with a knock-out party in March 2014. Situated in the previous Dr Feelgood venue, it features the familiar pawn shop trappings along with a life-sized vintage Ferris wheel and a DJ booth designed out of a Mack truck. DJ's, dancers and light shows keep the party going til 3am while rivers of alcohol flow from the 175ft bar.

CityPlace
CONCERT VENUE

(www.cityplace.com; 700 S Rosemary Ave; ☺10am-10pm Mon-Sat, noon-6pm Sun) This massive entertainment and shopping complex is the crown jewel of West Palm Beach's urban-renewal initiative. At its center is the **Harriet Himmel Theater** (☎561-318-7136; www.cityplace.com; 600 S Rosemary Ave), a beautiful 1926 Colonial Revival structure that previously housed the Methodist Church, and now puts on an exhaustive round of exhibitions, fashion shows and concerts. Besides that there's a swanky new bowling alley, a 20-screen cinema theater, dozens of restaurants and a slew of stores.

Palm Beach Dramaworks
THEATER

(☎561-514-4042; www.palmbeachdramaworks.org; 201 Clematis St) 'Theatre to Think About' is the tagline of this award-winning resident theater, which is committed to presenting underrated classic and contemporary plays from the likes of Lorca, Steinbeck, Pinter, Lorraine Hansberry and Horton Foote.

Respectable Street
LIVE MUSIC

(www.respectablestreet.com; 518 Clematis St) Respectables has kept South Florida jamming to great bands for two decades; it also organizes October's MoonFest, the city's best block party. Great DJs, strong drinks and a breezy chill-out patio are added bonuses. See if you can find the hole that the Red Hot Chili Peppers' Anthony Kiedis punched in the wall when they played here.

BB King's
LIVE MUSIC

(www.bbkingclubs.com; 550 S Rosemary Ave) One of bluesman BB King's stable of clubs, this Mississippi Delta–themed nightspot in CityPlace has a menu of (mediocre) Southern soul food and an excellent lineup of blues and jazz bands.

Shopping

Clematis St and CityPlace have tons of both chain and nonchain boutiques, home-decor shops and more. More hip is the up-and-coming Northwood Village artists community, which is well stocked with small galleries and antique stores.

Greenmarket
MARKET

(http://wpb.org/greenmarket; ☺9am-1pm Sat) Just north of the plaza at 2nd St and Narcissus Ave (where local schoolkids frolic in the fountains on hot afternoons), this delightful market offers treats ranging from locally grown avocados and orchids to organic coffee and dog treats on Saturday mornings.

Antiques Row
ANTIQUES

(S Dixie Hwy) Just south of town, this peerless market has more than 50 antiques collectors. You're sure to unearth an incredible find from a Palm Beach estate.

ℹ Information

The *Palm Beach Post* (www.palmbeachpost.com) is the largest paper. The visitor center publishes several vacation-planning guides, available online at www.palmbeachfl.com.

Post Office (640 Clematis St) Conveniently located.

Visitor Center (☎561-233-3000; www.palmbeachfl.com; 1555 Palm Beach Lakes Blvd) Extensive area information, maps and online guides.

ℹ Getting There & Around

Palm Beach International Airport (PBI; ☎561-471-7420; www.pbia.org; 1000 Palm Beach) is served by most major airlines and car-rental companies. It's about a mile west of I-95 on Belvedere Rd. **PalmTran** (www.palmtran.org) bus 44 runs between the airport, the train station and downtown ($2).

Greyhound (☎561-833-8534; www.greyhound.com; 215 S Tamarind Ave; ☺6am-10:45pm), **Tri-Rail** (☎800-875-7245; www.tri-rail.com; 203 S Tamarind Ave) and **Amtrak** (☎800-872-7245; www.amtrak.com; 209 S Tamarind Ave) share the same building, the historic Seaboard Train Station. PalmTran serves the station with bus 44 (from the airport).

Once you're settled, driving and parking is a cinch. There's also a cute and convenient (and free!) trolley running between Clematis St and CityPlace starting at 11am.

TREASURE COAST

The Treasure Coast gets its name for being the site of numerous treasure-laden shipwrecks over the years. In fact, today the Treasure Coast is where you'll find Florida's true jewels, in the form of unspoiled paradise.

Industrialist billionaire and philanthropist John D MacArthur (1897–1978) once owned almost everything from Palm Beach Gardens to Stuart, and he kept it mostly pristine during his life. Over time, he grew concerned that Florida's real-estate bonanza would compromise – or destroy – what he considered paradise. Therefore, in his will, he stated that thousands of acres would be kept wild, and the rest would be deeded out incrementally, in order to save the oceanfront property from Miami's fate. And you know what? His plan worked.

John D MacArthur State Park

While this state park (☑ 561-624-6952; www.macarthurbeach.org; 10900 Jack Nicklaus Dr; per vehicle/bicycle $5/2; ⊙ 8am-sunset) is one of the smallest in the region, it has among the best turtle-watching programs around. Loggerhead, green and leatherback turtles nest along the beach in June and July. It's home to several aquariums and a spectacular 1600ft boardwalk spanning the mangroves of Lake Worth Cove. The on-site nature center offers guided (single/double $20/35) and unguided (single/double $10/15 per hour) kayak trips.

In June and July, lucky visitors might catch a glimpse of hatching baby sea turtles during the ranger-led turtle walks, led nightly at 8:30pm.

Jupiter & Jupiter Island

Jupiter is a largely ritzy residential area, and one of the wealthiest communities in America. For visitors, it's best seen as a jumping-off point for exploring the area's fantastic parks, nature preserves and beaches. Unlike those of its southerly neighbors Palm Beach and Boca Raton, the beaches around here are largely untouched by condo development.

⊙ Sights & Activities

Jupiter Inlet Lighthouse   LIGHTHOUSE
(www.jupiterlighthouse.org; US 1 & Beach Rd, intersection Capt Armour's Way; adult/child $9/5; ⊙ 10am-5pm Tue-Sun) Built in 1860, this historic lighthouse hasn't missed a night of work in more than 100 years and is among the oldest lighthouses on the Atlantic coast. Visitors can climb the 108 steps to view the surrounding area and ocean. Tours to the lighthouse depart every half-hour. There's some interesting Seminole and pioneer Florida memorabilia in the small (and woefully disorganized) museum.

Hobe Sound National Wildlife Refuge   WILDLIFE RESERVE
(www.fws.gov/hobesound; US 1) A 1035 acre federally protected nature sanctuary, Hobe Sound has two sections: a small slice on the mainland, opposite the Jonathan Dickinson State Park; and the main refuge grounds at the northern end of Jupiter Island. The Jupiter Island section has 3.5 miles of beach (it's a favorite sea-turtle nesting ground), while the mainland section is a pine scrub forest. In June and July, nighttime turtle-watching walks occur on Tuesdays and Thursdays (reservations necessary), and birding trips can be arranged through the Hawley Education Center at Blowing Rocks Preserve.

Blowing Rocks Preserve   NATURE RESERVE
(574 S Beach Rd; admission $2; ⊙ 9am-4:30pm) This preserve encompasses a mile-long limestone outcrop riddled with holes, cracks and fissures. When the tide is high and there's a strong easterly wind (call for conditions), water spews up as if from a geyser. Bring a tripod and an empty memory card. Even when seas are calm, you can hike through four coastal biomes: shifting dune, coastal strand, interior mangrove wetlands and tropical coastal hammock.

Jonathan Dickinson State Park   PARK
(☑ 772-546-2771; www.floridastateparks.org/jonathandickinson; 16450 SE Federal Hwy; per vehicle/bicycle $6/2; ⊙ 8am-sunset) With almost 11,500 acres to explore, this is an excellent state park between US Hwy 1 and the Loxahatchee River. There's no ocean access in the park, but its attraction lies in its several habitats: pine flatwoods, cypress stands, swamp and increasingly endangered coastal sand-pine scrub. Ranger-led nature walks leave at 9am Sundays from the Cypress Creek Pavilion, and campfire programs are

JUNO BEACH

Take the scenic route north along A1A from John D Macarthur State Park to Jupiter and pass by pretty Juno Beach. If you're travelling with a four-legged companion, you can jump out here to enjoy one of the county's only **dog-friendly beaches** (from Xanadu Lane to Marcinski Rd).

Another reason to pass through is the **Loggerhead Marinelife Center** (☑ 561-627-8280; www.marinelife.org; 14200 US 1, Juno Beach; donations appreciated; ⊙ 10am-5pm Mon-Sat, 11am-5pm Sun) **FREE**, where you can view recovering sea turtle patients in specially designed outdoor tanks and see surgeons at work in the operating theater. Volunteers stand by turtle tanks with information on their charges: how they sustained their injuries, how they're healing and whether they're good or grumpy patients. It's a privilege to see and learn at such close quarters. All five species – greens, hawksbills, Kemp's ridleys, leatherbacks and loggerheads – frequent the local waters. Around 70 to 80 turtles are treated here and returned to the wild annually.

The center runs a host of educational programs, leads ecotours ($35) and hammock hikes through the dune system ($5), tells Hatchling Tales to younger kids (10:30am Wednesdays) and offers guided turtle walks (by reservation/walk-in $17/20) from Wednesday to Saturday evenings in June and July.

offered Saturday at dusk next to the Pine Grove campground.

You can rent canoes and kayaks from the **concession stand** (☑ 561-746-1466; www.floridaparktours.com; canoes/kayaks per 2hr $16/15; ⊙ 9am-5pm). Guided-tour boat rides of the Loxahatchee River are available throughout the day (adult/child $19/12) and there are also one-hour trail rides ($25).

Several short-loop hiking and bicycle trails can be explored. Most popular is the Kitching Creek Trail, just north of the boat landing, walkable in about 90 minutes. Visit www.clubscrub.org for details on cycling options.

Roger Dean Stadium   STADIUM
(☑ 561-775-1818;   www.rogerdeanstadium.com; 4751 Main St; tickets league/spring training $8.50/15) It may not be a 'nature' activity, but an afternoon here will get you outdoors. This small but immaculate stadium is home to spring-training action for the Miami Marlins, the St Louis Cardinals and various minor-league teams. Ticket prices vary; call for details.

**Palm Beach
International Raceway**   MOTORSPORTS
(www.racepbir.com; 17047 Bee Line Hwy) Located on 200 acres of wooded property, this motorsports park has a 2.25-mile 10-turn course and regular race events of all stripes. But the real fun here is the twice-weekly 'Test & Tune' on the NHRA-sanctioned 0.25-mile drag strip. Every Wednesday and Friday from 6pm to 11pm, you're allowed

to race your beater against another vehicle on the track. Just slip on the helmet you brought (mandatory if you plan to drive over 13.99mph), stage and burn rubber. After your run, pick up your time slip to see how your vehicle performed. It's $20 to race, $10 to watch.

Jupiter Outdoor Center   KAYAKING
(☑ 561-747-0063; www.jupiteroutdoorcenter.com; 1000 Coastal A1A; ⊙ 9am-5pm) The center rents kayaks and standup paddleboards (per half day $35/40) and organizes themed kayak trips (from $40) in the area, such as languid moonlight excursions and exploratory trips around Jupiter Inlet's mangroves.

🛏 Sleeping & Eating

Jupiter Waterfront Inn   HOTEL $$
(☑ 561-747-9085; www.jupiterwaterfrontinn.com; 18903 SE Federal Hwy; r $99-159; ❋ 🅿 🛜 🏊) As sunny and friendly as can be, this highway-side inn has huge rooms with flat-screen TVs, Intracoastal views and a marina for boaters. Decor is beachy, with Spanish tile floors and cheerful yellow walls. For romance, ask for a room with an in-suite Jacuzzi tub. The inn's own 240ft fishing pier is a big hit with anglers.

Jupiter Beach Resort   HOTEL $$$
(☑ 561-746-2511; www.jupiterbeachresort.com; 5 N A1A; r $190-680; 🅿 ❋ 🛜 🏊) This elegant, slightly stuffy Key-lime-and-chocolate destination offers rooms (and over-the-top penthouse suites) sporting British-colonial style and million-dollar views. Inside, the floors

are lined with Turkish marble; outside, the resort provides 1000ft of secluded beach, tennis courts and a heated swimming pool with a poolside bar.

★ **Jupiter Donut Factory**　　　SWEETS $
(📞561-741-5290; 141 Center St; per 1 doughnut $0.79-1.25, dozen $6.99; ⊙6am-2pm) These fresh-baked doughnuts are what doughnuts dream of being, so get here early so you don't miss out. Although opening hours are from 6am to 2pm, the doughnuts are usually greedily polished off by mid-morning. If you can't decide between Raspberry Jelly, Banana Coconut, S'mores or Red Velvet, just stick with the most popular order: the Bacon Maple Syrup.

Square Grouper　　　AMERICAN $
(www.squaregrouper.net; 1111 Love St; snacks $1-7; ⊙noon-midnight Sun-Thu, to 1am Fri & Sat) If this Old Florida dive looks familiar, it's because the video for the Alan Jackson–Jimmy Buffett tune 'It's Five O'Clock Somewhere' was shot here. Perched on the water, with an ample (sandy) dance floor, this place is an ultracasual gem in an otherwise well-heeled town. It's a bit hard to find – drive to the end of Love St and turn right.

★ **Little Moir's Food Shack**　　CARIBBEAN, SEAFOOD $$
(www.littlemoirsfoodshack.com; 103 S US 1; mains $9-24; ⊙11am-9pm Mon-Sat) If you didn't know to look, you'd walk right past this strip-mall hole-in-the-wall. But then you'd miss out on one of Florida's genuine food finds, a neo-Caribbean cafe serving a mouth-watering blend of global flavors: sweet-potato crusted fish, Jamaican pepper-pot soup, lobster egg rolls. The seafood is as fresh as you'd expect

(but so rarely find) from a seaside town, and the microbrew list is sure to please.

Food guru Mike Moir who runs the place also operates the first class **Leftovers Cafe** (📞561-627-6030; http://littlemoirs.com/leftovers; 451 University Blvd; mains $5-24; ⊙11am-9pm Mon-Sat), which serves a lighter menu of sandwiches, salads and sweets.

❶ Getting There & Around

Though I-95 is the quickest way through this area, do yourself a favor and get off the freeway. US Hwy 1 (US 1) runs up the coastline, and Hwy A1A jumps back and forth between the mainland (where it's the same as US 1) and various barrier islands.

Stuart & Around

Often overlooked in favor of its more famous southern neighbors, Stuart has long been a hush-hush destination for sporty millionaires and their gleaming yachts. Fishing is tops here, which explains Stuart's nickname: 'Sailfish Capital of the World.' It wasn't until the late 1980s, however, that Stuart got its first exit off I-95, which is when the wave of rich folk, leaving places like Boca, started coming by in earnest.

Though Stuart's retro, sherbet-colored downtown has some cute restaurants and boutiques, the real draws of the region are the adjacent beach areas of **Jensen Beach** and **Hutchinson Island**. Jensen Beach, on the mainland facing the Indian River Lagoon, caters to fishers and arty types, with a tiny downtown lined with craft shops and tackle stores. Just across the water by the bridge, narrow Hutchinson Island is where visitors go for sun and fun.

KAYAKING THE LOXAHATCHEE RIVER

One of two federally designated 'Wild and Scenic' rivers in the state, the free-flowing **Loxahatchee River** is home to a wide range of habitats, from tidal marsh riverines and dense mangrove communities to tidal flats and oyster bars. Translated as 'River of Turtles,' the coffee-colored river, which flows north, is home to countless shelled reptiles, as well as herons, ospreys, otters, raccoons, the occasional bobcat – and lots of alligators. For a great day exploring the various aquatic preserves here, nothing beats Riverbend Park's **Canoe Outfitters** (📞561-746-7053; www.canoeoutfittersofflorida.com; 9060 W Indiantown Rd, Jupiter; double canoes/single kayaks per day $42.50/37), which provides access to this lush waterway. From the launch, paddle to the right for thick, verdant waterways overhung with fallen branches and a small but thumping rapid; paddle to the left for open vistas and plentiful picnic areas. Canoes are good for families, but difficult to maneuver in this narrow waterway, so choose wisely. This terrific day out is gentle enough to be kid-friendly but eye-popping enough to appeal to the discerning adventurer.

⊙ Sights & Activities

Elliott Museum
MUSEUM

(☑ 407-225-1961; www.elliottmuseumfl.org; 825 NE Ocean Blvd, Hutchinson Island; adult/child $12/6; ⊙10am-5pm Mon-Sat) The eccentric Elliott collection is based in early 20th-century technology, and for good reason – the museum was founded by Harmon Elliott, the son of Sterling Elliott, who invented rack and pinion steering. Hence the spectacular collection of 54 antique cars, which are now displayed in a new $20-million gallery complete with robotic racking system, which ferries cars to the foreground and rotates them for viewing.

Other collections segue bizarrely from a 1910 Pelican hydro-airplane and a collection of outboard motors to artifacts detailing the history of prominent Martin County citizens. There's also the second-largest collection of autographed baseballs and baseball cards in the country.

Florida Oceanographic Coastal Science Center
AQUARIUM

(☑ 772-225-0505; www.floridaoceanographic.org; 890 NE Ocean Blvd; adult/child $12/6; ⊙10am-5pm Mon-Sat, noon-4pm Sun) This center is great for kids who'll be mesmerized by the four 300-gallon tropical-fish aquariums, a worm reef and touch tanks with crabs, sea cucumbers and starfish. There's an excellent menu of guided tours and nature programs, from guided nature walks at 10:15am (except Sundays) to daily stingray feedings to summer sea-turtle-spotting expeditions.

Hutchinson Island
BEACH

This long, skinny barrier island, which begins in Stuart and stretches north to Fort Pierce, features a stunning array of unspoiled beaches. All beaches have free access, and are excellent for walking, swimming and even a bit of snorkeling. The beaches get less touristed the further north you go.

St Lucie Inlet State Park
PARK

(☑ 772-219-1880; 4810 SE Cove Rd; admission per boat $2; ⊙8am-sunset) Accessible only by boat, the main part of this park protects 6 sq miles of reef in the Atlantic Ocean just off Jupiter Island. Twelve species of hard and soft coral inhabit the reef, so anchor on the sandy bottom. Snorkeling and scuba diving are permitted; depths range from 5ft to 35ft. Complementing the 2.7 miles of beaches are toilets and running water, piers and hiking trails. From the mainland at the eastern end

of Cove Rd, a 3300ft boardwalk runs from dock to beach.

Lady Stuart
FISHING

(☑ 772-286-1860; www.ladystuart.com; 555 NE Ocean Blvd, Stuart; adult/child $40/30) The crew will take you out, bait your hook, and clean and fillet any fish you catch. They make no guarantees of hooking dinner, but know where to sink their lines.

Hot Tuna Charters
FISHING

(☑ 772-334-0401; www.hottunacharters.com; half-/full day $450/650) Run by native Floridian Captain Wakeman, who boasts more than 20 years' experience and holds 10 world records on both fly and conventional tackle. Hot Tuna will help you find and catch stuff that swims.

🛏 Sleeping

Hutchinson Island has a handful of upscale resorts (the Marriott is the pick of the litter), while Jensen Beach caters to anglers. You'll find midprice chains and family-run budget motels on Federal Hwy in Stuart.

Savannas Recreation Area
CAMPGROUND $

(☑ 772-464-7855; www.stlucieco.gov/parks/savannas.htm; 1400 Midway Rd; tent sites $15-20; ⊙Nov-May) Covering 550 acres and five distinct biological communities – pine flatwoods, wet prairie, marsh, lake and scrub – the Savannas features both primitive and developed campsites.

★ Old Colorado Inn
HOTEL $$

(☑ 772-215-3437; www.oldcoloradoinn.com; 211 Colorado Ave, Stuart; r & ste $139-199; P 🛜) With its pastel-colored Key West vibe and easy charm, the excellent-value 1907 Colorado Inn is shaping up to be one of the best places to stay in the whole Southeast. Spacious studio rooms and suites come with gleaming wooden floors and ceilings, tasteful modern furnishings, grand beds and kitchenettes. Hosts Steven and Ashley brim with insightful tips on Stuart and the surrounding beaches.

River Palm Cottages & Fish Camp
COTTAGE $$

(☑ 772-334-0401; www.riverpalmcottages.com; 2425 NE Indian River Dr, Jensen Beach; winter $109-299, summer $89-239; P ❄ 🛜 🐾) Perched on Indian River, this complex has adorable cottages with kitchens, some with waterfront views and all sporting cool tiled floors and a breezy, Caribbean style. The peaceful grounds are lush with palm trees, guava and the exotic praying-hands banana tree. There's a private beach, a ping-pong table and a pier for watching sunsets.

Jensen Beach Inn   B&B **$$**
(☑772-334-1466; http://jensen-beach-inn.com; 1899 NE Jensen Beach Blvd; d $129-159, ste $179-209; ❋ 🐾) This old-fashioned B&B reminds us of classic European above-the-pub corner hotels, situated on the 2nd floor over an Irish restaurant in arty downtown Jensen Beach. With wood-paneled walls and chenille bedspreads, the six rooms have an appealing lodgelike feel.

✕ Eating

Fredgie's Hot Dog Wagon   FAST FOOD **$**
(3595 NE Indian River Dr, Jensen Beach; hot dogs from $2; ☺11am-4pm Wed-Sun) This vending cart has been dishing dogs for nearly two decades.

Crawdaddy's   CAJUN **$$**
(☑772-225-3444; www.crawdaddysrestaurant.org; 1949 NE Jensen Beach Blvd, Jensen Beach; mains $13-20; ☺11am-10pm Sun-Wed, to 11pm Thu-Sat) This place is a sliver of the French Quarter right near the beach. The menu is drenched in Louisiana tradition – think rum-soaked shrimp and a New Orleans picnic (for hungry seafood-lovers). A twinkling courtyard hosts live music on weekends.

Conchy Joe's   CARIBBEAN, AMERICAN **$$**
(www.conchyjoes.com; 3945 NE Indian River Dr, Jensen Beach; mains $10-22; ☺11:30am-10pm) Overlooking St Lucie River, drinks and pub grub at the palm-tree-filled bar are a surefire blast, especially when the band's jamming.

SNORKEL A SPANISH GALLEON

In 1715 a Spanish flotilla was decimated in a hurricane off the Florida coast. One of the ships, the Urca de Lima (☑850-245-6444) **FREE** went down (relatively) intact. Today, the wooden-hulled ship is partly exposed within snorkeling distance from the beach at Fort Pierce. To get here, exit Ocean Blvd (Hwy A1A) at Pepper Park and walk north along the beach about half a mile from the park boundary. The wreck is about 200yd from shore on the first offshore reef, under 10ft to 15ft of water.

11 Maple St   MODERN AMERICAN **$$$**
(☑772-334-7714; www.elevenmaple.com; 3224 NE Maple St, Jensen Beach; mains $32-45; ☺5:30-10pm Tue-Sat) This romantic spot, a series of rooms inside a historic cottage, has a daily changing menu of eclectic large and small plates, from roasted pompano with saffron essence to grilled elk tenderloin. For special-occasion dinners, this is your best bet short of driving south to Palm Beach.

🔒 Shopping

Historic downtown Stuart overflows with cute shops and antique stores. Jensen Beach is also tops for shopping, especially for arts and crafts – check out the galleries on Jensen Beach Blvd and Maple St.

ℹ Information

Chamber of Commerce (☑772-287-1088; www.stuartmartinchamber.org; 1650 S Kanner Hwy; ☺9am-4pm Mon, 8:30am-4:30pm Tue-Thu, to 1pm Fri) Stuart's Chamber of Commerce is about a mile south of town.

ℹ Getting There & Away

I-95 is the quickest way to and from this area. South of Stuart, US 1 runs up the coastline and then jogs west, into and through town. If you're headed between Stuart and Fort Pierce, the best route is the slow-but-scenic NE Indian River Dr.

Fort Pierce

Fort Pierce has a sleepy feel to it, but includes top sport fishing and some great beaches. Downtown, though newly renovated, often feels like a ghost town, with lots of vacancies and few people. Orange Ave is the main drag, far more vibrant than adjoining blocks. For sleeping options, Stuart and Jensen Beach are a better bet. For eating, there are a handful of waterfront places on Seaway Dr, and more on downtown's Orange Ave.

◉ Sights & Activities

Dolphin Watch Boat Tours   TOURS
(☑772-464-6673; http://dolphinwatchboattours.com; adult/child under 12 $40/30) Wild dolphins are spotted routinely in the Indian River Lagoon, occasionally from the riverbank. If you want to increase your chances of seeing them you need to get on the water. Captain Adam Pozniak seems to know instinctively where to find them on these two-

hour dolphin-spotting tours on his 25ft pontoon. He's also extremely knowledgeable about the lagoon, its flora and fauna, and offers ecotours in the Everglades as well.

Fort Pierce Inlet
State Recreation Area   PARK
(www.floridastateparks.org/fortpierceinlet; 905 Shorewinds Dr; per vehicle/bicycle $6/2; ☉8am-sunset) This 3400-acre park has everything you'd want in a waterfront recreation spot: sandy shores, verdant trails, mangrove swamps with a beautiful bird population and a family-friendly picnic area. It's also home to endangered beach stars, a low-lying sedge growing on the dunes and near the boardwalks, so stick to the sand, Bigfoot.

National Navy UDT-SEAL Museum MUSEUM
(www.navysealmuseum.com; 3300 Ocean Blvd; adult/child $8/4; ☉10am-4pm Mon Jan-Apr only, to 4pm Tue-Sat, noon-4pm Sun) The world's only museum dedicated to the elite warriors of Naval Special Warfare, this Hutchinson Island exhibit features once-top-secret tools and weapons used by the most elite combat forces of the US.

Manatee Observation Center NATURE CENTER
(www.manateecenter.com; 480 N Indian River Dr; admission $1; ☉10am-5pm Tue-Sat, noon-4pm Sun Oct-Jun, 10am-5pm Thu-Sat Jul-Sep; ⊞) A small center educating the public on the plight of the manatee. Videos and exhibits teach boaters how to avoid hurting the creatures – and the rest of us how our lifestyle has indirectly eradicated most of the manatee population. Manatee sightings are common-ish in winter in waters along the museum's observation deck.

❶ Getting There & Around

From Stuart, take I-95 or US 1 (a gorgeous drive that's highly recommended as a trip in itself) about 25 miles north. To get downtown from I-95, take the Orange Ave exit east, crossing US 1 (here called N 4th St).

Orlando & Walt Disney World

Best Places to Eat

➜ Ravenous Pig (p252)
➜ Yellow Dog Eats (p254)
➜ Mama Della's Ristorante (p304)
➜ Jiko (p287)
➜ Prato (p255)

Best Places to Stay

➜ Grande Lakes Orlando (p247)
➜ Bohemian Hotel Celebration (p250)
➜ Portofino Bay Hotel (p301)
➜ Alfond Inn (p249)
➜ Park Plaza Hotel (p249)

Why Go?

Play quidditch with Harry Potter, disappear into the Twilight Zone in a haunted elevator, whip through the air on a sea monster. In Orlando, the Theme Park Capital of the World, it's all about adrenaline-fueled fun wrapped up in the mystique of storytelling and fantasy. Walt Disney World, Universal Orlando Resort (including the Wizarding World of Harry Potter), SeaWorld and Discovery Cove cluster within 15 miles of one another, and Legoland is an hour's drive from downtown Orlando. These carefully constructed environments, dripping with illusion and magic, and filled with rides, shows and parades, promise escape from the everyday. Folks flock here by the thousands looking for just that. Sure, Orlando has a quieter side too, with world-class museums, excellent nature preserves and a burgeoning field-to-fork restaurant scene, but as wonderful as it may be, the city will always lie in the shadow of Cinderella's Castle and Hogwarts School of Witchcraft.

When to Go
Orlando

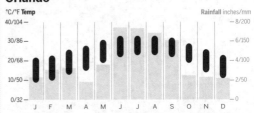

°C/°F **Temp**
40/104 —
30/86 —
20/68 —
10/50 —
0/32 —

Rainfall inches/mm
— 8/200
— 6/150
— 4/100
— 2/50
— 0

J F M A M J J A S O N D

Sep Theme-park crowds thin, accommodations rates drop, summer sizzle fades.

May Lull between spring break and summer vacation peaks; warm, before the rains.

Thanksgiving– mid-Dec Enjoy seasonal festivities; try to avoid soaring prices.

History

In 1824, three years after Florida became a US territory, swampy Mosquito County was established. The first US settlers arrived in 1837, and in 1838 the US military built Fort Gatlin as a base for the Seminole Indian Wars. Upon Florida statehood in 1845, Mosquito County changed names to the far more alluring Orange County. Orlando grew and in 1875 the 2-sq-mile city (population 85) was officially incorporated. With the arrival of the railroad in 1880, the region became a popular orange-growing and tourist center. WWII brought air bases and missile building, but it was the 1971 opening of Walt Disney World's Magic Kingdom that paved the way to the city's contemporary reputation as the theme-park capital of the US. Today, it is the USA's number-one travel destination, welcoming more than 57 million visitors in 2013 alone.

State & Regional Parks

Hundreds of lakes, thousands of acres of protected woodlands, wetlands and waterways, and several excellent state and regional parks offer easily accessible hiking, boating, biking and other outdoor activities. You can rent kayaks and canoes at both Wekiwa Springs State Park (p244) and Lake Louisa State Park (p244), and Orlando Wetlands Park (p245) is an excellent place for birding. For horseback riding, head to Rock Springs Run State Reserve (p245), about a half hour north of downtown Orlando. You don't have to be a hard-core outdoor enthusiast or go very far to take a peak into Florida's wilder side – within an hour of Walt Disney World, you can be paddling the calm waters of the Wekiva River, past alligators, turtles and heron, or walking along marvelously peaceful wilderness trails.

❶ Getting There & Away

AIR

Orlando International Airport (MCO; www.orlandoairports.net) Orlando's primary airport. Serviced by Disney's Magical Express (p293).

Orlando Sanford International Airport (☑407-585-4000; www.orlandosanfordairport.com; 1200 Red Cleveland Blvd) Small airport 30 minutes north of downtown Orlando and 45 minutes north of Walt Disney World.

BUS

A Greyhound bus originating in NYC, with stops including Washington, DC, and Daytona Beach, FL, terminates in Orlando (one way from $80 to $200, 24 hours).

CAR

Orlando lies 285 miles from Miami; the fastest and most direct route is a 4½-hour road trip via Florida's Turnpike. From Tampa it is an easy 60 miles along I-4. Both the Beachline Expwy and Hwy 50 will take you east to beaches on the Space Coast in just under an hour.

TRAIN

Amtrak's 97 *Silver Meteor* and 91 *Silver Star* from New York to Miami stop at Winter Park, downtown Orlando and Kissimmee. It's about a 22-hour ride from NYC (from $140). The daily *Auto Train* from Lorton, VA, terminates at Sanford, 30 miles north of downtown Orlando.

❶ Getting Around

TO & FROM THE AIRPORT

If you are flying into Orlando International Airport and are staying at a Walt Disney World resort, arrange in advance for complimentary luxury bus transportation to and from the airport through Disney's Magical Express (p293).

Legacy Towncar of Orlando (☑407-695-4413, 888-939-8227; www.legacytowncar.com) Prices include a 20-minute grocery-store stop. Round-trip to Universal, Walt Disney Word or International Dr costs $120 for a town car seating up to four people; $155 for a five- to nine-person van.

Orlando Airport Towncar (☑407-754-8166; www.orlandoairporttowncar.com) Greets you at baggage claim at Orlando International and Orlando Sanford Airports. Transport to Walt Disney World costs one way/return $60/120 for one to four people in a town car; $85/170 for one to six people in an SUV. It's about $20 less for transport to Universal Orlando Resort.

CAR & MOTORCYCLE

Hwy I-4 is the main north–south thoroughfare, though it's labeled east–west: to go north, take the I-4 east (toward Daytona Beach), and to go south, hop on the I-4 west (toward Tampa). Just about every place you'd want to go can be located through an I-4 exit number. From south to north, exits 62 through exit 87, you will find Walt Disney World, SeaWorld, Aquatica and Discovery Cove, Universal Orlando Resort, downtown Orlando and Thornton Park, Loch Haven Park and Winter Park.

Both Orlando International and Orlando Sanford International Airports, Walt Disney World and many hotels have car-rental agencies.

Orlando Harley-Davidson (☑407-423-0346; www.orlandoharley.com; per day $120-200) You must have a motorcycle endorsement on your license or valid proof of a motorcycle license. Multiple locations.

ORLANDO & WALT DISNEY WORLD

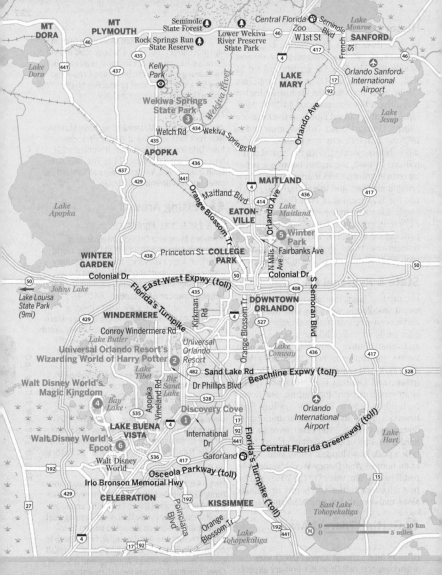

Orlando & Walt Disney World Highlights

1 Snorkeling among tropical fish and floating on the lazy river through the bird aviary at **Discovery Cove** (p236).

2 Wandering Hogsmeade's cobblestoned streets, and flying through Hogwarts at Universal Orlando Resort's **Wizarding World of Harry Potter** (p296).

3 Paddling quietly past alligators and blue herons on the Wekiva River at **Wekiwa Springs State Park** (p244).

4 Watching Magic Kingdom's **Main Street Electrical Parade** (p279) and sticking around for **Wishes Nighttime Spectacular** (p279) fireworks over Cinderella's Castle.

5 Poking through art museums, window-shopping and sampling some of Orlando's best farm-to-fork dining in **Winter Park** (p241).

6 Meeting Sleeping Beauty after sipping wine in Italy and watching the Beatles in England at Disney's **Epcot** (p269).

PUBLIC TRANSPORTATION

I-Ride Trolley (📞407-354-5656; www.iridetrolley.com; rides adult/child 3-9yr $2/1, passes 1/3/5/7/14 days $5/7/9/12/18; ⊙8am-10:30pm) Services International Dr, from south of SeaWorld north to the Universal Orlando Resort area. Buses run at 20- to 30-minute intervals and exact change is required.

Lymmo (www.golynx.com; free; ⊙6am-10pm Mon-Thu, to midnight Fri, 10am-midnight Sat, to 10pm Sun) Circles downtown Orlando for free.

Lynx (📞route info 407-841-8240; www.golynx.com; per ride/day/week $2/5/16, transfers free) Orlando's public bus covers greater Orlando, but service is limited after 8pm.

TAXI

Cabs sit outside the theme parks, Downtown Disney, resorts and other tourist centers, but otherwise you'll need to call to arrange a pick-up. A ride from the Disney area to downtown Orlando takes 30 minutes and costs about $60; from Universal Orlando Resort to Disney takes 15 minutes and costs $35. Just getting around *within* Walt Disney World can easily cost $30.

Casablanca Transportation (📞407-927-2773; www.casablancatransportation.com)

Mears Transportation (📞customer service 407-423-5566, reservations 855-463-2776; www.mearstransportation.com)

ORLANDO & AROUND

It's quite easy to get caught up in the isolated worlds of Disney or Universal Orlando, never venturing beyond their constructed environments, but do so and you will find Orlando has so much more. Lovely tree-lined neighborhoods, a rich performing-arts scene, and several fantastic gardens, nature preserves and museums in and around the city encourage a slower pace often passed over by visitors. Even if you're coming to Orlando for the theme parks, take a few days to jump off their spinning wheels of adrenaline-pumped fantasy to explore the quieter, gentler side of Orlando. You may be surprised to find that you enjoy the theme parks all that much more as a result.

⊙ Sights

⊙ Downtown Orlando

Thornton Park   NEIGHBORHOOD

Trendy Thornton Park borders Lake Eola to the east. Though it's only a few blocks, you'll find several good restaurants, a handful of

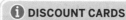

ⓘ DISCOUNT CARDS

The following are available online and in person at the Official Visitor Center (p260).

Orlando Magicard Shave expenses with this free discount book chock-full of coupons for attractions, transportation, hotels and restaurants.

Orlando FlexTicket (adult/child $324/304) Unlimited entrance to multiple theme and water parks over 14 consecutive days. The five-park pass covers Universal Orlando Resort (including both Universal Studios and Islands of Adventure), SeaWorld, Aquatica and Wet 'n Wild, as well as giving access to select live-music venues at CityWalk. Add Busch Gardens, in Tampa Bay (including free shuttle), for $38. Note that Disney does not participate in the FlexTicket.

neighborhood bars, and a weekend energy of 20-somethings and young families.

Orange County Regional History Center   MUSEUM

(Map p230; 📞407-836-8500; www.thehistorycenter.org; 65 E Central Blvd; adult/child 3-12yr/senior $10/3.50/6.50; ⊙10am-5pm Mon-Sat, from noon Sun; 👪) Orlando before Disney? Permanent exhibits cover prehistoric Florida, European exploration, race relations and citrus production, with a re-created pioneer home and 1927 courtroom.

Lake Eola Park   PARK

(Map p230; 📞407-246-2378; 195 N Rosalind Ave; ⊙6am-midnight; 👪) Pretty and shaded, this little city park sits between downtown Orlando and Thornton Park. A paved sidewalk circles the water; there's a waterfront playground; and you can rent swan paddleboats (per 30 minutes $15). On Saturday mornings, the park is home to the Orlando Farmers Market (p260).

Wells' Built Museum of African American History & Culture   MUSEUM

(Map p230; 📞407-245-7535; 511 W South St; adult/child $5/2; ⊙9am-5pm Mon-Fri) Dr Wells, one of Orlando's first African American doctors, came to Orlando in 1917. In 1921 he built a hotel for African Americans barred from Florida's segregated hotels, and soon after he built South Street Casino, a venue for

Downtown Orlando

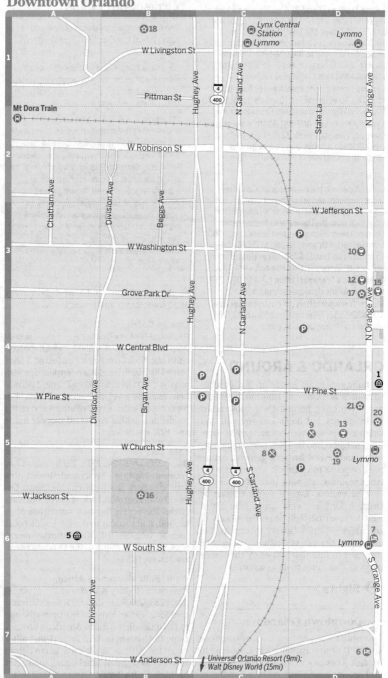

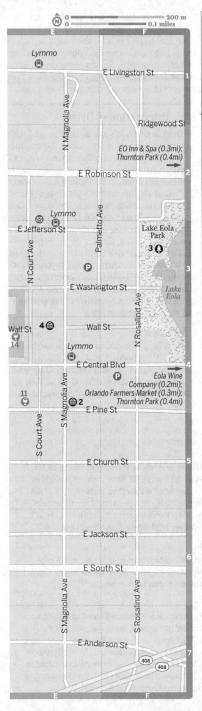

African American entertainers. This small museum sits in the original hotel.

Gallery at Avalon Island　　　　　　GALLERY
(Map p230; www.avalongallery.org; 39 S Magnolia Ave; ⊙11am-6pm Thu-Sat) FREE Contemporary art gallery housed in the oldest commercial building in Orlando (c 1886).

City Arts Factory　　　　　　　　GALLERY
(Map p230; ☑407-648-7060; www.cityartsfactory.com; 29 S Orange Ave; ⊙11am-6pm Mon-Sat) FREE Central hub to downtown Orlando's arts scene.

◎ Loch Haven Park

Picturesque Loch Haven Park, with 45 acres of parks, giant shade trees and three lakes, sits a couple miles north of downtown Orlando.

★ Orlando Museum of Art   MUSEUM

(☎ 407-896-4231; www.omart.org; 2416 N Mills Ave; adult/child $8/5; ◷ 10am-4pm Tue-Fri, from noon Sat & Sun; ⌖; ☐ Lynx 125) Founded in 1924, Orlando's grand and blindingly white center for the arts boasts a fantastic collection, and hosts an array of adult and family-friendly art events and classes. The popular First Thursday ($10), from 6pm to 9pm on the first Thursday of the month, celebrates local artists with regional work, live music and food from Orlando restaurants.

Mennello Museum of American Art   MUSEUM

(☎ 407-246-4278; www.mennellomuseum.com; 900 E Princeton St; adult/child 6-18yr $5/1; ◷ 10:30am-4:30pm Tue-Sat, from noon Sun; ⌖) Tiny but excellent lakeside art museum featuring the work of Earl Cunningham, whose brightly colored images, a fusion of pop and folk art, leap off the canvas. Visiting exhibits often feature American folk art.

Orlando Science Center   MUSEUM

(☎ 407-514-2000; www.osc.org; 777 E Princeton St; adult/child $19/13; ◷ 10am-5pm, closed Wed; ⌖; ☐ Lynx 125) Changing exhibits on dinosaurs, the human body, the solar system and more offer candy-coated science education geared toward children ages five to 12. A giant tree grows through the four-story atrium, at the base of which you'll find alligators and a natural science discovery room.

Unfortunately, many displays are too complicated to teach anything and too educational to be fun, and the result is a lot of kids just running around punching buttons. Check the website for screenings at the giant Cinedom Theater, as well as Science Live events like stingray feeding and experiments.

◉ International Drive

I-Drive is Orlando's tourist hub, packed with chain restaurants, bars, shops, hotels, motels and a handful of minor Orlando attractions. It parallels I-4 to its east, stretching 17 miles from Orlando Premium Outlets south to World Dr, just east of Walt Disney World. The couple miles between the convention center and Sand Lake Rd is a divided road, with palm trees, museums and a relatively pleasant walking district. From Sand Lake Rd north to the dead end at the outlet mall, it is Orlando tourism at full throttle, with $5.99 Disney T-shirts, an ice-cream stand shaped like a soft-serve cone and a miniature golf course advertising the opportunity to 'feed our live alligators.'

★ SeaWorld   THEME PARK

(Map p234; ☎ 888-800-5447; www.seaworldparks. com; 7007 Sea World Dr; adult/child $92/87, 14-day unlimited access incl with Discovery Cove ticket; ◷ 9am-7pm; ⌖; ☐ Lynx 8, 38, 50, 111, ☐ I-Ride Trolley Red Line Stop 33) On top of the leaping dol-

---

ORLANDO IN...

Two Days

Stay one night at a Universal Orlando Resort hotel, and hit the **Wizarding World of Harry Potter** (p296) one hour before the gates open to the public. After a day at Islands of Adventure and Universal Studios, head out for dinner at **Yellow Dog Eats** (p254). Move to a Disney resort and go to **Magic Kingdom** (p263) the next morning. Take the monorail for dinner at **'Ohana** (p287) or **Narcoossee's** (p287) and return to the park for Disney's **Main Street Electrical Parade** (p279) and **Wishes Nighttime Spectacular** (p279).

Four Days

Canoe and swim at **Wekiwa Springs State Park** (p244), float an inner tube at **Kelly Park** (p244) and eat dinner at **Cask & Larder** (p252). Spend a day at **Discovery Cove** (p236), and take in Downtown Disney's **Cirque du Soleil La Nouba** (p258).

Seven Days

Spend a morning at **Hollywood Studios** (p273), lunch at 50's **Prime Time Café** (p285) and take a boat to **Epcot** (p269). Don't miss **Soarin'** (p269); eat, drink and shop your way around the world; and catch **Illuminations** (p279). After a full day at **SeaWorld** (p232), go to dinner outside the gates at **Thai Thani** (p251) or head to **Celebration** (p250). Hit **Typhoon Lagoon** (p274) the next morning, and head to **Winter Park** (p254) for lunch. Go to **Charles Hosmer Morse Museum of American Art** (p241), take a **boat tour** (p242) and browse the gift shops. Finish the day with dinner and a movie at the **Enzian Theater** (p257).

phins, silly sea lions and splashing whales of SeaWorld's famous marine-animal shows, this park offers massive aquariums, opportunities to feed stingrays and dolphins, and two of the biggest thrill rides in town. While sea-animal encounters and shows remain as popular as ever, they have received criticism by animal welfare groups who claim the captivity of marine life is debilitating and stressful for the animals, and that this is exacerbated by human interaction.

If you do want to see the animals in action, check show and feeding times online before visiting, and plan your day accordingly.

Two sea-inspired roller coasters maximize the knuckle-whitening adrenaline rush with simple design twists. Kraken is a whiplash zip of twists, turns, inversion and plunges touted by aficionados as one of the most wicked coasters in Florida and beyond; it has no floor so your feet dangle free. On Manta, you lie horizontally, face down, several to a row, so that the coaster vaguely resembles a manta ray, and dive and fly through the air in this position, reaching speeds of almost 60mph. Neither of these hard-core coasters is for the faint hearted or weak bellied. SeaWorld's third and last thrill is a water ride. Journey to Atlantis begins in darkness, moving gently through an underwater world of neon and fluorescent coral and fish. Things turn macabre when the creepy evil mermaid beckons you into her world and up, up, up you go, through the steam, before the coaster plunges 60ft into the water.

Folks with little ones in tow should count on spending a couple of hours at Shamu's Happy Harbor, where six eye-candy rides, four stories of nets connected with slides and tunnels, and a water-spewing playground delight the under-10 crowd. Come first thing when the park opens and during Shamu shows, when crowds are thinnest and lines can dwindle down to nothing. To feed the stingrays at Stingray Lagoon, swing by anytime and pick up a box of fish ($7). Hold them between your index and middle finger, and place your hand in the water palm-up. When the rays go by, they vacuum them up. You can feed dolphins at Dolphin Cove ($7), but you can only do this at scheduled feeding times. Finally, Antarctica: Empire of the Penguin is a family-friendly ride through the South Pole that follows baby Puck and ends in the frigid air of a live penguin colony. If you would like personal interaction with the dolphins, sea

ORLANDO'S TOP 10 THEME PARK THRILLS

➡ Incredible Hulk Coaster (p294; Islands of Adventure)

➡ Harry Potter and the Forbidden Journey (p296; Islands of Adventure)

➡ Kraken (SeaWorld)

➡ Manta (SeaWorld)

➡ Dragon Challenge (p296; Islands of Adventure)

➡ Hollywood Rip Ride Rockit (p296; Universal Studios)

➡ Revenge of the Mummy (p297; Universal Studios)

➡ Twilight Zone Tower of Terror (p273; Hollywood Studios)

➡ Escape from Gringotts (p297; Universal Studios)

➡ Space Mountain (p267; Magic Kingdom)

lions, penguins and more, check the website for details on SeaWorld's Up Close Tours.

The park's most famous draw is the corny and melodramatic Shamu show. Other popular performances include Blue Horizons, an extravaganza of light, music, dolphins, birds and acrobats in costume. The show tells some sort of story of good and evil, with lots of splashing and drama. Kids like the goofy and slapstick humor of the Clyde & Seamore Take Pirate Island; this stars sea lions, otters and walruses in 'comedian' roles. The 30-minute water-themed A'Lure the Call of the Ocean is a bit like a dramatically pared-down Cirque du Soleil. It combines acrobats, elaborate costumes and a heap of special effects to tell the story of the sea sirens, the mythical creatures who lured Odysseus.

You won't starve at SeaWorld, but expect the usual mediocre and overpriced theme-park fare. The only option for advanced reservations is Sharks Underwater Grille – the bar is literally a tropical aquarium and you eat next to a giant aquarium of sharks.

Parking costs $15; you can reserve strollers (single/double $13/18), wheelchairs ($12) and Electric Conveyance Vehicle (ECV) mobility carts ($45) in advance; and there are kennel facilities ($15) with air-con for dogs. A record of shots and updated rabies is required, and you must return to walk and feed your pet.

ORLANDO & WALT DISNEY WORLD ORLANDO & AROUND

International Drive

0 — 1 km
0 — 0.5 miles

Conroy Rd/Conroy Windermere Rd

25

Lake Cane

Vineland Rd

Wizarding World of Harry Potter – Diagon Alley 5

Lake Marsha

17

19

Major Blvd

Universal Orlando Resort

33

Americana Blvd 32

Vineland Rd

Florida's Turnpike (toll)

W Oak Ridge Rd

30

Universal Studios 4

Wizarding World of Harry Potter – Hogsmeade 6 2

Islands of Adventure

Hollywood Way

Universal Blvd

S Kirkman Rd

International Dr

20

18

8

15

14

11

American Way

Bay Hill Golf Club (0.6mi)

Dr Phillips Blvd

Turkey Lake Rd

International Dr

Canada Ave

Universal Blvd

Sand Lake

Apopka Vineland Rd

Della Dr

23

27 24

W Sand Lake Rd

Spring Lake

28

Little Sand Lake

9

Sand Lake Rd

Big Sand Lake

10

22 16

ⓘ Official Visitor Center

29

12

35

21

Turkey Lake Rd

International Dr

Beachline Expwy (toll) 528

7

Grande Lakes Orlando (0.5mi)

SeaWorld 3

26

Discovery Cove 1

Central Florida Pkwy

Apopka Vineland Rd

Palm Pkwy

Lake Willis

International Dr

13

Vineland Ave

34

International Drive

See the website for vacation packages that include accommodations at partner hotels and information on Quick Queue Unlimited and Signature Show Seating (both from $19).

Aquatica   WATER PARK
(Map p234; ☎407-351-3600; www.aquaticaby-seaworld.com; 5800 Water Play Way; adult/child $56/41, advance online Splash & Save $19-28,

14-day unlimited access incl SeaWorld adult/child $119/114; ⊙9am-6pm; ; Lynx 8, 38, 50, 111, SeaWorld shuttle, I-Ride Trolley Red Line Stop 34) A clean and pretty water park with tropical greenery offering a vague sense of Polynesia and some animal-viewing twists. Come here to splash, bob, float and zoom in lazy rivers, splash zones, wave pools and slippery slides – that's what you do at water parks, and at Aquatica it's no different.

SeaWorld, which owns Aquatica, has come under scrutiny for its treatment of dolphins, and for their policies of keeping dolphins in captivity. Animal welfare organizations make compelling arguments against this practice.

The **Dolphin Plunge** spits you through a glass-enclosed tube through a tank of Commerson's dolphins; the problem is that a high-speed waterslide isn't the best way to see dolphins. You zoom through so fast and the stretch through the tank is so short that you're lucky if you catch a passing glance at the black-and-white cuties.

For little ones, the children's play areas are excellent. At **Walkabout Waters** buckets of water dump regularly over all kinds of brightly colored climbing structures and fountains, and **Kookaburra Cove** offers tiny slides and shallow water perfect for toddlers.

DISCOVERY COVE

At **Discovery Cove** (Map p234; ☎877-434-7268; www.discoverycove.com; 6000 Discovery Cove Way; tickets incl 14-day unlimited access to SeaWorld & Aquatica $169-280, incl dolphin swim $229-399, SeaVenture extra $59; ⊙8am-5:30pm, all-day experience, advance reservations required; ; Lynx 8, 38, 50, 111), guests spend the day snorkeling in a fish- and ray-filled reef, floating on a lazy river through an aviary, and simply relaxing in an intimate tropical sanctuary of white-sand beaches. Sure, this island getaway is all artificially made, but that's what Orlando does best. For an added price beyond the Resort Only package, you can swim with dolphins and walk along the sea floor.

Note that since the early 1990s, there has been a growing controversy regarding the ethics of dolphin captivity for the purposes of public display and human interaction. Both the Humane Society of the United States and the World Society for the Protection of Animals have come out strongly against the practice. If you'd like more information on the issues surrounding keeping dolphins in captivity, *The Case Against Marine Mammals in Captivity*, by Naomi Rose, is a good resource.

If you have signed up for a **Dolphin Swim**, you'll be given a time and place to meet your instructor when you arrive in the morning. Groups of about 10 gather under a thatched-roof tiki hut, are given a brief orientation and a wetsuit, and then head into the chilly lagoon with the dolphins. Each group is assigned a dolphin for hands-on interaction and a short one-on-one glide through the water. The minimum age is six, and children under 12 must be accompanied by a paying adult. Purchase the Dolphin Swim when you make your reservation.

The second add-on option is **SeaVenture**. Don a dive helmet for a walk along the reef among schools of saltwater fish, rays, sharks and other creatures, but don't worry – the more dangerous ones lie behind a glass barrier. Suitable for ages 10 and older; no Scuba certification required. The experience is limited to six people at a time and takes one hour, with 20 minutes of it spent underwater. As with the Dolphin Swim, you must purchase this experience when you make your reservation.

Beyond this, just kick back – wiggle your toes in the sand, stretch out in the sun with a beer and explore as the mood moves you. Discovery Cove is small, allowing only 1300 guests per day, and is completely secured with several lifeguards overseeing the swimming areas, making it suitable for families. You can snorkel in the lagoons whenever you'd like. At the aviary, the brightly colored feathered critters will eat out of your hand.

Though the price is steep, it includes a cafeteria breakfast and a more elaborate and tasty lunch, both served at a beachside patio; unlimited beer, soda and snacks; snorkel gear, a wetsuit, a locker, shower facilities, towels and sunscreen; parking; and unlimited admission to SeaWorld and Aquatica anytime within 14 days. Ticket prices shift according to availability, like airlines; it could cost $199 one day, $299 a few weeks later. You can change your date once you've made a reservation if there's availability, but you'll have to pay any price difference. See the website for current prices. Specially designed wheelchairs, outfitted with oversized tires for maneuvering on the beach, can be reserved in advance.

There are several decent fast-food restaurants and there's plenty of cold beer for sale. Picnic tables sit just outside the park gates, next to the bus drop-off area – you'll find complimentary cooler-size lockers near Guest Relations. Air-conditioned kennel facilities for dogs only ($15) are located outside the main entrance of SeaWorld. Aquatica participates in the Orlando Flex Ticket.

Titanic the Experience   MUSEUM
(Map p234; ☑407-248-1166; www.titanicshipofdreams.com; 7324 International Dr; adult/child 6-11yr $22/13; ☺10am-9pm Jun & Jul, to 8pm Mar & Aug, to 6pm rest of year; ⊞; ⊟ Lynx 8, 38, 42, 50, 58, ⊟ I-Ride Trolley Red Line Stop 13) Full-scale replicas of the doomed ship's interior and artifacts found at the bottom of the sea. Tour the galleries with period-dressed guides or wander through on your own. Kids especially love the dramatic and realistic interpretation of history – each passenger receives a boarding pass, with the name of a real passenger, and at the end of the experience (once the ship has sunk) you learn your fate.

WonderWorks   MUSEUM
(Map p234; ☑407-351-8800; www.wonderworksonline.com; 9067 International Dr; adult/child 4-12yr $25/20; ☺9am-midnight; ⊞; ⊟ Lynx 8, 38, 42, 50, 58, ⊟ I-Ride Trolley Red Line Stop 23 or Green Line Stop 12) Housed in a hard-to-miss, upside-down building, this bright, loud, frenetic landmark is a cross between a children's museum, a video arcade and an amusement park. Several stories of wall-to-wall interactive exhibits offer high-speed, multisensory education. Lie on a bed of nails, sit inside a hurricane simulator, and measure how high you can jump.

Younger children may find the pulse disorienting and frightening, but older ones will probably enjoy the cool stuff there is to do. There's also a 36ft indoor ropes course, a 4-D theater with changing shows, laser tag and the nightly Outta Control Magic Show.

Wet 'n Wild   WATER PARK
(Map p234; ☑407-351-1800; www.wetnwildorlando.com; 6200 International Dr; adult/child 3-9yr $48/42, afternoons half-price; ☺vary, call ahead; ⊞; ⊟ Lynx 8, 38, 42, 50, 58, ⊟ I-Ride Trolley Red Line Stop 9 or Green Line Stop 5) Though not the most aesthetically pleasing water park in Orlando, this is the place to come for high-speed thrills. If you can tolerate the lines for rides, their twists, spins, dips and dives won't disappoint. For little ones, the fantastic one-acre Blastaway Beach offers all kinds of interactive water-spewing features and pint-

sized slides. The park, owned by Universal Orlando Resort, is about a 10-minute walk from the theme parks. Parking costs $12. Wet 'n Wild participates in the Orlando Flex Ticket.

Ripley's Believe It or Not!   MUSEUM
(Map p234; ☑407-345-0501; www.ripleys.com/Orlando; 8201 International Dr; adult/child 4-12yr $17/11; ☺9:30am-midnight; ⊞; ⊟ Lynx 8, 38, 42, 50, 58, ⊟ I-Ride Trolley Red Line Stop 9) The 1933 World's Fair in Chicago introduced Ripley's collection of 'oddities and unusual people' to the public. While it may today offend 21st-century politically correct sensibilities, this 'odditorium' offers Ripley's vision with no holds barred. Twenty-first-century additions tend to focus on the creation of odd, such as a dog sculpture made out of clothes pins, rather than the finding of odd.

**World of Chocolate
Museum & Cafe**   MUSEUM
(Map p234; ☑407-778-4871; www.worldofchocolatemuseum.com; 11701 International Dr; adult/child 4-12yr $17/12; ☺10am-9pm; ⊞; ⊟ I-Ride Trolley Red Line Stop 37A) History of chocolate, giant chocolate sculptures and chocolate tasting. The cafe and shop do not require admission.

◉ Greater Orlando

★Gatorland   ZOO
(☑407-855-5496; www.gatorland.com; 14501 S Orange Blossom Trail/Hwy 17; adult/child $27/19; ☺10am-5pm; ⊞; ⊟ Lynx 108) With no fancy roller coasters or drenching water rides, this mom-and-pop park harkens back to Old Florida. It's small, it's silly and it's kitschy with, you guessed it, plenty of gators. A splintery wooden boardwalk winds past the hundreds of alligators in the breeding marsh and you can buy hot dogs to feed them.

Allow time to see all the rather tongue-in-cheek shows, charmingly free of special effects, dramatic music and spectacular light design. At the Jumparoo Show 10ft-long alligators leap almost entirely out of the water to grab whole chickens from the trainer. After the Gator Wrestling Show you can choose to get a photo of yourself sitting on a gator. Up-Close Encounters involves mysterious boxes holding animals the public has sent to the park. The trainers are too scared to open them, so they drag audience members down to help. The Screamin' Gator Zip Line (per two hours $70, including

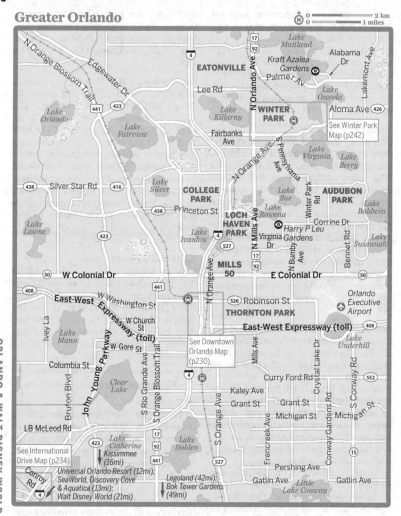

park admission) features five zip lines over the park. After a day of gators, head across the street to the excellent Private Island Ice-Cream (p255). Parking is free.

Audubon Center
for Birds of Prey
WILDLIFE RESERVE

(☑ 407-644-0190; http://fl.audubon.org/audubon-center-birds-prey; 1101 Audubon Way, Maitland; adult/child 3-12yr $5/4; ☺10am-4pm Tue-Sun; ⛱) Centered at a cool old house and very much off the beaten track, this little lakeside rehabilitation center for hawks, screech owls and other talon-toed feathered friends offers plenty of opportunities to see the birds up close, just hanging out on the trainers' arms. Look out for Trouble the bald eagle splashing and playing in his bathtub.

Fun Spot America –
Kissimmee
AMUSEMENT PARK

(Map p262; ☑ 407-397-2509; www.funspotattractions.com; 2850 Florida Plaza Blvd, Kissimmee; admission free, unlimited all-day rides adult/child under 54in $40/30; ☺10am-midnight; ⛱) FREE Whirling, swinging and twisting old-time carnival rides, including four go-kart tracks and a handful of kiddy options. There's no clever theming or simulated masterpieces, but it's fun, easy, and the lines aren't hours long. Thrill-seekers might want to try the 'world's tallest skycoaster,' a bungee-jumping-style experience with a 300ft free fall. Free parking.

A second park, **Fun Spot America – Orlando** (Map p234; ☑ 407-363-3867; www.funspotattractions.com; 5700 Fun Spot Way; admission free, unlimited all-day rides adult/child under 54in $40/30; ☺ 10am-midnight; ☐ I-Ride Trolley Red Line Stop 6), sits on International Drive, minutes from Universal Orlando Resort.

Green Meadows Farm   FARM
(☑ 407-846-0770; www.greenmeadowsfarm.com; 1368 S Poinciana Blvd; admission $23; ☺ 9:30am-4pm, final tour 2pm; ☀) Only 30 minutes' drive from Disney, this little farm makes a pleasant getaway to the countryside and an easy break from the theme-park energy. You can pet the animals, milk a cow, ride a pony, and

there's plenty of shade and grass, a picnic area and a playground. Note that you can only see the farm by two-hour tour.

To fully participate in everything offered, arrive by 2pm; if you come after that, they'll give you a truncated tour as time allows.

Central Florida Zoo   ZOO
(☑ 407-323-4450; www.centralfloridazoo.org; 3755 NW Hwy 17-92, Sanford; adult/child 3-9yr $15/11, zip line $18-48; ☺ 9am-5pm; ☀) Small but satisfying zoo set apart from the usual intensity of Orlando tourist attractions, with an excellent splash-play area, animal interactions and a zip line (from $18 to $48).

Audubon Park   NEIGHBORHOOD
(http://audubonparkgardens.com) Just south of Winter Park and anchored on the west by Leu Gardens, this quirky little residential pocket has a distinct urban-hip meets

ORLANDO FOR CHILDREN

The challenge for families vacationing in the Theme Park Capital of the World is digging through the overwhelming options and inflated rhetoric to find what best suits your time, budget and family. If time is limited, stick to Disney's iconic Magic Kingdom (p263) and the edgier, less-stressful Universal Orlando Resort, boasting the marvelously themed Wizarding World of Harry Potter (p297).

Though part of the Disney magic is how it magically makes your money disappear, there are plenty of inexpensive highlights in and around Orlando. Tubing at Kelly Park (p244), canoeing at Wekiwa Springs State Park (p244) and a visit to the lovely Bok Tower Gardens (p244) make perfect day trips. The free outdoor movie at Disney's Chip 'n' Dale Campfire Singalong (p271) is one of the best things at Disney.

Everything in Orlando is an opportunity to attract tourists, and eating is no exception. There are **character meals** both inside the parks and at resort hotels; **dinner shows** at Walt Disney World, Universal Orlando Resort and venues around town; and **themed restaurants** offering everything from dining under asteroid showers to burgers and milkshakes in a mock drive-in theater.

You may be ready for bed once the sun sets, obsessively checking your watch to see if it's time yet to collapse, but there's more fun to be had. With the exception of Animal Kingdom, all of Disney's theme parks offer **light shows** or **fireworks**; Orlando's performing-arts scene includes excellent **children's theater**, Disney's Cirque du Soleil La Nouba (p258) performs nightly, and Universal's Blue Man Group (p258) is full of silly shenanigans. Disney's BoardWalk, Downtown Disney and Universal Orlando Resort's CityWalk all make for a festive evening, with street performers and plenty of eye candy, but if you've had enough adrenaline for one day, kick back in small-town Celebration (p250) or Winter Park. Children appreciate the slow pace, and on a summer evening, after a day slogging through parks, sitting with a glass of wine while the children play in Celebration's lakefront fountain may just be heaven.

Sprinkle in the big-bang, high-energy fun judiciously. Yes, you might ride the Winnie the Pooh seven times in a row, and yes, you may never make it to the Finding Nemo musical in Animal Kingdom. If only we had gotten up earlier, if only we hadn't waited in line for that Mickey ice cream, if only we had scurried out of the park after the fireworks: if only, if only, if only we'd seen this, that and the other thing.

Forget it. There's too much, and you'll never win that game. In the end it's what you do that kids remember, not what you missed.

WINTER HAVEN

Legoland is sleepy Winter Haven's main draw, but you'll also find a handful of good restaurants in the small historic downtown. Lovely Bok Tower Gardens (p244) sits 15 miles to the southwest. Winter Haven is 30-mile drive south of Walt Disney World.

Legoland (☎ 863-318-5346; http://florida.legoland.com; 1 Legoland Way, Winter Haven; 1-/2-day tickets adult $84/99, child 9-12yr $75/92; ☺ 10am-5pm; ⊞; Legoland Shuttle) With manageable crowds and lines, and no bells and whistles, lakeside Legoland maintains an old-school vibe – you don't have to plan like a general to enjoy a day here, and though it feels a bit dated, it is strikingly stress free and relaxed. Rides and attractions, including the attached water park, are geared toward children ages two to 12. Booking online for a specific date can save you up to $15. Opening hours vary seasonally.

Highlights include **Coastercaurus**, a classic wooden roller coaster; **Flight School**, a coaster that zips you around with your feet dangling free; and **Miniland**, a Lego re-creation of iconic American landmarks and cities. There are a few remnants from the park's history as the site of Cypress Gardens (circa 1936), including lovely botanical gardens with the giant banyan tree and waterski shows, but the charm of that grande dame of Florida theme parks is largely absent. The Southern belles are Lego rather than real, the water-ski show centers on a bizarre and rather silly pirate theme, and the cartoon network's *Legends of Chima* inspires an entire section.

The best option for eating is the Lakeside Sandwich Co, just behind Pirates Cove, and the best snack is the park's signature Granny Apple Fries (french-fry-styled cinnamon-sugar-dusted fried apples).

A shuttle (round-trip $5) runs daily from Orlando Premium Outlets – Vineland (p259), near Walt Disney World, with multiple return times, but you must reserve a spot before 11:30am the day prior. You can rent strollers/wheelchairs/Electric Conveyance Vehicles ($10/12/37) and lockers (from $5 to $12). Parking costs $14.

Donut Man (☎ 863-293-4031; 1290 6th St, Winter Haven; donuts $2-4; ☺ 5am-10pm; ⊞) Classic roadside retro dive, with circa 1967 exterior, formica-counter dining and delicious doughnuts made daily – avoid the greasy breakfast sandwiches. Five miles from Legoland.

granola-crunchy vibe. There are a handful of recommended restaurants, bakeries and bars, as well as a good ice-cream shop, primarily clustered around the intersection of Corrine Dr and Winter Park Rd.

Maitland Art Center   ARTS CENTER
(☎ 407-539-2181; www.maitlandartcenter.org; 231 W Packwood Ave, Maitland; adult/child $3/2; ☺ 11am-4pm Tue-Sun) Founded as an art colony in 1937 and listed on the National Register of Historic Places, this lovely little spot provides classes and studio space to area artists, galleries where they can display their work, and peaceful gardens.

While here, check out the small history museum and telephone museum next door.

Old Town   AMUSEMENT PARK
(Map p262; ☎ 407-396-4888; www.myoldtownusa. com; 5770 W Irlo Bronson Memorial Hwy; admission free, per ride $2-6; ☺ noon-11pm; ℗ ⊞; ☐ Lynx 55, 56) Plopped among the exhaust, chain motels and the treeless landscape of Hwy 192, Old Town blends county fair and boardwalk

with a touch of 1950s Americana. There are classic carnival rides, a spooky haunted funeral parlor, kitschy shops, live rock and roll, and old car cruises (Wednesday, Friday and Saturday at 8:30pm). Though it feels a bit run-down, lines for rides are short and there's no admission charge. Opening hours vary; see the website for a calendar of events. Free parking.

Zora Neale Hurston
National Museum of Fine Arts   MUSEUM
(☎ 407-647-3307; www.zoranealehurstonmuseum. com; 227 E Kennedy Blvd, Eatonville; ☺ 9am-4pm Mon-Fri, 11am-1pm Sat) FREE Dedicated to Florida writer and anthropologist Zora Neale Hurston (1881–1960), born here in Eatonville and famous for her novel *Their Eyes Were Watching God*. This tiny one-room museum features changing exhibits of African American artists.

While the museum itself attracts folks with particular interests in the author, African American studies or a specific exhibit, the museum-sponsored **Zora Neale Hurston Festival of the Arts and Humanities** (www.zorafestival.org) attracts thousands for a multi-day family-friendly celebration every January.

⊙ Winter Park

Founded in 1858 and home to Rollins College, bucolic Winter Park concentrates some of Orlando's best-kept secrets – including several of Orlando's most talked about restaurants and field-to-fork favorites – into a few shaded, pedestrian-friendly streets. Shops, wine bars and sidewalk cafes line Park Ave.

★**Charles Hosmer Morse Museum of American Art** MUSEUM
(Map p242; ☑ 407-645-5311; www.morsemuseum.org; 445 N Park Ave, Winter Park; adult/child $5/free; ⊙ 9am-4pm Tue-Sat, from 1pm Sun, to 8pm Fri Nov-Apr; ☑) Internationally famous, this stunning and delightful museum houses the world's most comprehensive collection of Louis Comfort Tiffany art. Highlights include the chapel interior designed by the artist for the 1893 World's Columbian Exhibition in Chicago; 10 galleries filled with architectural and art objects from Tiffany's Long Island home, Laurelton Hall; and an installation of the Laurelton's Daffodil Terrace.

Cornell Fine Arts Museum MUSEUM
(Map p242; www.rollins.edu/cfam; Rollins College, 1000 Holt Ave, Winter Park; adult/child $5/free; ⊙ 10am-4pm Tue-Fri, noon-5pm Sat & Sun) This tiny lakeside museum on the campus of Rollins College houses an eclectic collection of historic and contemporary US art.

Kraft Azalea Gardens PARK
(1365 Alabama Dr, Winter Park; ⊙ 8am-dusk) Quiet lakeside park with enormous cypress trees. Particularly stunning January through March, when the azaleas burst into bloom. There's a dock, but no BBQs or picnic tables.

Albin Polasek Museum & Sculpture Gardens MUSEUM
(Map p242; www.polasek.org; 633 Osceola Ave, Winter Park; adult/child $5/free; ⊙ 10am-4pm Tue-Sat, from 1pm Sun) Listed on the National Register of Historic Places and perched on the shore of Lake Osceola, this small yellow villa was home to Czech sculptor Albin Polasek. The house serves as a small museum of his life and work, and the gardens house some of his sculptures.

Hannibal Square Heritage Center MUSEUM
(Map p242; ☑ 407-539-2860; www.hannibalsquareheritagecenter.org; 642 W New England Ave, Winter Park; ⊙ noon-4pm Tue & Wed, to 5pm Thu & Fri, 10am-2pm Sat) **FREE** As far back as 1881, Winter Park's Hannibal Sq was home to African Americans employed as carpenters, farmers and household help. The *Heritage Collection: Photographs and Oral Histories of West Winter Park 1900–1980,* on permanent display at this little museum, celebrates and preserves this community's culture and history.

🏃 Activities

Walt Disney World, a city in and of itself, offers bike rental and trails, water sports, fishing and several golf courses.

Cycling

Though the streets of Orlando are not particularly bike friendly, the city boasts a network of paved bike trails. Go to www.orlandosentinel.com/travel/bike-trails for trail maps.

West Orange Trail CYCLING
🖋 This 24-mile rural trail lies 20 miles west of downtown Orlando and passes through 10 miles of horse country.

West Orange Trail Bikes & Blades CYCLING
(☑ 407-877-0600; www.orlandobikerental.com; 17914 State Rd 438, Winter Garden; bikes per hour $6-10, per day $30-50, per week $99-149, delivery/pick-up $40; ⊙ 11am-5pm Mon-Fri, from 7:30am Sat & Sun) This bike shop lies 20 miles west of Orlando and sits at the beginning of the West Orange Trail. It offers bike rental and comprehensive information, both online and on-site, on biking in and around Orlando.

Orange Cycle CYCLING
(☑ 407-422-5552; www.orangecycleorlando.com; 2204 Edgewater Dr; ⊙ 7am-10pm Mon-Fri, 10am-5pm Sat) Provides printable maps to Orlando bike trails and is an excellent source of information for all things biking in and around Orlando. Sells and repairs bikes, but does not rent.

Water Sports

In addition to waterskiing and boating on 300-plus lakes, the calm waters of the Wekiva River offer easy paddling access to Old Florida and is one of two National Wild and Scenic Rivers in Florida.

Nature Adventures CANOEING
(☑ 407-884-4311; www.canoewekiva.com; 1800 Wekiwa Circle, Wekiwa Springs State Park, Apopka; 2hr canoe/kayak $17, per additional hour $3;

Winter Park

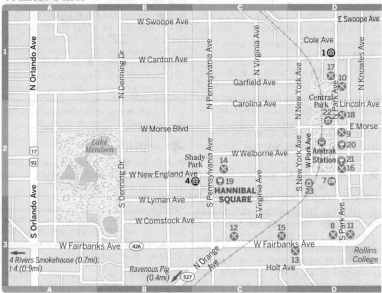

⊙8am-8pm; 🚲) Canoe and kayak rental at Wekiwa Springs State Park (p244). If you'd like to paddle to a primitive riverside campsite, this outfit can supply sleeping bags, tents, stoves, lanterns and coolers (cost for two days/one night $132).

Central Florida
Nature Adventures
KAYAKING

(☎352-589-7899; www.kayakcentralflorida.com; 2-3hr per person $60, 4-5hr $90; 🚲) Small-group nature tours make for a relaxing day paddling among the alligators, turtles, herons and egrets.

Buena Vista Watersports
WATER SPORTS

(☎407-239-6939; www.bvwatersports.com; 13245 Lake Bryan Dr; per hr kayak, canoe or paddleboard $25, jetski $105, pontoon $125; ⊙9am-6:30pm; 🚲) Just outside the Disney gates, with a low-key vibe. Water-skiing and tube riding include driver/instructor (per hour $95).

Scenic Boat Tour
BOAT TOUR

(Map p242; ☎407-644-4056; www.scenicboattours.com; 312 E Morse Blvd, Winter Park; adult/child $12/6; ⊙hourly 10am-4pm; 🚲) Hop on an 18-passenger pontoon and cruise through Winter Park's tropical canals and lakes,

past mansions, Rollins College and other sites.

Fishing

Central Florida is famous for its freshwater fishing, and the canals and lakes in and around Orlando offer some of the best.

Lake Tohopekaliga
FISHING

(Lake Toho; ☎Big Toho Marina 407-846-2124; www.bigtoho.com) Popular 35-sq-mile lake hosting several fishing tournaments. Half- and full-day guide services range in price from $150 to $350. Alternatively, rent a boat at the marina in downtown Kissimmee and throw in a line on your own.

Golf

Orlando boasts more than 60 golf courses. For details and packages, go to www.golfpacorlando.com. Call individual golf courses for information on club rental and twilight rates. Hours vary seasonally.

Dubsdread Golf Course
GOLF

(☎407-246-2551; www.historicaldubsdread.com; 549 W Par St; 9 holes $30-40, 18 holes $40-60) Old-school Orlando course opened in 1923. Sits in the College Park neighborhood, just west of I-4 and south of Winter Park.

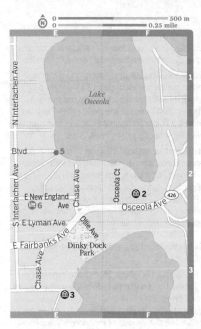

Bay Hill Golf Club GOLF
(☑ 407-876-2429; www.bayhill.com; 9000 Bay Hill Blvd) A regular on the PGA tour, this low-key course stretches over 270-acres.

Grand Cypress Golf Club GOLF
(Map p262; ☑ 407-239-1909; www.grandcypress. com; 1 N Jacaranda; green fees $120-175) Beautiful 45 holes, including an 18-hole Scottish links-style course, just outside Walt Disney World.

Ritz Carlton (Grande Lakes Orlando) GOLF
(☑ 407-393-4900; www.grandelakes.com; 4040 Central Florida Pkwy; 18 holes $175, Jan-May $115) Ask about no-charge family golf specials and off-season rates.

Adventure Sports

I Fly Orlando ADVENTURE SPORTS
(Map p234; ☑ 407-903-1150; wwww.iflyorlando. com; 8501 International Dr; adult/child 3-7yr/child 7-12yr $35/7/20, family package $240; ◎ 10:30am-9pm Mon-Fri; 🅿; 🚌 Lynx 8, 38, 42, 50, 58, 🚃 I-Ride Trolley Red Line Stop 8) Think you may like to jump out of a moving plane? Or does the thought give you the heebie-jeebies? This indoor skydiving experience sends you soaring free-form in a vertical wind tunnel, giving you a taste of the real thing.

ZoomAir Adventure Park ADVENTURE SPORTS
(☑ 407-330-0767; www.zoomair.us; Central Florida Zoo, Sanford; fees $19-50) Three zip-line and high-ropes games at the Central Florida Zoo (p239) are geared toward kids 10 and older. Stop after the Upland, or continue with the higher and more intense Rainforest. The Kids Course is 4ft above ground, and each course takes about an hour. Come early, as the courses backlog easily and it's frustrating to spend time hanging and waiting on the platforms.

★☆ Festivals & Events

Walt Disney World, Universal Orlando Resort and SeaWorld celebrate the holidays with seasonal shows and parades.

BEST OF ORLANDO OUTDOORS

After a few days of theme-park rides and lines, fried food, loud music, traffic and shopping, a jaunt beyond the pavement can soothe and rejuvenate even the most harried of spirits.

Wekiwa Springs State Park (☎ 407-884-2008; www.floridastateparks.org/wekiwasprings; 1800 Wekiwa Circle, Apopka; admission $6, campsites per person $5, hookups $24; ⊘ 7am-dusk) Cool off in the icy spring-fed swimming hole, hike miles of trails and paddle the tranquil, still waters of the Wekiva River. Nature Adventures (p241), inside the park, offers 2½-hour guided tours, rents kayaks and canoes (two hours $17, per additional hour $3) and supplies overnight camping supplies. Reserve primitive riverside campsites in advance.

Bok Tower Gardens (☎ 863-676-1408; www.boktowergardens.org; 1151 Tower Blvd, Lake Wales; adult/child $12/3, house tour $5; ⊘ 8am-6pm, last admission 5pm; ⊛) Designed by Frederick Law Olmstead Jr and showcasing the meticulously carved 205ft stone bell tower, this 250-acre National Historic Landmark features beautiful gardens, twice-daily carillon concerts, the Mediterranean-style Pinewood Estates (circa 1930s) and a garden cafe. Kids can pick up special paper at the entry and make a treasure hunt out of looking for the iron rubbing posts, each with a different animal to rub. The gardens hosts outdoor classical-music concerts ($25).

Bok Tower Gardens sits an hour south of Orlando, close to Legoland. Take I-4 west, exit 55 and proceed south on Hwy 27 for 23 miles.

Kelly Park (☎ 407-254-1902; 400 E Kelly Park Rd, Apopka; per vehicle $5; ⊘ 8am-7pm Mar-Oct, to 5pm Nov-Feb; ⊛) Pick up an inner tube ($5) at the bar a half mile before the entrance and float the shallow 1-mile stream formed by Rock Spring.

In the winter, your only company might be the otter swimming beside you, the turtles lounging and the deer grazing along the creek's edge, but crowds of locals give the park a raucous party atmosphere on warm weekends and during the summer. A small concession is open in the summer only. Kelly Park sits just beyond the northwest corner of Wekiwa Springs State Park, 20 miles northwest of downtown Orlando.

Lake Louisa State Park (☎ 352-394-3969; www.floridastatepark.org/lakelouisa; 7305 US 27, Clermont; admission $5, campsites per person $5, hookups $24, 6-person cabins $120; ⊘ 8am-sundown) Located 30 minutes west of Walt Disney World, Lake Louisa is an easy getaway from the theme-park overdrive. There are several peaceful lakes, lovely beaches and 25 miles of hiking trails through fields, woods and orange groves. For boating on Dixie Lake, you can rent three-person canoes and single-rider kayaks (from $15 to $30) at the ranger station.

Swimming is allowed in Lake Louisa only – take note of the signs about alligators, and keep your eyes open. Twenty cabins, each with two bedrooms (linen included), a fully

Thursday Gallery Hop CULTURE
(☎ 407-648-7060; www.orlandoslice.com) Downtown Orlando art and culture crawl, with live music and monthly themes at various venues from 6pm to 9pm on the third Thursday of the month.

Zora Neale Hurston Festival of the Arts and Humanities CULTURE
(www.zorafestival.org; Eatonville) African American music, art and culture festival.

Spring Training SPORTS
(www.springtrainingonline.com) From mid-Feb to April, bring a blanket, grab the Cracker Jacks and watch baseball like it was meant to be. The Atlanta Braves play at Walt Disney World's ESPN Center. The Houston Astros play at Osce-ola County Stadium (p259) in Kissimmee, with a move to Palm Beach Gardens in the pipeline.

Silverspurs Rodeo SPORTS
(☎ 321-697-3495; www.silverspursrodeo.com; adult/child under 10yr $15/free) Bull-riding, calf-roping and all things cowboy since 1944. Held in February and June.

Winter Park Sidewalk Art Festival CULTURE
(☎ 407-644-7207; www.wpsaf.org; Winter Park) In mid-March, more than 250 artists display work along the sidewalks of small-town Winter Park.

Florida Film Festival FILM
(☎ 407-629-1088; www.floridafilmfestival.com; 1300 S Orlando Ave, Maitland; films $11) Indie and alter-

equipped kitchen and front porches, offer lake views. Camping and cabin reservations can be made up to 11 months in advance.

Orlando Wetlands Park (☎407-568-1706; www.orlandowetlands.org; 25115 Wheeler Rd, Christmas; ☉sunrise to sunset, closed Nov 15-Feb 1; 🖐) Woodlands, lakes and marshes flush with migrating birds, alligator, deer and all kinds of other critters. There are 20 miles of hiking trails and dirt roads, as well as restrooms, picnic tables and charcoal grills at the main entrance. Biking is limited to unpaved berm roads. The park, 30 miles east of downtown Orlando, sits about halfway between Orlando and Titusvile, home to Canaveral National Seashore and the Kennedy Space Center.

Take Hwy 408 east, continue on Hwy 50 east, then north on Fort Christmas Rd past Fort Christmas, and right onto Wheeler Rd into the park.

Nature Conservancy's Disney Wilderness Preserve (☎407-935-0002; www.nature.org/florida; 2700 Scrub Jay Trail, Kissimmee; adult/child 6-17yr $3/2; ☉9am-5pm Mon-Fri; 🖐) Hidden within Orlando's sprawl, this undeveloped and little-visited 11,500-acre preserve is the result of laws that required Walt Disney World to compensate for the company's impact on (and devastation of) wetlands and sensitive natural habitats. The park's scrub, fields and woods are home to gopher tortoises, bald eagles, sandhill cranes and hundreds of other wildlife species.

Hike the 1-mile round-trip to Lake Russell, or continue onto the 2.5-mile loop. The park is located just south of Kissimmee, about 20 minutes from Walt Disney World.

Rock Springs Run Trail Rides (Cactus Jack's Trail Rides; ☎352-266-9326; www.rockspringsruntrailrides.com; 3700 County Rd 433, Sorrento; 1/1½/2hr rides $45/65/90) Guided trail rides through meadows, pine-scrub swampland and dense forests of Rock Springs Run State Reserve. Children must be age six and over to ride. Ask in advance which trail you'll be taking, as some simply follow the dirt road into the park and others venture deeper into the reserve. Take I-4 exit 101C. Head west, and it's about 8 miles on the left.

Harry P Leu Gardens (☎407-246-2620; www.leugardens.org; 1920 N Forest Ave, Audubon Park; adult/child 4-18yr $10/3; ☉9am-5pm, last admission 4pm) Camelias, roses, orange groves and desert plants, as well as plenty of grassy spots for a lakeside picnic. Pick up supplies at East End Market (p252), a half mile east of the entrance gate on Corrine Dr. Tours of Leu House, an 18th-century mansion, run every half hour from 10am to 3:30pm. See website for details on outdoor movies, storytelling and live music.

Rock Springs Run State Reserve (☎407-884-2008; www.floridastateparks.org/rockspringsrun; 30601 Country Rd 433, Sorrento; admission $3; ☉8am-6pm) This 14,000-acre reserve located 30 miles north of downtown Orlando offers 17 miles of hiking trails, and primitive riverside camping accessible by canoe or kayak only.

native movies organized through the hip Enzian (p257) theater in early April. Multifilm and event packages available from $50.

Orlando International Fringe Festival   CULTURE
(www.orlandofringe.org) Fourteen-day festival in May 'offering 100% unjuried, 100% uncensored, 100% accessible theater, music, dance and art.'

Gay Days   GAY & LESBIAN
(www.gaydays.com) More than 160,000 folks descend upon the city for a week of events in the theme parks and venues throughout town in the first week of June.

Orlando Film Festival   FILM
(www.orlandofilmfest.com) Indie films screen at the downtown Orlando cineplex in October.

Capital One Bowl   SPORTS
(☎407-440-5700; www.capitalonebowl.com; 1610 W Church St, Florida Citrus Bowl Stadium) Footfall fans decked out in their university's colors flock to Orlando for the New Year's Day parade and football game.

🛏 Sleeping

You'll find every conceivable motel and hotel chain in every nook and cranny of greater Orlando, plenty of cheap independent motels, particularly along Hwy 192 east of I-4, and a dizzying number of resorts ranging

---

ℹ️ HOUSE RENTALS

Most rentals will be in gated housing developments dedicated almost exclusively to vacation rentals or in time-share resorts. If you want to stay within the gates of Walt Disney World, you can rent Disney Vacation Club villas and condos at Disney resorts for far less than the rack rate. Search Lake Buena Vista, and scroll for Disney resorts.

All Star Vacation Homes (☎321-281-4966; www.allstarvacationhomes.com) Though the communities tend to look a little like 'Pleasantville,' many are within miles from Disney World and offer Disney-themed bedrooms.

Vacation Rental By Owner (www.vrbo.com) Reputable international source.

HomeAway (www.homeaway.com) House and condo rentals in the Orlando area and beyond.

---

from family-friendly mayhem to a lakeside nudist hideaway. Most hotels offer complimentary shuttles to the theme parks, but always ask about details as many require advance reservations, fill up easily and only run a couple of times a day. They can be miserably inconvenient. Walt Disney World and Universal Orlando both offer on-site resort hotels with all kinds of enticing perks.

Rack rates vary dramatically according to demand, change within the course of a week or even a day and can plummet for no apparent reason. Rates outside theme-park hubs are lowest from June through September and highest between Christmas and early January, and in March. Rates quoted are during high season.

🛏️ Downtown Orlando

EO Inn & Spa   BOUTIQUE HOTEL **$$**
(☎407-481-8485; www.eoinn.com; 227 N Eola Dr, Thornton Park; r $129-229; @ 🛜) Small and understated hotel on the northeastern shore of Lake Eola, with an easy walk to Thornton Park and downtown Orlando bars and restaurants. The rooms vary dramatically in size.

Aloft Orlando Downtown   BUSINESS HOTEL **$$**
(Map p230; ☎497-380-3500; www.aloftorlandodowntown.com; 500 S Orange Ave; r $150-240; P @ 🛜 ☒)

Open, streamlined and decidedly modern, although the carefully constructed minimalist decor results in rooms that feel oddly empty, uninviting and unfinished, and the sleek little pool sits unpleasantly on the main road. But it is one of the few hotels within an easy walk to downtown Orlando's bars and restaurants. Valet-only parking per day $20.

Westin Grand Bohemian   LUXURY HOTEL **$$$**
(Map p230; ☎407-313-9000; www.grandbohemianhotel.com; 325 S Orange Ave; r $179-299, ste $299-499, valet-only parking per day $24; P @ 🛜 ☒; 🍽Lymo) Downtown's most luxurious and elegant option has marble floors, a stunning art-deco bar with massive black pillars, weekend jazz and rich urban rooms. The small rooftop pool echoes 1950s Miami Beach.

🛏️ International Drive (Around Universal Orlando Resort & Seaworld)

Hilton Garden Inn International Drive North   MOTEL **$$**
(Map p234; ☎407-363-9332; www.hiltongardenorlando.com; 5877 American Way; r $100-225; @ 🛜 ☒; 🚋I-Trolley Red Line Stop 7) With an airy garden-style lobby, a poolside tiki bar and an on-site restaurant, this makes an excellent midrange option for visiting Universal Orlando. It's less than a mile to the parks and, although it sits on I-4, it's quiet and set apart from the chaos of International Dr.

Hilton Homewood Suites   MOTEL **$$**
(Map p234; ☎407-226-0669; http://homewoodsuites1.hilton.com; 5893 American Way; ste $120-160; @ 🛜 ☒; 🚋I-Ride Trolley Red Line Stop 7) Comfy beds and spacious suites, each with a fully equipped kitchen and a low-key feel that is lacking at comparable chain hotels in Orlando. There's a complimentary hot breakfast, a dinner buffet (weekdays) and a 24 hour snack shop. Great choice, particularly if you're going to Universal Orlando and don't want to stay on-site. The hotel sits a 15-minute walk from Universal Orlando Resort, though it's an unpleasant walk over the interstate.

Castle Hotel   HOTEL **$$**
(Map p234; ☎407-345-1511; www.castlehotelorlando.com; 8629 International Dr; r $140-270; P @ 🛜 ☒ 🐾; 🚋I-Ride Trolley Red Line Stop 20 or Green Line Stop 10) You can't miss the castlelike exterior of this International Dr landmark. Inside you'll find gilt, sparkle

and antler chandeliers, with rooms decorated in deep purple and red; outside, a small pool sits next to a modern and airy garden-inspired cafe. Wi-fi costs $15 per night, parking $15 oer day. There's a $150 nonrefundable fee for pets.

★ **Grande Lakes Orlando –**
JW Marriott & Ritz-Carlton   LUXURY HOTEL **$$$**
(✔ JW Marriott 407-206-2300, Ritz-Carlton 407-206-2400; www.grandelakes.com; Ritz-Carlton 4012 Central Florida Pkwy, JW Marriott 4040 Central Park Pkwy; r $299-400, ste from $350, resort fee per day $25; P @ 🕏 🏊) Two properties, one a Ritz and the other a Marriott, share facilities. The grounds, peaceful and elegant, with plenty of greenery and the best lazy river pool in Orlando, sit in a sheltered oasis of quiet and luxury. The spa is divine, the service impeccable, the food outstanding and most rooms have balconies overlooking the pool and golf course. Excellent for honeymooners and families alike, this hotel is the rare Orlando find that seamlessly combines child and adult friendly. Rates at the Marriott are generally a bit less than the Ritz. Self-/valet parking is $19/26.

🛏 **Around Walt Disney World**

Countless hotels, motels and resorts in Lake Buena Vista, Kissimmee and Celebration lie within a few miles of Walt Disney World. In addition to these recommended options, there's an excellent selection of chain motels along grassy Palm Pkwy just outside Disney's gates and a cluster of seven upscale chain hotels (www.downtowndisneyhotels.com) across from Downtown Disney.

Palm Lakefront Hostel   HOSTEL **$**
(✔ 407-396-1759; www.orlandohostels.com; 4840 W Irlo Bronson/Hwy 192, Kissimmee; dm/d/q $19/40/60; 🕏 🏊; 🚌 Lynx 56 & 55) This two-story roadside-motel-styed hostel sits among the traffic and chain restaurants of the Kissimmee strip. It doesn't look like much at first glance, but in the back, there's a grassy lakeside picnic and BBQ area, a quiet fishing dock and a little pool. The public bus just outside connects directly to Disney's Transportation & Ticket Center.

Embassy Suites
Lake Buena Vista South   HOTEL **$$**
(✔ 407-597-4000; https://embassysuites3.hilton.com; 4955 Kyngs Heath Rd, Kissimmee; r $110-225; @ 🕏 🏊) Comfortable and modern two-room suites, complimentary cooked-to-order breakfasts and evening cocktails, as well as an on-site travel agent, Hertz car-rental desk, a market with food basics and coin laundry. Built in 2013, this is an excellent choice in a city overflowing with mediocre, aging and overrated chains.

Barefoot Suites   MOTEL **$$**
(Map p262; ✔ 407-589-2127; www.thebarefoot-suites.com; 2750 Florida Plaza Blvd, Kissimmee; ste $83-200, resort fee per day $7; 🏊) Bright and spacious one- and two-bedroom suites in a yellow six-story building. Low-key, friendly, under-the-radar and close to Disney, with kitchens and washer/dryers.

Melia Orlando
Suite Hotel at Celebration   HOTEL **$$**
(Map p262; ✔ 888-956-3542, 407-964-7000; www.melia.com; 225 Celebration Pl, Celebration; ste $130-280, resort fee per day $17; 🕏 🏊) Stylishly contemporary, with a circular pool surrounding an island of palm trees. Earth-toned one- and two-bedroom suites have fully equipped kitchens, but the rooms feel tired and uninspired. Family suites sleep up to eight, and there is a distinct 'family-friendly' vibe to the pool area.

Melia Orlando sits just off I-4, an easy drive to Walt Disney World. It is not within walking distance to the eateries, shops and pleasant lake of downtown Celebration.

Hilton Orlando Bonnet Creek   RESORT **$$**
(Map p262; ✔ 407-597-3600; www.hiltonbonnetcreek.com; 14100 Bonnet Creek Resort Lane; r $130-300, resort fee per day $22; P @ 🕏 🏊) Surrounded by Walt Disney World and boasting a big pool with a lazy river and a slide, this quintessential full-service resort makes an excellent alternative to comparable resorts on Disney property. No, you won't enjoy the benefits of staying at a Disney hotel, but the quality more accurately mirrors the price. Self-/valet parking $16/24.

The on-site Harvest Cafe serves reasonably priced fresh and tasty fare, and children under 12 eat free for breakfast and dinner.

Wyndham Bonnet Creek Resort   RESORT **$$**
(Map p262; ✔ 407-238-3500; www.wyndhambonnetcreek.com; 9560 Via Encinas; ste from $150; ✳ 🕏 🏊) Great value and close to Disney, this Mediterranean-style resort has one-, two-, three- and four-bedroom suites, rooms with bunk-bed nooks that the kids will love, lazy rivers, a fountain splash area, several pools and all kinds of kid-friendly touches. Yet it manages to offer a quiet sanctuary

that parents will enjoy too. Try the excellent sushi at the award-winning on-site seafood restaurant.

★ **Villas of Grand Cypress** RESORT $$$
(Map p262; ☑887-330-7370, 407-239-4700; www.grandcypress.com; 1 N Jacaranda Blvd; r from $165, 1-/2-/3-/4-bedroom villas from $280/395/555/725, resort fee per day $22; ☎❄) Beautifully appointed rooms and villas, with natural cut stone, deep soaking tubs and outdoor patios, sit quietly along the Grand Cypress resort golf course. The least expensive option is the 'club suite,' a 650-sq-ft room with one king or two queen beds, a sleeper couch and a small patio. It feels cramped, but can work for a family of four.

The spacious villas boast private baths for each bedroom, living and dining rooms and fully equipped kitchens. There's a small and quiet swimming pool, plus complimentary bikes and helmets for peaceful rides through the golf course, and an on-demand door-to-door shuttle service from your villa to the Hyatt Grand Cypress across the street. Opt for breakfast elsewhere – the clubhouse dining is overpriced and mediocre.

Waldorf Astoria LUXURY HOTEL $$$
(Map p262; ☑407-597-5500; www.waldorfastoriaorlando.com; 14200 Bonnett Creek Resort Lane; r $200-400, ste $450-560, resort fee per day $25, valet-only parking $25; ☐@☎❄) Though this elegant classic doesn't offer the benefits of on-site Disney hotels, it's located within the gates of Walt Disney World and, unlike Disney luxury, the quality of its rooms, amenities and service is impeccable. There's an excellent buffet breakfast, two grandly styled pools bordering the golf course, a Guerlain spa and divine beds. Hilton Orlando Bonnet Creek (p247), which has a lazy river and pool slide, shares amenities with the Waldorf, and rooms and packages there cost a bit less.

Bus shuttle to Disney is complimentary but unreliable – it may make several stops on the way to or from your destination, stretching what should be a 15-minute ride closer to an hour, and so rendering null the benefit of close proximity to Disney.

**Hyatt Regency
Grand Cypress Resort** RESORT $$$
(Map p262; ☑407-239-1234; www.hyattgrandcypress.com; 1 Grand Cypress Blvd, Lake Buena Vista; r $169-350, resort fee per day $25; ☐@☎❄❄) Considering the proximity to Disney (just outside the gates), and the quality of the

rooms, service, grounds and amenities, this atrium-style resort is one of the best-value top-end options in Orlando. There are multiple pools, a waterfall set into a grotto, a splash play area and a winding slide, as well as a beachside lake with hammocks, sailboats and bicycles. Self-/valet parking is $12/22.

Shuttles go to Disney's Transportation & Ticket Center (from there you must connect with Disney transportation), to SeaWorld and to Universal Orlando Resort (an easy 10 minutes to the north; if driving, take Palm Pkwy and Turkey Lake Rd).

**Gaylord Palms Resort
& Convention Center** RESORT $$$
(Map p262; ☑407-586-0000; www.gaylordpalms.com; 6000 W Osceola Pkwy; r & ste $180-350, resort fee per day $20; ☐@☎❄) An enormous glass-topped atrium encompasses three recreations of Florida wilderness: the Everglades, St Augustine and Key West, each with live plantings, piped-in insect sounds and running water. This is, without a doubt, the most massive hotel in Orlando, with plenty of eye candy and energy, and it's popular as a conference center (expect corporate banners) and a family resort. Self-/valet parking is $18/24.

There's an on-site 'water park,' with poolside movies, waterslides and a zero entry pool, as well as an adults-only pool.

🛏 Greater Orlando

All kinds of chain motels cluster around Orlando International Airport – recommended options include **Springhill Suites** (www.marriott.com/springhill-suites/travel.mi) and **Homewood Suites** (http://homewoodsuites3.hilton.com), and the lovely little town of Winter Park, just north of downtown Orlando, boasts the Alfond Inn and Park Plaza Hotel, two of the city's best hotels.

Parliament House GAY & LESBIAN $
(☑407-425-7571; www.parliamenthouse.com; 410 N Orange Blossom Trail; r & ste $66-106; ☎❄) An exclusively gay and lesbian Orlando institution on the shores of Rock Lake. The resort has several bars, nightclubs and a legendary Wednesday-night drag show. Parliament House is located on Orange Blossom Trail, northwest of downtown Orlando.

★ **Bay Hill Club and Lodge** HOTEL $$
(☑888-422-9455, 407-876-2429; www.bayhill.com; 9000 Bay Hill Blvd; r $150-240; @☎❄) Quiet and genteel Bay Hill feels like a time warp; as though you're walking into a TV set or your

grandmother's photo album, into a time and place that is reassuringly calm and simple, and slightly bizarre. The staff is exceptionally gracious and accommodating, and handsome rooms are spread among a series of two-story buildings bordering the golf course.

Though the lodge seems to attract an older, golfing clientele, and there is nothing trendy or fancy about its pool and amenities, families will find Bay Hill's comforting co-coonlike atmosphere a welcoming oasis after a day tackling Orlando. Theme parks and restaurants are an easy drive, and the on-site dining room is reasonably priced (as far as Orlando resort dining goes) and surprisingly good. Try the flat-bread pizza. Bay Hill, set in a residential golf community and sporting only a small sign, is difficult to find. Head west from Apopka Vineland Rd on Bay Hill Blvd and look for it 1 mile on the right. There is no daily parking or resort fee.

Omni Orlando Resort at ChampionsGate RESORT $$
(☑407-390-6664; www.omnihotels.com; 1500 Masters Blvd, ChampionsGate; r $175-300, villas $560-750, resort fee per day $20; @ 🛜 ⛱ 👪) Buffered from noise and congestion by two golf courses, wetlands and plenty of green space. There's an adult-only pool, and a pleasantly landscaped family pool boasting a waterslide and an 850ft lazy river. Villas sleep between six and eight people. The resort lies about 12 miles south of Walt Disney World, just off I-4. self-/valet parking is $16/24.

There aren't many restaurants nearby and, unfortunately, the on-site Japanese restaurant is expensive and mediocre.

Hammock House CABIN $$
(☑352-266-9326; www.hammockhousewekiva. com; 30210 Wekiva River Rd, Sorrento; per night/ week $250/1250) Nestled in the woods along the banks of the Wekiva River, this simple three-bedroom cabin makes you feel like you're in the middle of nowhere. Hammock House lies 8 miles west of I-4 exit 101C, about 45 minutes' drive north of downtown Orlando; alternatively, it's a four-hour canoe float from Wekiwa Springs State Park (p244). Two-night minimum stay.

Hyatt Regency Orlando International Airport Hotel HOTEL $$
(☑407-825-1234; 9300 Jeff Fuqua Blvd; r $159; @ 🛜 ⛱) Located inside the main terminal of the Orlando International Airport. Has a nice rooftop pool.

🏘 Winter Park

★**Alfond Inn** BOUTIQUE HOTEL $$$
(Map p242; ☑407-998-8090; www.thealfond inn.com; 300 E New England Ave; r $170-$260; @ 🛜 ⛱ 👪) Contemporary white-walled elegance, a low-key welcoming vibe and a commitment to the arts combine to give this Winter Park gem a distinct style. Not only does it house the Alfond Collection of Contemporary Art, but all proceeds from hotel-room prices fund liberal-arts scholarships at nearby Rollins College. There's a lovely rooftop pool, an excellent restaurant (locally sourced ingredients) with courtyard tables, and well-appointed rooms.

★**Park Plaza Hotel** BOUTIQUE HOTEL $$$
(Map p242; ☑407-647-1072; www.parkplazahotel. com; 307 S Park Ave; r $180-220, ste $260-320; 🛜) Brick walls, spartan wood furniture, antiques and luscious white cotton bedding create a distinct arts-and-crafts sensibility at this historic two-story hotel. Rooms lining Park Ave share a narrow balcony, each with a private entrance and a few wicker chairs hidden from the street by hanging ferns, and are well worth the extra money.

The hotel does not allow children under five years old (not because they're snobby, but because of the thin walls).

🍴 Eating

🍽 Downtown & Thornton Park

Graffiti Junktion American Burger Bar BURGERS $
(☑407-426-9503; www.graffitijunktion.com; 900 E Washington St, Thornton Park; mains $6-13; ◷11am-2am) This little neon graffiti-covered happenin' hangout, with courtyard dining and regular drink specials, is all about massive burgers with attitude. Top yours with a fried egg, artichoke hearts, chili, avocado and more.

Benjamin French Bakery BAKERY $
(☑407-797-2293; www.benjaminfrenchbakery. com; 716 E Washington St, Thornton Park; pastries $4, mains $6-12; ◷8am-7pm Tue-Sat, to 6pm Sun) Bright little French bakery featuring rustic sandwiches, salads and omelets. Your best bet, though, is a pastry and coffee to go. Try the crusty homemade baguette or a coconut croissant.

Dexters of Thornton Park
AMERICAN **$$**

(☑ 407-648-2777; www.dexwine.com; 808 E Washington St, Thornton Park; mains $10-17; ⊙ 7am-10pm Mon-Thu, to 2am Fri, 11am-2am Sat, 10am-10pm Sun) Neighborhood restaurant with outdoor seating and wine by the flight, glass or bottle. The popular daily brunch includes interesting twists to breakfast mainstays, including pepper-jack grits, apple-pie french toast, duck bacon, and a selection of fruity mimosas including peach, mango and pineapple.

There are sister locations in Winter Park (Map p242; ☑ 407-629-1150; www.dexwine.com; 558 W New England Ave, Winter Park; ⊙ 11am-10pm Mon-Thu, to midnight Fri & Sat, 10am-10pm Sun) and in Lake Mary (17 miles north of Winter Park, I-4 exit 101).

Hamburger Mary's
BURGERS **$$**

(Map p230; ☑ 321-319-0600; www.hamburgermarys.com; 110 W Church St; mains $8-19; ⊙ 11am-10:30pm Sun-Thu, to 11:30 Fri & Sat) Downtown high-energy diner specializing in over-the-top burgers with sweet-potato fries and serious cocktails. There's a Broadway Brunch with show tunes, drag shows and all kinds of interactive entertainment.

Shari Sushi
JAPANESE **$$**

(☑ 407-420-9420; www.sharisushilounge.com; 621 E Central Blvd, Thornton Park; mains $14-24; ⊙ 5-10pm Sun-Wed, to 11pm Thu-Sat) Minimalist decor, huge sidewalk windows and a rather odd variety of tasty sushi, rolls and sashimi, but there's a limited selection of hot dishes. The elaborate drinks menu includes lemongrass *mojitos* and a cilantro-lime sake cocktail.

International Drive (Around Universal Orlando Resort & SeaWorld)

The 5-mile stretch of Sand Lake Rd from I-4 (at Whole Foods) west to Apopka Vineland Rd and including Dr Philips Blvd, is known as Restaurant Row. Here you'll find a concentration of restaurants and high-end chains more popular with locals than tourists, with everything from wine bars to cigar bars, sushi to burgers.

Five Guys Burgers and Fries
BURGERS **$**

(Map p234; ☑ 407-352-8899; www.fiveguys.com; 3042 W Sand Lake, Restaurant Row; mains $5-10; ⊙ 11am-10pm; ⊕) Sure, it's a fast-food burger

---

CELEBRATION

Built by Disney from the swamps in 1994, tiny Celebration is small-town America like you imagine it may have once been...before John Cheever, David Lynch and *Desperate Housewives* introduced irony; before strip malls; before leaf blowers. We could wonder what goes on behind closed doors, but why? Relax over coffee while the kids play in the splash fountain and watch the ducks. Sure, maybe it doesn't sound that exciting, but wasn't that day at Universal's Islands of Adventure exciting enough?

Celebration sits off Hwy 192, just east of I-4 and a few miles from Walt Disney World. The main attraction is the small lake, which has a manicured promenade circling its length and palm trees dotting the banks. The handful of pubs and restaurants in town, all within walking distance of Hotel Celebration and many with sidewalk seating, serve up a surprising variety of cuisine. It's a good spot to come if you're at Disney and want to eat off-site.

Bohemian Hotel Celebration (☑ 407-566-6000, 888-499-3800; www.celebrationhotel.com; 700 Bloom St; r $150-275, ste $250-350; ⛿❄@🛎🐾) Quiet and genteel, with what has to be the city's smallest pool perched on the patio next to the lake, downtown Celebration's only hotel offers handsome rooms and an old-world Key West sensibility. Perfect for anyone looking for something beyond the impersonality of a large resort and the chaos of bars, nightly entertainment and programmed children's activities, but close to Disney.

It's an easy drive to all the parks but feels years and miles away. There's no theme-park shuttle. Wi-fi costs an additional $15 per day and self-valet parking is $14/19. There is limited free street parking.

Sweet Escape (☑ 407-566-0603; www.sweetescapecelebration.com; 603 Market St; mains $5-12; ⊙ 7am-9pm; ⊕) Local hangout with tasty doughnuts, steel-cut oats, sandwiches and soup.

Seito Sushi (www.seitosushi.com; 671 Front St; mains $8-23; ⊙ 8am-10pm) Intimate and modern; offers *yakisoba* (yellow egg noodles), bento boxes and very good sushi.

joint chain. Sure, you can find them scattered through Florida and beyond. But this Obama favorite, an easy drive from Universal Orlando, has some of the best burgers and fries in town.

TooJays
DELI $

(Map p234; ☑ 407-355-0340; www.toojays.com; 7600 Dr Phillips Blvd, Restaurant Row; sandwiches $4-7; ☺ 8am-9pm Sun-Thu, to 10pm Fri & Sat; ⓜ) Excellent deli sandwiches to go, but nothing much in terms of ambience. If you feel a cold coming on, head here for quintessential homemade chicken noodle or matzo ball soup.

Johnny Rockets
DINER $

(Map p234; ☑ 407-903-0762; www.johnnyrockets. com; 9101 International Dr, No 1100, Pointe Orlando; mains $6-10; ☺ 11:30am-11pm Sun-Thu, to 2am Fri & Sat; ⓜ; ⌨ I-Ride Trolley Red Line 24 or Green Line 12) Straight out of *Happy Days*, with red vinyl seating, lots of chrome and flip-style jukeboxes on the tables; the Fonz would feel right at home at this burger-joint chain.

Thai Thani
THAI $$

(Map p234; ☑ 407-239-9733; www.thaithani.net; 11025 International Dr; mains $9-22; ☺ 11:30am-11pm; ⓜ; ⌨ I-Ride Trolley Red Line) Just past the gates to SeaWorld, Discovery Cove and Aquatica, this makes an ideal dinner choice after a day of dolphins and waterslides. It's friendly, cool and quiet, with gilded Thai decor and some tables with traditional floor seating. Good food, but watered-down spice – for a kick, ask for level 5.

Taverna Opa
GREEK $$

(Map p234; ☑ 407-351-8660; www.opaorlando.com; 9101 International Dr; mains $12-25; ☺ noon-2am; ☑; ⌨ I-Ride Trolley Red Line) Great spot for Greek classics, including plenty of vegetarian options and fresh hummus made tableside. Can get loud and crazy late-night, when the belly dancer shimmies and shakes from table to table and it isn't unusual for folks to climb onto the solid tables and kick up their heels. Nightly entertainment from 7pm.

Cafe Tu Tu Tango
TAPAS $$

(Map p234; ☑ 407-248-2222; www.cafetututango. com; 8625 International Dr; tapas $8-16; ☺ 11:30am-11pm Mon, Wed, Thu & Sun, to midnight Tue, Fri & Sat; ⌨ I-Ride Trolley Red Line Stop 20) Local artwork, all for sale, crams the adobe-style walls of this bright Spanish eatery. Relax on the patio with cajun chicken egg rolls and a plate of alligator bites, washed down with a pitcher of sangria.

On Tuesdays from 9pm to midnight, there's live music and $3 drinks.

Melting Pot
FONDUE $$

(Map p234; www.meltingpot.com/orlando; 7549 W Sand Lake Rd, Restaurant Row; mains $12-25; ☺ 5-10pm Mon-Thu, to 11pm Fri & Sat, 4-10pm Sun; ⓜ) Kids in particular love the novelty of a fondue dinner (cheese, beef, chicken, seafood and, of course, chocolate).

B-Line Diner
DINER $$

(Map p234; ☑ 407-284-1234; 9801 International Dr, Hyatt Regency; mains $8-20; ☺ 24hr; ⓜ) Inside the giant Hyatt Regency, a retro-styled cafe serving basic but good diner food 24/7.

✕ Around Walt Disney World

There are plenty of restaurants catering to Walt Disney World visitors in Lake Buena Vista and Kissimmee, but it's mostly chains and overhyped disappointments. If you're looking for a quiet evening away from the spinning wheel of Disney eye candy, head to nearby Celebration. Several restaurants and bars line the small lake, and they all have patio dining.

Havana's Cafe
CUBAN $

(Map p262; ☑ 407-238-5333; www.havanascubancuisine.com; 8544 Palm Pkwy; mains $6-13; ☺ 11:30am-10pm Tue-Sat, noon-9pm Sun, 5-10pm Mon) This simple and friendly mom-and-pop spot is a breath of fresh air among the ubiquitous chains, resort dining and high-octane Disney options. Call ahead for takeout.

Hemmingways
SEAFOOD $$$

(Map p262; ☑ 407-239-1234; www.grandcypress. hyatt.com; 1 Grand Cypress Blvd, Hyatt Regency Grand Cypress Resort; mains $29-40; ☺ 5-10pm) Quiet spot with airy Key West atmosphere. Try the particularly tasty crab cakes, with big chunks of lump crab and very little filler, and ask for a table on the screened-in porch.

Deep Blu Seafood Grille
SEAFOOD $$$

(Map p262; ☑ 407-390-2420; www.deepbluorlando. com; 14651 Chelonia Pkwy, Wyndham Grand Orlando Resort; sushi $7-28, mains $29-44; ☺ 5:30-10pm) Contemporary à la carte open-kitchen dining with local-harvest fish, a raw bar, mussels and crab. Shared sides include tempura broccoli, crab mac 'n' cheese and candy-roasted sweet potato. Though the food is excellent, it's pricey, and things add up – instead of a full meal, opt for some of Orlando's best sushi and a glass of wine at the bar.

FIELD-TO-FORK EATING IN ORLANDO

The hum of of the field-to-fork Orlando dining scene has developed into a strong and steady crescendo, making it easy to find locally sourced, creatively inspired and delicious food in a city that has built a reputation as a dark hole of national chains, fast food and overpriced theme-park fare. Craft cocktails and artisan beers are an important part of the experience, and it's not just for foodies or fat wallets either – we love the low-key authenticity that invites anyone who loves good food and quality spirits to come on in and enjoy.

Ravenous Pig (☑407-628-2333; www.theravenouspig.com; 1234 Orange Ave, Winter Park; mains $19-33; ⊙11:30am-2pm & 5:30-9:30pm Tue-Sat) The cornerstone of Orlando's locally sourced restaurant trend, with giant black-and-white photos hanging from exposed ceiling pipes and a handful of sidewalk tables. Start with the bacon-infused bourbon old-fashioned and a plate of Gruyère biscuits. Mains include a burger with truffle-oil fries, Florida seafood specialties, and quirky twists such as duck breast with 'dragon-tongue' beans.

Swine Hour (from 4pm to 5:30pm Tuesdays to Fridays) offers $4 draft beers, $8 cocktails and $4 pub-fare plates.

East End Market (☑231-236-3316; www.eastendmkt.com; 3201 Corrine Dr, Audubon Park; ⊙10am-7pm Tue-Sat, 11am-6pm Sun; ☑📶) Look for the raised vegetable beds and picnic tables outside this earthy organic-hip collection of locally sourced eateries and markets.

Inside there's Local Roots Farm Store, specializing in 'All Florida, All Year' and offering flights of Florida beer and wine at the tiny bar; La Bretxa, with wild-caught Florida seafood to take back to your BBQ; the excellent vegan raw-bar Skybird Juicebar & Experimental Kitchen; and more.

Dandelion Communitea Café (☑407-362-1864; http://dandelioncommunitea.com; 618 N Thornton Ave; mains $6-10; ⊙11am-10pm Mon-Sat, to 5pm Sun; ☑📶) Unabashedly crunchy and definitively organic, this pillar of the sprouts-and-tofu, green-tea and soy-milk dining scene serves up creative and excellent vegetarian fare in a refurbished old house that invites folks to sit down and hang out.

There's an informal fire pit, tables in the yard and microbrew beer; check the website for details on art openings, poetry readings and live music.

Smiling Bison (☑407-898-8580; www.thesmilingbison.com; 745 Bennett Rd, Audubon Park; mains $11-22; ⊙5pm-midnight Tue-Thu, to 2am Fri & Sat) Don't be turned off by the dive exterior and empty-lot surrounds of this spunky little unaffected delight tucked just beyond the congestion of E Colonial Dr. Famous for its bison burger, served on an English-muffin-like bun with homemade fries, the limited but changing menu also features excellent pizza and creative dishes with a nod to the South.

There are a few tables outside, and live jazz and the like most nights.

✗ Greater Orlando

Dozens of Vietnamese, Korean, Chinese and other Asian eateries cluster along several blocks of Orlando's Little Vietnam, a pocket of the Mills 50 neighborhood. The epicenter is the intersection of Mills Ave and Colonial Dr; from here, head east along Colonial and see what looks good. Favorites include **Lac Viet Bistro** (2021 E Colonial) and, for a Vietnamese-styled sub sandwich to go, the tiny **Banh Mi Nha Trang** (1216 E Colonial).

House of Pizza   PIZZERIA **$**
(☑407-447-7515; www.orlandohouseofpizza.com; 14650 Gatorland Dr; mains $5-12; ⊙11am-10pm Mon-Sat, noon-9pm Sun; 📶) It doesn't look like much more than your standard greasy pizza joint, but give it a chance. It's independently owned and has very good pizza, as well as bruschetta, pasta, sandwiches and more. Across the street from Gatorland.

Stardust Video & Coffee   CAFE **$**
(☑407-623-3393; www.stardustvideoandcoffee. wordpress.com; 1842 E Winter Park Rd, Audubon Park; mains $7-14; ⊙7am-midnight Mon-Fri, from 8am Sat & Sun; P☕☑📶) Hipster-hippie hangout by day, with folks hunkered down behind laptops and books; craft cocktail and artisan beer hot spot by night. There's a Sunday brunch, fresh-squeezed juices, plenty of

K Restaurant (407-872-2332; www.krestaurant.net; 1710 Edgewater Dr, College Park; mains $18-38; 11:30am-2pm & 6-10pm Tue-Fri, 6-9pm Mon, to 10pm Sat;) Chef and owner Kevin Fonzo, one of Orlando's most celebrated and established field-to-fork foodie stars, earns local and national accolades year after year, but this neighborhood favorite remains wonderfully unassuming. There's a wraparound porch, a lovely little terrace, and herbs and vegetables come from the on-site garden.

Try the stacked fried green tomatoes with crab.

Cask & Larder (Map p242; 321-280-4200; www.caskandlarder.com; 565 W Fairbanks Ave, Winter Park; mains $13-30; 5-10pm Mon-Sat, 10:30am-3pm Sun) From open and airy environs the Cask & Larder serves an innovative menu of locally sourced Southern fare, including charred okra, and country-fried red snapper with crawfish grits. Pop in for a flight of thinly sliced ham with pepper jelly and biscuits, raw oysters and a house-brewed beer or craft cocktail. From Monday to Saturday the bar is open from 4pm to midnight and has a late-night bar menu.

The 'whole cookery dinner' includes roast suckling pig, a butcher's feast, a low country boil (snapper, clams, oysters and shrimp), or ribs and rib eye, served family-style with seasonal sides and a dessert (per person $60 to $75; minimum 72 hours advance notice required).

Luma on Park (Map p242; 407-599-411; www.lumaonpark.com; 290 S Park Ave, Winter Park; mains $25-30; 5:30-10pm Mon-Thu, 11:30am-11pm Fri & Sat, to 9pm Sun) A must for upscale foodie delights, featuring rather complicated pairings such as 'red snapper with black and white quinoa, braised watermelon radish, English pea, delta asparagus and citrus olive tapenade.' The recommended $35 prix-fixe menu is offered Sunday, Monday and Tuesday only.

B&B Junction (407-513-4134; www.bbjunction.com; 2103 W Fairbanks Ave, Winter Park; 11am-10pm Mon-Thu, to 11pm Fri & Sat ;) Fast food, field-to-fork style – grass-fed beef, free-range turkey burgers, housemade pickles, gourmet mac 'n' cheese – and Florida beer on tap.

Rusty Spoon (Map p230; 407-401-8811; www.therustyspoon.com; 55 W Church St; mains $15-31; 11am-3pm Mon-Fri, 5-10pm Sun-Thu, to 11pm Fri & Sat;) Airy, handsome and inviting, with a brick wall covered in giant photos of farm animals, a trendy urban vibe and an emphasis on pub classics with delightful twists.

Fresh Cafe (Map p242; 321-295-7837; 535 W New England Ave, Winter Park; mains $9-18; 11am-3pm & 6-10pm Mon-Fri, 6-10pm Sat, 10:30am-3pm Sun;) Nestled in Winter Park's historic Hannibal Sq neighborhood, this little white-walled cafe lives up to its name. Everything feels, looks and tastes clean and fresh, from the cucumber-mint water to the peach, prosciutto and mozzarella salad and Thai curried mussels. Sidewalk seating makes for a perfect summer evening.

vegetarian options and, oddly, video rentals. Yes, videos. Paper lanterns and twinkly lights dangle from the ceiling and snapshot-style photographs hang haphazardly from the concrete walls.

Call for information on weekly live music and the Saturday farmers market.

Greek Corner Restaurant   GREEK $
(407-228-0303; www.thegreekcorner.net; 1600 N Orange Ave; mains $6-14; 11am-10pm Mon-Sat, to 8pm Sun) This little, white-walled cafe with a small patio sits across from Lake Ivanhoe and serves pretty good gyros, moussaka and other Greek specialties.

Peach Valley Cafe   DINER $
(Map p234; 407-522-2601; www.peachvalleyrestaurants.com; 5072 Dr Phillips Blvd; mains $6-12; 7am-2:30pm Mon-Fri, to 3:30pm Sat & Sun;) Florida chain that offers surprisingly varied and tasty classics, from apple fritters and banana pancakes to chopped Cobb salad and chicken potpie. This is a standard fried eggs kind of place – nothing fancy, but solid and reasonably priced.

Bikes, Beans & Bordeaux   CAFE $
(407-427-1440; www.bikesbeansandbordeaux.com; 3022 Corrine Dr, Audubon Park; mains $6-12; 7am-10pm Mon-Fri, from 8am Sat, 8am-3pm Sun;) The wine and beer list follows the

ORLANDO & WALT DISNEY WORLD ORLANDO & AROUND

ⓘ BUYING GROCERIES

While most Orlando hotel rooms have small refrigerators, only deluxe Disney hotels provide them free of charge.

Whole Foods Market Philips Crossing (Map p234; ☑ 407-355-7100; www.wholefoods-market.com/stores/orlando; 8003 Turkey Lake Rd; ⊙ 8am-10pm) Organic fare, a salad bar, brick-oven pizza and more. There's another store at 1989 Aloma Ave, Winter Park.

Fresh Market (Map p234; ☑ 407-294-1516; 5000 Dr Phillips Blvd; ⊙ 9am-9pm Mon-Sat, 10am-8pm Sun) Excellent grocery store with organic and local produce.

Garden Grocer (☑ 866-855-4350; www.gardengrocer.com) Easy-to-navigate website allows you to select photos of groceries, beer and wine for delivery.

Orlando Grocery Express (☑ 407-395-4700; www.orlandogroceryexpress.com) Groceries, beer and wine delivered to your hotel or rental home. There's a $40 minimum, and a $14 delivery fee for orders less than $200. Order by 5am one day prior to delivery.

international cycling season, with French Bordeaux during the Tour de France and so on. There's weekend live music, couches for lounging and local art. Try the hot feta dip or create your own flatbread concoction.

★ **Yellow Dog Eats** BARBECUE $$
(☑ 407-296-0609; www.yellowdogeats.com; 1236 Hempel Ave, Windermere; mains $7-14; ⊙ 11am-9pm; ☑ ⛟) Housed in what was once a general store, with a tin roof, courtyard dining, an old boys' school locker filled with bottled beer, and an eclectic mix of quirky dog-inspired decor, this laid-back boho Orlando gem serves up excellent barbecue. Try the Florida Cracker (pulled pork with Gouda, bacon and fried onions) with a side of Cuban black beans.

Though it feels like a drive into the boondocks to get here, don't be deterred – Yellow Dog is an easy 6 miles northwest of Universal Orlando Resort.

Eden Bar AMERICAN $$
(☑ 407-629-1088; www.enzian.org; 1300 S Orlando Ave, Maitland; mains $10-16; ⊙ 11am-11pm Sun-Thu, to 1am Fri & Sat; ☑) ⛟ Island-vibe outdoor dining under the giant cypress of the ultra-cool Enzian Theater (p257). The delightfully eclectic menu ranges from pear prosciutto pizza and quinoa stuffed peppers to fried chicken and country fried steak. Try the Mexican *mojito*.

White Wolf Café and Bar DINER $$
(☑ 407-895-9911; www.whitewolfcafe.com; 1829 N Orange Ave; mains $14-29; ⊙ 8am-9pm Mon-Fri, to 3pm Sun) Neighborhood diner cafe, with Tiffany-styled chandeliers, a massive wooden bar and a mishmash of antiques. Come for the stick-to-your bones breakfasts and a Bloody Mary.

Keke's Breakfast Cafe CAFE $$
(☑ 407-226-1400; www.kekes.com; 4192 Conroy Rd; mains $8-14; ⊙ 7am-2:30pm; ⛟) Orlando go-to spot for great breakfasts, including stuffed French toast, eggs Benedict and banana nut pancakes. Other Orlando locations include one in Winter Park (Map p242; ☑ 407-629-1400; www.kekes.com; 345 W Fairbanks Ave, Winter Park; mains $8-14; ⊙ 7am-2:30pm; ⛟) and in Restaurant Row (Map p234; ☑ 407-354-1440; www.kekes.com; 7512 Dr Phillips Blvd; mains $8-14; ⊙ 7am-2:30pm; ⛟).

🍴 Winter Park

Ethos Vegan Kitchen VEGAN $
(Map p242; ☑ 407-228-3898; www.ethosvegankitchen.com; 601b S New York Ave; mains $7-14; ⊙ 11am-11pm Mon-Fri; ☑) ⛟ Pizza with broccoli, banana peppers, zucchini and seitan; meat-free shepherd's pie; pecan-encrusted eggplant; homemade soups and various sandwiches with names such as A Fungus Among Us and the Hippie Wrap.

4 Rivers Smokehouse BARBECUE $$
(☑ 407-474-8377; www.4rsmokehouse.com; 1600 W Fairbanks Ave; mains $8-16; ⊙ 11am-8pm Mon-Thu, to 9pm Fri & Sat) Expect lines out the door at this regular contender for best barbecue in Orlando.

Briarpatch CAFE $$
(Map p242; ☑ 407-628-8651; 252 N Park Ave; mains $8-15; ⊙ 7am-5pm Mon-Fri, from 8am Sat; ⛟) Massive multilayer cakes and hearty breakfasts in whitewashed shabby-chic tearoom environs.

Orchid Thai Cuisine
THAI $$

(Map p242; ✆407-331-1400; www.orchidthai-winterpark.com; 305 N Park Ave; mains $8-15; ⏱11am-10pm Mon-Thu, to 11pm Fri & Sat, noon-9pm Sun; ✐) Contemporary, friendly and tasty. Don't miss the delectable 'Golden Thai Doughnuts,' dough balls fried with a sweet condensed-milk dressing and sprinkled with crushed peanuts.

Bosphorous Turkish Cuisine
TURKISH $$

(Map p242; ✆407-644-8609; www.bosphorous-restaurant.com; 108 S Park Ave; mains $8-21; ⏱11:30am-10pm Mon-Thu, to 11pm Sat & Sun; ✐) An interesting menu and good food make this a standout in a town of great restaurants. Try the *lahmacun* (Turkish pizza) or the *hunkar begendi,* an Ottoman dish with beef and eggplant.

BurgerFi
BURGERS $$

(Map p242; ✆407-622-2010; www.burgerfi.com; 538 S Park Ave; mains $8-14; ⏱11am-11pm, to midnight Fri & Sat; ⚑) Essentially a burger and hot-dog fast-food joint and a national chain, but oh so much better than that. Come for hormone- and antibiotic-free beef, quinoa burgers, Coke in a bottle, fresh-squeezed lemonade, parmesan-and-herb hand-cut fries, frozen custard, and beer and wine by the glass or bottle.

★Prato
ITALIAN $$$

(Map p242; ✆407-262-0050; www.prato-wp.com; 124 N Park Ave; mains $15-28; ⏱11:30am-11pm Wed-Sat, from 5:30pm Mon & Tue, to 10pm Sun) A hopping go-to spot, with high ceilings, exposed beams and a bar expanding the length of the room. Offers inspired interpretations of classic Italian dishes, house-cured meats and excellent wood-oven pizza ($15).

Drinking

Orlando *really* likes to drink, so whether your tastes lean toward a flight of wine at a sidewalk cafe, shots of tequila at a pulsing nightclub or a craft cocktail over a game

---

ORLANDO'S BAKERIES & ICE CREAM

Orlando's field-to-fork dining and craft cocktail trends include a wave of independently owned bakeries and ice-cream shops. Decadent cupcakes, artisan pies, vegan delights and ice cream that's literally made right in front of you.

Private Island Ice-Cream (✆407-433-9545; www.privateislandicecream.com; 14650 Gatorland Dr; ice creams $5; ⏱1-9pm Sun-Thu, to 10pm Fri & Sat; ⚑) Choose your flavors and watch as John takes that bowl of cream, shoots it with liquid nitrogen right before your eyes, and, *voila* – ice cream. Huge bowls of ice cream with unlimited mix-ins and toppings, ranging from homemade caramel and cookie dough to cayenne pepper; all cost a flat $5. Mom-and-pop favorite across the street from Gatorland.

Dessert Lady Café (Map p234; ✆407-999-5696; www.dessertlady.com; 7600 Dr Phillips Blvd, No 78, Restaurant Row; desserts $5-10; ⏱10am-6pm Mon-Sat; ⚑) Nationally acclaimed and a local favorite, this is where the old saying 'desserts to die for' comes from. Fruit cobbler, bourbon pecan pie, key-lime cake and more.

Bluebird Bakery (✆407-228-3822; www.bluebirdbakeshop.com; 3122 Corrine Dr, Audubon Park; pastries $2-4; ⏱7am-5pm Tue-Sat, 10am-4pm Sun; ⚑) Tiny retro Bluebird, named after the favorite bird of the owner's grandma, offers daily baked cupcakes and organic java. Flavors range from classic chocolate to quirky vanilla black pepper or sweet potato. Closes early if cupcakes run out.

Raphsodic Bakery (✆407-704-8615; www.raphsodic.com; 710 N Mills Ave; ⏱11am-7pm Mon-Thu, to 8pm Fri & Sat) Self-defined as an 'urban pastry art house,' this hot-spot vegan bakery serves up delicious and mostly organic cakes, cookies, cupcakes and pies, including gluten-free.

B Cupcakes (Map p242; ✆407-660-2253; www.bcupcake.com; 127 W Fairbanks Ave, Winter Park; ⏱10:30am-8pm Mon-Sat, noon-6pm Sun; ⚑) Decidedly modern with excellent cupcakes. Try the salted caramel.

P is for Pie (✆727-534-6869, 407-745-4743; www.crazyforpies.com; 2806 Corrine Dr, Audubon Park; ⏱11:30am-5pm Tue-Sat; ⚑) Clean-lined with an artisan twist to classic pies, offering mini and specialty pies.

of pool, you'll be satisfied. The downtown Orlando drinking scene can be a crazy *Girls Gone Wild* meets spring break scene, particularly on the weekends and late at night, with thumping music blaring into the streets and burly bouncers staffing the doors. Dozens of bars compete for tourist dollars along the convention hub of International Dr.

Neighborhood bars in Winter Park, Thornton Park and Audubon Park offer an altogether different vibe, with wine bars, acoustic live music, and outdoor cafes sporting water bowls for canine companions. Vintage cocktail bars pepper the greater Orlando area. Walt Disney World's Downtown Disney and Universal Orlando's CityWalk both have plenty of drinking and live music as well, as do their theme parks.

Downtown Orlando

Courtesy Bar
COCKTAIL BAR

(Map p230; ☑ 407-450-2041; 114 N Orange Ave; drinks from $5; ☺5pm-2am, from 7pm Sat, from 3pm Sun) Housed in a historic Orlando space, with brick walls and Jefferson filament bulbs, this old-school cocktail bar serves up high-quality spirits with fresh and quirky artisan twists such as Himalayan pink salt, fresh honeydew juice and dandelion-eucalyptus tincture. We don't even know what all of it means, but what delights! There's also an excellent selection of beer and wine.

Woods
COCKTAIL BAR

(Map p230; ☑ 407-203-1114; www.thewoods orlando.com; 49 N Orange Ave, 2nd fl Historic Rose Bldg; ☺5pm-2am Mon-Fri, from 7pm Sat) Craft cocktails hidden in a cozy smoke-free 2nd-floor setting, with exposed brick, a tree-trunk bar and an earthy feel.

Hanson's Shoe Repair
THEME BAR

(Map p230; ☑ 407-476-9446; 27 E Pine St; cocktails $13; ☺8pm-2am Tue-Thu & Sat, from 7pm Fri) In a city saturated with over-the-top theming from *Beauty and the Beast* to *Harry Potter*, it shouldn't be surprising that you can walk from 21st-century downtown Orlando into a Prohibition-era speakeasy, complete with secret passwords, historically accurate cocktails and bartenders sporting suspenders and bow ties.

To get in, call in advance. A recorded message will ask if your shoes have lost their spirit, and when you'd like to bring your shoes in for repair. If there's room, and it's

tiny so it often doesn't, staff will call you back with the password. Sure, it leans toward the gimmicky and cocktails are pricey, but this is Orlando, capital of the gimmicky and pricey.

Eola Wine Company
WINE BAR

(☑407-481-9100; www.eolawinecompany.com; 430 E Central Blvd, Thornton Park; ☺4pm-2am Mon-Fri, from noon Sat & Sun) A California-style menu of light foods designed to pair with wine or quirky independent-label beers. You can also get a flight of beer or bubbly, and the cheese plate includes a choice from 16 Spanish, French, Italian and US cheeses. There's a second location in Winter Park (Map p242; ☑407-647-9103; www.eolawinecompany.com; 136 S Park Ave, Winter Park; ☺4pm-2am Mon-Fri, from noon Sat & Sun).

Bösendorfer Lounge
LOUNGE

(Map p230; ☑407-313-9000; 325 S Orange Ave, Westin Grand Bohemian; ☺11am-2am) Zebra-fabric chairs, gilded mirrors, massive black pillars and marble floors ooze pomp and elegance. This hotel bar is popular for after-work drinks, and the lounge picks up with live jazz at 7pm. The name stems from the lounge's rare Bösendorfer piano.

Latitudes
BAR

(Map p230; ☑407-649-4270; www.churchstreet bars.com; 33 W Church St; ☺4:30pm-2am) Island-inspired rooftop bar, with tiki lanterns and city views. There are two more thumping bars below.

Wall Street Plaza
THEME BAR

(Map p230; ☑407-849-0471; www.wallstplaza.net; 25 Wall St Plaza) Eight raucous theme bars, sometimes with live music and always with drink specials, all in one plaza.

Independent Bar
CLUB

(Map p230; ☑407-839-0457; 68 N Orange Ave; cover $10; ☺10pm-3am Sun, Wed & Thu, from 9:30pm Fri & Sat) Hip, crowded and loud, with DJs spinning underground dance and alternative rock into the wee hours.

Pulse
GAY

(☑407-649-3888; www.pulseorlandoclub.com; 1912 S Orange Ave; cover $5) Ultramodern and sleek, with nightly live entertainment and drag shows.

International Drive

Funky Monkey Wine Company
WINE BAR

(Map p234; ☑417-418-9463; 9101 International Dr, Pointe Orlando; ☺4-10pm Mon-Thu, 11am-midnight

Fri & Sat, 4-9pm Sun; 🚃 I-Ride Trolley Red Line Stop 24 or Green Line Stop 12) Come for a glass of wine and weekend drag shows (9pm), but eat elsewhere.

Icebar
THEME BAR

(Map p234; ☑ 407-426-7555; www.icebarorlando.com; 8967 International Dr; entry at door/advance online $20/15; ⏱ 7pm-midnight Sun-Wed, to 1am Thu, to 2am Fri & Sat; 🚃 I-Trolley Red Line Stop 23 or Green Line Stop 11) More classic Orlando gimmicky fun. Step into the 27°F (-3°C) ice house, sit on the ice seat, admire the ice carvings, sip the icy drinks. Coat and gloves are provided at the door (for a fee), and the fire-room, bathrooms and other areas of the bar are kept at normal temperature.

Adults over 21 welcome anytime; folks aged between eight and 20 are allowed between 7pm and 9pm only.

Greater Orlando

Matador
COCKTAIL BAR

(☑ 407-872-0844; 724 Virginia Dr, Mills 50; ⏱ 7pm-2am) Deep red walls, a pool table and furniture you'd expect in your grandmother's parlor. Low-key vibe perfect for sipping that Bulleit Rye.

Red Light, Red Light Beer Parlour
BAR

(☑ 407-893-9832; www.redlightredlightbeerparlour.com; 2810 Corrine Dr, Audubon Park; ⏱ 5pm-2am) Beer aficionados will love the impressive offerings of craft beers on draft at this local hangout housed in a former air-conditioner repair shop.

Wally's Mills Ave Liquors
BAR

(☑ 407-896-6975; www.wallysonmills.com; 1001 N Mills Ave; ⏱ 7:30am-1am) It's been around since the early '50s, before Orlando became Disney, and while its peeling naked-women wallpaper could use some updating, it wouldn't be Wally's without it. Nothing flashy, nothing loud, just a tiny, windowless, smoky bar with a jukebox and cheap, strong drinks – as much a dark dive as you'll find anywhere. And yes, it opens at 7:30*am*.

Wednesday night is $3 microbrews, Monday is $2 PBR beer, and the attached package store sells beer, wine and liquor.

Winter Park

Wine Room
WINE BAR

(Map p242; ☑ 407-696-9463; www.thewineroomonline.com; 270 S Park Ave, Winter Park; tastings from $2.50; ⏱ 3pm-midnight Mon-Wed, from noon

Thu, 11am-1:30am Fri & Sat, 1-11pm Sun) Purchase a wine card and put as much money on it as you'd like. Then simply slide your card into the automated servers for whichever wine looks good, press the button for a taste or a full glass, and enjoy. More than 150 wines, arranged by region and type.

☆ Entertainment
Live Music

Beacham & the Social
LIVE MUSIC

(Map p230; ☑ 407-246-1419; www.thebeacham.com; 46 N Orange Ave; cover varies; ⏱ 9pm-3am) Both the Beacham and the more intimate and recommended Social next door are cornerstones of Orlando's nightclub and live-music scene. They host bands from punk to reggae on the weekends and hop all week long with music and dancing. Shows are designated 'all ages', '18 plus' or '21 plus'.

Will's Pub
LIVE MUSIC

(☑ 407-898-5070; www.willspub.org; 1042 N Mills Ave; tickets $8-16; ⏱ 4pm-2am Mon-Sat, from 6pm Sun) With $2 Pabst on tap, pinball and vintage pinups on the walls, this is Orlando's less-polished music scene but it enjoys a solid reputation as one of the best spots in town to catch local and nationally touring indie music. Smoke free; beer and wine only.

Tanqueray's
LIVE MUSIC

(Map p230; ☑ 407-649-8540; 100 S Orange Ave; ⏱ 11am-2am Mon-Fri, 6pm-2am Sat & Sun) A former bank vault, this underground smoky dive bar draws folks looking to hang out with friends over a beer. There's Guinness on tap, and you can catch weekend local bands, usually reggae or blues.

Cinemas

★ Enzian Theater
CINEMA

(☑ 407-629-0054; www.enzian.org; 1300 S Orlando Ave, Maitland; adult/child $10/8; ⏱ 5pm-midnight Tue-Fri, noon-midnight Sat & Sun) The envy of any college town, this clapboard-sided theater screens independent and classic films, and has the excellent Eden Bar (p254) restaurant, featuring primarily local and organic fare. Have a veggie burger and a beer on the patio underneath the cypress tree, or opt for table service in the theater.

Regal Point Orlando | Stadium & IMAX
CINEMA

(Map p234; ☑ 407-248-9045; www.regmovies.com; 9101 International Dr; adult/child $10/7) Cineplex in the tourist district of International Dr.

ON THE STAGE & UNDER THE STARS

There's more to Orlando than theme parks and techno-club-hopping. In addition to the following, Walt Disney World, Universal Orlando Resort and SeaWorld all have island-inspired luau; Disney and Universal Orlando resorts screen classic family films poolside for free; and there are all kinds of over-the-top kitschy dinner-show extravaganzas, including the swashbuckling *Pirates* and the detective-themed *Sleuth*.

Cirque du Soleil La Nouba (Map p262; ☑ 407-939-7600, 407-939-7328; www.cirquedu-soleil.com; Downtown Disney; adult $65-150, child $55-125; ⊙6pm & 9pm Tue-Sat) Disney's best live show features mind-boggling acrobatic feats expertly fused to light, stage and costume design to create a cohesive artistic vision. And of course, there's a silly Disney twist involving a princess and a frog. This is a small horseshoe theater, with roughly 20 rows from the stage to the top, and no balcony. Disney built the theater specifically to house La Nouba – there are no bad seats. See website for black-out dates.

Mad Cow Theatre (Map p230; ☑ 407-297-8788; www.madcowtheatre.com; 54 W Church, 2nd fl; tickets $18-30) A model of inspiring regional theater, with classic and modern performances in a downtown Orlando space.

Blue Man Group (Map p234; ☑ 407-258-3626, 407-363-8000; www.universalorlando.com; CityWalk; adult/child 3-9yr from $69/29; ⊙vary; 🚌Lynx 21, 37, 40, 🚇Universal) Originally an off-Broadway phenomenon in 1991, this high-energy comedy theatrical troupe at Universal Orlando Resort features all kinds of multisensory craziness – percussion 'instruments,' paintballs, marshmallows, modern dancing and general mayhem.

SAK Comedy Lab (Map p230; ☑ 407-648-0001; www.sakcomedylab.com; 29 S Orange Ave, City Arts Factory, 2nd fl; tickets $15, Tue & Wed 9pm $3; ⊙Tue-Sat) Excellent improv comedy in intimate downtown Orlando theater.

Orlando Ballet (☑ 407-426-1739; http://orlandoballet.org) Performs primarily at downtown Orlando's **Bob Carr Performing Arts Center** (Map p230; ☑ 407-246-4262; www.orlando venues.net). The **Family Series** productions (11am for 1 hour) include children-friendly classics such as *The Nutcracker, Beauty and the Beast* and *Snow White*.

Theatre Downtown (☑ 407-841-0083; www.theatredowntown.net; 2113 N Orange Ave; tickets $16-22) Repertory theater featuring original works from local playwrights, regional actors and classic productions. Located two blocks west of Loch Haven Park.

Orlando Philharmonic Orchestra (☑ 407-770-0071; https://orlandophil.org) Classics, pop, opera and more, including family-friendly events, performed at venues in and around Orlando, including outdoor performances at Loch Haven Park.

John & Rita Lowndes Shakespeare Center (☑ 407-447-1700; www.orlandoshakes.org; 812 E Rollins St, Loch Haven Park; tickets $20-35) Set on the shores of Lake Estelle in grassy Loch Haven Park, this lovely theater includes three intimate stages hosting professional classics such as *Pride and Prejudice* and *Beowulf*, excellent children's theater and up-and-coming playwrights' work.

Orlando Repertory Theater (☑ 407-896-7365; www.orlandorep.com; 1001 E Princeton St, Loch Haven Park; tickets $10-25) Performances for families and children run primarily in the afternoons or early evenings. Shows stretch the gamut of styles and content, including *Rudolph the Red Nosed Reindeer, Richard Scarry's Busytown* and *James and the Giant Peach*.

Popcorn Flicks in the Park (Map p242; ☑ 407-629-1088; www.enzian.org; 251 S Park Ave, Central Park, Winter Park; ⊙8pm 2nd Thu of the month; 🎬) Bring a picnic and a blanket, and kick back under the stars for a free outdoor film classic.

AMC Downtown Disney 24 – Dine-In Theatres CINEMA (Map p262; ☑ 888-262-4386; http://dinein. amctheatres.com; 1500 E Buena Vista Dr, Downtown Disney; tickets $7-16; 🎬) Several screens offer Fork and Screen Theater, where you can order meals and have them delivered to your seat, and the bar sells beer, wine and cocktails to take into the flick.

Universal Cineplex 20
CINEMA

(Map p234; ☑ 407-354-3374; www.amctheatres. com; CityWalk; adult/child $12/9; 🚇 Lynx 21, 37, 40, 🚌 Universal) On-site bar and restaurant. Parking costs $16; after 6pm, $3 parking.

Plaza Cinema Café 12
CINEMA

(Map p230; ☑ 407-558-2878; www.cobbtheatres. com; 155 S Orange Ave; adult/child $10.75/7.50) Downtown Orlando cineplex with full menu and bar.

Cinemark at Festival Bay
CINEMA

(Map p234; ☑ 407-352-1042; www.cinemark.com; 5150 International Dr, Festival Bay Mall; adult/child $10/7)

Sports

Amway Center
SPECTATOR SPORT

(Map p230; ☑ 407-440-7000; www.amwaycenter. com; 400 W Church St) The Orlando Magic (National Basketball Association), the Orlando Predators (Arena Football League) and the Orlando Solar Bears (East Coast Hockey League) play here.

Osceola County Stadium
BASEBALL

(☑ 407-697-3201; 631 Heritage Park Way, Kissimmee) The Houston Astros spring train at the Grapefruit League's smallest ballpark.

University of Central Florida Knights
SPECTATOR SPORT

(www.ucfknights.com; 4000 Central Florida Blvd, University of Central Florida; ticket prices vary) University of Florida takes its sport very seriously. Check the website for details on both men's and women's teams, including basketball, football, soccer and volleyball.

Orlando City
SOCCER

(www.orlandocitysoccer.com) Orlando's Major League Soccer team plays at several venues in and around Orlando.

ESPN's Wide World of Sports
SPECTATOR SPORT

(☑ 407-939-4263, Visitors Center 407-541-5600; http://espnwwos.disney.go.com; 700 S Victory Way, Walt Disney World) This 230-acre sports facility at Walt Disney World hosts Atlanta Braves spring training and hundreds of amateur and professional sporting events.

🔒 Shopping

Head to Winter Park for pleasant browsing, small-town American style, or to Downtown Disney for shopping on steroids.

Mall at Millenia
MALL

(Map p234; ☑ 407-363-3555; www.mallatmillenia.com; 4200 Conroy Rd; ⊙ 10am-9pm Mon-Sat, 11am-7pm Sun; 🚇 Lynx 24) Big hitters at this high-end mall include Anthropologie, Bloomingdales, Apple, Crate & Barrel and J Crew.

Orlando Premium Outlets – International Drive
MALL

(Map p234; ☑ 407-352-9600; www.premiumoutlets.com; 4951 International Dr; ⊙ 10am-11pm Mon-Sat, to 9pm Sun; 🚇 I-Ride Trolley Red Line, 🚇 Lynx 8, 42) All the usual discount-mall suspects.

Orlando Premium Outlets – Vineland Ave
MALL

(Map p234; ☑ 407-238-7787; www.premiumoutlets. com; 8200 Vineland Ave; ⊙ 10am-11pm Mon-Fri, to 9pm Sun) Popular outlet mall just outside Walt Disney World – you'll know you're close when you're stuck in stand-still traffic for upwards of a half hour for no apparent reason.

Eli's Orange World
FOOD

(☑ 407-396-1306; www.orangeworld192.com; 5395 W Irlo Bronson Memorial Hwy/Hwy 192; ⊙ 8am-9:45pm) Family-owned, friendly and plenty of samples of the iconic Florida fruit, as

---

ℹ BABY BASICS AT THE PARKS

Hitting Orlando's theme parks with a baby in tow? Children three years and younger do not pay admission. Once in the gates, a few things help navigate your day.

Child Swap (Walt Disney World and Universal Orlando Resort) Allows caregivers to wait in line together, and then take turns staying behind with a baby or child while the other rides. Perfect for families traveling with multiple-age children or for kids who want a parent to check out the scare-factor before riding. Other parks offer similar options, but can be a bit complicated, so ask the ride attendant.

Disney's Baby Care Centers (Disney theme parks) Toys and Disney cartoons. You can purchase diapers, over-the-counter children's medication and more, and there's a full kitchen.

SeaWorld's Baby Center (SeaWorld) The cute house with rocking chairs on the porch in Shamu's Happy Harbor, with similar facilities to Disney. Women only.

ORLANDO & WALT DISNEY WORLD ORLANDO & AROUND

well as jams and kitschy souvenirs. Look for the half-an-orange-shaped building on the Kissimmee strip.

Orlando Farmers Market
MARKET
(www.orlandofarmersmarket.com; Lake Eola; ☉10am-4pm Sun) Local produce and a beer and wine garden on the shores of downtown Orlando's Lake Eola.

Winter Park Farmers Market
MARKET
(Map p242; 200 W New England Ave, Winter Park; ☉7am-1pm Sat) Housed in a former train station.

ℹ️ Information

EMERGENCY
Call 911 in an emergency.
Police (☑407-246-2470, 321-235-5300; www.cityoforlando.net/police; 100 S Hughey Ave) Central downtown station.

MEDIA
Axis (http://axismag.com) *Orlando Sentinel*'s magazine covers music, art and the bar scene.
Orlando Arts Magazine (http://unitedarts.cc/magazine) Go-to source for arts and culture in Orlando, including a detailed calendar of events.
Orlando Sentinel (www.orlandosentinel.com) Daily city paper.
Orlando Weekly (http://orlandoweekly.com) Free weekly focuses on news, art and entertainment.

MEDICAL SERVICES
Arnold Palmer Hospital for Children (☑407-649-9111; 1414 Kuhl Ave; ☉24hr) Orlando's primary children's hospital. Located just east of I-4 at exit 81.
Centra Care Walk-In Medical (☑407-934-2273; www.centracare.org; ☉8am-midnight Mon-Fri, to 8pm Sat & Sun) Walk-in medical center with more than 20 locations.
Doctors on Call Services (DOCS; ☑407-399-3627; www.doctorsoncallservice.com; ☉24hr) Twenty-four-hour doctors on call to your hotel, including to Walt Disney World and Universal Orlando Resort.
Dr P Phillips Hospital (☑407-351-8500; 9400 Turkey Lake Rd; ☉24hr) Closest hospital to Universal Orlando Resort, SeaWorld and International Drive.
Florida Hospital Celebration Health (☑407-303-4000, 407-764-4000; www.floridahospital.com/celebration-health; 400 Celebration Pl, Kissimmee; ☉24hr) Closest hospital to Walt Disney World.

MONEY
Mall at Millenia Concierge (☑407-345-3555, 407-363-3555; www.mallatmillenia.com; 78 Conroy Rd, I-4 exit; ☉10am-9pm Mon-Sat, 11am-7pm Sun)

POST
Downtown Post Office (Map p230; ☑407-425-6464; www.usps.com; 51 E Jefferson St; ☉7am-5pm Mon-Fri)

TOURIST INFORMATION
Official Visitor Center (Map p234; ☑407-363-5872; www.visitorlando.com; 8723 International Dr; ☉8:30am-6pm) Legitimate discount attraction tickets and best source for information on theme parks, accommodations, outdoor activities, performing arts and more.

USEFUL WEBSITES
Autism at the Parks (www.autismattheparks.com) Advice and tips for vacationing with autistic children and adults at Walt Disney World, Universal Orlando Resort and SeaWorld.
Lonely Planet (www.lonelyplanet.com/usa/florida/orlando)
Orlando Magazine (www.orlandomagazine.com) Events and entertainment news.
ReserveOrlando (www.reserveorlando.com) Central booking agency.
Undercover Tourist (www.undercovertourist.com) Reputable and authorized source for theme-park tickets, car rental, theme-park crowd calendars and more.

WALT DISNEY WORLD

'Here in Florida, we have something special we never enjoyed at Disneyland...the blessing of size. There's enough land here to hold all the ideas and plans we can possibly imagine.'

Walt Disney

Minutes before the Magic Kingdom opens, Alice in Wonderland, Cinderella, Donald Duck and others stand where all can see them, sing 'Zippidee Doo Dah' and throw sparkly Mickey Mouse confetti into the crowds. They dash off on an open-windowed train, the gates open, and children, adults, honeymooners, grandparents and everyone in between enter the park, some strolling, others dashing down the impeccably clean Main Street toward Cinderella's Castle. That iconic image is as American as the Grand Canyon, a place as loaded with myth and promises of hope as the Statue of Liberty. If only for these few minutes, this is indeed the Happiest Place on Earth.

Yes, there will be lines with seemingly endless waiting and sure, you'll spend more money than you intended on a Mickey Mouse sweatshirt that you wouldn't have dreamed of buying before you came. That *Pirates of the Caribbean* ride may not be everything everyone said it'd be, and you may get stuck behind the guy who spreads his shopping bags and empty stroller parallel to the curb so your kids can't sit down to see the parade ('I got here first,' he growls). You'll return to the hotel exhausted and aching, vaguely dissatisfied with the day's meals, carrying your sleeping Belle, her face painted with now-smudging sparkles and her poofy yellow dress stained with ice cream, cotton candy and that green punch so tantalizingly named Tinker Bell and Friends. You swear that next time you'll take a real vacation... Until those last minutes before you fall asleep, when everything you need to do is done and you're finally relaxing in bed, your eyes closed. You see your child's face staring adoringly at Winnie the Pooh as he gives a big ol' bear hug, or your child's arms reaching out to grab the Donald Duck that pops out from the 3-D movie. And it's OK. That beach vacation can wait.

Walt Disney World itself is like a child. One minute, you think you can't take another cafeteria-style restaurant serving fried food and bad coffee or another second in an over-stuffed shuttle bus. And the next, it does something right: maybe it's the fireworks, maybe it's a particular turn in a particular ride, maybe it's the corny joke of the guy who drives the horse-drawn carriage down Main Street.

And all is forgiven.

History

When Disneyland opened in southern California, it took off in a huge way, fundamentally transforming the concept of theme parks. Walt Disney, however, was irritated at the hotels and concessions that were springing up in a manner that he felt was entirely parasitic. In 1965, after a secret four-year search, he bought 27,000 acres of swamp, field and woodland in central Florida. His vision was to create a family vacation destination and he wanted to control every aspect – hotels, restaurants, parking and transportation. He would never see the realization of his dreams; in 1966, at age 65, Walt Disney died of lung cancer. His brother Roy took over responsibility for development. Walt Disney World's Magic Kingdom opened in 1971, and three months later Roy died of a brain hemorrhage. Epcot opened in 1982, Hollywood Studios in 1989 and Animal Kingdom in 1998.

◉ Sights & Activities

Walt Disney World covers more than 40 sq miles, and includes four separate theme parks and two water parks, all connected by a complicated system of monorail, boat and bus, and intersected by highways and roads. Attractions, primarily in the form of rides, character interactions, movies and shows, are spread out among the six parks, resort hotels, and, to a far lesser extent, two entertainment districts.

Walt Disney World Tickets are called Magic Your Way. The minimal base ticket, which allows access to one theme park for one day, costs $99 for adults and $93 for children aged between three and nine years for Magic Kingdom, and $5 less for the three other theme parks. From that, you can add days and options either when you first purchase your ticket or any time within the 14 days after the ticket is first used. See p306 for more on tickets and pricing.

You must purchase tickets to enter the theme and water parks, but activities and entertainment at resort hotels and Disney's entertainment districts do not require park admission.

➡ **Magic Kingdom** (p263) Low on thrills and high on nostalgia, with Cinderella's Castle and nightly fireworks.

➡ **Epcot** (p269) A handful of rides on one side, country-based food, shopping and attractions on the other.

➡ **Animal Kingdom** (p270) Part zoo and part county fair, with a heavy dusting of Disney-styled Africa.

➡ **Hollywood Studios** (p273) Movie-based attractions and Pixar characters.

➡ **Typhoon Lagoon** (p274) Water park particularly excellent for families.

➡ **Blizzard Beach** (p274) Water park with high-speed twists and turns.

➡ **Disney's BoardWalk** (p275) Intimate waterfront boardwalk with a handful of shops, restaurants and entertainment; no admission fee.

➡ **Downtown Disney** (p275) Outdoor pedestrian mall with shops, bars, live music and entertainment; no admission fee.

Walt Disney World

Magic Kingdom 4

22

Bay Lake

South Lake

Floridian Pkwy

Seven Seas Lagoon

Disney's Magnolia Golf Course

Timberline Dr 30

W Wilderness Wy

Fort Wilderness Trl

25

43 27

Seven Seas Dr

Transportation & Ticket Center (TTC)

Disney's Oak Trail Golf Course

37

Disney's Palm Golf Course

Walt Disney World Speedway 15

Disney's Fort Wilderness Resort & Campground

32

AAA Car Care Center

24

Vista Blvd

World Dr

Bonnet Creek Pkwy

Best Friends Pet Care at Walt Disney World

Epcot Center Dr

29

Soarin' Epcot 3

5

World Showcase Lagoon

Epcot Resort Blvd

31

International Gateway: Epcot Back Entrance

40

Crescent Lake

7

Disney's BoardWalk

13

21

Chelonia

23

Disney's Hollywood Studios

12

2

14

Disney's Animal Kingdom 1

19

6

16

Blizzard Beach

World Dr

Osceola Pkwy

20

Victory Way

28

Hourglass Lake

Century Dr

530

192

18

W Buena Vista Dr

Exit 65

4

Irlo Bronson Memorial Hwy

ESPN Wide World of Sports

530 192

Exit 64B

Irlo Bronson Memorial

36

⊙ Magic Kingdom

When most people think of Walt Disney World, they're thinking of the **Magic Kingdom** (Map p262; ☏407-939-5277; www.disney-world.disney.go.com; 1180 Seven Seas Dr; adult/child 3-10yr $95/89; ☉9am-9pm, hours vary; 🚍Disney, 🚤Disney, monorail Disney). This is the Disney of commercials, of princesses and pirates, dreams come true and Tinkerbell; this is quintessential old-school Disney with classic rides such as It's a Small World and Space Mountain.

Enter the park under the railroad station and continue on down Main Street, USA, past the small-town America storefronts toward that most iconic of all things Disney, Cinderella's Castle. A horse-drawn carriage and an old-fashioned car run continuously from the park entrance to the castle (though most people walk), and from there paths lead to the six 'lands.'

Main Street, USA   LANDMARK
(Map p262; www.disneyworld.disney.go.com; theme park admission required; ☉9am-9pm, hours vary; 🚹; 🚍Disney, 🚤Disney, 🚌Lynx 50, 56, monorail Disney) Fashioned after Walt Disney's hometown of Marceline, MO, Main Street, USA, is best experienced with an aimless meander. Peruse the miniature dioramas of Peter Pan and Snow White in the street windows; pop in to catch the black-and-white movie reels of old Disney cartoons, and browse the hundreds of thousands of must-have Disney souvenirs.

Fantasyland   RIDE, SHOW
(Map p262; www.disneyworld.disney.go.com/new-fantasyland; theme park admission required; ☉9am-9pm, hours vary; 🚹; 🚍Disney, 🚤Disney, 🚌Lynx 50, 56, monorail Disney) Quintessential Disney, Fantasyland is the highlight of any Disney trip for both the eight-and-under crowd and grown-ups looking for a nostalgic taste of classic Disney. Tweens too cool for fairy tales and teens looking for thrills may turn up their noses. Disney began introducing all kinds of changes here in 2013, such as *Beauty and the Beast*–themed attractions and the new *Snow White*–themed coaster, the **Seven Dwarfs Mine Train**.

The Beast's castle houses Disney's Be Our Guest (p283), Disney's hottest themed restaurant and the only place in Magic Kingdom to buy alcoholic drinks.

Walt Disney World

Without a doubt the best 3-D show in Disney, **Mickey's PhilharMagic** takes Donald Duck on a whimsical adventure through classic Disney movies. Ride with him through the streets of Morocco on Aladdin's carpet and feel the champagne on your face when it pops open during *Beauty and the Beast*'s 'Be Our Guest.' Fun, silly and lighthearted, this is Disney at its best. **Dream Along with Mickey** is a high-octane musical performance that brings the villains, princesses, Mickey and Donald to the steps of Cinderella's Castle for dancing and dramatic twists. Check your *Times Guide* for show times.

It's A Small World, a sweet boat trip around the globe, has captivated children since the song and ride debuted at the 1964 New York World's Fair. Small boats gently glide through country after country, each decked out from floor to ceiling with elaborate and charmingly dated sets inhabited by hundreds of automated animals and children. While snide comments about how the song sticks irritatingly in your head for weeks have become a Disney cliché, there's something poignantly endearing, almost melancholy, in this simple ride. Little ones love it and the wait is rarely longer than 10 minutes.

Board a pirate ship and fly through fog and stars over London to Never Never Land on **Peter Pan's Flight**; take a sweet journey through the Hundred Acre Wood on the **Many Adventures of Winnie the Pooh** and ride through *The Little Mermaid* on **Under the Sea: Journey of the Little Mermaid**. At **Dumbo the Flying Elephant** toddlers love jumping on a Dumbo and riding slowly around and around, up and down, and thrill at the chance to control how high they go. Lines here can be unbelievably long and slow, and the ride is incredibly short – hit this when the park gates open. The **Mad Tea Party** is a basic spinning ride, and you and others in the teacup decide just how much you'll be twirling.

Fantasyland offers all kinds of excellent character-interaction opportunities. Watch a princess tale at the little stone grotto of **Fairytale Garden**; listen to Belle tell a story at **Enchanted Tales with Belle**; meet Ariel at **Ariel's Grotto** and Gaston by **Gaston's Tavern**; or hop in line and catch a handful of princesses, including *Frozen*'s Anna and Elsa, in **Fairytale Hall**. And of course, always keep an eye out for Cinderella, Mary Poppins, Alice in Wonderland and other favorites hanging out throughout Fantasyland.

ORLANDO & WALT DISNEY WORLD WALT DISNEY WORLD

BEST OF MAGIC KINGDOM

With the exception of Space Mountain, Splash Mountain and the scary introduction to the Haunted Mansion, these are all perfect for children. At time of publication, Fantasyland's Seven Dwarf's Mine Train had not yet been completed – this kid-friendly coaster promises to be a new Disney favorite.

Mickey's Philharmagic 3-D movie perfection.

Space Mountain Indoor roller coaster in the dark.

Pirates of the Caribbean Cruise through the world of pirates.

Haunted Mansion Slow-moving ride past light-hearted spooks.

Festival of Fantasy Daytime parade.

Dream Along with Mickey Outdoor show in front of Cinderella's Castle.

Dumbo the Flying Elephant A favorite with toddlers.

Mad Tea Party Quintessential Disney spinning.

It's a Small World Boat ride through the world – you know the song.

Many Adventures of Winnie the Pooh A must for fans of that honey-loving bear.

Peter Pan's Flight Gentle flight through the story and over London.

Jungle Cruise Disney silliness at its best.

Splash Mountain Classic water ride.

Monsters, Inc Laugh Floor Interactive comedy show.

Enchanted Tales with Belle Charming storytelling performance in Maurice's cottage.

Adventureland RIDE, SHOW
(Map p262; www.disneyworld.disney.go.com; theme park admission required; ⊙9am-9pm, hours vary; 🚹; 🚏 Disney, 🚢 Disney, 🚌 Lynx 50, 56, monorail Disney) Adventure Disney-style means pirates and jungles, magic carpets and tree houses, whimsical and silly representations of the exotic locales from storybooks and imagination. Don't miss **Pirates of the Caribbean** – the slow-moving boat through the dark and shadowy world of pirates remains one of the most popular attractions at Disney.

Drunken pirates sing pirate songs, sleep among the pigs and sneer over their empty whiskey bottles, but unless you're scared of the dark or growling pirates, it's a giggle not a scream. And Jack Sparrow looks so incredibly lifelike that you'll swear it's Johnny Depp himself. The silliness continues at **Jungle Cruise** (FastPass+; see p272), but this time the captain takes you past fake crocodiles, elephants and monkeys, all the while throwing out the cheesiest jokes in all of Disney World.

Kids love flying around on **Magic Carpets of Aladdin**, but skip the slow train of folks climbing 116 steps at **Swiss Family Treehouse**, a replica tree house of the shipwrecked family from the book and movie *The Swiss Family Robinson*. Animatronic birds sing and dance Hawaiian-style at the **Enchanted Tiki Room**, a silly and rather bizarre two-bit attraction that opened in 1963 and continues to enjoy a curious cult following. You won't find lines, and it makes for a perfect spot to relax out of the heat for a bit.

Frontierland RIDE, SHOW
(Map p262; www.disneyworld.disney.go.com; theme park admission required; ⊙9am-9pm, hours vary; 🚹; 🚏 Disney, 🚢 Disney, 🚌 Lynx 50, 56, monorail Disney) Wild West Disney-style. **Splash Mountain** depicts the misadventures of Brer Rabbit, Brer Bear and Brer Fox, complete with chatty frogs, singing ducks and other critters. The 40mph drop into the river makes for one of the biggest thrills in the park, and you will get very wet! With no steep drops or loop-dee-loops, mild **Big Thunder Mountain Railroad** coaster is a great choice for little ones.

The 'wildest ride in the wilderness' takes you through the desert mountain and a cave of bats, past cacti and hot-spring geysers. The line can feel never-ending, winding and winding more than you think, so this is a good attraction to reserve as one of your three FastPass+ choices.

Dubbed by many as a peaceful escape, **Tom Sawyer Island** is a disappointment. This was originally designed for California's Disneyland in 1955, and in its day, when Disney was smaller and children's expectations were lower, it was a place for adventure. Today, people mill about, not sure what to do and wondering why they waited so long in line to take a boat out here.

In the odd and strangely dated **Country Bear Jamboree**, stuffed bears emerge from the stage and sing corny country songs.

Tomorrowland   RIDE, SHOW
(Map p262; www.disneyworld.disney.go.com; theme park admission required; ⊘9am-9pm, hours vary; ⊞; ⊒Disney, ⊒Disney, ⊒Lynx 50, 56, monorail Disney) Though the theming as a Jetsons-inspired peek into the future falls flat, Tomorrowland holds a few wildly popular Disney highlights. Come first thing or use a FastPass+ for **Space Mountain**, an indoor coaster into the star-studded galaxies of outer space, and **Buzz Lightyear's Space Ranger Spin**, a cross between a ride and a video game.

At the interactive comedy-show **Monsters, Inc Laugh Floor**, monsters from the film must harness human laughter rather than screams, and they use audience members to do it. It's pretty funny, and every show is different. Kids can put the pedal to the metal on grand-prix-style cars at Indy Speedway, but the cars are fixed to the track and you don't control the steering. Note that kids must be 52in tall to 'drive' on their own, which pretty much eliminates this ride's target audience.

Liberty Square   RIDE, SHOW
(Map p262; www.disneyworld.disney.go.com; theme park admission required; ⊘9am-9pm, hours vary; ⊒Disney, ⊒Disney, ⊒Lynx 50, 56, monorail Disney) The ramblin' 19th-century mansion houses **Haunted Mansion**, another classic favorite piece of low-on-thrill and high-on-silly fun, and the only real ride in Liberty Sq. Cruise slowly past the haunted dining room, where apparitions dance across the stony floor, but beware of those hitchhiking ghosts – don't be surprised if they jump into your car uninvited.

While mostly it's lighthearted ghosty goofiness, kids may be frightened by spooky preride dramatics. All sorts of presidential memorabilia decorate the waiting area of the **Hall of Presidents**, where people are herded into a theater to watch a superpatriotic flick on US history, ending with every US president standing before you on stage.

BEST WAYS TO SEE WISHES NIGHTTIME SPECTACULAR

The best place to catch Magic Kingdom's nighttime parade is on the curb of Main Street, just past the entrance gates. You're perfectly situated to watch the postparade Wishes Nighttime Spectacular (p279) fireworks over the castle and can scurry out of the park afterwards, beating the crowds to the lines for the buses, boats and monorail. Settle someone with a book and their cell phone to save a spot at least one hour before the parade starts. Parades change throughout the year, as well as start times, so check online. Alternatively, skip the parade, escape the crowds and watch the sky from a distance.

Boat Bring a bottle of wine on a private Specialty Fireworks Cruise or, for a more swashbuckling experience, with songs, storytelling and a pirate captain, take the Pirates and Pals Fireworks Voyage.

Disney's Contemporary Resort Make reservations up to 180 days in advance for a hot-ticket meal at the rooftop California Grill (p287) or head up for a drink on its terrace. Get there an hour or more before the show though, as staff close the elevator to anyone without dinner reservations when the bar is full.

Disney's Grand Floridian Resort & Spa Grab a glass of wine at Narcoossee's (p287) and sit on the pier; for real seclusion, walk over to the grassy area in front of the lagoonside rooms.

Lagoon-view room Several deluxe Disney hotels, including Disney's Grand Floridian (p278), Disney's Contemporary Resort (p279) and Disney's Polynesian Resort (p279), offer rooms with a view of Magic Kingdom.

Disney's Polynesian Resort Sip a pink-umbrella drink on the beach.

TOP TIPS FOR A SUCCESSFUL DISNEY FAMILY VACATION

Disney expectations run high, and the reality of things can be disappointing. Long waits, and getting jostled and tugged through crowds and lines, can leave the kids, and you, exhausted. Plan ahead with scrupulous attention to detail. Make dinner reservations, plan when to go where based on parade and show schedules, decide in advance what attractions to tackle once you're there, and reserve FastPass+ selections. And then be prepared to throw all those plans out the window when the kids decide they want to sleep late and go down the hotel pool's slide again, and again. Plan like a general; travel like a gypsy. Here are some simple tips:

Buy tickets that cover more days than you think you'll need It's less expensive per day, and it gives the freedom to break up time at the theme parks with downtime in the pool or at low-key attractions beyond theme-park gates.

Stay at a Walt Disney World resort hotel While it's tempting to save money by staying elsewhere, the value of staying at a Walt Disney World resort lies in the convenience offered. Don't expect the quality of the room and amenities to match the price: you're paying for Walt Disney World, not for Ritz-like luxury.

Take advantage of My Disney Experience Reserve your 3 FastPass+ (p272) attractions up to 60 days in advance (30 days for nonresort guests) – this will give you three guaranteed short lines each day.

Stock up on snacks Even if it's nothing more than a loaf of bread and a jar of peanut butter, you'll save the irritation of waiting in line for bad, overpriced food.

Arrive at the park at least 30 minutes before gates open Don't window-shop or dawdle – just march quickly to the rides, and then kick back for the afternoon. If you can only manage this on one day of your trip, make it the day you're going to Magic Kingdom. Watch the opening ceremony and be one of the first into the park.

Speed up, slow down Yes, there's a time to hurry, as 10 minutes of pushing the pedal to the metal could save two hours waiting in line, but allow days to unfold according to the ebbs and flows of your children's moods.

Program Disney Dining into your cell phone While you'll want to make some plans well in advance, once you have a sense of where you'll be at meal time, call ☎ 407-939-3463 to make reservations at table-service restaurants at all four theme parks, Disney resort hotels and at Disney's two shopping districts. Also, check for last-minute cancellations to dinner shows or character meals. Just keep interrupting the recorded message by pressing '0' until you get a real human voice.

Rose Garden GARDENS
(Map p262; www.disneyworld.disney.go.com; theme park admission required; ⊙9am-9pm, hours vary; ☐ Disney, ☑ Disney, ☐ Lynx 50, 56, monorail Disney) For a bit of downtime, the covered waterside pavilion just off the bridge to the right of Cinderella's Castle makes a perfect place to pull out those goldfish snacks and take a quiet rest. Pictured but not labeled on the Magic Kingdom map. Look for this quiet treasure on your way into Tomorrowland.

❶ Getting There & Around

➤ The only direct way to get to Magic Kingdom is by water launch or monorail from Disney's Contemporary Resort, Disney's Grand Floridian or Disney's Polynesian Resort; by water launch from Disney's Fort Wilderness Resort and Disney's Wilderness Lodge; by passenger ferry or monorail from the Transportation & Ticket Center, or by bus from any Disney resort hotel.

➤ If you drive, you *must* park at the Transportation & Ticket Center and then take the monorail or the ferry to the park. With its massive parking lot and endless lines for bus shuttles, the Transportation & Ticket Center, however, can be unbearable. Grown men knock down toddlers in their efforts to catch the bus; harried parents scream at exhausted children; and it's a depressing and miserable way to end a magical day.

➤ Consider hopping the monorail or water launch to a Magic Kingdom resort and then taking a cab to your hotel. If you coordinate reserved breakfast or dinner at one of these resorts, and many offer character meals, this works particularly nicely, and you can park at resort hotels free of charge if you have restaurant reservations. Note that you can get to Magic Kingdom via monorail from Epcot, but you must switch trains at the Transportation & Ticket Center.

➡ A horse-drawn carriage or old-fashioned car carries folk back and forth down Main Street, USA, from the entrance gate to Cinderella's Castle. The open-air Walt Disney World Railroad follows the perimeter of the park and stops at Main Street, USA, and Frontierland.

◉ Epcot

With no roller coasters screeching overhead, no parades, no water rides and plenty of greenery, things run a bit slower here in **Epcot** (Map p262; ☑ 407-939-5277; www.disneyworld.disney.go.com; 200 Epcot Center Dr; adult/child 3-10yr $90/84; ◷ 9am-6pm, hours vary; ▣ Disney, ▣ Disney, monorail Disney), with a bit less va-voom, than in the rest of Walt Disney World. Slow down and enjoy. Smell the incense in Morocco, listen to the Beatles in the UK and sip miso in Japan.

The park is divided into two sections. **Future World** is where you'll find Epcot's only two thrill rides. It is comprised of several pavilions, each holding attractions, restaurants, character greeting spots, separated by grass, fountains and gardens. **World Showcase** comprises 11 re-created nations featuring country-specific food and shopping. Note that though Disney's Epcot map shows only one entrance, there are two. The main entrance, next to the bus and monorail stations, sits at the landmark geodesic dome of Spaceship Earth in Future World. The back entrance, labeled **International Gateway**, brings guests walking or catching a boat from Disney's BoardWalk, Hollywood Studios and Disney Epcot resort hotels into the UK. Both entrances have lockers, strollers and wheelchair rental.

Each nation in the World Showcase has live music, comedy or dancing shows; check your *Times Guide*. Little ones can cool off in the fountain just before the bridge from Future World to World Showcase.

★ World Showcase
ATTRACTION
(www.disneyworld.disney.go.com; theme park admission required; ◷ 9am-6pm, hours vary; ▣ Disney, ▣ Disney, monorail Disney) Who needs the hassle of a passport and jet lag when you can travel the world right here at Walt Disney World? World Showcase, one of two themed sections of Epcot, comprises 11 countries arranged around a lagoon. Watch

belly dancing in Morocco, eat pizza in Italy and buy personally engraved bottles of perfume in France, before settling down to watch fireworks about world peace and harmony. Disney was right. It truly is a small world after all.

Sure, this is quite a sanitized stereotypical vision of the world, but so what? This is, after all, a theme park. And who knows, an afternoon here might just inspire you to hop a plane and check out the real thing, and it certainly is a fun way to show kids a little something about the world.

The best way to experience the World Showcase is to simply wander as the mood moves you, poking through stores and restaurants, and catching what amounts to Bureau of Tourism promotional films and gentle rides through some of the countries. Donald Duck and his comrades take you through Mexico in **Gran Fiesta Tour Starring the Three Caballeros**; Norway's rather odd boat-ride **Maelstrom** meanders past Vikings, trolls and waterfalls; and the **American Adventure** show features audioanimatonic figures presenting a simplified interpretation of US history. The featured countries from left to right around the water are Mexico, Norway, China, Germany, Italy, the USA (The American Adventure), Japan, Morocco, France, the UK and Canada.

★ Soarin'
RIDE
(Map p262; www.disneyworld.disney.go.com; Future World; theme park admission required; ◷ 9am-6pm, hours vary; ▣ Disney, ▣ Disney, monorail Disney) Soar up and down, hover and accelerate as the giant screen in front of you takes you over California's citrus groves, golf courses, mountains, coasts, rivers and cities and, finally, into the fireworks over Cinderella's Castle at Disney Lane. You can smell the oranges, and your feet almost touch those surfers below.

While not at all scary in terms of speed or special effects, people with agoraphobia may feel a bit uneasy. Reserve a FastPass+ or hit this first thing in the morning, as it's one of the best rides at Disney for everyone from toddlers to grandparents. When you do finally get to the front of the line, ask for a front-row seat. Otherwise, feet dangling in front of you can ruin the effect.

Seas with Nemo & Friends Pavilion
RIDE, SHOW
(Map p262; www.disneyworld.disney.go.com; Future World; theme park admission required;

⊙9am-6pm, hours vary; 🖵 Disney, 🚇 Disney, monorial Disney) Kids under 10 won't want to miss the two *Nemo*-themed attractions at Epcot's Future World. Ride a clamshell through the ocean with Nemo on **Seas with Nemo & Friends** and talk face-to-face with Crush in the interactive **Turtle Talk with Crush**, a Disney highlight.

A small blue room with a large movie screen holds about 10 rows of benches with sitting room for kids in front. Crush talks to the children staring up at him, taking questions from the 'dude in the dark-blue shell' and cracking jokes about how sea grass gives him the bubbles. Dory shows up and gets squished against the screen by the whale, and there's plenty of silliness and giggling.

Test Track
RIDE

(Map p262; www.disneyworld.disney.go.com; Future World; theme park admission required; ⊙9am-6pm, hours vary; 🖵 Disney, 🚇 Disney, monorail Disney) Board a car and ride through heat, cold, speed, braking and crash tests. At one point a huge semi with blinding lights heads right for you, its horn blaring. When testing the acceleration, the car speeds up to 60mph within a very short distance, but there are few turns and no ups and downs like a roller coaster.

At the ride's entrance you can virtually design your own car, and at the exit you'll find all kinds of car-themed games and simulators.

Mission Space
RIDE

(Map p262; www.disneyworld.disney.go.com; Future World; theme park admission required; ⊙9am-6pm, hours vary; 🖵 Disney, 🚇 Disney, monorail Disney) One of two thrill rides at Future World, Epcot, Mission Space straps you into a tiny four-person spaceship cockpit and launches you into, you guessed it, space. While this is a simulated experience and not a high-speed ride, the special effects can be nauseating and the dire warnings are enough to scare away even the most steel-bellied folk. There are two options, one with less intensity than the other.

Club Cool
ATTRACTION

(Map p262; www.disneyworld.disney.go.com; Future World, Epcot; theme park admission required; ⊙9am-6pm, hours vary; 🖵 Disney, 🚇 Disney, monorail Disney) Free samples of soft drinks from other countries that aren't sold in the USA. Try Smart Watermelon from China, Vegitabeta from Japan and Beverley from Italy, among others.

Spaceship Earth
RIDE

(Map p262; www.disneyworld.disney.go.com; Future World; theme park admission required; ⊙9am-6pm, hours vary; 🖵 Disney, 🚇 Disney, monorail Disney) Inside the giant golf-ball landmark at the entrance to Disney's Epcot, Spaceship Earth is a strange, kitschy slow-moving ride through time that is surprisingly cool and enjoys a cult following.

Ellen's Energy Adventure
RIDE

(Map p262; 🖉 407-939-5277; www.disneyworld. disney.go.com; Future World; theme park admission required; ⊙9am-6pm, hours vary; 🖵 Disney, 🚇 Disney, monorail Disney) This 45-minute ride is the oddest attraction in Orlando, perhaps in the entire state of Florida. It begins with a movie during which Ellen DeGeneres dreams that she is playing *Jeopardy!* with Jamie Lee Curtis. Determined to outsmart her know-it-all opponent, Ellen joins Bill Nye the Science Guy on a trip through history to learn about energy sources. At this point, you board a 96-passenger vehicle and lurch slowly through the darkness into the Cretaceous period.

Giant dinosaurs stomp about menacingly and, in one particularly surreal display, a mannequin Ellen battles a ferocious one. After this jaunt through dinosaur-land, the movie preaches wind energy, hydro-energy and other alternative fuel sources, and concludes with Ellen's *Jeopardy!* victory. The whole thing is just very bizarre.

❶ Getting There & Around

➔ A pleasant, well-lit paved waterfront path or boat shuttle connects Epcot to Hollywood Studios, Disney's BoardWalk and Epcot resorts. The monorail runs a direct line between Epcot and the Transportation & Ticket Center; from there, catch a monorail or ferry to Magic Kingdom. Disney buses depart from Epcot's main gate to Disney resorts, Hollywood Studios and Animal Kingdom.

➔ Within the park, a boat shuttles folks to and from Morocco and Germany from two boat docks just outside Future World.

⊙ Animal Kingdom

Set apart from the rest of Disney both in miles and in tone, **Animal Kingdom** (Map p262; 🖉 407-939-5277; www.disneyworld.disney. go.com; 2101 Osceola Pkwy; adult/child $90/84; ⊙9am-6pm, hours vary; 🖵 Disney) attempts to blend theme park and zoo, carnival and African safari, all stirred together with a healthy dose of Disney characters, storytell-

MEETING DISNEY CHARACTERS

Folks of all ages pay a lot of money and spend hours in line to get their photo taken with Winnie the Pooh, Snow White, Donald Duck and other Disney favorites. It doesn't make much sense on paper, but somehow, once at Disney, even the most hard-hearted swoon. Go to www.disneyworld.disney.go.com to peruse opportunities to sidle up next to a princess, villain or furry friend, and note that character experiences in the resort hotels do not require theme-park tickets.

Disney Character Dining (☑ 407-939-3463; www.disneyworld.disney.go.com; Walt Disney World theme parks & resort hotels; per person $30-60) Make reservations up to six months (yes, six!) for any of the almost 15 character-dining meals at Disney World. These are not fine-dining experiences, nor are they intimate affairs – they can be rather loud and chaotic. Characters rotate around the room, stopping for a minute or so at each table to pose for a photograph and sign autographs.

Disney's Grand Floridian Resort (p278) features a buffet breakfast with Winnie the Pooh, Mary Poppins and Alice in Wonderland, as well as the **Perfectly Princess Tea Party**; there's a jam-packed breakfast and dinner with Goofy, Donald Duck and pals at **Chef Mickey's** in Disney's Contemporary Resort (p279); princesses mingle in Epcot's Norway at the **Akershus Royal Banquet**; and the 100 Acre Wood folk come to Magic Kingdom's **Crystal Palace** for three meals a day.

Character Spots (☑ 407-939-4277; www.disneyworld.disney.go.com; Walt Disney World theme parks; theme park admission required) Each Walt Disney World theme park has specific spots where Disney characters hang out, and you can simply hop in line (and wait and wait) to meet them and have your photo taken. Some character spots, such as Enchanted Tales with Belle, include a short performance. In addition, check your map and *Times Guide* for times and locations of scheduled character greetings, and always keep your eyes open – you never know who you'll see!

Lines at Animal Kingdom are usually shorter than at other parks, and many character spots can be reserved in advance as a FastPass+ choice through **My Disney Experience** (see p272).

Cinderella's Royal Table (Map p262; ☑ 407-934-2927; www.disneyworld.disney.go.com; Cinderella's Castle, Magic Kingdom; adult $60-75, child $36-45; ⊙ 8-10:40am, 11:45am-2:40pm, 4-10pm; 🖤 🔙; 🔙 Disney, 🔙 Disney, 🔙 Lynx 50, 56, monorailDisney) Cinderella greets guests and sits for a formal portrait (included in the price), and a sit-down meal with princesses is served upstairs. This is the only opportunity to eat inside the iconic castle – make reservations six months in advance. Hours vary.

Chip 'n' Dale Campfire Singalong (Map p262; ☑ 407-939-7529; www.disneyworld.disney.go.com; 4510 N Wilderness Trail, Disney's Fort Wilderness Resort; ⊙ 7pm winter, 8pm summer; 🔙 Disney, 🔙 Disney) One of Disney's best offerings, this intimate and low-key character experience offers singing and dancing with Chip and Dale, campfires for roasting marshmallows, and a free outdoor screening of a Disney film. Every night is a different movie, and Disney doesn't post a schedule on its website – call or search online.

Generously portioned s'more supplies cost $7, and though there there are split-log benches, it's better to bring a blanket and pillows to snuggle down on. Cars are not allowed in Fort Wilderness (p278); park at the first left after the entry gate, or take a Disney bus or boat to the resort, and catch a shuttle the few minutes to the Meadow Recreation Area.

ing and transformative magic. The result is, at times, quite odd. The two most popular rides are Kilimanjaro Safari and Expedition Everest, located at opposite ends of the park.

Short trails around Animal Kingdom's Discovery Island lead to quiet spots along the water, where a handful of benches make a great place to relax with a snack. Keep an eye out for animals such as tortoises and monkeys.

Oasis   ZOO
(Map p262; www.disneyworld.disney.go.com; theme park admission required; ⊙ 9am-6pm, hours vary; 🖤; 🔙 Disney) Oasis is the first themed section of Animal

MY DISNEY EXPERIENCE: FASTPASS+ & MAGICBAND

FastPass+ is designed to allow guests to plan their days in advance and reduce time spent waiting in line. It replaced the paper FastPass system in 2014. Visitors can reserve a specific time for up to three attractions per day through **My Disney Experience** (☎407-828-8739; www.disneyworld.disney.go.com), accessible online or by downloading the free mobile app.

Resort guests receive a MagicBand – a plastic wristband that serves as a room key, park entrance ticket, FastPass+ access and room charge. As soon as you make your room reservation, you can set up your My Disney Experience account and begin planning your day-by-day Disney itinerary. A MagicBand will be sent to you in advance, or it will be waiting for you when you check into your hotel. Your itinerary, including any changes you make online or through the mobile app, will automatically be stored in your wristband.

Once at the park, head to your reserved FastPass+ ride or attraction anytime within the preselected one-hour time frame. Go to the Fastpass+ entrance, scan your Magic-Band, and zip right onto the attraction with no more than a 15-minute wait. Though it's a simple system, there are some kinks, so a few tips can help you navigate it smoothly with optimal benefit.

➡ If you are staying at a Disney Resort, you can access My Disney Experience and start reserving FastPass+ attractions up to 60 days in advance; nonresort guests with purchased theme-park tickets can reserve FastPass+ attractions 30 days in advance.

➡ You can use Fastpass+ selections for rides, character greeting spots (where lines can rival the most popular rides), fireworks, parades and shows.

➡ Some parks use a tiered FastPass+ system – you must choose one attraction from group one, and two from group two.

➡ Make reservations for meals and character dining through My Disney Experience.

➡ Change your selections anytime through the website or mobile app. Once you've used the three prebooked FastPass+ attractions, you can add additional FastPass+ at on-site kiosks for free. But note you must use *all three* reserved selections before adding new ones.

➡ Do not waste your limited FastPass+ options on attractions that do not have long lines; carefullly consider your day's plan to maximize the benefits of this system. Disney planning websites offer all kinds of tips. At Magic Kingdom, lines for Peter Pan's Flight, Big Thunder Mountain Railroad, Enchanted Tales with Belle and Space Mountain can be painfully long. Use your FastPass+ for sequential afternoon times at three of these, and use the morning, when your patience and energy is stronger and the lines are shorter, for other attractions.

➡ Check the website or call for updated information, as the system is always in flux.

Kingdom. It has cool critters, including a giant anteater, but it's best to move along to other attractions and pause to enjoy the animals on your way out.

Discovery Island   SHOW
(Map p262; www.disneyworld.disney.go.com; theme park admission required; ⊙9am-6pm, hours vary; ▯Disney) The only attraction here is the *Bugs' Life*–themed **It's Tough to Be a Bug!**, a 4-D movie that includes periods of darkness, dry ice and flashing lights. Though it's a lot of fun and very cute, it can terrify little ones – you will definitely hear children crying by the end.

Africa   RIDE, SHOW
(Map p262; www.disneyworld.disney.go.com; theme park admission required; ⊙9am-6pm, hours vary; ▯Disney) Board a jeep and ride through the African Savannah on **Kilimanjaro Safaris**, pausing to look at zebras, lions, giraffes and more, all seemingly roaming free. This is one of the Animal Kingdom's most popular attractions, so come early or use your FastPass+. The **Festival of the Lion King**, a *Lion King*–themed song and dance performance, earns rave reviews, but we were underwhelmed.

The **Pagani Forest Exploration Trail** passes gorillas, hippos, a great bat display and a hive of naked mole rats – nothing more than you'd find in any zoo, but those mole rats sure are cute.

Asia
RIDE, SHOW

(Map p262; www.disneyworld.disney.go.com; theme park admission required; ⊙9am-6pm, hours vary; ▣Disney) Home to two of Animal Kingdom's three most popular rides: Expedition Everest, a great roller coaster with a yeti twist; and Kali River Rapids, a water ride. Owls and peregrine falcons dazzle audiences at Flights of Wonder. It's got some cheesy dialogue, but the animals are spectacular as they zoom around over your head.

Maharajah Jungle Trek is a self-guided path past Bengal tigers, huge fruit bats and Komodo dragons.

Dinoland
RIDE, ATTRACTION

(Map p262; www.disneyworld.disney.go.com; theme park admission required; ⊙9am-6pm, hours vary; ▣Disney) This bizarre Dinosaur-themed section seems more like a tired carnival than Disney Magic, with garish plastic dinosaurs, midway games and 'Trilo-Bite' snacks. But little ones will like the kids' coaster Primeval Whirl, and Dinosaur is a really fun water ride with a *Jurassic Park* twist. Be warned – a giant T-Rex pops out just before you plummet, and you will get wet.

Rafiki's Planet Watch
ZOO

(Map p262; www.disneyworld.disney.go.com; theme park admission required; ⊙9am-6pm, hours vary; ⊞; ▣Disney) Veterinarians care for sick and injured animals at the Conservation Station, and sometimes there are animal interactions. You can check out the adorable, fist-sized tamarin monkeys and pet sheep and goats at Affection Section. But ultimately, the Wildlife Express Train you take to get here might just be the best part of this Disney enigma.

ⓘ Getting There & Away

Disney buses stop at Animal Kingdom, but be warned that the ride here can be up to 45 minutes, maybe longer. There is parking just outside the park gates.

◉ Hollywood Studios

The least charming of Walt Disney World's theme parks, Hollywood Studios (Map p262; ☑407-939-5277; www.disneyworld.disney.go.com; 351 S Studio Dr; adult/child 3-10yr $90/84; ⊙9am-6pm, hours vary; ▣Disney, ▣Disney) offers none of the nostalgic charm of Magic Kingdom, the sophisticated delights of Epcot or the kitschy fun of Animal Kingdom. It's meant to conjure the heydays of Hollywood, with a replica of Graumann's Chinese Theatre and Hollywood Brown Derby, but most of the attractions find their inspiration from unabashed 21st-century energy. *Hannah Montana* souvenirs line store shelves, screams from the Tower of Terror echo through the

---

BEST OF HOLLYWOOD STUDIOS

Several Disney jewels sparkle through the filler and fluff at Hollywood Studios, including Sci-Fi Dine-In Theater (p285) and 50's Prime Time Cafe (p285), two of Disney's best themed dining experiences (reservations recommended). The first three attractions listed below are wildly popular – take advantage of FastPass+, but note that the current system will not let you reserve both Rock 'n' Roller Coaster and Toy Story Mania!.

Twilight Zone Tower of Terror (Sunset Blvd) Elevator free fall through a haunted hotel. This is classic Disney thrills.

Rock 'n' Roller Coaster (Sunset Blvd) Indoor roller coaster with headrest speakers blasting Aerosmith.

Toy Story Mania! (Pixar Pl) Ride-through 3-D video game.

Star Tours: The Adventure Continues (Echo Lake) Board the Star Speeder 1000 into the galaxy at this 3-D *Star Wars*–themed simulation ride.

Beauty and the Beast – Live on Stage (Sunset Blvd) Outdoor show of the princess tale; one of the best at Disney.

Voyage of the Little Mermaid (Animation Courtyard) Live musical with fluorescent sea critters and bubbles – beautifully executed but frustratingly short.

Legend of Captain Jack Sparrow (Mickey Ave) Walk-through *Pirates of the Caribbean* attraction features piratey special effects

park and *American Idol* wannabes line up daily to strut their stuff.

The 122ft Sorcerer's Hat serves as the park's primary focal point. Make a right onto Sunset Blvd to hit the roller coasters, the *Beauty and the Beast* show and Fantasmic (a nighttime spectacular), and left toward New York for the movie-based attractions, primarily in the form of shows.

You won't need a whole day here, but there are some Disney highlights – the best plan is to come first thing in the morning, linger for lunch, and then take off to relax by the pool or, if you have a Park Hopper ticket, catch a boat over to Epcot's World Showcase for the afternoon.

Animation Academy COURSE

(Map p262; www.disneyworld.disney.go.com; theme park admission required; ⊙from 10:30am, on the half hour; ⊛; ⛲Disney, ⛲Disney) Try your hand at drawing a Disney character during a short course hosted by a Disney animator. There are about 40 drafting tables, equipped with paper and pencil, and your drawing may be one of the best souvenirs of the trip!

Jedi Training Academy COURSE

(Map p262; www.disneyworld.disney.go.com; theme park admission required; ⊙from 9am, up to 12 times a day) Twelve little ones at a time don brown robes, pledge the sacred Jedi oath and grab a light saber for on-stage training by a Jedi Master. But it's first-come, first-served, so get to Hollywood Studios when gates open, and line up at the ABC Sound Studio to sign up for one of the many classes held throughout the day. Children aged four to 12.

ℹ Getting There & Away

➡ A paved waterfront walkway and a boat shuttle connect Hollywood Studios, Disney's BoardWalk, Disney Epcot resorts (BoardWalk Inn, Yacht & Beach Clubs, Swan & Dolphin) and Epcot. It is about a 25-minute walk from Epcot to Hollywood Studios and, though the path is pleasant, it is unsigned – head to Disney's BoardWalk and ask directions. Disney buses provide transportation to other parks, hotels and the Transportation & Ticket Center, sometimes requiring a transfer.

➡ You cannot take the monorail to Epcot and then walk or take a boat to Hollywood Studios unless you have a park hopper ticket. The monorail is at Epcot's front entrance, and access to Hollywood Studios is from Epcot's back entrance.

⊙ Typhoon Lagoon & Blizzard Beach

In addition to the four theme parks, Disney boasts two distinctly themed water parks. Of the two, Blizzard Beach boasts the better thrills and speed, but Typhoon Lagoon has the far superior wave pool, a fantastic lazy river and tots' play area, and plenty of room to splash on the beach.

Be prepared to spend upwards of 30 minutes in line for a ride that's over in less than a minute, and take those wait times seriously – if it says the wait is 60 minutes, it's 60 minutes. Yes, 60 minutes for *one* slide. Both parks have fast-food restaurants and an outdoor pool bar.

Disney's water-park hours vary seasonally and by the day, but are generally open from 10am to 5pm, and from 9am to 10pm in the summer. From late October through February one water park is closed for refurbishment.

Typhoon Lagoon WATER PARK

(Map p262; ☑407-560-4120, 407-939-5277; www.disneyworld.disney.go.com; 1145 Buena Vista Dr; adult/child $53/45, admission incl in Water Park Fun & More with Magic Your Way theme park ticket; ⊙hours vary; ⛲Disney) An abundance of palm trees, a zero-entry pool with a white sandy beach, high-speed slides and the best wave pool in Orlando make this one of the most beautiful water parks in Florida. Little ones will love floating along **Castaway Creek** and splashing at **Ketchakiddee Creek**.

Included in admission is snorkeling equipment for small-group swims with the tropical fish, stingrays, and leopard and bonnethead sharks in the 68°F (20°C) waters of **Shark Reef**.

Blizzard Beach WATER PARK

(Map p262; ☑407-560-3400, 407-939-5277; www.disneyworld.disney.go.com; 1534 Blizzard Beach Dr; adult/child $53/45, admission incl in Water Park Fun & More with Magic Your Way theme park ticket; ⊙hours vary; ⛲Disney) The newer of Disney's two water parks, themed as a melted Swiss ski resort complete with a ski lift, Blizzard Beach is the 1980s Vegas Strip hotel to Typhoon Lagoon's Bellagio. At its center sits **Mt Gushmore**, from which waterslides burst forth.

ℹ Information

Swimsuits with buckles or metal parts aren't allowed on most of the rides. Hours vary by day and by season; call the individual parks for current hours. From October through February, only one Disney water park is open at a time. Disney's two water parks are included in the price of a Water Park Fun & More ticket upgrade.

ⓘ Getting There & Away

Disney buses stop at both Typhoon Lagoon and Blizzard Beach, and there is complimentary self-parking at both parks.

👁 Disney's BoardWalk

Disney's BoardWalk   WATERFRONT
(Map p262; ☑407-939-5277; www.disneyworld. disney.go.com; 2101 Epcot Resorts Blvd; 🚌Disney, 🚤Disney) Far less harried and crowded than Downtown Disney, the very small Disney's BoardWalk area across from Epcot and along Crescent Lake echoes waterfront boardwalks of turn-of-the-century New England seaside resorts. On Thursday to Saturday evenings magicians, jugglers and musicians give a festive vibe, and there are a handful of good restaurants and bars. Pick up a doughnut or cute lil' Mickey Mouse cakes at the bakery, and toot around on a surrey-with-the-fringe-on-top bike.

ⓘ Information

Public areas at Disney's BoardWalk are open from 8am to 2am.

ⓘ Getting There & Away

A well-lit paved walking path (unsigned) and small boats connect Disney's BoardWalk to Epcot and Hollywood Studios, as well as to Disney Epcot resorts (BoardWalk Inn, Yacht & Beach Clubs and Swan & Dolphin). Disney buses stop at the BoardWalk Resort and there's also parking here – be sure to say you're visiting the BoardWalk, and you won't be charged.

👁 Downtown Disney

Stretching along the water, the Downtown Disney (Map p262; ☑407-939-6244; www.disneyworld.disney.go.com; 1490 E Buena Vista Dr; ⏰8:30am-2am; 🚌Disney, 🚤Disney, 🚌Lynx 50) outdoor pedestrian mall lures tourists with shops, restaurants, music venues and more shops. This is where you'll find AMC Downtown Disney 24 (p258), the stage show Cirque du Soleil La Nouba (p258), bowling and the largest Disney store in the world. There's a Disney-styled party atmosphere here, particularly on the weekends, with folks walking around sipping margaritas

from paper cups; street performers dancing on stilts; and parents pushing strollers loaded down with Disney shopping bags.

Note that Disney is in the midst of completely overhauling Downtown Disney, renaming it Disney Springs and revamping the restaurants, stores and offerings. The new Disney Springs is expected to be completed in 2016.

DisneyQuest Indoor
Interactive Theme Park   ARCADE
(Map p262; ☑407-828-3800; www.disneyworld. disney.go.com; adult/child $48/42, admission incl in Water Park Fun & More with Magic Your Way theme park ticket; ⏰11:30am-10pm Mon-Fri, to 11pm Sat & Sun; 🚻; 🚌Disney, 🚤Disney, 🚌Lynx 50) With five dizzying floors of exhibits designed to indulge video-game addicts, this 'interactive theme park' makes the perfect place to while away a rainy or hot afternoon. Virtual-reality attractions include a trip on Aladdin's magic carpet over Agrabah and a float down a river into the Mesozoic Age. You can design and 'ride' your own roller coaster, or simply lose yourself for hours in old-school video games and pinball machines.

Characters in Flight   RIDE
(Map p262; ☑407-939-7529; www.disney-world.disney.go.com; adult/child $18/12;

INTERACTIVE DISNEY

Two Disney parks offer self-paced treasure-hunt-styled experiences that attract fans of all ages.

Sorcerers of the Magic Kingdom
(Magic Kingdom) Join Merlin in his efforts to find and defeat Disney villains. Key cards activate hidden game portals throughout Magic Kingdom and the spell cards work magic. Stop by the firehouse by the main gate on Main Street to sign up.

Pirates Adventure – Treasure of the Seven Seas (Magic Kingdom) Pick up a talisman at the Crow's Nest (Adventureland) and help Captain Jack collect the pirate gold.

Agent P's World Showcase Adventure
(Epcot) Phineas and Ferb–themed game. Make the beer steins in Germany sing, the soldiers dance, and activate surprises from China to the UK.

⊙ 8:30am–midnight; 🚌 Disney, 🚢 Disney, 🚌 Lynx 50) Guests climb on board the basket of this massive tethered gas balloon and ascend 400ft into the air for 360-degree views.

ℹ️ Information

Public areas at Downtown Disney are open from 8am to 2am.

ℹ️ Getting There & Around

➡ Downtown Disney is accessible by boat from Downtown Disney resorts and by bus from everywhere else. There is complimentary self-parking, but no direct Disney transportation to any of the theme parks. Lynx bus 50 services Downtown Disney from downtown Orlando and SeaWorld.

➡ You can walk from one end of Downtown Disney to the other, or catch a boat shuttle.

🏃 Activities

In addition to the four theme parks, two water parks and two entertainment districts, Disney offers a dizzying array of recreational activities, most based at Disney hotels and none requiring theme park admission. Call **Walt Disney World Recreation** (📞 407-939-7529) for reservations and details on everything from water-skiing lessons to bike rental; for general information on activities at Walt Disney World, check www.disneyworld.disney.go.com.

Golf

Walt Disney World Golf　　　　GOLF
(📞 407-939-4653; www.golfwdw.com; green fees from $40; ⊙ hours vary) Reserve tee times for any of Disney's four golf courses (Lake Buena Vista, Magnolia, Oak Trail and Palm Golf Courses) either online or by phone up to 90 days in advance for resort guests, 60 days in advance for nonresort guests.

Winter Summerland
Miniature Golf　　　　MINIATURE GOLF
(Map p262; 📞 407-560-3000; www.disneyworld.disney.go.com; 1548 W Buena Vista; adult/child $14/12; ⊙ 10am–11pm) Holiday-inspired miniature golf next to Blizzard Beach.

Fantasia Gardens　　　　MINIATURE GOLF
(Map p262; 📞 407-560-4870; www.disneyworld.disney.go.com; 1205 Epcot Resorts Blvd; adult/child $14/12; ⊙ 10am–11pm) Sweet fairyland-themed course across from the Walt Disney World Dolphin Resort.

Tennis

Several resort hotels offer hard and clay courts. Call 📞 407-939-7529 to reserve a court anywhere in Walt Disney World; there is no charge if you are staying at a Disney hotel. Racquet and ball rental available.

Cycling

Trails along the shores of Disney's lagoons and alongside woods, resorts and golf courses make for some lovely family-friendly cycling. Most locations offer training wheels and baby seats.

Walt Disney World
Bicycle Rental　　　　BICYCLE RENTAL
(📞 407-939-7529; www.disneyworld.disney.go.com; select Disney World resorts; per hour/day $9/18, surrey bikes per 30min from $20) Seven bike rental places throughout Walt Disney World rent on a first-come, first-served basis. A few places, including Disney's BoardWalk, rent two-, four- and six-person surrey bikes, with four wheels, candy-striped tops and bench seats.

Horseback Riding

Carriage rides are available at Disney's Port Orleans Resort.

Fort Wilderness
Tri-Circle-D Ranch　　　　HORSEBACK RIDING
(Map p262; 📞 407-824-2832; www.disneyworld.disney.go.com; 4510 N Wilderness Trail, Disney's Fort Wilderness Resort & Campground; per 30min $10-45; 🚌 Disney, 🚢 Disney) Guided trail, pony, wagon, hay and carriage rides.

Water Sports

Typhoon Lagoon Surf Lessons　　　　SURFING
(Map p262; 📞 407-939-7873; www.disneyworld.disney.go.com; 1145 Buena Vista Dr, Typhoon Lagoon; $150; ⊙ 6:45am Tue & Thu, hours vary; 🚌 Disney) No, Orlando is not on the ocean, but that doesn't stop Disney. Typhoon Lagoon gives surf lessons before the water park opens to the public. Price includes 30 minutes on land and two hours in the water, and nonpaying family and friends are welcome to come watch. If you stick around after the park opens, you must purchase admission tickets.

Disney Boat Rental　　　　BOATING
(📞 403-939-7529; www.disneyworld.disney.go.com; select Disney resort hotels; rental from $11) Disney rents canoes, kayaks, Sunfish and catamaran sailboats, pedal boats and

motorized boats at several resort hotels, including Disney's Port Orleans, Disney's Caribbean Beach and Disney's Fort Wilderness. Consider reserving a pontoon to watch the fireworks over the Magic Kingdom Castle.

Sammy Duvall's
Watersports Centre   WATER SPORTS
(Map p262; ☑407-939-0754; www.sammyduvall. com; 4600 World Dr, Disney's Contemporary Resort; personal watercraft per hour $135, waterskiing, wakeboarding & tubing up to 5 people per hour $165; ☺10am-5pm; ☒Disney, ☒Disney, monorail Disney) Lessons, rentals and parasailing.

Motor Sports

Richard Petty
Driving Experience   MOTOR SPORTS
(Map p262; ☑407-939-7529; www.disneyworld. disney.go.com; Walt Disney World Speedway; prices vary; ☺9am-4pm) NASCAR wannabes can race Winston Cup–style cars around a real track. The **Ride Along Program** puts you shotgun in a stock car for three laps speeding up to 165mph.

☞ Tours

Disney Tours   GUIDED TOUR
(☑407-939-8687, VIP tours 407-560-4033; www. disneyworld.disney.go.com; prices vary) Disney offers all kinds of guided tours and specialty experiences, including the **Wild Africa Trek** private safari and back-stage Disney tours. For the ultimate in hassle-free touring, with front-of-the-line access to attractions and insider information on the park and its history, consider a **VIP tour** ($380 per hour per group of up to 10 people).

Note that tours inside theme parks require theme park admission in addition to the cost of the tour.

Keys to the Kingdom   WALKING TOUR
(☑407-939-8687; www.disneyworld.disney.go; Magic Kingdom; tours $79, theme park admission required; ☺8:30am, 9am & 9:30am) Quintessential Disney, this popular five-hour tour peaks into Magic Kingdom's underground tunnels and backstage secrets – no children allowed, so as not to destroy the magic!

✯ Festivals & Events

In November and December, millions of lights and hundreds of Christmas trees, specialty parades and holiday shows celebrate the season throughout Walt Disney World.

Epcot International
Flower & Garden Festival   GARDEN
(☑407-939-5277; www.disneyworld.disney.go.com; Epcot; theme park admission required; ☒Disney, monorail Disney) Spectacular Disney-themed topiary and garden displays from March to May, and all the countries in the World Pavilion celebrate spring with seasonal delicacies.

Star Wars Weekends   FILM
(www.disneyworld.disney.go.com; Hollywood Studios; theme park admission required; ☒Disney, ☒Disney) All kinds of *Star Wars*–themed events at Disney's Hollywood Studios on weekends from mid-May to mid-June.

Epcot International
Food & Wine Festival   FOOD
(☑407-939-5277; www.disneyworld.disney.go.com; Epcot; theme park admission required; ☒Disney, monorail Disney) Disney-fied food and drink from around the world from late September to early November. You need to pay park admission, and then pay anywhere from $3 to $10 for food samples of varying quality. This is a very popular event – come early, expect crowds, and allow at least a half a day.

Mickey's Not-So-Scary
Halloween Party   STREET CARNIVAL
(☑407-939-5277; www.disneyworld.disney.go.com; Magic Kingdom; adult/child $65/60, plus theme park admission; ☒Disney, ☒Disney, ☒Lynx 50, 56, monorail Disney) Characters decked out in costumes, trick-or-treating and Halloween-inspired fireworks, parade and events from September to October 31. Discounted tickets available as advanced online purchase.

Mickey's Very
Merry Christmas Party   CHRISTMAS
(☑407-939-5277; www.disneyworld.disney.go.com; Magic Kingdom; $52-63, plus theme park admission; ☒Disney, ☒Disney, ☒Lynx 50, 56, monorail Disney) Christmas songs, decorations and festivities Disney-style saturate Disney's Magic Kingdom park, including a Christmas parade, snowfall on Main Street and seasonal shows. Select nights 7pm to midnight November to December.

▭ Sleeping

Disney resort hotels are divided according to location (Magic Kingdom, Epcot, Animal Kingdom and Downtown Disney) and price (Value, Moderate, Deluxe and Deluxe Villas). Prices vary drastically according to season, week and day, and there are more than 20 different price variations throughout the year; to further complicate things, deluxe resorts can have upwards of 10 different 'room types' that vary according to location and amenities, rooms that sleep five or more aren't necessarily more expensive than suites, and Disney vacation packages include park tickets and shave room rates. Go to www.wdwinfo.com for an exhaustive chart of room options and exact prices for each season, and to www.disneyworld.disney.go.com to plug in specific dates and see package offerings. Most rooms sleep up to four, with no extra charge for children or cribs, and a handful offer themed rooms and bunk beds.

While deluxe resorts are the best Disney has to offer, don't expect the same bang for your buck as you'd get elsewhere. They do, however, offer multiroom suites and villas, upscale restaurants, children's programs and incredibly easy access to theme parks. You're paying for Disney theming and location convenience, not luxury. Epcot resorts offer walking access and pleasant boat transport to restaurants and entertainment at Disney's BoardWalk, Hollywood Studios and Epcot, while Magic Kingdom resorts are an easy boat or monorail ride to park gates.

It is important to take note of what transport is available to/from your chosen resort when planning your trip, as you can use Disney transportation to reach any attraction from any resort but *not everything is directly connected* – you will sometimes need to transfer to get from point A to point B. All Disney resorts offer bus transportation, but those offering boat and monorail transportation are far more convenient (and, except for camping at Fort Wilderness, more expensive).

Magic Kingdom

The number-one advantage to staying at one of these resorts on Bay Lake is that they are one easy monorail or boat ride from Magic Kingdom – they're the only hotels at Walt Disney World where you can get to classic Disney with no need for transfers. This may not sound like much, but when you're slogging home with three exhausted children or are desperate for a quick afternoon dip in the pool, it makes a world of difference. You can also take the monorail to Epcot, though you have to transfer at the Transportation & Ticket Center, and there are nonstop buses to Animal Kingdom and Hollywood Studios.

★ **Disney's Fort Wilderness Resort** CAMPGROUND, CABIN $$
(Map p262; ☏407-939-5277, 407-824-2900; www.disneyworld.disney.go.com; 4510 N Fort Wilderness Trail; tent sites value/regular/peak $55/79/91, RV sites $74/102/130, 6-person cabins $330/403/456; ✳@☋✉☃; ☐Disney, ☳Disney) Located in a huge shaded natural preserve, Fort Wilderness caters to kids and families with its hay rides, fishing and nightly campfire singalongs. Cabins sleep up to six and are hardly rustic, with cable TV and full kitchens, and while cars aren't allowed within the gates, you can rent a golf cart to toot around in.

Staff keep a strict eye on after-hours noise; the grounds are meticulously maintained; and there's a wonderfully casual and friendly state-park-like tone to the entire resort.

★ **Disney's Grand Floridian Resort & Spa** RESORT $$$
(Map p262; ☏407-824-3000, 407-939-5277; www.disneyworld.disney.go.com; 4401 Floridian Way; r value/regular/peak $550/606/714, 6-person ste from $1412; ᴾ✳@☋✉; ☐Disney, ☳Disney, monorail Disney) One easy monorail stop from Magic Kingdom, the Grand Floridian rides on its reputation as the grandest, most elegant property in Disney World, and it does indeed exude a welcome calm and charm. The four-story lobby, with a live orchestra playing jazz (and yes, Disney classics), oozes all the accoutrements of Old Florida class and style.

At its heart, though, this is Disney. Sparkling princesses ballroom-dance across the oriental rugs; exhausted children sit entranced by classic Disney cartoons; and babies cry. In contrast to the massive ferries from the Transportation & Ticket Center, small wooden boats shuttle folks back and forth to Magic Kingdom.

★ **Disney's Wilderness Lodge** RESORT $$$
(Map p262; ☏407-824-3200, 407-939-5277; www.disneyworld.disney.go.com; 901 Timberline Dr, Walt Disney World; r value/regular/peak $325/394/471, 6-person ste from $688; ᴾ✳☋✉; ☐Disney, ☳Disney) The handsome lobby's low-lit tipi chandeliers, hand-carved totem pole and dramatic 80ft fireplace echo national-park lodges of America's Old West. Though it's meant to feel as if you're in John Muir country, with its wooded surrounds and hidden lagoonside location, the fake geyser and singing waiters in the lobby restaurant dispel the illusion mighty quick.

Disney's Polynesian Resort RESORT $$$
(Map p262; ☑ 407-939-5277, 407-824-2000; www.
disneyworld.disney.go.com; 1600 Seven Seas Dr; r
value/regular/peak $482/554/637; P ✳ @ 🛜 ✖;
🖵 Disney, 🚊 Disney, monorail Disney) With
faux-bamboo decor, a jungle motif in the
lobby, and coconut-shell cups and shell
necklaces in the store, you just may think
you're in the South Pacific. The rounded
lagoonside pool features a slide, a zero en-
trance perfect for little ones and an excellent
view of Cinderella's Castle.

Disney's Contemporary Resort RESORT $$$
(Map p262; ☑ 407-939-5277, 407-824-1000; www.
disneyworld.disney.go.com; 4600 N World Dr; r
value/regular/peak $378/436/465, 6-person ste
from $1258; P ✳ @ 🛜 ✖; 🖵 Disney, 🚊 Disney,
monorail Disney) The granddaddy of Disney resorts, the Contemporary's futuristic
A-frame opened Walt Disney World in 1971
but feels uninspired and disappointing by
today's standards. Yes, it's cool to see the
monorail zip silently through the lobby, and
its withering grandeur evokes melancholy
sentimental attachment, but the years have
faded this iconic hotel's sparkle.

On the upside, you can't beat the location.
Balcony rooms front Magic Kingdom, an excellent top-floor restaurant lures folks with
its drop-dead views of Disney's fireworks,
and renovated streamlined suites in Bay
Lake Towers sleep five and are some of the
most handsome digs at Disney.

DISNEY PARADES, FIREWORKS & LIGHT SHOWS

It takes a little bit of planning to coordinate your schedule to hit Disney's parades and
nighttime spectaculars. Note that times vary according to day and season. In addition to
the following cornerstones, check www.disneyworld.disney.go.com for holiday celebrations and specialty parties.

Festival of Fantasy (www.disneyworld.disney.go.com; Magic Kingdom; theme park admission
required; ⊙ morning & afternoon daily, hours vary; 🖵 Disney, 🚊 Disney, 🖵 Lynx 50, 56, monorail
Disney) Introduced in 2014, with elaborate floats and dancing characters, including Dumbo, Peter Pan and Sleeping Beauty.

Illuminations (www.disneyworld.disney.go.com; Epcot; theme park admission required;
⊙ nightly, hours vary; 🖵 Disney, 🚊 Disney, 🖵 Lynx 50 & 56, monorail Disney) This fiery narrative, with a light show and fireworks, centers around a massive globe illuminated with
LED lights in the center of Epcot's World Showcase Lagoon.

Main Street Electrical Parade (www.disneyworld.disney.go.com; Magic Kingdom; theme
park admission required; ⊙ nightly, hours vary; 🖵 Disney, 🚊 Disney, 🖵 Lynx 50, 56, monorail
Disney) Thousands of twinkling lights, covering various floats and favorite Disney characters, glimmer and sparkle through the park. Highlights include a massive Pete and his
dragon and Alice in Wonderland on top of a giant mushroom.

Wishes Nighttime Spectacular (www.disneyworld.disney.go.com; Magic Kingdom; theme
park admission required; ⊙ 8pm, hours vary; 🖵 Disney, 🚊 Disney, 🖵 Lynx 50, 56, monorail Disney) Jiminy Cricket narrates this classic Disney display over Cinderella's Castle at Magic
Kingdom.

Celebrate the Magic (www.disneyworld.disney.go.com; Magic Kingdom; theme park admission required; ⊙ nightly, hours vary; 🖵 Disney, 🚊 Disney, 🖵 Lynx 50, 56, monorail Disney) Seasonally changing light-and-music show at Cinderella's Castle highlights Disney movies
and characters at Magic Kingdom.

Jammin' Jungle (www.disneyworld.disney.go.co; Animal Kingdom; theme park admission required; ⊙ daily, hours vary; 🖵 Disney) Huge folk-art animal puppets and Disney characters
in safari motif at Animal Kingdom.

Fantasmic (☑ 407-939-5277; www.disneyworld.disney.go.com; Hollywood Studios; theme park
admission required; ⊙ nightly; 🚹; 🖵 Disney, 🚊 Disney) Dramatic and overhyped water, music and light show centers on a vague, rather disconnected and confusing plot in which
Mickey Mouse proves victorious over a cast of Disney villians. Seating for the 25-minute
show begins 90 minutes in advance, and even though the outdoor ampitheater seats
more than 6000 people, it's always crowded.

DISNEY'S VALUE RESORTS

Five value resorts, the least expensive Disney properties available (not including camping), have thousands of motel-style rooms and suites; are garishly decorated according to their theme; connect to all the parks by bus only; and cater to families and traveling school groups – expect cheerleader teams practising in the courtyard, or a lobby of teenagers wearing matching jerseys. You will definitely feel the difference in price: instead of proper restaurants, there are food courts and snack bars, and things are particularly bright, hectic and loud. Some value resorts offer family suites with two bathrooms and a kitchenette.

Disney's Art of Animation Resort (Map p262; ☑ 407-938-7000, 407-939-5277; www. disneyworld.disney.go.com; 1850 Animation Way; r value/regular/peak $118/147/174, 6-person ste from $300; P ✿ @ ☎ ✾; ☐ Disney) Inspired by four animated Disney classics (*Finding Nemo, Lion King, Cars* and *Little Mermaid*), this dazzlingly bright hotel is the best bet for budget-conscious Disney travel. It's the newest of Disney's Value Resorts (finished in 2012).

Disney's All-Star Resorts (Map p262; ☑ 407-939-5277; www.disneyworld.disney.go.com; 1701, 1801 & 1901 W Buena Vista Dr; r value/regular/peak $96/123/152, 6-person ste from $240; ☐ Disney) Three self-contained hotels, three of Disney's five 'value' accommodations options, let you take your pick between movie, music and sports themes.

Disney's Pop Century Resort (Map p262; ☑ 407-938-4000, 407-939-5277; www.disneyworld.disney.go.com; 1050 Century Dr; r value/regular/peak $106/136/163; P ✿ @ ☎ ✾; ☐ Disney) Each section pays homage to a different decade of the late 20th century, with massive bowling pins that extend beyond the roof and giant Play-Doh.

🛌 Epcot

One of the best parts about this cluster of hotels on the shore of Crescent Lake is their easy access to restaurants and entertainment in Epcot, Hollywood Studios and Disney's BoardWalk. The area is pedestrian friendly, and it's a pleasant walk or an easy boat ride to Epcot and to Hollywood Studios.

★**Walt Disney World Swan & Dolphin Hotels** RESORT $$
(Map p262; ☑ Dolphin 407-934-4000, Swan 407-934-3000; www.swandolphin.com; 1200 & 1500 Epcot Resorts Blvd; r $160-380; ☐ Disney) These two Michael Graves–designed high-rise luxury hotels, which face each other on Disney property and share facilities, offer a distinctly toned-down Disney feel but all the Disney perks, including Disney transportation and Magic Hours (where a theme park opens early and closes late for guests at Disney hotels only).

Perched along the bay between Epcot and Hollywood Studios, these are the only non-Disney hotels next to a theme park. Online and last-minute deals can save literally hundreds of dollars.

Disney's Caribbean Beach Resort RESORT $$
(Map p262; ☑ 407-939-5277, 407-934-3400; www.disneyworld.disney.go.com; 900 Cayman Way; r value/regular/peak $182/211/237; ✿ ☎ ✾; ☐ Disney) A Disney taste of the islands means painted beds, pastel rooms, a food court that looks like a street festival during Carnival and a pool with a vague resemblance to ancient temple ruins. This hotel sits along 45-acre Barefoot Bay, and does not have convenient boat transportation to Epcot and Hollywood Studios.

Rooms, some pirate-themed, spread out among two-story motel-like buildings.

★**Disney's BoardWalk Inn** RESORT $$$
(Map p262; ☑ 407-939-5277, 407-939-6200; www.disneyworld.disney.go.com; 2101 Epcot Resorts Blvd; r value/regular/peak $411/477/569, 6-person ste & cottages from $756; P ✿ @ ☎ ✾; ☐ Disney) This resort embodies the seaside charm of Atlantic City in its heyday, with a waterfront the color of saltwater taffy, tandem bicycles with candy-striped awnings, and a splintery boardwalk. The lovely lobby features sea-green walls, hardwood floors and soft floral vintage seating areas. Elegant rooms have a terrace or balcony.

The resort is divided into two sections, the Inn and the Villas; the Inn, with cute picket-fenced suites, quiet pools and plenty of grass, is far nicer and subdued. Accommodations range from rooms sleeping up to five to two-bedroom cottages.

Disney's Yacht Club Resort & Disney's Beach Club Resort RESORT $$$
(Map p262; ☑ Beach Club 407-934-8000, Walt Disney World 407-939-5277, Yacht Club 407-934-7000; www.waltdisneyworld.disney.go.com; 1700 & 1800 Epcot Resorts Blvd; r value/regular/peak $400/465/554, 8-person ste from $1633; ✳ ☎ ✈; ⬚ Disney, ✤ Disney) These handsome sister resorts, pleasantly located along the water and a five-minute walk from Epcot, strive for old New England beachside charm. The pools, boasting sandy shores and a slide off the mast of a ship, earn rave reviews, but we found them cramped and in need of a face-lift.

🛏 Animal Kingdom
Along with Disney's value resorts, these are the most inconveniently located of all Disney hotels. They are the furthest from all the parks except Animal Kingdom and the only Disney transportation is by bus.

Disney's Coronado Springs Resort RESORT $$
(Map p262; ☑ 407-939-5277, 407-939-1000; www.disneyworld.disney.go.com; 1000 W Buena Vista Dr; r value/regular/peak $187/217/243, 6-person ste from $450; P ✳ @ ☎ ✈; ⬚ Disney) The Southwestern theme, evidenced in the warm pink-and-yellow guest rooms, the colored lights strung across the Pepper Market and the adobe-colored buildings, creates a low-key tone that sets this resort apart from other Disney hotels. Several pleasantly landscaped two-story buildings, some with their own private and quiet pools, sit along a central lake.

There's plenty of grass, and little beaches with hammocks hung between the palm trees sprinkle the shore. At the central pool, an open-air slide zooms down a Maya pyramid. Suites and casitas sleep up to six, and the hotel is popular for conventions.

Disney's Animal Kingdom Lodge RESORT $$$
(Map p262; ☑ 407-939-5277, 407-938-3000; www.disneyworld.disney.go.com; 2901 Osceola Blvd; r value/regular/peak $319/389/465, 6-/8-person ste from $930/1697; P ✳ @ ☎ ✈; ⬚ Disney) With an abutting 33-acre savanna parading a who's who of Noah's Ark past hotel windows and balconies, park rangers standing ready

to answer questions about the wildlife, and African-inspired food served at the recommended restaurants, this resort offers particularly fun and quirky theming.

Ask about storytelling and singing around the fire. If you want to see giraffes and ostriches out your room window, you'll have to reserve the more expensive savanna-view rooms, but anyone can enjoy the animals from the deck out back. Even if you're not staying here, swing by for a drink after an afternoon at Animal Kingdom.

🛏 Downtown Disney
While these hotels offer easy and pleasant boat access to Downtown Disney, the only Disney transportation to the theme parks and Disney's BoardWalk is by bus.

Disney's Port Orleans French Quarter and Riverside Resorts RESORT $$
(Map p262; ☑ French Quarter 407-934-5000, Riverside 407-934-6000; www.disneyworld.disney.go.com; 1251 Riverside; r value/regular/peak $182/211/237; P ✳ @ ☎ ✈; ⬚ Disney, ✤ Disney) Lush gardens and a jubilant Mardi Gras motif blend in an effort to create a Louisiana feel to these sister resorts. Though the result sometimes falls flat and the simple rooms feel dated, the resort is a mecca for activities and includes a sea-serpent waterslide, boat rental, horse-drawn-carriage rides and evening s'mores.

This is one of the biggest resorts at Disney; a boat connects the two properties, or it's a 15-minute walk.

Disney's Old Key West Resort RESORT $$$
(Map p262; ☑ 407-939-5277, 407-827-7700; www.disneyworld.disney.go.com; 1510 N Cove Rd; studios value/regular/peak $327/368/431, 1-bedroom villas $452/508/556, 2-bedroom villas $618/742/903, 3-bedroom villas $1381/1536/1739; P ✳ @ ☎ ✈; ⬚ Disney, ✤ Disney) Victoriana oozes from every gingerbread-accented pastel corner, every palm-tree enclave and from the azure blue waters. This is an 'all villa' resort. Studios sleep four; one- and two-bedroom villas sleep eight; and three-bedroom villas sleep 12.

🛏 Other Walt Disney World Options
Several Disney properties, including Disney's Old Key West and Tree House Villas at Saratoga Springs, participate in **Disney Vacation Club**, Disney's version of a

ORLANDO & WALT DISNEY WORLD WALT DISNEY WORLD

timeshare. Go to www.disneyvacationclub.
go.com for details.

Shades of Green Resort RESORT $$

(Map p262; ☑ 407-824-3400; www.shadesofgreen.
org; 1950 W Magnolia Palm Dr; r $90-150, ste $235-
250; ❋ ✖; ☐ Disney) In a category all of its
own, this full-service resort sits within Walt
Disney World but is owned by the Armed
Forces Recreation Center. A valid US military or Department of Defense ID is required at check-in, and rates are determined
according to rank.

Four Seasons Resort Orlando
at Walt Disney World RESORT $$$

(Map p262; ☑ 800-267-3046; www.fourseasons.
com; 10100 Dream Tree Blvd; r/ste from $435/430;
P ❋ @ ✈ ✖) All the luxury, quality and attention to detail you'd expect from a Four
Seasons resort, on the grounds of Walt Disney World but marvelously removed from
the Disney vortex.

✕ Eating

Expect lots of mediocre fast food, bad coffee and cafeteria cuisine at premium prices. Yes, it's difficult to find a decent meal
at Disney, despite the fact that there are
more than 100 restaurants here, and it gets
frustrating paying a lot of money for disappointing meals. Table-service restaurants
accept 'priority seating' reservations up
to 180 days in advance. Make reservations
at these and dozens more through Disney
Dining (☑ 407-939-3463), online at www.
disneyworld.disney.go.com or through My
Disney Experience (p272). If you don't have
a reservation and the line is long, try the
bar – many places have great bars with limited menus. Remember that restaurants in
the theme parks require theme park admission, but resort hotel restaurants do not.

In addition to plain old eating, Disney
offers character meals, three dinner shows
and specialty dining. Possibilities include
a private safari followed by an Africa dinner; lunch with a Disney 'imagineer'; and
dinner in Cinderella's Castle. See website
for details.

✕ Magic Kingdom

Eating at Magic Kingdom is less about
great food than theming, festive environs
and character dining opportunities. You
certainly won't starve, as there are snacks,

fast-food eateries and table-service restaurants at every turn, but there's little here
worth seeking out. If you're going to be at
the park and want a sit-down meal, make a
reservation at one of Disney's Magic Kingdom Resorts – Disney's Polynesian, Disney's
Contemporary, Disney's Grand Floridian
or Disney's Wilderness Lodge – they're any
easy hop on the monorail or by boat from
Magic Kingdom.

Sleepy Hollow AMERICAN $

(Map p262; www.disneyworld.disney.go.com; snacks
$3-6, theme park admission required; ⊙ 9am-park
closing; ☐ Disney, ⬆ Disney, ☐ Lynx 50, 56, monorail Disney) The best snack in the park is this
walk-up window's ice-cream sandwich with
oozing vanilla ice cream squished between
warm, fresh-baked chocolate-chip cookies.
Alternatively, try the Mickey Mouse waffles
sprinkled with powdered sugar. Look for
the brick house in Liberty Sq, just across the
bridge from Cinderella's Castle.

Gaston's Tavern AMERICAN $

(www.disneyworld.disney.go.com; mains $6-10,
theme park admission required; ⊙ 9am-park closing; ✈ ♿; ☐ Disney, ⬆ Disney, ☐ Lynx 50, 56, monorail Disney) Homage to that superego Gaston,
with pork shanks, giant cinnamon rolls and
hummus. It's an odd mix of quick-service
options, but the re-created tavern with the
giant portrait of Gaston is well done, and
the food is pretty good. Try Le Fou's Brew,
Disney's counter to Universal's run-away hit
Butterbeer.

Cheshire Cafe BAKERY $

(Map p262; www.disneyworld.disney.go.com;
cake-cups $4-10, theme park admission required;
⊙ 9am-park closing; ☐ Disney, ⬆ Disney, ☐ Lynx
50, 56, monorail Disney) Delectably sweet and
charmingly cute cake-cups, which are basically cupcake parfaits with several layers of
rich butter-cream frosting topped with *Alice
in Wonderland*–themed decorations, are
big enough to share.

Main Street Bakery BAKERY $

(Map p262; www.disneyworld.disney.go.com;
items $5-10, theme park admission required;
⊙ 9am-park closing; ☐ Disney, ⬆ Disney, ☐ Lynx
50, 56, monorail Disney) Few places require
good strong java more than Disney World,
and few places are as notorious for bad coffee as the Happiest Place on Earth. Pop in

here for Starbucks, a reliable exception to the rule.

Columbia Harbour House
AMERICAN **$**

(Map p262; www.disneyworld.disney.go.com; mains $7-12, theme park admission required; ◷ 11am-park closing; 🖥🚹; ▢ Disney, 🚹 Disney, ▢ Lynx 50, 56, monorail Disney) Decent vegetarian chili, unusually tasty chicken nuggets and a 'Garden Galley Salad' of mixed greens, chicken, pecans, pineapple and feta cheese.

Be Our Guest
AMERICAN **$$**

(Map p262; ☑ 407-939-3463; www.disneyworld. disney.go.com; mains lunch $9-14, dinner $18-32; ◷ 10:30am-2:30pm & 4-9:30pm, hours vary; 🖥🚹; ▢ Disney, 🚹 Disney, ▢ Lynx 50, 56, monorail Disney) Disney's newest and hottest restaurant, set inside the Beast's marvelously detailed castle, is a must for *Beauty and the Beast* fans. Options include braised pork, carved turkey and the most talked about dessert at Disney, the Master's Cupcake. But it's the attention to theming that is the real draw.

This is the only place in Magic Kingdom with alcohol – beer and wine only. Come for quick-service lunch when the door opens or expect upwards of two hours' wait; reservations are accepted for dinner only, but you'll need to make them as close to six months in advance as you can. The Beast makes regular appearances, and after your meal you can explore his castle and have your picture taken with him in his study.

✖ Epcot

Eating at Epcot is as much about the experience as the food, and many of the restaurants go overboard to create an atmosphere characteristic of their country. You can savor a glass of champagne or a flight of wine in France; order a stein at the tavern in Germany; or indulge in a blood-orange margarita in Mexico before heading to China for wonton soup. As one visitor said, perusing the menu of a fast-food eatery in Future World, 'I'm gonna wait and try something exotic over in Morocco.' None of the food is going to knock your socks off, but it's a lot of fun, and there are many very good options.

★ La Cava del Tequila
MEXICAN **$**

(Map p262; ☑ 407-939-3463; www.disneyworld. disney.go.com; tapas $6-12, theme park admission required; ◷ noon-park closing; ▢ Disney, 🚹 Disney, monorail Disney) Pop in for a cucumber, passion-fruit or blood-orange margarita. Can't decide? Try a flight of margaritas or shots. The menu features more than 70 types of tequila and a limited tapas menu, and it's a cozy, dark spot, with tiled floors, Mexican-styled murals and a beamed ceiling.

La Cava is connected to San Angel Inn, a full-service sit-down restaurant, but does not take reservations.

La Hacienda de San Angel
MEXICAN **$$**

(Map p262; ☑ 407-939-3463; www.disneyworld. disney.go.com; Epcot; mains $23-30, theme park admission required; ◷ 4pm-park closing; 🚹; ▢ Disney, 🚹 Disney, monorail Disney) Authentic

---

QUICK EATS: EPCOT'S WORLD SHOWCASE

Cantina de San Angel (Map p262; www.disneyworld.disney.go.com; mains $5-10, theme park admission required; ◷ 11am-park closing; 🖥📶; ▢ Disney, 🚹 Disney, monorail Disney) One of the best fast-food places in the park. Try the tacos, served with surprisingly tasty *pico de gallo* (fresh salsa of tomatoes, onion and jalapeños) and fresh avocado.

Les Halles Boulangerie Patisserie (Map p262; www.disneyworld.disney.go.com; pastries & sandwiches $2-10, theme park admission required; ◷ 9am-park closing; 🚹 Disney, 🚹 Disney, monorail Disney) Most folks come for cakes, éclairs and cookies, but it also sells French-bread pizza, quiche and those baguette sandwiches that are ubiquitous in the real France, as well as wine and champagne.

Yorkshire County Fish Shop (Map p262; www.disneyworld.disney.go.com; fish & chips $9, theme park admission required; ◷ 11am-park closing; 🖥🚹; ▢ Disney, 🚹 Disney, monorail Disney) Crispy fish with vinegar and Bass Ale at the walk-up window outside the pub in UK.

Yakitori House (Map p262; www.disneyworld.disney.go.com; mains $5-12, theme park admission required; ◷ 11am-park closing; 🖥📶; ▢ Disney, 🚹 Disney, monorail Disney) Next to the lavish temples of Japan; serves miso soup, teriyaki chicken and noodle dishes.

Mexican rather than Tex Mex, this lagoon-side eatery features corn tortillas made daily; mango and chipotle salsas; and on-the-rocks margaritas ranging from rose-infused Rosita to a classic with cactus lemongrass salt on the rim.

Via Napoli
PIZZERIA $$

(Map p262; ✆407-939-3463; www.disneyworld.disney.go.com; pizzas $13-22, theme park admission required; ⏱11:30am-park closing; 🛜📶; 🖥Disney, 🚋Disney, monorail Disney) The thin-crust pizza cooked in a wood-burning stove is quite tasty, and the toppings take things beyond run-of-the-mill pepperoni.

San Angel Inn
MEXICAN $$

(Map p262; ✆407-939-3463; www.disneyworld.disney.go.com; mains $17-28, theme park admission required; ⏱11:30am-park closing; 🛜📄📶; 🖥Disney, 🚋Disney, monorail Disney) Set inside an Aztec pyramid and surrounded by a re-created Mexican market, with perpetual night skies twinkling with Disney stars. Excellent chips with freshly made salsa and *pico de gallo* (fresh salsa of tomatoes, onion and jalapeños), solid Mexican fare, and rice pudding with raisins and cinnamon for dessert. Ask about vegetarian options.

Rose & Crown
ENGLISH $$

(Map p262; ✆407-939-3463; www.disneyworld.disney.go.com; mains $13-21, theme park admission required; ⏱11am-park closing; 🛜📶; 🖥Disney, 🚋Disney, monorail Disney) Housed in a British pub, this little spot serves up ploughman's lunch, steak, fish and chips, and a tasty vegetable curry. Wash it down with Bass on tap and head across the path for a garden concert of the Fab Four, or settle on the patio for the nightly light show Illuminations.

Chefs de France
FRENCH $$

(Map p262; ✆407-939-3463; www.disneyworld.disney.com; mains $19-35, theme park admission required; ⏱noon-3pm & 4:30-park closing; 📶; 🖥Disney, 🚋Disney, monorail Disney) Bright yellow and with lovely big windows, this bustling French brasserie features steak *frites* and other bistro classics. Four times a day, from Monday to Saturday, *Ratatouille's* Remy makes an appearance. He won't stop at every table, like a traditional character meal, but he dances about, stopping randomly to visit with folk.

Biergarten
GERMAN $$

(Map p262; ✆407-939-3463; www.disneyworld.disney.go.com; buffet lunch adult/child $20/11, buffet dinner $27/13, theme park admission required; ⏱11am-park closing; 🛜📶; 🖥Disney, 🚋Disney, monorail Disney) Satisfy a hearty appetite with traditional German foods (don't miss the pretzel bread) and a massive stein of brew. The restaurant interior is made to look like an old German village, with cobblestones, trees and a Bavarian oompah band in the evening.

Teppan Edo
JAPANESE $$

(Map p262; ✆407-939-3463; www.disneyworld.disney.go.com; mains $16-29, theme park admission required; ⏱11am-park closing; 📶; 🖥Disney, 🚋Disney, monorail Disney) Chefs toss the chicken, fling the chopsticks and frenetically slice and dice the veggies in this standard cook-in-front-of-you eatery next to Japan's gardens.

Le Cellier Steakhouse
STEAKHOUSE $$$

(Map p262; ✆407-939-3463; www.disneyworld.disney.go.com; mains $21-35, theme park admission required; ⏱11am-park closing; 🛜📶; 🖥Disney, 🚋Disney, monorail Disney) If you love meat, this place is for you. Try the buffalo. Dark and cavernous, with stone walls and lanterns, Le Cellier makes a good spot to escape the heat, but the dense sauces and decadent desserts might not be the best fuel to get you through the day.

Restaurant Marrakesh
MEDITERRANEAN $$$

(Map p262; ✆407-939-3463; www.disneyworld.disney.go.com; mains $21-36, theme park admission required; ⏱11:30am-park closing; 🛜📄📶; 🖥Disney, 🚋Disney, monorail Disney) Sparkling belly dancers shimmy and shake past the massive pillars and around the tables of the Sultan's Palace, magnificently decorated with mosaic tiles, rich velvets and sparkling gold. While the lamb kebabs, vegetable couscous and other basics are disappointing, the windowless elegance is a fun escape from the searing sun and kids love to join in the dancing.

✖ Animal Kingdom

Plenty of quick counter-service joints disguised behind African names and offering nods to a somewhat tribal feel define eating options at Animal Kingdom.

Flame Tree Barbecue
BARBECUE $$

(Map p262; www.disneyworld.disney.go.com; mains $8-18, theme park admission required; ⏱11am-6pm; 🛜📶; 🖥Disney) Counter-

DISNEY DINNER SHOWS

Disney's three dinner shows sell out early, so make your reservation for these up to 180 days in advance; you can cancel up to 48 hours in advance with no penalty. They are each held at a Disney resort, include beer and wine, and do not require theme park admission.

Hoop-Dee-Doo Musical Revue (Map p262; ☑ 407-939-3463, 407-824-2803; www.disney-world.disney.go.com; 4510 N Wilderness Trail, Disney's Fort Wilderness Resort; adult $55-70, child $28-36; ⊙ 4pm, 6:15pm & 8:30pm daily, hours vary; ➡; ☑ Disney, ☑ Disney) Nineteenth-century vaudeville show at Disney's Fort Wilderness Resort, with ribs delivered to your table in metal buckets, corny jokes, and the audience singing along to 'Hokey Pokey' and 'My Darling Clementine.' This is one of Disney's longest-running shows and is great fun, once you grab your washboard and get into the spirit of it all.

Mickey's Backyard Barbecue (Map p262; ☑ 407-939-3463, 407-824-1593; www.disney-world.disney.go.com; 4510 N Fort Wilderness Trail, Disney's Fort Wilderness Resort; adult $50-60, child $36-40; ⊙ 6:30pm; ➡; ☑ Disney, ☑ Disney) The only dinner theater with Disney characters. Join in on country-and-western singin', ho-down style stompin' and goofy Mickey antics at this Disney favorite.

Spirit of Aloha (Map p262; ☑ 407-939-3463; www.disneyworld.disney.go.com; 1600 Seven Seas Dr, Disney's Polynesian Resort; adult $60-75, child $30-40; ⊙ 5:15pm & 8:15pm; ☑ Disney, ☑ Disney, monorailDisney) Hula-clad men and women leap around the stage, dance and play with fire in this South Pacific–style luau at Disney's Polynesian Resort. Pulled pork, barbecue ribs and island-themed specialties like pineapple-coconut bread are served family-style.

service barbecue ribs and chicken, a favorite with in-the-know Disney fans.

Yak and Yeti
ASIAN $$

(Map p262; ☑ 407-939-3463, 407-824-9384; www.disneyworld.disney.go; mains $14-29, theme park admission required; ⊙ 11am-park closing; ☎➡➡; ☑ Disney) Sharing the name of Kathmandu's exclusive digs in the real Nepal, decorated with a vaguely Nepalese-infused decor, and serving pan-fried noodles, pot stickers, tempura and icy Tsingtao, this recommended getaway at the base of Mt Everest transports you from Disney to the Himalayas. The food is surprisingly good, and is one of the best bets for for eating inside the park.

✖ Hollywood Studios

Writer's Stop
BAKERY $

(Map p262; www.disneyworld.disney.go.com; mains $6-12, theme park admission required; ⊙ 9am-park closing; ☎➡; ☑ Disney, ☑ Disney) Decent coffee and sweets in a small shop designed to look like an independent bookstore. If it's not too crowded, the few comfy chairs around a TV screening Disney cartoons make a good place to rest.

★ Sci-Fi Dine-In Theater
AMERICAN $$

(Map p262; ☑ 407-939-3463; www.disneyworld.disney.go.com; mains $13-30, theme park admission required; ⊙ 11am-park closing; ➡; ☑ Disney, ☑ Disney) Burgers, ribs and glow-in-the-dark drinks served drive-in-movie style. Climb into your convertible cadillac, order from the car hop, sip on a Lunar Landing and sit back for a silly horror movie or sci-fi flick. This is Disney theming at its best.

There are a handful of picnic tables in the back, so if you want your table in a car, request one.

★ 50's Prime Time Café
AMERICAN $$

(Map p262; ☑ 407-939-3463; www.disneyworld.disney.go.com; mains $13-21, theme park admission required; ⊙ 11am-park closing; ☎➡; ☑ Disney, ☑ Disney) Step into a quintessential 1950s home for a home-cooked meal, including Grandma's Chicken-Pot-Pie, Aunt Liz's Golden Fried Chicken and Mom's Old-Fashioned Pot Roast, served up on a Formica tabletop. Waitresses in pink plaid and white aprons banter playfully and admonish those diners who don't finish their meals, putting their elbows on the table with a sassy 'shame, shame, shame.'

Hollywood Brown Derby Lounge   TAPAS $$

(Map p262; ☑ 407-939-3463; www.disneyworld.
disney.go.com; dishes $8-18; ☺ 11am-park closing;
🛜 🚻; ☐ Disney, ☻ Disney) Upscale small-bite
menu with lump-crab cocktail, mussels and
beef sliders, and an excellent selection of
cocktails. It's generally pretty easy to snag
a table at the bistro-style sidewalk patio, a
great place to relax and people-watch over
a flight of scotch, champagne, martinis
or margaritas, or order a drink to go. Not
exactly fast food, but reservations are not
accepted.

Hollywood Brown Derby   AMERICAN $$$

(Map p262; ☑ 407-939-3463; www.disneyworld.
disney.go.com; mains $18-32, theme park admis-
sion required; ☺ 11:30am-park closing; 🛜 🚻;
☐ Disney, ☻ Disney) Semi-upscale surround-
ings modeled after the LA original, with an
odd selection of gourmet eats ranging from
a noodle bowl with wok-fried coconut tofu
to Sam Adams–braised short ribs and, of
course, that Derby classic, the Cobb salad.
This is heavy fare, not the place for a quick
light lunch.

✗ Disney's BoardWalk

The lovely waterfront stretch around Disney's BoardWalk Inn, which has candy-
striped surrey bikes for rent, a bakery and a
microbrew pub, makes a relaxing spot for a
meal. It's an easy boat ride here from Epcot
or Hollywood Studios.

Flying Fish   SEAFOOD $$$

(Map p262; ☑ 407-939-3463, 407-939-2359;
www.disneyworld.disney.go.com; mains $26-39;
☺ 5-10pm; 🚻; ☻ Disney) Flying Fish, specializing in complicated and innovative seafood dishes, consistently ranks as one of the
best upscale dining spots at Disney. Make
reservations well in advance for the limit-
ed-seating five-course prix-fix wine-pairing
menu. Kids' meals are significantly less expensive (from $6 to $15),

Kouzzina by Cat Cora   GREEK $$$

(Map p262; ☑ 407-939-3463, 407-939-2380; www.
disneyworld.disney.go.com; mains $15-35; ☺ 7-
11am & 5-10:30pm; 🚻; ☻ Disney) Though it can
be rather loud and hectic, Kouzzina boasts
a particularly interesting menu. Pop in for
breakfast of blueberry-orange pancakes and
chicken sausage on your way to Hollywood
Studios, or cinnamon-stewed chicken and
chilled ouzo on your way home!

✗ Downtown Disney

Ghiradelli Soda Fountain
& Chocolate Shop   ICE CREAM $

(Map p262; www.disneyworld.disney.go.com; ice
creams $2-8; ☺ 10:30am-11:30pm; 🅿 🛜 🚻;
☐ Disney, ☻ Disney, ☐ Lynx 50) Decadent ice-
cream concoctions involving entire chocolate bars blended into milkshakes.

Earl of Sandwich   SANDWICHES $

(Map p262; www.disneyworld.disney.go.com; sandwiches $5-8; ☺ 8:30am-11pm; 🅿 🛜 🚻; ☐ Disney,
☻ Disney, ☐ Lynx 50) Surprisingly good toasted sandwiches ranging from basic to exotic.
One of the most satisfying lunches at Disney,
with plenty of bang for your buck; but in the
end, it's a fast-food sandwich chain.

Fresh-A-Peel   AMERICAN $

(Map p262; www.disneyworld.disney.go.com;
mains $5-12; ☺ 9:30am-11:30pm, to midnight Fri
& Sat; 🅿 🛜 🚻; ☐ Disney, ☻ Disney, ☐ Lynx 50)
With nitrate-free hot dogs served on whole-
grain buns, veggie burgers, turkey burgers
and 'popped chips,' this is the closest to
health food you'll find at Disney.

Paradiso 37   SOUTH AMERICAN $$

(Map p262; ☑ 407-934-3700; www.paradiso37.
com; mains $15-25; ☺ 11:30am-11pm Sun-Thu,
to midnight Fri & Sat; 🅿 🛜 🚻; ☐ Disney, ☻ Lynx
50) With more than 15 tequila flights on
the menu, an impressive cocktail list and a
menu representing 37 countries of North,
South and Central America (or so it claims),
this contemporary waterfront spot is one of
Downtown Disney's best bets.

Though Paradiso 37 is family friendly, with
an excellent 'little tykes' menu, the mood
becomes decidedly barlike as the night pro-
gresses, and there's live music on the weekends. Call directly for reservations – it often
has more flexibility and openings than Disney
Dining, and try for a seat on the back patio.

T-Rex Cafe   AMERICAN $$

(Map p262; ☑ 407-828-8739; www.disneyworld.dis-
ney.go.com; mains $12-24; ☺ 11am-11pm Sun-Thu,
to midnight Fri & Sat; 🅿 🛜 🚻; ☐ Disney, ☻ Disney,
☐ Lynx 50) Over-the-top multisensory overload, with massive autotronic dinosaurs,
volcanoes erupting, light shows and meteor
showers every 15 minutes. The menu features
Woolly Mammoth Chicken, Caveman Punch
and Chocolate Extinction – you get the idea.
Kids will love it and the food is better than
you might expect.

✕ Resort Hotels

★ 'Ohana
AMERICAN $$
(Map p262; ☑ 407-939-3463; www.disneyworld.
disney.go.com; 1600 Seven Seas Blvd, Disney's
Polynesian Resort; mains $15-30; ⊘ 7:30-11am &
5-10pm; ⊕; ⌨ Disney, ⛴ Disney, monorail Disney)
The Polynesian's signature restaurant evokes
a South Pacific feel with rock-art animals,
a huge oak-burning grill cooking up mas-
sive kebabs of meat, and demonstrations
of hula and limbo dancing, coconut racing
and other Polynesian-themed shenanigans.
The only thing on the menu is the all-you-
can-eat family-style kebabs and veggies, slid
off skewers directly onto the giant wok-like
platters on the table. Breakfast is a Lilo and
Stitch character meal.

★ Boma
BUFFET $$
(Map p262; ☑ 407-938-4744, 407-939-3463; www.
disneyworld.disney.go.com; 2901 Osceola Pkwy, Disney's Animal Kingdom Lodge; adult/child breakfast
$23/13, dinner $40/19; ⊘ 7:30-11am & 4:30-9:30pm;
⊕; ⌨ Disney) Several steps above Disney's usual buffet options, this African-inspired eatery
offers wood-roasted meats, interesting soups
like coconut curried chicken and plenty of salads. Handsomely furnished with dark woods,
decorated with African art and tapestries, and
flanked by garden-view windows on one side,
Boma offers not only good food but unusually
calm and pleasant surrounds.

Sanaa
AFRICAN $$
(Map p262; ☑ 407-939-3463; www.disneyworld.
disney.go.com; 3701 Osceola Pkwy, Kidani Village,
Disney's Animal Kingdom Lodge; mains $12-22;
⊘ 11:30am-3pm & 5-9:30pm; ⏚⊕; ⌨ Disney)
Lovely cafe with savanna views – giraffes,
ostriches and zebras graze out the window.
You almost forget you're in Orlando, but,
hey, that's Disney. Try slow-cooked and tan-
doori chicken, ribs, lamb or shrimp; the de-
licious salad sampler with tasty watermelon,
cucumber and fennel salad; and a mango
margarita.

★ Jiko
AFRICAN $$$
(☑ 407-938-4733, 407-939-3463; www.disney-
world.disney.go.com; 2901 Osceola Pkwy, Disney's
Animal Kingdom Lodge; mains $24-35; ⊘ 5:30-
10pm; ⏚⊕; ⌨ Disney) Excellent food, with
plenty of grains, vegetables and creative
twists, a tiny bar and rich African surrounds
make this a Disney favorite for both quality
and theming. You can relax with a glass of
wine on the hotel's back deck, alongside the
giraffes and other African beasts.

For a less-expensive option, enjoy an appetizer (the Taste of Africa features various
dips and crackers) at the bar. Swing by for
dinner, or at least a cocktail, after a day at
Animal Kingdom.

Victoria & Albert's
AMERICAN $$$
(Map p262; ☑ 407-939-3463; www.disneyworld.
disney.go.com; 4401 Floridian Way, Disney's Grand
Floridian Resort; prix fixe $135, wine pairing extra
$65; ⊘ 5-10:30pm) Indulge yourself in the
earthy, cream-colored Victorian-inspired de-
cor at this elegant restaurant, the crème de
la crème of Orlando's dining scene and one
of its most coveted reservations. The seven-
course meal, complete with crystal and live
cello music, oozes romance.

Dinner at the intimate Chef's Table or
Queen Victoria's room includes 10 courses.
This is the only place in Disney that does not
allow kids. If you have children, consider re-
serving a spot at Disney's Children Activity
Center (p290) at Disney's Polynesian Resort,
an easy two stops away on the monorail.

California Grill
AMERICAN $$$
(Map p262; ☑ 407-939-3463; www.disneyworld.
disney.go.com; 4600 World Dr, Disney's Contemporary Resort; mains $32-60; ⊘ 5-10pm; ⊕; ⌨ Dis-
ney, ⛴ Disney, monorail Disney) Earning consistent oohs and aahs from locals and repeat
Disney guests, this rooftop classic boasts
magnificent views of Magic Kingdom fireworks and offers everything from quirky sushi to triple-cheese flatbread. Reservations
are very difficult to secure, so make them as
close to 180 days in advance as possible.

Narcoossee's
SEAFOOD $$$
(Map p262; ☑ 407-939-3463; www.disneyworld.dis-
ney.go.com; 4401 Floridian Dr, Disney's Grand Florid-
ian Resort; mains $21-40; ⊘ 4:30-10pm; ⊕; ⌨ Dis-
ney, ⛴ Disney, monorail Disney) Muted waterfront
dining on the boat dock at the Grand Florid-
ian makes a convenient, relaxing and lovely
respite if you've been at Magic Kingdom for
the afternoon and want to return after dinner
for the parade and fireworks. Though offer-
ing primarily seafood, it also serves duck, filet
mignon and free-range chicken.

Artist Point
AMERICAN $$$
(Map p262; ☑ 407-939-3463; www.disneyworld.
disney.go.com; 901 Timberline Dr, Disney's Wilderness Lodge; mains $21-43; ⊘ 5:30-10pm; ⏚⊕;
⌨ Disney, ⛴ Disney) Handsome arts-and-crafts
decor with an American West twist and

Pacific Northwest fare, including roast venison and salmon, grilled buffalo and berry cobbler. The bar, reminiscent of an old lodge, opens earlier – take your apple martini to the outdoor patio.

Blue Zoo SEAFOOD $$$
(Map p262; ☑407-934-1111; www.swandolphinrestaurants.com; 1500 Epcot Resorts Blvd, Walt Disney World Dolphin Resort; mains $28-34; ☺5-11pm; 🛜; 🖵Disney, 🚢Disney) Floor-to-ceiling silver threads shimmer in columns at this flashy blue-infused hot spot, evoking a trendy, urban spin on the underwater theme. Excellent seafood makes this one of the few restaurants at Disney where you feel like *maybe* you've gotten your money's worth. A truncated menu in the bar offers less-expensive choices.

Citrico's MEDITERRANEAN $$$
(Map p262; ☑407-939-3463; www.disneyworld.disney.go.com; 4401 Floridian Way, Disney's Grand Floridian Resort; mains $18-34; ☺5:30-10pm; 🛗; 🖵Disney, 🚢Disney, monorail Disney) An extensive wine list and handsome northern California ambience set this low-key brasserie apart from other Disney restaurants; it falls between the hectic family style and self-consciously upscale style, and serves up tasty and fresh eclectic fare.

🍷 Drinking & Entertainment

Disney has enough drinking and entertainment options to keep you busy with something different every night of the week for a month straight. There's dueling pianos, margaritas to go, animal safaris, dinner with princesses, fireworks, light shows, vaudeville dinner theater, country-and-western dancing with Mickey, parades...the list goes on. At Disney, the problem is not finding something to do, but rather finding time to do nothing.

Downtown Disney and the much smaller Disney's BoardWalk are Walt Disney World's designated shopping, drinking and entertainment districts, but you'll find bars and sometimes live music at most Disney resorts and within the theme parks. Magic Kingdom sells beer and wine only, and the only place to find it is dinner at Be Our Guest (p283); and Epcot's World Showcase offers a tantalizing smorgasbord of spirits from around the world.

Go to www.buildabettermousetrip.com/activity-outdoormovie.php for a schedule of free outdoor screenings of Disney movies at Disney hotels, including the highly recommended Chip 'n' Dale Campfire Singalong (p271), at Disney's Fort Wilderness.

One of the best shows at Walt Disney World is Finding Nemo: The Musical in Animal Kingdom. Outside the theme parks, Cirque du Soleil La Nouba (p258) fuses gymnastic superfeats with dance, light, music... and Disney.

★Belle Vue Room BAR
(Map p262; ☑407-939-6200; www.disneyworld.disney.go.com; 2101 Epcot Resorts Blvd, Disney's BoardWalk Inn; ☺7-11am & 5pm-midnight) On the 2nd floor of Disney's BoardWalk Inn, this is an excellent place for a quiet drink. It's more like a sitting room than a bar: you can relax and play a board game, listen to classic radio shows like *Lone Ranger*, or simply take your drink to a rocking chair on the balcony and watch the comings and goings along Disney's Boardwalk.

Raglan Road PUB
(Map p262; ☑407-938-0300; www.raglanroad.com; Downtown Disney; ☺11am-midnight, live music from 4pm; 🛜🛗) Traditional Irish ditties. Irish dancing, solid tasty Irish fare, cozy pub decor and beer flights with Guinness, Harp, Smithwicks and Kilkenny complete the leprechaun mood.

Dawa Bar BAR
(Map p262; www.disneyworld.disney.go.com; Animal Kingdom; theme park admission required; ☺11am-park closing; 🛜🛗; 🖵Disney) The best place in Animal Kingdom for a cocktail. Sidle up to the thatch-roofed bar, order a sugarcane *mojito* and rest those Disney-weary bones.

Big River Grille & Brewing Works BREWERY
(Map p262; ☑407-560-0253; www.disneyworld.disney.go.com; Disney's BoardWalk; ☺11:30am-11pm) Open-air microbrewery with outdoor seating along the water.

ESPN Club SPORTS BAR
(Map p262; ☑407-939-5100; www.disneyworld.disney.go.com; Disney's BoardWalk; ☺11:30am-1am) So many TVs screening the hottest games that even in the bathroom you won't miss a single play.

Jellyrolls THEME BAR
(Map p262; ☑407-560-8770; www.disneyworld.disney.go.com; Disney's BoardWalk; admission $12; ☺7pm-2am) Comedians on dueling pianos encourage the audience to partake in all kinds of musical silliness and sing-alongs.

House of Blues   LIVE MUSIC
(Map p262; ☑ 407-934-2583; www.houseofblues.
com; Downtown Disney; ◷ 10am-11pm Mon-Thu,
to midnight Fri & Sat, 10:30am-11pm Sun; 🛜📶;
🖳 Disney, 🛥 Disney, 🚌 Lynx 50) Top acts visit
this national chain serving Southern cooking and blues. It's particularly popular for
the Sunday's Gospel Brunch buffet.

Atlantic Dance Hall   CLUB
(Map p262; www.disneyworld.disney.go.com; Disney's BoardWalk; ◷ 9pm-2am, admission over
21yr only) Blaring Top 40 tunes, dancing and
a massive screen with music videos by request. If you really want to shake your boo-
tie, this is your only Disney option, and it
tends to be relatively empty. Otherwise, no
reason to come here.

🛍 Shopping

While there are endless stores throughout
Walt Disney World, don't expect to find the
same things in all the parks and resorts.
Most stores are thematically oriented, so after the Star Wars ride you'll find lots of *Star
Wars* stuff; after the Winnie the Pooh ride
you'll find lots of *Winnie the Pooh* stuff; and
after the Indiana Jones ride you'll find, well,
an *Indiana Jones* fedora, of course. Unless
you're looking for something related to a
specific story, movie or character, the fun
of shopping at Walt Disney World is in the
browsing.

For questions about shopping at Disney,
including details on returning and exchanging items purchased at the parks or checking the status of something you had sent to
your home, call **Disney Parks Merchan-
dise Guest Services** (☑ 877-560-6477).

🏛 Theme Parks

For an international twist to your Disney souvenir, walk around the world at Epcot. Buy
a belly-dancer kit in Morocco, tartan shawls
and Mickey Mouse shortbread cookies in
the UK, and a pink bejeweled wine stopper
in France. Japan has a store filled with Hello Kitty items, and in Germany you can buy
Steiff animals and make your own dolls.

Classic Disney shops, with mouse-ear
Rice Krispies, crystal Donald Ducks and
princess-themed everything, line Magic
Kingdom's Main Street leading up to Cinderella's Castle, making this the best place for
quintessential and off-the-radar shopping
pleasures.

DON'T MISS

FINDING NEMO – THE MUSICAL

Finding Nemo: the Musical (Map
p262; www.disneyworld.disney.go.com;
Animal Kingdom; theme park admission
required; ◷ several shows daily; 📶; 🖳 Disney) Arguably the best show at Walt
Disney World and a favorite of both kids
and adults, this sophisticated musical
theater performance features massive
and elaborate puppets on stage and
down the aisles, incredible set design
and fantastic acting.

The music was composed by Robert
Lopez and Kirsten Anderson-Lopez, who
also wrote *Frozen*'s Academy Award–
winning *Let It Go*, and the spectacular
puppets were created by Michael Curry,
the creative and artistic force behind the
puppets in Broadway's *The Lion King*.

Bibbidee Bobbidee Boutique   CHILDREN
(Map p262; ☑ 407-939-7895; www.disneyworld.dis-
ney.go.com; Magic Kingdom; hair & make up from
$49; ◷ 10am-8pm, hours vary) Inside Cinder-
ella's Castle, fairy godmothers finalize your
kid's transformation from shorts and T-shirt
to bedazzling princess with fanciful hairstyl-
ing and make up.

Girls aged from three to 12 can choose
from the Coach (hair and make up from
$55), the Crown (add nails, from $60), the
Courtyard (add T-shirt and tutu, from $95)
or the Castle (hair, make up, nails, full costume and photograph, from $190). For boys,
there's the Knight Package (hair, a sword
and a shield, $15). It's a more expensive and
elaborate version of the spiky green hair or a
pink updo and Disney sequins ($10 to $20)
at the Harmony Barber Shop on Magic Kingdom's Main Street. There's a second Bibbidee
Bobbidee Boutique in Downtown Disney.

🏛 Downtown Disney

Once Upon a Toy   CHILDREN
(Map p262; ☑ 407-824-4321; www.disneyworld.
disney.go.com; Downtown Disney; ◷ 10am-11pm;
🖳 Disney, 🛥 Disney, 🚌 Lynx 50) Design a personalized My Little Pony, build your own
light saber and create your own tiara at one
of the best toy stores anywhere. You'll find
old-school classics such as Mr Potato Head
and Lincoln Logs, board games, action figures, stuffed animals and more.

Lego Imagination Center
CHILDREN

(Map p262; ☑407-828-0065; www.disneyworld. disney.go.com; Downtown Disney; ☺9am-11pm; ⊡Disney, ⊛Disney, ⊡Lynx 50) Life-size Lego creations, tables to create your own masterpieces and a wall of individually priced Lego pieces.

World of Disney
SOUVENIRS

(Map p262; ☑407-939-6224; www.disneyworld. disney.go.com; Downtown Disney; ☺9am-11pm; ⊡Disney, ⊛Disney, ⊡Lynx 50) Room after room of Disney everything at this Disney megasuperduper store.

ⓘ Information

CHILD CARE

Disney's Children Activity Center (☑407-939-3463; www.disneyworld.disney.com.go; select Disney resort hotels; per child per hour $12, 2hr minimum, incl dinner; ☺hours vary) Five Disney resorts offer excellent drop-off children's activity centers for children aged three to 12, with organized activities, toys, art supplies, meals and a Disney movie in the evening. This is particularly handy if you'd like to enjoy a quiet meal at a Disney resort, as you do not have to be a hotel guest to use the centers.

Activity centers include Simba's Cubhouse at Disney's Animal Kingdom Lodge; Neverland Club at Disney's Polynesian Resort; Cub's Den at Disney's Wilderness Lodge; Sandcastle Club at Disney's Beach Club Resort; and Camp Dolphin at Walt Disney World Dolphin Hotel. Reservations, recommended at all locations and required at Camp Dolphin, can be made up to 180 days in advance.

Kid's Nite Out (☑407-828-0920; www. kidsniteout.com; 1/2/3/4 kids per hour $16/18.50/21/23.50, 4hr minimum, plus $10 travel fee; ☺sitters available 24/7) Walt Disney World uses Kid's Nite Out for private in-room child care for children ages six months to 12 years. You can also hire a helper if you need an extra pair of hands when you're out and about, but note that you'll have to pay the caregiver's theme park ticket.

Credit cards only; reservations accepted up to three months in advance.

INTERNET ACCESS

Complimentary wi-fi is available throughout Walt Disney World parks, entertainment districts, theme parks, water parks and resort hotels. Select Walt Disney World Resort network, and call ☑407-827-2732 if you have technical problems.

KENNELS

With the exception of select campsites at Disney's Fort Wilderness Resort & Campground, pets are not allowed anywhere at Walt Disney World.

Best Friends Pet Care at Walt Disney World

(☑877-493-9738; www.bestfriendspetcare. com/waltdisneyworldresort.com; 2510 Bonnet Creek Pkwy; per day $18-72, overnight $38-78; ☺1hr before Walt Disney World parks open to 1hr after closing) Offers overnight boarding and day care for dogs, cats and 'pocket pets.' Rates vary depending on how many walks and extra perks you'd like, and are a bit less for guests staying at a Disney hotel.

Reservations and written proof of vaccination (DHLPP, rabies and Bordetella for dogs; FVRCP and rabies for cats) are required.

MAPS

The free *Walt Disney World Resort Map* has a transportation-network chart. You'll get a free map of each individual park, color coded according to thematically divided lands, and a *Times Guide*, with character greeting and show times, when you enter each park. Don't lose these because, strangely, they're not easily available beyond the entrance gate. Guest Services have multilanguage maps.

MEDICAL SERVICES

Medical facilities are located within each theme park and at both Disney water parks. The closest hospital is Florida Hospital Celebration Health (p260). If you need care at your hotel room, Doctors On Call Service (p260) provides medical service 24/7.

Lake Buena Vista Centra Care (☑407-934-2273, for pickup 407-938-0650; www. centracare.org/visitors; 12500 S Apopka Vineland; ☺8am-midnight Mon-Fri, to 8pm Sat & Sun) Nonemergency care medical facility, offering adult and pediatric care, x-rays, and free transportation to and from area hotels and attractions.

MONEY

You will find ATMs throughout Walt Disney World. Guest Services at each park offer limited currency exchange.

OPENING HOURS

Theme park hours change not only by season, but day to day within any given month. Generally, parks open at 8am or 9am and close sometime between 6pm and 10pm. Every day one of the four theme parks opens early or closes late for guests of Walt Disney World hotels only – these 'Magic Hours' are a major perk of staying at a Disney resort hotel.

PARKING

If you're staying at a Disney resort, parking at all the theme parks and hotels is free; otherwise, it costs $17 per day. Parking tickets bought at one park are good all day for all Disney parks. Parking lots sit directly outside the gates of all the parks except for Magic Kingdom; if you're driving to Magic Kingdom, you have to park at the Transportation & Ticket Center and take a monorail or ferry to the park. Parking at Downtown Disney, the water parks, ESPN Wide World of Sports and all the golf courses is free, but there is no transportation from these attractions to any of the four theme parks. Valet parking at deluxe hotels costs $20 per day.

STROLLER RENTAL

Strollers (single/double per day $15/31, multi-day $13/27) are available on a first-come, first-served basis at Disney's four theme parks and Downtown Disney, and you can also purchase umbrella strollers.

TICKETS

Magic Your Way The minimal Walt Disney World base ticket, which allows access to one theme park for one day, costs $99 for adults and $93 for children aged between three and nine years for Magic Kingdom, and $5 less for the three other theme parks. From that, you can add days and options either when you first purchase your ticket or any time within the 14 days after the ticket is first used.

Multiple Days up to 10 The per-day cost drops 50% if you buy a seven-day or longer base ticket. Multiple-day tickets allow unlimited admission to all four of Disney's theme parks (but not the water parks), so you can go in and out of a theme park as many times as you'd like, *but you can only go to one theme park a day*. Tickets can be used anytime within 14 consecutive days, and expire 14 days after their first use.

NUMBER OF DAYS	PRICE ($)
2	188
3	274
4	294
5	304
6	314
7	324
8	334
9	344
10	354

Children's admission costs $10 to $20 less than the adult multiday ticket.

Park Hopper ($40 to $60) Allows unlimited access to any of the four theme parks during the course of one day, so you can spend the morning at Magic Kingdom, the afternoon at Animal Kingdom and head to Epcot for the evening.

Water Park Fun & More ($60) Includes one admission to your choice of water parks Blizzard Beach (p274) and Typhoon Lagoon (p274), miniature golf courses Fantasia Gardens (p276) and Winter Summerland (p276), DisneyQuest Indoor Interactive Theme Park (p275; at Downtown Disney), ESPN's Wide World of Sports (p259), and Disney's Oak Trail Golf Course (with reserved tee time). You will be given one Fun Pass for each day of your Magic Your Way ticket, and you can use these passes to access whatever you'd like, whenever you'd like; for instance, if you have a five-day ticket and you add this option, you can go to a water park in the morning, golf in the afternoon and DisneyQuest in the evening, and you'll have used three of your five Fun passes. The price for this option is the same regardless of how many days your Magic Your Way base ticket includes.

No Expiration Unused days of multiple-day tickets do not expire after 14 days. Note this add-on option is not available for tickets purchased online: you must purchase by phone or at theme park front desks. The price varies from $22 if added to a two-day ticket, to $67 if added to a four-day ticket, to $213 if added to a 10-day ticket.

Water Park Fun & More and Park Hopper ($86) Buy these options together, and save some money.

Disney Dining Disney offers an incredibly complicated Disney Dining Plan to guests staying at a Disney resort hotel; see www.disneyworld.disney.go.com for prices. If you decide to purchase a dining plan, do not do so when you make your room reservation. You may not get a full refund of your dining plan if you need to cancel, and you can add a dining plan anytime up until the day you check into your hotel.

TOURIST INFORMATION

For on-site questions and reservations, head to Guest Services, just inside each theme park, or the concierge at any Disney resort hotel. Any time you call Disney, you'll be prompted to give all kinds of information they use for customer research. Keep pressing '0' – just cut them off mid-sentence – until they ask whether or not you're a Florida resident. You'll have to answer that question before you get a real human being.

Important Telephone Numbers

Walt Disney World (☎ 407-939-5277) Central number for all things Disney, including packages, tickets, room and dining reservations, and general questions about hours and scheduled events. They'll connect you to anything you need.

Walt Disney World Dining (☎ 407-939-3463) Book priority dining reservations up to 180 days in advance, including character meals, dinner shows and specialty dining. You can

ⓘ SCOOTER, STROLLER & WHEELCHAIR RENTAL

Tackling Orlando's theme parks requires a huge amount of walking and standing, and it's exhausting for all ages. Sure, you can rent at the parks, but they don't all take reservations and it's expensive. Instead, reserve one online and have it delivered to your hotel.

Magical Stroller Rentals (☑407-494-8806; www.magicalstrollerrental.com; 1/4/8/11-14 nights from $40/60/80/100)

Orlando Stroller Rental (☑800-281-0084; www.orlandostrollerrentals.com; 1/4/8/11-14 days from $40/60/80/100)

Walker Mobility (☑407-518-6000; www.walkermobility.com; strollers 1/4/8/11-14 days from $35/55/65/80, wheelchairs per day $30, scooters 2/3/4 days from $65/90/120)

also book online, by phone or through your My Disney Experience (p272) app.

Walt Disney World Recreation (☑407-939-7529) Horseback riding, boating and more.

Walt Disney World Tours (☑407-939-8687) Tours at all of Disney's four theme parks.

Walt Disney World Lost & Found (☑407-824-4245) Items are sent to this central location at the end of each day; also see Guest Services at individual parks.

UK telephone contacts My Disney Experience ☑0800 16 90 749; Dining ☑0800 16 90 748; Resort Hotel Reservations ☑0800 16 90 730.

TRAVELERS WITH DISABILITIES

The *Guidebook for Guests with Disabilities*, available at Guest Services at each park and on Disney's website, has maps and ride-by-ride guides with information on closed captioning, and accommodating wheelchairs and seeing-eye dogs. On many rides, folks in wheelchairs will be waved to the front of the line. You can borrow braille guides and audiotape guides from Guest Services and rent wheelchairs ($12) and ECVs ($50) at each of Disney's theme parks and at Downtown Disney. All chairs are first-come, first-served; reservations are not possible.

Public transportation is wheelchair accessible and select resort hotels offer features and services for guests with disabilities. Call ☑407-824-4321 or ☑407-827-5141 for further information.

USEFUL WEBSITES

Google anything to do with Disney, and you'll find pages of blogs and websites offering planning tips, advice and mind-boggling details on restaurants and attractions. It's easy to suffer information overload, but they can be helpful. Here are some comprehensive and reputable favorites.

Walt Disney World (www.disneyworld.disney.go.com) Official Disney World website.

Walt Disney World Information (www.wdwinfo.com) Exceptionally readable and thorough.

All Ears (www.allears.net) News, menus and more.

MouseSavers (www.mousesavers.com) Disney discounts.

Build a Better Mousetrip (www.buildabettermousetrip.com) Movie schedules and planning.

Kenny the Pirate (http://kennythepirate.com) Everything you need to know about meeting Disney characters.

Disney Food Blog (www.disneyfoodblog.com) All things Disney dining, including lists of where to satisfy specific dietary needs.

Mouse on Wheels (www.themouseonwheels.com) Guide to navigating Disney in a wheelchair.

ⓘ Getting There & Away

BUS

Orlando's Lynx (p229) bus 50 connects the downtown central station to Disney's Transportation & Ticket Center and Downtown Disney, but it's an hour ride. Bus 56 runs along Hwy 192, between Kissimmee and Disney's Transportation & Ticket Center. From there, you can connect to any theme park or hotel.

CAR & MOTORCYCLE

Disney lies 25 minutes' drive south of downtown Orlando. Take I-4 to well-signed exits 64, 65 or 67.

Alamos and National car rental is available inside the Walt Disney World Dolphin Resort.

AAA Car Care Center (☑407-824-0976, car-rental shuttle 407-824-3470; 1000 W Car Care Dr; ☉6am-8pm Mon-Fri, to 6pm Sat & Sun) Full-service garage, Car Care One services (roadside assistance including towing, flat tire and battery jump-starts) and Alamo and National car-rental desks. Free shuttles to/from Disney resort hotels provided.

SHUTTLE

Call one day in advance to arrange personalized transport to/from Universal Orlando Resort and SeaWorld with Mears Transportation (p229). It costs about $25 per round-trip per person.

TAXI

Taxis can be found at hotels, theme parks, the Transportation & Ticket Center and Downtown Disney.

ℹ Getting Around

The Disney transportation system utilizes boat, bus and a monorail to shuttle visitors to hotels, theme parks and other attractions within the resort. The Transportation & Ticket Center operates as the main hub of this system. Note that it can take an hour to get from point A to point B using the Disney transportation system, and there is not always a direct route. Pick up a copy of the *Walt Disney World Transportation Guide/Map* at the resorts or from Guest Services at the parks, or download it in advance.

TO & FROM AIRPORT

Disney's Magical Express (☎ 866-599-0951; www.disneyworld.disney.go.com) If you're staying at a Walt Disney World hotel and are arriving into the Orlando International Airport (as opposed to Sanford), arrange in advance for complimentary luggage handling and deluxe bus transportation.

They will send you baggage labels in advance, collect your luggage at the airport, and if during your stay you transfer from one Disney hotel to another, the resort will transfer your luggage while you're off for the day.

BOAT

Disney Water Launches & Ferries (www.disneyworld.disney.go.com) Complimentary Disney boats connect Magic Kingdom to Magic Kingdom resorts and the Transportation & Ticket Center, and Epcot resorts to Hollywood Studios, Disney's BoardWalk and Epcot.

Water launches circulate directly between Magic Kingdom and Disney's Grand Floridian Resort and Disney's Polynesian Resort; a second route connects Magic Kingdom to Disney's Contemporary Resort, Disney's Fort Wilderness Resort & Campground and Disney's Wilderness Lodge; and a third route, utilizing 600-passenger ferries, connects Magic Kingdom to the Transportation & Ticket Center.

Boats also loop between Epcot, Hollywood Studios, Disney's BoardWalk, Disney's Yacht & Beach Club Resorts, and Walt Disney World Swan & Dolphin Hotels.

Finally, boats connect Downtown Disney to Downtown Disney resort hotels

BUS

Disney Buses (www.disneyworld.disney.go.com) Everything at Disney is accessible by a free bus (city-bus style) from other areas, but not all destinations are directly connected.

Buses from Downtown Disney, for example, do not connect directly to any theme parks.

MONORAIL

Disney Monorail (www.disneyworld.disney.go.com) Three separate monorail routes service select locations within Walt Disney World. The Resort Monorail loops between the Transportation & Ticket Center, Disney's Polynesian Resort, Disney's Grand Floridian Resort, Magic Kingdom and Disney's Contemporary Resort. A second monorail route connects the Transportation & Ticket Center directly to Magic Kingdom; and a third route connects the Transportation & Ticket Center directly to Epcot.

UNIVERSAL ORLANDO RESORT

Pedestrian-friendly Universal Orlando Resort offers fantastic rides, excellent children's attractions and entertaining shows. It's comparable to Walt Disney World, but Universal does everything just a bit smarter, funnier and more smoothly, as well as being smaller and easier to navigate. Instead of the seven dwarfs, there's *The Simpsons*. Instead of Donald Duck and Mickey Mouse, there's Spider Man. Universal offers pure, unabashed, adrenaline-pumped full-speed-ahead fun for the entire family. It's got spunk; it's got spirit; it's got attitude.

The Universal Orlando Resort consists of two theme parks – Islands of Adventure, with the bulk of the thrill rides, and Universal Studios, with movie-based attractions and shows; one entertainment and dining district (CityWalk); and four resort hotels. Small wooden shuttle boats and pleasant walking paths connect the entire resort, and Universal Orlando Resort's Express Pass system (see p306) can almost eliminate the stresses of long lines and the need for military-style plans of attack.

Universal is constantly updating and rethinking its attractions, pushing the limits of ride engineering and incorporating new movies and shows into its repertoire – rides close and new ones open at a regular pace. In 2010 Universal opened the Wizarding World of Harry Potter – Hogsmeade, a magnificently themed section within the Islands of Adventure theme park, and in 2014 Universal unveiled its Universal Studios counterpart, Diagon Alley.

👁 Sights

👁 Islands of Adventure

⭐ **Islands of Adventure** (Map p234; www.universalorlando.com; 6000 Universal Blvd; adult 1/2 days $96/136, child $89/129, multiday & multipark tickets available; ⏱9am-6pm, hours vary; 🚌Lynx 21, 37, 40, 🚢Universal) is just plain fun. Scream-it-from-the-rooftops, no-holds-barred, laugh-out-loud kind of fun. Superheroes zoom by on motorcycles, roller coasters whiz overhead, and plenty of rides will get you soaked. The park is divided into distinctly themed areas, each with rides, play areas, dining and other attractions. Harry Potter attractions are split between Wizarding World of Harry Potter – Hog-smeade (p296), at Islands of Adventure, and Wizarding World of Harry Potter – Diagon Alley (p297), at Universal Studios.

Marvel Super Hero Island   RIDE
(Map p234; www.universalorlando.com; theme park admission required; ⏱9am-6pm, hours vary; 🚗; 🚌Lynx 21, 37, 40) Bright, loud and fast moving, Marvel Super Hero Island is sensory overload and a thrill-lover's paradise. Don't miss the motion simulator **Amazing Adventures of Spider-Man** (Express Pass recommended), where super villains rendered in incredible 3-D are on the loose, jumping on your car and chasing you around the streets of New York City, and the wild and crazy **Incredible Hulk Coaster** (Express Pass).

BEST OF UNIVERSAL ORLANDO RESORT

Universal and its top-notch ride engineers have designed some of the most incredible simulated rides you'll see anywhere. It out-thrills and out-wows Disney hands down. Technology and creativity combine with a sense of humor and a disarming childlike passion for fun and silliness to create attractions that leave you, quite simply, awed. On top of that, Universal's Express Pass system (p306) almost eliminates line anxiety on all but a few rides, and, if you're OK riding without your friends and family, many rides offer single-rider lines that are usually much shorter than the standard line – always ask.

Universal Studios

➜ **The Simpsons Ride** (p298) *The Simpsons* creators James Brooks and Matt Groening helped create this simulated experience.

➜ **Hollywood Rip Ride Rockit** (p296) Hard-core coaster where you select your own soundtrack.

➜ **Revenge of the Mummy** (p297) Indoor coaster with fire and mummies.

➜ **Men in Black Alien Attack** (p298) Interactive family ride puts you face-to-face with aliens.

➜ **Harry Potter and the Escape from Gringotts** (p297) Coaster through the massive Gringotts Bank.

➜ **Despicable Me: Minion Mayhem** (p299) Become one of Gru's minions in this Universal simulation – 3-D at its best.

➜ **Transformers: The Ride 3-D** (p296) A must for Transformers fans

Islands of Adventure

➜ **Harry Potter and the Forbidden Journey** (p296) Ride through Hogwarts, past the cold chill of Dementors and into a quidditch match.

➜ **Incredible Hulk Coaster** (p294) Screams from this crown-jewel coaster echo throughout the park.

➜ **Amazing Adventures of Spider-Man** (p294) Don 3-D glasses and ride into New York City with Marvel Comics' classic superhero.

➜ **Dragon Challenge** (p296) Twist, turn and loop, feet dangling free, on one of two high-speed roller coasters, the Chinese Fireball or the Hungarian Horntail.

➜ **Dudley Do-Right's Ripsaw Falls** (p295) Classic water ride with a 75ft plunge.

At **Dr Doom's Fearfall** (Express Pass), you rocket 150ft up in the air and free-fall down. Comic-book characters patrol this area, so keep an eye out for your favorites and check your map for scheduled Meet and Greet times with Spider Man himself.

Toon Lagoon   RIDE
(Map p234; www.universalorlando.com; theme park admission required; ⊘9am-6pm, hours vary; ♿; ⊟Lynx 21, 37, 40) Island of Adventure's sparkly, lighthearted cartoon-themed Toon Lagoon transports visitors to the days when lazy weekends included nothing more than mornings watching Popeye and afternoons playing in the sprinkler. This is where you'll find most of Universal's water attractions, including **Popeye and Bluto's Bilge-Rat Barges** (Express Pass), a favorite that's short on thrills but high on silly soaking fun; and **Dudley Do-Right's Ripsaw Falls** (Express Pass), a classic with a short but steep fall.

Be warned that you will get drenched, so protect phones and cameras, wear water-friendly shoes, and bring a change of clothes. If you forget, there are of course plenty of shops that sell towels, flip-flops and clothes.

Jurassic Park   RIDE
(Map p234; www.universalorlando.com; theme park admission required; ⊘9am-6pm, hours vary; ♿; ⊟Lynx 21, 37, 40) Oddly quiet, with no screams or loud music and no neon colors or hawking vendors, this oasis of palm trees, greenery and ferns offers a handful of attractions with a prehistoric twist. **Jurassic Park River Adventure** (Express Pass) floats you past friendly vegetarian dinosaurs, and all seems well and good until...things go wrong and those grass-munchin' cuties are replaced with the stuff of nightmares.

To escape the looming teeth of the giant T Rex, you plunge 85ft to the water below. Little children might be terrified by the creatures, the dark and the plunge, but if yours are tough-as-nails they'll love it. At **Pterandoon Flyers**, kids can float gently over the lush landscape and robotic dinosaurs of Jurassic Park. Note that you must be between 36in and 56in tall to fly, and adults can't fly without a kid. Waits can be upwards of an hour for the 80-second ride and there's no Express Pass.

Lost Continent   SHOW
(Map p234; www.universalorlando.com; theme park admission required; ⊘9am-6pm, hours vary; ♿; ⊟Lynx 21, 37, 40) Magic and myth from across the seas and the pages of fantasy books inspire this mystical corner of the park. Here you'll find dragons and unicorns, psychic readings and fortune-tellers. And don't be startled if that fountain talks to you as you walk past. The **Mystic Fountain** banters sassily, soaking children with its waterspouts when they least expect it and engaging them in silly conversation.

And no, no one is hiding with a remote control. This is a talking fountain. At the swashbuckling **Eighth Voyage of Sinbad Stunt Show** (Express Pass), Sinbad and his sidekick Kabob must rescue Princess Amoura from the terrible Miseria and, of course, Sinbad has to tumble and jump around to do it.

Seuss Landing   RIDE, SHOW
(Map p234; www.universalorlando.com; theme park admission required; ⊘9am-6pm, hours vary; ♿; ⊟Lynx 21, 37, 40) Anyone who has fallen asleep to the reading of *Green Eggs and Ham* or learned to read with *Sam I Am* knows the world of Dr Seuss: the fanciful creatures, the lyrical names, the rhyming stories. Here, realized in magnificently designed 3-D form, is Dr Seuss' imagination. The Lorax guards his truffula trees; Thing One and Thing Two make trouble; and creatures from all kinds of Seuss favorites adorn the shops and the rides.

ORLANDO & WALT DISNEY WORLD UNIVERSAL ORLANDO RESORT

WIZARDING WORLD OF HARRY POTTER

The hottest thing to hit Orlando since Cinderella's Castle, and further expanded in 2014, the magnificently whimsical Wizarding World of Harry Potter invites muggles into JK Rowling's imagination. Alan Gilmore and Stuart Craig, art director and production designer for the films, collaborated closely with the Universal Orlando Resort engineers to create what is without exception the most fantastically realized themed experience in Florida. The detail and authenticity tickle the fancy at every turn, from the screeches of the mandrakes in the shop windows to the groans of Moaning Myrtle in the bathroom; keep your eyes peeled for magical happenings.

The Wizarding World of Harry Potter is divided into two sections, each with rides, attractions and over-the-top detailed theming: Hogsmeade sits in Islands of Adventure and Diagon Alley is in Universal Studios. If you have a park-to-park ticket, you can ride the Hogwarts Express from one section to the other.

Wizarding World of Harry Potter – Hogsmeade (Map p234; ☑ 407-363-8000; www.universalorlando.com; Islands of Adventure; theme park admission required; ⊙ 9am-6pm, hours vary; 🚌 Lynx 21, 37, 40) Poke around among the cobbled streets and impossibly crooked buildings of Hogsmeade; munch on Cauldron Cakes; and mail a card via Owl Post – all in the shadow of Hogwarts Castle. Two of Orlando's best rides are here – Harry Potter and the Forbidden Journey and Dragon Challenge. Come first thing when the park gates open, before the lines get too long and the crowds become unbearable. Guests staying at Universal Orlando Resort hotels get one hour early admission.

Harry Potter and the Forbidden Journey Wind through the corridors of Hogwarts, past talking portraits, Dumbledore's office and other well-known locations, to one of the best rides in Orlando. You'll feel the cold chill of Dementors, escape a dragon attack, join a quidditch match and soar over the castle with Harry, Hermione and Ron. Though it's not a fast-moving thrill ride, this is scary stuff. Little ones can enjoy the castle but sit out the ride with a parent in the Child Swap waiting room. There's a single-rider line as well, but it's tricky to find – ask at the Hogwarts entrance.

Dragon Challenge Gut-churning dueling roller coasters twist and loop, narrowly avoiding each other; inspired by the first task of the Triwizard Tournament in *Harry Potter & the Goblet of Fire*.

Drink Moose Juice or Goose Juice; eat Green Eggs and Ham; and peruse shelves of Dr Seuss books before riding through *The Cat in the Hat* or around and around on an elephant-bird from *Horton Hears a Who*. Seuss Landing is one of the best places for little ones in all of Orlando's theme parks, bringing the spirit and energy of Dr Seuss' vision to life. So come on in, walk into his world and take a spin on a fish.

⊙ Universal Studios

Divided geographically by film-inspired and region-specific architecture and ambience, and themed as a Hollywood backlot, **Universal Studios** (Map p234; ☑ 407-363-8000; www.universalorlando.com; 1000 Universal Studios Plaza; per 1/2 days adult $96/136, child $89/129, multiday & multipark tickets available; ⊙ from 9am; 🚌 Lynx 21, 37, 40, 🚢 Universal) has shows and magnificently designed simulation-heavy rides dedicated to silver-screen and TV icons. Drink Duff beer, a Homer favorite, in Springville; ride the Hogwarts Express into Diagon Alley; and sidle up to Lucille Ball on Hollywood Blvd. And if you're looking for thrills, Hollywood Rip Ride Rockit and Revenge of the Mummy are two of Orlando's best coasters.

For some downtime, a fenced-in grassy area with shade trees, flowers and views across the lagoon sits just across from the entrance to Woody Woodpecker's KidZone. Spread out a blanket and enjoy a snack, or simply chill out. It makes an excellent meeting spot.

Production Central   RIDE, SHOW
(Map p234; www.universalorlando.com; theme park admission required; ⊙ from 9am; 👶; 🚌 Lynx 21, 37, 40) Home to two of Universal's most talked-about rides, the incredible 3-D simulation **Transformers: The Ride 3-D** (Express

Ollivanders Wand Shop Floor-to-ceiling shelves crammed with dusty wand boxes and a winding staircase set the scene for a 10-minute show that brings to life the iconic scene in which the wand chooses the wizard. Come first thing, as the line quickly extends upwards of an hour.

Flight of the Hippogriff (Express Pass) Family-friendly coaster passes over Hagrid's Hut; listen for Fang's barks and don't forget to bow to Buckbeak!

Honeydukes Sweet Shop Bertie Botts Every Flavor Beans, Chocolate Frogs, Rock Cakes and other *Harry Potter*–inspired goodies.

Owl Post & Owlery Buy Wizarding World stamps and send a card officially postmarked Hogsmeade.

Filch's Emporium of Confiscated Goods Souvenir shop featuring the Marauders Map on display.

Three Broomsticks & Hog's Head Tavern Surprisingly good shepherd's pie, pumpkin juice and Hogs Head Brew.

Dervish & Banges Magical supplies and Hogwarts robes for sale.

Wizarding World of Harry Potter – Diagon Alley (Map p234; www.universalorlando.com; Universal Studios; theme park admission required; ☺ from 9am; ☒ Lynx 21, 37, 40) Diagon Alley, lined with magical shops selling robes, quidditch supplies, wands, brooms and more, leads to the massive Gringotts Bank, home to Universal Studio's newest multisensory thrill ride, **Harry Potter and the Escape from Gringotts**. To get here, you must walk through Muggles' London at Universal Studios or, if you have a park-to-park ticket, ride the Hogwarts Express from Islands of Adventure's Hogsmeade to King's Cross Station. Wizarding World of Harry Potter – Diagon Alley opened in summer 2014.

Grab some bangers and mash at the **Leaky Cauldron**, a scoop of quirky wizarding-themed ice cream at **Florean Fortescue's Ice-Cream Parlor**, and wander down the 'darkest of dark places,' Knockturn Alley, to pick up tools of the Dark Arts at **Borgin and Burkes**.

Given the creative spirit and success of Islands of Adventure's Hogsmeade, Diagon Alley promises to be theme-park magic at its best. Lines and crowds will be insane – stay at a Universal Orlando Resort so you can enter Diagon Alley one hour before the park opens to the general public.

Pass) and the high-thrill coaster **Hollywood Rip Ride Rockit** (Express Pass). This roller coaster is not for the faint of heart – you *Rip* up to 65mph, *Ride* 17 stories above the theme park, around a loop-dee-loop, and down a crazy-steep drop, and *Rockit* to customized music.

At **Shrek 4-D** (Express Pass), Shrek and Donkey try to save Princess Fiona from a dragon. And that dragon is indeed fierce, probably too fierce for tiny tots – it pops out at you with red eyes, spitting fire into your face. Unfortunately, the nonsensical preshow spiel goes on too long.

New York RIDE, SHOW
(Map p234; www.universalorlando.com; theme park admission required; ☺ from 9am; ☒; ☒ Lynx 21, 37, 40) **Revenge of the Mummy** (Express Pass) combines roller-coaster speed and twists with in-your-face special effects. Head deep into ancient Egyptian catacombs in

near pitch black, but don't anger Imhotep the mummy – in his wrath he flings you past fire, water and more. The walk-through attraction **Twister...Ride It Out** (Express Pass) takes folks into a film set of a dilapidated Midwest America town, eerily quiet... until the storm rolls in.

A radio announces a severe storm warning, and slowly you see and feel the change in weather. The sign rattles above the old gas station, and tumbleweed blows across the set. You see a tornado developing, far off in the distant sky, and it's coming, closer and closer, louder and louder. Anyone who has felt the fear of living through a real tornado, or children who already wake up scared of them thanks to sirens, hours in the basement and the eerie blanket of tornado-breeding green skies, should think twice before going to this attraction.

ⓘ TOP TIPS FOR VISITING HARRY POTTER'S HOGSMEADE & DIAGON ALLEY

You haven't seen crowds and lines until you've seen Universal's Wizarding World of Harry Potter during high season. It can be upwards of five hours *just to enter* the *Harry Potter*–themed section, and then there are the lines for rides, restaurants and shops once you get in. It can be a nightmare. But don't be deterred: with a little bit of smart planning, a visit to Hogsmeade and Diagon Alley can be magnificently joyful, easy and stress free.

Stay at a Universal Orlando Resort Hotel *Harry Potter* attractions open one hour early for guests at all four on-site hotels. Arrive at least 30 minutes before the gates open to the general public, and do not dawdle.

Strategize Head to Islands of Adventure's Hogsmeade (p296) on one morning – hit Harry Potter and the Forbidden Journey, Dragon Challenge, Flight of the Hippogriff, and finally shops and restaurants (in that order). The other morning, zip straight to Universal Studio's Diagon Alley (p297), hop on Escape from Gringotts, and then explore at leisure. There is an Ollivanders Wand Shop in both parks – on one of the two days, make this your first stop.

Buy a park-to-park ticket This allows you to ride the Hogwarts Express between Diagon Alley and Hogsmeade.

Visit during low season Do not go Christmas through early January, March and summer.

Take advantage of Universal's 'return time' tickets If the Wizarding World of Harry Potter *does* reach capacity during your visit (usually after 10:30am), it only allows new guests to enter once others have left; this electronic ticket allows you to enjoy other attractions and return for entry into the Wizarding World within a specific window of time. Look for the blue banner directing you to the easy-to-use kiosks.

San Francisco RIDE, SHOW
(www.universalorlando.com; theme park admission required; ⊙ from 9am; 🚇; 🚌 Lynx 21, 37, 40) San Francisco, themed heavily around the city as the site of the massive 1906 earthquake and the inspiration behind the 1974 film *Earthquake*, is home to Chez Alcatraz (p303), a tiny and pleasant outdoor bar in Fisherman's Wharf; Lombard's (p303), one of the park's two restaurants that accept reservations; and a couple of outdoor shows. The only ride here is the mock-movie-making attraction **Disaster** (Express Pass), an unusual slow-moving ride that centers on narrative schtick and special effects rather than speed thrills.

A fast-talking Hollywood casting agent casting a disaster movie chooses a handful of audience members and gives them directions ('give me terror like Britney Spears is your babysitter'), and then each volunteer is filmed for a second or so. Everyone then heads to the 'set' and boards a subway train in the incredibly authentic replica of a San Francisco Bay Area Rapid Transit (BART) station. Suddenly, the big one hits: tracks buckle, the place crumbles and general mayhem ensues. Hint: 65,000 gallons of water are released and recycled every six minutes, but you don't get wet. And yes, you do see the footage of those volunteers.

World Expo RIDE, SHOW
(Map p234; www.universalorlando.com; theme park admission required; ⊙ from 9am; 🚌 Lynx 21, 37, 40) The main attraction here is **Men in Black Alien Attack** (Express Pass), a 3-D interactive video game that is a lot of fun but not at all scary. Your car swings and spins through a danger-laden downtown Manhattan, with all kinds of silly looking aliens all over the place, and you aim your lasers and shoot away to rack up points. Oddly, Universal is adamant that you put all bags in the complimentary locker before boarding.

Springfield RIDE
(Map p234; www.universalorlando.com; theme park admission required; ⊙ from 9am; 🚇; 🚌 Lynx 21, 37, 40) In 2013 Universal opened *The Simpsons*–themed Springfield, home to that iconic American TV family. Hang at Moe's Tavern, grab doughnuts at Lard Lad, and meet Krusty the Clown, Sideshow Bob and the Simpson family themselves. The child-friendly **Kang & Kodos' Twirl & Hurl** offers an interactive twist to whirling, and don't miss **The Simpsons Ride** (Express Pass).

It's one of the best simulated experiences at Universal, a highlight even if you're not a *Simpsons* fan. Kids will want to try Springfield's signature drink, a bubbling and steaming **Flaming Moe** that rivals the theming fun of *Harry Potter*'s Butterbeer and tastes surprisingly good! Sure, it's just an orange soda, but it's a pretty cool orange soda, the cup makes a good souvenir, and in the eyes of an eight-year-old, it's worth every penny of that seven bucks.

Woody Woodpecker's KidZone   RIDE, SHOW
(Map p234; www.universalorlando.com; theme park admission required; ⊙from 9am; ⊒ Lynx 21, 37, 40) Kid-friendly shows and rides, a fantastic water-play area and supercool foam-ball cannons – it rivals Islands of Adventure's Seuss Landing (p295) as a Universal favorite of the eight-and-under crowd.

Despicable Me: Minion Mayhem   RIDE
(www.universalorlando.com; theme park admission required; ⊙from 9am; ⊒ Lynx 21, 37, 40) Fans of *Despicable Me* won't want to miss the chance to become one of Gru's minions in this 3-D simulated ride, one of Universal's best 3-D experiences. There's lots of silliness, in the best of Minion traditions, and there's nothing particularly scary. Note that even Express Pass lines can soar upwards from 30 minutes, so come first thing.

Hollywood   RIDE, SHOW
(Map p234; www.universalstudios.com; theme park admission required; ⊙from 9am; ⊒ Lynx 21, 37, 40) With glorious 3-D film footage, live action stunts and 4-D special effects, **Ter-**minator 2: 3-D** (Express Pass) is complete sensory overload – delicious fun for some, overwhelming and scary for others. Fans of the famous redhead Lucille Ball will particularly enjoy **Lucy – A Tribute**, a biographical exhibit with *I Love Lucy* clips, costumes, photos and Lucy's letters.

If you're really into horror make up, **Universal Horror Make-Up Show** (Express Pass) may be a little too short and thin on substance. It's humorous, full of silly antics, but optical illusions could freak out kids if they're not really clear from the get-go that it's not real.

◉ CityWalk

Across the canal from the two theme parks is Universal's entertainment district, a semicircle pedestrian mall with restaurants, clubs, bars, a multiplex movie theater, miniature golf, shops and a fountain for kids to play in. Live music and mucho alcohol sums up the entertainment options here. Although nights can be packed with partying 20-somethings, bachelorette parties and general drunken mayhem, there's a distinct family-friendly vibe, and several bars have pretty good food.

✷ Festivals & Events

Universal's Superstar Parade   PARADE
(www.universalorlando.com; Universal Studios; theme park admission required; ⊛; ⊒ Lynx 21, 37, 40) Elaborate floats and lights featuring

MEETING CHARACTERS AT UNIVERSAL ORLANDO RESORT

Characters roaming Universal Studios and Islands of Adventure include Curious George, SpongeBob Square Pants, Lucille Ball and Marilyn Monroe, as well as the cast of characters from *The Simpsons, Shrek, Madagascar* and Dr Seuss books. Some favorites, such as Spider Man, have scheduled meet-and-greets, so be sure to check your park map for times and places. In addition, Universal offers three character dining options.

Superstar Character Breakfast (☑407-224-7554; www.universalorlando.com; Cafe La Bamba, Universal Studios; adult/chid $25/11, theme park admission required; ⊙9-11am; ⊒ Lynx 21, 37, 40) Breakfast with Gru and his minions, Dora the Explorer and others from the Universal Superstar Parade at Universal Studio's Cafe La Bamba. Note that once you make online reservations, you must call to confirm it.

Universal Orlando Resort Character Dinners (☑407-503-3463; www.universalorlandoresort.com; Universal Orlando Resort; ⊙hours vary) Several nights a week, Universal characters visit one of the resort hotel restaurants. Call for details, as they appear at a different hotel each night and it varies seasonally.

Universal Orlando Resort Character Breakfast (☑407-503-3463; www.universalorlandoresort.com; 6300 Hollywood Way, Royal Pacific Resort; adult/child $27/15; ⊙8am-noon Sun) Universal favorites mingle over Sunday brunch at Jake's American Bar, at the Royal Pacific Resort.

Dora and Diego, *Despicable Me* characters, SpongeBob and *Hop*'s EB. Held daily; times vary.

Mardi Gras   STREET CARNIVAL
(www.universalorlando.com; Universal Studios; theme park admission required; 🚌 Lynx 21, 37, 40) Parades, live music and Cajun food

mimic the iconic New Orleans street festival, Universal-style. Held February to June.

★**Halloween Horror Nights**   STREET CARNIVAL
(www.universalorlando.com; Universal Studios; $50-$75, plus theme park admission; 🚌 Lynx 21, 37, 40) Magnificently spooky haunted houses, gory thrills and over-the-top Halloween

---

UNIVERSAL FOR CHILDREN

The word on the street says that Universal Orlando Resort is great for teens and adults but doesn't offer much for kids under seven. This is simply not true. No, it doesn't have as much as Walt Disney World and you won't find Disney's nostalgic charm, but Universal Orlando Resort is a master at blending attractions for all ages into one easily digestible and navigable package of fun. Dr Seuss' Grinch, superheroes and all kinds of Universal favorites make appearances at theme parks, and characters from *Despicable Me* and other kid-friendly shows swing by hotel restaurants. CityWalk is very family friendly, despite its many bars and live music, with a sci-fi themed miniature golf course and a splash fountain, and the Wantilan Luau at Portofino Bay Hotel gives folks of all ages a taste of the islands.

Most of the kid-friendly attractions cluster at Universal Studios Woody Woodpecker's KidZone (p299), Islands of Adventure's Seuss Landing (p295) and Toon Lagoon (p295), and the Wizarding World of Harry Potter. Bring a change of clothes, as both parks have attractions designed to get kids wet!

Universal Studios

Barney Show Delightfully gentle theater-in-the-round live performance and sing-along.

Curious George Goes to Town Best tiny-tot water-play area in any of the theme parks, and a giant room of nerf balls to throw and shoot from cannons.

Woody Woodpecker's Nuthouse Coaster Gentle coaster for kids three and up.

Animal Actors on Location! Big stage show that highlights exploits of animal actors.

ET Adventure Board a bike and ride through the woods, the police in hot pursuit, before rising safely into the sky through outer space to ET's fanciful home planet. There are a few spooky spots – prepare kids for darkness, loud noises and steam – but there are no spins, speeds or plummets.

Islands of Adventure

One Fish, Two Fish, Red Fish, Blue Fish Ride a Seussian fish around, slowly up and down, with just enough spin to thrill.

Cara-Seuss-al Hop on a fanciful Seuss character.

Cat in the Hat Classic ride through a storybook.

High in the Sky Seuss Trolley Train Ride Soar gently over the park.

If I Ran the Zoo Colorful interactive play area with water-spurting triggers.

Me Ship, the Olive Kids crawl, climb and squirt on Popeye's playground ship and zoom down tunnel waterslides.

Popeye & Bluto's Bilge-Rat Barges Float, twist, bump and giggle along on a circular raft – no sharp falls but you will get drenched!

Hogwarts Little ones too young for the scary Harry Potter and the Forbidden Journey ride can simply walk through the magical charms of the most famous school of witchcraft and wizardry. The separate line for this isn't marked, so ask – Universal folks are most accommodating. Other kid-friendly highlights in the Wizarding World of Harry Potter (p296) are Ollivanders Wand Shop (10-minute show) and family coaster the Flight of the Hippogriff.

shows – watch for goblins, monsters and mummies roaming the streets, creeping up behind you, and remember, this is Universal, not Disney. It isn't Mickey-coated scares, and parents should think carefully before bringing children 13 and under.

Held on select nights in September and October. This is a very popular event and tickets are limited; advanced purchase recommended.

Macy's Holiday Parade   PARADE
(www.universalorlando.com; Universal Studios; theme park admission required; 🖳 Lynx 21, 37, 40) Echoes the real thing in New York City, with giant balloons, Santa Claus, Christmas music and a tree-lighting ceremony. Held on select nights in November and December.

Grinchmas   STREET CARNIVAL
(www.universalorlando.com; Islands of Adventure; theme park admission required; 🚼; 🖳 Lynx 21, 37, 40) A whimsical holiday spectacular at Seuss Landing pays homage to that classic Christmas story. At the center is a musical production of *How the Grinch Stole Christmas*. Held in December.

🏃 Activities

Hollywood Drive-In Golf   MINIATURE GOLF
(Map p234; ☑ 407-802-4848; www.hollywooddriveingolf.com; CityWalk; adult/child 18 holes $14/12, 36 holes $25/21; ⊙ 9am-2am; 🚼; 🖳 Lynx 21, 37, 40, 🚌 Universal) Putt through a flying saucer at the sci-fi themed **Invader from Planet Putt** course; opt for haunted-house shenanigans at **Haunting of Ghostly Greens** course; or try both. Best at dark, when the LED special-effects lighting enhances the spooky thrills and silly twists.

Golf Universal Orlando Resort   GOLF
(☑ Hard Rock Hotel Concierge 407-503-2200, Portofino Bay Hotel Concierge 407-503-1200, Royal Pacific 407-503-3200; www.universalorlando.com; select Orlando golf courses) Preferred tee times, complimentary transportation (for groups of four or more) and club rental at several of Orlando's premier golf courses. For deluxe hotel guests only.

🛌 Sleeping

Universal Orlando Resort boasts three excellent deluxe resort hotels. Staying at the resort eliminates all kinds of logistical hassles: it's a pleasant gardened walk or a quiet boat ride to the parks; all guests receive Unlimited Express Pass access to park attractions and pri-

ority dining; the Wizarding World of Harry Potter opens one hour early for all guests; and the Loews Loves Pets program welcomes Fido as a VIP. Generally less expensive than Walt Disney World's deluxe accommodations, they offer far superior service, food, decor, amenities and rooms. Ask about kids' suites, including the *Jurassic Park*–themed suites at Royal Pacific and Seuss- and Minion-inspired suites at Portofino Bay. In 2014 Universal opened Cabana Bay, a value resort with family suites: guests here enjoy early admission to Harry Potter fun, but do not receive Universal Express Passes.

Cabana Bay Beach Resort   RESORT $$
(Map p234; ☑ 407-503-4000; www.universalorlando.com; 6550 Adventure Way; r $115-150, ste $175-215; 🅿 ❄ 🛜 🏊; 🚌 Universal) Evoking the spirit of road trips c 1957, Universal's newest resort opened in March 2014 and has a beautifully themed hip retro-Florida vintage vibe. It offers moderate and value-priced accommodations. Family suites have kitchenettes and sleep six; and there are two pools, a bowling alley, a food court and a lazy river. Self-parking is $18.

While guests can enjoy early admission to Wizarding World of Harry Potter (a huge plus), they do not benefit from perks afforded to guests at the other three Universal Resorts, including Unlimited Express Pass, priority dining status and boat transportation to the parks. You must either walk the 20 minutes or take a Universal bus to the theme parks.

★ Portofino Bay Hotel   RESORT $$$
(Map p234; ☑ 407-503-1000; www.universalorlando.com; 5601 Universal Blvd; r & ste value/regular/peak from $285/315/365; 🅿 ❄ @ 🛜 🏊 🐾; 🚌 Universal) Sumptuous and elegant, with beautiful rooms, cobblestone streets and sidewalk cafes around a central lagoon, this resort evokes the relaxing charm of seaside Italy. There's a sandy zero-entrance family pool, the secluded Hillside pool, and the elegant Villa pool, as well as the Mandara Spa, evening waterside minstrel music and the excellent Mama Della's (p304). Rates include one hour early entrance to Wizarding World of Harry Potter and Unlimited Express Pass. Self-/valet parking is $18/25 per day.

Royal Pacific Resort   RESORT $$$
(Map p234; ☑ 407-503-3000; www.universalorlando.com; 6300 Hollywood Way; r & ste value/regular/

peak from $230/260/300; P✳@🛜🛉🐾; 🛁U-niversal) The glass-enclosed Orchid Court, with its reflecting pool, Balinese fountains and carved stone elephants splashing in the water, sits at the center of the airy lobby at this friendly South Pacific–inspired resort. The grounds are lovely, with lots of grass, tropical plantings, flowers, bamboo and palm trees, and the on-site restaurants are excellent. Rates include one hour early entrance to Wizarding World of Harry Potter and an Unlimited Express Pass. Self-/valet parking is $18/25 per day.

Though kids will love the family-friendly pool, with real sand, Ping-Pong and a fountain play area, adults may find it unusually loud and chaotic. Note that the rooms here tend to be smaller than those at other Universal hotels.

Hard Rock Hotel   RESORT $$$

(Map p234; ☑407-503-2000; www.universal orlando.com; 5800 Universal Blvd; r & ste value/regular/peak from $259/294/365; P✳@🛜🐾🛉; 🛁Universal) From the grand lawn with the massive guitar fountain at its entrance to the pumped-in underwater music at the pool, the modern and stylized Hard Rock embodies the pure essence and energy of rock-and-roll cool. Rates include one hour early entrance to Wizarding World of Harry Potter and an Unlimited Express Pass. Self-/valet parking is $18/25 per day.

There's a huge zero-entry pool with a waterslide and families mingle harmoniously alongside a young party crowd, but the loud live band that sometimes plays in the lobby and the rockin' vibe may be overkill for folk looking for a peaceful getaway. If you're looking for something more subdued, head to Portofino Bay (p301).

🍴 Eating & Drinking

The only sit-down restaurants in the theme parks that take advance reservations are Mythos Restaurant and Confisco Grille in Islands of Adventure, and Finnegan's Bar & Grill and Lombard's Seafood Grille in Universal Studios.

🍴 Islands of Adventure

All the usual fast-food suspects are sold throughout the park, but with a commitment to theme that you don't see elsewhere. Sip a Predator Rocks in the lush foliage of the Cretaceous period in Jurassic Park or grab a Hog's Head Brew in Hogsmeade.

★ Three Broomsticks   BRITISH $

(Map p234; www.universalorlando.com; mains $11-16, theme park admission required; ⊗8am-park closing; 🛉; 🚌Lynx 21, 37, 40) Fast-food styled British fare inspired by *Harry Potter*, with cottage pie and Cornish pasties, and rustic wooden bench seating. There's plenty of outdoor seating out back too, by the river.

Confisco Grille & Backwater Bar   AMERICAN $

(Map p234; ☑407-224-4012; www.universalorlando. com; mains $6-22, theme park admission required; ⊗11am-park closing; 🍴🛉; 🚌Lynx 21, 37, 40) Under-the-radar and often overlooked, the recommended Confisco Grille has outdoor seating, freshly made hummus, tasty wood-oven pizzas, and a full bar.

Mythos Restaurant   MEDITERRANEAN $$

(Map p234; ☑407-224-4012, 407-224-4534; www. universalorlando.com; mains $8-15, theme park admission required; ⊗11am-5pm; 🛉; 🚌Lynx 21, 37, 40) Housed in an ornate underwater grotto with giant windows and running water.

Hog's Head Pub   PUB

(Map p234; www.universalorlando.com; drinks $4-8, theme park admission required; ⊗11am-park closing; 🚌Lynx 21, 37, 40) Butterbear, frozen or frothy, real beer on tap, pumpkin cider and more. Keep an eye on that hog over the bar – he's more real than you think! If the lines at the Butterbeer carts outside are too long, head inside. Same thing, same price.

🍴 Universal Studios

You'll find a plethora of snack and drink stands, most serving icy beer. Take one to the outdoor shows, or just settle back on the grass or a bench by the water and watch the crowds go by.

Schwab's Pharmacy   ICE CREAM $

(Map p234; www.universalorlando.com; theme park admission required; ⊗11am-park closing; 🛉; 🚌Lynx 21, 37, 40) In the 1930s two brothers bought what would become a favorite lunch-counter hangout for struggling movie-star wannabes in Hollywood. They say Ava Gardner worked the soda fountain, Harold Arlin composed 'Over the Rainbow' here, and regulars included Marilyn Monroe, Clark Gable and Orson Welles. Grab some Ben and Jerry's at Universal's re-creation of the famous original.

Mel's Diner   BURGERS $
(Map p234; www.universalorlando.com; mains $6-
10, theme park admission required; ⏱11am-park
closing; ♿; 🖳Lynx 21, 37, 40, 🚤Universal) Classic
cars and rockin' bands outside, '50s diner
style inside. This is a fast-food eatery, not
much different really than your standard
McDonald's, but it's a lot more fun!

Finnegan's Bar & Grill   PUB $$
(Map p234; ☑407-224-3613; www.universalorlando.
com; mains $8-20, theme park admission required;
⏱11am-park closing; 🛜♿; 🖳Lynx 21, 37, 40) An
Irish pub with live acoustic music plopped
into the streets of New York. Serves Cornish
pasties and Scotch eggs, as well as Harp, Bass
and Guinness on tap.

Lombard's Seafood Grille   SEAFOOD $$
(Map p234; ☑407-224-3613, 407-224-6401; www.
universalorlando.com; mains $12-25, theme park
admission required; ⏱11am-park closing; 🛜♿;
🖳Lynx 21, 37, 40) Oriental rugs, a huge fish
tank and a solid seafood menu make a calm-
ing respite from the Universal Orlando's
energy.

★**Moe's Tavern**   THEME BAR
(Map p234; www.universalorlando.com; drinks
$3-9, theme park admission required; ⏱11am-
park closing; 🛜; 🖳Lynx 21, 37, 40) Brilliantly
themed *Simpsons* bar with Isotopes memorabilia, the Love Tester and Bart Simpson
crank-calling the red rotary phone; it's as
if you walked straight into your TV to find
yourself at Homer's favorite neighborhood
joint. Buy a Krusty Burger from the neighboring food court and sidle up for a Duff
Beer, Duff Lite or Duff Dry.

Chez Alcatraz   BAR
(Map p234; www.universalorlando.com; theme
park admission required; ⏱11am-park closing; 🛜;
🖳Lynx 21, 37, 40) Frozen *mojitos*, flatbread
and housemade potato chips on the waterfront at Fisherman's Wharf. With the sound
of the boats jingling at the docks, views over
the water to the *Simpsons*-themed Springfield and Bruce the infamous shark from
Jaws dangling as a photo-op, this little outdoor bar makes a pleasant spot to kick back
and relax.

Duff Brewery   BAR
(Map p234; www.universalorlando.com; snacks $5-
12, theme park admission required; ⏱11am-park
closing; 🛜; 🖳Lynx 21, 37, 40) Outdoor lagoon-
side bar serving Homer Simpson's beer of
choice, on tap or by the bottle, and Spring-

field's signature Flaming Moe. Look for the
topiary Seven Duffs out front.

🍴 CityWalk

At time of writing, Universal was in the
process of rolling out a revamped CityWalk.
Look for changes and all kinds of promis-
ing new restaurants, including sushi and
brick-oven pizza. Several eateries shift to become live-music venues at night, and charge
covers after 9pm. Purchase a CityWalk Party
Pass ($12; free with multiday theme park
admission) for unlimited all-night club and
bar access, and add a movie (extra $3) if you
like.

Jimmy Buffett's Margaritaville   CARIBBEAN $$
(Map p234; ☑407-224-2155; www.universal
orlando.com; mains $8-15, cover after 10pm $10;
⏱11:30am-2am; ♿; 🖳Lynx 21, 37, 40, 🚤Univer-
sal) Island-inspired festivity, with three bars,
patio dining and live music Jimmy Buffett–
style after 10pm. Try the tantalizing and
colorful margarita flight – four minidrinks,
frozen or on-the-rocks.

Check out the Lone Palm tiki bar on the
water across from Margaritaville – just look
for the plane (from Jimmy Buffett's own col-
lection) parked outside. It's a nice spot for
a drink.

Hard Rock Café   AMERICAN $$
(Map p234; ☑407-351-7625; www.universal
orlando.com; mains $12-22; ⏱11am-midnight; ♿;
🖳Lynx 21, 37, 40, 🚤Universal) Excellent burgers
and a rock-and-roll theme. Reservations not
accepted.

NBA City   AMERICAN $$
(Map p234; ☑407-363-5919; www.universalorlan-
do.com; mains $9-20; ⏱11am-10pm; ♿; 🖳Lynx
21, 37, 40, 🚤Universal) A giant basketball play-
er out front and endless basketball games on
screens throughout the restaurant. Come for
the theming fun, not for gourmet fare.

**Bob Marley –
A Tribute to Freedom**   JAMAICAN $$
(☑407-224-3663; www.universalorlando.com;
mains $8-16, cover after 9pm $7; ⏱restaurant
4-10pm Sun-Thu, to 11pm Fri & Sat, bar 9pm-2am;
🖳Lynx 21, 37, 40, 🚤Universal) Jerk-spiced chick-
en, monk stew, veggie patties with yucca
fries served in a replica of the reggae master's Jamaican home. There's live reggae in
the courtyard every evening, and after 9pm
you must be 21 to enter.

NASCAR Sports Grille AMERICAN $$
(Map p234; ☑ 407-224-7223; www.universalorlando.com; mains $9-18; ☉ 11am-10pm; 📶; ☐ Lynx 21, 37, 40, ☷ Universal) Featuring Nascar simulators and games, and basic American fare with a car-racing twist – try the Daytona Chiliburger or the Pit Crew Pulled Pork Sandwich. A must for NASCAR wannabes of all ages.

Pat O'Brien's THEME BAR
(Map p234; ☑ 407-224-2106; www.universalorlando.com; mains $8-17, cover after 9pm $7; ☉ 4pm-2am, piano bar from 5pm; ☐ Lynx 21, 37, 40, ☷ Universal) Bar with Cajun food, dueling pianos and a pleasant outdoor patio.

Red Coconut Club CLUB
(Map p234; ☑ 407-224-4233; www.universalorlando.com; cover $7; ☉ 8pm-2am Sun-Thu, from 6pm Fri & Sat; ☐ Lynx 21, 37, 40, ☷ Universal) Contemporary vibe, live bands, martini bar and rooftop balcony.

Groove CLUB
(Map p234; ☑ 407-224-4233; www.universalorlando.com; cover $5; ☉ 9pm-2am; ☐ Lynx 21, 37 ,40, ☷ Universal) Dance club with sleek blue neon walls, multiple bars, themed lounges and blaring music. Wednesday nights are 'teen nights' – you must be 15 to 19 years old to get in.

✕ Resort Hotels

Emack and Bolio's Marketplace ICE CREAM $
(Map p234; ☑ 407-503-2000; www.universalorlando.com; 5800 Universal Blvd, Hard Rock Hotel; ice creams $3-8; ☉ 6:30am-11pm; 🛜 📶; ☷ Universal) Originally from Boston, Emack and Bolio ice cream beats other national chains hands down. And of course, only at this bastion of rock and roll will you find Bye Bye Miss American Mud Pie.

★ Mama Della's Ristorante ITALIAN $$
(Map p234; ☑ 407-503-3463; www.universalorlando.com; 5601 Universal Blvd, Portofino Bay Hotel; mains $10-22; ☉ 5:30-11pm; ☑ 📶; ☷ Universal) Charming, cozy and friendly, with vintage wallpaper, dark wood and several rooms with romantic nooks. You really do feel like you're a welcomed guest at a private home nestled in Italy. Strolling musicians entertain tableside, and the simple Italian fare is both fresh and excellent; the service is efficient but relaxed.

Good wine, old-fashioned soda in a bottle, and a bowl of pasta at Mama Della's makes a very nice ending to a day at the parks, for both kids and adults.

Orchid Court Sushi Bar JAPANESE $$
(Map p234; ☑ 407-503-3000; www.universalorlando.com; 6300 Hollywood Way, Royal Pacific Resort; sushi $4-8, mains $12-20; ☉ 11am-11pm; 📶; ☷ Universal) This small, informal sushi bar oozes calm inside the light-and-airy, glass-enclosed lobby of the Royal Pacific Resort, decked out with cushioned couches and chairs. Try the cherry blossom saketini.

Kitchen AMERICAN $$$
(Map p234; ☑ 407-503-2430; www.universalorlando.com; 5800 Universal Blvd, Hard Rock Hotel; mains $15-30; ☉ 7am-10pm Mon-Fri, to 11pm Sat & Sun; 📶; ☷ Universal) Music paraphernalia and patio poolside dining. Come for flatbreads, steak and comfort food such as chicken potpie and roast chicken. Children can eat in the Kids' Crib, which has bean-bag chairs, cartoons and toys, while parents dine in the big-people restaurant.

Emeril's Tchoup Chop SEAFOOD $$$
(Map p234; ☑ 407-503-2467; www.emerilsrestaurants.com; 6300 Hollywood Way, Royal Pacific Resort; mains $15-30; ☉ 11:30am-2:30pm & 5-10pm; ☷ Universal) Island-inspired food, including plenty of seafood and Asian accents, prepared with the freshest ingredients. One of the best sit-down meals at the Universal Orlando Resort.

Palm Restaurant STEAKHOUSE $$$
(Map p234; ☑ 407-503-7256; www.universalorlando.com; 5800 Universal Studios Blvd, Hard Rock Hotel; mains $32-50, shared sides $12; ☉ 5-10pm; ☷ Universal) The original Palm opened in New York City in 1926, and though there are now more than 30 locations, it remains a family-owned bedrock American steakhouse. Classic cocktails, a steady din, and big plates of steak, lobster and Italian fare.

★ Velvet Bar LOUNGE
(Map p234; ☑ 407-504-2588, tickets & info 407-503-2401; www.hardrockhotelorlando.com; 5800 Universal Blvd, Hard Rock Hotel; ☉ 5pm-2am; ☷ Universal) Trendy and sleekly stylized, with hardwood floors, floor-to-ceiling windows, zebra-fabric chairs and excellent martinis. On the last Thursday of the month, the bar hosts Velvet Sessions, a rock-and-roll

cocktail party with themed drinks, live music and finger food.

☆ Entertainment

In addition to the following, CityWalk throbs with live music and clubs, and Universal Orlando hosts the Blue Man Group (p258).

Universal's Cinematic Spectacular CINEMA
(Map p234; ☑ dining reservations 407-224-7554; www.universalorlando.com; Universal Studios; theme park admission required; ☺ evenings, showtimes vary; ☐ Lynx 21, 37, 40) This dramatic film tribute narrated by Morgan Freeman combines fireworks, a water and light show, and clips from movie classics projected on a massive screen over the lagoon.

Universal offers two options for waterfront-view reserved seating for the show: Universal's Cinematic Spectacular Dining Experience (adult/child $45/13), which includes dinner at Lombard's Seafood Grille (p303) and a dessert buffet on the deck; and VIP seating at Duff Brewery ($15, including a cupcake and nonalcoholic drink).

Dive-In Movies CINEMA
(Portofino Bay, Hard Rock & Royal Pacific Hotels; ☺ dusk; ☒ Universal) Free family-friendly movies screened poolside at Universal Orlando's deluxe resort hotels. Details vary seasonally, and sometimes films are screened several nights a week.

Wantilan Luau DINNER SHOW
(Map p234; ☑ 407-503-3463; www.universalorlando.com; 6300 Hollywood Way, Royal Pacific Resort; adult $63-70, child under 12yr $35-40; ☺ 6pm Tue & Sat May-Aug, 6pm Sat only Sep-Apr; ☒ Universal) Pacific Island fire dancers shimmy and shake on stage while guests enjoy a tasty buffet of roast suckling pig, guava-barbecued short ribs and other Polynesian-influenced fare. The atmosphere is wonderfully casual and, like everything at Universal Orlando, this is simple unabashed silliness and fun. Unlimited mai tais, beer and wine are included in the price.

The Hawaiian warrior's roar can be rather scary and the fire a bit close for comfort in the eyes of little ones, but there's a pleasant grassy area next to the open-air dining theater where kids can muck about. Reservations accepted up to 60 days in advance.

CityWalk's Rising Star KARAOKE
(Map p234; ☑ 407-224-4233; www.universalorlando.com; CityWalk; cover $7; ☺ 8pm-2am; ☐ Lynx 21, 37, 40, ☒ Universal) Karaoke to live music, and talent contests.

Hard Rock Live LIVE MUSIC
(Map p234; ☑ 407-351-5483; www.hardrocklive.com; tickets $20-30; ☺ box office 10am-9pm; ☐ Lynx 21, 37, 40, ☒ Universal) This 3000-person-capacity landmark draws some fairly big rock-and-roll names and comedy acts. Full bar.

❶ Information

CHILD CARE
Kids' Camp (☑ Hard Rock 407-503-2200, Portofino Bay 407-503-1200, Royal Pacific 407-503-3200; www.universalorlando.com; Portofino Bay, Hard Rock & Royal Pacific Resorts; per child per hour $15; ☺ 5-11pm) Every week one deluxe Universal Orlando Resort hotel offers a drop-off child-care center, with DVDs, arts and crafts, organized activities and games, for children aged four through 12. Reservations recommended but not required, and you must be a guest at one of the four Universal Orlando Resort hotels. Optional dinner for an extra $15.

INTERNET ACCESS
Complimentary wi-fi is available throughout Universal Studios, at the Starbucks inside Islands of Adventure and at CityWalk, and at Universal Orlando Resort hotels (guests only, though ask about public access in hotel lobbies and pools).

KENNELS
Universal Orlando Resort Kennel (☑ 407-224-9509; www.universalorlando.com; Universal Orlando Resort; per pet per day $15; ☺ 7am-3am) Day boarding for dogs and cats, but you must return to walk your pet. Located on the left side of the RV/camper parking lot at Universal Orlando Resort parking lot. Note that pets are welcome at all on-site hotels except Cabana Bay.

LOCKERS
Available inside both Islands of Adventure and Universal Studios parks for $8 per day. Several rides require that all loose items, including backpacks and small purses, be secured in complimentary short-term lockers. If you are carrying something too big for the locker, you can take advantage of the Bag Swap option: wait in line together, one person rides while the other holds the bag, and then swap.

MAPS
Pick up a free map and an *Attractions & Show Times* guide, with a schedule of events, show times, and time and location of free character interactions, at each park entrance.

MEDICAL SERVICES

Each theme park has medical facilities. The closest hospital is Dr P Phillips Hospital (p260), an easy 5.5 miles south on Turkey Lake Rd.

OPENING HOURS

Theme park hours change seasonally and daily. Generally, parks open at 8am or 9am and close sometime between 6pm and 10pm. Guests at any of the four on-site hotels can enter the Wizarding World of Harry Potter one hour before the park opens.

PARKING

Parking for both theme parks and CityWalk is available inside a giant garage structure (self-/valet parking $17/30). Hotels charge per day for self-parking ($18) or valet ($25).

STROLLER & WHEELCHAIR RENTAL

Rent strollers, wheelchairs and ECVs at the entrance to each park, and manual wheelchairs at the Rotunda section of the parking lot. To reserve an ECV in advance, call ☎ 407-224-4423.

TICKETS

The following table shows the cost of tickets for adults to one or both Universal Orlando Resort Parks (Islands of Adventure and Universal Studios):

NUMBER OF DAYS	ONE PARK ($)	TWO PARKS ($)
1	96	136
2	136	176
3	146	186
4	156	196

➺ Children aged from three to nine enter for up to $12 less.

➺ Tickets are good anytime within 14 consecutive days, and multiple-day tickets include admission to paid venues in CityWalk. See website for Wet 'n Wild (p237) packages. Universal Orlando Resort participates in the Orlando Flex Ticket (see boxed text, p229) available online or in person at the Orlando Official Visitor Center (p260).

Express Pass Avoid lines at designated Islands of Adventure and Universal Studios rides by flashing your Express Pass at the separate Express Pass line. The standard one-day pass (for one park $35 to $70; for two parks $40 to $90) allows one-time Express Pass access to each attraction. Alternatively, purchase the bundled two-day Park-to-Park Ticket Plus Unlimited Express ($135 to $180), which includes admission to both parks and unlimited access to Express Pass rides. With this, you can go to any ride, any time you like, as often as you like. If you are staying at one of Universal Orlando's three deluxe resort hotels – Universal Orlando's Portofino Bay, Hard Rock or Royal Pacific Resorts – up to five guests in each room automatically receive an Unlimited Express Pass pass. A limited number of passes per day are available online or at the park gates. Check www.universalorlando.com for a calendar of prices and black-out dates. Note that Unlimited Express Passes are sold bundled to park admission online, but, if they're available, you can add them to an existing ticket at the park.

Universal Orlando Dining Plan Universal offers two prepaid dining packages: Dining Plan – Quick Service (adult/child $20/13) and Dining Plan $46/18), which include a broad selection of restaurants at Islands of Adventure, Universal Studios and CityWalk. Note the latter is available only as part of a vacation package. Check out the detailed online analysis at **Orlando Informer** (www.orlandoinformer.com/universal/dining-plan) for pros and cons.

TOURIST INFORMATION

Guest Services inside each park and at CityWalk can help with anything you need, and there are concierge desks at the four on-site hotels. Furthermore, the front desk of just about any Orlando area hotel provides Universal Orlando Resort tourist information.

Important Telephone Numbers

Universal Orlando Resort (☎ 407-363-8000) Central number for all things Universal.

Resort Hotel Reservations (☎ 888-273-1311, for vacation packages 888-343-3636) Accommodations at Universal's four on-site resort hotels.

Dining CityWalk & Theme Parks (☎ 407-224-9255) Advanced priority seating for CityWalk, Islands of Adventure and Universal Studios.

Dining Resort Hotels (☎ 407-503-3463) Advanced priority seating for Portofino Bay, Hard Rock and Royal Pacific Resorts.

Universal Orlando Resort Lost & Found (☎ 407-224-4233) Located inside Guest Services.

Guest Services (☎ 407-224-6350, 407-224-4233).

TRAVELERS WITH DISABILITIES

➺ The *Universal Orlando Rider's Guide*, available online at www.universalorlando.com and at Guest Services, includes ride requirements and attraction-accessibility details for travelers with disabilities. There are also sign-language-interpreting, closed-captioning and assistive-listening devices available at no extra charge, and large-print and braille maps. Telecommunications Device for the Deaf–equipped (TDD) telephones are located throughout the park.

➡ Wheelchairs and ECVs can be rented from the entrance to each park; ECVs can be reserved in advance (📞 407-224-4423). Rent manual wheelchairs at the Rotunda section of the parking lot.

USEFUL WEBSITES

Universal Orlando Resort (www.universalorlando.com) Official site for information, accommodation and tickets.

Orlando Informer (www.orlandoinformer.com) Excellent and detailed information on all things Universal, including park changes, money-saving tips, menus and a crowd calendar.

ℹ Getting There & Around

BOAT

Universal Orlando Water Taxis (www.universalorlando.com; 🕐 7am-2am, hours vary) Water taxis, which leave each point roughly every 15 minutes, shuttle regularly and directly between each of the three deluxe Universal hotels and CityWalk. From here, it's a five-minute walk across the canal to the theme parks.

CAR

From the I-4, take exit 74B or 75A and follow the signs. From International Dr, turn west at Wet 'n Wild onto Universal Blvd.

BUS

Lynx buses 21, 37 and 40 service the Universal Orlando Resort parking garage (40 runs directly from the downtown Orlando Amtrak station). International Dr's I-Ride Trolley (p229) stops at Universal Blvd (Wet n' Wild); from there, it is a 0.6-mile walk.

SHUTTLE

Most hotels just outside Universal Studios and along International Dr provide free shuttle service to the Universal Orlando Resort, but remember that many are first-come, first-served. If you intend to use hotel shuttles, always ask for details including how often they run and whether or not they take reservations. Shuttles to Universal Orlando Resort are direct – they will drop you off within a few minutes' walk of both parks and CityWalk. Resort hotels offer guests complimentary shuttle service to SeaWorld and Wet 'n Wild. Call Mears Transportation (p229) one day in advance to arrange personalized shuttle service to Disney.

WALKING

Universal Orlando's resort hotels, Islands of Adventure and Universal Studios theme parks and CityWalk are linked by well-lit and landscaped pedestrian walkways. It's a 10- to 15-minute walk from the theme parks and CityWalk to the deluxe resort hotels. Cabana Bay Beach Resort is about a 25-minute walk. Several hotels outside the park are within a 20-minute walk, but it's not a very pleasant journey.

The Space Coast

Best Places to Eat

➜ Dixie Crossroads (p313)

➜ Green Room Cafe (p318)

➜ Fat Snook (p319)

➜ Beachside Cafe (p321)

➜ Maison Martinique (p324)

Best Places to Stay

➜ Solrisa Inn (p318)

➜ Beach Place Guesthouses (p318)

➜ Port d'Hiver (p321)

➜ Seashell Suites (p321)

➜ Caribbean Court Boutique Hotel (p324)

Why Go?

More than 75 miles of barrier-island Atlantic Coast stretch from Canaveral National Seashore south to Vero Beach, encompassing undeveloped stretches of endless white sand, an entrenched surf culture and pockets of Old Florida.

The Kennedy Space Center and several small museums dedicated to the history, heroes and science of the United States' space program give the Space Coast its name, and the region's tourist hub of Cocoa Beach is the launching point for massive cruise ships. But beyond the 3D space movies, tiki-hut bars and surf shops, the Space Coast offers quintessential Florida wildlife for everyone from grandmas to toddlers. Kayak with manatees, camp on a private island or simply stroll along miles and miles of sandy white beaches – it's easy to find a quiet spot.

When to Go
Cocoa Beach

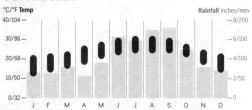

Jul Crowds diminish; prices drop; loggerhead sea turtles nest along miles of sandy coastline.

Apr More sunny days than any other month, and most spring-breakers have come and gone.

Fall Peak migratory-bird season and drier weather make for prime wildlife-spotting.

National & State Parks

Miles of the Space Coast are dedicated to national and state parks and wildlife refuges, including **Canaveral National Seashore** (part of the national park system), **Merritt Island National Wildlife Refuge** and **Sebastian Inlet State Park**. The Atlantic Ocean pounds along the eastern edge, while the calm, brackish waters of the Banana and Indian Rivers and Mosquito Lagoon separate the barrier island from the mainland to the west. See www.spacecoasthiking.com for area trail maps and detailed descriptions. Consult www.spacecoastbirding.com for the region's birding hot spots.

ⓘ Getting There & Around

AIR

Melbourne International Airport (☑ 321-723-6227; www.mlbair.com; 1 Air Terminal Pkwy) services Delta, Baer Air and US Airways. It is served by all the major rental-car companies and Greyhound buses. A SCAT bus stop is located outside the main terminal building.

Orlando International Airport and Sanford International Airport are about 50 minutes west of Cocoa Beach.

BUS

Space Coast Area Transit (SCAT; ☑ 321-633-1878; www.ridescat.com) operates a local bus service including a mainland route from Merritt Island south to Melbourne Beach, a beach trolley in Cocoa Beach and a bus running along Hwy A1A from Cocoa Beach to Indialantic. Surfboards and bikes are allowed on the bus, space permitting. **GoLineIRT** (☑ 772-569-0903; www.golineirt.com) services Sebastian Inlet south to Vero Beach, and **Greyhound** (☑ 321-723-4329; www.greyhound.com) buses stop along the mainland.

CAR

Three major roads run north and south: A1A along the beaches, US 1 on the mainland and paralleling the shore of the Indian River, and I-95 close to the western border of Brevard County. Seven bridges and causeways run east–west across the lagoon, the most important being Hwy 405 to the Kennedy Space Center, Hwy 528 (the Beachline) connecting Cape Canaveral to Orlando, and Hwy 520 between Cocoa Village and Cocoa Beach.

Major car-rental agencies have offices in Cocoa Beach, Melbourne and Vero Beach.

TRAIN

Amtrak trains run as far as Orlando.

Merritt Island

In 1958, in the aftermath of WWII, the US government selected the east coast of Florida as the base of its newly formed National Aeronautics and Space Administration (NASA). From here new-age captains would launch rockets, telescopes and shuttles into the orbiting circle of the earth to discover new worlds and galaxies. Thousands of acres of scrubland were commandeered at the northern end of Merritt Island; a third of it was cleared to form the new NASA base, while the remainder was given over to the US Fish and Wildlife Service to operate as the Merritt Island National Wildlife Refuge and the Canaveral National Seashore. The refuge and seashore provide the military with a secure and impenetrable buffer zone while also offering some 500 species of wildlife a pristine coastal habitat of saltwater marshes, hardwood hammocks, pine flatwoods and scrub.

Nowadays, this 43-mile strip of coast from the southern end of Cape Canaveral Air Station to the tip of Canaveral National Seashore is the longest stretch of undeveloped beach on Florida's Atlantic coast. It's also one of the most important turtle-nesting beaches in the US, with 7900 recorded nestings in 2013.

Kennedy Space Center

Since 1919, when physics professor Robert Goddard published *A Method of Reaching Extreme Altitudes*, erasing the line between science fiction and reality, NASA's engineers and astronauts have thrilled and amazed us with their moon landings, satellite launches and shuttle programs.

One of Florida's most visited sights, the more than 140,000-acre Kennedy Space Center was once a working space-flight facility, where shuttles were built and astronauts rocketed into the cosmos. With the termination of NASA's shuttle program in the summer of 2011, however, the Kennedy Space Center began the shift from a living museum to a historical one, although you can still see crew-less rockets and satellites launch from its pads (see www.spacecoast-launches.com for the schedule).

⊙ Sights

Admission to this all-day attraction covers most of the center, a guided bus tour to the

Space Coast Highlights

1 Watching a rocket launch from **Kennedy Space Center** (p311) and then seeing shuttle *Atlantis*, which flew 33 missions.

2 Kayaking with manatees and dolphins in the **Merritt Island National Wildlife Refuge** (p312).

3 Enjoying homegrown Florida shrimp at local institution **Dixie Crossroads** (p313) in Titusville.

4 Spotting nesting turtles and diving pelicans at **Canaveral National Seashore** (p313).

5 **Surfing** Florida's hottest waves or simply soaking up the scene at the **Cocoa Beach Pier** (p316).

6 Learning about conservation while zip-lining over alligator pits at the **Brevard Zoo** (p320).

7 Catching community theater and symphony in historic downtown **Melbourne** (p321).

8 Settling into the barefoot life in **Vero Beach** (p322), the quintessential beach escape.

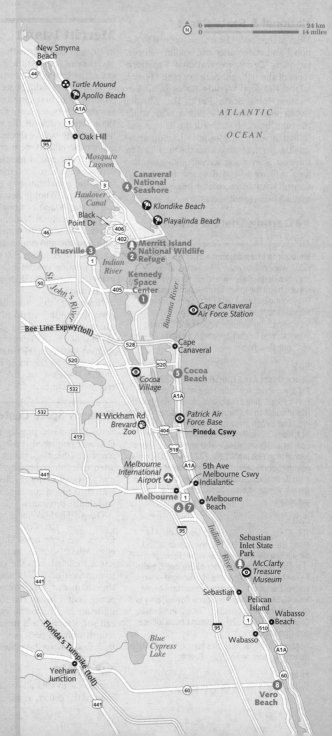

Apollo/Saturn V Center and entrance to the US Astronaut Hall of Fame (6 miles down the road). Alternatively, you can choose from combination tickets that fold in tours and activities such as Astronaut Encounters and the Astronaut Training Experience.

All attractions are wheelchair accessible, and complimentary strollers and wheelchairs are provided, as are air-conditioned kennels for pets.

Kennedy Space Center   MUSEUM
(📞866-737-5235; www.kennedyspacecenter.com; NASA Parkway, Merritt Island; adult/child 3-11yr $50/40; ⊙9am-7pm Apr-Aug, to 5pm Sep-Mar) Whether you're mildly interested in space or a die-hard sci-fi fan, a visit to the Space Center is awe inspiring. To get a good overview, start at the Early Space Exploration exhibit, progress to the 90-minute bus tour to the Apollo/Saturn V Center (where you'll find the best on-site cafe) and finish at the awesome new *Atlantis* exhibit, where you can walk beneath the heat-scorched fuselage of a shuttle that travelled over 126,000,000 miles through space on 33 missions.

➡ **Visitor Complex**

The surprisingly small Visitor Complex, with several exhibits showcasing the history and future of US space travel and research, is the heart of the Kennedy Space Center. Here you'll find the **Rocket Garden**, featuring replicas of classic rockets towering over the complex; the **Early Space Exploration exhibit**, which details the history of the US space program and the first manned space flights; and the hour-long **Astronaut Encounter**, where a real, live astronaut fields questions from the audience. Two delightful **IMAX films**, offering clear explanations of complicated science and cool footage of gravity-free life in space, delight folks of all ages. Astronauts pass tortillas through the air like Frisbees, toss M&Ms to each other and catch bubbles of water when they're thirsty. *Space Station 3D*, narrated by Tom Cruise, depicts the construction and operations of the International Space Station (ISS), and Leonardo DiCaprio narrates *Hubble 3D*, featuring truly awesome images (such as actual star nurseries!) captured from the Hubble telescope.

The stunningly beautiful **Astronaut Memorial**, a shiny granite wall standing four stories high, reflects both literally and figuratively on the personal and tragic stories behind the theme-park energy that perme-

🛈 KIDS' PLAY

Skip Kennedy Space Center's disappointing Children's Play Dome and cool off in the spurting fountain on the far corner of the Rocket Garden.

ates the center. Several stone panels display the photos and names of those who died in shuttle disasters.

➡ **Kennedy Space Center Tour**

This 90-minute bus tour is the only way to see beyond the Visitor Complex without paying for an add-on tour. The first stop is the **LC 39 Observation Gantry**, a 60ft observation tower with views of the twin launch pads. From here, the bus winds through the launch facilities to the **Apollo/Saturn V Center**, where you don't want to miss the multimedia show in the Firing Room. Video footage on three screens depicts America's first lunar mission, the 1968 launch of *Apollo VIII*, before ushering you through to an enormous hangar displaying the real *Apollo 14* Command Module and the 363ft *Saturn V* moon rocket. This 6.5-million-pound marvel of engineering boosted into space on November 9, 1967.

Tours depart every 15 minutes from 10am to 2:30pm. Look for the coach buses and long lines to the right when you enter the Visitor Complex.

➡ **Space Shuttle Atlantis**

Blasted by rocket fuel and streaked with space dust, space shuttle *Atlantis,* the final orbiter among NASA's fleet, is the latest and most impressive exhibit in the complex. Suspended in a specially designed, $100-million space, it hangs just a few feet out of reach nose down, payload doors open, as if its still orbiting the earth. It's a creative and dramatic display, preceded by a chest-swelling film that tells the story of the shuttle program from its inception in the 1960s to *Atlantis'* final mission in 2011. Around the shuttle interactive consoles invite visitors to try to land it or dock it to the International Space Station, touchscreens offer details of missions and crews, and there's a full-size replica of the Hubble Space Telescope and a not-very-scary 'shuttle launch experience'. Docents, many of whom worked on the shuttle program, are stationed around the exhibits to answer questions and tell tall space tales.

→ Add-on Experiences

Extended tours offer the opportunity to visit the **Air Force Space & Missile Museum**, the site of the first successful satellite launch in 1958, and **Firing Room 4**, from where all the shuttle launches were controlled. Great for kids, **Lunch with an Astronaut** offers a chance to hang out with a real astronaut, while the **Astronaut Training Experience (ATX)** is an action-oriented taste of training exercises and a team-based simulated mission. Families with kids aged seven to 14 need to sign up for the tamer ATX Family.

US Astronaut Hall of Fame   MUSEUM

(☑321-449-4444; www.kennedyspacecenter.com; NASA Parkway, Merritt Island; admission incl ticket to Kennedy Space Center; ⊘noon-5pm; ⚐) Six miles from the Kennedy Visitor Complex, this eye-candy museum features interactive exhibits and motion simulators dedicated to celebrating US astronauts. It is particularly fun for children, but families will need two days to cover attractions in both the Visitor Complex and the Hall of Fame. Tickets are valid for seven days.

ℹ Getting There & Away

Access to the Space Center is east across the NASA Parkway causeway on SR 405. There is no public transportation. Parking costs $10.

Merritt Island National Wildlife Refuge

Sharing a boundary with the Kennedy Space Center, the **Merritt Island National Wildlife Refuge** (☑321-861-0667; www.fws.gov/merrittisland; off FL-406; ⊘dawn-dusk) **FREE** is one of the most diverse natural habitats in America. The 140,000-acre wilderness ranges from saltwater marshes and estuaries to hardwood hammocks, pine flatwoods, scrub and coastal dunes that support more than 500 species of wildlife, 14 of which are listed as threatened or endangered. Between October and May the refuge is also filled with migrating and wintering birds; the best viewing is on Black Point Wildlife Dr during the early morning and after 4pm.

Be aware that the refuge closes for three days preceding a launch.

◉ Sights & Activities

Hiking along one of the refuge's seven **trails** is best during fall, winter and early spring. The shortest hike is 0.25 miles along a raised **boardwalk** behind the visitor center, while the longest is the 5-mile **Cruickshank Trail** that forms a loop around Black Point Marsh, making it an excellent place to view wading birds.

Black Point Wildlife Drive   DRIVING TOUR

(☑321-633-7245; off FL-406, Merritt Island Wildlife Refuge; per vehicle $5) One of the best places to see wildlife is on this self-guided, 7-mile drive through salt and freshwater marshes. A trail brochure detailing 12 stops and the habitats and wildlife found there is available at the entry point.

In season you'll see plenty of waterfowl, wading birds and raptors, including luridly colored roseate spoonbills and, if you're lucky, the endangered Florida scrub jay. Alligators, otters, bobcats and various species of reptile may also be visible in the early morning and at sunset. The drive takes approximately 40 minutes.

Mosquito Lagoon   KAYAKING, BOATING

(Merritt Island) Hugging the western side of the barrier-island strip, Mosquito Lagoon is an incredibly peaceful waterway connected to the ocean by the Ponce de Leon Inlet. At barely 4ft deep, it's a great place to paddle between island hammocks and dense mangroves observing the birds, manatees and dolphins.

A **manatee observation deck** can be found on the northeastern side of the **Haulover Canal**, which connects the lagoon to the Indian River. This also makes a great launch point for kayaks. Boat launches (requiring a Refuge Day Pass, $5) are available at Bairs Cove, Beacon 42 and the Bio Lab.

The lagoon is aptly named, so bring bug repellent.

A Day Away Kayak Tours   KAYAKING

(☑321-268-2655; www.adayawaykayaktours.com; adult/child day tours $30/20, night tours $34/26) Launching off from Haulover Canal, these kayak tours offer the opportunity of gliding alongside manatees and dolphins. On night tours the dark waters sparkle as comb jellyfish and bioluminescence illuminate cleaving paddle blades.

VALIANT AIR COMMAND WARBIRD MUSEUM

What started off as a hobby for 12 combat veterans has grown into a 1500-member-strong club and a fascinating **warbird museum** (☑ 321-268-1941; www.vacwarbirds.org; 6600 Tico Rd, Titusville; adult/military/child $18/15/5; ☺ 9am-5pm; ⊞) that celebrates the region's aviation heritage with an impressive stock of 40 classic planes.

A hall of memorabilia kicks off the tour, then you're free to roam through three hangars, one a restoration workshop and the other two housing vintage aircraft from WWII, Vietnam and the Korean War. The VAC's flagship, the *Tico Belle*, a 1942 C-47A that dropped paratroopers at the D-Day landings sits combat ready next to a restored *Top Gun*–style Grumman Wildcat that took over 30,000 hours to restore.

In March the museum hosts a family-friendly **Air Show** when combat veterans put on a three-hour aerial display and offer the next generation of ace pilots a chance to fly in a unique piece of history. Alternatively, drop by on the second Saturday of the month and enjoy a **fly-in breakfast** ($8; available 8am till 11am).

✕ Eating

There are no restaurants within the refuge. Instead, head back across the causeway on SR 406 to downtown Titusville.

★**Dixie Crossroads**   SEAFOOD $$
(☑ 321-268-5000; http://dixiecrossroads.com; 1475 Garden St, Titusville; mains $8-46; ☺ 11am-9pm Sun-Thu, to 10pm Fri & Sat; ⊞) Rodney Thompson developed the rock-shrimp fishery off Canaveral's coast in the early 1970s and in 1983 his daughter, Laurilee, opened the Dixie Crossroads Seafood Restaurant. The aim: to put local shrimp back on the Canaveral's tables, which are inundated with imports. Today this local landmark continues to serve up seasonal shrimp, including sweet, blush-coloured royal reds, succulent white shrimp and melt-in-your-mouth rock shrimp.

Shrimp are ordered by the dozen with accompaniments of sweet potato, grits and coleslaw. Other menu highlights include fresh Indian River red mullet, oysters and scallops. Despite the generous seating in the funky wooden chalet there's often a queue at peak times, so order a drink in the gazebo bar.

ℹ Information

Visitor Information Center (☑ 321-861-0667; www.fws.gov/merrittisland; GPS coordinates N 28°38′29.28, off FL-402; ☺ 9am-4pm Mon-Sat) This helpful center offers displays on the refuge's habitats and wildlife, information on conservation programs and hiking trail maps. You can also check out the schedule of bird tours (usually at 9am) and sign up for seasonal turtle-nesting tours along the Canaveral National Seashore.

Canaveral National Seashore

Part of America's national-park system, spectacular **Canaveral National Seashore** (☑ 321-267-1110; www.nps.gov/cana; Merritt Island; car/bike $5/1; ☺ 6am-6pm) includes 24 miles of undeveloped white-sand beach. Two roads squeeze along a skinny bridge of barrier island, one heading 6 miles south from the small beach town of New Smyrna Beach and another 6 miles north from Merritt Island National Wildlife Refuge. Each road dead-ends, leaving about 16 miles of wilderness beach between them.

The best time to visit the park is between November and April, when migrating birds flock to the beaches. During the drier months wildlife-viewing opportunities are also better and there are fewer mosquitos. Turtle-nesting tours run in June and July.

◎ Sights & Activities

Inexpressibly beautiful, Canaveral's three Atlantic beaches each have a distinct character as well as several historic sights. Remember, though, that these beaches are completely undeveloped and have very limited services. There are no designated picnic areas, food, phones or drinking water, so come prepared and remember to pack out all your trash. Pick up a map at the entrance gate, the **visitors center** (☑ 386-428-3384; www.nps.gov/cana; 7611 S Atlantic Ave, New Smyrna; ☺ 8am-6pm Oct-Mar, to 8pm Apr-Sep) or at Merrit Island National Wildlife Refuge. Lifeguards patrol Apollo and Playalinda beaches from 10am to 5pm from May 30 to September 1. Riptides can be particularly fierce here.

Campers can rent canoes ($25 per day) from the visitors center.

LOCAL KNOWLEDGE

FLORIDA SEAFOOD: A LOCAL'S GUIDE

Ironically, despite Florida's long history of commercial fishing, imported seafood has largely taken over local plates. We caught up with Cinthia Sandoval at the **Wild Ocean Seafood market** (www.wildoceanmarket.com; 688 S Park Ave, Titusville) – one of Cape Canaveral's last local fish houses – to see where we could track down the best Florida seafood.

Where are Canaveral's shrimpers? Shrimping off Florida's east coast started in the early 1900s and peaked in the 1970s. Coastal development, high fuel prices and low-cost, imported shrimp have since taken their toll and now the fleet is less than a third of its peak size and wild-caught, American shrimp accounts for less than 10% of the shrimp consumed in the US. Here at Wild Ocean we are committed to providing wild, locally caught, sustainable shrimp and seafood.

What's the Wild Ocean story? Wild Ocean evolved out of a multi-generational family that has been involved in the seafood business since the 1930s. Rodney Thompson started the Wild Ocean Seafood market and the Dixie Crossroads (p313) restaurant in the late 1960s as a direct sea-to-table experience. When Rodney retired, his two daughters, along with their business partners, split the business. Wild Ocean still supplies Dixie Crossroads as well as many other restaurants in Florida.

Describe the character of your best shrimp. It's difficult to pick the best shrimp since they all have different flavor profiles. One of the most unique species we carry is the royal red, which is caught at depths of 1200ft to 2000ft. They're dangerous to fish and have a unique tender texture and a salty, sweet flavor.

How can people find out more? There are over 80 species of harvestable Florida seafood. We believe in diversifying consumers' palates and therefore try to carry low trophic level fish as well as predatory species. We educate the public through tastings at our Titusville market, food festivals and events, and during our monthly **dock tours** ($5 per person), where you can see the daily catch come off the boats. Anyone interested can sign up on the events calendar online.

Turtle Mound
ARCHAEOLOGICAL SITE

Located at the northern end of Mosquito Lagoon, Turtle Mound is one of the largest shell middens on the Florida coast. It stands around 50ft high and consists of 1.5 million bushels (53 million liters) of oyster shells, the remains of an ancient Indian civilization that existed on these shores for five centuries prior to European contact. It can be reached via hiking trails from Apollo Beach and offers panoramic views over the park and ocean.

Eldora State House Museum
HISTORIC BUILDING

(⊙10am-4pm Sat & Sun) Eldora was a small waterfront community of around 100 citrus farmers and fishermen, many of them veterans of the Civil War, who settled here between 1877 and 1900. The town depended on the waterway for supplies, tourists and transport. It was fairly prosperous – at least prosperous enough for the construction of the colonial-revival Eldora House, which has now been renovated as a small house museum detailing the life of the settler community via photos, videos and artefacts.

To reach the house, take the Eldora Trail at parking area 8 in the North District. The trail winds through a coastal hammock to the shoreline of Mosquito Lagoon, where you'll find the house.

Apollo Beach
BEACH

This 6-mile beach, at the northern end of the park and immediately south of New Smyrna, attracts families. It has boardwalk access (wheelchair accessible), and a longer stretch of road along the dunes with fewer parking lots than at Playalinda. There are several hiking trails nearby, including the **Eldora Trail**. It feels more isolated and is perfect for cycling.

Klondike Beach
BEACH

The stretch between Apollo and Playalinda is as pristine as it gets: there are no roads and it's accessible only on foot or by bike (if you can ride on the beach). You need to obtain a back-country permit ($2 per person per day) from the entrance station before setting off.

Playalinda Beach
BEACH

At the southern end of Mosquito Lagoon, Playalinda is popular with surfers. Boardwalks provide beach access, but only 2 miles of park road parallel the dunes and there are more parking lots than at Apollo, with fewer opportunities to access the lagoon.

⟲ Tours

★ **Sea-Turtle Nesting Tours**   ECOTOUR
(🖉386-428-3384; adult/child 8-16yr $14/free; ☉8pm-midnight Jun & Jul) In the summer, rangers lead groups of up to 30 people on these nightly tours, with about a 75% chance of spotting the little guys. Reservations are required (beginning May 15 for June trips, June 15 for July trips); children under eight are not allowed.

Pontoon Boat Tours   BOAT TOURS
(🖉386-428-3384; per person $20) Two-hour ranger-led tours leave from the Visitor Information Center on Friday, Saturday and Sunday.

🛏 Sleeping

Required permits are available up to seven days in advance. Be sure to bring plenty of water. The park has canoes ($25 per day) available for rent to campers only from the Visitor Information Center.

Beach Camping   CAMPGROUND $
(sites $10, per 7 people or more $20) Two basic sites on Apollo Beach are available from November to late April.

Island Camping   CAMPGROUND $
(sites $10, per 7 people or more $20) Fourteen primitive campsites scattered throughout the islands in Mosquito Lagoon are available year-round.

❶ Information

Canaveral National Seashore Visitor Information Center (p313) is located just south of the North District entrance gate. Alternatively, the visitors center at Merritt Island National Wildlife Refuge can also provide information.

There is a fee station at both the North and South District entrances. There is a toilet at most beach parking areas.

Note that the park closes for three days preceding launches. For information on launch closures call 🖉321-867-4077.

❶ Getting There & Around

To get to the North District take I-95 to SR 44 (exit 249), head east to New Smyrna Beach, and then south on A1A 7 miles to the entrance gate. Access to the South District is 12 miles east of Titusville, through Merritt Island National Wildlife Refuge (I-95 exit 220 to SR 406). There is no public transportation to or within the park and no road access to Klondike Beach.

Cocoa Beach & Cape Canaveral
🖉321 / POP 21,130

In 1919 the first of three bridges to span the Intracoastal waterway was built connecting Cocoa Village to its namesake beach on the barrier island. Then, as now, day-trippers streamed across the bridge on their way to the oceanside boardwalk. As America raced to the moon in the wake of WWII, Cocoa Beach raced to keep up with growth, building dozens of motels and gaining a reputation as a party town. Cape Canaveral to the north evolved into a quieter residential community for space workers and their families.

In 1951 the US Army Corps of Engineers carved out an inlet at the cape to facilitate the shipping of goods to the Space Center. In the process it created the Thousand Islands from the dredged mud and laid the foundations for Port Canaveral, now the second busiest cruise port in the United States.

◉ Sights

Historic Cocoa Village is located on the mainland with the brasher, livelier Cocoa Beach and Port Canaveral across the causeway on the barrier island. In addition to the public beaches with seasonal lifeguards, stub-end streets access the ocean south from Ron Jon's to the air-force base.

Cocoa Village   NEIGHBORHOOD
Originally a trading post along the Indian River, Cocoa Village started serving tourists in the late 19th century when steamboat travelers disembarked along **Riverfront Park** to stretch their legs. Now the historic downtown offers a pleasant alternative to Cocoa Beach. Its main drag, Delannoy Ave, is lined with historic structures such as the **SF Travis Building**, which houses a hardware store (the village's oldest existing business).

THE SPACE COAST COCOA BEACH & CAPE CANAVERAL

Cocoa Beach

You'll also find several good cafes and upscale restaurants here, and there's a weekly **Farmers Market** (http://cocoamainstreet.com/projects/farmersmarket; Myrt Tharpe Sq; ⊘9am-3pm Wed).

Astronaut Memorial Planetarium & Observatory OBSERVATORY (☏321-433-7373; www.easternflorida.edu/community-resources/planetarium; Bldg 19, 1519 Clearlake Rd, Cocoa Village; shows adult/child under 12yr $8/5; ⊘exhibition hall 2-4pm Wed & 6.30-10pm Fri & Sat, shows from 7pm Fri & Sat, observatory 6.30-10pm Fri & Sat) Discover new galaxies and constellations in this 70ft domed planetarium that projects the night skies in startling detail enhanced with laser effects and accompanied by soaring soundtracks from Pink Floyd, Jimi Hendrix and the Beatles. On Friday and Saturday nights, volunteers help visitors navigate the real night sky through one of the largest telescopes in Florida, powerful enough to bring the rings of Saturn into focus and highlight lunar craters.

The planetarium is located on the campus of Brevard Community College, 10 minutes north of Cocoa Village off Clearlake Rd.

Cocoa Beach Pier PIER (www.cocoabeachpier.com; 401 Meade Ave; ⊘7-2am) Souvenir shops, restaurants and bars stretch along this 800ft pier built as a family attraction in 1962. It remains the focus of annual events such as the Easter Surfing

Festival. Fishing rods are available to rent for $15, and there's a $5 fee to fish on the pier with your own equipment.

Activities

Banana River, Indian River and Mosquito Lagoon lure water enthusiasts of all kinds, and as a prime surf spot Cocoa Beach is home to legendary surfing emporium Ron Jon's which stocks a surfer's every need. Nearby Cocoa Beach and Cape Canaveral are perfect for beginners, while the beaches at Patrick Air Force Base and Sebastian Inlet offer more challenging waves for experts.

At Port Canaveral a pleasant 1.5-mile cycle trail runs from Jetty Park to Rodney S Ketcham Park with access from North Atlantic Ave. Plenty of outlets around town rent bikes for $10 per two hours.

Jetty Park · PARK, BEACH
(www.jettyparkbeachandcampground.com; 9035 Campground Circle, Cape Canaveral; non-resident/resident per vehicle $10/5) Facing the distant Cape Canaveral Lighthouse, this 35-acre coastal park is a prime spot for sunbathing, fishing and watching cruise ships set sail. Chairs, umbrellas, kayaks and paddleboards can all be rented at the beach, which is patrolled by lifeguards. There are also grills, a playground and a couple of food concessions.

Ron Jon Surf Shop · WATER SPORTS
(321-799-8888; www.ronjonsurfshop.com; 4151 N Atlantic Ave, Cocoa Beach; 24hr) Rents just about anything water related, from fat-tired beach bikes ($15 daily) to surfboards ($30 daily). You can also sign up for surf school here ($65 per person for a one-hour lesson).

Sidney Fischer Park · BEACH
(Hwy A1A; parking $5) The closest beach to downtown Cocoa Beach, Fischer Park is crowded with surfers and cruise-ship crowds.

Lori Wilson Park · BEACH
(1500 N Atlantic Ave, Cocoa Beach) A 32-acre park with a mellow vibe and park-like facilities including wheelchair access, a playground, picnic tables and grills and a small dog-play area. Parking is free and plentiful.

Tours

Fin Expeditions · KAYAK TOUR
(321-698-7233; www.finexpeditions.com; 599 Ramp Rd; per person $30) Linger to watch a cormorant dry his wings, coast gently over horseshoe crabs and pause as Cinnamon explains the differences between mangrove species. The calm waters, stable boats and attentive and enthusiastic guides make this an excellent choice for families.

Indian River Queen · BOAT TOUR
(321-454-7414; www.indianriverqueen.com; Cocoa Village Marina, 90 Delannoy Ave; cruises $35-60) Take a trip back in time on this romantic paddleboat. The history-themed tour includes a narrated presentation on 19th-century Cocoa Village, when paddleboats were the norm and homesteaders hung a white cloth at the end of their pier to flag them down. Dinner and sunset booze cruises are also available. Check out the website for the schedule.

Grasshopper Airboat Eco Tours · AIRBOAT TOUR
(321-631-2990; www.airboatecotours.com; 5665 Lake Poinsett Rd; per person $42) Often referred to as the Central Florida Everglades, the marshy shallows of the St Johns River are packed with alligators and migrating birds. Hop on board with US Coast Guard Master Captain Rick for thrilling ecotours through the marshy shallows. Afternoon tours see the best alligator sunbathing.

CATCHING A WAVE

Eleven-time surfing world champion Kelly Slater, born and raised in Cocoa Beach, learned his moves in the Space Coast surf – this is arguably the best place in Florida to catch a wave. Surfing culture thrives around here. You'll have no problem finding a place to rent a board, and there are surfing events year-round. The **Ron Jon Easter Surf Festival**, the country's second-oldest surf competition, attracts 30,000-plus cool surfers, tanned beach bunnies and sunburned college kids.

The long-running **Ron Jon Surf School** (321-868-1980; www.cocoabeachsurfing-school.com; 150 E Columbia Lane, Cocoa Beach; per hr $50-65) offers lessons for everyone from groms (that's surf talk for beginners) to experts, and there are plenty of other schools. For children aged five to 17, Beach Place Guest House hosts week-long **Surf Art Camps** (321-799-3432; www.marymoonarts.com; per child $295; 9am-3pm Jun-Aug).

⭐ Festivals & Events

Easter Surf Festival SPORT
(www.eastersurffest.com; Cocoa Beach Pier) Ron Jon's Easter weekend surfing festival has been a tradition since 1964 and now draws crowds of more than 100,000 fans to watch some of the best surfers in the world.

Art of Sand CULTURE
(www.artofsand.org; Radisson Resort, 8701 Astronaut Blvd; adult/child $8/4) On the first weekend in April master sand artists from around the world congregate at the Radisson Resort in Cape Canaveral to compete for awards. Gates stay open for a month.

🛏 Sleeping

Of Cocoa Beach's many chain hotels, most located along a 2-mile stretch south from Ron Jon, the Doubletree sits directly on the beach and is separated a bit from the others.

Jetty Park CAMPGROUND $
(☎321-783-7111; www.jettyparkbeachandcampground.com; 400 Jetty Rd, Cape Canaveral; campsites $27-49, cabins $84; P 🤖 🛜 🎫) After extensive renovations in 2013, Jetty Park offers eight new cabins, fire pits for RV sites, a playground, two pavilions, 93 barbecue grills, beach access and a fishing pier.

Residence Inn Cape Canaveral HOTEL $$
(☎321-323-1100; www.marriott.com; 8959 Astronaut Blvd, Cape Canaveral; r $139-189; P 🌸 🛜 🎫) If you want to get away from the Cocoa Beach party scene, book into this comfortable Marriott hotel in Cape Canaveral. Rooms may be corporate, but they offer acres of space, comfortable beds and kitchenettes. Staff are also extremely accommodating and there's a pretty pool area. Popular with the pre-cruise crowd.

Surf Studio MOTEL $$
(☎321-783-7100; http://surf-studio.com; 1801 S Atlantic Ave, Cocoa Beach; r & ste $115-160; P 🌸 🛜 🎫 🎫) Friendly old-school, single-story, family-owned motel that sits on the ocean and offers basic doubles and apartments surrounded by grass and palms. One-bedroom apartments sleeping six cost $195 to $225; there's no charge for children under 10.

⭐ **Solrisa Inn** B&B $$$
(☎321-301-4419; http://solrisainn.com; 241 Indian River Dr, Cocoa Village; r $150-300, cottages $275-400; P 🌸 🛜 🎫) Solrisa sits on the banks of the Indian River and comes complete with a dock where guests sip sundowners and push off their paddle boats. Inside, the turn-of-the-century house unfolds in sunny Caribbean colors, and period floorboards gleam beneath Persian rugs. Accommodation is in three meticulously decorated rooms and a one-bedroom cottage that previously served as the cookhouse. Each room comes with its own deck and rocking chair.

⭐ **Beach Place Guesthouses** APARTMENT $$$
(☎321-783-4045; www.beachplaceguesthouses.com; 1445 S Atlantic Ave, Cocoa Beach; ste $195-395; P 🛜) A slice of heavenly relaxation in Cocoa Beach's partying beach scene, this laid-back two-story guesthouse in a residential neighborhood has roomy suites with hammocks and a lovely deck, all just steps from the dunes and beach.

🍴 Eating

⭐ **Green Room Cafe** VEGETARIAN $
(☎321-868-0203; http://greenroomcafecocoabeach.com; 222 N 1st St, Cocoa Beach; mains $6-12; ⏱10.30am-9pm Mon-Sat; 🍴) Focusing all its energies on the 'goodness within', this super cafe delights the health-conscious with fruit-combo açaí bowls, wheat- and gluten-free sandwiches, real fruit smoothies and homemade soups and wraps. If the 'Tower of Power' smoothie (sambazon, açai, peach, strawberry, honey and apple juice) fails to lift you the vibrant decor and friendly company will.

Ossorio CAFE $
(☎321-639-2423; 316 Brevard Ave, Cocoa Village; mains $7-9; ⏱8am-8.30pm Mon-Sat, 9am-6pm Sun) Fuel up pre- or post-beach at this sunny cafe, serving sandwiches, flatbread pizza, ice cream and coffee drinks.

⭐ **Seafood Atlantic** SEAFOOD $$
(☎321-784-0333; www.seafoodatlantic.org; 520 Glen Cheek Dr, Port Canaveral; mains $8-19; ⏱11am-6.30pm Mon & Wed, to 7.30pm Thu & Sun, to 8.30pm Fri & Sat) With deep roots in Canaveral's fishing industry, this restaurant (with outdoor deck) is one of the few places to serve locally sourced shrimp, crabs, mussels, clams, oysters and fish. If they're in, order a bucket of Florida's deep-sea golden crab, which has a deliciously moist and creamy texture. If you bring a cool bag you can also stock up at the market next door.

Slow and Low Barbecue
BARBECUE $$

(📞 321-783-6199; http://slowandlowbarbeque.com; 306 N Orlando Ave, Cocoa Beach; mains $7-15; ⏰ 11am-10pm Mon-Sat, from noon Sun) After a day on the beach, nothing satisfies better than a plate overflowing with barbecue ribs, fried okra, turnip greens and fried sweet potatoes. There's a daily happy hour and live music Thursday through Sunday.

Lone Cabbage Fish Camp
SEAFOOD $$

(📞 321-632-4199; www.twisterairboatrides.com; 8199 Hwy 520; mains $8-15; ⏰ 10am-9pm Sun-Thu, to 10pm Fri & Sat) Come to this Old Florida fish camp for cold beers, fried gator tail and sunset views over the Indian River. If you want, you can even scoot around the lagoon on its airboats (adult/child $22/15). You'll find it west of Cocoa Village on Hwy 520.

★ Fat Snook
SEAFOOD $$$

(📞 321-784-1190; http://thefatsnook.com; 2464 S Atlantic Ave, Cocoa Beach; mains $22-36; ⏰ 5:30-10pm) Hidden inside an uninspired building, tiny Fat Snook stands out as an oasis of fine cooking. Under the direction of Mona and John Foy, gourmet seafood is expertly prepared with unexpected herbs and spices influenced by Caribbean flavors.

The new sister restaurant, **Crush Eleven** (📞 321-634-1100; www.crusheleven.com/; 11 Riverside Drive, Cocoa Village; mains $8-26; ⏰ 5.30-9pm Mon-Sat, 11am-8.30 Sun), in Cocoa Village also gets top marks for its modern-American menu and crafted cocktails. Brunch on Sunday is the real highlight, with inventive dishes such as cilantro-lime crab cakes Benedict and carrot-cake pancakes.

Café Margaux
FRENCH, MEDITERRANEAN $$$

(📞 321-639-8343; http://margaux.com; 220 Brevard Ave, Cocoa Village; mains $15-45; ⏰ 11.30am-2pm & 5-9pm Mon-Sat) A longtime favorite of Cocoa Village regulars is this creative Mediterranean restaurant. Dine on the patio or in one of the themed dining rooms on sweet onion-crusted red snapper or braised veal scalloppini. To accompany your meal choose from a wine list that runs to 4000 labels.

🍷 Drinking & Entertainment

Beach Shack
LIVE MUSIC

(📞 321-783-2250; www.beachshackbar.com; 1 Minutemen Causeway; ⏰ 8pm-midnight Thu-Fri, 2pm-midnight Sat, 2-10pm Sun) A classic locals' bar with two pool tables, a beachfront patio, and blues Thursday to Sunday.

Coconuts on the Beach
BAR, RESTAURANT

(📞 321-784-1422; www.coconutsonthebeach.com; 2 Minutemen Causeway; mains $8-18; ⏰ 11am-10pm) Coconuts isn't just a name; it's a favored ingredient. The oceanfront 'party deck' hosts regular live music.

Mai Tiki Bar
BAR

(www.cocoabeachpier.com; Cocoa Beach Pier; ⏰ 11am-10pm) Kick back at this bar at the very tip of Cocoa Beach Pier and soak up the surfing-town mood.

Cocoa Village Playhouse
PERFORMING ARTS

(📞 321-636-5050; www.cocoavillageplayhouse.com; 300 Brevard Ave, Cocoa Village) Stages locally produced plays on the site of the ornate Aladdin Theatre (1924).

🛍 Shopping

Ron Jon Surf Shop
OUTDOOR EQUIPMENT

(www.ronjons.com; 4151 N Atlantic Ave; ⏰ 24hr) With live music, classic cars and a warehouse jammed with everything you could possibly need for a day at the beach, the massive 52,000-sq-ft Ron Jon is more than a store. And should you find yourself needing surf wax at 4am, no worries – it's open 24 hours a day.

Sunseed Food Co-op
FOOD & DRINK

(www.sunseedfoodcoop.com; 6615 N Atlantic Ave; ⏰ 9.30am-7pm Mon-Fri, 10am-6pm Sat & Sun) Swing by this healthy oasis for locally grown fruit, veggies, microbrew beers, wines and after-sun lotions.

Village Outfitters
OUTDOOR EQUIPMENT

(📞 321-633-7245; www.villageoutfitters.com; 229 Forrest Ave, Cocoa Village; ⏰ 10am-5pm Mon-Fri, 8.30am-4pm Sat) Outdoor and camping gear, as well as kayak rental.

ℹ Information

Go to www.cocoabeach.com for events, accommodations and more.

Space Coast Office of Tourism (📞 321-433-4470; www.visitspacecoast.com; 430 Brevard Ave, Cocoa Village; ⏰ 9am-5pm Mon-Sat) Inside the Bank of America, one block south of the Village Playhouse.

ℹ Getting There & Away

Three causeways – Hwy 528, Hwy 520 and Hwy 404 – cross Indian River, Merritt Island and Banana River to connect Cocoa Beach to the mainland. At Ron Jon's, Hwy 528 (also Minutemen Causeway) cuts south and becomes Hwy AIA (also Atlantic Ave), a north–south strip with chain hotels and restaurants, tourist shops and condos. Hwy A1A divides into two one-ways (southbound Orlando Ave and northbound Atlantic Ave) for a couple miles, reconnects and continues south along the barrier-island coast 53 miles to Vero Beach and beyond.

Melbourne & Indialantic

South of Cocoa Beach, Hwy A1A stretches along the barrier island 53 miles to Vero Beach, passing plenty of well-signed access to Atlantic beaches, state parks, small pockets of condos and long stretches of emptiness.

Indialantic, a blink-and-you-miss-it beach town 16 miles south of Cocoa Beach, isn't expansive, but it sure feels homey. You'll find a pizza place and a handful of other businesses, and the same surf and white sand, but it's worlds away from the Cocoa Beach rattle and hum.

On the mainland a few minutes west of Indialantic (look for signs on A1A), historic Melbourne offers a small-town feel with several good restaurants, coffee shops and bars. The original settlement was established by freed slaves and pineapple farmers who built homesteads on a small peninsula between Indian River and Crane Creek in the 1870s. A fire destroyed the burgeoning town in 1919 and a new downtown was resurrected along New Haven Ave, which remains much as it was in the 1920s.

◉ Sights & Activities

★ **Brevard Zoo**   ZOO
(🖉 321-254-9453; www.brevardzoo.org; 8225 N Wickham Rd, Melbourne; adult/child 2-12yr $16/12, Treetop Trek adult/small child $40/22; ⊙9:30am-5pm) For over 20 years this community-built zoo has set standards for imaginative design, immersive wildlife experiences, education and conservation. Since hammer-holding locals came out in force in March 1994 to start construction, the zoo's landscape has evolved via winding boardwalks through hardwood hammocks into distinct geographical zones featuring wildlife from Florida, South America, Africa and Australia. Specially designed enclosures merging with the undergrowth and free-flight aviaries give a real sense of wandering through a wilderness.

The zoo's best experiences are the kayak tours past gangly giraffes down the Nyami river and the Tree Top Trek, an aerial adventure course incorporating zip lines over wetland ponds and alligator pools.

Once you've got over the enjoyment of wandering around the zoo's unique environment, you'll begin to notice its dedication to the serious work of conservation and wildlife education. The Paws On children's area invites kids to build, explore and splash around on a real sand beach, engage in hookless fishing and pet the resident pigmy goats and alpacas. Volunteers work tirelessly to create oyster mats for the oyster-reef-regeneration project in Indian River; and the Wildlife Detective Training Academy encourages curiosity and inquiry in older kids through self-guided mystery tours designed around the zoo.

In addition, there are night hikes, a Junior Zoo Keeper's Club, summer camps, animal-adoption programs and well-attended community events, including the popular Boo at the Zoo Halloween celebration. For kids and animal lovers this may well outshine the Space Center.

Ryckman Park   PARK, PIER
(cnr Ocean Ave & Riverside Dr, Melbourne) Located in Melbourne's historic district, this family-friendly park features a large playground, bocce and basketball courts and the nationally registered Melbourne Beach Pier (1889). The latter extends into the fish-rich Indian River, making it a fantastic fishing spot.

Melbourne Beach   BEACH
(Ocean Park, Atlantic St, Melbourne) Backed by Ocean Park with its boardwalk, gazebo and showers, Melbourne Beach, along with its neighbour, Indialantic Beach (to the north), offers miles and miles of white, sandy shoreline unspoilt by high-rise condos and commercialism. Pick up picnic essentials at the Melbourne Beach Market (🖉 321-676-5225; 302 Ocean Ave; ⊙8am-8pm Mon-Sat, 9am-7pm Sun).

★ **Honest John's Fish Camp**   KAYAKING
(🖉 321-727-2923; www.honestjohnsfishcamp.com; 750 Mullet Creek Rd, Melbourne Beach; kayaks per hr/day $12/50, boats per half/full day $60/90; ⊙6am-6pm Wed-Mon) Rent kayaks and motor boats from this 1899 Florida Cracker homestead on the edge of Indian River. Set in an old citrus grove on Mullet Creek, it's a prime spot for fishing and spotting manatees. The camp is 10 miles south of Melbourne Beach.

Bob's Bicycle Shop
BICYCLE RENTAL

(☎ 321-725-2500; http://bobsbicycles.com; 113 5th Ave, Indialantic; per day/week $60/175; ⊙ 9.30am-6pm Mon-Sat, 11am-3pm Sun) Tool up with a super-cool Sun Cycle specially designed for riding on the beach.

🛏 Sleeping

Sea View Motel
MOTEL $$

(☎ 321-723-0566; www.seaviewmelbourne.com; 4215 S Hwy A1A, Melbourne Beach; r & ste $125-195; ❄🐾🐕) Located directly on the beach, this renovated 1950s motel has eight simple rooms with quilts, wood floors and fully equipped kitchens.

Crane Creek Inn
B&B $$

(☎ 321-768-6416; www.cranecreekinn.com; 907 E Melbourne Ave, Melbourne; r $165; 🅿❄🐾🐕) Two blocks from downtown Melbourne, this attractive 1925 home sits directly on Crane Creek, where manatees, dolphins and water birds can be seen. Rooms are furnished in period style with lazy ceiling fans and there is a hot tub and a two-person hammock beside the river.

★ Port d'Hiver
BOUTIQUE HOTEL $$$

(☎ 321-722-2727; www.portdhiver.com; 201 Ocean Ave, Melbourne Beach; r $279-329, ste $479-519; 🅿❄🐾🐕) Constructed in 1916, this cypress-built colonial-style beach house sits amid tall palms, hidden behind flowering bougainvillea and bright pink allamanda. Brick-paved courtyards connect the main house with seven cabana rooms and the carriage-house suite, and views of the Atlantic are complemented by artful interior decor incorporating French printed fabrics, candelabra chandeliers, antique dressers and four-poster beds.

★ Seashell Suites
RESORT $$$

(☎ 321-409-0500; www.seashellsuites.com; 8795 S Hwy A1A; r $225-245) 🐾 This low-key eco-resort has been designed to blend in with its pristine natural setting. With only eight two-bedroom suites, the atmosphere is intimate and environmental standards are high: there's a saltwater pool and cleaning agents are toxin free. Beach chairs, bikes, umbrellas, boogie boards and fishing supplies are all complimentary, and the digital library has a good stock of movies. Rates are reduced for weekly stays.

🍴 Eating

Ichabods Dockside
AMERICAN $

(☎ 321-952-9532; www.ichabodsbarandgrille-florida.com; 2210 Front St, Melbourne; mains $8-12; ⊙ 11am-11pm) Eddy Fisher's laid-back bar is a local favorite for its easy-going barside banter and top-quality burgers, grilled grouper wraps and mind-blowingly good buffalo wings.

El Ambia Cubano
CUBAN $

(www.elambiacubano.com; 950 E Melbourne Ave, Melbourne; mains $8-12; ⊙ 11am-10pm Mon-Sat) Conga stools, weekend salsa, jazz and acoustic guitar, and tasty family cooking in a tiny spot across from Crane Creek.

Beachside Cafe
CAFE $

(☎ 321-953-8444; www.thebeachsidecafe.com; 109 5th Ave, Indialantic; mains $6-12; ⊙ 7am-2pm; 🐾) It's worth the wait to grab a booth at this friendly downtown breakfast cafe, where Colleen regularly tops up coffee as locals scarf plates of stuffed French toast, griddled Belgian waffles and pastrami omelets.

Bizarro Famous NY Pizza
PIZZERIA $$

(☎ 321-724-4799; www.theoriginalbizzarro.com; 4 Wave Crest Ave, Indialantic; pizza $11-36; ⊙ 10am-10pm) This NY-style pizza joint sits magically beside the beach in Indialantic. Service is brusque – think 'the soup Nazi' but for pizza. But the spinach slice is divine with extra marinara sauce.

Scott's on Fifth
MEDITERRANEAN $$$

(☎ 321-729-9779; www.scottsonfifth.com; 141 5th Ave, Indialantic; mains $26-39; ⊙ 11am-2pm & 5.30-9pm Tue-Sun) This elegant restaurant on 5th Ave serves up European classics such as filet mignon, shrimp beurre blanc and Dijon-crusted rack of lamb. It's easy to miss as it's tucked behind a tiny storefront, and as there are only 12 tables you'll need to reserve in advance.

🍷 Drinking & Entertainment

While Cocoa Beach pays homage to the gods of commercialism, Melbourne prefers to pay its dues to those of culture with a thriving community arts, music and theatre scene.

On Friday and Saturday nights, **East New Haven Street** in downtown Melbourne is transformed into an urban block party. **Meg O'Malley's** (www.megomalleys.com; 812 E New Haven Ave; ⊙ 10.30-1am) Irish pub serves up 18¢ bowls of Parliament soup with Guinness and live music; **Main Street Pub** (http://main

streetpub.cc; 705 E New Haven Ave; ⊘11.30am-late Tue-Sat, from 4pm Mon & Sun) offers a good selection of beers and a nice deck; and the gay-friendly **Foo Bar** (816 E New Haven Ave; ⊘5pm-2am) draws an older crowd with an Asian-themed menu and cocktails.

Sand on the Beach   BAR
(http://sandonthebeach.com; 1005 Atlantic St, Melbourne Beach; ⊘8-2am) The only place where you can keep the sand between your toes and a margarita in your hand.

★Melbourne Civic Theatre   THEATER
(☑321-723-6935; www.mymct.org; 817 E Strawbridge Ave, Melbourne; tickets $25) The Space Coast's oldest community theater stages early Broadway productions and popular contemporary pieces in a tiny spot in La Galerie. They're a talented bunch and with only 90 seats in the auditorium it's an exciting space in which to experience live performances.

Henegar Center   ARTS CENTER, THEATER
(☑321-723-8698; www.henegar.org; 625 E New Haven Ave, Melbourne) Melbourne's one-time high school now houses a community arts center and a 500-seat proscenium-style theater where the resident Red Carpet Productions stages musicals and comedies.

Brevard Symphony Orchestra   CLASSICAL MUSIC
(☑321-242-2219; King Center, 3865 N Wickham, Melbourne) This 65-strong, not-for-profit orchestra has been bringing music to Melbourne residents for over 60 years and is one of the finest in the country. For the July 4 celebrations the symphony plays at the Cocoa Riverfront Park beneath a spectacular firework display.

Sebastian Inlet & Around

Continuing south along Hwy A1A, development trickles beyond sleepy Melbourne Beach. You'll find plenty of access to beaches, hiking and birding along both the Atlantic Coast and the Indian River. Just south of Sebastian Inlet State Park, mile after mile of tidy hedges and bike paths line the highway, hiding the upscale homes of northern Vero Beach.

⊙ Sights & Activities

The following recommended sights, all along Hwy A1A, are listed geographically from north to south.

Sebastian Inlet State Park   PARK
(☑321-984-4852; www.floridastateparks.org/sebastianinlet; 9700 South State Rd; cyclist/vehicle $2/8; ⊘dawn-dusk) Stretching along a narrow strip of the barrier island, this busy park, popular with fishermen, surfers, boaters and families, is divided into two sections by the inlet bridge. On the north side swimming is safe for children in the calm-water lagoon; on the south you'll find a **marina** (☑321-724-5424; www.sebastianinlet.com; 9502 South Hwy A1A; ⊘8am-5pm) with boat rental, a small fishing museum and an uninspiring campground ($28 per site).

In June and July you can join ranger-led nesting walks (reservations necessary).

McClarty Treasure Museum   MUSEUM
(☑772-589-2147; Hwy A1A; adult/child under 6yr $2/free; ⊘10am-4pm) In 1715 a Spanish ship carrying gold and treasures went down in a hurricane, and survivors built a makeshift camp. This small museum, featuring a 45-minute movie, dioramas and artifacts from the shipwreck, sits on the site of that wreck. Even today, folks looking for a pretty shell stumble upon treasures washed ashore. The museum is one mile south of Sebastian Inlet State Park.

★Pelican Island National Wildlife Refuge   WILDLIFE RESERVE
(☑772-581-5557; www.fws.gov/pelicanisland; Hwy A1A; ⊘7:30am-sunset) **FREE** Established in 1903 as a refuge for the endangered brown pelican, Pelican Island was America's first federal bird reservation, the forerunner of today's national-wildlife-refuge system. The preserve now encompasses 500 acres along the Indian River Lagoon as well as the 2.2-acre Pelican Island, which can be seen from the observation tower at the end of the **Centennial Trail**. The two trails loop 2.5 miles along the shore and are perfect for bike rides and long hikes.

Pelican Island itself can also be viewed by boat and there are several public boat ramps to access the refuge waters.

Vero Beach

☑772 / POP 15,220

Dubbed 'zero beach' by action-hungry folks in Cocoa Beach, this carefully zoned coastal town, with lovely grassy parks, wide, white, lifeguarded beaches and a pedestrian-friendly downtown, feels like a step into the past.

WHAT'S AILING THE INDIAN RIVER LAGOON?

The Indian River Lagoon is the largest marine nursery in the US and the most biologically diverse estuary in North America. Straddling temperate and subtropical zones, the lagoon (actually an ecosystem of three separate estuaries) stretches 156 miles from New Smyrna to Jupiter Inlet and is washed by tidal waters through six inlet channels. The resulting warm, shallow, soupy water is a dynamic environment for 4300 species of animal, plant and bird and exploring it is one of the true highlights of this coastline.

But all is not well in this natural paradise. Three consecutive years of heavy rain since 2011 have caused unprecedented run-off from Lake Okeechobee, lowered the salinity of the lagoon, flushed it with silt and drawn in high levels of nitrogen and phosphorous from industrial agriculture and domestic fertiliser. The result has been a 60% decline in seagrass beds (47,000 acres) and a blooming of red macro algae that is poisonous for many lagoon dwellers. The year 2013 saw a dramatic 'mortality event' among the lagoon's mammalian population, with 84 recorded dolphin deaths and over 120 dead manatees.

Local protests at the Lake Okeechobee run-off triggered a congressional briefing in Washington seeking federal money to fix the afflicted lagoon, but so far only the water district has committed $3.7 million and four teams of scientists to investigate what's going on; a full report is due in 2017. With an annual economic impact of $4 billion and thousands of livelihoods at stake, figuring out what's ailing the lagoon is the single biggest environmental and economic challenge facing the Sunshine State.

⊙ Sights & Activities

Though most are happy to lose themselves in the lull of beach life, Vero boasts a rich commitment to both the arts and the environment. For more information see www.verobeach.com.

★ **Vero Beach Museum of Art**　MUSEUM
(www.vbmuseum.org; 3001 Riverside Park Dr; adult/under 17yr $10/free; ☉10am-4:30pm Mon-Sat, from 1pm Sun) With changing fine-art exhibitions and regular outdoor jazz concerts, this sleek, white museum in Riverside Park could easily hold its own against any big-city heavy hitter. Look for signs on Hwy A1A.

McKee Botanical Gardens　GARDENS
(☑772-794-0601; www.mckeegarden.org; 350 US 1; adult/child $12/5; ☉10am-5pm Mon-Sat, noon-5pm Sun; ⊞) In Vero's early-1920s tourist heyday Waldo Sexton (of the eponymous Waldo's) and Arthur McKee joined forces to open the 80-acre McKee Jungle Gardens, which delighted visitors for decades until Disney stole the show in the 1970s. Much of the land was sold off for development, but passionate locals managed to save 18 acres of tropical garden, which now grows thick with native plants, palms and lily ponds.

Adventure Kayaking　KAYAKING
(☑772-567-0522; www.paddleflorida.com; adult/child under 12yr $45/25) Vero native Steve Cox runs daily Indian River kayak tours to Round and Pelican Islands, Sebastian River

and Blue Cypress Lake. Multi-day camp-and-kayak tours ($275 to $350) are also offered on Indian River and further afield to the Everglades.

★ **Sail Moonraker**　BOATING
(☑772-696-2941; www.sailmoonraker.com; Vero Beach Marina, 3611 Rio Vista Blvd; 2-6hr cruises for up to 6 guests $425-750; ⊞) Captain Bruce offers customized dolphin-watching, swimming and sunset cruises in Indian River Lagoon, excellent for children, grandparents and everyone in between, aboard his 40ft catamaran.

Environmental Learning Center　OUTDOORS
(☑772-589-5050; www.discoverelc.org; 255 Live Oak Dr; adult/child under 12yr $5/free; ☉10am-4pm Tue-Fri, 9am-noon Sat, 1-4pm Sun; ⊞) This 51-acre reserve, dedicated to educating folks about the fragile environment of the Indian River estuary, offers hands-on displays and a boardwalk through the mangroves. Check the website for details on EcoVentures, guided nature trips including canoe and pontoon boat trips and nature walks.

Orchid Island Bikes & Kayaks　BICYCLE RENTAL
(☑772-299-1286; www.orchidislandbikesandkayaks.com; 1175 Commerce Ave; bikes per day/week $19/54, kayaks s/tandem per half-day $69/99) Vero Beach is the perfect place to ditch the car for a bike, as even kids can easily pedal to restaurants, hotels and the beach. Rent kayaks and toodle around Indian River Lagoon.

🛏 Sleeping

⭐ Caribbean Court Boutique Hotel
BOUTIQUE HOTEL **$$**

(☑772-231-7211; www.thecaribbeancourt.com; 1601 S Ocean Dr; r & ste $139-230; P ❄ 🕸 🛜 🏊 🎿) In a quiet residential area a block off South Beach, this lovely spot expertly blends understated elegance with a casual beach vibe. Bougainvillea and palm trees hide a small garden pool, and handsome white-washed rooms with earthy accents have rattan furnishings, decorative tiled sinks, thick towels and a refrigerator stocked with goodies. Ask about weekday discounts.

South Beach Place
MOTEL **$$**

(☑772-231-5366; www.southbeachplacevero. com; 1705 S Ocean Dr; ste per day $125-175; 🛜 🎿) Old Florida with a facelift, this tasteful and bright two-story motel in Vero Beach sits in a particularly quiet stretch across from the beach. One-bedroom suites have a full kitchen.

🍴 Eating & Drinking

Barefoot Cafe
CAFE **$**

(☑772 770-1733; www.thebarefootcafe.com; 2036 14th Ave; sandwiches $5-10; ⊙8am-3pm Mon-Fri) Although it doesn't have a beachside location, this laid-back deli is a surf shack in its soul. Sandwiches, salads and wraps are homemade daily and include high-end ingredients such as ahi tuna, shiitake mushrooms and shredded asiago cheese.

Waldo's
SEAFOOD **$$**

(☑772-231-7091; www.waldosvero.net; Driftwood Resort, 3150 Ocean Dr; mains $10-22; P 🐾) Built out of driftwood by pioneering Vero settler Waldo Sexton in 1935, this is a Vero Beach institution for dinner and music for every-

one (from 9pm). Eat Cajun grouper wraps on the deck overlooking the ocean or prop up the rustic bar with the locals.

Lemon Tree
CAFE **$$**

(☑772-231-0858; 3125 Ocean Dr; mains $8-20; ⊙7am-9pm) Bright and busy, this cheerful downtown eatery is particularly popular for weekend brunch.

⭐ Maison Martinique
FRENCH **$$$**

(☑772-231-7299; Caribbean Court Boutique Hotel, 1603 S Ocean Dr; mains $24-42; ⊙5-10pm Tue-Sat) In Vero Beach, Maison Martinique offers outstanding French cuisine with first-rate service and intimate surrounds. On warm evenings, eat by the little pool; for something more casual, head to the romantic Havana piano bar upstairs.

Kilted Mermaid
PUB

(☑772-569-5533; www.kiltedmermaid.com; 1937 Old Dixie Hwy; ⊙5pm-1am Tue-Sun) Do as they say and 'drink outside the box' at this raucous local pub that serves over 80 craft and imported beers. Then order a cheese plate or chocolate fondue to keep the party going. There's an open mic on Wednesday, trivia on Thursday and live music every Friday and Saturday.

ℹ Getting There & Away

Vero Beach lies 53 miles south of Cocoa Beach on Hwy A1A. The closest international airports are in Orlando, 90 minutes to the northwest, West Palm Beach, 90 minutes to the south, and Melbourne, 30 minutes up the coast. **Vero Beach Shuttle** (☑772-834-1060; www.verobeachshuttle.com; Melbourne/Palm Beach/Orlando airport $95/130/175) provides an airport-shuttle service.

Northeast Florida

Best Places to Eat

➡ Collage (p344)

➡ High Tide at Snack Jacks (p335)

➡ Kelley's Courtyard Café (p356)

➡ Satchel's Pizza (p364)

➡ Cress (p359)

Best Places to Stay

➡ Ritz Carlton Amelia Island (p355)

➡ At Journey's End (p343)

➡ One Ocean (p351)

➡ Addison (p355)

➡ Shoreline & Cabana (p331)

Why Go?

Few regions highlight the diversity of Florida's geography and character as dramatically as the Northeast.

Near the Florida–Georgia border, Amelia Island is a gorgeous Southern belle, resplendent in nature's finest ornamentation. An hour to the south, Jacksonville, Florida's most populous city, is an urban sprawl of high-rises, highways and steel-girded bridges. Jacksonville's mellow beaches offer a refreshingly slower pace to their southern Atlantic counterparts. Incongruous and unique, nearby St Augustine, the oldest continuously occupied city in the US, has something for everyone – history, architecture, culture, a gamut of excellent dining and plenty of kid-friendly tourist schmaltz. The latter edges its way down to Daytona, 'the most famous beach in the world,' a proud party king, ever at the ready to whip off his shirt, down a beer with a shot of tequila and get all revved up for some r-r-r-racing: NASCAR, that is.

When to Go
Daytona Beach

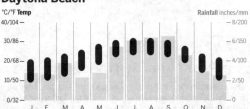

Mar & Apr ...or not to go. Spring break: boozed-up college students galore, especially in Daytona Beach.

Jun–Sep High season; temps range from balmy to sweltering.

Nov–Feb Cooler weather brings price fluctuations; you may have miles of coastline to yourself.

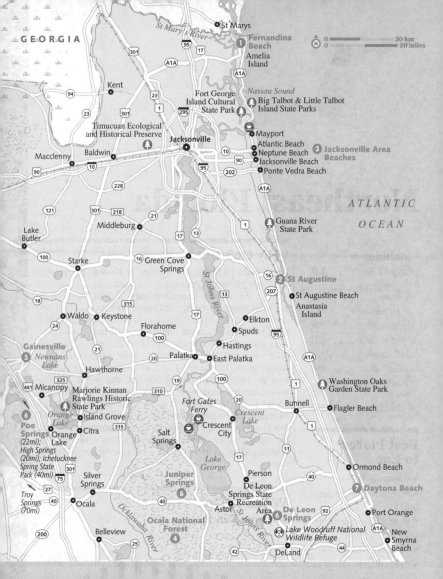

Northeast Florida Highlights

1 Relaxing on the porch of a Victorian B&B on Amelia Island's postcard-pretty **Fernandina Beach** (p353).

2 Exploring the unique Spanish-colonial architecture, fascinating museums and history in **St Augustine** (p335), America's oldest city.

3 Discovering how city bravado and beachside mellow coexist at the **Jacksonville area beaches** (p351).

4 Hiking and camping through pristine, wildlife-dense **Ocala National Forest** (p361).

5 Rocking out in **Gainesville** (p362), home of Florida's largest university, funky young thangs, cheap eats and cool bars.

6 Marveling at the cool azure waters of **Poe Springs** (p367), **De Leon Springs** (p359) and **Juniper Springs** (p361).

7 Driving along 'the world's most famous beach' then catching some NASCAR and downing some beer at **Daytona Beach** (p327).

ATLANTIC COAST

In 1902 speed catapulted Daytona Beach into the national psyche when playboy race-car drivers Ransom Olds (of Oldsmobile fame) and Alexander Winston waged a high-profile race along its unusually hard-packed sandy shore, reaching an unheard of top speed of 57mph. One year later, the Florida East Coast Automobile Association was founded, soon followed by the first Winter Speed Carnival – predecessor to today's Daytona 500. For the next 30 years Daytona Beach was where speed records were set and shattered. Stock-car racing came into vogue during the late 1930s; 'Race Weeks' packed beaches with fans and in 1947 NASCAR was born (see boxed text on p329).

Fortunately, there's a lot more to see and experience along this wonderful stretch of coastline than just the high-octane hype of Daytona. State Rd A1A heads north alongside the Atlantic Ocean through mellow Flagler Beach and on to historic St Augustine, where a one- or two-night sojourn is highly recommended. The road continues through affluent Ponte Vedra (headquarters of the PGA golf tour) and mega-urban Jacksonville's delightfully low-key strip of beaches, all the way to charming Amelia Island and the Florida–Georgia border. Along the way there's a plethora of picturesque islands and parks to explore, endless rugged coastline and a bunch of beachfront-mansion eye candy to boot.

Daytona Beach

Known for its wide, hard-packed white sandy beaches, for its gaudy carnival attractions, and as a mecca for leather-clad bikers, revheads and spring breakers, Daytona Beach is most famous as the birthplace of the ultra-Southern and mega-popular motorsport of NASCAR racing and as home of the Daytona 500. All this talk of racing has been known to inspire drivers to push the pedal to the metal. Police know this, of course, and quickly curtail any need for speed.

Anything but a wallflower, Daytona Beach draws a good-time crowd: it hosts one of the last spring breaks on the Atlantic Coast (tamer now than during its halcyon days); its population quintuples during speedweeks; and as many as half a million bikers roar into town for Bike Week in March and Biketoberfest in October. If balmy beer-soaked days and nights of motor racing, motorcycles and the men who love them are your thing, you might have found your heaven on earth. If not, move on.

If you can see past the garish beachside barricade of '70s high-rise blocks, nightclubs and tourist traps (if not quite literally), you might witness the phenomena of nesting sea turtles (in season) or explore a handful of interesting and worthwhile cultural attractions.

◉ Sights & Activities

★ Ponce de Leon Inlet Lighthouse & Museum   LIGHTHOUSE
(☑ 386-761-1821; www.ponceinlet.org; 4931 S Peninsula Dr, Ponce Inlet; adult/child $5/1.50; ☺ 10am-6pm Sep-May, to 9pm Jun-Aug) Those prone to vertigo may wish to forgo the 203-spiral-step climb to the top of Florida's tallest lighthouse and enjoy the interesting historical displays of the museum buildings instead. For everyone else, the views of the Atlantic Ocean from the top of the 53m structure, completed in 1887, are breathtaking. The lighthouse and museum are located 6 miles south of Daytona Beach.

★ Daytona International Speedway   RACETRACK
(☑ 800-748-7467; www.daytonainternationalspeedway.com; 1801 W International Speedway Blvd; tickets from $20) The Holy Grail of raceways has a diverse race schedule. Ticket prices skyrocket for good seats at big races, headlined by the Daytona 500 in February. It's worth wandering the massive stands for free on non-race days. First-come, first-served tram tours take in the track, pits and behind-the-scenes areas.

The 30-minute Speedway Tour (adult/child $16/10; ☺ 11:30am, 1:30pm, 3:30pm & 4pm) covers the basics. Die-hard revheads may wish to up the ante with the hour-long All Access Tour (adult/child $23/17; ☺ hourly 10am-3pm) or three-hour VIP Tour (tours $50; ☺ 1pm Tue, Thu, Sat); the latter covers everything NASCAR from the comfort of an air-conditioned coach. Real fanatics can indulge in the Richard Petty Driving Experience (p330), where you can either ride shotgun around the track or take a day to become the driver.

Daytona Beach   BEACH
(per car $5; ☺ beach driving 8am-7pm May-Oct, sunrise-sunset Nov-Apr) This perfectly planar stretch of sand was once the city's raceway. Sections of the beach still welcome drivers to the sands at a strictly enforced top speed

Daytona Beach

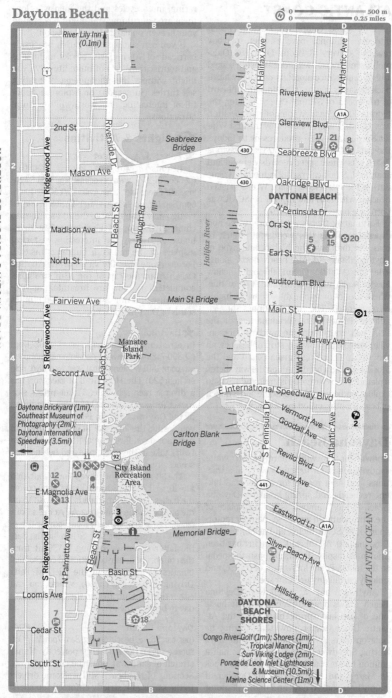

River Lily Inn
(0.1mi)

2nd St

Seabreeze
Bridge

N Ridgewood Ave

Riverside Dr

Mason Ave

N Beach St

Ballough Rd

Madison Ave

North St

Fairview Ave

Manatee
Island
Park

Second Ave

S Ridgewood Ave

N Beach St

Halifax River

Main St Bridge

Daytona Brickyard (1mi);
Southeast Museum of
Photography (2mi);
Daytona International
Speedway (3.5mi)

Carlton Blank
Bridge

City Island
Recreation
Area

E Magnolia Ave

S Ridgewood Ave

N Palmetto Ave

S Beach St

Memorial Bridge

Basin St

Loomis Ave

Cedar St

South St

N Halifax Ave

N Atlantic Ave

Riverview Blvd

Glenview Blvd

Seabreeze Blvd

Oakridge Blvd

DAYTONA BEACH

N Peninsula Dr

Ora St

Earl St

Auditorium Blvd

Main St

Harvey Ave

S Wild Olive Ave

E International Speedway Blvd

S Peninsula Dr

Vermont Ave
Goodall Ave

Revilo Blvd

Lenox Ave

S Atlantic Ave

Eastwood Ln

Silver Beach Ave

Hillside Ave

**DAYTONA
BEACH
SHORES**

Congo River Golf (1mi); Shores (1mi);
Tropical Manor (1mi);
Sun Viking Lodge (2mi);
Ponce de Leon Inlet Lighthouse
& Museum (10.5mi);
Marine Science Center (11mi)

ATLANTIC OCEAN

Daytona Beach

of 10mph. The most popular strip is a one-way stretch heading south between International Speedway Blvd and Dunlawton Ave. Beachside rentals for ATVs, fat-tired cruisers, recumbent trikes and all manner of water sports are ubiquitous. Of course, you're free to frolic anywhere on the beach, off the roadway.

Boardwalk & Pier WATERFRONT, PIER
(admission free; rides $3-5) Follow Main St E and you'll cross Daytona's sabal-palm-lined, ocean-fronting Boardwalk, bedecked with dollar-grabbing ice-cream shops, amusement arcades, rides and patios where you can sip beer from plastic cups. It's fun for the family with a side order of sleaze. Follow Main St further east toward the unmissable coral-colored pier, once a summer-vacation icon and still the longest in the US. Reopened after restoration in 2012, the 85-year-old wooden structure still feels a bit shabby, but perhaps that's to be expected when you jut 237m out into the wild Atlantic Ocean.

Marine Science Center AQUARIUM
(☑386-304-5545; www.marinesciencecenter.com; 100 Lighthouse Dr, Ponce Inlet; adult/child $5/2; ☺10am-4pm Tue-Sat, noon-4pm Sun; ⊛) We were impressed by this center's rescue, rehab and release programs for sea turtles and seabirds that nest on Daytona's beaches. It's a fun and environmentally conscious place where adults and kids can enjoy learning about our underwater friends. Exhibits include a 5000-gallon reef aquarium, a stingray touch pool and a bird-observation tower.

Museum of Arts & Sciences MUSEUM
(MOAS; ☑386-255-0285; www.moas.org; 352 S Nova Rd; adult/student/child $13/11/7; ☺9am-5pm Tue-Sat, from 11am Sun) This self-guided museum has a healthy dose of brain food for a fast and furious little town like Daytona.

NORTHEAST FLORIDA DAYTONA BEACH

NASCAR & THE AMERICAN SOUTH

During Prohibition, production of moonshine (corn liquor with a lightning-bolt kick) was integral to the Southern economy, and renegades filled up with cars speedy enough to outrun cops handled distribution. During their time off, they raced each other; when Prohibition was repealed the races continued. The most alluring venue was Daytona's Beach St track, where driver Bill France began promoting 'Race Weeks' that attracted thousands.

The sport exploded, though some automotive enthusiasts dismissed it as rednecks racing cars any mechanic could build. Mr France knew better and in 1947 set about transforming his obsession into a world-class sport: NASCAR, now the most-watched sport in America after football. It's hard to believe that it wasn't until as late as 1959 that racing was relocated from the beach itself to the Daytona International Speedway.

The appeal of NASCAR makes sense when you understand that dumping money at cars doesn't buy victory; winning relies on strategic driving skills and knowledge (when to pit, for example, or how many tires to change). Beneath those colorful product endorsements, the cars are everyday autos that conform to strict regulations to ensure the driver and pit crew – not the car – are tested.

VROOOM! DRIVE YOUR OWN RACE CAR

If merely watching NASCAR drivers streak around the track isn't adrenaline pumping enough, you can actually get in the car yourself via the **Richard Petty Driving Experience** (☎800-237-3889; www.drivepetty.com). Choose from several levels of death-defying action, from the three-lap passenger-seat Race Ride ($135) to the daylong Experience of a Lifetime ($2199), which puts you behind the wheel for 30 white-knuckle laps. The experience is held on a rotating basis on NASCAR tracks around the country; it usually lands in Daytona about three weekends out of the month – see the online calendar for details.

There's a delightful mishmash of everything from Cuban art and Coca-Cola memorabilia to train cars and teddy bears, and even the 13ft skeleton of a giant sloth. At the time of writing, work was almost complete on a brand new planetarium: the original had delighted locals for over 30 years.

Twenty minutes south of Daytona, **Gamble Place** (www.moas.org/gamble.place.html; 1819 Taylor Rd, Port Orange), the winter estate of the Gamble family (of Procter & Gamble fortune), lies in a sun-dappled glade. The restored cracker-style house and several whimsically named cottages (including a replica Snow White and the Seven Dwarfs house) are managed by MOAS and open on select dates: check the website for details.

Southeast Museum of Photography
MUSEUM

(☎386-506-4475; www.smponline.org; 1200 W International Speedway Blvd, Bldg 1200; ⊗11am-5pm Tue, Thu, Fri, 11am-7pm Wed, 1-5pm Sat & Sun) **FREE** We love this hidden treasure in Daytona, a service of the Daytona State College: it's the only museum in Florida dedicated solely to photography. This vibrant modern gallery with excellent lighting and facilities doesn't shy from provocative subjects in its rotating exhibitions. Best of all, it's free!

Jackie Robinson Ballpark & Museum
STADIUM

(☎386-257-3172; www.daytonacubs.com; 105 E Orange Ave; museum free, games in season from $7; ⊗9am-5pm; ⊞) 'The Jack' made history when, in 1946, the Montreal Royals, Jackie Robinson's team, were in Florida to play an exhibition against their parent club, the Brooklyn Dodgers: other Florida cities refused to let the game proceed due to segregation laws, but Daytona Beach cried, 'Play ball!' Robinson went on to be the first African American baseball player in the majors. The ballpark here was renamed in his honor in 1990. A small open-air museum tells the story.

Now home of the Daytona Cubs, a minor-league affiliate of the Chicago Cubs, the park, is situated on an island in the Halifax River and seats 4200 people.

Daytona Lagoon
WATER PARK

(☎386-254-5020; www.daytonalagoon.com; 601 Earl St; adult/child $28/21, all-inclusive pass $50; ⊗11am-11pm, shorter hours in winter; ⊞) Kids can burn off energy at this beachside water park, which has a tube float, a tidal-wave pool and a multilevel water playground, as well as arcade games, go-karts, laser tag, a climbing wall, an erupting volcano and a cannon blaster firing foam balls. Beware: some activities cost extra, unless you buy an all-inclusive pass.

Congo River Golf
MINI-GOLF

(☎386-258-6808; www.congoriver.com; 2100 S Atlantic Ave; adult/child $11/9; ⊗10am-11pm Sun-Thu, to midnight Fri & Sat; ⊞) Daytona's got plenty of mini-golf courses. But how many of them have live gators, dyed-blue waterfalls, a fake airplane and gem-panning?

⭐ Festivals & Events

February and March are mega in Daytona Beach. If you're not a NASCAR fan, biker or horny student, best to avoid town like the plague.

Budweiser Speedweeks
CAR RACING

(www.daytonainternationalspeedway.com) Over a week in February a bunch of races lead up to the big event, the Daytona 500. At the same time, 200,000 rowdy folks do a *lot* of partying.

Bike Week
MOTORCYCLES

(www.officialbikeweek.com) For 10 days in March, half a million bikers drool over each other's hogs and party round the clock. Locals run a 'death pool' predicting the number of casualties.

Spring Break
HOLIDAY

Over 100,000 exuberant, hormone-fueled youths from all corners of the US go off at the beach, in bars and clubs and on the streets. Keg stands galore. Early March.

Coke Zero 400
CAR RACING
(www.daytonainternationalspeedway.com) NASCAR fans fly the checkered flag at this 400-lap race during the July 4 weekend.

Biketoberfest
MOTORCYCLES
(www.officialbikeweek.com) Like Bike Week, but in mid-October. More drinking, bikes, burly blokes and busty babes. It generally begins the weekend following Columbus Day.

🛏 Sleeping

Accommodations here run the gamut: you can find everything from filthy fleabaggers to luxury suites – with a range of price tags. Prices soar during events: book well ahead if you're planning to attend, or juggle your dates if not. The Daytona Beach Area Convention & Visitors Bureau (p334) has the lowdown on all the beds in town. Most accommodations are located on Atlantic Ave, which is designated as North or South of Main St. As a general rule, the rowdier part of town centers on Main and heads north. South Atlantic Ave continues to Daytona Beach Shores, which is just that little bit quieter and a better choice for a more relaxing stay.

★ Shoreline & Cabana
MOTEL $
(☎ 386-252-1692; www.daytonashoreline.com; 2435 S Atlantic Ave, Daytona Beach Shores; cottage/ste from $59/79; ⓟ❋🌐❄📶) For a refreshing change from Daytona's high-rise impersonality, try this handful of quaint private suites and beachside cottages set among tropical gardens. All are tastefully and simply furnished, each has a full kitchen, and a variety of bedding configurations are available. The obligatory beachfront pool is provided. Exceptional value.

August Seven Inn
B&B $$
(☎ 386-248-8420; www.jpaugust.net; 1209 S Peninsula Dr; r $140-225; ⓟ❋🌐❄) The friendly innkeepers of this gorgeous B&B have stocked it with period antiques and stylish deco, creating a soothing haven from Daytona's typical NASCAR-and-spring-break carnival.

Hyatt Place
Daytona Beach Oceanfront
HOTEL $$
(☎ 386-944-2010; www.daytonabeach.place. hyatt.com; 3161 S Atlantic Ave, Daytona Beach Shores; r from $129; ⓟ❋🌐❄) Some of Day-

tona's freshest, funkiest and most functional rooms can be found here, in slightly less touristy Daytona Beach Shores. All rooms feature balconies, plush bedding, separate living and sleeping areas and a nifty panel to easily connect your laptop or iPod to the 42in panel TV. Hotel-wide wi-fi and a hot buffet breakfast are complimentary.

River Lily Inn
B&B $$
(☎ 386-253-5002; www.riverlilyinnbedandbreakfast.com; 558 Riverside Dr; r $125-220; ⓟ❋🌐❄) There's a grand piano in the living room, a heart-shaped pool in the backyard, Belgian waffles for breakfast and a fridge full of free Klondike bars for snacks. What more could you want in a B&B? Add to that a quiet location on an oak-shaded property overlooking the river, elegant rooms with high ceilings (some with private balconies), and friendly-as-can-be owners, and you've got the recipe for a perfect getaway.

Plaza Resort & Spa
RESORT $$
(☎ 855-327-5292; www.plazaresortandspa.com; 600 N Atlantic Ave; r from $109; ⓟ❋🌐❄) Built in 1908, Daytona's most historic resort underwent extensive renovations in 2013 but still maintains its old-world charm. If only the walls could talk! From the miles of honey-colored marble lining the lobby to the 42in plasma TVs and cloud-soft beds in the rooms, to the 15,000-sq-ft spa, this resort coos luxury. A variety of room types are available – not all face the ocean.

Tropical Manor
RESORT $$
(☎ 386-252-4920; www.tropicalmanor.com; 2237 S Atlantic Ave, Daytona Beach Shores; r $65-315; ⓟ❋🌐❄📶) This immaculate, family-friendly beachfront property is like a playful pastel vision of Candy Land: though

SCENIC DRIVE: TOMOKA STATE PARK

The 20-minute drive here from downtown Daytona Beach is almost as pleasant as the **park** (☎ 386-676-4050; www.floridastateparks.org/tomoka; 2099 N Beach St, Ormond Beach; per vehicle $5; ⏱ 8am-sunset) itself, a bird-watchers' heaven of former indigo fields turned hardwood forests. A canopy of trees overhangs the two-lane road like a green tunnel, letting in only the stray dapple of sunlight.

this might be too much for some. A variety of configurations from motel rooms to suites and cottages are available; many have kitchen facilities and no two rooms are the same.

Shores
RESORT $$

(☎ 386-767-7350; www.shoresresort.com; 2637 S Atlantic Ave, Daytona Beach Shores; r from $129; P ✳ ☞ ≋) One of Daytona's more elegant offerings, this chic, beachfront resort boasts on-site fine dining, a full-service spa and vibrant tiki bar. Rooms are plush and pastel with four-poster beds and balconies facing the ocean. Specials and packages are available online.

Sun Viking Lodge
RESORT $$

(☎ 800-815-2846;www.sunviking.com;2411SAtlantic Ave, Daytona Beach Shores; r/cottages from $79/115; P ✳ ≋ 🏠) Families continue to love this small private resort, favoring its swag of included attractions: two pools, a 60ft waterslide, beach access, shuffleboard, endless activities and a Viking theme. All rooms have a fridge and microwave, while suites and cottages offer separate sleeping and living areas and full kitchens.

Coquina Inn B&B
B&B $$

(☎ 386-254-4969; www.coquinainn.com; 544 S Palmetto Ave; r $99-139; P ✳ ☞) Shaded by an ancient oak, this sweet yellow-and-stone cottage smells of homemade cookies and looks like your grandma's house – in a good way

(painted flowers on the wall, snowy white quilts, holiday decorations). It's located in a quiet residential neighborhood near downtown.

Eating

It may feel like Daytona's a wasteland of fast food and biker bars, but there are quite a few restaurants that break out of the burgers-n-beer mold. The newly revitalized downtown has several good choices, while the beach remains fairly tourist trappy.

Cracked Egg Diner
BREAKFAST $

(☎ 386-788-6772; www.thecrackedeggdiner. com; 3280 S Atlantic Ave, Daytona Beach Shores; breakfast items $4-12; ☺ 7am-3pm; P) Best for breakfast, this cheery joint in Daytona Beach Shores has become so popular they've just annexed the building next door. Brainchild of brothers Chris and Kevin, one of whom will usually greet you at the door with a smile: the boys' mission is to deliver breakfast egg-cellence every time. We think they do a pretty fine job.

Dancing Avocado Kitchen
VEGETARIAN $

(☎ 386-947-2022; 110 S Beach St; mains $6-11.50; ☺ 8am-4pm Tue-Sat; ✍) Gluten-free and mostly vegetarian-friendly items feature at this colorful kitchen serving breakfasts, lunches and light meals, although you'll still find a spicy jerk chicken wrap among the tofu, hummus and liberal servings of fresh avocado. Healthy and delicious!

Daytona Brickyard
AMERICAN $

(☎ 386-253-2270; www.brickyardlounge.com; 747 W International Speedway Blvd; mains $7-17; ☺ 11am-10pm Mon-Sat, noon-8pm Sun; P) Sit cheek by jowl with bikers and speedway fiends at this beloved grease pit, in a one-of-a-kind A-frame building jammed to the hilt with racing memorabilia. Burgers, wings and T-bones are done to perfection, and the beer just keeps on flowin'.

★ Don Vito's
ITALIAN $$

(☎ 386-492-7935; www.donvitosrestaurant.com; 137 W International Speedway Blvd; pizza $12-21, pasta $10-14, mains $14-17; ☺ 4-9pm Tue-Sun; P) Diners flock to this unpretentious old-school ma-and-pa Italian joint for fresh home-baked breads and pizzas, rich pasta sauces and succulent ocean-fresh seafood prepared à la the old country. Speedy service with a smile and generous portions make for excellent value.

Ronin Sushi and Sake Bar
SUSHI $$

(☑ 386-252-6320; www.roninsushiandbar.com; 111 W International Speedway Blvd; sushi rolls from $8; ☺ 5pm-late; P) It's not brain science to work out that the best sushi joints can be found in seaside towns where fresh-from-the-boat seafood is in plentiful supply. This popular, atmospheric joint does American-style sushi rolls well, has a full bar with plenty of sake choices, and offers delicious small plates such as baked mussels and Kobe-beef sliders from the kitchen.

Zen Bistro
THAI $$

(☑ 386-248-0453;   www.zenbistrodaytona.com; 223 Magnolia Ave; lunch $8-11, dinner $12-20; ☺ 11am-3pm & 5-9pm Mon-Fri, 5-9pm Sat; P ☑) With alfresco dining, a fire pit and a bar, this is not your every-day Thai restaurant. Add to that delicious authentic curries, noodle and rice dishes cooked to your preferred degree of spiciness and finish it off with attentive, polite staff and you've found a wonderful alternative to Daytona's many fast-food outlets.

Aunt Catfish's on the River
SOUTHERN $$

(☑ 386-767-4768;   www.auntcatfishontheriver. com; 4009 Halifax Dr, Port Orange; mains $8-25; ☺ 11:30am-9pm Mon-Sat, from 9am Sun; P) Fresh-from-the-boat grouper and mahimahi lolling in butter or deeply and deliciously fried, as well as Southern-style Cajun-spiced catfish make this riverside seafood establishment insanely popular with tourists: table waits can be expected. It's just outside Daytona Beach in Port Orange.

The Cellar
ITALIAN $$$

(☑ 386-258-0011;   www.thecellarrestaurant.com; 220 Magnolia Ave; mains $19-39; ☺ 5-10pm Tue-Sun; P) Now you can tell your friends that you've dined in the summer mansion of 29th US president Warren G Harding! Harding is consistently ranked as one of the worst presidents in history; the restaurant rates much better – its classic, upscale Italian fare and elegant ambience have made it Daytona's go-to spot for special-occasion dinners.

Fusion 43
at the Rose Villa
MODERN AMERICAN $$$

(☑ 386-615-7673; www.fusion43.com; 43 West Granada Blvd, Ormond Beach; mains $19-34; ☺ 5-10pm Tue-Thu, to 11pm Fri & Sat; P) Intimate and delightful, this under-the-radar fine-dining bistro occupies this charming Victorian house and garden a few miles north of Daytona.

FREE CHOCOLATE? YES, PLEASE

Get your cacao fix at Angell & Phelps Chocolate Factory (☑ 386-252-6531; www.angellandphelps.com; 154 S Beach St; ☺ tours 10am, 11am, 1pm, 2pm, 3pm & 4pm Mon-Sat) FREE, a downtown Daytona tradition since 1925. Free 20-minute tours of the production area include a sweet taste of the goods. While you're here, snag a bag of chocolate-covered potato chips, chocolate gators or the factory's signature creation, a caramel, cashew and chocolate confection known as the HoneyBee. It's not high-end stuff, but only the grouchiest of food snobs will complain.

The eclectic menu has distinctly European and South American influences: dolmades and osso buco feature alongside tempura yellow beets and Brazilian shrimp-and-coconut stew. Highly recommended.

 Drinking & Entertainment

Daytona's entertainment scene skews pretty lowbrow – biker bars with rollicking live music (mostly along Main St), high-octane dance clubs (on or near Seabreeze Blvd – aka the 'Beachside Party District') and some good kitschy retro places.

Oyster Pub
PUB

(☑ 386-255-6348;   www.oysterpub.com; 555 Seabreeze Blvd; ☺ 11:30am-3am) Eternally happening, this sporty pub has a zillion TVs, tons of outdoor seating and all the fresh Gulf oysters you can gulp.

Froggy's Saloon
BAR

(☑ 386-253-0330; www.froggyssaloon.net; 800 Main St; ☺ 7am-3am) Outside this train wreck of a bar, a bone chopper gleams in the window. Inside, a sign asks, 'Ain't drinking fun?' You better believe they mean it: opening at 7am, this is Party Central for bikers and others who want to go bonkers. Expect to see flashing chicks, smoky beards, orgasm contests and more leather than on an African safari.

Mai Tai Bar
BAR

(☑ 386-947-2493;   www.maitaibar.com; 250 N Atlantic Ave; ☺ 4pm-2am Mon-Fri, from 11am Sat & Sun) A party-happy crowd downs crayon-colored rum drinks at this fun

Hawaiian-themed bar overlooking the Atlantic Ocean. Late-night happy hours (9pm to 1am Monday to Saturday, 4pm to midnight Sunday) are hard to argue with.

Ocean Deck BAR
(☑ 386-253-5224; www.oceandeck.com; 127 S Ocean Ave; ⊙ 11am-3am) No woman? No cry! Live reggae nightly at this beachfront restaurant by day, bar-club by night.

Razzles CLUB
(☑ 386-257-6236; www.razzlesnightclub.com; 611 Seabreeze Blvd; ⊙ 8pm-3am Wed-Sat) The reigning dance club, permanently thumping.

Blue Grotto CLUB
(☑ 386-255-6477; www.bluegrottodaytona.com; 125 Basin St; ⊙ 11am-9pm Sun-Wed, till late Thu-Sat) A late-twenty- through forty-something crowd dances like nobody's watching at this underwater-themed waterfront restaurant and nightclub, with grotto rock walls, aquarium windows and a light-up blue bar. Avoid the food.

Daytona Beach Bandshell LIVE MUSIC
(☑ 386-671-8250; www.daytonabandshell.com; 70 Boardwalk) Constructed in 1937 from coquina shell, this landmark venue with a killer beachfront location stages a free summer concert series and summer outdoor movies. Worth a look.

Cinematique of Daytona CINEMA
(☑ 386-252-3778; www.cinematique.org; 242 S Beach St; tickets $5-9; ⊙ box office 11am-10pm Tue-Sat, 1-4pm Sun) Home to the Daytona Beach Film Festival, Daytona's only arthouse cinema screens independent and foreign films and serves booze and snacks to your table/highboy/sofa in its intimate screening room.

🛍 Shopping

The Speedway gift shop hawks all things NASCAR, as do plenty of beachfront gift emporiums.

Daytona Flea & Farmers Market MARKET
(www.daytonafleamarket.com; 2987 Bellevue Ave; ⊙ 9am-5pm Fri-Sun) With over 1000 booths and 600 vendors, this gargantuan market is one of the world's largest. Fans of garage and car-boot sales will not want to miss this: allocate plenty of time. It's at the corner of US 92 at I-95, 1 mile west of the Speedway.

J&P Cycles Destination
Daytona Superstore MOTORCYCLES
(☑ 386-615-0950; www.jpcycles.com/pages/daytona; 253 Destination Daytona Lane, Ormond Beach; ⊙ 9am-6pm Mon-Sat, 10am-5pm Sun) Just north of Daytona Beach at the junction of I-95 and US 1, this is the place to go to gear up for Bike Week: you're bound to find something to make you look and feel the part among the 15,000 sq ft of aftermarket motorcycle accessories and clothing.

ℹ Information

Backstage Pass (www.backpassmag.com) Details local entertainment, in print and online formats.

Daytona Beach Area Convention & Visitors Bureau (☑ 386-255-0415; www.daytonabeach. com; 126 E Orange Ave; ⊙ 9am-5pm Mon-Fri) In person or online, the authority on all things Daytona Beach.

Daytona Beach Regional Library (☑ 386-257-6036; www.volusialibrary.org; 105 E Magnolia Ave; ⊙ 9am-7pm Mon-Thu, to 5pm Fri & Sat, 1-5pm Sun) Two hours' free internet access.

News-Journal (www.news-journalonline.com) The free online version of Daytona's daily rag.

FORT MATANZAS NATIONAL MONUMENT

The tiny, 1742-built **Fort Matanzas National Monument** (☑ 904-471-0116; www.nps. gov/foma; 8635 Hwy A1A; ⊙ 9am-5:30pm) **FREE** is located on Rattlesnake Island, near where Menéndez de Avilés executed hundreds of shipwrecked French soldiers and colonists when rations at St Augustine ran low. Today it makes a terrific excursion via a free 10-minute ferry that launches every hour (at half-past) from 9:30am to 4:30pm, weather permitting. Once there, the ranger provides an overview and lets you wander.

From Daytona, take I-95 north to exit 289. Exit right and follow Palm Coast Pkwy (a toll road) until you reach Hwy A1A. Turn left and follow A1A north to the monument, which will be on your left. The trip should take just under one hour.

To catch the 35-person ferry to the monument – the last free thing in Florida – go through the visitor center and out to the pier.

❶ Getting There & Around

Daytona Beach is close to the intersection of two major interstates, I-95 and I-4. I-95 is the quickest way to Jacksonville (about 90 miles) and Miami (260 miles), though Hwy A1A and US Hwy 1 are more scenic. Beville Rd, an east–west thoroughfare south of Daytona proper, becomes I-4 after crossing I-95; it's the fastest route to Orlando (55 miles).

Votran (☑386-756-7496; www.votran.org; adult/child under 6yr $1.25/free) Runs buses and trolleys throughout the city.

Daytona Beach International Airport (☑386-248-8030; www.flydaytonafirst.com; 700 Catalina Dr) Just south of the Speedway; is served by Delta and US Airways, and all major car-rental companies.

Greyhound (☑386-255-7076; www.greyhound.com; 138 S Ridgewood Ave) Has connections to most major cities in Florida, and beyond.

Flagler Beach & Around

Just 30 miles north of Daytona, isolated Flagler Beach is far removed from the towering hotels, dizzying lights and tire-tracked sands of its rowdy neighbor. On a 6-mile stretch of beach, this string of modest residences and smattering of shops has a three-story cap on buildings to preserve its spectacular sunrises and an end-of-the-earth feel.

Head on over to the **Flagler Beach Fishing Pier** (☑386-517-2436; www.cityofflaglerbeach.com; 105 S 2nd St; entry $1.50, fishing pole & permit $6; ⊙6am-midnight), where you can use a pole and some bait to try your luck against the deep blue sea by fishing off this historic landmark, or just walk the pier at a leisurely pace: it's breathtaking at sunrise. If you're a little more adventurous, why not see if you can catch some waves with a surfboard, bodyboard or skimboard rental from **Z Wave Surf Shop** (☑386-439-9283; www.zwavesurfshop.com; 400 S Hwy A1A; per hour/day $5/20): they also offer lessons to have you hanging five in no time at all.

If you're tired of getting sand in your undies, **Washington Oaks Gardens State Park** (☑386-446-6780; www.floridastateparks.org/washingtonoaks; 6400 N Oceanshore Blvd; per vehicle $5; ⊙8am-sunset) is a beautiful spot for a picnic, with its resplendent camellia- and bird-of-paradise-filled gardens, although we also highly recommend saving some greenbacks for a meal or a beer at **High Tide at Snack Jacks** (☑386-439-3344; www.snackjacks.com; 2805 Hwy A1A; mains $8-20; ⊙11am-9pm): cash only. The requisite valet parking (it's free) just adds to the fun of this wonderfully laid-back, open-to-the-elements beachfront bar and diner, loved by locals and visitors alike for its location, vibe and flavor. The original Jack's has been been providing local surfers with beer and nourishment since 1947, but you'd only know that by reading the menu: today it's as modern, clean and quirky as they come. There's free wi-fi and the fried seafood platter is decadent but covers all bases. Ah-maz-ing! Oh, and did we mention the view?

You might wish to spend a night or two at sleepy Flagler Beach, as an alternative to garish Daytona – you'll have miles of sandy shores largely to yourself. Of several inexpensive motels, the standout is the **Flagler Beach Motel** (☑386-517-6700; www.flaglerbeachmotelandvacationrentals.com; 1820 S Oceanshore Blvd; studio from $65, 2-bedroom from $130). Its spotless studio and one- and two-bedroom motel-style units – many with full kitchen facilities and views of the Atlantic – have been recently renovated, featuring artworks by local artists. Located across the road from the beach, this is a wonderful place to disappear for a while. Rooms have wi-fi and flat-screen TVs, and there's a pool!

If romance is on the agenda, you can't go past the **Island Cottage Oceanfront Inn & Spa** (☑386-439-0092; www.islandcottagevillas.com; 2316 S Oceanshore Blvd; r $175-329) for a little pampering and indulgence. The decor won't be to everyone's taste, but the level of attentive service offered is otherwise hard to come by and the included luxuries such as plush four-poster beds and double Jacuzzis aren't difficult to enjoy.

Nature lovers can camp beachside at **Gamble Rogers Memorial State Recreation Area** (☑386-517-2086; www.floridastateparks.org/gamblerogers; 3100 Hwy A1A; per vehicle $5, camping $28; ⊙8am-sunset), which straddles both sides of the A1A. Kayaks, canoes and bicycles are available for rent at the ranger station.

St Augustine

The oldest continuously occupied European settlement in the US, St Augustine was founded by the Spanish in 1565. Today, its 144-block National Historic Landmark District is a major tourist destination. For the most part, St Augustine exudes charm

Downtown St Augustine

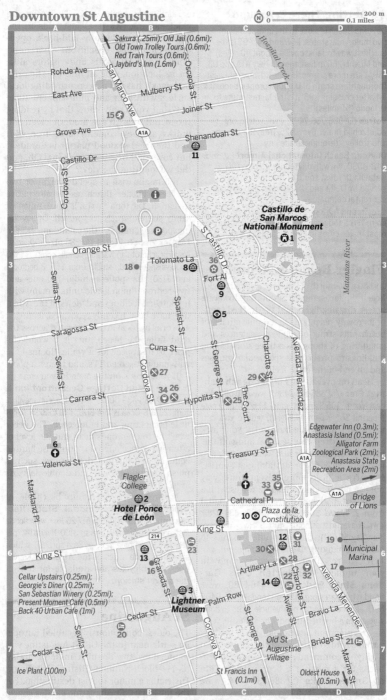

Sakura (.25mi); Old Jail (0.6mi);
Old Town Trolley Tours (0.6mi);
Red Train Tours (0.6mi);
Jaybird's Inn (1.6mi)

Rohde Ave

East Ave

Mulberry St

Joiner St

Osceola St

San Marco Ave

Hospital Creek

Grove Ave

Castillo Dr

Cordova St

Shenandoah St

11

A1A

Castillo de
San Marcos
National Monument

1

Orange St

Tolomato La

8

36

18

Fort Al

9

S Castillo Dr

5

Matanzas River

Sevilla St

Saragossa St

Cuna St

Spanish St

St George St

Charlotte St

Avenida Menéndez

Sevilla St

27

34 26

Carrera St

Hypolita St

25

The Court

29

Cordova St

Treasury St

24

Edgewater Inn (0.3mi);
Anastasia Island (0.5mi);
Alligator Farm
Zoological Park (2mi);
Anastasia State
Recreation Area (2mi)

6

Valencia St

Flagler
College

4

33 35

A1A

Cathedral Pl

7

2

Hotel Ponce
de León

10

Plaza de la
Constitución

A1A

Bridge
of Lions

Markland Pl

King St

214

12

31

19

Municipal
Marina

King St

13

23

30

28

Artillery La

32

17

Avenida Menéndez

Cellar Upstairs (0.25mi);
Georgie's Diner (0.25mi);
San Sebastian Winery (0.25mi);
Present Moment Café (0.5mi)
Back 40 Urban Cafe (1mi)

16

Granada St

3

Lightner
Museum

Palm Row

14

22

Charlotte St

Aviles St

Bravo La

Cedar St

20

St George St

Cordova St

Old St
Augustine
Village

Bridge St

21

Marine St

Cedar St

Sevilla St

Ice Plant (100m)

St Francis Inn
(0.1mi)

Oldest House
(0.5mi)

Downtown St Augustine

◎ Top Sights
1 Castillo de San Marcos National
  Monument C3
2 Hotel Ponce de León B5
3 Lightner Museum.................................... B6

◎ Sights
4 Cathedral Basilica of St Augustine........ C5
5 Colonial Quarter C4
6 Flagler Memorial Presbyterian
  Church.. A5
7 Government House C6
8 Oldest Wooden School House B3
9 Pirate & Treasure Museum C3
10 Plaza de la Constitución......................... C6
11 Ripley's Believe It or Not!...................... B2
12 Spanish Military Hospital
  Museum C6
13 Villa Zorayda Museum B6
14 Ximenez-Fatio House.............................. C6

◎ Activities, Courses & Tours
15 Solano Cycles... B1
16 St Augustine City Walks......................... B6
17 St Augustine Eco Tours D6
18 St Augustine Gold Tours......................... B3

19 Victory III Scenic Cruises D6

◎ Sleeping
20 At Journey's End B7
21 Bayfront Marin House D7
22 Casa de Solana C6
23 Casa Monica... B6
24 Pirate Haus Inn C5

◎ Eating
25 Bunnery Bakery & Café C4
26 Collage B4
27 Floridian... B4
28 Gaufres & Goods C6
29 Hyppo... C4
30 La Herencia Café C6

◎ Drinking & Nightlife
31 A1A Ale Works.. D6
32 JP Henley's... D6
33 Kookaburra C5
34 Scarlett O'Hara's B4
35 TradeWinds Lounge................................. C5

◎ Entertainment
36 Mill Top Tavern C3

and maintains its integrity, although there's no denying the presence of some tacky tourist traps in this working city: miniature theme parks, tour operators at almost every turn and horse-drawn carriages clip-clopping past townsfolk dressed in period costume. What makes St Augustine so genuinely endearing is the accessibility of its rich history via countless top-notch museums and the authenticity of its centuries-old architecture, monuments and narrow cobbled lanes. Unlike Florida's numerous historical theme parks, St Augustine is the real deal.

The people who live and work here do so because they're born into it and have become part of the fabric of this historic place, or, they've moved here because they're passionate about what they do and want to be a part of that history. For that reason, you'll find a stunning array of wonderful B&Bs, cozy cafes and lamp-lit pubs. While fine dining might not be the first thing that comes to mind at Florida's mention, it is certainly synonymous with St Augustine, whose charming one-off cafes and numerous impressive restaurants are the real deal too.

Plan to stay at least two nights if you can: you certainly won't run out of things to see, taste or learn.

◎ Sights

◎ Downtown St Augustine

All of St Augustine's historic district feels like a museum; there are literally dozens of separate attractions to choose from. Narrow little **Aviles St**, the oldest European-settled street in the country, and long, pedestrian-only **St George St** are both lined with galleries, cafes, museums and pubs, and are attractions in and of themselves.

★**Hotel Ponce de León** HISTORIC BUILDING
(☑904-823-3378; http://legacy.flagler.edu/pages/tours; 74 King St; tours adult/child $10/1; ☉tours hourly 10am-3pm in summer, 10am & 2pm during school year) Unmissable in town, this striking former luxury hotel, built in the 1880s, is now the world's most gorgeous dormitory, belonging to Flagler College who purchased and saved it in 1967. Guided tours are recommended to get a sense of the detail and history of this magnificent Spanish Renaissance building. At the very least, take a peek inside the lobby for free. Tours are occasionally cancelled for college functions: check the website for details.

★**Lightner Museum** MUSEUM
(☑904-824-2874; www.lightnermuseum.org; 75 King St; adult/child $10/5; ☉9am-5pm) Henry

Flagler's former Hotel Alcazar is now home to this wonderful museum, with a little bit of everything, from ornate Gilded Age furnishings to collections of marbles and cigar-box labels. The dramatic and imposing building itself is a must-see, dating back to 1887 and designed in the Spanish Renaissance Revival style by New York City architects Carrère and Hastings.

★ Castillo de San Marcos
National Monument   FORT
(☑ 904-829-6506; www.nps.gov/casa; 1 S Castillo Dr; adult/child $7/free; ⊙ 8:45am-5:15pm; ⊕) This incredibly photogenic fort is another atmospheric monument to longevity: it's the country's oldest masonry fort, completed by the Spanish in 1695. Park rangers lead programs hourly and shoot off cannons most weekends.

Villa Zorayda Museum   MUSEUM
(☑ 904-829-9887; www.villazorayda.com; 83 King St; adult/child $10/4; ⊙ 10am-5pm Mon-Sat, 11am-4pm Sun) Looking like a faux Spanish castle from a medieval theme park, this odd gray edifice was built in 1883 by an eccentric millionaire who was obsessed with Spain's 12th-century Alhambra Palace; it's made from a mix of concrete and local coquina shells. Today, it's an odd but engaging museum. The Moorish-style atrium and rooms contain quirky antiques and archaeological pieces: highlights include a 2400-year-old mummy's foot and an Egyptian 'Sacred Cat Rug.'

Ximenez-Fatio House   MUSEUM
(☑ 904-829-3575; www.ximenezfatiohouse.org; 20 Aviles St; adult/student $7/5; ⊙ 11am-4pm Tue-

Sat) Dating to 1798, this fascinating museum complex includes the main house building, the area's only detached kitchen building and a reconstructed washhouse. All are set on immaculately manicured grounds, dating to St Augustine's original town plan of 1572. Magnificently restored and chock-a-block full of artifacts and relics, the museum focuses primarily on the property's role as a boarding house/inn during the period 1826 to 1875.

Colonial Quarter   HISTORIC BUILDINGS
(☑ 904-342-2857; www.colonialquarter.com; 33 St George St; adult/child $13/7; ⊙ 10am-6pm) See how they did things back in the 18th century at this re-creation of Spanish Colonial St Augustine, complete with craftspeople demonstrating blacksmithing, leather working and other trades.

Discounted combination tickets including admission to the Pirate & Treasure Museum and the *First Colony* exhibit at Government House are available (adult/child $28/16).

Pirate & Treasure Museum   MUSEUM
(☑ 877-467-5863; www.thepiratemuseum.com; 12 S Castillo Dr; adult/child $13/7; ⊙ 10am-8pm; ⊕) Kids and big kids alike will enjoy this mash-up of theme park and museum: a celebration of all things pirate. As well as genuine historical treasures (including real gold) there's plenty of animatronic pirates, blasting cannons and a kid-friendly treasure hunt. Lots of fun.

Discounted combination tickets including admission to the Colonial Quarter and the *First Colony* exhibit at Government House are available (adult/child $28/16).

AMERICA'S OLDEST CITY

Timucua settled what is now St Augustine about 1000 BC, hunting alligators and cultivating corn and tobacco. In 1513, Spanish explorer Juan Ponce de León sighted land, came ashore and claimed La Florida (Land of Flowers) for Spain. In 1565 his compatriot Pedro Menéndez de Avilés arrived on the feast day of Augustine of Hippo, and accordingly christened the town San Augustín: 42 years prior to the founding of Jamestown (Virginia) and 55 years before that of Plymouth (Massachusetts).

Menéndez quickly established a military base against the French, who had established Fort Caroline near present-day Jacksonville. The French fleet did him the favor of getting stuck in a hurricane; Menéndez' men butchered the survivors. By the time Spain ceded Florida to the US in 1821, St Augustine had been sacked, looted, burned and occupied by pirates and Spanish, British, Georgian and South Carolinian forces.

Today the city's buildings, made of coquina – a DIY concrete made of sedimentary rock mixed with crushed shells – lend an enchanting quality to the slender streets. The city's long and colorful history is palpable, narrated vividly by what seems like innumerable museums, monuments and galleries.

THERE BE PIRATES

Notorious throughout the Caribbean and the Americas, pirates routinely ransacked St Augustine, given its vulnerable seaside location. Laying in wait along the coast, pirates would pounce on silver- and gold-laden fleets returning to Europe from Mexico and South America. When ships weren't around, they'd simply raid the town (which was home to the Spanish Royal Treasurer for Florida, no less).

Among the many brutal attacks on St Augustine was Sir Francis Drake's raid in June 1586, when he and his cohort pillaged the township before burning it down. Perhaps even more violent was Jamaican pirate Robert Searle's attack in 1668. After capturing a Spanish ship, Searle and crew went on a plundering and killing spree. No one was safe: one of Searle's victims was a five-year-old girl, whose ghost, it is said, haunted him to madness and ultimately suicide.

Both events are meticulously reenacted every year in St Augustine. Participants must conform to rigid requirements including no skull-and-crossbones emblems (they weren't used regularly by pirates until the early 1700s); no polyester or modern items of any kind, including eyeglasses and wristwatches; and no 'silly plumes.' If you're interested in participating, get thee to St Augustine in March (to reenact Searle's raid) or June (for Drake's). For more information, log on to www.searlesbucs.com.

Other local pirate activities include September's 'Talk Like a Pirate Day' (www.talklikeapirate.com), a global event that particularly shivers timbers in this place, and October/November's St Arrrgustine's Pirate Gathering (www.pirategathering.com).

Spanish Military Hospital Museum MUSEUM
(☑ 904-342-7730; www.spanishmilitaryhospital.com; 3 Aviles St; adult/child $7/5; ☺10am-6pm) Not for the faint of heart, guided tours of this museum discuss Colonial-era medical techniques in all their gory glory: amputations, leeching, the whole shebang. Housed in a reconstruction of the original hospital, the museum will make you very glad you're not a patient in 1791! Discounted tickets can be reserved online.

Ripley's Believe It or Not! MUSEUM
(☑ 904-824-1606; www.staugustine.ripleys.com; 19 San Marco Ave; adult/child $15/8; ☺9am-8pm; ⊛) Inside the old Castle Warden (1887), this is the first of the now-ubiquitous Ripley's 'Odditoriums.' Shrunken heads, a drum made from skulls and goofy pirate displays are par for the course here.

Government House HISTORIC BUILDING
(☑ 904-823-2212; www.staugustine.ufl.edu/govHouse.html; 48 King St; ☺10am-5pm) FREE A government building has stood on this site since 1598 and served as a residence, courthouse, administrative headquarters and post office. Today, it is maintained by the University of Florida as a public museum and exhibition space. Until October 2015, it houses the fascinating *First Colony* exhibit (adult/child $8/6), exploring the Spanish origins of present-day USA, beginning in St Augustine in 1565.

Discounted combination tickets including admission to the *First Colony* exhibit as well as the Colonial Quarter and Pirate & Treasure Museum are available (adult/child $28/16).

Oldest Wooden School House HISTORIC BUILDING
(☑ 904-824-0192; www.oldestwoodenschoolhouse.com; 14 St George St; adult/child $3/2; ☺9am-6pm) Built from red cedar and cypress, this 200-year-old building contains animatronic teachers and students, and provides a glimpse into 18th-century life and education. Naughty kids may be frightened into civility when they see the dungeon.

Plaza de la Constitution SQUARE
In the heart of downtown, this grassy square, the oldest public park in the US and a former marketplace for food (and slaves), has an attractive gazebo, some cannons, the remains of the town well and a monument to Confederate veterans.

Cathedral Basilica of St Augustine CHURCH
(☑ 904-824-2806; www.thefirstparish.org; 38 Cathedral Pl) With its magnificent bell tower lording it over the Plaza de la Constitution, this Spanish Mission–style cathedral is likely the country's first Catholic house of worship. Masses are held daily.

ST AUGUSTINE FOR CHILDREN

If visiting historical homes and shopping for antiques isn't quite your kids' cup of tea, don't wait for a temper tantrum to happen. St Augustine has plenty of diversions for the pint-sized traveler. Here are a few ideas:

➡ Shiver yer timbers at the Pirate & Treasure Museum (p338), though the scary animatronic pirates (like a cackling, decapitated Blackbeard) might scare the littlest travelers.

➡ Ride the choo-choos with the cherry-red St Augustine Sightseeing Trains (p342).

➡ Go waaaay beyond cherry-orange-lime at the Hyppo (p343), a wild and wacky popsicle shop with flavors like lavender lemonade and the Elvis Presley (banana, peanut butter, honey).

➡ Watch the soldiers in costumes and listen to the cannons fire at Castillo de San Marcos (p338).

➡ Squeal at the shrunken heads and other 'true' oddities at Ripley's Believe It or Not! (p339).

➡ See the scary gators devour their lunches at the Alligator Farm Zoological Park (p340).

Flagler Memorial Presbyterian Church CHURCH

(☏904-829-6451; www.memorialpcusa.org; 32 Sevilla St) Henry Flagler, his daughter and her stillborn child lie in the mausoleum at this church, Flagler's own magnificent Venetian-Renaissance edifice. The floor is Sienna marble, the wood is Santo Domingo mahogany and the pipe organ (played at 8:30am and 11am Sunday) is colossal. Services are held daily at 8:30am and 11am.

⊙ Around St Augustine

Old Jail HISTORIC BUILDING

(☏904-335-8982; 167 San Marco Ave; adult/child $9/5; ⊗8:30am-4:30pm) Built in 1891, this is the former town prison and residence of the town's first sheriff, Charles Joseph 'the terror' Perry (towering menacingly at 6ft 6in tall and weighing 300lb). Today, costumed 'deputies' escort visitors through cellblocks and detail the site's arresting history.

Oldest House MUSEUM

(☏904-824-2872; www.staugustinehistoricalsociety.org; 14 St Francis St; adult/student $8/4; ⊗9am-5pm) Also known as the González-Alvarez House, this is the oldest surviving Spanish-era home in Florida, dating to the early 1700s and sitting on a site occupied since the 1600s. The house is part of a complex that also contains two small historical museums and a lovely ornamental garden.

Mission of Nombre de Dios CHURCH

(☏904-824-2809; www.missionandshrine.org; 27 Ocean Ave; ⊗museum 10am-4pm Thu-Sat,

noon-4pm Sun) Just north of downtown on the A1A, the mission dates back to the earliest days of Spanish settlement. Today, the peaceful memorial gardens feature a replica of the original altar, a tiny ivy-shrouded chapel and a small museum.

Alligator Farm Zoological Park ZOO

(☏904-824-3337; www.alligatorfarm.com; 999 Anastasia Blvd; adult/child $23/12; ⊗9am-5pm, to 6pm summer; ⊕) Herpetophobes should run in the other direction of this facility – the only one on the planet with every species of crocodilian in residence. Nature lovers, on the other hand, will love it. Look for albino alligators, freaky gharials and seven different species of endangered monkey, including the world's smallest, the pygmy marmoset. There are talks and shows throughout the day; catch hungry alligators snapping their jaws at feeding times (noon and 3pm).

The park is a five-minute drive from downtown St Augustine along Anastasia Blvd.

Fountain of Youth HISTORIC SITE

(☏904-829-3168; www.fountainofyouthflorida.com; 11 Magnolia Ave; adult/child $12/8; ⊗9am-6pm) Insert tongue firmly in cheek and step right up for an acrid cup of eternal youth at this kitschy 'archaeological park.' As the story goes, Spanish explorer Juan Ponce de León came ashore here in 1513, and considered this freshwater stream the possible legendary Fountain of Youth. We know you'll find it hard not to see for yourself... just in case.

St Augustine Beach Area

Cross the Bridge of Lions and take Anastasia Blvd right out to the beach. The 7-mile stretch of St Augustine Beach is a great place to soak up rays, and the road fronting it has a small handful of hotels, family restaurants and bars.

St Augustine Lighthouse   LIGHTHOUSE
(☑ 904-829-0745; www.staugustinelighthouse. com; 81 Lighthouse Ave; adult/child $9.75/7.75; ⊙9am-6pm) The light produced by this 1870s striped lighthouse beams all the way downtown. A great place to bring kids over six and more than 44in tall (since all climbers must be able to ascend and descend the tower under their own power). A variety of special themed tours, such as the spooky 'Dark of the Moon' paranormal tour and the 'Lost Ships' archaeology tour, are held on a regular basis. Consult the website for what's on when.

St Augustine Beach   BEACH
There's a visitor information booth at the foot of **St Johns Pier**, where you can rent a rod and reel ($3 for two hours, $1 for each additional hour). About three blocks south of the pier, the end of A St has – as Florida goes – some fine waves.

Anastasia State Recreation Area   PARK
(☑ 904-461-2033; www.floridastateparks.org/anastasia; 1340 Hwy A1A; car/bike $8/2; ⊙8am-sunset) Locals come to escape the tourist hordes at this terrific beach and recreation area. There's also a **campground** (campsites $28) and rentals for all kinds of water sports.

Activities & Tours

★**St Augustine Gold Tours**   TOUR
(☑ 904-325-0547; www.staugustinegoldtours.com; 6 Cordova St; adult/child $20/10) Of the gamut of sightseeing tours in St Augustine, we prefer this new outfit, the brainchild of a retired British couple, both former legal eagles: you're assured a fascinating and articulate insight into St Augustine's history. Private and small group tours are conducted in a quiet electric vehicle that gets into places where the other tours can't.

★**St Augustine
Eco Tours**   KAYAKING, BOAT TOUR
(☑ 904-377-7245; www.staugustineecotours. com; 111 Avenida Menendez; adult/child $45/35; ⊙mid-morning & dusk) This eco-outfitter has certified naturalists who take kayakers on 3-mile ecology trips. If you don't feel like paddling, its 1½-hour boat tours explore the estuary and use hydrophones to search for bottlenose dolphins. A portion of profits goes to environmental organizations.

St Augustine City Walks   WALKING TOUR
(☑ 904-825-0087; www.staugcitywalks.com; 4 Granada St; tours $12-49; ⊙9am-8:30pm) Extremely fun walking tours of all kinds, from silly to serious. A variety of free tours are also available.

WORLD GOLF VILLAGE

The ultimate monument to a good walk spoiled, the **World Golf Village** (☑ 877-888-2002; www.worldgolfvillage.com; 1 World Golf Pl) is a massive golf resort, golf-course complex, golf museum and all-around golf-themed attraction.

Fans of the sport flock here to the **World Golf Hall of Fame** (☑ 904-940-4133; www. worldgolfhalloffame.org; adult/child $20/5; ⊙10am-6pm Mon-Sat, noon-6pm Sun), an 18-exhibit museum: the front nine covering the history of the sport and the back nine examining modern professional golf. Separating them is the Hall of Fame itself, with multimedia exhibits on inductees. Admission includes nine holes on a real grass putting green designed to PGA specifications, and an IMAX film.

Two legendary on-site courses, **King & Bear** and **Slammer & Squire**, are open for public tee times. If you're keen to improve your swing, two- to five-day **PGA Tour Golf Academy** (www.touracademy.com) packages start from $635; more expensive packages include accommodations at one of four on-site resorts. Private lessons start at $90 per hour.

Whether you're staying here or not, grab a burger from **Caddyshack** (☑ 904-940-3673; www.murraybroscaddyshack.com; 455 S Legacy Trail E106; mains $10-26; ⊙11:30am-10pm) restaurant and bar, named for the movie starring Bill Murray, who – along with his five brothers – owns it.

World Golf Village is just off I-95 via exit 323, about halfway between St Augustine and Jacksonville.

Old Town Trolley Tours

TOUR

(☑888-910-8687; www.trolleytours.com; 167 San Marco Ave; adult/child 6-12yr $25/10) Hop-on, hop-off narrated trolley tours. Tickets are valid for three consecutive days.

Red Train Tours

TOUR

(☑904-824-1606; www.ripleys.com/redtrains; 170 San Marco Ave; adult/child $23/10) Hop-on, hop-off narrated train tours with friendly, knowledgeable guides. Passes valid for three days.

Victory III Scenic Cruises

BOAT TOUR

(☑904-824-1806; www.scenic-cruise.com; 111 Avenida Menendez; adult/child $17/10; ⊙11am, 1pm, 2:45pm & 4:30pm year-round, plus evening cruises spring-fall) Narrated 1¼-hour waterfront cruises, leaving from the Municipal Marina, just south of the Bridge of Lions.

San Sebastian Winery

TOUR

(☑904-826-1594; www.sansebastianwinery.com; 157 King St; ⊙10am-6pm Mon-Sat, 11am-6pm Sun) FREE Free hour-long tours at this winery are capped with wine tastings and a video about Florida winemaking since the 1600s; if you're around in August, join the squishy fun during the annual grape-stomping competitions.

Pit Surfshop

SURFING

(☑904-471-4700; www.thepitsurfshop.com; 18 A St; lesson for 1 $70) Stop in at this place on St Augustine Beach for late-breaking surf conditions, to rent or buy a board, or to sink into the comfy couch in the screening room for a free, inspirational surf film. Lessons and surf camps are available.

Raging Water Sports

WATER SPORTS

(☑904-829-5001; www.ragingwatersports.com; 57 Comares Ave) Rents kayaks ($25 per hour), sailboats ($50 per hour), jet skis ($95 per hour) and motorboats (starting at $85 per hour). Located at Conch House Marina Resort.

🛏 Sleeping

For convenience and atmosphere, stay in the historic downtown area where there's a plenitude of classic B&Bs; check out the selection on www.staugustineinns.com. For larger rooms and cheaper prices, there's equally as many chain motels on San Marco Ave and Ponce de Leon Blvd. Otherwise, head to the beach. St Augustine is a popular weekend escape for Floridians – prices go up by about 30% on weekends and a minimum two-night stay is often required.

Pirate Haus Inn

HOSTEL $

(☑904-808-1999; www.piratehaus.com; 32 Treasury St; dm $25, r from $90; P ❋ 🕏 🐾) A-har me hearties! Although far from St Augustine's fanciest digs, this family-friendly European-style guesthouse-hostel may well be the cheapest and most cheerful: kids love it! Themed private rooms and dorms are squeaky clean, the location is hard to beat and who doesn't love fresh 'pirate pancakes' for breakfast? Staff speak a variety of languages.

Jaybird's Inn

MOTEL $$

(☑904-342-7938; www.jaybirdsinn.com; 2700 N Ponce de Leon Blvd; r inc breakfast $89-139) This older motel has been revamped to the highest of standards and modernity, with fresh and funky decor in an aquamarine color scheme that works. Beds are big and comfy, continental breakfast is included and free bikes will get you whizzing around in no time. There's an on-site restaurant as well. Go for the suite if it's available.

Edgewater Inn

MOTEL $$

(☑904-825-2697; www.stayatedgewater.com; 2 St Augustine Blvd; r $99-139) For something a little different, try this charming absolute waterfront motel across the bridge, overlooking St Augustine's historic downtown. Rooms are on the smaller side, but pleasantly decorated and recently refurbished. The waterfront rooms' sitting areas are unique in town, if not a little close together: great for the social traveler, not so great for the reclusive.

Casa de Solana

B&B $$

(☑904-824-3555; www.casadesolana.com; 21 Aviles St; r incl breakfast $169-209; P 🕏) Just off pedestrian-only Aviles St in the oldest part of town, this utterly charming little inn remains faithful to its early-1800s period decor. Rooms aren't the largest in town, but price and location make it a great deal. Rumors of a resident ghost might sway some potential guests.

The Conch House Marina Resort

MOTEL $$

(☑904-829-8646; www.conch-house.com; 57 Comares Ave; r $95-125; ❋ 🕏 ❧) Party-happy boaters love this festive Key West-y motel, with rooms facing the 200-slip marina, an always-packed patio bar, and a pool deck perfect for beer-sipping. It's minutes from either downtown or the beach.

Beachfront B&B

B&B $$

(☑904-461-8727; www.beachfrontbandb.com; 1 F St, St Augustine Beach; r $150-180; ❋ 🕏 ❧)

If you're looking to stay by the beach to avoid the tourist crowds, look no further. This sundrenched oceanfront beach house features canopy beds, rich pine floors and a private heated pool. Most rooms have private entrances and fireplaces for romantic wintry nights.

★**At Journey's End**   B&B $$$
(☑ 904-829-0076; www.atjourneysend.com; 89 Cedar St; r incl breakfast $159-209; P ❄ 🛜 🐾) Free from the granny-ish decor that haunts many St Augustine B&Bs, this pet-friendly, kid-friendly and gay-friendly spot is outfitted in a chic mix of antiques and modern furniture and run by friendly, knowledgeable hosts. Mouthwatering breakfasts and complimentary wi-fi, concierge services and beer, wine and soda throughout your stay are some of the inclusions that set Journey's End apart.

★**St Francis Inn**   INN $$$
(☑ 904-824-6068, 800-824-6062; www.stfrancis inn.com; 79 St George St; r incl breakfast $139-239; ❄ 🛜) St Augustine's oldest inn has been in continuous operation since 1791. Crushed-coquina-shell and ancient wood-beam architecture create a period ambience, abetted by open fireplaces, a maze of antique-filled nooks and crannies, beds with handmade quilts and a lush walled courtyard. Sumptuous buffet breakfasts, free local wine and complimentary evening desserts round out the picture. Guests also have day access to a beachfront cottage, perfect for a day away from the crowds.

Bayfront Marin House   INN $$$
(☑ 904-824-4301; www.bayfrontmarinhouse.com; 142 Avenida Menendez; r incl breakfast $179-219; ❄ 🛜 🏊) Created by joining three old houses, this buttercup-yellow waterfront inn is dominated by a bi-level wraparound porch with a commanding view of Matanzas Bay. Rooms are sumptuously decorated with four-poster beds and lots of rich brocades – for character, choose a room in the 1700s-era wing with cool crushed-coquina-shell walls, or enquire about the private Vilano Beach cottage.

Casa Monica   HISTORIC HOTEL $$$
(☑ 904-827-1888; www.casamonica.com; 95 Cordova St; r $179-379; P ❄ 🛜 🏊) 🐾 Built in 1888, this is *the* luxe hotel in town, with turrets and fountains adding to the Spanish-Moorish castle atmosphere. Rooms are appropriately richly appointed, with wrought-iron

triple-sheeted beds and Bose sound systems in every room. Some suites have decadent Jacuzzis and the location can't be beaten.

🍴 Eating

St Augustine has one of the best eating scenes in Florida, providing you know where to go and which overcrowded, overpriced tourist traps to avoid. Many Floridians visit for the weekend, just for the food. The listings below should help your tastebuds navigate their way around this tasty town.

Hyppo   POPSICLES $
(☑ 904-217-7853; www.thehyppo.com; 48 Charlotte St; popsicles $4; ⊙ 11am-10pm) On steamy St Augustine afternoons, seek out the Hyppo, a slip of a popsicle shop with an ever-changing whiteboard menu of outrageous flavors – pineapple-cilantro, rice pudding and Kick (an energising blend of espresso, green tea *and* chocolate). Keep your eyes open for anything containing datil pepper, a high-octane local chili beloved by Spanish settlers – it goes great with strawberry.

Back 40 Urban Cafe   CAFE $
(☑ 905-824-0227; www.back40cafe.com; 40 S Dixie Hwy; items $4-11; ⊙ 11am-9pm) The oldest city's newest secret, no longer! Flavored with the spices of Mexico and the Southwest this cozy, unpretentious joint is favored by locals for its cheap and tasty tacos, burgers and comfort foods. We couldn't go past the chili mac bowl. There's a good selection of cold beer too!

Bunnery Bakery & Café   BAKERY $
(☑ 904-829-6166; www.bunnerybakeryandcafe. com; 121 St George St; items $4-12; ⊙ 8am-4pm Mon-Fri, to 5pm Sat & Sun) The friendly staff at this family-owned bakery pour frosting on your cinnamon rolls to your individual specifications. Strudels, panini and fat, wedge-shaped scones are all hits, as are the noteworthy hot breakfasts. Expect major lines at noon, although it's always busy.

★**Present Moment Café**   VEGAN $$
(☑ 904-827-4499; www.thepresentmomentcafe. com; 224 W King St; mains $8-16; ⊙ 10am-9pm Mon-Sat; 🍴) Dishing up 'Kind Cuisine,' this folksy restaurant serves only vegan and raw food. To the delight (and surprise) of many patrons, the healthy, organic dishes created by this soulful cafe are bursting with flavor. If you need something a little bit naughty with your nice, why not have the gluten-free chocolate marble torte with drunken

banana for dessert? One to turn even the most die-hard carnivores on to food that's good for the soul and the planet.

Gas Full Service
MODERN AMERICAN $$

(☎904-217-0326; 9 Anastasia Blvd; mains $8-24; ☺11am-9pm Tue-Sat) Its increasing popularity as a lunch spot means you'll likely be vying for a table at this fantastic retro gas-station-esque cafe. The buzz is about the burgers: freshly baked buns, local beef, fried green tomatoes and crispy bacon all feature. How about the 'burger Benedict,' smothered in hollandaise? And did we mention waffle fries, Reuben egg rolls or the lobster corn dog...?

Floridian
MODERN AMERICAN $$

(☎904-829-0655; www.thefloridianstaug.com; 39 Cordova St; mains $13-22; ☺11am-3pm Wed-Mon, 5-9pm Mon-Thu, 5-10pm Fri & Sat) Oozing hipster-locavore earnestness, this farm-to-table restaurant serves whimsical neo-Southern creations in an oh-so-cool dining room. Although the service and general vibe might be a little too cool for school, it's hard to fault the food: fried green tomato bruschetta and seafood zucchini linguine pair perfectly. No reservations means long waits.

O'Steen's
SEAFOOD $$

(☎904-829-6974; www.osteensrestaurant.com; 205 Anastasia Blvd; mains $8-12; ☺11am-8:30pm Tue-Sat) Locals claim this seafood shack has the best shrimp on the East Coast, and having eaten our weight in shrimp, we think they're close to the mark. If you're allergic to shellfish, don't despair: the tilapia and catfish (broiled or fried) are pretty good too. O'Steen's ain't no secret, so prepare to wait for a table or plan to take-out and picnic.

Gypsy Cab Co
FUSION $$

(☎904-824-8244; www.gypsycab.com; 828 Anastasia Blvd; mains $12-22; ☺11am-10pm Mon-Fri, from 10:30am Sat & Sun) Across the bridge from downtown, this arty turquoise-and-purple bistro is a local fave for an eclectic menu spanning Italian pastas, French strip steaks, Asian tofu and Middle Eastern hummus platters.

Georgie's Diner
DINER $$

(☎904-819-9006; 100 Malaga St; mains $7-29; ☺7am-9pm) On the fringe of the historic downtown area, this shiny silver retro-look diner is best for big breakfasts and hearty Greek meals like gyro, souvlaki and calamari. Service is swift and smiley, despite the relatively constant stream of hungry patrons.

Gaufres & Goods
EUROPEAN $$

(☎904-829-5770; www.polishgreekrestaurant.com; 9a & 9b Aviles St; items $7-14; ☺9:30am-6pm Sun-Thu, to 9pm Fri & Sat) The flavors of Europe collide in this surprising addition to the St Augustine foodie scene, serving homestyle Polish and Greek favorites in the core of the historic downtown. It's a little overpriced and the decor is a tad drab, but if you're craving *pierogies* (dumplings), mussels, hearty soups or continental desserts and coffee, there's really no comparison – for miles.

Sakura
ASIAN FUSION $$

(☎904-819-5857; www.sakura-asian-restaurant.com; 120 San Marco Ave; mains $11-30; ☺11am-10pm) This pan-Asian restaurant serving sushi, sashimi, and a variety of Chinese and Thai dishes also has a hibachi grill and benefits from ocean-fresh ingredients. A low profile in this restaurant-heavy town means reasonable wait times. Combine that with great service and smart decor and you've got a remedy for those Asian cravings.

Mango Mango's
CARIBBEAN $$

(☎904-461-1077; www.mangomangos.com; 700 Hwy A1A, St Augustine Beach; mains $8-16; ☺11am-10pm) It's hard not to be charmed by this cheery lime-and-coral-colored beach bistro, with its menu of likable Caribbean-fusion fare – crunchy coconut shrimp, chicken with mango sauce, tons of sandwiches and wraps.

La Herencia Café
CUBAN $$

(☎904-829-9487; www.laherenciacafe.com; 4 Aviles St; mains $12-25; ☺8:30am-8pm Mon-Fri, to 10pm Sat & Sun) On St Aug's oldest street, this brightly painted Cuban cafe serves all-day breakfasts and killer Cuban sandwiches. Relax here with a cup of *café con leche,* just like in Old Havana.

★Collage
INTERNATIONAL $$$

(☎904-829-0055; www.collagestaug.com; 60 Hypolita St; mains $28-45; ☺5:30-9pm) This upscale dinner-only restaurant is renowned for its impeccable service, intimate atmosphere and the consistency of its cuisine: the menu makes the most of St Augustine's seaside locale and nearby local farms. It's all here: artisan salads, chicken, lamb, veal and pork, lobster, scallops and grouper. A subtle melange of global flavors enhance the natural goodness of the freshest produce.

🍷 Drinking & Entertainment

★ Ice Plant
BAR

(☑ 904-829-6553; www.iceplantbar.com; 110 Riberia St; ⏰ 5pm-2am) This super-cool bar in a former ice factory oozes style. Exposed concrete, raw brickwork and soaring windows are the backdrop upon which to imbibe some of Florida's finest cocktails. Small plates, bar snacks and mains also pack a punch. See and be seen.

Kookaburra
CAFE

(☑ 904-209-9391; www.kookaburrashop.com; 24 Cathedral Pl; ⏰ 7:30am-8pm) A little piece of Australia in the heart of Old Spanish St Augustine: who would have thought? Real Aussie meat pies and lamingtons do just fine for a quick snack, but the main draw is the barista coffee.

Cellar Upstairs
WINE BAR

(☑ 904-826-1594; www.sansebastianwinery. com; 157 King St; plates $6-14, wine by the glass $5-7; ⏰ 4pm-midnight Fri, noon-midnight Sat & Sun) On the grounds of the San Sebastian Winery (p342); head on up to this delightful rooftop patio for alfresco tasting plates, sandwiches, local wines and free live jazz (7pm to 11pm).

Scarlett O'Hara's
PUB

(☑ 904-824-6535; www.scarlettoharas.net; 70 Hypolita St; ⏰ 11am-1am) Good luck grabbing a rocking chair: the porch of this pine building is packed all day, every day. Built in 1879, today Scarlett's serves regulation pub grub, but it's got the magic ingredients – hopping happy hour, live entertainment nightly, hardworking staff, funky bar – that draw folks like spirits to a séance.

A1A Ale Works
PUB

(☑ 904-829-2977; www.a1aaleworks.com; 1 King St; ⏰ 11am-late) Who needs historical ambience with fine-crafted beer like this?

JP Henley's
PUB

(☑ 904-829-3337; www.jphenleys.com; 10 Marine St; ⏰ 11am-1am) With 50 beers on tap, 120 more in the bottle and over 75 bottles of wine, this place will appeal to even the most discriminating beer or wine snob. Great music, too.

TradeWinds Lounge
LOUNGE

(☑ 904-829-9336; www.tradewindslounge.com; 124 Charlotte St; ⏰ 11am-1am) Tiny bathrooms and big hairdos rule this nautical-themed dive. Smelling sweetly of stale beer, this classic divey bar has survived two locations and six decades. Crowds tumble out the door during happy hour, and there's live music – mostly Southern rock or '80s music – nightly. Smoky (for the moment), fun and old school.

Mill Top Tavern
LIVE MUSIC

(☑ 904-829-2329; www.milltop.com; 19½ St George St; ⏰ 11:30am-1am) Grooving to live music at the open-air Mill Top, on the 2nd story of a 19th-century mill that's hugged by a huge oak, is like hanging out in a treehouse – one that has a full bar and kitchen.

Café Eleven
LIVE MUSIC

(☑ 904-460-9311; www.originalcafe11.com; 501 Hwy A1A, St Augustine Beach; ⏰ 7am-9pm) At night, the tables of this slick beach cafe get shoved aside and the place transmogrifies into a theater for some of indie rock's biggest names.

🛍 Shopping

Meandering through the town's antique shops could take days; contact the **Antique Dealers Association of St Augustine** (www.adasta.org) for advice on collectibles.

St George Street
SHOPPING DISTRICT

This 11-block stretch of pedestrian shopping, eating and entertainment is the heart of Old Spanish St Augustine. Look for everything from souvenir shops hawking pirate shot glasses to elegant antiques stores.

Aviles Street
SHOPPING STREET

Opposite the plaza from St George St, this tiny pedestrian-only alleyway has some wonderfully dusty map shops and art galleries.

St Augustine Premium Outlets
MALL

(www.premiumoutlets.com; 2700 State Rd; ⏰ 9am-9pm Mon-Sat, to 6pm Sun) Name brands like Gap, Banana Republic, Nike and more, at steep discounts.

ℹ Information

INTERNET ACCESS

Public Library (☑ 904-827-6940; www.sjcpls. org; 1960 N Ponce de Leon Blvd; ⏰ 10am-8pm Mon-Wed, to 6pm Thu & Fri, to 5pm Sat) Free internet access.

MEDIA

St Augustine Record (www.staugustine.com) The daily has good visitor information on its website.

WORTH A TRIP

PALATKA

In its heyday, the village of Palatka (pronounced puhl-*at*-kuh), almost midway between St Augustine and Gainesville, was the furthest south you could travel by steamship, and boasted more than 7000 hotel rooms for wealthy snowbirds. Today, visitors are trickling back to this sweet, sleepy-verging-on-comatose town for fishing, for Memorial weekend's **blue-crab festival**, and simply to get away from the coastal crowds.

Spend a pleasant afternoon exploring the **Bronson-Mulholland House** (☑ 904-329-0140; www.bronsonmulhollandhouse.com; 100 Madison St; ⊘ 11am-4pm Thu & Fri, from 9am Sat & Sun, 8am-noon Mon) **FREE**, an 1854 historic mansion turned house museum, or crossing the swinging suspension footbridge through **Ravine Gardens State Park** (☑ 386-329-3721; www.floridastateparks.org/ravinegardens; 1600 Twigg St; per car $5; ⊘ 8am-sunset).

If you're feeling peckish, pull into **Angel's Dining Car** (☑ 386-325-3927; 209 Reid St; mains $2.50-8; ⊘ 6am-8pm Sun-Thu, to midnight Fri), Florida's oldest diner, serving cheeseburgers and Pusalow (an only-in-Palatka drink of chocolate milk with vanilla syrup and crushed ice) directly to patrons' cars since 1932.

Folio Weekly (www.folioweekly.com) This free magazine has events information, restaurant and bar listings every Tuesday.

TOURIST INFORMATION

Visitor Information Center (☑ 904-825-1000; www.ci.st-augustine.fl.us; 10 W Castillo Dr; ⊘ 8:30am-5:30pm) Helpful, period-dressed staff sell tour tickets and can advise you on everything St Augustinian.

❶ Getting There & Around

Driving from the north, take I-95 exit 318 and head east past US Hwy 1 to San Marcos Ave; turn right and you'll end up at the Old City Gate, just past the fort. Alternately, you can take Hwy A1A along the beach, which intersects with San Marco Ave, or US Hwy 1 south from Jacksonville. From the south, take exit 298, merge onto US 1 and follow it into town.

Cars are a nightmare downtown with one-way and pedestrian-only streets and severely limited parking; outside the city center, you'll need wheels. There's a massive car park at the Visitor Information Center.

If you're flying into Jacksonville, **Airport Express** (☑ 904-824-9400; www.airportexpresspickup.com) charges $65 to drop you downtown in a shuttle. For an additional $20, it'll take you to your hotel. Reservations required. Private services are also available.

The **Sunshine Bus Company** (☑ 904-209-3716; www.sunshinebus.net) runs from approximately 7am to 6pm and serves downtown, the beaches and the outlet malls, as well as many points in between ($1 one way).

To rent some wheels, try **Solano Cycles** (☑ 904-825-6766; www.solanocycle.com; 32 San Marco Ave) for bikes ($8/18 for 2/24 hours) and motor scooters ($30/75 for 2/24 hours).

Jacksonville

At a whopping 840 sq miles, Jacksonville is the largest city by area in the contiguous United States and the most populous in Florida. Sprawling along three meandering rivers, with sweeping bridges and twinkling city lights reflected in the water, it has a brash big-city charm. While its high-rises, corporate HQs and chain hotels can make Jacksonville feel a little soulless, its sweet Southern heart will reveal itself to the patient explorer.

Although to most visitors, Jacksonville (Jax) is an arrival or departure point for destinations further north or south, the city's museums and restored historic districts are worth a wander if you have the time. The Five Points and San Marco neighborhoods are both charming, walkable areas lined with bistros, boutiques and bars, and feel worlds away from the buzzing downtown.

The Jacksonville area beaches – a world unto themselves – are 30 to 50 minutes' drive from the city, depending on traffic and where you're coming from. Unless you need to be in the city, we recommend staying by the beach for its slower pace and all that space: you can always day-trip downtown, if you fancy.

◉ Sights

★ **Cummer Museum of Art & Gardens** MUSEUM
(☑ 904-356-6857; www.cummer.org; 829 Riverside Ave; adult/student $10/6; ⊘ 10am-9pm Tue, to 4pm Wed-Sat, noon-4pm Sun) This handsome museum, Jacksonville's premier cultural

space, has a genuinely excellent collection of American and European paintings, Asian decorative art and antiquities.

Jacksonville Zoological Gardens ZOO
(☎904-757-4463; www.jacksonvillezoo.org; 370 Zoo Pkwy; adult/child $16/11; ⊗9am-5pm Mon-Fri, to 6pm Sat & Sun; ⊛) Northeast Florida's only major zoo opened in 1914 with one deer; today, it's home to over 1800 exotic animals and hectares of beautiful gardens. Favored fauna from around the world include elephants, jaguars, rare Florida panthers, gators, kangaroos and komodo dragons. There's an elevated viewing platform that brings you face to nose with giraffes. The zoo is 15 minutes north of downtown off I-95.

Value tickets (adult/child $25/18) include general admission as well as entry to Butterfly Hollow, Stingray Bay and unlimited train and carousel rides.

Museum of Contemporary Art Jacksonville MUSEUM
(☎904-366-6911; www.mocajacksonville.org; 333 N Laura St; adult/child $8/5; ⊗11am-5pm Tue, Wed, Fri & Sat, 11am-9pm Thu, noon-5pm Sun) The focus of this ultramodern space extends beyond painting: get lost among contemporary sculpture, prints, photography and film. Check out www.jacksonvilleartwalk.com for details of the free MOCA-run Art Walk, held on the first Wednesday of every month from 5pm to 9pm: it has over 56 stops and is a great way to see the city.

Museum of Science & History MUSEUM
(☎904-396-6674; www.themosh.org; 1025 Museum Circle; adult/child admission $10/6, planetarium $5/3; ⊗10am-5pm Mon-Thu, to 8pm Fri, to 6pm Sat, noon-5pm Sun; ⊛) Packing kids? This awesomely named museum (MOSH) offers dinosaurs, all things science and exhibits on Jacksonville's cultural and natural history. Be sure to check out the Bryan Gooding Planetarium: it's the largest single-lens planetarium in the world. Shows and their times vary; check www.moshplanetarium.org for details.

Jacksonville Maritime Heritage Center MUSEUM
(☎904-355-1101; www.jacksonvillemaritimeheritagecenter.org; 2 Independent Dr; adult/child $3/1; ⊗11am-5pm Tue-Sat) For insight into how maritime history intertwines with this port city, this densely packed museum has an array of nautical artifacts, scale models and shipping logs.

Jacksonville Landing PROMENADE
(☎904-353-1188; www.jacksonvillelanding.com; 2 Independent Dr) At the foot of the high-rise downtown, this prominent shopping and entertainment district has about 40 mostly touristy shops surrounding a tip-top food court with outdoor tables and regular, free live entertainment.

Southbank Riverwalk PROMENADE
This 1.2-mile boardwalk, on the south side of the St Johns River, opposite downtown and Jacksonville Landing, has spectacular views of the city's skyline. Most nights yield head-shakingly beautiful scenes, but firework displays are a real blast. The Southbank Riverwalk connects the museums flanking Museum Circle and makes a pleasant promenade.

NORTHEAST FLORIDA JACKSONVILLE

ℹ JACKSONVILLE ORIENTATION

As big as it is, Jacksonville can be a bit tricky to navigate. A few things to know:

➡ Jacksonville is trisected by a very rough T formed by the St Johns River. Downtown Jacksonville is on the west side of the St Johns.

➡ I-95 comes in straight from the north to a junction just south of downtown with I-10. Follow I-10 east into downtown, where a maze of state highways offers access to surrounding areas.

➡ Three bridges cross the river and will take you to San Marco: Fuller Warren (I-10), Acosta (Hwy 13) and Main St Bridge.

➡ I-295 breaks off from I-95, forming a circle around the city.

➡ Though the city is enormous, most sites of interest to the visitor are concentrated along the St Johns River's narrowest point: downtown; Five Points, just south of downtown along the river; and the elegant San Marco Historical District along the southern shore.

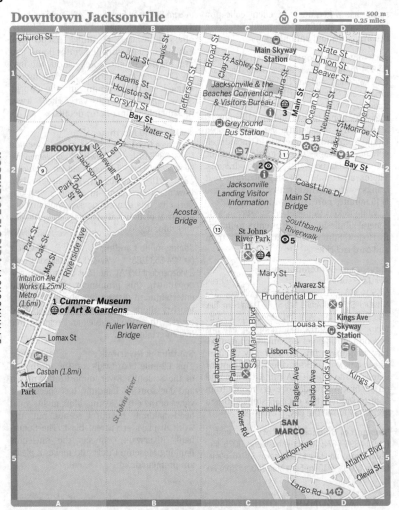

Downtown Jacksonville

🏃 Activities

With 72 golf courses in the greater area, there are plenty of opportunities to tee off. You can browse course summaries by visiting www.visitjacksonville.com.

👉 Tours

**Anheuser-Busch
Budweiser Brewery** TOUR
(☎800-342-5283; www.budweisertours.com; 111 Busch Dr; ⊙10am-4pm Mon-Sat) FREE Enjoy a free tour (and free beer if you're over 21).

🛏 Sleeping

Jacksonville suffers a serious dearth of interesting private hotels but there's a plethora of chain options dotted throughout the city and around highway interchanges: the cheapest rooms are along I-95 and I-10. It's nicer to stay by the beaches where there's camping, swanky resorts and well-priced beachfront chains.

Riverdale Inn B&B $$
(☎904-354-5080; www.riverdaleinn.com; 1521 Riverside Ave; r $110-190, ste $200-220; P❋☎) In the early 1900s this was one of 50 or so

mansions lining Riverside. Now there are only two left, and you're invited to enjoy the Riverdale's lovely rooms with full breakfast.

Omni Jacksonville Hotel　　　HOTEL $$
(☑904-355-6664; www.omnihotels.com; 245 Water St; r from $149; P ✽ ☏ ☯ ☺) Within sight of Jacksonville Landing, this stylish 354-room hotel has lavish, amenity-laden rooms, acres of marble, a heated rooftop pool and complimentary wi-fi.

Homewood Suites by Hilton Downtown　　　HOTEL $$
(☑904-396-6888; www.homewoodsuites.com; 1201 Kings Ave; r incl breakfast from $159; P ✽ @) These tasteful, modern suites in the central San Marco neighborhood feature full kitchens and all the comforts of home. Breakfast and high-speed internet are both complimentary.

✗ Eating

The Five Points neighborhood, southwest of downtown, and the San Marco neighborhood, across the river from downtown, have tons of trendy cafes and bars with outdoor seating. The city's suit-and-tie financial industry means lots of steakhouses and upscale bistros.

French Pantry　　　FRENCH $
(☑904-730-8696; 6301 Powers Ave; items $6-12; ☺11am-2pm Mon-Fri) The secret is well and truly out about this inconveniently located but thoroughly hopping weekday lunchonly joint serving fresh filled french rolls and panini, soups, salads and incredible pastries and desserts. Another downside is that folks line up to get in and the service

can get frustrating. If you're not fussy, grab the booty and devour it in your car.

★bb's　　　FUSION $$
(☑904-306-0100; www.bbsrestaurant.com; 1019 Hendricks Ave; mains $12-32; ☺11am-late Mon-Sat) This groovy establishment, with its molded-concrete bar, clean, modern lines and daily cheese selection champions fresh local produce, which is crafted into arty, flavorful dishes from scratch: a gourmand's delight. Suggested wine pairings keep things simple. Connoisseurs of dessert needn't look elsewhere – the chocolate ganache cake alone is worth the trip.

River City Brewing Company　　　SEAFOOD $$
(☑904-398-2299; www.rivercitybrew.com; 835 Museum Circle; mains $10-24; ☺11am-late Mon-Sat, 10:30am-2:30pm Sun) Jax's premier riverfront restaurant is the perfect place to quaff a microbrew and enjoy some upscale seafood overlooking the water. Prices are reasonable for the location and quality of the food. The Sunday Brunch Buffet (adult/child $23/15) is lots of fun.

Clark's Fish Camp　　　SOUTHERN $$
(☑904-268-3474; www.clarksfishcamp.com; 12903 Hood Landing Rd; mains $13-34; ☺4:30-9:30pm Mon-Thu, 4:30-10pm Fri, 11:30am-10pm Sat, 11:30am-9:30pm Sun) Sample Florida's Southern 'Cracker' cuisine surrounded by the surreal animal menagerie of 'America's largest private taxidermy collection,' which resembles the freakish love child of Tim Burton and Mr Kurtz from *Heart of Darkness*. Taxidermied monkeys prowl the ceiling. Leopards glare glassily from the corners. This swamp shack is unforgettable: gator,

smoked eel, fried snake and frogs legs all make menu appearances amid more prosaic offerings such as catfish and steak. It's far south of downtown Jacksonville.

If this grotesque menagerie puts you off your food, you can always sit outside by the murky water. But a word to the wise: don't feed the gators.

Casbah
MIDDLE EASTERN $$

(☑904-981-9966; www.thecasbahcafe.com; 3628 St Johns Ave; mains $8-15; ☺11am-2am) Upon spying the swords, camels and Moorish lanterns lining the walls, you'll wonder if a passport is required for entry to this divey local favorite featuring authentic Middle Eastern dishes, beer, music and belly dancing. For the scent sensitive, note that the cafe doubles as a hookah lounge with dozens of flavorful tobacco concoctions.

Bistro Aix
FRENCH $$$

(☑904-398-1949; www.bistrox.com; 1440 San Marco Blvd; mains $13-36; ☺11am-10pm Mon-Thu, to 11pm Fri, 5-11pm Sat, 5-9pm Sun) Dine with the fashionable food mavens on fusion-y Mediterranean dishes at Aix, whose menu bursts with global flavors. There are over 250 wines by the bottle, and 50 by the glass! Reservations recommended.

Drinking & Entertainment

Intuition Ale Works
BREWERY

(☑904-683-7720; www.intuitionaleworks.com; 720 King St; ☺3-11pm Tue-Fri, from 1pm Sat) Stop by for a pint or three in the taproom of this funky local brewery serving, you guessed it – beer only! Feel free to order pizza from the neighborhood when you get peckish. A must for beer fans.

Mark's
BAR

(☑904-355-5099; www.marksjax.com; 315 E Bay St; ☺4pm-late Tue-Fri, from 8pm Sat) Dress to impress at this upscale cocktail bar and nightclub. Midweek it's chatty and social but

---

GAY HOT SPOT: METRO

Metro (☑904-388-8719; www.metrojax. com; 849 Willow Branch Ave), Jacksonville's top gay entertainment complex, has a disco, a cruise bar, a piano bar, a games room with pinball machines, a smoke-free chill-out loft, a leathery boiler room and a show bar.

Friday and Saturday nights are reserved for dancing the night away.

Underbelly
LIVE MUSIC

(☑904-353-6067; www.underbellylive.com; 113 E Bay St; ☺11am-2am Mon-Fri, from 6pm Sat & Sun) Jax's hottest live-music venue in the heart of downtown beckons you to 'dig the pig.' Check the cool-as website for listings.

Florida Theatre
THEATER

(☑904-355-5661; www.floridatheatre.com; 1128 E Forsyth St) Home to Elvis' first indoor concert in 1956, which a local judge endured to ensure Presley was not overly suggestive, this opulent 1927 venue is an intimate place to catch big-name musicians, musicals and movies.

San Marco Theatre
CINEMA

(☑904-396-4845; www.sanmarcotheatre.com; 1996 San Marco Blvd) A landmark 1938 art-deco movie theater where you can order beer, wine, pizza and sandwiches while watching a flick.

❶ Information

There are a bunch of sources of information for Jacksonville and the surrounding areas.

Florida Times-Union (www.jacksonville.com) Conservative daily paper, in print and online; Friday's *Weekend* magazine features family-oriented events listings.

Folio Weekly (www.folioweekly.com) Free; with club, restaurant and events listings. Found all over town.

Jacksonville & the Beaches Convention & Visitors Bureau (☑800-733-2668; www. visitjacksonville.com; 208 N Laura St, Suite 102; ☺9am-5pm Mon-Fri) The Jacksonville & the Beaches Convention & Visitors Bureau has all there is to know about Jax and surrounds. There's also a branch at Jacksonville Landing (☑904-791-4305; 2 Independent Dr; ☺11am-3pm Mon-Thu, 10am-7pm Fri & Sat).

Jacksonville Public Library (☑904-630-2665; www.jpl.coj.net; 303 N Laura St; ☺10am-6pm Mon & Thu-Sat, 1-5pm Sun, 11am-7pm Tue & Wed; ☎) Free wi-fi and friendly staff.

❶ Getting There & Around

Jacksonville International Airport (JAX; ☑904-741-4902; www.flyjax.com), about 18 miles north of downtown on I-95, is served by major and regional airlines and car-rental companies. If you're not renting a car, a cab downtown costs around $35. Otherwise, follow the signs for shuttle services: there are numerous licensed providers and reservations aren't necessary.

The **Greyhound bus station** (☑904-356-9976; www.greyhound.com; 10 Pearl St) is at

LOCAL ODDITY: THE TREATY OAK

At first glance, it looks like a small forest is growing in the middle of the concrete on Jacksonville's south side. But upon closer inspection you'll see that the 'forest' is really one single enormous tree, with a trunk circumference of 25ft and a shade diameter of nearly 200ft. According to local lore, the live oak tree is the oldest thing in Jacksonville – its age is estimated to be 250 years. You'll find the super-tree in Jesse Ball duPont Park (1123 Prudential Dr).

the west end of downtown. The **Amtrak station** (☑ 904-766-5110; www.amtrak.com; 3570 Clifford Lane) is 5 miles northwest of downtown.

The **Jacksonville Transportation Authority** (☑ 904-630-3100; www.jtafla.com) runs buses and trolleys around town and the beaches (fare $1), as well as a scenic, if underused, river-crossing Skyway (monorail).

Jacksonville Area Beaches

The stretches of beach closest to Jacksonville are delightfully sparse. Moving from south to north, **Ponte Vedra Beach** is the posh home of the ATP and PGA golf tours: golf courses, resorts and mansions are here. Urban **Jacksonville Beach** is where to eat, drink and party, while cozy **Neptune Beach** is more subdued. And if you want some sand all to yourself, **Atlantic Beach**, with several entrances off Seminole Beach Rd, is sublime.

There's a nice, chilled vibe here: locals are mellower than their Southern Floridian counterparts. Jax Beach fits the Californian comparison more closely than the rest of Florida, despite the coastlines being on opposite sides!

◉ Sights & Activities

Most of the action is concentrated at Jacksonville Beach, which buzzes all summer (and most of the mild winter, too).

Jacksonville Beach Pier   PIER
(☑ 904-241-1515; www.jacksonvillebeachpier.com; 503 N 1st St, Jacksonville Beach; walk-on/fishing $1/4; ◷ 6am-10pm) Constructed from removable planks, allowing it to be dismantled in the event of a hurricane, the 1300ft pier has a bait shop, concessions and fish-cleaning stations. Bring drinks, cast your line and wait for a nibble.

Rent Beach Stuff   BICYCLE RENTAL
(☑ 904-305-6472; www.rentbeachstuff.com; 11 1st St N, Jacksonville Beach; ◷ 8am-6pm) The roads are flat and the towns are small: why not rent a bike? In addition to a bunch of other beach and water-sports equipment, these guys will deliver a 26in beach cruiser to your hotel for $30 per day.

⊨ Sleeping

Kathryn Abbey Hanna Park   CAMPGROUND $
(☑ 904-249-4700; 500 Wonderwood Dr, Atlantic Beach; sites $22) This pleasant park and shaded campground is a stone's throw from Atlantic Beach and has its own freshwater lake.

Sea Horse Oceanfront Inn   MOTEL $$
(☑ 800-881-2330; www.jacksonvilleoceanfronthotel.com; 120 Atlantic Blvd, Neptune Beach; r from $119; ❇ ❀ ⛱) Each room in this Pepto-Bismol-colored refurbished motel has a view of both the kidney-shaped pool and the ocean. This is definitely a cut above the average beach motel, with big flat-screen TVs and friendly management. Regulars return year after year.

Courtyard by Marriott Jacksonville Beach Oceanfront   HOTEL $$
(☑ 904-249-9071; www.marriott.com; 1617 1st St N, Jacksonville Beach; r from $169) Of the smattering of chain hotels in Jax Beach, we love this waterfront property for its practical, pleasant rooms and friendly, attentive staff. It's right on the beach and has everything you need to drop in and chill out.

Fig Tree B&B   B&B $$
(☑ 904-246-8855; www.figtreeinn.com; 185 4th Ave, Jacksonville Beach; r incl breakfast $145-175; ❇ @) This rustic cedar-shingle cottage conceals six rooms, including the quirky Bird Room, with a handmade willow-frame queen-size bed and willow reading chair. In addition to breakfast (fully cooked on weekends, self-serve weekdays), it does afternoon tea on the shady porch.

★ One Ocean   HOTEL $$$
(☑ 904-249-7402; www.oneoceanresort.com; 1 Ocean Blvd, Atlantic Beach; r from $180; ❇ ❀ ⛱)

This stylish resort hotel has been favored by A-list celebs for its low-key oceanfront locale. The grand lobby is modern and elegant: white marble, rippling iridescent walls and suited staff. Rooms follow suit with clean, contemporary lines and touches of silver, pewter and sea green – most have views. Complete your indulgence with a treatment in the day spa, followed by dinner at the Beaches' most elegant, oceanfront, fine-dining establishment, Azurea.

Lodge at Ponte Vedra RESORT $$$
(☑ 904-285-1111; www.pontevedra.com; 100 Ponte Vedra Blvd, Ponte Vedra Beach; r from $279; ✻ 🛜 🞓) 🏊 Well-heeled families love this opulent Mediterranean-style resort – a historic landmark – where kids play by the pool while the grown-ups enjoy a much-needed beachfront massage. Rooms and suites are plush and airy, with tasteful sage-and-sand decor and super-luxe granite-and-marble bathrooms.

✖ Eating & Drinking

Colonel Mustard's Phatburger BURGERS $
(☑ 904-247-5747; www.jaxbestburgers.com; 1722 3rd St N, Jacksonville Beach; burgers from $6; ☺ 8am-10pm) Even the kids get involved at this no-frills, friendly, family-owned-and-operated burger joint a few blocks back from the beach. It's cheap and cheery and guaranteed to please: although vegetarians will be disappointed. Breakfasts are as good as the burgers and the well-done fries and hash browns will sate even the most hard-ass *connaisseur du frites*.

Beach Road Chicken Dinners SOUTHERN $
(☑ 904-398-7980; www.beachroadchickendinners.com; 4132 Atlantic Blvd, Jacksonville; items $4-12; ☺ 11am-8:30pm Tue-Sat, to 6pm Sun) This

deliciously retro joint has been frying chicken since 1939. Tear off a chunk of tender thigh meat and wrap it up in a fluffy biscuit, and you'll understand why people line up every day at this much-loved shack.

Beach Hut Café SOUTHERN $
(☑ 904-249-3516; 1281 3rd St S, Jacksonville Beach; items $4-10; ☺ 6am-2:30pm) Don't let the strip-mall location deceive you: the food here is finger-lickin' good. Famous for its big, all-day Southern breakfasts, it draws *huge* lines – especially on weekends.

European Street CAFE $
(☑ 904-249-3001; www.europeanstreet.com; 992 Beach Blvd, Jacksonville; items $6-12; ☺ 10am-10pm) Sneak away from the beaches at this combination chocolatier, deli, bar (boasting 150 imported beers) and gourmet market, with a huge menu of salads, sandwiches and German fare.

Metro Diner DINER $$
(☑ 904-853-6817; www.metrodiner.com; 1534 N 3rd St, Jacksonville Beach; mains $9-16; ☺ 7am-2:30pm) Best for brunch in Jacksonville Beach, this tried-and-true diner has been in business since 1938. These days it's usually packed, especially on weekends. Benedicts for brunch, meatloaf, big fish sandwiches and chicken pot pie all feature.

Penthouse Lounge BAR
(☑ 904-270-0025; www.casamarinahotel.com; 691 N 1st St, Jacksonville Beach; ☺ 11am-late Tue-Fri, from 1pm Sat & Sun, from 4pm Mon; 🛜) Atop the restored 1925 Casa Marina hotel you'll find this compact yet happening beachfront bar with killer views and ambient tunes from its ample rooftop deck. There's a live DJ Thursday to Saturday nights.

FREEBIRD LIVE

Fans of local-boys-done-good Lynyrd Skynyrd will want to pay homage at **Freebird Live** (☑ 904-246-2473; www.freebirdlive.com; 200 N 1st St, Jacksonville Beach; ☺ 8pm-2am show nights), a two-story music venue with wide verandas owned by the Van Zant family. The band's founding lead singer Ronnie Van Zant and many of his bandmates died in a 1977 plane crash; his younger brother Johnny took his place when the band reformed a decade later.

With two original members still in the lineup, Skynyrd rocks this joint when they're not touring; there's plenty of memorabilia, too. But the Freebird is way more than a shrine. With an intimate stage and great acoustics, it has carved out a reputation as one of the nation's best small music venues. In addition to giving local talent a stage, past acts have included Willie Nelson, the Killers and George Clinton.

TALBOT & FORT GEORGE ISLANDS

The most scenic way to reach Amelia Island from Jacksonville's beaches offers plenty of reasons to stop along the way: exceptional kayaking, distinctive state parks, and riverbank and beachside camping galore. It's a wonderful day trip if you have wheels and time.

Heading north from the beaches along State Rd A1A, you'll have to jump on the **St Johns River Ferry** (☑904-241-9969; www.stjohnsriverferry.com; per car $5; ☺every half-hour 6am-7pm) in Mayport. Turn left on Fort George Rd to reach **Fort George Island Cultural State Park** (☑904-251-2320; www.floridastateparks.org/fortgeorgeisland; State Rd A1A S; ☺8am-sunset, visitor center 9am-5pm Wed-Sun) **FREE**. Although the exact location of the fort erected by the British in 1736 remains uncertain, the island still bears its name. In pre-WWII glory days, flappers flocked here to the ritzy Ribault Club, built in 1928, for lavish Gatsby-esque bashes. Now housing the visitor center, the meticulously restored mansion flaunts grand archways and three dozen sets of cypress French doors. It's the starting point of the 4.4-mile Saturiwa loop trail, which you can walk, bike or drive. Enormous shell middens date the island's habitation by the Timucua to over 4000 years ago.

Continuing on Fort George Rd to just outside the park's northern fringe, you'll come to **Kingsley Plantation** (☑904-251-3537; www.nps.gov/timu; 11676 Palmetto Ave; ☺9am-5pm) **FREE**, where you can tour portions of the oldest standing plantation house in Florida and the remains of 23 tabby-construction slave cabins. The main house is under near-constant restoration due to termites and humidity, but the sprawling shaded grounds and mangroves make a unique spot for a picnic. Be sure to engage a docent to learn about the colorful history of the site.

A short, shaded drive down Palmetto Ave will bring you back to the A1A: head north to **Little Talbot Island State Park** (☑904-251-2320; www.floridastateparks.org/littletalbotisland; 12157 Heckscher Dr; per vehicle $5, camping per night $24; ☺8am-sunset) and its 5 miles of pristine beaches, extraordinary wildlife (river otters, marsh rabbits, bobcats) and grand tidal fishing for mullet and sheepshead. Camping is available. Continuing north, you'll pull into the lone parking lot and deposit your fee in the blue envelope at the stark but lovely **Big Talbot Island State Park** (☑904-251-2320; www.floridastateparks.org/bigtalbotisland; State Rd A1A N; per vehicle $3; ☺8am-sunset). Take your camera on the short trail to Boneyard Beach, where salt-washed skeletons of live oak and cedar trees litter the white sand, framed by a 20ft bluff of eroded coastline.

Between the two islands, **Kayak Amelia** (☑904-251-0016; www.kayakamelia.com; 13030 Heckscher Dr; guided trips from $65, kayak rental per day from $49) will gear you up with your own kayak or canoe, or you can join in a guided ecotour. Moonlight paddles through the silvered marsh are a magical way to experience meditative waters. Kids are welcome, but call in advance to make arrangements.

The closest markets for munchies are near the ferry on Fort George Island, or on Amelia Island, whose delights await at the end of your drive.

❶ Information

Beaches Visitor Center (☑904-242-0024; www.jacksonvillebeach.org; 380 Pablo Ave, Jacksonville Beach; ☺10am-4:30pm Tue-Sat) Has information about the beaches.

❶ Getting There & Around

Traveling by car from Jacksonville, follow I-10 to Atlantic Beach, and Hwy 90 (Beach Blvd) directly to Jacksonville Beach. Coming from St Augustine, follow Hwy A1A due north.

The Jacksonville Transportation Authority (p351) operates buses from Jacksonville to the beaches ($1.50).

Amelia Island

History buffs adore this glorious sea island, just 13 miles from the Georgia border, which combines the moss-draped charm of the Deep South with the laid-back beach culture of Florida. It is believed the island's original inhabitants, the Timucua, arrived as early as 4000 years ago. Since that time, eight flags have flown over the island, starting with the French in 1562, followed by the Spanish, the English, the Spanish again, the Patriots, the Green Cross of Florida, the Mexican Rebels, the US, the Confederates, then the US again!

Vacationers have been flocking here since the 1890s, when Henry Flagler tamed the wild east coast, converting the area into a playground for the rich. The legacy of that golden era is evident in the central town of Fernandina Beach, whose 50 blocks of historic buildings, Victorian B&Bs, and restaurants housed in converted fishing cottages all help make Amelia Island one of the most charming finds in the US. Splurge on a few days here if you can.

Dotting the rest of the island are lush parks, green fairways and miles of unspoiled shoreline.

⊙ Sights & Activities

Strolling Fernandina Beach's bistro- and boutique-laden historical downtown is one of the island's main attractions.

Fort Clinch State Park   PARK
(✆904-277-7274; www.floridastateparks.org/fortclinch; 2601 Atlantic Ave; park pedestrian/car $2/6; ⊙park 8am-sunset, fort 9am-5pm) Although construction commenced in 1847, rapid technological advancements rendered Fort Clinch's masonry walls obsolete by as early as 1861, when the fort was taken easily by Confederate militia in the Civil War and later evacuated. Federal troops again occupied the fort during WWII. Today, the park offers a variety of activities, a half-mile-long fishing pier, serene beaches for shelling (of the non-military kind) and 6 miles of peaceful, unpaved trails for hiking and cycling.

On the first weekend of the month, authentically outfitted troops perform a reenactment of the Confederate evacuation that extends to cooking in the old kitchen's massive iron cauldron and sleeping on straw mats in the soldiers' barracks. Candlelight tours ($3) are a treat if you're here May to September.

Amelia Island Museum of History   MUSEUM
(✆904-261-7378; www.ameliamuseum.org; 233 S 3rd St; adult/student $7/4; ⊙10am-4pm Mon-Sat, 1-4pm Sun) Housed in the former city jail (1879–1975), Florida's only oral-history museum has tiny but informative exhibits exploring Native American history, the Spanish Mission period, the Civil War and historic preservation. A variety of tours are available, including the eight-flags tour (11am and 2pm Monday to Saturday and 2pm Sunday), providing lively interpre-

tations of the island's fascinating history, and architecture tours, pub crawls and cellphone walking tours ($5).

Kelly Seahorse Ranch   HORSEBACK RIDING
(✆904-491-5166; www.kellyranchinc.net; 7500 1st Coast Hwy; 1hr rides $70; ⊙10am, noon, 2pm & 4pm) This working ranch leads gentle beachside horseback-riding tours, suitable for new riders; call in advance for longer and more challenging trips. You don't need prior riding experience, but children must be at least 13 years old.

Egan's Creek Greenway   WALKING
(✆904-310-3363; 2500 Atlantic Ave) **FREE** A network of grassy trails covering over 300 acres, the Egan's Creek Greenway is the perfect place to spot alligators, snakes, bobcats and countless species of birds. Interpretive displays line the trails. Well soled, covered footwear is recommended.

Pipeline Surf Shop   SURFING
(✆904-277-3717; www.pipelinesurfshop.com; 2022 1st Ave; rentals from $35; ⊙9am-6pm) From fall through spring when nor'easters bluster through, surfable beach breaks are common, especially at Main Beach. Pipeline rents all kinds of boards and wetsuits, and gives surf lessons from beginner to advanced. It even runs SUP yoga classes: yoga on stand-up paddle boards!

☞ Tours

Amelia River Cruises   BOAT TOUR
(✆904-261-9972; www.ameliarivercruises.com; 1 N Front St; tours from $22) Hop aboard a 33ft riverboat to explore Amelia and nearby Cumberland Island, GA, stopping to marvel at plantation ruins and dense tracts of Spanish-moss-covered trees.

Old Towne Carriage Company   TOUR
(✆904-277-1555; www.ameliacarriagetours.com; 115 Beech St; half-hour rides adult/child $15/7) Horse carriages clip-clop through the historical downtown, offering half-hour or hourlong rides.

⊨ Sleeping

Fernandina Beach has a wealth of charming Victorian B&Bs and there are some opulent resorts on the island. That said, rooms don't come cheap and rates soar in peak summer and special events periods.

AFRICAN AMERICAN HERITAGE ON AMERICAN BEACH

Insurance magnate AL Lewis, Florida's first black millionaire, founded American Beach in 1935, creating the first black beach community on Florida's segregated shores. In its heyday American Beach catered to throngs of African Americans who arrived by busload to enjoy the beaches and African American–owned motels, restaurants and nightclubs, where shows with Ray Charles, Louis Armstrong and others made for some of the biggest bills in Florida. In 1964, however, Hurricane Dora destroyed many homes and businesses; shortly thereafter desegregation allowed African Americans to stroll the beaches closer to their homes. Recently, golf courses and gated communities have encroached upon what's left of American Beach, though beach access is possible via Lewis St, off Hwy A1A.

Fort Clinch State Park
CAMPGROUND $

(☏904-277-7274; www.floridastateparks.org/fort-clinch; 2601 Atlantic Ave; sites $26) Take your pick (if you're lucky) of riverside or oceanfront sites in this lovely and extremely popular park. The oak-and-moss-protected Amelia River sites are more private than the exposed beach sites. Be sure to make reservations well in advance.

★Addison
B&B $$

(☏904-277-1604; www.addisononamelia.com; 614 Ash St; r incl breakfast $195-260; ❋ 🅿) 🏊 Built in 1876, the Addison has modern upgrades (whirlpool tubs, deluge showers, Turkish-cotton towels and wi-fi) that'll trick you into thinking it was finished last week. The Addison's white, aqua and sage color scheme is bright and totally un-stuffy. Enjoy daily happy hours overlooking a delightful courtyard with the friendliest (and funniest) innkeepers on Amelia.

Eco-conscious guests take note: the inn's water- and energy-saving efforts have earned it a Green Lodging certification from the state.

Hampton Inn & Suites
HOTEL $$

(☏904-491-4911; www.hamptoninn.com; 19 S 2nd St; r from $139; ❋) Location can sometimes be everything: walk to all that downtown Fernandina Beach has to offer from this, the only significant chain hotel in the heart of the historic downtown, just steps from the harborfront. Offering excellent value in an expensive destination, guest rooms and suites feature comfy bedding, neutral furnishings and good showers. Optional kitchens add bang for the buck.

Fairbanks House
B&B $$

(☏904-277-0500; www.fairbankshouse.com; 227 S 7th St; r/ste/cottage incl breakfast from $185/265/230; ❋ 🛜 🅿) You could imagine Indiana Jones retiring to a place like this grand Gothic Victorian; it's stuffed to the gills with silk carpets, heavy leather-bound books and global knickknacks. Oversized guest rooms are individually styled to suit the period of the house. Suites, such as the upstairs wood-paneled Tower Suite, sleep five and allow private use of the glass cupola overlooking the oaks. Other guests will have to make do with the small pool and butterfly garden in the backyard.

★Ritz Carlton
HOTEL $$$

(☏904-277-1100; www.ritzcarlton.com/en/Properties/AmeliaIsland; 4750 Amelia Island Pkwy; r from $299) The height of luxury, decadence and impeccable service awaits at this unexpectedly located Ritz Carlton. Set on 13 miles of pristine beaches, with its own private 18-hole golf course and lavish rooms and suites furnished with casual elegance, this is a property for those with fat wallets, accustomed to the best in life, or for that very special vacation experience.

Hoyt House
B&B $$$

(☏904-277-4300, 800-432-2085; www.hoythouse.com; 804 Atlantic Ave; r incl breakfast from $229; ❋ 🛜 🅿) This stately, award-winning Victorian B&B perched on the edge of downtown boasts an enchanting gazebo that begs idle time with a cool drink. Ten rooms each have their own stylish mix of antiques and found treasures. Room service is available.

Elizabeth Pointe Lodge
B&B $$$

(☏904-277-4851; www.elizabethpointelodge.com; 98 S Fletcher Ave; r/ste from $240/390; ❋ 🛜) Atmosphere oozes from this eccentric yet stylish 1890s Nantucket-shingle-style maritime inn, perched on the ocean, 2 miles from downtown. Rocking-chair-laden porches offer the best seats on the island for beholding a sunrise. Classic, elegant rooms have plush,

WORTH A TRIP

CUMBERLAND ISLAND NATIONAL SEASHORE

The largest wilderness island in the US, Cumberland Island (☎912-882-4336; www.nps.gov/cuis; entry $4, sea camping $4) lies just over the Georgia state line. At 17.5 miles long and 3 miles wide, almost half of its 57 sq miles is marshland, mudflats and tidal creeks. Only 300 visitors at any given time are allowed on the island, accessible by a 45-minute ferry ride.

Ashore, rangers lead free one-hour tours concluding at the ruins of Thomas and Lucy Carnegie's 1884 mansion, Dungeness. Along the way rangers interpret the rich bird and animal life – including sandpipers, ospreys, painted buntings, nesting loggerhead turtles, armadillos and deer – and detail 4000 years of human history that spans the Timucua, British colonists and Spanish missionaries.

After the Civil War, freed slaves purchased parcels of land at the island's northern end and founded the First African Baptist Church in 1893. The tiny, 11-pew, white-painted wooden church was rebuilt in the 1930s, and the late John F Kennedy Jr and Carolyn Bessette were married in it in 1996. It's open to the public, but it's a hefty 15-mile hike from the ferry drop through moss-draped thickets.

The historic village of St Marys (www.stmaryswelcome.com) is the island's charming gateway: there are no shops on the island. Bring food, insect repellent and your camera! Accommodation options on the island range from an opulent mansion to rugged camping. Check the St Marys website for details.

Ferries (☎912-882-4335; www.nps.gov/cuis; round trip adult/senior/child $20/18/14) depart St Marys at 9am and 11:45am, returning at 10:15am and 4:45pm (an additional ferry runs at 2:45pm Wednesday to Saturday from March to November; no ferries run on Tuesday or Wednesday from December to February). Reservations are recommended.

From northern Florida, take I-95 north to St Marys Rd exit 1. Turn right onto GA-40/St Marys Rd E and follow it to the end.

chunky beds and oversized tubs (some are jetted). Adjacent to the main lodge, the new Ocean House has four luxury suites in a West Indian style. Families should enquire about the equally charming two-bedroom Miller Cottage.

Omni Amelia Island
Plantation Resort   RESORT $$$
(☎904-261-6161; www.omnihotels.com/Amelia Island; 39 Beach Lagoon; r from $269) Fresh from an $85-million renovation, this solid beachfront resort about 9 miles south of Fernandina Beach has a wide variety of dining options and an array of stylish, check-in and tune-out guest rooms and villas. It's perfect for those who prefer seclusion and amenities to the intimacy of Fernandina's homely B&Bs.

✗ Eating

Downtown Fernandina Beach has dozens of cute cafes and bistros.

T-Ray's Burger Station   BURGERS $
(202 S 8th St; mains $3-9; ⊙7am-3pm Mon-Fri, 8am-1pm Sat) Inside an Exxon gas station, this high-carb, high-fat, low-pretense diner and take-out joint is worth the cholesterol spike. Revered by locals, the big breakfasts

are just that, and daily specials sell out fast. Juicy burgers, chunky fries, fried shrimp and tender crab cakes all make the mouth water. Believe the hype: the line's there for a reason.

★**Kelley's Courtyard Café**   AMERICAN $$
(☎904-432-8213; www.kelleyscourtyardcafe.com; 19 S 3rd St; mains $8-26; ⊙11:30am-9pm Thu-Sat, Mon & Tue, 11:30am-3pm Wed) Run by lifelong locals, this charming, versatile cafe serves delicious home-style meals, prepared from only the freshest local ingredients, with a Southern, seaside bent. The delightful courtyard makes Kelley's family-friendly by day, yet perfect for casual, starlit romance by night. If you've never experienced a BBQ shrimp pizza – now is the time!

Café Karibo & Karibrew   FUSION $$
(☎904-277-5269; www.cafekaribo.com; 27 N 3rd St; mains $8-25; ⊙11am-9pm Tue-Sat, 11am-3pm Sun & Mon) This funky side-street favorite serves a large and eclectic menu of sandwiches, soups, salads and healthy treats in a sprawling two-story space with a shady patio hung with twinkling Christmas lights. Have a crabcake sandwich, or down a Sloppy Skip's Stout at the adjacent Karibrew brewpub, which has its own menu of global pub grub.

Le Clos
FRENCH $$$

(✆904-261-8100; www.leclos.com; 20 S 2nd St; mains $16-30; ⊘5:30-9:30pm Mon-Sat) Dine on classic French dishes with a light Florida twist – fish with citrus glazes, tender *steak frites*, shatteringly crisp crème brûlée – at this almost-too-cute-for-words but almost-too-busy-to-be-romantic patio bistro. Its reputation for ambience, quality meals and service excellence precedes it.

Merge
MODERN AMERICAN $$$

(✆904-277-8797; 510 S 8th St; meals $18-34; ⊘5-10pm) This classy, understated bistro tucked off the side of busy 8th St is gaining momentum as a local favorite. Those in the know rave about innovative and exquisite creations with a seafood leaning: scallops over braised rhubarb, cornmeal-breaded oysters in white cheddar cream... Think fresh and fabulous.

29 South
SOUTHERN $$$

(✆904-277-7919; 29 S 3rd St; mains $10-28; ⊘11:30am-2:30pm & 5:30-9:30pm Wed-Sat, 10am-2.30pm & 5:30-9:30pm Sun, 5:30-9:30pm Mon & Tue) Lobster corn dogs, sweet-tea-brined pork chops, homemade donut-bread pudding and coffee ice cream. Um...hello! In a pale-purple cottage, this neo-Southern bistro takes some risks and executes them well. It's casual yet classy and full of flavor.

🍸 Drinking & Nightlife

★ Palace Saloon
BAR

(✆904-491-3332; www.thepalacesaloon.com; 113-117 Centre St; ⊘noon-2am) Push through the swinging doors at the oldest continuously operated bar in Florida (since 1878), and the first thing you'll notice is the 40ft gas-lamp-lit bar. Knock back the saloon's rum-laced Pirate's Punch in dark, velvet-draped surroundings, curiously appealing to both bikers and Shakespeare buffs. At time of writing, patrons could still smoke inside. Nostalgic!

Green Turtle Tavern
BAR

(www.greenturtletavern.com; 14 S 3rd St; ⊘3pm-1am) You can't get much more laid-back or friendly than this colorful, peaced-out bar in a crooked little cottage with a wraparound porch. It serves cocktails, bourbon of all sorts and plenty of cold beer. Check out the dude playing guitar out front, if you're lucky.

Hammerhead Beach Bar
BAR

(✆904-491-7783; www.hammerheadbeachbar.com; 2045 S Fletcher Ave; ⊘10am-2am) There's nothing snooty about this booty bar, serving cheap drinks and plenty of them. With pool tables inside, two expansive decks with ocean views outside, occasional DJs and infamous 'bikini Sundays,' there's plenty of testosterone and sunshine to keep the boys and girls happy.

🛍 Shopping

Downtown Fernandina Beach features a dozen blocks lined with fudge shops, children's boutiques, candle stores and more. It's particularly noteworthy for antiques, especially nautical-themed goods.

Eight Flags Antiques Market
ANTIQUES

(✆904-277-8550; 605 Centre St; ⊘10am-6pm Mon-Sat, from noon Sun) Three dozen dealers in one large indoor space. Bargains can be found.

ℹ Information

Historic Downtown Visitor Center (✆904-277-0717; www.ameliaisland.com; 102 Centre St; ⊘10am-4pm) Reams of useful information and maps in the old railroad depot. A fun stop in itself.

Maritime Museum & Welcome Center (✆800-226-3542; www.fbmaritimemuseum.org; 17 S Front St; ⊘10am-4pm Wed-Sat, 1-4pm Sun) This small maritime museum on the harborfront provides a selection of local maps and pamphlets.

Nassau County Public Library (25 N 4th St; ⊘10am-6pm Tue, Wed, Fri & Sat, 10am-8pm Mon & Thu) Free internet access.

ℹ Getting There & Around

Hwy A1A splits in two directions on Amelia Island, one heading west toward I-95 and the other following the coast; both are well marked.

To get to Amelia the fastest route from the mainland is to take I-95 north to exit 373 and head east about 15 miles straight to the island.

Want a prettier route? Heading from Jacksonville Beach to the town of Mayport, catch the St Johns River Ferry (p353), which runs every 30 minutes to Fort George Island.

NORTH CENTRAL FLORIDA

Sprinkled between the thoroughbred-horse studs, the sprawling forest of Ocala and the funky college town of Gainesville, you'll discover crystal-clear springs, meandering back roads and small Victorian gingerbread towns reminiscent of a time before the tourism explosion. North Central Florida is more 'Southern' than Florida's South. Go figure!

Blue Spring State Park

The largest spring on the St Johns River, Blue Spring maintains a constant 72°F (22°C) . Between November and March it becomes the winter refuge for up to 200 West Indian manatees. The best time to see them is before 11am; there's a wheelchair-accessible path to the viewing platform. This tranquil state park (☑386-775-3663; www.floridastateparks.org/bluespring; 2100 W French Ave, Orange City; car/bike $6/2; ◷8am-sunset) is a revitalizing spot to swim (prohibited when manatees are present), snorkel or canoe. Campsites ($24), basic cabins ($95) and gear rentals are available.

You can also spend two hours cruising the peaceful waters with St Johns River Cruises (☑386-917-0724; www.sjrivercruises.com; 2100 West French Ave, Orange City; adult/child $22/16; ◷tours 10am & 1pm), whose nature tours offer a thoughtful insight into this fragile ecosystem.

Cassadaga

In 1894, 27-year-old New Yorker George Colby was suffering from tuberculosis. Seneca, Colby's Native American spirit guide, told him to head south to a lake and establish a spiritualist community, where he'd be healed. Colby did it, and Cassadaga (pronounced kassuh-*day*-guh) was born.

Today, Colby's camp – a collection of mainly 1920s cracker cottages – is a registered historic district, the oldest active religious community in the US, and home to the Southern Cassadaga Spiritualist Camp Meeting Association (☑386-228-3171; www.cassadaga.org; 1325 Stevens St), who believe in infinite intelligence, prophecy, healing and communicating with the dead. Some say the area is part of an energy vortex where the spirit and earth planes are exceptionally close, creating a 'portal' between the two. We've been to some weird places before, and Cassadaga is right up there.

You wouldn't find the town if you weren't looking for it. At a rural crossroads about 2 miles off the main drag, the tiny camp doesn't have an ATM or gas station. Scattered throughout the area are 30-some spiritual practitioners who offer a variety of 'psychic' readings, starting at around $50 for 30 minutes.

The camp's heart is the Cassadaga Camp Bookstore (☑386-228-2880; www.cassadaga.org; 1112 Stevens St; ◷10am-5pm Mon-Sat, 11.30am-5pm Sun), which sells New Age books, crystals and incense, and serves as the visitor center for the town. The whiteboard in the back room connects you with which psychics are working that day. The store also organizes historical tours of the village (1pm and 3pm Saturday, $15) and orb tours (8pm Saturday, $25), where photographers shoot glowing balls of light – reportedly spirits from another world. A $1 donation gets you a camp directory, allowing you to take a pretty good self-guided tour. Mandatory stop: spooky, serene Spirit Lake, where residents scatter the ashes of the departed.

The original Cassadaga Hotel (☑386-228-2323; www.cassadagahotel.net; 355 Cassadaga Rd; r from $55; ❇) burned down in 1926. Today, ghosts reportedly lurk in the shadows of the rebuilt hotel (sniff for Jack's cigar smoke, and listen for two girls terrorizing the upstairs halls). Looking like a rejected set from *The Shining*, the hotel is appropriately eerie: on the creepy vibe scale, this place is off the charts!

DeLand

While much of Florida seems frantic to cover itself in neon and high-rises, stoic DeLand shrugs that off as nonsense. Development is coming, but locals, intimate with the area and acutely aware of what's needed, are bringing it. The quaint, walkable Woodland Blvd, bisecting the east side of town from the west, is home to independent shops and restaurants – modern yet thoroughly small-town. Ancient oaks lean in to hug each other over city streets and Spanish moss dribbles from their branches. Picture-perfect Stetson University, with one of the prettiest campuses in America, forms the town's heart. This is Old Town Florida, and it feels so cozy. Ironically, DeLand was the first town in Florida to enjoy electricity.

Despite all this hometown goodness, risk-taking flows through DeLand's blood. In the 1870s New York baking-soda magnate Henry DeLand traveled down the St Johns River with a vision of founding the 'Athens of Florida.' That moniker has stuck, but these days, DeLand is most famous for skydiving – the tandem jump was invented here.

◉ Sights & Activities

Several historic buildings are open for tours. Check out the West Volusia Historical Society for info (www.delandhouse.com).

De Leon Springs State Park   PARK
(☑386-985-4212; www.floridastateparks.org/deleonsprings; 601 Ponce de Leon Blvd, De Leon Springs; car/bike $6/2; ☉8am-sunset) Fifteen minutes north of town, these natural springs flow into the 28-sq-mile Lake Woodruff National Wildlife Refuge and were used by Native Americans 6000 years ago. Today they're a popular developed swimming area, great for kids. Water-equipment rentals and boat tours are available: enquire at the Park Office. Experienced hikers can attack the robust, blue-blaze 4.2-mile Wild Persimmon Trail, meandering through oak hammocks, floodplains and open fields.

DeLand Hospital Museum   MUSEUM
(☑386-740-5800; www.delandhouse.com/hospital; 230 N Stone St; ☉9am-3pm Mon-Sat) FREE Lovers of things unusual will appreciate this quirky museum, housed in a former hospital. Its eight galleries and exhibits range from a somewhat unsettling 1920s operating room to the Hawtense Conrad Elephant Fantasyland – a collection of more than 1000 elephants.

Skydive DeLand   SKYDIVING
(☑386-738-3539; www.skydivedeland.com; 1600 Flightline Blvd; tandem jumps $179, freefall training & 1st jump $351) If plummeting toward earth at speeds of 120mph sounds like a whiz-bang time, you're in the right place. A short briefing and a seasoned professional strapped to your back is all it takes to experience the least-boring two minutes of your life above some glorious countryside with Skydive DeLand. Experienced skydivers can jump solo or advance their skills at this first-rate facility. It also offers freefall training so you can learn to jump on your own.

🛏 Sleeping & Eating

Most of the cheap hotels are along Hwy 17 (Woodland Blvd), north of New York Ave. There's camping nearby in Ocala National Forest.

DeLand Country Inn   B&B $
(☑386-736-4244; www.delandcountryinn.com; 228 West Howrie Ave; r incl breakfast $89-119; ❋🐾) Popular with skydivers, this sweet B&B is run by a lovely English couple, who'd

possibly like to redefine the acronym to read 'Best & British.' Six cosy rooms in the c 1883 guesthouse feature comforting echoes of Mother England. Of course, a full English breakfast is fried up daily!

Artisan Downtown   HOTEL $$
(☑386-873-4675; www.delandartisaninn.com; 215 S Woodland Blvd; r from $125; ❋🐾) This centrally located boutique hotel was fully renovated in 2013 and features the trendiest rooms in DeLand, with whirlpool baths and cozy sitting areas. The on-site bar and restaurant is a nice bonus, from which noise doesn't appear to be an issue.

Buttercup Bakery   BAKERY $
(197 E Church St; snacks $2-7; ☉7am-5pm Mon-Fri, 8am-3pm Sat) Inside this sunny yellow cottage the pastry cases are stacked high with luscious sweets: lemon-curd bars, white-chocolate-apricot bars, chocolate-chip bread pudding and more. It also serves organic coffee, tea and salad.

Cook's   AMERICAN $$
(☑386-734-4399; www.cooksbuffetdeland.com; 704 N Woodland Blvd; buffet from $10; ☉11am-8:30pm) It's hard not to enjoy a buffet when it is done well, with plenty of selections kept clean, fresh and warm. Cook's does just that. Roast meats, veggies, soups and salads from the buffet are complemented by a modest selection of à la carte deli sandwiches on freshly baked breads. Cheap and cheerful. Grandma will love it!

★ Cress   MODERN AMERICAN $$$
(☑386-734-3740; www.cressrestaurant.com; 103 W Indiana Ave; mains $19-32; ☉from 5:30pm Tue-Sat) Citified foodies have been known to trek to sleepy DeLand just to eat at this cutting-edge bistro, whose menu might

---

ROADSIDE ATTRACTION: US POSTAL MUSEUM & HOTEL

Philatelists (aka stamp collectors) will marvel at the collection of 'fancy cancels' (interesting postage-cancellation stamps) and vintage decorative envelopes at this quirky museum, in the lobby of the pleasant 1876 Heritage Inn (☑386-774-8849; www.1876heritageinn.com; 300 S Volusia Ave, Orange City; r $55; 🅿), just down the road from DeLand in Orange City.

offer such delights as local seafood *mofongo* (a classic Caribbean dish), Indonesian shrimp curry, and a salad of delicate pea tendrils with passion-fruit emulsion. Look for lots of fiery Indian flavors – chef Pulapaka was born in Mumbai, and ditched a career as a math professor to follow his passion for food.

ℹ Information

Welcome Center (☏ 386-734-4331; www. delandchamber.org; 336 N Woodland Blvd; ⊙8:30am-5pm Mon-Fri) Everything you ever wanted to know about DeLand but never thought to ask.

Ocala

Blanketed by velvety emerald paddocks where sleek-limbed horses neigh in the misty morning air, the outskirts of Greater Ocala look like the US Dept of Agriculture–certified 'Horse Capital of the World' *should* look. There are about 1200 horse farms in Marion County, with more than 45 breeds represented.

Downtown Ocala, however, ain't so grand – there's a reason locals call it 'Slocala.' But it's not the downtown you're here for – this rural city is surrounded by beautiful clear springs and the best backyard in Florida: Ocala National Forest.

◉ Sights & Activities

★**Don Garlits Museums**   MUSEUM
(☏877-271-3278; www.garlits.com; 13700 SW 16th Ave; adult/child $15/6; ⊙9am-5pm) Local Don 'Big Daddy' Garlits won 144 national events and 17 World Championship titles, shattering numerous records in his hand-built breakneck speedsters. A visit to Ocala isn't complete without checking out his twin museums. First up, the Museum of Drag Racing, where you'll see engine collections and an impressive lineup of about 150 dragsters. The adjacent Museum of Classic Cars houses a phenomenal collection of more than 70 autos, including a 1926 Model T and Don's two-toned 1950 Mercury, driven by the Fonz in *Happy Days*. Allow two hours to look around.

Silver Springs State Park   PARK
(☏352-236-7148; www.floridastateparks.org/silversprings; 5656 E Silver Springs Blvd; pedestrian/car $2/8; ⊙10am-5pm) In one of Florida's first amusement parks, glass-bottomed boats were invented here in 1878 to show visitors the natural springs and stunningly clear Silver River. Although the amusement side of things closed when the park was taken over by the state in 2013, the natural beauty and the boat tours (adult/child $10/9) over Mammoth Spring remain. The spring is the world's largest artesian limestone spring, gushing 550 million gallons of 99.8%-pure spring water per day.

Cactus Jack's Trail Rides   HORSEBACK RIDING
(☏352-266-9326; www.cactusjackstrailrides.com; 11008 S Hwy 475A; 1/2/3hr rides $45/65/80) You're in the horse capital of America, so saddle up and let Cactus Jack's take you trotting through shady forests and clover-green fields on the backs of their handsome quarter horses and thoroughbreds.

🛏 Sleeping & Eating

There's a cluster of cheap lodgings just south of downtown Ocala on Hwy 441 (S Pine Ave) and more within walking distance of Silver Springs.

Silver River State Park   CAMPGROUND $
(☏352-236-7148;   www.floridastateparks.org/silversprings; 1425 NE 58th Ave; sites $24, cabins $110; ❋ ❋) Pets are welcome at any of the 59 campsites nestled among the woods at this 5000-acre park. If you want something more sumptuous (but canine-free), try the park's fully equipped luxury cabins, which sleep up to six.

Hilton Ocala   HOTEL $$
(☏352-854-1400; www.hiltonocala.com; 3600 SW 36th Ave; r from $139; ❋ 🛜 ❋) Ocala's paddockside Hilton has its own Clydesdale horse, Buddy (and free horse cookies for you to feed him), who waits patiently to take guests on free carriage rides. There's a biweekly chocolate fountain and a jogging trail, too.

The Schnitzel Factory   GERMAN $$
(www.theschnitzelfactory.com; 1053 NE 14th St; mains $14-20; ⊙11am-8pm Tue-Sat) You'll find this little German restaurant in a strip mall in suburban Ocala does a roaring trade. The schnitzels aren't drool-worthy, but the '80s German music videos on the multiple LaserJuke screens could be the secret weapon. Oh, and the beer!

ℹ Information

Ocala & Marion County Visitors Center (www.ocalamarion.com; 112 N Magnolia Ave; ⊙9am-5pm Mon-Fri)

BARBERVILLE ROADSIDE YARD ART & PRODUCE

On Rte 40, plunked halfway between Ocala and Daytona and roughly one-third the way between DeLand and Palatka, nestled cozily beneath a Spanish-moss canopy, sits the king of roadside stands, **Barberville Roadside Yard Art & Produce** (☑386-749-3562; www.barbervilleroadside.com; 140 West State Rd 40, Barberville; ◷9am-7pm). Offering more than just fruits, veggies and honey, this open-air market fills 3 acres with mounds of fountains, wrought-iron furniture, gazing balls, ceramic drop-in sinks and old-fashioned peanut brittle. There's even an 8ft-tall aluminum rooster. Who doesn't need one of those?

❶ Getting There & Around

Greyhound (☑352-732-2677; www.greyhound.com; 529 NE 1st Ave) is in the Central Transfer Station, at the corner of NE 5th St, just a few blocks from downtown. The transfer station for **Amtrak** (☑352-629-9863; www.amtrak.com) is here, and so is **SunTran** (☑352-401-6999; www.suntran.com), whose buses can get you around town between roughly 6am and 7pm; bus trips cost $1.25.

Ocala National Forest

The oldest national forest east of the Mississippi River and the southernmost national forest in the continental US, the 625-sq-mile Ocala National Forest is one of Florida's most important natural treasures. An incredible ecological web, the park is a tangle of springs, biomes (sand-pine scrub, palmetto wilderness, subtropical forest) and endangered flora and fauna.

With 18 developed campgrounds and 24 primitive ones, 219 miles of trails and 600 lakes (30 for boating), there are endless opportunities for swimming, hiking, cycling, horseback riding, canoeing, bird- and wildlife-watching – or just meditating on how great it is that the government got here before the theme parks did.

Two highways cross the region: Hwy 19 runs north–south and Hwy 40 runs east–west.

🏃 Activities

Hiking Trails HIKING
(www.fs.usda.gov/activity/ocala/recreation) Also referred to as the Ocala Trail, roughly 61 miles of the Florida National Scenic Trail spears the center of the forest north–south. Marked with orange blazes, pickup points include Juniper Springs, Alexander Springs and Clearwater Lake recreation areas. Outside hunting season, hikers can camp anywhere 200ft from the trail, but if you prefer to commune with others you'll find spur trails to developed campgrounds every 10 to 12 miles.

The 8.5-mile St Francis Trail (blue blazes) winds through riverine and bayhead swamp to the abandoned 1880s pioneer town of St Francis on the St Johns River. No buildings remain, but you'll see the old logging railroad bed and levee built for rice growing.

Paisley Woods Bicycle Trail CYCLING
(www.pwbt.weebly.com) Passing through prairies and live-oak domes, the popular 22-mile Paisley Woods Bicycle Trail is yellow blazed. Its end points are Alexander Springs to the north and Clearwater Lake to the south, but it's shaped like a figure eight so you can do either half as a loop. Be sure to bring both a bike that can handle off-road conditions and plenty of water (none is available along the trail).

Juniper Springs Recreation Area OUTDOORS
(☑352-625-3147; www.juniper-springs.com; 26701 Hwy 40, Silver Springs; admission/campsites $6/23; ◷8am-8pm) Ocala National Forest's flagship recreation area was developed in the mid-1930s. Concessions sell groceries and firewood, and rent kayaks and canoes ($33.50 per day, 8am to 8pm) for making the 7-mile, palmetto- and cypress-lined run down Juniper Creek. There's a pickup and return shuttle at the end of the creek between 1:30pm and 4:40pm ($6 per person and $6 per boat). Swimming is sublime at Juniper Springs: the water is a crisp 72°F (22°C) year-round.

Salt Springs Recreation Area OUTDOORS
(☑352-685-2048; www.floridasprings.org/visit/map/salt-springs; 13851 N Hwy 19, Salt Springs; admission $5.50, campsites with/without hookups $26/19; ◷8am-8pm) Rumored to have curative powers, Salt Springs is a favorite with RV owners for its lovely shady areas.

Salt Springs Run Marina BOAT RENTAL
(☑352-685-2255; www.saltspringsmarina.com; 25711 NE 134th Pl, Salt Springs; ◷7am-4pm) Rent a variety of water vessels to cruise enormous

Lake Kerr: canoes ($25 per day), pontoon boats ($90/140 per four hours/day plus gas) or a 16ft Carolina Skiff ($36/50 per four hours/day plus gas).

Alexander Springs Recreation Area
OUTDOORS

(📞 352-669-3522; www.fs.usda.gov/recarea/oca-la/recarea/?recid=32209; 49525 County Rd 445, Altoona; admission/campsites $5.50/21; ⏰ 8am-8pm) This picturesque recreation area has one of the last untouched subtropical forests left in Florida. The stunning sapphire-blue freshwater spring attracts wildlife, swimmers, scuba divers (an extra $6.50 fee) and sunbathers. Canoe rental ($16/38 per two hours/daily) includes a welcome rehaul at the end of the 7-mile paddle.

ℹ️ Information

Rangers serve most of the area and all campgrounds have resident volunteers who are good sources of information. There's no single admission fee and no one number to call; day-use areas are generally open 8am to 8pm. Pick up free literature and maps or buy a topographical version at any of the visitor centers, all open 8am to 5pm.

Ocklawaha Visitor Center (📞 352-236-0288; 3199 NE Hwy 315, Silver Springs) Your first stop if you're coming from Ocala and Silver Springs.

Pittman Visitor Center (📞 352-669-7495; 45621 SR 19, Altoona) On the major throughway from Orlando and Mt Dora.

Salt Springs Visitor Center (📞 352-685-3070; 14100 N Hwy 19, Salt Springs) In Salt Springs, accessible from Jacksonville and Palatka.

ℹ️ Getting There & Away

Several different entrances can be used to access Ocala National Forest. From Orlando take Hwy 441 north to the Eustis turnoff and continue north on Hwy 19 (about 40 miles); from Daytona take Hwy 92 west to DeLand, then head north on Hwy 17 to Barberville and west on SR 40 (about 30 miles); from Ocala take Silver Springs Blvd due west about 6 miles to the forest's main entry.

Gainesville

Originally a whistle-stop along the Florida Railroad Company's line chugging from Cedar Key to Fernandina Beach, Gainesville soon thrived as a citrus-producing community until repeated frosts in the 1890s drove orange-growers south. Today it's an energetic, upbeat city, routinely ranked among the country's best places to live and play, and home to the nation's second-largest university, the sprawling University of Florida (UF). The campus itself is 2 miles from downtown, but the student vibe infuses the entire city, with loads of cheap eats, cool bars and fine galleries. The university also bequeathed the world Gatorade: the science department developed the sports drink to counteract the on-field dehydration of its football team, the Fightin' Gators, which has a huge following here (just try getting a room on game weekends).

The town is known for its thriving music scene – the most notable band to hail from Gainesville is Tom Petty and the Heartbreakers. Indie rock and punk rock rule clubs today, though music-lovers can find everything from bluegrass to hip-hop almost every night.

Gainesville is also a mecca for the outdoorsy. Surrounding the city are pristine wilderness areas and a succession of stunningly clear springs just aching to be tubed.

⊙ Sights & Activities

Gainesville has a unique citywide cell-phone audio tour – when you spot a placard, dial the number listed for information about historical and cultural sites.

★ Florida Museum of Natural History
MUSEUM

(📞 352-846-2000; www.flmnh.ufl.edu; 3215 Hull Rd; museum free, Butterfly Rainforest adult/child $10.50/6; ⏰ 10am-5pm Mon-Sat, 1-5pm Sun) The highlight of this excellent natural-history museum is the expansive Butterfly Rainforest. Hundreds of butterflies from 55 to 65 species flutter freely in the soaring, screened vivarium. As you stroll among waterfalls and tropical foliage, peek at scientists preparing specimens in the rearing lab of this, the world's largest butterfly research facility.

Kanapaha Botanical Gardens
GARDENS

(📞 352-372-4981; www.kanapaha.org; 4700 SW 58th Dr; adult/child $7/3.50; ⏰ 9am-5pm Mon-Wed & Fri, to dusk Sat & Sun; 🐾) ✎ Central Florida's lush native plants – azaleas, rare double-crowned cabbage palms, southern magnolias – are on proud display at this highly rated 62-acre garden, with hiking paths, a labyrinth, a children's koi pond and special herb and ginger gardens. Especially cool is the dense bamboo garden, whose dark groves look like fairy homes. Dogs are welcome.

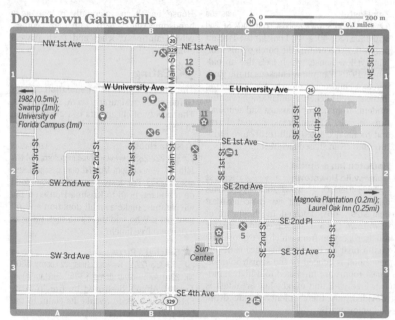

Downtown Gainesville

**Devil's Millhopper
State Geological Site** PARK
(☎352-955-2008; www.floridastateparks.org/
devilsmillhopper; 4732 Millhopper Rd; pedestrian/
car $2/4; ◎9am-5pm Wed-Sun) As the name
indicates, this is not your average park. The
site centers on a 120ft-deep, 500ft-wide
funnel-shaped rainforest which you enter
by descending a 232-step wooden staircase.
Water trickles down the slopes from the
surrounding springs; some of it flows into
a natural drain and ultimately to the Gulf
of Mexico. Rangers lead tours every Saturday at 10am. The park is about 20 minutes
northwest of downtown by car.

University of Florida UNIVERSITY
(UF; ☎352-392-3261; www.ufl.edu; Welcome
Center, cnr Museum Rd & Reitz Union Dr) The city
is dominated by the UF campus, one of the
largest in the country. Pop in to the Welcome
Center for tips on where best to wander
around to check out the student vibe.

Samuel P Harn Museum of Art GALLERY
(☎352-392-9826; www.harn.ufl.edu; 3259 Hull
Rd; ◎11am-5pm Tue-Fri, 10am-5pm Sat, 1-5pm
Sun) FREE Peer in at ancient Indian sculptures and contemporary paintings at this
excellent free art gallery on the University of
Florida campus.

🛏 Sleeping

Prices soar during football games and gradua-
tions, when a minimum stay may be required
and rooms fill rapidly. Many inexpensive motels are just east of UF, along SW 13th St or
on approach roads. Just east of downtown,
the historic district has a handful of elegant
B&Bs in restored Victorian homes.

NORTHEAST FLORIDA GAINESVILLE

Zen Hostel
HOSTEL **$**

(☎352-336-3613; www.zenhostel.com; 404 SE 2nd St; dm $25, r $35-40; ❊ ☎) Look for the Tibetan prayer flags decorating the porch of this rambling yellow house, which feels like an old-school 1970s commune: chickens in the yard, barefoot children, kombucha tea fermenting in the shared kitchen. Popular among visiting students from nearby massage and acupuncture schools, it's got creaky-floored dorms and rooms decorated with thrift-store furniture, and clean shared facilities.

Hampton Inn & Suites – Gainesville Downtown
HOTEL **$$**

(☎352-240-9300; www.hamptoninnandsuites gainesville.com; 101 SE 1st Ave; d incl breakfast from $129; ℗☎) Located in the heart of downtown Gainesville, you couldn't ask for a better location from which to explore this quaint district. The attractive facade of this new hotel is echoed in the stylish interior. Guest rooms are furnished to a high standard. Free wi-fi and a light hot breakfast is provided, and there's plenty to eat, drink and enjoy nearby.

Magnolia Plantation
B&B **$$**

(☎352-375-6653; www.magnoliabnb.com; 309 SE 7th St; r/cottages from $145/185; ❊☎) Lovingly restored, this French Second Empire–style mansion was unique to Gainesville when constructed by a woodworker in 1885. It's still unique today. The main house boasts five rooms, 10 fireplaces (check the detailing in those mantels) and snacks around the clock. Outside, a tangled hidden garden has a pond and chairs for relaxing.

Laurel Oak Inn
B&B **$$**

(☎352-373-4535; www.laureloakinn.com; 221 SE 7th St; r from $125; ❊☎) The 1885 Lassiter House has been splendidly redone as a handsome yellow B&B, with high ceilings, velvet fainting couches and fresh flowers everywhere.

✖ Eating

The heavy student population keeps Gainesville's restaurant scene on its toes. The variety of cheap eats is a great reason to visit.

Krishna House
VEGETARIAN

(☎352-222-2886; www.krishnalunch.com; 214 NW 14th St; ◷noon-3pm Mon-Fri during school sessions) **FREE** For tasty vegetarian soul food on a budget, head to Krishna House on the UF campus, make a small donation and fill your belly. Who said there's no such thing as a (karma) free lunch?

★Satchel's Pizza
PIZZA **$**

(☎352-335-7272; www.satchelspizza.com; 1800 NE 23rd Ave; menu items $3-15; ◷11am-10pm Tue-Sat) Almost destroyed by fire in 2012, Satchel's is back to restake its claim to the best pizza on Florida's east coast. Grab a seat at a mosaic courtyard table or in the back of a gutted 1965 Ford Falcon. Most nights there's live music in the Back 40 Bar, with its head-scratchingly eccentric collection of trash and treasure. Satchel's takes cash only; the fees from the on-site ATM go to charity. There's always a wait, so just kick back, down a beer and watch the peeps.

Maude's Classic Café
CAFE **$**

(☎352-336-9646; www.maudescafe.com; 101 SE 2nd Pl; items $4-9; ◷7am-11pm) This locally owned and operated boho hangout serves tea, coffee and cakes as well as themed sandwiches and salads such as 'When Harry Met Salad': you get the drift.

WINGED FURY AT THE BAT HOUSE

Across from Gainesville's little Lake Alice, adjacent to a student garden, stands what appears to be two oversized birdhouses. However, these stilted gray-roofed structures are actually the **Bat House** and the **Bat Barn** (www.flmnh.ufl.edu/bats), home to a family of Brazilian free-tailed bats. Built in 1991 after the flying mammals' poop began stinking up the campus, the population has since exploded to over 300,000. Each night just after sundown, the bats drop from their roost – at the amazing rate of 100 bats per second – and fly off to feed.

To witness this winged fury, follow University Ave west to Gale Lamerand Dr, turn left and head south to Museum Rd, between Village Dr and Radio Rd. The batshacks are on the north side of Museum Rd. There's a parking lot south of here, near Radio Rd, with a sidewalk leading to an observation area. Parking is free after 4:30 pm weekdays and all day on weekends.

WORTH A TRIP

MICANOPY

A must-do day trip from Gainesville, Micanopy (pronounced mickuh-noh-pee) is the oldest inland settlement in Florida. Starting out as an Indian trading post, today it's a trading post for antique hunters. Its moniker, 'the town that time forgot,' fits: hulking oaks dripping with Spanish moss converge over wide streets of stoic brick buildings. The half-mile main drag, NE Cholokka Blvd, looks like a movie set – *Doc Hollywood* was filmed here in 1991, and residents have never forgotten! Enjoy a leisurely browse through its dozen or so antique shops, galleries and cafes, and be sure to bring your camera.

Two miles north on Hwy 441, wild horses and bison roam the 33-sq-mile **Paynes Prairie Preserve State Park** (☑352-466-3397; www.floridastateparks.org/Paynesprairie; 100 Savannah Blvd; per vehicle $6; ⊙8am-sunset). This slightly eerie preserve's wet prairie, swamp, hammock and pine flatwoods have more than 34 trails, including the 16-mile Gainesville–Hawthorne Rail Trail, slicing through the northern section. The 3-mile La Chua Trail takes in the Alachua Sink and Alachua Lake, offering alligator- and sandhill-crane-spotting opportunities. Just north of the visitor center, climb the 50ft observation tower for panoramas. Campsites cost $18, and include water and electricity.

For pure luxury, nothing beats **Herlong Mansion** (☑352-466-3322; www.herlong.com; 402 NE Cholokka Blvd; r $119-189), sitting on the northern edge of Micanopy like a king surveying his fiefdom. It's impeccably manicured, and the mansion's 2nd floor boasts two endless porches, perfect for relaxing with a cool drink.

Manuel's Vintage Room   ITALIAN $$

(☑352-375-7372; www.manuelsvintageroom.com; 6 S Main St; mains $14-24; ⊙5-10pm Tue-Sun) Warm, intimate and friendly, Manuel's is the perfect spot for a romantic dinner in the heart of downtown. Pasta aplenty and dishes such as veal porcini and pork Milanese cooked to your liking are sure to satisfy.

The Top   FUSION $$

(☑352-376-1188; 30 N Main St; mains $8-24; ⊙5pm-2am Tue-Sat, 11am-11pm Sun; ☑) Combining 1950s kitsch, hunting-lodge decor and giant owl art, this place is both hip and comfortable. Vegetarians will thrill at the options here and everyone will appreciate the working photo booth in the back ($2). Just as popular for the nightlife as it is for food.

Emiliano's   CUBAN $$

(☑352-375-7381; www.emilianoscafe.com; 7 SE 1st Ave; mains $8-22; ⊙11am-10pm Mon-Sat, 10am-3pm Sun) A Gainesville standby, Emiliano's rocks a mid-century Cuban-Floridian vibe, with striped awnings, rattan chairs and salsa in the background. Go for Cuban classics like *ropa vieja* (pulled braised brisket) or fried plantains, or pick something a little more contemporary off the tapas menu.

Paramount Grill   MODERN AMERICAN $$$

(☑352-378-3398; www.paramountgrill.com; 12 SW 1st Ave; mains $14-28; ⊙11am-2pm & 5-10pm Tue-Fri, 5-10pm Sat-Mon, brunch 10am-3pm Sun) Very Scandinavian chic, with minimalist wood

tables and apple-green walls decorated with vintage sailor photos, this is the top spot for innovative upscale-casual eats in Gainesville. A globally influenced menu spans crab cakes, duck dishes and homemade ravioli.

Drinking & Entertainment

Live music is to Gainesville what mouse ears are to Orlando, and many bars double as music venues. For an up-to-the-minute overview of local music, visit www.gainesvillebands.com.

Stubbies & Steins   PUB

(☑352-384-1261; www.stubbiesandsteins.com; 9 W University Ave; ⊙5pm-2am) When Berkeley Hoflund visited Australia, she fell in love with the beer. Upon returning, she opened this awesomely quirky Australia-meets-Germany pub and restaurant, with a doorstopper beer menu of 400-plus brews representing 16 countries, and classic Bavarian chow like sausages and schnitzels.

2nd Street Speakeasy   BAR

(☑352-271-7569; www.2ndstreetspeakeasy.com; 21 SW 2nd St; ⊙8pm-2am Tue-Sun) If you're not paying attention, you'll cruise right past the dark door leading into Gainesville's chillest bar. Fringe-tipped crimson lamps, a mellow azure aquarium and cushy burgundy sofas are some of the cool features here. What's coolest, though, is that the volume of the lounge music is set so you can actually chat with people.

Swamp
BAR

(☑ 352-377-9267; www.swamprestaurant.com; 1642 W University Ave; ☉11am-2am) A college bar for a college town, with cheap pitchers and drunken frat boys galore, plus a pretty darn nice patio for daytime boozing. Gets wild on weekends.

Lillian's Music Store
LIVE MUSIC

(☑ 352-372-1010; 112 SE 1st Ave; ☉ 2pm-2am Mon-Sat, 3-11pm Sun) The crowd's a little older than in the clubs along University Ave, so they appreciate that elegant stained-glass partition and the 3ft-tall gorilla at the entrance. Monday night jam sessions really pack 'em in.

1982
LIVE MUSIC

(☑ 352-371-9836; www.1982bar.com; 919 W University Ave; ☉7:30pm-2am) Cramped, dingy and musty, this sweet spot boasts both local and national bands, and a great beer selection. If the band sucks, you can play classic Nintendo games on one of four TVs behind the bar. Duck Hunt FTW!

University Club
GAY & LESBIAN

(☑ 352-378-6814; www.ucnightclub.com; 18 E University Ave; ☉5pm-2am Sun-Fri, from 9pm Sat) Predominantly gay, but straight-friendly, this is the hub of the local gay and lesbian scene and is famous for its drag shows. The entrance is around back. DJs spin most nights, though karaoke is also a popular draw.

Hippodrome
THEATER

(☑ 352-375-4477; www.thehipp.org; 25 SE 2nd Pl; ☉box office noon-7pm Tue-Sun) In an imposing historic edifice (1911), the Hippodrome is the city's main cultural center, with a diverse theater and independent-cinema program.

ROADSIDE ATTRACTION: THE ORANGE SHOP

Follow the billboards to the hamlet of Citra, just outside Cross Creek, where you'll find the Orange Shop (☑352-595-3361; www.floridaorangeshop.com; 18545 US Hwy 301; ☉8am-5pm mid-Oct to May), a retro orange-themed souvenir shop hawking 10lb bags of Florida oranges, bottles of orange-blossom honey, orange marmalade, orange gel candies, novelty orange-shaped chewing gum and other kitschy Florida goodies. Visitors are treated to a free Dixie Cup of fresh-squeezed orange juice from the backyard grove.

---

❶ Information

You'll find free wi-fi coverage downtown around the Hippodrome.

Alachua County Library (☑ 352-334-3900; www.aclib.us; 401 E University Ave; ☉ 9:30am-9pm Mon-Thu, to 6pm Fri, to 5pm Sat, 1-5pm Sun) Free internet access.

Alachua County Visitors & Convention Bureau (☑ 352-374-5260; www.visitgainesville.com; 30 E University Ave; ☉9am-5pm Mon-Fri) Friendly staff are happy to welcome you to town and advise on the latest happenings.

Pride Community Center (☑ 352-377-8915; www.gainesvillepride.org; 3131 NW 13th St; ☉3-7pm Mon-Fri, noon-4pm Sat) For gay and lesbian info.

❶ Getting There & Around

Gainesville Regional Airport (☑ 352-373-0249; www.gra-gnv.com; 3880 NE 39th Ave), 10 miles northeast of downtown, is served by a handful of domestic carriers.

The **Greyhound bus station** (☑ 352-376-5252; www.greyhound.com; 101 NE 23rd Ave) is a mile or so north of downtown.

Gainesville Regional Transit System (RTS; ☑ 352-334-2600; www.go-rts.com; fares $1.50) services the city with buses.

Around Gainesville

Cross Creek

Near the rural hamlet of Cross Creek, swing by the **Marjorie Kinnan Rawlings Historic State Park** (☑ 352-466-3672; www.floridastateparks.org/MarjorieKinnanRawlings; 18700 S CR 325; per vehicle $3; ☉9am-5pm). Rawlings (1896–1953) was the author of the Pulitzer Prize–winning novel *The Yearling*, a coming-of-age story set in what's now Ocala National Forest. Her career flourished only after Max Perkins, Rawlings' (and also Ernest Hemingway's and F Scott Fitzgerald's) editor, told her that her letters about her friends and neighbors were more interesting than her gothic fiction, inspiring her to write *Cross Creek,* a book about her life in this area. Her former cracker-style home is open for **tours** (adult/child $3/2; ☉10am-4pm Thu-Sun, closed Aug & Sep) on the hour (except noon). You can stroll the orange groves, farmhouse and barn on your own – pick up a self-guided walking brochure from the car park.

Cross Creek's cedar-shingled **Yearling Restaurant** (☑352-466-3999; www.yearlingrestaurant.net; 14531 Hwy 325, Hawthorne; mains

$6-15; ⊘noon-8pm Thu-Sun) serves 'Cracker cuisine' like gator tail, hush puppies and catfish in an atmospheric wood-paneled dining room decorated with historical photos and paintings. It's worth a stop just to try its famous sour orange pie, one of our very most favorite treats in the entire state of Florida.

High Springs

Quaint High Springs, the 'friendliest town in Florida,' is a hub for antiquers, bikers and locals seeking a getaway. Main St, dotted with shops, galleries and restaurants, is the major north–south divider. Intersecting it, Hwy 441 (here called 1st Ave) is the east–west throughway.

The town is the gateway to superb natural springs. Follow CR-340 west for 2 miles to reach shallow **Poe Springs** (☑352-374-5245; www.floridasprings.org/visit/map/poe springs; 28800 NW 182nd Ave; ⊘9am-sunset) **FREE**, perfect for small children. It's one of the least crowded springs in the area – depending on the time of year, you could find yourself in blissful isolation. **Ginnie Springs** (☑386-454-7188; www.ginniespringsoutdoors.com; 7300 NE Ginnie Springs Rd; adult/child $12/3; ⊘8am-7pm summer, to 4pm winter) is more developed, with equipment for rent (kayaks/tubes $25/6 per day), a handful of campsites ($20) and even scuba diving in its clear waters.

Grady House Bed & Breakfast (☑386-454-2206; www.gradyhouse.com; 420 NW 1st Ave; r $115-155; Ⓟ🛈) has five rooms themed according to color: the Red Room has over 350 classic nudes gracing the walls; the Navy Room is styled nautically. The **Great Outdoors Restaurant** (☑386-454-1288; www.greatoutdoorsdining.com; 65 N Main St; mains $14-26; ⊘11am-9pm Tue-Sun) is a woodsy, lantern-lit steakhouse and saloon in the former downtown Opera House, with an inviting patio area for alfresco dining.

Ichetucknee Springs State Park

Relax in a giant inner tube and float through gin-clear waters at this popular **park** (☑386-

WRECK DIVING IN TROY SPRINGS

At the bottom of crystalline Troy Springs is something unexpected: the wreck of a Civil War steamboat. The Madison was deliberately sunk in 1863 to prevent her capture by Union troops; though her owner intended to raise her after the war, when he returned he found her body stripped by scavengers. Today, divers float over the Madison's ravaged skeleton, peering at her 150-year-old hull. Even snorkelers can have a gander – the water's so clear you can see 70ft straight down. Divers must be certified and bring a buddy. The springs are part of Troy Springs State Park, at 674 Troy Springs Rd in Branford, just east of Ichetucknee Springs. Park entry is $5 per car.

497-4690; www.floridastateparks.org/ichetucknee springs; 12087 SW US 27, Fort White; car $6, river use per person $5; ⊘8am-sunset), on the lazy, spring-fed Ichetucknee River.

Various water sports are available here, but tubing is certainly the most popular. Floats last from 45 minutes to 3½ hours, with scattered launch points along the river. The park runs regular trams bringing tubers to the river and also a free shuttle service (May to September) between the north and south entrances.

To minimize environmental impact, the number of tubers is limited to 750 a day; arrive early as capacity is often reached mid-morning. Use the south entrance: the shuttle service takes you to the launch points, allowing you to float back down to your car.

You'll see farmers advertising tube rental as you approach the park along Hwy 238 and 47 (the park itself does not rent tubes). Tubes are $5 and one- or two-person rafts cost $10 to $15. At the end of the day, leave your gear at the tube drop at the southern end of the park; it'll be returned.

Tampa Bay & Southwest Florida

Why Go?

To drive southwest Florida's Gulf Coast is to enter an impressionistic watercolor painting: first, there is the dazzling white quartz sand of its barrier-island beaches, whose turquoise waters darken to silver-mantled indigo as the fiery sun lowers to the horizon. Later, seen from the causeways, those same islands become a phosphorescent smear beneath the inky black night sky.

The Gulf Coast's beauty is its main attraction, but variety is a close second: from Tampa to St Petersburg to Sarasota to Naples, there is urban sophistication and exquisite cuisine. There are secluded islands, family-friendly resorts and Spring Break–style parties.

Here, Salvador Dalí's melting canvases, Ringling's Venetian Gothic palace and Chihuly's tentacled glass sculptures fit perfectly – all are bright entertainments to match wintering manatees, open-mouthed alligators and the peacock-colored, sequined costumes of twirling trapeze artists.

Best Places to Eat

➡ Indigenous (p401)

➡ Turtle Club (p424)

➡ Ristorante San Marco (p408)

➡ Columbia Restaurant (p374)

➡ Peg's Cantina (p390)

Best Places to Stay

➡ Dickens House (p385)

➡ Gasparilla Inn (p409)

➡ Inn at the Beach (p408)

➡ Hotel Ranola (p401)

➡ 'Tween Waters Inn (p419)

When to Go
Tampa Bay

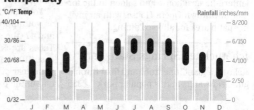

Mid-Feb–mid-Apr Peak season, ideal weather, high prices. Best for camping, hiking, manatees.

Jun-Sep Hot and rainy. Low season means beach bargains; some places close.

Nov-Dec Snowbirds arrive. Weather cools and dries; great off-season prices.

History

First established as Fort Brooke in 1824, Tampa was little more than a yellow-fever-plagued minor port for most of its early history. Then phosphate was discovered and Tampa's fortunes changed. In 1883, Henry B Plant built a railroad connecting Tampa with Jacksonville. And in 1886, the first in a wave of cigar manufacturers relocated from Key West to Tampa, in large part because of the easy railroad transportation north.

As in Florida generally, railroads led to increased tourism by northern 'snowbirds.' In 1885, inventor Thomas Alva Edison became one of the most famous, building a winter home in Fort Myers. In another budding winter resort, Sarasota, John Ringling located the winter home of his traveling circus in 1911. By the time the Tamiami Trail was completed in 1928 – connecting the region to Miami – Tampa and neighboring St Petersburg were Florida's third- and fourth-largest cities, respectively.

Then the Great Depression hit. Undermined by the advent of machine-rolled cigarettes, the cigar industry steadily declined (eventually folding entirely with the later 1959 US embargo of Cuba). After WWII, however, GIs who'd served at Tampa's Mac-Dill Field returned to settle down, and new arrivals flooded the region again, with the Tampa Bay area topping 3 million residents in 2007.

Since then, following the 2007–09 global recession, the Tampa Bay area and southwest coast have been defined by a slowdown. Lee County experienced the highest rate of foreclosures in the country and in 2012 the annual Floridian wage declined to 88% of the national average. As elsewhere in the Sunshine State, creating a long-term, sustainable recovery based on economic diversification into health, IT and manufacturing has become the region's mantra.

ⓘ Getting There & Away

AIR

Tampa International Airport (p516) is the main regional hub, 9 miles west of downtown Tampa. Smaller international airports are St Petersburg-Clearwater (p388), Sarasota-Bradenton (p403) and Southwest Florida International (p415) in Fort Myers.

BUS

Greyhound (p379) buses serve the main towns in the region.

CAR

Tampa is 84 miles due west of Orlando via I-4, and 255 miles west of Miami; take I-95 north to I-75 and head west across 'Alligator Alley' to Naples, then continue north on I-75.

TAMPA BAY AREA

Surrounding the gorgeous deep-water Tampa Bay are two major cities and a seemingly endless expanse of urban-suburban sprawl – forming the state's second-largest metropolitan area – which along the Gulf Coast is edged by some 35 miles of barrier-island beaches. Not many places in the country offer as much big-city sophistication mere minutes from so much dazzling sand. Yet since Miami is one of those that does, the bay area is rarely given its due. Both Tampa and St Petersburg burble with cultural and culinary excitement as they spruce up their historic districts and polish their arts institutions. The range of adventures on offer – from fine arts to world-class aquariums to hot nightclubs and dolphin cruises – make this a compelling region to explore.

Tampa

✎ 813 / POP 335,700

Sprawling and businesslike, Tampa lacks the iconic downtown skyline and cultural buzz that gives Miami its distinct persona. Therefore, it's surprising to learn that so many new museums, parks and gourmet South Tampa restaurants have popped up recently that the city is dangerously close to becoming stylish. In the heart of downtown, the revitalized Riverwalk along the Hillsborough River glitters with contemporary architecture and scenic green spaces. Plus, between the zoo, the aquarium, the children's museums and the theme parks, families have enough top-shelf entertainment to last a week. By evening Ybor City's streets transform into Southwest Florida's hottest bar and nightclub scene.

◎ Sights

Downtown, the attractive **Tampa Riverwalk** (www.thetampariverwalk.com) connects most sights. Located along the Hillsborough River, this undulating green space, with playgrounds and restrooms, makes a pretty walk from the museums edging Curtis Hixon Park, past the Convention Center, to the aquarium

Tampa Bay & Southwest Florida Highlights

1 Sampling craft beer and pondering Dali's *Hallucinogenic Toreador* (not necessarily in that order) in **St Petersburg** (p381).

2 Paddling the waterways of **Homosassa Springs Wildlife State Park** (p396) beside slow-moving manatees.

3 Juggling art and circus at Sarasota's **Ringling Museum Complex** (p398).

4 Finding Old Florida on **Anna Maria Island** (p404).

5 Exploring the history time-warp that is **Historic Spanish Point** (p406).

6 Freewheeling through forest and along the Intracoastal on the **Legacy Trail** (p407).

7 Hunting for shells with the kids on **Sanibel Island** (p417).

8 Getting lost on secluded Cayo Costa Island, mostly preserved as **Cayo Costa State Park** (p409).

9 Dolphin-spotting and dining in **Naples** (p420).

10 Admiring bald cypress and wood storks at **Corkscrew Swamp Sanctuary** (p420).

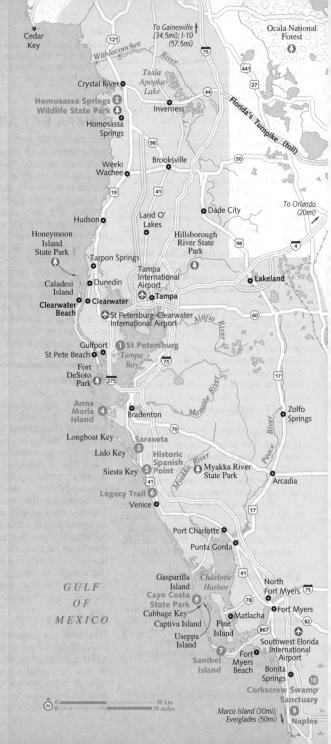

at the far end. Within downtown, the Franklin St Mall is a pedestrian-only corridor between Kennedy Blvd and Zack St that's lined with food carts and lunchtime eateries.

Ybor (ee-bore) City is a short car or trolley ride northeast of downtown. Like the illicit love child of Key West and Miami's Little Havana, this 19th-century district is a multiethnic neighborhood that hosts the Tampa Bay area's hippest party scene. It also preserves a strong Cuban, Spanish and Italian heritage from its days as the epicenter of Tampa's cigar industry. For a guided, 90-minute walking tour, reserve ahead with **Ybor City Historic Walking Tours** (☑813-505-6779; www.yborwalkingtours.com; adult/child $15/5); they typically run twice daily.

★**Florida Aquarium**   AQUARIUM
(☑813-273-4000; www.flaquarium.org; 701 Channelside Dr; adult/child $24/19; ⊗9:30am-5pm; ☀) Tampa's excellent aquarium is among the state's best. Cleverly designed, the re-created swamp lets you walk among herons and ibis as they prowl the mangroves. Programs let you swim with the fishes (and the sharks) or take a catamaran ecotour in Tampa Bay.

Tampa Museum of Art   MUSEUM
(☑813-274-8130; www.tampamuseum.org; 120 W Gasparilla Plaza; adult/student $10/5; ⊗11am-7pm Mon-Thu, to 8pm Fri, to 5pm Sat & Sun) Architect Stanley Saitowitz's dramatically cantilevered museum building appears to float above Curtis Hixon Park overlooking the Hillsborough River. Inside its sculptural shell six galleries house a permanent collection of Greek and Roman antiquities beside contemporary exhibitions of photography and new media. Its most recent show exhibited the work from Tampa's cutting-edge Graphicstudio, showcasing 110 printworks by 45 artists including Robert Rauschenberg, Louise Bourgeois, Chuck Close and Christian Marclay.

The museum's **Sono Café** (☑813-421-8384; mains $5-14; ⊗11am-6pm Mon-Thu, to 7pm Fri, to 5pm Sat & Sun), by the creative team behind Mise en Place (p374), is a great place for brunch or cocktails overlooking the river. The cafe is accessible through an admission-free entrance.

Tampa Bay History Center   MUSEUM
(☑813-228-0097; www.tampabayhistorycenter.org; 801 Old Water St; adult/child $13/8; ⊗10am-5pm) This first-rate history museum presents the region's Seminole and Miccosukee people, Cracker pioneers and cattle breeders, and Tampa's Cuban community and cigar industry. The cartography collection, spanning six centuries, dazzles.

Henry B Plant Museum   MUSEUM
(☑813-254-1891; www.plantmuseum.com; 401 W Kennedy Blvd; adult/child $10/5; ⊗10am-5pm Tue-Sat, from noon Sun) The silver minarets of Henry B Plant's 1891 Tampa Bay Hotel glint majestically, testimony to the vaunting ambitions of its creator who first brought the railroad to the city – and then extended it so guests could disembark straight into the lobby of his 511-room hotel. Never-before-seen-luxuries such as private baths, telephones and electricity became the talk of the town, as did the hotel's European decor of Venetian mirrors, French porcelain and exotic furnishings. Now part of the University of Tampa, one section re-creates the original hotel's gilded late-Victorian world.

At Christmas it is particularly atmospheric as rooms are decked out for the season with decorated trees, antique toys and Victorian ornaments.

Florida Museum of Photographic Arts   MUSEUM
(FMoPA; ☑813-221-2222; www.fmopa.org; The Cube, 400 N Ashley Dr; suggested donation $10; ⊗10am-5pm Tue-Thu & Sat, to 8pm Fri, noon-5pm Sun) This small, intimate photography museum is housed on the 2nd and 3rd story of the Cube, a five-story atrium, in downtown Tampa. In addition to a permanent collection from Harold Edgerton and Len Prince, temporary exhibits have included the work of Ansel Adams, Andy Warhol and contemporary photographers such as David Hilliard. Three-hour ($55), one day ($60) and multi-week photography courses are also offered.

Lowry Park Zoo   ZOO
(☑813-935-8552; www.lowryparkzoo.com; 1101 W Sligh Ave; adult/child $25/20; ⊗9:30am-5pm;

Downtown Tampa

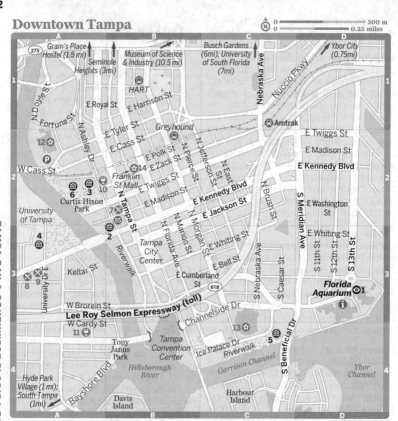

N 0 ————— 500 m
0 ————— 0.25 miles

Gram's Place
Hostel (1.5 mi)
Seminole
Heights (3mi)
Museum of Science
& Industry (10.5 mi)
Busch Gardens
(6mi); University
of South Florida
(7mi)
Ybor City
(0.75mi)

N Doyle St
N Fortune St
N Ashley Dr
E Royal St
E Harrison St
HART
E Tyler St
E Cass St
Greyhound
E Polk St
E Zack St
N Jefferson St
N Pierce St
Franklin
St Mall
E Twiggs St
E Madison St
E Kennedy Blvd
E Jackson St
N East St
N Tampa St
N Marion St
N Morgan St
N Florida Ave
Tampa
City
Center
E Whiting St
E Bell St
E Cumberland
St
Kellar St
University Dr E
Riverwalk
W Brorein St
Lee Roy Selmon Expressway (toll)
W Cardy St
Tony
Janus
Park
Tampa
Convention
Center
Channelside Dr
Ice Palace Dr
Riverwalk
Garrison Channel
S Beneficial Dr
S Caesar St
S Nebraska Ave
N Brush St
S Meridian Ave
S 11th St
S 12th St
S 13th St
Nebraska Ave
Nuccio Pkwy
Amtrak
E Twiggs St
E Madison St
E Kennedy Blvd
E Washington
St
E Whiting St
Florida
Aquarium
W Cass St
Curtis Hixon
Park
University
of Tampa
Hillsborough
River
Hyde Park
Village (1 mi);
South Tampa
(1mi)
Bayshore Blvd
Davis
Island
Harbour
Island
Ybor
Channel

TAMPA BAY & SOUTHWEST FLORIDA TAMPA

P 🚻) North of downtown, Tampa's zoo gets you as close to the animals as possible, with several free-flight aviaries, a camel ride, giraffe feeding, wallaby enclosure and rhino 'encounter.'

Glazer Children's Museum MUSEUM
(📞 813-443-3861; www.glazermuseum.org; 110 W Gasparilla Plaza; adult/child $15/9.50; ⊙ 10am-5pm Mon-Fri, to 6pm Sat, 1-6pm Sun; 🚻) This crayon-bright, interactive museum provides a creative play space for under 10s. Eager staff and tons of coolio fun; adjacent Curtis Hixon Park is picnic- and playground-friendly.

Museum of Science & Industry MUSEUM
(MOSI; 📞 813-987-6000; www.mosi.org; 4801 E Fowler Ave; adult/child $25/20; ⊙ 9am-5pm Mon-Fri, to 6pm Sat & Sun; P 🚻) There's something intriguing for all ages at this interactive science museum. Younger kids go straight to Kids in Charge, where a wealth of hands-on activities hides science beneath unadorned

play. The frank human body exhibit – with preserved fetuses and cautionary looks at pregnancy and health – is best for older kids. Don't miss the IMAX movie; it's included with admission.

From downtown, take I-275 north to exit 51, and go east on Fowler Ave.

Manatee Viewing Center WILDLIFE RESERVE
(📞 813-228-4289; www.tampaelectric.com/manatee; Big Bend Rd, Apollo Beach; ⊙ 10am-5pm 1 Nov-15 Apr) FREE One of Florida's more surreal wildlife encounters is spotting manatees in the warm-water discharge canals of coal-fired power plants. Yet these placid mammals show up here so reliably from November through April that this is now a protected sanctuary. Look for tarpon, rays and sharks, too. A snack bar, small exhibit, bathrooms and picnic tables round out the sight.

It's half an hour from downtown Tampa; take I-75 south to exit 246 and follow signs.

Downtown Tampa

◉ Top Sights
1	Florida Aquarium	D3

◉ Sights
2	Florida Museum of Photographic Arts	B3
3	Glazer Children's Museum	A2
4	Henry B Plant Museum	A3
5	Tampa Bay History Center	C4
6	Tampa Museum of Art	A2

⊗ Eating
7	L'Eden	B2
8	Mise en Place	A3
9	Oxford Exchange	A3
	Sono Café	(see 6)

◉ Drinking & Nightlife
10	Anise Global Gastrobar	A2
11	Four Green Fields	A4

◉ Entertainment
12	Straz Center for the Performing Arts	A2
13	Tampa Bay Times Forum	C4
14	Tampa Theatre	B2

Hyde Park NEIGHBORHOOD
(www.ehydepark.org) With Henry Plant's grand hotel invigorating Tampa's late-19th-century economy, expansion over the river was inevitable. **Old Hyde Park Village**, once given over to citrus groves, provided the perfect spot for the city's first suburb. Streetcar services along Swann St and Rome Ave existed as early as 1892. By 1909 the trolley trundled down the 5-mile **Bayshore Boulevard**, which is now lined with some of Tampa's fanciest homes and provides the city's most scenic walking and jogging routes in the city.

The Neighborhood Association provides a useful map of the district online.

Ybor City Museum State Park MUSEUM
(☑813-247-6323; www.ybormuseum.org; 1818 E 9th Ave; adult/child $4/free; ☺9am-5pm) This dusty, old-school history museum preserves a bygone era, with cigar-worker houses and wonderful photos. Best is the museum store; get expert cigar advice and pick-up its self-guided **walking tour** (☑813-428-0854; online/audio tour $10/20). The tour is narrated by 24 significant members of the community, including Rafael Martinez-Ybor, great-grandson of Ybor City's founder, and Casey Gonzmart, a fourth-generation member of the Columbia Restaurant clan.

☆ Festivals & Events

Gasparilla Pirate Festival CULTURE
(www.gasparillapiratefest.com; ☺Jan) On the last Saturday in January, pirates invade and parade in Tampa's version of Mardi Gras.

Florida State Fair CULTURE
(Florida State Expo; www.floridastatefair.com; ☺Feb) Classic Americana for more than 100 years; enjoy rides, food and livestock for two weeks in February.

Ybor City Heritage & Cigar Festival CULTURE
(☺Nov) Music and cigars mid-November.

⊨ Sleeping

Interesting, independent lodgings aren't Tampa's strong suit. Business travelers tend to aim for the high-end chains (such as Westin or Marriott) downtown, while travelers are best situated in Ybor City. An abundance of midrange chains are also north of downtown, close to Busch Gardens and the University of South Florida.

Gram's Place Hostel HOSTEL $
(☑813-221-0596; www.grams-inn-tampa.com; 3109 N Ola Ave; dm $23, r $25-60; ❈@☎) As charismatic as an aging rock star, Gram's is a tiny, welcoming hostel for international travelers who prefer personality over perfect linens. Dig the in-ground hot tub and Saturday night jams. Breakfast is not included, but there are two fully serviced kitchens. Gram's Place is in Tampa Heights, 2 miles north of the Museum of Art.

Hilton Garden Inn Ybor City HOTEL $$
(☑813-769-9267; www.hiltongardeninn.com; 1700 E 9th Ave; r $160-230; P❈@☎☀) The best option in Tampa is this attractive, efficient and friendly branch of the Hilton Garden chain located just a few blocks from 7th Ave. Rooms are vast and comfortable, there's a nice, private pool area, and the breakfast is generous and cooked to order. An on-call free shuttle is also available for those who want to head downtown.

Hampton Inn & Suites Ybor City HOTEL $$
(☑813-247-6700; www.hamptoninn.hilton.com; 1301 E 7th Ave; r $130-180; P❈☎☀) The red-brick Hampton Inn offers a good level of comfort, a free shuttle downtown and a tiny pool. Its location on 7th Ave means rooms at the front can be noisy.

Don Vicente de Ybor Historic Inn   HISTORIC HOTEL **$$**

(☎813-241-4545; www.donvicenteinn.com; 1915 Republica de Cuba; r incl breakfast $139-219; P❋❂) Slightly faded, the 1895 Don Vicente recalls Ybor City's glory days. Unfortunately, rooms are less warmly dramatic than the atmospheric Old World public spaces.

Epicurean Hotel   HOTEL **$$$**

(☎813-999-8700; www.epicureanhotel.com; 1207 S Howard Ave; r $180-280; P❋❂❖) Although part of the Marriott collection, the brand-new Epicurean in South Tampa is a collaboration between six businesses. Bern's Steak House (p375) chef, Chad Johnson, designed the menu of the Élevage restaurant and Dean Hurst plans cutting-edge cocktails at the Edge Social Drinkery rooftop bar. Then there's the Pi patisserie, a fine wine-and-food shop and a culinary classroom. It's hard to see how you'll find time to enjoy the health club, pool or full-service spa, although after all that gourmet gorging they'll be in high demand.

✗ Eating

Tampa has an excellent restaurant scene, though precious little is downtown. Ybor City is jam-packed with restaurants, particularly Spanish and Italian, while the Seminole Heights neighborhood (along Florida Ave) is an up-and-coming hipster hangout. Other good spots include gentrified Hyde Park Village, south of downtown, and design-savvy Palma Ceia. SoHo (South Howard Ave) in South Tampa has been dubbed 'restaurant row'; the stretch between Kennedy and Bayshore Blvds is prime.

✗ Downtown

Oxford Exchange   AMERICAN **$$**

(☎813-253-0222; www.oxfordexchange.com; 420 W Kennedy Blvd; mains $17-32; ⊘7:30am-5pm Mon-Wed & Fri, to 9pm Thu, 9am-5pm Sat, 9am-8pm Sun) Built in 1891 as a stable for the Plant Hotel, the re-imagined Oxford Exchange takes its inspiration from the venerable Wolseley in London. Chef Erin Guggino's American menu is served beneath sculptural palm fronds in a greenhouse atrium. There's also a tiny wood-paneled bookstore, a Buddy Brew coffee stand and TeBella bar. In 2014 it was granted a liquor license, which means an exciting new wine and cocktail menu powered by cold-pressed juices.

The restaurant recently opened for dinner on Thursday and Sunday evenings and is hoping to host a summer supper series.

L'Eden   FRENCH **$$**

(☎813-221-4795; www.dineatleden.com; 500 N Tampa St; mains $9-22; ⊘7am-3pm Mon-Tue, 7am-3pm & 5-11pm Wed-Sat) The sunny, southern Mediterranean menu at L'Eden reflects chef Gerard Jamgotchian's Marseillais roots. Flaky-crust quiches cradle a velvety mix of ham and cheese; crepes come drizzled with cheese or chocolate; and the show-stealing Nicoise salad is dressed in crunchy green beans and a signature vinaigrette. Breakfast is also good.

Mise en Place   MODERN AMERICAN **$$$**

(☎813-254-5373; www.miseonline.com; 442 W Kennedy Blvd; lunch $10-15, dinner $20-35; ⊘11:30am-2:30pm & 5:30-10pm Tue-Fri, 5:30-11pm Sat) This landmark Tampa restaurant has been a destination for romantic, sophisticated dining for more than 25 years. The menu emphasizes contemporary American cuisine with Floribbean accents, and constantly evolves with nods to culinary fashions without ever feeling pretentious or 'trendy.' Go all out with the great-value 'Get Blitzed' tasting menu ($55).

✗ Ybor City

Tre Amici @ the Bunker   CAFE **$**

(☎813-247-6964; www.yborbunker.com; 1907 19th St N; items $3-8; ⊘8am-4pm Mon-Wed, Fri & Sat, to 11pm Thu) Ybor City's hipster contingent wake up at this relaxed community coffeehouse, which offers a range of breakfast burritos, soups and sandwiches all day. Come evening, it hosts open mics, movie nights and even GLBT speed dating.

La Segunda Bakery   BAKERY **$**

(www.lasegundabakery.com; 2512 N 15th St; items $1-8; ⊘6:30am-5pm Mon-Fri, 7am-3pm Sat, 7am-1pm Sun) At 15th Ave and 15th St, just outside Ybor's main drag, this authentic Spanish bakery cranks out delicious breads and pastries, rich Cuban coffee and maybe Tampa's best Cuban sandwich. Here since 1915, it bustles every morning with a cross-section of Tampa society.

★ Columbia Restaurant   SPANISH **$$$**

(☎813-248-4961; www.columbiarestaurant.com; 2117 E 7th Ave; mains lunch $9-15, dinner $18-29; ⊘11am-10pm Mon-Thu, to 11pm Fri & Sat, noon-9pm Sun) Celebrating its centennial in 2015, this Spanish Cuban restaurant is the oldest in Florida. Occupying an entire block, it consists of 13 elegant dining rooms and romantic, fountain-centered courtyards. Many of the gloved waiters have been here a lifetime, and owner Richard Gonzmart is zealous about authentic Spanish and Cuban cuisine. Reserve ahead for twice-nightly flamenco and look out for one helluva good birthday party.

Seminole Heights & Around

★ Rooster & the Till   FUSION $$
(☎813-374-8940; www.roosterandthetill.com; 6500 N florida Ave; plates $8-19; ⊗3:30-10pm Mon-Thu, to 11pm Fri & Sat) With an impressive culinary pedigree behind them, Ferrell Alvarez and Ty Rodriguez launched Seminole Heights' most recent and ambitious farm-to-table restaurant. Don't come here for big portions or national brand beverages, instead come for small plates bursting with flavor. Try the Mangalitsa pork belly complemented by pickled apple and peppercorn honey, or smoked shimeji and oyster mushrooms with tart green tomato and Point Reyes blue cheese.

There's a wallet-friendly three-tier wine list with bottles at $25, $45 and $65.

Refinery   MODERN AMERICAN $$
(☎813-237-2000; www.thetamparefinery.com; 5137 N Florida Ave; mains $9-24; ⊗5-10pm Sun-Thu, to 11pm Fri & Sat, brunch 11am-2:30pm Sun; ☑) 🍴 This blue-collar gourmet joint promises chipped plates and no pretensions, just playful, delicious hyperlocal cuisine that cleverly mixes a sustainability ethic with a punk attitude. Owners Michelle and Greg Baker are among a tiny number of Florida restaurateurs who are known outside the area, thanks no doubt to Greg's three James Beard nominations. From 5pm to 7pm there are $5 chef plates.

Keep an eye out for the couple's next venture, Fodder & Shine, offering old Cracker cuisine influenced by the state's African American, Native American and Spanish roots.

Ella's Americana Folk Art Cafe   AMERICAN $$
(☎813-234-1000; www.ellasfolkartcafe.com; 5119 N Nebraska Ave; mains $11-22; ⊗5-11pm Tue-Thu, to midnight Fri & Sat, 11am-8pm Sun) After one too many Boozy Suzys the visionary outsider art on Ella's walls starts to make a lot of sense. But it's not just the eccentric art and

cocktails that keep locals loyal, it's the cozy vibe, the heartwarming soul food and the weekly roster of events from live music to doughnut and beer tasting evenings.

South Tampa

Wright's Gourmet House   SANDWICHES $
(www.wrightsgourmet.com; 1200 S Dale Mabry Hwy; sandwiches & salads $5-10; ⊗7am-6pm Mon-Fri, 8am-4pm Sat) From the outside this place looks like it could be a paint store. The inside isn't much better; green vinyl tablecloths and bare white walls. But the red velvet cake, pecan pie and monster sandwiches (try the beef martini with roast beef, wine-marinated mushrooms and bacon), well, these explain what all the fuss is about.

Piquant   FRENCH $$
(☎813-251-1777; 1633 W Snow Ave, Hyde Park Village; mains $9-18; ⊗8am-6pm Mon-Wed & Sun, to 10pm Thu-Sat; ☑) Hot-to-trot French pastries, French-inspired salads and sandwiches dominate the menu at this bakery in Hyde Park Village. The 'Power Salad' comes heaped with avocado, spinach, feta, chickpeas, shredded chicken and roasted red peppers atop a base of brown rice. Gluten-free and vegetarian options are also available.

★ Restaurant BT   FUSION $$$
(☎813-258-1916; www.restaurantbt.com; 2507 S MacDill Ave, Palma Ceia; mains lunch $10-15, dinner $23-32; ⊗11:30am-2:30pm & 5:30-10pm Mon-Thu, to 11pm Fri & Sat) 🍴 Chef Trina Nguyan-Batley has combined her high-fashion background and Vietnamese upbringing to create this ultrachic temple to sustainable, locavore gastronomy.

★ Bern's Steak House   STEAKHOUSE $$$
(☎813-251-2421; www.bernssteakhouse.com; 1208 S Howard Ave; mains $25-60; ⊗5-10pm Sun-Thu, to 11pm Fri & Sat) This legendary, nationally renowned steakhouse is an event as much as a meal. Dress up, order caviar and on-premises dry-aged beef, ask to tour the wine cellar and kitchens, and *don't* skip dessert in the specially designed Harry Waugh Dessert Room.

Sidebern's   EUROPEAN $$$
(☎813-258-2233; www.sideberns.com; 2208 W Morrison Ave; charcuterie plates $8-16, mains $30-48; ⊗5-10pm Mon-Thu, to 11pm Fri & Sat; ☑) 🍴 Don't feel like steak? This trendy alternative to Bern's Steak House offers inventive, big-city gourmet cuisine, locally sourced. Impeccable service. Run, don't walk, for the early

BUSCH GARDENS & ADVENTURE ISLAND

Orlando doesn't hold a monopoly on Florida theme parks. In Tampa, Busch Gardens presents two enormous thrill-seeker destinations: the Africa-themed Busch Gardens, which has some of the country's best roller coasters, and the adjacent Adventure Island water park. If you'll be visiting both, get combo tickets.

Both parks are about 7 miles north of downtown Tampa; take I-275 north to exit 50/ Busch Blvd and follow signs. Parking costs $13.

Busch Gardens

This **theme park** (✆888-800-5447; http://seaworldparks.com/en/buschgardens-tampa; 10165 McKinley Dr; adult/child 3-9yr $92/87, discounts online; ⏰10am-7pm) has 10 loosely named African zones, which flow together without much fuss. The entire park is walkable. Admission includes three types of fun: epic roller coasters and rides, animal encounters and various shows, performances and entertainment. All are spread throughout the park, so successful days require some planning: check show schedules before arriving and plan what rides and animals to visit around the shows. Coaster lines only get longer as the day goes on.

Egypt Home to the epic Cheetah Hunt, a low-to-the-ground scream-fest meant to mimic a cheetah's acceleration. Another top-notch ride is Montu, the southeast USA's largest inverted steel roller coaster. The Moroccan Palace Theater presents the headliner shows (such as Cirque du Soleil).

Serengeti Plain This 65-acre habitat mimics the African plains, with hundreds of free-roaming animals. You can view it from the Serengeti Railway train ride, but the main access is the Serengeti Safari Tour (from $19 to $39 per person), which lets you out of the truck to feed giraffes, and so on.

Morocco You'll find Gwazi, a huge but traditional wooden coaster, along with monkey and ape encounters. It's close to the other main animal exhibits in Egypt and Nairobi.

Nairobi Devoted mostly to animals, Nairobi has reptiles and nocturnal creatures in Curiosity Caverns, and Jambo Junction lets you pet a flamingo and eyeball cute critters. It's also the location of the Animal Care Center, which offers educational behind-the-scenes tours of vets at work with some of the park's 12,000 animals.

Timbuktu Smaller, carnival-like rides and arcades dominate Timbuktu. The 4D theater shows are a hoot: shameless 'interactive' fun where the seats goose and douse you.

---

evening specials (from 5pm to 7pm) when barrel-aged cocktails and wine cost $5 and appetizer plates $6.

🍷 Drinking & Nightlife

Restaurants with great bars include Mise en Place, SideBern's and the Sono Cafe in the Museum of Art. For nightlife, Ybor City is party central, though SoHo and Seminole Heights have a more grown-up vibe. Most clubs are open from 10pm to 3am Thursday to Saturday and charge a cover of between $10 and $30. Tampa Bay's alternative weekly is Creative Loafing (www.cltampa.com), with event and bar listings.

Ybor City is also the center of Tampa's GLBT life; to connect with it, check out the GaYbor District Coalition (www.gaybor.com) and Gay Tampa (www.tampabaygay.com).

Cigar City Brewing BREWERY
(✆813-348-6363; www.cigarcitybrewing.com; 3924 West Spruce St; ⏰11am-11pm Sun-Thu, to 1am Fri & Sat) This is Tampa's premier craft brewery. It has dozens of crafted brews on tap, some exclusive to the brewery. On Friday nights there are food trucks in the parking lot and you can take tours of the brewery for $5 (with one beer included).

You'll find it west of downtown, north off I-275.

Independent Bar BAR
(✆813-341-4883; www.independenttampa.com; 5016 N Florida Ave; ⏰noon-midnight Sun-Wed, to 1am Thu-Sat) If you appreciate craft brews, roll into this converted gas station, now a low-key hip bar in Seminole Heights. You can count on one or more local Cigar City Brews, and it serves some mean pub grub.

Pantopia The imaginary Pantopia with its Painted Camel bazaar and animal- and travel-themed dining options opened in 2014. At its center is the park's newest ride, Falcon's Fury, a 335ft-high freestanding drop tower that plunges riders earthwards at 60mph.

Congo The Kumba roller coaster is a long-standing favorite. It features three gulp-inducing loops and a 360-degree spiral. Recover on the Congo River Rapids, a water ride.

Jungala Designed for younger kids, Jungala has a fantastic climbing structure, a splash area and a zip-line ride, as well as encounters with tigers and orangutans.

Stanleyville Another all-star coaster, SheiKra is North America's first dive coaster, which plunges straight down and even goes underground.

Safari of Fun & Bird Gardens The *Sesame Street*–themed Safari of Fun has awesome fenced-in play and climbing structures and splash zones that will keep kids busy for hours. Don't miss the Elmo and Friends show; reserve ahead to dine with costumed characters. Adjacent Bird Gardens (the seed of the modern park) has the quintessential flock of flamingos and a walk-in aviary.

Adventure Island

This 30-acre **water park** (☎ 888-800-5447; www.adventureisland.com; 10001 McKinley Dr; adult/child 3-9yr $42/38; ☺ 10am-5pm) has everything a modern, top-flight water park requires: a long, lazy river, huge wave pool, bucket-dumping splash zones, swimming pool, sandy lounge areas and enough twisting, plunging, adrenaline-fueled waterslides to keep teens lining up till closing.

Sleeping & Eating

Within the park, cafes and food carts outnumber rides. They're merely adequate and get expensive, though; bring plenty of snacks, to save time and money.

Near Busch Gardens, at the corner of Busch Blvd and 30th St, you'll find several midrange chain hotels: Holiday Inn Express, La Quinta and Days Inn. While they may advertise being 'walkable' to the park, it is an *extremely* long walk that isn't recommended (especially with young kids). Just north of Busch Gardens, and across from University of South Florida, Fowler Ave also is home to a string of dependable midrange chains.

Anise Global Gastrobar COCKTAIL BAR
(☎ 813-225-4272; 777 N Ashley Dr; ☺ 4-10pm Mon-Thu, to midnight Fri, 11am-midnight Sat, 11am-10pm Sun) Located at the base of the soaring SkyPoint building, Anise has a long sleek bar and a short, smart cocktail list. Even mixers are taken seriously here, from Fever Tree Tonic to Mexican Coke (sweetened with sugar cane not high-fructose corn syrup). There's also a globetrotting wine list and an Asian-inspired tapas menu (from $8 to $11).

Four Green Fields IRISH PUB
(www.fourgreenfields.com/tampa; 205 W Platt St; ☺ 11am-3am Mon-Sat, noon-3am Sun) This thatch-roof, plaster-sided bit o' blarney in Hyde Park looks like a traditional Irish cottage, and the gregarious Irish staff, football shirts, draft Guinness and Irish menu (items from $11 to $13) will have you affecting your own Irish brogue.

Club Prana CLUB
(www.clubprana.com; 1619 E 7th Ave) Many nightclubs come and go, but Club Prana, rising five floors from its lounge to the rooftop Sky Bar, has stood the test of time.

☆ Entertainment

Arts Tampa Bay (www.artstampabay.com) maintains a regionwide cultural calendar.

Live Music & Performing Arts

★ **Skipper's Smokehouse** LIVE MUSIC
(☎ 813-971-0666; www.skipperssmokehouse.com; 910 Skipper Rd; cover $5-25; ☺ 11am-midnight Tue-Fri, from noon Sat, from 1pm Sun) Like it blew in from the Keys, Skipper's is a beloved, unpretentious open-air venue for blues, folk, reggae and gator-swamp rockabilly. It's 9 miles directly north of downtown on N Nebraska Ave.

Straz Center for
the Performing Arts PERFORMING ARTS

(☑813-229-7827; www.strazcenter.org; 1010 Mac-Innes Pl) This enormous, multivenue complex draws the gamut of fine-arts performances: touring Broadway shows, pop concerts, opera, ballet, drama and more.

Improv Comedy Theater COMEDY

(☑813-864-4000; www.improvtampa.com; 1600 E 8th Ave, Centro Ybor; tickets $10-30) This 21-plus comedy club in Ybor City brings the funny five nights a week with local and national acts.

Cinemas

★ Tampa Theatre CINEMA

(☑813-274-8981; www.tampatheatre.org; 711 N Franklin St; tickets $11) This historic 1926 theater in downtown is a gorgeous venue in which to see an independent film. The mighty Wurlitzer organ plays before most movies. Too bad showtimes are so limited: only one evening screening midweek and three on weekends. Look for special events.

Cinebistro CINEMA

(☑813-514-8300; www.cobbcinebistro.com; 1609 W Swann Ave, Hyde Park Village) Cross a trendy South Beach nightclub with a plush art-house cinema, and you get this: a snazzy lobby cocktail bar and upscale munchies (mains from $10 to $20) so you can nosh at your seat while you watch. It's movie-going with style.

Sports

The NFL's Tampa Bay Buccaneers play at Raymond James Stadium (☑813-350-6500; http://raymondjamesstadium.com; 4201 N Dale Mabry Hwy) from August (pre-season) to December, but single-game tickets are hard to come by; most games sell out.

The New York Yankees play spring-training baseball games in March at Steinbrenner Field (☑813-875-7753; www.steinbrennerfield.com; 1 Steinbrenner Dr), the 10,000-seat stadium modeled after the 'House that Ruth Built' (ie Yankee Stadium in New York). The Yankees' class-A minor-league team, the Tampa Yankees, plays at Legends Field from April to September.

The NHL's Tampa Bay Lightning play hockey at the newly renovated Tampa Bay Times Forum (☑813-301-6600; www.tampabaytimesforum.com; 401 Channelside Dr) from October to March. The forum also hosts basketball games, wrestling, football, concerts and ice shows.

College sports are followed avidly in Tampa: the USF Bulls (www.gousfbulls.com) field competitive football, baseball, basketball and other teams. Basketball teams play in the Sun Dome (www.sundomearena.com), and football games are held at Raymond James Stadium. Indeed, Tampa's biggest college-football event is the Outback Bowl (☑813-874-2695; www.outbackbowl.com; tickets $75), an NCAA (National College Athletic Association) football game held on New Year's Day.

🛍 Shopping

The most interesting street shopping is in Ybor City. The Columbia Restaurant (p374) gift shop has a notable selection of hand-painted Spanish ceramics. On 8th Ave between 15th and 17th Sts, Centro Ybor (www.centroybor.com) is an attractive shopping, dining and entertainment complex. In addition, the Ybor City Farmers Market (www.ybormarket.com; 8th Ave & 18th St, Centennial Park; ☺9am-3pm Sat) emphasizes arts and crafts.

SoHo (South Howard St) south of Platt is another trendy stretch with cool finds and boutiques.

La France VINTAGE

(☑813-248-1381; 1612 E 7th Ave, Ybor City; ☺11am-8pm Mon-Thu, to 10pm Fri & Sat, noon-7pm Sun) Thanks to an influx of wealthy snowbirds, Tampa has a thriving vintage scene. With four streetfront windows rotating displays of flapper dresses, ornamental umbrellas, feathered hats and men's leisure suits, La France is like a living museum without a cover charge. Inside you can browse racks of 1930s maxi-dresses, sparkling 1940s swing dresses and Mod suits from the '60s. Some items are newly made from period designs, while others come from estate sales and private sellers.

Inkwood Books BOOKS

(☑813-253-2638; www.inkwoodbooks.com; 216 S Armenia; ☺10am-9pm Mon-Thu, to 7pm Fri & Sat, 1-5pm Sun) In a small house close to Hyde Park, Tampa's best independent bookstore has a fantastic selection of new Florida titles, both nonfiction and mysteries, and wonderful children's books. It also hosts a whole roster of readings and signing events.

Hyde Park Village MALL

(www.hydeparkvillage.com; ☺10am-7pm) Tampa has its share of malls, but for upscale trends and fashion, seek out this outdoor complex, in the lovely Old Hyde Park neighborhood in South Tampa. You'll find it between Swann and Morrison Aves.

ℹ Information

DANGERS & ANNOYANCES

Tampa has big-city problems with homelessness, panhandlers and crime. Both downtown and Ybor City are safe in themselves, but they are bordered by tough neighborhoods; don't wander aimlessly. Panhandlers tend to gather on the median at stoplights and approach drivers; to end a solicitation, simply shake your head.

MEDIA

The Tampa Bay area has two major daily newspapers.

St Petersburg Times (www.tampabay.com)
Tampa Tribune (www.tbo.com)

MEDICAL SERVICES

Tampa General Hospital (☏ 813-844-7000; www.tgh.org; 1 Tampa General Circle, Davis Island; ☺ 24hr) South of downtown on Davis Island.

TOURIST INFORMATION

Tampa Bay Convention & Visitors Bureau (☏ 813-223-1111; www.visittampabay.com; 615 Channelside Dr; ☺ 10am-5:30pm Mon-Sat, 11am-5pm Sun) The visitor center has good free maps and lots of information. Book hotels directly through the website.

Visitor Center (☏ 813-241-8838; www.ybor. org; 1600 E 8th Ave; ☺ 10am-5pm Mon-Sat, from noon Sun) The **visitor center** in Ybor City provides an excellent introduction with walking-tour maps and info.

ℹ Getting There & Around

AIR

Tampa International Airport (p516) is the region's third busiest hub. It's located 8 miles west of downtown, off Hwy 589.

HART bus 30 ($2, 25 minutes, every 30 minutes) picks up and drops off at the Red Arrival Desk on the lower level of the airport; exact change is required.

All major car agencies have desks at the airport. By car, take the I-275 to N Ashley Dr, turn right and you're in downtown.

BUS

Greyhound (☏ 813-229-2174; www.greyhound.com; 610 E Polk St, Tampa) Serves the region and connects Tampa with Miami, Orlando, Sarasota and Gainesville.

Hillsborough Area Regional Transit (HART; ☏ 813-254-4278; www.gohart.org; 1211 N Marion St; fares $2) HART buses converge at the Marion Transit Center. Buses cost $2 one way, $2 for a HARTFlex van all-day pass. Routes service the zoo, Busch Gardens, the Henry Plant Museum and Ybor City.

In-Town Trolley (fare 25¢; ☺ 6am-8:30am & 3:30-6pm Mon-Fri) Within downtown, HART's inexpensive trolley runs up and down Florida Ave, Tampa St and Franklin St every 15 minutes.

YBOR CITY CIGARS

Tampa's revitalized historic cigar district has a rich heritage. But let's start further south. Due to its proximity to Cuba and its excellent tobacco, Key West had long been the cigar-making capital of the US. But when workers started organizing in Key West, the cigar barons figured that the only way to break the union's grip on their factories was to relocate them. In 1886, when Vicénte Martínez Ybor and Ignacio Haya moved their considerable cigar factories – the Principe de Gales (Prince of Wales) and La Flor de la Sanchez y Haya, respectively – to present-day Ybor City, it marked a turning point. Over the next 50 years, Ybor City turned into the cigar capital of the USA, synonymous with quality and epitomized by brands such as Tampa Sweethearts and Hav-a-Tampa. Anyone who loves cigars shouldn't miss Ybor City's annual cigar festival mid-November.

Today, the old Tampa Sweethearts factory still stands (at 1301 N 22nd St), but the most personalized experience is the Ybor City Museum walking tour, run by PhD Wallace Reyes. He has his own cigar label and currently holds the world record for rolling the longest cigar, more than a whopping 196ft.

The most knowledgeable (and legitimate) places to buy cigars in Ybor City:

Metropolitan Cigars (2014 E 7th Ave; ☺ 9:30am-8pm Mon-Fri, 10:30am-5:30pm Sat) The store itself is actually a humidor; perhaps the best cigar shop in Tampa Bay.

King Corona Cigar Factory (www.kingcoronacigars.com; 1523 E 7th Ave; ☺ 8am-midnight Mon-Wed, to 1am Thu, to 2am Fri, 10-2am Sat, noon-midnight Sun) The city's largest cigar emporium, complete with an old-fashioned cigar bar.

Gonzales y Martinez Cigar Company (2025 E 7th Ave; ☺ 11am-9pm Mon-Thu, to 11pm Fri & Sat) Within the Columbia Restaurant gift store.

Greater Tampa Bay

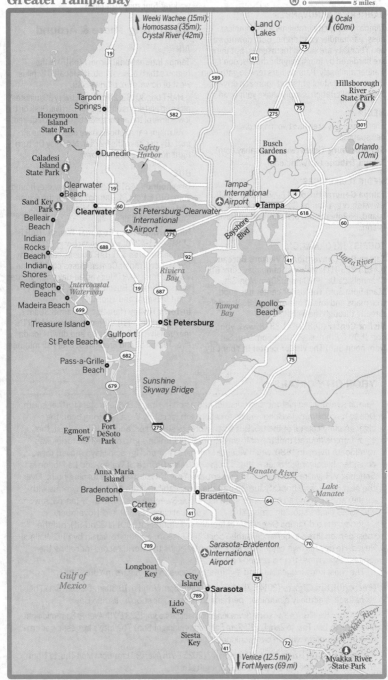

TECO Line Streetcars (www.tecolinestreetcar. org; adult/child $2.50/1.25; ⊙ noon-10pm Mon-Thu, 11-2am Fri & Sat, noon-8pm Sun) HART's old-fashioned electric streetcars connect downtown's Marion Transit Center with Ybor City, running every 20 minutes.

Between Tampa and Orlando, take I-4. The fastest route to Miami is via I-75 south, which turns east at Naples and meets I-95 south at Fort Lauderdale. Another option, with Everglades detours, is to pick up US 41 (Tamiami Trail) at Naples, and follow this directly to Miami.

TRAIN

Amtrak (⊘ 813-221-7600; www.amtrak.com; 601 N Nebraska Ave) Operates several daily shuttles between Tampa and Orlando ($12 to $26, 2 hours).

Hillsborough River State Park

When Tampa residents need a woodsy escape, they head to the fantastic 3400-acre Hillsborough River State Park (⊘ 813-987-6771; www.floridastateparks.org/hillsboroughriver; 15402 US 301 N; cyclist/car $2/6; ⊙ 8am-sunset; ⊡), just 12 miles (20 minutes) northeast of Tampa. For visiting families, it provides kid-friendly encounters with Florida's wilderness, and you'll find the region's best (nonbeach) camping.

In summer, no question the biggest draw is the giant half-acre swimming pool (per person $4, campers free; ⊙ 9am-5pm Memorial Day-Labor Day). On weekends, arrive by 8:30am or it might already be full (then you can't enter till someone leaves).

The flat, winding park roads make for scenic cycling (bike rental per hr/day $10/25), and there are more than 10 miles of equally easy hiking trails through pine flatwoods and cypress swamps.

The most evocative and fun activity, though, is canoeing (canoes per 2hr/full-day $25/50, kayaks per hr $15). Despite some small riffles, the lazy Hillsborough River lends itself to little paddlers. Who doesn't thrill to spotting raptors, deer, foxes and alligators gliding beneath torn curtains of Spanish moss? Early morning is best; animals are more active (and rentals can sell out).

The pretty 112-site campground (sites $24) has good facilities and solar-heated hot water, but not a lot of privacy. Spots along the river are prime, and camping is best (and busiest) during the October to March

dry season (book up to a year in advance). Midweek is always less busy.

From Tampa, take Fowler Ave/Hwy 582 east to US 301 N; it's about 9 miles.

St Petersburg

⊿ 727 / POP 244,750

Long known as little more than a bawdy spring-break party town and a retirement capital, St Petersburg is now forging a new name for itself as a culturally savvy Southern city. Spurred on by its redeveloped waterfront, revitalized historic district and stunning Dalí Museum, the downtown energy is creeping up Central Ave, spawning sophisticated restaurants, craft breweries, farmers markets and artsy galleries, all of which are attracting a younger professional crowd and a new wave of culturally curious travelers.

⊙ Sights

When taking in the sights, visitors can confine themselves to a walkable, T-shaped route: along Central Ave, mainly from 8th St to Bayshore Dr, and along Bayshore Dr from the Dalí Museum to the bayfront parks in the Old Northeast neighborhood. From here the pier juts out to sea. While the pier itself is open to walkers, the iconic, inverted pyramid amusement complex at its end is closed for redevelopment.

★ **Old Northeast**   NEIGHBORHOOD
The Old Northeast, or Coffee Pot Bayou, begins around 9th Ave NE and goes to 30th Ave NE; it extends inland from the bay to about 4th St. At about 10th Ave NE the North Shore Aquatic Complex (901 N Shore Dr NE; adult/child $5/4.50; ⊙ 9am-4pm Mon-Fri, 10am-4pm Sat, 1-4pm Sun) has three gorgeous swimming pools, including a kids' pool with waterslide. Adjacent grassy public parks include the Gizella Kopsick Palm Arboretum (⊙ sunrise-sunset) FREE, essentially an open 2-acre garden of more than 500 palms, all signed and lovingly landscaped. There are also large parking lots here and a long, white-sand swimming beach. Keep going along the paved trail, past pretty homes and private docks, all the way to small Coffee Pot Park, where manatees can occasionally be spotted.

Chihuly Collection   GALLERY
(⊘ 727-896-4527; www.moreanartscenter.org; 400 Beach Dr; adult/child $20/13; ⊙ 10am-5pm

St Petersburg

Mon-Sat, from noon Sun) Dale Chihuly's glass works are displayed at the Metropolitan Museum of Art in New York, the Victoria and Albert Museum (V&A) in London and the Louvre in Paris. But his permanent collection resides here in St Petersburg in an understated wood-and-marble gallery designed to off-set dramatic installations such as the *Ruby Red Icicle Chandelier* or the multicolored *Persians* ceiling.

Morean Arts Center ARTS CENTER
(☑727-822-7872; www.moreanartscenter.org; 719 Central Ave; ⊙10am-5pm Mon-Sat, from noon Sun) **FREE** This lively community arts center hosts interesting rotating exhibits in all media. If you love glass, don't miss Morean's attached **Hot Shop** (☑727-827-4527; adult/child $9/5; ⊙noon-5pm Mon-Sat) where full-blast glassmaking demonstrations occur every half-hour. Reserve ahead for a one-on-one 'hot glass experience' ($75) and take home your own creation.

St Petersburg Museum of Fine Arts MUSEUM
(☑727-896-2667; www.fine-arts.org; 255 Beach Dr NE; adult/child $17/10; ⊙10am-5pm Mon-Sat, to 8pm Thu, from noon Sun) The Museum of Fine Arts collection is as broad as the Dalí Museum's is deep, traversing the world's antiquities and following art's progression through nearly every era.

Florida Holocaust Museum MUSEUM
(☑727-820-0100; www.flholocaustmuseum.org; 55 5th St S; adult/student $16/8; ⊙10am-5pm) The understated exhibits of this Holocaust museum, one of the country's largest, present mid-20th-century events with moving directness. Temporary, contemporary art exhibits loosely related to the Holocaust and other human rights issues are also displayed here.

St Petersburg Museum of History MUSEUM
(☑727-894-1052; www.spmoh.org; 335 2nd Ave NE; adult/child 6-17yr $15/9; ⊙10am-5pm Wed-

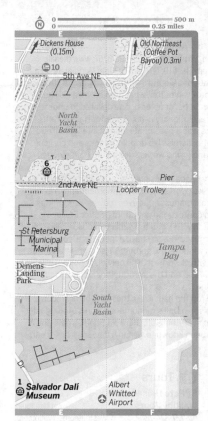

Sat, noon-5pm Sun) As city history museums go, St Pete's is intriguingly oddball: a real 3000-year-old mummy, a two-headed calf, a life-sized replica of a Benoist plane, plus exhibits on Tampa Bay Rays baseball, bay ecology and more.

🏃 Activities

★ **Weedon Island Preserve** HIKING, KAYAKING
(☑727-453-6500; www.weedonislandpreserve.org; 1800 Weedon Dr NE; ⊙7am-sunset) Like a patchwork quilt of variegated greens tossed out over Tampa Bay, this 3700-acre preserve protects a diverse aquatic and wetland ecosystem. At the heart of the preserve is the excellent **Cultural and Natural History Center** (open from 9am to 4pm) where you can browse exhibits about the natural environment and the early Weedon Island people. Sign-up also for interpretive hikes over miles of **boardwalk** or go it alone with the online map. Alternatively rent a kayak from

Sweetwater Kayaks and head out on the 4-mile **South Trail loop** through the idyllic mangrove islands.

The preserve is located on Riviera Bay, south off I-92.

Sweetwater Kayaks KAYAKING, PADDLEBOARDING
(☑727-570-4844; www.sweetwaterkayaks.wordpress.com; 10000 Gandy Blvd N; kayaks 1/4hr $17/40; ⊙10am-6pm Mon-Tue & Thu-Sat, 9am-3pm Sun) This local outfitter has the largest selection of seawater kayaks in the area.

DON'T MISS

SALVADOR DALÍ MUSEUM

The theatrical exterior of the Salvador Dalí Museum (☑727-823-3767; www.thedali. org; 1 Dali Blvd; adult/child 6-12yr $21/7, after 5pm Thu $10; ⊙10am-5:30pm Mon-Sat, to 8pm Thu, noon-5:30pm Sun) augurs great things: out of a wound in the towering white shoebox oozes the 75ft geodesic atrium Glass Enigma. Even better, what unfolds inside is like a blueprint of what a modern art museum should be, or at least, one devoted to understanding the life, art and impact of a single revolutionary artist. Salvador Dalí is often trivialized as a foppish visual trickster, but he was a passionate, daring intellectual and a true 20th-century visionary. Even those who dismiss his dripping clocks and curlicue mustache are swept away by this museum and grand works such as the *Hallucinogenic Toreador.*

The Dalí Museum's 20,000 sq ft of gallery space is designed specifically to display all 96 oil paintings in the collection, along with 'key works from every moment and in every medium': drawings, prints, sculptures, photos, manuscripts, even movies. Everything is arranged chronologically and explained in context. You get photographer Philippe Halsman's famous portraits (such as *Dalí Atomicus*), and the sublimely absurd and still shocking 1929 film *Un Chien Andalou*. The museum is so sharp it includes a 'contemplation area' with nothing but white walls and a window. The garden is also a great breather; it's small but, like everything, shot through with cleverness. The only disappointments: the kid-focused 'DillyDally with Dalí' activity room and the introductory film both feel perfunctory.

Excellent, free docent tours occur hourly (on the half hour); these are highly recommended to help crack open the rich symbolism in Dalí's monumental works. Audioguides are also free, but get snapped up fast. To top everything off, there's a Spanish cafe and a first rate gift store. Up to 3000 people have been known to visit in a day, so get here early or suffer waits for everything.

A knowledgeable staff also leads lessons in foundation skills, sea kayaking and paddleboard yoga, and heads up tours (with/without kayak rental $25/55) of Weedon Island Preserve and other nearby St Pete waterways.

Pinellas Trail　　　　　CYCLING, RUNNING
(www.pinellascounty.org/trailgd) This 47-mile county-maintained trail calls to dedicated urban cyclists and runners. A converted railway, the paved path starts along 1st Ave S and Bayshore Dr in St Petersburg and continues, through town, country and suburb, north to Tarpon Springs. Download trail maps and route details online.

Boyd Hill Nature Park　　　　　HIKING
(1101 Country Club Way S; adult/child $3/1.50; ⊙9am-7pm Tue-Fri & Sun, 7am-7pm Sat) A low-key, hidden oasis, Boyd Hill has nearly 4 miles of nature trails and boardwalks amid its 245 acres of pine flatwoods and swampy woodlands. Alligators, snowy egrets and bald eagles are among the wildlife you might see. From downtown, follow Martin Luther King Jr Blvd (9th St) south to 50th Ave and follow signs.

☞ Tours

St Pete Preservation Walking Tours　　　　　WALKING TOURS
(☑727-824-7802; www.stpetepreservation.org; tours $5; ⊙10am Sat Oct-Apr) Join these two-hour tours run by knowledgeable docents from the Preservation Society. Tours take in historic downtown architecture and well-preserved suburbs such as Old Northeast, Bahama Shores and Kenwood.

Allen's Aquatic Adventures　　　　　WATER SPORTS
(☑727-709-0088; www.allensaquaticadventures. com; sunset cruises adult/child $25/12.50) Wakeboarding, water-skiing, wake skating and skimming, you name it, Allen Clark can sort it for you. In addition, join him for Frisbee fun and adventures around the historic sites of Egmont Key (four people $200).

★ Festivals & Events

Grand Prix　　　　　SPORTS
(www.gpstpete.com; ⊙Mar) Grand Prix racing roars through downtown St Pete for four days in late March. Events are kicked off with the all-American Festival of States Parade.

Mainsail Arts Festival
CULTURE
(www.mainsailart.org; Vinoy Park; ☺Apr) Live music, food and kids' activities sit alongside 200 art-and-craft exhibitors at this two-day art extravaganza.

Tampa Bay Blues Festival
MUSIC
(www.tampabaybluesfest.com; Vinoy Park; ☺Apr) Three days of first-rate blues in early April.

International Folk Fair
CULTURE
(www.spiffs.org; Vinoy Park; ☺Nov) A three-day fair in early November showcasing different cultures through traditional foods, crafts and folk dancing.

🛏 Sleeping

With its impressive stock of period homes and newly minted waterfront hotels, St Petersburg has an excellent selection of accommodation. The Association of Bed & Breakfast Inns (www.spaabbi.com) is a good resource.

★ Dickens House
B&B $$
(☎727-822-8622; www.dickenshouse.com; 335 8th Ave NE; r $119-245; P❄@🖥) Five lushly designed rooms await in this passionately restored arts-and-crafts-style home. The gregarious, gay-friendly owner whips up a gourmet breakfast.

Watergarden Inn at the Bay
INN $$
(☎727-822-1700; www.innatthebay.com; 126 4th Ave N; r $130-190, ste $175-290; P❄🖥🏊) This fabulous 1910 inn carved from two old neighborhood houses offers 14 rooms and suites in a mature, half-acre garden. Outside a bright tropical palette and palm-fringed pool gives the complex a beachy Key West vibe, while inside four-poster beds, two-person Jacuzzis and fluffy robes conjure romance.

Hollander Hotel
BOUTIQUE HOTEL $$
(☎727-873-7900; www.hollanderhotel.com; 421 4th Ave N; r $98-140; P❄🖥) Stepping assuredly into St Pete's hotel scene the Hollander can do no wrong with its art-deco flavor, 130-ft porch, convivial Tap Room, full-service spa and serious Brew D Licious coffee shop. Common areas feature gorgeous period detailing and rooms retain a hint of 1930s romance with their polished wooden floors, lazy ceiling fans and cane furniture.

Larelle House
B&B $$
(☎727-490-3575; www.larellehouse.com; 237 6th Ave NE; r incl breakfast $149-189; 🖥) Larry and Ellen have decorated their 1907 Queen Anne house with heavy drapes, silk-print bedspreads and canopied two- and four-poster beds in homage to the Victorian era from which the house dates. Breakfast is a similarly studied three-course affair with fresh-cooked eggs served on fine china plates and orange juice in crystal glasses.

Renaissance Vinoy Resort
LUXURY HOTEL $$$
(☎727-894-1000; www.vinoyrenaissanceresort. com; 501 5th Ave NE; r $189-309; P❄@🖥🏊) St Pete's coral pink grande dame, the lavishly renovated 1925 Vinoy is a sumptuous concoction of period style and 21st-century comforts, including an 18-hole golf course, a private marina, 12 tennis courts, five restaurants and a 5000 sq ft fitness center. Take-note of off-season and online deals. It's worth it just for the gorgeous pool.

🍽 Eating

Beach Dr along the waterfront is a warm, friendly scene lined with attractive mid-range restaurants. The cafe at the Museum of Fine Arts (p382) is great for coffee, sandwiches and salads, while Marchand's at the Renaissance Vinoy Resort is worth a Sunday brunch splurge (from 11am to 2:30pm).

Coney Island Hot Dog
FAST FOOD $
(250 9th St N; items $2-3; ☺10am-7pm Mon-Fri, to 3:30pm Sat) Collectors of Americana and hot-dog fanatics: order two delicious chili dogs, slaw and a milkshake and savor the vinyl-booth charm of this authentic, unvarnished old St Pete institution. Cash only. Near 3rd Ave N.

DeLucia Italian Bakery Café
BAKERY $
(☎727-824-2874; 119 1st Ave N; pizza $10.50; ☺7am-9pm Mon-Sat, 7am-2pm Sun) With a master baker on hand to see that the pizza dough, bread and baked goods meet authentic Italian standards and baristas who have been trained by Illy, this new downtown bakery promises great things. Order a super-thin-crust pizza to share or just go for the cookies and a dark shot of Illy espresso.

Biff-Burger
BURGERS $
(www.biffburgers.com; 3939 49th St N; mains $3-8; ☺6am-10:30pm Mon-Thu, to midnight Fri & Sat, 7am-9:30pm Sun; 🚗) Once a national drive-in chain, the last standing Biff-Burger has morphed into a down-home, blue-collar institution. Under a tin roof you'll find an extremely long, double-sided bar

SUNSHINE SKYWAY BRIDGE

Supported by canary-yellow cables, the impressive, 4-mile Sunshine Skyway Bridge ($1.25 toll) spans Tampa Bay south of St Petersburg. It's worth the toll just to experience this dramatic arc over the bay. This bridge is actually a replacement for the original span, which was destroyed in 1980 when a boat, *Summit Venture*, rammed into its base. Bits of the old bridge now bookend the modern one and form what is proudly hailed as the 'world's largest fishing pier.'

At about 2 miles, the South Skyway Fishing Pier is the longest stretch. Both North and South piers offer dramatic bay-and-bridge views, especially at sunset, and there are bait shops with rentals for the anglers crowding the railings. To enter the piers, sightseeing costs $3 per car; fishing costs $4 per car plus $4 per person. Just want a quick peek? Free public parks are situated at each pier's base.

and thick-lacquered picnic tables. A wall of TV screens and various live musicians vie for your attention. For a buck and two bits (that is, $1.45), the Biff deluxe is the best burger around. Biker nights on Wednesdays and Saturdays are a scene.

Biff-Burger is far from downtown, 6 miles northwest of the Museum of Fine Arts, near 39th Ave N.

Alésia FRENCH, VIETNAMESE $$
(☑727-345-9701; http://alesiarestaurant.com; 7204 Central Ave; mains $7.50-18; ☺11:30am-2:30pm & 5:30-9pm Tue-Fri, from 10am Sat) Lovely Alésia with its big windows, laid-back soundtrack and umbrellaed courtyard is the brainchild of Sandra Ly-Flores, Erika Ly and Paul Hsu, who wanted to recreate the French Vietnamese cafes of their Parisian youth. Agonise over the selection of pastries tiered on the counter; breakfast on crepes or *croque monsieur*; and linger over bowls of spicy pho and plates of crunchy summer rolls. One thing's for sure: you'll probably be back.

You'll find it at the western end of Central Ave.

Meze 119 VEGETARIAN $$
(☑727-498-8627; www.meze119.com; 119 2nd St N; mains $7-14; ☺11am-9pm Sun-Thu, to 11pm Fri & Sat) Using Middle Eastern spices to create rich, complex flavors, this vegetarian restaurant satisfies even demanding omnivores with its wild mushroom, onion and cheese Flat Iron 'Stak' and couscous and raisin-stuffed acorn squash. Other popular standards include the multiflavor hummus plate and sautéed eggplant on open-faced pita bread.

Bella Brava ITALIAN $$
(☑727-895-5515; www.bellabrava.com; 204 Beach Dr NE; mains $7-20; ☺11:30am-10pm, to 11pm Fri & Sat, 3-9pm Sun) Anchoring the prime waterfront intersection, newly expanded Bella Brava continues to draw a noisy young, professional crowd with its contemporary Italian cooking, pizza menu and cocktail bar. There's also sidewalk seating on Beach Dr.

Moon Under Water INDIAN $$
(☑727-896-6160; www.themoonunderwater.com; 332 Beach Dr NE; mains $9-17; ☺11am-11pm, to midnight Fri & Sat) Sporting an upbeat, 19th-century British-colonial atmosphere, Moon Under Water serves admirably flavorful Indian curries; ask for a capsicum 'enhancer' to adjust the heat to your palate. The British side of the menu specializes in fish and chips, shepherd's pie and bangers and mash. Both imported British and local Cigar City brews are on tap.

Red Mesa Cantina & Lucha Bar MEXICAN $$
(☑727-896-8226; www.redmesacantina.com; 128 3rd St S; mains $10-17; ☺11am-10pm, to 11pm Fri & Sat) Rounding out St Pete's plethora of contemporary ethnic cuisine, Red Mesa dishes up tasty, updated Mexican mains, plus a range of interesting ceviches and tacos. Its Lucha Bar specializes in high-end tequilas and strong margaritas.

🍷 Drinking

The center of the action is Central Ave between 2nd and 3rd Sts, and within a block on all sides. Many restaurants also have lively bar scenes late, particularly Bella Brava and Lucha Bar. Kicking off each month, 'First Friday' is an evening block party and giant pub crawl with live music that takes place on Central Ave.

Canopy COCKTAIL BAR
(☑727-896-1080; www.thebirchwood.com; The Birchwood, 340 Beach Dr NE; ☺4pm-2am) The 5th-floor rooftop bar of the Birchwood Hotel is currently the hottest ticket in town for

late-night drinking thanks to its sexy ambience and panoramic views of Beach Dr. Couples loiter in the hope of snagging one of the private cabanas, while party-lovers lounge on long sofas warmed by the glow of fire pits.

Broken Tusk
BAR

(✆727-521-9514; 4685 28th St N; ☺11am-3am) Headed up by two of St Pete's best-known bartenders, Judah and Levi Love, this straight-friendly gay bar serves good, stiff drinks alongside pinball and pool, and the occasional drag and bingo night. During Saturday night 'Power Hour' (from 10pm to 11pm) all drinks are $3.

Ferg's Sports Bar & Grill
SPORTS BAR

(www.fergssportsbar.com; 1320 Central Ave; ☺11am-2am Mon-Sat, noon-11pm Sun) Next to Tropicana Field, this huge sports bar with lots of outdoor and deck seating is the place to be before, during or after a Tampa Bay Rays baseball game.

☆ Entertainment

For St Pete and some Tampa concert listings, check out *State Media* (www.state-media.com). Many St Petersburg bars offer live music, but the town has few DJ-fueled nightclubs.

★ Jannus Live
CONCERT VENUE

(✆727-565-0551; www.jannuslive.com; 16 2nd St N) Well-loved outdoor concert venue inside an intimate courtyard; national and local bands reverberate downtown.

Mahaffey Theater
PERFORMING ARTS

(✆727-892-5767; www.mahaffeytheater.com; 400 1st St S; tickets $15-70) The gorgeous, 2000-seat Mahaffey Theater hosts a wide range of performing arts, from touring comedy acts to Broadway, dance, orchestra and more.

State Theatre
CONCERT VENUE

(✆727-895-3045; www.statetheatreconcerts.com; 687 Central Ave; tickets $14-26) Up-and-coming bands of all stripes, and occasional national acts, play this restored art-deco theater (built in 1927).

Push Ultra Lounge
CLUB

(www.pushlounge.com; 128 3rd St S; ☺10pm-3am Fri & Sat) In a three-story brick building above Red Mesa Cantina, Push is St Pete's premier hip-hop nightclub.

Coliseum Ballroom
DANCE

(✆727-892-5202; www.stpete.org/coliseum; 535 4th Ave N; tea dances $7-10) This old-fashioned 1924 ballroom hosts occasional events and has regular tea dances on the first and third Wednesday every month.

ST PETE'S CRAFT BEER CRAZE

Since the opening of Dunedin Brewery across the bay in 1996 there's been a growing enthusiasm for locally produced craft beers in the Tampa Bay area. Tourism officials even started marketing a craft-beer trail from Tarpon Springs to Gulfport. Here are five of the best downtown breweries:

3 Daughters Brewing (✆727-495-6002; www.3dbrewing.com; 222 22nd St S; ☺2-9pm Mon-Thu, to 11pm Fri, noon-11pm Sat) A 30-barrel brewhouse with a range of styles from light sessions to barrel-aged stouts.

Ale & the Witch (✆727-821-2533; www.thealeandthewitch.com; 111 2nd Ave NE; ☺3pm-midnight) The 'Burg's favorite taphouse serving more than 32 craft beers and a $6 'witch flight' sample of four 4-ounce servings.

Brewers Tasting Room (✆727-873-3900; www.brewerstastingroom.com; 11270 4th St N; ☺3-11pm Tue-Thu, 11am-midnight Fri & Sat, to 11pm Sun) Experimental brewpub with a rotating lineup of beers made by homebrewers, accompanied by Cajun food and live music. Located 10 miles north of the Museum of Art.

★ Cycle Brewing (✆727-320-7954; 534 Central Ave; ☺3pm-midnight Mon-Thu, to 3am Fri, noon-3am Sat, noon-10pm Sun) Hipster brewhouse with sidewalk seating serving 12 rotating taps of world-class beer. No website but it's on Facebook.

Green Bench Brewing (✆727-800-9836; http://greenbenchbrewing.com; 1133 Baum Ave N; ☺2-10pm Tue-Thu, to midnight Fri, noon-midnight Sat, noon-10pm Sun) A red-brick garage now does duty as a 15-barrel brewhouse with a family-friendly beer garden.

American Stage
THEATER

(727-823-7529; www.americanstage.org; 163 3rd St N; tickets $29-59) One of the Tampa Bay area's most highly regarded regional theaters presents American classics and recent Tony winners (such as *August: Osage County* and *The Wiz*). Its 'In the Park' series presents Broadway musicals.

Florida Orchestra
CLASSICAL MUSIC

(7272-892-3337; www.floridaorchestra.com; 244 2nd Ave N, Suite 420; tickets $15-75) The Florida Orchestra's office is in St Petersburg, but it plays at Tampa's Straz Center as often as at Mahaffey downtown.

Tropicana Field
STADIUM

(www.raysbaseball.com; cnr 1st Ave S & 16th St S; tickets $9-85; ⊙9am-5pm) Home to the major-league Tampa Bay Rays, who play baseball from April to September. New renovations include a welcome 360-degree walkway around the ballpark from where fans can keep track of the action.

Huge parking lots line 10th St S near 1st Ave S.

🔒 Shopping

The main shopping corridor is along Central Ave between 5th and 8th Sts and between 10th and 13th Sts. This hip stretch doesn't lack for funky boutiques, art galleries and antique stores, which are best viewed during the monthly Art Walk (www.artwalkstpete. com; ⊙5-9pm) on the second Saturday of each month.

Downtown at 1st St N and 2nd Ave N the flash new Sundial St Pete (www.sundialstpete.com) shopping mall opens spring 2014 with upscale boutiques, entertainment and dining options housed around a plaza paved in Turkish travertine.

★ Haslam's Book Store
BOOKS

(727-822-8616; www.haslams.com; 2025 Central Ave; ⊙10am-6:30pm Mon-Sat, noon-5pm Sun) A half-block long, with a tremendous selection of new and used books and a fantastic Florida section, Haslam's claims to be the largest independent bookstore in the US Southeast.

Florida Craftsmen Gallery
ARTS & CRAFTS

(727-821-7391; www.floridacraftsmen.net; 501 Central Ave; ⊙10am-5:30pm Mon-Sat) A nonprofit association runs this gallery-store dedicated to Florida craftspeople. Find unusual, unique, high-quality ceramics, jewelry, glass, clothing and art.

Saturday Morning Market
MARKET

(www.saturdaymorningmarket.com; Al Lang Field, cnr 1st St & 1st Ave S; ⊙9am-2pm Oct-May) For a slice of local life, head down to the Al Lang Field parking lot on Saturday mornings when more than 200 vendors gather for the local farmers market. In summer (from June to September) it moves to the shadier location of Williams Park.

ℹ Information

MEDICAL SERVICES

All Children's Hospital (727-898-7451; www.allkids.org; 501 6th St S; ⊙24hr) The area's largest hospital.

Bayfront Medical Center (727-823-1234; www.bayfront.org; 701 6th St S; ⊙24hr) A convenient option downtown.

POST

Post Office (76 4th St N; ⊙8:30am-5pm Mon-Fri) This Mediterranean Revival building was the nation's first open-air post office, and it's a glorious thing. It contains an itty-bitty display case in the rear with postal paraphernalia such as stamps, inkwells and a numbering device. Mailing letters has never been so educational.

TOURIST INFORMATION

The **Tampa Bay Times** (www.tampabay.com) website is a useful resource. For the wider Clearwater area, check out www.visitstpeteclearwater.com.

St Petersburg Area Chamber of Commerce (727-821-4069; www.stpete.com; 100 2nd Ave N; ⊙9am-5pm Mon-Fri) Helpful, staffed chamber office has good maps and a driving guide.

St Pete Downtown Arts Association (www.stpetearts.org) Information on galleries, craftspeople and artists, plus a locator map.

ℹ Getting There & Around

AIR

St Petersburg-Clearwater International Airport (www.fly2pie.com; Roosevelt Blvd & Hwy 686, Clearwater) Mainly regional flights; two international services to Toronto and Halifax, Nova Scotia.

BUS

Downtown Looper (www.loopertrolley.com; fare 50¢; ⊙10am-5pm Sun-Thu, to midnight Fri & Sat) Old-fashioned trolley cars run a downtown circuit every 15 minutes; great for sightseeing.

Greyhound (727-898-1496; www.greyhound.com; 180 Dr Martin Luther King Jr St N; ⊙8:15-10am & 2:30-6:30pm Mon-Sun) Buses connect to Miami, Orlando and Tampa.

Pinellas Suncoast Transit Authority (PSTA; www.psta.net; 340 2nd Ave N; adult/student $2/1.25) St Petersburg buses serve the barrier-island beaches and Clearwater; unlimited-ride Go Cards cost $4.50 per day.

CAR

From Tampa, take I-275 south over the Howard Frankland Bridge. Reach downtown via either I-375 or I-175.

To Sarasota, continue on I-275 south over the Sunshine Skyway Bridge, which connects with I-75 and US 41 (Tamiami Trail).

To St Pete Beach, take I-275 to exit 17, and follow US 682/Pinellas Bayway. Or take Central Ave due west to Treasure Island Causeway or turn south on 66th St to the Corey Causeway.

To Clearwater Beach, go north on US 19 (34th St in St Petersburg) to Gulf to Bay Blvd; turn west and follow signs.

St Pete Beach & Barrier-Island Beaches

☑727 / POP 9350

Just 20 minutes from downtown St Petersburg, the legendary barrier-island beaches are the sandy soul of the peninsula. This 30-mile-long stretch of sun-faded towns and sun-kissed azure waters is the perfect antidote to city life and the primary destination of most vacationers. Winter and spring are the high seasons, particularly January through March. During these months, readiness is all: book rooms far in advance, and get up early to beat the traffic and to snag sometimes-elusive parking spaces.

While St Pete Beach is the biggest town, a string of communities offers variations on a theme.

◉ Sights & Activities

Barrier-island beaches are almost uniformly excellent in terms of their quality. Rather, they are distinguished by how amenable they are to day-trippers: some have much more public parking, better access, commerce and hotels, while others are largely residential. From south to north this stretch of beach passes through the sun-faded towns of Pass-a-Grille, St Pete Beach, Treasure Island, Madeira, Redington, Indian Shores, Indian Rocks and Belleair. Limited public parking at Bellair keeps day-trippers away, who are better served just north at Sand Key and Clearwater.

Parking meters cost $1.25 per hour; some lots have pay-and-display kiosks.

★ **Fort DeSoto Park** PARK, BEACH
(☑727-552-1862; www.pinellascounty.org/park; 3500 Pinellas Bayway S; ☺sunrise-sunset) **FREE**
Fort DeSoto's 1136-acres of unspoiled wilderness is unquestionably one of Florida's premier beach parks – with the accolades to prove it. It includes 7 miles of beaches, two fishing piers and an extensive nature trail hopping over five interconnected islands. Of its two swimming areas, the long, silky stretch of North Beach is the best. It's accessed by huge parking lots and offers grassy picnic areas, a cafe and gift store (open from 10am to 4pm weekdays and to 5pm weekends). The cafe organises bike ($10 per hour) and kayak ($23 per hour) rentals. East Beach, meanwhile, is smaller and coarser, and consequently less crowded.

The fort after which the park is named, and which dates from the 1898 Spanish American war, is in the southwest corner of Mullet Key, which was once inhabited by Tocobaga Native Americans. Union troops were later stationed here and on uninhabited Egmont Key (www.fws.gov/egmontkey) during the Civil War. You can visit Egmont's ruined Fort Dade by ferry (☑727-398-6577; www.hubbardsmarina.com/egmont; per person $20) from the park. Once there you can explore the fort and abandoned houses, say hello to the protected gopher tortoises, and go shelling and snorkeling (equipment hire $5) off the beach.

Fort DeSoto Park is signed off US 682/Pinellas Bayway (exit 17 off I-275). Parking costs $5.

Suncoast Seabird Sanctuary WILDLIFE RESERVE
(☑727-392-4291; www.seabirdsanctuary.com; 18328 Gulf Blvd, Indian Shores; admission by donation; ☺9am-sunset) The largest wild-bird hospital in North America, this sanctuary has up to 600 sea and land birds for public viewing at any one time, including a resident population of permanently injured birds. Thousands of birds are treated and released back to the wild annually.

John's Pass Village PIER
(☑727-394-0756; www.johnspass.com; 209 Boardwalk Pl E, Madeira Beach) For an industrial-strength concentration of Florida seaside tackiness, tie up the boat (er, park the car) at this former fishing village now transmogrified into an all-in-one, wharf-sized nautical tourist trap. Any kind of rental or boat trip is available: WaveRunners, pirate ships, dolphin cruises, parasailing, fishing charters, you name it. Watch pelicans scavenge below

GULFPORT

Don't tell anyone, but Gulfport is the cutest, quirkiest little beach town that's not on the barrier-island beaches. Nestled at peninsula's end within Boca Ciega Bay, this artists community exudes that elusive, easygoing, fun-loving attitude Florida made famous. The hard-to-resist spell is in full effect on sultry evenings when the trees along Beach Blvd glow with lights and the outdoor restaurants burble with laughter.

It doesn't compare to the barrier islands, of course, but Gulfport does have a beach with a playground and a shady picnic area. Beach Blvd, meanwhile, is a four-block stretch of funky boutiques and surprisingly good restaurants. Get the full dose of wry local sensibilities during the twice-monthly **art walk**, essentially a low-key street party; it happens every first Friday and third Saturday from 6pm to 10pm. The Tuesday morning **market** (from 9am to 2pm), lining Bayshore Dr, is another fun local shindig.

Peg's Cantina (☏727-328-2720; www.pegscantina.com; 3038 Beach Blvd; mains $10-16; ⏱5-9pm Wed-Thu, noon-9:30pm Tue, Fri & Sat, noon-9pm Sun) is ripe with Gulfport mojo. This brewpub in a woodsy bungalow perfectly pairs fanciful Mexican dishes with creamy hand-crafted beers (craft brewery Cycle Brewing (p387) was spawned here by Doug Dozark), ideally enjoyed in the wonderful gardens. Or, sit at the cozy bar and partake in a de facto beer class, sampling from the cornucopia of international selections from the beer fridge.

If you're tempted to spend the night, the historic **Peninsula Inn** (☏727-346-9800; www.innspa.net; 2937 Beach Blvd; r $130-180; ✻@🐾) has been renovated into a pretty, romantic choice. It also has a recommended restaurant, **Isabelle's**, which serves classic Southern cuisine with jazz on weekends.

For more information, visit www.gulfportflorida.us and www.gulfportma.com. To get there from St Petersburg, take I-275 exit 19 onto 22nd Ave S/Gulfport Blvd, and turn left onto Beach Blvd into town. From St Pete Beach, the Corey Causeway connects to Gulfport Blvd.

the fish-cutting stations. Wander the wooden boardwalk while dripping ice cream. Navigate the culinary Scylla and Charybdis of Hooters and Bubba Gump. It's no-regrets holiday fun.

★ **Pass-a-Grille Beach**　　BEACH
(www.pass-a-grillebeach.com; Gulf Blvd) The epic sliver of sand that is Pass-a-Grille Beach is the most idyllic barrier-island beach, backed only by beach houses and a long stretch of metered public parking. Here you can watch boats coming through Pass-a-Grille Channel, hop aboard the **Shell Key Shuttle** (www.shellkeyshuttle.com; Merry Pier, Pass-a-Grille; adult/child $25/12.50; ⏱shuttles 10am, noon & 2pm) to unspoiled **Shell Key,** and retire for eats and ice cream in the laid-back village center.

St Pete Beach　　BEACH
(www.stpetebeach.org; Gulf Blvd) Anchored by the huge, historic Moorish Mediterranean Don CeSar hotel, St Pete Beach is a long, double-wide strand with parasail booths and chair rentals seemingly every 50ft. It's crowded with families and spring breakers, who appreciate the big public parking lots, restaurants, bars and motels just steps away.

Treasure Island　　BEACH
(Gulf Blvd) Even wider than St Pete Beach and more jam-packed with fun-seekers, concessions and motels. Very built up, with lots of public access, volleyball courts and beachside tiki bars.

Indian Rocks Beach　　BEACH
(www.indian-rocks-beach.com; Gulf Blvd) A series of small lots and one larger lot with restrooms near 17th Ave make the quieter stretch of Indian Rocks Beach appealing to day-trippers. Located within two blocks of the main action is the only free 18-berth, public docks (from 7am to 9pm) on the Intracoastal Waterway.

🛏 Sleeping

If you don't want a beach-based vacation, Fort DeSoto, Pass-a-Grille and St Pete Beach are an easy day trip from St Petersburg. If, against all advice, you show up without a reservation, cruise Gulf Blvd in St Pete Beach and Treasure Island: the main drag is packed shoulder-to-shoulder with motels, hotels and condos. Low season nets steep discounts.

★ Fort DeSoto Park
Campground　　　　　　　　　　CAMPGROUND $

(☎727-582-2100; www.pinellascounty.org/park; 3500 Pinellas Bayway S; tent sites $34-36, RV sites $40-42; ⊙office 9am-6pm Sat-Thu, to 9pm Fri; P🐾) For tent camping, the Gulf Coast hardly offers better than the more than 200 sites here. Well shaded by thick-growing palms, many face the water, and there are good facilities, hot showers, a grassy field and small camp store, in addition to other park concessions. Online reservations can be made three months in advance, but a few first-come, first-served sites are made available every Friday.

★ Inn on the Beach
　　　　　　　　　　　　　　　　MOTEL $$

(☎727-360-8844; www.innonbeach.com; 1401 Gulf Way, Pass-a-Grille; r $115-250, cottages $185-295; P❄🐾) For a quiet, relaxing seaside getaway, these 12 rooms and four cottages are unqualified gems. With bright coral and teal accents, functional kitchenettes and lovely tile bathrooms, these quarters are a pleasure to return to in the evening; a couple of 2nd-floor rooms have luscious gulf views and the top-floor Ibis honeymoon suite is swoonworthy.

Laughing Lizard
　　　　　　　　　　　　　　　　B&B $$

(☎727-595-7006; www.laughinglizardbandb.com; 2211 Gulf Blvd, Indian Rocks Beach; r $185-220; P❄🐾) Bill Ockunzzi, the gregarious former mayor of Indian Rocks, has whipped up a perfectly funky and festive south-of-the-border-style B&B. The five rooms and one efficiency are each unique, filled with playful art, chunky crayon-colored tiles and bright quilts. Full hot breakfast, afternoon sangria and loaner kites are included.

Coconut Inn
　　　　　　　　　　　　　　　　INN $$

(☎727-367-1305; www.pagbeachinns.com; 113 11th Ave, Pass-a-Grille; r $135-235; P❄@🐾) The latest addition to Pass-a-Grille's beach scene is in keeping with the village's low-level, Old Florida vibe. The two-story clapboard house offers 11 homey studios with kitchenettes, some with lounge seating, others with balconies offering garden or gulf views. They're all set around a courtyard pool, although with complimentary beach chairs and bikes you won't have much time for swimming.

Bon-Aire Resort Motel
　　　　　　　　　　　　　　　　RESORT $$

(☎727-360-5596; www.bonaireresort.com; 4350 Gulf Blvd, St Pete Beach; r $75-230; P❄🐾) Family-owned and operated for more than 60 years, the Bon-Aire is one of St Pete's best kept secrets. Looking pretty much as it did when it was built in 1953, it sits on a wide beach with a variety of rooms, efficiencies and apartments dotted around mature, blooming gardens. Two pools, shuffleboard courts and the locally popular tiki bar, Sandbar Bill's (p392), keep loyal customers returning. Book ahead.

Postcard Inn
　　　　　　　　　　　　BOUTIQUE MOTEL $$

(☎727-367-2711; www.postcardinn.com; 6300 Gulf Blvd, St Pete Beach; r $130-230; P❄@🐾) For its vintage 1950s hang-10 style alone, the Postcard Inn leads the pack in St Pete Beach. The long, double-armed shell of a 1957 Colonial Gateway has been transformed into a designer-chic surf shack with surf-themed rooms sporting murals of wave riders in the curl. Some rooms have outdoor hammocks, and all surround the sizable pool, plus there are Ping-Pong tables, a tiki bar and direct access to the beach. The young, hip crowd matches this fun place.

Thunderbird Beach Resort
　　　　　　　　　　　　　　　　MOTEL $$

(☎727-367-1961; www.thunderbirdflorida.com; 10700 Gulf Blvd, Treasure Island; r & apt $130-200; P❄🐾) The art-deco sign has beckoned travelers since 1958, and the Thunderbird remains a reliable choice in the thick of the Treasure Island commercial corridor. Clean, standard decor eschews seaside kitsch for sage and coppery hues. The real amenities, though, are the pool, tiki bar and beach.

Loews Don CeSar Hotel
　　　　　　　　　　　　　　　　RESORT $$$

(☎727-360-1881; www.loewshotels.com/doncesar; 3400 Gulf Blvd, St Pete Beach; r $250-400; P❄@🐾) The magnificent, coral-pink Don CeSar shimmers like a mirage as you approach St Pete Beach from the causeway. Built in 1928, it's the sort of elegant seaside palace you imagine F Scott Fitzgerald spilling cocktails in, with chandelier-filled hallways and white cabanas by the glittering pool. Rooms are more relaxed roosts, and the full-service, four-diamond property has all you need: fine dining, European-style spa, kids programs and, most of all, its own sultry beach.

✗ Eating

★ Walt'z Fish Shak
　　　　　　　　　　　　　　　　SEAFOOD $

(☎727-395-0732; www.waltzfishshak.com; 224 Boardwalk Pl E, Madeira Beach; mains $4-12; ⊙5-9pm Tue-Fri, noon-3pm Sun) The MO at Walter Gerbase's fish shack is simple: the day's domestic-only catch (often featuring grouper, cobia and amberjack) is chalked on the board; you choose one grilled, fried or blackened and served with coleslaw, salad or raw veg. When they run out, that's it for the night. Get there early to grab a table and the best of the day's selection.

Sandbar Bill's
BURGERS $

(☑ 727-360-5596; 4350 Gulf Blvd, St Pete Beach; mains $5-10; ☺ 11am-late) Located right on the beach, the Bon-Aire Resort's tiki bar is a local favorite for chargrilled, hand-pattied burgers and rib-eye sandwiches. Not hungry? Jackie will keep you supplied with Rum Runners as the fiery Florida sun kisses the horizon. Watch out for marauding seagulls; they will take you down for a bite of that juicy burger.

La Casa del Pane
DELI, BAKERY $

(☑ 727-367-8322; 7110 Gulf Blvd, St Pete Beach; items $3-6; ☺ 8am-5pm Tue-Sat) With proprietors hailing from Altamura, the bread capital of Italy, it's hardly surprising that this local deli dishes up the best croissants, focaccia and pizza on the beach. The coffee's the real deal, too.

Paradise Grille
SEAFOOD $

(☑ 727-367-1495; 900 Gulf Way, Passe-a-Grille; items $6-10; ☺ 8am-10pm) With a deck right over the beach, cold beer and the best pound of shrimp on the beach, this is indeed a little slice of paradise. It also does a mean breakfast, and there's a craft market and live music on Fridays, Saturdays and Sundays.

★ Guppy's
SEAFOOD $$

(☑ 727-593-2032; www.3bestchefs.com; 1701 Gulf Blvd, Indian Rocks; lunch $9-14, dinner $13-25; ☺ 11:30am-10pm) For variety, quality and price, it's hard to beat Guppy's, which packs diners in nightly. Preparations are diverse, skillfully spanning styles (and budgets), from Italian cioppino to Hawaiian seared-ahi and Caribbean spice-rubbed grouper. The only problem: it doesn't take reservations, though its 'call-ahead seating' gets your name on the wait list before arrival.

Ted Peter's Famous Smoked Fish
SEAFOOD $$

(☑ 727-381-7931; www.tedpetersfish.com; 1350 Pasadena Ave, St Pete Beach; mains $6.50-19; ☺ 11:30am-7:30pm Wed-Mon) Since the 1950s, Ted Peter's has been smoking fresh salmon, mackerel, mahimahi and mullet in the little smokehouse here, then dishing it up whole or in sandwich spreads. You eat at outdoor picnic tables; nothing fancy. Cash only. Pasadena Ave is on the mainland side of the Corey Causeway.

★ Fetishes
FRENCH $$$

(☑ 727-363-3700; www.fetishesrestaurant.com; 6305 Gulf Blvd, St Pete Beach; mains $19-60; ☺ 5-10pm Tue-Sat) Under Bruce Caplan's eagle eye sumptuous classics such as steak Diane, duck à l'orange, coquilles St Jacques and sole meunière are sautéed, brandied and flambéed tableside for tongue-tingling flavor. Go the whole hog and splash out on a spicy, black-cherry flavored Silver Oak Alexander Valley cabernet from the glassed-in wine cellar.

Salt Rock Grill
SEAFOOD $$$

(☑ 727-593-7625; www.saltrockgrill.com; 19325 Gulf Blvd, Indian Shores; mains $15-40; ☺ 4-10pm Mon-Thu, to 11pm Fri & Sat, noon-10pm Sun) This contemporary, upscale harborside eatery puts everything on display: the basement wine cellar through a floor cutaway, the waterfront from sweeping windows and the outdoor deck, and the open kitchen's wood-fired grill, where seafood and steaks sizzle at a promised 1200°F (650°C).

▼ Drinking

Hurricane
BAR

(www.thehurricane.com; 807 Gulf Blvd, Pass-a-Grille; ☺ 7am-11pm Mon-Thu & Sun, to midnight Fri & Sat) Skip the mediocre restaurants and head straight to the rooftop bar for 360-degree views and the best sundowner spot on the beach.

Undertow Bar
BAR

(www.undertowbeachbar.com; 3850 Gulf Blvd; ☺ noon-3am) Locals, bikers and coeds all mingle along the three flagstone-topped bars to booze it up and flirt, day or night, on the edge of the sand. When live reggae or DJs aren't playing, country music dominates the jukebox.

❶ Information

St Petersburg/Clearwater Area Convention & Visitors Bureau (☑ 727-464-7200; www.visitstpeteclearwater.com; 13805 58th St N, Suite 2-200, Clearwater; ☺ 9am-5pm Mon-Fri) Inconveniently located adjacent to the airport but website is a good resource.

Tampa Bay Beaches Chamber of Commerce (☑ 727-360-6957; www.tampabaybeaches.com; 6990 Gulf Blvd, at 70th Ave; ☺ 9am-5pm Mon-Fri) Extremely helpful; excellent maps and advice.

❶ Getting There & Around

Suncoast Beach Trolleys (☑ 727-540-1900; www.psta.net; fare $2; ☺ 5am-10:10pm Mon-Thu & Sun, to midnight Fri & Sat) ply the entirety of Gulf Blvd, every 20 to 30 minutes, from Pass-a-Grille north to Sand Key, and connects with other peninsula trolley and bus services. All-day passes cost $4.50.

Clearwater & Clearwater Beach

📞 727 / POP 107,700

The psychological divide between the city of Clearwater and Clearwater Beach is wider than the harbor between them. A few details tell the story. First, the indefatigable Hooters restaurant chain was invented in Clearwater in 1983, and its burgers-and-babes dining concept certainly encapsulates the spring-break party scene. Meanwhile, the city has a stuck-in-amber, gray-suited, 1950s-era downtown that's dominated by the international spiritual headquarters of the Church of Scientology. The Clearwater Church, known as Flag Land Base, has occupied the historic Fort Harrison Hotel since the late 1970s, and has a further 66 properties in the city. None of this is open to the public, and Clearwater itself remains deeply ambivalent about being home to the largest concentration of Scientologists outside of Los Angeles.

⊙ Sights & Activities

★ **Clearwater Marine Aquarium** AQUARIUM
(📞 727-447-1790; www.seewinter.com; 249 Windward Passage; adult/child 3-12yr $20/15; ⊙ 9am-6pm) The home of Winter the dolphin, this non-profit aquarium is dedicated to rescuing and rehabilitating injured sea animals, such as dolphins, sea otters, fish, rays, and loggerhead and Kemp's ridley sea turtles. Though small, it provides unusually intimate encounters with these magnificent creatures, many of which are resident due to injuries that prevent their return to the wild. While the aquarium's mission is dedicated to the rescue, rehabilitation and release of injured sea animals, dolphin encounters and shows make up a large part of the aquarium's entertainment offerings, and some animal rights groups maintain that these can be harmful to dolphins.

Excellent conservation-focused movies, demonstrations and presentations are included with admission. Other behind-the-scenes tours and dolphin interactions, such as shadowing a professional trainer for the day (from $30 to $325), must be reserved ahead.

Pier 60 BEACH
(www.sunsetsatpier60.com; 1 Causeway Blvd, Clearwater Beach) In high season, Clearwater's long stretch of smooth, white sand becomes a scrum of sun-baked coeds and extended families. Hotels, resorts and raucous beach bars line the sand, particularly near Pier 60, where sunset is 'celebrated' each night with a festive menagerie of musicians, magicians, performers and trinket stands hawking their wares. On Coronado Dr across from the pier, activity booths offer parasailing, fishing, cruises and so on.

Sand Key Park & Beach BEACH
(www.pinellascounty.org/park; 1060 Gulf Blvd; ⊙ 7am-sunset) If you want a less-crowded beach day free of commercial folderol, head to this 65-acre, family-friendly beach park. It's at the northern tip of the barrier island to the south, just over the Clearwater Pass Bridge. The sand isn't nearly as fine as at Clearwater Beach, but it's a wide strand with decent shelling that's popular with local families. It has restrooms and outdoor showers, but bring lunch. Clearwater's Jolley Trolley stops here. Daily parking costs $5.

🛏 Sleeping

Chain lodgings dominate your choices. Reserve a year ahead for spring but, like at St Pete

---

WINTER IN CLEARWATER

The most famous celebrity in Clearwater these days is Winter, a tailless dolphin who's the subject of the 2011 Hollywood movie *Dolphin Tale*. Filmed on location at the Clearwater Marine Aquarium, the movie co-stars Morgan Freeman and Ashley Judd, and it tells Winter's truly amazing, heartwarming story: as a baby she was found caught in a crab trap and was injured so badly her tail flukes died and fell off. Yet Winter survived and has thrived despite her handicap.

In 2014 the original cast were reunited for a sequel, *Dolphin Tale 2*, in which the death of Winter's surrogate mother and poolmate, Panama, places Winter in danger of relocation (according to USDA regulations dolphins cannot be housed alone due to their social natures). Time is running out until the arrival of Hope, a rescued baby dolphin. For a maximal dose of inspiration the movie also features Bethany Hamilton, the pro-surfer who lost her arm to a 13ft tiger shark while surfing Kauai's North Shore. You can meet Winter and Hope (but sadly not Bethany) every day of the week at the Clearwater Marine Aquarium.

Beach, so many hotels vie for your business that a cruise along Gulfview Blvd usually turns up something. Resorts along South Beach typically cordon off their own slice of sand.

Cavalier Beach Resort — MOTEL $$
(☎727-442-9492; www.cavalierbeachresort.com; 64 Bay Esplanade; r $99-140; P☀🅿❄🐾) Amid the behemoths on the beach a few small, mom-and-pop places such as the Cavalier linger on. Run by Ellen, this 1950s motel is full of quirky details and retro furnishings. Years of experience mean her rooms are equipped with everything you'll ever need and service is attentive and personal.

Parker Manor Resort — MOTEL $$
(☎727-446-6562; www.parkermanor.com; 115 Brightwater Dr; r $95-135, 2-bed apt $160-180; P☀🅿❄🐾) On the harbor, but a walkable distance to the beach, this small, well-kept complex attracts an older crowd who enjoy playing billiards in the covered courtyard and lounging by the small pool. Suites are fully loaded for cooking and extended stays.

SandPearl Resort — RESORT $$$
(☎727-441-2425; www.sandpearl.com; 500 Mandalay Ave; r $250-450; P☀🅿❄🐾) Clearwater's SandPearl is an LEED Silver-certified beach resort within walking distance of Pier 60 and Clearwater's restaurant row. Following all the most fashionable trends, it touts an ecoconscious spa, boat slips, 253 sandy-hued rooms and suites with dark-wood furniture and Gulf-gazing balconies. Dining at the Caretta restaurant includes an organically sourced menu and sushi, while the Tate Island Grill serves pulled pork just inches from the sand.

✖ Eating

No one comes to Clearwater for the food, but rest assured, cheap to midrange meals are plentiful.

Frenchy's Original Cafe — SEAFOOD $$
(☎727-446-3607; www.frenchysonline.com; 41 Baymont, at Mandalay Ave; mains $8-15; ⊙11am-11pm) This beach-bum-casual hole-in-the-wall serves grouper sandwiches you'll dream about months later. These crusty beauties

---

DON'T MISS

HONEYMOON & CALADESI ISLANDS

Two of the best beaches in the US are just north of Clearwater: Honeymoon Island, which you can drive to (west on Curlew Rd/Hwy 586 from Dunedin), and the ferry-only Caladesi Island. In fact, the two islands were once part of a single barrier island, split in half during the hurricane of 1921. Together, they offer nearly a thousand acres of coastal wilderness not much changed from when Spanish explorers first surveyed this coast in the mid-1500s.

Honeymoon Island State Park (☎727-469-5942; www.floridastateparks.org/honeymoonisland; 1 Dunedin Causeway; car/cyclist $8/2; ⊙8am-sunset; 🐾), so named in the 1940s when marketeers pitched the island as the perfect getaway for newlyweds, is graced with the Gulf Coast's legendary white sand, a dog-friendly beach and warm aquamarine water. On the beach, the **Island Cafe** (☎727-260-5503; www.romantichoneymoonisland. com; ⊙9am-5pm) serves sandwiches, snacks and beer, and offers bicycle (per hour $20), kayak (per hour $10 to $20) and umbrella (per day $25) rentals. The park's **Nature Center** (☎727-738-2903; www.honeymoonnaturecenter.org; ⊙9am-5pm) has wildlife exhibits, and hiking trails lead through virgin slash pine and past nesting eagles and osprey in winter and spring. Outside of winter, mosquitoes are ravenous inland.

★**Caladesi Island State Park** (☎727-469-5918; www.floridastateparks.org/caladesiisland; boat/kayak $6/2; ⊙8am-sunset; FREE) directly to the south of Honeymoon is accessible only by boat and is virtually as nature made it: unspoiled and pristine. Consequently, it often tops national beach polls, and its 3 palm-lined miles of sugar-sand beaches should make the top of your list, too. Secluded and uncrowded it nevertheless boasts a 110-slip marina, kayak rentals, a tiny cafe, restrooms and showers. Though you can kayak to Caladesi from Honeymoon or Clearwater, it's far more relaxing to kayak the 3.5-mile mangrove trail while at Caladesi.

Caladesi Connection Ferry (☎727-734-1501; www.caladesiferry.org; adult/child $14/7) runs half-hourly ferries from Honeymoon Island beginning at 10am and ending around 4pm. Capacity is 62 people, and ferries often fill up. Also, officially you must catch a return ferry within four hours. If you're late, passengers with the correct return times board first.

on an onion roll go perfectly with its light-and-sweet pineapple coleslaw. Well-loved Frenchy's has four Clearwater locations.

Island Way Grill
SEAFOOD $$$

(☑727-461-6617; www.islandwaygrill.com; 20 Island Way; mains $15-40; ☺4-10pm Sun-Fri, noon-11pm Sat, 11am-10pm Sun; ☻) Eschew the beachfront seafood shacks and come to this contemporary restaurant overlooking the inner harbor. Wide windows and an expansive deck do justice to the sunset, and a moderately priced Asian-influenced menu is bound to please everyone, with a raw bar, a sushi bar, crab cakes, pastas, steaks and wok-seared fresh fish.

❶ Information

There is a Clearwater Beach **information booth** (☑727-442-3604; www.visitclearwaterflorida.com; 1 Causeway Blvd; ☺10am-7pm) at the base of Pier 60; for more, visit www.beachchamber.com.

❶ Getting There & Around

Driving from the peninsula, take Hwy 19 to Hwy 60/Gulf to Bay Blvd, and follow it west to Memorial Causeway and the beach. Be warned: beach traffic is a nightmare. If you're coming for sun and fun, ditch the car as soon as you can and walk.

Greyhound (www.greyhound.com; 2811 Gulf to Bay Blvd, Clearwater) Buses run between Tampa and Clearwater; take PSTA's Suncoast Beach Trolley to the beach.

Jolley Trolley (☑727-445-1200; www.clearwaterjolleytrolley.com; 483 Mandalay Ave; adult/reduced $2/1; ☺10am-10pm Sun-Thu, to midnight Fri & Sat) Tootles around Clearwater Beach and south to Sand Key. A day pass costs $4.50.

Suncoast Beach Trolley (☑727-540-1900; www.psta.net; 14840 49th Ave N; adult/reduced $2/1; ☺5am-10pm Sun-Thu, to midnight Fri & Sat) PSTA's Suncoast Beach Trolley connects downtown Clearwater, Clearwater Beach and the barrier-island beaches south to Pass-a-Grille.

NORTH OF TAMPA

Florida's Nature Coast tracks south from the Panhandle through a largely rural landscape of parkland, preserves and estuaries. As such, it retains more of that oft-promised but hard-to-find Old Florida atmosphere with its moss-draped rivers, warm-water springs and quiet creeks and bays filled with scallops and tarpon. North of Clearwater, the main high-

way through the area is US 19, which runs through small towns full of boat dealers and bait shops all the way to Cedar Key on Waccasassa Bay. When travelling its length, its highly recommended to travel with a boat or kayak, as its one thing to see these amazing rivers and creeks, but quite another to get out on their crystal-clear waters.

Weeki Wachee Springs

☑352 / POP 12

Were the 'City of Mermaids' ever to close up shop, a bit of Florida's soul would be lost forever. The 'city' of Weeki Wachee is almost entirely constituted by this **state park** (☑352-592-5656; www.weekiwachee.com; 6131 Commercial Way, Spring Hill; adult/child 6-12yr $13/8; ☺9am-5:30pm) and is dedicated to its underwater **mermaid show** that has entertained families since 1947. Esther Williams, Danny Thomas and Elvis Presley have all sat in the glass-paneled underwater theater and watched as pink-tailed mermaids perform pirouettes while turtles and fish swim past. The three daily half-hour shows (at 11am, 1:30pm and 3pm) remain gleeful celebrations of nostalgic kitsch, particularly the mainstay, *The Little Mermaid*. While there's no mystery to the trick – the mermaids hold air hoses as they swim and gulp air as needed – there's an undeniable theatrical magic to their effortless performances. The park also offers animal shows, a sedate **riverboat cruise** and a modest, weekend-only **water park**, plus picnic areas. Perfect for an afternoon's entertainment.

The springs are about 45 miles north of Clearwater via US 19. It's about 45 minutes from Tampa; take I-75 north to Hwy 50 then head west.

★**Paddling Adventures**
KAYAKING

(☑352-597-8484; www.paddlingadventures.com; kayaks $30-35; ☺8am-2pm) Kayaking or canoeing the Weeki Wachee River is one of the region's best paddles. Weeki Wachee's spring – a 100ft hole that pumps about 170 million gallons of water daily – is actually the headwater of the crystal-clear river. The 7-mile route includes beach areas with good swimming and rope swings, plus you'll see lots of fish and even manatees in winter and spring. Trips take three to four hours, and include pickup service. Reserve a week ahead, especially for weekends.

Follow the signs to Paddling Adventures from the back of the Weeki Wachee parking lot.

TAMPA BAY & SOUTHWEST FLORIDA WEEKI WACHEE SPRINGS

Homosassa Springs

☎352 / POP 13,800

As any fly fisherman will tell you, the Homosassa River is a popular feeding ground for the Silver King of the sea world, Atlantic tarpon. On any given day you'll see the river dotted with 20 to 30 flat boats as anglers sit in hushed concentration hoping to see one roll to the surface. The tarpon begin to run in the last weeks of April and fade out in July; dozens of outlets offer half- and full-day trips. If the cut and thrust of landing a giant tarpon isn't for you, the warm waters of the river are also a favorite hangout for slow-moving West Indian manatees between October and March. To view them visit the Homosassa Springs Wildlife State Park, signed along US 19. The park is quieter than Crystal River.

To reach the center of Homosassa leave US 19 along Hwy 490/W Yulee Rd (just south of the park) and enter an Old Florida time warp, where live oaks dripping in Spanish moss curtain a roadway dotted with local eateries and funky galleries.

Sights & Activities

★Homosassa Springs Wildlife State Park PARK

(☎352-628-5343; www.floridastateparks.org/homosassasprings; 4150 S Suncoast Blvd; adult/child 6-12yr $13/5; ⊙9am-5:30pm) This state park is essentially an old-school outdoor Florida animal encounter that features Florida's wealth of headliner species: American alligators, black bears, whooping cranes, Florida panthers, tiny Key deer and – especially – manatees. Homosassa's highlight is an underwater observatory directly over the springs, where through glass windows you can eyeball enormous schools of some 10,000 fish and ponderous manatees nibbling lettuce.

Various animal presentations happen daily, but time your visit for the manatee program (11:30am, 1:30pm and 3:30pm). The park itself is a short, narrated boat ride from the visitor center.

Homosassa Inshore Fishing FISHING

(☎352-621-9284; www.homosassainshorefishing.com; half-/full-day $350/400) Captain William Toney is a fourth-generation Homosassa fisherman specializing in red fish, trout and tarpon fishing. You can't get a better guide.

Sleeping

MacRae's MOTEL $$

(☎352-628-2602; www.macraesofhomosassa.com; 5300 S Cherokee Way; r $85-125; ❄📶) MacRae's is a good sleeping option 3 miles from the Homosassa Springs park off W Yulee Rd. It's a fisher's paradise of pseudo log cabins and has 22 rooms (some with kitchens) complete with front-porch rockers. MacRae's also operates the riverfront **Tiki Bar**, which is perfectly perched for exceptional afternoon drinks. You can come to MacRae's to do nothing but sleep and read, or you can arrange tarpon fishing trips, airboat tours and kayak rentals from its marina.

Crystal River

☎352 / POP 3100

Florida has some 700 freshwater springs, 33 of which are categorized as first magnitude, meaning they discharge at least 100 cubic feet of water per second. The Nature Coast boasts several of these high-volume springs, the largest of which are the 30-odd springs that feed Kings Bay, near the town of Crystal River. Maintaining an average temperature of 72°F (22.5°C), the water attracts upwards of 400 manatees (and many more tourists) during the winter months between October and March. Were it not for the manatees, Crystal River, like Homosassa and Cedar Key, would be a low-key fishing community.

Crystal River National Wildlife Refuge WILDLIFE RESERVE

(☎352-563-2088; www.fws.gov/crystalriver; 1502 SE Kings Bay Dr; ⊙8am-5:30pm Mon-Fri) The winter home of more than 20% of Florida's West Indian manatee population, this wildlife refuge protects almost the whole of Kings Bay. Up to 560 of these gentle, endangered sea creatures have been counted in a single January day, and like any wildlife spectacle, this draws crowds of onlookers. Nearly 40 commercial operators offer rentals and guided tours, via every type of nautical conveyance, and the chance to swim with wild manatees. Many conservationists advise against the latter (or touching manatees), however, arguing this causes the animals undue stress. Certainly, in season, the corralled manatees and crowded bay are a far cry from any natural wildlife interaction, which is better gained by taking one of the area's top-notch paddle tours.

There is no public viewing area on land; the only access to the refuge is by boat. The best place to begin is the refuge **headquarters** (from 8am to 4pm), which has tons of excellent information and a list of approved operators. Also, although manatees live in Kings Bay year-round, the population dwindles to a few dozen between April and September.

Nature Coast
Canoe & Kayak Trail
KAYAKING, CANOEING

This trail is 20 miles long and carves a protected path through the rich estuarine ecosystem. It begins on the Salt River off Crystal River, then meanders east on the Homosassa River finally cutting south to the mouth of the Chassahowitzka River. As part of the Great Florida Birding Trail, the early stages of the route are rich with birdlife and you'll likely spot pelicans, gulls, hawks, bald eagles, cormorants, storks and other wading birds. Particularly good is the 5.3-mile **Ozello Trail**, which passes through the **St Martins Aquatic Preserve**.

Beware, this is not a beginners trail and much of the paddle is remote, so come prepared with a GPS and file a float plan. Otherwise, hire a guide.

To reach Ozello and the aquatic preserve follow Hwy 494W through Crystal River State Park.

★Aardvark's Florida Kayak Company
KAYAKING

(☑ 352-795-5650; www.floridakayakcompany.com; 707 N Citrus Ave; tours $50-85) Rents kayaks and canoes, as well as guiding excellent eco-tours to Kings Bay, Chassahowitzka, Ozello backcountry and Rainbow River. Guided tours are led by knowledgeable wildlife biologists, naturalists and a former park ranger.

Nature Coast Kayak Tours
KAYAKING

(☑ 352-795-9877; www.naturecoastkayaktours. com; 8153 W Justin Lane; per person $40) Small kayak-only tours with Tracy Colson, a conservation-minded no-touch advocate. Tours explore the unspoilt waterways of the Chassahowitzka and Withlacoochee rivers, Ozello and Lake Rousseau.

SOUTH OF TAMPA

People who prefer Florida's Gulf side over its Atlantic one generally fall in love with this stretch of sun-kissed coastline from Sarasota to Naples. These two affluent, cultured towns set the tone for the whole region, where visits sway between soporific beach days and art-museum meanders, fine dining and designer cocktails. With their rowdy bars and casual fun, Siesta Key and Fort Myers Beach are slight exceptions, but even they don't reach the same pitch of spring break hysteria just north. No, in this region you'll remember hunting prehistoric shark's teeth in Venice and jewel-like tulip shells in Sanibel, a night at the circus in Sarasota and buying art in Matlacha.

Sarasota

☑ 941 / POP 51,900

Entire vacations can be spent soaking up the sights and pretty beaches of sophisticated Sarasota, but this city took its time to become the culturally rich place it is today. Even after marauding Spanish explorers expelled the native Calusa people from this coastline in the 15th century, the land lay virtually empty. That is until the Seminole Wars inspired the Armed Occupation Act (1842), which deeded 160 acres and six months' provisions to anyone who would settle here and bear arms to protect their farms. Sailing boats and steamships were the only connection to the outside world, until the Tampa railroad came to town in 1902. Only then, as Sarasota grew popular as a winter resort among affluent Northerners, were the city's first arts institutions established. One of those early tourists was circus magnate John Ringling, who decided to relocate his circus here, building himself a winter residence, art museum and college, and setting the struggling town on course to become the welcoming, well-to-do bastion of the arts it is today.

As the 1920s roared on, Ringling scooped up more property across the causeway in St Armands Circle and development crept up the dazzling barrier island beaches from south to north: lively, low-rise Siesta Key through upscale Longboat Key to slow, sweet, family-friendly Anna Maria Island.

◉ Sights & Activities

Sarasota isn't that big, but sights are spread out and not well served by public transportation. You'll also want your own car to explore the Keys; while Lido and St Armands are really just extensions of downtown, Anna Maria Island is 16 miles north.

Take note, many cultural institutions take a break during the summer months.

Sarasota

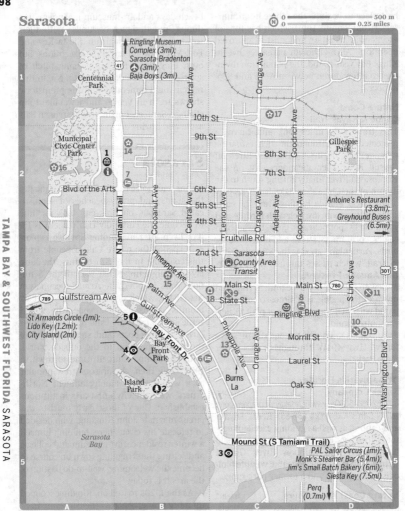

Ringling Museum Complex (3mi); Sarasota-Bradenton (3mi); Baja Boys (3mi)

★ **Ringling Museum Complex** MUSEUM
(☑941-359-5700; www.ringling.org; 5401 Bay Shore
Rd; adult/child 6-17yr $25/5; ☺10am-5pm daily, to
8pm Thu; ♿) The 66-acre winter estate of railroad, real-estate and circus baron John Ringling and his wife, Mable, is one of the Gulf
Coast's premier attractions and incorporates
their personal collection of artworks in what
is now Florida's state art museum. Nearby,
Ringling's Circus Museum documents his theatrical successes, while their lavish Venetian
Gothic home, Cà d'Zan, reveals the impresa-
rio's extravagant tastes. To get the best out of
the complex, don't miss the PBS-produced

film on Ringling's life, which is screened in
the Asolo Repertory Theatre (p402).

➡ **John & Mable Ringling Museum of Art**
The Ringlings aspired to become serious
art connoisseurs, and they amassed an impressive collection of 14th- to 18th-century
European tapestries and paintings. Housed
in a grand Mediterranean-style palazzo, the
museum covers 21 galleries showcasing many
Spanish and baroque works, and includes a
world-renowned collection of Rubens canvases including the *Triumph of the Eucharist*
cycle. One wing presents rotating exhibits
of contemporary art, and in 2011 the Sear-

Sarasota

ing Wing opened *Joseph's Coat,* a stunning 3000-sq-ft James Turrell–designed 'Sky Space.'

➡ Cà d'Zan

Ringling's winter home Cà d'Zan (1924–26), or 'House of John,' displays an unmistakable theatrical flair evocative of his two favorite Venetian hotels, the Danieli and the Bauer Grunwald. Ceilings are painted masterpieces, especially Willy Pogany's *Dancers of Nations* in the ballroom, and even the patio's zigzag marble that fronts Sarasota Bay dazzles. Self-guided tours include the 1st floor's kitchens, tap room and opulent public spaces, while guided tours ($5) add the 2nd floor's stupendous bedrooms and bathrooms.

➡ Circus Museum

This is actually several museums in one, and they are as delightful as the circus itself. One building preserves the hand-carved animal wagons, calliopes and artifacts from Ringling Bros' original traveling show. Other exhibits trace the evolution of the circus from sideshow to Cirque du Soleil. Yet in the center ring, so to speak, is the miniature Howard Bros Circus: a truly epic recreation at 1/12th scale of the entire Ringling Bros and Barnum & Bailey Circus in action. This intricately detailed work occupies its own building, and is mostly the 50-year labor of love of one man, Howard Tibbels.

★**Mote Marine Laboratory**   AQUARIUM
(☑941-388-4441; www.mote.org; 1600 Ken Thompson Pkwy, City Island; adult/child $20/15; ☺10am-5pm) A research facility first and an aquarium second, the Mote is one of the world's leading organizations for shark study, and glimpsing its work is a highlight: marvel at seahorse 'fry' born that very day, and time your visit for shark training. Above-average exhibits include a preserved giant squid (37ft long when caught), a stingray touch tank, a dramatic shark tank, and a separate building with intimate encounters with sea turtles, manatees and dolphins. An interactive immersion theater is perfect for kids. Note that animal welfare groups suggest interaction with dolphins and other sea mammals held in captivity creates stress for these creatures.

Adjacent to Mote, Save Our Seabirds displays a wide range of rescued seabirds in outdoor cages. Sarasota Bay Explorers (p400) is also based here. To get here, go to St Armands Circle, take John Ringling Blvd north to Ken Thompson Pkwy and follow to the end.

Marie Selby Botanical Gardens   GARDENS
(☑941-366-5731; www.selby.org; 811 S Palm Ave; adult/child 4-11yr $19/6; ☺10am-5pm) If you visit just one botanical garden in Florida, choose Selby, which has the world's largest scientific collection of orchids and bromeliads – more than 20,000 species. Emblematic of Florida, these plants are the sideshow freaks of the plant kingdom, propagating in such a bizarre fashion it boggles the mind. In addition, Selby's genteel outdoor gardens are exceptionally well landscaped and relaxing, with 80-year-old banyan trees, koi ponds and splendid bay views. Art exhibits, a cafe and an enticing plant shop complete the experience.

St Armands Circle   SQUARE
(www.starmandscircleassoc.com) Conceived by John Ringling in the 1920s, St Armands Circle is essentially an upscale outdoor shopping mall surrounded by posh residences on St Armands Key. Yet even more than downtown, this traffic circle is Sarasota's social center; it's where everyone strolls in the early evening, window shopping while enjoying a

Kilwin's waffle cone. Numerous restaurants, from diners to fine dining, serve all day.

The circle is also an unavoidable traffic chokepoint; mid-morning and late-afternoon beach commutes are worst.

Marina Jack
WATERFRONT, PORT

(🕿 941-955-9488; www.marinajacks.com; 2 Marina Plaza) Sarasota's plush deep-water marina is within walking distance of downtown and is well served with alfresco and fine-dining restaurants, and numerous sight-seeing cruises and private charters. Head here for boat rentals, water sports, sailing and fishing charters.

Island Park
PARK

Sarasota's marina is notable for Island Park, an attractive green space poking into the harbor: it has a great playground and play fountain; restrooms, tree-shaded benches, a restaurant and tiki bar; and kayak, Wave-Runner and boat rentals. A short stroll north along the waterfront is **Unconditional Surrender**, a towering statue of WWII's most famous kiss.

Art Center Sarasota
GALLERY

(🕿 941-365-2032; www.artsarasota.org; 707 N Tamiami Trail; donation $3; ⊙10am-4pm Tue-Sat) This community-oriented nonprofit gallery has four exhibition spaces that mix local and out-of-town artists. In winter, **family days** (per family $5) let kids get creative.

Tours

Sarasota Bay Explorers
BOAT TOUR

(🕿 941-388-4200; www.sarasotabayexplorers. com; 1600 Ken Thompson Pkwy, Mote Marine Laboratory) 🐾 Under the supervision of marine biologists, boat cruises trawl a net and then examine the sponges, sea horses and various fish you catch. The marine safari (adult/child $45/40) heads out to Lido Key

and nearby sandbars where participants get out into the grass flats to commune with crabs, sea horses and sea stars under the guidance of a marine biologist. It also offers guided kayak tours (adult/child $55/45). To get to Mote Marine Laboratory, head to St Armands Circle, take John Ringling Blvd north to Ken Thompson Pkwy; follow to end.

✺✺ Festivals & Events

Art & Craft Festivals
ARTS

(www.artfestival.com; ⊙late Mar) For two days in late March, an explosion of art and craft stalls dominates downtown Sarasota. The same happens in Siesta Village in late April.

Sarasota Film Festival
FILM

(www.sarasotafilmfestival.com; ⊙Apr) If you enjoy seeing serious independent films and wearing your flip-flops to free outdoor screenings at the beach, then head to Sarasota's ten-day film festival.

Ringling International Arts Festival
PERFORMING ARTS

(www.ringlingartsfestival.org; ⊙mid-Oct) For a week in mid-October, Ringling partners with NYC's Baryshnikov Arts Center to bring international dance, theater and music to Sarasota.

Sarasota Chalk Festival
ARTS

(http://chalkfestival.org; ⊙Nov) Come and gawp at the phenomenal artistry on display on South Pineapple Ave and Burns Sq in November.

🛏 Sleeping

Staying downtown in Sarasota is cheaper than staying at the beach, and it's only 3 miles to St Armands Circle and 6 miles to Siesta Key.

KIDS CIRCUS

The only actual circus in Sarasota is performed by kids, and it's worth planning a trip around. The **PAL Sailor Circus** (🕿 941-361-6350; www.sailorcircus.org; 2075 Bahia Vista St; tickets $10-16; ⊙late Dec, Mar & Apr; 👪), founded in 1949, is truly unique: it's an extra-curricular activity for Sarasota County students, who gear up for two big shows a year: during the December holidays, and for 10 days in late March and April. They call it 'The Greatest Little Show on Earth,' but don't be fooled: there is nothing little about this show, which includes high wire and trapeze, hand balancing and unicycles, and innumerable mid-air ballets while dangling from tissues, rings and bars.

If you miss the show, consider arranging a tour; customized individually, they include the big tent, costume shop, museum and – hopefully – attending practice. Please bring your own kids; just know they will nurture, forever after, dreams of running away to the circus.

★**Hotel Ranola** BOUTIQUE HOTEL **$$**
(☑941-951-0111; www.hotelranola.com; 118 Indian
Pl; r $109-155, ste $209-270; P✳☎) The nine
rooms feel like a designer's brownstone
apartment: free-spirited and effortlessly art-
ful, but with real working kitchens. It's ur-
ban funk, walkable to downtown Sarasota.

Hotel Indigo HOTEL **$$**
(☑941-487-3800; www.srqhotel.com; 1223
Blvd of the Arts; r $140-230; P✳@☎✈✈)
Boutique-style chain that's reliable and at-
tractive, as well as being close to downtown.
Good off-season discounts.

Cypress B&B **$$$**
(☑941-955-4683; www.cypressbb.com; 621 Gulf
Stream Ave S; r $150-290; P✳☎) For a roman-
tic getaway, the Cypress is dreamy. The ar-
tistic owners have individualized each room,
though a Victorian seaside mood prevails,
with wicker bed frames, Oriental rugs over
hardwood floors, palm-frond fans and mod-
ern art. A full hot breakfast and afternoon
cocktails can bookend trips to the beach.
Children are discouraged.

✖ Eating

From taco trucks to Indian comfort curries
and Korean BBQ, Sarasota has an exciting,
multiethnic eating scene and a strong lo-
cavore tradition. Log on to www.dineorigi-
nal.com for details of independent, locally
owned restaurants and the annual **Forks &
Corks food festival** in January.

Farmers Market MARKET **$**
(www.sarasotafarmersmarket.org; 1420 State St;
⊙7am-1pm Sat) This farmers market is one of
the best in the state.

★**Jim's Small Batch Bakery** BAKERY, CAFE **$**
(☑941-922-2253; 2336 Gulf Gate Dr; items $1-
10; ⊙8am-4pm Mon-Fri, 9am-3pm Sat) Real
small-batch, scratch baking makes Jim's a
delicious stop for breakfast and lunch.
All-butter hand-laminated croissants, can-
died bacon BLTs, creamy quiches and cups
of soup for a dollar.

Baja Boys MEXICAN **$**
(☑941-726-9302; 8451 N Tamiami Trail; items $7-9;
⊙11am-2pm Mon-Fri, 8:30am-1:30pm Sat) Warm
tortillas, lightly fried fish, shredded organ-
ic chicken and homemade guacamole, no
wonder Baja Boys won best bay food truck
in 2013.

Morton's Gourmet Market MARKET **$**
(www.mortonsmarket.com; 1924 S Osprey Ave;
mains $4-10; ⊙8am-8pm Mon-Sat, 10am-6pm
Sun) This chichi grocery store is a must-stop
for Siesta Key–bound gourmands dreaming
of that perfect beach picnic: simply partake
of Morton's unusually wide selection of take-
out salads, sandwiches, sushi and mains.
About 15 blocks south of downtown.

Blue Dolphin DINER **$**
(www.bluedolphincafe.com; 470 John Ringling Blvd;
mains $7-10; ⊙7am-3pm) On St Armands Cir-
cle, this small, casual diner is a go-to destina-
tion for a prebeach breakfast or quick lunch.

Main Bar Sandwich Shop SANDWICHES **$**
(www.themainbar.com; 1944 Main St; sandwiches
from $7; ⊙10am-4pm Mon-Sat; ♿) The Main
Bar is a Sarasota classic: an old-school, booth-
filled, diner-style deli founded by retired cir-
cus performers whose photos blanket the
walls. It offers a ton of sandwiches, but – no
kidding – order the 'famous' Italian, which
instantly transports you to Brooklyn c 1958.

Madison Avenue Cafe & Deli CAFE **$$**
(☑941-388-3354; www.madisoncafesarasota.
com; 28 Blvd of the Presidents, St Armands Circle; items $10-12; ⊙8am-5pm; ☎☑) One of
the most popular places on the Circle, this
upscale cafe has outdoor seating and a
generous menu of sandwiches, wraps and
salads. Everything is made fresh to order,
and sandwiches come bursting with deli
meats, crunchy veg and thick slabs of cheese.

Monk's Steamer Bar SEAFOOD **$$**
(☑941-927-3388; www.monkssteamerbar.com;
6690 Superior Ave; mains $7-30; ⊙4pm-1am Mon-
Fri, 3pm-1am Sat & Sun) Order a spicy oyster
shooter (a Bloody Mary with an oyster in it)
or oyster 'Monkafellas' (baked with signature
toppings) and watch bar staff expertly shuck
the gnarly shells in front of you. Or guzzle
2lb of sweet, steamed mussels or Cajun craw-
dads (crayfish) before lining up for a game
of pool at this ever-popular local sports bar.

★**Indigenous** MODERN AMERICAN **$$$**
(☑941-706-4740; www.indigenoussarasota.
com; 239 S Links Ave; mains $14-26; ⊙5:30-9pm
Tue-Sat) Focusing on the popular farm-to-
table movement, chef Steve Phelps whips
up innovative American creations such as
American-harvested shrimp with grits *lyon-
naise* (grits blended with caramelized on-
ions, butter, eggs and Parmesan) and Mote
marine sturgeon with sweet potatoes. It's a

lot of fun, too, housed in a funky, Old-Florida bungalow with a broad deck and an intimate 'wine cottage' serving biodynamic and small-production wine labels.

Antoine's Restaurant EUROPEAN $$$
(☑941-377-2020; www.antoinessarasota.com; 5020 Fruitville Rd; mains $16-32; ☺4-10pm) Despite its inauspicious location (in a former KFC), Antoine's is a small, charming French bistro with a clubby vibe serving elegant dishes such as scallop risotto with a candied, tangerine sauce. But this isn't faddish fusion food: owner Christian Zebier hails from Belgium and the restaurant reflects his classic European style. Save room for the Belgian chocolate desserts; you won't regret it.

Marina Jack's Restaurant SEAFOOD $$$
(☑941-365-4232; www.marinajacks.com; 2 Marina Plaza; sandwiches $9-13, mains $25-34; ☺11:30am-10pm) Anchoring the marina is this well-loved multilevel, multivenue eatery that offers something for everyone, but most especially that quintessential harbor-at-sunset ambience. Be serenaded by steel drums in the relaxed downstairs cafe and lounge, with expansive outdoor seating, tropical cocktails and an easy-on-the-wallet menu. The Bayfront dining room upstairs positions every formally laid table before curving, two-story windows and serves upscale surf-and-turf; make reservations.

Drinking

Why doesn't downtown Sarasota have a nightlife? In the evening, everyone is strolling St Armands Circle or Ocean Blvd in Siesta Village, a five-block stretch of seaside eats and drinks. Siesta's warm, friendly scene doesn't get rowdy till late.

For events and the local scene, visit This Week in Sarasota (www.thisweekinsarasota. com).

Perq CAFE
(☑941-955-8101; www.perqcoffeebar.com; 1821 Hillview St; ☺7am-5:30pm Mon-Fri, 8am-5:30pm Sat & Sun) Sophisticated brewing methods and sourcing of single-original beans make Perq the best coffee bar in Sarasota.

Jack Dusty BAR
(Ritz-Carlton; ☑941-309-2000; 1111 Ritz-Carlton Dr; ☺7am-11pm) The Ritz-Carlton's new gold-trimmed restaurant features one of the sexiest drinking dens in town, with a central glass-and-stone bar, small plates of Mote Marina caviar and oysters, and terrace

seating with water views. The bar is headed up by mixologist Roy Roig, hot from Miami, who devises nautically themed cocktails such as the Purser's Bane and Starboard Swizzle.

Old Salty Dog BAR
(www.theoldsaltydog.com; 1601 Ken Thompson Pkwy, City Island; ☺11am-9:30pm) At the City Island marina across from the Mote, Old Salty Dog is a perfect end to a day or start to an evening. Unwind with a brew and some above-average fish and chips on the breezy outdoor deck (mains from $7 to $16).

☆ Entertainment

Burns Court Cinema CINEMA
(☑941-955-3456; 506 Burns Lane) This wee theater in an alleyway off Pineapple Ave presents independent and foreign films. It's run by the Sarasota Film Society (SFS; www. filmsociety.org), which screens more than 40 of the year's best international films in November during the annual 10-day CINE-World Film Festival.

Players Theatre THEATER
(☑941-365-2494; www.theplayers.org; 838 N Tamiami Trail; tickets from $20) This highly regarded nonprofit community theater stages popular Broadway musicals, new plays and collaborations.

Westcoast Black Theater Troupe THEATER
(☑941-366-1505; www.wbttsrq.org; 1646 10th Way; tickets $20-40) One of only two African American theater ventures in Florida, WBTT has a reputation for high-quality musicals and thought-provoking dramas. Through the company's mentorship numerous national and international careers have been launched.

Asolo Repertory Theatre THEATER
(☑941-351-8000; www.asolorep.org; 5555 N Tamiami Trail; tickets $20-50; ☺Nov-Jul) This lauded regional theater company is also an acting conservatory (in partnership with Florida State University). It presents a mix of commissioned works, classics and current Tony-winning dramas on two main stages. The Sarasota Ballet (www.sarasotaballet.org) also performs here.

Van Wezel Performing Arts Hall PERFORMING ARTS
(☑941-953-3368; www.vanwezel.org; 777 N Tamiami Trail; tickets $25-80) This city-run arts hall hosts crowd-pleasing favorites, from touring

Broadway musicals to magicians, modern dance, pops orchestras and more.

Sarasota Opera House OPERA
(☑941-366-8450; www.sarasotaopera.org; 61 N Pineapple Ave; tickets $20-100; ⊘Feb-Mar) This elegant, 1000-seat Mediterranean Revival venue was built in 1926, and the two-month winter opera season is a serious affair.

🔒 Shopping

In downtown Sarasota, Main St, Pineapple Ave and Palm Ave form the main shopping district, with lots of fun and trendy stores. St Armands Circle is another shopping hot spot.

Towles Court Artist Colony ARTS & CRAFTS
(www.towlescourt.com; 1938 Adams Lane; ⊘11am-4pm Tue-Sat) A dozen or so hip galleries occupy quirky, parrot-colored bungalows in this artists colony. The most lively time to be here is the late-opening night on the third Friday of each month (6pm to 10pm). Outside of this, individual gallery hours can be whimsical.

Book Bazaar/Parker's Books BOOKS
(☑941-366-2898; 1488 Main St; ⊘10am-5pm Mon-Sat) Huge used bookstore perfect for cheap beach reading.

ℹ️ Information

Arts & Cultural Alliance (www.sarasotaarts. org) All-encompassing event info.
Sarasota Herald-Tribune (www.heraldtribune. com) The main daily owned by the *New York Times*.
Sarasota Memorial Hospital (☑941-917-9000; www.smh.com; 1700 S Tamiami Trail; ⊘24hr) The area's biggest hospital.
Sarasota Visitor Information Center (☑941-957-1877; www.sarasotafl.org; 701 N Tamiami Trail; ⊘10am-5pm Mon-Sat; 🛜) Very friendly office with tons of info; sells good maps.

ℹ️ Getting There & Around

Sarasota is roughly 60 miles south of Tampa and about 75 miles north of Fort Myers. The main roads into town are Tamiami Trail/US 41 and I-75.
Greyhound (☑941-955-5735; www.greyhound. com; 19 E Rd; ⊘7am-9pm) Connects Sarasota and Miami, Fort Myers and Tampa.
Sarasota-Bradenton International Airport (SRQ; ☑941-359-2777; www.srq-airport.com; 6000 Airport Circle) Served by many major airlines. Go north on Hwy 41, and right on University Ave.

Sarasota County Area Transit (SCAT; ☑941-861-5000; www.scgov.net/SCAT; cnr 1st St & Lemon Ave; fare $1.25; ⊘6am-6:30pm Mon-Sat) Buses have no transfers and a very limited Sunday service. Bus 4 connects Ringling Blvd with Armands Circle and Lido Key Beach; bus 11 heads to Siesta Key.

Sarasota Keys

For sun-worshippers and salty dogs alike, Sarasota's Keys offer an irresistible combination of fabulous beaches, laid-back living and endless watery pursuits. Geographically, the Keys are a series of barrier islands that stretch 35 miles from south of Sarasota north to Anna Maria Island across the causeway from Bradenton. Each has its own distinct identity, but all offer access to miles of glorious beach.

⊙ Sights & Activities

Siesta Key ISLAND, BEACH
At 8 miles long, Siesta Key is the area's most popular beach hangout with a family-friendly village and a public beach of pure quartz sand so fine it's like confectioner's sugar. The enormous parking lot (at the corner of Beach Rd and Beach Way) has an information booth dispensing info on all types of activities and water sports (parasailing, jet-ski rental, kayaks, bikes and more), plus nice facilities, a snack bar and covered eating areas.

For a quieter experience, head to Turtle Beach. The sun and teal waters are the same, but it's several miles south of the action and the narrow ash-gray sand beach isn't half as fine, so few prefer it. Not so the sea turtles, who nest here from May through October.

SCAT bus 11 serves Siesta Key from downtown Sarasota.

Lido Key ISLAND, BEACH
Just a hop, skip and jump across St Armands Circle, Lido Key is barely 15 minutes' drive from downtown Sarasota. Lido Beach is an excellent, wide stretch of white sand backed by a number of nature trails. Street and lot parking is free, so expect crowds. A pavilion at the parking lot has food, restrooms and even a small lap swimming pool (400 Benjamin Franklin Dr; adult/child 4-11yr $4/2; ⊘10am-4:45pm Tue-Sun). About a mile south is South Lido Beach, whose grills and grassy lawns are extremely popular with picnicking families; strong currents here discourage swimming.

SCAT bus 4 serves Lido Key from downtown Sarasota.

CORTEZ FISHING VILLAGE

Ever since the 1700s fishermen have been harvesting mullet in Cortez, now one of the few remaining wild fisheries in the US. Sandwiched between Anna Maria Island and Palma Sola Bay on the mainland, the village is a perfect time-warp with old boats and crab traps drying on the lawns of wooden bungalows. Ethan Hawke played poor boy Pip here to Gwyneth Paltrow's Estella in the 1998 adaptation of *Great Expectations*.

Head down to the water and you'll find the **Star Fish Company** (✆941-794-1243; http://starfishcompany.com; 12306 46th Ave W , Cortez; mains $3-15; ⏰11:30am-8pm Tue-Sat, to 3pm Sun & Mon; ⊛), a commercial fish house that's been selling wholesale fish since the 1920s. It now has a rustic restaurant that sits out over the dock with views of Jewel Fish Key and Net House, out in the bay. If there's smoked mullet on the menu, be sure to order it with a side of cheese grits.

Longboat Key
ISLAND, BEACH

Once a quiet fishing village, the 12 long miles of Longboat Key are now lined with upscale resorts and condos. A few teeny-tiny public parking lots don't offer much access for day-trippers. **Beer Can Island** (aka Greer Island), at the northern tip of Longboat, is one of the area's prettiest beaches.

★Anna Maria Island
ISLAND, BEACH

The perfect antidote to party-loving Siesta Key, Anna Maria Island appears beached in a 1950s time warp, with sun-faded clapboard houses, teenagers hanging outside ice-cream stores and a clutch of good seafood restaurants. The island is made up of three beach towns: at the southern end is Bradenton Beach, mid-island is Holmes Beach, which is considered the hub, and at the northern tip is Anna Maria village.

The best beaches are to the south and north. Southern **Coquina Beach** has plenty of pavilions, lifeguards and restrooms, and is backed by a stand of Australian pines through which the **Coquina Bay Walk** meanders. To the north, **Anna Maria Bayfront Park** sits on Tampa Bay, offering views of the Sunshine Skyway Bridge, a playground and restrooms. The latter is within walking distance of the **City Pier** and the center of Anna Maria.

Siesta Sports Rentals
CYCLING, KAYAKING

(✆941-346-1797; www.siestasportsrentals.com; 6551 Midnight Pass Rd; ⏰9am-5pm) South of Siesta Village, just south of the Stickney Point Bridge, this rental shop has bikes, kayaks, scooters, four-person surreys, beach gear, baby equipment and more.

🛏 Sleeping

Many people opt for house rental on Anna Maria Island, and there are dozens of providers. Check www.annamariaisland accommodations.com.

Turtle Beach Campground
CAMPGROUND $

(✆941-349-3839; www.scgove.net/turtlebeach-campground; 8862 Midnight Pass Rd, Siesta Key; campsites $32-60; P🛜) This park campground is small, caters to RVs, has zero privacy and doesn't allow campfires, but it's well worth camping here to be mere steps from Turtle Beach and a quick drive from Sarasota.

Hayley's Motel
MOTEL $$

(✆941-778-5405; www.haleysmotel.com; 8102 Gulf Dr, Anna Maria Island; r $169-219; P❄🛜☀) Owner-operated Hayley's offers motel rooms, one bedroom suites and buckets of 1950s charm. Super-quaint and competitively priced for Anna Maria. You'll find it about a block back from Holmes Beach. There's a $50 fee for pets, but note that the beaches on Anna Maria don't allow dogs.

★Harrington House
B&B $$$

(✆941-778-5444; www.harringtonhouse.com; 5626 Gulf Dr, Anna Maria Island; ste $179-359, bungalows $209-399; P❄🛜☀) Sneak away to this beachside B&B and fantasize about your own little seaside paradise. Made up of three former beach houses, the B&B's guest suites and bungalows have sun porches overlooking an idyllic beach. Common rooms ooze Old Florida charm with their wing-back armchairs, mahogany sideboards and candelabra lights. Children under 12 are discouraged.

Siesta Key Inn
APARTMENTS $$$

(✆941-349-4999; www.siestakeyinn.com; 1017 Point of Rocks Rd, Siesta Key; Feb-Apr $269-329, May-Jan $179-249; P❄🛜☀) Recently refurbished these beachy suites sit within a tropical garden a few steps from the shore and the Crescent Beach shops. And when they say these suites are fully equipped, they mean it. Aside from the usual beach chairs and towels, you'll find beach coolers, beach toys, car seats, snorkeling equipment and even inline skates.

Sunsets on the Key APARTMENTS $$$
(☑941-312-9797; www.sunsetsonthekey.com; 5203 Avenida Navarre, Siesta Key; mid-Dec–Apr $230-340, May–mid-Dec $149-209; P❄🐾🛜⛱) In Siesta Village, eight well-kept, rigorously clean condo apartments are run like a hotel.

✖️ Eating

Ginny's & Jane E's CAFE $
(☑941-778-3170; www.ginnysandjanees.com; 9807 Gulf Dr, Anna Maria Island; items $2-12; ⊙8am-5pm; 🛜) Browse the web or shop for vintage furniture, flip-flops, and outsider art and trinkets while you wait for your server to cut off a hunk of Connie Wolgast's pecan pie and rustle up a sandwich for the beach. Ginny's & Jane E's is a unique cafe, coffee-and-ice-cream bar and vintage-finds store housed in the old village grocery. And don't feel shy: sit down at the tables and sofas with other beachcombers; this place is made for socializing.

Lélu Coffee Lounge CAFE $
(☑941-346-5358; www.lelucoffee.com; 5251 Ocean Blvd, Siesta Key; items $5.50-13; ⊙7:30am-10pm Mon-Sat, 8:30am-5pm Sun) Look no further than this retro coffee lounge for laid-back lounging over your early-morning espresso or Island Coconut Mocha. Surfboards dangle from the ceiling; comfortable sofas beckon; and there's a short menu of fruit smoothies, 'samiches' and smashed omelets stuffed with produce from the farmers market. Come nightfall there's a martini bar, open mic and jazz events.

Siesta Key Farmers Market MARKET $
(www.siestafarmersmarket.com; Davidson's Plaza, Ocean Blvd; ⊙9am-2pm Sun) Focusing on locally grown produce, the Siesta Key Farmers Market is a great place to pick up groceries.

Dry Dock SEAFOOD $$
(☑941-383-0102; drydockwaterfrontgrill.com; 412 Gulf of Mexico Dr, Longboat Key; mains $7-19; ⊙11am-9pm Mon-Sat, 4:30-9pm Sun) With a deck overhanging the water and panoramic views from its upstairs dining room impeded only by shady palm fronds, it's hard to beat Dry Dock for waterside dining. Match that with excellent blackened grouper sandwiches, a half-pound chargrilled burger and

Caribbean shrimp tacos and you'll see why the wait time is usually around 40 minutes. Don't stress; just grab a beer, take a seat in one of the Adirondack chairs and watch the pelicans on the pilings.

Blasé Café & Martini Bar ITALIAN $$
(☑941-349-9822; www.theblasecafe.com; 5253 Ocean Blvd, Siesta Key; mains $15-23; ⊙3pm-1am) At the end of Siesta Village, Blasé combines the artful vibe of an urban wine bar with a seaside casual bistro. The menu of pastas and mains is fine, but taste much better with a dry martini or generous pour of Cabernet.

★ Beach Bistro MODERN AMERICAN $$$
(☑941-778-6444; www.beachbistro.com; 6600 Gulf Dr, Anna Maria Island; mains $20-60; ⊙5-10pm) Sean Murphy's Beach Bistro is Anna Maria's best date night. Perfectly executed Floridian dishes showcase the best locally and nationally sourced farm products, including fresh line-caught seafood, Hudson Valley *foie gras* and prime USA beef tenderloin. The Bistro Bouillabaisse is legendary, stacked with lobster tail, jumbo shrimp, shellfish and calamari and stewed in a fresh tomato, saffron and anise flavored broth.

Cottage FUSION, SEAFOOD $$$
(☑941-312-9300; www.cottagesiestakey.com; 153 Avenida Messina, Siesta Key; tapas $9-15, mains $20-30; ⊙11am-10pm Sun-Thu, to midnight Fri & Sat) Siesta Key's hottest restaurant is headed up by dynamic chef Larry Eppler, whose exciting fusion menu not only includes mouthwatering sushi, but sophisticated tapas including slow-braised Korean short ribs and walu sashimi on a chilled block of Himalayan sea salt drizzled with pistachio aioli. Pair with a frozen *mojito*. Perfection.

🍸 Drinking

Siesta Key Oyster Bar BAR
(www.skob.com; 5238 Ocean Blvd, Siesta Village; ⊙11am-midnight Sun-Thu, to 1:30am Fri & Sat) At SKOB, the tilting rafters are tacked with dollar bills – yes, it's that kind of place. Live music.

Beach Club BAR
(www.beachclubsiestakey.com; 5151 Ocean Blvd, Siesta Village; ⊙11am-2am) Cavernous bar with pool tables, a stage, a great white shark and Sunday bikini contests. Live music.

Gilligan's Island Bar & Grill BAR
(www.gilligansislandbar.net; 5253 Ocean Blvd, Siesta Village; ⊙11:30am-2am) Classic Florida

DON'T MISS

HISTORIC SPANISH POINT

There were never any Spaniards at Historic Spanish Point (☎941-966-5214; www.historicspanishpoint.org; 337 N Tamiami Trail , Osprey; adult/child 5-12yr $12/5; ⊙9am-5pm Mon-Sat, noon-5pm Sun). Instead the name derives from a friendly Spanish trader who tipped off settlers John and Eliza Webb about the idyllic location when they were searching for land to farm in 1867. He did them a big favor, as the site is one of the prettiest in Sarasota County. The narrow peninsula stretches out into Little Sarasota Bay. It's an undulating landscape of prehistoric shell middens covered in tropical foliage.

Not surprisingly the Webbs were very happy here. Eventually they accumulated the entire 30-acre peninsula, which they planted with citrus they shipped to market in Cedar Key and Key West. Wander the 1-mile trail (tours via electric cart are also available) around the site and you can see the wooden packing-house, Mary's Chapel, the Webb-family cemetery and Frank Guptill's beautiful wooden homestead, which he built for his wife Lizzie Webb Guptill.

The Webbs farmed the land for more than 40 years before it was purchased by Bertha Palmer in 1910. Luckily for Spanish Point, wealthy Bertha, widow of Potter Palmer, a prominent Chicago real-estate developer and cofounder of Marshall Field and Company, treasured the beauty of the place when she selected it as the anchor of her 350-acre winter estate. She left intact the shell middens as well as the Webb homestead, outbuildings and chapel while developing her gardens in keeping with the tropical landscape. Now pergolas, classic Greek columns, lawns and flower gardens punctuate the wild foliage.

To cap it all, between 1959 and 1962 the Smithsonian Institution partially excavated one of the shell middens. You can enter the mound and see what the layers of shell deposits and prehistoric paraphernalia look like from the inside. It's the only such site in Florida and is quite fascinating. Viewed altogether, the Point offers a unique narrative of Florida's prehistoric and pioneering history.

thatched-roof tiki-bar vibe, with VW bus, outdoor courtyard and deadly fishbowl cocktails. Live music.

ℹ Information

Anna Maria Island Chamber of Commerce
(☎941-778-1541; www.annamariaislandchamber.org; 5313 Gulf Dr N, Holmes Beach; ⊙9am-5pm Mon-Fri) Provides info on accommodation, activity providers and island events.

Siesta Key Chamber of Commerce (☎941-349-3800; www.siestakeychamber.com; 5118 Ocean Blvd, Siesta Key; ⊙9am-5pm Mon-Fri, to noon Sat) Tracks daily hotel availability and will help you find a room.

Simply Siesta Key (www.simplysiestakey.com) A comprehensive, online resource.

Myakka River State Park

Florida's oldest resident – the 200-million-year-old American alligator – is the star of this 57-sq-mile wildlife preserve (☎941-361-6511; www.myakkariver.org; 13208 State Rd 72, Sarasota; car/bike $6/2; ⊙8am-sunset). Between 500 and 1000 alligators make their home in Myakka's slow-moving river and its shallow, lily-filled lakes. You can get up close and

personal via canoe, kayak and pontoon-style airboat. During mating season in April and May, the guttural love songs of the males ring out across the waters.

The extensive park offers much more besides: its hammocks, marshes, pine flatwoods and prairies are home to a great variety of birds and wildlife, and 38 miles of trails crisscross the terrain. In winter, airboat trips (adult/child $12/6) depart at 10am, 11:30am, 1pm and 2:30pm; call for summer times. Winter-only wildlife trams run at 1pm and 2:30pm and cost the same.

A camp store and cafe are located at the Myakka Outpost (☎941-923-1120; www.myakkaoutpost.com; canoes/bikes $20/15; ⊙9:30am-5pm Mon-Fri, 8:30am-6pm Sat & Sun), from where you can also organize tours, and kayak and bike rentals. The recommended campground (sites $26) is prime during dry season, from January to April; avoid rainy, buggy summer. The five cabins (per night $70) have kitchens, air con and linens; book through Reserve America (☎800-326-3521; www.reserveamerica.com).

To reach the park from Sarasota, take US 41 south to Hwy 72/Clark Rd and head east for about 14 miles; the park is about 9 miles east of I-75.

Venice

📞 941 / POP 20,750

About the only resemblance Venice has to its Italian namesake is that it's an island in the sea. Venice has scenic, tan-sand beaches but is otherwise an extremely quiet seaside town that's most popular with retirees and families with young kids, who enjoy hunting for shark's teeth. It also appeals to budget-minded travelers looking for a low-key getaway – far from the condos and hard-drinking beach bars elsewhere. Here, entertainment pretty much begins and ends with saluting the tangerine sun's nightly descent into the shimmering ocean.

From US 41/Tamiami Trail, Venice Ave heads west directly to Venice Beach. About five blocks east of the beach, the main downtown commercial district lies along W Venice Ave between US 41 and Harbor Dr.

🏃 Activities

All Venice-area beaches have free parking.

Venice Beach   BEACH
Where W Venice Ave dead-ends you'll find a covered beach pavilion with restrooms and a snack bar. There's free yoga on the sand daily at 9am, and free acoustic music from Saturday to Wednesday at around 5pm. Sea turtles nest on Venice Beach from May to October.

Venice Pier   BEACH
Off Harbor Dr 1.5 miles south of W Venice Ave, this long, wide beach with a huge parking lot is the most popular, especially for sunset. The adjacent pier, which has a bait shack and fish tables, is well equipped for fishing. Modest surf near the pier encourages boogie boarding; at the pier's base, Sharky's provides food and drink.

Caspersen Beach   BEACH
Another 1.5 miles south of Venice Pier along Harbor Dr, Caspersen is famous for the fossilized prehistoric sharks' teeth that wash up. Most teeth are the size of a fingernail, but occasionally finger-long specimens are found. Its attractive, palmetto-backed sand, playground and paved bike path also make Caspersen popular; there are facilities but no concessions (kiosks).

Nokomis Beach   BEACH
(www.nokomisbeachflorida.com; 100 Casey Key Rd, Nokomis) North of Venice on Casey Key, Nokomis is yet another attractive, low-key beach. Its 'minimalist'-style beach pavilion is an intriguing architectural bauble; it has nice facilities but no concessions (so bring lunch). Also, at sundown on Wednesday and Saturday nights things get genuinely groovy: the Nokomis Beach Drum Circle gathers and its rhythm draws upwards of several hundred folks. To get to Nokomis Beach take US 41 N to Albee Rd W.

Warm Mineral Springs   SPA
(📞 941-426-1692; www.scgov.net/warmmineralsprings; 12200 San Servando Ave; adult/child $20/10; ⊙9am-5pm) Was this warm mineral spring the actual fountain of youth Ponce de León was hunting? So they say. And it's an appropriate fable for this Old Florida throwback. The spring's 87°F (30.5°C) waters, which have the highest mineral content of any in the US, have long been a favored health tonic by elderly Eastern

VENICE TO SARASOTA: THE LEGACY TRAIL

Voted the best-kept secret in Sarasota County by *Herald Tribune* readers, the Legacy Trail (www.scgov.net; ⊙6am-sunset) is a gorgeous 20-mile bike ride, running from Caspersen Beach in Venice to Palmer Ranches just east of downtown Sarasota. Cutting through a landscape of suburban backyards, forested state park and traversing the Intracoastal Waterway over three trestle bridges, it offers a pleasant variety of scenery, with well-planned rest stops every mile along the trail. In addition, the trail traverses the 1400-acre Oscar Scherer State Park (www.floridastateparks.org/oscarscherer; 1843 S Tamiami Trail, Osprey; per car/cyclist $8/2; ⊙8am-sunset), which has another 15 miles of sandy off-road tracks, lake swimming and a handy campsite (per tent $26) midway along the route.

There are eight trailheads. The best section runs between the Venice Train Depot (303 E Venice Ave) and Osprey Junction (939 E Bay St, Osprey), where you could finish with a visit to gorgeous Historic Spanish Point.

Europeans. The refurbished spa, changing areas and vegetarian cafe, not to mention the free yoga, pilates and water-aerobics classes, are attracting a new generation of wellness fanatics. From US 41 east of North Port, head north 1 mile on Ortiz Blvd.

🛏 Sleeping

Banyan House   B&B $$
(☑ 941-484-1385; www.banyanhouse.com; 519 S Harbor Dr; r $145-197; P ✱ 🐾 🛜 ≋) A charming bed and breakfast in one of Venice's grand old homes. It has a heated pool, a lemon-yellow sun room, a billiards room and a hammock beneath the namesake banyan tree.

★ Inn at the Beach   RESORT $$$
(☑ 941-484-8471; www.innatthebeach.com; 725 W Venice Ave; r $225-350, ste $353-515; ✱ @ 🛜 ≋) Right across from the beach and a perfect choice for an extended stay, this well-managed hotel-style resort worries the details so you don't have to. Each room's attractive palette of cream yellow, burnt umber and sage avoids seaside clichés, and the fully functional kitchenettes are a pleasure to cook in. Excellent amenities include Continental breakfast, and complimentary water and snacks all day. Multinight stays get good discounts.

✕ Eating

Stroll W Venice Ave west of US 41 and you'll pass bakeries, an Irish pub, an ice creamery and other modest eateries, along with all the boutiques and gift shops you could need.

Robbi's Reef   SEAFOOD $$
(www.robbisreef.com; 775 Hwy 41 By-Pass S; mains $8-15; ◷ 11am-9pm Tue-Sat) This perfect simulacrum of a harbor seafood shack is incongruously in a strip mall a half mile south of Venice Ave. From the walls crammed with fishing photos to the flagstone bar to the unpretentious, delicious cooking, you'd swear you were at the docks. Fish tacos and Bayou Willy's pasta get high marks.

Sharky's on the Pier   SEAFOOD $$
(☑ 941-488-1456; www.sharkeysonthepier.com; 1600 Harbor Dr S; mains $10-27; ◷ 11:30am-10pm, to midnight Fri & Sat) With the prime sunset spot at the Venice Pier, Sharky's doesn't have to try too hard. It's a typical middle-of-the-road seafood restaurant with a tiki bar positioned for the evening's magic moment.

For those more concerned with what's on their plate, head upstairs to **Fins** (☑ 941-786-

3068; www.finsatsharkys.com; sushi $8-16, mains $26-36; ◷ noon-2:30pm & 4-10pm) for well-executed sushi, prime cuts of mesquite charcoal-grilled meat and sophisticated seafood dishes such as golden tilefish in a macadamia crust and a mango-ginger sauce.

★ Ristorante San Marco   ITALIAN $$$
(☑ 941-254-6565; http://sanmarcovenice.com; 305 W Venice Ave; ◷ 11am-2:30pm & 5-9pm) Superlative southern Italian cuisine served in a romantic art-filled dining room. All breads and pastas are made on-site and daily specials showcase seasonal ingredients. Reservations advised.

ℹ Information

Venice Chamber of Commerce (☑ 941-488-2236; www.venicechamber.com; 597 S Tamiami Trail; ◷ 8:30am-5pm Mon-Fri) This helpful office provides good, free maps.

Charlotte Harbor & Barrier Islands

Between Charlotte Harbor and Fort Myers a chain of little islands dots the Gulf waterways. Once inhabited by Native Americans from the Calusa tribe, who survived off the abundance of shell fishing, the islands later developed a romantic reputation as the hideout for pirates. The most famous of these was José Gaspar, who called himself Gasparilla. He roamed the Gulf Coast plundering treasure and seizing beautiful women, whom he held captive on so-called Captiva Island. Cabbage Key, Useppa and Cayo Costa are accessible only by boat and make for good day trips, while upscale Gasparilla and the largely residential Pine Island are connected to the mainland via causeways. Further south, the two most well known islands, Sanibel and Captiva, are accessed over three arcing causeways south of Fort Myers.

Gasparilla Island

Of all the rum-smuggling, treasure plundering pirates to have set foot in southwest Florida, José Gaspar, better known as Gasparilla, is the most notorious. He set up his headquarters at **Boca Grande** on Gasparilla Island, so the story goes, where he built a palmetto palace and furnished it with the treasures he swiped from his high-seas adventures. Serious historians may doubt his

'CHEESEBURGER IN PARADISE': CABBAGE KEY INN

As all Parrotheads know, Jimmy Buffett's famous song 'Cheeseburger in Paradise' was allegedly inspired by a meal at the **Cabbage Key Inn** (☑239-283-2278; www.cabbagekey.com; r $100-150, cottages $180-405; ☺7:30-9am, 11:30am-3pm & 6-8:30pm). Truth be told, the burger is only average, and it wouldn't be worth writing a song about if it weren't served on this 100-acre, mangrove-fringed key in the Gulf of Mexico, which somehow makes everything more special. Built atop a Calusa shell mound, and originally the 1938 home of writer Mary Roberts Rinehart, the inn has the romantic air of a secluded semi-tropical port for global wayfarers – one that receives ferry loads of tourists every lunchtime. The bar is certainly a sight: the walls are matted and spongy with perhaps $80,000 in signed $1 bills, including framed bills from ex-president Jimmy Carter and, of course, Mr Buffett himself. Bills flutter to the floor daily, which the inn collects, annually donating $10,000 to charity.

Staying in one of the inn's six rooms or seven cottages is definitely the best experience. All are Old Florida atmospheric with pretty touches (Rinehart and Dollhouse are favorites), but they aren't resort-plush: no TVs, no pool and wi-fi only in the restaurant. But you're not exactly marooned: the inn serves powerful cocktails and full dinner nightly (from $16 to $29, and they'll cook your catch), but make reservations. Most people visit for lunch (from $9 to $11); we'd recommend the blackened mahimahi, but we know what you'll probably order.

To get here, Tropic Star (p410) has ferries that include lunch at Cabbage Key, or you can rent your own boat or book a private water taxi on Pine Island or Captiva Island.

existence, but Boca Grande continues to woo the great and the good who come to chase the glint of silver scales on the monstrous Atlantic tarpon that swim in its passes.

Despite its popularity as a blue-blooded bolt-hole, Boca Grande has a quaint fishing-village feel and is a great destination for families. It has miles of undeveloped white-sand beaches encompassed within the **Gasparilla Island State Park** (☑941-964-0375; www.floridastateparks.org/gasparillaisland; 880 Belcher Rd; per car/pedestrian $3/2; ☺8am-sunset).

🏃 Activities

Boca Grande Fishing Guides Association   FISHING
(www.bocagrandefishing.com) Fisherfolk should contact the Boca Grande Fishing Guides Association to get out on the water.

Boca Boat Cruises   CRUISE
(☑941-964-1333; www.bocaboat.com; cruises $39-59) For those less interested in catching fish but keen to get out on the water, Boca Boat Cruises offers charters and tours.

🛏 Sleeping

★Gasparilla Inn   HISTORIC HOTEL $$$
(☑941-964-4500; www.gasparillainn.com; 500 Palm Ave, Boca Grande; r $235-480; 🅿☀🛜🏊) Retire beneath the pillared Georgian entrance of this historic 1913 hotel and you'll

be transported to a more genteel age. Bell boys and butlers are on hand to attend to your every need and rooms offer splendidly unpretentious coral-and-pistachio-accented comfort. Days will no doubt drift by in a blur of golf, tennis, fishing and seaplane tours.

Anchor Inn   INN $$$
(☑941-964-2700; www.anchorinnbocagrande.com; 450 4th St E; r $175-240; 🅿☀🛜🏊) This historic 1925 home passes for the budget option in Boca Grande. With only four suites, book far, far in advance.

❶ Getting There & Away

To reach Gasparilla Island, head southwest of Hwy 41 on Hwy 776, which merges with Gasparilla Rd. The toll over the causeway costs $6.

Cayo Costa Island

As slim as a supermodel and just as lovely, Cayo Costa Island is almost entirely preserved as the 2500-acre **Cayo Costa State Park** (☑941-964-0375; www.floridastateparks.org/cayocosta; admission $2; ☺8am-sunset). While its pale, ash-colored sand may not be as fine as other beaches, its idyllic solitude and bathtub-warm azure waters are without peer. Bring a snorkel mask to help scour sandbars for shells and huge conchs – delightfully, many still house colorful occupants (who, by law, must be left there).

Cycle dirt roads to more-distant beaches; hike interior island trails; and kayak mangroves. The ranger station near the dock sells water and firewood, and rents bikes and kayaks, but otherwise bring everything you need.

The 30-site campground (per tent $22) is exposed and hot, with fire-pit grills, restrooms and showers, but sleeping on this beach is its own reward. Twelve plain cabins (per night $40) have bunk beds with vinyl-covered mattresses. January to April is best; by May, the heat and no-see-ums (biting midges) become unpleasant.

The only access is by boat, which doubles as a scenic nature-and-dolphin cruise. Tropic Star ferries depart from Pine Island, Captiva and Punta Gorda on Charlotte Harbor.

Pine Island

☑ 239 / POP 1800

The 17-mile-long Pine Island, the region's largest, is a mangrove island with no sandy beaches to call its own, but offers relaxing, quiet lodgings for anglers, kayakers and romantics fleeing the tourist hordes. It encompasses several communities: Matlacha, the island's center, with a small amount of commerce and funky Old Florida art galleries; the northern communities of Pineland and Bokeelia, where you can find boat and fishing charters; and the largely residential St James City at the southern tip. Pine Island is a great jumping-off point for all-day adventures among the region's tarpon-rich waterways and gorgeous barrier islands.

⊙ Sights & Activities

Matlacha   VILLAGE
The tiny fishing village of Matlacha (pronounced mat-la-shay) straddles the drawbridge to Pine Island and provides a quirky window into local life. In addition to its unpretentious fresh-seafood markets and restaurants, a collection of old fishing huts have been transformed into gift shops that sit like a clutch of chattering Day-Glo-painted tropical birds.

Matlacha Bridge   FISHING
They call this causeway between Cape Coral and Matlacha the 'fishingest bridge in the US,' sitting as it does at the center of several dynamic tidal flows. Anglers are here literally 24/7, especially during tarpon season.

Tropic Star   BOAT TOUR
(☑ 239-283-0015; www.cayocostaferry.com; Jug Creek Marina, Bokeelia) Cruises and ferries to Cayo Costa depart from Jug Creek Marina. Ferries (adult/child $32/25) take an hour; other options include stops at Cabbage Key for lunch (adult/child $27/20). It also offers private water taxis (per hour $150), which are much faster and offer island-hopping to Useppa and Gasparilla Island.

Gulf Coast Kayak   KAYAKING
(☑ 239-283-1125; www.gulfcoastkayak.com; 4530 NW Pine Island Rd) In Matlacha, just past the drawbridge, Gulf Coast offers several kayak tours (per person $56) in the wildlife-rich Matlacha Pass Aquatic Preserve. You can also rent a canoe or kayak (half-/full day $35/50) and paddle yourself. Want to kayak *to* Cayo Costa? Talk to them.

🛏 Sleeping

★ **Inn on the Bay**   B&B $$
(☑ 239-283-7510; www.webbwiz.com/inn; 12251 Shoreview Dr, Matlacha; r $99-199; 🅿❄🕾) You'll receive a warm welcome from Bill and Diana, the resident osprey and visiting manatees when you stay at this friendly inn that has great views over the water to distant Bokeelia. All four rooms are decorated with funky fishing art and vibrant craftwork. Ask for room 2 from where you'll be at eye-level with the neighboring osprey's nest. It's well located for all the action in Matlacha.

Tarpon Lodge   INN $$
(☑ 239-283-3999; www.tarponlodge.com; 13771 Waterfront Dr, Pineland; r $125-190; 🅿❄🕾) The atmosphere at this genteel 1926 fishing inn seems barely to have changed since the door opened. Rooms have a comfortable, retro feel while the dining room has a clubby vibe thanks to its gleaming wooden interior and black-and-white portraits of previous angling patrons. The family also manages the rental cottages on Cabbage Key Island, and you can book any number of cruises or fishing trips through the lodge.

🍴 Eating

Most eateries are to be found in Matlacha and along Stringfellow Rd.

★ **Perfect Cup**   BREAKFAST $
(☑ 239-283-4447; 4548 Pine Island Rd, Matlacha; mains $5-10; ⊗6am-3pm Mon-Sat, 7am-2pm Sun) A genuine local gathering place, Perfect Cup

offers just that: a bottomless mug of flavorful house-roasted coffee ($2) to go with its top-quality diner-style fare – creative omelets, French toast and pancakes.

Andy's Island Seafood   MARKET $
(www.andysislandseafood.com; 4330 Pine Island Rd, Matlacha; items $8-14; ☺10am-6pm Mon-Sat, to 4pm Sun) This lime-green shack offers a great selection of fresh seafood to cook, as well as succulent grouper sandwiches, crab cakes and chowder for lunch. It's so popular you'll find Andy's lunch trucks popping up on other islands.

Reds   AMERICAN, SEAFOOD $$
(☑239-283-4412;   www.redsfreshseafood.com; 10880 Stringfellow Rd, Bokeelia; mains $8-28; ☺4-9pm Sun-Thu, to 10pm Fri & Sat; ☻) This enormous, barn-like restaurant is perpetually buzzing with the chatter of happy eaters who plough through pounds of coconut crab cakes, Boom Boom shrimp and homegrown Pine Island clams. Do as they do and order tried-and-tested classics. The blackened grouper and baby back ribs are winners; the Big Bomber burrito not so much.

🔒 Shopping

⭐ **Lovegrove Gallery**   ARTS & CRAFTS
(☑239-283-6453; www.leomalovegrove.com; 4637 Pine Island Rd, Matlacha; ☺11am-5pm Fri-Mon) If Matlacha is unexpectedly groovy for such a sun-faded fishing village, you can thank artist Leoma Lovegrove. Her gallery has transformed a fishing shack into a whimsical vision of tile mosaics and paintings, with a loopy 'Tropical Waterways Garden' in back. Now the whole block is a bona fide slice of roadside Americana, with unusual gift and craft shops.

ℹ Information

For more information, visit www.pineisland-chamber.org and www.floridascreativecoast.com.

ℹ Getting There & Around

Pine Island is due west of North Fort Myers and is not accessible by public transportation. By car, take US 41 to Pine Island Rd (Hwy 78), and head west.

Boat charters and water taxis are available at Pineland and Matlacha Marinas.

ℹ THE GREAT CALUSA BLUEWAY

With almost 200 miles of kayaking routes, the Great Calusa Blueway (www.calusablueway.com) is like a watery circulation system that snakes throughout Lee County, much of it hugging the coast of Pine Island, and extending further afield to the shores of Cayo Costa, Captiva and Sanibel Islands, Fort Myers Beach and down to Bonita Springs. The warm, calm waters are a joy to paddle, and there's a lot you miss on land that's only visible by boat. Check the website for 'trails' and where they can be accessed.

Fort Myers

☑239 / POP 62,300

Nestled inland along the Caloosahatchee River, and separated from Fort Myers Beach by several miles of urban sprawl, the city of Fort Myers is often defined by what it's not: it's not an upscale, arty beach town like Sarasota or Naples, and it's not as urbanely sophisticated as Tampa or St Petersburg. While it isn't a city to base a trip around, it's worth a trip to browse its brick-lined main street and visit Thomas Edison's winter home and laboratory.

◉ Sights & Activities

Most of Fort Myers' sights are in a compact area near the US 41 bridge along the river. The historic district is a six-block grid of streets along 1st St between Broadway and Lee St, extending to the riverfront.

⭐ **Edison & Ford Winter Estates**   MUSEUM
(☑239-334-7419;   www.edisonfordwinterestates.org; 2350 McGregor Blvd; adult/child $20/11; ☺9am-5:30pm) Florida's snowbirds can be easy to mock, but not this pair. Thomas Edison built his winter home in 1885 and lived in Florida seasonally until his death in 1931. Edison's friend Henry Ford built his adjacent bungalow in 1916. Together, and sometimes side by side in Edison's lab, these two inventors, businessmen and neighbors changed our world. The museum does an excellent job of presenting the overwhelming scope of their achievements.

Edison, Ford and Harvey Firestone were dedicated 'tin-can tourists' who enjoyed driving and camping across America together,

Fort Myers

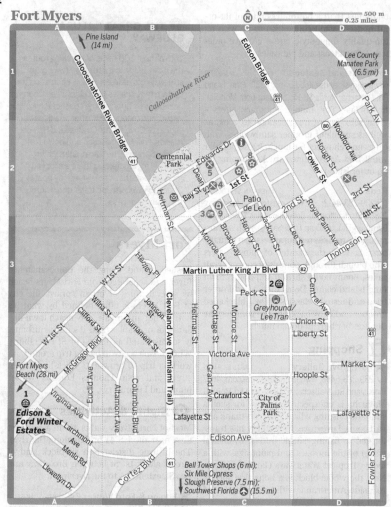

and exhibits chronicle their journeys and how these fed their refinements of the automobile. Indeed, the main purpose of Edison's Fort Myers lab was to develop a domestic source of rubber (primarily using goldenrod plants) for auto manufacturing, although he then went on to file 1093 patents for things like the lightbulb, the phonograph, wafflemakers and sprocketed celluloid film.

The rich botanical gardens and genteel homes very nearly glow, and are decked out with historical goodies and period furniture. Don't forgo the self-guided audio tour of the estates (guided tours cost $5 extra).

Six Mile Cypress
Slough Preserve   NATURE RESERVE
(239-533-7550; www.sloughpreserve.org; 7791 Penzance Blvd; parking per hr/day $1/5; dawn-dusk) FREE A 2000-acre slough (pronounced 'slew'), this park is a great place to experience southwest Florida's flora and fauna. A 1.2-mile boardwalk trail is staffed by volunteers who help explain the epiphytes, cypress knees, migrating birds and nesting alligators you'll find. Wildlife-watchers should target the winter dry season. The wet summer season is also dramatic of course: at its peak, the entire slough becomes a forested stream up to 3ft deep. The nature

center (open from 10am to 4pm Tuesday to Sunday) has excellent displays and offers free guided walks.

From Fort Myers, go south on Cleveland Ave/US 41, east on Colonial Blvd/Hwy 884, then south for 3 miles on Ortiz Ave (which becomes Six Mile Cypress Pkwy).

Southwest Florida Museum of History   MUSEUM
(☑239-321-7430; www.swflmuseumofhistory.com; 2031 Jackson St; adult/child 3-18yr $9.50/5; ☺10am-5pm Tue-Sat; 👪) Crammed with artifacts, this small museum leapfrogs from the giant sloths of the Pleistocene Era to the twisted props of downed WWII fighter jets in a veritable blink. Along the way, iron cannons and Calusa dugout canoes, a Cracker house and an iron lung provide snapshots of Florida through the ages. If you have kids, get combo tickets with the Imaginarium.

Lee County Manatee Park   WILDLIFE RESERVE
(☑239-690-5030; www.leeparks.org; 10901 State Rd 80; parking per hr/day $2/5; ☺8am-sunset daily) **FREE** November through March, manatees flock up the Orange River to this warm-water discharge canal from the nearby power plant. The waterway is now a protected sanctuary, with a landscaped park and playground in addition to viewing platforms at water's edge, where manatees swim almost at arm's reach. **Calusa Blueway Outfitters** (☑239-481-4600; www.calusabluewayoutfitters.com; 10901 Palm Beach Blvd) rents kayaks.

The park is signed off Hwy 80, about 6.5 miles from downtown Fort Myers, and 1.5 miles east of I-75.

🚩 Tours

Classic Air Ventures   AIR TOUR
(☑941-505-9226; http://coastalbiplanetours.com; 605 Danley Dr; per 2 people $280-380; ☺10am-5:30pm Mon-Sat Oct-May) At Page Field, off Cleveland Ave, just south of downtown Fort Myers, Classic Air operates restored 1940s open-cockpit biplanes (that's right, goggles, leather helmet and all). It offers three different flights from 35 to 60 minutes in length.

✷ Festivals & Events

Edison Festival of Light   CULTURE
(www.edisonfestival.org; ☺Feb) For two weeks around Edison's birthday on February 11, Fort Myers offers dozens of mostly free events including street fairs, antique-car shows, music and the best school-sponsored science fair you'll ever see. Everything culminates in the enormous Parade of Light.

🛏 Sleeping & Eating

Some of the area's best budget options are the midrange chain hotels that line S Cleveland Ave near the airport: try the popular Hampton Inn and Homewood Suites (www.hilton.com).

For dining, the historic downtown has plenty of attractive choices. The upscale Bell Tower Shops, at S Cleveland Ave and Cypress Lake Dr, also has several.

Hotel Indigo   HOTEL $$
(☑239-337-3446; www.hotelindigo.com/fortmyers-fl; 1520 Broadway; r $120-240; ✻@🛜🏊) Now anchoring the downtown historic district, this boutique chain makes an attractive, reliable stay. The 67 rooms have powder-blue comforters, wall murals, a mix of wood floors and carpets, and snazzy glass-door showers. The kicker is the small rooftop pool and bar, with panoramic views of the scenic riverfront. Valet parking costs $14.

Wisteria Tea Room   CAFE $
(☑239-689-4436; http://wisteriatearoom.com; 2512 2nd St; lunch items $5-12, afternoon tea $9-24; ☺11am-3pm Mon-Sat) Housed in a remodeled Florida bungalow with gleaming wooden floors, this quaint tearoom is a favorite ladies lunch spot. Beat them to it, as the thick slabs of quiche, homemade meatloaf sandwich and fragrant asparagus soup are excellent. And that's to say nothing of the outstanding

savory teas, which come with tiers of apricot scones and dollops of Devonshire cream.

Spirits of Bacchus   TAPAS $$

(☑239-689-2675; www.spiritsofbacchus.com; 1406 Hendry St; small plates $7-12; ☺4pm-late Mon-Fri, 6-8pm Sat,1-8pm Sun) This stylish exposed-brick saloon is a favorite Fort Myers watering hole. It serves a range of fancy tapas, sandwiches and bar food, along with wine and cocktails. Nosh and slosh your way through an evening on the vine-wrapped patio.

City Tavern   AMERICAN $$

(☑239-226-1133; www.mycitytavern.com; 2206 Bay St; mains $8-16; ☺11am-11pm Sun-Wed, to 2am Thu-Sat) This former dive bar may have retained the TVs, darts board and pool table, but TV chef Brian Duffy has revamped its tired menu and brew list to include packed *muffaletta* and Cuban sandwiches, and craft brews.

Farmers Market Restaurant   SOUTHERN $$

(☑239-334-1687; http://farmersmarketrestaurant. com; 2736 Edison Ave; mains $12-14; ☺6am-8pm) Pleasing diners with its simple Southern comfort food since 1950s, this modest place has a loyal local following. It's nothing fancy, but if you're hankering after some fried chicken and mustard greens and whitefish and grits, this is the place for you. It's a five-minute drive southwest of downtown.

Cantina Laredo   MEXICAN $$

(☑239-415-4424; www.cantinalaredo.com; 5200 Big Pine Way, Bell Tower Shops; mains $12-23; ☺11am-10pm Sun-Thu, noon-11pm Fri & Sat) Maybe it's the margarita talking, but this atmospheric Mexican chain does everything right: sharp service, low and romantic lighting, top-shelf tequila, Mexican beer on tap and guacamole made fresh tableside. The *poblano asado* (steak-wrapped *poblano* pepper) is delicious. From downtown, it's a 15-minute drive south along S Cleveland Ave to Bell Tower Shops.

🍸 Drinking & Entertainment

The historic downtown, in and around 1st St, is plenty active come nightfall; definitely cruise the restaurants and bars in Patio de Leon, a courtyard off Hendry St near 1st St. The district becomes a veritable street party twice every month: for the Fort Myers Art Walk (www.fortmyersartwalk.com) on the first Friday of the month and the Music Walk (www.fortmyersmusicwalk.com) on the third Saturday of the month.

Theater

⭐ **Arcade Theatre**   THEATER

(☑239-332-4488; www.floridarep.org; 2267 1st St; tickets $17-40; ☺Oct-May) The 1908 Arcade Theatre is home to the **Florida Repertory Theatre**, one of the best regional theaters in the state. It produces popular comedies, musicals and recent Tony winners, such as *The Seafarer*.

Davis Art Center   PERFORMING ARTS

(☑239-333-1933; www.sbdac.com; 2301 1st St; ☺Oct-Jun) This downtown performance space produces an eclectic slate of drama, children's theater, dance, music and film.

Sports

March in Fort Myers means major-league baseball's spring training. **Boston Red Sox** (www.redsox.com) fans literally camp out for tickets to **JetBlue Park** (www.leeparks. org; 11500 Fenway S Dr) on Hwy 876. The **Minnesota Twins** (www.mntwins.com) play in Hammond Stadium at **Lee County Sports Complex** (14100 Six Mile Cypress Pkwy), just southwest of the intersection of Daniels Pkwy and Six Mile Cypress Pkwy. During the regular season, the Fort Myers Miracles (the Minnesota Twins' class A minor-league baseball team) play here.

🛍 Shopping

Franklin Shops   ARTS & CRAFTS

(www.thefranklinshops.com; 2200 1st St; ☺10am-8pm Mon-Sat, noon-7pm Sun) Riding Fort Myers' upsurge in artsy cool, this gift store and gallery represents more than 60 local artists and businesses, including Leoma Lovegrove and Bert's of Matlacha. Great for only-in-southwest-Florida gifts.

ℹ Information

Greater Fort Myers Chamber of Commerce (☑239-332-3624; www.fortmyers.org; 2310 Edwards Dr; ☺9am-5pm Mon-Fri) Lots of info and can help you find a room.

Lee Memorial Hospital (☑239-343-2000; www.leememorial.org; 2776 Cleveland Ave; ☺24hr) The area's largest hospital.

ℹ Getting There & Around

A car is essential. US 41/S Cleveland Ave is the main north–south artery. From downtown, both Summerlin Rd/Hwy 869 and McGregor Blvd/Hwy 867 eventually merge and lead to Sanibel Island; they also connect with San Carlos Blvd/Hwy 865 to Fort Myers Beach.

Greyhound (www.greyhound.com; 2250 Peck St) Connects Fort Myers to Miami, Orlando and Tampa.

Southwest Florida International Airport (RSW; ✈ 239-590-4800; http://flylcpa.com; 11000 Terminal Access Rd) Take I-75 from Fort Myers and exit 131/Daniels Pkwy. This is also the main airport for nearby Naples.

LeeTran (www.rideleetran.com; 2250 Widman Way; ride $1.25) Routes run to Fort Myers Beach and Pine Island, but not to Sanibel or Captiva Islands.

Fort Myers Beach

✈ 239 / POP 6300

Like Clearwater Beach and St Pete Beach, Fort Myers Beach foments a party atmosphere year-round, and spring unfolds like one long-running street festival slash fraternity bash. And yet, situated on the 7-mile-long Estero Island, Fort Myers Beach has sand and space enough to accommodate all needs and ages. In the north, the so-called Times Sq area is a walkable concentration that verily epitomizes 'sun-bleached seaside party town.' Head south and the beachfront becomes more residential, less crowded and much quieter.

🏃 Activities

Fort Myers Beach BEACH
Fort Myers Beach is long, long, long. The southern end is dominated by condos, with very little public access. The low-key middle has a large number of end-of-road access points with tiny metered lots. The northern Times Sq area, right where the causeway dumps visitors, has large paid lots (per day from $5 to $10) and is typically packed and loud, with beach bars pumping out the music. Parasail and water-sport concessions congregate thickly here, and a bait house on the pier rents fishing rods.

Bowditch Point Park PARK, BEACH
(✈ 239-765-6794; www.leeparks.org; 50 Estero Blvd; ⊙ 7am-sunset) At the island's northernmost tip, Bowditch is a favorite with families and picnickers. The small parking lot (per hour $2) fills up fast, so come early. There's a good snack bar, free boat dockage, kayak and paddleboard rentals. You'll also find a butterfly garden, expansive picnic areas and a replenished beach that narrows around the tip. It's a good place to view dolphins fishing in the Matanzas Pass and there's a paddle launch onto the Great Calusa Blueway (p411) paddling trail.

The beach can be reached by the local buses that run along Estero Blvd.

Lovers Key State Park BEACH
(✈ 239-463-4588; www.floridastateparks.org/loverskey; 8700 Estero Blvd; car/bike $8/2; ⊙ 8am-sunset) In the mood for a good hike, bike or kayak, with a chance to spot manatees in spring and summer? Come to Lovers Key, just south (and over a bridge) from Estero Island. Canals and 2.6 miles of trails around inner islands provide head-clearing quietude and bird-watching. The long, narrow beach is excellent for shelling, but erosion can make it too slim to lay a towel at high tide. There're a snack bar, rental concessions and nice facilities; a tram shuttles between beach and parking lot.

🎉 Festivals & Events

Fort Myers Beach Shrimp Festival FOOD
(www.fortmyersbeachshrimpfestival.com; ⊙ Mar) For two weekends in early March, Fort Myers celebrates the glorious Gulf pink shrimp with parades, beauty queens, craft fairs and lots of cooking.

American Sandsculpting Championship CULTURE
(www.fmbsandsculpting.com; ⊙ Nov) Four-day national sand-sculpting event, with amateur and pro divisions, during the first weekend in November.

🛏 Sleeping

You'll pay extra to be near the bars, restaurants and party crowds of Times Sq. For those seeking quieter accommodation, head south.

Dolphin Inn MOTEL $
(✈ 239-463-6049; www.dolphininn.net; 6555 Estero Blvd; r $80-140; ❀ @ 🎧 🐕) This vintage Old Florida motel is best if you get one of the newly renovated rooms. However, all rooms sport no-fuss furniture and have full kitchens; the best are bayside, overlooking a scenic residential harbor where manatees play. Amenities include a sizable L-shaped pool, communal grills, loaner kayaks, a DVD library and cheap bike rental.

★ **Mango Street Inn** B&B $$
(✈ 239-233-8542; www.mangostreetinn.com; 126 Mango St; r $95-165; ❀ 🎧 🐕) Mango Street's affable husband-and-wife owners have created a winning seaside B&B: its eclectic, idiosyncratic decor is funky and memorable but relaxed enough to feel homey. The six rooms with full kitchens hug an interior

courtyard that has a wood deck and pretty pergola. It's a short walk to the beach, and the B&B has loaner bikes and beach gear. Most memorable, though, is the gourmet breakfast; Dan is a Cajun-trained chef.

Manatee Bay Inn INN $$
([☎]239-463-6906; www.manateebayinn.com; 932 Third St; r $115-209; [P][※][🐾][🏊]) Situated a block back from Times Sq with views over a sleepy inlet, Manatee Bay offers the best of both worlds. By day you can position yourself on one of the sun loungers on the deck overhanging the water and by night stroll down to Times Sq for cocktails, eats and fun. The six suites are decorated in tropical style and come equipped with kitchens, beach paraphernalia and outdoor BBQs.

★ Edison Beach House HOTEL $$$
([☎]239-463-1530; www.edisonbeachhouse.com; 830 Estero Blvd; r $145-415; [※][🐾][🏊]) This all-suite hotel was designed smartly from the ground up and proudly maintains impeccable standards. Attractive decor and rattan furniture are pleasing and all suites frame perfect ocean views from nice balconies. The more sizable rooms are comfortable for longer stays. Fully equipped kitchens feature good-quality appliances; each room has a washer-dryer. It's beachside near the pier, and walkable to Times Sq.

✕ Eating & Drinking

Most of the action is centered on Times Sq, which is rife with middling eateries and seafood joints, several with live-music bars that can become quite raucous after sunset.

Heavenly Biscuit BREAKFAST $
(110 Mango St; items $3-8; ⊙8am-noon Mon, 7:30am-2pm Tue-Sun) This unassuming shack offers two genuine delights: sumptuous fresh-baked buttermilk biscuits – overflowing with eggs, cheese and bacon – and delectable cinnamon rolls. Eat directly off the waxed paper on the tiny porch or get it to go; you can build a bigger breakfast with grits and home fries. It's nothing fancy or highbrow, just a simple thing done right.

Smokin' Oyster Brewery SEAFOOD $$
([☎]239-463-3474; www.smokinoyster.com; 340 Old San Carlos Blvd; $6-14; ⊙11am-11pm) You can rock up in your bathing suit and flip-flops at this open-air beach bar just steps from Fort Myers Beach. Order a platter of oysters or a bucket of steamed shrimp, corn and red potatoes. Caught your own? Bring it along and

they'll cook it for you. Every evening there's live music, and happy hour runs from 3pm to 5:30pm.

Doc Ford's SEAFOOD $$
([☎]239-765-9660; www.docfords.com; 708 Fisherman's Wharf; mains $10-22; ⊙11am-10pm, bar till late) Part-owner Randy Wayne White once lived on the marina here, and he named this scenic wharf eatery after his beloved mystery-novel protagonist, marine biologist Doc Ford. The wood-sided building with spacious decks, big windows and multiple bars emphasizes Floribbean flavors and a Latin American spice rack. It's on the mainland at the base of the causeway bridge.

Beached Whale SEAFOOD $$
([☎]239-463-5505; www.thebeachedwhale.com; 1249 Estero Blvd; mains $10-18; ⊙11am-2am) The breezy upstairs deck is a long-standing favorite for a reliable sunset meal with gulf views; go for either grilled seafood or sticky-sweet barbecue. An older crowd creates a friendly vibe in this unpretentious local watering hole, which has live music and gets rowdier later in the evening.

Fresh Catch Bistro SEAFOOD $$$
([☎]239-463-2600; www.freshcatchbistro.com; 3040 Estero Beach Blvd; mains $14-50) This nautically themed bistro is a cut above other seafood restaurants on the beach. Inside, a wall of windows frames stunning sunsets or lightning streaks across the waves, and a vaulted wooden roof arcs over linen-dressed tables. Here diners tuck in to Pine Islands clams on ice, Point Judith calamari fried with mild cherry peppers and grouper sandwiches with a side of Cajun rémoulade and apple fennel slaw.

ⓘ Information

Greater Fort Myers Beach Chamber of Commerce ([☎]239-454-7500; www.fortmyersbeachchamber.org; 17200 San Carlos Blvd; ⊙9am-5pm Mon-Fri, 10am-5pm Sat, 10am-3pm Sun) On the mainland, about 2 miles north of the Sky Bridge. It maintains a list of hotel vacancies.

ⓘ Getting There & Around

The main drag, Estero Blvd, runs the island's length, from Bowditch Point Park in the north to Lover's Key State Park.

Key West Express ([☎]239-463-5733; www.seakeywestexpress.com; 1200 Main St; single fare adult/child $86/20) Offers daily sailings to the Keys, departing at 8:30am from a dock on the mainland (take a left just prior to the causeway). The trip takes 3½ hours, so you may want to consider an overnight stay.

LeeTran Trolley (www.rideleetran.com; adult/reduced $1.25/0.60; ☺ 6:30am-9:25pm) Plies the island's length daily, and connects to Fort Myers buses at Summerlin Sq on the mainland.

Sanibel & Captiva Islands

☑ 239 / POP SANIBEL 6500: CAPTIVA 580

By preference and by design, island life on Sanibel and Captiva is informal and egalitarian, and riches are rarely flaunted. Even Captiva's mansions are hidden behind thick foliage and sport playful names such as 'Seas the Day.' Development on Sanibel has been carefully managed: the northern half is almost entirely protected within the JN 'Ding' Darling National Wildlife Refuge. While there are hotels aplenty, the beachfront is free of commercial-and-condo blight. Plus, public beach access is limited to a handful of spread-out parking lots, so there is no crush of day-trippers in one place.

There is no 'downtown.' On Sanibel, businesses and restaurants are spread leisurely along the inner-island corridor: Periwinkle Way, which becomes Sanibel-Captiva Rd. On Captiva, the tiny village is confined to a single street, Andy Rosse Lane. There are no traffic lights and the preferred mode of transport is the family-friendly bike.

☺ Sights

The quality of **shelling** on Sanibel is so high that dedicated hunters are identified by their hunchbacked 'Sanibel stoop.' If you're serious, buy a scoop net, get a shell guide from the visitor center and peruse the blog www.iloveshelling.com.

Fourteen miles of largely public-access beaches offer you lots of room to choose from. Most beaches except Blind Pass have restrooms; none of the beaches have concessions or snack bars. Parking is $2 per hour.

JN 'Ding' Darling
National Wildlife Refuge   WILDLIFE RESERVE
(☑ 239-472-1100;   www.fws.gov/dingdarling;   1 Wildlife Dr; car/cyclist $5/1; ☺ 7am-7pm Sat-Thu Apr-Oct, to 5:30pm Nov-Mar) Named for cartoonist Jay Norwood 'Ding' Darling, an environmentalist who helped establish more than 300 sanctuaries across the USA, this 6300-acre refuge is home to an abundance of seabirds and wildlife, including alligators, night herons, red-shouldered hawks, spotted sandpipers, roseate spoonbills, pelicans and anhinga. The refuge's 5-mile **Wildlife Drive** provides easy access, but bring binoculars; flocks sometimes sit at expansive distances. Only a few very short walks lead into the mangroves. For the best, most intimate experience, canoe or kayak Tarpon Bay.

Don't miss the free **visitors center** (open from 9am to 5pm), which has excellent exhibits on refuge life and Darling himself. Naturalist-narrated Wildlife Drive tram tours depart from the visitor-center parking lot, usually on the hour from 10am to 4pm.

Bowman's Beach   BEACH
(1700 Bowman's Beach Rd) Bowman's Beach is the quintessential Sanibel beach, a bright dollop of coast with soft white sand, supplied with a playground and excellent facilities. It's remote in the sense that it rarely feels crowded, except perhaps at the height of tourist season. Alphabet cones, angel wings, lightning whelks and horse conch shells all glitter on the powder. Excellent views to the west make for magical sunsets.

'No nude sunbathing' signs are meant to dissuade scofflaws from doing just that at the distant west end.

Lighthouse Beach   BEACH
(112 Periwinkle Way) The most photogenic of the beaches, Lighthouse Beach sports Sanibel's historic metal lighthouse (1884) on the eastern tip of the island. There's also a T-dock, off which pelicans dive-bomb, and a short boardwalk around the point. Park in the lot and walk over a bridge to the narrow beach.

Turner & Blind Pass Beaches   BEACH
(Sanibel-Captiva Rd) Every shell in the Gulf seems to make it a mission to wash up on either Blind Pass Beach or Turner Beach, two short stretches on either side of the Captiva Island Bridge. Turner Beach really rocks during amazing sunsets over the Gulf.

Captiva Beach   BEACH
(14790 Captiva Dr) Besides looking directly out onto heart-melting Gulf sunsets, Captiva Beach has lovely sand and is located close to several romantic restaurants. Arrive early if you want to park in the small lot or come by bike.

Bailey-Matthews Shell Museum   MUSEUM
(☑ 239-395-2233;   www.shellmuseum.org;   3075 Sanibel-Captiva Rd, Sanibel; adult/child 5-16yr $9/5; ☺ 10am-5pm) Like a mermaid's jewelry box, this museum is dedicated to shells, yet it's much more than a covetous display of treasures. It's a crisply presented natural history of

the sea, detailing the life and times of the bivalves, mollusks and other creatures who reside inside their calcium homes. It also shows the role of these animals and shells in human culture, medicine and cuisine. Fascinating videos show living creatures. It's nearly a must after a day spent combing the beaches.

Sanibel Historical Village   HISTORIC SITE
(☎239-472-4648; www.sanibelmuseum.org; 950 Dunlop Rd; adult/child $10/free; ◷10am-1pm Wed-Sat May-Aug, to 4pm Nov-Apr) Well polished by the enthusiasm of local volunteers, this museum and collection of nine historic buildings preserves Sanibel's pioneer past. It gives a piquant taste of settler life, with a general store, post office, cottage and more.

🏃 Activities

Nearly all of Sanibel's main roads are paralleled by paved bike paths; on Captiva, main roads have bike lanes. Bikes have preference at road crossings, and they scoot by auto backups and full parking lots at public beaches. So rent a bike and forget your worries.

Billy's Rentals   BICYCLE RENTAL
(☎239-472-5248; www.billysrentals.com; 1470 Periwinkle Way, Sanibel; bikes per 2hr/day $5/15; ◷8:30am-5pm) Billy's rents every type of wheeled contrivance, including joggers, tandems, surreys, scooters and more. From Monday to Saturday, by reservation, it also offers three daily segway tours (per person $60) at 9am, 11:30am and 2pm.

Tarpon Bay Explorers   KAYAKING
(☎239-472-8900; www.tarponbayexplorers.com; 900 Tarpon Bay Rd, Sanibel; ◷8am-6pm) Within the Darling refuge, this outfitter rents canoes and kayaks ($25 for two hours) for easy, self-guided paddles in Tarpon Bay, a perfect place for young paddlers. Guided kayak trips (adult from $30 to $40, child from $20 to $25) are also excellent, and there's a range of other trips and deck talks. Reserve ahead or come early, as trips book up.

'Tween Waters Marina   KAYAKING
(☎239-472-5161; www.tween-waters.com; 15951 Captiva Rd, Captiva; ◷7:30am-5:30pm) For a more-involved kayak, target Buck Key off Captiva. 'Tween Waters Marina, at the 'Tween Waters Inn, can set you up with rentals ($25 for two hours) and guided kayak tours ($40).

Sanibel Recreation Center   HEALTH & FITNESS
(☎239-472-0345; www.mysanibel.com; 3880 Sanibel-Captiva Rd, Sanibel; per person/family $12/20; ◷6:30am-8pm Mon-Thu, to 6:30pm Fri, 8am-5pm Sat & Sun) Want resort amenities without paying resort prices? Frequent this pristine rec center. It has a lap pool, kids' pool with waterslide, extensive exercise room, four tennis courts and an indoor games room, and all classes are included in the day fee. Call for open-swim hours, which vary.

👉 Tours

Boats and cruises are nearly as ubiquitous as shells on the islands.

Sanibel Marina   BOAT TOUR
(☎239-472-2723; www.sanibelmarina.com; 634 N Yachtsman Dr) The main small-boat harbor on Sanibel has a ton of boat rentals (from $125) and charters (from $350).

McCarthy's Marina   CRUISE
(☎239-472-5200; www.mccarthysmarina.com; 11401 Andy Rosse Lane, Captiva) This is where **Captiva Cruises** (☎239-472-5300; www.captivacruises.com; 11400 Andy Rosse Lane) departs from. It offers everything from dolphin and sunset cruises (from $25) to various island excursions, such as Cayo Costa ($35), Cabbage Key ($40) and Boca Grande ($50) on Gasparilla Island.

🎉 Festivals & Events

Sanibel Music Festival   MUSIC
(www.sanibelmusicfestival.org; ◷Mar) A classical- and chamber-music festival that draws international musicians for a month-long concert series every Tuesday and Saturday in March.

'Ding' Darling Days   CULTURE
(www.dingdarlingsociety.org/dingdarlingdays.php; ◷Oct) A week-long celebration of the wildlife refuge, with birding tours, workshops and guest speakers.

Sanibel Luminary Fest   CULTURE
(◷Dec) Sanibel's signature street fair occurs the first weekend of December, when paper luminaries line the island's bike paths.

🛏 Sleeping

As elsewhere, low season sees a huge drop in rates.

If you're interested in a one-week vacation rental, contact **Sanibel & Captiva Accommodations** (☎800-656-9111; www.sanibelaccom.com).

Tarpon Tale Inn   MOTEL $$
(☎239-472-0939; www.tarpontale.com; 367 Periwinkle Way, Sanibel; r $99-260; 🅿@🛜🐾) The five charming tile-floored rooms evoke a bright blue-and-white seaside mood and are

TAMPA BAY & SOUTHWEST FLORIDA SANIBEL & CAPTIVA ISLANDS

well located for Sanibel's Old Town; each has its own shady porch and tree-strung hammock. On offer are two efficiencies and three rooms with full kitchens. With communal hot tub and loaner bikes, it does a nice imitation of a B&B without the breakfast.

Sandpiper Inn   INN $$
(☑239-472-1529; www.palmviewsanibel.com; 720 Donax St, Sanibel; r $99-199; P❋❄) Set a block back from the water and in close proximity to the shops and restaurants on Periwinkle Way, this Old Florida inn offers good value for Sanibel. Each of the one-bedroom units has a bedroom, a functional (if dated) kitchen and a spacious sitting area decked out in tropical colors.

⭐'Tween Waters Inn   RESORT $$$
(☑239-472-5161; www.tween-waters.com; 15951 Captiva Dr, Captiva; r $185-285, ste $270-410, cottages $265-460; ❋@❄❋❋) For great resort value on Captiva, choose 'Tween Waters Inn. Rooms are attractive roosts with rattan furnishings, granite counters, rainfall showerheads and Tommy Bahama–style decor. All have balconies; those directly facing the Gulf are splendid, and tidy little cottages are romantic. Families make good use of the big pool, tennis courts, full-service marina and spa. Multinight discounts are attractive.

Blue Dolphin Cottages   MOTEL $$$
(☑239-472-1600; www.bluedolphincottages.com; 4227 W Gulf Dr, Sanibel; r $135-285; ❋❄) On a secluded stretch of Gulf Dr, Blue Dolphin has 11 duplex rooms set within pretty gardens right on the beach. Most have full kitchens, and all have well-kept, easy-clean, standard seaside decor. It's worth paying that bit extra for the deluxe efficiencies. Communal grills face the water, and Continental breakfast is included.

Mitchell's Sandcastles   MOTEL $$$
(☑239-472-1282; www.mitchellssandcastles.com; 3951 W Gulf Dr; r $160-280; P❋❄❋❋) Mitchell's is a Gulf Dr getaway choice right on the beach. Its 25 rooms are strictly standard, but each has full kitchen and its own grill. The range of amenities appeals to families: a small pool, tennis court, fitness center, and loaner kayaks and bikes.

✖ Eating

Sanibel Bean   CAFE $
(www.sanibelbean.com; 2240 Periwinkle Way, Sanibel; mains $5-9; ⊘7am-9pm; ❄❋) Popular lo-

cal hangout with an extensive cafe menu of quick, cheap eats.

Over Easy Cafe   CAFE $$
(☑239-472-2625; www.overeasycafesanibel.com; 630 Tarpon Bay Rd, at Periwinkle Way, Sanibel; mains $8-14; ⊘7am-3pm; ❋) Despite Provence-style decor, the menu offers strictly top-quality diner fare, including eggs every which way. Add fluffy pancakes, good coffee and friendly, efficient service, and this becomes Sanibel's go-to morning choice – so expect a wait. In summer, it also opens for dinner from Tuesday to Saturday.

Lazy Flamingo   SEAFOOD $$
(☑239-472-5353; www.lazyflamingo.com; 6520 Pine Ave, Sanibel Island; mains $6-15; ⊘11am-midnight; ❋) Look for the Pepto Bismol–pink shack just before Blind Pass and you'll have found the friendly Lazy Flamingo. This is where locals go for blackened grouper sandwiches, conch fritters and ragingly spicy Dead Parrot Wings. It ain't fancy, but it's family-friendly and the shrimp-boat decor, outdoor tables and scallop-shaped plates are no-fuss fun.

There's another outlet at the other end of the island at 1036 Periwinkle Way.

Mucky Duck   PUB $$
(www.muckyduck.com; 11546 Andy Rosse Lane, Captiva; mains $10-25; ⊘11:30am-3pm & 5-9:30pm Mon-Sat) The unpretentious, shingle-roofed Mucky Duck is perfectly positioned for Captiva sunsets, and devoted locals jockey for beach chairs and picnic tables each evening. The extended menu offers more than just pub grub, with pasta, steak, chicken and seafood. Really, though, it's the friendly bar and toes-in-the-sand Gulf views that keep 'em coming.

⭐Mad Hatter Restaurant   AMERICAN $$$
(☑239-472-0033; www.madhatterrestaurant.com; 6467 Sanibel-Captiva Rd, Sanibel; mains $29-45; ⊘6-9pm) 🍴 Vacationing Manhattan and Miami urbanites flock to what is widely regarded as Sanibel's best locavore gourmet restaurant. Contemporary seafood is the central focus, with creative appetizers such as oysters and a seafood martini, while mains emphasize bouillabaisse, crab cakes, pan-seared grouper and so on. As the name suggests, it's not stuffy, but it's for culinary mavens whose concern is quality, whatever the price.

★ **Sweet Melissa's Cafe** AMERICAN $$$
(☑239-472-1956; www.sweetmelissascafe.net;
1625 Periwinkle Way, Sanibel; tapas $9-16, mains
$26-34; ⊙11:30am-2:30pm & 5-9pm Mon-Fri,
5-9pm Sat) From menu to mood, Sweet Melissa's offers well-balanced, relaxed refinement.
Dishes are creative without trying too hard,
and most mains can be served tapas size,
which encourages experimenting. Try the
shrimp with grits, seared scallops over curried cauliflower, grilled romaine and the
refreshing watermelon salad. Service is attentive and the atmosphere upbeat.

Gramma Dot's SEAFOOD $$$
(☑239-472-8138; www.sanibelmarina.com/gramma.html; N Yachtsman Dr, Sanibel Marina; lunch $11-
15, dinner $19-25; ⊙11:30am-8pm) Pull up a bar
stool next to the charter-boat captains at this
longtime Sanibel Marina favorite. Enjoy a no-
fuss fried-oyster sandwich, mesquite-grilled
grouper or the coconut shrimp, plus Caesar
salad several ways. A great lunch stop.

ⓘ Information

Sanibel & Captiva Islands Chamber of Commerce (☑239-472-1080; www.sanibel-captiva.
org; 1159 Causeway Rd, Sanibel; ⊙9am-5pm;
🐾) One of the more helpful visitor centers
around; keeps an updated hotel-vacancy list
with dedicated hotel hotline.

ⓘ Getting There & Around

Driving is the only way to come and go. The Sanibel
Causeway (Hwy 867) charges an entrance toll
(cars/motorcycles $6/2). Sanibel is 12 miles long,
and Captiva 5 miles, but low speed limits and traffic
make them seem longer. The main drag is Periwinkle Way, which becomes Sanibel-Captiva Rd.

Corkscrew Swamp Sanctuary

The crown jewel in the National Audubon
Society's sanctuary collection, the **Corkscrew Swamp Sanctuary** (☑239-348-9151;
www.corkscrew.audubon.org; 375 Sanctuary Rd W;
adult/child 6-18yr $12/4; ⊙7am-5:30pm Oct–mid-
Apr) provides an intimate exploration of six
pristine native habitats, including sawgrass,
slash pine and marsh, along a shady 2.25-
mile boardwalk trail. The centerpiece is
North America's oldest virgin bald-cypress
forest, with majestic specimens more than
600 years old and 130ft tall. Abundant wildlife includes nesting alligators, night herons,
endangered wood storks and trees full of

ibis. However, two rare species, when spotted, make the news: the famed ghost orchid
and the elusive Florida panther. Volunteers
help point out wildlife, and signage is excellent; the visitor center rents binoculars ($3).
Corkscrew is as good as the Everglades.

The preserve is southeast of Fort Myers
and northeast of Naples; take I-75 exit 111
and head east on Hwy 846/Imokalee Rd to
Sanctuary Rd; follow signs. Bring repellent
for deer flies in late spring.

Naples

☑239 / POP 19,550

For upscale romance and the prettiest, most
serene city beach in southwest Florida, come
to Naples, the Gulf Coast's answer to Palm
Beach. As on Sanibel and Captiva Islands, development along the shoreline has been kept
residential. The soft white sand is backed only
by narrow dunes and half-hidden mansions.
More than that, though, Naples is a cultured,
sophisticated town, stylish and privileged,
but also welcoming and fun-loving. Families,
teens, couture-wearing matrons, middle-aged
executives and smartly dressed young couples all mix and mingle as they stroll downtown's 5th Ave on a balmy evening. Travelers
sometimes complain that Naples is expensive, but it's equally true that you can spend
as much elsewhere for a whole lot less.

⊙ Sights

Downtown Naples is laid out on a grid.
There are two primary retail corridors: the
main one is 5th Ave between 9th St S/US
41 and W Lake Dr. Pretty, picnic-friendly
Cambier Park (cnr 8th St S & 6th Ave S) is here.
The other retail district runs along 3rd St
S between Broad Ave S and 14th St S; this
area, called **Third St South**, forms the heart
of Old Naples. Throughout the area there's
a mix of Mediterranean Revival and board-and-batten Cracker cottages. From spring to
fall the Old Naples district hosts a range of
events: music, art and a Saturday-morning
farmers market. See the online calendar at
www.thirdstreetsouth.com.

All downtown parking (off-beach) is free.

★ **Baker Museum** MUSEUM
(☑239-597-1900; www.artisnaples.org; 5833 Pelican Bay Blvd; adult/child $10/free; ⊙10am-8pm
Tue, to 4pm Wed-Sat, noon-4pm Sun) The pride
of Naples, this engaging, sophisticated art
museum is part of the Artis–Naples campus,
which includes the fabulous Philharmonic

Center next door. Devoted to 20th-century modernism, particularly American abstract expressionism, the museum hosts an exciting round of temporary shows, ranging from sculpture and photography, to papercraft and the eccentric postmodern *Wunderkammern* (cabinets of curiosity) of collector Ronny Van de Velde. In 2015 the museum hopes to host its first international exhibition of 140 major works from the Écoles des Beaux-Arts in Paris exploring the theme of Gods and Heroes.

On the last Wednesday of each month, between 6pm and 9pm, the popular 'Art After Hours' allows visitors to explore the museum for free. To accompany, there's live music and free docent tours.

★**Naples Botanical Gardens**　　GARDENS
(☑239-643-7275; www.naplesgarden.org; 4820 Bayshore Dr; adult/child 4-14 $13/8; ⊙9am-5pm) This outstanding botanical garden styles itself as 'a place of bliss, a region of supreme delight.' And after spending some time wandering its 2.5-mile trail through six cultivated gardens you'll rapidly find your inner zen. Children particularly delight in the garden supplied with a thatched-roof tree house, a butterfly house and an interactive fountain, while adults get all dreamy-eyed contemplating the giant lily pads in the Brazilian Garden.

Other highlights include the Florida Garden, designed by Naples' own Ellin Goetz, which features an extensive wildflower meadow encircled by sabal palms (Florida's state tree) and garden rooms providing locals with useful planting tips. The Naples Garden Club has found a home here, too, and offers on-site advice and a variety of programs.

Still in the works is a 12,000-sq-ft visitors center, which is currently being built using the highest level of sustainable innovation in construction. On completion it will house botanical and environmental science laboratories to be shared with Florida Gulf Coast University, as well as extensive visitor facilities.

Golisano Children's Museum of Naples　　MUSEUM
(C'MON; ☑239-514-0084; www.cmon.org; 📷) Designed by kids (and child psychologists) for kids, it's hardly surprising that this interactive children's museum is a big hit. At its center a trolley takes kids to different exhibits, including a virtual pond, where they can observe fish and growing water plants, and a produce market, where fruit and veg are sorted and sold to other kid 'customers.' Best of all is the Journey Through the Everglades with its boardwalk winding up into a 'tree'

overlooking a mangrove maze of 20 pods. It has hands-on learning experiences, enhanced by light and sound installations signaling different day and night experiences.

The state-of-the-art building also incorporates the all-organic Garden Café.

Naples Zoo at Caribbean Gardens　　ZOO
(☑239-262-5409; www.napleszoo.com; 1590 Goodlette-Frank Rd; adult/child 3-12yr $20/13; ⊙9am-5pm) Caribbean Gardens is an Old Florida attraction that's been updated into a modest zoo. Though it lacks some big-ticket species, it has narrated boat rides in a lake to visit free-roaming, island-bound monkeys and some unique species such as honey badgers and the Madagascan fosa, which looks something like a short-legged cougar. All presentations are included in admission.

Naples Nature Center　　NATURE RESERVE
(☑239-262-0304; www.conservancy.org/nature-center; 1450 Merrihue Dr; adult/child 3-12 $13/9; ⊙9:30am-4:30pm Mon-Sat) One of Florida's premier nature-conservancy and advocacy nonprofits, the Conservancy of Southwest Florida is a must-visit destination for anyone interested in Florida's environment and its preservation. While the new Discovery Center immerses visitors in southwest Florida environments, with informative films, displays and a rare peak into the avian nursery, the 21-acre park offers pleasant boardwalk trails and naturalist boat rides.

Palm Cottage　　HISTORIC BUILDING
(☑239-261-8164; www.napleshistoricalsociety.org/palm-cottage; 137 12th Ave S; adult/child $10/free; ⊙1-4pm Tue-Sat) One of the last tabby-mortar cottages in Collier County, this quaint cottage was built in 1895 for Henry Watterson, the editor of the *Louisville Courier Journal*. It then offered overflow accommodation for the Old Naples Hotel, hosting movie stars such as Hedy Lamarr. After more recent renovations it now houses the Naples Historical Society, which offers engaging guided tours of the house, alongside lectures by authors and artists in the adjacent **Norris Gardens**, on the first and third Thursday of the month.

🏃 **Activities**

Naples has 9 miles of idyllic white-sand beaches. At the end of 12th Ave S, the historic pier is a locus of activity.

Naples Municipal Beach　　BEACH
(12th Ave S & Gulf Shore Blvd) Naples city beach is a long, dreamy white strand that succeeds

DON'T MISS

THE DOLPHIN STUDY

Just south of Naples, neighboring **Marco Island** provides a gateway to the estuarine labyrinth of the Ten Thousand Islands. One of the best ways to explore the marine ecosystem is with the **Dolphin Study** (☏212-209-3370; www.dolphin-study.com; 951 Bald Eagle Dr, Marco Island; per person $59), a long-term scientific study of the behavior and movements of southwestern Florida's bottlenose dolphins. Using photo ID of dorsal fins, tour participants have the opportunity to get involved in sighting, counting and confirming individual sightings, data which is then shared with the Mote Marine Laboratory (p399) in Sarasota.

Passing around a heavy photo album of dorsal fins, naturalist Kent Morse points out bite marks and tears that will help you tell the difference between Ripples, Nibbles and Flag. While close enough to ID the different dolphins, the catamaran always keeps a respectful distance. Sometimes whole pods are sighted nosing around the mangroves or playing in family groups. If you spot a dolphin not already catalogued, you may even get to name it. Along the way, you'll stop at some of the most remote and beautiful, unbridged barrier islands such as shell-tastic **Keewaydin**.

Tours last three hours and depart from Marco River Marina.

in feeling lively but rarely overcrowded. At the end of 12th Ave S, the 1000ft **pier** is a symbol of civic pride, having been destroyed by fire and hurricane and reconstructed each time. Parking is spread out in small lots between 7th Ave N and 17th Ave S, each with 10 to 15 spots of mixed resident and metered parking ($1.50 per hour); be sure to park at meters only or you'll be ticketed. You'll find restrooms and a larger parking lot at the pier.

Lowdermilk Park   BEACH, PARK
(cnr Banyan Blvd & Gulf Shore Blvd) North of Old Naples, this is a family-friendly beach park with picnic tables, vending machines, restrooms, and volleyball courts showcasing some of the best players around. If you're a world-class player visiting from, say, Hawaii, you might be able to join them. Otherwise, just watch the buff bods. Bring quarters for the parking meters.

Clam Pass County Park   BEACH, PARK
(☉8am-sunset) This county park covers 35 acres of coastal habitat, including a 0.75-mile boardwalk through a mangrove forest that leads out to a powdery white-sand beach. It's next to Naples Grand Beach Resort, which runs both the water-sports rentals and the free tram that travels between the large parking lot ($8 per day) and the well-groomed beach. It's a favorite with families and young adults. The snack bar serves beer and cocktails.

Delnor-Wiggins Pass State Park BEACH, PARK
(☏239-597-6196; www.floridastateparks.org/Delnorwiggins; 11135 Gulf Shore Dr; car/bike $6/2;

☉8am-sunset) This lovely state park and beach extends for a mile from the mouth of the Cocohatchee River. It boasts gorgeous white sands, which are protected during turtle-nesting season (from May to October). There's an **observation tower** at the north end, but swimming is best south of the pass's fast-moving waters. The beach is supplied with food concessions (at parking lot 4), showers, and has every item you might need for a day in the sun for hire. Afternoon winds attract kiteboarders and there's great snorkeling at a reef just offshore.

From US 41, take 111th Ave/Hwy 846.

☞ Tours

★**Naples Trolley Tours**   TOUR
(☏239-262-7205; www.naplestrolleytours.com; 1010 6th Ave S; adult/child 4-12yr $27/13; ☉9:30am-5:30pm) Hop-on, hop-off narrated trolley tours make a 1¾-hour circuit through the city daily. Segway tours are also offered.

⚘ Festivals & Events

Naples Winter Wine Festival   FOOD
(www.napleswinefestival.com; ☉Jan) This multiday event features celebrity wine tastings, chef-hosted dinners and a high-yielding auction – the proceeds of which go to benefit 20 childrens charities in Collier County.

🛏 Sleeping

Naples specializes in top-end lodgings, but an economical sleep can be had. Visit outside February to mid-April and you'll find prices drop dramatically, often by half.

Lemon Tree Inn
MOTEL **$$**

(☑ 239-262-1414; www.lemontreeinn.com; 250 9th St S; r $80-169; ✸@🛜☒) Value for money is high at the Lemon Tree, where 34 clean and brightly decorated rooms (some with passable kitchenettes) form a U around pretty, private gardens. Screened porches, free lemonade and Continental breakfasts are nice, but most of all, you'll treasure being walking distance to the 5th Ave corridor.

Gondolier
INN **$$**

(☑ 239-262-4858; www.gondolierinnnaples.com; 407 8th Ave S; r $80-180; ℗✸🛜) This classic 1950s Googie-style bungalow with sharp angles, overhanging roof and kitsch Gondolier signage is well located on a quiet street in Old Naples. Rooms are of a similar vintage and have hand-hewn kitchens and period furniture. Better still, it's just a few blocks' walk to the beach.

Cove Inn
APARTMENTS **$$**

(☑ 239-262-7161; www.coveinnnaples.com; 900 Broad Ave S; r $90-250; ✸@🛜☒) The individually owned condo units of this marina hotel are something of a gamble: most are surprisingly attractive, up-to-date, tile-floored, rattan-furnished rooms with peaceful harbor views. A few await 21st-century face-lifts and feel as tired as the building's bleached exterior. Request an updated unit to enjoy one of Naples' better-value accommodations.

★ Escalante
BOUTIQUE HOTEL **$$$**

(☑ 239-659-3466; www.hotelescalante.com; 290 Fifth Ave S; r $175-455) Hidden in plain sight at 5th Ave and Third St, the wonderful Escalante is a boutique hotel crafted in the fashion of a Tuscan villa. Rooms and suites are nestled behind luxuriant foliage and flowering pergolas, and feature plantation-style furniture, European linens and Gilchrist & Soames bath products. A sustainable garden supplies the veranda restaurant, and there's a full-service spa and golf cart service to the beach. It's very private and terribly romantic.

Inn on 5th
HOTEL **$$$**

(☑ 239-403-8777; www.innonfifth.com; 699 5th Ave S; r $180-500; ✸@🛜☒) This well-polished, Mediterranean-style luxury hotel provides an unbeatable location in the midst of 5th Ave. Stylish rooms are more corporate-perfect than historic-romantic, but who complains about pillowtop mattresses and glass-walled tile showers? Full-service amenities include a 2nd-floor heated pool, business and fitness centers, and an indulgent spa. Free valet parking.

Eating

Naples has one of the region's friendliest downtowns for evening strolls. In high season, 5th Ave sidewalks are crowded and bars typically serve past midnight. More restaurants cluster on 3rd St S in Old Naples.

Food & Thought
MARKET, CAFE **$**

(☑ 239-213-2222; www.foodandthought.com; 2132 Tamiami Trail N; $3-10; ⊙7am-8pm Mon-Sat; ✔) You won't find anything that isn't 100% organic on the shelves of this market or in its ever busy cafe. Vegetarians will delight in the artfully layered raw basil lasagna.

★ The Café
CAFE, JUICE BAR **$$**

(☑ 239-430-6555; www.thecafeon5th.com; 821 5th Ave S; 7:30am-4pm Oct-Apr, to 3pm May-Sep; ✔) You could easily walk past this unassuming cafe, but then you'd be missing out on a superlative breakfast of fluffy, organic eggs, grilled Canadian bacon and perfectly toasted artisan bread. And that's just the standard; Ironman oatmeal topped with flaxseeds, almonds, raisins and apples, acai bowls, crepes and lox bagels topped with pale-pink salmon satisfy healthier cravings. Lunch is a similarly well-executed affair with classic burgers, vegetarian wraps and salads, and an extensive menu of fresh juices and smoothies.

IM Tapas
SPANISH **$$**

(☑ 239-403-8272; http://imtapas.com; 965 4th Ave N; tapas $9-18; ⊙from 5:30pm Mon-Sat) Off the beaten path in a strip mall, this simply decorated, romantic Spanish restaurant serves Madrid-worthy tapas. The mother-daughter team presents contemporary interpretations of classics such as salt cod, Serrano ham, *angula* (baby eels), and shrimp with garlic. Even seemingly simple dishes such as wild leeks are elegant and heavenly.

Campiello
ITALIAN **$$**

(☑ 239-435-1166; www.campiello.damico.com; 1177 3rd St S; lunch $14-22, dinner $15-40; ⊙11:30am-3pm & 5-10pm, to 10:30pm Fri & Sat) Campiello hits you with the perfect one-two combo: an attractive, umbrella-shaded patio for stylish alfresco dining along the 3rd St shopping corridor, and Italian cuisine priced for all budgets. Go light with a wood-fired pizza or a housemade pasta, or tuck into rich versions of osso bucco or Kobe steak. Live jazz from Wednesday to Saturday evenings make it a popular hangout. Reservations recommended.

DETOUR TO THE EVERGLADES

If you've traveled as far south as Naples, you really owe it to yourself to visit the Everglades. Heading west on the Tamiami Trail/Hwy 41, you can be in Everglades City in half an hour, Big Cypress in 45 minutes and Shark Valley in 75 minutes.

★ **Turtle Club**   SEAFOOD, AMERICAN $$$
(☑ 239-592-6557; www.theturtleclubrestaurant. com; Vanderbilt Beach Resort, 9225 Gulf Shore Dr; mains $9-42; ☉ 11am-2:30pm & 5-9pm) How do you compete with the show-stopping sunsets on the Gulf of Mexico? The Turtle Club at the Vanderbilt Resort tries hard with kickass cocktails and a short, sharp seafood menu rocking Pine Island lump crab, shrimp and crab Napoleon with mango and jicama, and the best cold-water oysters on the market. Get there *early* if you want to snag a place on the beach.

Mereday's Fine Dining   MODERN AMERICAN $$$
(☑ 239-732-0784; www.meredaysnaples.com; Naples Bay Resort, 1500 5th Ave S; 2-/3-/4-courses $55/75/95; ☉ 5-9pm) Probably the finest dining experience in Naples is Charles Mereday's restaurant hidden in the Naples Bay Resort. Choose two, three or four courses from the prix-fixe menu. Sit back and enjoy superlative classics with a contemporary twist such as shrimp and stoneground cheddar grits, escargot with *pistou* (garlic, basil and olive oil sauce) and mangrove mahimahi with cauliflower couscous and *sauce vierge* (olive oil, basil, chopped tomatoes and lemon juice).

Cafe Lurcat   FUSION $$$
(☑ 239-213-3357; www.cafelurcat.com; 494 5th Ave; dinner $24-39; ☉ 5-10pm) Slip into your sexiest clothes for Naples' hippest, most stylish scene. The cafe upstairs has formal dining beneath a vaulted ceiling with a Chagall-inspired mural. The trendy downstairs lounge features low leather banquettes, an under-lit glass bar and live jazz on weekends. The tapas menu is served in both areas, and features eclectic takes on Chinese BBQ, sea bass in miso and great salads. The bar stays open until midnight.

☆ Entertainment

★ **Naples Philharmonic**   CLASSICAL MUSIC
(☑ 239-597-1900; www.artisnaples.org; 5833 Pelican Bay Blvd) Naples' 85-piece Philharmonic Orchestra is increasingly recognized as one of the country's best young orchestras. Adrey Boreyko was named as music director in 2013. The season runs from June to September, but the Artis complex within which it lives runs a year-round schedule of concerts and performances, including many events for children.

Sugden Community Theatre   THEATER
(☑ 239-263-7990; www.naplesplayers.org; 701 5th Ave; tickets $35; ☉ box office 10am-4pm Mon-Fri, to 1pm Sat) Home of the Naples Players, the Sugden boasts two state-of-the-art stages on whose boards it enacts seven main-stage performances and four studio productions each year, including four KidzAct performances. It's well attended so book ahead.

🛍 Shopping

For upscale boutiques and other ritzy shopping, stroll Old Naples' **3rd St S Shops** (www.thirdstreetsouth.com) or wander 5th Ave S. For seaside trinkets, pink flamingos and 'Mommy needs a timeout' T-shirts, head to **Tin City** (www.tin-city.com; 1200 5th Ave S), a jaunty harborside tourist trap.

Farmers Market   MARKET
(cnr 3rd St S & Gordon Dr; ☉ 7:30-11:30am Sat) At one of the region's best farmers markets, you can find organic produce and lots of artisan products – bread, soaps, jams, woven baskets and more.

ℹ Information

Greater Naples Chamber of Commerce
(☑ 239-262-6141; www.napleschamber.org; 900 5th Ave S; ☉ 9am-5pm Mon-Sat) Will help with accommodations; good maps, internet access and acres of brochures.

Third St Concierge Kiosk (☑ 239-434-6533; www.thirdstreetsouth.com; Camargo Park, 3rd St S; ☉ 9am-5pm Mon-Fri, 10am-5pm Sun) What's in Old Naples? This friendly outdoor kiosk is glad you asked.

ℹ Getting There & Around

A car is essential; ample and free downtown parking makes things easy. Naples is about 40 miles southwest of Fort Myers via I-75.

Collier Area Transit (CAT; www.colliergov.net; fares $1.50; ☉ 6am-7:30pm) Buses serve the greater Naples area. The Marco Express costs $2.50.

Greyhound (☑ 239-774-5660; www.greyhound. com; 2669 Davis Blvd; ☉ 8:15-10:30am & 1:30-4:15pm Mon-Sat) Connects Naples to Miami, Orlando and Tampa.

The Panhandle

Best Places to Eat

➡ Up the Creek Raw Bar (p449)

➡ Indian Pass Raw Bar (p448)

➡ Peg Leg Pete's (p436)

➡ Five Sisters Blues Cafe (p435)

➡ Firefly (p446)

Best Places to Stay

➡ WaterColor Inn & Resort (p442)

➡ Water Street Hotel (p449)

➡ Hibiscus Coffee & Guesthouse (p442)

➡ Aunt Martha's Bed & Breakfast (p440)

➡ Island Hotel (p462)

Why Go?

Take the best bits of the Deep South – friendly ('howdy y'all!') people, a molasses-slow pace, oak-lined roads and fried green tomatoes – then add sugar-white beaches, clear natural springs and bountiful seafood and you're beginning to conjure up the magnificent, diverse and highly underrated Florida Panhandle: so overlooked in the bigger Florida picture that we almost want to keep it to ourselves.

Dig your toes into the endless miles of impossible white sands and azure waters of the Gulf Coast, gallery-hop in pretty Pensacola with its surprising wealth of history and understated class, fish the primeval Steinhatchee, explore the rugged wilderness of St Vincent Island and be sure to bunker down for some slow, balmy nights in charming Apalachicola. Too chilled? Head on over to gaudy Panama City Beach and suck down Jell-O shots with the spring-breakers.

Consider it road-trip heaven.

When to Go
Pensacola

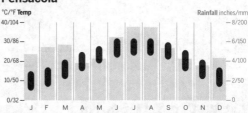

| **Mar & Apr** Spring-breakers descend upon the gulf to party. | **May–Oct** Steamy temps: accommodations fill fast. Sweltering heat eases: vacationing families depart. | **Nov–Feb** Low season: the Panhandle is all yours at bargain rates. |

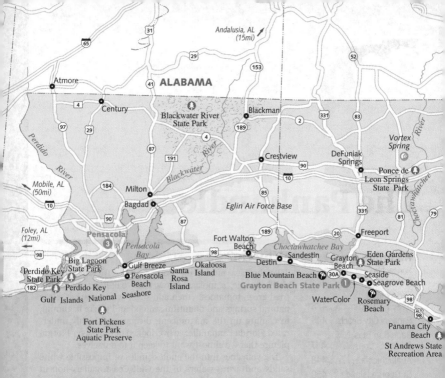

The Panhandle Highlights

1 Feasting your eyes on the luminous gulf waters of **Grayton Beach State Park** (p441), home to the country's most beautiful beaches.

2 Embracing your inner romantic in **Apalachicola** (p448), the gulf's most charming town.

3 Marveling at the death-defying maneuvres of **Blue Angels** (p432), then getting hands-on with the amazing exhibits at the **National Museum of Naval Aviation** (p432) in Pensacola.

4 Getting laid-back in **Cedar**

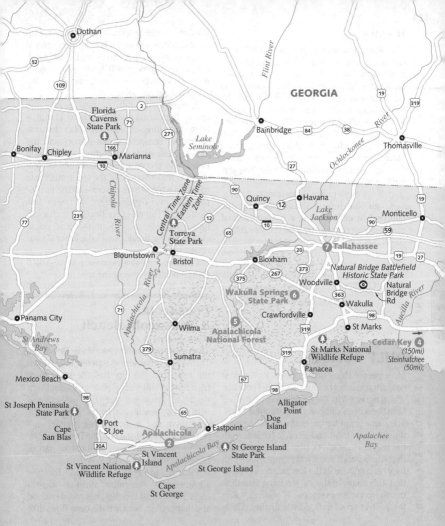

History

The area that would become Tallahassee (meaning 'abandoned fields') was first inhabited by Native Americans of the Apalachee tribes, who cleared out and were felled by disease after the region was settled by Spaniards in 1539, with explorer Hernando de Soto leading the way. After the US Territory of Florida was founded in 1821, Tallahassee was chosen as the state capital; a plantation economy soon developed – as did the city's reckless reputation, with frequent knife and gun fights leading to the formation of the city's police department.

A rail line linked Tallahassee with the gulf port in 1837, making it the commercial center of the region. And, by the late 1800s, cotton estates were snapped up by wealthy northerners, who turned them into hunting retreats. Eventually, environmentalists reacted against the man-versus-beast behavior of the hunters, which led to the establishment of groundbreaking ecological efforts in the region.

GULF COAST

Most people think of the state's south when conjuring images of Florida's famed beaches, which may be why the eastern half of the Gulf Coast has been dubbed the Forgotten Coast. The name is apt for the entire shoreline here, unless you're local and already familiar with the region's magical beauty. That's not to say that the beaches are always empty, although they certainly are in the low season. It's more that this many miles of stunning coastline means room for everyone. If you can't find the perfect spot, walk a little further. These northern, gulfside spits are spectacular, with sand that's as soft and white as ultra-refined sugar, gently rolling dunes and clear, calm, turquoise waters that'll make you wonder why you've ever vacationed anywhere else. We're not exaggerating.

Alongside all this natural beauty are towns that burst with Southern charm – from the lure of Apalachicola's historic district to Pensacola's rich history and the almost unfeasible perfection of Grayton Beach and the planned community of Seaside. On the other end of the spectrum, some will love what others describe as the not-so-pleasant over-development of towns like Destin and Panama City Beach, which swell into a maelstrom of hormones and booze during spring break. Avoid the latter if your constitution so dictates.

Chances are, whatever your fancy, you'll find your ideal place in the sun.

Pensacola & Pensacola Beach

☏ 850 / POP 52,340

The Deep South meets Florida in Pensacola. The Alabama border is just a few miles down the road and the city has the small-town friendliness and sleepy pace of its Southern neighbor. Pensacola keeps things colorful with lively beaches, a sultry, Spanish-style downtown and a thrumming military culture: southwest of the city, the Pensacola Naval Air Station has been an intrinsic part of Pensacola's identity since WWII.

Visitors to Pensacola come for the all-American blue-collar vacation experience: white-sand beaches, bountiful seafood and happening bars where beer flows like

THE OIL SPILL

On April 20, 2010, 40 miles off the coast of Louisiana, a BP oil rig called Deepwater Horizon exploded, killing 11 workers and touching off one of the worst environmental disasters in American history. In the three months it took to stymie the gushing well, nearly 5 million barrels of crude oil were released into the Gulf of Mexico, poisoning sea life and causing inestimable harm to the fishing and tourism industries along the coasts of Texas, Louisiana, Mississippi, Alabama and Florida.

Though the globs of oil that once washed up on Gulf Coast beaches are now hard to imagine, the damage has been done: many coastal businesses did not survive the economic thrashing, and many tourists have remained wary of eating local seafood (though tests run by the National Oceanographic and Atmospheric Administration continue to show no sign of contaminants in fish and shrimp).

In 2014 the tourism boom seems to have returned, but chat with any Gulf Coaster and they'll tell you that the psychological scars remain.

THE PANHANDLE FOR CHILDREN

The down-to-earth Panhandle is one of Florida's most family-friendly regions, with laid-back beaches, aquariums, amusement parks, ice-cream shops and fudge museums. Traveling families will appreciate Destin and Panama City Beach for their range of attractions. For the kidlets, we recommend:

➜ Manning your own fighter jet and watching the dazzling Blue Angels formation flying at the National Museum of Naval Aviation (p432) in Pensacola.

➜ Watching the dolphins frolic at Destin's long-established Gulfarium (p439).

➜ Exercising the gray matter at Panama City Beach's hyperstimulating, wacky WonderWorks (p444) and Ripley's Believe It or Not! (p445).

➜ Checking out cool, interactive exhibits on dinosaurs or bugs or ships at the **Mary Brogan Museum of Art & Science** (Map p456; ☑ 850-513-0700; www.thebrogan.org; 350 S Duval St; adult/child $7.50/5; ☺ 10am-5pm Mon-Sat, from 1pm Sun; ⊞) in Tallahassee, the state capital.

➜ Learning about Pensacola's rich history at the hands-on Pensacola Children's Museum (p429).

water. During March and April, things reach fever pitch when droves of students descend for the week-long bacchanalia of spring break. Beware.

Others will appreciate the city's cultured, historical side. Since Pensacola's permanent settlement in 1698, flags belonging to Spain, France, Britain, the Confederacy and the US have flown over the city, earning it the moniker, 'City of Five Flags.' Traces of the past are evident in Pensacola's architecture, historical sites and museums.

Downtown, centered on Palafox St, lies north of the waterfront. Across the Pensacola Bay Bridge from here is the mostly residential peninsula of Gulf Breeze. Cross one more bridge, the Bob Sikes (toll $1), to reach magnificent Pensacola Beach, the ultimate destination for most visitors. Kick off your shoes, dig your toes into the sand, and, ahhh...relax!

◉ Sights & Activities

◉ Pensacola

Historic Pensacola Village HISTORIC BUILDINGS
(Map p434; ☑ 850-595-5985; www.historicpensacola.org; 205 E Zaragoza St; adult/child $6/3; ☺ 10am-4pm Tue-Sat, tours 11am, 1pm & 2:30pm) You might be surprised to learn that Pensacola's rich colonial history spans over 450 years. This fascinating and attractive village is a self-contained enclave of photogenic historic homes turned museums: it's the perfect starting point for familiarizing yourself with

the city. Admission is good for one week and includes a guided tour and entrance to each building.

Pensacola Museum of Art MUSEUM
(Map p434; ☑ 850-432-6247; www.pensacolamuseum.org; 407 S Jefferson St; adult/student $5/3; ☺ 10am-5pm Tue-Fri, from noon Sat) In the city's old jail (1908), this lovely art museum features an impressive, growing collection of major 20th- and 21st-century artists, spanning cubism, realism, pop art and folk art.

Pensacola Children's Museum MUSEUM
(Map p434; ☑ 850-595-1559; 115 E Zaragoza St; admission $3; ☺ 10am-4pm Tue-Sat) Learn about the over 450 years of local history and have some fun along the way in this compact museum occupying two floors of the historic (and allegedly haunted) Arbona building. The first hands-on level is aimed at youngsters up to nine years old, while the 2nd floor has a little more to offer older kids, including dress-ups!

**Pensacola Scenic
Bluffs Highway** SCENIC DRIVE
This 11-mile stretch of road, which winds around the precipice of the highest point along the Gulf Coast, makes for a peaceful drive or slightly challenging bike ride. You'll see stunning views of Escambia Bay and pass a notable crumbling brick chimney – part of the steam-power plant for the Hyer-Knowles lumber mill in the 1850s – the only remnant of what was the first major industrial belt in the area.

Pensacola Area

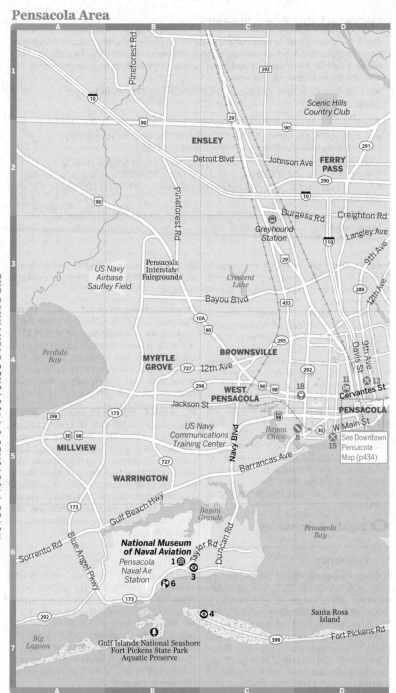

Pineforest Rd

Scenic Hills
Country Club

ENSLEY

Detroit Blvd

Johnson Ave

FERRY
PASS

Greyhound
Station

Burgess Rd

Creighton Rd

Langley Ave

US Navy
Airbase
Saufley Field

Pensacola
Interstate
Fairgrounds

Crescent
Lake

Bayou Blvd

Perdido
Bay

MYRTLE
GROVE

12th Ave

BROWNSVILLE

WEST
PENSACOLA

18

11

13

Cervantes St

PENSACOLA

Jackson St

Navy Blvd

Bayou
Chico

8

See Downtown
Pensacola
Map (p434)

W Main St

15

MILLVIEW

US Navy
Communications
Training Center

Barrancas Ave

WARRINGTON

Gulf Beach Hwy

Bayou
Grande

Pensacola
Bay

Sorrento Rd

Blue Angel Pkwy

National Museum
of Naval Aviation

Pensacola
Naval Air
Station

1

3

6

Taylor Rd

Duncan Rd

4

Santa Rosa
Island

Fort Pickens Rd

Big
Lagoon

Gulf Islands National Seashore
Fort Pickens State Park
Aquatic Preserve

399

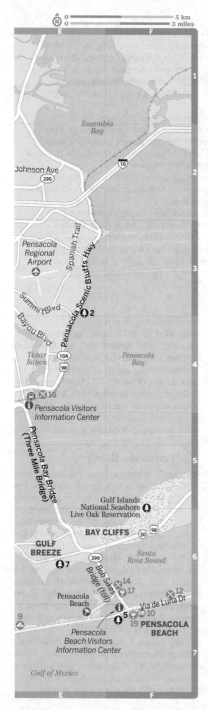

Bay Bluffs Park   PARK

(Map p430; Scenic Hwy) Off Pensacola Scenic Bluffs Hwy, this beautiful park is a 32-acre oasis of wooden boardwalks that lead you along the side of the steep bluffs, through clutches of live oaks, pines, Florida rosemary and holly down to the empty beach below.

◎ Naval Air Station Pensacola

Every US WWII pilot was trained at the Naval Air Station Pensacola (NAS), known as 'the cradle of naval aviation.' Today, some 6000 young aviators train here, and the base is a major part of Pensacola's social fabric. Southwest of downtown Pensacola, NAS has a number of interesting attractions for visitors. To get here, take Hwy 295 to the NAS entrance, south of the bridge at the end of Navy Blvd, across Bayou Grande. You'll be stopped at the gate for a security check of your car, so be sure to bring photo ID.

BLUE ANGELS

To maintain its profile after WWII, and to reinforce its recruitment drive, the US Navy gathered some of its most elite pilots to form the **Blue Angels** (☑850-452-2583; www.blueangels.navy.mil; 390 San Carlos Rd, Suite A), a flight-demonstration squadron traveling to air shows around the country. The name caught on during the original team's trip to New York in 1946, when one of the pilots saw the name of the city's Blue Angel nightclub in the *New Yorker*.

These days performing for about 15 million people a year, 'the Blues' (never 'the Angels'), their C130 Hercules support aircraft named Fat Albert and their all-Marine support crew visit about 35 show sites a year. Six jets execute precision maneuvers, including death-defying rolls and loops, and two F/A-18s undertake solo flights; the show culminates in all six planes flying in trademark delta formation.

Each of the Blues does a two-year tour of duty, staggered to rotate every two years. In addition to the six pilots (which always include one Marine) is a narrator, who'll then move up through the ranks, and an events coordinator.

The Blues practice frequently (as would you if you were doing 500mph stunts in a quarter of a million dollars worth of aircraft): you can see take-off (a jet-assisted, near-vertical incline by way of rocket propellant) on Tuesday and Wednesday at 8:30am between March and November (weather permitting); Wednesday sessions are followed by pilot autographs. It's best to arrive between 7:30am and 8am. Bleachers are available for the first 1000 spectators; BYO coffee and lawn chairs. The viewing area is behind the National Museum of Naval Aviation parking lot.

★**National Museum
of Naval Aviation**   MUSEUM
(Map p430; ☑850-452-3604; www.navalaviationmuseum.org; 1750 Radford Blvd; ⊙9am-5pm Mon-Fri; ⛟) FREE A visit to Pensacola is not complete without a trip to this enormous collection of military aircraft muscle and artifacts. Adults and children alike will be fascinated by the range of planes on display: over 150! That's before we even get to the high-tech stuff like flight simulators and an IMAX theatre. You can watch the Blue Angels (p432) practice their death-defying air show at 8:30am most Tuesdays and Wednesdays between March and November. Best of all – it's free!

**Fort Barrancas
& Advanced Redoubt**   LANDMARK
(Map p430; ☑850-934-2600; www.nps.gov/guis/planyourvisit/fort-barrancas; 3182 Taylor Rd; ⊙8:30am-3:45pm Nov-Feb, 9:30am-4:45pm Mar-Oct) FREE On a dramatic bluff overlooking Pensacola Bay, 19th-century Fort Barrancas was built by slaves atop an abandoned 18th-century Spanish fort. The fort, now part of the National Park Service, has endless dark passageways to explore but not much in the way of displays. A half-mile away via a walking trail lie the ruins of Advanced Redoubt, a Civil War–era fort. **Tours** operate on Saturday only, at 2pm for Barrancas and 11am for Advanced Redoubt.

Pensacola Lighthouse   LIGHTHOUSE
(Map p430; ☑850-393-1561; www.pensacolalighthouse.org; 2081 Radford Blvd; adult/child $6/4; ⊙10am-5:30pm Mon-Sat, from noon Sun) Be on the lookout for ghosts of lighthouse-keepers past as you climb the 177 steps of this 160ft, 1859 lighthouse, rumored to be haunted. The views are quite stunning, as you might expect. If you're afraid of heights, you can hang back and take a look at the adjacent museum.

⊙ Pensacola Beach

Distinctly separate from Pensacola itself, Pensacola Beach is a paradise of powdery white sand, gentle, warm waters and a string of mellow beachfront hotels. The beach occupies nearly 8 miles of the 40-mile-long Santa Rosa barrier island, surrounded by the Santa Rosa Sound and the Gulf of Mexico to the north and south, and by the federally protected Gulf Islands National Seashore on either side. Though determined residents have protected much of the barrier island from development, there is change afoot, as several high-rise condos have recently created a bit of a Gulf Coast skyline.

The area is a major hub for local entertainment and special events, including Mardi Gras celebrations, a triathlon, wine tastings, a summer music series, parades and the annual Blue Angels (p432) air show in July.

Gulf Islands National Seashore PARK

(Map p430; ☑ 850-934-2600; www.nps.gov/guis; 7-day pass pedestrian/cyclist/car $3/3/8; ⊙ sunrise-sunset) We're pleased to say that no visible signs of damage from the devastating 2010 Deepwater Horizon oil spill remain on this stunning 150-mile stretch of mostly undeveloped white-sand beach jointly maintained by Mississippi and Florida. Aim for the **Naval Live Oaks** section for a calm, familyfriendly beach, or head to the easy-access **Pensacola Beach**.

Fort Pickens HISTORIC SITE

(Map p430; ☑ 850-934-2600; www.nps.gov/guis/planyourvisit/fort-pickens; 1400 Fort Pickens Rd; 7-day pass pedestrian/cyclist/car $3/3/8; ⊙ sunrise-sunset; ⊕) Part of the Gulf Islands National Seashore (p433), this 1834 historic fort perched at the western extent of the Santa Rosa barrier island has survived wars and scores of hurricanes to remain a fascinating and scenic excursion. Pick up a self-guided tour map from the visitor center.

Shoreline Park UFO Spotting PARK

(Map p430; 700 Shoreline Dr, Gulf Breeze) Maybe it's activity from the nearby Pensacola Naval Air Station, but this stretch of the gulf has apparently had hundreds of UFO sightings in the past few decades, with reports right along the coast. Local skywatchers (including members of the Mutual UFO Network) gather at this park with binoculars and lawn chairs in the hope of a close encounter: as good a reason as any to spread out a beach blanket and gaze at the stars.

Lanier Sailing Academy SAILING

(Map p434; ☑ 850-432-3199; www.laniersail.com/al/pensacola-3; 997 S Palafox St; sailboat rentals from $245; ⊙ 9am-5pm Tue-Sun) Conditions at Pensacola Bay are perfect for sailing, and this award-winning school offers a variety of courses. Those in the know can rent a Capri 22 from $245 daily.

MBT Divers DIVING

(Map p430; ☑ 850-455-7702; www.mbtdivers.com; 3920 Barrancas Ave; courses from $199; ⊙ 8am-6pm Mon-Sat, to 3pm Sun) The *Oriskany* CV/CVA-34 aircraft carrier, at approximately 900ft long and 150ft tall, was the largest vessel ever sunk as an artificial reef when it was submerged in 2007 off Pensacola Beach. This professional outfitter will gear up and help experienced divers plan their dive. A variety of dive courses are also available, including an exclusive Oriskany class.

⌂ Sleeping

You'll find plenty of budget and midrange chains on N Palafox St in Pensacola. Consider basing yourself in a waterfront hotel at Pensacola Beach and day-tripping into Pensacola.

Pensacola

Solé Inn MOTEL $

(Map p434; ☑ 850-470-9298; www.soleinnandsuites.com; 200 N Palafox St; r inc breakfast from $89; ❈ 🞥 ≋) Just north of downtown, this renovated motel goes for a 1960s mod look, with a black-and-white color scheme, animal-print accents and acrylic bubble lamps. Rooms aren't huge, but price, location and originality make up for the lack of space. There's free wi-fi and a complimentary continental breakfast.

Noble Manor B&B B&B $$

(Map p430; ☑ 850-434-9544; www.noblemanor.com; 110 W Strong St; r incl breakfast $145-160) Located in the North Hill historic district, this restored 1905 Tudor revival home is now a charming B&B with four handsome guestrooms that blend modern and traditional styling. There's a romantic private carriage house by the hot tub out back. We like the Olivia Rose suite with its tempting freestanding soaker tub.

Crowne Plaza Pensacola Grand HOTEL $$

(Map p434; ☑ 850-433-3336; www.crowneplaza.com/Pensacola; 200 E Gregory St; d from $145) Built atop the historic 1912 L&N Rail passenger terminal, which now serves as the hotel lobby, furnished with period antiques, this refurbished hotel has spacious, modern guestrooms, many with excellent views of the surrounding area. It's situated in a convenient spot between downtown and the Pensacola Bay Bridge.

Pensacola Victorian B&B B&B $$

(Map p434; ☑ 850-434-2818; www.pensacolavictorian.com; 203 W Gregory St; r inc breakfast $85-125; 🅿 ❈ ≋) This stately 1892 Queen Anne building offers four lovingly maintained guest rooms. The standout is Suzanne's Room, with its hardwood floors, blue toile prints and clawfoot tub. It's about a mile north of downtown Pensacola.

Downtown Pensacola

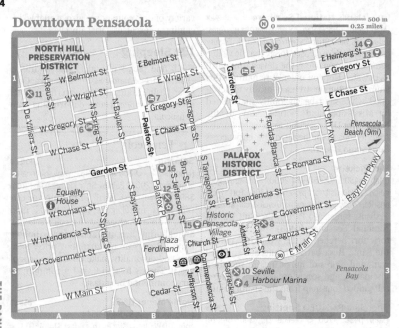

N 0 ——————— 500 m
0 ——————— 0.25 miles

Downtown Pensacola

Pensacola Beach

Fort Pickens Campground CAMPGROUND $
(Map p430; ☎850-934-2656; www.nps.gov/guis; Fort Pickens entrance to Gulf Islands National Seashore; tent & RV sites $26; 🖾) Amid the windblown trees across from the beach, these two pleasant campgrounds are popular with RV-ers, though you'll see the odd tent or two. There are fire pits, a bathhouse and a small camp store. Park entrance fees to Gulf Islands National Seashore (p433) must be paid separately.

Paradise Inn MOTEL $
(☎850-932-2319; www.paradiseinn-pb.com; 21 Via de Luna Dr; r from $59; 🅿❄🛜🏊) Across from the beach, this sherbet-colored motel is a lively, cheery place thanks to its popular bar and grill (ask for a quiet room near the parking lot). Compact quarters are spick and span with tiled floors and brightly painted walls. Online specials offer even better value.

★**Holiday Inn Resort** HOTEL $$
(Map p430; ☎850-932-5331; www.holidayinn-resortpensacolabeach.com; 14 Via de Luna Dr; r

from $95; ■) This fresh, recently renovated beachfront hotel has cool, inviting rooms with ultra-comfy beds, flat-screen TVs and great showers. Oceanfront rooms have spacious balconies overhanging the soft, white sands and the cool turquoise waters below. Suites and kids suites are available, and the pool is killer. Friendly, obliging staff help seal the deal. Excellent value.

Margaritaville Beach Hotel　　HOTEL **$$$**
(☑ 850-916-9755; www.margaritavillehotel.com; 165 Fort Pickens Rd; r from $219; ❋ 🕸 ■) Jimmy Buffett, of Vegas' Margaritaville fame, isn't known for his good taste, however, this elegant beachfront hotel certainly challenges that reputation. The 162 spacious rooms are styled in crisp whites and aquas, with arty murals and huge flat-panel TVs. Downstairs, a sleek grown-up crowd swans around the lobby and sips cocktails by the pool.

✖ Eating

✖ Pensacola

S Palafox St has scads of bars and cafes with outdoor seating. Many of Pensacola's more popular restaurants have long waits, even on weeknights – go early, or plan to hang out at the bar for an hour or so. Try to make reservations if you can.

Joe Patti's　　SEAFOOD MARKET **$**
(Map p430; ☑ 850-432-3315; www.joepattis.com; 534 South B St, at Main St; items from $2.50; ☉7:30am-7pm Mon-Sat, to 6pm Sun) At this beloved seafood emporium, get dock-fresh fish and seafood, prepared picnic food and sushi.

End of the Line Cafe　　VEGAN **$**
(Map p434; ☑ 850-429-0336; www.eotlcafe.com; 610 E Wright St; items $7-11; ☉10am-10pm Tue-Sat, 11am-2pm Sun; 🕸🐾) A funky, fair-trade cafe with velour and vinyl lounges, this is the place for such casual vegan fare as tempeh Reubens and tofu BLTs, as well as cooking classes and cultural events, like the big open-mike night on the second Friday of the month. There's also free wi-fi.

My Favorite Things　　CAFE **$**
(Map p430; ☑ 850-346-1707; www.myfavorite thingstoo.com; 2183 E Cervantes S; mains $7-14; ☉10am-3pm Tue-Fri, 9am-5pm Sat, to 3pm Sun) This delightfully rustic cafe on the edge of town serves equally delightful soups, sandwiches, salads and a small selection of simple seafood mains like grilled shrimp and pan-seared scallops. Best, however, are the breakfasts: fluffy omelets, decadent French toast and eggs Benedict with Canadian bacon: as it should be.

★**Five Sisters Blues Cafe**　　CAFE **$$**
(Map p434; ☑ 850-912-4856; www.fivesisters bluescafe.com; 421 W Belmont St; mains $7-18; ☉11am-9pm Tue-Thu, to late Fri & Sat, to 5pm Sun) Come get your weekly dose of soulful blues (Thursday to Sunday) and good ole Southern cuisine (crab cakes, fried green tomatoes, seafood gumbo) at this smart, classic diner in the heart of Pensacola. Even more fun – if you can get a table – are the Sunday jazz brunches: chicken and Belgian waffles, shrimp over grits and crab-cake Benedicts.

★**Tin Cow**　　MODERN AMERICAN **$$**
(Map p434; ☑ 850-466-2103; www.thetincow. com; 102 S Palafox Pl; burgers $4-16; ☉11am-3am) Burger fans can't leave town without sampling the oozy, mountainous delight that is the Tin Cow burger: choose from signature suggestions or enjoy the freedom of building your own. With a tasty and original starter menu – blue balls (yes), truffle Parmesan fries and fried pickle spears – a stocked fridge of craft beers and sweet shakes, this joint is popular, cool and fun.

**Fish House
& Atlas Oyster House**　　SEAFOOD **$$**
(Map p434; ☑ 850-470-0003; www.greatsouthern-restaurants.com; 600 S Barracks St; mains $12-23; ☉11am-late) These twin seafood restaurants overlooking the harbor are always packed. The more upscale Fish House has a dark wood interior and prepares fish every possible way. Atlas is best for slurping oysters or sipping vino on the porch. Both are known for their grits a ya ya – spicy gulf shrimp, bacon and garlicky veggies over steaming Gouda-cheese grits. Weekend happy hours throb with crowds and live music.

Dharma Blue　　INTERNATIONAL **$$**
(Map p434; ☑ 850-433-1275; www.dharmablue. com; 300 S Alcaniz St; mains $10-30; ☉11am-4pm & 5-9:30pm Mon-Sat; 🎵) The eclectic menu of this compact local favorite ranges from semolina-dusted calamari and grilled duck to mouthwatering sushi, the latter being the most popular. A casual, welcoming vibe extends from the charming, cozy, chandelier-adorned interior to the sunny patio out front.

Bonnelli's Cafe Italia ITALIAN $$

(Map p430; ☑ 850-466-3002; www.bonnelliscafeita-lia.com; 1217 N 9th Ave; pastas from $11, mains from $17; ⊙ 5-10pm Tue-Sat) When you've got the Italian urge, Bonnelli's delivers, though not literally. All your favorites are represented: chunky meatballs, cheesy pizzas, creamy pastas, baked ziti and stuffed eggplant. Meals are hearty and well priced. Dinner only.

✕ Pensacola Beach

Beach Pops POPSICLES $

(Map p430; ☑ 850-677-9177; 49 Via de Luna Dr; from $2; ⊙ 9am-5pm) Sweet treats that are good to eat (and drink): popsicles and smoothies that are all natural, gluten free, and organic too.

Dog House Deli DINER $

(Map p430; ☑ 850-916-4993; www.doghousedeli.com; 35 Via de Luna Dr; items from $2.75; ⊙ 7:30am-9pm) For cheap and easy beachfront eats, try this local favorite, in business for over 35 years, serving a range of signature or build-your-own dogs as well as a tasty breakfast menu.

★ **Peg Leg Pete's** SEAFOOD $$

(☑ 850-932-4139; www.peglegpetes.com; 1010 Fort Pickens Rd; mains $9-30; ⊙ 11am-10pm; ☑) Ahar me hearties...pop into Pete's for almost-beachfront oysters any way you like, fat grouper sandwiches, crab legs and jumbo sea scallops. There's nothing fancy about the woodsy, somewhat grungy sea-shanty decor,

but the service is swift and smiley, despite how busy it gets.

Native Café AMERICAN $$

(Map p430; ☑ 850-934-4848; www.thenativecafe.com; 45a Via de Luna Dr; mains $5-16; ⊙ 7:30am-3pm) This funky breakfast and lunch spot, 'owned and operated by friendly natives,' is a welcome addition to the fried-fish stretch. Try a shrimp po'boy, grilled chicken sandwich, fish tacos, rice and beans, or seafood gumbo – or, for a cheap morning jump start, eggs Benedict or pancakes.

Grand Marlin SEAFOOD $$$

(Map p430; ☑ 850-677-9153; www.thegrandmarlin.com; 400 Pensacola Beach Rd; mains $11-35; ⊙ 11am-10pm Mon-Sat, from 10am Sun) This versatile seafood restaurant and oyster bar gives you the best of both worlds: enjoy a more casual alfresco atmosphere on the best-for-sunset patio, or treat yourself to formal fine-dining indoors. Either way, expect excellent service and oceanic delights like blue crab, lobster mac and cheese (yum!) and fresh-from-the-boat seafood cooked any way you like.

☕ Drinking & Entertainment

In season, the beachside bars have more of a spring-break vibe (tequila and sozzled new drinkers); downtown offerings tend to be slightly more sophisticated. Many restaurants have their own bars. Check out www.pnj.com/entertainment for music listings.

GAY & LESBIAN PENSACOLA

While the Panhandle isn't best known for its progressive values, Pensacola, a small, bright spot for gay culture, is the exception. On the last weekend in May, members of the LGBTQ community descend upon the city for the annual **Gay Memorial Day** (www.memorialweekendpensacola.com), a three-day fiesta of DJ soirees, all-night beach parties, drag shows and general fun and frivolity: crowds reach as many as 50,000, so book ahead!

The Panhandle's signature gay bar (406 East Wright St) pulls in a mixed, though male-heavy, crowd for dancing, drinks and drag shows. The complex is made up of the **Other-side**, a casual video bar, open daily, and **Emerald City**, the nightclub-show venue, open from 9pm Wednesday to Monday.

For those who like their men manly, check out the **Roundup** (Map p434; ☑ 850-433-8482; www.theroundup.net; 560 E Heinberg St; ⊙ 2pm-3am), a niche-y neighborhood hangout with a killer furry-friendly patio. Ladies are welcome, but cowboys, tradies and bikers are always flavor of the month. There's a Facebook page for events listings.

For the lowdown on what's gay in town, or if you need a friend, check out the local LGBTQ community center, **Equality House** (Map p434; ☑ 850-685-2881; 18 S Devilliers St), which organizes film screenings, speakers and other community events.

Pensacola

⭐ **Seville Quarter** CLUB
(Map p434; www.sevillequarter.com; 130 E Government St; ⊙7am-2:30am) Taking up an entire city block, this massive entertainment complex contains seven separate eating, drinking and music venues, along with an HG Wells-ian 1890s decor.

Elbow Room PUB
(Map p430; ☑850-434-0300; 2213 W Cervantes St; ⊙4pm-2am Mon-Fri, from 6pm Sat & Sun) Although it doesn't have much external visual appeal, this funky, dark, retro dive-bar in suburban Pensacola houses a whole world of fun. The folks who work and play here are friendly and mellow; you should be too.

McGuire's Irish Pub PUB
(Map p434; ☑850-433-6789; www.mcguiresirishpub.com; 600 E Gregory St; ⊙11am-1am) This ginormous Irish theme park of a pub gets rowdy around 9pm and is super popular at dinnertime: the pub grub is top notch. Don't try to pay for your drinks with one of the thousands of dollar bills hanging from the ceiling – a local recently found himself in the slammer that way!

Vinyl Music Hall LIVE MUSIC
(Map p434; ☑850-607-6758; www.vinylmusichall.com; 2 S Palafox Pl; ⊙box office noon-5pm Mon-Fri) Pensacola's best venue for live music. Check the website for listings.

Saenger Theatre THEATER
(Map p434; ☑850-595-3880; www.pensacolasaenger.com; 118 S Palafox Pl; ⊙box office 10am-4pm) This Spanish baroque beauty was reconstructed in 1925 using bricks from the Pensacola Opera House, which was destroyed in a 1916 hurricane. It now hosts popular musicals and top-billing music acts and is home to the Pensacola Symphony Orchestra and the Pensacola Opera.

Pensacola Beach

Bamboo Willie's BAR
(Map p430; ☑850-916-9888; www.bamboowillies.com; 400 Quietwater Beach Rd; ⊙11am-late) An open-air bar right on the boardwalk in Pensacola Beach, this is the spot to get twisted in a variety of ways, with signature frozen cocktails from the Bushwacker to the 190 Octane (don't ask – just drink).

Sidelines Sports Bar BAR
(Map p430; ☑850-934-3660; www.sidelinespensacola.com; 2 Via de Luna Dr; ⊙11am-10pm) This popular almost-beachfront sports bar heaves during spring break. The rest of the year it's the best place in town to down a beer and watch the game.

ℹ Information

The local daily is the *Pensacola News Journal* (www.pnj.com). National Public Radio (NPR) is syndicated locally on WUWF 88.1FM.

Pensacola Visitors Information Center (Map p430; ☑800-874-1234; www.visitpensacola.com; 1401 E Gregory St; ⊙8am-5pm Mon-Fri, 9am-4pm Sat, 10am-4pm Sun) Come to the foot of the Pensacola Bay Bridge for a bounty of tourist information, knowledgeable staff and a free internet kiosk.

Pensacola Beach Visitors Information Center (Map p430; ☑850-932-1500; www.visitpensacolabeach.com; 735 Pensacola Beach Blvd) On the right as soon as you enter Pensacola Beach; this is a small place with some useful maps and brochures about goings-on, road closures (due to storms) and anything else beach oriented.

Public Library (☑850-436-5060; mywfpl.com; 239 N Spring St; ⊙10am-8pm Mon-Thu, to 4pm Fri & Sat) Free internet.

ℹ Getting There & Around

Pensacola Regional Airport (Map p430; ☑850-436-5000; www.flypensacola.com; 2430 Airport Blvd) is served by most major US airlines. Primary direct connections include Atlanta, Charlotte, Dallas and Houston. It's 4 miles northeast of downtown off 9th Ave on Airport Blvd. A taxi costs about $20 to downtown and $35 to the beach. Try **Yellow Cab** (☑850-433-3333; www.yellowcabpensacola.com).

The **Greyhound station** (Map p430; ☑850-476-4800; www.greyhound.com; 505 W Burgess Rd) is located north of the downtown area. **Escambia County Transit** (ECAT; ☑850-595-3228; www.goecat.com; rides $1.75) has a limited bus service around Pensacola. A free trolley connects downtown Pensacola and the beach between Memorial Day weekend and the end of September.

I-10 is the major east–west thoroughfare used by buses, and many pass down Palafox St.

INTERSTATE MULLET TOSS

Every year in the last full weekend in April, locals gather on both sides of the Florida–Alabama state line for a time-honored tradition: the mullet toss. The idea – apart from a very fine excuse for a party – is to see who can throw their (dead) mullet (an abundant local fish) the furthest across the border from Florida into Alabama. People have developed their own techniques: tail first, head first, or breaking its spine and bending it in half for better aerodynamics.

The mullet toss is organized by Perdido Key's **Flora-Bama Lounge, Package and Oyster Bar** (☑850-492-0611; www.florabama.com; 17401 Perdido Key Dr; ⊙11am-2:30am), a legendary bar and roadhouse just east of the state line. Out-there events are a hallmark of the Flora-Bama – it also hosts the annual Polar Bear Dip (with a free drink if you brave the winter seas) and the **Frank Brown International Songwriters' Festival** (frank-brownsongwriters.com; ⊙Nov). Flora-Bama has tried to get mullet tossing into the *Guinness Book of World Records*, but its time hasn't come – yet.

Hurricane Ivan sadly did a number on the Flora-Bama, but after years of fundraising and beer-fueled rebuilding parties, the lounge rose again in April 2011. So if you miss the mullet toss, still do stop by for a rowdy night of live music, booze and a mean plate of fried pickles!

Perdido Key

☑850

About 12 miles southwest of Pensacola, off Hwy 292 (which becomes Hwy 182), the easternmost Florida piece of the Gulf Islands National Seashore spans Perdido Key's crystalline waters. These dunes are home to the endangered Perdido Key beach mouse, which blends in well with the white-quartz sands here. There are two coastal state parks in the area: **Perdido Key State Park** (☑850-492-1595; www.floridastateparks.org/perdidokey; 12301 Gulf Beach Hwy; admission per vehicle $3; ⊙8am-sunset) and, on the northern side of the lagoon between Perdido Key and the mainland, **Big Lagoon State Park** (☑850-492-1595; www.floridastateparks.org/biglagoon; 12301 Gulf Beach Hwy; admission per vehicle $6; ⊙8am-sunset), with great crabbing in the lagoon's shallows. (You'll find several free beach areas along the stretch of Perdido Key town, too.)

The town of Perdido Key is centered not on hotels but on condo resorts, all requiring multinight stays, and there are few restaurants or bars – the notable exception is the venerable Flora-Bama Lounge. There are also a handful of seafood spots along the main drag. Visitors can stay in Pensacola, or 3 miles west in Orange Beach, AL.

Perdido Key runs right to the state line. From here, you can follow Hwy 182 straight into Alabama and take Hwy 59/US 90 north to connect with I-10.

If you're arriving in Perdido Key on Hwy 182 from the west, welcome to Florida.

Fort Walton Beach & Destin

☑850 / POP FORT WALTON BEACH 20,300, DESTIN 12,800

With a rich Native American history, these neighboring resort towns are larger than Pensacola Beach but slightly less developed than nearby Panama City Beach. Driving along Hwy 98 from Pensacola Beach, Fort Walton Beach comes first, with its stilted holiday shacks, beachfront mansions and long-time residents. Continuing east, across the Brooks and then the Marler Bridge, Destin, which has the odd claim of appealing to retirees, families *and* spring-breakers, begins to look like an endless chain of strip malls, high-rise condos and mini-amusement parks. Both towns offer luminous waters, white sand and plenty of food, drink and merriment.

Deep-sea fishing is an entrenched part of the area's tradition, with an offshore shelf dropping to depths of 100ft about 10 miles off Destin's east pass. Locals call their town the 'world's luckiest fishing village' – not that it looks much like a village any more.

Between the towns, which bend around Choctawhatchee Bay like two crab claws, lies pristine beachfront owned by the US Air Force, whose largest base, Eglin, is here.

⊙ Sights & Activities

Fishing, snorkeling, dolphin-watching and party-boat cruises are all popular activities in the area.

Indian Temple
Mound & Museum
ARCHAEOLOGICAL SITE

(☑850-833-9595; fwb.org/museums/indian-temple-mound-museum; 139 Miracle Strip Pkwy SE, Fort Walton Beach; ☺10am-4:30pm Mon-Sat Jun-Aug, noon-4:30pm Mon-Fri, from 10am Sat Sep-May) FREE One of the most sacred sites for local Native American culture to this day, the 17ft-tall, 223ft-wide ceremonial and political temple mound, built with 500,000 basket loads of earth and representing what is probably the largest prehistoric earthwork on the Gulf Coast, dates back to somewhere between AD 800 and 1500. On top of the mound you'll find a recreated temple housing a small exhibition center.

The museum offers an extensive overview of 12,000 years of Native American history, and houses flutes, ceramics and artifacts fashioned from stone, bone and shells, as well as a comprehensive research library.

Okaloosa Island Pier
& Boardwalk
LANDMARK

(☑850-244-1023; www.okaloosaislandpier.com; 1030 Miracle Strip Pkwy E, Fort Walton Beach; walk-on $2, fishing adult/child $7.50/4.50; ☺24hr Apr-Oct, 5am-9pm Nov-Mar) Stretching out almost a quarter of a mile into the Atlantic, this popular recreational-fishing pier is open 24 hours in the summer and is illuminated for night fishing. Rental gear is available (from $7) and there are no fishing-license requirements. Otherwise, the pier and adjacent boardwalk are perfect for a leisurely stroll.

Gulfarium
AQUARIUM

(☑850-243-9046; www.gulfarium.com; 1010 Miracle Strip Pkwy SE, Fort Walton Beach; adult/child $20/12; ☺9am-4:30pm; 🖪) This aquarium has been entertaining folks since 1955 with its myriad shows and activities, and it has a wide range of animal encounters (at additional cost), such as Discover Stingrays and the Dolphin Splash Encounter. Animal-welfare groups say that interactions in captivity are detrimental to dolphins' wellbeing; Gulfarium says that it is protecting these graceful mammals and educating the public about them. We'll let you decide. You must be aged eight or over to swim with the dolphins.

US Air Force Armament Museum
MUSEUM

(☑850-651-1808; www.afarmamentmuseum.com; 100 Museum Dr, Eglin Air Force Base; ☺9:30am-4:30pm Mon-Sat) FREE One for military buffs. The exterior of this hangar-style museum, flanked by fighter planes, appears small, but inside are extensive weapons displays including a frightening F-105 Thunderchief missile, a Warthog simulator, and a detailed history of Eglin base, the largest in the US. The museum is about 9 miles northeast of Fort Walton Beach.

Destin Boardwalk
& HarborWalk Village
MARINA

(☑850-424-1232; www.destinboardwalk.com; 102 Harbor Blvd, Destin) This tourist mecca of timeshare condos, boutiques, restaurants, nightclubs and a marina is worth a stroll, especially if you have kids. Most of the area's tour operators (including private fishing charters) have kiosks here and there are plenty of activities to enjoy, albeit at tourist prices.

Southern Star Dolphin Cruises
CRUISE

(☑850-837-7741; www.dolphin-sstar.com; 100 Harbor Blvd, Suite A, Destin; adult/child $29/15.50; ☺9am-6pm Mon-Sat) This environmentally conscious operator has been sailing for over 20 years, observing the bottlenose dolphins that live in these temperate waters. Two-hour cruises operate year-round from an 80ft glass-bottom boat. Check the website for schedules.

ScubaTech
DIVING

(☑850-837-2822; www.scubatechnwfl.com; 301 Hwy 98 E; snorkeling from $30, scuba diving from $90; ☺9am-4pm) Take advantage of the region's great diving with this competent outfitter. A four-hour, two-tank, 58ft to 90ft dive is $90; a complete gear package including fins, mask and snorkel costs $65. Two-hour snorkeling trips including gear and wetsuit cost $30.

Just Chute Me
PARASAILING

(☑850-650-4630; www.parasaildestin.com; 500 Harbor Blvd, Destin; per person from $35; ☺8am-7pm Feb-Oct) Calm waters and stunning vistas make the gulf a great place for parasailing. This professional operator takes beginners into the great blue yonder above to gaze at the great blue wonder below.

🛌 Sleeping

Chain hotels of all stripes line Hwy 98.

Henderson Beach State Park
CAMPGROUND $

(☑850-837-7550; www.floridastateparks.org/hendersonbeach; 17000 Emerald Coast Pkwy, Destin; tent & RV sites $30, day use $6) This coastal paradise has 54 very private sites and good restrooms amid twisted scrub pines, with a three-quarter-mile nature walk through the dune system. It's better suited to RVs than tents.

★ Aunt Martha's Bed & Breakfast B&B $$
(☎850-243-6702; www.auntmarthasbedandbreak-fast.com; 315 Shell Ave SE, Fort Walton Beach; r incl breakfast $105-115; ✳🖥) A short walk from downtown, this charming inn overlooks the Intracoastal. Elegant, unfussy rooms with big brass beds look out into the leafy branches of live oak trees. The common area has a baby grand piano, a well-stocked library and French doors that open onto a breezy veranda. Martha's Southern breakfasts – crawfish quiche, ham and cheese grits, stuffed French toast, you name it – are a veritable feast.

Candlewood Suites Destin-Sandestin MOTEL $$
(☎850-337-3770; www.candlewooddestin.com; 11396 Hwy 98, Destin; d from $89; 🖥) Smart, practical rooms and extra-courteous staff make this modern highway hotel at the eastern extent of town a good-value offering. All rooms have kitchen facilities, comfy bedding and free wi-fi.

Henderson Park Inn INN $$
(☎866-398-4432; www.hendersonparkinn.com; 2700 Hwy 98, Destin; r from $169; ✳🖥🏊🏊) This classy shingled inn has 36 tastefully decorated rooms with high-end Egyptian cotton linens, and thoughtful touches like chocolates on your pillow. Breakfast, lunch, drinks and snacks are all included, making this a popular spot with honeymooners.

✖ Eating

Stewby's Seafood Shanty SEAFOOD $
(☎850-586-7001; www.stewbys.com; 427 Race-track Road NW, Fort Walton Beach; items $3-15; ⊙10am-9pm) Off the main drag, en route to Eglin base, this unpretentious, predominantly takeout restaurant is famed for its seafood gumbo and signature sandwiches, based on recipes passed down over the generations. Increasing popularity means longer waits, but the food is both top notch and affordable.

Donut Hole Café & Bakery BAKERY $
(☎850-837-8824; 635 Harbor Blvd, Destin; items from $4; ⊙6am-10pm) This simple bakery-diner is a local favorite, serving sit-down breakfasts, fluffy takeout buttermilk donuts and bakery items. Folks come from near and far for the generous wedges of decadent Key lime pie.

Boathouse Oyster Bar SEAFOOD $
(☎850-837-3645; www.boathouseoysterbar.com; 228 Hwy 98 E, Destin; items $4-18; ⊙11am-late) What looks like a waterfront shed is the most happening little place in Destin, with live music from country to jazz and phenomenal Apalachicola oysters, crawfish and seafood gumbo.

Dewey Destin's SEAFOOD $$
(☎850-837-7525; www.destinseafood.com; 202 Harbor Blvd, Destin; mains $9-22; ⊙from 11am) Refreshingly human-scale compared to some of the corporate-behemoth restaurants on Destin's main strip, this longtime local favorite serves up simple but delicious fried and steamed seafood platters and cool rum drinks in a crowded old beach shack decorated with vintage Florida photos. There's now a second location (☎850-837-7575; 9 Calhoun Ave, Destin; mains $9-22; ⊙from 11am) overlooking Crab Island.

Bay Café FRENCH $$
(☎850-344-7822; www.baycafewaterfront.com; 233 Alconese Ave, Fort Walton Beach; mains $16-28; ⊙11am-10pm Mon-Sat, to 3pm Sun) Foie gras, pan-seared scallops and filet mignon all feature on the menu of this *très jolie* French cafe on the waterfront beneath the shadow of the Brooks Bridge. Loved by locals for over 30 years, the cafe has an indoor-outdoor patio with wonderful views of the bay, and an extensive wine list.

★ Louisiana Lagniappe SEAFOOD $$$
(☎850-837-0881; www.thelouisianalagniappe.com/destin; 775 Gulf Shore Dr, Destin; mains $18-39; ⊙5-9pm Mon-Fri, to 10pm Sat & Sun) Real N'awlins cooking can be found right here in Destin, overlooking the water. Ocean-fresh seafood is presented in a style unique to New Orleans and the deep South: grouper, crab and lobster feature heavily. Attentive servers ensure you'll understand the subtleties of each dish before you order. Starched white tablecloths and stunning sunsets complete the picture. Highly recommended.

🍷 Drinking & Entertainment

HarborWalk Village and Okaloosa Island Boardwalk have plenty of nightlife, with busy, tourist-oriented pubs and restaurants overlooking the water.

Props Craft Brewery BREWERY
(☎850-586-7117; www.propsbrewery.com; 255 Miracle Strip Pkwy SE, Fort Walton Beach; ⊙11am-11pm) If you're looking for a friendly, unas-

suming spot to down a cold, locally brewed craft beer, check out some sport on the big screen or hang in the beer garden to mingle with the folks who call the Gulf Coast home, search no further.

AJ's Club Bimini   CLUB
(📞850-837-1913; www.ajs-destin.com/club-bimini; 116 Harbor Blvd, Destin; ⊙9pm-late) This tiki palace is dedicated to pleasure, with multiple tiers of dining and dancing. The bar also arranges daily sunset cruises on its luxury schooner.

🛍 Shopping

Silver Sands Outlets   MALL
(📞850-654-9771; www.silversandsoutlet.com; 10562 Emerald Coast Pkwy, Destin; ⊙10am-9pm Mon-Sat, to 6pm Sun) Over 100 premium outlet stores make up this attractive and easy-to-wander shopping paradise with current and last-season brand-name items at heavily discounted prices.

ℹ Information

Servicing the area is the **Emerald Coast Visitors Welcome Center** (📞850-651-7131, 800-322-3319; www.destin-fwb.com; 1540 Miracle Strip Pkwy, Destin; ⊙8am-5pm Mon-Fri, 10am-4pm Sat & Sun). Additional info can be found online at the Destin Area Chamber of Commerce website (www.destinchamber.com) and at www.destin-ation.com.

ℹ Getting There & Around

Destin is about 45 miles west of Panama City Beach and about 47 miles east of Pensacola, along Hwy 98. The **Okaloosa Regional Airport** (www.flyvps.com) serves the Destin–Fort Walton area, with direct services to many US cities, including Chicago and Tampa, with American Eagle, Vision, Delta, Continental and US Airways.

Okaloosa County Transit (www.rideoct.org) runs a shuttle service four times daily from 8am to 7pm Monday to Saturday in winter, and eight times daily from 8am to 10pm in summer (fares $1).

Beaches of South Walton & Scenic Highway 30A

📞850
Sandwiched between Destin and Panama City along Scenic Hwy 30A, these 15 unincorporated communities make up what is collectively known as Santa Rosa Beach or the Beaches of South Walton. Each town has its own identity, although most are masterplanned resort towns with architecture following set themes. All lie along an incredibly gorgeous stretch of gulf that's been dubbed the Emerald Coast. Driving the 30A along this stretch is an absolute must: peer between the dream homes and beachfront townhouses for glimpses of their million-dollar views, or park the car to wander around boutiques and cafes.

If you only make two stops, we recommend delightful Grayton Beach, which feels as though it was settled by old-school hippies who came into money (stay a night here if you can) and the almost inconceivably pretty village of Seaside (p443). Other places to wish you lived are the whimsically named community of WaterColor, Moroccan-themed Alys Beach and the Dutch-inspired hamlet of Rosemary Beach. For more information, check out www.discover30a.com.

The area is ideally suited for cyclists. You can explore the area along the 19-mile paved Timpoochee Trail, which parallels Scenic Hwy 30A; the 8-mile Longleaf Pine Greenway hiking and cycling trail, paralleling Hwy 30A inland from just east of SR 395 to just before SR 393; and the Eastern Lake Trail, which starts in Deer Lake State Park and links up with the western end of the Longleaf Pine Greenway.

Otherwise, if you prefer four wheels to two, allow at least two hours to drive the short stretch of the 30A between Destin and Panama City Beach, even if you're not planning to stop: speed limits are low, kids and cars are plentiful and the beaches are mesmerizing.

◉ Sights & Activities

Grayton Beach State Park   PARK
(📞850-267-8300; www.floridastateparks.org/graytonbeach; 357 Main Rd, Santa Rosa Beach; vehicle $5; ⊙8am-sunset) The beauty of this state park, a 1133-acre stretch of marble-colored dunes rolling down to the water's edge, is genuinely mind-blowing. It sits nestled against the wealthy but down-to-earth community of Grayton Beach, home to the famed Red Bar and to the quirky Dog Wall – a mural on which residents paint portraits of their dogs. Locals flock here for nightly sunsets and to wakeboard on the unique coastal dune lakes that shimmer across the sand from the gulf.

The park also contains the Grayton Beach Nature Trail (start your self-guided tour at the gate), which runs from the eastern side of the parking lot through the dunes, magnolias and pine flatwoods and onto a boardwalk to a return trail along the beach.

Eden Gardens State Park PARK

(☑850-267-8320; www.floridastateparks.org/
edengardens; 181 Eden Gardens Rd, Santa Rosa
Beach; admission $4, tours adult/child $4/2;
☺8am-sunset, tours 10am-3pm Mon-Thu) Inland
from 30A on a peninsula jutting into Choctawhatchee Bay, manicured gardens and
lawns front the 1800s estate home of the
Wesleys, a wealthy Florida timber family.
The white-columned house was purchased
and renovated in 1963 by Lois Maxon, who
turned it into a showcase for Louis XVI
furniture and many other heirlooms and
antiques. Visitors can relax in the oak-lined
grounds or the lovely picnic area by the
water.

Big Daddy's BICYCLE RENTAL

(☑850-622-1165; www.bigdaddysbikes.com; 2217
W County Hwy 30A, Santa Rosa Beach) 'Dangerously Optimistic since 1998,' the Daddy
will get you wheelin' down this picturesque
coastal road, or on the beach itself, in no
time at all. A plethora of two-wheeled rentals start at $26 per day, and include helmet,
lock and free delivery to and pickup from
most locations on Hwy 30A.

30-A Bike Rentals BICYCLE RENTAL

(☑850-865-7433; www.30Abikerentals.net; 5399 E
County Hwy 30A, Santa Rosa Beach) Bike rental,
including free delivery and pickup to most
locations on the highway, starting at $20
a day.

🛏 Sleeping

Accommodations on this section of the
30A vary from beachside camping to intimate guesthouses, a luxury resort and a
wide selection of jaw-droppingly beautiful
private-home and condo rentals. For the
latter, try www.graytoncoastrentals.com,
www.30avacationrentals.com and www.
cottagerentalagency.com. Book your rooms
ahead of time, or consider staying in Destin
or Panama City if you're on a budget.

Grayton Beach State Park CAMPGROUND $

(☑850-267-8300; www.floridastateparks.org/
graytonbeach; 357 Main Park Rd, Santa Rosa Beach;
tent & RV sites $24, cabins $110-130) It might be
tricky to make spending the rest of your
life here in paradise a reality, but it doesn't
mean you can't afford to stay here for a short
time. Cheap as chips camping and compact,
cozy cabins make a taste of Grayton Beach
living – albeit in the rough – a possibility for
everybody.

★ Hibiscus Coffee & Guesthouse GUESTHOUSE $$

(☑850-231-2733; www.hibiscusflorida.com; 85
Defuniak St, Grayton Beach; r from $115, 🌐🛜)
Tucked into a tree-studded corner of the
area's oldest township, you'll find this delightfully chilled-out garden guesthouse. A
variety of self-contained rooms and apartments are done up with tropical prints and
funky folk paintings, like an arty friend's
beach house. If you're just day-tripping,
why not stop by for tasty, healthy multigrain
pancakes or a mango smoothie in the on-
site vegetarian cafe (items from $4; ☺7:30-
11:30am): it's so very Grayton Beach.

★ WaterColor Inn & Resort RESORT $$$

(☑866-426-2656; www.watercolorresort.com; 4
Goldenrod Circle, WaterColor; r from $250) This
lauded, full-service luxury resort designed
by architect David Rockwell occupies almost
500 acres of beachfront land. Contemporary
rooms feature soft linens in seaside tones,
large windows and balconies. Many have
ocean views or are steps from the beach. No
fewer than six gorgeous pools and the stunning waters of the gulf invite you to soothe
away any tensions and relax into a truly rest-
ful vacation.

Pensione BOUTIQUE HOTEL $$$

(☑866-348-8952; www.rosemarybeach.com/
pensione-rosemary-beach; 78 Main St, Rosemary
Beach; r from $195; 🌐🛜) As its name sug-
gests, this recently renovated private hotel
in downtown Rosemary Beach is styled like
a European inn. There's no lobby, and the 11
guest rooms are quiet and individually decorated, with mod-cons like free wi-fi, Blu-
ray players, flat-screen TVs and Keurig cof-
feemakers. Guests receive complimentary
access to the local racquet club and fitness
center.

🍴 Eating & Drinking

Grayton Beach, Seaside and Rosemary
Beach all have fun downtown areas with
several restaurants and nightlife spots.

Rose Bros CAFE

(www.rbsodafountain.com; 78 Main St, Rosemary
Beach; items from $3; ☺7am-9pm Mon-Sat)
Refreshment is the theme of this smart
yet casual Rosemary Beach cafe and soda
fountain: ice cream, milkshakes, hot dogs
and burgers all feature on a simple menu
designed with comfort and ease in mind.

LIFE IN A BUBBLE: SEASIDE

If you need some help designing your dream board, come and spend some time – an hour, or an afternoon or evening, if you can – photographing this close-to-perfect designer community that might make you feel as though you've stumbled into a movie. Jim Carrey fans especially will probably feel a strong sense of déjà vu: the 1998 film *The Truman Show* about the unwitting star of a popular reality-TV series, set in an annoyingly perfect place, was filmed almost entirely here.

Unlike the film, Seaside is idyllic without being annoying. Lauded as the country's first planned community, it was created in 1981 with input from a range of accomplished architects and has been hailed as a model for New Urbanism. It didn't quite take off as the year-round place to live, as expected, but it has become a largely seasonal community of summer homes for wealthy folk from other parts of the country.

If you come in the low season (November to April), it'll seem even more surreal than usual: if you go for an evening stroll you may be the only one on the streets or the beach. Other times there's plenty of life here and people seem genuinely friendly. Consider it a side effect of living in paradise.

There's a hip book and music shop, **Sundog Books** (☑850-231-5481; www.sundog-books.com; 89 Central Sq; ⊙9am-9pm), carrying great literature, coffee-table pieces and uber-cool tracks. Nearby are a handful of excellent eateries, some small private art galleries and – the pièce de résistance – one of the most stunning beaches on the coast.

The grassy town square, under renovation at time of writing, has always been a popular spot to sit and people-watch. You won't be able to miss the irresistibly photogenic group of vintage silver Airstream trailers that form a kind of food court in the center of town, hawking everything from decadent cupcakes to vitamin-laden juices. Unless you're gluten and dairy intolerant, we dare you to go past our favorite of these food trucks, the **Meltdown on 30A** (☑850-231-0952; 2235 E County Hwy 30A; items from $5; ⊙8:30am-10pm), a vendor of oozy grilled-cheese deliciousness (we couldn't resist the avocado-and-bacon-jam creation). It also serves cheese-tastic breakfast biscuits and grits till 11am. Eat in the shade or on the beach – cheap, cheery and...did we mention the cheese?

It's refreshingly reasonably priced for such a tourist-centric locale.

Cowgirl Kitchen TEX-MEX $
(☑850-213-0058; www.cowgirlkitchen.com; 54 Main St, Rosemary Beach; mains $6-15; ⊙8am-9pm; 🐾) A longtime favorite for casual Tex-Mex bites like burritos, nachos, tacos galore and spicy chicken salads, in the center of cute, walkable downtown Rosemary Beach. The well-priced menu also features a variety of signature pizzas, which can be downed with a beer while watching the game on the big-screen TV.

Red Bar PUB $$
(☑850-231-1008; www.theredbar.com; 70 Hotz Ave, Grayton Beach; dinner mains $14-25; ⊙11am-3pm & 5-10pm, bar open till late) There's live music most nights at this hippy, homely, funky local fave, housed in the old general store. It draws friendly mobs who hunker down for beers, goss and good tunes, or to tuck into a small selection of well-prepared dishes, like crab cakes, shrimp-stuffed eggplant and manicotti.

★ **Cafe Thirty-A** AMERICAN $$$
(☑850-231-2166; www.cafethirtya.com; 3899 E Scenic Hwy 30A, Santa Rosa Beach; mains $14-38) Set in a modern, Frank Lloyd Wright–esque townhouse, this smart-casual fine-dining establishment feels good from the moment you walk through the door. Seafood delights include Maine lobster in paradise and wood-oven-roasted grouper, but you can enjoy a filet mignon cooked to perfection or pan-roasted chicken if you just gotta have some turf with your surf.

Fish out of Water SEAFOOD $$$
(☑850-534-5050; 34 Goldenrod Circle, Water-Color; mains $18-40; ⊙8-11am Mon, 8-11am & 5:30-9pm Tue-Sun) With a menu focusing on local bounty – roasted black grouper, steamed red snapper, fresh Apalachicola oysters – a dining room oozing understated good taste and alfresco dining on the breathtaking sunset deck, this is a destination restaurant. For the experience minus the sunset (and the dent in the wallet), come for breakfast.

Bud & Alley's
AMERICAN $$$

(☏850-231-5900; www.budandalleys.com; 2236 East County Rd 30A, Seaside; mains $25-34; ⊙11am-9:30pm) This landmark seafood restaurant, with dining room and rooftop tables overlooking the gulf, is a seriously happening place to be – especially at sunset, when locals and visitors gather to cheer on the sky while enjoying cold beers and such excellent dishes as seared halibut and grilled shrimp and grits. Weekends bring live world, jazz and funk music. Some critics argue that the food doesn't justify the price, but we think the view and the vibe just might.

❶ Information

Beaches of South Walton Tourist Center

(☏800-822-6877; www.beachesofsouthwalton.com; cnr Hwys 331 & 98; ⊙8am-4:30pm) The tourist center is inland, between SR 283 and SR 83. There's also a bulletin board with tourist brochures on the eastern end of Seaside Town Sq.

Panama City Beach

☏850 / POP 11,800

While much of the Panhandle's charms spring from its mellow Old Florida roots, don't expect to find any of those vibes in Panama City Beach, an overdeveloped gulf-front pocket about 10 miles west of unremarkable Panama City. PCB (as the locals call it) has embraced a transformation from 1970s resort town to overcommercialized condo hot spot. Families come here for cheap vacays, retirees move here to live out their days, and youngsters flock to get smashed in the sunshine.

Architecturally dire high-rises spring up from the beachfront and block both sunlight and vistas for those on the streets below, which are lined with more strip malls, chain hotels, amusement arcades, uninspiring restaurants and dive bars than good taste allows. From March to May the place goes bonkers as a spring-break destination, when students from 150 colleges east of the Mississippi roar into town to drink and party till they puke.

That said, PCB's beaches remain dazzling for swimming, fishing and diving, with dozens of natural, historic and artificial reefs attracting spectacular marine life. The city's tourism boom means cheap rooms close to the more inspiring stretch of Hwy 30A between here and Destin, where affordable beds are in short supply. In the low season, beachfront bargains can be found.

Panama City Beach is one for wannabe spring-breakers, and families on a budget with hard-to-entertain kids – outside spring-break season, of course!

◉ Sights & Activities

There's plenty to do in PCB, especially for the young and young at heart. Cinemas, mini-golf, shopping and amusement arcades are in plentiful supply, and there is a handful of fun attractions.

Something of a scuba-diver's paradise, the area has more than a dozen boats offshore, including a 441ft WWII Liberty ship and numerous tugs, earning the place its nickname 'Wreck Capital of the South.' There are more than 50 artificial reefs made from bridge spans, barges and a host of other sunken structures, as well as natural coral reefs. Visibility varies from 10ft to 80ft, averaging around 40ft. In winter, the average water temperature is 60°F (16°C), rising to 87°F (31°C) in summer.

★ Shell Island
PARK

(☏850-233-0504; www.shellislandshuttle.com; 4607 State Park Lane, Panama City; round-trip adult/child $17/9; ⊙9am-5pm Mar-Sep) Offshore from St Andrews State Park, this sandy 'desert' island is fantastic for sunbathing, swimming and snorkelling. There are neither facilities nor shade: wear a hat and plenty of sunscreen. To get here, buy tickets for the Shell Island Shuttle at Pier Marketplace in the park; there's a trolley service to the boat. Snorkelling and kayak rentals are available. Check the website for details and schedules.

St Andrews State Park
PARK

(☏850-233-5140; www.floridastateparks.org/standrews; 4607 State Park Lane, Panama City; vehicle/pedestrian $8/2; ⊙8am-sunset) This peaceful 1260-acre park is graced with nature trails, swimming beaches and wildlife, including foxes, coyotes, snakes, seabirds and alligators (fear not: gators live in freshwater, and the swimming areas – including the kiddie pool's 4ft-deep water, near the jetties – are in the ocean). Excellent waterfront campsites are available year-round for $28. You can still see the circular cannon platforms from when this area was used as a military reservation during WWII; look for them on the beach near the jetties.

WonderWorks
MUSEUM

(☏850-249-7000; www.wonderworkspcb.com; 9910 Front Beach Rd, Panama City Beach; adult/

child $24/19, laser tag extra $8; ⊙9am-10pm;) Designed to look like an upside-down building (complete with an upside-down lawn and palm trees), this wacky interactive museum and fun center is impossible to miss – even if you want to! While hands-on exhibits like a spinning g-force bike, an obstacle climbing course and virtual-reality soccer may give some grown-ups a migraine, kids will have a blast: literally, in the case of the laser-tag maze!

Bear Creek Feline Center ANIMAL RESCUE
(✆850-722-9927; www.bearcreekfelinecenter.org; 8822 Tracy Way, Panama City; suggested donation $50; ⊙tours by appointment) Outside Panama City, this unique facility with an emphasis on conservation, preservation and education provides 'forever homes' for a total of 24 exotic felines from around the world. Each cat is assigned to an individual handler, and if getting up close and personal with majestic panthers, bobcats and lynxes gets you purring, a visit to the center is a must. Tours are by appointment only. The center is about 14 miles north of Panama City, and 24 miles inland.

Museum of Man in the Sea MUSEUM
(✆850-235-4101; www.maninthesea.org; 17314 Panama City Beach Pkwy, Panama City Beach; adult/child $5/free; ⊙10am-5pm Wed-Sat) Owned by the Institute of Diving, this museum takes a close look at the sport. Interactive exhibits let you crank up a Siebe pump, climb into a Beaver Mark IV submersible, check out models of underwater laboratory Sealab III and find out how diving bells really work. There's also a cool collection of old diving suits and a sea-life-filled aquarium.

Ripley's Believe It or Not! MUSEUM
(✆850-230-6113; www.ripleyspanamacitybeach. com; 9907 Front Beach Rd, Panama City Beach; adult/child $16/11; ⊙9am-9pm;) Love it or hate it, the ubiquitous Ripley's is very Panama City Beach – loud, crowded, tacky-but-fun. In a building designed to look like a ship, the 'Odditorium' features bizarro exhibits like a replica of the world's tallest man and an Amazonian shrunken head (believe it? Or not?). There's also laser tag (locals love it!) and an IMAX with seats that shake.

Gulf World Marine Park AQUARIUM
(✆850-234-5271; www.gulfworldmarinepark.com; 15412 Front Beach Rd, Panama City Beach; adult/child $20/12; ⊙9:30am-5pm, later in summer & holidays) Open since 1969, this aquarium is a good place to get up close and personal with our marine friends: swim with dolphins programs, including classroom sessions, start at $175. (Animal-welfare groups believe that interacting with captive sea creatures is harmful to the animals. Gulf World states that its policy is one of protection and education. Ultimately, the choice is yours.) Children must be over five to swim with the dolphins.

Dive Locker DIVING
(✆850-230-8006; www.divelocker.net; 106 Thomas Dr, Panama City Beach; ⊙8am-6pm) This well-respected outfitter and dive school knows all the local reefs. Basic supervised dives start at $84, gear included. Three-day open-water-certification courses cost $325. Check the website for the lowdown on what's on offer.

🛏 Sleeping

A plentiful supply of beds means there's usually something for everyone in Panama City Beach – or for everyone's budget, anyway. In terms of taste, there's nothing particularly noteworthy. The code words 'family-friendly' or 'families only' mean you'll avoid spring-breakers, in season. Rates vary dramatically between quieter winter months and heaving summers, and they spike during spring break (March to May). For a complete guide to hotels and resorts, visit www. pcbeach.org.

Driftwood Lodge HOTEL $
(✆850-234-6601; www.driftwoodpcb.com; 15811 Front Beach Rd, Panama City Beach; d from $89) An absolute beachfront location with two pools and a variety of spotless, no-frills room types make this family-friendly motel an excellent budget choice. Minimum stays are sometimes required during busy periods: check with the hotel for details.

Holiday Inn Resort HOTEL $$
(✆850-234-1111; www.hipcbeach.com; 11127 Front Beach Rd, Panama City Beach; r from $99) This half-moon-shaped beachfront mega-hotel has large, recently refurbished rooms, although it's impossible to fully shake its '70s *Boogie Nights* vibe. It's got something for everyone, from party-hearty spring-breakers to holidaying families and lonely solos looking for love. The sheer hulking size of the place means good deals can usually be found.

Bay Point Wyndham Resort HOTEL $$
(✆850-236-6000; www.baypointwyndham.com; 4114 Jan Cooley Dr, Panama City Beach; r from $99;

✳ 🛜 🅿) One of the more comfortable bases in PCB is this pleasantly appointed resort, featuring views of St Andrews Bay, two golf courses, water-sports rentals, a lovely pool, three on-site restaurants and a full-service spa. Rooms are cozy, modern and airy.

Wisteria Inn
MOTEL $$

(📞 850-234-0557; www.wisteria-inn.com; 20404 Front Beach Rd, Panama City Beach; d from $99; 🅿 ✳ 🅿 🅿) This sweet little 15-room motel has a variety of tastefully themed rooms from South Beach to the Far East, as well as poolside mimosa hours and an 'adults only' policy that discourages spring-breakers. It's also very pet-friendly: keep that in mind if you're allergic to four-legged friends.

✗ Eating & Drinking

People don't flock to Panama City Beach for the cuisine, although restaurants and eateries aren't in short supply. Waiting for a table at one of the beachside's many massive restaurants is an endurance sport. Downtown Panama City, to the east, has more low-key offerings and less waiting, but you'll have to drive.

Andy's Flour Power Bakery
BAKERY $

(📞 850-230-0014; www.andysflourpower.com; 3123 Thomas Dr, Panama City; items from $3; ⏰ 7am-2pm) Come for hands-down the best breakfasts in town: fluffy rolled omelets cooked to perfection, cheesy grits, breakfast frittata, Belgian waffles and, of course, bacon and eggs, any way you like 'em. Locals are known to start the day with breakfast here and come back for lunch: tasty New York deli–style sandwiches galore on freshly baked breads. Highly recommended.

Pineapple Willy's
CARIBBEAN $$

(📞 850-235-1225; www.pwillys.com; 9875 S Thomas Dr, Panama City Beach; mains $10-28; ⏰ 11am-late) Ask for a table on the restaurant pier for breezy beachside dining. Famed for its signature drinks and its house special, Jack Daniels barbecue ribs, this is a monster venue popular with a younger crowd.

★ Firefly
MODERN AMERICAN $$$

(📞 850-249-3359; www.fireflypcb.com; 535 Richard Jackson Blvd, Panama City Beach; mains $23-42; ⏰ 5-10pm) This uber-atmospheric, casual fine-dining establishment glistens with hundreds of fairy lights and beckons with

---

WORTH A TRIP

MEXICO BEACH

For an alternative to the expense of the Beaches of South Walton and the mania of Panama City Beach, consider the delightfully old-school outpost of Mexico Beach, located midway between Panama City and Port St Joe, a few miles past gargantuan Tyndall Air Force Base. There's not much to do here but relax and enjoy the peace, quiet and slower pace of this sweet little hamlet: shacks by the beach, fish and chips, folks playing in the streets. And if the kids get bored, it's only a half-hour drive to the hustle and bustle of PCB.

For a place to rest your weary head, consider the authentically retro, beachfront **El Govenor Motel** (📞 850-648-5757; www.elgovenormotel.net; Hwy 98; d from $69). Rooms are dated but clean and some have kitchen facilities. All have balconies overlooking the gulf. The motel is also home to the most appealing pool bar in the world. If you're looking for something a little more homely, yet exotic, try the **Driftwood Inn** (📞 850-648-5126; www.driftwoodinn.com; 2105 Hwy 98; d from $110), with its manicured gardens, gift shop, resident pets and combination of tidy hotel-style rooms and oceanfront cottages. Otherwise, a variety of private vacation rentals are available: many are absolute beachfront and enjoy unforgettable sunsets. Try www.gulfcoastvacationrentals.com for private listings.

Mexico Beach is a great place to self-cater, with many accommodation options featuring functional kitchens. Of the smattering of local eateries, we liked **Fish House Restaurant** (📞 850-648-8950; www.fishhousemexicobeach.com; 3006 Hwy 98; mains $9-28; ⏰ 11am-9pm Mon-Fri, 7am-9pm Sat & Sun) for low-key, family-friendly fish and chips and fry-up breakfasts. You can't go past the killer shrimp basket, overflowing with golden battered shrimp and fries for just $7 between 11am and 4pm. And there's something for everyone at **Toucan's** (📞 850-648-8207; www.toucansmexicobeachfl.com; 719 Hwy 98; ⏰ 11am-11pm), a beachfront sports bar, tiki bar and seafood grill. Best of all, the killer sunsets are free and go down particularly well with cold beer.

seafood dishes like sesame tempura shrimp, andouille crusted snapper and a wide variety of sushi and sashimi. It's good enough for the US president – Obama has dined here, and the regulars won't let you forget it.

Don't be turned off by the price of the mains: there's a bunch of well-priced appetizers and weekly happy hours are offered. Check the website for details.

Tootsie's Orchid Lounge   LOUNGE, LIVE MUSIC
(☑ 850-236-3459; www.tootsies.net; 700 S Pier Park Dr, Panama City Beach; ☉ 10am-late) It lacks the dusty character of the Nashville original, but the non-stop live country music is still plenty boot-stompin' for y'all.

🔒 Shopping

Pier Park   MALL
(☑ 850-236-9974; www.simon.com/mall/pier-park; 600 Pier Park Dr, Panama City Beach; ☉ 10am-9pm Mon-Sat, noon-6pm Sun) Popular with families, this sprawling outdoor mall and entertainment zone has endless chain stores for clothing, accessories and snack foods, and several touristy restaurants and bars.

ℹ️ Information

Panama City Beach Convention & Visitors Bureau (☑ 850-233-6503; www.visitpanamacitybeach.com; 17001 Panama City Beach Pkwy, Panama City Beach; ☉ 8am-5pm) Come for maps, brochures and the lowdown on what's up and coming in town.

Panama City Beach Chamber of Commerce (☑ 850-235-1159; www.pcbeach.org; 309 Richard Jackson Blvd, Suite 101, Panama City Beach; ☉ 9am-5pm Mon-Fri, to 2pm Sat) This handy information office has touch-screen kiosks with information on where to sleep, shop and play.

Panama City Beach Public Library (☑ 850-235-5055; www.nwrls.lib.fl.us; 12500 Hutchison Blvd, Panama City Beach; ☉ 9am-6pm Mon-Wed, to 5pm Thu & Fri, to 4pm Sat) Provides free internet access.

ℹ️ Getting There & Around

The **Northwest Florida Beaches International Airport** (PFN; ☑ 850-763-6751; www.iflybeaches.com; 6300 West Bay Pkwy, Panama City) is served by Delta and Southwest, with daily nonstop flights to Atlanta, Baltimore, Houston, Nashville and St Louis.

For bus services connecting throughout the continental USA, head to the **Greyhound** (☑ 850-785-6111; www.greyhound.com; 917 Harrison Ave, Panama City) bus station, al-

though it's not the most inviting of places for visitors to arrive or depart!

By car, Panama City Beach is almost halfway between Tallahassee (about 130 miles) and Pensacola (95 miles). Coming along the coast, Hwy 98 takes you into town; from I-10 take either Hwy 231 or Hwy 79 south.

The **Bay Town Trolley** (☑ 850-769-0557; www.baytowntrolley.org; tickets $1.50) runs in Panama City Beach. The service continues to add stops to its coverage, but its schedule is still limited to Monday to Friday between 6am and 8pm.

Classic Rentals (☑ 850-235-1519; www.classicrentalsinc.com; 13226 Front Beach Rd, Panama City Beach; ☉ 8am-5pm) rents scooters (half/full day $20/35) and old-school Harleys (half/full day $75/125).

Cape San Blas & Port St Joe

☑ 850 / POP 3500

Delicate Cape San Blas curls around St Joseph Bay at the southwestern end of the bulge in the Panhandle, starting on the mainland at Port St Joe and ending at its undeveloped, 10-mile-long tip with **St Joseph Peninsula State Park** (☑ 850-227-1327; www.floridastateparks.org/stjoseph; 8899 Cape San Blas Rd; vehicle $6, campsites $24, cabins $100; ☉ 8am-sunset). The sugar-sand beaches stretch for 2516 acres along grassy, undulating dunes, edging wilderness trails and the 13-mile **Loggerhead Run Bike Path**, named for the turtles that inhabit the island, which is perfect for cyclists, joggers or bladers.

The state park is one of the most prized camping spots along the Gulf Coast, home to 119 sites in two separate developed grounds. You can stay in seclusion in just-renovated loft-style timber cabins with queen beds and walkways leading from your back door to the water (bring your own towels). At the peninsula's northern extremity, primitive camping is allowed in designated areas of the wilderness preserve in the park, a sojourning point for migratory birds and butterflies. You'll need to bring everything, including water and a camp stove, as no fires are allowed. Pets are not permitted anywhere in the park.

There is a lovely place to picnic right at the start of the cape, though – **Salinas Park** (Cape San Blas Rd), where you can stroll an over-dunes boardwalk, take a dip in the gulf or just sit and enjoy the waterfront breezes before continuing on with your journey.

INDIAN PASS RAW BAR

On a desolate stretch of 30A just outside Port St Joe, this old wooden building might look like an abandoned general store. But look a little closer, and you'll see pickup trucks parked two deep in the back lot, and note the twang of guitar music coming from the porch. This is **Indian Pass Raw Bar** (☑ 850-227-1670; www.indianpassrawbar.com; 8391 Indian Pass Rd; mains $10-17; ☉ noon-9pm Tue-Sat), a family tradition serving the area for over 100 years and one of the true classics of old Florida Gulf culture. Inside, grab a beer from the cooler (on the honor system) and take a seat at a share table, if you can find a spot. The menu, posted above the bar, is simple: oysters three ways (raw, steamed or baked with Parmesan cheese), crab legs and a handful of shrimp dishes. Please, get the oysters – even if you think you don't like the salty bivalves, you'll be surprised at the sweetness of these guys, drawn just this morning from the waters of nearby Apalachicola. Stay for a slice of Key lime pie and impromptu line dancing on the porch. If you're lucky, Jimmy will be firing up the drum grill out front with his specialty drunken chicken.

Across the bay, which has gentle rip- and current-free swimming, the town of **Port St Joe** was once known as 'sin city' for the casinos and bordellos that greeted seafarers. Note the switch in time zones from Central to Eastern here: even though Port St Joe is west of some Central time communities, it goes by Eastern Time. The Florida Constitution was originally drafted here in 1838, but scarlet fever and hurricanes combined to stymie its progression as one of Florida's boom towns. These days it's in something of a transition as industry, particularly paper mills, gives way to tourism, with a small historic district showing fledgling signs of renewal.

A really pleasant Panhandle overnight stop is the **Port Inn** (☑ 850-229-7678; www.portinnfl.com; 501 Monument Ave/Hwy 98, Port St Joe; r from $80; ❄ 🛜 🐾), with front-row seats for the sunsets over the bay. A timber porch with rocking chairs runs the full length of this lovely inn, which has bay-view rooms with sisal carpet, wicker furniture and sparkling baths. Its Thirsty Goat lounge bar is a nice, mellow spot to wind up your evening with a cold brew.

For something a little more lively and atmospheric, enjoy live music nightly inside or on the poop deck at the **Lookout Lounge** (☑ 850-647-8310; www.lookoutlounge.com; 602 Nautilus Dr, Port St Joe; ☉ 5pm-late). Enjoy a cold one as the sun slides gently beneath the horizon and you feel, ahh, oh so good to be alive.

Apalachicola

☑ 850 / POP 2260

Slow, mellow and delightfully preserved, Apalachicola is one of the gulf's most appealing villages and a key Panhandle destination, with a sultry Southern vibe and plenty of excellent accommodation and dining options.

Perched on the edge of a broad bay, the oak-shaded town combines an old-fashioned fishing-based economy with a new wave of bistros, art galleries, eclectic boutiques, and B&Bs in renovated old mansions: it's hugely popular as a romantic weekend getaway – stroll through the Historic District at sunset and you'll understand why.

Don't even think of leaving without trying one of the area's famous oysters – Apalachicola Bay is one of the best known producers. Essentially, the oysters are all the same, but half the fun is finding out which of the myriad local restaurants serve them freshest or have the most original and delicious seasonings. (We gave it our all researching it for you.)

☉ Sights

The sights below – and 35 in total – are well marked on a chamber of commerce historic walking tour guide and map, available free from the chamber office and most B&Bs. Apalachicola's main drag is Ave E, and the entire Historic District is easily walked and is lined with interesting shops and restaurants.

John Gorrie State Museum   MUSEUM

(☑ 850-653-9347; www.floridastateparks.org/JohnGorrieMuseum; 46 6th St; admission $2; ☉ 9am-5pm Thu-Mon) Dr John Gorrie (1803–55), one of Apalachicola's most famous sons, developed an ice-making machine to keep yellow-fever patients cool during an epidemic. He died poor and unknown, unaware of how his invention laid the groundwork for modern refrigeration and air conditioning. This tiny museum commemorates him.

THE PANHANDLE APALACHICOLA

Raney House
HISTORIC BUILDING

(☑ 850-653-1700; 128 Market St; donations welcome; ☺1-4pm Sun-Thu, 10am-4pm Fri & Sat) **FREE** Sitting behind a white-picket fence and a facade of grand columns, this small museum occupies the former 1838 Southern-style plantation home of two-time mayor of Apalachicola David Raney.

Trinity Episcopal Church
CHURCH

(☑ 850-653-9550; 79 6th St) This handsome church was built in New York state and cut into sections, which were shipped down the Atlantic Coast and around the Keys before making their way to this spot where the church was reassembled in 1836.

Grady Market
MARKET

(☑ 850-653-4099; www.jegrady.com; 76 Water St; ☺10am-5:30pm Mon-Sat) Built in the late 1880s and rebuilt after a fire in 1900, this hulking brick space was originally a ship's chandlery and general store, as well as the home of a French consulate. Today it's a sprawling market of antiques traders and galleries running the gamut from textiles to painting and sculpture.

☞ Tours

Backwater Guide Service
BOAT TOUR

(☑ 850-899-0063; www.backwaterguideservice. com; tours $175-350; ☺by appointment) Offers private wildlife-spotting boat tours, where alligators, wading birds and willowy trees are the main attractions, and fishing charters with the promise of snagging your own red fish or speckled trout for grilling.

🛏 Sleeping

★ Water Street Hotel
HOTEL $$

(☑ 850-653-3700; www.waterstreethotel.com; 329 Water St; r from $129) Fabulous, modern yet classically styled one- and two-bedroom suites with full kitchens, four-poster beds and broad covered porches overlooking the Apalachicola River await at this delightful new boutique hotel and marina located a short walk from downtown.

Coombs House Inn
B&B $$

(☑ 850-653-9199; www.coombshouseinn.com; 80 6th St; r incl breakfast from $129; ❈ 🤶) This stunning yellow Victorian inn was built in 1905 and features black-cypress wall paneling, nine fireplaces, a carved oak staircase, leaded glass windows and beadboard ceilings. Settle into one of the fabulous rooms and be sure to join the other guests for nightly wine socials in the dining room, where a lavish breakfast is also served each morning.

Apalachicola River Inn
INN $$

(☑ 850-653-8139; www.apalachicolariverinn.com; 123 Water St; r incl breakfast from $149; ❈ 🤶) Strung with Christmas lights that twinkle across Apalachicola Bay, this waterfront inn has tasteful, old-fashioned rooms in pastel shades, many with water views. The on-site restaurant, **Caroline's River Dining**, is one of the best places in town for breakfast (it's open to the general public as well as guests).

House of Tartts
GUESTHOUSE $$

(☑ 850-653-4687; www.houseoftartts.com; 50 Ave F; r $120-135, carriage house $215; ❈) With creaky wooden floors, fireplaces and rustic log cabin-ish walls, this charmingly low-key guesthouse feels every bit of its 125-plus years. A shared kitchen and a lack of daily housekeeping make this seem more like staying at a friend's house than staying at a B&B. The carriage house is great value for families.

Gibson Inn
INN $$

(☑ 850-653-2191; www.gibsoninn.com; 51 Ave C; r from $120; ❈) This grand 1907 cracker-style inn has 30 somewhat creaky rooms with bright colors and high antique beds. Ask for a 2nd-floor room that opens onto the sprawling veranda – or, if you're game, request reputedly haunted room 309. The hotel restaurant **Ira's** does wonderful home-style dinners.

✗ Eating & Drinking

The Historic District is packed with cute cafes and bistros; nightlife pretty much consists of watching the moon dance over the bay.

★ Up the Creek Raw Bar
SEAFOOD $$

(☑ 850-653-2525; www.upthecreekrawbar.com; 313 Water St; mains $7-20; ☺noon-9pm) We reckon these are the 'best' oysters in town. There's a variety of toppers, but we loved the 'classic': lightly cooked with Colby-Jack cheese, chopped jalapeños and bacon – a great way to introduce oyster virgins to the bivalve. Oh, and the crab and lobster bisque is to die for! Order at the counter and pull up a pew in the shade-house or on the deck.

A bunch of tasty burgers and salads are available. You just can't beat the combination of the food, the view and a cold beer.

Owl Cafe & Tap Room   MODERN AMERICAN $$

(☑850-653-9888; www.owlcafeflorida.com; 15 Ave D; mains $16-28; ⏲11am-10pm Mon-Sat, 10:30am-3pm Sun) Everyone is catered to in this local favorite, with casual fine dining in the upstairs cafe and wine room and craft beers and tap-room-only offerings below. The eclectic menu both includes and deviates from the seafood theme: vegetarian pastas, pork tenderloin, chicken marsala and jumbo gulf shrimp all make appearances. Brunches are spectacular.

AJ's Neighborhood Bar & Grill   DINER $$

(☑850-653-2571; www.ajsapa.com; 120 Martin Luther King Jr Ave; mains $9-32; ⏲11am-10pm Tue-Sun) De-licious homestyle Southern fare (soul food and seafood) is cooked to order at this friendly, family-run diner just outside the downtown area. Choose from wings, crab cakes, mullet and grouper cooked as you like it, as well as tender fried chicken and tasty sides like mac and cheese, green beans and garlic mash. Mmm-mmm!

Tamara's Café Floridita   SOUTH AMERICAN $$$

(☑850-697-4111; www.tamarascafe.com; 17 Ave E; mains $16-32; ⏲8:30am-10pm) In the heart of town, Tamara's popular cuisine is influenced by the spices of her native Venezuela, in dishes like grilled, herbed pork chop with shrimp and scallops in a creamy tomato-tarragon sauce, and margarita chicken sautéed in honey, tequila and lime glaze with scallops.

❶ Information

Apalachicola Bay Chamber of Commerce
(☑850-653-9419; www.apalachicolabay.org; 122 Commerce St; ⏲9am-5pm Mon-Fri) Offers bucketloads of tourist information, oyster facts, downtown walking maps and helpful advice.

❶ Getting There & Around

Hwy 98 (which becomes Market St) brings you into town from either direction. It's easy (and delightful) to wander around downtown, but you'll need a car to explore the greater area.

St George Island

☑850 / POP 300

Located just over a 4-mile causeway from Apalachicola's neighbor Eastpoint, this 28-mile-long barrier island is home to white-sand beaches, bay forests, salt marshes and an inoffensive mix of summer homes and condos. It's a great place for shelling, kayaking, sailing or swimming. At the end of every street on the island you'll find public beach access and, generally, plentiful parking. St George Island State Park sits at the island's northeastern point; Little St George Island lies southwest.

◉ Sights & Activities

St George Island State Park   PARK
(☑850-927-2111; www.floridastateparks.org/stgeorgeisland; vehicle $6, tent & RV sites $24; ⏲8am-dusk) The island at its undeveloped best is found here, in the 9 miles of glorious beach and sand dunes that make up this pristine park. A 2.5-mile nature trail offers exceptional birding opportunities and throughout the park boardwalks lead to shell-sprinkled beaches, with shallow waters perfect for canoeing, kayaking, and fishing for flounder and whiting. See loggerhead sea turtles from May, when they come ashore to dig nests and lay their eggs, yielding hatchlings that race into the gulf.

Camping is permitted at one of the 60 powered campsites, or at the Gap Point primitive campsites, accessible by boat or a 2.5-mile hike.

**Apalachicola National
Estuarine Research Reserve**   RESEARCH CENTER
Just over the bridge from Apalachicola, in Eastpoint, the Apalachicola National Estuarine Research Reserve provides a great overview of its research site, which encompasses over 385 sq miles in Apalachicola Bay, with giant aquariums simulating different habitats. A half-mile boardwalk leads down to the river, where you'll find a free telescope on a turret.

St George Lighthouse   LIGHTHOUSE
(www.stgeorgelight.org; adult/child $5/3; ⏲10am-5pm Mon-Wed, Fri & Sat, noon-5pm Sun) Originally built in 1858, this little lighthouse was painstakingly reconstructed in 2008 after collapsing into the sea due to erosion in 2005. Today you can climb the 92 steps to the top for glorious water views.

Journeys   BOAT TOUR, KAYAK TOUR
(☑850-927-3259; www.sgislandjourneys.com; 240 E 3rd St) This outfitter leads boat and kayak tours (from $50), and rents kayaks ($60 per day), sailboats ($100 per day) and catamarans ($275 per day). All are ideal ways to make the voyage to Cape St George.

ST VINCENT ISLAND & AROUND

Just a few minutes from Apalachicola but accessible only by boat lies pristine **St Vincent Island** (☑850-653-8808; www.fws.gov/saintvincent). Its pearly dunes reveal 5000-year-old geological records, while its pine forests and wetlands teem with endangered species such as red wolves, sea turtles, bald eagles and peregrine falcons. Fishing's permitted on lakes except when bald eagles are nesting (generally in winter). For those sick of the high-rises and bikini-clad crowds of the gulf beaches, it's the perfect getaway for a day of hiking and solitude. To get here, hop aboard the **St Vincent Island Shuttle** (☑850-229-1065; www.stvincentisland.com; adult/child $10/7), which can also take your bike ($20), or rent you one of its own ($25, including boat trip). Phone for schedules and reservations.

On the mainland near Apalachicola's shrimping-boat docks, the **St Vincent National Wildlife Refuge Visitors Center** (☑850-653-8808; www.fws.gov/saintvincent; 479 Market St; ⊙10am-3:30pm Mon-Thu) **FREE** has interactive exhibits and information.

🛏 Sleeping

Most visitors to the island rent cottages, which can be anything from a humble beach shack to a multi-story mansion: try www.st-georgeislandvacationproperties.com. Hotels are limited to the two options below.

St George Inn　　　　　　　INN **$**
(☑850-927-2903; www.stgeorgeinn.com; 135 Franklin Blvd; r from $85; ❄🅿🛜🏊) One of the few historic structures on an island lined with new condo development, this rambling clapboard inn has comfy if creaky rooms and numerous cozy sitting areas filled with dog-eared books.

Buccaneer Inn　　　　　　MOTEL **$**
(☑800-847-2091; www.buccinn.com; 160 W Gorrie Dr; r from $70; ❄🛜🏊) Right on the gulf, rooms here are like those of a basic, design-challenged motel – dated green carpet, painted cinderblock walls. But all are clean, bright and surprisingly spacious, and some have kitchenettes.

🍴 Eating & Drinking

As with accommodations, eating options are surprisingly limited on the island, as many families cook for themselves. If you're day-tripping here, you may want to pack a picnic.

Blue Parrot Oceanfront Café　SEAFOOD **$$**
(☑850-927-2987; www.blueparrotcafe.net; 68 W Gorrie Dr; mains $9-26; ⊙11am-9pm) Out the back of this relaxed and breezy gulf-front cafe-bar, locals sip rum runners and down oversized po'boys and delicious crab cakes.

Eddy Teach's　　　　　　　　　BAR
(☑850-927-5050; www.eddyteachs.com; 37 E Pine Ave; ⊙11am-11pm) Though not on the beachfront, Eddy's is the best place in town to down a beer on the sunny patio, kick back to some live tunes or get a little rowdy. The bar food is pretty worthy also.

❶ Getting There & Around

From the dock-lined town of Eastpoint on Hwy 98, 7 miles east of Apalachicola, follow the 4-mile-long causeway onto the island until you reach Gulf Beach Dr, also known as Front Beach Dr, at the end. Turning left brings you to the state park; a right turn takes you toward Government Cut, which separates Little St George Island.

If you want to ditch the car, **Island Adventures** (☑850-927-3655; sgislandadventures.com; 105 E Gulf Beach Dr) rents bikes for just $10 a day.

Inland Panhandle

Though most of the attractions around here are indeed on the gulf, there are a couple of spots inland that are worth going out of your way for.

Florida Caverns State Park

Just over an hour from Tallahassee or Panama City, on Hwy 166, the 1300-acre **Florida Caverns State Park** (☑850-482-9598; www.floridastateparks.org/floridacaverns; 3345 Caverns Rd, Marianna; vehicle $5, cave tours adult/child $8/5, camping $20; ⊙8am-sunset) on the Chipola River has fascinating caves unique to Florida. Eerie stalactites, stalagmites and flowstone (formed by water flowing over rock) fill the lighted caves, along with calcified shapes created over centuries as calcite has bubbled through the stone. You can take a 45-minute guided tour, available from 9am to 4pm daily, with a volunteer – who will surely mention the quirky names they've come up with to describe the various formations, from 'wedding cake' to 'bacon.' Outside, the Blue Hole swimming area makes for a fun – if freezing – dip.

DeFuniak Springs

Switzerland has one (near Zurich) and the Florida Panhandle has the other: the Walton County seat of DeFuniak Springs is home to one of just two almost perfectly round lakes in the world. It's popularly thought that the lake was created by a meteorite crashing to Earth eons ago, but there's no final scientific word on its formation. Ringing the lake's approximately mile-long circumference along Circle Dr is the town's historic district, with 39 Victorian buildings in various states of restoration or disrepair. Stroll around the lake and check out the ghostly downtown: there's not much to do in this sleepy ol' town, and that's precisely its charm.

Fifteen minutes down the road, the far lovelier **Ponce de Leon Springs State Park** ([J]850-836-4281; www.florida stateparks.org/poncedeleonsprings; 2860 Ponce de Leon Springs Rd, Ponce de Leon; vehicle $4; ☺8am-sunset) features one of Florida's loveliest and least touristed springs. The spring has clear, almost luminescent waters, like something from a fairy tale, and is studded with knobby trees and surrounded by ladders for easy swimming access. Two short trails skirt the bank of nearby Blackwater Creek. The water temperature remains a constant 68°F (20°C).

The only noteworthy accommodations in the area is the charming **Hotel DeFuniak** ([J]850-892-4383; www.hoteldefuniak.com; 400 Nelson Ave, DeFuniak Springs; r from $99; [❄]), a 1920s downtown hotel with 12 atmospheric rooms bedecked with vintage telephones and pedestal sinks. On-site restaurant **Bogey's** has a menu featuring fish, veal and scampi and a committed, wine-loving local clientele.

DeFuniak Springs is 50 miles west of the Florida Caverns and Marianna along I-10, or 47 miles north of Destin on Hwy 331.

TALLAHASSEE & THE BIG BEND

Florida's gracious state capital, blanketed by moss-draped live oaks and infused with a blend of historic and university cultures, sits inland at the edge of what's known as the Big Bend region – a little-traveled arc of the Florida coastline that curves around the Gulf of Mexico. Within it you'll find remote fishing communities, freshwater springs, picturesque islands and the edges of the Apalachicola National Forest.

Tallahassee

[J] 850 / POP 187,000

Florida's capital, cradled between gently rising hills and nestled beneath tree-canopied roadways, is a calm and gracious city, far more Southern, culturally speaking, than the majority of the state it administers. Geographically it's closer to Atlanta than it is to Miami, and culturally, like Jacksonville, its citizens consider themselves Southern, which is inversely the case the further south you travel.

Despite the city's two major universities (Florida State and Florida Agricultural and Mechanical University) and its status as a government center, the pace here is slower than syrup. That said, there are a handful of interesting museums and outlying attractions that will appeal to history and nature buffs and could easily detain a visitor for at least a day or two.

◉ Sights

★**Tallahassee Automobile & Collectibles Museum**   MUSEUM
([J]850-942-0137; www.tacm.com; 6800 Mahan Dr; adult/child $16/11; ☺8am-5pm Mon-Fri, from 10am Sat, from noon Sun) Adults and kids alike will revel in this fascinating, pristine collection of more than 130 unique and historical automobiles from around the world. Top that with collections of boats, motorcycles, books, pianos and sports memorabilia and you've got a full day on your hands. The museum is about 8 miles northeast of downtown, off I-10.

★**Tallahassee Museum of History & Natural Science**   MUSEUM
(Map p454; [J]850-575-8684; www.tallahasseemuseum.org; 3945 Museum Rd; adult/child $9/6; ☺9am-5pm Mon-Sat, from 11am Sun) Occupying 52 acres of pristine manicured gardens and

wilderness on the outskirts of Tallahassee, near the airport, this stunning natural-history museum features living exhibits of Floridian flora and fauna and has delighted visitors for over 50 years. Be sure to check out the otters in their new home or try zip-lining above the canopy in the fun-for-most, scary-for-others Tree to Tree Adventures – a variety of scenarios are available, from $25.

Florida Historic Capitol Museum MUSEUM
(Map p456; ☑ 850-487-1902; www.flhistoriccapitol.gov; 400 S Monroe St; ⊙9am-4:30pm Mon-Fri, from 10am Sat, from noon Sun) FREE Adorned by candy-striped awnings and topped with a reproduction of the original glass dome, the 1902 Florida capitol building now houses this interesting political museum, including a restored House of Representatives chamber and governor's reception area, numerous portraits, and exhibits on immigration, state development and the infamous 2000 US presidential election.

Florida State Capitol NOTABLE BUILDING
(Map p456; www.myfloridacapitol.com; cnr S Duval & W Pensacola Sts; ⊙8am-5pm Mon-Fri) FREE The stark and imposing 22-story Florida State Capitol's top-floor observation deck affords wonderful 360-degree views of the city and its edge of rolling green hills that stretch to the horizon. In session the capitol is a hive of activity, with politicians, staffers and lobby groups buzzing in and around its honeycombed corridors.

Museum of Florida History MUSEUM
(Map p456; ☑ 850-245-6400; www.museumoffloridahistory.com; 500 S Bronough St; ⊙9am-4:30pm Mon-Fri, from 10am Sat, from noon Sun) FREE Here it is: Florida's history splayed out in fun, crisp exhibits, from mastodon skeletons to Florida's Paleo-Indians and Spanish shipwrecks, the Civil War to 'tin-can tourism.'

Mission San Luis HISTORIC SITE
(Map p454; ☑ 850-245-6406; www.missionsanluis.org; 2100 W Tennessee St; adult/child $5/2; ⊙10am-4pm Tue-Sun) This 60-acre site is home to a 17th-century Spanish and Apalachee mission that's been wonderfully reconstructed, especially the soaring Council House. Good tours included with admission provide a fascinating taste of 300 years ago.

Knott House Museum HISTORIC BUILDING
(Map p456; ☑ 850-922-2459; www.museumoffloridahistory.com; 301 E Park Ave; ⊙1-4pm Wed-Fri, 10am-4pm Sat) FREE This stately, white, col-

HIDDEN GEM: SOUTHEASTERN REGIONAL BLACK ARCHIVES RESEARCH CENTER & MUSEUM

Universally referred to by its acronym, FAMU (fam-you), the **Florida Agricultural & Mechanical University** (Map p454; www.famu.edu; 1500 Wahnish Way) was founded in 1887 as the State Normal College for Colored Students, with 15 students and two instructors. Today it's home to a population of about 10,000 students of all races, as well as the **Southeastern Regional Black Archives Research Center & Museum** (Map p454; ☑ 850-599-3020; www.famu.edu/BlackArchives; 445 Gamble St; ⊙9am-5pm Mon-Fri) FREE. A forerunner in research on African American influence on US history and culture, the center and museum holds one of the country's largest collections of African American and African artifacts as well as a huge collection of papers, photographs, paintings and documents pertaining to black American life.

umned 1843 house, affiliated with the history museum, is a quirky attraction. Occupied during the Civil War by Confederate and then Union troops before the Emancipation Proclamation was read here in 1865, it's otherwise known as 'the house that rhymes.' That's because in 1928 it was bought by politico William V Knott, whose poet wife, Luella, attached verses on the evils of drink to many of the furnishings.

🏃 Activities

Tallahassee-St Marks Historic Railroad State Trail CYCLING
(☑ 850-519-6594; www.floridastateparks.org/tallahasseestmarks; 1358 Old Woodville Rd, Crawfordville; ⊙8am-sunset) FREE The ultimate treat for runners, skaters and cyclists, this trail has 16 miles of smooth pavement shooting due south to the gulf-port town of St Marks and not a car or traffic light in sight. It's easy and flat for all riders, sitting on a coastal plain and shaded at many points by canopies of gracious live oaks.

More experienced riders may opt for forest trails, like the rugged 7.5-mile **Munson Hills Loop trail**, navigating sand dunes and a towering pine forest.

THE PANHANDLE TALLAHASSEE

Tallahassee

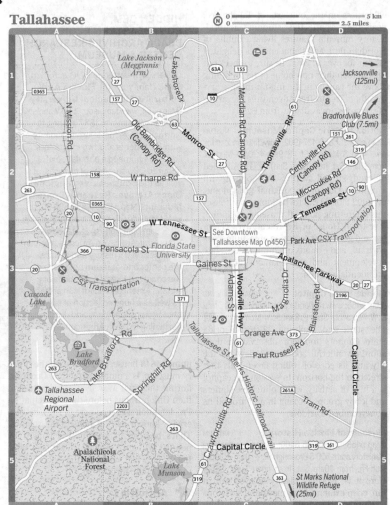

THE PANHANDLE TALLAHASSEE

See Downtown
Tallahassee Map (p456)

Leon County Canopy Roads SCENIC DRIVE
(www.leoncountyfl.gov/PUBWORKS/oper/can-opy) Tallahassee's famed oak- and moss-shrouded canopy roads make for lovely afternoon drives and rides. Roads include Old St Augustine Rd, Centerville Rd, Meridian Rd, Miccosukee Rd and Old Bainbridge Rd. Check the website for info and a map.

Great Bicycle Shop BICYCLE RENTAL
(Map p454; ☎ 850-224-7461; www.greatbicycle.com; 1909 Thomasville Rd; ⏱ 10am-5pm Mon-Sat, noon-4pm Sun) This professional outfitter will rent you a bike to cruise around the many excellent bike paths. Rentals start at $35 per day.

🛏 Sleeping

With just a couple of charming exceptions, you'll find that Tallahassee's hotels are mostly midrange chains, clumped at exits along I-10 or along Monroe St between I-10 and downtown. Be sure to book well ahead during the legislative session and football games, when prices peak.

Four Points Tallahassee Downtown HOTEL $$
(Map p456; ☎ 850-422-0071; www.fourpointstalla-hasseedowntown.com; 316 W Tennessee St; d from $159) Discounted prepaid rates are available online for this comfortable, central hotel that

Tallahassee

looks a little like a massive blue cigar. With an emphasis on service and style, guestrooms feature floor-to-ceiling windows and most have great neighborhood views. The pool area is a nice place to while away an afternoon.

Hotel Duval　　　　　　　　　HOTEL $$
(Map p456; ☑ 850-224-6000; www.hotelduval. com; 415 N Monroe St; r from $169; P❄✿☎) Slick, sleek and ultra modern, this centrally located 117-room hotel has all the mod-cons. The rooftop bar and lounge is open until 2am most nights, and **Shula's 347 Grill**, a fancy chain steakhouse, is off the lobby.

aloft Tallahassee Downtown　　HOTEL $$
(Map p456; ☑ 850-513-0313; www.alofttallahassee. com; 200 N Monroe St; r from $119) Tallahassee's newest digs have a prime downtown location and funky, functional rooms. Baths feature counter-to-ceiling mirrors and lots of space for all the makeup in the world. Beds are uber-comfy, and free high-speed internet is included.

Governor's Inn　　　　　　　　HOTEL $$
(Map p456; ☑ 850-681-6855; www.thegovinn.com; 209 S Adams St; r $149-209; P❄☎) In a stellar downtown location, this warm, inviting inn has everything from single rooms to two-level loft suites, plus a daily cocktail hour.

Little English Guesthouse　　　B&B $$
(Map p454; ☑ 850-907-9777; www.littleenglishguest-house.com; 737 Timberlane Rd; r incl breakfast from $89; ❄✿☎) In a peaceful residential neighborhood 20 minutes from downtown Tallahassee, London-bred Tracey has turned her suburban house into a homey three-room B&B, complete with a friendly golden retriever.

✗ Eating

Kool Beanz Café　　　　　　　FUSION $$
(Map p454; ☑ 850-224-2466; www.koolbeanz-cafe. com; 921 Thomasville Rd; mains $17-24; ☺11am-10pm Mon-Fri, 5:30-10pm Sat, 10:30am-2pm Sun) It's got a corny name but a wonderfully eclectic and homey vibe – plus great, creative fare. The menu changes daily, but you can count on finding anything from hummus plates to jerk-spiced scallops to duck in blueberry-ginger sauce.

China Delight　　　　　　　　CHINESE $$
(Map p456; ☑ 850-222-8898; www.chinadelight-tallahassee.com; 220 W Tennessee St; dishes $7-26; ☺11am-10pm Mon-Sat) If you've had more Southern cooking and seafood than you can handle, you might find this no-frills downtown Chinese joint a welcome relief. Prices are reasonable, servings are generous and all the usual suspects are represented: the best Peking duck in town, beef with broccoli, chunky egg rolls and *ma po* tofu.

Reangthai　　　　　　　　　　THAI $$
(Map p454; ☑ 850-386-7898; www.reangthai.com; 2740 Capital Circle NE; mains $14-22; ☺11am-2pm & 5-10pm Tue-Fri, 5-10pm Mon & Sat) The real deal, and elegant despite its suburban strip-mall setting, Reangthai serves the kind of spicy, fish-saucy, explode-in-your-mouth cuisine so many American Thai restaurants shy away from. Worth the drive.

Andrew's　　　　　　　　　AMERICAN $$
(Map p456; ☑ 850-222-3444; www.andrewsdown-town.com; 228 S Adams St; mains $9-36; ☺11:30am-10pm) Downtown's see-and-be-seen political hot spot. At this split-level place, the downstairs (Andrew's Capital Grill and Bar) serves casual burgers and beer, while upstairs (Andrew's 228) serves upscale neo-Tuscan dishes.

Bella Bella　　　　　　　　　ITALIAN $$
(☑ 850-412-1114;　　www.bellabellatallahassee. com; 123 E 5th Ave; mains $14-19; ☺11am-10pm Mon-Fri, 5-10pm Sat) Come for authentic Italian cuisine in a hip, modern setting: a refreshing change from the old-school ma-and-pa joints that we also love. For a 'great

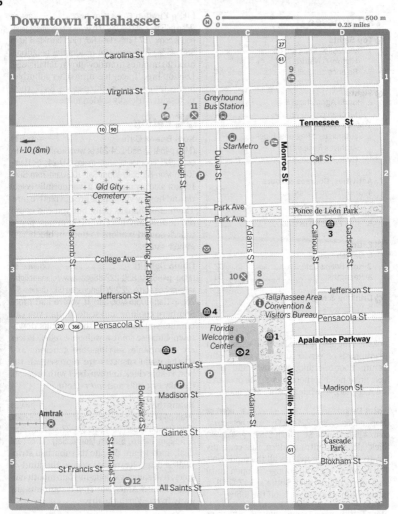

Downtown Tallahassee

beginning' try the bruschetta and stuffed mushrooms, then move on to creamy pastas or shrimp scampi or chicken Parmesan.

Catfish Pad SOUTHERN $$
(Map p454; ☑ 850-575-0053; www.catfishpadwest.com; 4229 W Pensacola St; mains $8-18; ⊙ 11am-9pm Mon-Sat) There's no doubt you're in the South at this home-style seafood joint in Tallahassee's western suburbs. Go for a plate of cornmeal-battered catfish with a side of grits, chased down with a cup of sweet tea: about as authentic as it gets.

Drinking & Entertainment

Most of the frat bars (and there are many) are in and around Tennessee St between Copeland St and Dewey St. There are a few good options around town too. For a comprehensive guide to cultural events in town, such as lectures and art exhibits, be sure to visit the handy online calendar at www.morethanyouthought.com.

Fermentation Lounge BAR
(Map p456; ☑ 850-727-4033; 113 All Saints St; ⊙ 5pm-1am) Sandwiched between the universities, this cool little bar packs a punch, with a chilled vibe attracting an unusual mix of punters from all walks of life and, more importantly, an ever-changing selection of most excellent craft beers and tasty bar snacks.

Waterworks BAR
(Map p454; ☑ 850-224-1887; 1133 Thomasville Rd; ⊙ 5pm-2am) This popular, gay-friendly place in Midtown has a Polynesian tiki-bar theme, and packs 'em in with nights of live jazz and Latin salsa as well as rotating DJs.

Bradfordville Blues Club LIVE MUSIC
(☑ 850-906-0766; www.bradfordvilleblues.com; 7152 Moses Lane, off Bradfordville Rd; tickets $5-25; ⊙ 10pm Fri & Sat, 8:30pm some Thu, check online) Down the end of a dirt road lit by tiki torches you'll find a bonfire raging under the live oaks at this hidden-away juke joint that hosts excellent national blues acts.

ℹ Information

Florida Welcome Center (☑ 850-488-6167; www.visitflorida.com; cnr Pensacola St & Duval St; ⊙ 8am-5pm Mon-Fri) In the new Florida State Capitol, this is a must-visit resource.

Tallahassee Area Convention & Visitors Bureau (☑ 850-606-2305; www.visittallahassee.com; 106 E Jefferson St; ⊙ 8am-5pm Mon-Fri) Runs the excellent visitor information center, with brochures on walking and driving tours.

Leroy Collins Leon County Public Library (☑ 850-606-2665; www.leoncountyfl.gov/library; 200 W Park Ave; ⊙ 10am-9pm Mon-Thu, to 6pm Fri, 10am-5pm Sat, 1-6pm Sun) Plenty of free online computers; enter the parking lot from Call St.

Post Office (216 W College Ave) Close to the center.

ℹ Getting There & Around

Tallahassee is 98 miles from Panama City Beach, 135 miles from Jacksonville, 192 miles from Pensacola, 120 miles from Gainesville and 470 miles from Miami. The main access road is I-10; to reach the Gulf Coast, follow Hwy 319 south to Hwy 98.

The tiny **Tallahassee Regional Airport** (☑ 850-891-7802; www.talgov.com/airport; 3300 Capital Circle SW) is served by American and Delta for US domestic and international connections, and Silver Airways for direct flights to Tampa and Orlando. It's about 5 miles southwest of downtown, off Hwy 263. There's no public transportation. Some hotels have shuttles, but otherwise a taxi to downtown costs upwards of $25: try **Yellow Cab** (☑ 850-580-8080).

The **Greyhound bus station** (☑ 850-222-4249; www.greyhound.com; 112 W Tennessee St) is at the corner of Duval, opposite the downtown StarMetro transfer center.

StarMetro (☑ 850-891-5200; www.talgov.com/starmetro; single ride $1.25, daily unlimited $3) is the local bus service around the greater Tallahassee area and has a main transfer point downtown on Tennessee St at Adams St. Fares are $1.25.

Around Tallahassee

You'll find historic sites, natural wonders and an abundance of antiquing opportunities in the fascinatingly diverse area surrounding Florida's capital.

Wakulla Springs State Park

Glowing an otherworldly aqua and overhung with Spanish moss, the natural spring at the center of the 6000-acre **Wakulla Springs State Park** (☑ 850-561-7276; www.floridastateparks.org/wakullasprings; 550 Wakulla Park Dr; vehicle/pedestrian $6/2; ⊙ 8am-sunset) feels like something from the set of an exotic adventure movie, and indeed parts of *Tarzan* and *The Creature from the Black Lagoon* were filmed here. Gushing 1.2 billion gallons of water daily, the spring is deep and ancient: the remains of at least 10 ice-age mammals have been found.

You can swim in the deep, gin-clear waters or dive off the elevated platform. But don't miss the chance to take a 40-minute guided boat tour (adult/child $8/5; ⊙11am-3pm), which glides under moss-draped bald cypress trees and past an array of creatures, including precious manatees (in season), alligators, tribes of red-bellied turtles and graceful wading birds.

Time has stood still at the faded 1937 Wakulla Springs Lodge (☑850-421-2000; www.wakullaspringslodge.com; 465 Wakulla Park Dr; r $85-125), a charming Spanish-style building with an enormous faux-stone fireplace in the lobby. Its 27 basic, scruffy rooms have original marble floors, walk-in wardrobes and no TVs. The lodge's grandiose Ball Room Restaurant (☑850-421-2000; mains $14-27; ⊙7:30am-2pm & 5-9pm), named for financier Edward Ball, who built the lodge, is a favorite dining spot with Tallahassee locals – try the fried chicken and the famous bean soup.

St Marks National Wildlife Refuge

About 25 miles southeast of Tallahassee you'll find the St Marks National Wildlife Refuge (☑850-925-6121; www.fws.gov/saintmarks; 1255 Lighthouse Rd, St Marks; ⊙8am-sunset), established in 1931 to provide a winter habitat for migratory birds. It spans a whopping 70,000 acres and has approximately 43 miles of gulf shoreline along its coastal boundary. Within the park's protected marshes, rivers, estuaries and islands, a diverse range of flora and fauna thrives. It's a wildlife photographer's dream, with beautiful contrasts between land, sea and sky.

Be sure to start your visit with a trip to the visitor center for information on the park's numerous walking and hiking trails and the lowdown on just how many species of critter live here. If you only have time for a short visit, follow Lighthouse Rd all the way to the coast to enjoy Florida's most photographed lighthouse, completed in 1842 and still a functioning beacon today.

Apalachicola National Forest

☑850

The largest of Florida's three national forests, the Apalachicola National Forest (325 John Knox Rd; day-use areas $5; ⊙8am-sunset) occupies almost 938 sq miles – more than half a million acres – of the Panhandle from just

west of Tallahassee to the Apalachicola River. It's made up of lowlands, pines, cypress hammocks and oaks, and dozens of species call the area home, including mink, gray and red foxes, coyotes, six bat species, beavers, woodpeckers, alligators, Florida black bears and the elusive Florida panther. A total of 68.7 miles of the Florida National Scenic Trail extends through the forest as well.

You can sunbathe on the white-sand shores or swim in the waters of Silver Lake (close to Tallahassee in the northeastern part of the forest on Forest Rd 370), Wright Lake (Forest Rd 379 in the southwest of the forest) and Camel Lake (off Hwy 12 in the northwest of the forest), all of which have facilities and picnic areas.

There are also plentiful opportunities for canoeing along the forest's rivers and waterways. Information on canoeing in the area and canoe rental is available from the ranger stations, or visit the excellent website for Florida Greenways & Trails System (www.dep.state.fl.us/gwt/guide), which has maps and updated lists of outfitters in the surrounding towns. Canoe rental costs $25 to $35 per day.

Powerboats are allowed on the rivers but not on the glassy lakes.

⊙ Sights & Activities

Fort Gadsden Historic Site   HISTORIC SITE
This is the former location of an 1814 British fort manned by African American and Native American soldiers armed and trained by the British to defend against Spain's hold on Florida. The fort was blown to pieces two years later, killing more than 200 people, but its rebuilt fortification would later be used by Confederate troops. These days it's a green, serene picnic area, with an interpretive trail detailing its history. From Hwy 65, turn west on Forest Rd 129, then south on Forest Rd 129B.

Leon Sinks Geological Area   PARK
(vehicle $3; ⊙8am-sunset) More than 6 miles of trails and boardwalks marked with interpretive signs wind past sinks and swamps in this fascinating park. Be sure to stay on the trails, as the karst (terrain affected by the dissolution of the underlying limestone bedrock) here is still evolving, and new sinkholes could appear any time. At Big Dismal Sink you'll see ferns, dogwoods and dozens of other lush plants descending its steep walls. The sinks are at the eastern end of the forest, just west of Hwy 319, about 10 miles south of Tallahassee.

QUINCY & HAVANA

Half an hour from Tallahassee, these two charming villages make nice day-trips from the capital. Quincy, nicknamed 'Cola-Cola Town,' struck it rich in the early 20th century by investing, en masse, in Coke stock. There's an original 1905 Coca-Cola mural on E Jefferson St, and 36 blocks of stunning historic homes built on the dividends of America's favorite soft drink. Havana, 12 miles down the road, is a former cigar-making town (hence the name) known for its antiques shops, which make for a pleasant afternoon of exploring. Most are concentrated around 2nd St, and most are only open Wednesday to Sunday.

If you find yourself here for the night, Quincy's 1843 **Allison House Inn** (☑ 888-904-2511; www.allisonhouseinn.com; 215 North Madison St; r $85-155; 🅿 🛜) has six peaceful, antique-y rooms downtown. A few blocks away, **McFarlin House Bed & Breakfast Inn** (☑ 850-524-0640; www.mcfarlinhouse.com; 305 E King St; r $99-249; 🅿) is a turreted 1895 Queen Anne with nine museum-piece (if froofy) rooms and a sweet communal deck.

Florida National Scenic Trail   HIKING
(www.dep.state.fl.us/gwt/guide) Roughly 74 miles of the Florida National Scenic Trail cuts a northwest–southeast swath through the Apalachicola National Forest. Prepare to get soaked if you opt for the **Bradwell Bay Wilderness** section, which involves some waist-deep swamp tramping. You can pick up the trail at the southeastern gateway, just east of Forest Rd 356 on Hwy 319, or at the northwestern corner on Hwy 12.

Munson Hills Loop   CYCLING
On the eastern side of the Apalachicola National Forest is the 7.5-mile Munson Hills Loop bicycle trail, which spurs to the Tallahassee-St Marks Historic Railroad State Trail. Experienced off-road cyclists can tackle this area made up of hammock, dunes, hills and brush, though its soft sand can make this a challenging route. If you run out of steam halfway through, take the Tall Pine Shortcut out of the trail, roughly at the halfway point, for a total distance of 4.5 miles.

🛏 Sleeping

None of the campgrounds have hookups. For developed camping ($10 per site), head to **Camel Lake** and **Wright Lake**, which have full bathrooms with hot showers, shelters and picnic tables.

Less developed campgrounds ($4 per site) with drinking water and vault toilets include **Hickory Landing** (from Sumatra, take Hwy 65 south; turn right on Forest Rd 101 and left on 101B), while primitive camping areas (with drinking water but no toilets) include **Wood Lake** (from Sopchoppy, take Hwy 375 to Hwy 22 west, then take Hwy 340 south to Hwy 338).

ℹ Information

Apalachicola Ranger Station (☑ 850-643-2282; 11152 NW SR-20, Bristol) The western half of the forest is controlled by the Apalachicola Ranger Station, northwest of the forest near the intersection of Hwys 12 and 20, just south of Bristol.

Wakulla Ranger Station (☑ 850-926-3561; 57 Taff Dr, Crawfordville) The eastern half of the forest is managed by the Wakulla Ranger Station, just off Hwy 319 behind the Winn Dixie in Crawfordville.

Steinhatchee

☑ 352 / POP 1500

Talk about unexpected Florida! Steinhatchee (*steen*-hatch-ee) is an under-the-radar fishing haven that sits in a secret crevice of the Big Bend beneath towering pines, mossy oaks and pink, juicy sunsets. The hamlet's claim to fame is its scallop season, which runs from July to early September and brings up to 1000 boats on its opening day to the otherwise peaceful waters of Dead Man's Bay. The season is kind of like a twisted Easter egg hunt, with locals and visitors taking a mesh bag, donning a snorkel and mask, and snatching up their own seafood as they swim. Locals will often clean your catch in exchange for half the meat.

🏃 Activities

Fishing and scalloping is where it's at: depending on the season, cobia, sea trout, mackerel, tarpon and the famous scallops are plentiful. For a full list of fishing guides, charter operators and boat-rental services, check out www.steinhatcheeriverchamber.org.

River Haven Marina   EQUIPMENT RENTAL
(☑ 352-498-0709; www.riverhavenmarinaandmotel.com; 1110 Riverside Dr; ⊙9am-5pm) Rent a

variety of fishing boats (from $80 per half-day) and kayaks including pickup and dropoff ($30/40 single/tandem per half-day): great for exploring the maze of waterways.

Reel Song Charters
FISHING CHARTER

(☎ 352-895-7544; www.reelsongcharters.com) For a guided fishing charter with locals who know the waters, try this outfit specializing in near-shore and flats fishing for trout, red fish and scallops. Trips cost from $400 per day for up to four people.

Big Bend Charters
FISHING CHARTER

(☎ 352-210-3050; www.bigbendcharters.com) In-shore and offshore fishing charters start at $400 for four people.

🛏 Sleeping & Eating

Steinhatchee River Inn Motel
MOTEL $

(☎ 352-498-4049; www.steinhatcheeriverinn.net; 1111 Riverside Dr; r from $79; ❋ 🐾 🛜 ☀) This classic motel-style inn has decent-size rooms and is close to the marina. Some rooms have kitchens, and all have TVs, coffeemakers, wi-fi and refrigerators.

Steinhatchee Landing
RESORT $$

(☎ 352-498-3513; www.steinhatcheelanding.com; 203 Ryland Circle; cottages from $150; ❋ 🛜 ☀) This cute-as-a-button riverside resort community has one- through four-bedroom self-catering cottages clustered around a loop road, with a pool, country store, spa, and lusciously manicured grounds bursting with hibiscus and palms. A two-night minimum stay is often required.

Roy's
SEAFOOD $$

(☎ 352-498-5000; www.roys-restaurant.com; 100 1st Ave; mains $15-25; ☉ 11am-9pm) Since 1969, Roy's, which sits overlooking the gulf, has been a favorite for seafood. The standard style is fried, but if you ask they'll serve it spiced and broiled, nestled up to sides that include heaping portions of grits, fries, baked potatoes and hush puppies.

ℹ Information

There's no visitor information center, but information is available online at www.steinhatcheeriverchamber.org.

ℹ Getting There & Away

Coming from either the north or south, take Hwy 19 (also called Hwy 19/27 and Hwy 19/98) to the crossroads with a blinking light, then drive west on Hwy 51 to the end, about 12 miles.

Manatee Springs State Park

Between Cedar Key and Steinhatchee, **Manatee Springs State Park** (☎ 352-493-6072; www.floridastateparks.org/manateesprings; 11650 NW 115th St; vehicle $6; ☉ 8am-sundown) is worth a stop, especially for a dip into the 72°F (22°C) crystalline waters of the beautiful spring.

You can also scuba dive (bring your own gear and buddy, and register at the office) at the springhead, which gushes 117 million gallons of water per day, or canoe or kayak along the spring run (boat rentals $8 to $10 hourly). Scuba diving, canoeing and kayaking can be organized through the park office. On dry land – which is a uniquely spongy combo of sand and limestone shaded by tupelo, cypress and pine trees – there's the 8.5-mile-long **North End hiking-cycling trail** on your right as you enter the park. Camping ($2 per site) is also available at 94 shady spots with picnic tables and ground grills. A highlight here is the wheelchair-accessible raised timber boardwalk that traces the narrow spring down to the Suwannee River as it flows to the gulf and out to sea.

Ranger programs include guided canoe journeys, moonlight hikes, nature walks and occasional covered-wagon rides. Contact the park office for details.

Cedar Key

☎ 352 / POP 950

Jutting 3 miles into the Gulf of Mexico, this windswept and isolated island has a bit of a wild-frontier feel: an enchantingly ramshackle downtown of historic buildings, roadhouses with parking lots full of Harleys, long stretches of uninhabited bayou, meadows and bay. The otherworldly landscape sings with marshes that reflect candy-colored sunsets, and tiny hills offering sweeping island views. Cedar Key is just one of 100 islands (13 of which are part of the Cedar Keys National Wildlife Refuge) that make up this coastal community, which is gloriously abundant with wildlife and friendly, small-town vibes.

As the western terminus of the trans-Florida railroad in the late 1800s, Cedar Key was one of Florida's largest towns, second only to St Augustine. Its primary industry was wood (for Faber pencils), which eventually deforested the islands; an 1896 hurricane destroyed what was left. Consequently, the trees here are less than 100 years old. Aquaculture has recently revived the town's economy: spurred by government subsidies when net fishing was banned, it's now the largest clam-farming region in the country.

◉ Sights & Activities

Cedar Keys
National Wildlife Refuge WILDLIFE RESERVE
(☑ 352-493-0238; www.fws.gov/cedarkeys; ⊙8am-sunset) Home to 250 species of bird (including ibises, pelicans, egrets, herons and double-crested cormorants), 10 species of reptile and one romantic lighthouse, the 13 islands in this refuge can only be reached by boat. The islands' interiors are generally closed to the public, but during daylight hours you can access most of the white-sand beaches, which provide great opportunities for both fishing and manatee viewing.

Cedar Key Museum State Park MUSEUM
(☑ 352-543-5350; www.floridastateparks.org/cedarkeymuseum; 12231 SW 166th St; admission $2; ⊙10am-5pm Thu-Mon) This eclectic museum features the historic house, remodeled to its 1902 state, of St Clair Whitman. A main player

in both the pencil factory and the local fiber mill, he arrived in the area in 1882 and started collecting everything he saw: insects, butterflies, glass, sea glass, bottles and infinite varieties of seashell. After your visit, enjoy a bucolic walk on the surrounding nature trails.

Cedar Key
Historical Society Museum MUSEUM
(☑ 352-543-5549; 609 2nd St; adult/child $1/50¢; ⊙1-4pm Sun-Fri, 11am-5pm Sat) This small museum packs a punch with its wonderful exhibits of Native American, Civil War and seafood-industry artifacts, and especially for its extensive collection of Cedar Key historic photographs.

Kayak Cedar Keys KAYAKING
(☑ 352-543-9447; www.kayakcedarkeys.com; tours from $60; ⊙10am-4pm) The waterways and estuaries in and around Cedar Key make for superb kayaking. This outfitter will rent you gear (kayaks from $25 for three hours) and can arrange to take you to offshore clam beds.

☞ Tours

Tidewater Tours BOAT TOUR
(☑ 352-543-9523; www.tidewatertours.com) Tidewater Tours runs two-hour nature tours

THE PANHANDLE CEDAR KEY

UPON THE SUWANNEE RIVER

Flowing 207 miles, the Suwannee River was immortalized by Stephen Foster in Florida's state song, 'Old Folks at Home.' Foster himself never set eyes on the river but thought 'Suwannee' (or 'Swannee', as his map apparently stated, hence his corruption of the spelling) sounded suitably Southern. As it happened he was right; the river winds through wild Spanish-moss-draped countryside from the far north of the state to the Gulf of Mexico in the curve of the Big Bend. See it for yourself along the **Suwannee River Wilderness Trail** (www.suwanneeriver.com), which covers 169 miles of the river to the gulf, with nine 'hubs' – cabins – spaced one day's paddle apart. They book up fast, so reserve as early as possible. River camps along the banks of the trail are also in the pipeline.

The trail starts at the **Stephen Foster State Folk Cultural Center** (☑ 386-397-2733; www.floridastateparks.org/stephenfoster; Hwy 41 N, White Springs; vehicle $5, camp sites $20, cabins $100; ⊙park 8am-sunset, museum 9am-5pm), north of White Springs. With lush green hills and monolithic live oak trees, the park has a museum of Florida history that you'd swear is a 19th-century plantation. The three-day **Florida Folk Festival**, a celebration of traditional Floridian music, crafts, food and culture, takes place here every Memorial Day weekend. Next door to the park, canoe rentals are available from **American Canoe Adventures** (☑ 386-397-1309; www.aca1.com; 10610 Bridge St, White Springs; ⊙10am-4pm), which offers day trips ($35 to $60, depending on mileage and terrain) where you're transported upstream and then paddle down. Overnight canoe rentals are $25.

The **Suwannee River State Park** (☑ 386-362-2746; www.floridastateparks.org/suwanneeriver; 20185 CR 132, Live Oak; vehicle $5, camp sites $22, cabins $100; ⊙8am-sunset), at the confluence of the Withlacoochee and Suwannee Rivers, has Civil War fortifications. Camping is available, as well as basic cabins which sleep up to six people. The park is 13 miles west of Live Oak, just off US 90 – follow the signs.

of the islands for $26, and rents pontoons and skiffs for solo exploration (from $60 for three hours) – be sure to time your visit to avoid getting stuck on the mudflats.

🛏 Sleeping & Eating

There are plenty of cute, family-run motels in the area. Dock St – a little spit of land jutting into the bay just across from downtown – is crowded with pubs and seafood restaurants and takes on a raucous character on busy nights.

★ Island Hotel   HOTEL $$
(📞352-543-5111;   www.islandhotel-cedarkey.com; 224 2nd St, at B St; r $80-135; 🌂 🕸) A night in this old-fashioned, 1859 tabby shell and oak building will relax you for sure. Listed on the National Register of Historic Places, it has 10 simple and romantic rooms with original hand-cut wooden walls, a wraparound balcony with rocking chairs, a history of notable guests including John Muir and President Grover Cleveland and, by all reports, as many as 13 resident ghosts.

Faraway Inn   MOTEL $$
(📞352-543-5330; www.farawayinn.com; cnr 3rd & G Sts; motel r from $80, cottages from $150; 🌂 🕸 🐾 🐕) Overlooking a silent, glassy stretch of bay, this funky little motel complex has rooms and cottages decorated in driftwood art and brightly colored prints. Guests chill on waterfront porch swings for mind-blowing sunsets.

Tony's   SEAFOOD $$
(📞352-543-0022; www.tonyschowder.com; 597 2nd St; mains $8-28; ⊙11am-9pm) Creamy, whole-clam-studded clam chowder – Tony's claim to fame – is truly superlative, and a reason to visit this otherwise mediocre seafood restaurant in a downtown storefront.

Pickled Pelican   PUB $$
(📞352-543-5654; 360 Dock St; mains $8-16; ⊙11am-9pm Mon-Sat, to 4pm Sun; 🍴) Probably the most popular of the Dock St eateries, this 2nd-floor pub specializes in beachy bar food: fried pickles, burgers, fish sandwiches.

ℹ Information

Cedar Keys Chamber of Commerce (📞352-543-5600; www.cedarkey.org; 525 2nd St; ⊙10am-3pm Thu-Mon) The source in town for all things local.

Library (📞352-543-5777; www.levycounty. org/cd_library.aspx; 466 2nd St; ⊙10am-4pm Mon, Wed & Thu, 4-8pm Tue, 10am-1pm Sat) One of the few spots you'll find free internet access.

Post Office (518 2nd St; ⊙9am-5pm Mon-Fri, to 1pm Sat)

ℹ Getting There & Around

There's no public transportation to Cedar Key, but driving is easy: take Hwy 19/98 or I-75 to Hwy 24 and follow it southwest to the end.

You'll see locals zipping around in golf ('gulf') carts, which are perfect for traversing the little island; try **Cedar Key Gulf Kart Company** (📞352-543-5090; www.gulfkartcompany.com; cnr 1st & A St; carts per 2hr/day from $25/55).

Understand Florida

Florida Today

Florida is undergoing seismic shifts in demographics, state identity, and – if the environment doesn't improve – state topography, thanks to immigration, economic recession and resurgence, and climate change. These developments, and how the state will adapt and respond to them, will shape life in the Sunshine State for the foreseeable future. In the meantime, the state is constantly re-evaluating and evolving her tourism infrastructure to accommodate an ever-increasing amount of visitors.

Best on Film

Scarface (1983) Al Pacino.
The Birdcage (1996) Robin Williams and Nathan Lane as gay lovers.
Sunshine State (2002) Florida developers vs mermaid.
Adaptation (2002) Surreal adaptation of *The Orchid Thief*.

Best in Print

Pilgrim in the Land of Alligators (Jeff Klinkenberg) Profiles of wacky Floridians.
Salvaging the Real Florida (Bill Belleville) Moving nature essays on a fragile landscape.
Paradise Screwed (Carl Hiaasen) *Miami Herald* columns of biting sarcasm and outrage.
Weird Florida (Charlie Carlson) Too easy. Like shooting two-headed fish in a barrel.

Wild Etiquette

Wildflowers Never pick them, especially orchids.
Beaches Never approach nesting sea turtles or hatchling runs. Adhere to lights-out policies.
Coral reefs Don't touch them when snorkeling or diving.
Dolphins & manatees Admire but don't touch, chase or feed them.
Alligators Never feed – they bite.

Preserving the Peninsula

One of Florida's deepest cultural fault lines runs across the debate over development versus conservation. For years, development held sway in the state, which has long had one of the most robust housing markets in the country, and not coincidentally, one of the fastest growing populations. As of this writing, Florida was poised to overtake New York as the third-most populous state in the country.

All of those people need places to live, and in Florida, the need for housing and businesses has traditionally taken precedence over preservation. But a new check on growth has emerged that even some of the most gung-ho developers are noting. In the environmental debates of the 21st century, low-lying Florida is on the ecological frontlines of the climate change and water table debates.

Florida is a largely below-sea-level peninsula, and the ocean is rising even as the peninsula is crumbling. The culprits behind the crumble are artificial canals and waterways dredged in the early 20th century. Those public works directed water away from the Everglades and the South Florida aquifer, eroding the wetlands and depleting freshwater reserves. State leaders seem to have recognized how untenable the situation is, and as of the time of research, it seems that the Florida legislature may have the political will to redirect the natural flow of run-off water from Lake Okeechobee.

While the interior of the state is trying to re-establish a base of water, coastal areas are trying to ward water away. Rising sea levels can be traced to climate change; rains in Miami that would have been an afterthought a decade ago are now flooding main thoroughfares. Local governments are moving forward with climate change plans to deter the worst fallout of a potential ecological disaster.

A House Divided

From Stand Your Ground laws to political redistricting, some of the most intense debates over American rights and responsibilities occur in Florida. This has always been a place where settlers tried to bend the world to fit their dreams, from Disney World emerging from Central Florida to Miami sprouting from a swamp. This can-do attitude usually comes hand in hand with a pro-business environment that stresses deregulation and individual liberty over public welfare. The frontier mentality that feeds this attitude has traditionally incubated in Florida's sprawling suburbs and agricultural zones.

But as Florida's city spaces grow, so do city ideals, values and policy priorities such as public infrastructure and mass transit. Governor Rick Scott's decision to void a high-speed train between Orlando and Tampa was seen as fiscal prudence by supporters from the countryside and exurbs, but urban opponents felt like a chance at alleviating the state's ubiquitous car culture had been squandered.

As these debates rage, the rifts between rural, white, culturally conservative North Florida and multiethnic South Florida are deepening. South Floridians feel political redistricting, seen by some as gerrymandering, has led to them being frozen out of the Florida statehouse; while the state is consistently a toss-up between Democrats and Republicans at the national level, at the state level Republicans have carved out numerous small districts and as a result dominate the legislature.

On the other hand, North Floridians feel like they are being demographically eclipsed by the increasingly ethnically diverse southern part of the state. The irony is that the children of those immigrants tend to Americanize quickly, and some would likely lean conservative if the anti-immigrant rhetoric coming from the American right wasn't so fiery. These kinds of views were what caused Pablo Pantoja, director of the Republican National Party's Hispanic Outreach program in Florida, to defect to the Democratic Party in 2013.

POPULATION: **19.32 MILLION**

AREA: **65,755 SQ MILES**

GDP: **$748 BILLION**

GDP GROWTH: **+2.4%**

INFLATION: **1.74%**

UNEMPLOYMENT: **6.2%**

if Florida were 100 people

75 would be White   1 would be
16 would be Black   Native American
2 would be Asian   6 would be other

*According to the US Census Bureau, Hispanics may be of any race so are included in applicable race categories

belief systems

(% of population)

40
Protestant

26
Roman Catholic

3
Jewish

15
Others

16
Nonreligious

population per sq mile

USA   FLORIDA   MIAMI

☥ ≈ 90 people

History

Florida has the oldest recorded history of any US state, and it might qualify as the most bizarre too. Something about this swampy peninsula invites exaggeration and inflames desire, then gleefully bedevils those who pursue their visions. Spanish explorers chased rumors of golden cities, yet only a funhouse mirror separates them from Disney and its promised Magic Kingdom. The constant in this state is wild-eyed speculation, great tides of immigration, and inevitably, a crash. It certainly makes for great storytelling.

First Inhabitants & Seminoles

Florida's original inhabitants never organized into large, cohesive tribes. For some 11,500 years, they remained split into numerous small chiefdoms or villages, becoming more settled and agricultural in the north and remaining more nomadic and warlike in the south.

Seminole & Indian Resources

Ah-Tah-Thi-Ki Museum (www. ahtahthiki.com)

The Museum (www.flamuseum. com)

Heritage of the Ancient Ones (www.ancient native.org)

The Apalachee in Florida's Panhandle developed the most complex agriculture-based society, but other tribes included the Timucua in northern Florida, the Tequesta along the central Atlantic Coast, and the fierce Calusa in southern Florida. Legends say it was a poison-tipped Calusa arrow that killed Spanish explorer Ponce de León.

The most striking evidence of these early cultures is shell mounds or middens. Florida's ancestral peoples ate well, and their discarded shells reached 30ft high and themselves became the foundations of villages, as at Mound Key.

When the Spanish arrived in the 1500s, the indigenous population numbered perhaps 250,000. Over the next 200 years, European diseases killed 80% of them. The rest were killed by war or sold into slavery, so that by the mid-1700s virtually none of Florida's original inhabitants were left.

However, as the 18th century unfolded, Muscogee and other tribes from the north migrated into Florida, driven by or enlisted in the partisan European feuds for New World territory. These tribes intermingled and intermarried, and in the late 1700s they were joined by numerous runaway African American slaves, whom they welcomed into their society.

TIMELINE	10,000 BC	AD 500	1513
	After crossing the Bering Strait from Siberia some 50,000 years earlier, humans arrive in Florida, hunting mastodon and saber-toothed tigers, at the end of the last ice age.	Indigenous peoples settle in year-round villages and begin farming, cultivating the 'three sisters' of corn, beans and squash, plus pumpkins, lemons and sunflowers.	Ponce de León discovers Florida, landing south of Cape Canaveral, believing it to be an island. Since it's Easter time, he names it La Florida, 'The Flowery Land' or 'Feast of Flowers.'

At some point, these independent, fugitive, mixed peoples occupying Florida's interior were dubbed 'Seminoles,' a corruption of the Spanish word *cimarrones,* meaning 'free people' or 'wild ones.' Defying European rule and ethnic category, they were soon considered too free for the newly independent United States, who brought war to them.

Five Flags: Florida Gets Passed Around

All Floridian schoolchildren are taught that Florida has been ruled by five flags: those of Spain, France, Britain, the US and the Confederacy.

Spain claimed Florida in 1513 when explorer Ponce de León arrived. Five more Spanish expeditions followed (and one French, raising its flag on the St Johns River), but established until 1565, when St Augustine was

THE UNCONQUERED SEMINOLES

The US waged war on Florida's Seminoles three times. The First Seminole War, from 1817 to 1818, was instigated by Andrew Jackson, who ruthlessly attacked the Seminoles as punishment for sheltering runaway slaves and attacking US settlers. Trouble was, Florida was controlled by Spain. After Jackson took over Pensacola, Spain protested this foreign military incursion, forcing Jackson to halt.

In 1830, now President Andrew Jackson (aka Old Hickory), passed the Indian Removal Act, which aimed to move all Native Americans west of the Mississippi River. Some Seminoles agreed to give up their lands and move to reservations, but not all. In 1835 US troops arrived to enforce agreements and resistance, led by Osceola a Seminole leader, attacked an army detachment, triggering the Second Seminole War.

The war was fought guerrilla style by 2000 or so Seminoles in swamps and hammocks, and it's considered one of the most deadly and costly Indian wars in US history. In October 1837, Osceola was captured under a flag of truce and later died in captivity, but the Seminoles kept fighting. In 1842 the US finally called off its army, having spent $20 million and seen the deaths of 1500 US soldiers.

Thousands of Seminoles had been killed or marched to reservations, but hundreds survived and took refuge in the Everglades. In 1855 a US army survey team went looking for them, but the Seminoles killed them first. The resulting backlash turned into the Third Seminole War, which ended after Chief Billy Bowlegs was paid to go west in 1858.

But 200 to 300 Seminoles refused to sign a peace treaty and slipped away again into the Everglades. Technically, these Seminoles never surrendered and remain the only 'unconquered' Native American tribe.

In the 1910s, brutally impoverished, the Seminoles discovered that tourists would pay to watch them in their temporary camps, and soon 'Seminole villages' were a mainstay of Florida tourist attractions, often featuring alligator wrestling and Seminole 'weddings.'

In 1957 the US officially recognized the **Seminole Tribe** (www.semtribe.com), and in 1962, the **Miccosukee Tribe** (www.miccosukee.com).

1539	1565	1702	1776
Hernando de Soto arrives in Florida with 800 men, seeking rumored cities of gold. He fights Native Americans and camps near Tallahassee but, finding no precious metals, keeps marching west.	Pedro Menéndez de Avilés founds St Augustine, which becomes the first permanent European settlement in the New World and is the oldest city in the continental US.	In their ongoing struggle with Spain and France over New World colonies, the British burn St Augustine to the ground; two years later they destroy 13 Spanish missions in Florida.	The American Revolution begins, but Florida's two colonies don't rebel. They remain loyal to the British crown, and soon English Tories flood south into Florida to escape the fighting.

settled. A malarial, easily pillaged outpost that produced little income, St Augustine truly succeeded at only one thing: spreading the Catholic religion. Spanish missionaries founded 31 missions across Florida, converting and schooling Native Americans, occasionally with notable civility.

In 1698 Spain established a permanent military fort at Pensacola, which was thence variously captured and recaptured by the Spanish, French, English and North Americans for a century.

Spain found itself on the losing side of the 1754–63 French and Indian War, having backed France in its fight with England. Afterward, Spain bartered with the English, giving them Florida in return for the captured Havana. Almost immediately, the 3000 or so Spaniards in Florida gratefully boarded boats for Cuba.

The British held Florida for 20 years and did marginally well, producing indigo, rice, oranges and timber. But in 1783, as Britain and the US were tidying up accounts after the close of the American Revolution, Britain handed Florida back to Spain – which this time had supported the winning side, the US.

The second Spanish period, from 1783 to 1819, was marked by one colossal misjudgment. Spain needed settlers, and quickly, so it vigorously promoted immigration to Florida, but this backfired when, by 1810, those immigrants (mainly North American settlers) started demanding 'independence' from Spain. Within a decade, Spain threw up its hands. It gave Florida back to the US for cash in a treaty formalized in 1822. In 1845 Florida became the 27th state of the US, but in 16 short years, it would reconsider that relationship and raise its fifth flag.

From Civil War to Civil Rights

In 1838 the Florida territory was home to about 48,000 people, of whom 21,000 were African American slaves. By 1860, 15 years after statehood, Florida's population was 140,000, of whom 40% were slaves, most of them working on highly profitable cotton plantations.

Thus, unsurprisingly, when Abraham Lincoln was elected president on an antislavery platform, Florida joined the Confederacy of southern states that seceded from the Union in 1861. During the ensuing Civil War, which lasted until 1865, only moderate fighting occurred in Florida.

Afterward, from 1865 to 1877, the US government imposed 'Reconstruction' on all ex-Confederate states. Reconstruction protected the rights of freed slaves, and led to 19 African Americans becoming elected to Florida's state congress. Yet this radical social and political upheaval led to a furious backlash.

When federal troops finally left, Florida 'unreconstructed' in a hurry, adopting a series of Jim Crow laws that segregated and disenfranchised African Americans in every sphere of life – in

Alleged Fountains of Youth
....
Fountain of Youth Archaeological Park, St Augustine
....
De Leon Springs State Park, DeLand
....
Warm Mineral Springs, Venice

Best Florida Histories
....
The New History of Florida, Michael Gannon
....
The Everglades: River of Grass, Marjory Stoneman Douglas
....
Dreamers, Schemers and Scalawags, Stuart B McIver
....
The Enduring Seminoles, Patsy West
....
Miami Babylon, Gerald Posner

1816–58	1823	1835	1845
The three Seminole Wars pit the United States against the Seminoles and allies, including escaped slaves. Although most Seminoles are exiled, small bands remain in the Everglades.	Tallahassee is established as Florida's territorial capital because it's halfway between Pensacola and St Augustine. Later attempts to move the state capital fail.	In attacks coordinated by Seminole leader Osceola, Seminoles destroy five sugar plantations on Christmas Day and soon after kill 100 US soldiers marching near Tampa, launching the Second Seminole War.	Florida is admitted to the Union as the 27th state. Since it is a slave state, its admission is balanced by that of Iowa, a free state.

restaurants and parks, on beaches and buses – while a poll tax kept African Americans and the poor from voting. From then until the 1950s, African Americans field hands in turpentine camps and cane fields worked under a forced-labor 'peonage' system, in which they couldn't leave till their wages paid off their debts, which of course never happened.

The Ku Klux Klan thrived, its popularity peaking in the 1920s, when Florida led the country in lynchings. Racial hysteria and violence were commonplace; most infamously, a white mob razed the entire town of Rosewood in 1923.

In 1954 the US Supreme Court ended legal segregation in the US with Brown v Board of Education, but in 1957 Florida's Supreme Court rejected

BLACK MARKET FLORIDA

In 1919, when the US passed the 18th Amendment – making liquor illegal and inaugurating Prohibition – bootleggers discovered something that previous generations of slaves and Seminoles knew well: Florida is a good place to hide.

Almost immediately Florida became, as the saying went, 'wet as a frog,' and soon fleets of ships and airplanes were bringing in Cuban and Jamaican rum to be hidden in coves and dispersed nationwide.

Interestingly, Florida rumrunning was conducted mostly by local 'mom-and-pop' operations, not the mob, despite the occasional vacationing mobster, such as Al Capone. In this way, Prohibition really drove home the benefits of a thriving black market. When times were good, as in the 1920s, all that (illicit) money got launder-...um...pumped into real estate, making the good times unbelievably great. When hard times hit in the 1930s, out-of-work farmers could still make bathtub gin and pay the bills. Because of this often-explicit understanding, Miami bars served drinks with impunity throughout the 1920s, and local police simply kept walking.

In the 1960s and '70s, the story was repeated with marijuana. Down-on-their-luck commercial fisherman made a mint smuggling plastic-wrapped bails of pot, and suddenly Florida was asking, 'Recession? What recession?' West Florida experienced a condo boom.

In the 1980s cocaine became the drug of choice. But this time the smugglers were Colombian cartels, and they did business with a gun, not a handshake. Bloody shootouts on Miami streets shocked Floridians (and inspired the *Miami Vice* TV show), but it didn't slow the estimated $10-billion drug business – and did you notice Miami's new skyline? In the 1980s so much cash choked Miami banks that smuggling currency itself became an industry – along with smuggling out guns to Latin America and smuggling in rare birds, flowers, and Cuban cigars.

By the 1990s the cartels were finished and banking laws were stricter, but some still believed that smuggling remained Florida's number-one industry.

1861	1889	1894–5	1912
Voting 62 to seven, Florida secedes from the US and raises its fifth flag, that of the Confederacy. Florida's farms and cattle provide vital Confederate supplies during the ensuing Civil War.	Key West becomes the largest, most populous city in Florida largely due to the wrecking industry – salvaging cargo from ships that sink in the treacherous surrounding waters.	The Great Freeze ruins citrus crops across the agricultural belt in Central Florida. Settlers begin moving to South Florida seeking warmer climes and longer growing seasons.	'Flagler's Folly,' Henry Flagler's 128-mile overseas railroad connecting the Florida Keys, reaches Key West. It's hailed as the 'Eighth Wonder of the World' but is destroyed by a 1935 hurricane.

this decision, declaring it 'null and void.' This sparked protests but little change until 1964, when a series of demonstrations, some led by Martin Luther King, Jr, and race riots rocked St Augustine and helped spur passage of the national Civil Rights Act of 1964.

More race riots blazed across Florida cities in 1967 and 1968, after which racial conflict eased as Florida belatedly and begrudgingly desegregated itself. Florida's racial wounds healed equally slowly – as evidenced by more race riots in the early 1980s. Today, despite much progress and the fact that Florida is one of the nation's most ethnically diverse states, these wounds still haven't completely healed.

Draining Swamps & Laying Rail

By the middle of the 19th century, the top half of Florida was reasonably well explored, but South Florida was still an oozing, mosquito-plagued swamp. So, in the 1870s, Florida inaugurated its first building boom by adopting laissez-faire economic policies centered on three things: unrestricted private development, minimal taxes and land grants for railroads.

In 10 years, from 1881 to 1891, Florida's railroad miles quintupled, from 550 to 2566. Most of this track crisscrossed northern and central Florida, where the people were, but one rail line went south to nowhere. In 1886, railroad magnate Henry Flagler started building a railroad down the coast on the spectacular gamble that once he built it, people would come.

In 1896 Flagler's line stopped at the squalid village of Fort Dallas, which incorporated as the city of Miami that same year. Then, people came, and kept coming, and Flagler is largely credited with founding every town from West Palm Beach to Miami.

It's hard to do justice to what happened next, but it was madness, pure and simple – far crazier than Ponce's dream of eternal waters. Why, all South Florida needed was to get rid of that pesky *swamp*, and then it really *would* be paradise: a land of eternal sunshine and profit.

In 1900 Governor Napoleon Bonaparte Broward, envisioning an 'Empire of the Everglades,' set in motion a frenzy of canal building. Over the next 70 years, some 1800 miles of canals and levees were etched across Florida's porous limestone. These earthworks drained about half the Everglades (about 1.5 million acres) below Lake Okeechobee, replacing it with farms, cattle ranches, orange groves, sugarcane and suburbs.

From 1920 to 1925 the South Florida land boom swept the nation. In 1915 Miami Beach was a sand bar; by 1925 it had 56 hotels, 178 apartment buildings and three golf courses. In 1920 Miami had one skyscraper; by 1925, 30 were under construction. In 1925 alone, 2.5 million people moved to Florida. Real-estate speculators sold undeveloped land, undredged land, and then just the airy paper promises of land. Everything went like hotcakes.

Historic Resorts & Mansions

Tampa Bay Hotel, Henry B Plant Museum, Tampa

Hotel Ponce de León, St Augustine

The Breakers, Palm Beach

Whitehall Mansion, Flagler Museum, Palm Beach

Biltmore Hotel, Coral Gables

1923	1926	1933–40	1935
The African American town of Rosewood, in Levy County, is wiped off the map by a white lynch mob; former residents are scattered and resettle elsewhere.	A major hurricane flattens and floods South Florida. Nearly 400 people die, most drowning when Lake Okeechobee bursts its dike. Two years later another hurricane kills 2000 people.	New Deal public-works projects employ 40,000 Floridians and help save Florida from the Depression. Most notable construction project is the Overseas Hwy through the Keys, replacing Flagler's railroad.	'Swami of the Swamp' Dick Pope opens Cypress Gardens, the USA's first theme park, with water-ski stunts, topiary and Southern belles. Allegedly, this inspires Walt Disney to create California's Disneyland.

Then, two hurricanes struck, in 1926 and 1928, and the party ended. The coup de grâce was the October 1929 stock-market crash, which took everyone's money. Like the nation, Florida plunged into the Depression, though the state rode it out better than most due to New Deal public works, tourism, and a highly profitable foray into rumrunning.

Tin-Can Tourists, Retirees & a Big-Eared Mouse

For the record, tourism is Florida's number-one industry, and this doesn't count retirees (the tourists who never leave).

Tourism didn't become a force in Florida until the 1890s, when Flagler built his coastal railroad and his exclusive Miami Beach resorts. In the 1920s, middle-class 'tin-can tourists' arrived via the new Dixie Hwy – driving Model Ts, sleeping in campers and cooking their own food.

In the 1930s, to get those tourists spending, savvy promoters created the first 'theme parks': Cypress Gardens and Silver Springs. But it wasn't until after WWII that Florida tourism exploded. During the war, Miami was a major military training ground, and afterward many of those GIs returned with their families to enjoy Florida's sandy beaches at leisure.

In addition, after the war social security kicked in, and the nation's aging middle class migrated south to enjoy their first taste of retirement. As old folks will, they came slowly but steadily, at a rate of a thousand a week till they numbered in the hundreds of thousands and then millions. Many came from the East Coast, and quite a few were Jewish: by 1960, Miami Beach was 80% Jewish, creating a famous ethnic enclave.

Then one day in 1963, so the story goes, Walt Disney flew over central Florida, spotted the intersection of I-4 and the Florida Turnpike, and said, 'That's it.' In secret, he bought 43 sq miles of Orlando-area wetlands. Afterward, like an expert alligator wrestler, Disney successfully negotiated with the state of Florida and was granted unprecedented and unique municipal powers to build his tourist mecca.

Exempt from a host of state laws and building codes and largely self-governing, Disney World opened in 1971. How big did it become? In 1950 Florida received 4.5 million tourists, not quite twice its population. By the 1980s Disney alone was drawing 40 million visitors a year, or four times the state population.

Disney had the Midas touch. In the shadow of the Magic Kingdom, Florida's old-school attractions – Weeki Wachee, Seminole Village, Busch Gardens; all the places made famous through billboards and postcards – seemed hokey, small-time. The rules of tourism had changed forever.

The Florida State Archives website (www.florida memory.com) presents a fascinating collection of historical documents (a 1586 map of St Augustine, Civil War letters), plus oodles of great photos, both historic and contemporary.

1941–45	1942	1946	1946
US enters WWII. Two million men and women receive basic training in South Florida. At one point, the army commandeers 85% of Miami Beach's hotels to house personnel.	From January to August, German U-boats sink over two dozen tankers and ships off Florida's coast. By war's end, Florida holds nearly 3000 German POWs in 15 labor camps.	The development of modern air conditioning, coupled with a post-war economic boom, opens the door to thousands of transplants settling in the state.	Frozen concentrated orange juice is invented. As the nation's top orange producer, this event leads to Florida's orange boom, giving birth to the orange millionaires of the '50s and '60s.

Viva Cuba Libre!

South Florida has often had a more intimate relationship with Cuba than with the rest of the US. Spain originally ruled Florida from Havana, and in the 20th century so many Cuban exiles sought refuge in Miami that they dubbed it the 'Exile Capital.' Later, as immigration expanded, Miami simply became the 'Capital of Latin America.'

From 1868 to 1902, during Cuba's long struggle for independence from Spain, Cuban exiles settled in Key West and Tampa, giving birth to Ybor City and its cigar-rolling industry. After independence, many Cubans returned home, but the economic ties they'd forged remained. Then, in 1959, Fidel Castro's revolution (plotted partly in Miami hotels) overthrew the Batista dictatorship. This triggered a several-year exodus of over 600,000 Cubans to Miami, most of them white, wealthy, educated professionals.

In April 1961 Castro declared Cuba a communist nation, setting the future course for US–Cuban relations. The next day President Kennedy approved the ill-fated Bay of Pigs invasion, which failed to overthrow Castro, and in October 1962 Kennedy blockaded Cuba to protest the presence of Russian nuclear missiles. Khrushchev famously 'blinked' and removed the missiles, but not before the US secretly agreed never to invade Cuba again.

None of this sat well with Miami's Cuban exiles, who agitated for the US to free Cuba (chanting '*Viva Cuba libre*': long live free Cuba). Between 1960 and 1980, a million Cubans emigrated – 10% of the island's population; by 1980, 60% of Miami was Cuban. Meanwhile, the US and Cuba wielded immigration policies like cudgels to kneecap each other.

The Cuban exiles disparaged assimilation (and sometimes the US), because the dream of return animated their lives. Miami became two parallel cities, Cuban and North American, that rarely spoke each other's language.

In the 1980s and 1990s, poorer immigrants flooded Miami from all over the Latin world – particularly El Salvador, Nicaragua, Mexico, Colombia, Venezuela, the Dominican Republic and Haiti. These groups did not always mix easily or embrace each other, but they found success in a city that already conducted business in Spanish. By the mid-1990s, South Florida was exporting $25 billion in goods to Latin America, and Miami's Cubans were more economically powerful than Cuba itself.

Today, Miami's Cubans are firmly entrenched, and those of the younger generation no longer consider themselves exiles.

At the height of the industry in the 1940s, Florida's sugarcane fields produced one of every five teaspoons of sugar consumed in the US.

After WWII, the advent of effective bug spray and affordable air-conditioning did more for Florida tourism than anything else. With these two technological advancements, Florida's subtropical climate was finally safe for delicate Yankee skin.

1947	1961	1969	1971
Everglades National Park is established, successfully culminating a 19-year effort, led by Ernest Coe and Marjory Stoneman Douglas, to protect the Everglades from the harm done by dredging and draining.	Brigade 2506, a 1300-strong volunteer army, invades Cuba's Bay of Pigs on April 16. President Kennedy withholds air support, leading to Brigade 2506's immediate defeat and capture by Fidel Castro.	*Apollo 11* lifts off from Cape Canaveral, landing on the moon on July 20, winning the space race with the Russians. Five more lunar-bound rockets take off through 1972.	Walt Disney World in Orlando opens and around 10,000 people arrive on the first day. The park attracts 10 million visitors during its first year.

Hurricanes, the Everglades & Elections

Florida has a habit of selling itself too well. The precarious foundation of its paradise was driven home in 1992 when Hurricane Andrew ripped across South Florida, leaving a wake of destruction that stunned the state and the nation. Plus, mounting evidence of rampant pollution – fish kills, dying mangroves, murky bays – appeared like the bill for a century of unchecked sprawl, population growth and industrial nonchalance.

Newcomers were trampling the very features they were coming for. From 1930 to 1980, Florida's population growth rate was 564%. Florida had gone from the least-populated to the fourth-most-populated state and its infrastructure was woefully inadequate, with too few police, overcrowded prisons, traffic jams, ugly strip malls and some of the nation's worst schools.

In particular, saving the Everglades became more than another environmental crusade. It was a moral test: would Florida really squander one of the earth's wonders over subdivisions and a quick buck? Remarkably, legislation was passed: the Florida Forever Act and the Comprehensive Everglades Restoration Plan were both signed into law in 2000. Meanwhile, the actual implementation of Everglades restoration has been delayed and held up by bureaucracy and politicking at the federal, state and local levels.

Yet 2000 became even more emblematic of Florida's deeply divided self. That year's tight presidential election between Republican George W Bush and Democrat Al Gore hung on Florida's result. However, Florida's breathtakingly narrow vote in favor of Bush unraveled into a fiasco of 'irregularities,' including defective ballots, wrongly purged voter rolls and mysterious election-day roadblocks. After months of legal challenges and partial recounts, Florida's vote was finally approved, but its reputation had been tarnished.

As the 21st century dawned, Florida's historic tensions – between its mantra of growth and development and the unsustainable demands that this placed on society and nature – seemed as entrenched and intractable as ever.

It's all too easy to mock Florida for its bumbling 2000 presidential vote, but the HBO movie *Recount* (2008) doesn't. Instead, it cogently shows what happened and unearths the political grudges that shadowed an honest recount.

Southernmost Schisms

The beginning of this century was a politically polarizing time across much of the United States, and Florida, being in many ways a microcosm of the nation as a whole, was not immune to the trend. If anything, Florida's ideological divisions were exacerbated by deep boundaries that run along its geographic and ethnic lines.

While the governorship has remained securely in Republican hands since 1999, the state itself is a toss-up in every presidential election (it

May 1980	1980	1984	1992
In the McDuffie trial, white cops are acquitted of wrongdoing in the death of a black man, igniting racial tensions and Miami's Liberty City riots, killing 18 people.	Castro declares the Cuban port of Mariel 'open.' The USA's ensuing Mariel Boatlift rescues 125,000 *Marielitos*, who face intense discrimination in Miami.	TV show *Miami Vice* debuts, combining music-video sensibilities, pastel fashions, blighted South Beach locations and cynical undercover cops battling gun-wielding Miami cocaine cartels.	On August 24, Hurricane Andrew devastates Dade County, leaving 41 people dead, over 200,000 homeless and causing $15.5 billion in damage.

narrowly broke for George W Bush twice and Barack Obama twice). This is largely due to redistricting practices, widely seen as gerrymandering (ie drawing voting districts to bolster a political party's performance), which have driven a deep rift between the state's political camps. That said, past governors such as Jeb Bush (George W Bush's younger brother; 1999-2007) and Charlie Crist (2007-2011) toed the centrist line within the Republican policy universe, generally skewing towards conservative economics and lenient policies regarding immigration.

Indeed, Crist, who supports same sex marriage but is also pro-gun ownership, made the relatively rare American political move of defection, joining the Democratic Party in 2012. That he did so a month after Barack Obama's re-election did not help his reputation as a political

TRAYVON MARTIN & STAND YOUR GROUND

One of the most divisive racial and political incidents of the early 21st century began in Florida. On the night of February 26, 2012, 17-year old African American Trayvon Martin walked to his temporary home in the Central Florida town of Sanford. Martin, clad in a hoodie, was carrying a pack of Skittles and some Arizona Iced Tea. To get home quickly, he cut across yards in a gated community. Following him was George Zimmerman, a 28-year-old mixed-race Hispanic and neighborhood watch coordinator. Against the advice of police, Zimmerman confronted Martin, leading to an altercation. In the subsequent fight Zimmerman received head and facial injuries, and shot and killed the unarmed Martin.

Zimmerman was taken into police custody and released; under Florida's recently passed Stand Your Ground law, police did not believe he had committed a crime. Under the Stand Your Ground statue, in a self-defense incident a victim does not have to exercise the traditional 'Duty to Retreat' common across American legal code, which states that someone who kills in self defense must have exhausted their opportunities to avoid conflict.

Media attention and a subsequent national outcry led to Zimmerman being re-arrested on a charge of second-degree (ie non-premeditated) murder on April 11, 2012. A trial in the summer of 2013 found Zimmerman not guilty. The decision outraged many, who felt Zimmerman had (literally) gotten away with the murder of an unarmed teenager. On the flip side, gun-rights advocates believed Zimmerman had exercised his rights to self defense during the course of an assault.

The role of 'Stand Your Ground' was invoked and discussed by pundits and commentators, even though Zimmerman's legal team did not utilize Stand Your Ground in their defensive arguments. Nonetheless, there were calls for boycotts of Florida tourism over the law. To date, these boycotts have not had much impact on travel in the state. For an excellent overview of the impact of the legislation, read the June 2012 investigation into the law carried out by the *Tampa Bay Times*.

1999	2000	2000–2010	2004
On Thanksgiving, five-year-old Elián Gonzalez is rescued at sea, his Cuban mother having died en route. Despite wild protests by Miami's Cuban exiles, the US returns Elián to his father in Cuba.	Before the presidential election, Florida mistakenly purges thousands of legitimate voters from rolls. George W Bush then narrowly defeats Al Gore by 537 votes in Florida to win the presidency.	High-rise architecture sweeps Miami; during this period, 20 of the city's 25 tallest buildings are erected, a trend some call the 'Manhattanization' of Miami.	Florida records its worst hurricane season ever when four storms – Charley, Frances, Ivan and Jeanne – strike the state over two months, causing 130 deaths and $22 billion in damage.

opportunist, although defenders say he is merely flexible and open to changing his position on past issues. His ouster and political conversion came amid the 2008 financial crisis, which particularly devastated the Florida housing market.

Rick Scott settled into the gubernatorial office in Tallahassee in 2011 and has been instrumental in setting the state's political compass since. An unabashedly anti-regulation businessman (prior to election, Scott had been a CEO and venture capitalist with a net worth of $218 million), he has also been sympathetic to Everglades protection policies, which speaks to the very delicate balancing act Scott maintains on a daily basis. He must constantly both diffuse and harness the tension between the white, conservative northern end of the state, the more liberal and Latin American south, and the mishmash of identities and interests that lays in between. A Florida of Stand Your Ground, Everglades restoration, climate-change denial and climate-change preparation policy is today's Florida in all its glorious contradictions.

2008	2010	2014	2014
Wanting greater influence in the Democratic presidential nomination, Florida moves its primary up to January. The Democratic party strips Florida of its delegates, so its votes don't count.	In the Gulf, *Deepwater Horizon*'s offshore oil spill becomes the worst in US history. Oil only affects Panhandle beaches, but Florida tourism plummets, with losses estimated at $3 billion.	Everglades restoration plans get green lights from the state, including conservative politicians, but are then delayed due to bureaucratic gridlock and postponements from the Army Corps of Engineers.	The 0.75-mile Port of Miami Tunnel, which connects the MacArthur Causeway on Watson Island with the Port of Miami on Dodge Island, is scheduled to open.

People & Culture

Florida's people and culture are a compelling mix of accents and rhythms, of pastel hues and Caribbean spices, of rebel yells and Latin hip-hop, of Jewish retirees and Miami Beach millionaires. Florida is, in a word, diverse. Like the prehistoric swamp at its heart, it is both fascinatingly complex and too fluid to pin down, making for a very intriguing place to explore. Is there tension? Absolutely. But that tension drives a social dynamic that is undoubtedly one of the most unique in the country.

'Crackers' got their name most likely for the cracking of whips during cattle drives, though some say it was for the cracking of corn to make cornmeal, grits or moonshine. For a witty, affectionate look at what makes a Cracker, pick up *Cracker: The Cracker Culture in Florida History* by Dana Ste Claire.

Portrait of a Peninsula

Pessimists contend that the state is so socially and culturally fractured that it will never have a coherent identity. Optimists, strangely enough, say nearly the same thing. Like an overpraised but insecure beauty queen, Florida is almost too popular for its own good, and it can never quite decide if the continual influx of newcomers and immigrants is its saving grace or what will eventually strain society to breaking point.

In terms of geography, Florida is a Southern state. Yet culturally, only Florida's northern half is truly of the South. The Panhandle, Jacksonville and the rural north welcome those who speak with that distinctive Southern drawl, serve sweet tea as a matter of course and still remember the Civil War. Here, the stereotype of the NASCAR-loving redneck with a Confederate-flag bumper sticker on a mud-splattered pickup truck remains the occasional reality.

But central Florida and the Tampa Bay area were a favored destination for Midwesterners, and here you often find plain-spoken, Protestant worker-bee sobriety. East Coast Yankees, once mocked as willing dupes for any old piece of swamp, have carved a definable presence in South Florida – such as in the Atlantic Coast's Jewish retirement communities, in callused, urban Miami, and in the sophisticated towns of the southern Gulf Coast.

Rural Florida, meanwhile, whether north or south, can still evoke America's western frontier. In the 19th century, after the West was won, Florida became one of the last places where pioneers could simply plant stakes and make a life. These pioneers became Florida's 'Crackers,' the poor farmers, cowhands and outlaws who traded life's comforts for independence on their terms. Sometimes any Florida pioneer is called a Cracker, but that's not quite right: the original Crackers scratched out a living in the backwoods (in the Keys, Crackers became Conchs). They were migrant field hands, not plantation owners, and with their lawless squatting, make-do creativity, vagrancy and carousing, they weren't regarded kindly by respectable townsfolk. But today, all native Floridians like to feel they too share that same streak of fierce, undomesticated self-reliance.

And yet, stand in parts of Miami and even Tampa and you won't feel like you're in the US at all, but tropical Latin America. The air is filled with Spanish, the majority of people are Roman Catholic, and the politics of Cuba, Haiti or Colombia animate conversations.

Ultimately, Florida satisfies and defies expectations all at once, and is a study in contrasts. From Cuban lawyers to itinerant construction works, from fixed-income retirees to gay South Beach restaurateurs, it's one of the USA's more bizarre dinner parties come to life.

However, most residents do have something in common: in Florida, nearly everybody is from someplace else. Nearly everyone was a newcomer and, one and all, they wholeheartedly agree on two things: today's newcomers are going to ruin Florida, and wasn't it great to beat them here?

Immigrants & the Capital of Latin America

Like Texas and California, modern Florida has been largely redefined by successive waves of Hispanic immigrants from Latin America. What sets Florida apart is the teeming diversity of its Latinos and their self-sufficient, economically powerful, politicized, Spanish-speaking presence.

How pervasive is Spanish? One in four Floridians speak a language other than English at home, and three-quarters of these speak Spanish. Further, nearly half of these Spanish-speakers admit they don't speak English very well – because they don't need to. This is a sore point with some Anglo Floridians, perhaps because it's incontrovertible evidence that Florida's Latinos are enjoying America's capitalism without necessarily having to adopt its culture or language.

Florida's Cuban exile community (concentrated in Little Havana and Hialeah Park), who began arriving in Miami in the 1960s following Castro's Cuban revolution, created this from the start. Educated and wealthy, these Cubans ran their own businesses, published their own newspapers and developed a Spanish-speaking city within a city. Their success aggravated Florida's African American population, who, at the moment the civil rights movement was opening the doors to economic opportunity, found themselves outmaneuvered for jobs by Hispanic newcomers.

Then Latinos kept arriving nonstop, ranging from the very poorest to the wealthiest. In Miami they found a Spanish-speaking infrastructure to help them, while sometimes being shunned by the insular Cuban exiles who preceded them.

Today, every Latin American country is represented in South Florida. Nicaraguans arrived in the 1980s, fleeing war in their country, and now number over 100,000. Miami's Little Haiti is home to more than 70,000 Haitians, the largest community in the US. There are 80,000 Brazilians, and large communities of Mexicans, Venezuelans, Colombians, Peruvians, Salvadorans, Jamaicans, Bahamians and more. This has led to significant in-migration around South Florida, as groups displace each other and shift to more fertile ground.

IMMIGRATION BY THE NUMBERS

For the past 70 years the story of Florida has been population growth, which has been driven mostly by immigration. Before WWII Florida was the least populated state (with under two million), and today it is the fourth most populated, with 18.8 million in 2010.

Florida's growth rate has been astonishing – it was 44% in the 1970s. While it's been steadily declining since, growth was still more than 17% for the 21st century's first decade, twice the national average. That equaled nearly three million new residents from 2000 to 2010. Florida ranks fourth in the nation for the largest minority population (7.9 million), as well as for the largest number and percentage of foreign-born residents (3.5 million people, who make up 18%). In Miami the foreign-born population exceeds 60%, which is easily tops among large US cities.

Finally, Florida is home to an estimated 700,000 illegal immigrants, and stemming this tide is currently a hot-button issue.

The children of Cuban exiles are now called YUCAs, 'young urban Cuban Americans,' while the next generation of Latinos has been dubbed Generation Ñ (pronounced enyey), embodying a hybrid culture. For instance, the traditional Cuban *quinceañera* (or *quince*; celebrating a girl's coming of age at 15) is still celebrated in Miami, but instead of a community-wide party, kids now plan trips. With each other, young Latinos slip seamlessly between English and Spanish, typically within the same sentence, reverting to Spanish or old-school Cuban in front of relatives.

Florida has also welcomed smaller waves of Asian immigrants from China, Indonesia, Thailand and Vietnam. And, of course, South Florida is famous for its Jewish immigrants, not all of whom are over 65 or even from the US. There is a distinctly Latin flavor to South Florida Judaism, as Cuban and Latin Jews have joined those from the US East Coast, Europe and Russia. Overall, Florida is home to 850,000 Jews, with two-thirds living in the Greater Miami area.

Life in Florida

Let's get this out of the way first: Florida is indeed the nation's oldest state. It has the highest percentage of people over 65 (over 17%), which pulls the state's median age up to nearly 41, or four years higher than the national average. In fact, ever since WWII South Florida has been 'God's waiting room' – the land of the retiree.

But the truth is, most immigrants to the state (whether from within the US or abroad) are aged 20 to 30, and they don't come for the early-bird buffet. They come because of Florida's historically low cost of living and its usually robust job and real-estate markets.

When times are good, what they find is that there are plenty of low- to mid-wage construction, tourist and service-sector jobs, and if they can buy one of those new-built condos or tract homes, they're money ahead, as Florida home values usually outpace the nation's. But in bad times when real estate falters – and in Florida, no matter how many warnings people get, the real-estate market does eventually falter – home values plummet, construction jobs dry up and service-sector wages can't keep up with the bills. Thus, those 20- to 30-year-olds also leave the state in the highest numbers.

In recent years, the growing wealth gap in America has made it increasingly difficult for middle-income earners to afford rent (let alone a mortgage) in Florida's growing urban areas. While businesses have always been able to fall back on cheap migrant labor from Latin America, the Caribbean and Eastern Europe, there has also usually been an accompanying nucleus of lifer service-industry professionals. Said professionals are increasingly finding Florida unaffordable, though, which bears the question: how can a state that is supported by tourism survive without folks who can afford what the tourism industry pays?

Florida's urban and rural divides are extreme. Urban sprawl, particularly around Miami, Orlando and Tampa, is universally loathed – because who likes traffic jams and cookie-cutter sameness? Well, some folks like the sameness; Florida wouldn't be famous for her suburbs and shopping malls if people didn't occupy them. In addition new immigrants tend to gravitate to the suburbs – the green lawns predictably rejected by so many Americans seeking a new urbanism are seen as signs of a high quality of life for émigrés from Haiti and Cuba. In any case, almost everyone really does have a tan. It's nearly unavoidable: 80% of Floridians live within 10 miles of the coast because that's why everyone came – the beach.

Profiles of Peoples

'Voices of the Apalachicola,' by Faith Eidse

'Jews of South Florida,' by Andrea Greenbaum

'Cuban Miami,' by Robert M Levine and Moisés Asís

So, along the peninsula's urbanized edges, everyone rubs up against each other: racial, ethnic and class tensions are a constant fact of life, but they have also calmed tremendously in recent decades. In general, tolerance (if not acceptance) of diversity is the norm, while tolerance of visitors is the rule. After all, they pay the bills.

But wilderness and rural life define much of interior and northern Florida: here, small working-class towns can be as white, old-fashioned and conservative as Miami is multiracial, gaudy and permissive. This is one reason why it's so hard to predict Florida elections and why sometimes they turn on a handful of votes.

A large military presence in the Florida Panhandle makes for an area that is generally quite conservative in its politics but, thanks to overseas rotations is a bit more cosmopolitan than the deep piney villages of the north Florida interior.

Floridians at Play

Floridians are passionate about sports. If you let them, they'll fervently talk baseball, football, basketball and NASCAR through dinner, dessert and drinks on the porch.

For the majority of Floridians, college football is the true religion. Florida has three of the country's best collegiate teams – the University of Miami Hurricanes, the University of Florida Gators (in Gainesville) and the Florida State University Seminoles (in Tallahassee). Between them these teams have won nine national championships but, if anything, they are even more competitive with each other. It's hardly an exaggeration to say that beating an in-state rival is – at least for fans, who take deep pleasure in *hating* their rivals – almost more important than winning all the other games. If you want to cause a scene in Florida, tell an FSU student how much you love the Gators, or mention to a UF student how great the 'Noles are.

Florida also boasts three pro football teams: the Miami Dolphins, Tampa Bay Buccaneers and Jacksonville Jaguars. There's a reason college football is so popular in Florida; In recent years all three

PEOPLE & CULTURE FLORIDIANS AT PLAY

When former *David Letterman* writer Rodney Rothman burned out, he decided to test drive 'retirement' in Boca Raton – at age 28. A good Jewish boy, Rothman crafts a very personal anthropological study of the unsentimental world of Florida retirees in *Early Bird: A Memoir of Premature Retirement*.

CELEBRATING FLORIDA HERITAGE & CULTURE

Florida's diversity really comes alive in its many cultural festivals. Here are a handful worth planning a trip around.

Zora Neale Hurston Festival of the Arts & Humanities (www.zorafestival.org; Eatonville) For 20 years, Zora Neale Hurston's hometown has honored her with this African American cultural festival, culminating in a lively three-day street fair. Runs for one week in late January–early February.

Carnaval Miami (www.carnaval-miami.org) The Calle Ocho festival in Little Havana, which runs for 10 days in early March, is the USA's biggest Hispanic street fair. There are domino tournaments, cooking contests, Latin-music concerts and more.

Florida Folk Festival (www.floridastateparks.org/folkfest; White Springs) Since 1953 the Stephen Foster State Folk Cultural Center has held this enormous heritage festival, with hundreds of Florida musicians – from gospel singers to banjo pickers – plus storytellers and Seminole craft demonstrations. Held on Memorial Day weekend.

Goombay Festival (www.goombayfestivalcoconutgrove.com; Miami) One of the nation's largest multicultural festivals celebrates Miami's Bahamian immigrants with tons of Caribbean music, dancing and food. Held over four days in early June.

Barberville Jamboree (www.pioneersettlement.org; Barberville) On the first weekend of November, the Pioneer Settlement for the Creative Arts hosts Florida's best pioneer-heritage festival, with folk music and authentic demonstrations of Cracker life.

professional teams have (sorry, it must be said) royally sucked. The Jaguars in particular seem to have made it a point of pride to be consistently the worst team in the NFL. Florida has two pro basketball teams, the Orlando Magic and Miami Heat. The Heat, who won back-to-back NBA championships in 2012 and 2013, are loved in Miami and pretty much loathed everywhere else. The Stanley Cup–winning Tampa Bay Lightning is one of several pro and semipro ice-hockey teams in the state, including the Miami-based Florida Panthers.

Major-league baseball's spring training creates a frenzy of excitement from February each year, when 15 pro teams practice across southern Florida. The stadiums then host minor-league teams, while two pro teams are based here: the Miami Marlins and the Tampa Bay Rays (in St Petersburg). The Minnesota Twins and Boston Red Sox both have their training facilities in Fort Myers.

NASCAR originated among liquor bootleggers who needed fast cars to escape the law – and who later raced against each other. Fast outgrowing its Southern redneck roots to become popular across the US, NASCAR is near and dear to Floridians and hosts regular events in Daytona.

Imported sports also flourish in Florida. One is the dangerous Basque game of jai alai, which is popular with Miami's cigar-smoking wagering types. Another is cricket, thanks to the Miami region's large Jamaican and West Indian population.

> In *Dream State*, bawdy, gimlet-eyed journalist Diane Roberts weaves her family's biography with Florida's history to create a compelling, unique, hilarious masterpiece. Roberts is like the troublemaking cousin at Florida's family reunion, dishing the dirt everyone else is too polite to discuss.

Religion

Florida is not just another notch in the South's evangelical Bible Belt. It's actually considerably more diverse religiously than its neighboring states.

In Florida, religious affiliations split less along urban/rural lines than along northern/southern ones. About 40% of Florida is Protestant, and about 25% of Protestants are Evangelicals, who tend to be supporters of the religious right. However, these conservative Protestants are much more concentrated in northern Florida, nearer their Southern neighbors.

The majority of the state's Roman Catholics (who make up 26% of the population) and Jews (3%) live in South Florida. In South Florida, Jews make up 12% of the population, the second-highest percentage after the New York metro area. The high Catholic population reflects South Florida's wealth of Latin American immigrants.

South Florida also has a growing Muslim population, and it has a noticeable number of adherents of Santeria, a mix of West African and Catholic beliefs, and *vodou* (voodoo), mainly practiced by Haitians.

Further, about 16% of Floridians say that they have no religious affiliation. That doesn't mean they lack spiritual beliefs; it just means their beliefs don't fit census categories. For instance, one of Florida's most famous religious communities is Cassadaga (www.cassadaga.org), a home for Spiritualists for more than 100 years.

> Florida real estate is a continual Ponzi scheme. For a heartfelt look at the human cost when the Florida real-estate market collapsed in 2007, read *Exiles in Eden* by Paul Reyes, a reporter who joined the family business of 'trashing out' foreclosed homes.

The Arts

Florida has a well-earned reputation as a welcoming port for all manner of kitsch and low-brow entertainment. It invented the theme park, spring break, *Miami Vice* and its own absurdist, black-comic semitropical crime noir. But there's so much more. Should we dismiss Florida's contributions to high culture just because the colors are always sunshine bright? At their best, Florida traditions are simultaneously homegrown and cosmopolitan, and vibrate with the surreal, mercurial truths of everyday life in this alligator-infested, hurricane-troubled peninsula.

Literature

Beginning in the 1930s, Florida cleared its throat and developed its own bona fide literary voice, courtesy mainly of three writers. The most famous was Ernest Hemingway, who settled in Key West in 1928 to write, fish and drink, not necessarily in that order. 'Papa' wrote *For Whom the Bell Tolls* and *A Farewell to Arms* here, but he only set one novel in Florida, *To Have and Have Not* (1937), thus making his life more Floridian than his writing.

The honor of 'most Floridian writer' is generally bestowed on Marjorie Kinnan Rawlings, who lived in Cross Creek between Gainesville and Ocala. She turned her sympathetic, keen eye on Florida's pioneers – the Crackers who populated 'the invisible Florida' – and on the elemental beauty of the state's swampy wilderness. Her novel *The Yearling* (1938) won the Pulitzer Prize, and *Cross Creek* (1942) is a much-lauded autobiographical novel. Her original homestead is now a museum.

Rounding out the trio is Zora Neale Hurston, an African American writer who was born in all-black Eatonville, near Orlando. Hurston became a major figure in New York's Harlem Renaissance of the 1930s, and her most famous novel, *Their Eyes Were Watching God* (1937), evokes the suffering of Florida's rural African Americans, particularly women. In *Seraph on the Suwanee* (1948) Hurston portrays the marriage of two white Florida Crackers. Controversial in her time, Hurston died in obscurity and poverty.

Another famous depiction of Florida's pioneers is Patrick Smith's *A Land Remembered* (1984), a sprawling, multigenerational saga that highlights the Civil War. Meanwhile Peter Matthiessen's *Shadow Country* (2008) is an epic literary masterpiece. A trilogy revised into a single work, *Shadow Country* fictionalizes the true story of EJ Watson, a turn-of-the-century Everglades plume hunter who murdered his employees and was in turn murdered by the townsfolk.

Florida writing is perhaps most famous for its eccentric take on hard-boiled crime noir fiction. Carl Hiaasen almost singlehandedly defines the genre; his stories are hilarious bubbling gumbos of misfits and murderers, who collide in plots of thinly disguised environmentalism, in which the bad guys are developers and their true crimes are against nature. Some other popular authors are Randy Wayne White, John D MacDonald, James Hall and Tim Dorsey.

You can count among Florida's snowbirds some of the USA's best writers, such as Robert Frost, Stephen King, Isaac Bashevis Singer and Annie Dillard, and every January the US literati holds court at the annual Key West Literary Seminar.

FLORIDA PULP

Florida mystery writers love to tickle the swampy underbelly of the Sunshine State. This list focuses on early novels of famous series. Grab one and hit the beach for another murderous day in paradise.

➤ *Rum Punch* (Elmore Leonard, 1992) Leonard is the undisputed master of intricate plots, crackling dialogue and terrific bad guys. Set in Miami, *Rum Punch* inspired Tarantino's movie *Jackie Brown*.

➤ *Double Whammy* (Carl Hiaasen, 1987) Hiaasen perfected his absurdist, black-comic rage in his second novel; you'll laugh till you cry. *Skinny Dip* and *Hoot* are also Hiaasen gems.

➤ *The Girl in the Plain Brown Wrapper* (John D MacDonald, 1968) The godfather of Florida crime fiction introduces us to Travis McGee, who saves a girl from suicide and gets trouble as thanks.

➤ *Sanibel Flats* (Randy Wayne White, 1990) With crisp prose and tight plotting, White introduces his much-beloved 'retired' NSA agent/marine biologist Doc Ford.

➤ *Miami Blues* (Charles Willeford, 1984) Willeford first made it big with this addictive novel about a denture-wearing detective's chase after a quirky criminal.

➤ *Cold Case Squad* (Edna Buchanan, 2004) Miami police sergeant Craig Burch leads the cold-case squad after killers whose 'trails vanished long ago like footprints on a sea-washed beach.'

➤ *Torpedo Juice* (Tim Dorsey, 2005) Zany Serge A Storms only kills people who really deserve it – people who disrespect Florida – as he searches for love in the Keys.

➤ *Tropical Depression* (Laurence Shames, 1996) Shames is off-the-wall silly. Here, an inept Jersey bra magnate seeks to find himself in Key West. Yeah, right.

Florida's modern novelists tend to favor supernatural, even monstrously absurd Southern Gothic styles, none more so than Harry Crews; try *All We Need of Hell* (1987) and *Celebration* (1999). Two more cult favorites are *Ninety-two in the Shade* (1973) by Thomas McGaune and *Mile Zero* (1990) by Thomas Sanchez, both writerly, dreamlike Key West fantasies. Also don't miss Russell Banks' *Continental Drift* (1985), about the tragic intersection of a burned-out New Hampshire man and a Haitian woman in unforgiving Miami.

Most recently, Karen Russell's *Swamplandia!* (2011), about the travails of a family of alligator wrestlers, marries Hiaasen-style characters with swamp-drenched magical realism.

Naked Came the Manatee (1998) is a collaborative mystery novel by a constellation of famous Florida writers: Carl Hiaasen, Dave Barry, Elmore Leonard, James Hall, Edna Buchanan and more. It's like nibbling a delectable box of cyanide-laced chocolates.

Cinema & Television

Get this: Jacksonville almost became Hollywood. In the 1910s, Jacksonville had 30 production companies – far more than Hollywood – who were using its palm-tree-lined beaches as 'exotic' backdrops for 120 silent films. Yet even as Laurel and Hardy were becoming famous in one-reeler slapstick comedies, religiously conservative Jacksonville decided to run those wild movie types out of town. Then Florida's 1926 real-estate bust (and the talkies) killed what remained of Florida moviemaking.

Still, it was a close call, and you can see why: Florida, like California, has always fostered dreams and fantasies. Only in Florida they come to life as theme parks.

Actually, Hollywood has returned to Florida time and again to film both TV shows and movies. Some of the more notable popular films include the Marx Bros farce *Cocoanuts*, *Creature from the Black Lagoon* (filmed at Wakulla Springs), *The Truman Show* (filmed at Seaside), *Ulee's Gold*, *Donnie Brasco*, *Get Shorty*, *Hoot* and *Miami Blues*.

Florida, as the setting, has been a main character in a number of TV shows. In the 1960s the most famous were *Flipper*, about a boy and his dolphin, and *I Dream of Jeannie*. Set in Cocoa Beach, *Jeannie* was Florida all over: an astronaut discovers a pinup-gorgeous female genie in a bottle, only she never quite fulfills his wishes in the way he wants.

In the 1980s Miami was never the same after *Miami Vice* hit the air. This groundbreaking cop drama made it OK to wear sport coats over T-shirts and helped inspire the renovation of South Beach's then-dilapidated historic district. The popular, more recent *CSI: Miami* owed a debt to actor Don Johnson and *Miami Vice*.

What's fascinating about modern Miami cinematic media is its willingness to peer past the pastel and deco. Of course, shows such as *Miami Vice* were always comfortable with Miami's seedy side. but recent forays into film and television are looking at the savagery and darkness that seem to lurk side by side with the glittery celebrity facade. Shows such as *Dexter* have dipped past Miami's glamor directly into her bucket of weirdness.

It's also worth noting that Miami is one of the centers of American Spanish-language media, especially film and television. The first Spanish-language presidential debate in the United States was hosted at the University of Miami on Univision, while Spanish-language network Telemundo is based in Hialeah, a suburb of Miami.

Music

Florida's musical heritage is as rich and satisfyingly diverse as its cuisine. Folk and blues are deep-running currents in Florida music, and pioneers Ray Charles and Cannonball Adderley both hailed from the state. For folk, visit the **Spirit of the Suwannee Music Park** (www.musicliveshere.com), near Suwannee River State Park, while Tallahassee has a notable blues scene.

Florida's state song, 'Old Folks at Home,' was written by Stephen Foster in 1851. Best known for the refrain 'Waaaay down upon the Suwanee River...,' on the one hand it is a lament of an exile for his home, but on the other hand it quite explicitly a nostalgic missive by a slave who longs for his old plantation. In recent decades, Florida has sought to modernize the lyrics so that the song's sentimental paean to Old Florida is sanitized of its inherent racism, but some argue it should be retired nonetheless.

Florida definitely knows how to rock. Bo Diddley, after helping define rock and roll, settled near Gainesville for the second half of his life. North Florida is one of the wombs of that particularly American sub-genre of the musical catalog: Southern rock. The style is characterized by roots-laden references to old-school honky tonk overlaid with sometimes folksy, sometimes rowdy lyrics. Tom Petty, Lynyrd Skynyrd and the Allman Brothers form Florida's holy Southern-rock trio.

The 1960 movie of Glendon Swarthout's novel *Where the Boys Are* is largely responsible for spring break as we know it today. It's a bawdy, cautionary coming-of-age tale about four Midwest coeds visiting Fort Lauderdale for sun, sand and sex.

PERFORMING ARTS

Iconic American playwright Tennessee Williams called Key West home on and off for over 30 years, but Florida doesn't have much of a homegrown theater or dance tradition. However, several South Florida cities offer top-drawer performing arts and some spectacular stages.

Naturally, Miami leads the way. The Miami City Ballet, a Balanchine company, is one of the nation's largest. The statewide **Florida Dance Association** (www.floridadanceassociation.org) promotes dance performances and education. Miami's showstopper is the Adrienne Arsht Center for the Performing Arts, but also don't miss the New World Center. Tampa and St Petersburg also have large, lauded performing-arts centers.

For good regional theater, head for Miami, Sarasota, Orlando and even Fort Myers.

In more recent years, bands including Matchbox Twenty, Dashboard Confessional, Radical Face and Iron & Wine have gotten their start in Florida. Indie-rock sounds are strong across the state, from the expected college towns such as Gainesville to the perhaps unexpected Latin streetscape of Miami.

The popular musician who most often defines Florida is Jimmy Buffett, whose heart lives in Key West, wherever his band may roam. His fans, known as Parrotheads, are a particularly faithful (some might say obsessed) bunch. If you've never heard Buffet's music, it's basically crowd-pleasing beach tunes with a gentle, anti-authoritarian bent – anarchy via sandals and piña coladas, if you will. In a state where musical tastes tend to divide along sharp cultural fault lines, Buffet's easy-going guitar riffs are a bridge between camps. The more conservative side of the state appreciates his yacht-y swagger, while liberals like his gentle advocacy for environmentalism.

Orlando (by way of mogul and now jailbird Lou Pearlman) bestowed upon the world a special genre of music: the boy bands of 'N Sync and Backstreet Boys. In fact, in many ways Orlando via Disney is responsible for shaping the soundscape of much of the world's teen and tween-focused pop music; Miley Cyrus and Britney Spears may not be from Florida, but they perfected the art of mass marketability via trained Disney handlers and taste makers. While the aim of pop is to create a universal sound that cuts across borders, Florida's native beat works its way into the most globally marketed Orlando albums, from Hollywood native Victoria Justice's mallrat anthems to Boca Raton–born Ariana Grande's Latin-spiced dance numbers.

Rap and hip-hop have flourished in Tampa and Miami, from old-school 2 Live Crew to Trick Daddy, Rick Ross, DJ Khaled and Pitbull, the most visible link between North American hip-hop and Latin American reggaeton. The latter has its roots in Panama and Puerto Rico, and blends rap with Jamaican dancehall, Trinidadian soca, salsa and electronica.

Miami, of course is a tasty mélange of Cuban salsa, Jamaican reggae, Dominican merengue and Spanish flamenco, plus mambo, rumba, cha-cha, calypso and more. Gloria Estefan & the Miami Sound Machine launched a revival of Cuban music in the 1970s, when they mixed Latin beats with disco with 'Conga.' While disco has thankfully waned, Latin music has not; for a taste of Miami-style hip-hop, check out Los Primeros. The best times to see ensemble Cuban bands – often with up to 20 musicians and singers – is during celebrations such as Carnaval Miami.

Electric music is ubiquitous across South Florida, especially in Miami, which celebrates the genre with two of its biggest festivals: the Ultra Music Festival and the Winter Music Conference, both of which kick off in March (the two festivals essentially piggyback off of one another).

Architecture

Like its literature, Florida's architecture has some distinctive homegrown strains. These run from the old – the Spanish-colonial and Revival styles of St Augustine – to the aggressively modern, as in Miami and particularly South Beach.

At the turn of the century, Henry Flagler was instrumental in promoting a particularly Floridian Spanish-Moorish fantasia, which, as historian Michael Gannon writes, combined 'the stately architecture of Rome, the tiled rooftops of Spain, the dreamy beauty of Venice, [and] the tropical casualness of Algiers.' Prime examples are the monumental Hotel Ponce de León in St Augustine (now Flagler College), Whitehall Mansion in Palm Beach (now Flagler Museum) and Miami's awesome George Merrick–designed Coral Gables.

Two of the best film festivals in the US are the Miami International Film Festival (www.miamifilmfestival.com; March), a showcase for Latin cinema, and the up-and-coming Florida Film Festival (www.floridafilmfestival.com; April) in Orlando.

The Florida Division of Cultural Affairs (www.florida-arts.org) is a great resource for statewide arts organizations and agencies. Its Florida Artists Hall of Fame memorializes the Sunshine State's creative legacy.

THE FLORIDA HIGHWAYMEN

Beginning in the 1950s, about two dozen largely self-taught African American painters made a modest living selling vivid, impressionistic 'Florida-scapes' on wood and Masonite for about $20 a pop. They sold these romantic visions of raw swamps and technicolor sunsets from the trunks of their cars along I-95 and A1A, a practice that eventually gave them their name.

The Highwaymen were mentored and encouraged by AE 'Beanie' Backus, a white artist and teacher in Fort Pierce. Considered the 'dean' of Florida landscape art, Beanie was also largely self-taught, often preferring the rough strokes of a palette knife over a brush. Backus and his contemporaries from the '50s and '60s are also referred to as the Indian River School, a reference to the famous Hudson River School of naturalist landscape painters.

Today, this outsider art is highly revered and collected. To learn more, pick up Gary Monroe's excellent book *The Highwaymen;* visit the **Highwaymen website** (www.florida highwaymenpaintings.com); and check out the **AE Backus Museum & Gallery** (www. backusgallery.com) in Fort Pierce.

Miami Beach got swept up in the art-deco movement in the 1920s and '30s (which Florida transformed into 'tropical deco'), and today it has the largest collection of art-deco buildings in the US. These languished until the mid-1980s, when their rounded corners and glass bricks were dusted off and spruced up with new coats of pastel-pink and aquamarine paint.

Florida's vernacular architecture is the oft-maligned 'Cracker house.' However, these pioneer homesteads were cleverly designed to maximize comfort in a pre-air-conditioning, subtropical climate. Raised off the ground with windows and doors positioned for cross-ventilation, they had extra-wide gables and porches for shade, and metal roofs to reflect the sun. They weren't pretty, but they worked. A great example is Marjorie Kinnan Rawlings' home in Cross Creek.

Painting & Visual Arts

Florida has an affinity for modern art, and modern artists find that Florida allows them to indulge their whims. In 1983 Bulgarian artist Christo 'wrapped' 11 islands in Biscayne Bay in flamingo-colored fabric, so that they floated in the water like giant discarded flowers, dwarfing the urban skyline. Everyone loved it; it was so Miami.

But then so was Spencer Tunick when he posed 140 naked women on hot-pink rafts in the Sagamore hotel pool in 2007, and Roberto Behar and Rosario Marquardt when they plunked salmon-colored *The Living Room* in the Design District. Whatever the reasons, cartoon-hued silly-happy grandeur and exhibitionism seem Miami's calling cards. That certainly applies to Brazilian-born Romero Britto, whose art graces several buildings, such as the Miami Children's Museum. Miami's prominence in the contemporary-art world was cemented in 2002 when the Art Basel festival arrived. Now, without question, Miami's gallery scene is unmatched outside of LA and Manhattan.

Some say Florida's affinity for bright colors started with the Florida Highwaymen and their supersaturated Florida landscapes. Another famous self-taught folk artist was Earl Cunningham, sometimes nicknamed 'Grandpa Moses' for his naive portraits of a bygone Florida world.

And Florida does not lack for high-quality art museums. In addition to Miami, other notable locations are Fort Lauderdale, West Palm Beach, St Petersburg, Tampa, Sarasota, Naples and even Orlando.

Folk Art & Florida Funkiness

Mennello Museum of American Art, Orlando

Richard Bickel Photography, Apalachicola

Lovegrove Gallery, Matlacha

Fort East Martello Museum & Gardens, Key West

Big Cypress Gallery, Everglades National Park

Food & Drink

The treasures of the ocean, the citrus-scented whiff of farmland and an immigrant population give Florida serious culinary cred. On the flip side, strip malls, an all-too-American emphasis on reliability over adventure and a bad habit of cloning, rather than creating trends, are all marks against Florida's gastronomic reputation. Where does the truth lie? In the middle. In the meantime, gourmets can genuflect before celebrity chefs, while gourmands hunt Florida's delicacies, such as boiled peanuts, frogs legs and gator.

Destination Dining

In Miami, you can find classic Cuban brands that are no longer sold in Cuba itself – such as Hatuey beer, La Llave coffee and Gilda crackers.

Florida has a rich culinary heritage, but the state wasn't known as a place for good restaurants until the 1990s, when a wave of gourmet chefs transformed the Miami dining scene. They dedicated themselves to pleasing sophisticated urban palates by spicing up menus with South Florida's unique combination of Cuban, Caribbean and Latin American influences, which came to be dubbed Floribbean cuisine.

Today, Miami remains the epicenter of all things gourmet, and it has the greatest selection of ethnic cuisines. It's a town that is highly susceptible to buzzword-of-the-moment dining trends; at the time of writing, farm-to-table cuisine and an affected focus on rustic simplicity was all the rage.

The ripples of Miami dining have since spread statewide. In big cities and anywhere moneyed tourists and snowbirds linger, you will find upscale restaurants and skilled chefs plying their trade, often in contemporary dining rooms framing ocean views.

North of Miami and Miami Beach, Fort Lauderdale, Palm Beach and West Palm Beach offer the well-heeled foodie oodles of fun. Key West is, as in all things, more laid-back, but its dining scene is notably stocked with creative-fusion cool, and for a town of its size, it possesses a surfeit of excellent dining options.

The southern Gulf Coast is similarly satisfying: Tampa and St Petersburg are riding the cusp of a culinary renaissance, with everything from Old World Iberian to locavore-inspired modern gastronomy. Skip south through the rich beach towns of Sarasota, Sanibel Island and Naples, and a memorable meal is a reservation away.

As you go north, robust Southern cuisine comes to dominate, and high-end dining favors classic Italian, French and seafood. Though lack-

---

FLORIBBEAN CUISINE

OK, somebody worked hard to come up with 'Floribbean' – a term for Florida's tantalizing gourmet mélange of just-caught seafood, tropical fruits and eye-watering peppers, all dressed up with some combination of Nicaraguan, Salvadoran, Caribbean, Haitian, Cajun, Cuban and even Southern influences. Some call it 'fusion,' 'Nuevo Latino,' 'New World,' 'nouvelle Floridian' or 'palm-tree cuisine,' and it could refer to anything from a ceviche of lime, conch, sweet peppers and scotch bonnets to grilled grouper with mango, *adobo* and fried plantains.

ing gourmet 'scenes,' great choices are sprinkled in Jacksonville and Tallahassee. Along the Atlantic Coast, Amelia Island and St Augustine are foodie havens, and there's plenty of fresh, upscale seafood in Panhandle resort towns.

In general, Florida offers two kinds of tourism destinations, and in a similar vein, it offers two kinds of eating options. In the more typical beach and tourism towns you'll find family-friendly eateries that emphasize big portions and cheap prices. The more upscale you get, the more rarefied the atmosphere, but with that said, this is always Florida. You'll see people showing up for nice dinners in sandals (almost) everywhere.

Bounty of the Sea

Florida has always fed itself from the sea, which lies within arm's reach of nearly every point of the state. In a country where oysters are served in the rolling plains of Nebraska, there's no excuse not to have seafood in water-bound Florida. If it swims or crawls in the ocean, you can bet some enterprising local has shelled or scaled it, battered it, dropped it in a fryer and put it on a menu next to two plastic cups of tartar and cocktail sauce.

Grouper is far and away the most popular fish. Grouper sandwiches are to Florida what the cheesesteak is to Philadelphia or pizza to Manhattan – a defining, iconic dish, and the standard by which many places are measured. Hunting the perfect grilled or fried grouper sandwich is an

South Florida Food Blogs

Jan Norris (www. jannorris.com)

Short Order (http://blogs. miaminewtimes. com/shortorder)

Meatless Miami (www.meatless miami.com)

FOOD & DRINK BOUNTY OF THE SEA

FLORIDA SPECIALTIES

From north to south, here's a list of dishes strange and sublime, but 100% Florida; try not to leave without trying them at least once.

Boiled peanuts In rural north Florida, they take green or immature peanuts and boil them until they're nice and mushy, sometimes spicing them up with Cajun or other seasonings. Sure, they feel weird in the mouth, but they're surprisingly addictive.

Tarpon Springs Greek salad We don't know why, but in Tarpon Springs, Greek restaurants started hiding a dollop of potato salad inside a regulation Greek salad – now you can find this odd combination throughout central Florida.

Alligator Alligator tastes like a cross between fish and pork. The meat comes from the tail, and is usually served as deep-fried nuggets, which overwhelms the delicate flavor and can make it chewy. Try it grilled. Most alligator is legally harvested on farms and is often sold in grocery stores. It's also healthier than chicken, with as much protein but half the fat, fewer calories and less cholesterol.

Frogs legs Those who know say the 'best' legs come from the Everglades; definitely ask, since you want to avoid imported ones from India, which are smaller and disparaged as 'flavorless.'

Peel-and-eat shrimp A decidedly old-school, Old Florida treat, peel-and-eat shrimp are served boiled and pink in their shells. There's an art to ripping off the legs and stripping down the shells to get to the sweet meat underneath, which is inevitably overwhelmed by a nice dunk in cocktail sauce.

Stone crabs The first recycled crustacean: only one claw is taken from a stone crab – the rest is tossed back in the sea (the claw regrows in 12 to 18 months, and crabs plucked again are called 'retreads'). The claws are so perishable that they're always cooked before selling. October through April is less a 'season' than a stone-crab frenzy. Joe Weiss of Miami Beach is credited with starting it all.

Key lime pie Key limes are yellow, and that's the color of an authentic Key lime pie, which is a custard of Key lime juice, sweetened condensed milk and egg yolks in a cracker crust, then topped with meringue. Avoid any slice that's green or stands ramrod straight.

obsessive Floridian quest (by the way, the issue of fried versus grilled has been known to provoke fights. Well, not really, but it could), as is finding the creamiest bowl of chowder.

Of course, a huge range of other fish are offered. Other popular species include snapper (with dozens of varieties), mahimahi (which is sometimes labeled as dolphin, to the hilarious consternation of many a tourist) and catfish.

Florida really shines when it comes to crustaceans: try pink shrimp and rock shrimp, and don't miss soft-shell blue crab – Florida is well known for her blue-crab hatcheries, making them available fresh year-round. Locals will boil their crabs, as is common across the American South, but a plethora of Northeastern transplants means crabs are also steamed. Try them side by side and determine which method you like best.

Winter (October to April) is the season for Florida spiny lobster and stone crab (out of season both will be frozen). Florida lobster is all tail, without the large claws of its Maine cousin, and stone crab is heavenly sweet, served steamed with butter or the ubiquitous mustard sauce. Usually, only the stone-crab claw is served; the arms are ripped off the poor creatures and then they're tossed back into the water, where the arm is re-grown and the whole process kicks off again the next year. We know this could be read as a sad metaphor for the futility of our mortal condition, but that claw meat really is good.

Finally, the Keys popularized conch (a giant sea snail); now fished out, most conch is from the Bahamas. It has a slightly rubbery texture and a lovely, savory flavor. From July to September, Steinhatchee is the place for fresh scallops, and in fall/winter, Apalachicola Bay produces 90% of Florida's small but flavorful oysters.

Florida Cookbooks

Cross Creek Cookery, Marjorie Kinnan Rawlings

New World Cuisine, Allen Susser

Miami Spice: The New Florida Cuisine, Steve Raichlen

The Florida Cookbook: From Gulf Coast Gumbo to Key Lime Pie, Jeanne Voltz and Caroline Stuart

Florida Bounty, Eric and Sandra Jacobs

Cuban & Latin American Cuisine

Cuban food, once considered 'exotic,' is itself a mix of Caribbean, African and Latin American influences, and in Tampa and Miami, it's a staple of everyday life. Sidle up to a Cuban *loncheria* (snack bar) and order a *pan cubano:* a buttered, grilled baguette stuffed with ham, roast pork, cheese, mustard and pickles.

Integral to many Cuban dishes are *mojo* (a garlicky vinaigrette, sprinkled on sandwiches), *adobo* (a meat marinade of garlic, salt, cumin, oregano and sour orange juice) and *sofrito* (a stew-starter mix of garlic, onion and chili peppers). Cuban food may seem foreign and strange, but it's actually quite accessible to even the most conservative palette; this is basically meat-and-starch cuisine, with an emphasis on huge portions. Main-course meats are typically accompanied by rice and beans and fried plantains.

With its large number of Central and Latin American immigrants, the Miami area offers plenty of authentic ethnic eateries. Seek out Haitian *griot* (marinated fried pork), Jamaican jerk chicken, Brazilian barbecue, Central American *gallo pinto* (red beans and rice) and Nicaraguan *tres leches* ('three milks' cake).

In the morning, try a Cuban coffee, also known as *café cubano* or *cortadito*. This hot shot of liquid gold is essentially sweetened espresso, while *café con leche* is just *café au lait* with a different accent: equal parts coffee and hot milk.

Another Cuban treat is *guarapo,* or fresh-squeezed sugarcane juice. Cuban snack bars serve the greenish liquid straight or poured over crushed ice, and it's essential to an authentic *mojito*. It also sometimes finds its way into *batidos,* a milky, refreshing Latin American fruit smoothie.

Southern Cooking

The further north you travel, the more Southern the cooking gets in Florida. This is the sort of cuisine that makes up in fat what it may lack in refinement. 'Meat and three' is Southern restaurant lingo for a main meat – such as fried chicken, catfish, barbecued ribs, chicken-fried steak or even chitlins (hog's intestines) – and three sides: perhaps some combination of hush puppies, cheese grits (a sort of cornmeal polenta), cornbread, coleslaw, mashed potatoes, black-eyed peas, collard greens or buttery corn. End with pecan pie, and that's living. Po' boys are merely Southern hoagies, usually filled with fried nuggets of goodness.

Cracker cooking is Florida's rough-and-tumble variation on Southern cuisine, but with more reptiles and amphibians. And you'll find a good deal of Cajun and Creole as well, which mix in spicy gumbos and bisques from Louisiana's neighboring swamps. These days, Southern food isn't confined to North Florida. Fancy variations on the theme – haute Southern, if you will – are all the rage from Jacksonville to Key West.

Southern Floridian cooking is epitomized by writer Marjorie Kinnan Rawlings' famous cookbook *Cross Creek Cookery*. Near Rawlings' former home, the Yearling Restaurant (p366) is a good place to try Southern Floridian (ie North Florida) food.

Iced tea is so ubiquitous it's called the 'wine of the South,' but watch out for 'sweet tea,' which is an almost entirely different Southern drink – tea so sugary your eyes will cross. You may want to specify that your tea come unsweetened if you don't fancy a trip to the dentist.

> If you love farmers' markets, visit the website of the Florida Dept of Agriculture (www.florida-agriculture.com), which has listings for farmers' markets across the state.

SUNSHINE STATE FOOD FESTIVALS

Many of Florida's food festivals have the tumultuous air of county fairs, with carnival rides, music, parades, beauty pageants and any number of wacky, only-in-Florida happenings.

Food Fest! by Joan Steinbacher is the definitive guide; her companion website (www.foodfestguide.com) lists festivals for the coming three months.

Everglades Seafood Festival (www.evergladesseafoodfestival.com) Everglades City; three-day weekend, early February. Not just seafood, but gator, frogs legs and snakes, oh my!

Swamp Cabbage Festival (www.swampcabbagefestival.org) LaBelle; three-day weekend, late February. Armadillo races and crowning of the Miss Swamp Cabbage Queen.

Grant Seafood Festival (www.grantseafoodfestival.com) Grant; two-day weekend, early March. This small Space Coast town throws one of Florida's biggest seafood parties.

Florida Strawberry Festival (www.flstrawberryfestival.com) Plant City; 11 days, early March. Since 1930, more than half a million folks come annually to pluck, eat and honor the mighty berry.

Carnaval Miami (www.carnaval-miami.org) Miami; two weeks, early March. Negotiate drag queens and in-line skaters to reach the Cuban Calle Ocho food booths.

Isle of Eight Flags Shrimp Festival (www.shrimpfestival.com) Amelia Island; three-day weekend, early May. Avast, you scurvy dog! Pirates invade for shrimp and a juried art show.

Palatka Blue Crab Festival (www.bluecrabfestival.com) Palatka; four-day Memorial Day weekend. Hosts the state championship for chowder and gumbo. Yes, it's that good.

Florida Seafood Festival (www.floridaseafoodfestival.com) Apalachicola; two days, early November. Stand way, way back at its signature oyster-shucking and -eating contests.

Ribfest (www.ribfest.org) St Petersburg; three days, mid-November. Three words: ribs, rock, Harleys.

From Farm (& Grove) to Table

Florida has worked long and hard to become an agricultural powerhouse, and it's famous for its citrus. The state is the nation's largest producer of oranges, grapefruits, tangerines and limes, not to mention mangoes and sugarcane. Scads of bananas, strawberries, coconuts, avocados (once called 'alligator pears'), and the gamut of tropical fruits and vegetables are also grown in Florida. The major agricultural region is around Lake Okeechobee, with field upon field and grove upon grove as far as the eye can see.

With the advent of the USA's locavore, farm-to-table movement, Florida started featuring vegetables in its cooking and promoting its freshness on the plate. Florida's regional highlights – its Southern and Latin American cuisines – do not usually emphasize greens or vegetarianism. But today, most restaurants with upscale or gourmet pretensions promote the local sources of their produce and offer appealing choices for vegetarians.

That said, old habits die hard. The further you get outside of places such as Miami, Orlando, Sanibel, Fort Lauderdale, St Petersburg and college towns, the fewer the dedicated vegetarian restaurants. In many rural areas and in parts of North Florida, vegetarians can be forced to choose among iceberg-lettuce salads and pastas.

One indigenous local delicacy is heart of palm, or 'swamp cabbage,' which has a delicate, sweet crunch. The heart of the sabal palm, Florida's state tree, it was a mainstay for Florida pioneers. Try it if you can find it served fresh (don't bother if it's canned; it won't be from Florida).

Edible Communities (www.ediblecommunities.com) is a regional magazine series that celebrates and supports local, sustainable farming, culinary artisans and seasonal produce. It publishes editions (print and online) for Orlando and South Florida.

Libations

Is it the heat or the humidity? With the exception of the occasional teetotaling dry town, Florida's embrace of liquor is prodigious, even epic. And as you ponder this legacy – from Prohibition-era rumrunners, spring-break hedonists and drive-through liquor stores to Ernest Hemingway and Jimmy Buffett – it can seem that quantity trumps quality most of the time.

Yet as with Florida's cuisine, so with its bars. Surely, Anheuser-Busch's Jacksonville brewery will never go out of business, but Tampa also boasts several handcrafted local microbreweries. Daytona's beaches may be littered with gallon-size hurricane glasses, but Miami mixologists hone their reputations with their designer takes on martinis and *mojitos*.

Indeed, Cuban bartenders became celebrities in the 1920s for what they did with all that sugarcane and citrus: the two classics are the Cuba libre (rum, lime and cola) and the *mojito* (rum, sugar, mint, lime and club soda), traditionally served with *chicharrones* (deep-fried pork rinds).

As for Hemingway, he favored piña coladas, lots of them. Jimmy Buffett memorialized the margarita – so that now every sweaty beach bar along the peninsula claims to make the 'best.' Welcome, good friends, to Margaritaville.

Coinciding with modern refrigeration, frozen concentrated orange juice was invented in Florida in 1946: this popularized orange juice as a year-round drink and created a generation of 'orange millionaires.'

Outdoor Activities

Florida doesn't have mountains, valleys, cliffs, or snow. What *does* she have? Water, and lots of it – freshwater, saltwater, rainwater, springwater, swamp water. Florida's peninsula bends with more than 1200 miles of coastline, which include more than 660 miles of the best beaches in the US. Plus: coral reefs, prehistoric swamps and forests, all teeming with Ice Age flora and dinosaur-era fauna. In short, Florida doesn't have everything, but her surreal, watery landscape still provides one of the greatest shows on Earth.

Hiking & Camping

One thing Florida hikers never have to worry about is elevation gain. But the weather more than makes up for it. If your destination is South Florida, it's best to hike and camp from November through March. This is Florida's 'dry season,' when rain, temperatures, humidity and mosquitoes decrease to tolerable levels. In summer, hike before noon to avoid the midday heat and afternoon thundershowers.

The **Florida National Scenic Trail** (www.fs.usda.gov/fnst) is one of 11 national scenic trails and covers 1400 not-yet-contiguous miles. It runs north from the swamps of Big Cypress National Preserve; around Lake Okeechobee; through the Ocala National Forest; and then west to the Gulf Islands National Seashore near Pensacola. All the parks above are filled with great hikes.

Other prime hiking areas include the remote pine wilderness, karst terrain and limestone sinkholes of Apalachicola National Forest and Paynes Prairie Preserve State Park. Wekiwa Springs State Park rewards hikers, paddlers and snorkelers.

South Florida swamps tend to favor 1- to 2-mile boardwalk trails; these are excellent, and almost always wheelchair accessible. But to really explore the wetlands, get in a kayak or canoe. In the Everglades, you can also embark on 'wet walks,' which are wading trips deep into the blackwater heart of the swamps. It may seem like folly to tread through the same waters that alligators and crocodiles prowl, but wet walks have been conducted unabated for well over a decade.

Prized camping spots include the shady riverside at Stephen Foster Folk Culture Center State Park; the Ocala National Forest; the Panhandle's

---

Great Hiking & Camping Guides

....

30 Eco-Trips in Florida (2005), Holly Ambrose

....

Hiker's Guide to the Sunshine State (2005), Sandra Friend

....

The Best in Tent Camping: Florida (2010), John Malloy

TREAD LIGHTLY, EXPLORE SAFELY

These days, it should go without saying that any wilderness, even a swamp, is a fragile place. Practicing 'Leave No Trace' ethics (see www.lnt.org for comprehensive advice) boils down to staying on the trail, cleaning up your own mess, and observing nature rather than plucking or feeding it.

As you enjoy Florida's natural bounty, take care of yourself, too. Carry lots of water – up to a gallon per person per day – and always be prepared for rain. Line backpacks with plastic bags, and carry rain gear and extra clothes for when (not if) you get soaked. Reid Tillery's *Surviving the Wilds of Florida* is a helpful guide, while Tillery's website **Florida Adventuring** (www.floridaadventuring.com) covers backcountry essentials.

St Joseph State Park; Myakka River State Park; the 'chickees' (raised platforms) that dot the waterways of the Everglades and the 10,000 Islands; and in the Florida Keys, Bahia Honda State Park.

Just be warned: mosquitoes are an unavoidable reality, especially during the spring and summer months. Sunscreen is a must when hiking in Florida, but a good bug repellent (and insect-proof clothes) comes a close second.

A great all-in-one paddling guide – with everything from the state's best water trails to nitty-gritty advice about weather, equipment and supplies – is *Paddler's Guide to the Sunshine State* (2001) by Sandy Huff.

Swimming & Springs

Florida's beaches are the best in the continental United States, and incredibly diverse, so let's start with two questions: Do you prefer sunrise or sunset? Do you prefer surfing and boogie boarding or sunbathing and sandcastles? For sunrise and surfing, hit the bigger, east-facing waves of the Atlantic Coast; for sandcastles at sunset, choose the soporific, west-facing waters of the Gulf Coast and the Panhandle.

Would you prefer if we get a little more nuanced with our sand and surf judgment? Fair enough. There are a few other elements of beach-going we can certainly address: namely, the 'beach as casual escape' versus 'family destination' versus 'spring-break boozefest' versus 'sexy spot to show off your fashion sense and spot celebrities.' If you're into the last of those iterations of beach, head for Palm Beach, Fort Lauderdale and Miami Beach. These are the spots where you'll see the stars and models decked out in swimwear. Those searching for a casual beach escape or a trip for the family may be better served by the tepid, calm waters of the Gulf; Sanibel Island, off the coast of Fort Myers, may have the most family-friendly beaches in the state. You'll also feel less pressure to look stunning in your skivvies compared to Southeast Florida and Miami. If you're into straight-up partying and a spring-break atmosphere, set your compass to Panama City and Daytona Beach, and kiss your liver goodbye. Fair warning: while the Florida Keys seem like they would possess excellent swaths of sand, they are in fact mangrove islands with few natural beaches to speak of (larger private resorts do tend to create their own artificial beaches).

Beyond that, your main concern is how close to or far from other people you want to be. Even in the most hyper-developed condo canyons of South Florida, it is possible to find state and local parks that provide a

GET YOUR BOARD ON

Eleven-time world-champion surfer Kelly Slater is from Cocoa Beach, and four-time women's champion Lisa Anderson is from Ormond Beach. Both first learned how to carve in Space Coast waves, in the shadow of rockets, and Slater honed his aerials at Sebastian Inlet.

All of which is to say that while Florida's surf may be considered 'small' by Californian and Hawaiian standards, Florida's surfing community and history are not. Plus, Florida makes up in wave quantity what it may lack in wave size.

Nearly the entire Atlantic Coast has rideable waves, but the best spots are gathered along the Space Coast, which has surf lessons, rentals and popular competitions: shoot for Cocoa Beach, Indialantic, Sebastian Inlet and Playalinda Beach. However, you'll find tiny, longboard-friendly peelers from Fort Lauderdale down to Miami's South Beach, although the presence of the Bahamas offshore prevents Miami from being a truly great surfing destination. In general, you'll find the big waves end at around Jupiter Beach.

Florida's northern Atlantic Coast is less attractive, partly due to chilly winter water, but consistent, 2ft to 3ft surf can be had at Daytona Beach; from Flagler Beach up to St Augustine; and around Amelia Island.

relative degree of natural isolation. With few exceptions, Florida's beaches are safe places to swim; the most dangerous surf will occur just before and after a storm. Also, stingrays in summer and occasional jellyfish can trouble swimmers (look for lifeguard-posted warnings).

Don't overlook Florida's lakes, rivers and springs. Taking a dip in one of Florida's 700 freshwater springs – each 72°F (22°C) and, when healthy, clear as glass – is unforgettable. There are too many to list, but good swimming destinations are the Suwannee River, the Ichetucknee River and Ponce de Leon Springs State Park.

Canoeing & Kayaking

To really experience Florida's swamps and rivers, its estuaries and inlets, its lagoons and barrier islands, you need a watercraft, preferably the kind you paddle. The intimate quiet of dipping among mangroves, cruising alligators and startled ibis stirs wonder in the soul.

The winter 'dry' season is best for paddling. That's because 'dry' in Florida is still pretty darn wet. So why come during the dry season? Because evaporation and receding waterlines force wildlife into highly visible concentrations amid the state's waterways and pools. In summer, canoe near cool, freshwater springs and swimming beaches, because you'll be dreaming about them.

In terms of rivers, the 207-mile Suwannee River is quintessential Florida: a meandering, muddy ribbon (ideal for multiday trips) decorated with 60 clear blue springs that runs from Georgia's Okefenokee Swamp to the Gulf of Mexico. About 170 miles are an official **wilderness trail** (www.floridastateparks.org/wilderness), and the section near Big Shoals State Park actually has some Class III rapids – woo-hoo!

Other unforgettable rivers include: the Atlantic Coast's 'Wild and Scenic' Loxahatchee River; Orlando's 'Wild and Scenic' Wekiva River; and the Tampa region's placid Hillsborough River and the alligator-packed Myakka River.

You'll tell your grandchildren about kayaking Everglades National Park; Hell's Bay paddling trail is heavenly. The nearby 10,000 Islands are just as amazing, and nothing beats sleeping in the Everglades in a 'chickee' (a wooden platform raised above the waterline). A truly great Florida adventure – indeed, one of the most unique wilderness experiences in North America – is paddling through the mangrove ecosystem that fringes the entirety of the southern Florida coast.

And don't forget the coasts. You'll kick yourself if you don't kayak Miami's Bill Baggs Cape Florida State Park; Tampa Bay's Caladesi Island; Sanibel Island's JN 'Ding' Darling National Wildlife Refuge; and the Big Bend's Cedar Key. There's even an entire 'blueway' – a collection of charted streams and rivers – within Lee County in southwest Florida.

On Florida's Atlantic Coast, more mangroves, water birds, dolphins and manatees await at Canaveral National Seashore, particularly Mosquito Lagoon, and also seek out Indian River Lagoon. Big and Little Talbot Islands provide more intercoastal magic.

Diving & Snorkeling

For diving and snorkeling, most already know about Florida's superlative coral reefs and wreck diving, but northern Florida is also known as the 'Cave Diving Capital of the US.' The peninsula's limestone has more holes than Swiss cheese, and most are burbling goblets of diamond-clear (if chilly) water.

Many diving spots line the Suwannee River: try **Peacock Springs State Park** (www.floridastateparks.org/peacocksprings), one of the continent's largest underwater cave systems; **Troy Springs State Park** (www.floridastateparks.org/troyspring); and Manatee Springs State Park. Another

LIFE'S A BEACH

Florida's best beach? Why not ask us to choose a favorite child? It's impossible! Each beach has its own personality, its own wondrous qualities. But visitors do have to make decisions. For the best beaches by coastline, see below. For a list based on 'science,' consult Dr Beach (www.drbeach.org).

Best Gulf Coast Beaches

→ Siesta Key Beach (p403)

→ Fort DeSoto Park (p389)

→ Honeymoon Island State Park (p394)

→ Sanibel Island (p417)

→ Naples Municipal Beach (p421)

→ Fort Myers Beach (p415)

Best Atlantic Coast Beaches

→ Apollo Beach (p314)

→ Bahia Honda State Park (p168)

→ Bill Baggs Cape Florida State Park (p83)

→ Fort Lauderdale (p189)

→ Lake Worth Beach (p204)

→ Hutchinson Island (p223)

→ Vero Beach (p322)

Best Panhandle Beaches

→ Grayton Beach State Park (p441)

→ St George Island State Park (p450)

→ Pensacola Beach (p428)

fun dive is Blue Spring State Park, near Orlando. Note that you need to be cavern certified to dive a spring (an open-water certification won't do), and solo diving is usually not allowed. But local dive shops can help with both. One place that offers certification courses is Vortex Spring.

Every Florida spring has prime snorkeling. At times, the clarity of the water is disconcerting, as if you were floating on air; every creature and school of fish all the way to the bottom feels just out of reach, so that, as William Bartram once wrote, 'the trout swims by the very nose of the alligator and laughs in his face.'

If you prefer coral reefs teeming with rainbow-bright tropical fish, you're in luck…Florida has the continent's largest coral-reef system. The two best spots are John Pennekamp Coral Reef State Park, located in Key Largo (the uppermost of the Florida Keys) and Biscayne National Park, located south of Miami, at the tip of the Florida mainland. Biscayne is actually the only national park in the US park service system to exist primarily under the waves – 95% of the park is located underwater. If you travel further along the Keys, you won't be disappointed at Bahia Honda State Park or Key West.

Wreck diving in Florida is equally epic, and some are even accessible to snorkelers. So many Spanish galleons sank off the Emerald Coast, near Panama City Beach, that it's dubbed the 'Wreck Capital of the South.' But also check out wreck dives in Pensacola, Sebastian Inlet State Park, Troy Springs, Fort Lauderdale, Biscayne National Park and Key West, a town that historically supported itself off the industry of wrecking, or salvaging sunken ships and their cargo.

Named for its abundant sea turtles, the Dry Tortugas are well worth the effort to reach them.

Biking

Florida is too flat for mountain biking, but there are plenty of off-road opportunities, along with hundreds of miles of paved trails for those who prefer to keep their ride clean. As with hiking, avoid biking in summer, unless you like getting hot and sweaty.

Top off-roading spots include **Big Shoals State Park** (www.floridastateparks.org/bigshoals), with 25 miles of trails along the Suwannee River, and Paynes Prairie Preserve State Park, with 20 miles of trails through its bizarre landscape. Also recommended are the Ocala National Forest and the Apalachicola National Forest, particularly the sandy Munson Hills Loop.

With so many paved biking trails, it's hard to choose. To dip among the Panhandle's sugar-sand beaches, take the 19-mile Timpoochee Trail, which parallels Hwy 30A. In Tallahassee, the 16-mile Tallahassee-St Marks Historic Railroad State Trail shoots you right to the Gulf. Both paved and off-road trails encircle Lake Okeechobee, which is a great way to take in the surrounding countryside. Two of the most unforgettable paved trails? Palm Beach's Lake Trail, aka the 'Trail of Conspicuous Consumption' for all the mansions and yachts, and the 15-mile Shark Valley Tram Road Trail, which pierces the Everglades' gator-infested sawgrass river.

For more-involved overland adventures, do the Florida Keys Overseas Heritage Trail, which mirrors the Keys Hwy for 70 noncontiguous miles, and the urban-and-coastal Pinellas Trail, which runs 43 miles from St Petersburg to Tarpon Springs.

In Florida's many beach towns, it's easy to find beach-cruiser-style bicycle rentals. These heavy-duty vehicles are made for lazy cycling along flat boardwalks – a perfect casual exercise for travelers who may be a little out of shape.

Fishing

The world may contain seven seas, but there's only one Fishing Capital of the World: Florida. No, this isn't typically overwrought Floridian hype. Fishing here is the best the US offers, and for variety and abundance, nowhere else on the globe can claim an indisputable advantage.

In Florida's abundant rivers and lakes, largemouth bass are the main prize. Prime spots, with good access and facilities, are **Lake Manatee State Park** (www.floridastateparks.org/lakemanatee), south of St Petersburg; for fly-fishing, Myakka River State Park; and **Jacksonville** (www.jacksonvillefishing.com), which has charters to the St Johns River and Lake George for freshwater fishing and to the bay for ocean fishing, plus kayak fishing.

Near-shore saltwater fishing means redfish and mighty tarpon, snook, spotted sea trout and much more, up and down both coasts. The jetties at Sebastian Inlet are a mecca for shore anglers on the Atlantic Coast, while on the Gulf, Tampa's Skyway Fishing Pier is dubbed the world's longest fishing pier.

In the Keys, Bahia Honda and Old Seven Mile Bridge on Pigeon Key are other shore-fishing highlights.

However, as 'Papa' Hemingway would tell you, the real fishing is offshore, where majestic sailfish leap and thrash. Bluefish and mahimahi are other popular deep-water fish. For offshore charters, head for Stuart, Fort Lauderdale, Lauderdale-by-the-Sea, Destin, Steinhatchee and

OUTDOOR ACTIVITIES BIKING

Wildlife-Watching Resources

Florida Fish & Wildlife Conservation Commission (www.myfwc.com)

Audubon of Florida (www.audubonofflorida.org)

Great Florida Birding Trail (www.floridabirdingtrail.com)

Florida Wildlife Viewing (www.floridawildlifeviewing.com)

Florida mystery writer Randy Wayne White has created an angler's delight with his *Ultimate Tarpon Book* (2010), a celebration of Florida's legendary big-game fish, with 'contributions' from Hemingway, Teddy Roosevelt, Zane Grey and others.

Miami. The best strategy is to walk the harborside, talking with captains, until you find one who speaks to your experience and interests.

Note that you usually need a license to fish, and there are a slew of regulations about what you can catch.

Sailing

If you like the wind in your sails, Florida is your place. Miami is a sailing sweet spot, with plenty of marinas for renting or berthing your own boat – Key Biscayne is a particular gem. Fort Lauderdale is chock-full of boating options. In Key West, you can sail on a schooner with real cannons, though tour operators are plentiful throughout the Keys. To learn how to sail, check out Pensacola's Lanier Sailing Academy.

Golf

Fun fact: With more than 1250 courses (and counting), Florida has the most golf courses of any US state. Whether or not this is related to Florida's high number of wealthy retirees isn't known, but one thing is certain, if you want to tee up, you won't have to look far.

Towns that are notable for golf include Palm Beach, Naples, Fort Myers, Orlando, Jacksonville, Miami and St Augustine. Near St Augustine is the World Golf Hall of Fame.

For a comprehensive list of Florida courses, see **Florida Golf** (www.fgolf.com).

Theme parks have most of Florida's adrenaline-pumping thrill rides. Then there's DeLand, where the tandem jump was invented and which today remains an epicenter of skydiving. Get jumping at www.skydivedeland.com.

Landscapes & Wildlife

Naturalist Marjory Stoneman Douglas called Florida 'a long pointed spoon' that is as 'familiar as the map of North America itself.' On that map, the shapely Floridian peninsula represents one of the most ecologically diverse regions in the world. Eons ago, a limestone landmass settled just north of the Tropic of Cancer. A confluence of porous rock and climate gave rise to a watery world of uncommon abundance – one that could be undone by humanity in a geological eye blink.

The Land

Florida is many things, but elevated it is decidedly not. This state is as flat as a pancake, or as Douglas says, like a spoon of freshwater resting delicately in a bowl of saltwater – a spongy brick of limestone hugged by the Atlantic Ocean and the Gulf of Mexico. The highest point, the Panhandle's Britton Hill, has to stretch to reach 350ft, which isn't half as tall as the buildings of downtown Miami. This makes Florida officially the nation's flattest state, despite being 22nd in total area with 58,560 sq miles.

However, over 4000 of those square miles are water; lakes and springs pepper the map like bullet holes in a road sign. That shotgun-sized hole in the south is Lake Okeechobee, the second-largest freshwater lake in North America. Sounds impressive, but the bottom of the lake is only a few feet above sea level, and it's so shallow you can practically wade across.

Every year Lake Okeechobee ever so gently floods the southern tip of the peninsula. Or it wants to; canals divert much of the flow to either irrigation fields or Florida's bracketing major bodies of water – ie the Gulf of Mexico and the Atlantic Ocean. But were the water to follow the natural lay of the land, it would flow down: from its center, the state of Florida inclines about 6in every 6 miles until finally, the peninsula can't keep its head above water anymore. What was an unelevated plane peters out into the 10,000 Islands and the Florida Keys, which end with a flourish in the Gulf of Mexico. Key West, the last in the chain, is the southernmost point in the continental United States.

Incidentally, when the waters of Okeechobee *do* flood the South Florida plane, they interact with the local grasslands and limestone to create a wilderness unlike any other: the Everglades. They also fill up the freshwater aquifers that are required for maintaining human existence in the ever-urbanizing Miami area. Today, numerous plans, which seem to fall prey to private interest and bureaucratic roadblocks, are being discussed for restoring the original flow of water from Central to South Florida, an act that would revitalize the 'Glades and, to some degree, address the water supply needs of Greater Miami.

What really sets Florida apart, though, is that it occupies a subtropical transition zone between northern temperate and southern tropical climates. This is key to the coast's florid coral-reef system, the largest in North America, and the key to Florida's attention-getting collection of surreal swamps, botanical oddities and monstrous critters. The

Great Nature Guides

....

'The Living Gulf Coast' (2011) by Charles Sobczak

....

'Priceless Florida' (2004) by Ellie Whitney, D Bruce Means & Anne Rudloe

....

'Seashore Plants of South Florida & the Caribbean' (1994) by David W Nellis

FLORIDA'S MANATEES

It's hard to believe Florida's West Indian manatees were ever mistaken for mermaids, but it's easy to see their attraction: these gentle, curious, colossal mammals are as sweetly lovable as 10ft, 1000lb teddy bears. Solitary and playful, they have been known to 'surf' waves, and every winter, from November to March, they migrate into the warmer waters of Florida's freshwater estuaries, rivers and springs. Like humans, manatees will die if trapped in 62°F (17°C) water for 24 hours, and in winter Florida's eternally 72°F (22°C) springs are balmy spas.

Florida residents for over 45 million years, these shy herbivores have absolutely no defenses except their size (they can reach 13ft and 3000lb), and they don't do much, spending most of each day resting and eating the equivalent of 10% of their body weight. Rarely moving faster than a languid saunter, manatees even reproduce slowly; females birth one calf every two to five years. The exception to their docility? Mating. Males are notorious for their aggressive sex drive.

Florida's manatees have been under some form of protection since 1893, and they were included in the first federal endangered-species list in 1967. Manatees were once hunted for their meat, but today collisions with boats are a leading cause of manatee death, accounting for over 20% annually. Propeller scars are so ubiquitous among the living they are the chief identifying tool of scientists.

Population counts are notoriously difficult and unreliable. In 2013 a bloom of red tide algae in Southwest Florida and illnesses caused the death of over 800 manatees – a whopping 16% of the total population of these gentle giants. At the time of writing there were at least 4800 manatees left in the state.

Everglades gets the most press and as an International Biosphere, World Heritage Site and National Park, this 'river of grass' deserves it.

But while the Everglades are gorgeous, there is far more waiting to be discovered. The Keys are dollops of intensely beautiful mangrove forest biomes. The white-sand beaches of the Gulf Coast have been gently lapped over geological millennia into wide ribbons of sugar studded with prehistoric shells. The Panhandle's Apalachicola River basin has been called a 'Garden of Eden,' in which Ice Age plants survive in lost ravines and where more species of amphibians and reptiles hop and slither than anywhere else in the US. The Indian River Lagoon estuary, stretching 156 miles along the Atlantic Coast, is the most diverse on the continent. And across North Florida, the pockmarked and honeycombed limestone (called karst terrain) holds the Florida Aquifer, which is fed solely by rain and bubbles up like liquid diamonds in more than 700 freshwater springs.

To learn about the incredible efforts to save the whooping crane, visit Operation Migration (www.operationmigration.org), a nonprofit organisation run by Bill Lishman, whose techniques inspired the film *Fly Away Home*. Another resource is www.bringbackthecranes.org.

Wildlife

With swamps full of gators, rivers full of snakes, manatees in mangroves, sea turtles on beaches, and giant flocks of seabirds taking wing at once, how is it, again, that a squeaky-voiced mouse became Florida's headliner?

Birds

Nearly 500 avian species have been documented in the state, including some of the world's most magnificent migratory waterbirds: ibis, egrets, great blue herons, white pelicans and whooping cranes. This makes Florida the ultimate bird-watcher's paradise.

Nearly 350 species spend time in the Everglades, the prime bird-watching spot in Florida. But you don't have to brave the swamp. Completed in 2006, the **Great Florida Birding Trail** (www.floridabirdingtrail.com) runs 2000 miles and includes nearly 500 bird-watching sites. Nine of these are 'gateway' sites, with staffed visitor centers and free 'loan' binoculars; see the website for downloadable guides and look for brown road signs when driving.

Among the largest birds, white pelicans arrive in winter (October to April), while brown pelicans, the only pelican to dive for its food, lives here year-round. To see the striking pale-pink roseate spoonbill, a member of the ibis family, visit JN 'Ding' Darling National Wildlife Refuge, the wintering site for a third of the US roseate spoonbill population.

About 5000 nonmigratory sandhill cranes are joined by 25,000 migratory cousins each winter. White whooping cranes, which at up to 5ft tall are the tallest bird in North America, are nearly extinct; about 100 winter on Florida's Gulf Coast near Homosassa.

Songbirds and raptors fill Florida skies, too. The state has more than 1000 mated pairs of bald eagles, the most in the southern US. Peregrine falcons, which can dive up to 150mph, also migrate through in spring and fall.

Back in the day, birds were both legally hunted and poached for their gorgeous feathers, which were molded, shaped and accessorized into fashion accoutrements. Miami-based journalist and Everglades advocate Marjory Stoneman Douglas wrote about this practice and the subsequent loss of avian life, a move which laid the foundation for both wilderness protection and wildlife conservation in the state.

Audubon of Florida (www.audubonofflorida.org) is perhaps Florida's leading conservation organization. It has tons of birding and ecological information, and it publishes *Florida Naturalist* magazine.

Land Mammals

Florida's most endangered mammal is the Florida panther. Before European contact, perhaps 1500 roamed the state. The first panther bounty ($5 a scalp) was passed in 1832, and over the next 130 years they were hunted relentlessly. Though hunting was stopped in 1958, it was too late for panthers to survive on their own. Without a captive breeding program, begun in 1991, the Florida panther would now be extinct and with only around 120 known to exist, they're not out of the swamp yet. The biggest killers of panthers are motor vehicles. Every year a handful – sometimes more – of panthers are killed on roads; pay particular attention to speed limits posted in areas such as the Tamiami Trail, which cuts through Everglades National Park and the Big Cypress Preserve.

You're not likely to see a panther, but black bears have recovered to a population of around 3000. As their forests diminish, bears are occasionally seen traipsing through suburbs in northern Florida.

Easy to find, white-tailed deer are a common species that troubles landscaping. Endemic to the Keys are Key deer, a Honey-I-Shrunk-the-Ungulate subspecies. Less than 3ft tall and lighter than a 10-year-old boy, they live mostly on Big Pine Key.

Although they are ostensibly native to the American West, the adaptable coyote has been spotted across Florida, appearing as far south as the Florida Keys. Hopefully they won't swim too much further or else they'll end up on Big Pine Key, home of the aforementioned Key deer.

The critically endangered red wolf once roamed the bottomlands, marshes and flooded forests of the American eastern seaboard, particularly the southeast. Due to hunting and habitat loss the red wolf was almost wiped out, but a breeding population has been established at the St Vincent National Wildlife Refuge, located off the coast of the Panhandle.

Marine Mammals

Florida's coastal waters are home to 21 species of dolphins and whales. By far the most common is the bottlenose dolphin, which is highly social, extremely intelligent and frequently encountered around the entire peninsula. Bottlenose dolphins are also the species most often seen in captivity.

LANDSCAPES & WILDLIFE WILDLIFE

The North Atlantic population of about 300 right whales comes to winter calving grounds off the Atlantic Coast near Jacksonville. These giant animals can be over 50ft long and are the most endangered species of whale.

Winter is also the season for manatees, which seek out Florida's warm-water springs and power-plant discharge canals, beginning in November. These lovable, lumbering creatures are another iconic Florida species whose conservation both galvanizes and divides state residents.

Reptiles & Amphibians

Boasting an estimated 184 species, Florida has the nation's largest collection of reptiles and amphibians and, unfortunately, it's growing. No, we're not anti-reptile, but invasive scaly species are wreaking havoc with Florida's native, delicate ecosystem. Uninvited guests arrive regularly, many establishing themselves after being released by pet owners. Some of the more dangerous, problematic and invasive species include Burmese pythons, black and green iguanas and Nile monitor lizards.

The American alligator is Florida's poster species, and they are ubiquitous in Central and South Florida. They don't pose much of a threat to humans unless you do something irredeemably stupid, like feed or provoke them. With that said, you may want to keep small children and pets away from unfamiliar inland bodies of water. South Florida is also home to the only North American population of American crocodile. Florida's crocs number around 1500; they prefer saltwater, and to distinguish them from gators, check their smile – a croc's snout is more tapered and its teeth stick out.

Turtles, frogs and snakes love Florida, and nothing is cuter than watching bright skinks, lizards and anoles skittering over porches and sidewalks. Cute doesn't always describe the state's 44 species of snakes – though Floridian promoters emphasize that only six species are poisonous, and only four of those are common. Feel better? Of the baddies, three are rattlesnakes (diamondback, pygmy, canebrake) and the others

---

KEEPERS OF THE EVERGLADES

Anyone who has dipped a paddle among the sawgrass and hardwood hammocks of Everglades National Park wouldn't quibble with the American alligators' Florida sobriquet, 'Keepers of the Everglades.' With their snouts, eyeballs, and pebbled backs so still they hardly ripple the water's surface, alligators have watched over the Glades for more than 200 million years.

It's impossible to count Florida's wild alligators, but estimates are that 1.5 million lumber among the state's lakes, rivers and golf courses. No longer officially endangered, they remain protected because they resemble the still-endangered American crocodile. Alligator served in restaurants typically comes from licensed alligator farms, though since 1988 Florida has conducted an annual alligator harvest, open to nonresidents, that allows two alligators per person.

Alligators are alpha predators that keep the rest of the food chain in check, and their 'gator holes' become vital water cups in the dry season and during droughts, aiding the entire wetlands ecosystem. Alligators, which live for about 30 years, can grow up to 14ft long and weigh 1000lb.

A vocal courtship begins in April, and mating takes place in May and June. By late June, females begin laying nests of 30 to 45 eggs, which incubate for two months before hatching. On average, only four alligators per nest survive to adulthood.

Alligators hunt in water, often close to shore; typically, they run on land to flee, not to chase. In Florida, an estimated 15 to 20 nonfatal attacks on humans occur each year, and there have been 22 fatal attacks since 1948.

Some estimate an alligator's top short-distance land speed at 30mph, but it's a myth that you must zigzag to avoid them. The best advice is to run in a straight line as fast as your little legs can go.

are copperheads, cottonmouths and coral snakes. The diamondback is the biggest (up to 7ft), most aggressive and most dangerous. But rest assured, while cottonmouths live in and around water, most Florida water snakes are not cottonmouths. Whew!

Sea Turtles

Most sea-turtle nesting in continental US occurs in Florida. Predominantly three species create over 80,000 nests annually, mostly on southern Atlantic Coast beaches but extending to all Gulf Coast beaches. Most are loggerhead, then far fewer green and leatherback, and historically hawksbill and Kemp's ridley as well; all five species are endangered or threatened. The leatherback is the largest, attaining 10ft and 2000lb in size.

During the May-to-October nesting season, sea turtles deposit from 80 to 120 eggs in each nest. The eggs incubate for about two months, and then the hatchlings emerge all at once and make for the ocean. Contrary to myth, hatchlings don't need the moon to find their way to the sea. However, they can become hopelessly confused by artificial lights and noisy human audiences. For the best, least-disruptive experience, join a sanctioned turtle watch; for a list, visit www.myfwc.com/seaturtle, then click on 'Educational Information' and 'Where to View Sea Turtles.'

Plants

The diversity of the peninsula's flora, including over 4000 species of plants, is unmatched in the continental US. Florida contains the southern extent of temperate ecosystems and the northern extent of tropical ones, which blend and merge in a bewildering, fluid taxonomy of environments. Interestingly, most of the world at this latitude is a desert, which Florida definitely is not.

Wetlands & Swamps

It takes special kinds of plants to thrive in the humid, waterlogged, sometimes-salty marshes, sloughs, swales, seeps, basins, marl prairies and swamps of Florida, and several hundred specialized native plants evolved to do so. Much of the Everglades is dominated by vast expanses of sawgrass, which is actually a sedge with fine toothlike edges that can reach 10ft high. South Florida is a symphony of sedges, grasses and rushes. These hardy water-tolerant species provide abundant seeds to feed birds and animals, protect fish in shallow water, and pad wetlands for birds and alligators.

The strangest plants are the submerged and immersed species that grow in, under and out of the water. Free-floating species include bladderwort and coontail, a species that lives, flowers and is pollinated entirely underwater. Florida's swamps are abundant with rooted plants that have floating leaves, including the pretty American lotus, water lilies and spatterdock (if you love quaint names, you'll love Florida botany!). Another common immersed plant, bur marigolds, can paint whole prairies yellow.

Across Florida, whenever land rises just enough to create drier islands, tracts, hills and hillocks, dense tree-filled hammocks occur; ecological zones can shift as dramatically in 1ft in Florida as they do in 1000ft elsewhere. These hammocks go by many names depending on location and type. Tropical hammocks typically mix tropical hardwoods and palms with semideciduous and evergreen trees such as live oak.

Another dramatic, beautiful tree in Florida's swamps is the bald cypress, the most flood-tolerant tree. It can grow 150ft tall, with buttressed, wide trunks and roots with 'knees' that poke above the drenched soil.

LANDSCAPES & WILDLIFE WILDLIFE

Naturalist Doug Alderson helped create the Big Bend Paddling Trail, and in his book *Waters Less Traveled* (2005) he describes his adventures: dodging pygmy rattlesnakes, meeting Shitty Bill, discussing Kemp's ridley turtles and pondering manatee farts.

In Florida, even the plants bite: the Panhandle has the most species of carnivorous plants in the US – a result of its nutrient-poor sandy soil.

Cypress domes are a particular type of swamp, which arise when a watery depression occurs in a pine flatwood.

Forests, Scrubs & Flatwoods

Florida's northern forests, particularly in the Panhandle, are an epicenter of plant and animal biodiversity, just as much as its southern swamps. Here, the continent's temperate forests of hickory, elm, ash, maple, magnolia and locust trees combine with the various pine, gum and oak trees that are common throughout Florida along with the sawgrass, cypress and cabbage palms of southern Florida. The wet but temperate Apalachicola forest supports 40 kinds of trees and more insect species than scientists can count.

Central and Northern Florida were once covered in longleaf and slash-pine forests, both prized for timber and pine gum. Today, due to logging, only 2% of old-growth longleaf forests remain. Faster-growing slash pine has now largely replaced longleaf pine in Florida's second-growth forests.

Scrubs are found throughout Florida; they are typically old dunes with well-drained sandy soil. In central Florida (along the Lake Wales Ridge), scrubs are the oldest plant communities, with the highest number of endemic and rare species. Sand pines, scrub oak, rosemary and lichens predominate.

Scrubs often blend into sandy pine flatwoods, which typically have a sparse longleaf or slash-pine overstory and an understory of grasses and/or saw palmetto. Saw palmetto is a vital Florida plant: its fruit is an important food for bears and deer (and an herbal medicine), it provides shelter for panthers and snakes, and its flower is an important source of honey. It's named for its sharp saw-toothed leaf stems.

Visit the website of the Florida Native Plant Society (www.fnps.org), a nonprofit conservation organization, for updates on preservation issues and invasive species and for a nice overview of Florida's native plants and ecosystems.

Mangroves & Coastal Dunes

Where not shaved smooth by sand, Southern Florida's coastline is often covered with a three-day stubble of mangroves. Mangroves are not a single species; the name refers to all tropical trees and shrubs that have adapted to loose wet soil, saltwater, and periodic root submergence. Mangroves have also developed 'live birth,' germinating their seeds while they're still

GHOST HUNTERS

Florida has more species of orchids than any other state in the US, and orchids are themselves the largest family of flowering plants in the world, with perhaps 25,000 species. On the dial of botanical fascination, orchids rank highly, and the Florida orchid that inspires the most intense devotion is the rare ghost orchid.

This bizarre epiphytic flower has no leaves and usually only one bloom, which is of course deathly white with two long thin drooping petals that curl like a handlebar mustache. The ghost orchid is pollinated in the dead of night by the giant sphinx moth, which is the only insect with a proboscis long enough to reach down the ghost orchid's 5in-long nectar spur.

The exact locations of ghost orchids are kept secret for fear of poachers, who, as Susan Orlean's book The Orchid Thief makes clear, are a real threat to their survival. But the flower's general whereabouts are common knowledge: South Florida's approximately 2000 ghost orchids are almost all in Big Cypress National Preserve and Fakahatchee Strand Preserve State Park. Of course, these parks are home to a great many other wild orchids, as are Everglades National Park, Myakka River State Park and Corkscrew Swamp Sanctuary.

To learn more, see Florida's Native Orchids (www.flnativeorchids.com) and Ghost Orchid Info (www.ghostorchid.info), and visit Sarasota's Marie Selby Botanical Gardens.

attached to the parent tree. Of the over 50 species of mangroves worldwide, only three predominate in Florida: red, black and white.

Mangroves play a vital role on the peninsula, and their destruction usually sets off a domino-effect of ecological damage. Mangroves 'stabilize' coastal land, trapping sand, silt and sediment. As this builds up, new land is created, which ironically strangles the mangroves themselves. Mangroves mitigate the storm surge and damaging winds of hurricanes, and they anchor tidal and estuary communities, providing vital wildlife habitats.

Coastal dunes are typically home to grasses and shrubs, saw palmetto and occasionally pines and cabbage palm (or sabal palm, the Florida state tree). Sea oats, with large plumes that trap wind-blown sand, are important for stabilizing dunes, while coastal hammocks welcome the wiggly gumbo-limbo tree, whose red peeling bark has earned it the nickname the 'tourist tree.'

National, State & Regional Parks

About 26% of Florida's land lies in public hands, which breaks down to three national forests, 11 national parks, 28 national wildlife refuges (including the first, Pelican Island), and 160 state parks. Attendance is up, with over 20 million folks visiting state parks annually, and Florida's state parks have twice been voted the nation's best.

Florida's parks are easy to explore. For more information, see the websites of the following organizations:

Florida State Parks (www.floridastateparks.org)
National Forests, Florida (www.fs.usda.gov/florida)
National Park Service (www.nps.gov/drto)
National Wildlife Refuges, Florida (www.fws.gov/southeast/maps/fl.html)
Recreation.gov (www.recreation.gov) National campground reservations.
Florida Fish & Wildlife Commission (www.myfwc.com) Manages Florida's mostly undeveloped Wildlife Management Areas (WMA); the website is an excellent resource for wildlife-viewing, as well as boating, hunting, fishing and permits.

Environmental Issues

Florida's environmental problems are the inevitable result of its century-long love affair with land development, population growth and tourism, and addressing them is especially urgent given Florida's uniquely diverse natural world. These complex, intertwined environmental impacts include erosion of wetlands, depletion of the aquifer, rampant pollution (particularly of waters), invasive species, endangered species and widespread habitat destruction. There is nary an acre of Florida that escapes concern.

In the last decade, Florida has enacted several significant conservation efforts. In 2000, the state passed the Florida Forever Act (www.supportfloridaforever.org), a 10-year, $3 billion conservation program that in 2008 was renewed for another 10 years. It also passed the multibillion-dollar Comprehensive Everglades Restoration Plan (CERP; www.evergladesplan.org) and the associated Central Everglades Planning Project. Unfortunately, implementation of the latter plan has been delayed due to a lack of approval from Federal agencies such as the Army Corps of Engineers.

Signs of other progress can be encouraging. For instance, phosphorous levels in the Everglades have been seriously reduced, and the Kissimmee River is a model of restoration: within a few years of backfilling the canal that had restricted its flow, the river's floodplain is again a humid marsh full of waterbirds and alligators. Also, in 2010 the state completed a purchase of 300 sq miles of Lake Okeechobee sugarcane fields from US Sugar,

The Florida chapter of the Nature Conservancy (www.nature.org) has been instrumental in the Florida Forever legislation. Check the web for updates and conservation issues.

LANDSCAPES & WILDLIFE NATIONAL, STATE & REGIONAL PARKS

intending to convert them back to swamp. Along with plans to bridge 6.5 miles of the Tamiami Trail, the lake may once again water the Glades.

However, Lake Okeechobee, controlled by Hoover Dike since 1928, is full of toxic sludge which gets stirred up during hurricanes and causes 'red tides,' or algal blooms that kill fish. Red tides occur naturally, but they are also sparked by pollution and unnatural water flows.

Studies have found that half of the state's lakes and waterways are too polluted for fishing. Though industrial pollution has been curtailed, pollution from residential development (sewage, fertilizer runoff) more than compensates. This is distressing Florida's freshwater springs, which can turn murky with algae. Plus, as the groundwater gets pumped out to slake homeowners' thirsts, the springs are shrinking and the drying limestone honeycomb underfoot sometimes collapses, causing sinkholes that swallow cars and homes.

Residential development continues almost unabated. The Miami–Fort Lauderdale–West Palm Beach corridor (the USA's sixth-largest urban area) is, as developers say, 'built out,' so developers are targeting the Panhandle and central Florida. Projections for the next 50 years show unrelenting urban sprawl up and down both coasts and across Central Florida.

Then there's the rising seas due to global warming. Here, the low-lying Florida Keys are a 'canary in a coalmine', being watched worldwide for impacts. In another century, some quip, South Florida's coastline could be a modern-day Atlantis, with its most expensive real estate underwater.

A KINDER, GENTLER WILDERNESS ENCOUNTER

While yesterday's glass-bottom boats and alligator wrestling have evolved into today's swamp-buggy rides and manatee encounters, the question remains: just because you can do something, does that mean you should? In Florida, everyone can be involved in protecting nature just by considering the best ways to experience it without harming it in the process.

For most activities, there isn't a single right answer; specific impacts are often debated. However, here are a few guidelines:

Airboats and swamp buggies While airboats have a much lighter 'footprint' than big-wheeled buggies, both are motorized (and loud) and have far larger impacts than canoes for exploring wetlands. As a rule, nonmotorized activities are least damaging.

Dolphin encounters Captive dolphins are, for better or worse, usually already acclimated to humans. However, when encountering wild dolphins in the ocean, it is illegal by federal law to feed, pursue or touch them. Keep in mind that habituating any wild animal to humans can lead to the animal's death, since approaching humans often results in conflict and accidents (as with boats).

Manatee swims When swimming near manatees, a federally protected endangered species, look but don't touch. 'Passive observation' is the standard. Harassment is a rampant problem that may lead to stricter 'no touch' legislation.

Feeding wild animals In a word, don't. Friendly animals such as deer and manatees may come to rely on human food (to their detriment), while feeding bears and alligators just encourages them to hunt you.

Sea-turtle nesting sites It's a federal crime to approach nesting sea turtles or hatchling runs. Most nesting beaches have warning signs and a nighttime 'lights out' policy. If you do encounter turtles on the beach, keep your distance and don't take flash photos.

Coral-reef etiquette Coral polyps are living organisms and touching or breaking coral creates openings for infection and disease. To prevent reef damage, never touch the coral. It's that simple.

Survival Guide

Directory A–Z

Accommodations

Our reviews (and rates) use the following room types:

➤ single occupancy (s)

➤ double occupancy (d)

➤ room (r), same rate for one or two people

➤ dorm bed (dm)

➤ suite (ste)

➤ apartment (apt)

Many places have certain rooms that cost above or below their standard rates, and seasonal/holiday fluctuations can see rates rise and fall dramatically, especially in Orlando and tourist beach towns. Specific advice for the best rates varies by region, and is included throughout. On the one hand, booking in advance for high-season tourist hot spots (like beaches and Orlando resorts) can be essential to ensure the room you want. On the other, enquiring at the last minute, or even same-day, can yield amazing discounts on any rooms still available.

B&Bs & Inns

These accommodations vary from small, comfy houses with shared bath (least expensive) to romantic, antique-filled historic homes and opulent mansions with private bath (most expensive). Properties focusing on upscale romance may discourage children. Also, inns and B&Bs often require a minimum stay of two or three days on weekends and advance reservations. Always call ahead to confirm policies (regarding kids, pets, smoking) and bath arrangements: many lower end B&Bs will have shared baths, although anywhere charging more than $100 per night should include private facilities. As a general rule, any property calling themselves a B&B will provide a full cooked breakfast for one or two guests. Properties designating themselves as an inn may not include breakfast. If you're opting for this type of accommodation, the breakfast is often one of the best perks, so be sure to confirm what's included before your stay!

Camping

Three types of campgrounds are available: undeveloped or primitive ($10 per night), public or powered ($15 to $25) and privately owned ($25 and up). In general, Florida campgrounds are quite safe. Undeveloped campgrounds are just that (undeveloped), while most public campgrounds have toilets, showers and drinking water. Reserve state-park sites in advance (yes, you need to!) by calling ☎800-326-3521 or visiting www.reserveamerica.com.

Most privately owned campgrounds are geared to RVs (recreational vehi-

---

SLEEPING PRICE RANGES

The following price ranges refer to a standard double room at high season rates, unless rates are distinguished as winter/summer or high/low season. Note that 'high season' can mean summer or winter depending on the region. Unless otherwise stated, rates do not include breakfast, bathrooms are private and all lodging is open year-round. Rates don't include taxes, which vary considerably between towns; in fact, hotels almost never include taxes and fees in their rate quotes, so always ask for the total rate with tax. Florida's sales tax is 6%, and some communities tack on more. States, cities and towns also usually levy taxes on hotel rooms, which can increase the final bill by 10% to 12%.

$ less than $100

$$ $100–200

$$$ more than $200

PRACTICALITIES

→ **Electricity** Voltage is 110/120V, 60 cycles.

→ **Measurements** Distances are measured in feet, yards and miles; weights are tallied in ounces, pounds and tons.

→ **Newspapers** Florida has three major daily newspapers: *Miami Herald* (in Spanish, *El Nuevo Herald*), *Orlando Sentinel* and the *St Petersburg Times*.

→ **Smoking** Florida bans smoking in all enclosed workplaces, including restaurants and shops, but excluding 'stand-alone' bars (that don't emphasize food) and designated hotel smoking rooms.

→ **Time** Most of Florida is in the US Eastern Time Zone: noon in Miami equals 9am in San Francisco and 5pm in London. West of the Apalachicola River, the Panhandle is in the US Central Time Zone, one hour behind the rest of the state. During daylight-saving time, clocks 'spring forward' one hour in March and 'fall back' one hour in November.

→ **TV** Florida receives all the major US TV and cable networks: **Florida Smart** (www.floridasmart.com/news) lists them by region. Video systems use the NTSC color TV standard.

cles; motor homes) but will also have a small section available for tent campers. Expect tons of amenities, like swimming pools, laundry facilities, convenience stores and bars. **Kampgrounds of America** (KOA; www.koa.com) is a national network of private campgrounds; its Kamping Kabins have air-con and kitchens.

A growing trend is free camping (or 'framping'), where you're able to legally sleep in your car or camper, or pitch a tent on public land. Sites can be as un-glamorous as casino car parks, or as picturesque as a soft grassy knoll by a billowing brook. Note, you can't just pitch a tent wherever you want, and you can be fined by the police if you're sleeping in the wrong place. One of the best resources for frampers is www.freecampsites.net.

Hostels

In most hostels, group dorms are segregated by sex and you'll be sharing a bath-

room; occasionally alcohol is banned. About half the hostels throughout Florida are affiliated with **Hostelling International USA** (HI-USA; ☏301-495-1240, reservations 888-464-4872; www.hiusa.org). You don't have to be a member to stay, but you'll pay a slightly higher rate; you can join HI by phone, online or at most youth hostels. From the US, you can book many HI hostels through its toll-free reservations service.

Try www.hostels.com for listings of Florida's many independent hostels. Most have comparable rates and conditions to HI hostels, and some are better.

Hotels

We have tried to highlight independently owned hotels in this guide, but in many towns, members of hotel chains offer the best value in terms of comfort, location and price. The calling-card of chain hotels is reliability: acceptable cleanliness, unremarkable yet inoffensive decor, a comfortable bed and a good shower. Air-conditioning, mini-refrigerator, microwave, hair dryer, safe and, increasingly, flat-screen TVs and free wi-fi are now standard amenities in most midrange chains. A recent trend, most evident in Miami and beach resorts, is an emergence of funky new brands, such as **aloft** (www.starwoodhotels.com/alofthotels), which are owned by more recognizable hotel chains striving for a share of the boutique market.

High-end hotel chains like Four Seasons and Ritz-Carlton overwhelm guests with their high levels of luxury and service: Les Clefs d'Or concierges, valet parking, 24-hour room service, dry cleaning, health clubs and decadent day spas. These special touches are reflected in the room rates. If you're paying for these five-star properties and finding they're not delivering on any of their promises, you have every right to speak politely with the front-desk manager to have your concerns addressed – you deserve only the best.

You'll find plenty of boutique and specialty hotels in places such as Miami's South Beach and Palm Beach. While all large chain hotels have toll-free reservation numbers, you may find better savings by calling the

BOOK YOUR STAY ONLINE

For more accommodations reviews by Lonely Planet authors, check out http://lonelyplanet.com/usa/florida/hotels. You'll find independent reviews, as well as recommendations on the best places to stay. Best of all, you can book online.

hotel directly, or paying up-front using the hotel website or a third-party booking site.

Note that it is customary to tip in most hotels of any size or stature in the US. Anywhere between $1 and $5 is appreciated for the porter who carries your bags, the bellhop who greets you by name daily, and the driver of the 'free' airport shuttle. Some people find it a nice gesture to leave a greenback or two on the pillow for the housekeeping staff. Conversely, if you're given attitude or any sense of entitlement by any hotel staff member, do feel free to save your bucks for the bar.

Chain-owned hotels in-clude the following:

Four Seasons (☏800-819-5053; www.fourseasons.com)

Hilton (☏800-445-8667; www.hilton.com)

Holiday Inn (☏888-465-4329; www.holidayinn.com)

Marriott (☏888-236-2427; www.marriott.com)

Radisson (☏888-201-1718; www.radisson.com)

Ritz-Carlton (☏800-542-8680; www.ritzcarlton.com)

Sheraton (☏800-325-3535; www.starwoodhotels.com/sheraton)

Wyndham (☏877-999-3223; www.wyndham.com)

Motels

Budget and midrange motels remain prevalent in Florida; these 'drive-up rooms' are often near highway exits and along a town's main road. Many are still independently owned, and thus quality varies tremendously. Some are much better inside than their exteriors suggest: ask to see a room first if you're unsure. Most strive for the same level of amenities and cleanliness as a budget-chain hotel.

A motel's 'rack rates' can be more open to haggling, but not always. Demand is the final arbiter, though simply asking about any specials can sometimes inspire a discount.

The most common motel chains with a presence in Florida include:

Best Western (☏800-780-7234; www.bestwestern.com)

Choice Hotels (☏877-424-6423; www.choicehotels.com)

Motel 6 (☏800-466-8356; www.motel6.com)

Red Roof Inn (☏800-733-7663; www.redroof.com)

Super 8 (☏800-454-3213; www.super8.com)

Resorts

Florida resorts, much like Disney World, aim to be so all-encompassing you'll never need, or want, to leave. Included are all manner of fitness and sports facilities, pools, spas, restaurants, bars and so on. Many also have on-site babysitting services. However, some also tack an extra 'resort fee' onto rates, so always ask.

Activities

For an introduction to all the things you can do in Florida, see the Outdoor Activities chapter (p491).

Biking

Note that the state organi-zations listed under Hiking & Camping also discuss biking trails. Florida law requires that all cyclists under 16 must wear a helmet (under 18 in national parks).

Bike Florida (www.bikeflorida.org) Nonprofit organization pro-moting safe cycling and organized rides, with good biking links.

Florida Bicycle Asso-ciation (www.floridabicycle.org) Advocacy organization pro-viding tons of advice, a statewide list of cycling clubs, and links to off-road-cycling organizations, racing clubs, a touring calendar and more.

Canoeing & Kayaking

Water-trail and kayaking in-formation is also provided by the Florida State Parks and Florida Greenways & Trails websites listed under Hiking & Camping. Here are more resources:

American Canoe Asso-ciation (ACA; www.ameri-cancanoe.org) ACA publishes a newsletter, has a water-trails database and organizes courses.

Florida Professional Paddlesports Association (www.paddleflausa.com) Pro-vides a list of affiliated member kayak outfitters.

Kayak Online (www.kayakonline.com) A good resource for kayak gear, with links to Florida outfitters.

Diving

Ocean diving in Florida requires an Open Water I certificate, and Florida has plenty of certification programs (with good weather, they take three days). To dive in freshwater springs, you need a separate cave-diving certification, and this is also offered through-out the state.

National Association for Underwater Instruction (NAUI; www.naui.org) Informa-tion on dive certifications and a list of NAUI-certified Florida dive instructors.

Professional Diving Instructors Corporation (PDIC; www.pdic-intl.com) Similar to NAUI, with its own list of PDIC-certified Florida dive instructors.

Fishing

All non-residents 16 and over need a fishing license to fish and crab, and Florida offers several short-term options. There are lots of regulations about what and how much you can catch, and where. Locals can give you details, but please do the right thing and review the official word on what's OK and what's not; visit the Florida Fish & Wildlife Conservation Com-mission website.

Florida Fish & Wildlife Conservation Commis-sion (FWC; www.myfwc.com) The official source for all fishing regulations and licenses (purchase online or by phone). Also has boating and hunting information.

Florida Fishing Capital of the World (www.visit-florida.com/fishing) State-run all-purpose fishing advice and information.

Florida Sportsman (www.floridasportsman.com) Get the lowdown on sport fishing, tournaments, charters and gear, and detailed regional advice.

Hiking & Camping

For advice on low-impact hiking and camping, visit **Leave No Trace** (www.lnt.org). For a rich introduction to Florida trails, see **Florida Hikes** (www.floridahikes.com).

For short hikes in national, state or regional parks, free park maps are perfectly adequate. Most outdoor stores and ranger stations sell good topographical (topo) maps.

Florida Greenways & Trails (www.visitflorida.com/trails) The Florida Dept of Environmental Protection has downloadable hiking, biking and kayaking trail descriptions.

Florida State Parks (www.floridastateparks.org) Comprehensive state-park information and all cabin and camping reservations.

Florida Trail Association (www.floridatrail.org) Maintains the Florida National Scenic Trail (FNST); a wealth of online advice, descriptions and maps.

Florida Trails Network (www.floridatrailsnetwork.com) The state's main database of current and future trails.

Rails-to-Trails Conservancy (www.railstotrails.org) Converts abandoned railroad corridors into public biking and hiking trails; has a Florida chapter and reviews trails at www.traillink.com.

Recreation.gov (www.recreation.gov) Reserve camping at all national parks and forests.

National Geographic (www.nationalgeographic.com) Custom and GPS maps.

Trails.com (www.trails.com) Create custom, downloadable topo maps.

US Geological Survey (USGS; 888-275-8747; www.store.usgs.gov) Your online one-stop shop for maps and geological surveys of all US states.

Surfing

Looking for lessons, surf reports or competitions? Start here:

Florida Surfing (www.floridasurfing.com) Instructors, contests, webcams, weather, equipment, history: it's all here.

Florida Surfing Association (FSA; www.floridasurfing.org) Manages Florida's surf competitions; also runs the surf school at Jacksonville Beach.

Surf Guru (www.surfguru.com) East Coast Florida surf reports.

Surfer (www.surfermag.com) *Surfer*'s travel reports cover Florida and just about every break in the USA.

Discount Cards

There are no discount cards specific to Florida. It's a *very* competitive tourist destination, so persistence, patience and thorough research often pays dividends.

Being a member of certain groups also gives access to discounts (usually about 10%) at many hotels, museums and sights. Simply carry the appropriate ID.

Students Any student ID is typically honored; international students might consider an **International Student Identity Card** (ISIC; www.isiccard.com).

Seniors Generally refers to those 65 and older, but sometimes those 60 and older. Join the **American Association of Retired Persons** (AARP; 888-687-2277; www.aarp.org) for more travel bargains.

Electricity

110V/60Hz

110V/60Hz

Food

To whet your appetite for all things culinary and beverage-related in Florida, see the Food & Drink chapter (p486).

EATING PRICE RANGES

The following price ranges refer to a typical dinner main course. The Florida state sales and use tax is 6%, which will be added to the total of your bill. Some counties and municipalities may charge an additional percentage, but this is the exception and not the rule. For good to excellent service, always tip 15% to 25% of the total bill.

For Miami and Orlando:

$ less than $15

$$ $15–30

$$$ more than $30

Elsewhere:

$ less than $10

$$ $10–20

$$$ more than $20

Gay & Lesbian Travelers

Florida is not uniformly anything, and it's not uniformly embracing of gay life. The state is largely tolerant, particularly in major tourist destinations, beaches and cities, but this tolerance does not always extend into the more rural and Southern areas of northern Florida. However, where Florida does embrace gay life, it does so with a big flamboyant bear hug. Miami and South Beach are as 'out' as it's possible to be, with some massive gay festivals. Fort Lauderdale, West Palm Beach and Key West have long supported vibrant gay communities and are now regarded as some of the 'gayest' destinations in the world. Notable gay scenes and communities also exist in Orlando, Jacksonville, Pensacola, and, to far lesser degrees, in Daytona Beach, Tampa and Sarasota.

Good gay-and-lesbian resources include the following:

Damron (https://damron. com) Damron, an expert in LGBT travel, offers a searchable database of LGBT-friendly and specific travel listings. Publishes popular national guidebooks, including *Women's Traveller*, *Men's Travel Guide* and *Damron Accommodations*.

Gay Cities (www.gaycities. com) Everything gay about every major city in the US and beyond.

Gay Yellow Network (www.glyp.com) City-based yellow-page listings include six Florida cities.

Gayosphere (www.gay-osphere.com) The new website from the creators of Fun Maps, bringing you all the naughty and nice hot spots for gay travelers in Florida's major cities and beyond.

Out Traveler (www.out-traveler.com) Travel magazine specializing in gay travel.

Purple Roofs (www.purple-roofs.com) Lists queer accommodations, travel agencies and tours worldwide.

Health

Florida (and the USA generally) has a high level of hygiene, so infectious diseases are not a significant concern for most travelers. There are no required vaccines, and tap water is safe to drink. Despite Florida's plethora of intimidating wildlife, the main concerns for travelers are sunburn and mosquito bites – as well as arriving with adequate health insurance in case of accidents.

Animal & Spider Bites

Florida's critters can be cute, but they can also bite and sting. Here are a few to watch out for:

Alligators and snakes Neither attack humans unless startled or threatened. If you encounter them, simply back away calmly. Florida has several venomous snakes, so always immediately seek treatment if bitten.

Bears and wildcats Florida is home to a small population of black bears and predatory felines such as the lynx and Florida panther: one of the rarest and most endangered species on the planet. All are generally incredibly hard to spot and live deep in wilderness areas. Should you be lucky (or unlucky) enough to encounter these critters in the wild, stay calm, do not provoke the animal and don't be afraid to make a little noise (talking, jiggling keys) to alert the animal of your presence. In the rare and unfortunate event of an attack, do your best to defend yourself and retreat to a covered position as soon as possible.

Jellyfish and stingrays Florida beaches can see both; avoid swimming when they are present (lifeguards often post warnings). Treat stings immediately; they hurt but aren't dangerous.

Spiders Florida is home to two venomous spiders – the black widow and the brown recluse. Seek immediate treatment if bitten by any spider.

Health Care

In general, if you have a medical emergency, go to the emergency room of the nearest hospital. If the problem isn't urgent, call a nearby hospital and ask for a referral to a local physician; this is usually cheaper than a trip to the emergency room. Stand-alone, moneymaking urgent-care centers provide good service, but can be the most expensive option.

Pharmacies (called drugstores) are abundantly supplied. However, some medications that are available over the counter in other countries require a prescription in the US. If you don't have insurance to cover the cost of prescriptions, these can be shockingly expensive.

Health Insurance

The US offers some of the finest health care in the world. The problem is that it can be prohibitively expensive. It's essential to purchase travel health insurance if your policy doesn't cover you when you're abroad.

Citizens of some Canadian provinces may have a certain level of reciprocal health cover within the US: check with your provincial health-care provider before traveling. Citizens from all other nations should not even think about travel to the States without adequate travel insurance covering medical care. Find out in advance whether your insurance plan will make payments directly to the providers or if they will reimburse you later for any overseas health expenditures.

Accidents and unforeseen illnesses do happen and horror stories are common of people's vacations turning into nightmares when they're hit with hefty hospital bills for seemingly innocuous concerns. On a more serious note, hospital bills for car accidents, falls or serious medical emergencies can run into the tens of thousands of dollars. Look for an insurance policy that provides at least $1 million of medical coverage. Policies with unlimited medical coverage are also available at a higher premium, but are usually not necessary. You may be surprised at how inexpensive good insurance can be.

Bring any medications you may need in their original containers, clearly labeled. A signed, dated letter from

your physician that describes all of your medical conditions and medications (including generic names) is also a good idea.

Infectious Diseases

In addition to more-common ailments, there are several infectious diseases that are unknown or uncommon outside North America. Most are acquired by mosquito or tick bites.

Giardiasis Also known as traveler's diarrhea. A parasitic infection of the small intestines, typically contracted by drinking feces-contaminated fresh water. Never drink untreated stream, lake or pond water. Easily treated with antibiotics.

HIV/AIDS HIV infection occurs in the US, as do all sexually transmitted diseases: incidences of syphilis are on the rise. Use condoms for all sexual encounters.

Lyme Disease Though more common in the US northeast than Florida, Lyme disease occurs here. It is transmitted by infected deer ticks, and is signaled by a bull's-eye rash at the bite and flulike symptoms. Treat promptly with antibiotics. Removing ticks within 36 hours can avoid infection.

Rabies Though rare, the rabies virus can be contracted from the bite of any infected animal; bats are most common, and their bites are not always obvious. If bitten by any animal, consult with a doctor, since rabies is fatal if untreated.

West Nile Virus Extremely rare in Florida, West Nile Virus is transmitted by culex mosquitoes. Most infections are mild or asymptomatic, but serious symptoms and even death can occur. There is no treatment for West Nile Virus. For the latest update on affected areas, see the **US Geological Survey disease maps** (http://diseasemaps.usgs.gov).

Useful Websites

Consult your government's travel health website before departure, if one is available. There is a vast wealth of

travel-health advice on the internet.

Good sources include the following:

MD Travel Health (www.mdtravelhealth.com) Provides complete, updated and free travel-health recommendations for every country.

World Health Organization (www.who.int/ith) The superb book *International Travel and Health* is available free online.

Insurance

It's expensive to get sick, crash a car or have things stolen from you in the US. Make sure you have adequate coverage before arriving. To insure yourself for items that may be stolen from your car, consult your homeowner's (or renter's) insurance policy or invest in travel insurance.

Worldwide travel insurance is available at www.lonelyplanet.com/travel-insurance. You can buy, extend and claim online anytime – even if you're already on the road.

Internet Access

The USA and Florida are wired. Nearly every hotel and many restaurants and businesses offer high-speed internet access. With few exceptions, most hotels and motels offer in-room wi-fi: generally free of charge, but do check for connection rates.

Many cafes and all McDonald's offer free wi-fi and most transportation hubs are wi-fi hot spots. Public libraries provide free internet terminals, though sometimes you must get a temporary nonresident library card ($10).

For a list of wi-fi hot spots (plus tech and access info), visit **Wi-Fi Alliance** (www.wi-fi.org) and **Wi-Fi Free Spot** (www.wififreespot.com).

INTERNATIONAL VISITORS

Entering the Region

A passport is required for all foreign citizens. Unless eligible under the Visa Waiver Program, foreign travelers must also have a tourist visa.

Travelers entering under the Visa Waiver Program must register with the US government's program, **ESTA** (https://esta.cbp.dhs.gov), at least three days before arriving; earlier is better, since if denied, travelers must get a visa. Registration is valid for two years.

Upon arriving in the US, all foreign visitors must register in the US-Visit program, which entails having two index fingers scanned and a digital photo taken. For information on US-Visit, see the **Dept of Homeland Security** (www.dhs.gov/us-visit) website.

Visas

All visitors should reconfirm entry requirements and visa guidelines before arriving. You can get visa information through www.usa.gov, but the **US State Dept** (www.travel.state.gov) maintains the most comprehensive visa information, with lists of consulates and downloadable application forms. **US Citizenship & Immigration Services** (USCIS; www.uscis.gov) mainly serves immigrants, not temporary visitors.

The **Visa Waiver Program** allows citizens of three dozen countries to enter the USA for stays of 90 days or less without first obtaining a US visa. See the ESTA website for a current list. Under this program you must have a nonrefundable return ticket and an 'e-passport' with digital chip. Passports issued/renewed before October 26, 2006, must be machine-readable.

Visitors who don't qualify for the Visa Waiver Program need a visa. Basic requirements are a valid passport, recent photo, travel details and often proof of financial stability. Students and adult males also must fill out supplemental travel documents.

The validity period for a US visitor visa depends on your home country. The length of time you'll be allowed to stay in the USA is determined by US officials at the port of entry. To stay longer than the date stamped on your passport, visit a local **USCIS** (www.uscis.gov) office.

Customs

For a complete, up-to-date list of customs regulations, visit the website of **US Customs & Border Protection** (www.cbp.gov). Each visitor is allowed to bring into the US duty-free 1L of liquor (if you're 21 or older) and 200 cigarettes (if you're 18 or older) and up to $100 in gifts and purchases.

Embassies & Consulates

To find a US embassy in another country, visit www.usembassy.gov. Most foreign embassies in the US have their main consulates in Washington, DC, but some have representation in Miami. Except for the Italian consulate, the following consulates are all in Miami:

Brazilian Consulate (☎305-285-6200; http://miami.itamaraty.gov.br/en-us; 80 SW 8th St, Suite 2600)

Canadian Consulate (☎305-579-1600; http://can-am.gc.ca/miami/menu.aspx; 200 S Biscayne Blvd, Suite 1600)

French Consulate (☎305-403-4150; www.consulfrance-miami.org; 1395 Brickell Ave, Suite 1050)

German Consulate (☎305-358-0290; www.germany.info; 100 N Biscayne Blvd, Suite 2200)

Italian Consulate (☎305-374-6322; www.consmiami.esteri.it/Consolato_Miami; 4000 Ponce de Leon Blvd, Suite 590, Coral Gables)

Mexican Consulate (☎786-268-4900; http://consulmex.sre.gob.mx/miami; 1399 SW 1st Ave)

Netherlands Consulate (☎877-388-2443; http://miami.the-netherlands.org; 701 Brickell Ave, Suite 500)

UK Consulate (☎305-400-6400; http://ukinusa.fco.gov.uk/florida; 1001 Brickell Bay Dr, Suite 2800)

Legal Matters

In everyday matters, if you are stopped by the police, note that there is no system for paying traffic tickets or other fines on the spot. The patrol officer will explain your options to you; there is usually a 30-day period to pay fines by mail.

If you're arrested, you are allowed to remain silent, though never walk away from an officer; you are entitled to have access to an attorney. The legal system presumes you're innocent until proven guilty. All persons who are arrested have the right to make one phone call. If you don't have a lawyer or family member to help you, call your embassy or consulate. The police will give you the number on request.

Drinking & Driving

To purchase alcohol, you need to present a photo ID to prove your age. Despite what you sometimes see, it's illegal to walk with an open alcoholic drink on the street. More importantly, don't drive with an 'open container'; any liquor in a car must be unopened or else stored in the trunk. If you're stopped while driving with an open container, police will treat you as if you were drinking and driving. Refusing a breathalyzer, urine or blood test is treated as if you'd taken the test and failed. A DUI (driving under the influence) conviction is a serious offense, subject to stiff fines and even imprisonment.

Money

Prices quoted in this book are in US dollars ($).

The ease and availability of ATMs have largely negated the need for traveler's checks. However, traveler's checks in US dollars are accepted like cash at most midrange and top-end businesses (but rarely at budget places). Personal checks not drawn on US banks are generally not accepted. Exchange foreign currency at international airports and most large banks in Miami, Orlando, Tampa and other Florida cities.

Major credit cards are widely accepted, and they are required for car rentals. Most ATM withdrawals using out-of-state cards incur surcharges of $2 or so.

Tipping

Tipping is standard practice across America. In restaurants, for satisfactory to excellent service, tipping 15% to 25% of the bill is expected; less is OK at informal diners. Bartenders expect $1 per drink; cafe baristas a little change in the jar. Taxi drivers and hairdressers expect 10% to 15%. Skycaps at airports and porters at nice hotels expect $1 a bag or so. If you spend several nights in a hotel, it's polite to leave a few dollars for the cleaning staff.

Opening Hours

Standard business hours are as follows:

Banks 8:30am to 4:30pm Monday to Thursday, to 5:30pm Friday; sometimes 9am to 12:30pm Saturday.

Bars Most bars 5pm to midnight; to 2am Friday and Saturday.

Businesses 9am to 5pm Monday to Friday.

Post offices 9am to 5pm Monday to Friday; sometimes 9am to noon Saturday.

Restaurants Breakfast 7am to 10:30am Monday to Friday; brunch 9am to 2pm Saturday and Sunday; lunch 11:30am to 2:30pm Monday to Friday; dinner 5pm to 9:30pm, later Friday and Saturday.

Shops 10am to 6pm Monday to Saturday, noon to 5pm Sunday; shopping malls keep extended hours.

Photography

All camera supplies (print and slide film, digital memory, camera batteries) are readily available in local drugstores, which also usually provide inexpensive film developing (including one-hour service) and burning of photo CDs and DVDs.

Don't pack unprocessed film (including the roll in your camera) into checked luggage because exposure to high-powered X-ray equipment will cause it to fog. As an added precaution, 'hand check' film separately from carry-on bags at airport security checkpoints.

When photographing people, politeness is usually all that's needed (though street performers appreciate a tip).

For a primer on taking good shots, consult *Lonely Planet's Guide to Travel Photography*.

Post

The **US Postal Service** (USPS; ☎800-275-8777; www.usps.com) is reliable and inexpensive. For exact rates, refer to www.postcalc.usps.com.

You can have mail sent to you 'c/o General Delivery' at most big post offices (it's usually held for 30 days). Most hotels will also hold mail for incoming guests.

Public Holidays

On the following national public holidays, banks, schools and government offices (including post offices) are closed, and transportation, museums and other services operate on a Sunday schedule. Many stores, however, maintain regular business hours. Holidays falling on a weekend are usually observed the following Monday.

New Year's Day January 1

Martin Luther King, Jr Day Third Monday in January

Presidents Day Third Monday in February

Easter March or April

Memorial Day Last Monday in May

Independence Day July 4

Labor Day First Monday in September

Columbus Day Second Monday in October

Veterans Day November 11

Thanksgiving Fourth Thursday in November

Christmas Day December 25

Safe Travel

When it comes to crime, there is Miami, and there is the rest of Florida. As a rule, Miami suffers the same urban problems facing other major US cities such as New York and Los Angeles, but it is no worse than others. The rest of Florida tends to have lower crime rates than the rest of the nation, but any tourist town is a magnet for petty theft and car break-ins.

If you need any kind of emergency assistance, such as police, ambulance or fire-fighters, call ✆911. This is a free call from any phone.

Hurricanes

Florida hurricane season extends from June through November, but the peak is September and October. Relatively speaking, very few Atlantic Ocean and Gulf of Mexico storms become hurricanes, and fewer still are accurate enough to hit Florida, but the devastation they wreak when they do can be enormous. Travelers should take all hurricane alerts, warnings and evacuation orders seriously.

Hurricanes are generally sighted well in advance, allowing time to prepare. When a hurricane threatens, listen to radio and TV news reports. For more information on storms and preparedness, contact the following:

Florida Division of Emergency Management (www.floridadisaster.org) Hurricane preparedness.

Florida Emergency Hotline (✆800-342-3557) Updated storm warning information.

National Weather Service (www.nws.noaa.gov)

Telephone

Always dial '1' before toll-free (✆800, ✆888 etc) and domestic long-distance numbers. Some toll-free numbers only work within the US. For local directory assistance, dial ✆411.

To make international calls from the US, dial ✆011 + country code + area code + number. For international operator assistance, dial ✆0. To call the US from abroad, the international country code for the USA is ✆1.

Pay phones are readily found in major cities, but are becoming rarer. Local calls cost 50¢. Private prepaid phonecards are available from convenience stores, supermarkets and drugstores.

Most of the USA's cell-phone systems are incompatible with the GSM 900/1800 standard used throughout Europe and Asia. Check with your service provider about using your phone in the US. In terms of coverage, Verizon has the most extensive network, but AT&T, Sprint and T-Mobile are decent. Cellular coverage is generally excellent, except in the Everglades and parts of rural northern Florida.

Tourist Information

Most Florida towns have some sort of tourist information center that provides local information; be aware that chambers of commerce typically only list chamber members, not all the town's hotels and businesses. This guide provides visitor center information throughout.

To order a packet of Florida information prior to coming, contact **Visit Florida** (www.visitflorida.com).

Travelers with Disabilities

Because of the high number of senior residents in Florida, most public buildings are wheelchair accessible and have appropriate restroom facilities. Transportation services are generally accessible to all, and telephone companies provide relay operators for the hearing impaired. Many banks provide ATM instructions in braille, curb ramps are common and many busy intersections have audible crossing signals.

A number of organizations specialize in the needs of disabled travelers:

Access-Able Travel Source (www.access-able.com) An excellent website with many links.

Flying Wheels Travel (✆507-451-5005; http://flyingwheelstravel.com) A full-service travel agency specializing in disabled travel.

Mobility International USA (www.miusa.org) Advises disabled travelers on mobility issues and runs an educational exchange program.

Travelin' Talk Network (www.travelintalk.net) Run by the same people as Access-Able Travel Source; a global network of service providers.

Volunteering

Volunteering can be a great way to break up a long trip, and it provides memorable opportunities to interact with locals and the land in ways you never would when just passing through.

Volunteer Florida (www.volunteerflorida.org), the primary state-run organization, coordinates volunteer

---

GOVERNMENT TRAVEL ADVICE

Australia (www.smartraveller.gov.au)

Canada (www.hc-sc.gc.ca/index-eng.php)

Germany (www.auswaertiges-amt.de)

New Zealand (www.safetravel.govt.nz)

UK (www.fco.gov.uk)

USA (www.travel.state.gov)

---

centers across the state. Though it's aimed at Floridians, casual visitors can find situations that match their time and interests.

Florida's state parks would not function without volunteers. Each park coordinates its own volunteers, and most also have the support of an all-volunteer 'friends' organization (officially called Citizen Support Organizations). Links and contact information are on the website of **Florida State Parks** (www.floridastateparks.org/getinvolved/volunteer.cfm)

Finally, **Habitat for Humanity** (☏305-634-3628; www.miamihabitat.org; 3800 NW 22nd Ave, Miami) does a ton of work in Florida, building homes and helping the homeless.

Women Travelers

Women traveling by themselves or in a group should encounter no particular problems unique to Florida. Indeed, there are a number of excellent resources to help traveling women.

The community resource **Journeywoman** (www.journeywoman.com) facilitates women exchanging travel tips, with links to resources.

These two national advocacy groups might also be helpful:

➡ **National Organization for Women** (NOW; ☏202-628-8669; www.now.org)

➡ **Planned Parenthood** (☏800-230-7526; www.plannedparenthood.org)

In terms of safety issues, single women need to exhibit the same street smarts as any solo traveler, but they are sometimes more often the target of unwanted attention or harassment. Some women like to carry a whistle, mace or cayenne-pepper spray in case of assault. These sprays are legal to carry and use in Florida, but only in self-defense. Federal law prohibits them being carried on planes.

If you are assaulted, you can call the **police** (☏911) or a rape-crisis hotline; telephone books have listings of local organizations, or contact the 24-hour **National Sexual Assault Hotline** (☏800-656-4673; www.rainn.org), or go straight to a hospital. Police can sometimes be insensitive with assault victims, while a rape-crisis center or hospital will advocate on behalf of victims and can act as a link to other services, including the police.

Work

Seasonal service jobs in tourist beach towns and theme parks are common and often easy to get, if low-paying.

If you are a foreigner in the USA with a standard non-immigrant visitors visa, you are expressly forbidden to take paid work in the USA and will be deported if you're caught working illegally. In addition, employers are required to establish the bona fides of their employees or face fines. In particular, southern Florida is notorious for large numbers of foreigners working illegally, and immigration officers are vigilant.

To work legally, foreigners need to apply for a work visa before leaving home. For non-student jobs, temporary or permanent, you need to be sponsored by a US employer, who will arrange an H-category visa. These are not easy to obtain.

Student-exchange visitors need a J1 visa, which the following organizations will help arrange:

American Institute for Foreign Study (AIFS; ☏866-906-2437; www.aifs.com)

BUNAC (☏203-264-0901; www.bunac.org) British Universities North American Club.

Camp America (☏800-727-8233; www.campamerica.aifs.com)

Council on International Educational Exchange (CIEE; ☏800-407-8839; www.ciee.org)

InterExchange (☏212-924-0446; www.interexchange.org) Camp and au-pair programs.

Transportation

GETTING THERE & AWAY

Nearly all international travelers to Florida arrive by air, while most US travelers prefer air or car. Florida is bordered by Alabama to the west and north, and Georgia to the north. Major interstates into Florida are the I-10 from the west (Alabama), and the I-75 and I-95 from the north (Georgia).

Getting to Florida by bus is a distant third option, and by train an even more distant fourth. Major regional hubs in Florida include Miami, Fort Lauderdale, Orlando, Tampa and Jacksonville.

Flights, cars and tours can be booked online at lonelyplanet.com/bookings.

Air

Unless you live in or near Florida and have your own wheels, flying to the region and then renting a car is the most time-efficient option. Depending on your plans, you'll be missing out on lots of the best bits without the freedom and convenience of a vehicle.

Airports & Airlines

Whether you're coming from within the US or from abroad, the entire state is well served by air, with a number of domestic and international airlines operating services into Florida.

Major airports:

Orlando International Airport (MCO; ☑407-825-2001; www.orlandoairports. net; 1 Jeff Fuqua Blvd) Handles more passengers than any other airport in Florida. Serves Walt Disney World, the Space Coast and the Orlando area.

Miami International Airport (MIA; ☑305-876-7000; www.miami-airport.com; 2100 NW 42nd Ave) One of Florida's busiest international airports. It serves metro Miami, the Ever-glades and the Keys, and is a hub for American, Delta and US Airways.

Fort Lauderdale-Hollywood International Airport (FLL; ☑866-435-9355; www.broward.org/airport; 320 Terminal Dr) Serves metro Fort Lauderdale and Broward County. It's about 30 miles north of Miami: be sure to check flights into Fort Lauderdale as they are often cheaper or have availability when flights into Miami are full.

Tampa International Airport (TPA; ☑813-870-8700; www.tampaairport.com; 4100 George J Bean Pkwy) Florida's third-busiest airport is located 6 miles southwest of downtown Tampa and serves the Tampa Bay and St Petersburg metro area.

Other airports with international traffic include Daytona Beach (DAB) and Jacksonville (JAX).

Most cities have airports and offer services to other US cities; these include Palm Beach (PBI; actually in

---

CLIMATE CHANGE & TRAVEL

Every form of transportation that relies on carbon-based fuel generates CO_2, the main cause of human-induced climate change. Modern travel is dependent on aeroplanes which might use less fuel per kilometer per person than most cars but travel much greater distances. The altitude at which aircraft emit gases (including CO_2) and particles also contributes to their climate change impact. Many websites offer 'carbon calculators' that allow people to estimate the carbon emissions generated by their journey and, for those who wish to do so, to offset the impact of the greenhouse gases emitted with contributions to portfolios of climate-friendly initiatives throughout the world. Lonely Planet offsets the carbon footprint of all staff and author travel.

West Palm Beach), Sarasota (SRQ), Tallahassee (TLH), Gainesville (GNV), Fort Myers (RSW), Pensacola (PNS) and Key West (EYW).

Tickets

It helps to know that in the US there are a number of APEX (Advance Purchase Excursion) fares of 7, 14, 21 and 28 days available, which can really save you money. It is prudent to compare flights into the state between the handful of significant airline hubs. The distance between Orlando, Fort Lauderdale and Miami, for example, is not so great, yet each city has a major airport. Rates can sometimes fluctuate widely between these destinations, depending on season and demand. If you're lucky, you could save money by flying into one airport and out of the other, or, flying into an airport a little further from your destination, and driving. The combination of Miami and Fort Lauderdale often works well in this regard.

Land

Bus

For bus trips, **Greyhound** (☎800-231-2222; www.greyhound.com) is the main long-distance operator in the US. It serves Florida from most major cities. It also has the only scheduled statewide service.

CAR TRAVEL TIMES

Sample distances and times from various points in the US to Miami:

CITY	DISTANCE (MILES)	DURATION (HR)
Atlanta	660	10½
Chicago	1380	23
Los Angeles	2750	44
New York City	1280	22
Washington, DC	1050	17

Standard long-distance fares can be relatively high; bargain airfares can undercut buses on long-distance routes, and on shorter routes, renting a car can be cheaper. Nonetheless, discounted (even half-price) long-distance bus trips are often available by purchasing tickets online seven to 14 days in advance. Then, once in Florida, you can rent a car to get around. Inquire about multiday passes.

Car & Motorcycle

Driving to Florida is easy; there are no international borders or entry issues. Incorporating Florida into a larger USA road trip is very common, and having a car while in Florida is often a necessity: there's lots of ground to cover and some of the most interesting places and state parks are only accessible by car.

BUS FARES

Sample one-way advance-purchase and standard fares between Miami and some major US cities:

CITY	FARE (ADVANCE/STANDARD)	DURATION (HR)	FREQUENCY (PER DAY)
Atlanta	$82/148	16-18	4-6
New Orleans	$139/154	23-24	3-4
New York City	$166/184	33-35	4-6
Washington, DC	$154/178	27-29	4-6

Train

From the East Coast, **Amtrak** (☎800-872-7245; www.amtrak.com) makes a comfortable, affordable option for getting to Florida. Amtrak's *Silver Service* (which includes *Silver Meteor* and *Silver Star* trains) runs between New York and Miami, with services that include Jacksonville, Orlando, Tampa, West Palm Beach and Fort Lauderdale, plus smaller Florida towns in between.

There is no direct service to Florida from Los Angeles, New Orleans, Chicago or the Midwest. Trains from these destinations connect to the *Silver Service* route, but the transfer adds a day or so to your travel time.

Amtrak's *Auto Train* takes you and your car from the Washington, DC, area to the Orlando area; this saves you gas, the drive and having to pay for a rental car. The fare for your vehicle isn't cheap, though, depending on its size and weight. The *Auto Train* leaves daily from Lorton, VA, and goes only to Sanford, FL. It takes about 18 hours, leaving in the afternoon and arriving the next morning. On the *Auto Train*, you pay for your passage, cabin and car separately. Book tickets in advance. Children, seniors and military personnel receive discounts. See p518 for sample train fares.

TRAIN FARES

Sample one-way fares (from low to high season) and durations from NYC to points in Florida:

FROM	TO	FARE	DURATION (HR)
New York City	Jacksonville	$172-291	18-20
New York City	Miami	$185-314	28-31
New York City	Orlando	$175-297	22-23
New York City	Tampa	$176-299	26

Sea

Florida is nearly completely surrounded by the ocean, and it's a major cruise-ship port. Fort Lauderdale is the largest transatlantic harbor in the US. Adventurous types can always sign up as crew members for a chance to travel the high seas.

GETTING AROUND

Once you reach Florida, traveling by car is the best way of getting around – it allows you to reach areas not otherwise served by public transportation.

Air

The US airline industry is reliable and safe, and serves Florida extremely well, both from the rest of the country and within Florida. However, the industry's continuing financial troubles have resulted in a series of high-profile mergers in recent years: Midwest joined Frontier; Orlando-based Air Tran merged into Southwest; Continental merged with United, and the American Airlines merger with US Airways to form the world's largest airline was finalized in 2014.

In general, this has led to the abolition of some routes, fewer flights, fuller airplanes, less perks, more fees and higher fares. Airport security screening procedures also keep evolving; allow extra time.

Air service between Florida's four main airports – Fort Lauderdale, Miami, Orlando International and Tampa – is frequent and direct. Smaller destinations such as Key West, Fort Myers, Pensacola, Jacksonville, Tallahassee and West Palm Beach are served, but less frequently, indirectly and at higher fares.

Airlines in Florida

Domestic airlines operating in Florida:

American (AA; ☑800-433-7300; www.aa.com) Has a Miami hub and service to and between major Florida cities.

Cape Air (9K; www.flycapeair.com) Convenient connections between Fort Myers and Key West.

Delta (DL; ☑800-455-2720; www.delta.com) International carrier to main Florida cities, plus flights from Miami to Orlando and Tampa.

Frontier (F9; ☑800-432-1359; www.frontierairlines.com) Services Tampa, Orlando and Fort Lauderdale from Denver, Minneapolis and the Midwest.

JetBlue (JB; ☑800-538-2583; www.jetblue.com) Serves Orlando, Fort Lauderdale and smaller Florida cities from the East and West Coast.

Southwest (WN; ☑800-435-9792; www.southwest.com) One of the US' leading low-cost carriers, offering free baggage and, at times, extremely low fares.

Spirit (NK; ☑801-401-2220; www.spiritair.com) Florida-based discount carrier serving Florida cities from East Coast US, Caribbean, and Central and South America.

United (UA; ☑800-824-6400; www.united.com) International flights to Orlando and Miami; domestic flights to and between key Florida cities.

Air Passes

International travelers who plan on doing a lot of flying, both in and out of the region, might consider buying an air pass. Air passes are available only to non-US citizens, and must be purchased in conjunction with an international ticket.

Conditions and cost structures can be complicated, but all include a certain number of domestic flights (from three to 10) that must be used within a set time frame, generally between 30 and 60 days. In most cases, you must plan your itinerary in advance, but dates (and even destinations) can sometimes be left open. Talk with a travel agent to determine if an air pass would save you money based on your plans.

The two main airline alliances offering air passes are **Star Alliance** (www.staralliance.com) and **One World** (www.oneworld.com).

Bicycle

Regional bicycle touring is very popular. Flat countryside and scenic coastlines make for great itineraries. However, target winter to spring; summer is unbearably hot and humid for long-distance biking.

Some Florida biking organizations organize bike tours. Renting a bicycle is easy throughout Florida.

Some other things to keep in mind:

Helmet laws Helmets are required for anyone aged 16 and younger. Adults are not required to wear helmets, but should for safety.

Road rules Bikes must obey auto rules; ride on the right-hand side of the road, with traffic, not on sidewalks.

Transporting your bike to Florida Bikes are considered checked luggage on airplanes, but often must be boxed and fees can be high (more than $200).

Theft Bring and use a sturdy lock (U-type is best). Theft is common, especially in Miami Beach.

For more information and assistance, a few organizations can help:

Better World Club (☑866-238-1137; www.betterworldclub. com) Offers a bicycle roadside assistance program.

International Bicycle Fund (www.ibike.org) Comprehensive overview of bike regulations by airline, and lots of advice.

League of American Bicyclists (www.bikeleague.org) General advice, plus lists of local cycle clubs and repair shops.

Boat

Florida is a world center for two major types of boat transportation: privately owned yachts and cruise ships.

Each coastal city has sightseeing boats that cruise harbors and coastlines. It really pays (in memories) to get out on the water. Water-taxi services along Intracoastal Waterways are a feature in Fort Lauderdale and around Sanibel Island and Pine Island on the Gulf.

Cruises

Florida is a huge destination and departure point for cruises of all kinds. Miami likes to brag that it's the 'cruise capital of the world,' and Walt Disney World runs its own **Disney Cruise Line** (☑800-951-3532; www.disneycruise. disney.go.com), which has a number of three- to seven-night cruises throughout the Caribbean, including to

Disney's own private island, Castaway Cay.

For specials on other multinight and multiday cruises, see the following:

Cruise.com (www.cruise.com)

CruiseWeb (www.cruiseweb.com)

Vacations to Go (www.vacations togo.com)

CruisesOnly (www.cruisesonly. com)

Florida's main ports:

Port Canaveral (www. portcanaveral.com) On the Atlantic Coast near the Kennedy Space Center; gives Miami a run for its money.

Port Everglades (www. porteverglades.net) Near Fort Lauderdale, and the third-busiest Florida port.

Port of Miami (☑305-347-4800; www.miamidade.gov/ portofmiami) At the world's largest cruise-ship port, the most common trips offered are to the Bahamas, the Caribbean, Key West and Mexico.

Port of Tampa (www.tam-paport.com) On the Gulf Coast; rapidly gaining a foothold in the cruise market.

Major cruise companies:

Carnival Cruise Lines (☑800-764-7419; www.carnival. com)

Norwegian Cruise Line (☑866-234-7350; www.ncl. com)

Royal Caribbean (☑866-562-7625; www.royalcaribbean. com)

Bus

The only statewide bus service is by **Greyhound** (☑800-231-2222; www.grey-hound.com), which connects all major and mid-sized Florida cities, but not always smaller towns (even some popular beach towns). Regional or city-run buses cover their more limited areas much better; used together, these bus systems make travel by bus possible, but time-consuming.

It's always a bit cheaper to take a Greyhound bus during the week than on the weekend. Fares for children are usually about half the adult fare.

GREYHOUND BUS FARES

To get you started, here are some round-trip Greyhound bus fares and travel times around Florida:

FROM	TO	FARE	DURATION (HR)
Daytona Beach	St Augustine	$29	1
Fort Lauderdale	Melbourne	$58	4
Jacksonville	Tallahassee	$54	3
Melbourne	Daytona Beach	$34	3½
Miami	Key West	$58	4½
Miami	Naples	$46	3
Panama City	Pensacola	$49	3
St Augustine	Jacksonville	$24	1
Naples	Tampa	$59	5
Tampa	Orlando	$38	2
Tallahassee	Panama City	$39	2½

Car & Motorcycle

By far the most convenient and popular way to travel around Florida is by car. While it's quite possible to avoid using a car on single-destination trips – to Miami, to Orlando theme parks or to a self-contained beach resort – relying on public transit can be inconvenient for even limited regional touring. Even smaller, tourist-friendly towns such as Naples, Sarasota or St Augustine can be frustrating to negotiate without a car. Motorcycles are also popular in Florida, given the flat roads and warm weather (summer rain excepted).

Automobile Associations

The **American Automobile Association** (AAA; ☑800-874-7532; www.aaa.com) has reciprocal agreements with several international auto clubs (check with AAA and bring your membership card). For members, AAA offers travel insurance, tour books, diagnostic centers for used-car buyers and a greater number of regional offices, and it advocates politically for the auto industry. It also has a handy online route planner that can help you calculate the exact mileage and estimated fuel costs of your intended itinerary.

An ecofriendly alternative is the **Better World Club** (☑866-238-1137; www.betterworldclub.com), which donates 1% of earnings to assist environmental cleanup; offers ecologically sensitive choices for services; and advocates politically for environmental causes. Better World also has a roadside-assistance program for bicycles.

In both organizations, the central member benefit is 24-hour emergency roadside assistance anywhere in the USA. Both clubs also offer trip planning and free maps, travel-agency services, car insurance and a range of discounts (car rentals, hotels etc).

Driver's License

Foreign visitors can legally drive in the USA for up to 12 months with their home driver's license. However, getting an International Driving Permit (IDP) is recommended; this will have more credibility with US traffic police, especially if your home license doesn't have a photo or is in a foreign language. Your automobile association at home can issue an IDP, valid for one year, for a small fee. You must carry your home license together with the IDP at all times. To drive a motorcycle, you need either a valid US state motorcycle license or an IDP specially endorsed for motorcycles.

Insurance

Don't put the key into the ignition if you don't have insurance: it's legally required, and you risk financial ruin without it if there's an accident. If you already have auto insurance (even overseas), or if you buy travel insurance, make sure that the policy has adequate liability coverage for a rental car in Florida; it probably does, but check.

Rental-car companies will provide liability insurance, but most charge extra for the privilege. Always ask. Collision-damage insurance for the vehicle is almost never included in the US. Instead, the provider will offer an optional Collision Damage Waiver (CDW) or Loss Damage Waiver (LDW), usually with an initial deductible of $100 to $500. For an extra premium, you can usually get this deductible covered as well. However, most credit cards now offer collision-damage coverage for rental cars if you rent for 15 days or less and charge the total rental to your card. This is a good way to avoid paying extra fees to the rental company, but note that if there's an accident, you sometimes must pay the rental car company first and then seek reimbursement from the credit-card company. Check your credit-card policy. Paying extra for some or all of this insurance increases the cost of a rental car by as much as $10 to $30 a day.

Travel insurance, either specific paid policies or free insurance provided by your credit-card company (when your travel arrangements are purchased on their credit cards), often includes cover for rental-car insurances up to the full amount of any deductible. If you plan on renting a vehicle for any significant period of time, the cost of travel insurance, which includes coverage for rental vehicles, is often way cheaper than purchasing the optional insurance from the car-rental company directly. Be prudent and do your research to avoid getting a shock when you go to sign your car-rental contract and discover all the additional charges.

Rental

CAR

Car rental is a very competitive business. Most rental companies require that you have a major credit card; that you be at least 25 years old; and that you have a valid driver's license (your home license will do). Some national companies may rent to drivers between the ages of 21 and 24 for an additional charge. Those under 21 are usually not permitted to rent at all.

Additional drivers are not usually covered under the base rate and an additional daily surcharge will be applied. If someone other than the parties authorised on the rental contract is driving the vehicle and has an accident, all paid insurances will be void: you don't want this to happen. If anyone else is likely to drive the vehicle, they need to be present at the time of collection and are required to submit their driver's license and pay the extra fee. If the additional driver is not able to be present at the time of collection, it is possible to drive into any branch of the rental company and add the additional driver on to your rental agreement at a later date. Charges may be backdated to the day of collection.

Good independent agencies are listed by **Car Rental Express** (www.carrentalexpress.com), which rates and compares independent agencies in US cities; it's particularly useful for searching out cheaper long-term rentals.

National car-rental companies include the following:

Alamo (☑877-222-9075; www.alamo.com)

Avis (☑800-331-2112; www.avis.com)

Budget (☑800-527-0700; www.budget.com)

Dollar (☑800-800-4000; www.dollar.com)

Enterprise (☑800-261-7331; www.enterprise.com)

Hertz (☑800-654-3131; www.hertz.com)

National (☑800-468-3334; www.nationalcar.com)

Rent-a-Wreck (☑877-877-0700; www.rentawreck.com)

Thrifty (☑800-367-2277; www.thrifty.com)

Rental cars are readily available at all airport locations and many downtown city locations. With advance reservations for a small car, the daily rate with unlimited mileage is about $35 to $55, while typical weekly rates are $200 to $400, plus myriad taxes and fees. If you rent from a downtown location, you can save money by avoiding the exorbitant airport fees.

An alternative in Miami is **Zipcar** (www.zipcar.com), a car-sharing service that charges hourly and daily rental fees with free gas, insurance and limited mileage included; prepayment is required.

Note that one-way rentals (picking up in one city and dropping off in another) will often incur a prohibitive one-way drop fee. Experimenting with your routing, or returning the vehicle to the same or a nearby city to where you collected your vehicle, may help avoid this penalty. Also check if the location that you're collecting the car from is franchised or centrally owned: sometimes the latter will help get any one-way fees waived.

MOTORCYCLE

To straddle a Harley across Florida, contact **EagleRider** (☑888-900-9901; www.eaglerider.com), which has offices in Daytona Beach, Fort Lauderdale, Miami, St Augustine and Orlando. It offers a wide range of models, which start at $150 a day, plus liability insurance. Adult riders (over 21) are not required by Florida law to wear a helmet, but you should for your own safety.

MOTORHOME (RV)

Forget hotels. Drive your own. Touring Florida by recreational vehicle (RV) can be as low-key or as over-the-top as you wish.

After settling on the vehicle's size, consider the impact of gas prices, gas mileage, additional mileage costs, insurance and refundable deposits; these can add up quickly. Typically, RVs don't come with unlimited mileage, so estimate your mileage up front to calculate the true rental cost.

Inquire about motorhome relocations: sometimes, you can get amazing deals where you're effectively being paid to move the vehicle between cities for its owner – but you'll need to be extremely flexible with your dates and routes.

Adventures On Wheels (☑800-943-3579; www.wheels9.com) Office in Miami.

CruiseAmerica (☑800-671-8042; www.cruiseamerica.com) The largest national RV-rental firm has offices across South Florida.

Recreational Vehicle Rental Association (☑703-591-7130; www.rvda.org) Good resource for RV information and advice, and helps find rental locations.

Road Rules

If you're new to Florida or US roads, here are some basics:

➡ The maximum speed limit on interstates is 75mph, but that drops to 65mph and 55mph in urban areas. Pay attention to the posted signs. City-street speed limits vary between 15mph and 45mph.

➡ Florida police officers are strict with speed-limit enforcement, and speeding tickets are expensive. If caught going over the speed limit by 10mph, the fine is $155. Conversely, you may be fined if you're driving too slowly on an interstate.

➡ All passengers in a car must wear seat belts; the fine for not wearing a seat belt is $30. All children under three must be in a child safety seat.

➡ As in the rest of the US, drive on the right-hand side of the road. On highways, pass in the left-hand lane (but anxious drivers often pass wherever space allows).

➡ Right turns on a red light are permitted after a full stop. At four-way stop signs, the car that reaches the intersection first has right of way. In a tie, the car on the right has right of way.

Hitchhiking

Hitchhiking is never entirely safe in any country, and we don't recommend it. Travelers who decide to hitch should understand that they are taking a small but potentially serious risk. People who do choose to hitch will be safer if they go in pairs and if they let someone know where they are planning to go. Be sure to ask the driver where he or she is going rather than telling the person where you want to go.

Local Transportation

Bus

Local bus services are available in most cities; along the coasts, service typically connects downtown to at least one or two beach communities. Some cities (such as Tampa and Jacksonsville) have high-frequency trolleys circling downtown, while some coastal stretches are linked by seasonal trolleys that ferry beach-goers between towns (such as between St Pete Beach and Clearwater).

Fares generally cost between $1 and $2. Exact change upon boarding is usually required, though some buses take $1 bills. Transfers – slips of paper that will allow you to change buses – range from free to 25¢. Hours of operation differ from city to city, but generally buses run from approximately 6am to 10pm.

Metro

Walt Disney World has a monorail and Tampa has an old-fashioned, one-line streetcar, but the only real metro systems are in and near Miami. In Miami, a driverless Metromover circles downtown and connects with Metrorail, which connects downtown north to Hialeah and south to Kendall.

Meanwhile, north of Miami, Hollywood, Fort Lauderdale and West Palm Beach (and the towns between them) are well connected by Tri-Rail's double-decker commuter trains. Tri-Rail runs all the way to Miami, but the full trip takes longer than driving.

Train

Amtrak (☑800-872-7245; www.amtrak.com) trains run between a number of Florida cities. For the purpose of getting around Florida, its service is extremely limited, and yet for certain trips its trains can be very easy and inexpensive. In essence, daily trains run between Jacksonville, Orlando and Miami, with one line branching off to Tampa. In addition, the Thruway Motorcoach (or bus) service gets Amtrak passengers to Daytona Beach, St Petersburg and Fort Myers.

Behind the Scenes

SEND US YOUR FEEDBACK

We love to hear from travelers – your comments keep us on our toes and help make our books better. Our well-traveled team reads every word on what you loved or loathed about this book. Although we cannot reply individually to your submissions, we always guarantee that your feedback goes straight to the appropriate authors, in time for the next edition. Each person who sends us information is thanked in the next edition – the most useful submissions are rewarded with a selection of digital PDF chapters.

Visit **lonelyplanet.com/contact** to submit your updates and suggestions or to ask for help. Our award-winning website also features inspirational travel stories, news and discussions.

Note: We may edit, reproduce and incorporate your comments in Lonely Planet products such as guidebooks, websites and digital products, so let us know if you don't want your comments reproduced or your name acknowledged. For a copy of our privacy policy visit lonelyplanet.com/privacy.

OUR READERS

Many thanks to the travelers who used the last edition and wrote to us with helpful hints, useful advice and interesting anecdotes: Anneke Abma, Emily Brock, Cécile Brouwer, Victor Bryant, Vanessa Dowsett, Lan Jiang, Mikael Lypinski, Frank McIntyre, Christina Minna, Lechat Jean Philippe, Peter Rytz, Laura van Eerten.

AUTHOR THANKS
Adam Karlin

To my crew: Paula, Benedict and Jennifer, for giving me a painless turn at the coordinating author's helm; my editors, Jo and Dora, for being understanding, accommodating and supportive; Jaime Levenshon and Bethany Martinez, for an amazing crash-course in Miami dining; my parents, for their unflagging support; Eggy and Gizmo, who have made writing from home more zoo-keeping, cuddling joy than chore; Rachel Houge, my lovely wife, for the same, for her humor, smiles and laughter, and for following me whenever I paddle too close to crocodiles; and to my daughter, who is on the way, and to whom I whisper the hope of new roads, and I promise all the world to explore.

Jennifer Rasin Denniston

Thank you to my co-authors Adam and Paula, to Dora Whitaker, Alison Lyall and Dianne Schallmeiner, and to Karla Zimmerman. Big thanks to Denielle Cox, Jimmy Clarity and Jennifer Hodges for their gracious help with everything Universal Orlando. Finally, love and thanks to my husband Rhawn and my daughters Anna and Harper, who are always happy to hit the road and 'check things out', and who always bring a sense of humor, a critical eye and a spirit of adventure.

Paula Hardy

A huge thank you to the Krasnys, particularly Keith, Mary, Glenn and Robin, for their crazy hospitality and invaluable insights. Thanks also to Marcia Gaedcke and Jackie Barker at the Titusville Chamber, Dawna Thorstad, Mike Merrifield, the staff at Brevard Zoo, Mike Crego and Jim Jozefowicz, Kathie Smith and the folks at Visit Florida. Thanks also to Dora and Jo at Lonely Planet, Larry for teaching me to surf (badly) and Cinthia Sandoval for excellent food tips. And thanks, as always, to Rob for endless grouper sandwiches and always knowing the best beaches.

Benedict Walker

Heartfelt thanks to my two families: the Walkers in Australia, and the Cowies in Canada – without your love, trust and support, who knows where I'd be now; to my mum, Trish Walker, for always believing in me and never giving up on me – I am your number-one fan; to my friends in Australia, Canada, Japan and the US, who never get as much of my time or love as they deserve, but hang in there with me anyway; and to Luca, Felix and Mila, my godkids – I lo-ve you! Follow your dreams. Tremendous gratitude for Lonely Planet and Stage and Screen Travel: for keeping me in work, with food in my belly and a smile on my face. I'm the luckiest man alive.

ACKNOWLEDGEMENTS

Climate map data adapted from Peel MC, Finlayson BL & McMahon TA (2007) 'Updated World Map of the Köppen-Geiger Climate Classification', *Hydrology and Earth System Sciences*, 11, 163344.

Cover photograph: Lifeguard hut, Fort Lauderdale Beach, Florida, Pietro Canali / 4Corners ©.

THIS BOOK

This 7th edition of Lonely Planet's *Florida* guidebook was researched and written by Adam Karlin, Jennifer Rasin Denniston, Paula Hardy and Benedict Walker. The 6th edition was written by Jeff Campbell, Jennifer Rasin Denniston, Adam Karlin and Emily Matchar; the 5th edition was written by Jeff Campbell, Becca Blond, Jennifer Rasin Denniston, Beth Greenfield, Adam Karlin and Willy Volk. This guidebook was commissioned in Lonely Planet's London office, and was produced by the following:

Destination Editors
Jo Cooke, Alexander Howard, Dora Whitaker

Product Editor
Elizabeth Jones

Book Designer
Virginia Moreno

Senior Cartographer
Alison Lyall

Assisting Editors Sarah Bailey, Nigel Chin, Katie Connolly, Penny Cordner, Kate Mathews, Charlotte Orr, Susan Paterson, Gabrielle Stefanos, Jeanette Wall, Tracy Whitmey

Assisting Cartographers
Anita Banh, Mark Griffiths, Valentina Kremenchutskaya, Anthony Phelan, Julie Sheridan, Diana Von Holdt

Cover Researcher
Naomi Parker

Thanks to Sasha Baskett, Briohny Hooper, Indra Kilfoyle, Clara Monitto, Claire Naylor, Karyn Noble, Katie O'Connell, Martine Power, Dianne Schallmeiner, John Taufa, Angela Tinson, Amanda Williamson, Juan Winata.

Index

Map Legend

Sights
- Beach
- Bird Sanctuary
- Buddhist
- Castle/Palace
- Christian
- Confucian
- Hindu
- Islamic
- Jain
- Jewish
- Monument
- Museum/Gallery/Historic Building
- Ruin
- Sento Hot Baths/Onsen
- Shinto
- Sikh
- Taoist
- Winery/Vineyard
- Zoo/Wildlife Sanctuary
- Other Sight

Activities, Courses & Tours
- Bodysurfing
- Diving
- Canoeing/Kayaking
- Course/Tour
- Skiing
- Snorkeling
- Surfing
- Swimming/Pool
- Walking
- Windsurfing
- Other Activity

Sleeping
- Sleeping
- Camping

Eating
- Eating

Drinking & Nightlife
- Drinking & Nightlife
- Cafe

Entertainment
- Entertainment

Shopping
- Shopping

Information
- Bank
- Embassy/Consulate
- Hospital/Medical
- Internet
- Police
- Post Office
- Telephone
- Toilet
- Tourist Information
- Other Information

Geographic
- Beach
- Hut/Shelter
- Lighthouse
- Lookout
- Mountain/Volcano
- Oasis
- Park
- Pass
- Picnic Area
- Waterfall

Population
- Capital (National)
- Capital (State/Province)
- City/Large Town
- Town/Village

Transport
- Airport
- BART station
- Border crossing
- Boston T station
- Bus
- Cable car/Funicular
- Cycling
- Ferry
- Metro/Muni station
- Monorail
- Parking
- Petrol station
- Subway/SkyTrain station
- Taxi
- Train station/Railway
- Tram
- Underground station
- Other Transport

Note: Not all symbols displayed above appear on the maps in this book

Routes
- Tollway
- Freeway
- Primary
- Secondary
- Tertiary
- Lane
- Unsealed road
- Road under construction
- Plaza/Mall
- Steps
- Tunnel
- Pedestrian overpass
- Walking Tour
- Walking Tour detour
- Path/Walking Trail

Boundaries
- International
- State/Province
- Disputed
- Regional/Suburb
- Marine Park
- Cliff
- Wall

Hydrography
- River, Creek
- Intermittent River
- Canal
- Water
- Dry/Salt/Intermittent Lake
- Reef

Areas
- Airport/Runway
- Beach/Desert
- Cemetery (Christian)
- Cemetery (Other)
- Glacier
- Mudflat
- Park/Forest
- Sight (Building)
- Sportsground
- Swamp/Mangrove

OUR STORY

A beat-up old car, a few dollars in the pocket and a sense of adventure. In 1972 that's all Tony and Maureen Wheeler needed for the trip of a lifetime – across Europe and Asia overland to Australia. It took several months, and at the end – broke but inspired – they sat at their kitchen table writing and stapling together their first travel guide, *Across Asia on the Cheap*. Within a week they'd sold 1500 copies. Lonely Planet was born.

Today, Lonely Planet has offices in Franklin, London, Melbourne, Oakland, Beijing and Delhi, with more than 600 staff and writers. We share Tony's belief that 'a great guidebook should do three things: inform, educate and amuse'.

OUR WRITERS

Adam Karlin

Coordinating Author, Miami, The Everglades, Florida Keys & Key West, Understand Florida Adam's grandmother sheltered him from winter weather in West Palm Beach throughout his childhood, and he worked for a stint at the *Key West Citizen*, covering hyperbolic politicians, Cuban exiles, mosquito-control initiatives and trailer park evictions. It was the sort of journalism gig you supplement with a try at being a local-radio DJ and a few nights' bouncing at Keys bars. After that adventure, Adam went on to Lonely Planet, where he has written or co-authored well over 40 guidebooks, including three editions of *Florida* and *Miami & the Keys*.

Jennifer Rasin Denniston

Theme Park Trip Planner, Travel with Children, Orlando & Walt Disney World Jennifer, her geologist husband Rhawn, and their two daughters Anna and Harper spend three or four months every year road-tripping through the US and beyond, including annual weeks-long trips to Florida. They've explored beaches from the Panhandle to the Keys, kayaked Space Coast estuaries and searched the Gulf Coast for ice-age fossils, screamed hands-free on coasters and sidled up to Cinderella.

Paula Hardy

Southeast Florida, The Space Coast, Tampa Bay & Southwest Florida Born in Kenya, based in London and married to a man who's lived half his life on Gulf Coast islands, Paula has spent an awful lot of days at the beach. Who can complain? When not squabbling over shells or the merits of grouper sandwiches with her second half, she's authored over 30 guidebooks for Lonely Planet, including contributions to *New England*, *USA* and *Eastern USA*. When not researching Lonely Planet guidebooks, Paula writes about culture, travel and food for a variety of websites and travel publications. You can find her tweeting @paula6hardy.

Benedict Walker

Northeast Florida, The Panhandle, Directory A–Z, Transportation Born in Newcastle, Australia, Ben is living the dream, exploring the wilds and the wild things of Florida, Canada, Japan and Australia. Ben dog-eared his first Lonely Planet guide *(Japan)* when he was 14. When he grew up, he'd write chapters for the same book: a dream come true. A Communications graduate, then travel agent by trade, Ben speaks fluent Japanese. He's co-written and directed a play, toured with rock stars and fancies himself as a photographer. Writing for Lonely Planet means that 'home' equals living out of a suitcase between Australia, Canada, Japan and the US, but he loves and is grateful for every second.

Published by Lonely Planet Publications Pty Ltd
ABN 36 005 607 983
7th edition – January 2015
ISBN 978 1 74220 752 0
© Lonely Planet 2015   Photographs © as indicated 2015
10 9 8 7 6 5 4 3 2 1
Printed in China